MARKETING
MANAGEMENT

FOURTEENTH CANADIAN EDITION

PHILIP KOTLER,
NORTHWESTERN UNIVERSITY

KEVIN LANE KELLER,
DARTMOUTH COLLEGE

SUBRAMANIAN SIVARAMAKRISHNAN,
UNIVERSITY OF MANITOBA

PEGGY H. CUNNINGHAM,
DALHOUSIE UNIVERSITY

Toronto

Vice-President, Editorial Director: Gary Bennett
Editor-in-Chief: Nicole Lukach
Acquisitions Editor: Nick Durie
Senior Marketing Manager: Leigh-Anne Graham
Developmental Editor: Patti Altridge
Project Manager: Lesley Deugo
Production Editor: Susan Broadhurst
Copy Editor: Marnie Lamb
Proofreaders: Kelli Howey, Susan Bindernagel
Compositor: Christine Velakis
Photo Researcher/Permissions Editor: Danny Meldung/Photo Affairs
Manufacturing Manager: Susan Johnson
Art Director: Julia Hall
Cover and Interior Designer: Julia Hall

Credits and acknowledgments for material borrowed from other sources and reproduced, with permission, in this textbook appear on the appropriate page within text, or on page 716.

If you purchased this book outside the United States or Canada, you should be aware that it has been imported without the approval of the publisher or the author.

Library and Archives Canada Cataloguing in Publication
    Marketing management / Philip Kotler ... [et al.]. -- Canadian 14th ed.

Includes bibliographical references and indexes.
ISBN 978-0-13-216107-7

    1. Marketing--Management--Textbooks. I. Kotler, Philip

HF5415.13.M36 2013   658.8   C2011-906230-55

ISBN 978-0-13-216107-7

ABOUT THE AUTHORS

Philip Kotler is one of the world's leading authorities on marketing. He is the S. C. Johnson & Son Distinguished Professor of International Marketing at the Kellogg School of Management, Northwestern University. He received his master's degree at the University of Chicago and his Ph.D. at MIT, both in economics. He did post-doctoral work in mathematics at Harvard University and in behavioural science at the University of Chicago.

Dr. Kotler is the co-author of *Principles of Marketing* and *Marketing: An Introduction*. His *Strategic Marketing for Nonprofit Organizations*, now in its seventh edition, is the best seller in that specialized area. Dr. Kotler's other books include *Marketing Models; The New Competition; Marketing Professional Services; Strategic Marketing for Educational Institutions; Marketing for Health Care Organizations; Marketing Congregations; High Visibility; Social Marketing; Marketing Places; The Marketing of Nations; Marketing for Hospitality and Tourism; Standing Room Only—Strategies for Marketing the Performing Arts; Museum Strategy and Marketing; Marketing Moves; Kotler on Marketing; Lateral Marketing: Ten Deadly Marketing Sins;* and *Corporate Social Responsibility*.

In addition, he has published more than 100 articles in leading journals, including the *Harvard Business Review, Sloan Management Review, Business Horizons, California Management Review,* the *Journal of Marketing,* the *Journal of Marketing Research, Management Science,* the *Journal of Business Strategy,* and *Futurist.* He is the only three-time winner of the coveted Alpha Kappa Psi award for the best annual article published in the *Journal of Marketing.*

Professor Kotler was the first recipient of the American Marketing Association's (AMA) Distinguished Marketing Educator Award (1985). The European Association of Marketing Consultants and Sales Trainers awarded him their Prize for Marketing Excellence. He was chosen as the Leader in Marketing Thought by the Academic Members of the AMA in a 1975 survey. He also received the 1978 Paul Converse Award of the AMA, honouring his original contribution to marketing. In 1995, the Sales and Marketing Executives International (SMEI) named him Marketer of the Year. In 2002, Professor Kotler received the Distinguished Educator Award from the Academy of Marketing Science. He has received honorary doctoral degrees from Stockholm University, the University of Zurich, Athens University of Economics and Business, DePaul University, the Cracow School of Business and Economics, Groupe H.E.C. in Paris, the Budapest School of Economic Science and Public Administration, and the University of Economics and Business Administration in Vienna.

Professor Kotler has been a consultant to many major U.S. and foreign companies, including IBM, General Electric, AT&T, Honeywell, Bank of America, Merck, SAS Airlines, Michelin, and others in the areas of marketing strategy and planning, marketing organization, and international marketing.

He has been Chairman of the College of Marketing of the Institute of Management Sciences, a Director of the American Marketing Association, a Trustee of the Marketing Science Institute, a Director of the MAC Group, a member of the Yankelovich Advisory Board, and a member of the Copernicus Advisory Board. He was a member of the Board of Governors of the School of the Art Institute of Chicago and a member of the Advisory Board of the Drucker Foundation. He has travelled extensively throughout Europe, Asia, and South America, advising and lecturing to many companies about global marketing opportunities.

Kevin Lane Keller is widely recognized as one of the top marketing academics of the last 25 years. He is the E. B. Osborn Professor of Marketing at the Tuck School of Business at Dartmouth College. Professor Keller has degrees from Cornell, Carnegie-Mellon, and Duke universities. At Dartmouth, he teaches MBA courses on marketing management and strategic brand management and lectures in executive programs on those topics.

Previously, Professor Keller was on the faculty of the Graduate School of Business at Stanford University, where he also served as the head of the marketing group. Additionally, he has been on the marketing faculty at the University of California at Berkeley and the University of North Carolina at Chapel Hill, has been a visiting professor at Duke University and the Australian Graduate School of Management, and has two years of industry experience as Marketing Consultant for Bank of America.

Professor Keller's general area of expertise lies in marketing strategy and planning, and branding. His specific research interest is in how understanding theories and concepts related to consumer behaviour can improve marketing strategies. His research has been published in three of the major marketing journals: the *Journal of Marketing*, the *Journal of Marketing Research*, and the *Journal of Consumer Research*. He also has served on the Editorial Review Boards of those journals. With more than 90 published papers, his research has been extensively cited and has received numerous awards.

Professor Keller is acknowledged as one of the international leaders in the study of brands and branding. His textbook on those subjects, *Strategic Brand Management*, has been adopted at top business schools and leading firms around the world and has been heralded as the "bible of branding."

Actively involved with industry, he has worked on a host of different types of marketing projects. He has served as a consultant and adviser to marketers for some of the world's most successful brands, including Accenture, American Express, Disney, Ford, Intel, Levi Strauss, Procter & Gamble, and Samsung. Additional brand consulting activities have been with other top companies such as Allstate, Beiersdorf (Nivea), BlueCross BlueShield, Campbell's, Colgate, Eli Lilly, ExxonMobil, General Mills, GfK, Goodyear, Intuit, Johnson & Johnson, Kodak, L.L.Bean, Mayo Clinic, Nordstrom, Ocean Spray, Red Hat, SAB Miller, Shell Oil, Starbucks, Unilever, and Young & Rubicam. He has also served as an academic trustee for the Marketing Science Institute.

A popular and highly sought-after speaker, he has made speeches and conducted marketing seminars to top executives in a variety of forums. Some of his senior management and marketing training clients have included such diverse business organizations as Cisco, Coca-Cola, Deutsche Telekom, GE, Google, IBM, Macy's, Microsoft, Nestle, Novartis, and Wyeth. He has lectured all over the world, from Seoul to Johannesburg, from Sydney to Stockholm, and from Sao Paulo to Mumbai. He has served as keynote speaker at conferences with hundreds to thousands of participants.

An avid sports, music, and film enthusiast, in his so-called spare time he has helped to manage and market, as well as serve as executive producer for, one of Australia's great rock and roll treasures, The Church, as well as American power-pop legends Dwight Twilley and Tommy Keene. Additionally, he is the Principal Investor and Marketing Advisor for Second Motion Records. He is also on the Board of Directors for The Doug Flutie, Jr. Foundation for Autism and the Montshire Museum of Science. Professor Keller lives in Etna, New Hampshire, with his wife, Punam (also a Tuck marketing professor), and his two daughters, Carolyn and Allison.

Subramanian (Subbu) Sivaramakrishnan is Associate Professor of Marketing at the I. H. Asper School of Business, University of Manitoba. Subbu received his Ph.D. in Marketing from Penn State University; his MBA from Bharathiar University, India; and a bachelor's of science degree in Mathematics from Madras Christian College, India.

Subbu has received several awards for teaching. He received the CMA Merit Award for Research, Teaching, and Service and the Asper Associates' Award for Teaching from the University of Manitoba. He was also honoured with an Award for Innovative Teaching by the University of Arkansas at Pine Bluff and an Outstanding Teaching Award by Penn State University. Besides teaching in Canada and the United States, Subbu teaches regularly in Executive Education and MBA programs in Spain (where he has taught for 22 consecutive years), Taiwan, Singapore, and India. In addition to co-authoring *Marketing Management* (13th and 14th Canadian editions), he has co-authored *Marketing Research Essentials*, Canadian edition.

Subbu's research is primarily in the area of consumer behaviour. His research interests extend to knowledge management by organizations and to online marketing. His recent publications have appeared in the *International Journal of Research in Marketing*, *Journal of Product & Brand Management*, *Journal of Interactive Marketing*, *Journal of Strategic Marketing*, and *Journal of International Consumer Marketing*. Subbu is the recipient of three large federal research grants from the Social Sciences and Humanities Research Council of Canada.

Besides academic work, Subbu has conducted a number of pro bono marketing research studies for organizations such as the Canadian Museum for Human Rights, Royal Winnipeg Ballet, Winnipeg Art Gallery, Investors Group, MTS, Manitoba Hydro, Festival du Voyageur, Manitoba Museum, and Labatt Breweries, as well as for many local community service organizations.

Subbu lives in Winnipeg with his wife, Kala, and children, Varsha and Varun. He is a compulsive photographer and loves singing. He also plays competitive badminton and cricket and has the not-so-coveted distinction of being the oldest member on his teams!

Dr. Peggy Cunningham is the Dean of the Faculty of Management at Dalhousie University and the R. A. Jodrey Chair. Dr. Cunningham received her Ph.D. from Texas A&M University, her MBA from the University of Calgary, and her bachelor's degree from Queen's University. She has published in the *California Management Review*, the *Journal of Business Ethics*, the *Journal of the Academy of Marketing Science*, the *Journal of Advertising*, and the *Journal of International Marketing* among others. She has co-authored numerous Canadian editions of *Principles of Marketing* (Pearson Publishing, 3rd to 9th edtions) and *Marketing Management* (11th to 14th editions). Her teaching and research focus on ethics, corporate social responsibility, and partnerships within the field of marketing. Peggy is an acclaimed and awarded teaching professor. Her awards include the PriceWaterhouseCoopers Leaders in Management Education award, the Academy of Marketing Science's Outstanding Teacher, and the Frank Knox Award for Teaching Excellence. She has written more than 40 cases in the areas of branding, ethics, and corporate social responsibility. She advises a number of Canadian corporations on marketing and corporate social responsibility. She is an avid sailor and hiker and enjoys golf and tennis. She lives in Halifax with her husband, Paul. Her daughter is a marketing professional who works with an international packaged goods company.

This book is dedicated to my wife and best friend, Nancy, with love. **PK**

This book is dedicated to my wife, Punam, and my two daughters, Carolyn and Allison, with much love and thanks. **KLK**

This book is dedicated to my students, whose enthusiasm inspires me every day. **SS**

This book is dedicated to my family, who have always been my strongest supporters. **PC**

BRIEF CONTENTS

CONTENTS

PART 8   CREATING SUCCESSFUL LONG-TERM GROWTH   524

CHAPTER 20   INTRODUCING NEW MARKET OFFERINGS   524

PREFACE

WHAT'S NEW IN THE 14TH EDITION

The overriding goal of the revision for the 14th edition of *Marketing Management* was to create as comprehensive, current, and engaging an MBA marketing textbook as possible. Where appropriate, new material was added, old material was updated, and material that was no longer relevant or necessary was deleted. *Marketing Management*, 14th edition, allows those instructors who used the 13th edition to build on what they learned and did while at the same time offering a text that is unsurpassed in breadth, depth, and relevance for students experiencing it for the first time.

The successful across-chapter reorganization into eight parts that began with the 12th edition of *Marketing Management* has been preserved, as have many of the favourably received within-chapter features that have been introduced over the years, such as topical chapter openers, in-text boxes highlighting noteworthy companies or issues, and the Marketing Insight and Marketing Memo boxes that provide in-depth conceptual and practical commentary.

Significant changes to the 14th edition include the following:

- Brand new opening vignettes in each chapter set the stage for the chapter material to follow. By covering topical Canadian brands and companies, the vignettes are great for starting classroom discussion.

- Almost half of the in-text boxes are new. These boxes provide vivid illustrations of chapter concepts using actual companies and situations. The boxes cover a variety of products, services, and markets, and many have accompanying illustrations in the form of ads or product shots.

- The end-of-chapter section now includes a Marketing Excellence mini-case that highlights innovative, insightful marketing accomplishments by organizations. Each case includes questions that promote classroom discussion and student analysis.

- Dramatic changes in the marketing environment have occurred in recent years—in particular, in the economic, natural, and technological environments. Throughout the 14th edition, these three areas are addressed, sometimes via new subsections in chapters, with emphasis on evolving topics such as marketing during economic downturns and recessions, the rise of sustainability and "green" marketing, the extensive use of social media, and the increasing reliance on mobile devices. These new marketing realities make it more important than ever for marketers to be holistic in what they do, the overriding theme of this text.

- Forecasting has been moved to Chapter 3, where it fits well with the material on the marketing environment.

- Chapter 5 was retitled "Creating Long-Term Loyalty Relationships" to better reflect its stronger area of emphasis.

- Chapters 10 and 11 were reorganized and material was swapped. Chapter 11 was also retitled "Competitive Dynamics" to acknowledge the significant material added on marketing in an economic downturn.

- Chapter 19, on personal communications, received a significant update with much new material to reflect the changing social media landscape and communications environment.

WHAT IS MARKETING MANAGEMENT ALL ABOUT?

Marketing Management is the leading marketing text because its content and organization consistently reflect changes in marketing theory and practice. The very first edition of *Marketing Management*, published in 1967, introduced the concept that companies must be customer and market driven. But there was little mention of what have now become fundamental topics such as segmentation, targeting, and positioning. Concepts such as brand equity, customer value analysis, database marketing, e-commerce, value networks, hybrid channels, supply chain management, and integrated marketing communications were not even part of the marketing vocabulary then. *Marketing Management* continues to reflect the changes in the marketing discipline over the past 40 years.

Firms now sell goods and services through a variety of direct and indirect channels. Mass advertising is not nearly as effective as it was, so marketers are exploring new forms of communication, such as experiential, entertainment, and viral marketing. Customers are telling companies what types of product or services they want and when, where, and how they want to buy them. They are increasingly reporting to other consumers what they think of specific companies and products—using email, blogs, podcasts, and other digital media to do so. Company messages are becoming a smaller fraction of the total "conversation" about products and services.

In response, companies have shifted gears from managing product portfolios to managing *customer* portfolios, compiling databases on individual customers so they can understand them better and construct individualized offerings and messages. They are doing less product and service standardization and more niching and customization. They are replacing monologues with customer dialogues. They are improving their methods of measuring customer profitability and customer lifetime value. They are intent on measuring the return on their marketing investment and its impact on shareholder value. They are also concerned with the ethical and social implications of their marketing decisions.

As companies change, so does their marketing organization. Marketing is no longer a company department charged with a limited number of tasks—it is a company-wide undertaking. It drives the company's vision, mission, and strategic planning. Marketing includes decisions such as who the company wants as its customers, which of the customers' needs to satisfy, what products and services to offer, what prices to set, what communications to send and receive, what channels of distribution to use, and what partnerships to develop. Marketing succeeds only when all departments work together to achieve goals: when engineering designs the right products; finance furnishes the required funds; purchasing buys high-quality materials; production makes high-quality products on time; and accounting measures the profitability of different customers, products, and areas.

To address all of these different shifts, good marketers are practising holistic marketing. *Holistic marketing* is the development, design, and implementation of marketing programs, processes, and activities that recognize the breadth and interdependencies of today's marketing environment. Four key dimensions of holistic marketing are:

1. **Internal marketing**—ensuring everyone in the organization embraces appropriate marketing principles, especially senior management.
2. **Integrated marketing**—ensuring that multiple means of creating, delivering, and communicating value are employed and combined in the best way.
3. **Relationship marketing**—having rich, multifaceted relationships with customers, channel members, and other marketing partners.
4. **Performance marketing**—understanding returns to the business from marketing activities and programs, as well as addressing broader concerns and their legal, ethical, social, and environmental effects.

These four dimensions are woven throughout the book and at times spelled out explicitly. The text specifically addresses the following tasks that constitute modern marketing management in the 21st century:

1. Developing marketing strategies and plans
2. Capturing marketing insights and performance
3. Connecting with customers
4. Building strong brands
5. Shaping the market offerings
6. Delivering and communicating value
7. Creating successful long-term growth

WHAT MAKES MARKETING MANAGEMENT THE MARKETING LEADER?

Marketing is of interest to everyone, whether they are marketing goods, services, properties, persons, places, events, information, ideas, or organizations. As it has maintained its respected position among students, educators, and business people, *Marketing Management* has kept up to date and contemporary. Students (and instructors) feel that the book is talking directly to them in terms of both content and delivery.

Marketing Management owes its marketplace success to its ability to maximize three dimensions that characterize the best marketing texts—depth, breadth, and relevance—as measured by the following criteria:

- *Depth.* Does the book have solid academic grounding? Does it contain important theoretical concepts, models, and frameworks? Does it provide conceptual guidance to solve practical problems?

- *Breadth.* Does the book cover all of the right topics? Does it provide the proper amount of emphasis on those topics?

- *Relevance.* Does the book engage the reader? Is it interesting to read? Does it have a lot of compelling examples?

The 14th edition builds on the fundamental strengths of past editions that collectively distinguish it from all other marketing management texts:

- *Managerial orientation.* The book focuses on the major decisions that marketing managers and top management face in their efforts to harmonize the organization's objectives, capabilities, and resources with marketplace needs and opportunities.

- *Analytical approach. Marketing Management* presents conceptual tools and frameworks for analyzing recurring problems in marketing management. Cases and examples illustrate effective marketing principles, strategies, and practices.

- *Multidisciplinary perspective.* The book draws on the rich findings of various scientific disciplines—economics, behavioural science, management theory, and mathematics—for fundamental concepts and tools directly applicable to marketing challenges.

- *Universal applications.* The book applies strategic thinking to the complete spectrum of marketing: products, services, persons, places, information, ideas, and causes; consumer and business markets; profit and nonprofit organizations; domestic and foreign companies; small and large firms; manufacturing and intermediary businesses; and low-tech and high-tech industries.

- *Comprehensive and balanced coverage. Marketing Management* covers all of the topics an informed marketing manager needs to understand to execute strategic, tactical, and administrative marketing.

INSTRUCTOR SUPPLEMENTS

Instructor supplements are available for download from a password-protected section of Pearson Education Canada's online catalogue (**vig.pearsoned.ca**). Navigate to your book's catalogue page to view a list of the supplements that are available. See your local sales representative for details and access.

INSTRUCTOR'S RESOURCE MANUAL The Instructor's Resource Manual includes chapter/summary overviews, key teaching objectives, answers to end-of-chapter materials, Harvard Business School case suggestions, exercises, projects, and detailed lecture outlines. The feature "Professors on the Go!" was created with the busy professor in mind. It brings key material upfront, where an instructor who is short on time can find key points and assignments that can be incorporated into the lecture, without having to page through all of the material provided for each chapter.

MYTEST for *Marketing Management,* 14th Canadian Edition, from Pearson Education Canada is a powerful assessment generation program that helps instructors easily create and print quizzes, tests, and exams, as well as homework or practice handouts. Questions and tests can be authored online, allowing instructors ultimate flexibility and the ability to efficiently manage assessments at any time, from anywhere.

TEST ITEM FILE The Test Item File, in Word format, contains more than 3000 multiple-choice, true-false, short-answer, and essay questions, with page reference and difficulty level provided for each question. The testbank includes an entire section of application questions. These real-life situations take students beyond basic chapter concepts and vocabulary and ask them to apply marketing skills.

POWERPOINT PRESENTATIONS cover the key concepts and figures in each chapter.

IMAGE LIBRARY provides electronic versions of the figures and tables that appear in the text.

COURSESMART goes beyond traditional expectations, providing instant online access to the textbooks and course materials you need at a lower cost for students. And even as students save money, you can save time and hassle with a digital eTextbook that allows you to search for the most relevant content at the very moment you need it. Whether it's evaluating textbooks or creating lecture notes to help students with difficult concepts, CourseSmart can make life a little easier. See how when you visit **www.coursesmart.com/ instructors.**

TECHNOLOGY SPECIALISTS Pearson's Technology Specialists work with faculty and campus course designers to ensure that Pearson technology products, assessment tools, and online course materials are tailored to meet your specific needs. This highly qualified team is dedicated to helping schools take full advantage of a wide range of educational resources, by assisting in the integration of a variety of instructional materials and media formats. Your local Pearson Education sales representative can provide you with more details on this service program.

MARKETING MANAGEMENT CASES Pearson Custom Library can provide instructors and students with all of the cases and articles needed to enhance and maximize learning in a marketing course. Instructors can create Custom CoursePacks or Custom CaseBooks. Resources include top-tier cases from Darden, Harvard, Ivey, NACRA, and Thunderbird, plus full access to a database of articles. For details on how to order these value-priced packages, contact your local Pearson representative.

MARKETING MANAGEMENT VIDEO GALLERY Make your classroom "newsworthy." Pearson has updated the *Marketing Management* video library for the 14th edition. A full library of video segments accompanies this edition, featuring issue-focused footage such as interviews with top executives, industry research analysts, and marketing and advertising campaign experts and objective reporting by real news anchors. A full video guide—including synopses, discussion questions, and teaching suggestions—is available on the IRC (online and on CD-ROM) to accompany the video library. Contact your local Pearson representative for more information.

THE MARKETING PLAN HANDBOOK, 4TH EDITION, WITH MARKETING PLAN PRO Marketing Plan Pro is a highly rated commercial software program that guides students through the entire marketing plan process. The software is totally interactive and features 10 sample marketing plans, step-by-step guides, and customizable charts. Customize your marketing plan to fit your marketing needs by following easy-to-use plan wizards. Follow the clearly outlined steps from strategy to implementation. Click to print and your text, spreadsheet, and charts come together to create a powerful marketing plan. The new *The Marketing Plan Handbook,* by Marian Burk Wood, supplements the in-text marketing plan material with an in-depth guide to what student marketers really need to know. A structured learning process leads to a complete and actionable marketing plan. Also included are timely real-world examples that illustrate key points, sample marketing plans, and Internet resources. The Handbook and Marketing Plan Pro software are available as value-pack items at a discounted price. Contact your local Pearson representative for more information.

CBC/PEARSON CANADA LIBRARY This supplement features video segments and accompanying cases.

PEARSON CUSTOM LIBRARY For enrolments of at least 25 students, you can create your own textbook by choosing the chapters that best suit your own course needs. To begin building your custom text, visit **www.pearsoncustomlibrary.com.** You may also work with a dedicated Pearson Custom editor to create your ideal text—publishing your own original content or mixing and matching Pearson content. Contact your local Pearson Representative to get started.

STUDENT SUPPLEMENTS

COMPANION WEBSITE This site offers students valuable resources including quizzes, Internet exercises, and more at **www.pearsoned.ca/kotler.**

COURSESMART FOR STUDENTS CourseSmart goes beyond traditional expectations, providing instant online access to the textbooks and course materials you need at an average savings of 60 percent. With instant access from any computer and the ability to search your text, you'll find the content you need quickly, no matter where you are. And with online tools like highlighting and note-taking, you can save time and study efficiently. See all the benefits at **www.coursesmart.com/students.**

ACKNOWLEDGMENTS

Without excellent students and exciting and productive colleagues, no instructor or author can stay vibrant and connected. We wish to thank the following colleagues at other schools who have reviewed past editions of this book, including:

- Bryan Barbieri, Concordia University
- Emin Civi, University of New Brunswick (Saint John)
- Anthony Francescucci, Ryerson University
- Ray Friedman, Lethbridge College
- Ingrid Kajzer Mitchell, Royal Roads
- Anshuman Khare, Athabasca University
- Bhasker Mukerji, St. Francis Xavier University
- Robert J. Palmer, Williams School of Business
- Reg Sheppard, University of New Brunswick (Fredericton)
- Dwight R. Thomas, Athabasca University

I really appreciate the amazing research assistance provided by Chelsea Peters, Maia Schor, Alix Kendall, and Jaysa Nachtigall. I could not have completed this book without their contributions. I enjoyed working with the Pearson team—Don Thompson, Nick Durie, Patti Altridge, Susan Broadhurst, Marnie Lamb, and Lesley Deugo—all of whom showed great professionalism and patience and provided support throughout the authoring and production processes. I am very grateful to my wife, Kala, who made numerous sacrifices to give me the time to write, and to my children, Varsha and Varun, who gave up a lot of "Daddy Time" for the same reason. I really appreciate my family in India for being so understanding when I spent much more time before the computer than with them during a recent visit. My acknowledgments would not be complete without recognizing the inspiration I receive from my brother-in-law L.V.V. Iyer, who constantly motivates me to write books. Thanks again to all of you!

Subramanian (Subbu) Sivaramakrishnan
Associate Professor, Department of Marketing
I. H. Asper School of Business
University of Manitoba

Chapter 1 | Defining Marketing for the 21st Century

Chapter 2 | Developing Marketing Strategies and Plans

In This Chapter, We Will Address the Following **Questions**

1. Why is marketing important?

2. What is the scope of marketing?

3. What are some core marketing concepts?

4. How has marketing management changed in recent years?

5. What are the tasks necessary for successful marketing management?

The Dairy Farmers of Canada used an unusual marketing campaign to generate interest among youngsters in an otherwise boring product.

Defining Marketing for the 21st Century

Formally or informally, people and organizations engage in a vast number of activities we could call marketing. Good marketing has become increasingly vital for success. But what constitutes good marketing and what can be marketed are constantly evolving and changing. Even many commodity products require marketing.

Effective marketing can take a relatively uninteresting mainstream product and make it attention grabbing and exciting for its intended target market. Take, for example, the campaign launched by the Dairy Farmers of Canada (DFC), a national organization representing over 13 000 dairy farms committed to supplying nutritious, high-quality 100 percent Canadian milk. Recently, the DFC has been trying to get teenagers more interested in milk with its "Get a Load of Milk" campaign specifically targeted toward the teen market. The initiatives range from Facebook advertisements, to over a hundred different quirky five-second commercials, to the first ever 3-D advertising campaign in Canada.

A main component of the DFC campaign is its funky www.getaloadofmilk.ca website, an animated and interactive portal designed with the youngster in mind. The website includes teen-friendly features such as free downloads from the iTunes store, cell phone and iPod apps, a host of YouTube videos, contests to win a trip to a Marvel red carpet event, and online games. Features such as these particularly encourage teens and tweens to visit the website and also convey a message that "milk is cool," an idea not commonly held by these age groups.

The Facebook advertisements specifically target Canadian teenagers, inviting them to download an application that emits a range of goofy "moos" when a little button is clicked. The DFC also organized the "Great Canadian Moo Contest" on June 3, 2009, to set a world record for the most moos clicked in a 24-hour period. The campaign went viral and over a million moos were generated, making the contest a resounding success.

With some research and lots of creative thinking, the DFC has taken milk, a simple product that many would consider boring, and turned it into something fun and exciting. The DFC has geared its "Get a Load of Milk" campaign to the intended teenage market ingeniously, fetching it the 2009 International Milk Promotions Trophy—a worldwide award given to the best campaign for a dairy product.[1]

Good marketing is no accident, but a result of careful planning and execution using state-of-the-art tools and techniques. It becomes both an art and a science as marketers strive to find creative new solutions to often-complex challenges amid profound changes in the twenty-first-century marketing environment. In this book, we describe how top marketers balance discipline and imagination to address these new marketing realities. In the first chapter, we lay the foundation by reviewing important marketing concepts, tools, frameworks, and issues.

THE IMPORTANCE OF MARKETING

The first decade of the twenty-first century challenged firms to prosper financially and even to survive in the face of an unforgiving economic environment. Marketing is playing a key role in addressing those challenges. Finance, operations, accounting, and other business functions won't really matter without sufficient demand for products and services so that the firm can make a profit. In other words, there must be a top line for there to be a bottom line. Thus, financial success often depends on marketing ability.

Marketing's broader importance extends to society as a whole. Marketing has helped introduce and gain acceptance of new products that have eased or enriched people's lives. It can inspire enhancements in existing products as marketers innovate to improve their position in the marketplace. Successful marketing builds demand for products and services, which, in turn, creates jobs. By contributing to the bottom line, successful marketing also allows firms to more fully engage in socially responsible activities.[2]

CEOs recognize the role of marketing in building strong brands and a loyal customer base, intangible assets that contribute heavily to the value of a firm. Consumer goods makers, health-care insurers, non-profit organizations, and industrial product manufacturers all trumpet their latest marketing achievements. Many companies now have a chief marketing officer (CMO) to put marketing on a more equal footing with other C-level executives, such as the chief financial officer (CFO) or chief information officer (CIO).[3]

Making the right marketing decisions isn't always easy. One survey of more than a thousand senior marketing and sales executives revealed that although 83 percent felt that marketing and sales capabilities were a top priority for their organization's success, in rating their actual marketing effectiveness only 6 percent felt that they were doing an "extremely good" job.[4]

Marketers must decide what features to design into a new product or service; what prices to set; where to sell products or offer services; and how much to spend on advertising, sales, the Internet, or mobile marketing. They must make those decisions in an Internet-fuelled environment where consumers, competition, technology, and economic forces change rapidly, and the consequences of the marketer's words and actions can quickly multiply.

Domino's

When two employees in Conover, North Carolina, posted a YouTube video showing themselves preparing sandwiches while putting cheese up their noses and violating other health-code standards, Domino's learned an important lesson about PR and brand communications in a modern era. Once it found the employees—who claimed the video was just a gag and the sandwiches were never delivered—the company fired them. In just a few days, however, there had been more than a million downloads of the video and a wave of negative publicity. When research showed that perception of quality for the brand had turned from positive to negative in that short time, the firm aggressively took action through social media such as Twitter and YouTube.[5]

As Domino's learned, in an era of connectivity, it is important to respond swiftly and decisively. While marketers were coming to grips with this increasingly wired world, the economic recession of 2008–2009 brought budget cuts and intense pressure from senior management to make every marketing dollar count. More than ever, marketers need to understand and adapt to the latest marketplace developments. At greatest risk are firms that fail to carefully monitor their customers and competitors; to continuously improve their value offerings and marketing strategies; or to satisfy their employees, stockholders, suppliers, and channel partners in the process.

Skillful marketing is a never-ending pursuit. Consider how some top firms drive business:

- In an attempt to draw customers away from competitors Tim Hortons and Starbucks, McDonald's Canada, during certain weeks, has been offering customers free Premium Roast Coffee, with no purchase necessary.
- eBay promoted its "Let's Make a Daily Deal" holiday promotion by recreating the famous 1970s TV game show *Let's Make a Deal* in Times Square, adding an online component so people outside New York City could play.
- Johnson & Johnson launched BabyCenter.com to help new parents. Its success is thought to have contributed to subscription slumps experienced by parenting magazines.

Good marketers are always seeking new ways to satisfy customers and beat competition.[6]

THE SCOPE OF MARKETING

To prepare to be a marketer, you need to understand what marketing is, how it works, who does it, and what is marketed.

What Is Marketing?

Marketing is about identifying and meeting human and social needs. One of the shortest good definitions of marketing is "meeting needs profitably." When eBay recognized that people were unable to locate some of the items they desired most, it created an online auction clearing house. When IKEA noticed that people wanted good furnishings at substantially lower prices, it created knockdown furniture. These two firms demonstrated marketing savvy and turned a private or social need into a profitable business opportunity.

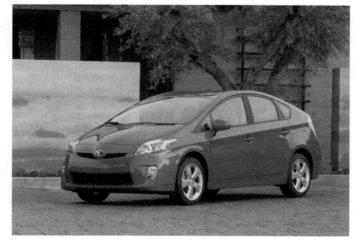

The Toyota Prius has been successful because it was developed based on careful study of consumers' needs and wants.

The American Marketing Association offers the following formal definition: *Marketing is the activity, set of institutions, and processes for creating, communicating, delivering, and exchanging offerings that have value for customers, clients, partners, and society at large.*[7] Coping with these exchange processes calls for a considerable amount of work and skill. *Marketing management* takes place when at least one party to a potential exchange thinks about the means of achieving desired responses from other parties. Thus we see **marketing management** as *the art and science of choosing target markets and getting, keeping, and growing customers through creating, delivering, and communicating superior customer value.*

We can distinguish between a social and a managerial definition of marketing. A social definition shows the role marketing plays in society; for example, one marketer has said that marketing's role is to "deliver a higher standard of living." Here is a social definition that serves our purpose: *Marketing is a societal process by which individuals and groups obtain what they need and want through creating, offering, and freely exchanging products and services of value with others.*

Managers sometimes think of marketing as "the art of selling products," but many people are surprised when they hear that selling is *not* the most important part of marketing! Selling is only the tip of the marketing iceberg. Peter Drucker, a leading management theorist, puts it this way:

> There will always, one can assume, be need for some selling. But the aim of marketing is to make selling superfluous. The aim of marketing is to know and understand the customer so well that the product or service fits him and sells itself. Ideally, marketing should result in a customer who is ready to buy. All that should be needed then is to make the product or service available.[8]

When Nintendo designed its Wii game system, when Canon launched its ELPH digital camera line, and when Toyota introduced its Prius hybrid automobile, these manufacturers were swamped with orders because they had designed the right product, based on doing careful marketing homework.

What Is Marketed?

Marketers market ten main types of entities: goods, services, events, experiences, persons, places, properties, organizations, information, and ideas. Let's take a quick look at these categories.

GOODS Physical goods constitute the bulk of most countries' production and marketing efforts. For example, despite Canada's history as a resource-based economy, primary industries (agriculture, fishing, forestry, hunting, mining, oil and gas extraction) constituted only 6.5 percent of the gross domestic product (GDP) in 2010 while manufacturing made up 12.9 percent of GDP.[9] Each year, companies market billions of fresh, canned, bagged, and frozen food products and millions of cars, refrigerators, televisions, machines, and other mainstays of a modern economy.

SERVICES As economies advance, a growing proportion of their activities focuses on the production of services. The Canadian economy today produces a 72:28 services-to-goods mix.[10] Services include the work of airlines, hotels, car rental firms, health-care institutions, barbers and beauticians, maintenance and repair people, accountants, bankers, lawyers, engineers, software programmers, and management consultants. Many market offerings mix goods and services, such as restaurants and airlines.

EVENTS Marketers promote time-based events, such as major trade shows, artistic performances, and company anniversaries. Global sporting events such as the Olympics and the World Cup are promoted aggressively to both companies and fans.

EXPERIENCES By orchestrating several services and goods, a firm can create, stage, and market experiences. Walt Disney World's Magic Kingdom allows customers to visit a fairy kingdom, a pirate ship, or a haunted house. There is also a market for customized experiences, such as a week at a hockey camp with retired hockey greats, a four-day rock-and-roll fantasy camp, or a climb up Mount Everest.[11]

PERSONS Artists, musicians, CEOs, physicians, high-profile lawyers and financiers, and other professionals all get help from celebrity marketers.[12] Some people have done a masterful job of marketing themselves—David Beckham, Oprah Winfrey, and the Rolling Stones. Management consultant Tom Peters, a master at self-branding, has advised each person to become a "brand."

PLACES Cities, provinces, regions, and whole nations compete to attract tourists, residents, factories, and company headquarters.[13] Place marketers include economic development specialists, real estate agents, commercial banks, local business associations, and advertising and public relations agencies. The Las Vegas Convention & Visitors Authority succeeded with its provocative ad campaign, "What Happens Here, Stays Here," portraying Las Vegas as "an adult playground." In the recession of 2008, however, convention attendance declined. Concerned about its potentially out-of-step racy reputation, the authority took out a full-page *BusinessWeek* ad to defend its ability to host serious business meetings.[14] Unfortunately, the 2009 summer box office blockbuster *The Hangover,* set in a debauched Las Vegas, likely did not help the city position itself as a choice business and tourist destination. By contrast, the Government of British Columbia was able to piggyback on the popularity of the 2010 Winter Olympics to build tourism in the province.

Government of British Columbia

In 2010, while advertisements for the Vancouver Olympics graced television screens, newspapers, webpages, and promotional material across the world, the Government of British Columbia saw the opportunity to promote tourism in the province. Pairing scenes of British Columbia with home-grown celebrities such as actor Michael J. Fox, actress Kim Cattrall of *Sex and the City,* singer Sarah McLachlan, NBA icon Steve Nash, and actor Eric McCormack, the "You Gotta Be Here" campaign attempted to showcase the natural beauty and opportunities in the province. Pairing the advertisements with the Olympic Games resulted in an estimated 1 billion views of the 30-second TV commercial and over 200 million hits for the online version, creating a widespread awareness of the awesome tourism attractions British Columbia has to offer.[15]

PROPERTIES Properties are intangible rights of ownership to either real property (real estate) or financial property (stocks and bonds). They are bought and sold, and these exchanges require marketing. Real estate agents work for property owners or sellers, or they buy and sell residential or commercial real estate. Investment companies and banks market securities to both institutional and individual investors.

Michael J. Fox has been instrumental in promoting tourism in Canada.

ORGANIZATIONS Organizations work to build a strong, favourable, and unique **image** in the minds of their target publics. In the United Kingdom, Tesco's "Every Little Helps" marketing program reflects the food marketer's attention to detail in everything it does, within the store and in the community and environment. The campaign has vaulted Tesco to the top of the U.K. supermarket chain industry. Universities, museums, performing arts organizations, corporations, and nonprofits all use marketing to boost their public images and compete for audiences and funds.

INFORMATION The production, packaging, and distribution of information are major industries.[16] Information is essentially what books, schools, and universities produce, market, and distribute at a price to parents, students, and communities. The former CEO of Siemens Medical Solutions USA, Tom McCausland, says, "[our product] is not necessarily an X-ray or an MRI, but information. Our business is really health care information technology, and our end product is really an electronic patient record: information on lab tests, pathology, and drugs as well as voice dictation."[17]

IDEAS Every market offering includes a basic idea. Charles Revson of Revlon once observed, "In the factory we make cosmetics; in the drugstore we sell hope." Products and services are platforms for delivering some idea or benefit. Social marketers are busy promoting such ideas as "Friends Don't Let Friends Drive Drunk" and "A Mind Is a Terrible Thing to Waste."

Who Markets?

MARKETERS AND PROSPECTS A **marketer** is someone who seeks a response—attention, a purchase, a vote, a donation—from another party, called the **prospect**. If two parties are seeking to sell something to each other, we call them both marketers.

Marketers are skilled at stimulating demand for their products, but that's a limited view of what they do. Just as production and logistics professionals are responsible for supply management, marketers are responsible for demand management. They seek to influence the level, timing, and composition of demand to meet the organization's objectives. Eight demand states are possible:

1. **Negative demand**—Consumers dislike the product and may even pay to avoid it.

2. **Nonexistent demand**—Consumers may be unaware of or uninterested in the product.

3. **Latent demand**—Consumers may share a strong need that cannot be satisfied by an existing product.

4. **Declining demand**—Consumers begin to buy the product less frequently or not at all.

5. **Irregular demand**—Consumer purchases vary on a seasonal, monthly, weekly, daily, or even hourly basis.

6. **Full demand**—Consumers are adequately buying all products put into the marketplace.

7. **Overfull demand**—More consumers would like to buy the product than can be satisfied.

8. **Unwholesome demand**—Consumers may be attracted to products that have undesirable social consequences.

In each case, marketers must identify the underlying cause(s) of the demand state and determine a plan of action to shift demand to a more desired state.

MARKETS Traditionally, a market was a physical place where buyers and sellers gathered to buy and sell goods. Economists describe a market as a collection of buyers and sellers who transact over a particular product or product class (such as the housing market or the grain market).

Five basic markets and their connecting flows are shown in Figure 1.1. Manufacturers go to resource markets (raw material markets, labour markets, money markets); buy resources and turn them into goods and services; and sell finished products to intermediaries, who sell them to consumers. Consumers sell their labour and receive money with which they pay for goods and services. The government collects tax revenues to buy goods from resource, manufacturer, and intermediary markets and uses these goods and services to provide public services. Each nation's economy and the global economy consist of interacting sets of markets linked through exchange processes.

Marketers use the term **market** to cover various groupings of customers. They view sellers as constituting the industry and buyers as constituting the market. They talk about need markets (the diet-seeking market), product markets (the shoe market), demographic markets (the youth market), and geographic markets (the Chinese market); or they extend the concept to cover voter markets, labour markets, and donor markets, for instance.

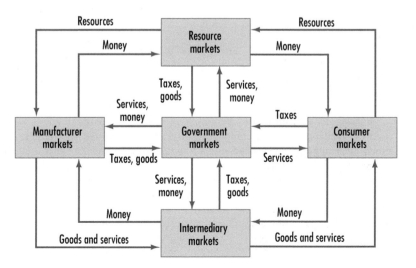

FIGURE 1.1

Structures of Flows in a Modern Exchange Economy

FIGURE 1.2

A Simple Marketing System

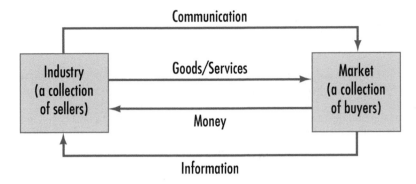

Figure 1.2 shows the relationship between the industry and the market. Sellers and buyers are connected by four flows. Sellers send goods and services and communications such as ads and direct mail to the market; in return, they receive money and information such as customer attitudes and sales data. The inner loop shows an exchange of money for goods and services; the outer loop shows an exchange of information.

KEY CUSTOMER MARKETS Consider the following key customer markets: consumer, business, global, and nonprofit and governmental.

Consumer Markets Companies selling mass consumer goods and services, such as juices, cosmetics, athletic shoes, and air travel, spend a great deal of time establishing a strong **brand image** by developing a superior product and packaging, ensuring its availability, and backing it with engaging communications and reliable service.

Business Markets Companies selling business goods and services often face well-informed professional buyers skilled at evaluating competitive offerings. Business buyers buy goods to make or resell a product to others at a profit. Business marketers must demonstrate how their products will help achieve higher revenue or lower costs. Advertising can play a role, but the sales force, the price, and the company's reputation may play a greater one.

Global Markets Companies in the global marketplace must decide which countries to enter; how to enter each country (as an exporter, licensor, joint venture partner, contract manufacturer, or solo manufacturer); how to adapt product and service features to each country; how to price products in each country; and how to design communications for different cultures. They face different requirements for buying and disposing of property; cultural, language, legal, and political differences; and currency fluctuations. Yet the payoff can be huge.

Nonprofit and Governmental Markets Companies selling to nonprofit organizations with limited purchasing power, such as churches, universities, charitable organizations, and government agencies, need to price carefully. Lower selling prices affect the features and quality the seller can build into the offering. Much government purchasing calls for bids, and buyers often focus on practical solutions and favour the lowest bid in the absence of extenuating factors.[18]

MARKETPLACES, MARKETSPACES, AND METAMARKETS The *marketplace* is physical, such as a store you shop in; the *marketspace* is digital, as when you shop on the Internet.[19] Northwestern University's Mohan Sawhney has proposed the concept of a *metamarket* to describe a cluster of complementary products and services closely related in the minds of consumers, but spread across a diverse set of industries.

Metamarkets are the result of marketers packaging a system that simplifies carrying out these related product–service activities. The automobile metamarket consists of automobile manufacturers, new and used car dealers, financing companies, insurance companies, mechanics, spare parts dealers, service shops, auto magazines, classified auto ads in newspapers, and auto sites on the Internet.

A car buyer will engage many parts of this metamarket, creating an opportunity for *metamediaries* to assist him or her in moving seamlessly through these parts. Edmunds (www.edmunds.com) lets a car buyer find the stated features and prices of different automobiles and easily click to other sites to search for the lowest-price dealer for financing, accessories, and used cars. Metamediaries also serve other metamarkets, such as home ownership, parenting and baby care, and weddings.[20]

CORE MARKETING CONCEPTS

To understand the marketing function, we need to understand the following core set of concepts.

Needs, Wants, and Demands

Needs are basic human requirements, such as air, food, water, clothing, and shelter. Humans also have strong needs for recreation, education, and entertainment. These needs become *wants* when they are directed to specific objects that might satisfy the need. A Canadian consumer needs food but may want to eat pancakes with maple syrup. A person in Afghanistan needs food but may want rice, lamb, and carrots. Wants are shaped by our society.

Demands are wants for specific products backed by an ability to pay. Many people want a Mercedes; only a few are able to buy one. Companies must measure not only how many people want their product, but also how many are willing and able to buy it.

These distinctions shed light on the frequent criticism that "marketers create needs" or "marketers get people to buy things they don't want." Marketers do not create needs: needs pre-exist marketers. Marketers, along with other societal factors, influence wants. They might promote the idea that a Mercedes would satisfy a person's need for social status. They do not, however, create the need for social status.

Some customers have needs of which they are not fully conscious or that they cannot articulate. What does it mean when the customer asks for a "powerful" lawn mower or a "peaceful" hotel? The marketer must probe further. We can distinguish five types of needs:

1. Stated needs (The customer wants an inexpensive car.)

2. Real needs (The customer wants a car whose operating cost, not initial price, is low.)

3. Unstated needs (The customer expects good service from the dealer.)

4. Delight needs (The customer would like the dealer to include an onboard GPS navigation system.)

5. Secret needs (The customer wants friends to see him or her as a savvy consumer.)

Responding only to the stated need may shortchange the customer.[21] Consumers did not know much about cell phones when they were first introduced, and Nokia and Ericsson fought to shape consumer perceptions of them. To gain an edge, companies must help customers learn what they want.

Target Markets, Positioning, and Segmentation

Not everyone likes the same cereal, restaurant, university, or movie. Therefore, marketers start by dividing the market into segments. By examining demographic, psychographic, and behavioural differences among buyers, marketers identify and profile distinct groups of buyers who might prefer or require varying product and service mixes.

After identifying market segments, the marketer decides which present the greatest opportunities—which are the *target markets,* as exemplified by the law firm MNP LLP.

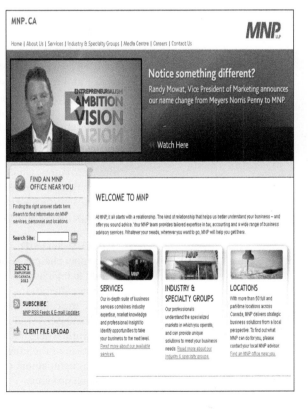

Even law firms such as MNP LLP segment markets and target certain segments.

MNP LLP

Established in 1945, Calgary-based MNP LLP has grown to be the seventh-largest accounting firm in Canada, with over 50 offices across the country. By establishing close relationships with clients and providing services designed around each client's needs, the firm continues to be successful. MNP LLP offers personalized services and solutions in a variety of areas, such as insurance, accounting, corporate finance, tax, risk management, and investigative services. The firm's success relies on the ability to provide specialized services to specific market segments, such as Hutterite colonies, Aboriginal communities, agri-businesses, credit unions, and the forestry sector. MNP LLP markets itself by highlighting the benefit of working with a firm that can tailor its services to the client's unique needs.[22]

Offerings and Brands

Companies address customer needs by putting forth a **value proposition**, a set of benefits that satisfy those needs. The intangible value proposition is made physical by an *offering*, which can be a combination of products, services, information, and experiences.

A *brand* is an offering from a known source. A brand name such as McDonald's carries many associations in people's minds that make up its image: hamburgers, cleanliness, convenience, courteous service, and golden arches. All companies strive to build a brand image with as many strong, favourable, and unique brand associations as possible. For example, lululemon has been successful in building a brand that signifies high-quality, trendy activewear.

lululemon

British Columbia–based lululemon athletica opened its first store in Vancouver in 1998 and has since grown to over 100 store locations in Canada, the United States, Hong Kong, and Australia. The company is focused on creating comfortable yoga-inspired activewear, and many innovative marketing tactics have driven lululemon to reap significant financial gains in just a few years. With a cute brand name, recognizable logo, and attractive shopping bags (decorated with inspiring, attention-grabbing one-liners), lululemon seems to have found a way to market its unique product line, attract new customers, and retain existing customers while offering quality products at moderately high prices. The success of the company is evident in its financial performance, with revenues of over $700 million in 2010, nearly 400 percent of what it made four years prior.[23]

Value and Satisfaction

The buyer chooses the offerings he or she perceives to deliver the most *value,* the sum of the tangible and intangible benefits and costs to him or her. Value, a central marketing concept, is primarily a combination of quality, service, and price (qsp), called the *customer value triad*. Value perceptions increase with quality and service but decrease with price.

We can think of marketing as the identification, creation, communication, delivery, and monitoring of customer value. *Satisfaction* reflects a person's judgment of a product's perceived performance in relationship to expectations. If the performance falls short of expectations, the customer is disappointed. If it matches expectations, the customer is satisfied. If it exceeds them, the customer is delighted.

Marketing Channels

To reach a target market, the marketer uses three kinds of marketing channels. *Communication channels* deliver and receive messages from target buyers and include newspapers, magazines, radio, television, mail, telephone, billboards, posters, flyers, CDs, and the Internet. Beyond these, firms communicate through the look of their retail stores and websites and other media. Marketers are increasingly adding dialogue channels such as email, blogs, and toll-free numbers to familiar monologue channels such as ads.

The marketer uses *distribution channels* to display, sell, or deliver the physical product or service to the buyer or user. These channels may be direct via the Internet, mail, cell phone, or telephone, or indirect with distributors, wholesalers, retailers, and agents as intermediaries.

To carry out **transactions** with potential buyers, the marketer also uses *service channels* that include warehouses, transportation companies, banks, and insurance companies. Marketers clearly face a design challenge in choosing the best mix of communication, distribution, and service channels for their offerings.

Supply Chain

The supply chain is a longer channel stretching from raw materials to components to finished products carried to final buyers. The supply chain for coffee may start with Ethiopian farmers who plant, tend, and pick the coffee beans, selling their harvest to wholesalers or perhaps a Fair Trade co-operative. If sold through the co-operative, the coffee is washed, dried, and packaged for shipment by an Alternative Trading Organization (ATO) that pays a minimum of $1.26 a pound. The ATO transports the coffee to another part of the world where the ATO can sell it directly or via retail channels. Each company captures only a certain percentage of the total value generated by the supply chain's value-delivery system. When a company acquires competitors or expands upstream or downstream, its aim is to capture a higher percentage of supply chain value.

Competition

Competition includes all the actual and potential rival offerings and substitutes a buyer might consider. A consumer looking for entertainment after dinner on a Friday can go to a movie theatre owned by Cineplex or its rival, watch a movie on cable or satellite either through its regular programming or pay-per-view, rent a movie at Rogers Video, buy it from a movie retailer, or watch it online through a service such as Netflix. Or the consumer may choose to go to a hockey game, ballet, opera, concert, or casino. Clearly, Cineplex Entertainment would be thinking too narrowly about its competition if it thought only of other movie theatres. In the long run, Cineplex is more likely to be hurt by substitutes than by other movie theatres.

Marketing Environment

The marketing environment consists of the task environment and the broad environment. The *task environment* includes the actors engaged in producing, distributing, and promoting the offering. These are the company, suppliers, distributors, dealers, and target customers. In the supplier group are material suppliers and service suppliers, such as marketing research agencies, advertising agencies, banking and insurance companies, transportation companies, and telecommunications companies. Distributors and dealers include agents, brokers, manufacturer representatives, and others who facilitate finding and selling to customers.

The *broad environment* consists of six components: demographic environment, economic environment, social-cultural environment, natural environment, technological environment, and political-legal environment. Marketers must pay close attention to the trends and developments in these and adjust their marketing strategies as needed. Constantly emerging are new opportunities that await the right marketing savvy and ingenuity. Here are two good examples.

TerraCycle

After finding that some of his friend's indoor herbal plants flourished with a fertilizer made by feeding table scraps to red wiggler worms in a composting bin, TerraCycle founder Tom Szaky came up with an idea for a business. TerraCycle is devoted to "upcycling," finding new ways to use nonrecyclable waste materials. Plastic bags become sturdy totes, yogurt cups become plant holders, and cookie wrappers become notebook covers, all distributed by major retailers such as Home Depot, Whole Foods, and Walmart. The firm also has partnerships with Kraft, Target, Honest Tea, Stonyfield Farm, and others. Schools, churches, wineries, and nonprofits provide space to store donated used bottles, corks, and candy wrappers. For each item collected, TerraCycle makes a donation to a charity (typically 2 cents).[24]

Allrecipes.com

Allrecipes.com has cooked up a winning online formula by blending recipes posted by individuals with those provided by corporations promoting their own products such as Kraft cheese or Campbell's soup. After almost a 50 percent increase in site visits and unique visitors in 2009, the website overtook the Food Network's recipe site as the market leader. With tens of thousands of posted recipes, Allrecipes.com thrives on people's willingness to share recipes and the satisfaction they feel if their recipe becomes popular with others. The viral nature of the site's success is obvious—it doesn't spend any money on advertising! Users tend to think of it as "their" site—not something with a big company behind it.[25]

THE NEW MARKETING REALITIES

We can say with some confidence that the marketplace isn't what it used to be. It is dramatically different from what it was even ten years ago.

Major Societal Forces

Today, major and sometimes interlinking societal forces have created new marketing behaviours, opportunities, and challenges. Here are 12 key forces:

- *Network information technology.* The digital revolution has created an Information Age that promises to lead to more accurate levels of production, more targeted communications, and more relevant pricing.

- *Globalization.* Technological advances in transportation, shipping, and communication have made it easier for companies to market in, and consumers to buy in, almost any country in the world. International travel has continued to grow as more people work and play in other countries.

- *Deregulation.* Many countries have deregulated industries to create greater competition and growth opportunities. Canada has been among these countries and has deregulated industries such as airlines, natural gas, and post-secondary education.

- *Privatization.* Many countries have converted public companies to private ownership and management to increase their efficiency, such as the massive telecom company Telefónica CTC in Chile and the international airline British Airways in the United Kingdom.

- *Heightened competition.* Intense competition among domestic and foreign brands raises marketing costs and shrinks profit margins. Brand manufacturers are further buffeted by powerful retailers that market their own store brands. Many strong brands have become megabrands and extend into a wide variety of related product categories, presenting a significant competitive threat.

- *Industry convergence.* Industry boundaries are blurring as companies recognize new opportunities at the intersection of two or more industries. The computing and consumer electronics industries are converging, for example, as Apple, Sony, and Samsung release a stream of entertainment devices from MP3 players to plasma TVs and camcorders. Digital technology fuels this massive convergence.[26]

- *Retail transformation.* Store-based retailers face competition from catalogue houses; direct-mail firms; newspaper, magazine, and TV direct-to-customer ads; home shopping TV; and e-commerce. In response, entrepreneurial retailers are building entertainment into their stores with coffee bars, demonstrations, and performances, marketing an experience rather than a product assortment, as in the new Apple Stores that have opened throughout Canada.

- *Disintermediation.* The amazing success of early dot-coms such as AOL, Amazon.com, Yahoo!, eBay, and E*TRADE created *disintermediation* in the delivery of products and services by intervening in the traditional flow of goods through distribution channels. These firms struck terror into the hearts of established manufacturers and retailers. In response, traditional companies engaged in *reintermediation* and became "**brick-and-click**" retailers, adding online services to their offerings. Some became stronger contenders than **pure-click** firms, because the brick-and-click retailers had a larger pool of resources to work with and established brand names.

Modern retailers increasingly emphasize in-store experiences for their customers, as does Bass Pro Shops.

- *Consumer buying power.* In part, due to disintermediation via the Internet, consumers have substantially increased their buying power. From the home, office, or cell phone, they can compare product prices and features and order goods online from anywhere in the world 24 hours a day, 7 days a week, bypassing limited local offerings and realizing significant price savings. Even business buyers can run a *reverse auction* in which sellers compete to capture their business. They can readily join others to aggregate their purchases and achieve deeper volume discounts.

- *Consumer information.* Consumers can collect information in as much breadth and depth as they want about practically anything. They can access online encyclopedias, dictionaries, medical information, movie ratings, consumer reports, newspapers, and other information sources in many languages from anywhere in the world. Personal connections and user-generated content thrive on social media such as Facebook, Flickr (photos), Digg (news stories), Wikipedia (encyclopedia), and YouTube (videos).[27] Social networking sites—such as Dogster for dog lovers, TripAdvisor for ardent travellers, and Moterus for bikers—bring together consumers with a common interest. At www.edmunds.com auto enthusiasts talk about chrome rims, the latest BMW model, and where to find a great local mechanic.[28]

- *Consumer participation.* Consumers have found an amplified voice to influence peer and public opinion. In recognition, companies are inviting them to participate in designing and even marketing offerings to heighten their sense of connection and ownership. Consumers see their favourite companies as workshops from which they can draw out the offerings they want.

■ *Consumer resistance.* Many customers today feel there are fewer real product differences, so they show less brand loyalty and become more price- and quality-sensitive in their search for value, and less tolerant of undesired marketing. A Yankelovich study found record levels of marketing resistance from consumers; the majority reported negative opinions about marketing and advertising and said they avoid products they feel are overmarketed.[29]

New Company Capabilities

These major societal forces create complex challenges for marketers, but they have also generated a new set of capabilities to help companies cope and respond:

■ *Marketers can use the Internet as a powerful information and sales channel.* The Internet augments marketers' geographical reach to inform customers and promote products worldwide. A website can list products and services, history, business philosophy, job opportunities, and other information of interest. In 2006, a Montgomery, Alabama, flea market gained national popularity when owner Sammy Stephens's rap-style advertisement spread virally through the Internet. Created for $1500, the advertisement was viewed more than 100 000 times on YouTube and landed Stephens on *The Ellen DeGeneres Show*. Stephens now sells T-shirts, ring tones, and other **branded** merchandise through his website; advises retailers about advertising; and hosts hundreds of visitors from all over the world at his store each month.[30]

■ *Marketers can collect fuller and richer information about markets, customers, prospects, and competitors.* Marketers can conduct fresh marketing research by using the Internet to arrange focus groups, send out questionnaires, and gather primary data in several other ways. They can assemble information about individual customers' purchases, preferences, demographics, and profitability. The drugstore chain CVS uses loyalty-card data to better understand what consumers purchase, the frequency of store visits, and other buying preferences. Its ExtraCare program netted an extra 30 million shoppers and $12 billion a year in revenue across 4000 stores.[31]

■ *Marketers can tap into social media to amplify their brand message.* Marketers can feed information and updates to consumers via blogs and other postings, support online communities, and create their own stops on the Internet superhighway. Dell Corporation's @DellOutlet Twitter account has more than 600 000 followers. Between June 2007 and June 2009, Dell took in more than $2 million in revenue from coupons provided through Twitter, and another $1 million from people who started at Twitter and went on to buy a new computer on the company's website.[32]

■ *Marketers can facilitate and speed external communication among customers.* Marketers can also create or benefit from online and offline buzz through brand advocates and user communities. Word-of-mouth marketing agency BzzAgent has assembled a nationwide volunteer army of 600 000 consumers who join promotional programs for products and services they deem worth talking about.[33] In 2005, Dunkin' Donuts hired BzzAgent to help launch a new espresso beverage, Latte Lite. Three thousand trained volunteers (called BzzAgents) in 12 test markets experienced the Latte Lite, formed their opinions, engaged in natural conversations about the product, and reported back to BzzAgent via the company's reporting interface. After four weeks, product sales had increased by more than 15 percent in test markets.[34]

■ *Marketers can send ads, coupons, samples, and information to customers who have requested them or given the company permission to send them.* Microtarget marketing and two-way communication are easier thanks to the proliferation of special-interest magazines, TV channels, and Internet newsgroups. Extranets linking suppliers and distributors let firms send and receive information, place orders, and make payments more efficiently. The company can also interact with each customer individually to personalize messages, services, and the relationship.

■ *Marketers can reach consumers on the move with mobile marketing.* Using GPS technology, marketers can pinpoint consumers' exact location and send them messages at the mall with coupons good only that day, a reminder of an item on their wish list, and a relevant perk (buy this book today and get a free coffee at the bookstore's coffee shop). Location-based advertising is attractive because it reaches consumers closer to the point of sale. Firms can also advertise on video iPods and reach consumers on their cell phones through mobile marketing.[35]

■ *Companies can make and sell individually differentiated goods.* Thanks to advances in factory customization, computer technology, and database marketing software, customers can buy M&M candies, TABASCO jugs, or Maker's Mark bottles with their names on them; Wheaties boxes or Jones Soda cans with their picture on the front; and Heinz ketchup bottles with customized messages.[36] BMW's technology allows buyers to design their own car models from among 350 variations, with 500 options, 90 exterior colours, and 170 trims. The company claims that 80 percent of the cars bought in Europe and up to 30 percent bought in the United States are built to order.

- *Companies can improve purchasing, recruiting, training, and internal and external communications.* Firms can recruit new employees online, and many have Internet training products for their employees, dealers, and agents. Retailer Patagonia has joined Walt Disney, General Motors, and McDonald's in embracing corporate blogging to communicate with the public and employees. Patagonia's "The Cleanest Line" posts environmental news, reports the results of its sponsored athletes, and posts pictures and descriptions of employees' favourite outdoor locations.[37]

- *Companies can facilitate and speed up internal communication among their employees by using the Internet as a private intranet.* Employees can query one another, seek advice, and download or upload needed information from and to the company's main computer. Seeking a single online employee portal that transcended business units, General Motors launched a platform called mySocrates in 2006, consisting of announcements, news, links, and historical information. GM credits the portal with $17.4 million in cost savings to date.[38]

- *Companies can improve their cost efficiency by skillful use of the Internet.* Corporate buyers can achieve substantial savings by using the Internet to compare sellers' prices and purchase materials at auction, or by posting their own terms in reverse auctions. Companies can improve logistics and operations to reap substantial cost savings while improving accuracy and service quality.

Marketing in Practice

Not surprisingly, these new marketing forces and capabilities have profoundly changed marketing management. In theory, the marketing *planning* process consists of analyzing marketing opportunities, selecting target markets, designing marketing strategies, developing marketing programs, and managing the marketing effort. In practice, however, in the highly competitive marketplaces that are more often the norm, marketing planning is more fluid and is continuously refreshed.

Companies must always move forward with marketing programs, innovate products and services, stay in touch with customer needs, and seek new advantages rather than rely on past strengths. This is especially true of incorporating the Internet into marketing plans. Marketers must try to balance increased spending on search advertising, social media, direct email, and text/SMS marketing efforts with appropriate spending on traditional marketing communications. But they must do so in tough economic times, when accountability has become a top priority and returns on investment are expected from every marketing activity. "Marketing Insight: Marketing in an Age of Turbulence" offers some recommendations for adjusting to new marketing realities.

THE NEW CMO The rapidly changing marketing environment is putting even greater demands on marketing executives. A well-publicized survey revealed that the average CMO tenure at U.S. companies is about 28 months, well below the average tenure of CEOs (54 months) or other C-level positions. One explanation is that the role of marketing—and thus management expectations—varies widely among firms. Harvard's Gail McGovern and John Quelch find tremendous variability in CMO responsibilities and job descriptions.[39]

Another challenge CMOs face is that the success factors for top marketers are many and varied. CMOs must have strong quantitative skills but also well-honed qualitative skills; they must have an independent, entrepreneurial attitude but also work in close harmony with other departments such as sales; and they must capture the voice and point of view of consumers yet have a keen bottom-line understanding of how marketing creates value within their organization.[40] One survey asked 200 senior-level marketing executives which innate and learned qualities were most important; here are their answers:[41]

- Innate Qualities
  - Risk taker
  - Willingness to make decisions
  - Problem-solving ability
  - Change agent
  - Results-oriented

- Learned Qualities
  - Global experience
  - Multichannel expertise
  - Cross-industry experience
  - Digital focus
  - Operational knowledge

Perhaps the most important role for any CMO is to infuse a customer perspective and orientation in business decisions affecting any customer *touch point* (where a customer directly or indirectly interacts with the company in some form). The CMO of lodging franchisor Choice Hotels International, Chris Malone, is responsible for directing virtually all customer-facing efforts for the firm, including the following:[42]

- Directing advertising, loyalty programs, and direct response
- Guiding the company's central reservations systems, including its call centres, website, and relationships with outside travel vendors such as Travelocity and Orbitz
- Heading the company's global group sales efforts with organizations such as AAA, AARP, and professional sports teams

The severe economic recession of 2008–2009 caused marketers to rethink the best practices of management. Philip Kotler and John Caslione see management entering a new Age of Turbulence in which chaos, risk, and uncertainty characterize many industries, markets, and companies. According to them, turbulence is the new normal, punctuated by periodic and intermittent spurts of prosperity and downturn—including extended downturns amounting to recession or even depression. They see many new challenges in the foreseeable future, and unlike in past recessions, there may be no assurance that a return to past management practices would ever be successful again.

According to Kotler and Caslione, marketers should always be ready to activate automatic responses when turbulence whips up and chaos reigns. They recommend marketers keep these eight factors in mind as they create "*chaotics* marketing strategies"

1. *Secure your market share from core customer segments.* This is not a time to get greedy, so get your core customer segments firmly secured, and be prepared to ward off attacks from competitors seeking your most profitable and loyal customers.

2. *Push aggressively for greater market share from competitors.* All companies fight for market share, and in turbulent and chaotic times, many have been weakened. Slashing marketing budgets and sales travel expenses is a sure sign a competitor is buckling under pressure. Push aggressively to add to your core customer segments at the expense of your weakened competitors.

3. *Research customers more now because their needs and wants are in flux.* Everyone is under pressure during times of turbulence and chaos, and all customers—even those in your core segments whom you know so well—are changing. Stay close to them as never before. Research them more than ever. Don't find yourself using old, tried-and-true marketing messages that no longer resonate with them.

4. *Minimally maintain, but seek to increase, your marketing budget.* With your competitors aggressively marketing to your core customers, this is the worst time to think about cutting anything in your marketing budget that targets them. In fact, you need to add to it, or take money away from forays into totally new customer segments. It's time to secure the home front.

5. *Focus on all that's safe and emphasize core values.* When turbulence is scaring everyone in the market, most customers flee to higher ground. They need to feel the safety and security of your company and your products and services. Do everything possible to tell them that continuing to do business with you is safe, and to sell them products and services that keep making them feel safe.

6. *Quickly drop programs that aren't working for you.* Your marketing budgets will always be scrutinized, in good times and bad times. If anyone is to cut one of your programs, let it be you, before anyone else spots any ineffective ones. If you're not watching, rest assured someone else is, including your peers whose budgets couldn't be protected from the axe.

7. *Don't discount your best brands.* Discounting your established and most successful brands tells the market two things: your prices were too high before, and your products won't be worth the price in the future once the discounts are gone. If you want to appeal to more frugal customers, create a new brand with lower prices. This lets value-conscious customers stay close to you, without alienating those still willing to pay for your higher-priced brands. Once the turbulence subsides, you may consider discontinuing the value product line—or not.

8. *Save the strong; lose the weak.* In turbulent markets, your strongest brands and products must become even stronger. There's no time or money to be wasted on marginal brands or products that lack strong value propositions and a solid customer base. Appeal to safety and value to reinforce strong brands and product and service offerings. Remember, your brands can never be strong enough, especially against the waves of a turbulent economy.

Source: Based on Philip Kotler and John A. Caslione, *Chaotics: The Business of Managing and Marketing in the Age of Turbulence* (New York: AMACOM, 2009), pp. 151–153.

MARKETING IN THE ORGANIZATION Although an effective CMO is crucial, increasingly marketing is *not* done by only the marketing department. Because marketing must affect every aspect of the customer experience, marketers must properly manage all possible touch points—store layouts, package designs, product functions, employee training, and shipping and logistics methods. Marketing must also be influential in key general management activities, such as product innovation and new-business development. To create a strong marketing organization, marketers must think like executives in other departments, and executives in other departments must think more like marketers.[43]

As the late David Packard of Hewlett-Packard observed, "Marketing is far too important to leave to the marketing department." Companies now know that every employee has an impact on the customer and must see the customer as the source of the company's prosperity. So they're beginning to emphasize interdepartmental teamwork to manage key processes. They're also emphasizing the smooth management of core business processes, such as new-product realization, customer acquisition and retention, and order fulfillment.

COMPANY ORIENTATION TOWARD THE MARKETPLACE

Given these new marketing realities, what philosophy should guide a company's marketing efforts? Increasingly, marketers operate consistent with the holistic marketing concept. Let's first review the evolution of earlier marketing ideas.

The Production Concept

The **production concept** is one of the oldest concepts in business. It holds that consumers prefer products that are widely available and inexpensive. Managers of production-oriented businesses concentrate on achieving high production efficiency, low costs, and mass distribution. This orientation makes sense in developing countries such as China, where the largest PC manufacturer, Legend (principal owner of Lenovo Group), and domestic appliances giant Haier take advantage of the country's huge and inexpensive labour pool to dominate the market. Marketers also use the production concept when they want to expand the market.[44]

The Product Concept

The **product concept** proposes that consumers favour products offering the most quality, performance, or innovative features. However, managers are sometimes caught in a love affair with their products. They might commit the "better mousetrap" fallacy, believing that a better product will by itself lead people to beat a path to their door. A new or improved product will not necessarily be successful unless it's priced, distributed, advertised, and sold properly.

The Selling Concept

The **selling concept** holds that consumers and businesses, if left alone, won't buy enough of the organization's products. It is practised most aggressively with unsought goods—goods buyers don't normally think of buying, such as insurance and cemetery plots—and when firms with overcapacity aim to sell what they make, rather than make what the market wants. Marketing based on hard selling is risky. It assumes customers coaxed into buying a product not only won't return or bad-mouth it or complain to consumer organizations but might even buy it again.

The Marketing Concept

The **marketing concept** emerged in the mid-1950s[45] as a customer-centred, sense-and-respond philosophy. The job is to find not the right customers for your products, but the right products for your customers. Dell doesn't prepare a perfect computer for its target market. Rather, it provides product platforms on which each person customizes the features he or she desires in the computer.

The marketing concept holds that the key to achieving organizational goals is being more effective than competitors in creating, delivering, and communicating superior customer value to your target markets. Harvard's Theodore Levitt drew a perceptive contrast between the selling and marketing concepts:

> Selling focuses on the needs of the seller; marketing on the needs of the buyer. Selling is preoccupied with the seller's need to convert his product into cash; marketing with the idea of satisfying the needs of the customer by means of the product and the whole cluster of things associated with creating, delivering, and finally consuming it.[46]

Several scholars found that companies embracing this new marketing concept achieved superior performance.[47]

The Holistic Marketing Concept

Without question, the trends and forces that have defined the first decade of the twenty-first century are leading business firms to a new set of beliefs and practices. Today's marketers recognize the need to have a more complete, cohesive approach that goes beyond traditional applications of the marketing concept. "Marketing Memo: Marketing Right and Wrong" suggests where companies go wrong—and how they can get it right—in their marketing.

The **holistic marketing concept** is based on the development, design, and implementation of marketing programs, processes, and activities that recognize their breadth and interdependencies. Holistic marketing acknowledges that everything matters in marketing—and that a broad, integrated perspective is often necessary. Holistic marketing thus recognizes and reconciles the scope and complexities of marketing activities.

Figure 1.3 provides a schematic overview of four broad components characterizing holistic marketing: relationship marketing, integrated marketing, internal marketing, and performance marketing. We'll examine these major themes throughout this book. Successful companies change their marketing with the changes in their marketplace—and marketspace.

Relationship Marketing

Increasingly, a key goal of marketing is to develop deep, enduring relationships with people and organizations that directly or indirectly affect the success of the firm's marketing activities. **Relationship marketing** aims to build mutually satisfying long-term relationships with key constituents in order to earn and retain their business.[48]

Four key constituents for relationship marketing are customers, employees, marketing partners (channels, suppliers, distributors, dealers, agencies), and members of the financial community (shareholders, investors, analysts). Marketers must create prosperity among all these constituents and balance the returns to all key stakeholders. To develop strong relationships with them requires understanding their capabilities and resources, needs, goals, and desires.

The ultimate outcome of relationship marketing is a unique company asset called a **marketing network**, consisting of the company and its supporting stakeholders—customers, employees, suppliers, distributors, retailers, and others—with whom it has built mutually profitable business relationships. The operating principle is simple: build an effective network of relationships with key stakeholders, and profits will follow.[49] Thus, more companies are choosing to own brands rather than physical assets and are subcontracting activities to firms that can do them better and more cheaply, while retaining core activities at home.

Companies are also shaping separate offers, services, and messages to *individual customers,* based on information about past transactions, demographics, psychographics, and media and distribution preferences. By focusing on their most profitable customers, products, and channels, these firms hope to achieve

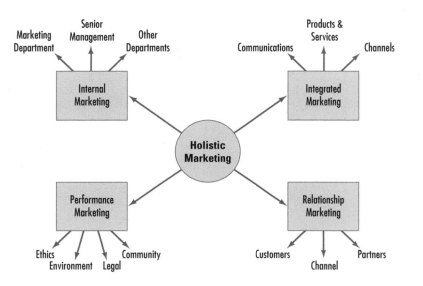

FIGURE 1.3

Holistic Marketing Dimensions

MARKETING **MEMO** | MARKETING RIGHT AND WRONG

The Ten Deadly Sins of Marketing

1. The company is not sufficiently market focused and customer driven.
2. The company does not fully understand its target customers.
3. The company needs to better define and monitor its competitors.
4. The company has not properly managed its relationships with its stakeholders.
5. The company is not good at finding new opportunities.
6. The company's marketing plans and planning process are deficient.
7. The company's product and service policies need tightening.
8. The company's brand-building and communications skills are weak.
9. The company is not well-organized to carry on effective and efficient marketing.
10. The company has not made maximum use of technology.

The Ten Commandments of Marketing

1. The company segments the market, chooses the best segments, and develops a strong position in each chosen segment.
2. The company maps its customers' needs, perceptions, preferences, and behaviour, and motivates its stakeholders to obsess about serving and satisfying the customers.
3. The company knows its major competitors and their strengths and weaknesses.
4. The company builds partners out of its stakeholders and generously rewards them.
5. The company develops systems for identifying opportunities, ranking them, and choosing the best ones.
6. The company manages a marketing planning system that leads to insightful long-term and short-term plans.
7. The company exercises strong control over its product and service mix.
8. The company builds strong brands by using the most cost-effective communication and promotion tools.
9. The company builds marketing leadership and a team spirit among its various departments.
10. The company constantly adds technology that gives it a competitive advantage in the marketplace.

Source: Adapted from Philip Kotler, *Ten Deadly Marketing Sins* (Hoboken, NJ: John Wiley & Sons, 2004), pp. 10, 145–148. Reprinted with permission of John Wiley & Sons, Inc.

---

profitable growth and to capture a larger share of each customer's expenditures by building high customer loyalty. They estimate individual customer lifetime value and design their market offerings and prices to make a profit over the customer's lifetime.

These activities fall under what Columbia Business School professor Larry Selden and his wife and business consulting partner, Yoko Sugiura Selden, call "customer centricity." The Seldens offer the Royal Bank of Canada as an example.

Royal Bank of Canada

Thinking of its business in terms of customer segments rather than product segments, Royal Bank of Canada (RBC) has put each of its roughly 11 million clients into meaningful segments whose profitability it can measure. In the process, it discovered a sizeable subsegment of customers hidden within its broader categories of "wealth preservers" and "wealth accumulators." Dubbed "snowbirds," these individuals spent a number of months each winter in Florida, where they were experiencing difficulties establishing credit as well as missing their Canadian communities, particularly the familiarity of the French-Canadian accent and fluency in French. To meet their unique needs, RBC created a Canadian banking experience in Florida.[50]

Because attracting a new customer may cost five times as much as retaining an existing one, relationship marketing also emphasizes customer retention. Companies build customer share by offering a larger variety of goods to existing customers and training employees in cross-selling and up-selling. Manitoba Telecom Services does that effectively.

Manitoba Telecom Services

Manitoba Telecom Services (MTS) has several competitors for each of the services it provides. In the land line phone, TV, and Internet service, MTS competes primarily with Shaw Communications, which provides all of these services. In the area of cell phone service, there are several national competitors, such as Telus, Rogers, Fido, and Koodo Mobile. MTS competes with companies such as ADT, API, and Chubb in the security and monitoring market. In an attempt to attract and retain the customer, MTS uses the pricing strategy of "bundling." This allows the customer to get a bundle discount if he or she gets two or more services with MTS. The discount gets higher with each service the customer adds to the bundle, thereby encouraging the customer to get all services with MTS. No other provider in Manitoba currently offers all the services that MTS does, giving the company a competitive advantage in the province.[51]

Marketing must skillfully conduct not only customer relationship management (CRM), but partner relationship management (PRM) as well. Companies are deepening their partnering arrangements with key suppliers and distributors, seeing them as partners in delivering value to final customers so everybody benefits.

Integrated Marketing

Integrated marketing occurs when the marketer devises marketing activities and assembles marketing programs to create, communicate, and deliver value for consumers such that the whole is greater than the sum of its parts. Two key themes are that (1) many different marketing activities can create, communicate, and deliver value; and (2) marketers should design and implement any one marketing activity with all other activities in mind. When a hospital buys an MRI system from General Electric's medical systems division, for instance, it expects good installation, maintenance, and training services to go with the purchase.

All company communications also must be integrated. Using an integrated communication strategy means choosing communication options that reinforce and complement each other. A marketer might selectively employ television, radio, and print advertising; public relations and events; and website communications so that each contributes on its own as well as improves the effectiveness of the others. Each must also deliver a consistent brand message at every contact.

When BMW launched the modernized MINI Cooper in 2002, it employed an integrated marketing strategy in North America that included a broad mix of media: billboards, posters, Internet, print, PR, product placement, and grassroots campaigns. Many media were linked to a cleverly designed website with product and dealer information. The car was placed atop Ford Excursion SUVs at 21 auto shows across the United States, was used as seats in a sports stadium, and appeared in *Playboy* magazine as a centrefold. The imaginative integrated campaign built a six-month waiting list for the MINI Cooper.

The company must also develop an integrated channel strategy. It should assess each channel option for its direct effect on product sales and brand equity, as well as its indirect effect through interactions with other channel options. Marketers must weigh the trade-off between having too many channels (leading to conflict among channel members and/or a lack of support) and too few (resulting in market opportunities being overlooked).

Online marketing activities are increasingly prominent in building brands and sales. Created for $300 000 and no additional promotional expense, the Carnival Connections site made it easy for cruise fans to compare notes on destinations and onboard entertainment from casinos to conga lines. In a few short months, 2000 of the site's 13 000 registered users planned trips aboard Carnival's 22 ships, generating an estimated $1.6 million in revenue for the company.[52]

Internal Marketing

Internal marketing, an element of holistic marketing, is the task of hiring, training, and motivating able employees who want to serve customers well. It ensures that everyone in the organization embraces appropriate marketing principles, especially senior management. Smart marketers recognize that marketing activities *within* the company can be as important as—or even more important than—those directed outside the company. It makes no sense to promise excellent service before the company's staff is ready to provide it.

Marketing is no longer the responsibility of a single department—it is a company-wide undertaking that drives the company's vision, mission, and strategic planning.[53] It succeeds only when all departments work together to achieve customer goals (see Table 1.1): when engineering designs the right products, finance furnishes the right amount of funding, purchasing buys the right materials, production makes the right products in the right time horizon, and accounting measures profitability in the right ways. Such interdepartmental harmony can only truly coalesce, however, when management clearly communicates a vision of how the company's marketing orientation and philosophy serve customers. The following example highlights some of the potential challenge in integrating marketing:

The marketing vice-president of a major European airline wants to increase the airline's traffic share. His strategy is to build up customer satisfaction by providing better food, cleaner cabins,

---

TABLE 1.1 | ASSESSING WHICH COMPANY DEPARTMENTS ARE CUSTOMER-MINDED

R&D

- They spend time meeting customers and listening to their problems.
- They welcome the involvement of marketing, manufacturing, and other departments to each new project.
- They benchmark competitors' products and seek "best of class" solutions.
- They solicit customer reactions and suggestions as the project progresses.
- They continuously improve and refine the product on the basis of market feedback.

Purchasing

- They proactively search for the best suppliers.
- They build long-term relationships with fewer but more reliable, high-quality suppliers.
- They don't compromise quality for price savings.

Manufacturing

- They invite customers to visit and tour their plants.
- They visit customer plants.
- They willingly work overtime to meet promised delivery schedules.
- They continuously search for ways to produce goods faster and/or at lower cost.
- They continuously improve product quality, aiming for zero defects.
- They meet customer requirements for "customization" where possible.

Marketing

- They study customer needs and wants in well-defined market segments.
- They allocate marketing effort in relation to the long-run profit potential of the targeted segments.
- They develop winning offers for each target segment.
- They measure company image and customer satisfaction on a continuous basis.
- They continuously gather and evaluate ideas for new products, product improvements, and services.

- They urge all company departments and employees to be customer centered.

Sales

- They have specialized knowledge of the customer's industry.
- They strive to give the customer "the best solution."
- They make only promises that they can keep.
- They feed back customers' needs and ideas to those in charge of product development.
- They serve the same customers for a long period of time.

Logistics

- They set a high standard for service delivery time and meet this standard consistently.
- They operate a knowledgeable and friendly customer service department that can answer questions, handle complaints, and resolve problems in a satisfactory and timely manner.

Accounting

- They prepare periodic "profitability" reports by product, market segment, geographic areas (regions, sales territories), order sizes, channels, and individual customers.
- They prepare invoices tailored to customer needs and answer customer queries courteously and quickly.

Finance

- They understand and support marketing expenditures (e.g., image advertising) that produce long-term customer preference and loyalty.
- They tailor the financial package to the customer's financial requirements.
- They make quick decisions on customer creditworthiness.

Public Relations

- They send out favorable news about the company and "damage control" unfavorable news.
- They act as an internal customer and public advocate for better company policies and practices.

---

better-trained cabin crews, and lower fares, yet he has no authority in these matters. The catering department chooses food that keeps food costs down; the maintenance department uses inexpensive cleaning services; the human resources department hires people without regard to whether they are naturally friendly; the finance department sets the fares. Because these departments generally take a cost or production point of view, the vice-president of marketing is stymied in his efforts to create an integrated marketing program.

Internal marketing requires vertical alignment with senior management and horizontal alignment with other departments, so that everyone understands, appreciates, and supports the marketing effort. "Marketing Insight: Measuring Internal Marketing Orientation" provides a measurement scale to assess the extent of internal marketing within an organization.

Performance Marketing

Performance marketing requires understanding the financial and nonfinancial returns to business and society from marketing activities and programs. Top marketers are increasingly going beyond sales revenue to examine the marketing scorecard and interpret what is happening to market share, customer loss rate, customer satisfaction, product quality, and other measures. They are also considering the legal, ethical, social, and environmental effects of marketing activities and programs.

MARKETING **INSIGHT** | MEASURING INTERNAL MARKETING ORIENTATION

Lings and Greenley (2005) developed and validated a 16-item scale to measure an organization's extent of internal marketing. Their research identified five major factors that comprise internal market orientation. The items under each factor are measured on a 'Strongly Disagree' to 'Strongly Agree' scale.

Factor 1: Formal Face-to-Face Information Generation

1. Management meets with our employees at least once a year to find out what expectations they have of their jobs for the future.
2. We have regular staff appraisals in which we discuss what employees want.
3. Management interacts directly with our employees to find out how to make them more satisfied.

Factor 2: Formal Written Information Generation

4. We survey our employees at least once a year to assess the quality of employment.
5. We often talk with our survey people to identify influences on our employees' behavior.
6. We do a lot of internal market research.

Factor 3: Informal Information Generation

7. When at work, I try to find out my employees' real feelings about their jobs.
8. When at work, I regularly talk to my staff to find out about their work.
9. When at work, if I notice one of my employees is acting differently to normal, I will try to find out if there is a problem that is causing a change in behavior.
10. When at work, I try to find out what employees want from the company.

Factor 4: Information Dissemination

11. I regularly report back to my staff about issues that affect their working environment.
12. I regularly meet with all my staff to report about issues relating to the whole organization.
13. We have regular staff meetings with employees at all levels attending.

Factor 5: Responsiveness

14. We make changes to what we do when employee feedback indicates that they are dissatisfied with the status quo.
15. When we find that employees would like us to modify their conditions of employment, the departments make concerted efforts to do so.
16. When we find out that employees are unhappy with our supervision or management, we take corrective action.

Source: Ian N. Lings, Gordon E. Greenley, "Measuring Internal Market Orientation," *Journal of Service Research*, 7(3), pp. 290–305, copyright © 2005 by SAGE Publications. Reprinted by Permission of SAGE Publications.

FINANCIAL ACCOUNTABILITY Marketers are increasingly asked to justify their investments in financial and profitability terms, as well as in terms of building the brand and growing the customer base.[54] They're employing a broader variety of financial measures to assess the direct and indirect value their marketing efforts create and recognizing that much of their firms' market value comes from intangible assets, particularly brands, customer base, employees, distributor and supplier relations, and intellectual capital. Marketing metrics can help firms quantify and compare their marketing performance along a broad set of dimensions. Marketing research and statistical analysis assess the financial efficiency and effectiveness of different marketing activities. Finally, firms can employ processes and systems to make sure they maximize the value from analyzing these different metrics.

SOCIAL RESPONSIBILITY MARKETING Because the effects of marketing extend beyond the company and the customer to society as a whole, marketers must consider the ethical, environmental, legal, and social context of their role and activities.[55]

The organization's task is thus to determine the needs, wants, and interests of target markets and satisfy them more effectively and efficiently than competitors while preserving or enhancing consumers' and society's long-term well-being. LG Electronics, Toshiba, and NEC Display Solutions offer electronic recycling programs, for instance, often providing consumers with prepaid postage to return old items. Retailers such as Staples, Best Buy, and Mountain Equipment Co-op offer similar programs in their stores.

Table 1.2 displays some different types of corporate social initiatives, illustrated by McDonald's.[56]

As goods become more commoditized, and consumers grow more socially conscious, some companies—including The Body Shop, Bullfrog Power, and Ecotel Hotels—incorporate social responsibility as a way to differentiate themselves from competitors, build consumer preference, and achieve notable sales and profit gains. When they founded Ben & Jerry's, Ben Cohen and Jerry Greenfield embraced the performance marketing concept by dividing the traditional financial bottom line into a "double bottom line" that also measured the environmental impact of their products and processes. That later expanded into a "triple bottom line," to represent the social impacts, negative and positive, of the firm's entire range of business activities.[57] Stonyfield Farm is another company that makes social responsibility a priority.

TABLE 1.2 | CORPORATE SOCIAL INITIATIVES

Type	Description	Example
Corporate social marketing	Supporting behaviour-change campaigns	Promotion of the Stairway to Health program in Canada, a fun and easy way to get employees active in the workplace.
Cause marketing	Promoting social issues through efforts such as sponsorships, licensing agreements, and advertising	Sponsorship of Forest (a gorilla) at Sydney's Zoo—a ten-year sponsorship commitment, aimed at preserving this endangered species.
Cause-related marketing	Donating a percentage of revenues to a specific cause based on the revenue occurring during the announced period of support	Earmarking of $1 for Ronald McDonald Children's Charities from the sale of every Big Mac and pizza sold on McHappy Day
Corporate philanthropy	Making gifts of money, goods, or time to help nonprofit organizations, groups, or individuals	Contributions to Ronald McDonald House Charities.
Corporate community involvement	Providing in-kind or volunteer services in the community	Catering meals for firefighters in the December 1997 bushfires in Australia.
Socially responsible business practices	Adapting and conducting business practices that protect the environment and human and animal rights	Requirement that suppliers increase the amount of living space for laying hens on factory farms

Sources: "McDonald's Canada: Local Community Programs," www.mcdonalds.ca/en/community; Philip Kotler and Nancy Lee, *Corporate Social Responsibility: Doing the Most Good for Your Company and Your Cause* (Hoboken, NJ: Wiley, 2004). Copyright © 2005 by Philip Kotler and Nancy Lee. Used by permission of John Wiley & Sons, Inc.

Stonyfield

Social responsibility has been at the core of Stonyfield Farm—makers of all-natural organic yogurts—from the start. Stonyfield's suppliers eschew the productivity practices of agribusiness, including the use of antibiotics, growth hormones, pesticides, and fertilizers. After calculating the amount of energy used to run its plant, Stonyfield decided to make an equivalent investment in environmental projects such as reforestation and wind farms. The company stopped using plastic lids on its yogurt, saving about a million pounds of plastic a year, and added on-package messages about the perils of global warming, hormones, and genetically modified foods. It makes low-fat versions of its products, and adds cultures or dietary supplements to help the immune system fight off illness. The attitudes and beliefs Stonyfield adopted have not hurt its financial performance as it has become the number-three yogurt brand in the United States.[58] Since 2006 Stonyfield yogurt has been produced in Canada by Danone. The yogurt is made in Quebec and sold from coast to coast in Canada.[59]

UPDATING THE FOUR Ps

E. Jerome McCarthy classified various marketing activities into *marketing-mix* tools of four broad kinds, which he called *the four Ps* of marketing: product, price, place, and promotion.[60] The marketing variables under each P are shown in Figure 1.4.

Given the breadth, complexity, and richness of marketing, however—as exemplified by holistic marketing—clearly these four Ps are not the whole story anymore. If we update them to reflect the holistic marketing concept, we arrive at a more representative set that encompasses modern marketing realities: people, processes, programs, and performance, as in Figure 1.5.

People reflects, in part, internal marketing and the fact that employees are critical to marketing success. Marketing will be only as good as the people inside the organization. *People* also reflects the fact that marketers must view consumers as people to understand their lives more broadly, and not just how they shop for and consume products and services.

Processes reflects all the creativity, discipline, and structure brought to marketing management. Marketers must avoid ad hoc planning and decision making and ensure that state-of-the-art marketing ideas and concepts play an appropriate role in all they do. Only by instituting the right set of processes to guide activities and programs can a firm engage in mutually beneficial long-term relationships. Another

FIGURE 1.4

The Four P Components of the Marketing Mix

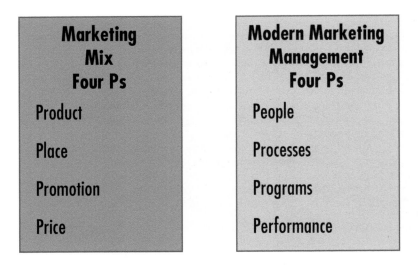

important set of processes guides the firm in imaginatively generating insights and breakthrough products, services, and marketing activities.

Programs reflects all of the firm's consumer-directed activities. It encompasses the old four Ps as well as a range of other marketing activities that might not fit as neatly into the old view of marketing. Regardless of whether they are online or offline, traditional or nontraditional, these activities must be integrated such that their whole is greater than the sum of their parts and they accomplish multiple objectives for the firm.

We define *performance* as in holistic marketing, to capture the range of possible outcome measures that have financial and nonfinancial implications (profitability as well as brand and customer equity), and implications beyond the company itself (social responsibility: legal, ethical, and community related).

Finally, these new four Ps actually apply to *all* disciplines within the company, and by thinking this way, managers grow more closely aligned with the rest of the company.

MARKETING MANAGEMENT TASKS

With the holistic marketing philosophy as a backdrop, we can identify a specific set of tasks that make up successful marketing management and marketing leadership. We'll use the following situation to illustrate these tasks in the context of the book plan. ("Marketing Memo: Marketers' Frequently Asked Questions" is a good checklist for the questions marketing managers ask, all of which we examine in this book.)

Zeus Inc. (name disguised) operates in several industries, including chemicals, cameras, and film. The company is organized into strategic business units. Corporate management is considering what to do with its Atlas camera division, which produces a range of 35mm and digital cameras. Although Zeus has a sizeable share and is producing revenue, the 35mm market is rapidly declining. In the much faster-growing digital camera segment, Zeus faces strong competition and has been slow to gain sales. Zeus's corporate management wants Atlas's marketing group to produce a strong turnaround plan for the division.

Developing Marketing Strategies and Plans

The first task facing Atlas is to identify its potential long-run opportunities, given its market experience and core competencies (see Chapter 2). Atlas can design its cameras with better features. It can make a line of video cameras, or it can use its core competency in optics to design a line of binoculars and telescopes. Whichever direction it chooses, it must develop concrete marketing plans that specify the marketing strategy and tactics going forward.

Capturing Marketing Insights

Atlas needs a reliable marketing information system to closely monitor its marketing environment so that it can continuously assess market potential and forecast demand. Its microenvironment consists of all the players who affect its ability to produce and sell cameras—suppliers, marketing intermediaries, customers, and competitors. Its macroenvironment includes demographic, economic, social-cultural, natural, technological, and political-legal forces that affect sales and profits (see Chapter 3).

Atlas also needs a dependable marketing research system. To transform strategy into programs, marketing managers must make basic decisions about their expenditures, activities, and budget allocations (Chapter 4).

Connecting with Customers

Atlas must consider how to best create value for its chosen target markets and develop strong, profitable, long-term relationships with customers (see Chapter 5). To do so, it needs to understand consumer markets (see Chapter 6). Who buys cameras and why? What features and prices are they looking for, and where do they shop? Atlas also sells cameras to business markets, including large corporations, professional firms, retailers, and government agencies (see Chapter 7), where purchasing agents or buying committees make the decisions. Atlas needs to gain a full understanding of how organizational buyers buy. It needs a sales force well-trained in presenting product benefits.

Atlas will not want to market to all possible customers. It must divide the market into major market segments, evaluate each one, and target those it can best serve (see Chapter 8).

Building Strong Brands

Atlas must understand the strengths and weaknesses of the Zeus brand as customers see it (see Chapter 9). Is its 35mm film heritage a handicap in the digital camera market? Suppose Atlas decides to focus on the consumer market and develop a positioning strategy (see Chapter 10). Should it position itself as the "Cadillac" brand, offering superior cameras at a premium price with excellent service and strong advertising? Should it build a simple, low-priced camera aimed at more price-conscious consumers? Or something in between?

Atlas must also pay close attention to competitors (see Chapter 11), anticipating their moves and knowing how to react quickly and decisively. It may want to initiate some surprise moves, in which case it needs to anticipate how its competitors will respond.

Shaping the Market Offerings

At the heart of the marketing program is the product—the firm's tangible offering to the market, which includes the product quality, design, features, and packaging (see Chapter 12). To gain a competitive advantage, Atlas may provide leasing, delivery, repair, and training as part of its product offering (see Chapter 13).

MARKETING **MEMO** | MARKETERS' FREQUENTLY ASKED QUESTIONS

1. How can we spot and choose the right market segment(s)?
2. How can we differentiate our offerings?
3. How should we respond to customers who buy on price?
4. How can we compete against lower-cost, lower-price competitors?
5. How far can we go in customizing our offering for each customer?
6. How can we grow our business?
7. How can we build stronger brands?
8. How can we reduce the cost of customer acquisition?
9. How can we keep our customers loyal longer?
10. How can we tell which customers are more important?
11. How can we measure the payback from advertising, sales promotion, and public relations?
12. How can we improve sales force productivity?
13. How can we establish multiple channels and yet manage channel conflict?
14. How can we get the other company departments to be more customer oriented?

A critical marketing decision relates to price (see Chapter 14). Atlas must decide on the price, any discounts, allowances, and credit terms. Its price should match well with the offer's perceived value; otherwise, buyers will turn to competitors' products.

Delivering Value

Atlas must also determine how to properly deliver to the target market the value embodied in its products and services. Channel activities include those the company undertakes to make the product accessible and available to target customers (see Chapter 15). Atlas must identify, recruit, and link various marketing facilitators to supply its products and services efficiently to the target market. It must understand the various types of retailers, wholesalers, and physical-distribution firms and how they make their decisions (see Chapter 16).

Communicating Value

Atlas must also adequately communicate to the target market the value embodied by its products and services. It will need an integrated marketing communication program that maximizes the individual and collective contribution of all communication activities (see Chapter 17). Atlas needs to set up mass communication programs consisting of advertising, sales promotion, events, and public relations (see Chapter 18). It also needs to plan more personal communications, in the form of direct and interactive marketing, as well as hire, train, and motivate salespeople (see Chapter 19).

Creating Successful Long-Term Growth

Based on its product positioning, Atlas must initiate new-product development, testing, and launching as part of its long-term view (see Chapter 20). The strategy should take into account changing global opportunities and challenges (see Chapter 21).

Finally, Atlas must build a marketing organization capable of implementing the marketing plan (see Chapter 22). Because surprises and disappointments can occur as marketing plans unfold, Atlas will need feedback and control to understand the efficiency and effectiveness of its marketing activities and how it can improve them.

SUMMARY

1. Marketing is an organizational function and a set of processes for creating, communicating, and delivering value to customers and for managing customer relationships in ways that benefit the organization and its stakeholders. Marketing management is the art and science of choosing target markets and getting, keeping, and growing customers through creating, delivering, and communicating superior customer value.

2. Marketers are skilled at managing demand: they seek to influence its level, timing, and composition for goods, services, events, experiences, persons, places, properties, organizations, information, and ideas. They also operate in four different marketplaces: consumer, business, global, and nonprofit and governmental.

3. Marketing is not done only by the marketing department. Marketing needs to affect every aspect of the customer experience. To create a strong marketing organization, marketers must think like executives in other departments, and executives in other departments must think more like marketers.

4. Today's marketplace is fundamentally different as a result of major societal forces that have resulted in many new consumer and company capabilities. These forces have created new opportunities and challenges and changed marketing management significantly as companies seek new ways to achieve marketing excellence.

5. There are five competing concepts under which organizations can choose to conduct their business: the production concept, the product concept, the selling concept, the marketing concept, and the holistic marketing concept. The first three are of limited use today.

6. The holistic marketing concept is based on the development, design, and implementation of marketing programs, processes, and activities that recognize their breadth and interdependencies. Holistic marketing recognizes that everything matters in marketing and that a broad, integrated perspective is often necessary. Four components of holistic marketing are relationship marketing, integrated marketing, internal marketing, and performance marketing.

7. The set of tasks necessary for successful marketing management includes developing marketing strategies and plans, capturing marketing insights, connecting with customers, building strong brands, shaping the market offerings, delivering and communicating value, and creating long-term growth.

APPLICATIONS

Marketing Debate: Does Marketing Create or Satisfy Needs?

Marketing has often been defined in terms of satisfying customers' needs and wants. Critics, however, maintain that marketing goes beyond that and creates needs and wants that did not exist before. They feel marketers encourage consumers to spend more money than they should on goods and services they do not really need.

Take a position: Marketing shapes consumer needs and wants *versus* Marketing merely reflects the needs and wants of consumers.

Marketing Discussion: Shifts in Marketing

Consider the broad shifts in marketing. Do any themes emerge in them? Can you relate the shifts to the major societal forces? Which force has contributed to which shift?

MARKETING EXCELLENCE | FORD MOTOR COMPANY OF CANADA

The end of the last decade was one the world economy would rather forget. The subprime mortgage crisis in the United States and bursting of the housing bubble caused economic failure of financial institutions and set off a global recession affecting businesses around the world. Two of the so-called "Big Three" automakers in Canada—Daimler-Chrysler and General Motors—needed government assistance to the tune of over $10 billion from the Government of Canada, and far more from the American government for their U.S. operations in order to avoid bankruptcy. The only one of the Big Three in Canada that did not seek a government bailout to maintain operations was the Ford Motor Company of Canada.

Less than a decade ago, Ford was ranked 23rd in the J.D. Power and Associates Initial Quality Study, which measures consumer issues with a vehicle during the first three months of ownership. When the study was repeated in 2010, Ford had earned the distinction as the top initial quality brand among all nonluxury automakers. So, what is behind this rapid rise to the top, and why was Ford able to endure the recession better than its two major North American rivals?

First of all, Ford has gone beyond the norm in the automotive industry by going directly to consumers to help design their cars. Consumer feedback is key to the Ford business model, and some consumers are even invited to "drive" concept cars, courtesy of a virtual reality machine. Ford Canada has also paired up with other subsidiaries of the Ford Motor Company from around the world to share these responses from their customers, and the best practices emerging from these discussions are implemented worldwide. By utilizing consumer feedback to their advantage, Ford has come up with innovative new design ideas that not only appeal to the average consumer, but also help save manufacturing costs. Design innovations such as the ONE Ford DNA have up to 80 percent of vehicles produced using the same parts.

A second reason for Ford's success is the company's marketing campaign, in which Ford challenges the consumer to "Drive One" and see the new look of Ford. The campaign attempts to illustrate Ford's commitment to customers, the environment, and quality, and consumers are responding to the challenge.

Ford Motor Company North America went from a net loss of $14.78 billion in 2008 to a net profit of $2.72 billion in 2009, a swing of over $17 billion, and Ford does not plan to stop there. Additional plans are in the works to incorporate some of the more successful ideas, such as the fuel-saving EcoBoost engine, into more vehicles. According to Paul Roy,

Director of Marketing Plans at Ford Canada, the goal is to have these engines in 80 percent of Ford vehicles by 2012.

The advances in technology are far from over, and new ideas such as the SmartGauge are being advanced constantly. This revolutionary gauge, installed in Ford's hybrid vehicles, tells drivers how efficiently they are driving their car. It uses a simple picture of a plant, from which leaves grow or fall off depending on how efficiently or inefficiently the driver is operating the car. The Automobile Journalists' Association of Canada recognized Ford in 2010 by awarding the company with the Best New Green Technology designation for SmartGauge.

In previous years, domestic vehicles produced in Canada and the United States have been compared unfavourably in quality to manufacturers from Japan such as Honda or Toyota, but Ford has been working hard to shake off that stigma. "We're at a statistical dead heat with the Japanese," says Adrian Vido, Director of Global Manufacturing Quality. "Our goal by 2012 is to differentiate ourselves from the rest of the competition."

Ford has realized a stunning turnaround in just a few short years. Through a combination of customer-focused marketing approaches, Ford has been able to turn consumer wants into a reality that not only increases car sales, but cuts costs as well. This approach has made Ford one of the top manufacturers in the Canadian auto industry, and the company is working harder than ever to make sure it is not unseated from that spot anytime soon.

QUESTIONS

1. How would you describe Ford's company orientation?

2. What steps can Ford take to be a socially responsible marketer?

3. If any of the Big Three automakers go bankrupt, which stakeholders would be adversely affected in the process?

4. In your opinion, should the Canadian government have loaned money to GM and Chrysler to bail them out during the recent recession? Why or why not?

Sources: "ONE Ford: Ford Motor Company / 2009 Annual Report," http://www.annualreports.com/HostedData/AnnualReports/PDFArchive/f2009.pdf (viewed August 26, 2011); Johnathan Katz, "U.S. Automakers Back on Top," Industry Week, August 2010, p. 20; "The Ford Story as Seen by Jeremy Cato and Michael Vaughn," Ford Motor Company of Canada: News and Media, www.ford.ca/app/fo/en/our_company/news_and_media.do (viewed September 14, 2010); David Friend, "Embattled Industries Ask Federal Government for Help After Auto Bailout," The Canadian Press, June 7, 2009; Automobile Journalists Association of Canada, "AJAC—Canadian Car of the Year Winners (by Year)," www.ajac.ca/web/ccoty/previous_byyear.asp (viewed September 14, 2010).

Chapter 2

aeroplan

BIN
627421

Aeroplan Number
234 567 980

Code
1

John Sample

Groupe Aeroplan Inc. must continuously design and implement marketing activities at many levels to keep it ahead of its rivals.

In This Chapter, We Will Address the Following **Questions**

1. How does marketing affect customer value?

2. How is strategic planning carried out at different levels of the organization?

3. What does a marketing plan include?

Developing Marketing Strategies and Plans

The key ingredients of the marketing management process

are insightful, creative strategies and plans that can guide marketing activities. Developing the right marketing strategy over time requires a blend of discipline and flexibility. Firms must stick to a strategy but also constantly improve it. Marketers must also develop strategies for a range of products and services within the organization.

Aeroplan is headquartered in Montreal and is a loyalty marketing program. Originally created by Air Canada in 1984 as a frequent flyer program, today Aeroplan has over 5 million active members, and has evolved into an independent loyalty marketing company that offers its members benefits when they buy products and services from firms like Esso, Sobeys, and Home Hardware, in addition to Air Canada.

David Klein, Aeroplan's vice-president of marketing planning and program development, notes, "The last few years, we've seen the competitive environment really ramp up." Thus, Aeroplan can never rest on its past success. The number of loyalty programs has been growing as many firms seek to retain their customers and build strong relationships with them. The travel-related subsector of the market is no exception. AIR MILES has long been Aeroplan's chief competitor, but there are more and more programs offered by credit companies and banks that work with various airlines and travel programs. A new competitor to Aeroplan is the loyalty program offered by WestJet Airlines Ltd. In April 2010, WestJet announced its long-awaited loyalty program, through which travellers can accumulate WestJet dollars by using a co-branded RBC MasterCard. Like WestJet, Aeroplan has an alliance with a credit card company to increase the value it can deliver to its members. Aeroplan works with CIBC and they jointly offer customers benefits through the CIBC Aerogold Visa Infinite credit card. Other rivals include American Express AeroplanPlus Platinum, and Toronto-Dominion Bank's TD First Class Travel Visa Infinite and TD Platinum Travel.

To constantly increase the value Aeroplan offers its members, it constantly looks for rewards other than free travel. Aeroplan analyzes its vast database to better understand the shopping patterns of its customers so that it can give its loyalty members rewards they want. Thus, today members can earn rewards that include not only airline seats, but also vacation packages, hotel rooms, car rentals, merchandise, and experiential rewards such as gourmet getaways, tickets to sports events, and even spa packages.

To hold ground in such an intensely competitive environment, Aeroplan launched a new $2 million campaign. The first task of the campaign was to make it clear to current and potential members alike that Aeroplan delivers more value than its rivals. One half-page ad reads, "We put more people in more reward seats than any other Canadian loyalty program." Another stresses that "we give you more flexibility than any other Canadian loyalty program," while a third reads, "26 Star Alliance airlines means more ways to get outta town."

Aeroplan is also looking for more international growth as competition heats up in its home marketplace. Germany, France, Spain, and Japan are among the countries where Groupe Aeroplan may expand, says Rupert Duchesne, president and CEO of Groupe

Aeroplan Inc. "The markets where we think this works are essentially markets that are similar to Canada, the U.K. and Italy—they're big homogenous economies. Ideally, these markets have one or two airlines, four or five big retail banks and significant retail competitors with 'sophisticated' product offerings."

Aeroplan's efforts have been a success to date. Veritas Investment Research compared Aeroplan's rewards program against that of its rivals and found that it came out the clear winner. Veritas is a research-only firm with an independent voice; it doesn't have business relationships with the companies it analyzes. Aeroplan took the top spot because of the value members earn for each dollar spent using the CIBC Aerogold Visa Infinite card, because of the levels of customer satisfaction, and because Aeroplan's members would recommend the program to their friends.[1]

This chapter begins by examining some of the strategic marketing implications in creating customer value. We'll look at several perspectives on planning and describe how to draw up a formal marketing plan.

MARKETING AND CUSTOMER VALUE

Marketing involves satisfying consumers' needs and wants. The task of any business is to deliver customer value at a profit. In a hypercompetitive economy with increasingly rational buyers faced with abundant choices, a company can win only by fine-tuning the value-delivery process and choosing, providing, and communicating superior value.

The Value-Delivery Process

The traditional view of marketing is that the firm makes something and then sells it, with marketing taking place in the selling process. Companies that subscribe to this view have the best chance of succeeding in economies marked by goods shortages where consumers are not fussy about quality, features, or style—for example, with basic staple goods in developing markets.

The traditional view will not work in economies with many different types of people, each with individual wants, perceptions, preferences, and buying criteria. The smart competitor must design and deliver offerings for well-defined target markets. This realization inspired a new view of business processes that places marketing at the *beginning* of planning. Instead of emphasizing making and selling, companies now see themselves as part of a value-delivery process.

The sequence of value creation and delivery can be divided into three phases.[2] The first phase, *choosing the value,* represents the "homework" marketing must do before any product exists. The marketing staff must segment the market, select the appropriate market target, and develop the offering's value positioning. The formula "segmentation, targeting, positioning" is the essence of strategic marketing. Once the business unit has chosen the value, the second phase is *providing the value.* Marketing must determine specific product features, prices, and distribution. The task in the third phase is *communicating the value* by utilizing the sales force, sales promotion, advertising, and other promotional tools to inform and promote the product. Each of these value phases has cost implications.

The Value Chain

Michael Porter of Harvard has proposed the **value chain** as a tool for identifying ways to create more customer value.[3] According to this model, every firm is a synthesis of activities performed to design, produce, market, deliver, and support its product. The value chain identifies nine strategically relevant activities that create value and cost in a specific business.

The *primary activities* are (1) inbound logistics, or bringing materials into the business; (2) operations, or converting materials into final products; (3) outbound logistics, or shipping out final products; (4) marketing, which includes sales; and (5) service. Specialized departments handle the *support activities*—(1) procurement, (2) technology development, (3) human resource management, and (4) firm infrastructure. (Infrastructure covers the costs of general management, planning, finance, accounting, legal, and government affairs.)

The firm's task is to examine its costs and performance in each value-creating activity and to look for ways to improve it. The firm should estimate its competitors' costs and performances as *benchmarks* against which to compare its own costs and performance. It should go further and study the "best of class" practices of the world's best companies. We can identify best-practice companies by consulting customers, suppliers, distributors, financial analysts, trade associations, and magazines to see whom they rate as doing the best job. Even the best companies can benchmark, against other industries if necessary, to improve their performance. To support its corporate goal to be more innovative, GE has benchmarked against P&G and is also developing its own best practices.[4]

The firm's success depends not only on how well each department performs its work, but also on how well the various departmental activities are coordinated to conduct *core business processes*.[5] These core business processes include the following:

- *The market-sensing process.* All the activities involved in gathering market intelligence, disseminating it within the organization, and acting on the information.

- *The new offering–realization process.* All the activities involved in researching, developing, and launching new high-quality offerings quickly and within budget.

- *The customer-acquisition process.* All the activities involved in defining target markets and prospecting for new customers.

- *The customer relationship management process.* All the activities involved in building deeper understanding with, relationships with, and offerings to individual customers.

- *The fulfillment management process.* All the activities involved in receiving and approving orders, shipping the goods on time, and collecting payment.

Strong companies are also re-engineering their workflows and building cross-functional teams responsible for each process.[6] At Xerox, a Customer Operations Group links sales, shipping, installation, service, and billing so that these activities flow smoothly into one another. Winning companies are those that excel at managing core business processes through cross-functional teams. AT&T, LexisNexis, and Pratt & Whitney have reorganized their employees into cross-functional teams; cross-functional teams are also found in nonprofits and government organizations.

To be successful, a firm also needs to look for competitive advantages beyond its own operations into the value chains of suppliers, distributors, and customers. Many companies today have partnered with specific suppliers and distributors to create a superior **value-delivery network** (also called a **supply chain**). One example is lululemon.

lululemon athletica

The Canadian-based yoga-apparel retail phenomenon lululemon has learned the importance of an efficient and responsive supply chain the hard way. It grew so fast in both Canada and the United States that its supply chain couldn't keep up with demand, and its stores kept running out of products. For example, when it opened its Chicago store the shelves were emptied of running outfits just when a big marathon was being held. In 2010, lululemon formed a partnership with Vitech Business Group, Inc., and will use the firm's voice technology for picking items from warehouses, sending them to the right stores, and cross docking. Vitech's VP of sales and marketing, Andrew Wright, said that lululemon athletica has "embraced voice as a technology that will offer them great efficiencies as they continue their fast paced growth. Partnering with Vitech to use our supply chain knowledge and experience to implement Vocollect's Voice techonology will give them the edge they need to be a leader in the athletic apparel market." lululemon sees this move as a major step toward increasing productivity at its distribution centres.[7]

Core Competencies

Traditionally, companies owned and controlled most of the resources that entered their businesses—labour power, materials, machines, information, and energy—but this situation is changing. Many companies today outsource less-critical resources if they can be obtained at better quality or lower cost. India has developed a reputation as a country that can provide ample outsourcing support.

The key is to own and nurture the resources and competencies that make up the essence of the business. A **core competency** has three characteristics: (1) it is a source of competitive advantage in that it makes a significant contribution to perceived customer benefits, (2) it has applications in a wide variety of markets, and (3) it is difficult for competitors to imitate.[8]

Competitive advantage also accrues to companies that possess *distinctive capabilities* or excellence in broader business processes. Whereas core competencies tend to refer to areas of special technical and production expertise, *distinctive capabilities* tend to describe excellence in broader business processes. Consider the Hospital for Sick Children, located in Toronto.

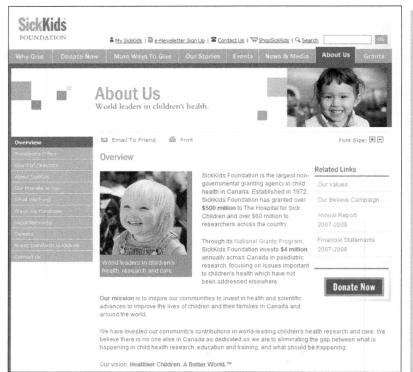

Hospital for Sick Children

The vision of the Toronto-based Hospital for Sick Children (SickKids) is "Healthier Children. A Better World.™" SickKids is recognized as one of the world's foremost pediatric health-care institutions, and its success is due to the integration of its three core competencies: patient care, research, and education. As Canada's most research-intensive hospital, SickKids has generated discoveries that have helped children globally. SickKids' competencies make it one of the best and most recognized children's health-care and research institutions in the world. It continuously works to improve its core competencies by attracting and retaining world-class faculty and research trainees; creating state-of-the-art, high-quality, large-scale shared facilities; capitalizing on intellectual property and technology-commercialization opportunities; maximizing opportunities for discovery and innovation; developing internationally competitive, cutting-edge infrastructure; and providing exceptional training and development opportunities. To help the hospital build even more upon its strengths, Myron and Berna Garron gave the hospital a transformational gift of $30 million in 2010. "We are privileged to support one of the most respected children's hospitals in the world," said the donors. "Our son was treated for cancer at SickKids for many years and we will never forget the dedication and level of care he received. We are confident this gift will lead to more positive outcomes for cancer patients and their families." This gift will allow SickKids to help more children survive their cancer diagnosis.[9]

SickKids Foundation has leveraged the many distinctive capabilities of The Hospital for Sick Children so it can live up to its promise of being a world leader in children's health.

Competitive advantage ultimately derives from how well the company has fitted its core competencies and distinctive capabilities into tightly interlocking "activity systems." Companies such as Transat A.T., Dell, and IKEA are hard to imitate because their activity systems can't be copied by competitors.

Business realignment may be necessary to maximize core competencies. Realignment has three steps: (1) (re)defining the business concept or "big idea," (2) (re)shaping the business scope, and (3) (re)positioning the company's brand identity. Consider what the Argos football team is doing to realign its business.

The Argos

In the face of growing competition for fans who are harder to drag away from other forms of entertainment, an unlikely partnership has been founded. The CFL's Toronto Argonauts and the NFL's Buffalo Bills are joining forces to promote football in southern Ontario. Average attendance at Argos games has been disappointing, at around 20 000 despite the team's winning record. The two teams are collaborating with Football Canada to stage Football Week in Toronto. Its aim is to strengthen the recognition of both brands, build more excitement around the game, and appeal to fans on both sides of the border. Toronto Argonauts president Bob Nicholson said he doesn't feel threatened by the Bills and he believes that working with the NFL team will help his club strengthen its hold in its home city.[10]

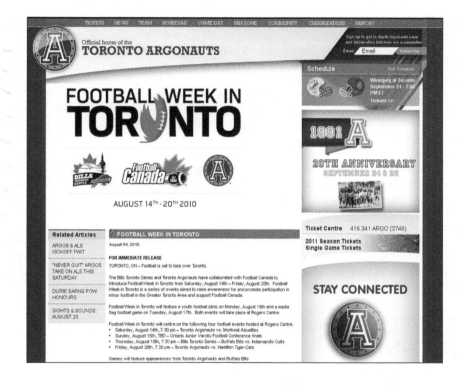

The Argos recently partnered with the Buffalo Bills to promote football in southern Ontario.

A Holistic Marketing Orientation and Customer Value

One view of holistic marketing is as "integrating the value exploration, value creation, and value-delivery activities with the purpose of building long-term, mutually satisfying relationships and co-prosperity among key stakeholders."[11] According to this view, holistic marketers succeed by managing a superior value chain that delivers a high level of product quality, service, and speed. Holistic marketers achieve profitable growth by expanding customer share, building customer loyalty, and capturing customer lifetime value.

The holistic marketing framework is designed to address three key management questions:

1. *Value exploration.* How can a company identify new value opportunities?
2. *Value creation.* How can a company efficiently create more promising new value offerings?
3. *Value delivery.* How can a company use its capabilities and infrastructure to deliver the new value offerings more efficiently?

The Central Role of Strategic Planning

Successful marketing thus requires having capabilities such as understanding customer value, creating customer value, delivering customer value, capturing customer value, and sustaining customer value. Only a handful of companies stand out as master marketers: Canadian Tire, Molson, Tim Hortons, Bombardier, Procter & Gamble, WestJet Airlines, Nike, Disney, Enterprise Rent-A-Car, Walmart, McDonald's, and several Asian (Sony, Toyota, and Canon) and European (IKEA, Club Med, Bang & Olufsen, Nokia, Tesco, and Virgin) companies. These companies focus on the customer and are organized to respond effectively to changing customer needs. They all have well-staffed marketing departments, and all their other departments—manufacturing, finance, research and development, personnel, purchasing—also accept the concept that the customer is king.

To ensure that the proper activities are selected and executed, strategic planning is paramount. Strategic planning calls for action in three key areas: The first is managing a company's businesses as an investment portfolio. The second involves assessing each business's strength by considering the market's growth rate and the company's position and fit in that market. The third is establishing a strategy. For each business, the company must develop a game plan for achieving long-run objectives.

To understand marketing management, we must understand strategic planning at different organizational levels. Most large companies consist of four organizational levels: the corporate level, the division level, the business-unit level, and the product level. Corporate headquarters is responsible for designing a corporate strategic plan to guide the whole enterprise; it makes decisions on the amount of resources to allocate to each division, as well as on which businesses to start or eliminate. Each division establishes a plan covering the allocation of funds to each business unit within the division. Each business unit develops a strategic plan to carry that business unit into a profitable future. Finally, each product level (product line, brand) within a business unit develops a marketing plan for achieving its objectives in its product market.

The **marketing plan** is the central instrument for directing and coordinating the marketing effort. The marketing plan operates at two levels: strategic and tactical. The **strategic marketing plan** lays out the target markets and the value proposition that will be offered, based on an analysis of the best market opportunities. The **tactical marketing plan** specifies the marketing tactics, including product features, promotion, merchandising, pricing, sales channels, and service.

Today, teams develop the marketing plan with inputs and sign-offs from every important function. Management then implements these plans at the appropriate levels of the organization, monitors results, and takes necessary corrective action. The complete planning, implementation, and control cycle is shown in Figure 2.1. We next consider planning at each of the four levels of the organization.

CORPORATE AND DIVISION STRATEGIC PLANNING

Some corporations give their business units a lot of freedom to set their own sales and profit goals and strategies. Others set goals for their business units but let them develop their own strategies. Still others set the goals and participate in developing individual business-unit strategies.

All corporate headquarters undertake four planning activities:

1. Defining the corporate mission
2. Establishing strategic business units (SBUs)
3. Assigning resources to each SBU
4. Assessing growth opportunities

We'll briefly look at each process.

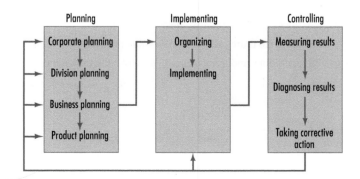

FIGURE 2.1

The Strategic-Planning, Implementation, and Control Processes

Defining the Corporate Mission

An organization exists to accomplish something: to make cars, lend money, provide a night's lodging, and so on. Its specific mission or purpose is usually clear when the business starts. Over time, the mission may change to take advantage of new opportunities or respond to new market conditions, as was the case with Aviva.

Aviva Canada Inc.

Aviva Canada Inc., Canada's second-largest home, auto, and business insurance group, is on a mission to change how people think about insurance in Canada. Its market research showed that Canadians were frustrated and dissatisfied with the current state of the insurance industry, believing that no firm really listened to them. Aviva decided to change such perceptions and earn consumers' trust through a series of unique initiatives. It began by opening up a dialogue with Canadians. It made a revolutionary move and offered the country's first national money-back Claims Service Satisfaction Guarantee. It offered new products and worked to improve services including a 24/7 claims line. It launched a new website, changeinsurance.ca, and a funny ad campaign to better position itself. Paul Fletcher, Senior Vice President, Brand Marketing, Aviva Canada Inc., noted, "Canadians have called for change. We've heard them loud and clear. It's time to change insurance and Aviva is committed to do just that in partnership with Canadians."[12]

To define its mission, the company should address Peter Drucker's classic questions:[13] What is our business? Who is the customer? What is of value to the customer? What will our business be? What should our business be? These simple-sounding questions are among the most difficult the company will ever have to answer. Successful companies continuously raise these questions and answer them thoughtfully and thoroughly.

Organizations develop **mission statements** to share with managers, employees, and (in many cases) customers. A clear, thoughtful mission statement provides employees with a shared sense of purpose, direction, and opportunity. Mission statements are at their best when they are guided by a vision, an almost "impossible dream" that provides a direction for the company for the next 10 to 20 years. Fred Smith wanted to deliver mail anywhere in the United States before 10:30 A.M. the next day, so he created FedEx. Almost 30 years ago, Graeme McRae, founder of Bioniche, a biopharmaceutical company headquartered in Belleville, Ontario, wanted to improve the quality of life for both humans and animals through innovative research and therapeutics. Today, the company has developed a cattle vaccine that prevents the shedding of e-coli (which can contaminate water supplies) and a human bladder-cancer drug that is undergoing clinical trials. In 2007, Bioniche was recognized as one of the Top 10 Life Sciences Companies in Canada, and in 2010, it received its second award as one of the Top 50 Best Small and Medium Employers in Canada.[14]

Good mission statements have five major characteristics:

1. *They focus on a limited number of goals.* The statement "we want to produce the highest-quality products, offer the most service, achieve the widest distribution, and sell at the lowest prices" claims too much.

2. *They stress the company's major policies and values.* They narrow the range of individual discretion so employees act consistently on important issues.

3. *They define the major competitive spheres within which the company will operate.* Table 2.1 summarizes some key competitive dimensions for mission statements.

4. *They take a long-term view.* Management should change the mission only when it ceases to be relevant.

5. *They are as short, memorable, and meaningful as possible.* Marketing consultant Guy Kawasaki advocates developing three- to four-word corporate mantras rather than mission statements, like "Enriching Women's Lives" for Mary Kay.[15]

TABLE 2.1 | DEFINING COMPETITIVE TERRITORY AND BOUNDARIES

- **Industry** The range of industries in which a company will operate. Some companies will operate only in one industry; some only in a set of related industries; some only in industrial goods, consumer goods, or services; and some in any industry.
  - DuPont prefers to operate in the industrial market, whereas Dow is willing to operate in the industrial and consumer markets.

- **Products and applications** The range of products and applications a company will supply.
  - Bioniche Life Sciences of Belleville, Ontario, has three major lines of products organized according to the market they apply to: animal health products, human health products, and products aimed at food safety.[16]

- **Competence** The range of technological and other core competencies that a company will master and leverage.
  - Japan's NEC has built its core competencies in computing, communications, and components to support production of laptop computers, television receivers, and handheld telephones.

- **Market segment** The type of market or customers a company will serve.
  - Aston Martin makes only high-performance sports cars. Gerber serves primarily the baby market.

- **Vertical** The vertical sphere is the number of channel levels—from raw material to final product and distribution—in which a company will participate.
  - At one extreme are companies with a large vertical scope; at one time, Ford owned its own rubber plantations, sheep farms, glass-manufacturing plants, and steel foundries. At the other extreme are "hollow corporations" or "pure marketing companies" consisting of a person with a phone, fax, computer, and desk, and who contracts out every service, including design, manufacture, marketing, and physical distribution.

- **Geographical** The range of regions, countries, or country groups in which a company will operate.
  - At one extreme are companies that operate in a specific city. At the other are multinationals, such as Unilever and Caterpillar, that operate in almost every country in the world.

Compare the rather vague mission statements on the left with Google's mission statement and philosophy on the right.

To build total brand value by innovating to deliver customer value and customer leadership faster, better, and more completely than our competition.

We build brands and make the world a little happier by bringing our best to you.

Google Mission
To organize the world's information and make it universally accessible and useful.

Google Philosophy
Never settle for the best.
1. Focus on the user and all else will follow.
2. It's best to do one thing really, really well.
3. Fast is better than slow.
4. Democracy on the Web works.
5. You don't need to be at your desk to need an answer.
6. You can make money without doing evil.
7. There is always more information out there.
8. The need for information crosses all borders.
9. You can be serious without a suit.
10. Great just isn't good enough.[17]

Establishing Strategic Business Units

Companies often define their businesses in terms of products: they are in the "auto business" or the "clothing business." *Market definitions* of a business, however, describe the business as a customer-satisfying process, not a goods-producing process. Products are transient; basic needs and customer groups endure forever. Transportation is a need: the horse and carriage, the automobile, the railroad, the airline, and the truck are products that meet that need.

Viewing businesses in terms of customer needs can suggest additional growth opportunities. Table 2.2 gives several examples of companies that have moved from a product to a market definition of their business, highlighting the difference between a target market definition and a strategic market definition.

TABLE 2.2	PRODUCT-ORIENTED VERSUS MARKET-ORIENTED DEFINITIONS OF A BUSINESS	
Company	**Product Definition**	**Market Definition**
VIA Rail	We run a railroad.	We are a people mover.
Xerox	We make copying equipment.	We help improve office productivity.
Imperial Oil	We sell gasoline.	We supply energy.
Salter Street Films	We make movies and television programs.	We market thoughtful entertainment.
Encyclopaedia Britannica	We sell encyclopedias.	We distribute information.
Carrier	We make air conditioners and furnaces.	We provide climate control in the home.

A *target market definition* tends to focus on selling a product or service to a current market. Pepsi could define its target market as everyone who drinks carbonated soft drinks, and competitors would therefore be other carbonated soft drink companies. A *strategic market definition,* however, also focuses on the potential market. If Pepsi considered everyone who might drink something to quench his or her thirst, its competition would include noncarbonated soft drinks, bottled water, fruit juices, tea, and coffee. To better compete, Pepsi might decide to sell additional beverages with promising growth rates.

A business can be defined in terms of three dimensions: customer groups, customer needs, and technology.[18] Consider a small company that defines its business as designing incandescent lighting systems for television studios. Its customer group is television studios; the customer need is lighting; and the technology is incandescent lighting. The company might want to expand. It could make lighting for other customer groups, such as homes, factories, and offices; or it could supply other services needed by television studios, such as heating, ventilation, or air conditioning. It could design other lighting technologies for television studios, such as infrared or ultraviolet lighting.

Large companies normally manage quite different businesses, each requiring its own strategy. Bombardier has two core businesses: aerospace and transportation. It operates eight **strategic business units (SBUs)** under the aerospace umbrella and six units under transportation. An SBU has three characteristics:

1. It is a single business or collection of related businesses that can be planned separately from the rest of the company.

2. It has its own set of competitors.

3. It has a manager who is responsible for strategic planning and profit performance and who controls most of the factors affecting profit.

The purpose of identifying the company's SBUs is to develop separate strategies and assign appropriate funding. Senior management knows that

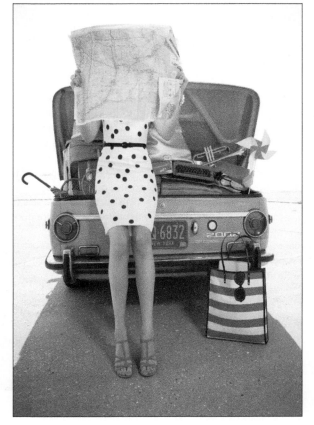

The Kate Spade brand allows Liz Claiborne to attract a more youthful customer.

its portfolio of businesses usually includes a number of "yesterday's has-beens" as well as "tomorrow's breadwinners."[19] Liz Claiborne has put more emphasis on some of its younger businesses, such as Juicy Couture, Lucky Brand Jeans, Mexx, and Kate Spade, while selling businesses without the same buzz (Ellen Tracy, Sigrid Olsen, and Laundry). The Campbell Soup Company has out-paced the stock market for close to a decade by developing or keeping only products that ranked number one or number two in the categories of simple meals, baked snacks, and veggie-based drinks and that had a strong emphasis on value, nutrition, and convenience.[20] See how Shaw Communications Inc.'s many SBUs work to its advantage.

Shaw Communications Inc.

Shaw Communications Inc. is a diversified communications and media company, providing consumers with broadband cable television, high-speed Internet, home phone, telecommunications services (through Shaw Business Solutions), satellite direct-to-home services (through Shaw Direct), and engaging programming content (through Shaw Media).[21] Each of these is operated as a strategic business unit, and because the company is diversified into various business units, it is better able to weather economic downturns. When one unit is negatively affected, others remain stable or grow.

Assigning Resources to Each SBU[22]

Once it has defined SBUs, management must decide how to allocate corporate resources to each. Several portfolio-planning models provide ways to make investment decisions. The GE/McKinsey Matrix classifies each SBU by the extent of its competitive advantage and the attractiveness of its industry. Management can decide to grow, "harvest" or draw cash from, or hold on to the business. Another model, BCG's Growth-Share Matrix, uses relative market share and annual rate of market growth as criteria to make investment decisions, classifying SBUs as dogs, cash cows, question marks, or stars.

Portfolio-planning models like these have fallen out of favour as oversimplified and subjective. Newer methods rely on shareholder value analysis, and on whether the market value of a company is greater with an SBU or without it (whether it is sold or spun off). These value calculations assess the potential of a business based on growth opportunities from global expansion, repositioning or retargeting, and strategic outsourcing.

Assessing Growth Opportunities

Assessing growth opportunities involves planning new businesses, downsizing, or terminating older businesses. If there is a gap between future desired sales and projected sales, corporate management will have to develop or acquire new businesses to fill it.

Figure 2.2 illustrates this strategic-planning gap for Musicale (name disguised), a major manufacturer of blank compact discs. The lowest curve projects the expected sales over the next five years from the current business portfolio. The highest curve describes desired sales over the same period. Evidently, the company wants to grow much faster than its current businesses will permit. How can it fill the strategic-planning gap?

The first option is to identify opportunities to achieve further growth within current businesses (intensive opportunities). The second is to identify opportunities to build or acquire businesses that are related to current businesses (integrative opportunities). The third is to identify opportunities to add attractive businesses that are unrelated to current businesses (diversification opportunities).

FIGURE 2.2

The Strategic-Planning Gap

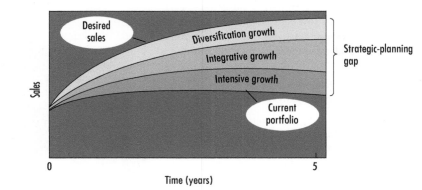

INTENSIVE GROWTH Corporate management's first course of action should be a review of opportunities for improving existing businesses. One useful framework for detecting new intensive-growth opportunities is a "product-market expansion grid."[23] It considers the strategic growth opportunities for a firm in terms of current and new products and markets.

The company first considers whether it could gain more market share with its current products in their current markets (market-penetration strategy). Next it considers whether it can find or develop new markets for its current products (market-development strategy). Then it considers whether it can develop new products of potential interest to its current markets (product-development strategy). Later it will also review opportunities to develop new products for new markets (diversification strategy). Consider how ESPN has employed growth opportunities.[24]

ESPN

ESPN (the Entertainment and Sports Programming Network) was launched in 1978 with a single satellite, broadcasting regional sports and obscure international sporting contests such as the "World's Strongest Man." Through its singular focus on providing sports programming and news, it grew into the biggest name in sports. In the early 1990s, the company crafted a well-thought-out plan: wherever sports fans watched, read, and discussed sports, ESPN would be there. It pursued this strategy by expanding its brand into a number of new categories and by 2009 encompassed 10 cable channels, a website, a magazine, a restaurant chain (ESPNzone), more than 600 local radio affiliates, original movies and television series, book publishing, a sports merchandise catalogue and online store, music and video games, and a mobile service. ESPN continues to expand its brand footprint. Its failed seven-month foray into the fiercely competitive cell phone market in 2006 left it undaunted. It transitioned from a service provider to a content provider in 2007 and partnered with Verizon Wireless to launch ESPN MVP. Now owned by The Walt Disney Company, ESPN earns US$5 billion a year in revenue, but perhaps the greatest tribute to the power of its brand came from one male focus group respondent: "If ESPN was a woman, I'd marry her."

How might Musicale use three major intensive-growth strategies—market penetration, market development, and product development—to increase its sales? If using market penetration, Musicale could try to encourage its current customers to buy more by demonstrating the benefits of using compact discs for data storage in addition to recording music. Musicale could try to attract competitors' customers in the existing market if it noticed major weaknesses in competitors' product or marketing programs. Finally, Musicale could try to convince nonusers in the market of compact discs to start using them.

How can Musicale use a market-development strategy? First, it might try to identify potential user groups in adjacent sales areas. If Musicale has been selling compact discs only to consumer markets, it might go after office and factory markets. Second, Musicale might seek additional distribution channels to reach new markets. If it has been selling its discs only through stereo-equipment dealers, it might add mass-merchandising channels. Third, the company might consider selling in new locations in its home country or abroad.

Management should also consider new-product possibilities. Musicale could develop new features, such as additional data storage capabilities or greater durability. It could offer the CD at two or more quality levels, or it could research an alternative technology such as flash drives.

By examining these intensive growth strategies, management may discover several ways to grow. Still, that growth may not be enough. In that case, management must also look for integrative-growth opportunities.

INTEGRATIVE GROWTH A business's sales and profits may be increased through backward, forward, or horizontal integration within its industry. For example, drug company giant Merck has gone beyond just developing and selling ethical pharmaceuticals. It purchased Medco, a mail-order pharmaceutical distributor, in 1993; formed a joint venture with DuPont to establish more basic research; and formed another joint venture with Johnson & Johnson to bring some of its ethical products to the over-the-counter market.

Horizontal mergers and alliances don't always work out. The merger between Sears and Kmart didn't solve either retailer's problems.[25] Media companies have long reaped the benefits of integrative growth, however.

Corus Entertainment

Corus Entertainment is one of Canada's most successful integrated media and entertainment companies. It was built from the media assets originally owned by Shaw Communications, and spun off as a separate, publicly traded company in 1999. Since then, it has grown remarkably through strategic acquisitions. Its television services include YTV, Treehouse, Nickelodeon (Canada), TELETOON, TELETOON Retro, W Network, CosmoTV, VIVA, W Movies, CMT (Canada), Sundance Channel (Canada), DUSK, Telelatino, Western Canada's pay TV service Movie Central, HBO Canada in the West, and three local over-the-air television stations. It is also a leader in Canadian radio, with 49 stations clustered predominantly in major Canadian markets. Corus takes prides in its many companies and brands that deliver compelling, engaging, interactive, and informative content to millions of people every day.[26]

How might Musicale achieve integrative growth? The company might acquire one or more of its suppliers (such as plastic-material producers) to gain more control or generate more profit (backward integration). It might acquire some wholesalers or retailers, especially if they are highly profitable (forward integration). Finally, Musicale might acquire one or more competitors, provided that the government does not bar this move (horizontal integration). However, these new sources may still not deliver the desired sales volume. In that case, the company must consider diversification.

DIVERSIFICATION GROWTH Diversification growth makes sense when good opportunities can be found outside the present businesses. A good opportunity is one in which the industry is highly attractive and the company has the right mix of business strengths to be successful. For example, from its origins as an animated film producer, Walt Disney Company has moved into licensing characters for merchandised goods, entered the broadcast industry with its own Disney Channel as well as ABC and ESPN acquisitions, and developed theme parks and vacation and resort properties.

Several types of diversification are possible for Musicale. First, the company could choose a concentric strategy and seek new products that have technological or marketing synergies with existing product lines, even though the new products themselves may appeal to a different group of customers. It might start a mini-disc manufacturing operation because it knows how to manufacture compact discs. Second, the company might use a horizontal strategy to search for new products that could appeal to current customers even though the new products are technologically unrelated to its current product line. Musicale might produce compact disc cases, even though producing them requires a different manufacturing process. Finally, the company might seek new businesses that have no relationship to its current technology, products, or markets (a conglomerate strategy) and consider making application software or personal organizers.

DOWNSIZING AND DIVESTING OLDER BUSINESSES Weak businesses require a disproportionate amount of managerial attention. Companies must carefully prune, harvest, or divest themselves of tired old businesses in order to release needed resources to other uses and reduce costs. In 2004, Bombardier sold one of its "heritage assets," the recreational-products division, maker of its famous Sea-Doo personal watercraft and Ski-Doo snowmobiles. The sale took place as a recovery measure so the company could have the flexibility to focus on its rail-equipment and aerospace businesses.

Organization and Organizational Culture

Strategic planning is done within the context of the organization. A company's **organization** consists of its structures, policies, and corporate culture, all of which can become dysfunctional in a rapidly changing business environment. Whereas structures and policies can be changed (with difficulty), the company's culture is very hard to change. Yet changing a corporate culture is often the key to successfully implementing a new strategy.

What exactly is a **corporate culture**? Most businesspeople would be hard-pressed to find words to describe this elusive concept, which some define as "the shared experiences, stories, beliefs, and norms that characterize an organization." Yet, walk into any company and the first thing that strikes you is the corporate culture: the way people are dressed, how they talk to one another, and the way they greet customers.

A customer-centric culture can affect all aspects of an organization. Sometimes corporate culture develops organically and is transmitted directly from the CEO's personality and habits to company employees.

Mike Lazaridis, president and co-CEO of BlackBerry producer Research In Motion (headquartered in Waterloo, Ontario), is a scientist in his own right, winning an Academy Award for technical achievement in film. He hosts a weekly, innovation-centred "Vision Series" at company headquarters to focus on new research and company goals. As he states, "I think we have a culture of innovation here, and [engineers] have absolute access to me. I live a life that tries to promote innovation."[27]

Marketing Innovation

Innovation in marketing is critical. The traditional view is that senior management hammers out the strategy and hands it down. Gary Hamel offers the contrasting view that imaginative ideas on strategy exist in many places within a company.[28] Senior management should identify and encourage fresh ideas from three groups who tend to be underrepresented in strategy making: employees with youthful perspectives; employees who are far removed from company headquarters; and employees who are new to the industry. Each group is capable of challenging company orthodoxy and stimulating new ideas.

German-based Reckitt Benckiser has been an innovator in the staid household cleaning products industry by generating 40 percent of sales from products under three years old. Its multinational staff is encouraged to dig deep into consumer habits and is well-rewarded for excellent performance. "Marketing Insight: Different Approaches to Innovative Marketing" describes how some leading companies approach innovation.

MARKETING **INSIGHT**	DIFFERENT APPROACHES TO INNOVATIVE MARKETING

When IBM surveyed top CEOs and government leaders about their agenda priorities, their answers about innovation were revealing. Business-model innovation and coming up with unique ways of doing things scored high. IBM's own drive for business-model innovation led to much collaboration, both within IBM itself and externally with companies, governments, and educational institutions. CEO Samuel Palmisano noted how the breakthrough Cell processor, based on the company's Power architecture, would not have happened without collaboration with Sony and Nintendo, as well as competitors Toshiba and Microsoft.

Procter & Gamble has similarly set a goal for 50 percent of the company's new products to come from outside P&G's labs—from inventors, scientists, and suppliers whose new-product ideas can be developed in-house.

The research of business guru Jim Collins emphasizes the importance of systematic, broad-based innovation: "Always looking for the one big breakthrough, the one big idea, is contrary to what we found: To build a truly great company, it's decision upon decision, action upon action, day upon day, month upon month.... It's cumulative momentum and no one decision defines a great company." He cites the success of Walt Disney with theme parks and Walmart with retailing as examples of companies which were successful after having executed a big idea brilliantly over such a long period of time.

Northwestern's Mohan Sawhney and his colleagues outline 12 dimensions of business innovation that make up the "innovation radar" (see Table 2.3) and suggest that business innovation is about increasing customer *value*, not just creating new *things*; business innovation comes in many flavours and can take place on any dimension of a business system; and business innovation is systematic and requires careful consideration of all aspects of a business.

Finally, to find breakthrough ideas, some companies find ways to immerse a range of employees in solving marketing problems. Samsung's Value Innovation Program (VIP) isolates product-development teams of engineers, designers, and planners with a timetable and end date in the company's centre just south of Seoul, Korea, while 50 specialists help guide the teams' activities. To help make tough trade-offs, team members draw "value curves" that rank attributes such as a product's sound or picture quality on a scale from one to five. To develop a new car, BMW similarly mobilizes specialists in engineering, design, production, marketing, purchasing, and finance at its Research and Innovation Center or Project House.

Sources: Steve Hamm, "Innovation: The View from the Top," *BusinessWeek*, April 3, 2006, pp. 52–53; Jena McGregor, "The World's Most Innovative Companies," *BusinessWeek*, April 24, 2006, pp. 63–74; Rich Karlgard, "Digital Rules," *Forbes*, March 13, 2006, p. 31; Jennifer Rooney and Jim Collins, "Being Great Is Not Just a Matter of Big Ideas," *Point*, June 2006, p. 20; Moon Ihlwan, "Camp Samsung," *BusinessWeek*, July 3, 2006, pp. 46–47; Mohanbir Sawhney, Robert C. Wolcott, and Inigo Arroniz, "The 12 Different Ways for Companies to Innovate," *MIT Sloan Management Review*, Spring 2006, pp. 75–85.

TABLE 2.3	THE 12 DIMENSIONS OF BUSINESS INNOVATION	
Dimension	**Definition**	**Examples**
Offerings (WHAT)	Develop innovative new products or services.	■ Gillette Mach3Turbo razor ■ Apple iPad for web, email, photo, and video use
Platform	Use common components oor building blocks to create derivative offerings.	■ General Motors OnStar telematics platform derivative ■ Disney animated movies
Solutions	Create integrated and customized offerings that solve end-to-end customer problems.	■ UPS logistics services Supply Chain Solutions ■ DuPont Building Innovations for construction
Customers (WHO)	Discover unmet customer needs or identify underserved customer segments.	■ Enterprise Rent-A-Car focus on replacement-car renters ■ Bullfrog Power focus on "green power"
Customer Experience	Redesign customer interactions across all touch points and all moments of contact.	■ ING Direct retail-banking concept ■ Second Cup's "store as neighbourhood oasis" concept
Value Capture	Redefine how company gets paid or create innovative new revenue streams.	■ Google paid search ■ Blockbuster revenue sharing with movie distributors
Processes (HOW)	Redesign core operating processes to improve efficiency and effectiveness.	■ Toyota Production System for operations ■ General Electric Design for Six Sigma (DFSS)
Organization	Change form, function, or activity scope of the firm.	■ Cisco partner-centric networked virtual organization ■ Procter & Gamble front-back hybrid organization for customer focus
Supply Chain	Think differently about sourcing and fulfillment.	■ Moen ProjectNet for collaborative design with suppliers ■ General Motors Celta use of integrated supply and online sales
Presence (WHERE)	Create new distribution channels or innovative points of presence, including the places where offerings can be bought or used by customers.	■ Starbucks music-CD sales in coffee stores ■ Diebold RemoteTeller System for banking
Networking	Create network-centric intelligent and integrated offerings.	■ Otis Remote Elevator Monitoring service ■ Bell Canada's Intelligent Systems
Brand	Leverage a brand into new domains.	■ Virgin Group "branded venture capital" ■ Yahoo! as a lifestyle brand

Source: Mohanbir Sawhney, Robert C. Wolcott, and Inigo Arroniz, "The 12 Different Ways for Companies to Innovate," *MIT Sloan Management Review*, Spring 2006, p. 78. From *MIT Sloan Management Review* © 2006 by Massachusetts Institute of Technology. All rights reserved. Distributed by Tribune Media Services.

Firms develop strategy by identifying and selecting among different views of the future. The Royal Dutch/Shell Group has pioneered **scenario analysis**, which develops plausible representations of a firm's possible future using assumptions about forces driving the market and different uncertainties. Managers think through each scenario with the question "What will we do if it happens?" They then adopt one scenario as the most probable and watch for signposts that might confirm or disconfirm it.[29] Consider the challenges faced by the movie industry.

Movie Industry

The success of Netflix in the United States and the ease of watching longer-form entertainment or playing games on broadband Internet helped produce a 6.8 percent decrease in DVD sales. (Netflix started offering online services in Canada in September 2010, but many found the selection disappointing.) The recent emergence of Redbox and its thousands of kiosks renting movies for $1 a day poses yet another threat to the movie business and DVD sales. Film studios clearly need to prepare for the day when films are primarily sold not

Netflix and Redbox kiosks have film studios rethinking their pricing and distribution strategies.

through physical distribution but through satellite and cable companies' video-on-demand services. Although studios make 70 percent on a typical $4.99 cable viewing versus 30 percent on the sale of a DVD, sales of DVDs still generate 70 percent of film profits. To increase electronic distribution without destroying their DVD business, studios are experimenting with new approaches. Some, such as Warner Bros., are releasing a DVD at the same time as online and cable versions of a movie. Disney has emphasized its parent-friendly Disney-branded films, which generate higher DVD sales and are easy to cross-promote at the company's theme parks, on its TV channels, and in its stores. Paramount chose to debut *Jackass 2.5* on Blockbuster's site for free to create buzz and interest. Film studios are considering all possible scenarios as they rethink their business model in a world where the DVD no longer will reign as king.[30]

BUSINESS UNIT STRATEGIC PLANNING

The business unit strategic-planning process consists of the steps shown in Figure 2.3. We examine each step in the sections that follow.

The Business Mission

Each business unit needs to define its specific mission within the broader company mission. Thus, a lighting-equipment company that serves television studios might define its mission as "to target major television studios and become their vendor of choice for lighting technologies that represent the most advanced and reliable studio lighting arrangements." Notice that this mission does not attempt to win business from smaller television studios, offer the lowest price, or venture into nonlighting products.

SWOT Analysis

The overall evaluation of a company's strengths, weaknesses, opportunities, and threats is called SWOT analysis. It's a way of monitoring the external and internal marketing environment.

EXTERNAL ENVIRONMENT (OPPORTUNITY AND THREAT) ANALYSIS A business unit has to monitor key *macroenvironment forces* (demographic-economic, natural, technological, political-legal, social-cultural) and significant *microenvironment actors* (customers, competitors, suppliers, distributors, dealers) that affect its ability to earn profits. The business unit should set up a marketing intelligence system to track trends and important developments. For each trend or development, management needs to identify the associated opportunities and threats.

Good marketing is the art of finding, developing, and profiting from opportunities.[31] A **marketing opportunity** is an area of buyer need and interest in which there is a high probability that a company can profitably satisfy that need. There are three main sources of market opportunities.[32] The first is to supply something in short supply. This requires little marketing talent, as the need is fairly obvious. The second is to supply an existing product or service in a new or superior way. There are several ways to uncover possible product or service improvements: by asking consumers for their suggestions (*problem-detection method*); by asking consumers to imagine an ideal version of the product or service (*ideal method*); and by asking consumers to chart their steps in acquiring, using, and disposing of a product (*consumption-chain method*). The third source often leads to a totally new product or service.

Opportunities can take many forms and marketers have to be good at spotting them. Consider the following:

FIGURE 2.3

The Business Unit Strategic-Planning Process

- A company may benefit from converging industry trends and introduce hybrid products or services that are new to the market. Example: At least five major cell phone manufacturers released phones with digital-photo capabilities.

- A company may make a buying process more convenient or efficient. Example: Consumers can now use the Internet to find more books than ever and search for the lowest price with a few clicks.

- A company can meet the need for more information and advice. Example: Guru.com facilitates finding professional experts in a wide range of fields.

- A company can customize a product or service that was formerly offered only in a standard form. Example: P&G's Reflect.com website is capable of producing a customized skin-care or hair-care product to meet a customer's need.

- A company can introduce a new capability. Example: Consumers can now create and edit digital iMovies with the iMac and upload them to an Apple web server to share with friends around the world.

- A company may be able to deliver a product or a service faster. Example: FedEx discovered a way to deliver mail and packages much more quickly than the U.S. Postal Service.

- A company may be able to offer a product at a much lower price. Example: Pharmaceutical firms have created generic versions of brand-name drugs.

To evaluate opportunities, companies can use **Market Opportunity Analysis (MOA)** to determine the attractiveness and probability of success, asking themselves the following questions:

1. Can the benefits involved in the opportunity be articulated convincingly to a defined target market(s)?

2. Can the target market(s) be located and reached with cost-effective media and trade channels?

3. Does the company possess or have access to the critical capabilities and resources needed to deliver the customer benefits?

4. Can the company deliver the benefits better than any actual or potential competitors?

5. Will the financial rate of return meet or exceed the company's required threshold for investment?

In the opportunity matrix in Figure 2.4(a), the best marketing opportunities facing the lighting-equipment company are listed in the upper-left cell (#1). The opportunities in the lower-right cell (#4) are too minor to consider. The opportunities in the upper-right cell (#2) and lower-left cell (#3) should be monitored in the event that any improve in attractiveness and success probability.

An **environmental threat** is a challenge posed by an unfavourable trend or development that would lead, in the absence of defensive marketing action, to lower sales or profit. Threats should be classified according to seriousness and probability of occurrence. Figure 2.4(b) illustrates the threat matrix facing the lighting-equipment company. The threats in the upper-left cell are major because they can seriously hurt the company and they have a high probability of occurrence. To deal with them, the company needs contingency plans that spell out changes it can make before or during the threat. The threats in the lower-right cell are very minor and can be ignored. The threats in the upper-right and lower-left cells need to be monitored carefully in the event that they grow more serious.

INTERNAL ENVIRONMENT (STRENGTHS/WEAKNESSES) ANALYSIS It is one thing to find attractive opportunities and another to be able to take advantage of them. Each business needs to evaluate its internal strengths and weaknesses relative to those of its competition. Loblaws, for example, when compared with Walmart's new grocery business, has the advantage of great locations in the heart of most Canadian cities and strong private brands, but it is weaker when it comes to the management of inventory and suppliers. Businesses can evaluate their own strengths and weaknesses by using a form like the one shown in "Marketing Memo: Checklist for Strengths/Weaknesses Analysis."

Clearly, the business does not have to correct all its weaknesses, nor should it gloat about all its strengths. The big question is whether the business should limit itself to those opportunities where it possesses the required strengths or whether it should consider opportunities that mean it might have to acquire or develop certain strengths. For example, managers at Texas Instruments (TI) were split between those who wanted TI to stick to industrial electronics (where it has clear strength) and those who wanted the company to continue introducing consumer products (where it lacks some required marketing strengths).

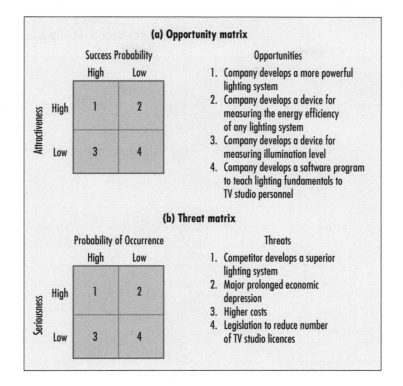

FIGURE 2.4

Opportunity and Threat Matrices

Goal Formulation

Once the company has performed a SWOT analysis, it can proceed to develop specific goals for the planning period. This stage of the process is called **goal formulation**. Managers use the term *goals* to describe objectives that are specific with respect to magnitude and time.

Most business units pursue a mix of objectives, including profitability, sales growth, market share improvement, risk containment, innovation, and reputation. The business unit sets these objectives and then manages by objectives (MBO). For an MBO system to work, the unit's objectives must meet four criteria:

1. *They must be arranged hierarchically, from the most to the least important.* For example, the business unit's key objective for the period may be to increase the rate of return on investment. Managers can increase profit by increasing revenue and reducing expenses. Revenue can be increased by increasing market share and prices.

2. *Objectives should be stated quantitatively whenever possible.* The objective "increase the return on investment (ROI)" is better stated as the goal "increase ROI to 15 percent within two years."

3. *Goals should be realistic.* They should arise from an analysis of the business unit's opportunities and strengths, not from wishful thinking.

4. *Objectives must be consistent.* It is not possible to maximize both sales and profits simultaneously.

Other important trade-offs include short-term profit versus long-term growth, deep penetration of existing markets versus development of new markets, profit goals versus nonprofit goals, and high growth versus low risk. Each choice in this set of trade-offs calls for a different marketing strategy.[33]

Many believe that adopting the goal of strong market share growth may mean having to forgo strong short-term profits. Volkswagen has 15 times the annual revenue of Porsche—but Porsche's profit margins are 7 times bigger than Volkswagen's. Other successful companies, such as Google, Microsoft, and Samsung, have maximized profitability *and* growth.

Strategy Formulation

Goals indicate what a business unit wants to achieve; **strategy** is a game plan for getting there. Every business must design a strategy for achieving its goals, consisting of a *marketing strategy* and a compatible *technology strategy* and *sourcing strategy*.

MARKETING **MEMO**		CHECKLIST FOR STRENGTHS/WEAKNESSES ANALYSIS						

	Performance					Importance		
	Major Strength	Minor Strength	Neutral	Minor Weakness	Major Weakness	High	Med	Low
Marketing								
1. Company reputation	____	____	____	____	____	____	____	____
2. Market share	____	____	____	____	____	____	____	____
3. Customer satisfaction	____	____	____	____	____	____	____	____
4. Customer retention	____	____	____	____	____	____	____	____
5. Product quality	____	____	____	____	____	____	____	____
6. Service quality	____	____	____	____	____	____	____	____
7. Pricing effectiveness	____	____	____	____	____	____	____	____
8. Distribution effectiveness	____	____	____	____	____	____	____	____
9. Promotion effectiveness	____	____	____	____	____	____	____	____
10. Sales force effectiveness	____	____	____	____	____	____	____	____
11. Innovation effectiveness	____	____	____	____	____	____	____	____
12. Geographical coverage	____	____	____	____	____	____	____	____
Finance								
13. Cost or availability of capital	____	____	____	____	____	____	____	____
14. Cash flow	____	____	____	____	____	____	____	____
15. Financial stability	____	____	____	____	____	____	____	____
Manufacturing								
16. Facilities	____	____	____	____	____	____	____	____
17. Economies of scale	____	____	____	____	____	____	____	____
18. Capacity	____	____	____	____	____	____	____	____
19. Able, dedicated workforce	____	____	____	____	____	____	____	____
20. Ability to produce on time	____	____	____	____	____	____	____	____
21. Technical manufacturing skill	____	____	____	____	____	____	____	____
Organization								
22. Visionary, capable leadership	____	____	____	____	____	____	____	____
23. Dedicated employees	____	____	____	____	____	____	____	____
24. Entrepreneurial orientation	____	____	____	____	____	____	____	____
25. Flexible or responsive	____	____	____	____	____	____	____	____

PORTER'S GENERIC STRATEGIES Michael Porter has proposed three generic strategies that provide a good starting point for strategic thinking: overall-cost leadership, differentiation, and focus.[34]

■ *Overall-cost leadership.* Firms pursuing this strategy must be good at engineering, purchasing, manufacturing, and physical distribution. They need less skill in marketing. The problem with this strategy is that other firms will compete with still-lower costs and hurt the firm that rested its whole future on cost.

■ *Differentiation.* The business concentrates on achieving superior performance in an important customer-benefit area valued by a large part of the market. Thus, the firm seeking quality leadership, for example, must make products with the best components, put them together expertly, inspect them carefully, and effectively communicate their quality.

■ *Focus.* The business focuses on one or more narrow market segments. The firm gets to know these segments intimately and pursues either cost leadership or differentiation within the target segment.

The online air-travel industry provides a good example of these three strategies: Travelocity is pursuing a differentiation strategy by offering the most comprehensive range of services to the traveller. Lowestfare is pursuing a lowest-cost strategy; and Last Minute is pursuing a niche strategy in focusing on travellers who have the flexibility to travel on very short notice.

According to Porter, firms pursuing the same strategy directed to the same target market constitute a **strategic group**.[35] The firm that carries out that strategy best will make the most profits. Firms that do not pursue a clear strategy and try to be good on all strategic dimensions do the worst. Eaton's fell upon hard times because it did not stand out in its industry as lowest in cost, highest in **perceived value**, or best in serving some market segment.

Porter draws a distinction between operational effectiveness and strategy. Competitors can quickly copy an operationally effective company using benchmarking and other tools, thus diminishing the advantage of operational effectiveness. Porter defines strategy as "the creation of a unique and valuable position involving a different set of activities." A company can claim that it has a strategy when it "performs different activities from rivals or performs similar activities in different ways."

STRATEGIC ALLIANCES Companies are also discovering that they need strategic partners if they hope to be effective. Even giant companies—AT&T, Philips, Nokia—often cannot achieve leadership, either nationally or globally, without forming alliances with domestic or multinational companies that complement or leverage their capabilities and resources.

Just doing business in another country may require the firm to license its product, form a joint venture with a local firm, or buy from local suppliers to meet "domestic content" requirements. As a result, many firms are rapidly developing global strategic networks, and victory is going to those who build the better global network. The Star Alliance, for example, joins Air Canada with 26 other airlines, including Lufthansa, United Airlines, Mexicana, Austrian Airlines, British Midland, Singapore Airlines, SAS, Thai Airways, Varig, Air New Zealand, and South African Airways, to form a huge global partnership that allows travellers to make nearly seamless connections to hundreds of destinations.

To operate on a global scale, many companies, like Air Canada, find they need to be part of a strategic alliance.

Many strategic alliances take the form of marketing alliances. These fall into four major categories:

1. *Product or service alliances.* One company licenses another to produce its product, or two companies jointly market their complementary products or a new product. For instance, Bell Canada and Microsoft—two service businesses—have joined together in a marketing alliance, Sympatico/MSN.

2. *Promotional alliances.* One company agrees to carry a promotion for another company's product or service. For example, the Aeroplan rewards program promotes the products and services of its partners, including Fairmont hotels, Home Hardware, Avis car rental, Rogers magazines, and Primus telephone and Internet service.[36]

3. *Logistics alliances.* One company offers logistical services for another company's product. For example, Warner Music Group and Sub Pop Records created the Alternative Distribution Alliance (ADA) in 1993 as a joint venture to distribute and manufacture records owned by independent labels. ADA is the leading indie distribution company in the United States for both physical and digital product.

4. *Pricing collaborations.* One or more companies join in a special pricing collaboration. Hotel and rental car companies often offer mutual price discounts.

Companies need to give creative thought to finding partners that might complement their strengths and offset their weaknesses. Well-managed alliances allow companies to obtain a greater sales impact at less cost. To keep their strategic alliances thriving, corporations have begun to develop organizational structures to support them and have come to view the ability to form and manage partnerships as core skills (called **partner relationship management, PRM**).[37]

In many industries, such as the pharmaceutical, biotech, and telecommunications industries, companies are starting to make partnership a core competency. After years of growth through acquisition and buying interests in two dozen companies, the world's biggest wireless telecom operator, Vodafone, has looked outside the company for partners to help it leverage its existing assets.[38]

Vodafone

To spur more innovation and growth, Vodafone has embraced open source software and open platforms that allow it to tap into the creativity and skills of others. With its web portal called Betavine, amateur or professional software developers can create and test their latest mobile applications on any network, not just Vodafone's. While these developers retain intellectual property rights, Vodafone gains early exposure to the latest trends and ensures that innovations are compatible with its network. Some of the new apps include real-time train arrivals and departures, movie show times, and an Amazon.com widget with personalized details. With 289 million customers in 27 countries, the $35 billion company hasn't had trouble finding help from interested corporate partners either. Dell has collaborated with Vodafone to design laptops and low-priced netbooks with built-in wireless broadband access over Vodafone's networks.

Program Formulation and Implementation

Even a great marketing strategy can be sabotaged by poor implementation. If the unit has decided to attain technological leadership, it must plan programs to strengthen its R&D department, gather technological intelligence, develop leading-edge products, train the technical sales force, and develop ads to communicate its technological leadership.

Once the marketing programs are formulated, the marketing people must estimate their costs. Questions arise: Is participating in a particular trade show worthwhile? Will a specific sales contest pay for itself? Will hiring another salesperson contribute to the bottom line? Activity-based cost (ABC) accounting should be applied to each marketing program to determine whether it is likely to produce results sufficient to justify the cost.[39]

Today's businesses are increasingly recognizing that unless they nurture other stakeholders—customers, employees, suppliers, distributors—the business may never earn sufficient profits for the shareholders. For example, it might aim to delight its customers, perform well for its employees, and deliver a threshold level of satisfaction to its suppliers. In setting these levels, a company must be careful not to violate the various stakeholder groups' sense of fairness about their relative treatment.[40]

There is a dynamic relationship connecting the stakeholder groups. A smart company creates a high level of employee satisfaction, which leads to higher effort, which leads to higher-quality products and services, which creates higher customer satisfaction, which leads to more repeat business, which leads to higher growth and profits, which leads to high shareholder satisfaction, which leads to more investment, and so on. This is the virtuous circle that spells profits and growth. According to McKinsey & Company, strategy is only one of seven elements in successful business practice (referred to as the seven Ss).[41] The first three elements—strategy, structure, and systems—are considered the "hardware" of success. The next four—style, skills, staffing, and shared values—are the "software."

The first "soft" element, *style,* means company employees share a common way of thinking and behaving. The second, *skills,* means employees have the skills needed to carry out the company's strategy. *Staffing* means the company has hired able people, trained them well, and assigned them to the right jobs. The fourth element, *shared values,* means employees share the same guiding values. When these elements are present, companies are usually more successful at strategy implementation.[42]

Feedback and Control

A company's strategic fit with the environment will inevitably erode because the market environment changes faster than the company's seven Ss. Thus, a company might remain efficient while it loses effectiveness. Peter Drucker pointed out that it is more important to "do the right thing" (effectiveness) than "to do things right" (efficiency). The most successful companies excel at both.

Once an organization fails to respond to a changed environment, recapturing its lost position becomes increasingly hard. Consider KB Toys. Founded in 1922 as a candy wholesaler, the company successfully reinvented itself many times, first by shifting its focus to discounted toys and then by anticipating the growth of shopping malls. The firm became the second-largest toy retailer in the world but ultimately crumbled due to competition from big-box retailers and its failed acquisition of eToys. The company declared bankruptcy in 1994 but re-emerged in the late 1990s—only to again file bankruptcy and liquidate its assets in late 2008.

Organizations, especially large ones, are subject to inertia. It is difficult to change one part without adjusting everything else. Yet organizations can be changed through strong leadership, preferably in advance of a crisis. The key to organizational health is willingness to examine the changing environment and to adopt new goals and behaviours.

PRODUCT PLANNING: THE NATURE AND CONTENTS OF A MARKETING PLAN

Working within the plans set by the levels above them, product managers come up with marketing plans for individual products, lines, brands, channels, or customer groups. Each product level (product line, brand) must develop a marketing plan for achieving its goals. A **marketing plan** is a written document that summarizes what the marketer has learned about the marketplace and indicates how the firm plans to reach its marketing objectives.[43] It contains tactical guidelines for the marketing programs and financial allocations over the planning period.[44]

A marketing plan is one of the most important outputs of the marketing process. It provides direction and focus for a brand, product, or company. Nonprofit organizations use marketing plans to guide their fund-raising and outreach efforts, and government agencies use them to build public awareness of nutrition and stimulate tourism.

More limited in scope than a business plan, the marketing plan documents how the organization will achieve its strategic objectives through specific marketing strategies and tactics, with the customer as the starting point. It is also linked to the plans of other departments. Suppose a marketing plan calls for selling 200 000 units annually. The production department must gear up to make that many units, finance must arrange funding to cover the expenses, human resources must be ready to hire and train staff, and so on. Without the appropriate level of organizational support and resources, no marketing plan can succeed.

Marketing plans are becoming more customer- and competitor-oriented, better reasoned, and more realistic than in the past. The plans draw more inputs from all the functions and are team developed. Marketing executives increasingly see themselves as professional managers first and specialists second. Planning is becoming a continuous process to respond to rapidly changing market conditions.

Although the exact length and layout varies from company to company, most marketing plans cover one year and vary in length from under 5 to over 50 pages. Smaller businesses may create shorter or less formal marketing plans, whereas corporations generally require highly structured documents. To guide implementation effectively, every part of the plan must be described in considerable detail. Sometimes a company will post its marketing plan on an internal website so everyone can consult specific sections and collaborate on changes. The most frequently cited shortcomings of current marketing plans, according to marketing executives, are lack of realism, insufficient competitive analysis, and a short-run focus. (See "Marketing Memo: Marketing Plan Criteria" for some guideline questions to ask in developing marketing plans.)

What, then, does a marketing plan look like? What does it contain? A marketing plan usually contains the following sections:

■ *Executive summary and table of contents.* The marketing plan should open with a brief summary of the main goals and recommendations. The executive summary permits senior management to grasp the plan's major thrust. The summary should be followed by a table of contents that outlines the rest of the plan and all the supporting rationale and operational detail.

■ *Situation analysis.* This section presents relevant background data on sales, costs, the market, competitors, and the various forces in the macroenvironment. How is the market defined, how big is it, and how fast is it growing? What are the relevant trends affecting the market? What is the product offering and what are the critical issues facing the company? Pertinent historical information can be included to provide context. All this information is used to carry out a SWOT (strengths, weaknesses, opportunities, threats) analysis.

■ *Marketing strategy.* Here the product manager defines the mission and marketing and financial objectives. The manager also defines those groups and needs that the market offerings are intended to satisfy. The manager then establishes the product line's competitive positioning, which will inform the game plan to accomplish the plan's objectives. All this is done with inputs from other organizational areas, such as purchasing, manufacturing, sales, finance, and human resources, to ensure that the company can provide proper support for effective implementation.

■ *Financial projections.* Financial projections include a sales forecast, an expense forecast, and a break-even analysis. On the revenue side, the projections show the forecast sales volume by month and product category. On the expense side, the projections show the expected costs of marketing broken down into finer categories. The **break-even analysis** shows how many units must be sold monthly to offset the monthly fixed costs and average per-unit variable costs. A more complex method of estimating profit is risk analysis. **Risk analysis** involves obtaining three estimates (optimistic, pessimistic, and most likely) for each uncertain variable affecting profitability, under an assumed marketing environment and marketing strategy for the planning period. A computer simulates possible outcomes and computes a distribution showing the range of possible rates of return and their probabilities.[45]

■ *Implementation controls.* The last section of the marketing plan outlines the controls for monitoring and adjusting implementation of the plan. Typically, the goals and budget are spelled out for each month or quarter so management can review each period's results and take corrective action as needed. A number of different internal and external measures will need to be taken to assess progress and suggest possible modifications. Some organizations include contingency plans outlining the steps management would take in response to specific environmental developments, such as price wars or strikes.

MARKETING **MEMO** | MARKETING PLAN CRITERIA

Here are some questions to ask in evaluating a marketing plan.

1. *Is the plan simple?* Is it easy to understand and act on? Does it communicate its content easily and practically?

2. *Is the plan specific?* Are its objectives concrete and measurable? Does it include specific actions and activities, each with specific dates of completion, specific persons responsible, and specific budgets?

3. *Is the plan realistic?* Are the sales goals, expense budgets, and milestone dates realistic? Has a frank and honest self-critique been conducted to raise possible concerns and objections?

4. *Is the plan complete?* Does it include all the necessary elements?

Source: Tim Berry and Doug Wilson, *On Target: The Book on Marketing Plans* (Eugene, OR: Palo Alto Software, 2000).

The Role of Research

To develop innovative products, successful strategies, and action programs, marketers need up-to-date information about the environment, the competition, and the selected market segments. Often, analysis of internal data is the starting point for assessing the current marketing situation, supplemented by marketing intelligence and research investigating the overall market, the competition, key issues, threats, and opportunities. As the plan is put into effect, marketers use research to measure progress toward objectives and identify areas for improvement. Finally, marketing research helps marketers learn more about their customers' requirements, expectations, perceptions, satisfaction, and loyalty. Thus, the marketing plan should outline what marketing research will be conducted and when, as well as how the findings will be applied.

The Role of Relationships

Although the marketing plan shows how the company will establish and maintain profitable customer relationships, it also affects both internal and external relationships. First, it influences how marketing personnel work with each other and with other departments to deliver value and satisfy customers. Second, it affects how the company works with suppliers, distributors, and partners to achieve the plan's objectives. Third, it influences the company's dealings with other stakeholders, including government regulators, the media, and the community at large. Marketers must consider all these relationships when developing a marketing plan.

From Marketing Plan to Marketing Action

Most companies create yearly marketing plans. Marketers start planning well in advance of the implementation date to allow time for marketing research, analysis, management review, and coordination between departments. As each action program begins, they monitor ongoing results, investigate any deviation from plans, and take corrective steps as needed. Some prepare contingency plans; marketers must be ready to update and adapt marketing plans at any time.

The marketing plan should define how progress toward objectives will be measured. Managers typically use budgets, schedules, and marketing metrics for monitoring and evaluating results. With budgets, they can compare planned expenditures with actual expenditures for a given period. Schedules allow management to see when tasks were supposed to be completed and when they actually were. Marketing metrics track actual outcomes of marketing programs to see whether the company is moving forward toward its objectives.

SAMPLE MARKETING PLAN: PEGASUS SPORTS INTERNATIONAL*

1.0 EXECUTIVE SUMMARY

Pegasus Sports International is a start-up aftermarket inline skating-accessory manufacturer. In addition to its aftermarket products, Pegasus is developing SkateTours, a service that takes clients out, in conjunction with a local skate shop, and provides them with an afternoon of skating using inline skates and some of Pegasus' other accessories such as SkateSails. The aftermarket skate-accessory market has been largely ignored. Although there are several major manufacturers of the skates themselves, the accessory market has not been addressed. This provides Pegasus with an extraordinary opportunity for market growth. Skating is a booming sport. Currently most of the skating is recreational. There are, however, a growing number of skating competitions, including team-orientated competitions such as skate hockey, as well as individual competitions such as speed skate racing. Pegasus will work to grow these markets as well as develop the skate transportation market, a more utilitarian use of skating. Several of Pegasus' current products have patents pending and local market research indicates that there is great demand for these products. Pegasus will achieve fast, significant market penetration through a solid business model, long-range planning, and a strong management team that will be able to execute this exciting opportunity. The three principals on the management team have over 30 years of combined personal and industry experience. This extensive experience provides Pegasus with the empirical information as well as the passion to provide the skating market with much-needed aftermarket products. Pegasus will sell its products initially through its website. This "Dell" direct-to-the-consumer approach will allow Pegasus to achieve higher margins and maintain a close relationship with customers, which is essential for producing products that have true market demand. By the end of the year, Pegasus also will have developed relationships with different skate shops and will begin to sell some of its products through retailers.

1.1 TABLE OF CONTENTS

*Palo Alto Software, Inc.

2.0 SITUATION ANALYSIS

Pegasus is entering its first year of operation. Its products have been well received, and marketing will be key to developing brand and product awareness and growing the customer base. Pegasus International offers several different aftermarket skating accessories, serving the growing inline skating industry.

2.1 MARKET SUMMARY

Pegasus possesses good information about the market and knows a great deal about the common attributes of the most-prized customer. This information will be leveraged to better understand who is served, what their specific needs are, and how Pegasus can better communicate with them.

Target Markets
- Recreational
- Fitness
- Speed
- Hockey
- Extreme

2.1.1 Market Demographics

The profile of the typical Pegasus customer includes the following geographic, demographic, and behaviour factors:

Geographics
- Pegasus has no set geographic target area. By leveraging the expansive reach of the Internet and multiple delivery services, Pegasus can serve both domestic and international customers.
- The total targeted population is 31 million users.

Demographics
- Male and female users, with an almost equal ratio between the two.
- Ages 13–46, with 48 percent clustering around the ages 23–34. The recreational users tend to cover the widest age range, including young users through active adults. The fitness users tend to be ages 20–40. The speed users tend to be in their late 20s and early 30s. The hockey players are generally in their teens through their early 20s, as are the extreme segment.
- Of the users who are over 20, 65 percent have an undergraduate degree or substantial undergraduate coursework.
- The adult users have a median personal income of $47 000.

Behaviour Factors
- Users enjoy fitness activities not as a means to a healthy life, but as an intrinsically enjoyable activity.
- Users spend money on gear, typically sports equipment.
- Users have active lifestyles that include some sort of recreation at least two to three times a week.

2.1.2 Market Needs

Pegasus is providing the skating community with a wide range of accessories for all variations of skating. Pegasus seeks to fulfill the following benefits that are important to its customers:

- *Quality craftsmanship.* The customers work hard for their money and do not enjoy spending it on disposable products that work only for a year or two.
- *Well-thought-out designs.* The skating market has not been addressed by well-thought-out products that serve skaters' needs. Pegasus' industry experience and personal dedication to the sport will provide Pegasus with the information needed to produce insightfully designed products.
- *Customer service.* Exemplary service is required to build a sustainable business that has a loyal customer base.

2.1.3 Market Trends

Pegasus will distinguish itself by marketing products not previously available to skaters. The emphasis in the past has been to sell skates and very few replacement parts. The number of skaters is not restricted to any one single country, continent, or age group, so there is a world market. Pegasus has products for virtually every group of skaters. The fastest-growing segment of this sport is the fitness skater. Therefore, the marketing is being directed to service this group. BladeBoots will enable users to enter establishments without having to remove their skates. BladeBoots will be aimed at the recreational skater, the largest segment. SkateAids, on the other hand, are great for everyone.

The sport of skating will also grow through SkateSailing. This sport is primarily for the medium-to-advanced skater. The growth potential for this sport is tremendous. The sails that Pegasus has manufactured have been sold in Europe, following a pattern similar to windsurfing. Windsurfing originated in Santa Monica, California, but did not take off until it had already grown big in Europe.

Another trend is group skating. More and more groups are getting together on skate excursions in cities all over the world. For example, San Francisco has night group-skating that numbers in the hundreds of people. The market trends are showing continued growth in all aspects of skating.

2.1.4 Market Growth

With the price of skates going down due to competition from so many skate companies, the market has had steady growth throughout the world, although sales have slowed down in some markets. Sales for 2011 are projected to be $31 million. Table 2.1 shows the projected growth rates over the next four years. Growth rates should be steady as more and more people are discovering—and in many cases rediscovering—the health benefits and fun of skating.

2.2 SWOT ANALYSIS

The following SWOT analysis captures the key strengths and weaknesses within the company and describes the opportunities and threats facing Pegasus.

2.2.1 Strengths

- In-depth industry experience and insight
- Creative yet practical product designers
- The use of a highly efficient, flexible business model utilizing direct customer sales and distribution

2.2.2 Weaknesses

- Reliance on outside capital necessary to grow the business
- Lack of retailers who can work face-to-face with customers to generate brand and product awareness
- Difficulty in developing brand awareness because it is a start-up company

2.2.3 Opportunities

- Participation within a growing industry
- Decreased product costs through economies of scale
- Ability to leverage other industry participants' marketing efforts to help grow the general market

2.2.4 Threats

- Future/potential competition from an already established market participant
- A slump in the economy that could have a negative effect on people's spending of discretionary income on fitness/recreational products
- The release of a study that questions the safety of skating or the inability to prevent major skating-induced traumas

2.3 COMPETITION

Pegasus Sports International is forming its own market. Although there are a few companies that do make sails and foils that a few

TABLE 2.1	TARGET-MARKET FORECAST						
				Target-Market Forecast			
Potential Customers	Growth	2011	2012	2013	2014	2015	CAGR*
Recreational	10%	19 142 500	21 056 750	23 162 425	25 478 668	28 026 535	10.00%
Fitness	15%	6 820 000	7 843 000	9 019 450	10 372 368	11 928 223	15.00%
Speed	10%	387 500	426 250	468 875	515 763	567 339	10.00%
Hockey	6%	2 480 000	2 628 800	2 786 528	2 953 720	3 130 943	6.00%
Extreme	4%	2 170 000	2 256 800	2 347 072	2 440 955	2 538 593	4.00%
Total	10.48%	31 000 000	34 211 600	37 784 350	41 761 474	46 191 633	10.48%

*Compound Annual Growth Rate

skaters are using, Pegasus' are the only ones that are truly designed for and by skaters. The few competitors' sails on the market are not designed for skating, but for windsurfing or for skateboards. In the case of foils, storage and carrying are not practical. There are different indirect competitors which are manufacturers of the actual skates. After many years in the market, these companies have yet to become direct competitors by manufacturing accessories for the skates that they make.

2.4 PRODUCT OFFERING

Pegasus Sports International now offers several products:

- The first product that has been developed is BladeBoots, covers for the wheels and frame of inline skates that enable skaters to enter places that normally would not allow them in with skates on. BladeBoots come with a small pouch and belt that converts to a well-designed skate carrier.
- The second product is SkateSails. These sails are designed specifically for use while skating. Feedback that Pegasus has received from skaters indicates skatesailing could become a very popular sport. Trademarking this product is currently in progress.
- The third product, SkateAid, will be in production by the end of the year. Other ideas for products are under development, but will not be disclosed until Pegasus can protect them through pending patent applications.

2.5 KEYS TO SUCCESS

The keys to success are designing and producing products that meet market demand. In addition, Pegasus must ensure total customer satisfaction. If these keys to success are obtained, Pegasus will become a profitable, sustainable company.

2.6 CRITICAL ISSUES

As a start-up business, Pegasus is still in the early stages. The critical issues are for Pegasus to:

- Establish itself as the premier skating-accessory company.
- Pursue controlled growth with payroll expenses that never exceed the revenue base. This will help protect against recessions.
- Constantly monitor customer satisfaction, ensuring that the growth strategy will never compromise service and satisfaction levels.

3.0 MARKETING STRATEGY

The key to the marketing strategy is focusing on the speed, health and fitness, and recreational segments of skaters. Pegasus can cover about 80 percent of the skating market because it produces products geared toward each segment. Pegasus is able to address all of the different segments within the market because, although each segment is distinct in terms of its users and equipment, Pegasus' products are useful to all of the different segments.

3.1 MISSION

Pegasus Sports International's mission is to provide the customer with the finest skating accessories available. We exist to attract and maintain customers. With a strict adherence to this maxim, success will be ensured. Our services and products will exceed the expectations of the customers.

3.2 MARKETING OBJECTIVES

- Maintain positive, strong growth each quarter (notwithstanding seasonal sales patterns).
- Achieve a steady increase in market penetration.
- Decrease customer acquisition costs by 1.5 percent per quarter.

3.3 FINANCIAL OBJECTIVES

- Increase the profit margin by 1 percent per quarter through efficiency and economy-of-scale gains.
- Maintain a significant research and development budget (as a percentage relative to sales) to spur future product developments.
- A double- to triple-digit growth rate for the first three years.

3.4 TARGET MARKETS

With a world skating market that's over 31 million and steadily growing (statistics released by the Sporting Goods Manufacturers Association), the niche has been created. Pegasus' aim is to expand this market by promoting SkateSailing, a new sport that is popular in both Santa Monica and Venice Beach in California. The Sporting Goods Manufacturers Association survey indicates that skating now has more participation than football, softball, skiing, and snowboarding combined. The breakdown of participation of skating is as follows: 1+ percent speed (growing), 8 percent hockey (declining), 7 percent extreme/aggressive (declining), 22 percent fitness (nearly 7 million—the fastest growing), and 61 percent recreational (first-timers). Our products are targeting the fitness and recreational groups because they are the fastest growing. These groups are gearing themselves toward health and fitness, and combined, they can easily grow to 85 percent (or 26 million) of the market in the next five years.

3.5 POSITIONING

Pegasus will position itself as the premier aftermarket skating-accessory company. This positioning will be achieved by leveraging Pegasus' competitive edge: industry experience and passion. Pegasus is a skating company formed by skaters for skaters.

Pegasus' management is able to use its vast experience and personal passion for the sport to develop innovative, useful accessories for a broad range of skaters.

3.6 STRATEGIES

The single objective is to position Pegasus as the premier skating-accessory manufacturer, serving both the domestic and international markets. The marketing strategy will seek first to create customer awareness of the offered products and services and then to develop the customer base. The message that Pegasus will seek to communicate is that Pegasus offers the best-designed, most useful skating accessories. This message will be communicated through a variety of methods. The first will be the Pegasus website. The website will provide a rich source of product information and offer consumers the opportunity to purchase products. A lot of time and money will be invested in the site to provide customers with a perception of total professionalism and the utility of Pegasus' products and services.

The second marketing method will be advertisements placed in numerous industry magazines. The skating industry is supported by several different glossy magazines designed to promote the industry as a whole. In addition, a number of smaller periodicals serve the smaller market segments within the skating industry. The last method of communication is the use of printed sales literature. The two previously mentioned marketing methods will create demand for the sales literature that will be sent to customers. The cost of the sales literature will be fairly minimal because it will use already-compiled information from the website.

3.7 MARKETING MIX

Pegasus' marketing is comprised of the following approaches to pricing, distribution, advertising and promotion, and customer service:

- *Pricing.* This will be based on a per-product retail price.
- *Distribution.* Initially, Pegasus will use a direct-to-consumer distribution model. Over time, Pegasus will use retailers as well.
- *Advertising and promotion.* Several different methods will be used for the advertising effort.
- *Customer service.* Pegasus will strive to achieve benchmarked levels of customer care.

3.8 MARKETING RESEARCH

Pegasus is blessed with the good fortune of being located in the centre of the skating world: Venice, California. Pegasus will be able to leverage this opportune location by working with many of the different skaters who live in the area. Pegasus was able to test all of its products not only with its principals, who are accomplished skaters, but also with the many other dedicated and "newbie" users located in Venice. The extensive product testing by a wide variety of users provided Pegasus with valuable product feedback and has led to several design improvements.

4.0 FINANCIALS

This section offers a financial overview of Pegasus related to marketing activities. It addresses break-even analysis, sales forecast, and expense forecast and indicates how these activities link to the marketing strategy.

4.1 BREAK-EVEN ANALYSIS

The break-even analysis (Table 4.1) indicates that $7 760 will be required in monthly sales revenue to reach the break-even point.

TABLE 4.1	BREAK-EVEN ANALYSIS	
Break-Even Analysis:		
Monthly Units Break-Even		62
Monthly Sales Break-Even		$ 7 760
Assumptions:		
Average Per-Unit Revenue		$125.62
Average Per-Unit Variable Cost		$ 22.61
Estimated Monthly Fixed Cost		$ 6 363

4.2 SALES FORECAST

Pegasus feels that the sales-forecast figures are conservative (Table 4.2). Pegasus will steadily increase sales as the advertising budget allows. Although the target-market forecast (Table 2.1) listed all of the potential customers divided into separate groups, the sales forecast groups customers into two categories: recreational and competitive. Reducing the number of categories allows the reader to quickly discern information, making the chart more functional.

Monthly-Sales Forecast

TABLE 4.2	SALES FORECAST		
	Sales Forecast		
Sales	**2011**	**2012**	**2013**
Recreational	$455 740	$598 877	$687 765
Competitive	$72 918	$95 820	$110 042
Total Sales	$528 658	$694 697	$797 807
Direct Cost of Sales	**2011**	**2012**	**2013**
Recreational	$82 033	$107 798	$123 798
Competitive	$13 125	$17 248	$19 808
Subtotal Cost of Sales	$95 159	$125 046	$143 605

4.3 EXPENSE FORECAST

The expense forecast (Table 4.3) will be used as a tool to keep the department on target and provide indicators when corrections/modifications are needed for the proper implementation of the marketing plan.

Monthly-Expense Budget

TABLE 4.3	MARKETING EXPENSE BUDGET		
Marketing Expense Budget	**2011**	**2012**	**2013**
Website	$25 000	$8 000	$10 000
Advertisements	$8 050	$15 000	$20 000
Printed Material	$1 725	$2 000	$3 000
Total Sales and Marketing Expenses	$34 775	$25 000	$33 000
Percent of Sales	6.58%	3.60%	4.14%
Contribution Margin	$398 725	$544 652	$621 202
Contribution Margin/Sales	75.42%	78.40%	77.86%

5.0 CONTROLS

The purpose of Pegasus' marketing plan is to serve as a guide for the organization. The following areas will be monitored to gauge performance:

- Revenue: monthly and annual
- Expenses: monthly and annual
- Customer satisfaction
- New product development

5.1 IMPLEMENTATION

The following milestones (Table 5.1) identify the key marketing programs. It is important to accomplish each one on time and on budget.

5.2 MARKETING ORGANIZATION

Stan Blade will be responsible for the marketing activities.

5.3 CONTINGENCY PLANNING

Difficulties and Risks

- Problems generating visibility, a function of being an Internet-based start-up organization.
- An entry into the market by an already established market competitor

Worst-Case Risks Include

- Determining that the business cannot support itself on an ongoing basis
- Having to liquidate equipment or intellectual capital to cover liabilities

Milestones

TABLE 5.1	MILESTONES					
Milestones	**Start Date**	**End Date**	**Plan Budget**	**Manager**	**Department**
Marketing-plan completion	1/1/11	2/1/11	$0	Stan	Marketing
Website completion	1/1/11	3/15/11	$20 400	outside firm	Marketing
Advertising campaign #1	1/1/11	6/30/11	$3 500	Stan	Marketing
Advertising campaign #2	3/1/1	12/30/11	$4 550	Stan	Marketing
Development of the retail channel	1/1/11	11/30/11	$0	Stan	Marketing
Totals			$28 450		

SUMMARY

1. The value-delivery process involves choosing (or identifying), providing (or delivering), and communicating superior value. The value chain is a tool for identifying key activities that create value and costs in a specific business.

2. Strong companies develop superior capabilities in managing core business processes such as new-product realization, inventory management, and customer acquisition and retention. Managing these core processes effectively means creating a marketing network in which the company works closely with all parties in the production and distribution chain, from suppliers of raw materials to retail distributors. Companies no longer compete—marketing networks do.

3. Holistic marketing maximizes value exploration by understanding the relationships among the customer's cognitive space, the company's competence space, and a collaborator's resource space. A company can maximize value creation by identifying new customer benefits from the customer's cognitive space, utilizing core competencies from its business domain, and selecting and managing business partners from its collaborative networks. It can maximize value delivery by becoming proficient at customer relationship management, internal resource management, and business partnership management.

4. Market-oriented strategic planning is the managerial process of developing and maintaining a viable fit between an organization's objectives, skills, and resources and its changing market opportunities. The aim of strategic planning is to shape the company's businesses and products so that they yield target profits and growth. Strategic planning takes place at four levels: corporate, division, business unit, and product.

5. The corporate strategy establishes the framework within which the divisions and business units prepare their strategic plans. Setting a corporate strategy entails four activities: defining the corporate mission, establishing strategic business units (SBUs), assigning resources to each SBU based on its market attractiveness and business strength, and planning new businesses and assessing growth opportunities.

6. Strategic planning for individual businesses entails the following activities: defining the business mission, analyzing external opportunities and threats, analyzing internal strengths and weaknesses, formulating goals, formulating strategy, formulating supporting programs, implementing the programs, and gathering feedback and exercising control.

7. Each product level within a business unit must develop a marketing plan for achieving its goals. The marketing plan is one of the most important outputs of the marketing process.

APPLICATIONS

Marketing Debate: What Good Is a Mission Statement?

Mission statements are often the product of much deliberation and discussion. At the same time, critics claim that mission statements sometimes lack "teeth" and specificity, or do not vary much from firm to firm and make the same empty promises.

Take a position: Mission statements are critical to a successful marketing organization *versus* Mission statements rarely provide useful marketing value.

Marketing Discussion

Consider Porter's value chain and the holistic marketing model. What implications do they have for marketing planning? How would you structure a marketing plan to incorporate some of their concepts?

MARKETING **EXCELLENCE** | CISCO

Cisco Systems is the worldwide leading supplier of networking equipment for the Internet. The company sells hardware (routers and switches), software, and services that make most of the Internet work. Cisco was founded in 1984 by a husband and wife team who worked in the computer operations department at Stanford University. They named the company cisco—with a lowercase c, short for San Francisco, and developed a logo that resembled the Golden Gate Bridge, over which they frequently travelled.

Cisco went public in 1990 and the two founders left the company shortly thereafter, due to conflicting interests with the new president and CEO. Over the next decade, the company grew exponentially, led by new products such as patented routers, switches, platforms, and modems—products which significantly contributed to the backbone of the Internet. Cisco opened its first international offices in London and France in 1991, followed by offices in Canada, Japan, Belgium, Mexico, and Hong Kong. During the 1990s, Cisco acquired and successfully integrated 49 companies into its core business. As a result, the company's market capitalization grew faster than for any company in history—from US$1 billion to US$300 billion between 1991 and 1999. In March 2000, Cisco became the most valuable company in the world, with market capitalization peaking at US$582 billion or US$82 per share.

By the end of the twentieth century, although the company was extremely successful, brand awareness was low—Cisco was known to many for its stock price rather than for what it actually did. Cisco developed partnerships with Sony, Matsushita, and US West to co-brand its modems with the Cisco logo in hopes of building its name recognition and brand value. In addition, the company launched its first television spots as part of a campaign entitled "Are You Ready?" In the ads, children and adults from around the world delivered facts about the power of the Internet and challenged viewers to ponder "Are You Ready?"

Surviving the Internet bust, the company reorganized in 2001 into 11 new technology groups and a marketing organization, which planned to communicate the company's product line and competitive advantages better than it had in the past. In 2003, Cisco introduced a new marketing message, "This Is the Power of the Network. Now." The international campaign targeted corporate executives and highlighted Cisco's critical role in a complicated, technological system by using a soft-sell approach. Television commercials explained how Cisco's systems change people's lives around the world and an eight-page print ad spread didn't mention Cisco's name until the third page. Marilyn Mersereau, Cisco's vice-president of corporate marketing, explained, "Clever advertising involves the reader in something that's thought-provoking and provocative and doesn't slam the brand name into you from the first page."

The year 2003 brought new opportunities as Cisco entered the consumer segment with the acquisition of Linksys, a home and small-office network gear maker. By 2004, Cisco offered several home entertainment solutions, including wireless capabilities for music, printing, and video. Since previous marketing strategies had targeted corporate and IT decision makers, the company launched a rebranding campaign in 2006, to increase awareness among consumers and help increase the overall value of Cisco's brand. "The Human Network" campaign tried to "humanize" the technology giant by repositioning it as more than just a supplier of switches and routers and communicating its critical role in connecting people through technology. The initial results were positive. Cisco's revenues increased 41 percent from 2006 to 2008, led by sales increases in both home and business use. By the end of 2008, Cisco's revenue topped US$39.5 billion and *BusinessWeek* ranked it the 18th biggest global brand.

With its entrance into the consumer market, Cisco has had to develop unique ways to connect with consumers. One recent development is *Cisco Connected Sports*, a platform that turns sports stadiums into digitally connected interactive venues. To celebrate its 25th anniversary in 2010, Cisco Canada launched a program titled "Transformational Canadians," which recognized 24 notable people who helped transform the lives of others.

Today, Cisco continues to acquire companies—over 40 between 2004 and 2010—that help it expand into newer markets such as consumer electronics, business collaboration software, and computer servers. These acquisitions align with Cisco's goal of increasing overall Internet traffic, which ultimately drives demand for its networking hardware products. However, by entering into these new markets, Cisco has gained new competitors such as Microsoft, IBM, and Hewlett-Packard. To compete against them, it reaches out to both consumers and businesses in its advertising efforts, including tapping into social media such as Facebook, Twitter, and blogs.

QUESTIONS

1. How is building a brand in a business-to-business context different from doing so in the consumer market?
2. Is Cisco's plan to reach out to consumers a viable one? Why or why not?

Sources: Marguerite Reardon, "Cisco Spends Millions on Becoming Household Name," *CNET*, October 5, 2006; Michelle Kessler, "Tech Giants Build Bridge to Consumers," *USA Today*, March 13, 2006; Marla Matzer, "Cisco Faces the Masses," *Los Angeles Times*, August 20, 1998; David R. Baker, "New Ad Campaign for Cisco," *San Francisco Chronicle*, February 18, 2003; Bobby White, "Expanding into Consumer Electronics, Cisco Aims to Jazz Up Its Stodgy Image," *Wall Street Journal*, September 6, 2006, p. B1; Burt Helm, "Best Global Brands," *BusinessWeek*, September 18, 2008; Ashlee Vance, "Cisco Buys Norwegian Firm for $3 Billion," *New York Times*, October 1, 2009; Jennifer Leggio, "10 Fortune 500 Companies Doing Social Media Right," *ZDNet*, September 28, 2009.

Chapter 3 | Collecting Information and Forecasting Demand

Chapter 4 | Conducting Marketing Research

Matt & Nat has responded to new trends in the macroenvironment by introducing a vegan line of stylish fashion accessories.

In This Chapter, We Will Address the Following **Questions**

1. What are the components of a modern marketing information system?

2. What are useful internal records for such a system?

3. What makes up a marketing intelligence system?

4. What are some influential macroenvironment developments?

5. How can companies accurately measure and forecast demand?

Collecting Information and Forecasting Demand

Making marketing decisions in a fast-changing world is both an art and a science. To provide context, insight, and inspiration for marketing decision making, companies must possess comprehensive, up-to-date information about macro trends, as well as about microeffects particular to their business. Holistic marketers recognize that the marketing environment is constantly presenting new opportunities and threats, and they understand the importance of continuously monitoring, forecasting, and adapting to that environment.

The demand for animal cruelty–free products has been a popular topic of discussion for a number of years. A relatively recent trend is that of customers preferring ecofriendly products. Recognizing these two separate trends that often relate to the same customer, Inder Bedi decided to take advantage of both with one philosophy. Bedi is the president of Montreal-based Matt & Nat—a company that makes stylish handbags, wallets, backpacks, briefcases, and other items with no animal products and containing at least one recycled material. Matt & Nat is a vegan line of fashion accessories with a strict zero-tolerance policy, an aspect that Bedi pushes to the forefront to differentiate his brand from the competition. Celebrities such as Charlize Theron, Natalie Portman, and Sir Paul McCartney love the vegan philosophy of the brand and are just some of the celebrities who have endorsed the brand publicly and helped bring about its success.

Consumers do not consider only traditional factors such as quality and price while making purchase decisions anymore. Whether the company follows ethical business practices is becoming increasingly important in choosing brands. In fact, research shows that about 15 percent of Canadians are willing to pay a premium for ecofriendly options, and this proportion is growing. Businesses such as Inder Bedi's have been quick to recognize trends such as this and capitalize on them.[1]

Firms are adjusting the way they do business, for more reasons than just the economy. Virtually every industry has been touched by dramatic shifts in the technological, demographic, social-cultural, natural, and political-legal environments. In this chapter, we consider how firms can develop processes to identify and track important macroenvironment trends. We also outline how marketers can develop good sales forecasts. Chapter 4 will review how they conduct more customized research on specific marketing problems.

COMPONENTS OF A MODERN MARKETING INFORMATION SYSTEM

The major responsibility for identifying significant marketplace changes falls to the company's marketers. Marketers have two advantages for performing the task: disciplined methods for collecting information, and time spent interacting with customers and observing competitors and other outside groups. Some firms have marketing information systems that provide rich detail about buyer wants, preferences, and behaviour. See how a marketing information system effected a change in DuPont's marketing.

DuPont

DuPont commissioned marketing studies to uncover personal pillow behaviour for its Dacron Polyester unit, which supplies filling to pillow makers and sells its own Comforel brand. One challenge is that people don't give up their old pillows: 37 percent of one sample described their relationship with their pillow as being like that of an "old married couple," and an additional 13 percent said their pillow was like a "childhood friend." Respondents fell into distinct groups in terms of pillow behaviour: stackers (23 percent), plumpers (20 percent), rollers or folders (16 percent), cuddlers (16 percent), and smashers, who pound their pillows into a more comfy shape (10 percent). Women were more likely to plump, men to fold. The prevalence of stackers led the company to sell more pillows packaged as pairs, as well as to market different levels of softness or firmness.[2]

Marketers also have extensive information about how consumption patterns vary across and within countries. On a per capita basis, for example, the Swiss consume the most chocolate, the Czechs the most beer, the Portuguese the most wine, and the Greeks the most cigarettes.

Table 3.1 summarizes these and other comparisons across countries. Consider regional differences within Canada: those in Ontario are more likely to use public transportation than those in New Brunswick, those in Nova Scotia spend much more on pets compared with those in Quebec, per capita alcohol consumption by the Northwest Territories is over twice that of Prince Edward Island, and Albertans smoke much more than neighbouring British Columbians.[3]

Organizations with quality information can choose their markets better, develop better offerings, and execute better marketing planning. Parks Canada periodically surveys park visitors to understand their needs and preferences. For instance, one survey found that some visitors to specific national parks placed less value on modern-day comforts in park areas, but relished the peace and quiet of the outdoors. The same survey also found that American visitors were far more likely to patronize hotels and restaurants within park areas than Canadians, who preferred to camp and cook their meals outdoors. Information such as this allows Parks Canada to better design its offerings to suit its clientele.[4]

Every firm must organize and distribute a continuous flow of information to its marketing managers. A **marketing information system (MIS)** consists of people, equipment, and procedures to gather, sort, analyze, evaluate, and distribute needed, timely, and accurate information to marketing decision makers. It

Parks Canada surveys visitors to serve their needs better.

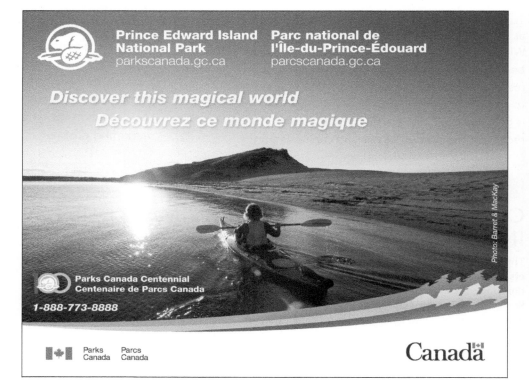

TABLE 3.1	A GLOBAL PROFILE OF EXTREMES	
Highest fertility rate	Niger	6.88 children per woman
Highest education expenditure as percent of GDP	Kiribati	17.8% of GDP
Highest number of cell phone subscribers	China	547 286 000
Largest number of airports	United States	14 951 airports
Highest military expenditure as percent of GDP	Oman	11.40% of GDP
Largest refugee population	Pakistan	21 075 000 people
Highest divorce rate	Aruba	4.4 divorces per 1000 population
Highest colour TV ownership per 100 households	United Arab Emirates	99.7 TVs
Cell phone subscribers per capita	Lithuania	138.1 subscribers per 100 people
Highest cinema attendance	India	1 473 400 000 cinema visits
Biggest beer drinkers per capita	Czech Republic	81.9 litres per capita
Biggest wine drinkers per capita	Portugal	33.1 litres per capita
Highest number of smokers per capita	Greece	8.2 cigarettes per person per day
Highest GDP per person	Luxembourg	$87 490
Largest aid donors as percentage of GDP	Sweden	1.03% of GDP
Most economically dependent on agriculture	Liberia	66% of GDP
Highest population in workforce	Cayman Islands	69.20%
Highest percent of women in workforce	Belarus	53.30%
Most crowded road networks	Qatar	283.6 vehicles per km of road
Most deaths in road accidents	South Africa	31 killed per 100 000 population
Most tourist arrivals	France	79 083 000
Highest life expectancy	Andorra	83.5 years
Highest diabetes rate	United Arab Emirates	19.5% of population aged 20–79

Sources: *CIA World Fact Book*, www.cia.gov/library/publications/the-world-factbook/geos/xx.html (viewed July 24, 2009); *The Economist's Pocket World in Figures*, 2009 edition, www.economist.com.

relies on internal company records, marketing intelligence activities, and marketing research. We'll discuss the first two components here, and the third one in the next chapter.

The company's marketing information system should be a mixture of what managers think they need, what they really need, and what is economically feasible. An internal MIS committee can interview a cross-section of marketing managers to discover their information needs.

Table 3.2 displays some useful questions to ask them.

TABLE 3.2	INFORMATION NEEDS PROBES

1. What decisions do you regularly make?
2. What information do you need to make these decisions?
3. What information do you regularly get?
4. What special studies do you periodically request?
5. What information would you want that you are not getting now?
6. What information would you want daily? Weekly? Monthly? Yearly?
7. What online or offline newsletters, briefings, blogs, reports, or magazines would you like to see on a regular basis?
8. What topics would you like to be kept informed of?
9. What data analysis and reporting programs would you want?
10. What are the four most helpful improvements that could be made in the present marketing information system?

INTERNAL RECORDS

To spot important opportunities and potential problems, marketing managers rely on internal reports of orders, sales, prices, costs, inventory levels, receivables, and payables.

The Order-to-Payment Cycle

The heart of the internal records system is the order-to-payment cycle. Sales representatives, dealers, and customers send orders to the firm. The sales department prepares invoices, transmits copies to various departments, and back-orders out-of-stock items. Shipped items generate shipping and billing documents that go to various departments. Because customers favour firms that can promise timely delivery, companies need to perform these steps quickly and accurately. Many use the Internet and extranets to improve the speed, accuracy, and efficiency of the order-to-payment cycle.

Sales Information Systems

Marketing managers need timely and accurate reports on current sales. Walmart operates a sales and inventory data warehouse that captures data on every item for every customer, in every store, every day, and refreshes it every hour. Consider the experience of Panasonic.

Panasonic

Panasonic makes digital cameras, plasma televisions, and other consumer electronics. After missing revenue goals, the company decided to adopt a vendor-managed inventory solution. Inventory distribution then came in line with consumption, and availability of products to customers jumped from 70 percent to 95 percent. The average weeks that product supply sat in Panasonic's channels went from 25 weeks to just 5 weeks within a year, and unit sales of the targeted plasma television rose from 20 000 to approximately 100 000. Best Buy, the initial retailer covered by the vendor-managed inventory model, has since elevated Panasonic from a Tier 3 Supplier to a Tier 1 "Go-To" Brand for plasma televisions.[5]

Companies that make good use of "cookies," records of website usage stored on personal browsers, are smart users of targeted marketing. Many consumers are happy to co-operate: A recent survey showed that 49 percent of individuals agreed that cookies are important to them when using the Internet. Not only do they *not* delete cookies, but they also expect customized marketing appeals and deals once they accept them.

Companies must carefully interpret the sales data, however, so as not to draw the wrong conclusions. Michael Dell gave this illustration: "If you have three yellow Mustangs sitting on a dealer's lot and a customer wants a red one, the salesman may be really good at figuring out how to sell the yellow Mustang. So the yellow Mustang gets sold, and a signal gets sent back to the factory that, hey, people want yellow Mustangs."[6]

Databases, Data Warehousing, and Data Mining

Companies organize their information into customer, product, and salesperson databases—and then combine their data. The customer database will contain every customer's name, address, past transactions, and sometimes even demographics and psychographics (activities, interests, and opinions). Instead of sending a mass "carpet bombing" mailing of a new offer to every customer in its database, a company will rank its customers according to factors such as purchase recency, frequency, and monetary value (RFM) and send the offer to only the highest-scoring customers. Besides saving on mailing expenses, such data analysis can often achieve a double-digit response rate, as Sobeys experienced.

Sobeys

The number-two player in Canada's fiercely competitive grocery retailing sector, Sobeys, has been using data-mining techniques to refocus its brand strategy. Consumer loyalty is low and competition is high in the grocery retail industry. With the help of data mining, Sobeys was able to segment its customers into five categories based on price consciousness, life stage, lifestyle choices, tendency to entertain, and duration of shopping trips. The company was then able to develop strategies to target those segments based on their unique needs and wants. Using the data collected through its loyalty program, Sobeys was able to use its new data-mining platform to send out 1.4 million different combinations of highly customized loyalty offerings to customers on its email list. Average direct-mail coupon redemption is about 2 percent or lower, while Sobeys' targeted and customized mailings have resulted in double-digit redemptions.[7]

Companies make these data easily accessible to their decision makers. Analysts can mine the data and garner fresh insights into neglected customer segments, recent customer trends, and other useful information. Managers can cross-tabulate customer information with product and salesperson information to yield still-deeper insights. PC Financial wished to run a print catalogue campaign with the objective of getting customers to redeem loyalty points for general merchandise. Using PC Financial's in-house database and 1000 input variables, Angoss Software Corporation was able to data mine those customers most likely to respond to the campaign. With this, PC Financial was able to reduce its mailings and target just 20 percent of its customers who were most likely to respond, resulting in savings of over $250 000.[8]

To manage all the different databases efficiently and effectively, firms are using business integration software (see "Marketing Insight: Getting the Most Out of Customer Databases with CRM").

MARKETING **INSIGHT**	GETTING THE MOST OUT OF CUSTOMER DATABASES WITH CRM

In today's fiercely competitive environment, finding and keeping customers is more critical than ever. Companies, realizing that the financial benefit of retaining existing customers is greater than that of finding new ones, are increasingly relying on data mining to keep their customers satisfied.

One of the hottest trends in data mining began during the nineties when formal and systematic customer relationship management (CRM) came to the forefront. This new technology focused on building relationships with the firm's customers by analyzing their behaviour. CRM allowed companies to better utilize customer data they already possessed to uncover new-product opportunities, target customers more efficiently, and improve profitability. For instance, in some cases response rates to direct mail sent to customers reached 40 percent, far exceeding industry standards.

The system, however, has several drawbacks that management must consider prior to and during implementation. Two notable disadvantages are the considerable cost and the level of complexity. Forrester Research found that large companies could spend between US$15 million and US$30 million per year on CRM software. Similarly, the Meta Group estimates that, despite the heavy expenditure involved, 55 to 70 percent of CRM projects fail to meet their objectives. Implementing CRM can demand corporate reorganization and requires executives to wholeheartedly buy into the system prior to implementation. Such demands have led many companies to choose alternative routes to keep their customers satisfied.

That is not to say that many companies have not experienced significant success from their CRM systems. One such example is The Limited, the parent company of several brands including Victoria's Secret, Bath & Body Works, and La Senza. The Limited, upon investing in analytical CRM software, reported that increased cross-selling among its brands yielded a return on investment of 400 percent. Canadian companies such as Petro-Canada, London Drugs, and Royal Bank have also undertaken the expensive technological and conceptual changes that adoption of CRM requires and have found the systems to be beneficial. For instance, following the CRM implementation, Petro-Canada's 700 retail locations became capable of preparing profit and loss statements within just five days following month-end.

CRM is not just for large corporations—many small businesses have successfully implemented CRM and reaped its benefits. Martack Specialties Ltd. of Burlington, Ontario, manufacturer of products such as whiteboards and chalkboards, found that its productivity increased 50 percent and sales went up 15 percent within a year of implementing a CRM system. Similarly, B.C.-based Corporate Cleaning Services found its customer response time shortened following its adoption of CRM. For instance, its on-site crew can now send pictures of the client's flooring and carpeting to support staff who can identify the ideal cleaning approach for those surfaces almost immediately. This has increased customer satisfaction and employee morale.

With the considerable success experienced by many companies that have implemented a CRM system, it comes as no surprise that many more continue to pursue CRM—although with varying success.

Sources: Viren Joshi and Richard Verity, "No Frills–CRM," *strategy+business Resilience Report,* July 29, 2004; Lesley Young, "Cutting through All the Hype about CRM," *Marketing Direct,* February 12, 2001; "Microsoft Dynamics AX Success Story: Petro-Canada," www.ideaca.com/customers/success_petrocanada.aspx (viewed May 10, 2011); "Marktack Specialties Ltd.: Organizational Overhaul Increases Sales, Productivity and Customer Service Levels," www.maximizer.com/about/customers/max_martack.html (viewed March 16, 2008); "Corporate Cleaning Services: Maximizer CRM: Customer Success Story," www.maximizer.com.

MARKETING INTELLIGENCE

The Marketing Intelligence System

A **marketing intelligence system** is a set of procedures and sources that managers use to obtain everyday information about developments in the marketing environment. The internal records system supplies *results* data, but the marketing intelligence system supplies *happenings* data. Marketing managers collect marketing intelligence in a variety of different ways, such as by reading books, newspapers, and trade publications; talking to customers, suppliers, and distributors; monitoring social media on the Internet; and meeting with other company managers.

Before the Internet, sometimes you just had to go out in the field, literally, and watch the competition. This is what oil and gas entrepreneur T. Boone Pickens did. Describing how he learned about a rival's drilling activity, Pickens recalls, "We would have someone who would watch [the rival's] drilling floor from a half mile away with field glasses. Our competitor didn't like it but there wasn't anything they could do about it. Our spotters would watch the joints and drill pipe. They would count them; each [drill] joint was 30 feet long. By adding up all the joints, you would be able to tally the depth of the well." Pickens knew that the deeper the well, the more costly it would be for his rival to get the oil or gas up to the surface, and this information provided him with an immediate competitive advantage. [9]

Marketing intelligence gathering must be legal and ethical. In 2006, KPMG was awarded $1.7 million in damages paid by the private intelligence firm Diligence. Diligence had illegally infiltrated KPMG to acquire an audit of a Bermuda-based investment firm for a Russian conglomerate. Diligence's co-founder posed as a British intelligence officer and convinced a member of the audit team to share confidential documents. [10]

A company can take eight possible actions to improve the quantity and quality of its marketing intelligence. After describing the first seven, we devote special attention to the eighth, collecting marketing intelligence on the Internet.

■ *Train and motivate the sales force to spot and report new developments.* The company must "sell" its sales force on their importance as intelligence gatherers. Grace Performance Chemicals, a division of W. R. Grace, supplies materials and chemicals to the construction and packaging industries. Its sales reps were instructed to observe the innovative ways customers used its products in order to suggest possible new products. Some were using Grace waterproofing materials to soundproof their cars and patch boots and tents. Seven new-product ideas emerged, worth millions in sales. [11]

■ *Motivate distributors, retailers, and other intermediaries to pass along important intelligence.* Marketing intermediaries are often closer to the customer and competition and can offer helpful insights. ConAgra has initiated a study with some of its retailers, such as Safeway, Kroger, and Walmart, to study how and why people buy its foods. Finding that shoppers who bought their Orville Redenbacher and Act II brands of popcorn tended to also buy Coke, ConAgra worked with the retailers to develop in-store displays for both products. Combining retailers' data with its own qualitative insights, ConAgra learned that many mothers switched to time-saving meals and snacks when school started. It launched its "Seasons of Mom" campaign to help grocers adjust to seasonal shifts in household needs. [12]

■ *Hire external experts to collect intelligence.* Many companies hire specialists to gather marketing intelligence. [13] Service providers and retailers send mystery shoppers to their stores to assess cleanliness of facilities, product quality, and the way employees treat customers. Health-care facilities' use of mystery patients has led to improved estimates of wait times, better explanations of medical procedures, and less-stressful programming on the waiting room TV. [14]

■ *Network internally and externally.* The firm can purchase competitors' products, attend open houses and trade shows, read competitors' published reports, attend stockholders' meetings, talk to employees, collect competitors' ads, consult with suppliers, and look up news stories about competitors.

■ *Set up a customer advisory panel.* Members of advisory panels might include the company's largest, most outspoken, most sophisticated, or most representative customers. For example, GlaxoSmithKline sponsors an online community devoted to weight loss and says it is learning far more than it could have gleaned from focus groups, on topics from packaging its weight-loss pill to where to place in-store marketing. [15]

■ *Take advantage of government-related data resources.* Statistics Canada provides an in-depth look at the population swings, demographic groups, regional migrations, and changing family structure of the estimated 34 million people in Canada (as of July 1, 2008). Census marketer Nielsen Claritas cross-references census figures with consumer surveys and its own grassroots research for clients such as The Weather Channel, BMW, and Sovereign Bank. Partnering with "list houses" that provide customer phone and address information, Nielsen Claritas can help firms select and purchase mailing lists with specific clusters.[16]

■ *Purchase information from outside research firms and vendors.* Well-known data suppliers include firms such as Nielsen Canada and Ipsos Canada. They collect information about product sales in a variety of categories and consumer exposure to various media. They also gather consumer-panel data much more cheaply than marketers manage to on their own. Biz360 and its online content partners, for example, provide real-time coverage and analysis of news media and consumer opinion information from over 70 000 traditional and social media sources (print, broadcast, websites, blogs, and message boards).[17]

Collecting Marketing Intelligence on the Internet

Thanks to the explosion of outlets available on the Internet, online customer review boards, discussion forums, chat rooms, and blogs can distribute one customer's experiences or evaluation to other potential buyers and, of course, to marketers seeking information about the consumers and the competition. There are five main ways marketers can research competitors' product strengths and weaknesses online:[18]

■ *Independent customer goods and service review forums.* Independent forums include websites such as Epinions.com, RateItAll.com, ConsumerReview.com, and Bizrate.com. Bizrate.com collects millions of consumer reviews of stores and products each year from two sources: its 1.3 million volunteer members, and feedback from stores that allow Bizrate.com to collect information directly from their customers as they make purchases.

■ *Distributor or sales agent feedback sites.* Feedback sites offer positive and negative product or service reviews, but the stores or distributors have built the sites themselves. Amazon.ca offers an interactive feedback opportunity through which buyers, readers, editors, and others can review all products on the site, especially books. Elance.com is an online professional services provider that allows contractors to describe their experience and level of satisfaction with subcontractors.

■ *Combo sites offering customer reviews and expert opinions.* Combination sites are concentrated in industries like financial services and high-tech products that require professional knowledge. ZDNet.com, an online advisor on technology products, offers customer comments and evaluations based on ease of use, features, and stability, along with expert reviews. The advantage is that a product supplier can compare experts' opinions with those of consumers.

■ *Customer complaint sites.* Customer complaint forums are designed mainly for dissatisfied customers. PlanetFeedback.com allows customers to voice unfavourable experiences with specific companies. Another site, Complaints.com, lets customers vent their frustrations with particular firms or offerings.

■ *Public blogs.* Tens of millions of blogs and social networks exist online, offering personal opinions, reviews, ratings, and recommendations on virtually any topic—and their numbers continue to grow. Firms such as Nielsen's BuzzMetrics and Scout Labs analyze blogs and social networks to provide insights into consumer sentiment.

Communicating and Acting on Marketing Intelligence

In some companies, the staff scans the Internet and major publications, abstracts relevant news, and disseminates a news bulletin to marketing managers. The competitive intelligence function works best when it is closely coordinated with the decision-making process.[19]

Given the speed of the Internet, it is important to act quickly on information gleaned online. Here are two companies that benefited from a proactive approach to online information:[20]

■ When ticket broker StubHub detected a sudden surge of negative sentiment about its brand after confusion arose about refunds for a rain-delayed Yankees–Red Sox game, it jumped in to offer appropriate discounts and credits. The director of customer service observed, "This [episode] is a canary in a coal mine for us."

■ When Coke's monitoring software spotted a Twitter post that went to 10 000 followers from an upset consumer who couldn't redeem a prize from a MyCoke rewards program, Coke quickly posted an apology on his Twitter profile and offered to help resolve the situation. After the consumer got the prize, he changed his Twitter avatar to a photo of himself holding a Coke bottle.

ANALYZING THE MACROENVIRONMENT

Successful companies recognize and respond profitably to unmet needs and trends.

Needs and Trends

Enterprising individuals and companies manage to create new solutions to unmet needs. Dockers was created to meet the needs of baby boomers who could no longer fit into their jeans and wanted a physically and psychologically comfortable pair of pants. Let's distinguish among fads, trends, and megatrends.

- A **fad** is "unpredictable, short-lived, and without social, economic, and political significance." A company can cash in on a fad such as Crocs clogs, Elmo TMX dolls, and Pokémon gifts and toys, but getting it right requires luck and good timing.[21]

- A direction or sequence of events with momentum and durability, a **trend** is more predictable and durable than a fad; trends reveal the shape of the future and can provide strategic direction. For example, the percentage of people who value physical fitness and well-being has risen steadily. Yoga is experiencing a rebirth. Vancouver-based lululemon was born to serve people following this trend, particularly upscale young women in the under-30 group.

- A **megatrend** is a "large social, economic, political, and technological change [that] is slow to form, and once in place, influences us for some time—between seven and ten years, or longer."[22]

To help marketers spot cultural shifts that might bring new opportunities or threats, several firms offer social-cultural forecasts. The Yankelovich MONITOR interviews 2500 people in the United States each year and has tracked 35 social value and lifestyle trends since 1971, such as "anti-bigness," "mysticism," "living for today," "away from possessions," and "sensuousness." A new market opportunity doesn't guarantee success, of course, even if the new product is technically feasible. Market research is necessary to determine an opportunity's profit potential.

See how Starbucks recognized macroenvironment changes that presented a new market opportunity.

Starbucks VIA

The demographics and behaviour of coffee drinkers in North America are changing, and companies such as Starbucks are changing with them. Starbucks began in 1971 in Seattle and since then has changed and grown to adapt to coffee drinkers' tastes and lifestyles. Due to the recent recession and economic downturn, brewing coffee at home has become a more economical way for consumers to get their daily coffee without breaking their wallet. In 2009, the Starbucks Corporation launched an instant coffee called the Starbucks VIA Ready Brew, designed for those who want good coffee but have neither the equipment nor the time to make it. Made with high-quality coffee beans, Starbucks VIA promises coffee shop–quality coffee at home, for a fraction of the price. VIA's success is evident, with sales surpassing the $100 million mark less than a year following its launch.[23]

Identifying the Major Forces

The end of the first decade of the new century brought a series of new challenges: the steep decline of the stock market, which affected savings, investment, and retirement funds; increasing unemployment; corporate scandals; stronger indications of global warming and other signs of deterioration in the national environment; and, of course, the rise of terrorism. These dramatic events were accompanied by the continuation of many existing trends that have already profoundly influenced the global landscape.[24]

Firms must monitor six major forces in the broad environment: demographic, economic, social-cultural, natural, technological, and political-legal. We'll describe them separately, but remember that their interactions will lead to new opportunities and threats. For example, explosive population growth (demographic) leads to more resource depletion and pollution (natural), which leads consumers to call for more laws (political-legal), which stimulate new technological solutions and products (technological) that, if they are affordable (economic), may actually change attitudes and behaviour (social-cultural).

The Demographic Environment

Demographic developments often move at a fairly predictable pace. The main one marketers monitor is *population,* including the size and growth rate of population in cities, regions, and nations; age distribution and ethnic mix; educational levels; household patterns; and regional characteristics and movements.

TABLE 3.3	THE WORLD AS A VILLAGE

If the world were a village of 100 people:

- 61 villagers would be Asian (of that, 20 would be Chinese and 17 would be Indian), 14 would be African, 11 would be European, 8 would be Latin or South American, 5 would be North American, and only one of the villagers would be from Australia, Oceania, or Antarctica.
- At least 18 villagers would be unable to read or write but 33 would have cellular phones and 16 would be online on the Internet.
- 18 villagers would be under 10 years of age and 11 would be over 60 years old. There would be an equal number of males and females.
- There would be 18 cars in the village.
- 63 villagers would have inadequate sanitation.
- 32 villagers would be Christians, 20 would be Muslims, 14 would be Hindus, 6 would be Buddhists, 16 would be non-religious, and the remaining 12 would be members of other religions.
- 30 villagers would be unemployed or underemployed, while of those 70 who would work, 28 would work in agriculture (primary sector), 14 would work in industry (secondary sector), and the remaining 28 would work in the service sector (tertiary sector).
- 53 villagers would live on less than two U.S. dollars a day. One villager would have AIDS, 26 villagers would smoke, and 14 villagers would be obese.
- By the end of a year, one villager would die and two new villagers would be born so the population would climb to 101.

Source: David J. Smith and Shelagh Armstrong, *If the World Were a Village: A Book about the World's People*, 2nd ed. (Tonawanda, NY: Kids Can Press, 2002).

WORLDWIDE POPULATION GROWTH World population growth is explosive: earth's population totalled 6.8 billion in 2010 and will exceed 9 billion by 2040.[25]

Table 3.3 offers an interesting perspective.[26]

Population growth is highest in countries and communities that can least afford it. Developing regions of the world currently account for 84 percent of the world population and are growing at 1 percent to 2 percent per year; the population in developed countries is growing at only 0.3 percent.[27] In developing countries, modern medicine is lowering the death rate, but the birth rate remains fairly stable.

A growing population does not mean growing markets unless there is sufficient purchasing power. Care and education of children can raise the standard of living but are nearly impossible to accomplish in most developing countries. Nonetheless, companies that carefully analyze these markets can find major opportunities. Sometimes the lessons from developing markets are helping businesses in developed markets. See "Marketing Insight: Finding Gold at the Bottom of the Pyramid."

POPULATION AGE MIX Mexico has a very young population and rapid population growth. At the other extreme is Italy, with one of the world's oldest populations. Milk, diapers, school supplies, and toys will be more important products in Mexico than in Italy.

There is a global trend toward an aging population. In 1950, there were only 131 million people 65 and older; in 1995, their number had almost tripled to 371 million. By 2050, one of ten people worldwide will be 65 or older. In 2010, Canadian baby boomers—those approximately in the 50 to 64 age range—represented a market close to 6.9 million, about 20 percent of the population. In 2009, Canadian seniors (those 65 and over) represented 14 percent of the nation's population. This number is expected to rise to about 24 percent over the next 25 years, at which time the median age of the population in Canada will range between 42 and 45 years compared with the median of 39.5 in 2009.[28] See how universities such as the University of Toronto are responding to the rapid growth of older adults.

University of Toronto

Recognizing an aging Canadian population, the University of Toronto (U of T) saw an opportunity to attract more mature and mid-career professionals to its continuing education programs. Largely made up of active baby boomers, this lucrative market looks for a new career after retirement or some mental stimulation for an aging mind. Continuing education programs were traditionally the forte of public and private colleges, but universities are now actively seeking mature students, with remarkable success. Many universities have been offering continuing education classes for years, but with the population demographic shifting toward the older segments, the U of T saw potential for growth in its own programs. In 2007, the university created a new visual identity for the school and ran brand awareness campaigns through 2011. These included new course catalogues and publications and ads in local newspapers. Enrolment has grown by 75 percent for these courses since the strategy was first implemented.[29]

Marketers generally divide the population into six age groups: preschool children, school-age children, teens, young adults age 20 to 40, middle-aged adults 40 to 65, and older adults 65 and older. Some marketers focus on **cohorts**, groups of individuals born during the same time period and who travel through life together. The defining moments they experience as they come of age and become adults (roughly ages 17 through 24) can stay with them for a lifetime and influence their values, preferences, and buying behaviours.

ETHNIC AND OTHER MARKETS Ethnic and racial diversity varies across countries. At one extreme is Japan, where almost everyone is Japanese; at the other is Canada, where over 6 million people—nearly 20 percent of the population—were born in another country. Visible minorities (defined as non-Caucasian

---

MARKETING **INSIGHT** | FINDING GOLD AT THE BOTTOM OF THE PYRAMID

Business writer C. K. Prahalad believes that much innovation can come from developments in emerging markets such as China and India. He estimates there are 5 billion unserved and underserved people at the so-called "bottom of the pyramid." One study showed that 4 billion people live on $2 or less a day. Firms operating in those markets have had to learn how to do more with less.

In Bangalore, India, Narayana Hrudayalaya Hospital charges a flat fee of $1500 for heart bypass surgery that costs 50 times as much in the United States. The hospital has low labour and operating expenses and an assembly-line view of care that has specialists focus on their own area. The approach works—the hospital's mortality rates are half those of U.S. hospitals. Narayana also operates on hundreds of infants for free and profitably insures 2.5 million poor Indians against serious illness for 11 cents a month.

Overseas firms are also finding creative solutions in developing countries. In Brazil, India, Eastern Europe, and other markets, Microsoft launched its pay-as-you-go FlexGo program, which allows users to prepay to use a fully loaded PC for only as long as wanted or needed without having to pay the full price the PC would normally command. When the payment runs out, the PC stops operating and the user prepays again to restart it.

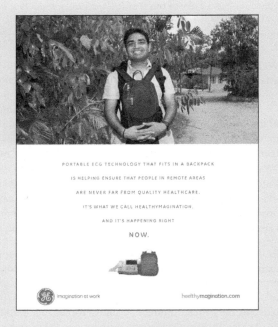

Other firms find "reverse innovation" advantages by developing products in countries like China and India and then distributing them globally. After GE successfully introduced a $1000 handheld electrocardiogram device for rural India and a portable, PC-based ultrasound machine for rural China, it began to sell them in the United States. Nestlé repositioned its low-fat Maggi brand dried noodles—a popular, low-priced meal for rural Pakistan and India—as a budget-friendly health food in Australia and New Zealand.

Sources: C. K. Prahalad, *The Fortune at the Bottom of the Pyramid* (Upper Saddle River, NJ: Wharton School Publishing, 2010); Bill Breen, "C. K. Prahalad: Pyramid Schemer," *Fast Company*, March 2007, p. 79; Pete Engardio, "Business Prophet: How C. K. Prahalad Is Changing the Way CEOs Think," *BusinessWeek*, January 23, 2006, pp. 68–73; Reena Jane, "Inspiration from Emerging Economies," *BusinessWeek*, March 23 and 30, 2009, pp. 38–41; Jeffrey R. Immelt, Vijay Govindarajan, and Chris Trimble, "How GE Is Disrupting Itself," *Harvard Business Review*, October 2009, pp. 56–65; Peter J. Williamson and Ming Zeng, "Value-for-Money Strategies for Recessionary Times," *Harvard Business Review*, March 2009, pp. 66–74.

and non-Aboriginal) in Canada have grown substantially since 2001. Over a quarter million immigrants make Canada their home each year, of which 58 percent are from Asia. As of the 2006 census, the Canadian population was about 80 percent white, 7 percent Asian, 4 percent Aboriginal, and 4 percent South Asian; visible ethnic minorities surpassed the 5 million mark for the first time and this number is expected to increase steeply over the next ten years.

Migration patterns are also changing. For instance, whereas Chinese immigrants used to come mainly from Hong Kong, today they come from mainland China and so speak Mandarin instead of Cantonese. The Chinese and South Asian populations have been growing rapidly and are expected to rise by about 50 percent to 1.8 million each by 2017. South Asians now account for a quarter of all ethnic minorities. The diversity of this community is witnessed by the range of languages spoken: Punjabi, Hindi, Urdu, Gujarati, Sinhalese, Tamil, Bengali, and English. The fastest-growing ethnic groups, however, are West Asians, Koreans, and Arabs, with their populations expected to increase between now and 2017 by 150 percent, 120 percent, and 118 percent, respectively.[30]

Data show immigrants' preference for urban life, possibly dictated by employment. The vast majority (96 percent) of immigrants in Canada live in metropolitan areas, compared with only 68 percent of the total population. Visible minorities represent about 43 percent of the population in Toronto, 42 percent in Vancouver, 22 percent in Calgary, and 16 percent in Montreal. Toronto is Canada's most diverse city—in fact, the United Nations has proclaimed it the most ethnically diverse city in the world. To understand where Toronto's population is headed, just consider the following statistics. Each year, nearly half of the over 250 000 landed immigrants entering Canada settle in Toronto. If this trend continues, nearly 1 out of every 2 Torontonians will belong to a visible minority by the end of the decade.

Marketing to new immigrants is both an opportunity and a challenge. It must be remembered that when people arrive in a new country, they often have few or no preconceptions of where to buy furniture or appliances, what car to buy, whether or not to buy insurance, or even what personal hygiene products are used by people in that country. They are new consumers looking for information. Culturally sensitive firms have an opportunity to build relationships and develop brand loyalty. This is evidenced in the increasing number of Canadian businesses with signage in multiple languages and personnel who speak Mandarin, Punjabi, or Arabic, for example.

Marketers must be careful not to overgeneralize about ethnic groups. Asian Canadians, for example, are not a homogeneous group. The identities and values of East Indians, Sri Lankans, Filipinos, Chinese, and Koreans are as different from each other as they are from Canadians of European background. Stereotypes must be avoided when approaching visible minorities, especially if they are second-generation Canadians. Research has shown that people become integrated into Canada's cultural mainstream in a single generation.

The needs of visible minorities are often underserved. Asian consumers, for example, often complain that the off-the-rack clothing found in most Canadian stores does not fit them well. Even the colours are wrong for Asian complexions. A more serious concern is that small Asian Canadians often find that they experience side effects when they take the recommended dosages of over-the-counter drugs.

Some firms are starting to listen to these voices. Until recently, many black women had to mix their own cosmetics shades to obtain the right tones, but now Revlon Canada offers a line of products specifically for black women. Neilson Dairy has launched Soy Delight, a product that is an alternative to milk for lactose-intolerant Asians. And when Nike, a global sponsor of the World Cup soccer tournament, wanted to promote its affiliation in Canada, it turned toward the Italian and Portuguese communities of Toronto. In Nike's view, they represented the most passionate devotees of the sport in Canada.[31]

The French-Canadian minority deserves special attention because of its large size and its dispersion through several provinces. Comprising 80 percent of Quebec households and 19 percent of Canadian households, this minority (6.8 million) cannot be ignored by national marketers.[32] Canada is officially a bilingual country, and Canadian marketers need to be sensitive to cultural differences between English- and French-speaking Canadians. French Canadians have traditionally emphasized family, home, and church, but in recent decades, a growing secularism has weakened these ties in favour of materialism and nationalism. The question of whether French-Canadian consumers are becoming more like other Canadians is debatable. But most marketers would agree that existing differences make it hazardous to employ a uniform promotional strategy across Canada. Differences in lifestyle, attitudes, and product usage make separate copy strategies and media decisions essential.

Diversity goes beyond ethnic markets. Persons with disabilities constitute almost 15 percent of Canada's population. The majority of these people are employed (65 percent of men, 50 percent of women). Since 60 percent of these people report requiring help for performing everyday activities, they are often a prime market for delivery and home-care services.[33]

EDUCATIONAL GROUPS The population in any society falls into five educational groups: illiterates, high-school dropouts, high-school diplomas, college degrees, and professional degrees. Over two-thirds of the world's 785 million illiterate adults are found in only eight countries (India, China, Bangladesh, Pakistan, Nigeria, Ethiopia, Indonesia, and Egypt); of all illiterate adults in the world, two-thirds are women.[34] Canada categorizes the population aged 25 to 64 into six educational groups: people with less than a high-school diploma (15 percent of the population); people with a high-school diploma (24 percent); people with a certificate from a trade school or community college (12 percent); people with a college or other non-university diploma (20 percent); people with a university certificate below a bachelor's level (5 percent); and people with a university degree or diploma (23 percent). Canada has one of the world's highest percentages of citizens (60 percent) who have some post-secondary education. The large number of educated people in Canada drives strong demand for high-quality books, magazines, and travel, and creates a good supply of skilled employees.

HOUSEHOLD PATTERNS The traditional household consists of a husband, wife, and children (and sometimes grandparents). Yet in Canada today, household living arrangements are becoming more diverse. Of Canada's 12.4 million households reported in the 2006 census, couples with children still made up the largest proportion: 31.4 percent of the total. However, single-person households made up the next-largest segment at 26.8 percent, couples with no children made up another 26.1 percent, and other family-household types totalled 15.8 percent. More people are divorcing or separating, choosing not to marry, marrying later, or marrying without the intention to have children. The number of common-law couples increased nearly 19 percent between 2001 and 2006, compared with only a 3.5 percent growth in married couples. Moreover, the nature of a couple is in itself changing, considering that the number of same-sex couples increased nearly 33 percent from 2001 to 2006, compared with only a 6 percent increase in opposite-sex couples during the same period.

Furthermore, the number of children people are having is declining. This, in combination with a growing number of single-parent homes, has resulted in a decline in the average family size from 3.7 persons in 1971 to 3.0 persons in 2006.[35] Each household type has a distinctive set of needs and buying habits. For example, people in the SSWD group (single, separated, widowed, divorced) need smaller apartments; inexpensive and smaller appliances, furniture, and furnishings; and smaller-sized food packages. Marketers must increasingly consider the special needs of nontraditional households because they are now growing more rapidly than traditional households.

The gay market is thought to be a particularly lucrative segment. In 2003 and 2005, Statistics Canada conducted surveys that asked people about sexual orientation. Among Canadians aged 18 to 59, 1.9 percent identified themselves as gay, lesbian, or bisexual. The data showed that adult men were twice as likely to be gay than bisexual. Adult women, however, were more likely to be bisexual than lesbian.[36] However, the numbers from these surveys are thought to underestimate the actual gay and lesbian population, given, for example, that academics and marketing experts estimate that the gay and lesbian population ranges between 4 percent and 8 percent of the total North American population, with an even higher percentage in urban areas.[37] The gay and lesbian market in Canada is estimated to be worth a mind-blowing $100 billion.[38]

The Economic Environment

The available purchasing power in an economy depends on current income, prices, savings, debt, and credit availability. As the recent economic downturn vividly demonstrated, trends affecting purchasing power can have a strong impact on business, especially for companies whose products are geared to high-income and price-sensitive consumers. Conversely, a recessionary economy in one country can present an opportunity for businesses from another country, as the following example shows.

Joe Fresh Clothing

After five successful years of offering affordable, fashion-forward clothing through Loblaws grocery stores across Canada, Joe Fresh decided to expand into the United States in the fall of 2011. "Go big or go home" was the motto for Joe Fresh executives, choosing the cutthroat retail and real estate market in Manhattan, NY, to build four stand-alone Joe Fresh stores. Given the strong Canadian dollar and strong domestic economy, Joe Fresh saw an opportunity to take a chance in the U.S. market. In addition, U.S. real estate prices overall are more attractive and attainable to Canadians than they once were. Marketing research from Synovate Canada confirmed that U.S. buyers were looking for more "cheap chic" clothing, due to a still-recovering economy. Well-prepared to take on this new and challenging market, Joe Fresh forged ahead by purchasing a 1954 five-storey building near the New York Public Library for its flagship store.[39]

CONSUMER PSYCHOLOGY Did new consumer spending patterns during the 2008–2009 global recession reflect short-term, temporary adjustments or long-term, permanent changes?[40] Some experts believed the recession had fundamentally shaken consumers' faith in the economy and their personal financial situations. "Mindless" spending would be out; willingness to comparison shop, haggle, and use discounts would become the norm. Others maintained that tighter spending reflected a mere economic constraint and not a fundamental behavioural change. Thus, consumers' aspirations would stay the same, and spending would resume when the economy improved.

Identifying the more likely long-term scenario—especially with the coveted 18- to 34-year-old age group—would help to direct how marketers spend their money. After six months of research and development in the baby boomer market, Starwood launched a "style at a steal" initiative to offer affordable but stylish hotel alternatives to its high-end W, Sheraton, and Westin chains. Targeting an audience seeking both thrift and luxury, it introduced two new low-cost chains: Aloft, designed to reflect the urban cool of loft apartments, and Element, suites with every "element" of modern daily lives, including healthy food choices and spa-like bathrooms.[41]

INCOME DISTRIBUTION There are four types of industrial structures: *subsistence economies* like Papua New Guinea, with few opportunities for marketers; *raw material–exporting economies* like the Democratic Republic of Congo (copper) and Saudi Arabia (oil), with good markets for equipment, tools, supplies, and luxury goods for the rich; *industrializing economies* like India, Brazil, and the Philippines, where a new rich class and a growing middle class demand new types of goods; and *industrial economies* like Western Europe, with rich markets for all sorts of goods.

Marketers often distinguish countries using five income-distribution patterns: (1) very low incomes; (2) mostly low incomes; (3) very low, very high incomes; (4) low, medium, high incomes; and (5) mostly medium incomes. Consider the market for the Lamborghini, an automobile costing more than $150 000. The market would be very small in countries with type 1 or 2 income patterns. One of the largest single markets for Lamborghinis is Portugal (income pattern 3)—one of the poorer countries in Western Europe, but with enough wealthy families to afford expensive cars.

INCOME, SAVINGS, DEBT, AND CREDIT Consumer expenditures are affected by income levels, savings rates, debt practices, and credit availability. Over the past ten years in Canada, savings rates have been declining. In addition, with consistently lower interest rates and a more relaxed attitude toward consumer debt, the amount of household indebtedness is on the rise. This is consistent with the increasing availability of credit in Canada. The number of credit cards in circulation was over 55 million in 2005 with 50 percent of Canadian families owing $2400 or more as credit card debt.[42] Even though that debt is on the rise and saving is down, overall household net worth in Canada has continued to increase. This means that while Canadians are saving less and spending more, their total assets still outpace their liabilities. This suggests that as long as net worth grows faster than liabilities, an increasing level of household debt is sustainable, providing the ability of households to service this debt remains stable.

An economic issue of increasing importance is the migration of manufacturers and service jobs offshore. From India, Infosys provides outsourcing services for Cisco, Nordstrom, Microsoft, and others. The 25 000 employees the fast-growing $4 billion company hires every year receive technical, team, and communication training in Infosys's $120 million facility outside Bangalore.[43]

The Social-Cultural Environment

From our social-cultural environment we absorb, almost unconsciously, a world view that defines our relationships to ourselves, others, organizations, society, nature, and the universe.

- *Views of ourselves.* People vary in the relative emphasis they place on self-gratification. During the 1960s and 1970s, "pleasure seekers" sought fun, change, and escape. Others sought "self-realization." Today, some are adopting more conservative behaviours and ambitions (see Table 3.4 for favourite consumer leisure-time activities and how they have changed, or not, in recent years).

- *Views of others.* People are concerned about the homeless, crime and victims, and other social problems. At the same time, they seek those like themselves for long-lasting relationships, suggesting a growing market for social-support products and services such as health clubs, cruises, and religious activity as well as "social surrogates" like television, video games, and social networking sites.

- *Views of organizations.* After a wave of layoffs and corporate scandals, organizational loyalty has declined.[44] Companies need new ways to win back consumer and employee confidence. They need to ensure they are good corporate citizens and that their consumer messages are honest.[45]

- *Views of society.* Some people defend society (preservers), some run it (makers), some take what they can from it (takers), some want to change it (changers), some are looking for something deeper

TABLE 3.4	FAVOURITE LEISURE-TIME ACTIVITIES		
		1995 %| 2008 %
Reading		28	30
TV watching		25	24
Spending time with family/kids		12	20
Going to movies		8	8
Fishing		10	7
Computer activities		2	7
Gardening		9	5
Renting movies		5	5
Walking		8	6
Exercise (aerobics, weights)		2	8

Source: Harris Interactive, "Spontaneous, Unaided Responses to: 'What Are Your Two or Three Most Favorite Leisure-Time Activities?'" www.harrisinteractive.com/harris_poll/index.asp?PID=980. Base: All Adults.

(seekers), and still others want to leave it (escapers). Consumption patterns often reflect these social attitudes. Makers are high achievers who eat, dress, and live well. Changers usually live more frugally, drive smaller cars, and wear simpler clothes. Escapers and seekers are a major market for movies, music, surfing, and camping.

■ *Views of nature.* Business has responded to increased awareness of nature's fragility and finiteness by producing wider varieties of camping, hiking, boating, and fishing gear such as boots, tents, back-packs, and accessories.

■ *Views of the universe.* Many North Americans are monotheistic, although religious conviction and practice have waned through the years or been redirected into an interest in evangelical movements or Eastern religions, mysticism, the occult, and the human potential movement.

Other cultural characteristics of interest to marketers are the high persistence of core cultural values and the existence of subcultures. Let's look at both.

HIGH PERSISTENCE OF CORE CULTURAL VALUES Most people in Canada still believe in work-ing, getting married, giving to charity, and being honest. *Core beliefs* and values are passed from parents to children and reinforced by social institutions—schools, churches, businesses, and governments. *Secondary beliefs* and values are more open to change. Believing in the institution of marriage is a core belief; believing people should marry early is a secondary belief.

Marketers have some chance of changing secondary values, but little chance of changing core values. The nonprofit organization Mothers Against Drunk Drivers (MADD) does not try to stop the sale of alcohol but promotes lower legal blood-alcohol levels for driving and limited operating hours for businesses that sell alcohol.

Although core values are fairly persistent, cultural swings do take place. In the 1960s, hippies, the Beatles, Elvis Presley, and other cultural phenomena had a major impact on hairstyles, clothing, sexual norms, and life goals. Today's young people are influenced by new heroes and activities: the Montreal-based indie pop band Arcade Fire, the NHL's Sidney Crosby, and snowboarder and skateboarder Shaun White.

Research has shown that Canadians and Americans, especially those who live along the border between the two countries, hold many values in common. Both believe in freedom, equality, and striving for happiness, mature love, self-respect, and true friendship. Canadian researcher and author Michael Adams notes, however, that Canadians operate with a set of social values fundamentally different from those of Americans, and marketers need to be sensitive to these differences.

For example, Americans are much more outer-directed and risk-taking, yet are more concerned with maintaining social order and tradition. In contrast, Canadians are more inner-directed and security-seeking, yet are more socially liberal and tolerant of individual diversity. Americans celebrate those who have lived the American Dream—working hard, taking chances, and striking it rich—so visual markers of success, such as expensive cars, homes, and vacations, become important indicators of one's status in the social hierarchy. Canadians, on the other hand, believe in greater interdependence, achieving equitable balances, and the "fair" distribution of wealth.[46]

Canadians also are less trusting of business and are more skeptical of advertising. Canadians, therefore, seek to do business with companies perceived as being more ethical. Adams believes that this difference in social values results in more understated consumption. As Canadians, we focus less on what products and brands say about us and more on what the products do for us. Canadians, therefore, prefer smaller, more affordable, and more practical cars. It was for this reason that BMW chose to subtly change its slogan "The Ultimate Driving Machine" to "The Ultimate Driving Experience" for Canada.[47]

EXISTENCE OF SUBCULTURES Each society contains **subcultures**, groups with shared values, beliefs, preferences, and behaviours emerging from their special life experiences or circumstances. Marketers have always loved teenagers because they are trendsetters in fashion, music, entertainment, ideas, and attitudes. Attract someone as a teen, and you will likely keep the person as a customer later in life. Frito-Lay, which draws 15 percent of its sales from teens, noted a rise in chip snacking by grown-ups. "We think it's because we brought them in as teenagers," said Frito-Lay's marketing director.[48]

The Natural Environment

In Western Europe, "green" parties have pressed for public action to reduce industrial pollution. In North America, experts have documented ecological deterioration, and groups such as the Green Party of Canada, Sierra Club, and Friends of the Earth carry these concerns into political and social action.

Environmental regulations hit certain industries hard. Steel companies and public utilities have invested billions of dollars in pollution-control equipment and environmentally friendly fuels, making hybrid cars, low-flow toilets and showers, organic foods, and green office buildings everyday realities. Opportunities await those who can reconcile prosperity with environmental protection. Consider these solutions to concerns about air quality:[49]

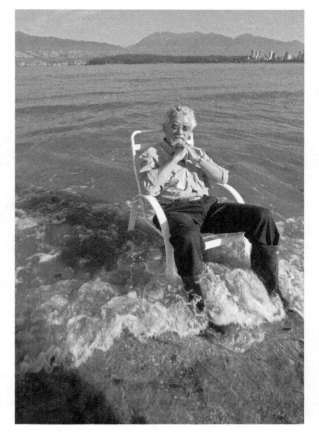

David Suzuki, a long-time Canadian activist, has been working with the government, businesses, and individuals to conserve the environment.

- Nearly a quarter of the carbon dioxide that makes up about 80 percent of all greenhouse gases comes from electrical power plants. Bullfrog Power provides "green power" in several Canadian provinces, with environmentally friendly electricity generated from wind and hydro facilities.

- Transportation is second only to electricity generation as a contributor to global warming, accounting for roughly a fifth of carbon emissions. Vancouver-based Westport Innovations developed a conversion technology—high-pressure direct injection—that allows diesel engines to run on cleaner-burning liquid natural gas, reducing greenhouse emissions by a fourth.

- Due to millions of rural cooking fires, parts of Southern Asia suffer extremely poor air quality. A person cooking over an open wood or kerosene fire inhales the equivalent of two packs of cigarettes a day. Illinois-based Sun Ovens International makes family-sized and institutional solar ovens that use mirrors to redirect the sun's rays into an insulated box. Used in 130 countries, the oven both saves money and reduces greenhouse gas emissions.

Corporate environmentalism recognizes the need to integrate environmental issues into the firm's strategic plans. Trenwds in the natural environment for marketers to be aware of include the shortage of raw materials, especially water; the increased cost of energy; the increased pollution levels; and the changing role of governments. (See also "Marketing Insight: The Green Marketing Revolution.")[50]

- The earth's raw materials consist of the infinite, the finite renewable, and the finite nonrenewable. Firms whose products require *finite nonrenewable resources*—oil, coal, platinum, zinc, silver—face substantial cost increases as depletion approaches. Firms that can develop substitute materials have an excellent opportunity.

- One finite nonrenewable resource, oil, has created serious problems for the world economy. As oil prices soar, companies search for practical means to harness solar, nuclear, wind, and other alternative energies.

- Some industrial activity will inevitably damage the natural environment, creating a large market for pollution-control solutions such as scrubbers, recycling centres, and landfill systems as well as for alternative ways to produce and package goods.

- Many poor nations are doing little about pollution, lacking the funds or the political will. It is in the richer nations' interests to help them control their pollution, but even richer nations today lack the necessary funds.

An increasing number of companies are responding to the trends in the natural environment and the associated consumer response to them, as the following example shows.

Enterprise Rent-A-Car

Operating in Canada since 1993, Enterprise quickly became Canada's largest car rental company, employing over 2800 Canadians nationwide. In response to rising oil prices, Enterprise started promoting an electric-car culture, realizing that future success depends on a steady supply of cars and fuels that are socially acceptable. Heading in that direction, Enterprise began by adding the electric-powered Nissan LEAF to its fleet in 2009 and continued its commitment in 2011 by adding the Chevrolet Volt. The introduction of electric vehicles is just one of Enterprise Holdings', the parent company's, several initiatives, which include a customer carbon-offset program, a pledge to plant 50 million trees over the next 50 years, the use of biodiesel fuel in its airport shuttle buses, and a commitment to alternative fuels research.[51]

The Technological Environment

It is the essence of market capitalism to be dynamic and tolerate the creative destructiveness of technology as the price of progress. Transistors hurt the vacuum-tube industry, and autos hurt the railroads. Television hurt the newspapers, and the Internet hurt them both.

When old industries fight or ignore new technologies, their businesses decline. Tower Records had ample warning that its music retail business would be hurt by Internet downloads of music (as well as the growing number of discount music retailers). Its failure to respond led to the liquidation of all its domestic physical stores in 2006.

Major new technologies stimulate the economy's growth rate. Unfortunately, between innovations, an economy can stagnate. Minor innovations fill the gap—new supermarket products such as frozen waffles, body washes, and energy bars might pop up—but while lower risk, they can also divert research effort away from major breakthroughs.

A Statistics Canada study revealed that more than 70 percent of successful new companies are high-tech in that they innovate, use advanced technologies, employ skilled workers, or emphasize training. They operate in all sectors of the economy, including publishing and farm services, not just in those industries usually thought of as high-tech, such as biotechnology and information technology. For example, the dairy-farming industry has adopted very high-tech processes. Technology is what helps one or two farmers manage dozens or hundreds of highly productive dairy cattle. From computer-generated algorithms for designing feeding programs, to laboratory testing for determining the digestibility of feed ingredients, to sophisticated instruments and databases that track milk production, technology is used in all aspects of milk production.[52]

Innovation's long-run consequences are not always foreseeable. The contraceptive pill reduced family size and thus increased discretionary incomes, also raising spending on vacation travel, durable goods, and luxury items. Cell phones, video games, and the Internet are reducing attention to traditional media, as well as face-to-face social interaction as people listen to music or watch a movie on their cell phones.

Marketers should monitor the following technology trends: the accelerating pace of change, unlimited opportunities for innovation, varying R&D budgets, and increased regulation of technological change.

Text messaging is profoundly changing how consumers choose to communicate.

ACCELERATING PACE OF CHANGE More ideas than ever are in the works, and the time between idea and implementation is shrinking. So is the time between introduction and peak production. For example, a staggering 10 billion applications were downloaded from the Apple App Store barely two-and-a-half years following its launch in July 2008.[53]

UNLIMITED OPPORTUNITIES FOR INNOVATION Some of the most exciting work today is taking place in biotechnology, computers, microelectronics, telecommunications, robotics, and designer materials. Researchers are working on AIDS vaccines, safer contraceptives, and nonfattening foods. They are developing new classes of antibiotics to fight ultra-resistant infections, superheating furnaces to reduce trash to raw materials, and building miniature water-treatment plants for remote locations.[54]

VARYING R&D BUDGETS In 2008, business spending on research amounted to 1 percent of Canada's GDP, significantly below the average spending of 1.6 percent by the 30 Organisation for Economic Co-operation and Development (OECD) member countries.[55] Canada was a dismal 27th out of the 30 OECD countries in government funding for business research. On the positive side, Canada ranked 2nd in tax incentives for R&D, trailing only Korea. A pattern noticed over the past few years is that non-OECD countries such as China, Russia, India, Brazil, and South Africa have made considerable increases to their research spending whereas the OECD countries on average have decreased theirs.[56]

INCREASED REGULATION OF TECHNOLOGICAL CHANGE Safety and health regulations have increased for most product categories and the government has expanded its agencies' powers to investigate and ban potentially unsafe products. Canada has a complex web of legislation. Consider, for example, some of the legislation focused on food safety. Agriculture and Agri-Food Canada is responsible for the safety of food products, but Health Canada also has a food- and product-safety division. Health Canada also administers the nutrition labelling regulations for food products. To complicate matters further, the Department of Justice regulates the Food and Drug Act and the Hazardous Products Act. The Canadian Standards Association (www.csa.ca), a not-for-profit organization, also works with business, government, and consumers to develop standards to enhance public safety and health. Marketers must be aware of these regulations when proposing, developing, and launching new products.

The Political-Legal Environment

The political and legal environment consists of laws, government agencies, and pressure groups that influence various organizations and individuals. Sometimes these laws create new business opportunities. Mandatory recycling laws have boosted the recycling industry and launched dozens of new companies making new products from recycled materials. Two major trends are the increase in business legislation and the growth of special-interest groups.

INCREASE IN BUSINESS LEGISLATION Business legislation is intended to protect companies from unfair competition, protect consumers from unfair business practices, protect society from unbridled business behaviour, and charge businesses with the social costs of their products or production processes. Each new law may also have the unintended effect of sapping initiative and slowing growth.

The European Commission has established new laws covering competitive behaviour, product standards, product liability, and commercial transactions for the 27 member nations of the European Union. Canada has many consumer protection laws such as the Competition Act covering competition, product safety and liability, fair trade and credit practices, and packaging and labelling, but many countries' laws are stronger.[57] Norway bans several forms of sales promotion—trading stamps, contests, and premiums— as inappropriate or unfair. Thailand requires food processors selling national brands to market low-price brands also, so low-income consumers can find economy brands. In India, food companies need special approval to launch duplicate brands, such as another cola drink or brand of rice. As more transactions take place in cyberspace, marketers must establish new ways to do business ethically.

GROWTH OF SPECIAL-INTEREST GROUPS Political action committees (PACs) lobby government officials and pressure business executives to respect the rights of consumers, women, senior citizens, minorities, and gays and lesbians. Insurance companies directly or indirectly affect the design of smoke detectors; scientific groups affect the design of spray products. Many companies have established public affairs departments to deal with these groups and issues. The **consumerist movement** organized citizens and government to strengthen the rights and powers of buyers in relationship to sellers. Consumerists have won the right to know the real cost of a loan, the true cost per standard unit of competing brands (unit pricing), the basic ingredients and true benefits of a product, and the nutritional quality and freshness of food.

Privacy issues and identity theft will remain public policy hot buttons as long as consumers are willing to swap personal information for customized products—from marketers they trust.[58] Consumers worry that they will be robbed or cheated, that private information will be used against them, that they will be bombarded by solicitations, and that children will be targeted.[59] Wise companies establish consumer affairs departments to formulate policies and resolve complaints.

MARKETING **INSIGHT**   THE GREEN MARKETING REVOLUTION

Nowadays, terms such as "climate change," "global warming," and "greenhouse gas emissions" have become common lingo for most people around the world. In line with the growing number of issues concerning the environment is the growing ecological awareness of consumers. A survey of 20 countries by Synovate and BBC showed that over two-thirds (68 percent) of the world's population is concerned about climate change. In correlation with this, a recent survey found that 53 percent of Canadian moms have switched to buying ecofriendly household products. As research by GfK Roper Consulting shows, consumer expectations as to corporate behaviour toward the environment have significantly changed, and in many cases these expectations are higher than the demands consumers place on themselves. Consumers vary, however, in their environmental sensitivity and can be categorized into five groups based on their degree of commitment (see Figure 3.1). Interestingly, although some marketers assume that younger people are more concerned about the environment than older consumers, some research suggests that older consumers actually take their eco-responsibilities more seriously.

In the past, the "green marketing" programs launched by companies around specific products were not always entirely successful, for several possible reasons. Consumers might have thought that the product was inferior because it was green, or that it was not even really green to begin with. Those green products that were successful, however, persuaded consumers that in buying green products, they were acting in their own and society's long-run interest at the same time. Some examples were organic foods that were seen as healthier, tastier, and safer, and energy-efficient appliances that were seen as costing less to run.

- *Genuine Greens* (15%): This segment is the most likely to think and act green. Some may be true environmental activists, but most probably fall more under the category of strong advocates. This group sees few barriers to behaving green and may be open to partnering with marketers on environmental initiatives.
- *Not Me Greens* (18%): This segment expresses very pro-green attitudes, but its behaviors are only moderate, perhaps because these people perceive lots of barriers to living green. There may be a sense among this group that the issue is too big for them to handle, and they may need encouragement to take action.
- *Go-with-the-Flow Greens* (17%): This group engages in some green behaviors—mostly the "easy" ones such as recycling. But being green is not a priority for them, and they seem to take the path of least resistance. This group may only take action when it's convenient for them.
- *Dream Greens* (13%): This segment cares a great deal about the environment, but doesn't seem to have the knowledge or resources to take action. This group may offer the greatest opportunity to act green if given the chance.
- *Business First Greens* (23%): This segment's perspective is that the environment is not a huge concern and that business and industry is doing its part to help. This may explain why they don't feel the need to take action themselves—even as they cite lots of barriers to doing so.
- *Mean Greens* (13%): This group claims to be knowledgeable about environmental issues, but does not express pro-green attitudes or behaviors. Indeed, it is practically hostile toward pro-environmental ideas. This segment has chosen to reject prevailing notions about environmental protection and may even be viewed as a potential threat to green initiatives.

FIGURE 3.1

Consumer Environmental Segments

Source: GfK Roper Green Gauge® 2007, GfK Roper Consulting, New York, NY.

There are some expert recommendations as to how to avoid "green marketing myopia" by focusing on consumer value positioning, calibration of consumer knowledge, and the credibility of product claims. One challenge with green marketing is the difficulty consumers have in understanding the environmental benefits of products, leading to many accusations of "greenwashing" where products are not nearly as green and environmentally beneficial as their marketing might suggest.

Although there have been green products emphasizing their natural benefits for years—Tom's of Maine, Burt's Bees, Stonyfield Farm, and Seventh Generation to name just a few—products offering environmental benefits are becoming more mainstream. Part of the success of Clorox Green Works cleaning products, launched in January 2008, was that Clorox found the sweet spot of a target market wanting to take smaller steps toward a greener lifestyle and matched that with a green product with a very modest price premium and sold through a grassroots marketing program.

Environmental concerns are affecting how virtually every major organization does its business: Walt Disney Corp. has pledged to reduce its solid waste by 2013, conserve millions of litres of water, invest in renewable energy, and become completely carbon neutral (reaching 50 percent of that goal by 2012); Best Buy has expanded its recycling program for electronics; Caterpillar announced plans to reduce the GHG emissions of its entire product line by 20 percent by 2020; and several Canadian provinces have offered a tax credit or rebate for buying a "green" car.

Toyota, HP, IKEA, Procter & Gamble, and Walmart have all been linked to high-profile environmental and sustainability programs. Some other marketers, fearing harsh scrutiny or unrealistic expectations, keep a lower profile. Even though Nike uses recycled sneakers in its soles of new shoes, they chose not to publicize that fact so that they can keep their focus on performance and winning. The rules of the game in green marketing are changing rapidly as both consumers and companies respond to problems and proposed solutions to the significant environmental problems that exist.

Sources: Jerry Adler, "Going Green," *Newsweek*, July 17, 2006, pp. 43–52; Jacquelyn A. Ottman, Edwin R. Stafford, and Cathy L. Hartman, "Avoiding Green Marketing Myopia," *Environment*, June 2006, pp. 22–36; Jill Meredith Ginsberg and Paul N. Bloom, "Choosing the Right Green Marketing Strategy," *MIT Sloan Management Review*, Fall 2004, pp. 79–84; Jacquelyn Ottman, *Green Marketing: Opportunity for Innovation,* 2nd ed. (New York: BookSurge Publishing, 2004); Mark Dolliver, "Deflating a Myth," *Brandweek*, May 12, 2008, pp. 30–31; "Canadian Moms Global Leaders When It Comes to the Environment," Canada Newswire, March 30, 2011; "Winner: Corporate Sustainability, Walt Disney Worldwide," *Travel and Leisure*, November 2009, p. 106; "The Greenest Big Companies in America," *Newsweek*, September 28, 2009, pp. 34–53; Sarah Mahoney, "Best Buy Connects Green with Thrift," *Media Post News: Marketing Daily*, January 28, 2009; Reena Jana, "Nike Quietly Goes Green," *BusinessWeek*, June 11, 2009.

FORECASTING AND DEMAND MEASUREMENT

Understanding the marketing environment and conducting marketing research (described in Chapter 4) can help to identify marketing opportunities. The company must then measure and forecast the size, growth, and profit potential of each new opportunity. Sales forecasts prepared by marketing are used by finance to raise cash for investment and operations; by manufacturing to establish capacity and output; by purchasing to acquire the right amount of supplies; and by human resources to hire the needed workers. If the forecast is off the mark, the company will face excess or inadequate inventory. Since the forecast is based on estimates of demand, managers need to define what they mean by market demand. Although DuPont's Performance Materials group knows that DuPont Tyvek has 70 percent of the $100 million market for air-barrier membranes, the group sees greater opportunity with more products and services to tap into the entire $7 billion U.S. home construction market.[60]

The Measures of Market Demand

Companies can prepare as many as 90 different types of demand estimates for six different product levels, five space levels, and three time periods (see Figure 3.2). Each demand measure serves a specific purpose. A company might forecast short-run demand to order raw materials, plan production, and borrow cash. It might forecast regional demand to decide whether to set up regional distribution.

There are many productive ways to break down the market:

- The **potential market** is the set of consumers with a sufficient level of interest in a market offer. However, their interest is not enough to define a market unless they also have sufficient income and access to the product.

- The **available market** is the set of consumers who have interest, income, *and* access to a particular offer. The company or government may restrict sales to certain groups; a particular state might ban

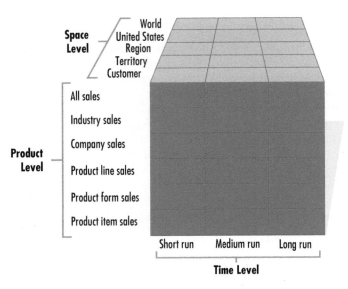

FIGURE 3.2

Ninety Types of Demand
Measurement (6×5×3)

motorcycle sales to anyone under 21 years of age. Eligible adults constitute the *qualified available market*—the set of consumers who have interest, income, access, and qualifications for the market offer.

- The **target market** is the part of the qualified available market the company decides to pursue. The company might concentrate its marketing and distribution effort on the East Coast.

- The **penetrated market** is the set of consumers who are buying the company's product.

These definitions are a useful tool for market planning. If the company isn't satisfied with its current sales, it can try to attract a larger percentage of buyers from its target market. It can lower the qualifications for potential buyers. It can expand its available market by opening distribution elsewhere or lowering its price, or it can reposition itself in the minds of its customers. Consider the case of Loblaw Companies.

Loblaw Companies

Loblaw Companies Limited, Canada's largest food distributor, recently fell upon hard times due to competition from rival chains. The company posted a $219 million loss in 2006. To combat the fall, Galen Weston, Jr., was named executive chairman and given the task of turning around the struggling grocery franchise. In 2007, Weston became spokesperson for the President's Choice (PC) brand and launched a new campaign in an effort to reposition the brand and the organization as a whole. The repositioning strategy included adopting a more customer-focused approach to doing business as well as focusing on social issues. The brand has implemented this strategy by introducing products such as 99-cent reusable shopping bags to help limit waste and creating the Blue Menu brand, which specializes in healthier food choices. PC has also begun to cater more to ethnic groups and focus heavily on fair-trade products, all in an effort to better meet the needs of its customers. The transformation of Loblaw is exemplified by its turnaround and rising profits, from $336 million in 2007 to $681 million in 2010.[61]

A Vocabulary for Demand Measurement

The major concepts in demand measurement are market demand and company demand. Within each, we distinguish among a demand function, a sales forecast, and a potential.

MARKET DEMAND The marketer's first step in evaluating marketing opportunities is to estimate total market demand. **Market demand** for a product is the total volume that would be bought by a defined customer group in a defined geographical area in a defined time period in a defined marketing environment under a defined marketing program.

Market demand is not a fixed number, but rather a function of the stated conditions. For this reason, we call it the *market demand function*. Its dependence on underlying conditions is illustrated in Figure 3.3(a). The horizontal axis shows different possible levels of industry marketing expenditure in a given time period. The vertical axis shows the resulting demand level. The curve represents the estimated market demand associated with varying levels of marketing expenditure.

Some base sales—called the *market minimum* and labelled Q_1 in the figure—would take place without any demand-stimulating expenditures. Higher marketing expenditures would yield higher levels of demand, first at an increasing rate, then at a decreasing rate. Take fruit juices. Given the indirect competition they face from other types of beverages, we would expect increased marketing expenditures to help fruit juice products stand out and increase demand and sales. Marketing expenditures beyond a certain level would not stimulate much further demand, suggesting an upper limit called the *market potential* and labelled Q_2 in the figure.

The distance between the market minimum and the market potential shows the overall *marketing sensitivity of demand*. We can think of two extreme types of markets, the expansible and the nonexpansible. An *expansible market,* such as the market for racquetball playing, is very much affected in size by the level of industry marketing expenditures. In terms of Figure 3.3(a), the distance between Q_1 and Q_2 is relatively large. A *nonexpansible market*—for example, the market for weekly trash or garbage removal—is *not* much affected by the level of marketing expenditures; the distance between Q_1 and Q_2 is relatively small. Organizations selling in a nonexpansible market must accept the market's size—the level of *primary demand* for the product class—and direct their efforts toward winning a larger **market share** for their product, that is, a higher level of selective demand for their product.

It pays to compare the current and potential levels of market demand. The result is the **market-penetration index.** A low index indicates substantial growth potential for all the firms. A high index suggests it will be expensive to attract the few remaining prospects. Generally, price competition increases and margins fall when the market-penetration index is already high.

Comparing current and potential market shares yields a firm's **share-penetration index**. If this index is low, the company can greatly expand its share. Holding it back could be low brand awareness, low availability, benefit deficiencies, or high price. A firm should calculate the share-penetration increases from removing each factor, to see which investments produce the greatest improvement.[62]

Remember that the market demand function is not a picture of market demand over time. Rather, it shows alternative current forecasts of market demand associated with possible levels of industry marketing effort.

MARKET FORECAST Only one level of industry marketing expenditure will actually occur. The market demand corresponding to this level is called the **market forecast.**

MARKET POTENTIAL The market forecast shows *expected* market demand, not maximum market demand. For the latter, we need to visualize the level of market demand resulting from a very high level of industry marketing expenditure, where further increases in marketing effort would have little effect. **Market potential** is the limit approached by market demand as industry marketing expenditures approach infinity for a given marketing environment.

The phrase "for a given market environment" is crucial. Consider the market potential for automobiles. It's higher during prosperity than during a recession. The dependence of market potential on the environment is illustrated in Figure 3.3(b). Market analysts distinguish between the position of the market demand function and movement along it. Companies cannot do anything about the position of the market

FIGURE 3.3

Market Demand Functions

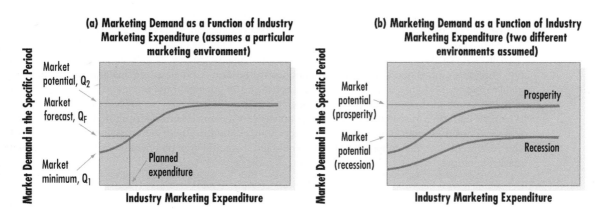

(a) Marketing Demand as a Function of Industry Marketing Expenditure (assumes a particular marketing environment)

Market Demand in the Specific Period

Market potential, Q_2
Market forecast, Q_F
Market minimum, Q_1
Planned expenditure
Industry Marketing Expenditure

(b) Marketing Demand as a Function of Industry Marketing Expenditure (two different environments assumed)

Market Demand in the Specific Period

Market potential (prosperity)
Market potential (recession)
Prosperity
Recession
Industry Marketing Expenditure

demand function, which is determined by the marketing environment. However, they influence their particular location on the function when they decide how much to spend on marketing.

Companies interested in market potential have a special interest in the **product-penetration percentage**, the percentage of ownership or use of a product or service in a population. Companies assume that the lower the product-penetration percentage, the higher the market potential, although this also assumes everyone will eventually be in the market for every product.

COMPANY DEMAND **Company demand** is the company's estimated share of market demand at alternative levels of company marketing effort in a given time period. It depends on how the company's products, services, prices, and communications are perceived relative to the competitors'. Other things equal, the company's market share depends on the relative scale and effectiveness of its market expenditures. Marketing model builders have developed sales response functions to measure how a company's sales are affected by its marketing expenditure level, marketing mix, and marketing effectiveness.[63]

COMPANY SALES FORECAST Once marketers have estimated company demand, their next task is to choose a level of marketing effort. The **company sales forecast** is the expected level of company sales based on a chosen marketing plan and an assumed marketing environment.

We represent the company sales forecast graphically with sales on the vertical axis and marketing effort on the horizontal axis, as in Figure 3.3. We often hear that the company should develop its marketing plan on the basis of its sales forecast. This forecast-to-plan sequence is valid if *forecast* means an estimate of national economic activity, or if company demand is nonexpansible. The sequence is not valid, however, where market demand is expansible or where *forecast* means an estimate of company sales. The company sales forecast does not establish a basis for deciding what to spend on marketing. On the contrary, the sales forecast is the result of an assumed marketing expenditure plan.

Two other concepts are important here. A **sales quota** is the sales goal set for a product line, company division, or sales representative. It is primarily a managerial device for defining and stimulating sales effort, often set slightly higher than estimated sales to stretch the sales force's effort.

A **sales budget** is a conservative estimate of the expected volume of sales, primarily for making current purchasing, production, and cash flow decisions. It's based on the need to avoid excessive risk and is generally set slightly lower than the sales forecast.

COMPANY SALES POTENTIAL **Company sales potential** is the sales limit approached by company demand as company marketing effort increases relative to that of competitors. The absolute limit of company demand is, of course, the market potential. The two would be equal if the company got 100 percent of the market. In most cases, company sales potential is less than the market potential, even when company marketing expenditures increase considerably. Each competitor has a hard core of loyal buyers unresponsive to other companies' efforts to woo them.

Estimating Current Demand

We are now ready to examine practical methods for estimating current market demand. Marketing executives want to estimate total market potential, area market potential, and total industry sales and market shares.

TOTAL MARKET POTENTIAL **Total market potential** is the maximum sales available to all firms in an industry during a given period, under a given level of industry marketing effort and environmental conditions. A common way to estimate total market potential is to multiply the potential number of buyers by the average quantity each purchases, times the price.

If 12 million Canadians buy books each year, the average book buyer buys three books a year, and the average price of a book is $20, then the total market potential for books is $720 million (12 million $\times$ 3 $\times$ $20). The most difficult component to estimate is the number of buyers for the specific product or market. One can always start with the total population in the nation, say, 32 million people. The next step is to eliminate groups that obviously would not buy the product. Let us assume that illiterate people and children under 12 do not buy books, and they constitute 20 percent of the population. This means that only 80 percent of the population, or approximately 25.6 million people, would be in the suspect pool. We might do further research and find that people of low income and low education do not buy books, and they constitute over 30 percent of the suspect pool. Eliminating them, we arrive at a prospect pool of approximately 17.9 million book buyers. We would use this number of potential buyers to calculate total market potential.

A variation on this method is the *chain-ratio method,* which multiplies a base number by several adjusting percentages. Suppose a brewery is interested in estimating the market potential for a new light beer especially designed to accompany food. The brewery can make an estimate with the following calculation:

Demand for the new light beer	×	Population	×	Average percentage of personal discretionary income per capita spent on food	×	Average percentage of amount spent on food that is spent on beverages	×	Average percentage of amount spent on beverages that is spent on alcoholic beverages	×	Average percentage of amount spent on alcoholic beverages that is spent on beer	×	Expected percentage of amount spent on beer that will be spent on light beer

AREA MARKET POTENTIAL Because companies must allocate their marketing budget optimally among their best territories, they need to estimate the market potential of different cities, provinces, and nations. Two major methods are the market-buildup method, used primarily by business marketers, and the multiple-factor index method, used primarily by consumer marketers.

Market-Buildup Method The **market-buildup method** calls for identifying all the potential buyers in each market and estimating their potential purchases. It produces accurate results if we have a list of all potential buyers and a good estimate of what each will buy. Unfortunately, this information is not always easy to gather.

Consider a machine-tool company that wants to estimate the market potential for its wood lathe in the Montreal area. Its first step is to identify all potential buyers of wood lathes in the area, primarily manufacturing establishments that shape or ream wood as part of their operations. The company could compile a list from a directory of all manufacturing establishments in the area. Then it could estimate the number of lathes each industry might purchase, based on the number of lathes per thousand employees or per $1 million of sales in that industry.

An efficient method of estimating area market potentials makes use of the *North American Industry Classification System (NAICS),* developed by the U.S. Bureau of the Census in conjunction with the Canadian and Mexican governments.[64] The NAICS classifies all manufacturing into 20 major industry sectors and further breaks each sector into a six-digit, hierarchical structure as in the following example.

51	Industry sector (information)
513	Industry subsector (broadcasting and telecommunications)
5133	Industry group (telecommunications)
51332	Industry (wireless telecommunications carriers, except satellite)
513321	National industry (U.S. paging)

For each six-digit NAICS number, a company can purchase CD-ROMs of business directories that provide complete company profiles of millions of establishments, subclassified by location, number of employees, annual sales, and net worth.

To use the NAICS, the lathe manufacturer must first determine the six-digit NAICS codes that represent products whose manufacturers are likely to require lathe machines. To get a full picture of all six-digit NAICS industries that might use lathes, the company can (1) determine past customers' NAICS codes, (2) go through the NAICS manual and check off all the six-digit industries that might have an interest in lathes, or (3) mail questionnaires to a wide range of companies inquiring about their interest in wood lathes.

The company's next task is to determine an appropriate base for estimating the number of lathes each industry will use. Suppose customer industry sales are the most appropriate base. Once the company estimates the rate of lathe ownership relative to the customer industry's sales, it can compute the market potential.

Multiple-Factor Index Method Like business marketers, consumer companies also need to estimate area market potentials, but since their customers are too numerous to list, they commonly use a straightforward index. A drug manufacturer might assume the market potential for drugs is directly related to population size. If the province of British Columbia has 13.3 percent of the Canadian population, the company might assume that B.C. will be a market for 13.3 percent of total drugs sold in Canada.

A single factor, however, is rarely a complete indicator of sales opportunity. Regional drug sales are also influenced by per capita income and the number of physicians per 10 000 people. Thus, it makes sense to develop a multiple-factor index, with each factor assigned a specific weight. The numbers are the weights attached to each variable. For example, suppose B.C. has 12.8 percent of the Canadian disposable personal income, 11.7 percent of Canadian retail sales, and 13.3 percent of Canadian population, and the respective weights are 0.5, 0.3, and 0.2. The buying-power index for B.C. would be 12.57 [= 0.5(12.8) + 0.3(11.7) + 0.2(13.3)]. Thus, 12.57 percent of the nation's drug sales might be expected to take place in B.C.

The weights in the buying-power index are somewhat arbitrary, and companies can assign others if appropriate. A manufacturer might adjust the market potential for additional factors, such as competitors' presence, local promotional costs, seasonal factors, and market idiosyncrasies.

Many companies compute other area indices as a guide to allocating marketing resources. Suppose the drug company is reviewing the six cities listed in Table 3.5. The first two columns show its percentage of brand and category sales in these six cities. The third column shows the **brand development index (BDI)**, which is the index of brand sales to category sales. Montreal, for example, has a BDI of 114 because the brand is relatively more developed than the category in Montreal. Toronto has a BDI of 65, which means that the brand is relatively underdeveloped in Toronto.

Normally, the lower the BDI, the higher the market opportunity, in that there is room to grow the brand. However, other marketers would argue the opposite, that marketing funds should go into the brand's strongest markets—where it might be important to reinforce loyalty or more easily capture additional brand share.[65]

After the company decides on the city-by-city allocation of its budget, it can refine each city allocation down to census tracts or postal code centres. *Census tracts* are small, locally defined statistical areas in metropolitan areas and some other counties. They generally have stable boundaries and a population of about 4000. Postal code centres are a little larger than neighbourhoods. Data on population size, median family income, and other characteristics are available for these geographical units. Marketers have found these data extremely useful for identifying high-potential retail areas within large cities and for buying mailing lists to use in direct-mail campaigns (see Chapter 19).

INDUSTRY SALES AND MARKET SHARES Besides estimating total potential and area potential, a company needs to know the actual industry sales taking place in its market. This means identifying competitors and estimating their sales.

The industry trade association will often collect and publish total industry sales, although it usually does not list individual company sales separately. With this information, however, each company can evaluate its own performance against the industry's. If a company's sales are increasing by 5 percent a year and industry sales are increasing by 10 percent, the company is losing its relative standing in the industry.

Another way to estimate sales is to buy reports from a marketing research firm that audits total sales and brand sales. Nielsen Media Research audits retail sales in various supermarket and drugstore product categories. A company can purchase this information and compare its performance to the total industry or any competitor to see whether it is gaining or losing share, overall or brand by brand. Because distributors typically will not supply information about how much of competitors' products they are selling, business-to-business marketers operate with less knowledge of their market share results.

Estimating Future Demand

The few products or services that lend themselves to easy forecasting generally enjoy an absolute level or a fairly constant trend, and competition that is either nonexistent (public utilities) or stable (pure oligopolies). In most markets, in contrast, good forecasting is a key factor in success.

TABLE 3.5	CALCULATING THE BRAND DEVELOPMENT INDEX (BDI)		
Territory	(a) % of Brand Sales	(b) % of Category Sales	BDI (a ÷ b) × 100
Montreal	3.09	2.71	114
Toronto	6.74	10.41	65
Vancouver	3.49	3.85	91
Halifax	0.97	0.81	120
Winnipeg	1.13	0.81	140
Calgary	3.12	3.00	104

Companies commonly prepare a macroeconomic forecast first, followed by an industry forecast, followed by a company sales forecast. The macroeconomic forecast projects inflation, unemployment, interest rates, consumer spending, business investment, government expenditures, net exports, and other variables. The end result is a forecast of gross domestic product (GDP), which the firm uses, along with other environmental indicators, to forecast industry sales. The company derives its sales forecast by assuming it will win a certain market share.

How do firms develop their forecasts? They may create their own or buy forecasts from outside sources such as marketing research firms, which interview customers, distributors, and other knowledgeable parties. Specialized forecasting firms produce long-range forecasts of particular macroenvironmental components, such as population, natural resources, and technology. Examples are IHS Global Insight (a merger of Data Resources and Wharton Econometric Forecasting Associates), Forrester Research, and the Gartner Group. The Economic Services Group of the Conference Board of Canada specializes in developing economic and forecasting models for Canadian companies. Canada's banks also perform economic forecasts, many of which are placed online. (For example, see TD Bank's Economic Group forecast at www.td.com/economics.)

All forecasts are built on one of three information bases: what people say, what people do, or what people have done. Using what people say requires surveying buyers' intentions, composites of sales force opinions, and expert opinion. Building a forecast on what people do means putting the product into a test market to measure buyer response. To use the final basis—what people have done—firms analyze records of past buying behaviour or use time-series analysis or statistical demand analysis. For further insight into sales forecasting methods, see "Marketing Memo: Fifteen Common Sales Forecasting Methods."

SURVEY OF BUYERS' INTENTIONS **Forecasting** is the art of anticipating what buyers are likely to do under a given set of conditions. For major consumer durables such as appliances, research organizations conduct periodic surveys of consumer buying intentions, ask questions like *Do you intend to buy an automobile within the next six months?* and put the answers on a **purchase probability scale**:

0.00	0.20	0.40	0.60	0.80	1.00
No chance	Slight possibility	Fair possibility	Good possibility	High possibility	Certain

Surveys also inquire into consumers' present and future personal finances and expectations about the economy. They combine bits of information into a consumer confidence measure (the Conference Board does this) or a consumer sentiment measure (the Survey Research Center of the University of Michigan does this).

For business buying, research firms can carry out buyer-intention surveys for plant, equipment, and materials, usually falling within a 10 percent margin of error. These surveys are useful in estimating demand for industrial products, consumer durables, product purchases where advanced planning is required, and new products. The survey's value increases to the extent that buyers are few, the cost of reaching them is low, and they have clear intentions they willingly disclose and implement.

COMPOSITE OF SALES FORCE OPINIONS When buyer interviewing is impractical, the company may ask its sales representatives to estimate their future sales. Few companies use these estimates without making some adjustments, however. Sales representatives might be pessimistic or optimistic, they might not know how their company's marketing plans will influence future sales in their territory, and they might deliberately underestimate demand so the company will set a low sales quota. To encourage better estimating, the company could offer incentives or assistance, such as information about marketing plans or past forecasts compared with actual sales.

Sales force forecasts yield a number of benefits. Sales reps might have better insight into developing trends than any other group, and forecasting might give them greater confidence in their sales quotas and more incentive to achieve them. A "grassroots" forecasting procedure provides detailed estimates broken down by product, territory, customer, and sales rep.

EXPERT OPINION Companies can also obtain forecasts from experts, including dealers, distributors, suppliers, marketing consultants, and trade associations. Dealer estimates are subject to the same strengths and weaknesses as sales force estimates. Many companies buy economic and industry forecasts from well-known economic-forecasting firms that have more data available and more forecasting expertise.

Occasionally, companies will invite a group of experts to prepare a forecast. The experts exchange views and produce an estimate as a group *(group-discussion method)* or individually, in which case another analyst might combine them into a single estimate *(pooling of individual estimates)*. Further rounds of estimating and refining follow (the Delphi method).[66]

MARKETING MEMO | FIFTEEN COMMON SALES FORECASTING METHODS

Judgment Methods

1. Naïve Extrapolation: a simple assumption about the sales during the next time period, or a simple subjective extension of the results of current events.

2. Sales Force Composite: a compilation of estimates by salespeople (or dealers) of expected sales in their territories, adjusted for presumed biases and expected changes.

3. Jury of Executive Opinion: the consensus of predictions by a group of experts, often from a variety of functional areas within a company.

4. Delphi Technique: a successive series of sales estimates independently developed by a group of experts, each member of which at each step in the process, uses a summary of the group's previous results to formulate new estimates.

5. Historical Analogy: Predictions based on elements of past events that are analogous to the present situation.

Counting Methods

6. Market Testing: representative buyers' responses to new offerings, tested, and extrapolated to estimate the products' future prospects.

7. Consumer Market Survey: purchase intentions data gathered from prospective buyers.

Time Series Methods

8. Moving Averages: recent sales figures averaged to predict future sales.

9. Exponential Smoothing: an estimate for the coming period based on a constantly weighted combination of the forecast sales estimate for the previous period and the most recent outcome.

10. Time Series Extrapolation: a prediction of outcomes derived from a function fitted to a data series that uses time as an independent variable.

11. Decomposition: a prediction of expected outcomes from trend, seasonal, cyclical, and random components, which are isolated from a data series.

12. Box-Jenkins: a complex, computer-based iterative procedure that produces an integrated moving average model, adjusts for seasonal and trend factors, estimates weighting parameters, tests the model, and repeats the cycle as appropriate.

Association or Causal Methods

13. Correlation: predictions of values based on historic patterns of covariation between sales and another variable.

14. Regression: estimates produced from a predictive equation derived from fitting a trend line or curve to past data on sales and variables affecting it.

15. Leading Indicators: forecasts generated from one or more variables systematically related to sales.

Source: David M. Georgoff and Robert G. Murdick, "Manager's Guide to Forecasting," *Harvard Business Review*, Jan/Feb 1986, 64(1), pp. 110–120.

PAST-SALES ANALYSIS Firms can develop sales forecasts on the basis of past sales. *Time-series analysis* breaks past time series into four components (trend, cycle, seasonal, and erratic) and projects them into the future. *Exponential smoothing* projects the next period's sales by combining an average of past sales and the most recent sales, giving more weight to the latter. *Statistical demand analysis* measures the impact of a set of causal factors (such as income, marketing expenditures, and price) on the sales level. Finally, *econometric analysis* builds sets of equations that describe a system and statistically derives the different parameters that make up the equations statistically.

MARKET-TEST METHOD When buyers don't plan their purchases carefully, or experts are unavailable or unreliable, a direct-market test can help forecast new-product sales or established product sales in a new distribution channel or territory. (We discuss market testing in detail in Chapter 20.)

SUMMARY

1. To carry out their analysis, planning, implementation, and control responsibilities, marketing managers need a marketing information system (MIS). The role of the MIS is to assess the managers' information needs, develop the needed information, and distribute that information in a timely manner.

2. An MIS has three components: (1) an internal records system, which includes information on the order-to-payment cycle and sales information systems; (2) a marketing intelligence system, a set of procedures and sources used by managers to obtain everyday information about pertinent developments in the marketing environment; and (3) a marketing research system that allows for the systematic design, collection, analysis, and reporting of data and findings relevant to a specific marketing situation.

3. Marketers find many opportunities by identifying trends (directions or sequences of events that have some momentum and durability) and megatrends (major social, economic, political, and technological changes that have long-lasting influence).

4. Within the rapidly changing global picture, marketers must monitor six major environmental forces: demographic, economic, social-cultural, natural, technological, and political-legal.

5. In the demographic environment, marketers must be aware of worldwide population growth; changing mixes of age, ethnic composition, and educational levels; the rise of nontraditional families; and large geographic shifts in population.

6. In the economic arena, marketers need to focus on income distribution and levels of savings, debt, and credit availability.

7. In the social-cultural arena, marketers must understand people's views of themselves, others, organizations, society, nature, and the universe. They must market products that correspond to society's core and secondary values and address the needs of different subcultures within a society.

8. In the natural environment, marketers need to be aware of the public's increased concern about the health of the environment. As a result, many marketers are now embracing sustainability and green marketing programs that provide better environmental solutions.

9. In the technological arena, marketers should take account of the accelerating pace of technological change, opportunities for innovation, varying R&D budgets, and the increased governmental regulation brought about by technological change.

10. In the political-legal environment, marketers must work within the many laws regulating business practices and with various special-interest groups.

11. There are two types of demand: market demand and company demand. To estimate current demand, companies attempt to determine total market potential, area market potential, industry sales, and market share. To estimate future demand, companies survey buyers' intentions, solicit their sales force's input, gather expert opinions, analyze past sales, or engage in market testing. Mathematical models, advanced statistical techniques, and computerized data collection procedures are essential to all types of demand and sales forecasting.

APPLICATIONS

Marketing Debate: Is Consumer Behaviour More a Function of a Person's Age or Generation?

One of the widely debated issues in developing marketing programs that target certain age groups is how much consumers change over time. Some marketers maintain that age differences are critical and that the needs and wants of a 25-year-old in 2010 are not that different from those of a 25-year-old in 1980. Others argue that cohort and generation effects are critical, and that marketing programs must therefore suit the times.

Take a position: Age differences are fundamentally more important than cohort effects *versus* Cohort effects can dominate age differences.

Marketing Discussion: Age Targeting

What brands and products do you feel successfully "speak to you" and effectively target your age group? Why? Which ones do not? What could they do better?

MARKETING **EXCELLENCE** | CANADIAN TOURISM COMMISSION

The Canadian Tourism Commission (CTC) knows a thing or two about finding new market opportunities internationally. Committed to maintaining Canada's status as the world's number-one country brand, the CTC uses research to design its marketing strategy to attract visitors. The CTC's research program has gained a global reputation for its innovative approach to tourism. Market trends, industry research, and future market outlook are all continuously monitored for changes that may affect strategy and return on investment.

Potential markets are carefully analyzed by demographics, economic conditions, spending patterns, trends, and social influences. The CTC uses an integrated communications plan to market the Canada brand across countries that show the highest return on investment potential. For example, the CTC added India, with a population at about 1.2 billion, as an emerging market for Canadian tourism. Indian outbound traffic has grown more than 20 percent over the last few years, ranking among the top five tourism-generating markets in many countries. Fluency in the English language, a positive trade relationship, growing economic prosperity, and a large affluent middle class make India an attractive target market for the CTC moving forward.

The CTC also monitors environmental factors that influence the tourism industry, such as foreign exchange rates, economic conditions, political stability, and oil prices. A strong Canadian dollar inflates the cost of boarding, lodging, and admission to attractions for visitors. However, airfares have become less expensive than in previous years and have made Canada a more affordable tourism destination. Political changes, like Canada's being granted Approved Destination Status (ADS) by the Chinese government in 2010, opened Canada's doors to the world's largest outbound tourism market. Anticipating this political change, the CTC rolled out a prepared post-ADS strategy and welcomed the first Chinese tour groups two months later. The CTC expects a 50 percent increase in Chinese visitors by 2015, representing an additional $300 million per year in tourism revenue.

By continuously gathering information on markets and environmental factors to design its marketing programs, the CTC is not only attracting new visitors to Canada—it is doing so at an ROI of 101 percent. In other words, for every dollar spent on CTC core campaigns, $101 is generated in tourism revenue, not to mention the thousands of jobs created or protected in the Canadian tourism industry.

QUESTIONS

1. The CTC conducts extensive research before targeting a new market. Is it always necessary to gather data before every marketing decision? Are there trade-offs?

2. Identify current challenges in the global economic and political environment that would limit the CTC's ability to promote tourism in Canada.

3. Discuss the role of technological advances in aiding the CTC's success.

Sources: Canadian Tourism Commission, "Canadian Tourism Commission—2010 Corporate Brochure," http://en-corporate.canada.travel/sites/Corporate/flash/CorporateBrochure-en/flippingbook.swf (viewed February 21, 2011); Canadian Tourism Commission Corporate website, http://en-corporate.canada.travel/Corporate/Flyout.page?id=356&fid=353 (viewed February 21, 2011); Canadian Tourism Commission, "U.S. and Overseas Travel to Canada, Short-Term Competitive Outlook: Third Quarter of 2011," April 2011.

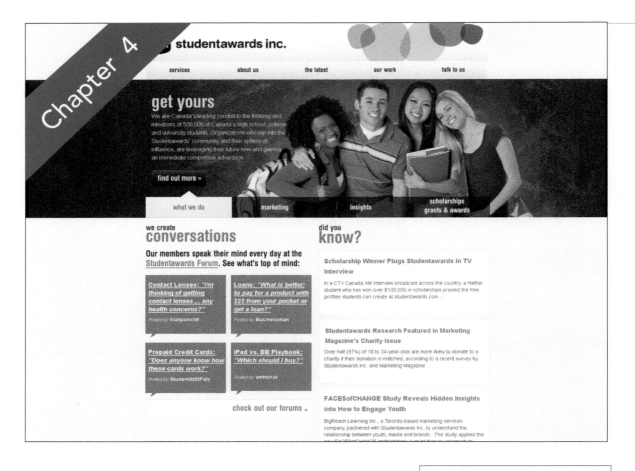

Studentawards Inc. uses research extensively to serve its student and corporate clients better.

In This Chapter, We Will Address the Following **Questions**

1. What constitutes good marketing research?

2. What are the best metrics for measuring marketing productivity?

3. How can marketers assess their return on investment for marketing expenditures?

Conducting Marketing Research

Good marketers need insights to help them interpret past
performance as well as plan future activities. To make the best possible tactical decisions in the short run and strategic decisions in the long run, they need timely, accurate, and actionable information about consumers, competition, and their brands. Discovering a consumer insight and understanding its marketing implications can often lead to a successful product launch or spur the growth of a brand.

The average post-secondary student in Canada graduates with $24 500 of debt. Recognizing student financial need across the country, Toronto-based Studentawards Inc. set out on a mission: to provide students with quick and easy access to information on educational scholarships, bursaries, grants, fellowships, and other types of financial assistance. To help students find the funding they need, Studentawards Inc. established a website (www.studentawards.com) offering free scholarship suggestions to online members based on their location, school, interests, and more. Financial assistance is easy to find, apply for, and receive, ranging in value from $50 to $350 000.

Once students become a member of the website and create a profile, Studentawards not only has information on a valuable target market but also gets a channel to communicate with them. Besides providing a service to students, Studentawards also helps its corporate clients link with students for marketing campaigns that may include opportunities for its student members. In addition to access to hundreds of thousands of Canadian students, Studentawards is also able to provide its corporate clients with useful consumer data on this lucrative market.

Studentawards' "Students as Consumers" 2009 study revealed valuable insights on the purchasing priorities of Canada's student market over the 2009–2010 school year. Over 5000 high-school, college, and university students provided data on their fall 2009 back-to-school purchases. The data collected were then analyzed by categories such as gender, province, and current level of institution (high school, college, or university). The study revealed average monthly expenses for students across all levels of institution to be $1107. In addition, the study included aspects such as how much research was done prior to buying, whether any advertising or promotions played a role, and what the students' monthly budgets are for the year.

Studentawards Inc. provides companies with an attractive marketing opportunity by not only collecting a wealth of up-to-date data on the student consumer market, but also giving access to a 600 000 student member database. The unique service that Studentawards has to offer has attracted large corporations such as Scotiabank, Apple Canada, VIA Rail, Microsoft, Bell Mobility, and Wendy's Restaurants of Canada. A commitment to developing relationships with hundreds of thousands of Canadian students and to performing ongoing research on this young, attractive market is expected to carry Studentawards Inc. toward further growth and success.[1]

In this chapter, we review the steps in the marketing research process. We also consider how marketers can develop effective metrics for measuring marketing productivity.

THE MARKETING RESEARCH SYSTEM

Marketing managers often commission formal marketing studies of specific problems and opportunities. They may request a market survey, a product-preference test, a sales forecast by region, or an advertising evaluation. It's the job of the marketing researcher to produce insight into the customer's attitudes and buying behaviour. **Marketing insights** provide diagnostic information about how and why we observe certain effects in the marketplace, and what that means to marketers.[2]

Good marketing insights often form the basis of successful marketing programs. When an extensive consumer research study of U.S. retail shoppers by Walmart revealed that the store's key competitive advantages were the functional benefit of "offers low prices" and the emotional benefit of "makes me feel like a smart shopper," its marketers used those insights to develop their "Save Money, Live Better" campaign. Gillette's Venus razor has become the most successful female shaving line ever—holding more than 50 percent of the global women's shaving market—as a result of insightful consumer research that led to product design, packaging, and advertising cues that better satisfied female shaving needs.[3]

Venus Razor

As part of a $300 million budget for the development of its first razor designed solely for women, Gillette conducted extensive consumer research and performed numerous market tests. The razor, called Venus, was a marked departure from previous women's razor designs, which had essentially been coloured or repackaged versions of men's razors. After research revealed that women change their grip on a razor about 30 times during each shaving session, Gillette designed the Venus with a wide, sculpted rubberized handle offering superior grip and control, and an oval-shaped blade in a storage case that could stick to shower walls. Research also indicated that women were reluctant to leave the shower in order to replace a dull blade, so the case was made to hold spare blade cartridges. When Gillette research later revealed four distinct segments of women shavers—perfect shave seekers (no missed hairs), skin pamperers, pragmatic functionalists, and EZ seekers—the company designed Venus products for each of them.

Gaining marketing insights is crucial for marketing success. If marketers lack consumer insights, they often get in trouble. When Tropicana redesigned its orange juice packaging, dropping the iconic image of an orange skewered by a straw, it failed to adequately test for consumer reactions, with disastrous results. Sales dropped by 20 percent, and Tropicana reinstated the old package design after only a few months.[4]

We define **marketing research** as the systematic design, collection, analysis, and reporting of data and findings relevant to a specific marketing situation facing the company. Spending on marketing research was nearly US$29 billion globally in 2009, according to ESOMAR, the world association of opinion and market research professionals.[5] Most large companies have their own marketing research departments, which often play crucial roles within the organization. Procter & Gamble's Consumer & Market Knowledge (CMK) market research function has dedicated CMK groups working for P&G businesses around the world to improve both their brand strategies and program execution, as well as a relatively smaller, centralized corporate CMK group that focuses on a variety of big-picture concerns that transcend any specific line of business.

Marketing research, however, is not limited to large companies with big budgets and marketing research departments. Often at much smaller companies, everyone carries out marketing research—including the customers. Small companies can also hire the services of a marketing research firm or conduct research in creative and affordable ways, such as the following:

1. *Engaging students or professors to design and carry out projects*—Companies such as GE, Hilton Hotels, IBM, Mars, and Whirlpool engage in "crowdcasting" and are sponsors of competitions such as the Innovation Challenge, where top MBA students compete in teams. The payoff to the students is experience and visibility; the payoff to the companies is a fresh set of eyes to solve problems at a fraction of what consultants would charge.[6]

2. *Using the Internet*—A company can collect considerable information at very little cost by examining competitors' websites, monitoring chat rooms, and accessing published data.

3. *Checking out rivals*—Many small businesses, such as restaurants, hotels, or specialty retailers, routinely visit competitors to learn about changes they have made.

4. *Tapping into marketing partner expertise*—Marketing research firms, ad agencies, distributors, and other marketing partners may be able to share relevant market knowledge they have accumulated.

Those partners targeting small or medium-sized businesses may be especially helpful. For example, to promote more shipping to China, UPS conducted several in-depth surveys of the Chinese market to portray its complexities but also its opportunities for even small and medium-sized businesses.[7]

Most companies use a combination of marketing research resources to study their industries, competitors, audiences, and channel strategies. Companies normally budget marketing research at 1 percent to 2 percent of company sales and spend a large percentage of that on the services of outside firms. Marketing research firms fall into three categories:

1. *Syndicated-service research firms*—These firms gather consumer and trade information, which they sell for a fee. Examples include the Nielsen Company, Ipsos, TNS Canada, NRG, and IRI.

2. *Custom marketing research firms*—These firms are hired to carry out specific projects. They design the study and report the findings.

3. *Specialty-line marketing research firms*—These firms provide specialized research services. The best example is the field-service firm, which sells field interviewing services to other firms.

To take advantage of all these different resources and practices, good marketers adopt a formal marketing research process.

THE MARKETING RESEARCH PROCESS

Effective marketing research follows the six steps shown in Figure 4.1. We illustrate them in the following situation.[8]

Air Canada is constantly looking for new ways to serve its passengers; it was the first airline in the world to offer telephone handsets within arm's reach on all its aircraft. The airline constantly reviews many new ideas to improve its operations and customer satisfaction. For example, Air Canada has been examining how to cater to its first-class passengers on long-haul flights, many of whom are businesspeople whose high-priced tickets pay most of the freight. Among these ideas are (1) to supply an Internet connection with limited access to webpages and email, (2) to offer 24 channels of satellite TV, and (3) to offer a 50-CD audio system that lets each passenger create a customized playlist of music and movies to enjoy during the flight. The marketing research manager was assigned to investigate how first-class passengers would rate these services and how much extra they would be willing to pay if a charge were made. He was asked to focus specifically on the Internet connection. One estimate says that airlines might realize revenues of $70 billion over the next decade from in-flight Internet access if enough first-class passengers would be willing to pay $25 for it. Air Canada could thus recover its costs in a reasonable time. Making the connection available would cost the airline $90 000 per plane.[9]

Step 1: Define the Problem, the Decision Alternatives, and the Research Objectives

Marketing managers must be careful not to define the problem too broadly or too narrowly for the marketing researcher. A marketing manager who says, "Find out everything you can about first-class air travellers' needs," will collect a lot of unnecessary information. One who says, "Find out whether enough passengers aboard a B747 flying direct between Vancouver and Tokyo would be willing to pay $25 for an Internet connection for Air Canada to break even in one year on the cost of offering this service," is taking too narrow a view of the problem.

The marketing researcher might even ask, "Why does the Internet connection have to be priced at $25 as opposed to $15, $35, or some other price? Why does Air Canada have to break even on the cost of the service, especially if it attracts new customers?" Another relevant question to ask is, "How important is it to be first in the market, and how long can the company sustain its lead?"

The marketing manager and marketing researcher agreed to define the problem as follows: "Will offering an in-flight Internet service create enough incremental preference and profit for Air Canada to justify its cost against other possible investments in service enhancements Air Canada might make?" To help in designing the research, management should first spell out the decisions it might face and then work backward. Suppose management outlines these decisions: (1) Should Air Canada offer an Internet connection? (2) If so, should we offer the service to first class only, or include business class and possibly economy class? (3) What price(s) should we charge? (4) On what types of planes and lengths of trips should we offer the service?

FIGURE 4.1

The Marketing Research Process

Define the problem and research objectives

↓

Develop the research plan

↓

Collect the information

↓

Analyze the information

↓

Present the findings

↓

Make the decision

Now management and marketing researchers are ready to set specific research objectives: (1) What types of first-class passengers would respond most to using an in-flight Internet service? (2) How many first-class passengers are likely to use the Internet service at different price levels? (3) How many extra first-class passengers might choose Air Canada because of this new service? (4) How much long-term goodwill will this service add to Air Canada's image? (5) How important is Internet service to first-class passengers relative to other services, such as a power plug or enhanced entertainment?

Not all research projects can be this specific. Some research is *exploratory*—its goal is to shed light on the real nature of the problem and to suggest possible solutions or new ideas. Some research is *descriptive*—it seeks to quantify demand, such as how many first-class passengers would purchase in-flight Internet service at $25. Some research is *causal*—its purpose is to test a cause-and-effect relationship.

Step 2: Develop the Research Plan

The second stage of marketing research is where we develop the most efficient plan for gathering the needed information and what that will cost. Suppose Air Canada made a prior estimate that launching in-flight Internet service would yield a long-term profit of $50 000. If the manager believes that doing the marketing research will lead to an improved pricing and promotional plan and a long-term profit of $90 000, he should be willing to spend up to $40 000 on this research. If the research will cost more than $40 000, it's not worth doing.[10]

To design a research plan, we need to make decisions about the data sources, research approaches, research instruments, sampling plan, and contact methods.

DATA SOURCES The researcher can gather secondary data, primary data, or both. *Secondary data* are data that were collected for another purpose and already exist somewhere. *Primary data* are data freshly gathered for a specific purpose or for a specific research project.

Researchers usually start their investigation by examining some of the rich variety of low-cost and readily available secondary data, to see whether they can partly or wholly solve the problem without collecting costly primary data. For instance, auto advertisers looking to get a better return on their online car ads might purchase a copy of J. D. Power and Associates' semi-annual *Power Auto Online Media Study*, a survey that gives insights into who buys specific brands and where on the web advertisers can find them.[11]

When the needed data don't exist or are dated, inaccurate, incomplete, or unreliable, the researcher will need to collect primary data. Most marketing research projects do include some primary-data collection.

RESEARCH APPROACHES Marketers collect primary data in five main ways: through observation, focus groups, surveys, behavioural data, and experiments.

Observational Research Researchers can gather fresh data by observing the relevant actors and settings unobtrusively as the actors shop or consume products.[12] Sometimes researchers equip consumers with pagers and instruct them to write down what they're doing whenever prompted, or they hold informal interview sessions at a café or bar. Photographs can also provide a wealth of detailed information.

Ethnographic research is a particular observational research approach that uses concepts and tools from anthropology and other social science disciplines to provide deep cultural understanding of how people live and work.[13] The goal is to immerse the researcher into consumers' lives to uncover unarticulated desires that might not surface in any other form of research.[14] Firms such as Fujitsu Laboratories, Herman Miller, IBM, Intel, Steelcase, and Xerox have embraced ethnographic research to design breakthrough products. Here are three specific examples:

- Bank of America's ethnographic research that followed female baby boomers at home and while they shopped yielded two insights—women rounded up financial transactions because it was more convenient, and those with children found it difficult to save. Subsequent research led to the launch of "Keep the Change," a debit card program that rounded purchases up to the nearest dollar amount and automatically transferred the added difference from a chequing to a savings account. Since the launch, 2.5 million customers have signed up for the program, opening 800 000 new chequing accounts and 3 million new savings accounts in the process.[15]

- Frito-Lay Canada conducted ethnographic research over several weeks, interacting with and observing a group of eighth-graders to see how they communicate with each other. The company learned that kids are so used to text messaging that they use abbreviations even when speaking face-to-face—a finding that would not have surfaced in a focus group or survey. Research such as this was responsible for Frito-Lay's subsequent "inNw?" (which stands for "if not now, when?") campaign to launch its Doritos Black Pepper Jack flavour.[16]

■ When package design firm 4sight, Inc., was hired by PepsiCo to come up with a new design for Gatorade's 64-ounce package, its team initially assumed the package functioned as a family pack to be used for multiple servings to multiple users in the household. In watching moms in their homes, however, team members were surprised to find them taking the jug out of the refrigerator—for example, after a hard workout—and chugging it right there on the spot! That insight led to a totally different package design, one that could be easily gripped and grabbed.[17]

Ethnographic research isn't limited to consumer companies in developed markets. In a business-to-business setting, GE's ethnographic research into the plastic-fibre industry revealed to the firm that it wasn't in a commodity business driven by price, as it had assumed. Instead, it was in an artisanal industry, with customers who wanted collaborations at the earliest stages of development. GE completely reoriented the way it interacted with the companies in the industry as a result. In developing markets, ethnographic research also can be very useful, especially in far-flung rural areas, given that marketers often do not know these consumers as well.[18]

Air Canada researchers might meander around first-class lounges to hear how travellers talk about the different carriers and their features or sit next to passengers on planes. They can fly on competitors' planes to observe in-flight service.

Focus-Group Research A **focus group** is a gathering of six to ten people carefully selected by researchers based on certain demographic, psychographic, or other considerations and brought together to discuss various topics of interest at length. Participants are normally paid a small sum for attending. A professional research moderator provides questions and probes based on the marketing managers' discussion guide or agenda. In focus groups, moderators try to discern consumers' real motivations and why they say and do certain things. They typically record the sessions, and marketing managers often remain behind two-way mirrors in the next room. To allow for more in-depth discussion with participants, focus groups are trending smaller in size.[19]

Focus-group research is a useful exploratory step, but researchers must avoid generalizing from focus-group participants to the whole market, because the sample size is too small and the sample is not drawn randomly. Some marketers feel the research setting is too contrived and prefer to seek other means of collecting information that they believe are less artificial. "Marketing Memo: Conducting Informative Focus Groups" has some practical tips to improve the quality of focus groups.

In the Air Canada research, the moderator might start with a broad question, such as "How do you feel about first-class air travel?" Questions then move to how people view the different airlines, different existing services, and different proposed services, specifically Internet service.

Survey Research Companies undertake surveys to assess people's knowledge, beliefs, preferences, and satisfaction and to measure these in the general population. A company such as Air Canada might prepare its own survey instrument to gather the information it needs, or it might add questions to an omnibus survey that carries the questions of several companies at a much lower cost. It can also pose the questions to an ongoing consumer panel run by itself or another company. It may do a mall intercept study by having researchers approach people in a shopping mall and ask them questions.

As we'll discuss in more detail later in this chapter, many marketers are taking their surveys online where they can easily develop, administer, and collect email and web-based questionnaires. However they conduct their surveys—online, by phone, or in person—companies must feel that the information they're getting from the mounds of data makes it all worthwhile. San Francisco–based Wells Fargo bank collects more than 50 000 customer surveys each month through its bank branches. It has used customers' comments to begin more stringent new wait-time standards designed to improve customer satisfaction.

An important marketing research tool is focus groups.

Of course, by putting out so many surveys each month, companies may run the risk of creating "survey burnout" and seeing response rates plummet. Keeping a survey short and simple and contacting customers no more than once a month are two keys to drawing people into the data collection effort. Offering incentives is another way companies get consumers to respond. Both Gap and Jack in the Box offer coupons for discounts on merchandise or the chance to win a cash prize.[20]

Behavioural Research Customers leave traces of their purchasing behaviour in store scanning data, catalogue purchases, and customer databases. Marketers can learn much by analyzing these data. Actual purchases reflect consumers' preferences and often are more reliable than statements they offer to market researchers. For example, grocery shopping data show that high-income people don't necessarily buy the

---

| MARKETING **MEMO** | CONDUCTING INFORMATIVE FOCUS GROUPS |

Focus groups allow marketers to observe how and why consumers accept or reject concepts, ideas, or any specific notion. The key to using focus groups successfully is to listen and observe. Marketers should eliminate their own biases as much as possible. Although many useful insights can emerge from thoughtfully run focus groups, questions can arise about their validity, especially in today's complex marketing environment.

There are many challenges to conducting a good focus group. Some researchers believe that consumers have been so bombarded with ads, they unconsciously (or perhaps cynically) parrot back what they've already heard instead of what they really think. There's always a concern that participants are just trying to maintain their self-image and public persona or have a need to identify with the other members of the group. Participants also may not be willing to acknowledge in public—or may not even recognize—their behaviour patterns and motivations. And the "loudmouth" or "know-it-all" problem often crops up when one highly opinionated person drowns out the rest of the group. Getting the right participants is crucial, but it may be expensive to recruit qualified subjects who meet the sampling criteria ($3000 to $5000 per group).

Even when marketers use multiple focus groups, it may be difficult to generalize the results to a broader population. For example, within the United States, focus-group findings often vary from region to region. One firm specializing in focus-group research claimed the best city to conduct groups was Minneapolis, because there it could get a sample of fairly well-educated people who were honest and forthcoming with their opinions. Many marketers interpret focus groups in New York and other northeastern cities carefully, because the people in these areas tend to be highly critical and generally don't report that they like much.

Participants must feel as relaxed as possible and strongly motivated to be truthful. Physical surroundings can be crucial to achieving the right atmosphere. At one agency an executive noted, "We wondered why people always seemed grumpy and negative—people were resistant to any idea we showed them." Finally, in one session a fight broke out between participants. The problem was the room itself: cramped, stifling, forbidding. "It was a cross between a hospital room and a police interrogation room." To fix the problem, the agency gave the room a make-over. Other firms are adapting the look of the room to fit the theme of the topic, such as designing the room to look like a playroom when speaking to children.

To allow for more interactivity among focus group members, some researchers are incorporating pre-session homework assignments such as diaries, photography, and videography. An area of increasing interest is online focus groups. These may cost less than a fourth of a traditional in-person focus group. Online focus groups also offer the advantages of being less intrusive, allowing geographically diverse subjects to participate, and yielding fast results. They are useful at collecting reactions to focused topics such as a specific new product concept.

Proponents of traditional focus groups, on the other hand, maintain that in-person focus groups allow marketers to be immersed in the research process, get a close-up look at people's emotional and physical reactions, and ensure that sensitive materials are not leaked. Marketers can also make spontaneous adjustments to the flow of discussion and delve deeply into more complex topics, such as alternative creative concepts for a new ad campaign.

Regardless of the particular form it takes, the beauty of a focus group, as one marketing executive noted, is that "it's still the most cost-effective, quickest, dirtiest way to get information in rapid time on an idea." In analyzing the pros and cons, Wharton's Americus Reed might have said it best: "A focus group is like a chain saw. If you know what you're doing, it's very useful and effective. If you don't, you could lose a limb."

Sources: Naomi R. Henderson, "Beyond Top of Mind," *Marketing Research,* September 1, 2005; Rebecca Harris, "Do Focus Groups Have a Future?" *Marketing,* June 6, 2005, p. 17; Linda Tischler, "Every Move You Make," *Fast Company,* April 2004, pp. 73–75; Alison Stein Wellner, "The New Science of Focus Groups," *American Demographics,* March 2003, pp. 29–33; Dennis Rook, "Out-of-Focus Groups," *Marketing Research,* 15, no. 2 (Summer 2003): 11; Dennis W. Rook, "Loss of Vision: Focus Groups Fail to Connect Theory, Current Practice," *Marketing News,* September 15, 2003, p. 40; Sarah Jeffrey Kasner, "Fistfights and Feng Shui," *Boston Globe,* July 21, 2001; Piet Levy, "In with the Old, In Spite of the New," *Marketing News,* May 30, 2009, p. 19.

more expensive brands, contrary to what they might state in interviews; and many low-income people buy some expensive brands. And as Chapter 3 described, there is a wealth of online data to collect from consumers. Clearly, Air Canada can learn many useful things about its passengers by analyzing ticket purchase records and online behaviour. Cineplex has learned a fair bit about moviegoers by analyzing its SCENE data.

Cineplex

SCENE is an entertainment rewards program, which began with Cineplex Entertainment and Scotiabank. The program allows members to turn everyday purchases into free movie tickets and other rewards. The debit-rewards program provided both Scotiabank and Cineplex with an insight into what the 18- to 45-year-old market was purchasing, as well as which movies they were going to. Thanks to the SCENE database, Cineplex can determine where moviegoers spend their money, who the high-spending customers are, and what movies they prefer, which can be very useful in determining what to offer the different market segments.[21]

Experimental Research The most scientifically valid research is **experimental research**, designed to capture cause-and-effect relationships by eliminating competing explanations of the observed findings. If the experiment is well designed and executed, research and marketing managers can have confidence in the conclusions. Experiments call for selecting matched groups of subjects, subjecting them to different treatments, controlling extraneous variables, and checking whether observed response differences are statistically significant. If we can eliminate or control extraneous factors, we can relate the observed effects to the variations in the treatments or stimuli.

Air Canada might introduce in-flight Internet service on one of its regular flights from Vancouver to Tokyo and charge $25 one week and $15 the next week. If the plane carried approximately the same number of first-class passengers each week and the particular weeks made no difference, the airline could relate any significant difference in the number of passengers using the service to the different prices charged.

RESEARCH INSTRUMENTS Marketing researchers have a choice of three main research instruments in collecting primary data: questionnaires, qualitative measures, and technological devices.

Questionnaires A **questionnaire** consists of a set of questions presented to respondents. Because of its flexibility, it is by far the most common instrument used to collect primary data. Researchers need to carefully develop, test, and debug questionnaires before administering them on a large scale. The form, wording, and sequence of the questions can all influence the responses. *Closed-end questions* specify all the possible answers and provide answers that are easier to interpret and tabulate. *Open-end questions* allow respondents to answer in their own words and often reveal more about how people think. They are especially useful in exploratory research, where the researcher is looking for insight into how people think rather than measuring how many people think a certain way, as the Pantene example below illustrates.

Pantene

Proctor & Gamble's Pantene Pro-V hair-care products recently underwent some changes in order to tackle what its target market fears most—the bad hair day. In order to reinvent the product and image, Pantene conducted research to discover women's specific emotions when it came to their hair. The researchers used a questionnaire to measure how women's hair affects their mood. Before washing their hair, subjects used words such as "hostile," "ashamed," and "irritable" to describe their moods when they experience a bad hair day. After trying Pantene, users reported that they felt positive emotions such as "excited," "proud," and "interested." Using this research, P&G discovered that Pantene could do more than wash women's hair—it could change their moods as well![22]

Table 4.1 provides examples of both types of questions; also see "Marketing Memo: Questionnaire Dos and Don'ts."

Qualitative Measures Some marketers prefer more qualitative methods for gauging consumer opinion, because consumer actions don't always match their answers to survey questions. *Qualitative research techniques* are relatively unstructured measurement approaches that permit a range of possible responses. Their variety is limited only by the creativity of the marketing researcher.

Because of the freedom it affords both researchers in their probes and consumers in their responses, qualitative research can often be an especially useful first step in exploring consumers' brand and product perceptions. It is indirect in nature, so consumers may be less guarded and reveal more about themselves in the process.

Qualitative research does have its drawbacks. Marketers must temper the in-depth insights that emerge with the fact that the samples are often very small and cannot necessarily be generalized to broader populations. And different researchers examining the same qualitative results may draw very different conclusions.

Nevertheless, there is increasing interest in using qualitative methods. "Marketing Insight: Getting into the Heads of Consumers" describes the pioneering ZMET approach. Here are some other popular

TABLE 4.1 | TYPES OF QUESTIONS

Name	Description	Example
A. Closed-end Questions		
Dichotomous	A question with two possible answers.	In arranging this trip, did you personally phone Air Canada? Yes No
Multiple choice	A question with three or more answers.	With whom are you travelling on this flight? ☐ No one ☐ Children only ☐ Spouse ☐ Business associates/friends/relatives ☐ Spouse and children ☐ An organized tour group
Likert scale	A statement with which the respondent shows the amount of agreement/disagreement.	Small airlines generally give better service than large ones. Strongly disagree 1___ Disagree 2___ Neither agree nor disagree 3___ Agree 4___ Strongly agree 5___
Semantic differential	A scale connecting two bipolar words. The respondent selects the point that represents his or her opinion.	Air Canada Large ----------Small Experienced ----------Inexperienced Modern----------Old-fashioned
Importance scale	A scale that rates the importance of some attribute.	Airline food service to me is Extremely important 1___ Very important 2___ Somewhat important 3___ Not very important 4___ Not at all important 5___
Rating scale	A scale that rates some attribute from "poor" to "excellent."	Air Canada in-flight service is Excellent 1___ Very Good 2___ Good 3___ Fair 4___ Poor 5___
Intention-to-buy scale	A scale that describes the respondent's intention to buy.	If an in-flight telephone were available on a long flight, I would Definitely buy 1___ Probably buy 2___ Not sure 3___ Probably not buy 4___ Definitely not buy 5___
B. Open-end Questions		
Completely unstructured	A question that respondents can answer in an almost unlimited number of ways.	What is your opinion of Air Canada?
Word association	Words are presented, one at a time, and respondents mention the first word that comes to mind.	What is the first word that comes to your mind when you hear the following? Airline _____ Air Canada _____ Travel _____
Sentence completion	An incomplete sentence is presented and respondents complete the sentence.	When I choose an airline, the most important consideration in my decision is _____.
Story completion	An incomplete story is presented, and respondents are asked to complete it.	"I flew Air Canada a few days ago. I noticed that the exterior and interior of the plane had very bright colours. This aroused in me the following thoughts and feelings. . . ." Now complete the story.
Picture	A picture of two characters is presented, with one making a statement. Respondents are asked to identify with the other and fill in the empty balloon.	
Thematic Apperception Test (TAT)	A picture is presented and respondents are asked to make up a story about what they think is happening or may happen in the picture.	

MARKETING **MEMO** | QUESTIONNAIRE DOS AND DON'TS

1. *Ensure that questions are without bias.* Don't lead the respondent into an answer.

2. *Make the questions as simple as possible.* Questions that include multiple ideas or two questions in one will confuse respondents.

3. *Make the questions specific.* Sometimes it's advisable to add memory cues. For example, be specific with time periods.

4. *Avoid jargon or shorthand.* Avoid trade jargon, acronyms, and initials not in everyday use.

5. *Steer clear of sophisticated or uncommon words.* Use only words in common speech.

6. *Avoid ambiguous words.* Words such as "usually" or "frequently" have no specific meaning.

7. *Avoid questions with a negative in them.* It is better to say, "Do you ever... ?" than "Do you never... ?"

8. *Avoid hypothetical questions.* It's difficult to answer questions about imaginary situations. Answers aren't necessarily reliable.

9. *Do not use words that could be misheard.* This is especially important when administering the interview over the telephone. "What is your opinion of sects?" could yield interesting but not necessarily relevant answers.

10. *Desensitize questions by using response bands.* To ask people their age or ask companies about employee turnover rates, offer a range of response bands instead of precise numbers.

11. *Ensure that fixed responses do not overlap.* Categories used in fixed-response questions should be distinct and not overlap.

12. *Allow for the answer "other" in fixed-response questions.* Precoded answers should always allow for a response other than those listed.

Source: Adapted from Paul Hague and Peter Jackson, *Market Research: A Guide to Planning, Methodology, and Evaluation* (London: Kogan Page, 1999). See also Hans Baumgartner and Jan-Benedict E. M. Steenkamp, "Response Styles in Marketing Research: A Cross-National Investigation," *Journal of Marketing Research*, May 2001, pp. 143–156.

---

qualitative research approaches to get inside consumers' minds and find out what they think or feel about brands and products:[23]

1. *Word associations*—Ask subjects what words come to mind when they hear the brand's name. "What does the Aldo name mean to you? Tell me what comes to mind when you think of Aldo shoes." The primary purpose of free-association tasks is to identify the range of possible brand associations in consumers' minds.

2. *Projective techniques*—Give people an incomplete stimulus and ask them to complete it, or give them an ambiguous stimulus and ask them to make sense of it. One approach is "bubble exercises" in which empty bubbles, like those found in cartoons, appear in scenes of people buying or using certain products or services. Subjects fill in the bubble, indicating what they believe is happening or being said. Another technique is comparison tasks in which people compare brands to people, countries, animals, activities, fabrics, occupations, cars, magazines, vegetables, nationalities, or even other brands.

3. *Visualization*—Visualization requires people to create a collage from magazine photos or drawings to depict their perceptions.

4. *Brand personification*—Ask subjects what kind of person they think of when the brand is mentioned: "If the brand were to come alive as a person, what would it be like, what would it do, where would it live, what would it wear, who would it talk to if it went to a party (and what would it talk about)?" For example, when Labatt Ice used Alexander Godunov as brand spokesperson in its advertising, marketers found that consumers viewed his personality to be inconsistent with that of the Labatt brand's, which was that of a confident, credible male.[24]

5. *Laddering*—A series of increasingly more specific "why" questions can reveal consumer motivation and consumers' deeper, more abstract goals. Ask why someone wants to buy a Nokia cell phone. "They look well built" (attribute). "Why is it important that the phone be well built?" "It suggests Nokia is reliable" (a functional benefit). "Why is reliability important?" "Because my colleagues or

| MARKETING **INSIGHT** | GETTING INTO THE HEADS OF CONSUMERS |

Harvard Business School marketing professor Gerald Zaltman, with some of his research colleagues, has developed an in-depth methodology to uncover what consumers truly think and feel about products, services, brands, and other things. The basic assumption behind the Zaltman Metaphor Elicitation Technique (ZMET) is that most thoughts and feelings are unconscious and shaped by a set of "deep metaphors." **Deep metaphors** are basic frames or orientations that consumers have toward the world around them. Largely unconscious and universal, deep metaphors recast everything someone thinks, hears, says, or does. According to Zaltman, there are seven main metaphors:

1. *Balance:* justice equilibrium and the interplay of elements
2. *Transformation:* changes in substance and circumstance
3. *Journey:* the meeting of past, present, and future
4. *Container:* inclusion, exclusion, and other boundaries
5. *Connection:* the need to relate to oneself and others
6. *Resource:* acquisitions and their consequences
7. *Control:* sense of mastery, vulnerability, and well-being

The ZMET technique works by first asking participants in advance to select a minimum of 12 images from their own sources (magazines, catalogues, family photo albums) to represent their thoughts and feelings about the research topic. In a one-on-one interview, the study administrator uses advanced interview techniques to explore the images with the participant and reveal hidden meanings. Finally, the participants use a computer program to create a collage with these images that communicates their subconscious thoughts and feelings about the topic. The results often profoundly influence marketing actions, as the following three examples illustrate:

- In a ZMET study about pantyhose for marketers at DuPont, some respondents' pictures showed fence posts encased in plastic wrap or steel bands strangling trees, suggesting that pantyhose are tight and inconvenient. But another picture showed tall flowers in a vase, suggesting that the product made a woman feel thin, tall, and sexy. The love-hate relationship in these and other pictures suggested a more complicated product relationship than the DuPont marketers had assumed.

- A ZMET study of Nestlé Crunch revealed that—besides the obvious associations to a small indulgence in a busy world, a source of quick energy, and something that just tasted good—the candy bar was also seen as a powerful reminder of pleasant childhood memories.

- When Motorola conducted a ZMET study of a proposed new security system, study participants selected images of what they felt when they were secure. The Motorola researchers were struck by how many images of dogs showed up, suggesting that it might be appropriate to position the product as a companion.

Sources: Gerald Zaltman and Lindsay Zaltman, *Marketing Metaphoria: What Deep Metaphors Reveal about the Minds of Consumers* (Boston: Harvard Business School Press, 2008); Daniel H. Pink, "Metaphor Marketing," *Fast Company*, March–April 1998, pp. 214–229; Brad Wieners, "Getting Inside—Way Inside—Your Customer's Head," *Business 2.0*, April 2003, pp. 54–55; Glenn L. Christensen and Jerry C. Olson, "Mapping Consumers' Mental Models with ZMET," *Psychology & Marketing, 19*, no. 6 (June 2002): 477–502; Emily Eakin, "Penetrating the Mind by Metaphor," *New York Times*, February 23, 2002.

family can be sure to reach me" (an emotional benefit). "Why must you be available to them at all times?" "I can help them if they're in trouble" (brand essence). The brand makes this person feel like a Good Samaritan, ready to help others.

Marketers don't necessarily have to choose between qualitative and quantitative measures, however, and many marketers use both approaches, recognizing that their pros and cons can offset each other. For example, companies can recruit someone from an online panel to participate in an in-home-use test in which the subject is sent a product and told to capture his or her reactions and intentions with both a video diary and an online survey.[25]

Technological Devices There has been much interest in recent years in various technological devices. Galvanometers can measure the interest or emotions aroused by exposure to a specific ad or picture. The tachistoscope flashes an ad to a subject with an exposure interval that may range from less than one hundredth of a second to several seconds. After each exposure, the respondent describes everything he or she recalls. Eye cameras study respondents' eye movements to see where their eyes land first, how long they linger on a given item, and so on.

Technology has now advanced to such a degree that marketers can use devices such as skin sensors, brain wave scanners, and full body scanners to get consumer responses.[26] Some researchers study eye movements and brain activity of web surfers to see which ads grab their attention.[27] "Marketing Insight: Understanding Brain Science" provides a glimpse into some new marketing research frontiers in the study of the brain.

Technology has replaced the diaries that participants in media surveys used to keep. Audiometers attached to television sets in participating homes now record when the set is on and to which channel it is tuned. Electronic devices can record the number of radio programs a person is exposed to during the day, or, using Global Positioning System (GPS) technology, how many billboards a person may walk or drive by during a day.

SAMPLING PLAN   After deciding on the research approach and instruments, the marketing researcher must design a sampling plan. This calls for three decisions:

1. *Sampling unit: Whom should we survey?* In the Air Canada survey, should the sampling unit consist of first-class business travellers, first-class vacation travellers, or both? Should it include travellers under age 18? Both traveller and spouse? Once they have determined the sampling unit, marketers must develop a sampling frame so everyone in the target population has an equal or known chance of being sampled.

2. *Sample size: How many people should we survey?* Large samples give more reliable results, but it's not necessary to sample the entire target population to achieve reliable results. Samples of less than 1 percent of a population can often provide good reliability, with a credible sampling procedure.

3. *Sampling procedure: How should we choose the respondents?* Probability sampling allows marketers to calculate confidence limits for sampling error and makes the sample more representative. Thus, after choosing the sample, marketers could conclude that "the interval five to seven trips per year has 95 chances in 100 of containing the true number of trips taken annually by first-class passengers flying between Vancouver and Tokyo."

CONTACT METHODS   Now the marketing researcher must decide how to contact the subjects: by mail, by telephone, in person, or online.

Mail Contacts The *mail questionnaire* is one way to reach people who would not give personal interviews or whose responses might be biased or distorted by the interviewers. Mail questionnaires require simple and clearly worded questions. Unfortunately, the response rate is usually low or slow.

Telephone Contacts *Telephone interviewing* is a good method for gathering information quickly; the interviewer is also able to clarify questions if respondents do not understand them. Interviews must be brief and not too personal. Although the response rate has typically been higher than for mailed questionnaires, telephone interviewing in Canada is getting more difficult because of consumers' growing antipathy toward telemarketers.

Conducting telephone surveys has also been affected by Canada's implementation of the National Do Not Call List (DNCL), which prohibits telemarketers from calling those on the national registry. However, the DNCL may help the marketing research industry because it reduces the number of telemarketing calls households receive, which in turn improves the quality and response rate of telephone surveys being conducted by marketing researchers.[28]

In other parts of the world, such restrictive legislation does not exist. Because cell phone penetration in Africa has risen from just 1 in 50 people in 2000 to almost one-third of the population in 2008, cell phones in Africa are used to convene focus groups in rural areas and to interact via text messages.[29]

Using sophisticated equipment and methods, neuroscience researchers are studying how brain activity is affected by consumer marketing.

| MARKETING **INSIGHT** | UNDERSTANDING BRAIN SCIENCE |

As an alternative to traditional consumer research, some researchers have begun to develop sophisticated techniques from neuroscience that monitor brain activity to better gauge consumer responses to marketing. The term *neuro-marketing* describes brain research on the effect of marketing stimuli. Firms with names such as NeuroFocus and EmSense are using EEG (electroencephalograph) technology to correlate brand activity with physiological cues such as skin temperature or eye movement and thus gauge how people react to ads.

Researchers studying the brain have found different results from those of conventional research methods. One group of researchers at UCLA used functional magnetic resonance imaging (fMRI) to measure how consumers' brains responded to the 2006 Super Bowl advertisements. They found that the ads for which subjects displayed the highest brain activity were different from the ads with the highest stated preferences. Other research found little effect from product placement unless the products in question played an integral role in the storyline.

One major research finding to emerge from neurological consumer research is that many purchase decisions appear to be characterized less by the logical weighing of variables and more "as a largely unconscious habitual process, as distinct from the rational, conscious, information-processing model of economists and traditional marketing textbooks." Even basic decisions, such as the purchase of gasoline, seem to be influenced by brain activity at the subrational level.

Neurological research has been used to measure the type of emotional response consumers exhibit when presented with marketing stimuli. A group of researchers in England used an EEG to monitor cognitive functions related to memory recall and attentiveness for 12 different regions of the brain as subjects were exposed to advertising. Brain wave activity in different regions indicated different emotional responses. For example, heightened activity in the left prefrontal cortex is characteristic of an "approach" response to an ad and indicates an attraction to the stimulus. In contrast, a spike in brain activity in the right prefrontal cortex is indicative of a strong revulsion to the stimulus. In yet another part of the brain, the degree of memory formation activity correlates with purchase intent. Other research has shown that people activate different regions of the brain in assessing the personality traits of people than they do when assessing brands.

By adding neurological techniques to their research arsenal, marketers are trying to move toward a more complete picture of what goes on inside consumers' heads. Although it may be able to offer different insights from conventional techniques, neurological research at this point is very costly, running as much as $100 000 or even more per project. Given the complexity of the human brain, however, many researchers caution that neurological research should not form the sole basis for marketing decisions. These research activities have not been universally accepted. The measurement devices to capture brain activity can be highly obtrusive, such as with skull caps studded with electrodes, creating artificial exposure conditions. Others question whether they offer unambiguous implications for marketing strategy. Brian Knutson, a professor of neuroscience and psychology at Stanford University, compares the use of EEG to "standing outside a baseball stadium and listening to the crowd to figure out what happened." Other critics worry that if the methods do become successful, they will only lead to more marketing manipulation by companies. Despite all this controversy, marketers' endless pursuit of deeper insights about consumers' response to marketing virtually guarantees continued interest in neuromarketing.

Sources: Carolyn Yoon, Angela H. Gutchess, Fred Feinberg, and Thad A. Polk, "A Functional Magnetic Resonance Imaging Study of Neural Dissociations between Brand and Person Judgments," *Journal of Consumer Research*, 33 (June 2006): 31–40; Daryl Travis, "Tap Buyers' Emotions for Marketing Success," *Marketing News*, February 1, 2006, pp. 21–22; Deborah L. Vence, "Pick Someone's Brain," *Marketing News*, May 1, 2006, pp. 11–13; Martin Lindstrom, *Buyology: Truth and Lies about Why We Buy* (New York: Doubleday, 2008); Tom Abate, "Coming to a Marketer Near You: Brain Scanning," *San Francisco Chronicle*, May 19, 2008; Brian Sternberg, "How Couch Potatoes Watch TV Could Hold Clues for Advertisers," *Boston Globe*, September 6, 2009, pp. G1, G3.

Personal Contacts *Personal interviewing* is the most versatile method. The interviewer can ask more questions and record additional observations about the respondent, such as dress and body language. At the same time, however, personal interviewing is the most expensive method, is subject to interviewer bias, and requires more administrative planning and supervision. Personal interviewing takes two forms. In *arranged interviews,* marketers contact respondents for an appointment and often offer a small payment or incentive. In *intercept interviews,* researchers stop people at a shopping mall or busy street corner and request an interview on the spot. Intercept interviews must be quick, and they run the risk of including nonprobability samples.

Online Contacts An approach of increasing importance, the Internet offers many ways to do research. Over 80 percent of Canadian households and 95 percent of businesses are online. Furthermore, 92 percent of Canadian households have broadband access, that is, their neighbourhood is broadband Internet-ready.[30] Therefore, it is not surprising that nearly half of all surveys conducted nowadays are online.[31] A company can embed a questionnaire on its website and offer an incentive to answer it, or it can place a banner on a frequently visited site such as Facebook, inviting people to answer some questions and possibly win a prize. Online product testing, in which companies float trial balloons for new products, is also growing and providing information much faster than traditional new-product marketing research techniques.

Marketers can also host a real-time consumer panel or virtual focus group or sponsor a chat room, bulletin board, or blog and introduce questions from time to time. They can ask customers to brainstorm or have followers of the company on Twitter rate an idea. Online communities and networks of customers serve as a resource for a wide variety of companies. Insights from Kraft-sponsored online communities helped the company develop its popular line of 100-calorie snacks.[32] Here are two other examples:

- Del Monte tapped into its 400-member, handpicked online community called "I Love My Dog" when it was considering a new breakfast treat for dogs. The consensus request was for something with a bacon-and-egg taste and an extra dose of vitamins and minerals. Continuing to work with the online community throughout the product development, the company introduced fortified Snausages Breakfast Bites in half the time usually required to launch a new product.[33]

- InterContinental Hotel Group uses both surveys and communities to gather data on customer satisfaction. Online surveys provide actionable and speedy results to correct customer service issues; the online community provides a sounding board for more in-depth, longer-term research objectives.[34]

Online research was estimated to make up 33 percent of all survey-based research in 2006, and Internet-based questionnaires also accounted for nearly one-third of U.S. spending on market research surveys in the same year.[35] There are many other ways to use the Internet as a research tool. The company can learn about individuals who visit its site by tracking how they *clickstream* through the website and move to other sites. It can post different prices, use different headlines, and offer different product features on different websites or at different times to learn the relative effectiveness of its offerings.

Yet, as popular as online research methods are, smart companies are choosing to use them to augment rather than replace more traditional methods. At Kraft Foods, online research is a supplement to traditional research, says Seth Diamond, director of consumer insights and strategy. "Online is not a solution in and of itself to all of our business challenges," he says, "but it does expand our toolkit."[36]

There are a number of pros and cons to online research.[37] Here are some advantages:

- *Online research is inexpensive.* A typical email survey can cost between 20 percent and 50 percent less than what a conventional survey costs, and return rates can be as high as 50 percent.

- *Online research is fast.* Online surveys are fast because the survey can automatically direct respondents to applicable questions and transmit results immediately. One estimate says an online survey can generate 75 to 80 percent of the targeted response in 48 hours, compared with a telephone survey, which can require 70 days to obtain 150 interviews.

- *People tend to be honest and thoughtful online.* People may be more open about their opinions when they can respond privately and not to another person who they feel might be judging them, especially on sensitive topics (such as "how often do you bathe or shower?"). Because they choose when and where they take the survey and how much time to devote to each question, they may be more relaxed, introspective, and candid.

- *Online research is versatile.* Increased broadband penetration offers online research even more flexibility and capabilities. For instance, virtual reality software lets visitors inspect 3-D models of products such as cameras, cars, and medical equipment and manipulate product characteristics. Even at the basic tactile level, online surveys can make answering a questionnaire easier and more fun than paper-and-pencil versions. Online community blogs allow customer participants to interact with each other.

Some disadvantages include the following:

- *Samples can be small and skewed.* Some 30 percent of households were without broadband Internet access in Canada in 2009.[38] The percentage is even higher among lower-income groups; in rural areas; and in most parts of Asia, Latin America, and Central and Eastern Europe, where socioeconomic and education levels also differ.[39] Although it's certain that more and more people will go online, online market researchers must find creative ways to reach population segments on the other side of the digital divide. One option is to combine offline sources with online findings. Providing temporary Internet access at locations such as malls and recreation centres is another strategy. Some research firms use statistical models to fill in the gaps in market research left by offline consumer segments.

■ *Online panels and communities can suffer from excessive turnover.* Members may become bored with the company's efforts and flee. Or perhaps even worse, they may stay but only half-heartedly participate. Panel and community organizers are taking steps to address the quality of the panel and the data they provide by raising recruiting standards, downplaying incentives, and carefully monitoring participation and engagement levels. New features, events, and other activities must be constantly added to keep members interested and engaged.[40]

■ *Online market research can suffer from technological problems and inconsistencies.* Problems can arise with online surveys because browser software varies. The web designer's final product may look very different on the research subject's screen.

Online researchers have also begun to use text messaging in various ways—to conduct a chat with a respondent, to probe more deeply with a member of an online focus group, or to direct respondents to a website.[41] Text messaging is also a useful way to get teenagers to open up on topics.

Step 3: Collect the Information

The data collection phase of marketing research is generally the most expensive and the most prone to error. Marketers may conduct surveys in homes, over the phone, via the Internet, or at a central interviewing location like a shopping mall. Four major problems arise in surveys. Some respondents will be away from home or otherwise inaccessible and must be contacted again or replaced. Other respondents will refuse to co-operate. Still others will give biased or dishonest answers. Finally, some interviewers will be biased or dishonest.

Internationally, one of the biggest obstacles to collecting information is the need to achieve consistency.[42] Latin American respondents may be uncomfortable with the impersonal nature of the Internet and need interactive elements in a survey so that they feel they're talking to a real person. Respondents in Asia, on the other hand, may feel more pressure to conform and may therefore not be as forthcoming in focus groups as online. Sometimes the solution may be as simple as ensuring the right language is used.

Step 4: Analyze the Information

The next step in the process is to extract findings by tabulating the data and developing summary measures. The researchers now compute averages and measures of dispersion for the major variables and apply some advanced statistical techniques and decision models in the hope of discovering additional findings. They may test different hypotheses and theories, applying sensitivity analysis to test assumptions and the strength of the conclusions.

Step 5: Present the Findings

As the next-to-last step, the researcher presents findings relevant to the major marketing decisions facing management. Researchers increasingly are being asked to play a more proactive, consulting role in translating data and information into insights and recommendations.[43] They're also considering ways to present research findings in as understandable and compelling a fashion as possible. "Marketing Insight: Bringing Marketing Research to Life with Personas" describes an approach that some researchers are using to maximize the impact of their consumer research findings.

The main survey findings for the Air Canada case showed the following:

1. Passengers' chief reason for using in-flight Internet service would be to stay connected and receive and send emails. Some would also pass the time surfing the web. This entertainment capability would require expensive broadband Internet access, but passengers stated that they would be able to charge the cost and their companies would pay.

2. At $25, about 5 out of 10 first-class passengers would use Internet service during a flight; about 6 would use it at $15. Thus, a fee of $15 would produce less revenue ($90 = 6 × $15) than $25 ($125 = 5 × $25). Assuming the same flight takes place 365 days a year, Air Canada could collect $45 625 (= $125 × 365) annually. Given an investment of $90 000, it would take two years to break even.

3. Offering in-flight Internet service would strengthen the public's image of Air Canada as an innovative and progressive airline. Air Canada would gain some new passengers and customer goodwill.

Step 6: Make the Decision

The Air Canada managers who commissioned the research need to weigh the evidence. If their confidence in the findings is low, they may decide against introducing the in-flight Internet service. If they are predisposed to launching the service, the findings support their inclination. They may even decide to study the issues further and do more research. The decision is theirs, but rigorous research provides them with insight into the problem (see Table 4.2).[44]

During the winter of 2010, Air Canada tested its in-flight Internet access with the Gogo Wi-Fi service on some of its transborder flights. The service was made available for US$9.95 for laptops and $7.95 for handheld devices. Based on positive feedback from passengers and usage levels of the service, Air Canada decided to make the service available on all flights in Canada and to the United States from mid-2011.[45]

Some organizations use marketing decision support systems to help their marketing managers make better decisions. MIT's John Little defines a **marketing decision support system (MDSS)** as a coordinated collection of data, systems, tools, and techniques, with supporting software and hardware, by which an organization gathers and interprets relevant information from business and environment and turns it into a basis for marketing action.[46] Once a year, *Marketing News* lists hundreds of current marketing and sales software programs that assist in designing marketing research studies, segmenting markets, setting prices and advertising budgets, analyzing media, and planning sales force activity.[47]

TABLE 4.2 | THE SEVEN CHARACTERISTICS OF GOOD MARKETING RESEARCH

1. Scientific method	Effective marketing research uses the principles of the scientific method: careful observation, formulation of hypotheses, prediction, and testing.
2. Research creativity	In an award-winning research study to reposition Cheetos snacks, researchers dressed up in a brand mascot Chester Cheetah suit and walked around the streets of San Francisco. The response the character encountered led to the realization that even adults loved the fun and playfulness of Cheetos. The resulting repositioning led to a double-digit sales increase despite a tough business environment.[48]
3. Multiple methods	Marketing researchers shy away from overreliance on any one method. They recognize the value of using two or three methods to increase confidence in the results.
4. Interdependence of models and data	Marketing researchers recognize that data are interpreted from underlying models that guide the type of information sought.
5. Value and cost of information	Marketing researchers show concern for estimating the value of information against its cost. Costs are typically easy to determine, but the value of research is harder to quantify. It depends on the reliability and validity of the findings and management's willingness to accept and act on those findings.
6. Healthy skepticism	Marketing researchers show a healthy skepticism toward glib assumptions made by managers about how a market works. They are alert to the problems caused by marketing myths.
7. Ethical marketing	Marketing research benefits both the sponsoring company and its customers. The misuse of marketing research can harm or annoy consumers, increasing resentment at what consumers regard as an invasion of their privacy or a disguised sales pitch.

| MARKETING **INSIGHT** | BRINGING MARKETING RESEARCH TO LIFE WITH PERSONAS |

To bring all the information and insights they have gained about their target market to life, some researchers are employing personas. *Personas* are detailed profiles of one or perhaps a few hypothetical target market consumers, imagined in terms of demographic, psychographic, geographic, or other descriptive attitudinal or behavioural information. Researchers may use photos, images, names, or short bios to help convey the particulars of the persona.

The rationale behind personas is to provide exemplars or archetypes of how the target customer looks, acts, and feels, archetypes that are as true to life as possible, to ensure marketers within the organization fully understand and appreciate their target market and therefore incorporate a target customer point of view in all their marketing decision making. Consider some applications:

■ Chrysler designed rooms for two fictional characters—28-year-old single male Roberto Moore and 30-year-old pharmaceutical rep Jenny Sieverson—and decorated them to reflect the personality, lifestyles, and brand choices of these key targets for the Dodge Caliber and Jeep Compass.

■ Specialty tool and equipment maker Campbell Hausfeld relied on the many retailers it supplied, including Home Depot and Lowe's, to help it keep in touch with consumers. After developing eight consumer profiles, including a female do-it-yourselfer and an elderly consumer, the firm was able to successfully launch new products such as drills that weighed less or that included a level for picture hanging.

■ Unilever's biggest and most successful hair-care launch, for Sunsilk, was aided by insights into the target consumer the company dubbed "Katie." The Katie persona outlined the twenty-something female's hair-care needs, but also her perceptions and attitudes and the way she dealt with her everyday life "dramas."

Although personas provide vivid information to aid marketing decision making, marketers also have to be careful to not overgeneralize. Any target market may have a range of consumers who vary along a number of key dimensions. To accommodate these potential differences, researchers sometimes employ two to six personas. Best Buy used multiple personas to help redesign and relaunch GeekSquad.com, the online site of its fast-growing national computer-support service. Using quantitative, qualitative, and observational research, the firm developed five online customer personas to guide its web redesign efforts:

■ "Jill"—a suburban mom who uses technology and her computer daily and depends on the Geek Squad as an outsourced service akin to a landscaper or plumber.

■ "Charlie"—a 50-plus male who is curious about and interested in technology but needs an unintimidating guide.

■ "Daryl"—a technologically savvy hands-on experimenter who occasionally needs a helping hand with his tech projects.

■ "Luis"—a time-pressed small-business owner whose primary goal is to complete tasks as expediently as possible.

■ "Nick"—a prospective Geek Squad agent who views the site critically and needs to be challenged.

To satisfy Charlie, a prominent 911 button was added to the upper right-hand corner in case a crisis arose, but to satisfy Nick, Best Buy created a whole channel devoted to geek information.

Sources: Dale Buss, "Reflections of Reality," *Point*, June 2006, pp. 10–11; Todd Wasserman, "Unilever, Whirlpool Get Personal with Personas," *Brandweek*, September 18, 2006, p. 13; Daniel B. Honigman, "Persona-fication," *Marketing News*, April 1, 2008, p. 8; Rick Roth, "Take Back Control of the Purchase," *Advertising Age*, September 3, 2007, p. 13; Lisa Sanders, "Major Marketers Get Wise to the Power of Assigning Personas," *Advertising Age*, April 9, 2007, p. 36.

Overcoming Barriers to the Use of Marketing Research

In spite of the rapid growth of marketing research, many companies still fail to use it sufficiently or correctly.[49] They may not understand what all marketing research is capable of and not provide the researcher with the right problem definition and information from which to work. They may also have unrealistic expectations about what researchers can offer. Failure to use marketing research properly has led to numerous gaffes, including the following historic one.

Star Wars

In the 1970s, a successful marketing research executive left General Foods to try a daring gambit: bringing market research to Hollywood, to give film studios access to the same research that had spurred General Foods' success. A major film studio handed him a science fiction film proposal and asked him to research and predict its success or failure. His views would inform the studio's decision about whether to back the film. The research executive concluded the film would fail. For one, he argued, Watergate had made the United States less trusting of institutions and, as a result, its citizens in the 1970s prized realism and authenticity over science fiction. This particular film also had the word "war" in its title; he reasoned that viewers, suffering from post-Vietnam hangover, would stay away in droves. The film was *Star Wars*, which eventually grossed over $4.3 billion in box office receipts alone. What this researcher delivered was information, not insight. He failed to study the script itself, to see that it was a fundamentally human story—of love, conflict, loss, and redemption—that happened to play out against the backdrop of space.[50]

MEASURING MARKETING PRODUCTIVITY

Marketers are facing increased pressure to provide clear, quantifiable evidence to senior management as to how their marketing expenditures help the firm to achieve its goals and financial objectives. Although we can easily quantify marketing expenses and investments as inputs in the short run, the resulting outputs such as broader **brand awareness**, enhanced brand image, greater customer loyalty, and improved new-product prospects may take months or even years to manifest themselves. Moreover, a whole host of internal changes within the organization and external changes in the marketing environment may coincide with the marketing expenditures, making it hard to isolate the effects of any particular marketing activity.[51]

Nevertheless, an important task of marketing research is to assess the efficiency and effectiveness of marketing activities. In one survey, 65 percent of marketers indicated that return on marketing investment was a concern.[52] A recent survey of the nation's leading technology CMOs revealed that over 80 percent of the companies surveyed expressed dissatisfaction with their ability to benchmark their marketing program's business impact and value.[53]

Marketing research can help address this increased need for accountability. Two complementary approaches to measuring marketing productivity are (1) *marketing metrics* to assess marketing effects, and (2) *marketing-mix modelling* to estimate causal relationships and measure how marketing activity affects outcomes. *Marketing dashboards* are a structured way to disseminate the insights gleaned from these two approaches within the organization.

Marketing Metrics

Marketers employ a wide variety of measures to assess marketing effects.[54] **Marketing metrics** is the set of measures that helps them quantify, compare, and interpret their marketing performance. Here is how two marketing executives look at marketing metrics to better understand marketing ROI at their companies:[55]

- The CMO of Mary Kay, Rhonda Shasteen, focuses on four long-term brand-strength metrics—market awareness, consideration, trial, and 12-month beauty consultant productivity—as well as a number of short-term program-specific metrics like ad impressions, website traffic, and purchase conversion.

- The Virgin America VP of marketing, Porter Gale, looks at a broad set of online metrics—cost per acquisition, cost per click, and cost per thousand page impressions (CPM). She also looks at total dollars driven by natural and paid search and online display advertising, and she tracks results and other metrics from the offline world.

There are many different marketing measures; marketers choose one or more based on the particular issue they face or the problem they must solve. An advocate of simple, relevant metrics, the University of Virginia's Paul Farris draws an analogy to the way a Boeing 747 jet pilot decides what information to use from the vast array of instruments in the cockpit to fly the plane:[56]

Aircraft pilots have protocols. When they are sitting on the tarmac warming their engines waiting to take off, they are looking at certain things. When they are taxiing, they look at others. When they are in flight, they look at still others. There is a sequence of knowing when to pay attention to which metrics, which lets them have their cake and eat it too, in terms of the simplicity and complexity trade-off.

TABLE 4.3 | SAMPLE MARKETING METRICS

I. External	II. Internal
Awareness	Awareness of goals
Market share (volume or value)	Commitment to goals
Relative price (market share value/volume)	Active innovation support
Number of complaints (level of dissatisfaction)	Resource adequacy
Consumer satisfaction	Staffing/skill levels
Distribution/availability	Desire to learn
Total number of customers	Willingness to change
Perceived quality/esteem	Freedom to fail
Loyalty/retention	Autonomy
Relative perceived quality	Relative employee satisfaction

Source: Tim Ambler, "What Does Marketing Success Look Like?" *Marketing Management*, Spring 2001, pp. 13–18. Reprinted with permission from *Marketing Management*, published by the American Marketing Association.

London Business School's Tim Ambler suggests that if firms think they are already measuring marketing performance adequately, they should ask themselves five questions:[57]

1. Do you routinely research consumer behaviour (retention, acquisition, usage) and why consumers behave that way (awareness, satisfaction, perceived quality)?

2. Do you routinely report the results of this research to the board in a format integrated with financial marketing metrics?

3. In those reports, do you compare the results with the levels previously forecast in the business plans?

4. Do you also compare them with the levels achieved by your key competitor using the same indicators?

5. Do you adjust short-term performance according to the change in your marketing-based asset(s)?

Ambler says firms must give priority to measuring and reporting marketing performance through marketing metrics. He believes they can split evaluation into two parts: (1) short-term results and (2) changes in brand equity. Short-term results often reflect profit-and-loss concerns as shown by sales turnover, shareholder value, or some combination of the two. Brand equity measures could include customer awareness, attitudes, and behaviours; market share; relative price premium; number of complaints; distribution and availability; total number of customers; perceived quality; and loyalty and retention.[58]

Companies can also monitor an extensive set of internal metrics, such as innovation. For example, 3M tracks the proportion of sales resulting from its recent innovations. Ambler also recommends developing employee measures and metrics, arguing that "end users are the ultimate customers, but your own staff are your first; you need to measure the health of the internal market."

Table 4.3 summarizes a list of popular internal and external marketing metrics from Ambler's survey in the United Kingdom.[59]

Carefully measuring the effects of a marketing activity or program helps ensure managers make the right decisions going forward.

Alberta-based Servus Credit Union organized a contest to pick a representative who could create a greater connection of the credit union with the 25-and-under demographic group. The winner of the 2011/ 2012 "Young & Free Alberta" program, Dex Dunford, was hired as the new spokesperson. As part of his job, Dex maintains a daily blog on the Young & Free Alberta website, creates interesting videos, and connects with young Albertans through Facebook. The point of this campaign is to understand what the 17- to 25-year-old market is looking for when it comes to financial services and make the Servus Credit Union a financial institution that they can relate to. The program has had great success, generating over 2 million online entries, over 2000 new accounts, and over $4 million in new deposits.[60]

Marketing-Mix Modelling

Marketing accountability also means that marketers must more precisely estimate the effects of different marketing investments. *Marketing-mix models* analyze data from a variety of sources, such as retailer scan-

Giving you a **voice**, a head start and useful information

Dex Dunford
Young & Free
Alberta Spokester

YOUNG & FREE®
ALBERTA

Powered by

servus
credit union

Canada's Servus Credit Union used research to validate the effects of the spokesperson for its Young & Free Alberta Spokester program. Dex Dunford, shown here, was the 2011/2012 contest winner.

ner data, company shipment data, pricing data, media data, and promotion spending data, to understand more precisely the effects of specific marketing activities.[61] To deepen understanding, marketers can conduct multivariate analyses, such as regression analysis, to sort through how each marketing element influences marketing outcomes such as brand sales or market share.[62]

Especially popular with packaged-goods marketers such as Procter & Gamble, Clorox, and Colgate, the findings from marketing-mix modelling help allocate or reallocate expenditures. Analyses explore which part of ad budgets are wasted, what optimal spending levels are, and what minimum investment levels should be.[63]

Although marketing-mix modelling helps to isolate effects, it is less effective at assessing how different marketing elements work in combination. Wharton's Dave Reibstein also notes three other shortcomings:[64]

- Marketing-mix modelling focuses on incremental growth instead of baseline sales or long-term effects.

- The integration of important metrics such as customer satisfaction, awareness, and brand equity into marketing-mix modelling is limited.

- Marketing-mix modelling generally fails to incorporate metrics related to competitors, the trade, or the sales force (the average business spends far more on the sales force and trade promotion than on advertising or consumer promotion).

Marketing Dashboards

Firms are also employing organizational processes and systems to make sure they maximize the value of all these different metrics. Management can assemble a summary set of relevant internal and external measures in a *marketing dashboard* for synthesis and interpretation. Marketing dashboards are like the instrument panel in a car or plane, visually displaying real-time indicators to ensure proper functioning. They are only as good as the information on which they're based, but sophisticated visualization tools are helping bring data alive to improve understanding and analysis.[65]

Some companies are also appointing marketing controllers to review budget items and expenses. Increasingly, these controllers are using business intelligence software to create digital versions of marketing dashboards that aggregate data from disparate internal and external sources.

As input to the marketing dashboard, companies should include two key market-based scorecards that reflect performance and provide possible early warning signals:

- A **customer-performance scorecard** records how well the company is doing year after year on such customer-based measures as those shown in Table 4.4. Management should set target goals for each measure and take action when results get out of bounds.

- A **stakeholder-performance scorecard** tracks the satisfaction of various constituencies who have a critical interest in and impact on the company's performance: employees, suppliers, banks, distributors, retailers, and stockholders. Again, management should take action when one or more groups register increased or above-norm levels of dissatisfaction.[66]

TABLE 4.4	SAMPLE CUSTOMER-PERFORMANCE SCORECARD MEASURES

- Percentage of new customers to average number of customers
- Percentage of lost customers to average number of customers
- Percentage of win-back customers to average number of customers
- Percentage of customers falling into very dissatisfied, dissatisfied, neutral, satisfied, and very satisfied categories
- Percentage of customers who say they would repurchase the product
- Percentage of customers who say they would recommend the product to others
- Percentage of target market customers who have brand awareness or recall
- Percentage of customers who say that the company's product is the most preferred in its category
- Percentage of customers who correctly identify the brand's intended positioning and differentiation
- Average perception of company's product quality relative to chief competitor
- Average perception of company's service quality relative to chief competitor

Some executives worry that they'll miss the big picture if they focus too much on a set of numbers on a dashboard. Some critics are concerned about privacy and the pressure the technique places on employees. But most experts feel the rewards offset the risks.[67] "Marketing Insight: Marketing Dashboards to Improve Effectiveness and Efficiency" provides practical advice about the development of these marketing tools.

MARKETING **INSIGHT**	MARKETING DASHBOARDS TO IMPROVE EFFECTIVENESS AND EFFICIENCY

Marketing consultant Pat LaPointe sees marketing dashboards as providing all the up-to-the-minute information necessary to run the business operations for a company—such as sales versus forecast, distribution channel effectiveness, brand equity evolution, and human-capital development. According to LaPointe, an effective dashboard will focus thinking, improve internal communications, and reveal where marketing investments are paying off and where they aren't.

LaPointe observes four common measurement "pathways" marketers are pursuing today (see Figure 4.2):

- The *customer metrics pathway* looks at how prospects become customers, from awareness to preference to trial to repeat purchase, or some less linear model. This area also examines how the customer experience contributes to the perception of value and competitive advantage.

- The *unit metrics pathway* reflects what marketers know about sales of product/service units—how much is sold by product line and/or by geography; the marketing cost per unit sold as an efficiency yardstick; and where and how margin is optimized in terms of characteristics of the product line or distribution channel.

- The *cash-flow metrics pathway* focuses on how well marketing expenditures are achieving short-term returns. Program and campaign ROI models measure the immediate impact or net present value of profits expected from a given investment.

- The *brand metrics pathway* tracks the development of the longer-term impact of marketing through brand equity measures that assess both the perceptual health of the brand from customer and prospective customer perspectives as well as the overall financial health of the brand.

LaPointe feels a marketing dashboard can present insights from all the pathways in a graphically related view that helps management see subtle links between them. A well-constructed dashboard can have a series of tabs that allow the user to toggle easily between different "families" of metrics organized by customer, product, experience, brand, channels, efficiency, organizational development, or macroenvironmental factors. Each tab presents the three or four most insightful metrics, with data filtered by business unit, geography, or customer segment based on the users' needs. (See Figure 4.3 for a sample brand metrics page.)

Ideally, the number of metrics presented in the marketing dashboard would be reduced to a handful of key drivers over time. Meanwhile, the process of developing and refining the marketing dashboard will undoubtedly raise and resolve many key questions about the business.

Source: Adapted from Pat LaPointe, *Marketing by the Dashboard Light* (Association of National Advertisers, 2005), www.marketingnpv.com.

FIGURE 4.2

Marketing Measurement
Pathway

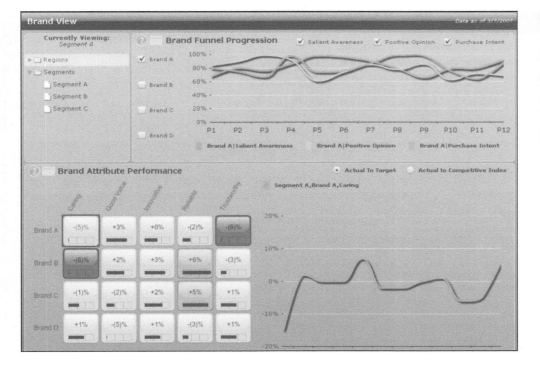

FIGURE 4.3

Example of a Marketing
Dashboard

Source: Adapted from Patrick
LaPointe, *Marketing by the
Dashboard Light—How to Get
More Insight, Foresight, and
Accountability from Your Marketing
Investments.* © 2005, Patrick
LaPointe.

SUMMARY

1. Companies can conduct their own marketing research or hire other companies to do it for them. Good marketing research is characterized by the scientific method, creativity, multiple research methods, accurate model building, cost-benefit analysis, healthy skepticism, and an ethical focus.

2. The marketing research process consists of defining the problem, decision alternatives, and research objectives; developing the research plan; collecting the information; analyzing the information; presenting the findings to management; and making the decision.

3. In conducting research, firms must decide whether to collect their own data or use data that already exist. They must also choose a research approach (observational, focus group, survey, behavioural data, or experimental) and research instruments (questionnaires, qualitative measures, or technological devices). In addition, they must decide on a sampling plan and contact methods (by mail, by phone, in person, or online).

4. Two complementary approaches to measuring marketing productivity are (1) marketing metrics to assess marketing effects, and (2) marketing-mix modelling to estimate causal relationships and measure how marketing activity affects outcomes. Marketing dashboards are a structured way to disseminate the insights gleaned from these two approaches within the organization.

APPLICATIONS

Marketing Debate: What Is the Best Type of Marketing Research?

Many market researchers have their favourite research approaches or techniques, although different researchers often have different preferences. Some researchers maintain that the only way to really learn about consumers or brands is through in-depth, qualitative research. Others contend that the only legitimate and defensible form of marketing research uses quantitative measures.

Take a position: The best marketing research is quantitative in nature *versus* The best marketing research is qualitative in nature.

Marketing Discussion: Survey Quality

When was the last time you participated in a survey? How helpful do you think the information you provided was? How could the research have been done differently to make it more effective?

| MARKETING **EXCELLENCE** | AUTO21 AND SMARTPHONES |

A significant problem faced by many organizations when doing research projects is the time it takes to collect, input, and analyze the data. The transportation department of the Government of Canada, Transport Canada, periodically conducts surveys on the driving habits of Canadians. The results of traditional research (research done with paper-and-pencil questionnaires) often take up to two years to be published, besides causing a significant dent in the research budget. Paper-and-pencil questionnaires have to be administered to respondents and data entered into the computer by hand, and only then can the data be analyzed. This length of time limits the usefulness of results, as they may not be relevant to the situation in Canada by the time the report is available. These time and cost issues limit the frequency of such studies and how actionable the results are.

The University of Windsor and AUTO21 (a national network of nearly 200 researchers from government, universities, and industry and who conduct auto-related research) have found a unique solution: Research In Motion's BlackBerry smartphone. "We wanted a mobile approach so data would be easily, accurately collected and downloaded into a database, which would save a lot of time and eliminate the cost of manual data entry," explains Dr. Anne Snowdon, associate professor at the University of Windsor and AUTO21 project leader.

One AUTO21 project involved collecting data from automobile drivers about their use of child restraints, at 200 road intersections across the country. The research team decided to use a smartphone for data collection rather than the traditional paper-and-pencil approach. By utilizing smartphones, researchers have cut down the time from data collection to final report submission to a mere four to five months. Using a mobile device in such a study has several advantages. Responses to questionnaires are collected electronically and transmitted immediately to a central database, where they are automatically entered into a statistical analysis software package, drastically cutting down the time for data entry and also eliminating errors resulting from misinterpretation of handwriting. This process also cuts down on costs, as it is no longer necessary to hire a team to input data from piles of questionnaires. In addition, the electronic version of the questionnaire automatically skips over to the next appropriate question based on the response given to a question, reducing interviewing time and data collection errors. Logistically, having to carry a smartphone rather than bundles of questionnaires and writing instruments is more practical, especially considering the data collectors will be spending several hours at a time stopping and interviewing drivers at road intersections. By utilizing smartphones to conduct a study such as the "Roadside Survey on Child Seat Safety," Transport Canada gets better results in a much shorter time frame and at a lower cost to Canadian taxpayers.

The usefulness of this innovative way of collecting data is being noticed by other organizations. For example, the Global Health Research Foundation used smartphones to collect data on malaria cases from remote regions of Uganda, where sending paper questionnaires back and forth by mail was not a feasible option. Similarly, the World Health Organization is looking into smartphone data collection where the traditional paper-and-pencil route has been problematic for making quick decisions, such as during catastrophes. "A BlackBerry solution can get that accurate data into people's hands when it's most needed," according to Dr. Snowdon, who has also started a project using the smartphone data collection system to collect patient fall data during stays at hospitals. The aim of this study is to use the data more quickly to create programs to help ensure the safety of patients.

QUESTIONS

1. Can smartphones be used for qualitative research? Justify your answer.

2. In measuring use of seat belts while driving, which would you prefer—observational research or survey? What are the pros and cons of each?

3. Can you think of devices other than smartphones that can reduce data collection time?

Sources: "Case Study: BlackBerry Solution Used for Roadside Surveys on Child Seat Safety," http://na.blackberry.com/eng/newsroom/success/uwindsor.jsp (viewed September 22, 2010); Todd R. Weiss, "Smartphones Help Collect Data on Malaria Cases in Remote Uganda," *Computerworld*, January 8, 2010.

Chapter 5

Sobeys builds customer loyalty through its popular Club Sobeys program.

In This Chapter, We Will Address the Following **Questions**

1. What are customer value, satisfaction, and loyalty, and how can companies deliver them?

2. What is the lifetime value of customers, and how can marketers maximize it?

3. How can companies attract and retain the right customers and cultivate strong customer relationships?

4. What are the pros and cons of database marketing?

Creating Long–term Loyalty Relationships

Today, companies face their toughest competition ever.

Moving from a product-and-sales philosophy to a holistic marketing philosophy, however, gives them a better chance of outperforming the competition. The cornerstone of a well-conceived holistic marketing orientation is strong customer relationships. Marketers must connect with customers—informing, engaging, and maybe even energizing them in the process. Customer-centred companies are adept at building customer relationships, not just products. Companies such as Sobeys, well-aware that acquiring a new customer is much more expensive than retaining an existing one, try to retain customers through attractive loyalty programs.

Sobeys Inc., a major Canadian grocery chain with over 1300 stores in ten provinces, has devised the Club Sobeys program, which aims at building customer loyalty. Although major competitors Safeway and Real Canadian Superstore have loyalty programs, the one offered by Sobeys has features that make it more attractive than theirs. Launched in September 2008, the program enrolled more than a million members in just six weeks—considered quite a feat in the retail industry.

The Club Sobeys program has a number of ways in which customers can earn points and redeem them for cash off their grocery bill or for products from the rewards catalogue. Besides giving members a discount on certain products each week, Sobeys marks select products with bonus points to enable shoppers to collect more points. Club Sobeys members who are enrolled in Air Canada's Aeroplan program are given the option of converting their points into Aeroplan Miles. In just the first year of the program, Club Sobeys members amassed 122 million Aeroplan Miles. Sobeys has teamed up with the Bank of Montreal by offering a BMO Club Sobeys MasterCard, which provides two points for every dollar spent in Sobeys as well as one point for every dollar spent on other purchases using the MasterCard. The chain also offers periodic special promotions to make its loyalty program even more attractive. For example, one promotion entered anyone who paid for groceries at Sobeys with the BMO Club Sobeys MasterCard into a draw for one of 25 prizes of $1000 off his or her credit card balance. Another promotion offered free groceries for a whole year.

The Club Sobeys program provides the company with a benefit not obvious to customers. Every time a customer uses the Sobeys card while checking out, details of that purchase go into a database. Although researchers may not be interested in examining the data at the individual level, at the aggregate level it gives them valuable insights into the purchasing habits of consumers who shop at that location. This enables the store to fine-tune its product selection, prices, and promotions to suit its clientele, which in turn improves customer satisfaction and builds customer loyalty.[1]

As the Club Sobeys example shows, successful marketers are those who carefully manage their customer base. In this chapter, we spell out in detail the ways they can go about winning customers and beating competitors. The answer lies largely in doing a better job of meeting or exceeding customer expectations.

FIGURE 5.1

Traditional Organization versus
Modern Customer-Oriented
Organization

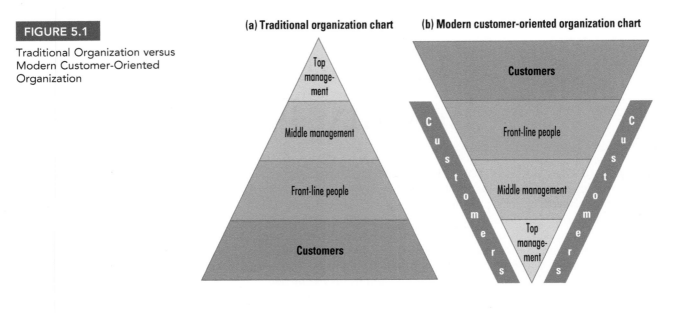

BUILDING CUSTOMER VALUE, SATISFACTION, AND LOYALTY

Creating loyal customers is at the heart of every business.[2] As marketing experts Don Peppers and Martha Rogers say:[3]

> The only value your company will ever create is the value that comes from customers—the ones you have now and the ones you will have in the future. Businesses succeed by getting, keeping, and growing customers. Customers are the only reason you build factories, hire employees, schedule meetings, lay fiber-optic lines, or engage in any business activity. Without customers, you don't have a business.

Managers who believe that the customer is the company's only true "profit centre" consider the traditional organization chart in Figure 5.1(a)—a pyramid with the president at the top, management in the middle, and front-line people and customers at the bottom—obsolete.[4]

Successful marketing companies invert the chart, as in Figure 5.1(b). At the top are customers; next in importance are front-line people who meet, serve, and satisfy customers; under them are the middle managers, whose job is to support the front-line people so that they can serve customers well; and at the base is top management, whose job is to hire and support good middle managers. We have added customers along the sides of Figure 5.1(b) to indicate that managers at every level must be personally involved in knowing, meeting, and serving customers.

Some companies have been founded with the customer-on-top business model, and customer advocacy has been their strategy—and competitive advantage—all along. Today, with the rise of digital technologies such as the Internet, increasingly informed consumers expect companies to do more than connect with them, more than satisfy them, and even more than delight them. They expect companies to *listen* and *respond* to them.[5]

When Office Depot added customer reviews to its website in 2008, revenue and sales conversion increased significantly. The company also incorporated review-related terms to its paid search advertising campaign. As a result of these efforts, website revenue and the number of new buyers visiting the site both increased by more than 150 percent.[6]

Customer-Perceived Value

Consumers are better educated and informed than ever, and they have the tools to verify companies' claims and seek out superior alternatives.[7] Consider the following example.

Dell

Dell rode to success by offering low-priced computers, logistical efficiency, and after-sales service. The firm's maniacal focus on low costs has been a key ingredient in its success. When the company shifted its customer-service call centres to India and the Philippines to cut costs, however, understaffing frequently led to 30-minute waits for customers. Almost half the calls required at least one transfer. To discourage customer calls, Dell even removed its toll-free service number from its website. With customer satisfaction slipping, and competitors matching Dell's product quality and prices and offering improved service, Dell's market share and stock price both declined sharply. Dell ended up hiring more North American call centre employees. "The team was managing cost instead of managing service and quality," Michael Dell confesses.[8]

How then do customers ultimately make choices? They tend to be value maximizers, within the bounds of search costs and limited knowledge, mobility, and income. Customers estimate which offer they believe—for whatever reason—will deliver the most perceived value and they act on it (Figure 5.2). Whether the offer lives up to expectations affects customer satisfaction and the probability that the customer will purchase the product again. In one 2008 survey asking U.S. consumers "Does [Brand X] give good value for what you pay?" the highest-scoring brands included Craftsman tools, Discovery Channel, History Channel, Google, and Rubbermaid.[9]

Customer-perceived value (CPV) is the difference between the prospective customer's evaluation of all the benefits and all the costs of an offering and the perceived alternatives. **Total customer benefit** is the perceived monetary value of the bundle of economic, functional, and psychological benefits customers expect from a given market offering because of the product, service, people, and image. **Total customer cost** is the perceived bundle of costs customers expect to incur in evaluating, obtaining, using, and disposing of the given market offering, including monetary, time, energy, and psychological costs.

Customer-perceived value is thus based on the difference between the benefits the customer gets and the costs he or she assumes for different choices. The marketer can increase the value of the customer offering by raising economic, functional, or emotional benefits and/or reducing one or more costs. The customer choosing between two value offerings, V1 and V2, will favour V1 if the ratio V1:V2 is larger than one, favour V2 if the ratio is smaller than one, and be indifferent if the ratio equals one.

APPLYING VALUE CONCEPTS Suppose the buyer for a large construction company wants to buy a tractor for residential construction from either Caterpillar or Komatsu. He wants the tractor to deliver certain levels of reliability, durability, performance, and resale value. The competing salespeople carefully describe their respective offers. The buyer decides Caterpillar has greater product benefits based on his perceptions of those attributes. He also perceives differences in the accompanying services—delivery, training, and maintenance—and decides Caterpillar provides better service as well as more knowledgeable and responsive staff. Finally, he places higher value on Caterpillar's corporate image and reputation. He adds up all the economic, functional, and psychological benefits from these four sources—product, services, personnel, and image—and perceives Caterpillar as delivering greater customer benefits.

Does he buy the Caterpillar tractor? Not necessarily. He also examines his total cost of transacting with Caterpillar versus Komatsu, which consists of more than money. As Adam Smith observed over two centuries ago in *The Wealth of Nations,* "The real price of anything is the toil and trouble of acquiring it." Total customer cost also includes the buyer's time, energy, and psychological costs expended in product acquisition, usage, maintenance, ownership, and disposal. The buyer evaluates these elements together with the monetary cost to form a total customer cost. Then he considers whether Caterpillar's total customer cost is too high compared with total customer benefits. If it is, he might choose Komatsu. The buyer will choose whichever source delivers the highest perceived value.

Now let's use this decision-making theory to help Caterpillar succeed in selling to this buyer. Caterpillar can improve its offer in three ways. First, it can increase total customer benefit by improving economic, functional, and psychological benefits of its product, services, people, and/or image. Second, it can reduce the buyer's nonmonetary costs by reducing the time, energy, and psychological investment. Third, it can reduce its product's monetary cost to the buyer.

Suppose Caterpillar concludes that the buyer sees its offer as worth $20 000. Further, suppose Caterpillar's cost of producing the tractor is $14 000. This means Caterpillar's offer generates $6000 over its cost, so the firm needs to charge between $14 000 and $20 000. If it charges less than $14 000, it won't cover its costs; if it charges more, it will price itself out of the market.

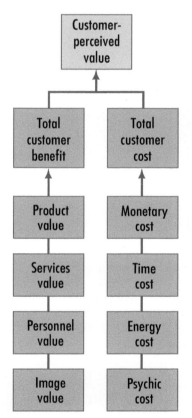

FIGURE 5.2

Determinants of Customer-Perceived Value

Caterpillar's price will determine how much value it delivers to the buyer and how much flows to Caterpillar. If it charges $19 000, it is creating $1000 of customer-perceived value and keeping $5000 for itself. The lower Caterpillar sets its price, the higher the customer-perceived value and, therefore, the higher the customer's incentive to purchase. To win the sale, the firm must offer more customer-perceived value than Komatsu does.[10] Caterpillar is well-aware of the importance of taking a broad view of **customer value**.

Caterpillar

Caterpillar has become a leading firm by maximizing total customer value in the construction-equipment industry, despite challenges from a number of able competitors, such as John Deere, Case, Komatsu, Volvo, and Hitachi. Caterpillar produces high-performance equipment known for reliability and durability—key purchase considerations in heavy industrial equipment. The firm also makes it easy for customers to find the right product by providing a full line of construction equipment and a wide range of financial terms. Caterpillar maintains the largest number of independent construction-equipment dealers in the industry. These dealers all carry a complete line of Caterpillar products and are typically better trained and perform more reliably than competitors' dealers. Caterpillar has also built a worldwide parts-and-service system second to none in the industry. Customers recognize all the value Caterpillar creates in its offerings, allowing the firm to command a premium price 10 percent to 20 percent higher than competitors. Caterpillar's biggest challenges are a re-energized Komatsu, which has made a strong push in China, and some supply chain issues in introducing new products.[11]

Very often, managers conduct a **customer value analysis** to reveal the company's strengths and weaknesses relative to those of various competitors. The steps in this analysis are the following:

1. *Identify the major attributes and benefits customers value.* Customers are asked what attributes, benefits, and performance levels they look for in choosing a product and vendors. Attributes and benefits should be defined broadly to encompass all the inputs to customers' decisions.

2. *Assess the quantitative importance of the different attributes and benefits.* Customers are asked to rate the importance of different attributes and benefits. If their ratings diverge too much, the marketer should cluster them into different segments.

3. *Assess the company's and competitors' performances on the different customer values against their rated importance.* Customers describe where they see the company's and competitors' performances on each attribute and benefit.

4. *Examine how customers in a specific segment rate the company's performance against a specific major competitor on an individual attribute or benefit basis.* If the company's offer exceeds the competitor's offer on all important attributes and benefits, the company can charge a higher price (thereby earning higher profits), or it can charge the same price and gain more market share.

Caterpillar's market success is partly a result of how well the firm creates customer value.

5. *Monitor customer values over time.* The company must periodically redo its studies of customer values and competitors' standings as the economy, technology, and features change.

CHOICE PROCESSES AND IMPLICATIONS Some marketers might argue that the process we have described is too rational. Suppose the customer chooses the Komatsu tractor. How can we explain this choice? Here are three possibilities:

1. *The buyer might be under orders to buy at the lowest price.* The Caterpillar salesperson's task is then to convince the buyer's manager that buying on price alone will result in lower long-term profits and customer value.

2. *The buyer will retire before the company realizes the Komatsu tractor is more expensive to operate.* The buyer will look good in the short run; he is maximizing personal benefit. The Caterpillar salesperson's task is to convince other people in the customer company that Caterpillar delivers greater customer value.

3. *The buyer enjoys a long-term friendship with the Komatsu salesperson.* In this case, Caterpillar's salesperson needs to show the buyer that the Komatsu tractor will draw complaints from the tractor operators when they discover its high fuel cost and need for frequent repairs.

The point is clear: buyers operate under various constraints and occasionally make choices that give more weight to their personal benefit than to the company's benefit.

Customer-perceived value is a useful framework that applies to many situations and yields rich insights. It suggests that the seller must assess the total customer benefit and total customer cost associated with each competitor's offer in order to know how his or her offer rates in the buyer's mind. It also implies that the seller at a disadvantage has two alternatives: increase total customer benefit or decrease total customer cost. The former calls for strengthening or augmenting the economical, functional, and psychological benefits of the offering's product, services, personnel, and image. The latter calls for reducing the buyer's costs by reducing the price or cost of ownership and maintenance, simplifying the ordering and delivery process, or absorbing some buyer risk by offering a warranty.[12]

DELIVERING HIGH CUSTOMER VALUE Consumers have varying degrees of loyalty to specific brands, stores, and companies. Oliver defines **loyalty** as "a deeply held commitment to rebuy or repatronize a preferred product or service in the future despite situational influences and marketing efforts having the potential to cause switching behavior."[13]

Table 5.1 displays brands with the greatest degree of customer loyalty according to one 2010 survey.

TABLE 5.1	TOP 25 BRANDS IN CUSTOMER LOYALTY		
Brand	**Category**	**Rankings**	
		2010	**2009**
Apple iPhone	Wireless Handset	1	1
Clairol (hair colour)	Hair Colour	2	NA
Samsung	Wireless Handset	3	2
Mary Kay	Cosmetics (Mass Merchandiser)	4	7
Grey Goose	Vodka	5	6
Clinique (cosmetics: luxury)	Cosmetics (Luxury)	6	19
AVIS	Car Rental	7	8
Walmart	Retail Store (Discount)	8	5
Google	Search Engine	9	3
Amazon.com	Online Book/Music	10	10
Bing	Search Engine	11	NA
J.Crew	Retail Store (Apparel)	12	23
AT&T Wireless	Wireless Phone	13	123
Discover Card	Credit Card	14	121
Verizon Wireless	Wireless Phone	15	21
Intercontinental Hotels	Hotel (Luxury)	16	103
Cheerios	Breakfast Cereal: Kids	17	71
Dunkin' Donuts	Coffee	18	54
Home Depot	Retail Store (Home Improvement)	19	192
Domino's Pizza	Pizza	20	156
Barilla	Pasta Sauce	21	NA
Canon	MFP Copier	22	44
Nike	Athletic Footwear	23	178
Coors Light	Beer (Light)	24	63
Acer	Computer (Netbook)	25	NA

Source: *2011 Brand Keys Loyalty Leaders List,* www.brandkeys.com.

The **value proposition** consists of the whole cluster of benefits the company promises to deliver; it is more than the core positioning of the offering. For example, Volvo's core positioning has been "safety," but the buyer is promised more than just a safe car; other benefits include good performance, design, and safety for the environment. The value proposition is thus a promise about the experience customers can expect from the company's market offering and their relationship with the supplier. Whether the promise is kept depends on the company's ability to manage its value-delivery system.[14] The **value-delivery system** includes all the experiences the customer will have on the way to obtaining and using the offering. At the heart of a good value delivery system is a set of core business processes that help deliver distinctive consumer value.[15]

THE FIRST CAR TO STOP TRAFFIC. AND ITSELF.

INTRODUCING THE NEW VOLVO XC60 WITH CITY SAFETY.

Volvo. for life

Although safety is Volvo's core position, the value proposition the firm offers customers includes other benefits too.

Total Customer Satisfaction

In general, **satisfaction** is a person's feelings of pleasure or disappointment that result from comparing a product's perceived performance (or outcome) with his or her expectations.[16] If the performance falls short of expectations, the customer is dissatisfied. If it matches expectations, the customer is satisfied. If it exceeds expectations, the customer is highly satisfied or delighted.[17] Customer assessments of product performance depend on many factors, especially the type of loyalty relationship the customer has with the brand.[18] Consumers often form more favourable perceptions of a product with a brand they already feel positive about.

Although the customer-centred firm seeks to create high customer satisfaction, that is not its ultimate goal. Increasing customer satisfaction by lowering price or increasing services may result in lower profits. The company might be able to increase its profitability by means other than increased satisfaction (for example, by improving manufacturing processes or investing more in R&D). Also, the company has many stakeholders, including employees, dealers, suppliers, and stockholders. Spending more to increase customer satisfaction might divert funds from increasing the satisfaction of other partners. Ultimately, the company must try to deliver a high level of customer satisfaction subject to also delivering acceptable levels to other stakeholders, given its total resources.[19]

How do buyers form their expectations? Expectations result from past buying experience, friends' and associates' advice, and marketers' and competitors' information and promises. If marketers raise expectations too high, the buyer is likely to be disappointed. If it sets expectations too low, it won't attract enough buyers (although it will satisfy those who do buy).[20] Some of today's most successful companies are raising expectations and delivering performances to match. Korean automaker Kia found success in the United States by launching low-cost, high-quality cars with enough reliability to offer ten-year, 100 000 mile warranties. See how Buckley's ensures ongoing customer satisfaction despite a negative product feature.

Buckley's Cough Syrup

In 1920, a Toronto pharmacist, William Buckley, began marketing his Buckley's cough syrup. In 1986, William's son Frank decided to promote the two main features of this unique cough-and-cold medicine—its bad taste and its effectiveness. Famous for its unique formula, the Buckley's name is especially known for the "It Tastes Awful. And It Works" slogan. Despite the bad taste and the disgusted face the Buckley's advertisements portray, the brand has built a loyal customer base, primarily due to its effectiveness in relieving coughs. The confidence the brand has in its own quality allows it the liberty of poking fun at its own product's taste without the fear of losing customers.[21]

Monitoring Satisfaction

Many companies are systematically measuring how well they treat customers, identifying the factors shaping satisfaction, and changing operations and marketing as a result.[22]

Wise firms measure customer satisfaction regularly, because it is one key to customer retention.[23] A highly satisfied customer generally stays loyal longer, buys more as the company introduces new and upgraded products, talks favourably to others about the company and its products, pays less attention to competing brands and is less sensitive to price, offers product or service ideas to the company, and costs less to serve than new customers because transactions can become routine.[24] Greater customer satisfaction has also been linked to higher returns and lower risk in the stock market.[25]

The link between customer satisfaction and customer loyalty is not proportional, however. Suppose customer satisfaction is rated on a scale from one to five. At a very low level of satisfaction (level one), customers are likely to abandon the company and even bad-mouth it. At levels two to four, customers are fairly satisfied but still find it easy to switch when a better offer comes along. At level five, the customer is very likely to repurchase and even spread good word of mouth about the company. High satisfaction or delight creates an emotional bond with the brand or company, not just a rational preference. Xerox's senior management found its "completely satisfied" customers were six times more likely to repurchase Xerox products over the following 18 months than even its "very satisfied" customers.[26]

The company needs to recognize, however, that customers vary in how they define good performance. Good delivery could mean early delivery, on-time delivery, or order completeness, and two customers can report being "highly satisfied" for different reasons. One may be easily satisfied most of the time and the other might be hard to please but was pleased on this occasion.[27]

MEASUREMENT TECHNIQUES *Periodic surveys* can track customer satisfaction directly and ask additional questions to measure repurchase intention and the respondent's likelihood or willingness to recommend the company and brand to others. Harley-Davidson Canada has been surveying 10 000 customers annually over the past ten years on their customer satisfaction with their motorcycle and with Harley's retail network. With commitment such as this, it is no wonder that 75 percent of Harley-Davidson owners make repeat purchases.[28] For more information on surveys, see "Marketing Insight: Net Promoter and Customer Satisfaction."

Companies need to monitor their competitors' performance too. They can monitor their *customer loss rate* and contact customers who have stopped buying or who have switched to another supplier to find out why. Finally, as described in Chapter 3, companies can hire *mystery shoppers* to pose as potential buyers and report on strong and weak points experienced in buying the company's and competitors' products. Managers themselves can enter company and competitor sales situations where they are unknown and experience first-hand the treatment they receive, or they can phone their own company with questions and complaints to see how employees handle the calls.

INFLUENCE OF CUSTOMER SATISFACTION For customer-centred companies, customer satisfaction is both a goal and a marketing tool. Companies need to be especially concerned with their customer satisfaction level today because the Internet provides a tool for consumers to quickly spread both good and bad word of mouth to the rest of the world. Some customers set up their own websites to air grievances and galvanize protest, targeting high-profile brands such as United Airlines, Home Depot, and Mercedes-Benz.[29]

The University of Michigan's Claes Fornell has developed the American Customer Satisfaction Index (ACSI) to measure consumers' perceived satisfaction with different firms, industries, economic sectors, and national economies.[30] Table 5.2 displays some of the 2009 leaders.

Companies that do achieve high customer satisfaction ratings make sure their target market knows it. Once they achieved number one status in their category on J. D. Power's customer satisfaction ratings, Hyundai, American Express, and Lexus communicated that fact.

A survey conducted by *Canadian Business* magazine some years ago found that some of the best and worst customer satisfaction levels were found within the same industries, illustrating just how effective customer satisfaction can be as a tool for differentiating oneself against competitors. In financial services, credit unions were found to have 82 percent satisfaction, while the range of satisfaction for the big five banks was between 38 and 47 percent. The biggest gap was in the Canadian airline industry, where Air Canada fetched a rating of 16 percent satisfaction (the lowest in the survey, scoring even lower than the Canada Revenue Agency), while WestJet came in at 89 percent (the highest rating in the survey).[31]

CUSTOMER COMPLAINTS Some companies think they're getting a sense of customer satisfaction by tallying complaints, but studies show that while customers are dissatisfied with their purchases about 25 percent of the time, only about 5 percent complain. The other 95 percent either feel complaining is not worth the effort or don't know how or to whom to complain. They just stop buying.[32]

MARKETING **INSIGHT**	NET PROMOTER AND CUSTOMER SATISFACTION

Many companies make measuring customer satisfaction a top priority, but how should they go about doing it? Bain's Frederick Reichheld suggests that only one customer question really matters: "How likely is it that you would recommend this product or service to a friend or colleague?" According to Reichheld, a customer's willingness to recommend results from how well the customer is treated by front-line employees, which in turn is determined by all the functional areas that contribute to a customer's experience.[33]

Reichheld was inspired in part by the experiences of Enterprise Rent-A-Car. When the company cut its customer satisfaction survey in 1998 from 18 questions to 2—one about the quality of the rental experience and the other about the likelihood customers would rent from the company again—it found those who gave the highest ratings to their rental experience were three times as likely to rent again as those who gave the second-highest rating. The firm also found that diagnostic information managers collected from dissatisfied customers helped it fine-tune its operations.

In a typical Net Promoter survey that follows Reichheld's thinking, customers are asked to rate their likelihood to recommend on a 0- to 10-point scale. Marketers then subtract detractors (those who gave a 0 to 6) from promoters (those who gave a 9 or 10) to arrive at the Net Promoter Score (NPS). Customers who rate the brand with a 7 or 8 are deemed passively satisfied and are not included. A typical set of NPS scores falls in the 10 percent to 30 percent range, but world-class companies can score over 50 percent. Some firms with top NPS scores include USAA (89 percent), Apple (77 percent), Amazon.com (74 percent), Costco.com (73 percent), and Google (71 percent).

Reichheld is gaining believers. GE, American Express, and Microsoft, among others, have all adopted the NPS metric, and GE has tied 20 percent of its managers' bonuses to its NPS scores. When the European unit of GE Healthcare scored low, follow-up research revealed that response times to customers were a major problem. After it overhauled its call centre and put more specialists in the field, GE Healthcare's Net Promoter scores jumped 10 to 15 points. BearingPoint found that clients who gave GE Healthcare high Net Promoter scores showed the highest revenue growth.

Reichheld says he developed NPS in response to overly complicated—and thus ineffective—customer surveys. So it's not surprising that client firms praise its simplicity and strong relationship to financial performance. When Intuit applied Net Promoter to its TurboTax product, feedback revealed dissatisfaction with the software's rebate procedure. After Intuit dropped the proof-of-purchase requirement, sales jumped 6 percent.

Net Promoter is not without critics. One comprehensive academic study of 21 firms and more than 15 000 consumers in Norway failed to find any superiority of Net Promoter over other metrics such as the ACSI measure, discussed later in this chapter.

Sources: Fred Reichheld, *The Ultimate Question: Driving Good Profits and True Growth* (Cambridge, MA: Harvard Business School Press, 2006); Jena McGregor, "Would You Recommend Us?" *BusinessWeek*, January 30, 2006, pp. 94–95; Kathryn Kranhold, "Client-Satisfaction Tool Takes Root," *Wall Street Journal*, July 10, 2006; Fred Reichheld, "The One Number You Need to Grow," *Harvard Business Review*, December 2003; Timothy L. Keiningham, Bruce Cooil, Tor Wallin Andreassen, and Lerzan Aksoy, "A Longitudinal Examination of Net Promoter and Firm Revenue Growth," *Journal of Marketing*, 71 (July 2007): 39–51; Neil A. Morgan and Lopo Leotte Rego, "The Value of Different Customer Satisfaction and Loyalty Metrics in Predicting Business Performance," *Marketing Science, 25*, no. 5 (September–October 2006): 426–439; Timothy L. Keiningham, Lerzan Aksoy, Bruce Cooil, and Tor W. Andreassen, "Linking Customer Loyalty to Growth," *MIT Sloan Management Review*, Summer 2008, pp. 51–57; Timothy L. Keiningham, Lerzan Aksoy, Bruce Cooil, and Tor W. Andreassen, "Commentary on 'The Value of Different Customer Satisfaction and Loyalty Metrics in Predicting Business Performance,'" *Marketing Science, 27*, no. 3 (May–June 2008): 531–532.

Of the customers who register a complaint, 54 percent to 70 percent will do business with the organization again if their complaint is resolved. The figure goes up to a staggering 95 percent if the customer feels the complaint was resolved *quickly*. Customers whose complaints are satisfactorily resolved tell an average of 5 people about the good treatment they received.[34] The average dissatisfied customer, however, gripes to 11 people. If each of these tells still other people, the number exposed to bad word of mouth may grow exponentially.

No matter how perfectly designed and implemented a marketing program is, mistakes will happen. The best thing a company can do is make it easy for customers to complain. Suggestion forms, toll-free numbers, websites, and email addresses allow for quick, two-way communication. The 3M Company claims that over two-thirds of its product improvement ideas come from listening to customer complaints.

Given the potential downside of having an unhappy customer, it's critical that marketers deal with negative experiences properly.[35] Beyond that, the following procedures can help to recover customer goodwill:[36]

TABLE 5.2	2009 ACSI SCORES BY INDUSTRY	
Industry	Firm	Score
Airlines	Southwest Airlines	81
Apparel	Jones Apparel	84
Automobiles & Light Vehicles	Lexus & BMW	87
Banks	Wachovia	76
Breweries	Molson Coors Brewing	83
Cable & Satellite TV	DIRECTV	71
Cellular Telephones	Nokia	74
Cigarettes	Philip Morris	79
Department & Discount Stores	Nordstrom & Kohl's	80
Energy Utilities	Sempra Energy	80
Express Delivery	FedEx	84
Fixed Line Telephone Service	Cox Communications	74
Food Manufacturing	H.J. Heinz	89
Health Insurance	Blue Cross and Blue Shield	73
Hotels	Hilton Hotels	79
Internet Brokerage	Fidelity Investments	80
Internet News & Information	MSNBC.com	76
Internet Portals & Search Engines	Google	86
Internet Travel	Expedia	77
Life Insurance	Prudential Financial	79
Personal Care & Cleaning Products	Clorox	87
Personal Computers	Apple	85
Soft Drinks	Dr Pepper Snapple	87
Supermarkets	Publix	82
Wireless Telephone Service	Verizon Wireless	74

Source: ACSI LLC, www.theacsi.org. Used with permission.

1. Set up a 7-day, 24-hour toll-free hotline (by phone, fax, or email) to receive and act on customer complaints.

2. Contact the complaining customer as quickly as possible. The slower the company is to respond, the more dissatisfaction may grow and lead to negative word of mouth.

3. Accept responsibility for the customer's disappointment; don't blame the customer.

4. Use customer service people who are empathic.

5. Resolve the complaint swiftly and to the customer's satisfaction. Some complaining customers are not looking for compensation so much as a sign that the company cares.

Product and Service Quality

Satisfaction will also depend on product and service quality. What exactly is quality? Various experts have defined it as "fitness for use," "conformance to requirements," and "freedom from variation." We will use the American Society for Quality's definition: **quality** is the totality of features and characteristics of a product or service that bear on its ability to satisfy stated or implied needs.[37] This is clearly a customer-centred definition. We can say the seller has delivered quality whenever its product or service meets or exceeds the customers' expectations.

A company that satisfies most of its customers' needs most of the time is called a quality company, but we need to distinguish between *conformance* quality and *performance* quality (or grade). A Lexus provides higher performance quality than a Hyundai: the Lexus rides smoother, goes faster, and lasts longer. Yet both a Lexus and a Hyundai deliver the same conformance quality if all the units deliver their respective promised quality.

MARKETING **MEMO** | MARKETING AND TOTAL QUALITY

Marketers play several roles in helping their companies define and deliver high-quality goods and services to target customers:

- They correctly identify customers' needs and requirements.
- They communicate customer expectations properly to product designers.
- They make sure customers' orders are filled correctly and on time.
- They check that customers have received proper instructions, training, and technical assistance in the use of the product.
- They stay in touch with customers after the sale to ensure they are, and remain, satisfied.
- They gather customer ideas for product and service improvements and convey them to the appropriate departments.

When marketers do all this, they make substantial contributions to total quality management and customer satisfaction, as well as to customer and company profitability.

IMPACT OF QUALITY Product and service quality, customer satisfaction, and company profitability are intimately connected. Higher levels of quality result in higher levels of customer satisfaction, which support higher prices and (often) lower costs. Studies have shown a high correlation between relative product quality and company profitability.[38] The drive to produce goods that are superior in world markets has led some countries—and groups of countries—to recognize or award prizes to companies that exemplify the best quality practices, such as the Deming Prize in Japan, the Malcolm Baldrige National Quality Award in the United States, the European Quality Award, and the Canada Awards for Excellence.

Companies that have lowered costs to cut corners have paid the price when the quality of the customer experience suffers.[39] When Northwest Airlines stopped offering free magazines, pillows, movies, and even minibags of pretzels on domestic flights, it also raised prices and reduced its flight schedule. As one frequent flier noted, "Northwest acts low cost without *being* low cost." Not surprisingly, Northwest came in last of all top U.S. airlines in both the ACS index and J. D. Power's customer satisfaction poll soon thereafter.

Quality is clearly the key to value creation and customer satisfaction. **Total quality** is everyone's job, just as marketing is everyone's job. "Marketing Memo: Marketing and Total Quality" outlines the role of marketing in maximizing total quality for the firm.

MAXIMIZING CUSTOMER LIFETIME VALUE

Ultimately, marketing is the art of attracting and keeping profitable customers. Yet every company loses money on some of its customers. The well-known 80–20 rule states that 80 percent or more of the company's profits come from the top 20 percent of its customers. Some cases may be more extreme—the most profitable 20 percent of customers (on a per capita basis) may contribute as much as 150 percent to 300 percent of profitability. The least profitable 10 percent to 20 percent, on the other hand, can actually reduce profits between 50 percent to 200 percent per account, with the middle 60 percent to 70 percent breaking even.[40] The implication is that a company could improve its profits by "firing" its worst customers.

It's not always the company's largest customers, who can demand considerable service and deep discounts, who yield the most profit. The smallest customers pay full price and receive minimal service, but the costs of transacting with them can reduce their profitability. Midsize customers who receive good service and pay nearly full price are often the most profitable.

Customer Profitability

A **profitable customer** is a person, household, or company that over time yields a revenue stream exceeding by an acceptable amount the company's cost stream for attracting, selling, and serving that customer. Note the emphasis is on the *lifetime* stream of revenue and cost, not the profit from a particular transaction.[41] Marketers can assess customer profitability individually, by market segment, or by channel.

Many companies measure customer satisfaction, but few measure individual customer profitability.[42] Banks claim this is a difficult task, because each customer uses different banking services

FIGURE 5.3

Customer–Product Profitability Analysis

Sources: Thomas M. Petro, "Profitability: The Fifth 'P' of Marketing," *Bank Marketing* (September 1990): 48–52; "Who Are Your Best Customers?" *Bank Marketing* (October 1990): 48–52.

and the transactions are logged in different departments. However, the number of unprofitable customers in their customer base has appalled banks that have succeeded in linking customer transactions. Some report losing money on over 45 percent of their retail customers.

CUSTOMER PROFITABILITY ANALYSIS A useful type of profitability analysis is shown in Figure 5.3. Customers are arrayed along the columns and products along the rows. Each cell contains a symbol representing the profitability of selling that product to that customer. Customer 1 is very profitable; he buys two profit-making products (P_1 and P_2). Customer 2 yields mixed profitability; he buys one profitable product (P_1) and one unprofitable product (P_3). Customer 3 is a losing customer because he buys one profitable product (P_1) and two unprofitable products (P_3 and P_4).

What can the company do about customers 2 and 3? (1) It can raise the price of its less profitable products or eliminate them, or (2) it can try to sell customers 2 and 3 its profit-making products. Unprofitable customers who defect should not concern the company. In fact, the company should encourage them to switch to competitors.

Customer profitability analysis (CPA) is best conducted with the tools of an accounting technique called **activity-based costing (ABC)**. ABC accounting tries to identify the real costs associated with serving each customer—the costs of products and services based on the resources they consume. The company estimates all revenue coming from the customer, less all costs.

With ABC, the costs should include the cost not only of making and distributing the products and services, but also of taking phone calls from the customer, travelling to visit the customer, paying for entertainment and gifts—all the company's resources that go into serving that customer. ABC also allocates indirect costs like clerical costs, office expenses, and supplies to the activities that use them, rather than in some proportion to direct costs. Both variable and overhead costs are tagged back to each customer.

Companies that fail to measure their costs correctly are also not measuring their profit correctly and are likely to misallocate their marketing effort. The key to effectively employing ABC is to define and judge "activities" properly. One time-based solution calculates the cost of one minute of overhead and then decides how much of this cost each activity uses.[43]

Measuring Customer Lifetime Value

The case for maximizing long-term customer profitability is captured in the concept of customer lifetime value.[44] **Customer lifetime value (CLV)** describes the net present value of the stream of future profits expected over the customer's lifetime purchases. The company must subtract from its expected revenues the expected costs of attracting, selling, and servicing the account of that customer, applying the appropriate discount rate (say, between 10 percent and 20 percent, depending on cost of capital and risk attitudes). Lifetime value calculations for a product or service can add up to tens of thousands of dollars or even into six figures.[45]

Many methods exist to measure CLV.[46] "Marketing Memo: Calculating Customer Lifetime Value" illustrates one. CLV calculations provide a formal quantitative framework for planning customer investment and help marketers adopt a long-term perspective. One challenge, however, is to arrive at reliable cost and revenue estimates. Marketers who use CLV concepts must also take into account the short-term, brand-building marketing activities that help increase customer loyalty.

| MARKETING **MEMO** | CALCULATING CUSTOMER LIFETIME VALUE |

Researchers and practitioners have used many different approaches for modelling and estimating CLV. Researchers Don Lehmann and Sunil Gupta recommend summing the present values of the profits from the customer for the period that the customer remains loyal minus the cost to acquire the customer. They illustrated this concept with the following formula:

$$CLV = \sum_{t=0}^{T} \frac{(p_t - c_t)r_t}{(1+i)^t} - AC$$

where, p_t = price paid by a consumer at time t,

c_t = direct cost of servicing the customer at time t,

i = discount rate or cost of capital for the firm,

r_t = probability of customer repeat buying or being "alive" at time t,

AC = acquisition cost, and

T = time horizon for estimating CLV.

A key decision is what time horizon to use for estimating CLV. Typically, three to five years is reasonable. With this information and estimates of other variables, we can calculate CLV using spreadsheet analysis.

Gupta and Lehmann illustrate their approach by calculating the CLV of 100 customers over a 10-year period (see Table 5.3). In this example, the firm acquires 100 customers with an acquisition cost per customer of $40. Therefore, in year 0, it spends $4000. Some of these customers defect each year. The present value of the profits from this cohort of customers over 10 years is $13 286.52. The net CLV (after deducting acquisition costs) is $9286.52, or $92.87 per customer.

Using an infinite time horizon avoids having to select an arbitrary time horizon for calculating CLV. In the case of an infinite time horizon, if margins (price minus cost) and retention rates stay constant over time, the future CLV of an existing customer simplifies to the following:

$$CLV = \sum_{t=1}^{\infty} \frac{mr^t}{(1+i)^t} = m\frac{r}{(1+i-r)}$$

In other words, CLV simply becomes margin (m) times a *margin multiple* [$r/(1 + i - r)$].

Table 5.4 shows the margin multiple for various combinations of r and i and a simple way to estimate CLV of a customer. When retention rate is 80 percent and the discount rate is 12 percent, the margin multiple is about two and a half. Therefore, the future CLV of an existing customer in this scenario is simply his or her annual margin multiplied by 2.5.

Sources: Sunil Gupta and Donald R. Lehmann, "Models of Customer Value," in *Handbook of Marketing Decision Models*, edited by Berend Wierenga (Berlin: Springer Science and Business Media, 2007); Sunil Gupta and Donald R. Lehmann, "Customers as Assets," *Journal of Interactive Marketing*, 17, no. 1 (Winter 2006): 9–24; Sunil Gupta and Donald R. Lehmann, *Managing Customers as Investments* (Upper Saddle River, NJ: Wharton School Publishing, 2005); Peter Fader, Bruce Hardie, and Ka Lee, "RFM and CLV: Using Iso-Value Curves for Customer Base Analysis," *Journal of Marketing Research*, 42, no. 4 (November 2005): 415–430; Sunil Gupta, Donald R. Lehmann, and Jennifer Ames Stuart, "Valuing Customers," *Journal of Marketing Research*, 41, no. 1 (February 2004): 7–18; Werner J. Reinartz and V. Kumar, "On the Profitability of Long-Life Customers in a Noncontractual Setting: An Empirical Investigation and Implications for Marketing," *Journal of Marketing, 64* (October 2000): 17–35.

CULTIVATING CUSTOMER RELATIONSHIPS

Companies are using information about customers to enact precision marketing designed to build strong long-term relationships.[47] Information is easy to differentiate, customize, personalize, and dispatch over networks at incredible speed.

But information cuts both ways. For instance, customers now have a quick and easy means of doing comparison shopping through sites such as Bizrate.com, Shopping.com, and PriceGrabber.com. The Internet also facilitates communication between customers. Websites such as Epinions.com and

TABLE 5.3 | **A HYPOTHETICAL EXAMPLE TO ILLUSTRATE CLV CALCULATIONS**

	Year 0	Year 1	Year 2	Year 3	Year 4	Year 5	Year 6	Year 7	Year 8	Year 9	Year 10
Number of Customers	100	90	80	72	60	48	34	23	12	6	2
Revenue per Customer		100	110	120	125	130	135	140	142	143	145
Variable Cost per Customer		70	72	75	76	78	79	80	81	82	83
Margin per Customer		30	38	45	49	52	56	60	61	61	62
Acquisition Cost per Customer	40										
Total Cost or Profit	−4 000	2 700	3 040	3 240	2 940	2 496	1 904	1 380	732	366	124
Present Value	−4 000	2 454.55	2 512.40	2 434.26	2 008.06	1 549.82	1 074.7	708.16	341.48	155.22	47.81

TABLE 5.4 | **MARGIN MULTIPLE**

Retention Rate	Discount Rate			
	10%	12%	14%	16%
60%	1.20	1.15	1.11	1.07
70%	1.75	1.67	1.59	1.52
80%	2.67	2.50	2.35	2.22
90%	4.50	4.09	3.75	3.46

Yelp.com enable customers to share information about their experiences with various products and services. Customer empowerment has become a way of life for many companies that have had to adjust to a power shift in their customer relationships.

Customer Relationship Management

Customer relationship management (CRM) is the process of carefully managing detailed information about individual customers and all customer "touch points" to maximize loyalty.[48] A *customer touch point* is any occasion on which a customer encounters the brand and product—from actual experience to personal or mass communications to casual observation. For a hotel, the touch points include reservations, check-in and checkout, frequent-stay programs, room service, business services, exercise facilities, laundry service, restaurants, and bars. The Four Seasons relies on personal touches, such as a staff that always addresses guests by name; high-powered employees who understand the needs of sophisticated business travellers; and at least one best-in-region facility, such as a premier restaurant or spa.[49]

CRM enables companies to provide excellent real-time customer service through the effective use of individual account information. Based on what they know about each valued customer, companies can customize market offerings, services, programs, messages, and media. CRM is important because a major driver of company profitability is the aggregate value of the company's customer base.[50]

PERSONALIZING MARKETING The widespread usage of the Internet allows marketers to abandon the mass market practices that built brand powerhouses in the 1950s, 1960s, and 1970s for new approaches that are a throwback to marketing practices from a century ago, when merchants literally knew their customers by name. *Personalizing marketing* is about making sure the brand and its marketing are as relevant as possible to as many customers as possible—a challenge, given that no two customers are identical.

An increasingly essential ingredient for the best relationship marketing today is the right technology. GE Plastics could not target its email effectively to different customers if it were not for advances in database software. Dell could not customize computer ordering for its global corporate customers without advances in web technology. Companies are using email, websites, call centres, databases, and database software to foster continuous contact between company and customer.

E-commerce companies looking to attract and retain customers are discovering that personalization goes beyond creating customized information.[51] For example, the Lands' End Live website offers visitors the opportunity to talk with a customer service representative. Nordstrom takes a similar approach to ensure that online buyers are as satisfied with the company's customer service as in-store visitors. Domino's has put the customer in charge of ordering a pizza delivery every step of the way.

Domino's

Domino's has introduced a new "build-your-own-pizza" feature on its website that allows customers to watch a simulated photographic version of their pizza as they select a size, choose a sauce, and add toppings. The website also shows exactly what the completed pizza would cost, and lets customers track orders from when the pizza enters the oven to when it leaves the store. Domino's also introduced a new point-of-sale system that streamlined the logistics of online and phone orders. This system improved accuracy, increased repeat visits, and boosted revenues and profits.[52]

Companies are also recognizing the importance of the personal component to CRM and what happens once customers make actual contact with the company. Employees can create strong bonds with customers by individualizing and personalizing relationships. In essence, thoughtful companies turn their customers into clients. Here is the distinction:

> Customers may be nameless to the institution; clients cannot be nameless. Customers are served as part of the mass or as part of larger segments; clients are served on an individual basis. Customers are served by anyone who happens to be available; clients are served by the professional assigned to them.[53]

Firms such as Giant Tiger know about the importance of making a personal connection with the customer.

Giant Tiger

Owned by the North West Company, Giant Tiger is focused on friendly service and quality products at discount prices. Employees are trained on the "eleven-foot rule," which is that whenever a customer is within eleven feet, the employee should greet the customer in a friendly manner and offer assistance. If the customer asks for assistance, the employee is trained to walk the customer over to the desired product as opposed to pointing to a section of the store. The little extra effort of these two-minute walks builds customer relationships to last so that customers become loyal customers. Return visits by customers actively contribute to the sales of North West, which reports approximately $1.5 billion in sales annually.[54]

To adapt to customers' increased desire for personalization, marketers have embraced concepts such as permission marketing and one-to-one marketing.

Permission marketing, the practice of marketing to consumers only after gaining their expressed permission, is based on the premise that marketers can no longer use "interruption marketing" via mass media campaigns. According to Seth Godin, a pioneer in the technique, marketers can develop stronger consumer relationships by respecting consumers' wishes and sending messages only when consumers express a willingness to become more involved with the brand.[55] Godin believes permission marketing works because it is "anticipated, personal, and relevant."

Permission marketing, like other personalization approaches, presumes consumers know what they want. But in many cases, consumers have undefined, ambiguous, or conflicting preferences. "Participatory marketing" may be a more appropriate concept than permission marketing, because marketers and consumers need to work together to find out how the firm can best satisfy consumers.

Don Peppers and Martha Rogers outline a four-step framework for *one-to-one marketing* that can be adapted to CRM marketing as follows:[56]

1. *Identify your prospects and customers.* Don't go after everyone. Build, maintain, and mine a rich customer database with information from all the channels and customer touch points.

2. *Differentiate customers in terms of (1) their needs and (2) their value to your company.* Spend proportionately more effort on the most valuable customers (MVCs). Apply activity-based costing and calculate customer lifetime value. Estimate net present value of all future profits from purchases, margin levels, and referrals, less customer-specific servicing costs.

3. *Interact with individual customers to improve your knowledge about their individual needs and to build stronger relationships.* Formulate customized offerings you can communicate in a personalized way.

4. *Customize products, services, and messages to each customer.* Facilitate customer interaction through the company contact centre and website.

One-to-one marketing is not for every company: It works best for firms that normally collect a great deal of individual customer information and carry a lot of products that can be cross-sold, need periodic replacement or upgrading, and offer high value. For others, the required investment in information collection, hardware, and software may exceed the payout. With automobiles that can cost over $100 000, Aston Martin engages in one-to-one marketing with a select group of customers. High-end dealerships offer separate owners-only clubroom sections and weekend getaways to test drive new models.[57]

CUSTOMER EMPOWERMENT Often seen as the flag-bearer for marketing best practices, P&G's former chairman, A. G. Lafley, created shock waves with his Association of National Advertisers' speech in October 2006. "The power is with the consumer," proclaimed Lafley, and "marketers and retailers are scrambling to keep up with her. Consumers are beginning in a very real sense to own our brands and participate in their creation. We need to learn to let go." In support of his contention, Lafley pointed out how a teenager had created an animated spot for Pringles snacks that was posted on YouTube; how Pantene, the hair-care products company, had created a campaign that encouraged women to cut their hair and donate the clippings to make wigs for cancer patients; and how sales of Cover Girl Outlast lipstick increased 25 percent after the firm put mirrored ads in women's restrooms asking, "Is your lipstick still on?" and ran targeted five-second TV ads with the same theme.[58]

Other marketers have begun to advocate a "bottom-up" grassroots approach to marketing, rather than the more traditional "top-down" approach in which marketers feel they are calling the shots. Burger King has launched attention-getting, edgy campaigns in recent years ("Whopper Freakout," "Subservient Chicken," and "Wake Up with the King") on consumer-friendly new media such as YouTube, MySpace, video games, and iPods. Allowing the customer to take charge just makes sense for a brand whose slogan is "Have It Your Way" and whose main rival, McDonald's, already owns the more staid family market.

Marketers are helping consumers become evangelists for brands by providing them with resources and opportunities to demonstrate their passion. Doritos held a contest to let consumers name its next flavour. Converse asked amateur filmmakers to submit 30-second short films that demonstrated their inspiration from the iconic sneaker brand. The best of the 1800 submissions were showcased in the Converse Gallery website, and the best of the best became TV commercials. Sales of shoes via the website doubled in the month after the gallery's launch.[59]

Even business-to-business firms are getting into the action. PAETEC provides telecommunications services to hotels, universities, and other companies. It has grown into a $500 million company in six years, and its growth is due entirely to customer evangelism. PAETEC's primary marketing strategy: invite current customers and key prospects to dine on PAETEC's tab and meet one another. No boring PowerPoint presentations here, just customers talking about their telecommunications challenges and their unfiltered experiences being PAETEC customers. Prospects are sold on the company by other customers.[60]

Although much has been made of the newly empowered consumer—in charge, setting the direction of the brand, and playing a much bigger role in how it is marketed—it's still true that only *some consumers* want to get involved with *some of the brands* they use and, even then, only *some of the time*. Consumers have lives, jobs, families, hobbies, goals, and commitments, and many things matter more to them than the brands they purchase and consume. Understanding how to best market a brand given such diversity is crucially important.

CUSTOMER REVIEWS AND RECOMMENDATIONS Although the strongest influence on consumer choice remains "recommended by relative/friend," an increasingly important decision factor is "recommendations from consumers." With increasing mistrust of some companies and their advertising, online customer ratings and reviews are playing an important role for Internet retailers such as Amazon.com and Shop.com.

Online pet food retailer PETCO actually started using consumer product ratings and reviews in emails and banner ads, finding the click-through rate increased considerably as a result.[61] Brick-and-mortar retailers such as Staples and Cabela's are also recognizing the power of consumer reviews and have begun to display them in their stores.[62]

Despite consumer acceptance of such reviews, however, their quality and integrity is always in question. In one famous example, over a period of seven years, the co-founder and CEO of Whole Foods Market reportedly posted more than 1100 entries on Yahoo! Finance's online bulletin board under a pseudonym, praising his company and criticizing competitors.

Some sites offer summaries of reviews to provide a range of product evaluations. Metacritic aggregates music, game, TV, and movie reviews from leading critics—often from more than 100 publications—averaged into a single 1 to 100 score. Review sites are important in the video game industry because of the influence they wield and the product's high selling price—often $50 to $60. Some game companies tie bonuses for their developers to game scores on the more popular sites. If a major new release doesn't make the 85-plus cutoff, the publisher's stock price may even drop.[63]

Bloggers who review products or services have become important because they may have thousands of followers; blogs are often among the top links returned in online searches for certain brands or categories. A company's PR department may track popular blogs via online services such as Google alerts, BlogPulse, and Technorati. Firms also court the favour of key bloggers via free samples, advance information, and special treatment. Most bloggers disclose when they are given free samples by companies.

For smaller brands with limited media budgets, online word of mouth is critical. To generate prelaunch buzz for one of its new hot cereals, organic food maker Amy's Kitchen shipped out samples before its release to several of the 50 or so vegan, gluten-free, or vegetarian food bloggers the company tracks. When favourable reviews appeared on these blogs, the company was besieged by emails asking where the cereal could be bought.[64]

Negative reviews actually can be surprisingly helpful. A January 2007 Forrester study of 10 000 consumers of Amazon.com's electronics and home and garden products found that 50 percent found negative reviews helpful. Most consumers purchased the products regardless of negative comments because they felt the comments reflected personal tastes and opinions that differed from their own. Because consumers can better learn the advantages and disadvantages of products through negative reviews, fewer product returns may result, saving retailers and producers money.[65]

Online retailers often add their own recommendations, "If you like that black purse, you'll love this red blouse." One source estimated that recommendation systems contribute 10 percent to 30 percent of an online retailer's sales. Specialized software tools help online retailers facilitate customer "discovery" or unplanned purchases. When Blockbuster adopted one such system, cancellation rates fell and subscribers nearly doubled the number of movies on their order lists.[66]

At the same time, online companies need to make sure their attempts to create relationships with customers don't backfire, as when customers are bombarded by computer-generated recommendations that consistently miss the mark. Buy a lot of baby gifts on Amazon.com, and your personalized recommendations suddenly don't look so personal! E-tailers need to recognize the limitations of online personalization at the same time that they try harder to find technology and processes that really work.

Attracting and Retaining Customers

Companies seeking to expand their profits and sales must spend considerable time and resources searching for new customers. To generate leads, they develop ads and place them in media that will reach new prospects, send direct mail and emails to possible new prospects, send their salespeople to participate in trade shows where they might find new leads, purchase names from list brokers, and so on.

Different acquisition methods yield customers with varying CLVs. One study showed that customers acquired through the offer of a 35 percent discount had about one-half the long-term value of customers acquired without any discount.[67] Campaigns that target loyal customers by reinforcing the benefits they enjoy also often attract new customers. Two-thirds of the considerable growth spurred by U.K. mobile communication leader O2's loyalty strategy was attributed to recruitment of new customers, the remainder from reduced defection.[68]

Many businesses team up with third-party loyalty programs to attract customers. See how the SPC Card helps attract customers.

SPC Card

The SPC Card (Student Price Card) is a discount card for students in Canada that has grown into the largest student customer-loyalty program in North America. For just $9, students have access to discounts and sales benefits from over 120 national retailers. For example, card holders are entitled to a free bag of popcorn with every rental or purchase at Blockbuster. The card quickly pays for itself in the savings students receive. With the addition of stores, membership with the SPC Card has soared to nearly a million members. Spccard.ca includes an interactive map that enables members to search for participating stores in their area.[69]

REDUCING DEFECTION It is not enough to attract new customers; the company must also keep them and increase their business.[70] Too many companies suffer from high **customer churn** or defection. Adding customers here is like adding water to a leaking bucket.

Cellular carriers and cable TV operators are plagued by "spinners," customers who switch carriers at least three times a year looking for the best deal. Many carriers lose 25 percent of their subscribers each year, at an estimated cost of $2 billion to $4 billion. Some of the dissatisfaction defecting customers cite comes from unmet needs and expectations, poor product/service quality and high complexity, and billing errors.[71]

To reduce the defection rate, the company must do the following:

1. *Define and measure its retention rate.* For a magazine, subscription renewal rate is a good measure of retention. For a college, it could be first- to second-year retention rate, or class graduation rate.

2. *Distinguish the causes of customer attrition and identify those that can be managed better.* Not much can be done about customers who leave the region or go out of business, but much can be done about those driven away by poor service, shoddy products, or high prices.[72]

3. *Compare the lost customer's lifetime value with the costs of reducing the defection rate.* As long as the cost to discourage defection is lower than the lost profit, spend the money to try to retain the customer.

RETENTION DYNAMICS Figure 5.4 shows the main steps in attracting and retaining customers in terms of a funnel and some sample customer responses to measure customer progress through the funnel. The **marketing funnel** identifies the percentage of the potential target market at each stage in the decision process, from merely aware to highly loyal. Consumers must move through each stage before becoming loyal customers. Some marketers extend the funnel to include loyal customers who are brand advocates or even partners with the firm.

By calculating *conversion rates*—the percentage of customers at one stage who move to the next—the funnel allows marketers to identify any bottleneck stage or barrier to building a loyal customer franchise. If the percentage of recent users is significantly lower than triers, for instance, something might be wrong with the product or service that prevents repeat buying.

FIGURE 5.4

The Marketing Funnel

The funnel also emphasizes how important it is not just to attract new customers, but to retain and cultivate existing ones. Satisfied customers are the company's *customer relationship capital.* If the company were sold, the acquiring company would pay not only for the plant and equipment and brand name, but also for the delivered *customer base,* the number and value of customers who will do business with the new firm. Consider these data about customer retention:[73]

- Acquiring new customers can cost five times more than satisfying and retaining current ones. It requires a great deal of effort to induce satisfied customers to switch from their current suppliers.
- The average company loses 10 percent of its customers each year.
- A 5 percent reduction in the customer defection rate can increase profits by 25 percent to 85 percent, depending on the industry.
- Profit rate tends to increase over the life of the retained customer due to increased purchases, referrals, price premiums, and reduced operating costs to service.

MANAGING THE CUSTOMER BASE Customer profitability analysis and the marketing funnel help marketers decide how to manage groups of customers that vary in loyalty, profitability, and other factors.[74] A key driver of shareholder value is the aggregate value of the customer base. Winning companies improve that value by excelling at strategies like the following:

- *Reducing the rate of customer defection.* Selecting and training employees to be knowledgeable and friendly increases the likelihood that customers' shopping questions will be answered satisfactorily. Whole Foods, the world's largest retailer of natural and organic foods, woos customers with a commitment to market the best foods and a team concept for employees.
- *Increasing the longevity of the customer relationship.* The more engaged with the company, the more likely a customer is to stick around. Nearly 65 percent of new Honda purchases replace an older Honda. Drivers cited Honda's reputation for creating safe vehicles with high resale value.
- *Enhancing the growth potential of each customer through "share of wallet," cross-selling, and up-selling.*[75] Sales from existing customers can be increased with new offerings and opportunities. Harley-Davidson sells more than motorcycles and accessories like gloves, leather jackets, helmets, and sunglasses. Its dealerships sell more than 3000 items of clothing—some even have fitting rooms. Licensed goods sold by others range from predictable items (shot glasses, cue balls, and Zippo cigarette lighters) to more surprising (cologne, dolls, and cell phones).
- *Making low-profit customers more profitable or terminating them.* To avoid the direct need for termination, marketers can encourage unprofitable customers to buy more or in larger quantities, forgo certain features or services, or pay higher amounts or fees.[76] Banks, phone companies, and travel agencies all now charge for once-free services to ensure minimum revenue levels. Firms can also discourage those with questionable profitability prospects. Progressive Insurance screens customers and diverts the potentially unprofitable to competitors.[77] "Free" customers who pay little or nothing and are subsidized by paying customers—as in print and online media, employment and dating services, and shopping malls—may still create useful direct and indirect network effects, however, an important function.[78]
- *Focusing disproportionate effort on high-profit customers.* The most profitable customers can be treated in a special way. Thoughtful gestures such as birthday greetings, small gifts, or invitations to special sports or arts events can send them a strong positive signal.

Building Loyalty

Creating a strong, tight connection to customers is the dream of any marketer and often the key to long-term marketing success. Companies that want to form such bonds should heed some specific considerations (see Figure 5.5). One set of researchers sees retention-building activities as adding financial benefits, social benefits, or structural ties.[79] The following sections explain three types of marketing activities companies are using to improve loyalty and retention.

INTERACTING WITH CUSTOMERS Listening to customers is crucial to customer relationship management. Some companies have created an ongoing mechanism that keeps their marketers permanently plugged in to front-line customer feedback.

- Deere & Company, which makes John Deere tractors and has a superb record of customer loyalty—nearly 98 percent annual retention in some product areas—has used retired employees to interview defectors and customers.[80]

- Create superior products, services, and experiences for the target market.
- Get cross-departmental participation in planning and managing the customer satisfaction and retention process.
- Integrate the "Voice of the Customer" to capture customers' stated and unstated needs or requirements in all business decisions.
- Organize and make accessible a database of information on individual customer needs, preferences, contacts, purchase frequency, and satisfaction.
- Make it easy for customers to reach appropriate company staff and express their needs, perceptions, and complaints.
- Assess the potential of frequency programs and club marketing programs.
- Run award programs recognizing outstanding employees.

FIGURE 5.5

Forming Strong Customer Bonds

- Boston Pizza introduced gluten-free pizza to its menu, added several thin-crust options, and lowered the level of sodium in most of its menu items, reaffirming its position as one of the most innovative pizza chains in Canada.[81]
- Build-A-Bear Workshop uses a "Cub Advisory Board" as a feedback and decision-input body. The board is made up of twenty 5- to 16-year-olds who review new-product ideas and give a "paws up or down." Many products in the stores are customer ideas.[82]

But listening is only part of the story. It is also important to be a customer advocate and, as much as possible, take the customers' side and understand their point of view.[83] USAA Insurance's legendary quality of service has led to the highest customer satisfaction in the industry. USAA subscribers will often tell stories about how the company looks out for them, even counselling them not to take out more insurance than they need. With such levels of trust, USAA enjoys high customer loyalty and significant cross-selling opportunities.[84]

DEVELOPING LOYALTY PROGRAMS **Frequency programs (FPs)** are designed to reward customers who buy frequently and in substantial amounts.[85] Such programs can help build long-term loyalty with high-CLV customers, creating cross-selling opportunities in the process. Pioneered by the airlines, hotels, and credit card companies, FPs now exist in many other industries. Most supermarket chains offer price club cards that grant discounts on certain items.[86]

In Canada, there are many widely recognized rewards programs, such as the AIR MILES card, which allows shoppers to redeem earned miles for flights and merchandise; the Shoppers Optimum card, which allows users to accumulate points to apply toward free goods at Shoppers Drug Mart; the CIBC Aerogold Visa, which allows users to accumulate Aeroplan points for Air Canada and Star Alliance flights; the President's Choice Financial MasterCard, which allows users to accumulate points to purchase groceries at Loblaws stores; and the HBC Rewards card, which allows users to accumulate points with purchases from The Bay, Zellers, and Home Outfitters. The list goes on and on.

Typically, the first company to introduce an FP in an industry gains the most benefit, especially if competitors are slow to respond. After competitors react, FPs can become a financial burden to all the offering companies, but some companies are more efficient and creative in managing them. Some FPs generate rewards in a way that locks customers in and creates significant costs to switching. FPs can also produce a psychological boost and a feeling of being special and elite that customers value.[87] For example, airlines run tiered loyalty programs in which they offer different levels of rewards to different travellers (e.g., Aeroplan Prestige, Aeroplan Elite, Aeroplan Super-Elite). Elite or Super-Elite status comes with a number of benefits such as free access to Star Alliance airport lounges, priority boarding, priority seating, extra baggage allowance, and upgrades to business class seats.

Club membership programs can be open to everyone who purchases a product or service, or limited to an affinity group of those willing to pay a small fee. Although open clubs are good for building a database or snagging customers from competitors, limited-membership clubs are more powerful long-term loyalty builders. Fees and membership conditions prevent those with only a fleeting interest in a company's products from joining. These clubs attract and keep those customers responsible for the largest portion of business. Such clubs are not only for the major national chains, as the Red River Co-op has demonstrated.

Red River Co-op

At the Red River Co-op, a Winnipeg petroleum company, members are the owners. At the end of each fiscal year, the co-operative returns a portion of each member's purchases in the form of equity dividends. Unlike competitor gas station chains that give immediate cents off per litre or reward points, Red River Co-op's loyalty program (equity) rewards customers at the end of the year with a lump sum cash refund based on the Co-op's profits. This has worked well both for the co-op and its members. With over 200 000 members, the chain grosses over $350 million annually, with the average member receiving a cheque for $162 in 2010.[88]

CREATING INSTITUTIONAL TIES The company may supply customers with special equipment or computer links that help them manage orders, payroll, and inventory. Customers are less inclined to switch to another supplier when it means high capital costs, high search costs, or the loss of loyal-customer discounts. A good example is McKesson Corporation, a leading pharmaceutical wholesaler, which invested millions of dollars in EDI (Electronic Data Interchange) capabilities to help independent pharmacies manage inventory, order-entry processes, and shelf space. Another example is Milliken & Company, which provides proprietary software programs, marketing research, sales training, and sales leads to loyal customers.

Win-Backs

Regardless of how hard companies may try, some customers inevitably become inactive or drop out. The challenge is to reactivate them through win-back strategies.[89] It's often easier to reattract ex-customers (because the company knows their names and histories) than to find new ones. Exit interviews and lost-customer surveys can uncover sources of dissatisfaction and help win back only those with strong profit potential.[90]

Red River Co-op's loyal customers are also owners.

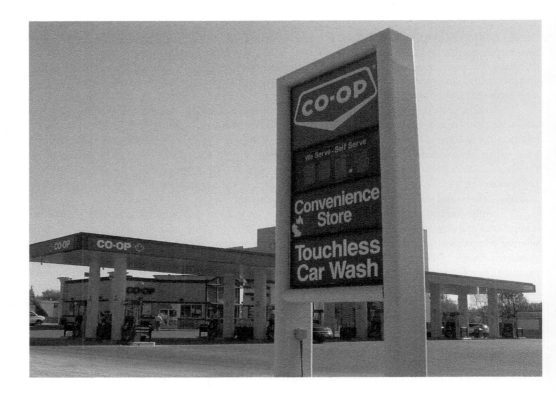

CUSTOMER DATABASES AND DATABASE MARKETING

Marketers must know their customers.[91] And in order to know the customer, the company must collect information and store it in a database from which to conduct database marketing. A **customer database** is an organized collection of comprehensive information about individual customers or prospects that is current, accessible, and actionable for lead generation, lead qualification, sale of a product or service, or maintenance of customer relationships. **Database marketing** is the process of building, maintaining, and using customer databases and other databases (products, suppliers, resellers) to contact, transact, and build customer relationships.

Customer Databases

Many companies confuse a customer mailing list with a customer database. A **customer mailing list** is simply a set of names, addresses, and telephone numbers. A customer database contains much more information, accumulated through customer transactions, registration information, telephone queries, cookies, and every customer contact.

Ideally, a customer database also contains the consumer's past purchases, demographics (age, income, family members, birthdays), psychographics (activities, interests, and opinions), mediagraphics (preferred media), and other useful information. The catalogue company Fingerhut possesses some 1400 pieces of information about each of the 30 million households in its massive customer database. And the Royal Bank of Canada has individual data on its 10 million customers and is able to model the lifetime value of individual customers, their potential interest in different offerings, and their vulnerability to attrition.

Ideally, a **business database** contains business customers' past purchases; past volumes, prices, and profits; buyer team member names (and ages, birthdays, hobbies, and favourite foods); the status of current contracts; an estimate of the supplier's share of the customer's business; competitive suppliers; an assessment of competitive strengths and weaknesses in selling and servicing the account; and relevant customer buying practices, patterns, and policies.

A Latin American unit of the Swiss pharmaceutical firm Novartis keeps data on 100 000 of Argentina's farmers, knows their crop protection chemical purchases, groups them by value, and treats each group differently.

Data Warehouses and Data Mining

Savvy companies capture information every time a customer comes into contact with any of their departments, whether the contact is a customer purchase, a customer-requested service call, an online query, or a mail-in rebate card.[92] Banks and credit card companies, telephone companies, catalogue marketers, and many other companies have a great deal of information about their customers, including not only addresses and phone numbers, but also transactions and enhanced data on age, family size, income, and other demographic information.

These data are collected by the company's contact centre and organized into a **data warehouse** where marketers can capture, query, and analyze them to draw inferences about an individual customer's needs and responses. Telemarketers can respond to customer inquiries based on a complete picture of the customer relationship, and customized marketing activities can be directed to individual customers. See how dunnhumby, a marketing research firm, has helped its clients understand their customers' individual needs.

dunnhumby

British research firm dunnhumby has increased the profitability of struggling retailers by gleaning insights from their loyalty program data and credit card transactions. The firm helped British supermarket giant Tesco tailor coupons and special discounts to its loyalty card shoppers. Tesco decided against dropping a poor-selling type of bread after dunnhumby's analysis revealed that the bread was a "destination product" for a loyal cohort that would shop elsewhere if it disappeared. Other major clients have included Kroger, Macy's, and Home Depot. For a major European catalogue company, dunnhumby found that not only did shoppers with different body types prefer different clothing styles, they also shopped at different times of the year: slimmer consumers tended to buy early in a new season, whereas larger folks tended to take fewer risks and wait until later in the season to see what would be popular.[93]

Through **data mining**, marketing statisticians can extract from the mass of data useful information about individuals, trends, and segments. Data mining uses sophisticated statistical and mathematical techniques such as cluster analysis, automatic interaction detection, predictive modelling, and neural networking. Some observers believe a proprietary database can provide a company with a significant competitive advantage.[94] See Figure 5.6 for some examples.

In general, companies can use their databases in five ways:

1. *To identify prospects*—Many companies generate sales leads by advertising their product or service. The ads generally contain a response feature, such as a business reply card or toll-free phone number, and the company builds its database from customer responses. It sorts through the database to identify the best prospects, then contacts them by mail or phone to try to convert them into customers.

2. *To decide which customers should receive a particular offer*—Companies interested in selling, up-selling, and cross-selling set up criteria describing the ideal target customer for a particular offer. Then they search their customer databases for those who most closely resemble the ideal. By noting response rates, a company can improve its targeting precision. Following a sale, it can set up an automatic sequence of activities: One week later send a thank-you note; five weeks later send a new offer; ten weeks later (if customer has not responded) phone and offer a special discount.

3. *To deepen customer loyalty*—Companies can build interest and enthusiasm by remembering customer preferences and sending appropriate gifts, discount coupons, and interesting reading material.

4. *To reactivate customer purchases*—Automatic mailing programs (automatic marketing) can send out birthday or anniversary cards, holiday shopping reminders, or off-season promotions. The database can help the company make attractive or timely offers.

5. *To avoid serious customer mistakes*—A major bank confessed to a number of mistakes it had made by not using its customer database well. In one case, the bank charged a customer a penalty for late payment on his mortgage, failing to note he headed a company that was a major depositor in this bank. The customer quit the bank. In a second case, two different staff members of the bank phoned the same mortgage customer offering a home equity loan at different prices. Neither knew the other had made the call. In a third case, the bank gave a premium customer only standard service in another country.

The Downside of Database Marketing and CRM

Database marketing is most frequently used by business marketers and service providers that normally and easily collect a lot of customer data, like hotels, banks, airlines, and insurance, credit card, and phone companies. Other types of companies in the best position to invest in CRM are those that do a lot of cross-selling and up-selling (such as GE and Amazon.com) or whose customers have highly differentiated needs and are of highly differentiated value to the company. Packaged-goods retailers and consumer packaged-goods companies use database marketing less frequently, though some (such as Kraft, Quaker Oats, Ralston Purina, and Nabisco) have built databases for certain brands. Some businesses cited as CRM successes include Enterprise Rent-A-Car, Fidelity Investments, Lexus, Intuit, and Capital One.[95]

Having covered the upside of database marketing, we also need to cover the downside. Five main problems can prevent a firm from effectively using CRM:

1. *Some situations are just not conducive to database management.* Building a customer database may not be worthwhile when (1) the product is a once-in-a-lifetime purchase (a grand piano); (2) customers show little loyalty to a brand (there is lots of customer churn); (3) the unit sale is very small (a candy bar) so CLV is low; (4) the cost of gathering information is too high; and (5) there is no direct contact between the seller and ultimate buyer.

2. *Building and maintaining a customer database requires a large, well-placed investment in computer hardware, database software, analytical programs, communication links, and skilled staff.* It's difficult to collect the right data, especially to capture all the occasions of company interaction with individual customers. Deloitte Consulting found that 70 percent of firms found little or no improvement from implementing CRM because the CRM system was poorly designed, it became too expensive, users didn't make much use of it or report much benefit, and collaborators ignored the system. Sometimes companies mistakenly concentrate on customer contact processes without making corresponding changes in internal structures and systems.[96]

Qwest Twice a year, Qwest sifts through its customer list looking for customers that have the potential to be more profitable. The company's database contains as many as 200 observations about each customer's calling patterns. By looking at demographic profiles, plus the mix of local versus long-distance calls or whether a consumer has voice mail, Qwest can estimate potential spending. Next, the company determines how much of the customer's likely telecom budget is already coming its way. Armed with that knowledge, Qwest sets a cutoff point for how much to spend on marketing to this customer.

Royal Caribbean Royal Caribbean uses its database to offer spur-of-the-moment cruise packages to fill all the berths on its ships. It focuses on retired people and single people because they are more able to make quick commitments. Fewer empty berths mean maximized profits for the cruise line.

Fingerhut The skillful use of database marketing and relationship building has made catalogue house Fingerhut one of the nation's largest direct-mail marketers. Not only is its database full of demographic details such as age, marital status, and number of children, but it also tracks customers' hobbies, interests, and birthdays. Fingerhut tailors mail offers based on what each customer is likely to buy. Fingerhut stays in continuous touch with customers through regular and special promotions, such as annual sweepstakes, free gifts, and deferred billing. Now the company has applied its database marketing to its websites.

Mars Mars is a market leader not only in candy, but also in pet food. In Germany, Mars has compiled the names of virtually every cat-owning family by contacting veterinarians and by advertising a free booklet titled "How to Take Care of Your Cat." Those who request the booklet fill out a questionnaire, so Mars knows the cat's name, age, and birthday. Mars now sends a birthday card to each cat each year, along with a new cat-food sample or money-saving coupons for Mars brands.

American Express It is no wonder that, at its secret location in Phoenix, security guards watch over American Express's 500 billion bytes of data on how its customers have used the company's 35 million green, gold, and platinum charge cards. Amex uses the database to include precisely targeted offers in its monthly mailing of millions of customer bills.

FIGURE 5.6

Examples of Database Marketing

3. *It may be difficult to get everyone in the company to be customer oriented and use the available information.* Employees find it far easier to carry on traditional transaction marketing than to practise CRM. Effective database marketing requires managing and training employees as well as dealers and suppliers.

4. *Not all customers want a relationship with the company.* Some may resent knowing that the company has collected that much personal information about them. Online companies should explain their privacy policies and give consumers the right not to have their information stored. Canada's RBC Financial Group has been a forerunner in this regard; it implemented a privacy code back in 1987. European countries do not look favourably on database marketing and are protective of consumers' private information. The European Union passed a law handicapping the growth of database marketing in its 27 member countries. Predictably, the United States and Canada have responded to the privacy issue very differently. While the United States opted for industry self-regulation, Canadian federal and provincial governments believed more controls were needed. The Personal Information Protection and Electronic Documents Act (PIPEDA) regulates how organizations collect, use, and disclose personal information. In keeping up with the times, the act covers electronic documents as well (for more information, visit the Office of the Privacy Commissioner of Canada website at www.priv.gc.ca). "Marketing Insight: The Behavioural Targeting Controversy" reviews some privacy and security issues.

5. *The assumptions behind CRM may not always hold true.*[97] High-volume customers often know their value to a company and can leverage it to extract premium service and/or price discounts, so that it may not cost the firm less to serve them. Loyal customers may expect and demand more and resent any attempt to charge full prices. They may also be jealous of attention lavished on other cus-

tomers. When eBay began to chase big corporate customers such as IBM, Disney, and Sears, some mom-and-pop businesses that helped build the brand felt abandoned.[98] Loyal customers also may not necessarily be the best ambassadors for the brand. One study found those who scored high on behavioural loyalty and bought a lot of a company's products were less active word-of-mouth marketers than customers who scored high on attitudinal loyalty and expressed greater commitment to the firm.

Thus, the benefits of database marketing do not come without significant costs and risks, not only in collecting the original customer data, but also in maintaining and mining them. When it works, a data warehouse yields more than it costs, but the data must be in good condition, and the discovered relationships must be valid and acceptable to consumers.

MARKETING **INSIGHT** | THE BEHAVIOURAL TARGETING CONTROVERSY

The emergence of *behavioural targeting* is allowing companies to track the online behaviour of target customers and find the best match between ads and prospects. Tracking an individual's Internet usage behaviour relies on cookies—randomly assigned numbers, codes, and data that are stored on the user's computer hard drive and reveal which sites have been visited, the amount of time spent there, which products or pages were viewed, which search terms were entered, and so on.

Most behavioural targeting is carried out by online ad networks owned by large Internet firms such as Google or AOL, as well as by some Internet service providers (ISPs). These online ad networks—such as AdBrite, which has more than 70 000 sites in its online marketplace—use cookies to track consumers' movements through all their affiliated sites. A new customer signing up with Microsoft for a free Hotmail email account, for example, is required to give the company his or her name, age, gender, and postal code. Microsoft can then combine those facts with information such as observed online behaviour and characteristics of the area in which the customer lives, to help advertisers better understand whether, when, and how to contact that customer. Although Microsoft must be careful to preserve consumer privacy—the company claims it won't purchase an individual's income history—it can still provide advertising clients with behavioural targeting information.

For example, Microsoft can help a DiningIn franchisee zero in on working moms aged 30 to 40 in a given neighbourhood with ads designed to reach them before 10 A.M., when they're most likely to be planning their evening meal. Or if a person clicks on three websites related to auto insurance and then visits an unrelated site for sports or entertainment, auto insurance ads may show up on that site, in addition to the auto insurance sites. This practice ensures that ads are readily apparent for a potential customer likely to be in the market. Microsoft claims behavioural targeting can increase the likelihood a visitor clicks an ad by as much as 76 percent.

Proponents of behavioural targeting maintain that consumers see more relevant ads in this way. Because the ads are more effective as a result, greater ad revenue is available to support free online content. Spending on behavioural targeting is projected to grow to $4.4 billion or 8.6 percent of total online ad spending by 2012.

Proponents of behavioural targeting also maintain that many consumers lack full understanding of different tracking practices and would be less concerned if they knew exactly how it worked. Proponents' claims of anonymity and privacy, however, have been weakened by events such as a leak at AOL of online behavioural data in 2006 for 650 000 users and overly aggressive attempts to institute data capture procedures at Facebook and various ISPs.

Sources: Elisabeth Sullivan, "Behave," *Marketing News,* September 15, 2008, pp. 12–15; Stephanie Clifford, "Two-Thirds of Americans Object to Online Tracking," *New York Times,* September 30, 2009; Jessica Mintz, "Microsoft Adds Behavioral Targeting," *Associated Press,* December 28, 2006; Becky Ebenkamp, "Behavior Issues," *Brandweek,* October 20, 2008, pp. 21–25; Brian Morrissey, "Connect the Thoughts," *Adweek Media,* June 29, 2009, pp. 10–11; Laurie Birkett, "The Cookie That Won't Crumble," *Forbes,* January 18, 2010, p. 32; Alden M. Hayashi, "How *Not* to Market on the Web," *MIT Sloan Management Review,* Winter 2010, pp. 14–15.

SUMMARY

1. Customers are value maximizers. They form an expectation of value and act on it. Buyers will buy from the firm that they perceive to offer the highest customer-perceived value, defined as the difference between total customer benefits and total customer cost.

2. A buyer's satisfaction is a function of the product's perceived performance and the buyer's expectations. Recognizing that high satisfaction leads to high customer loyalty, companies must ensure that they meet and exceed customer expectations.

3. Losing profitable customers can dramatically affect a firm's profits. The cost of attracting a new customer is estimated to be five times the cost of keeping a current customer happy. The key to retaining customers is relationship marketing.

4. Quality is the totality of features and characteristics of a product or service that bear on its ability to satisfy stated or implied needs. Marketers play a key role in achieving high levels of total quality so that firms remain solvent and profitable.

5. Marketing managers must calculate customer lifetime values of their customer base to understand their profit implications. They must also determine ways to increase the value of the customer base.

6. Companies are also becoming skilled in customer relationship management (CRM), which focuses on developing programs to attract and retain the right customers and meeting the individual needs of those valued customers.

7. Customer relationship management often requires building a customer database and data mining to detect trends, segments, and individual needs. A number of significant risks also exist, so marketers must proceed thoughtfully.

APPLICATIONS

Marketing Debate: Online versus Offline Privacy

As more firms practise relationship marketing and develop customer databases, privacy issues are emerging as an important topic. Consumers and public interest groups are scrutinizing—and sometimes criticizing—the privacy policies of firms and raising concerns about potential theft of online credit card information or other potentially sensitive or confidential financial information. Others maintain online privacy fears are unfounded and that security issues are as much a concern offline. They argue that the opportunity to steal information exists virtually everywhere, and it's up to consumers to protect their interests.

Take a position: Privacy is a bigger issue online than offline *versus* Privacy is no different online than offline.

Marketing Discussion: Using CLV

Consider customer lifetime value (CLV). Choose a business and show how you would go about developing a quantitative formulation that captures the concept. How would that business change if it totally embraced the customer equity concept and maximized CLV?

Canadians go to the movies over 100 million times collectively each year, and almost 70 percent of the time, they go to a Cineplex Entertainment theatre. Attendance at Cineplex movie theatres has been growing above the national average, and a large part of it can be attributed to Cineplex's SCENE, the first-ever Canadian entertainment rewards program. Launched in January 2007, SCENE members get discounts on concessions and earn points redeemable for movie tickets, concessions, and other merchandise.

Membership in the SCENE program has averaged 10 000 to 15 000 new members each week, and reached the 2 million mark in less than two years after its launch. The program itself has also expanded, allowing customers to redeem points for DVDs, Blu-rays, and music, and get discounts at some restaurants. SCENE has teamed up with Scotiabank, giving members the option to apply for a SCENE debit or VISA card, which allows them to accumulate rewards points faster when they pay with the card.

The SCENE program allows Cineplex to see where consumers are spending their money, identify emerging trends, and target the marketing strategy more effectively. The majority of the customer base is under the age of 30, which translates into huge potential revenues if the company can continue to attract these young consumers to movies. "It's about capturing customer data and understanding consumer behaviour, using that to make better decisions that help you drive sales and increase profits," according to Shawn Bloom, general manager for SCENE. "For Scotiabank, the primary objective was about the youth market; they wanted a way to appeal to the 18 to 45-year-olds and give them a reason to think about Scotiabank."

The results of SCENE have far exceeded the expectations set by Cineplex. Concession revenues were expected to dip slightly due to the 10 percent discount members receive. Instead, concession revenue per patron increased to $4.12—the highest ever by a Canadian theatre. Attendance at Cineplex theatres has risen by almost 8 million visits per year to approximately 70 million visits. The uniqueness of SCENE has allowed Cineplex continued growth and success, and doesn't appear to be slowing down any time soon. With thousands of new members joining every week, Cineplex is obtaining more and more data on how to better serve its customers' needs and, ultimately, its own.

QUESTIONS

1. How can Cineplex calculate the customer lifetime value of a moviegoer?

2. From a customer relationship management perspective, what are some patterns that Cineplex can analyze from its SCENE database? How can it act on those patterns?

3. What are some ethical considerations in collecting and analyzing such data?

Sources: "SCENE Reaches Two Million Members: SCENE Celebrates by Bringing Back a Fan Favourite to the Big Screen," *Marketwire*, November 30, 2009; Carey Toane, "Canada's Love Affair with Loyalty," *Strategy*, August 1, 2010, p. 40; "Cineplex Galaxy Income Fund Annual Report 2009," (Toronto: Cineplex Entertainment); "SCENE—About Us," www.scene.ca/aboutus.aspx (viewed September 17, 2010); "Motion Picture Theatres: 2008 Highlights," *Statistics Canada Service Bulletin*, May 20, 2010.

Chapter 6

In This Chapter, We Will Address the Following **Questions**

1. How do consumer characteristics influence buying behaviour?

2. What major psychological processes influence consumer responses to the marketing program?

3. How do consumers make purchasing decisions?

4. In what ways do consumers stray from a deliberative, rational decision process?

HBC recognized Canadians' need to connect with each other during the 2010 Winter Olympics and capitalized on it with its red mittens.

Analyzing Consumer Markets

The aim of marketing is to meet and satisfy target customers'

needs and wants better than competitors. Marketers must have a thorough understanding of how consumers think, feel, and act, and offer clear value to each and every target consumer.

Anyone who saw the coverage of the Vancouver 2010 Winter Olympics could not have missed seeing thousands of Canadians wearing their heart, not on their sleeves, but on their hands: the woolly red Olympic mittens. Canadians showed their support for the Olympics and Canadian athletes by purchasing 3.5 million pairs of the mittens, produced by the Hudson's Bay Company. Net proceeds from the sales went toward funding the Own the Podium 2010 initiative that provided Canadian athletes with the best equipment and training possible. The mittens rapidly became one of the most sought-after and enduring symbols of the 2010 Winter Games. But what was it about those red mittens?

A large part of the product's success was the need it satisfied in consumers: promoting belonging and patriotism. Canadians felt more connected to each other during the Vancouver 2010 Games than at any other time in recent years. The affordable red mittens with the Olympic rings stitched on the outside and a white maple leaf sewn on each palm were viewed as a unifying element that brought together Olympic torchbearers, Canadian athletes, and Canadian fans, whether they were cheering in the stands, from their homes, or from abroad. The colours of the collection, red and white, were strategically chosen to ring a chord with the patriotic hearts of Canadians. Those wearing the mittens felt connected to others sporting them—family members, friends, or even strangers passing by on the street. During the Christmas holiday season, the popularity of the mittens soared, both as a gift item and as a practical, fun way to keep hands warm.

A marketing campaign should consider the need the product satisfies and the influences on a buyer's decision-making process. The Hudson's Bay Company and the Vancouver 2010 Olympics organizing committee recognized the patriotic appeal the red mittens would have and capitalized on it by combining Canadian heritage values with the vast publicity the mittens got through Olympic media coverage to come up with a very successful product that was both symbolic and functional.[1]

Successful marketing requires that

companies fully connect with their customers. Adopting a holistic marketing orientation means understanding customers—gaining a 360-degree view of both their daily lives and the changes that occur during their lifetimes so that the right products are always marketed to the right customers in the right way. This chapter explores individual consumer buying dynamics; the next chapter explores the buying dynamics of business buyers.

WHAT INFLUENCES CONSUMER BEHAVIOUR?

Consumer behaviour is the study of how individuals, groups, and organizations select, buy, use, and dispose of goods, services, ideas, or experiences to satisfy their needs and wants.[2] Marketers must fully understand both the theory and the reality of consumer behaviour. Table 6.1 provides a snapshot profile of Canadians' consumption.

A consumer's buying behaviour is influenced by cultural, social, and personal factors. Of these, cultural factors exert the broadest and deepest influence.

Cultural Factors

Culture, subculture, and social class are particularly important influences on consumer buying behaviour. **Culture** is the fundamental determinant of a person's wants and behaviour. Through family and other key institutions, a child growing up in Canada is exposed to values such as achievement and success, activity, efficiency and practicality, progress, material comfort, individualism, freedom, external comfort, humanitarianism, and youthfulness.[3] A child growing up in another country might have a different view of self, relationship to others, and rituals. Marketers must closely attend to cultural values in every country to understand how to best market their existing products and find opportunities for new products.

The culturally based, shared understanding of certain symbols can provide marketers with powerful communication tools. Savvy marketers are using such Canadian icons as the Canadian flag, Canadian wildlife, and Mounties to help tie their products to the sense of pride many Canadians take in their country and its products. Companies such as Roots, Petro-Canada, Molson, Tim Hortons, and Air Canada follow this practice.[4]

Each culture consists of smaller **subcultures** that provide more specific identification and socialization for their members. Subcultures include nationalities, religions, racial groups, and geographic regions.

TABLE 6.1	CANADIAN CONSUMER ALMANAC		
EXPENDITURES			
Average Canadian outlays for goods and services in 2009		**$**	**%**
Personal income taxes		$14 399	20.2
Shelter		$14 095	19.8
Transportation		$9 753	13.7
Food		$7 262	10.2
Recreation		$3 843	5.4
Personal insurance payments and pension contributions		$4 269	6.0
Household operation		$3 428	4.8
Clothing		$2 841	4.0
Household furnishings and equipment		$1 896	2.7
Health care		$2 004	2.8
Tobacco products and alcoholic beverages		$1 506	2.1
Gifts of money and contributions		$1 715	2.4
Education		$1 238	1.7
Miscellaneous		$1 180	1.7
Personal care		$1 200	1.7
Games of chance (net amount)		$255	0.4
Reading materials and other printed matter		$232	0.3
TOTAL EXPENDITURE		$71 117	100

Source: "Average Household Expenditures, by Province and Territory," *Statistics Canada*, CANSIM Table 203-0001, December 17, 2010.

Companies have capitalized on well-thought-out multicultural marketing strategies in recent years (see "Marketing Insight: Marketing to Quebec and French-Canadian Consumers"). When subcultures grow large and affluent enough, companies such as Loblaw often design specialized marketing programs to serve them.

Loblaw and T&T

In an effort to tap into the growing immigrant Asian market in Canada, Loblaw Industries acquired the Asian supermarket chain T&T for $225 million in 2009. The chain from British Columbia combines traditional Asian products like barbecued duck and dumplings with a Western store layout of wide aisles and bright lighting. For Loblaw Industries, this acquisition is a way to reach a very important customer base; ethnic households spend up to 23 percent more on groceries compared with the rest of Canada, with the East Asian community buying over $5 billion of groceries each year. The company is already reaping the benefits of targeting the Asian market, with its revenues rising 2 percent in just a few months following the acquisition.[5]

Virtually all human societies exhibit *social stratification*, most often in the form of **social classes**, relatively homogeneous and enduring divisions in a society, hierarchically ordered and with members who share similar values, interests, and behaviour. One classic depiction of social classes defined seven ascending levels: (1) lower lowers, (2) upper lowers, (3) working class, (4) middle class, (5) upper middles, (6) lower uppers, and (7) upper uppers.[6]

Social class members show distinct product and brand preferences in many areas, including clothing, home furnishings, leisure activities, and automobiles. They also differ in media preferences; upper-class consumers often prefer magazines and books, and lower-class consumers often prefer television. Even within a category such as TV, upper-class consumers may show greater preference for news and drama, whereas lower-class consumers may lean toward reality shows and sports. There are also language differences—advertising copy and dialogue must ring true to the targeted social class. Companies such as Facebook are well-aware of the need to adapt to different cultures and languages, as shown in "Marketing Insight: Facebook."

REGIONALISM   Canada is an increasingly regionalized country, and the way people think, act, and buy varies greatly from one region to the next. The sheer size of the country and its varied geographic features and climate have certainly shaped regional character and personality. For example, Atlantic Canada is

---

MARKETING **INSIGHT**	FACEBOOK

Facebook has been so popular that its founder Mark Zuckerberg was named the 2010 *TIME* Person of the Year. With over 500 million active users and over 70 translations of the website, Facebook remains the most popular social networking site worldwide. After receiving feedback that many French Canadians wanted a version of Facebook that was more in line with Quebec French, Facebook developed a French-Canadian version of the social networking site. Facebook also developed an application that allowed people to comment and give their opinion on the translation by voting on the headings that they preferred. Some of the transitions from European French to the French-Canadian version were adaptations, such as changing the European "collège" and "lycée" to more Canadian words such as "cégep" and "école secondaire."

Sources: Canadian Press, "Facebook Launches French Canadian Version," *Marketing*, April 07, 2009, www.marketingmag.ca/english/news/media/article.jsp?content=20090407_142124_6412 (viewed September 18, 2010); "Press Room: Statistics," 2010, www.facebook.com/press/info.php?statistics (viewed September 18, 2010).

Quebec has long prided itself on being a distinct society. Marketers must be aware of Quebec's uniqueness if they are to be successful in the province. Quebec is characterized by unique laws, a different mix of indigenous and national businesses and industries, and attitudes and values distinct from those in the rest of Canada. According to the 2006 census data, 79 percent of the nearly 7.5 million Quebecers claim French as their mother tongue. In contrast, 7.7 percent claim English as their native language, with the remaining 13.3 percent having a different native tongue or a combination of French and English.

Known for their "joie de vivre," a large part of Quebec's population (49 percent or 3.6 million people) lived in the Montreal area in 2006. Montreal has a large number of high-tech industries, is the second-largest metropolitan area in Canada (behind Toronto), and is the second-largest French-speaking city in the world. However, one must not assume that the population of the Montreal region is homogeneous and made up only of French Canadians. Bilingualism is very common and the population is quite diverse as a result of immigration. According to the 2006 census, 20.6 percent of Montrealers are immigrants.

As a means of perpetuating its French culture and affirming the province's French-speaking identity, Quebec governments have passed legislation to ensure the use of French in various areas of public life. This is most evident in the education system, where the majority of schools are French speaking, although a few English schools exist.

Marketers who want to appeal to Quebec consumers need to do more than communicate in French using dictionary translations of words. Take a successful campaign by the Bank of Montreal that used the tagline "Profitez." You wouldn't fully understand the campaign if you used only a dictionary-based interpretation of the word. You'd find translations that said *profitez* means "profit from," "to profit," "to earn," or "something profitable." However, for Quebec consumers the meaning is more nuanced. They translate it as "make the most of it," "enjoy," or "take advantage," and the expression is strongly associated with the enjoyment of life—meanings that make the campaign more powerful and rich. Language and the meanings derived from it are very cultural and context-based. Furthermore, research has revealed differences in the activities, interests, opinions, and consumption habits of French-Canadian and English-Canadian consumers. French Canadians value their European roots, their rich and diverse cultural venues, gourmet food, and fine wines. As a result, Montreal is known as one of the trendiest centres in the world. Additionally, French-Canadian women are more family-oriented and fashion-conscious than women in the rest of Canada. Such differences are partly derived from their Latin cultural roots.

Demographic and socioeconomic differences also exist: education and income are both lower in Quebec than in Ontario. The legal environment is also different for marketers in Quebec. Besides strict language laws, there are stronger restrictions on advertising to children, with Quebec having some of the strictest regulations in the country. To be successful in French Canada, marketers must develop appeals that take these differences into account. For example, while many marketers use national symbols to appeal to their customers, Quebec's separatist sentiments make this practice unwise.

Quebec also has a distinct business and retail climate. Lavo Group, for example, is a packaged-goods manufacturer whose products rival those of Procter & Gamble and Colgate in the province. Many Québécois buy such Lavo products as La Parisienne laundry detergent and fabric softener instead of Tide and Downy, Hertel liquid cleanser instead of Mr. Clean, and Old Dutch powdered cleanser instead of Comet.

Because of differences such as these, many advertisers develop unique campaigns designed just for the Quebec marketplace. For example, research conducted by S. C. Johnson revealed that even attitudes toward cleaning vary between English and French Canada. While English Canadians just want to get the job done and see cleaning as a necessary evil, people in Quebec get a sense of pride and accomplishment after they clean. Using this research, S. C. Johnson designed a highly successful campaign for its cleaning products that centred on the distinctly Québécois custom of moving day: July 1, the date on which renters move from one apartment to another because leases in Quebec traditionally expire on June 30.

Regardless of the specific approach a company takes, one thing is clear: it is extremely important for the company to understand the culture and language of Québécois. This goes further than knowing the subtleties of the French language—it requires having a deep understanding of Québécois consumers, including key insights into their culture, lifestyle, motivations, and attitudes.

Sources: "Population by Mother Tongue, by Province and Territory (2006 Census)," *Statistics Canada*, December 11, 2007, www40.statcan.gc.ca/l01/cst01/demo11b-eng.htm; Samson Okalow, "Vive la Difference: Does That Mean I Have to Have a Separate Campaign?" *Strategy*, October 15, 2004, p. 31; Nicolette Flemming, "The True Meaning of 'Profitez,'" *Marketing*, June 10, 2002, p. 31; Helena Katz, "Johnson Sharpens Its Quebec Strategy," *Marketing*, October 12, 1998, p. 3.

largely defined by its proximity to and historical relationship with the sea. Equally, the isolation imposed by the mountain barrier, along with the abundance and grandeur of British Columbia's natural environment, has shaped the outlook of that region's residents. Immigration has also had a differential effect on the different regions within Canada. The economy of each region furthers these differences. The rise and decline of such tradable commodities as fish, timber, wheat, minerals, and petroleum have affected the mindsets and buying behaviour of people living within Canada's different regions. In particular, regional inequalities that resulted from fluctuating resource economies contributed to the rise of regional grievances, stereotypes, and dependencies that became part of each region's identity. However, many analysts today disagree with the view that regional disparities in outlook and behaviour are a simple byproduct of economics and geography. Instead they argue that these marked regional differences result from social relationships. In particular, disparities in political power have driven increased regionalism. The emergence of a new social class in Quebec—a new middle class of educated francophone professionals whose aspirations were blocked by the lack of opportunities for their skills within the old Quebec, with its backward state, its outdated, Church-administered social programs, and its Anglo-dominated business sector—is credited with giving birth to this trend. However, Quebec is not alone. In Alberta, a more regional identity has also emerged as the province has striven to become more politically assertive and pro-business. Alberta also focuses on a set of issues centred on energy and taxation policies that are quite different from those at the top of the political agenda in the other provinces.[7]

Social Factors

In addition to cultural factors, social factors such as reference groups, family, and social roles and statuses affect our buying behaviour.

REFERENCE GROUPS A person's **reference groups** are all the groups that have a direct (face-to-face) or indirect influence on his or her attitudes or behaviour. Groups having a direct influence are called **membership groups**. Some of these are **primary groups** with whom the person interacts fairly continuously and informally, such as family, friends, neighbours, and co-workers. People also belong to **secondary groups**, such as religious, professional, and trade-union groups, which tend to be more formal and require less continuous interaction.

Reference groups influence members in at least three ways. They expose an individual to new behaviours and lifestyles, they influence attitudes and self-concept, and they create pressures for conformity that may affect product and brand choices. People are also influenced by groups to which they do *not* belong. **Aspirational groups** are those a person hopes to join; **dissociative groups** are those whose values or behaviour an individual rejects.

Where reference group influence is strong, marketers must determine how to reach and influence the group's opinion leaders. An **opinion leader** is the person who offers informal advice or information about a specific product or product category, such as which of several brands is best or how a particular product may be used.[8] Opinion leaders are often highly confident, socially active, and frequent users of the category. Marketers try to reach them by identifying their demographic and psychographic characteristics, identifying the media they read, and directing messages to them.

Clothing companies such as Hot Topic, which hope to appeal to the fickle and fashion-conscious youth market, have used music in a concerted effort to monitor opinion leaders' style and behaviour.

Hot Topic

With over 600 stores in malls in 49 states and Puerto Rico, Hot Topic has been hugely successful at using anti-establishment style in its fashions. The chain also sells books, comics, jewellery, CDs, records, posters, and other paraphernalia. Hot Topic's slogan, "Everything about the Music," reflects its operating premise: whether a teen is into rock, pop-punk, emo, acid rap, rave, or rockabilly—or even more obscure musical tastes—Hot Topic has the right T-shirt. To keep up with music trends, all Hot Topic staffers, from the CEO to the music-obsessed salespeople (80 percent of whom are under 25), regularly attend concerts by up-and-coming and established bands to scout who's wearing what. Each store looks more like a campus student centre than a shop—loud music plays and dark walls have bulletin boards displaying concert flyers and staff music picks. Hot Topic also hosts free acoustic shows, called Local Static, showcasing local bands. Hot Topic can catch trends and launch hip new clothing and hard-to-find pop culture merchandise in six to eight weeks, literally months before traditional competitors using off-shore suppliers.[9]

FAMILY The family is the most important consumer buying organization in society, and family members constitute the most influential primary reference group.[10] There are two families in the buyer's life. The **family of orientation** consists of parents and siblings. From parents a person acquires an orientation toward religion, politics, and economics and a sense of personal ambition, self-worth, and love.[11] Even if the buyer no longer interacts very much with his or her parents, parental influence on behaviour can be significant. Almost 40 percent of families have auto insurance with the same company as the husband's parents.

A more direct influence on everyday buying behaviour is the **family of procreation**—namely, the person's spouse and children. In Canada, husband–wife engagement in purchases has traditionally varied widely by product category. The wife has usually acted as the family's main purchasing agent, especially for food, sundries, and staple clothing items. Now traditional purchasing roles are changing, and marketers would be wise to see both men and women as possible targets. *Canadian Grocer* magazine estimates that 25 to 30 percent of men now shop for groceries. Some males are forced into the role of shopper by demographic and lifestyle changes such as late marriage and high divorce rates, but most take on the role as a result of being part of a time-pressed, two-income household.[12]

For expensive products and services such as cars, vacations, or housing, the vast majority of husbands and wives engage in joint decision making.[13] Men and women may respond differently to marketing messages, however.[14] Research has shown that women value connections and relationships with family and friends and place a higher priority on people than on companies. Men, on the other hand, relate more to competition and place a high priority on action.[15]

Marketers are taking more direct aim at women with new products such as Quaker's Nutrition for Women cereals and Crest Rejuvenating Effects toothpaste. In 2003, Sherwin-Williams launched a Dutch Boy easy-to-use "Twist and Pour" paint can targeted specifically at women. Priced $2 higher than the same paint in traditional metal containers, the new product helped the company triple its revenue.[16] Corus Entertainment in Canada is another organization that is actively pursuing the women's market.

Corus Entertainment

Studies showed that Canadian women tend to be loyal to their favourite programs, and spend more time watching TV than men. Corus Entertainment is one of Canada's largest media companies, with a major standing in television, radio, and kids' entertainment. Recognizing the importance of the female market and that advertisers are willing to pay more for a female audience, Corus launched a television channel designed specifically for women. Focusing on women aged 18 to 49 who are a prime target for many products, the W Channel showcases movies for and about women in all genres, from romance to comedy to thrillers.[17]

Another shift in buying patterns is an increase in the amount of dollars spent and the direct and indirect influence wielded by children and teens. Direct influence describes children's hints, requests, and demands—"I want to go to McDonald's." Indirect influence means that parents know the brands, product choices, and preferences of their children without hints or outright requests ("I think Jake and Emma would want to go to McDonald's").

Research has shown that more than two-thirds of 13- to 21-year-olds make or influence family purchase decisions on audio/video equipment, software, and vacation destinations.[18] In total, these teens and young adults spend over $120 billion a year. They report that to make sure they buy the right products, they watch what their friends say and do as much as what they see or hear in an ad or are told by a salesperson in a store.[19]

Television can be especially powerful in reaching children, and marketers are using it to target them at younger ages than ever before with product tie-ins for just about everything—Disney character pyjamas, retro G. I. Joe toys and action figures, Harry Potter backpacks, and *High School Musical* playsets.

By the time children are around 2 years old, they can often recognize characters, logos, and specific brands. They can distinguish between advertising and programming by about ages 6 or 7. A year or so later, they can understand the concept of persuasive intent on the part of advertisers. By 9 or 10, they can perceive the discrepancies between message and product.[20]

The Canadian Marketing Association makes it clear that special care must be taken by marketers seeking to target the children's market. However, marketing to children is not new and can often become controversial, as the following Walmart example shows.

Walmart and geoGIRL

In March 2011, Walmart began to carry the geoGIRL line of makeup products targeted at tween girls. The line of about 70 beauty items, including mascara, foundation, eye shadow, lip treatment, and skin cleansers, comes in ecofriendly packaging made to be held by smaller hands. Besides enhancing beauty, the geoGIRL line boasts of having anti-aging ingredients—in products that are aimed at 8- to 12-year-olds! Walmart may have hit all the right buttons to appeal to the young audience—beauty, environmental awareness, and low price. But many question whether Walmart has taken its marketing too far in encouraging tweens to wear makeup. Although the geoGIRL brand is not the first one to target kids with such products, treating tweens as being older and teaching them to become conscious of their facial appearance at such a young age is certainly questionable.[21]

ROLES AND STATUS We each participate in many groups—family, clubs, organizations. Groups often are an important source of information and help to define norms for behaviour. We can define a person's position in each group in terms of role and status. A **role** consists of the activities a person is expected to perform. Each role in turn connotes a **status**. A senior vice-president of marketing may be seen as having more status than a sales manager, and a sales manager may be seen as having more status than an office clerk. People choose products that reflect and communicate their role and their actual or desired status in society. Marketers must be aware of the status symbol potential of products and brands.

Personal Factors

Personal characteristics that influence a buyer's decision include age and stage in the life cycle, occupation and economic circumstances, personality and self-concept, and lifestyle and values. Because many of these have a direct impact on consumer behaviour, it is important for marketers to follow them closely.

Walmart may have gone too far by targeting tweens with its geoGIRL line of cosmetics.

AGE AND STAGE IN THE LIFE CYCLE Our taste in food, clothes, furniture, and recreation is often related to our age. Consumption is also shaped by the *family life cycle* and the number, age, and gender of people in the household at any point in time. In "Marketing Insight: InTouchLink," see how a company recognizes the unique needs of seniors to cater to that market.

Canadian households are also increasingly fragmented. The traditional family of four with a husband, wife, and two kids makes up a much smaller percentage of total households than it once did. The average Canadian household size, as per the 2006 census, was 2.5 persons.[22]

MARKETING **INSIGHT** | INTOUCHLINK

With the Internet becoming a major channel for people to communicate and stay organized, InTouchLink developed a product to make using a computer and the Internet more user-friendly for seniors. The online market has room to grow among the nearly 5 million Canadian seniors, with a third of them not using the Internet. The Toronto-based company has created easy-to-use software. InTouchLink enables seniors or those who are intimidated by computers to go online, get connected, and experience the Internet, all via a very senior-friendly interface. The system is intuitive, simple, and developed specifically for seniors, taking into consideration their age-related constraints and preferences.

Sources: Marc Saltzman, "Canadian Company Making Web Surfing Easier for Seniors," August 18, 2010, www.sync-blog.com/sync/2010/08/canadian-company-making-web-surfing-easier-for-seniors.html (viewed September 17, 2010); "Internet Use by Individuals, by Selected Frequency of Use and Age," *Statistics Canada*, CANSIM Table 358-0129, May 10, 2010.

In addition, *psychological* life-cycle stages may matter. Adults experience certain "passages" or "transformations" as they go through life.[23] Their behaviour as they go through these passages, such as becoming a parent, is not necessarily fixed but changes with the times.

Marketers should also consider *critical life events or transitions*—marriage, childbirth, illness, relocation, divorce, first job, career change, retirement, death of a spouse—as giving rise to new needs. These changes should alert service providers—banks, lawyers, and marriage, employment, and bereavement counsellors—to ways they can help.

OCCUPATION AND ECONOMIC CIRCUMSTANCES Occupation also influences consumption patterns. Marketers try to identify the occupational groups that have above-average interest in their products and services and even tailor products for certain occupational groups: computer software companies, for example, design different products for brand managers, engineers, lawyers, and physicians.

As the recent recession clearly indicated, both product and brand choice are greatly affected by economic circumstances: spendable income (level, stability, and time pattern), savings and assets (including the percentage that is liquid), debts, borrowing power, and attitudes toward spending and saving. Luxury-goods makers, such as Gucci, Prada, and Burberry, are vulnerable to an economic downturn. If economic indicators point to a recession, marketers can take steps to redesign, reposition, and reprice their products or introduce or increase the emphasis on discount brands so that they can continue to offer value to target customers. Some firms are well-positioned to take advantage of good and bad economic times to begin with.

PERSONALITY AND SELF-CONCEPT Each person has personality characteristics that influence his or her buying behaviour. By **personality**, we mean a set of distinguishing human psychological traits that lead to relatively consistent and enduring responses to environmental stimuli (including buying behaviour). We often describe personality in terms of such traits as self-confidence, dominance, autonomy, deference, sociability, defensiveness, and adaptability.[24] Personality can be a useful variable in analyzing consumer brand choices. Brands also have personalities, and consumers are likely to choose brands whose personalities match their own. We define **brand personality** as the specific mix of human traits that we can attribute to a particular brand.

Stanford's Jennifer Aaker researched brand personalities and identified the following traits:[25]

1. Sincerity (down-to-earth, honest, wholesome, and cheerful)
2. Excitement (daring, spirited, imaginative, and up-to-date)
3. Competence (reliable, intelligent, and successful)
4. Sophistication (upper-class and charming)
5. Ruggedness (outdoorsy and tough)

Aaker analyzed some well-known brands and found that a number tended to be strong on one particular trait: Levi's on "ruggedness," MTV on "excitement," CNN on "competence," and Campbell's on "sincerity." These brands will, in theory, attract users who display the same traits. A brand personality may have several attributes: Levi's suggests a personality that is also youthful, rebellious, authentic, and American.

A cross-cultural study exploring the generalizability of Aaker's scale outside the United States found three of the five factors applied in Japan and Spain, but a "peacefulness" dimension replaced "ruggedness" both in Japan and Spain, and a "passion" dimension emerged in Spain instead of "competence."[26] Research on brand personality in Korea revealed two culture-specific factors—"passive likeableness" and "ascendancy"—reflecting the importance of Confucian values in Korea's social and economic systems.[27]

Consumers often choose and use brands with a brand personality consistent with their *actual self-concept* (how we view ourselves), although the match may instead be based on the consumer's *ideal self-concept* (how we would like to view ourselves) or even on *others' self-concept* (how we think others see us).[28] These effects may also be more pronounced for publicly consumed products than for privately consumed goods.[29] On the other hand, consumers who are high "self-monitors"—that is, sensitive to how others see them—are more likely to choose brands whose personalities fit the consumption situation.[30] Finally, often consumers have multiple aspects of self (serious professional, caring family member, active fun-lover) that may be evoked differently in different situations or around different types of people.

LIFESTYLE AND VALUES People from the same subculture, social class, and occupation may lead quite different lifestyles. A **lifestyle** is a person's pattern of living in the world as expressed in activities, interests, and opinions. It portrays the whole person interacting with his or her environment. Marketers search for relationships between their products and lifestyle groups. A computer manufacturer might find that most computer buyers are achievement-oriented and then aim the brand more clearly at the achiever lifestyle. Here's an example of one of the latest lifestyle trends that businesses are targeting.

LOHAS

Consumers who worry about the environment, want products to be produced in a sustainable way, and spend money to advance their personal development and potential have been named "LOHAS." The name is an acronym standing for *lifestyles of health and sustainability*. The market for LOHAS products encompasses things like organic foods, energy-efficient appliances and solar panels, alternative medicine, yoga DVDs, and eco-tourism. Rather than looking at discrete product categories like cars or organic foods, it is more important to look at the common factors linking these product groups—for example, at cars, energy, and household products that are perceived as better for the environment and society. Companies like Loblaw serve this emerging segment by offering alternative products such as organic foods and reusable cloth shopping bags. It is estimated that the U.S. market for LOHAS products well exceeds US$200 billion. It is also estimated that about 20 percent of adult consumers in the United States are LOHAS consumers.[31]

Table 6.2 breaks the LOHAS demographic into six segments with estimated size, and product and service interests.

Lifestyles are shaped partly by whether consumers are *money constrained* or *time constrained*. Companies aiming to serve money-constrained consumers will create lower-cost products and services. By appealing to thrifty consumers, Walmart has become the largest company in the world. Its "Everyday Low Prices" have wrung tens of billions of dollars out of the retail supply chain, passing the larger part of savings along to shoppers in the form of rock-bottom bargain prices.

Consumers who experience time famine are prone to **multitasking**, doing two or more things at the same time. They will also pay others to perform tasks because time is more important to them than money. Companies aiming to serve them will create convenient products and services for this group.

In some categories, notably food processing, companies targeting time-constrained consumers need to be aware that these very same people want to believe they're *not* operating within time constraints. Marketers call those who seek both convenience and some involvement in the cooking process the "convenience involvement segment." See how Hamburger Helper has changed its strategy to appeal to these customers.

TABLE 6.2 | LOHAS MARKET SEGMENTS

Personal Health	**Natural Lifestyles**
Natural, organic products	Indoor and outdoor furnishings
Nutritional products	Organic cleaning supplies
Integrative health care	Compact fluorescent lights
Dietary supplements	Social change philanthropy
Mind body spirit products	Apparel
U.S. Market—$118.03 billion	**U.S. Market—$10.6 billion**
Green Building	**Alternative Transportation**
Home certification	Hybrid vehicles
Energy Star appliances	Biodiesel fuel
Sustainable flooring	Car sharing programs
Renewable energy systems	**U.S. Market—$6.12 billion**
Wood alternatives	
U.S. Market—$50 billion	
Eco-Tourism	**Alternative Energy**
Eco-tourism travel	Renewable energy credits
Eco-adventure travel	Green pricing
U.S. Market—$24.17 billion	**U.S. Market—$380 million**

Source: Reprinted by permission of LOHAS, http://www.lohas.com/.

Hamburger Helper

Launched in 1971 in response to tough economic times, the inexpensive pasta-and-powdered-mix Hamburger Helper was designed to quickly and inexpensively stretch a pound of meat into a family meal. With an estimated 44 percent of evening meals prepared in under 30 minutes and strong competition from fast-food drive-through windows, restaurant deliveries, and precooked grocery store dishes, Hamburger Helper's days of prosperity might seem numbered. Market researchers found, however, that some consumers don't want the fastest microwaveable solution possible—they also want to feel good about how they prepare a meal. In fact, on average, they prefer to use at least one pot or pan and 15 minutes of time. To remain attractive to this segment, marketers of Hamburger Helper are always introducing new flavours to tap into changing consumer taste trends. Not surprisingly, the latest economic downturn saw U.S. sales of the brand rise 9 percent in 2009.[32]

Consumer decisions are also influenced by **core values**, the belief systems that underlie attitudes and behaviours. Core values go much deeper than behaviour or attitude and determine, at a basic level, people's choices and desires over the long term. Marketers who target consumers on the basis of their values believe that with appeals to people's inner selves, it is possible to influence their outer selves—their purchase behaviour.

KEY PSYCHOLOGICAL PROCESSES

The starting point for understanding consumer behaviour is the stimulus-response model shown in Figure 6.1. Marketing and environmental stimuli enter the consumer's consciousness, and a set of psychological processes combine with certain consumer characteristics to result in decision processes and purchase decisions. The marketer's task is to understand what happens in the consumer's consciousness between the arrival of the outside marketing stimuli and the ultimate purchase decisions. Five key psychological processes—motivation, perception, learning, emotions, and memory—fundamentally influence consumer responses.[33]

Motivation: Freud, Maslow, Herzberg

We all have many needs at any given time. Some needs are *biogenic;* they arise from physiological states of tension, such as hunger, thirst, or discomfort. Other needs are *psychogenic;* they arise from psychological states of tension, such as the need for recognition, esteem, or belonging. A need becomes a **motive** when it is aroused to a sufficient level of intensity to drive us to act. Motivation has both direction—we select one goal over another—and intensity—we pursue the goal with more or less vigour.

FIGURE 6.1

Model of Consumer Behaviour

Three of the best-known theories of human motivation—those of Sigmund Freud, Abraham Maslow, and Frederick Herzberg—carry quite different implications for consumer analysis and marketing strategy.

FREUD'S THEORY Sigmund Freud assumed that the psychological forces shaping people's behaviour are largely unconscious, and that a person cannot fully understand his or her own motivations. Someone who examines specific brands will react not only to their stated capabilities, but also to other, less conscious cues such as shape, size, weight, material, colour, and brand name. A technique called *laddering* lets us trace a person's motivations from the stated instrumental ones to the more terminal ones. Then the marketer can decide at what level to develop the message and appeal.[34]

Motivation researchers often collect in-depth interviews with a few dozen consumers to uncover deeper motives triggered by a product. They use various *projective techniques* such as word association, sentence completion, picture interpretation, and role playing, many pioneered by Ernest Dichter, a Viennese psychologist who settled in the United States.[35]

Today, motivational researchers continue the tradition of Freudian interpretation. Jan Callebaut identifies different motives a product can satisfy. For example, whiskey can meet the need for social relaxation, status, or fun. Different whiskey brands need to be motivationally positioned in one of these three appeals.[36] Another motivation researcher, Clotaire Rapaille, works on breaking the "code" behind product behaviour.[37] See how Chrysler's marketers used this technique.

Chrysler

When Chrysler decided to offer a new sedan, it had already done a great deal of traditional market research that suggested North American consumers wanted excellent gas mileage, safety, and prices. However, it was only through qualitative research that Chrysler discovered what cultural anthropologist Clotaire Rapaille calls "the code"—the unconscious meaning people give to a particular market offering. First, interviewers took on the role of "a visitor from another planet," asking participants to help them understand the product in question. Then, participants told stories about the product, and finally, after a relaxation exercise, they wrote about their first experiences with it. In this way, Chrysler learned that "cookie-cutter" sedans were "off-code," and it used information from the sessions to create the PT Cruiser. With its highly distinctive retro design, this sedan was one of the most successful U.S. car launches in recent history.[38]

MASLOW'S THEORY Abraham Maslow sought to explain why people are driven by particular needs at particular times.[39] His answer is that human needs are arranged in a hierarchy from most to least pressing—physiological needs, safety needs, social needs, esteem needs, and self-actualization needs (see Figure 6.2). People will try to satisfy their most important need first and then try to satisfy the next most important. For example, a starving man (need 1) will not take an interest in the latest happenings in the art world (need 5), nor in how he is viewed by others (need 3 or 4), nor even in whether he is breathing clean air (need 2), but when he has enough food and water, the next most important need will become salient.

HERZBERG'S THEORY Frederick Herzberg developed a two-factor theory that distinguishes *dissatisfiers* (factors that cause dissatisfaction) from *satisfiers* (factors that cause satisfaction).[40] The absence of dissatisfiers is not enough to motivate a purchase; satisfiers must be present. For example, a computer that does not come with a warranty would be a dissatisfier. Yet the presence of a product warranty would not act as a satisfier or motivator of a purchase, because it is not a source of intrinsic satisfaction. Ease of use would be a satisfier.

Herzberg's theory has two implications. First, sellers should do their best to avoid dissatisfiers (for example, a poor training manual or a poor service policy). Although these things will not sell a product, they might easily unsell it. Second, the seller should identify the major satisfiers or motivators of purchase in the market and then supply them.

Perception

A motivated person is ready to act—*how* is influenced by his or her perception of the situation. In marketing, perceptions are more important than reality, because perceptions affect consumers' actual behaviour. **Perception** is the process by which we select, organize, and interpret information inputs to create a meaningful picture of the world.[41] It depends not only on physical stimuli, but also on the stimuli's relationship to the surrounding environment and on conditions within each of us. One person might perceive

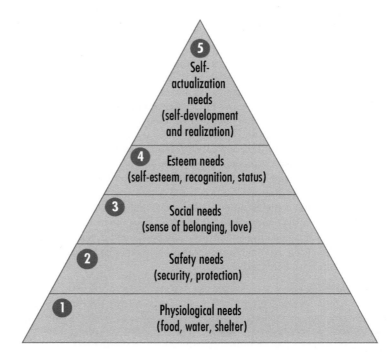

FIGURE 6.2

Maslow's Hierarchy of Needs

Source: *MASLOW, ABRAHAM H.; FRAGER, ROBERT D.; FADIMAN, JAMES, MOTIVATION AND PERSONALITY, 3rd Ed.,* © 1987. Adapted and Electronically reproduced by permission of Pearson Education, Inc., Upper Saddle River, New Jersey.

a fast-talking salesperson as aggressive and insincere; another, as intelligent and helpful. Each will respond to the salesperson differently.

People emerge with different perceptions of the same object because of three perceptual processes: selective attention, selective distortion, and selective retention.

SELECTIVE ATTENTION Attention is the allocation of processing capacity to some stimulus. Voluntary attention is something purposeful; involuntary attention is grabbed by someone or something. It's estimated that the average person may be exposed to over 1500 ads or brand communications a day. Because we cannot possibly attend to all these, we screen most stimuli out—a process called **selective attention**. Selective attention means that marketers must work hard to attract consumers' notice. The real challenge is to explain which stimuli people will notice. Here are some findings:

1. *People are more likely to notice stimuli that relate to a current need.* A person who is motivated to buy a computer will notice computer ads and be less likely to notice DVD ads.

2. *People are more likely to notice stimuli they anticipate.* You are more likely to notice computers than radios in a computer store because you don't expect the store to carry radios.

3. *People are more likely to notice stimuli whose deviations are large in relationship to the normal size of the stimuli.* You are more likely to notice an ad offering $100 off the list price of a computer than one offering $5 off.

Though we screen out much, we are influenced by unexpected stimuli, such as sudden offers in the mail, over the phone, or from a salesperson. Marketers may attempt to promote their offers intrusively in order to bypass selective attention filters.

SELECTIVE DISTORTION Even noticed stimuli don't always come across in the way the senders intended. **Selective distortion** is the tendency to interpret information in a way that fits our preconceptions. Consumers will often distort information to be consistent with prior brand and product beliefs and expectations.[42]

For a stark demonstration of the power of consumer brand beliefs, consider that in blind taste tests, one group of consumers samples a product without knowing which brand it is, while another group knows. Invariably, the groups have different opinions, despite consuming *exactly the same product.*

When consumers report different opinions of branded and unbranded versions of identical products, it must be the case that their brand and product beliefs, created by whatever means (past experiences, marketing activity for the brand, or the like), have somehow changed their product perceptions. We can find examples with virtually every type of product.[43] When Coors changed its label from "Banquet Beer" to "Original Draft," consumers claimed the taste had changed even though the formulation had not.

Selective distortion can work to the advantage of marketers with strong brands when consumers distort neutral or ambiguous brand information to make it more positive. In other words, coffee may seem to taste better, a car may seem to drive more smoothly, the wait in a bank line may seem shorter, depending on the brand.

SELECTIVE RETENTION Most of us don't remember much of the information to which we're exposed, but we do retain information that supports our attitudes and beliefs. Because of **selective retention**, we're likely to remember good points about a product we like and forget good points about competing products. Selective retention again works to the advantage of strong brands. It also explains why marketers need to use repetition—to make sure their message is not overlooked.

SUBLIMINAL PERCEPTION The selective perception mechanisms require consumers' active engagement and thought. A topic that has fascinated armchair marketers for ages is **subliminal perception**. They argue that marketers embed covert, subliminal messages in ads or packaging. Consumers are not consciously aware of them, yet they affect behaviour. Although it's clear that mental processes include many subtle subconscious effects,[44] no evidence supports the notion that marketers can systematically control consumers at that level, especially enough to change moderately important or strongly held beliefs.[45]

Learning

When we act, we learn. **Learning** induces changes in our behaviour arising from experience. Most human behaviour is learned, although much learning is incidental. Learning theorists believe learning is produced through the interplay of drives, stimuli, cues, responses, and reinforcement. Two popular approaches to learning are classical conditioning and operant (instrumental) conditioning.

A **drive** is a strong internal stimulus impelling action. **Cues** are minor stimuli that determine when, where, and how a person responds. Suppose you buy an HP computer. If your experience is rewarding, your response to computers and HP will be positively reinforced. Later, when you want to buy a printer, you may assume that because it makes good computers, HP also makes good printers. In other words, you *generalize* your response to similar stimuli. A countertendency to generalization is discrimination. **Discrimination** means we have learned to recognize differences in sets of similar stimuli and can adjust our responses accordingly.

Learning theory teaches marketers that they can build demand for a product by associating it with strong drives, using motivating cues, and providing positive reinforcement. A new company can enter the market by appealing to the same drives competitors use and by providing similar cues, because buyers are more likely to **transfer** loyalty to similar brands (generalization); or the company might design its brand to appeal to a different set of drives and offer strong cue inducements to switch (discrimination).

Some researchers prefer more active, cognitive approaches when learning depends on the inferences or interpretations consumers make about outcomes. (Was an unfavourable consumer experience due to a bad product, or did the consumer fail to follow instructions properly?) The **hedonic bias** occurs when people have a general tendency to attribute success to themselves and failure to external causes. Consumers are thus more likely to blame a product than themselves, putting pressure on marketers to carefully explicate product functions in well-designed packaging and labels, instructive ads and websites, and so on.

Emotions

Consumer response is not all cognitive and rational; much may be emotional and invoke different kinds of feelings. A brand or product may make a consumer feel proud, excited, or confident. An ad may create feelings of amusement, disgust, or wonder.

Here are two recent examples that recognize the power of emotions in consumer decision making:

■ For years, specialty foam mattress leader Tempur-Pedic famously used infomercials showing that a wine glass on its mattress did not spill even as people bounced up and down on the bed. To create a stronger emotional connection, the company began a broader-based media campaign in 2007 that positioned the mattress as a wellness brand and "the nighttime therapy for body and mind."[46]

■ Reckitt Benckiser and Procter & Gamble launched advertising approaches in 2009 for Woolite and Tide, respectively, that tapped not into the detergents' performance benefits but into the emotional connection—and challenges—of laundry. Based on research showing that one in three working women recognize that they ruined some of their clothes in the wash over the last year, Reckitt Benckiser launched an online and in-store "Find the Look, Keep the Look" style guide for Woolite for "finding fashion and keeping it looking fabulous without breaking the bank." Based on the premise that a detergent should do more than clean, P&G positioned new Tide Total Care as preserving clothing and keeping the "7 signs of beautiful clothes," including shape, softness, and finish.[47]

Memory

Cognitive psychologists distinguish between **short-term memory (STM)**—a temporary and limited repository of information—and **long-term memory (LTM)**—a more permanent, essentially unlimited repository. All the information and experiences we encounter as we go through life can end up in our long-term memory.

Most widely accepted views of long-term memory structure assume we form some kind of associative model.[48] For example, the **associative network memory model** views LTM as a set of nodes and links. *Nodes* are stored information connected by *links* that vary in strength. Any type of information can be stored in the memory network, including verbal, visual, abstract, and contextual. A spreading activation process from node to node determines how much we retrieve and what information we can actually recall in any given situation. When a node becomes activated because we're encoding external information (when we read or hear a word or phrase) or retrieving internal information from LTM (when we think about some concept), other nodes are also activated if they're strongly enough associated with that node.

In this model, we can think of consumer brand knowledge as a node in memory with a variety of linked associations. The strength and organization of these associations will be important determinants of the information we can recall about the brand. Brand associations consist of all brand-related thoughts, feelings, perceptions, images, experiences, beliefs, attitudes, and so on that become linked to the brand node.

We can think of marketing as a way of making sure consumers have product and service experiences to create the right brand knowledge structures and maintain them in memory. Companies such as Procter & Gamble like to create mental maps of consumers that depict their knowledge of a particular brand in terms of the key associations likely to be triggered in a marketing setting, and their relative strength, favourableness, and uniqueness to consumers. Figure 6.3 displays a very simple mental map highlighting brand beliefs for a hypothetical consumer of the Dole brand.

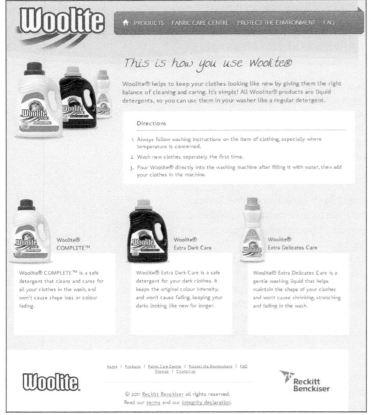

Woolite's style guide focuses on the emotional benefits of choosing and preserving the right look in clothes for women.

MEMORY PROCESSES Memory is a very constructive process, because we don't remember information and events completely and accurately. Often we remember bits and pieces and fill in the rest based on whatever else we know. "Marketing Insight: Made to Stick" offers some practical tips for how marketers can ensure their ideas—inside or outside the company—are remembered and have impact.

Memory encoding describes how and where information gets into memory. The strength of the resulting association depends on how much we process the information at encoding (how much we think about it, for instance) and in what way.[49] In general, the more attention we pay to the meaning of information during encoding, the stronger the resulting associations in memory will be.[50] Advertising research in a field setting suggests that high levels of repetition for an uninvolving, unpersuasive ad, for example, are unlikely to have as much sales impact as lower levels of repetition for an involving, persuasive ad.[51]

Memory retrieval is the way information gets out of memory. Three facts are important about memory retrieval:

1. The presence of other product information in memory can produce interference effects and cause us to either overlook or confuse new data. One marketing challenge in a category crowded with many competitors—for example, airlines, financial services, and insurance companies—is that consumers may mix up brands.

2. The time between exposure to information and encoding has been shown generally to produce only gradual decay. Cognitive psychologists believe memory is extremely durable, so once information becomes stored in memory, its strength of association decays very slowly.[52]

3. Information may be *available* in memory but not be *accessible* for recall without the proper retrieval cues or reminders. The effectiveness of retrieval cues is one reason marketing *inside* a supermarket or any retail store is so critical—the actual product packaging, the use of in-store mini-billboard displays, and so on. The information they contain and the reminders they provide of advertising or other information already conveyed outside the store will be prime determinants of consumer decision making.

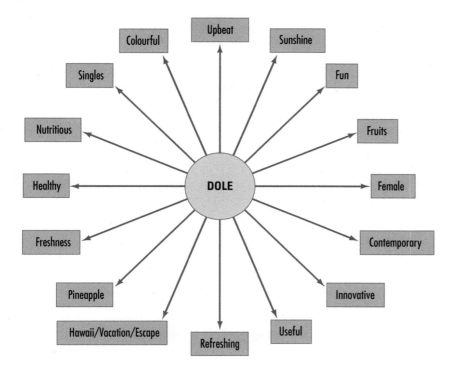

FIGURE 6.3

Hypothetical Dole Mental Map

THE BUYING-DECISION PROCESS: THE FIVE-STAGE MODEL

The basic psychological processes we've reviewed play an important role in consumers' actual buying decisions.[53]

Table 6.3 provides a list of some key consumer behaviour questions marketers should ask in terms of who, what, when, where, how, and why.

TABLE 6.3	UNDERSTANDING CONSUMER BEHAVIOUR
Who buys our product or service?	
Who makes the decision to buy the product?	
Who influences the decision to buy the product?	
How is the purchase decision made? Who assumes what role?	
What does the customer buy? What needs must be satisfied?	
Why do customers buy a particular brand?	
Where do they go or look to buy the product or service?	
When do they buy? Any seasonality factors?	
How is our product perceived by customers?	
What are customers' attitudes toward our product?	
What social factors might influence the purchase decision?	
Do customers' lifestyles influence their decisions?	
How do personal or demographic factors influence the purchase decision?	

Source: Based on figure 1.7 from George Belch and Michael Belch, *Advertising and Promotion: An Integrated Marketing Communications Perspective*, 8th ed. (Homewood, IL: Irwin, 2009).

MARKETING **INSIGHT** | MADE TO STICK

Picking up on a concept first introduced by Malcolm Gladwell in his book *The Tipping Point*, brothers Chip and Dan Heath set out to uncover what makes an idea sticky and catch on with an audience. Considering a wide range of ideas from diverse sources—urban legends, conspiracy theories, public policy mandates, and product design—they identified six traits that characterize all great ideas and used the acronym "SUCCES" to organize them:

1. Simple—find the core of any idea. Take an idea and distill it down, whittling away everything that is not essential. "WestJet is THE low-fare airline."

2. Unexpected—grab people's attention by surprising them. Nordstrom's customer service is legendary because it unexpectedly exceeds customers' already high expectations by going beyond helping them buy to addressing their personal situations—ironing shirts before meetings, keeping cars warm while they shop, or wrapping presents actually bought at Macy's.

3. Concrete—make sure any idea can be easily grasped and remembered later. Boeing successfully designed the 727 airplane by giving its thousands of engineers a very specific goal—the plane had to seat 131 passengers, be able to fly nonstop from New York to Miami, and land on runway 4-22 at LaGuardia, which could not be used by large planes.

4. Credibility—give an idea believability. Indian overnight delivery service Safexpress was able to overcome doubts about its capabilities by describing to a Bollywood film studio how it had flawlessly delivered 69 000 copies of the latest *Harry Potter* novel to bookstores all over the country by 8 A.M. on the morning of its release.

5. Emotion—help people see the importance of an idea. Research on fact-based versus appeal-to-emotion antismoking ads has demonstrated that emotional appeals are more compelling and memorable.

6. Stories—empower people to use an idea through narrative. Research again shows how narratives evoke mental stimulation, and visualization of events makes recall and further learning easier.

The Heaths believe great ideas are made, not born, via these traits. One example is the Subway ad campaign starring Jared—who lost 100 pounds in three months by eating two subs a day—that helped to raise Subway's sales 18 percent in one year. According to the Heaths, the idea scores high on all six dimensions of stickiness:

1. Simple—weight loss

2. Unexpected—weight loss by eating fast food

3. Concrete—weight loss by eating two Subway subs daily

4. Credibility—a documented loss of 100 pounds

5. Emotion—a triumph over difficult weight problems

6. Stories—a personal account of how eating two Subway subs led to an incredible weight loss

---

Sources: Chip Heath and Dan Heath, *Made to Stick: Why Some Ideas Survive and Others Die...* (New York: Random House, 2007); Malcolm Gladwell, *The Tipping Point: How Little Things Can Make a Big Difference* (New York: Little, Brown and Company, 2000); Barbara Kiviat, "Are You Sticky?" *TIME*, October 29, 2006; Justin Ewers, "Making It Stick," *U.S. News & World Report*, January 21, 2007; Mike Hofman, "Chip and Dan Heath: Marketing Made Sticky," *Inc*, January 1, 2007.

Smart companies try to fully understand customers' buying-decision process—all the experiences in learning, choosing, using, and even disposing of a product.[54] Marketing scholars have developed a "stage model" of the process (see Figure 6.4). The consumer typically passes through five stages: problem recognition, information search, evaluation of alternatives, purchase decision, and post-purchase behaviour. Clearly, the buying process starts long before the actual purchase and has consequences long afterward.[55]

Consumers don't always pass through all five stages—they may skip or reverse some. When you buy your regular brand of toothpaste, you go directly from the need to the purchase decision, skipping information search and evaluation. The model in Figure 6.4 provides a good frame of reference, however, because it captures the full range of considerations that arise when a consumer faces a highly involving new purchase.[56] Later in the chapter, we will consider other ways consumers make decisions that are less calculated.

Problem Recognition

The buying process starts when the buyer recognizes a problem or need triggered by internal or external stimuli. With an internal stimulus, one of the person's normal needs—hunger, thirst, sex—rises to a threshold level and becomes a drive. A need can also be aroused by an external stimulus. A person may admire a friend's new car or see a television ad for a Hawaiian vacation, which inspires thoughts about the possibility of making a purchase.

Marketers need to identify the circumstances that trigger a particular need by gathering information from a number of consumers. They can then develop marketing strategies that spark consumer interest. Particularly for discretionary purchases, such as luxury goods, vacation packages, and entertainment options, marketers may need to increase consumer motivation so that a potential purchase gets serious consideration.

Information Search

Surprisingly, consumers often search for limited amounts of information. Surveys have shown that for durables, half of all consumers look at only one store, and only 30 percent look at more than one brand of appliances. We can distinguish between two levels of engagement in the search. The milder search state is called *heightened attention*. At this level, a person simply becomes more receptive to information about a product. At the next level, the person may enter an *active information search:* looking for reading material, phoning friends, going online, and visiting stores to learn about the product.

INFORMATION SOURCES Major information sources to which consumers will turn fall into four groups:

- *Personal.* Family, friends, neighbours, acquaintances
- *Commercial.* Advertising, websites, salespersons, dealers, packaging, displays
- *Public.* Mass media, consumer rating organizations
- *Experiential.* Handling, examining, using the product

The relative amount and influence of these sources vary with the product category and the buyer's characteristics. Generally speaking, although consumers receive the greatest amount of information about a product from commercial—that is, marketer-dominated—sources, the most effective information often comes from personal or experiential sources, or public sources that are independent authorities.

Each source performs a different function in influencing the buying decision. Commercial sources normally perform an information function, whereas personal sources perform a legitimizing or evaluation function. For example, physicians often learn of new drugs from commercial sources but turn to other doctors for evaluations.

SEARCH DYNAMICS By gathering information, the consumer learns about competing brands and their features. The first box in Figure 6.5 shows the *total set* of brands available. The individual consumer will come to know a subset of these, the *awareness set.* Only some, the *consideration set,* will meet initial buying criteria. As the consumer gathers more information, just a few, the *choice set,* will remain strong contenders. The consumer makes a final choice from these.[57]

Marketers need to identify the hierarchy of attributes that guide consumer decision making in order to understand different competitive forces and how these various sets get formed. This process of identifying the hierarchy is called **market partitioning**. Years ago, most car buyers first decided on the manufacturer and then on one of its car divisions (*brand-dominant hierarchy*). A buyer might favour General Motors cars and, within this set, Chevrolet. Today, many buyers decide first on the nation from which they want to buy a car (*nation-dominant hierarchy*). Buyers may first decide they want to buy a German car, then an Audi, and then the A4 model of Audi.

The hierarchy of attributes also can reveal customer segments. Buyers who first decide on price are price dominant; those who first decide on the type of car (sports, passenger, hybrid) are type dominant; those who choose the brand first are brand dominant. Type/price/brand-dominant consumers make up one segment; price/brand/type buyers make up another. Each may have distinct demographics, psychographics, and mediagraphics, and different awareness, consideration, and choice sets.[58]

Figure 6.5 makes it clear that a company must strategize to get its brand into the prospect's awareness, consideration, and choice sets. If a food store owner arranges yogurt first by brand (such as Danone and Yoplait) and then by flavour within each brand, consumers will tend to select their flavours from the same brand. However, if all the strawberry yogurts are together, then all the vanilla, and so forth, consumers

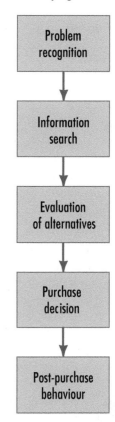

FIGURE 6.4

Five-Stage Model of the Consumer Buying Process

Problem recognition

↓

Information search

↓

Evaluation of alternatives

↓

Purchase decision

↓

Post-purchase behaviour

will probably choose which flavours they want first, and then choose the brand name they want for that particular flavour. Australian supermarkets arrange meats by the way they might be cooked, and stores use more descriptive labels, such as "a 10-minute herbed beef roast." The result is that Australians buy a greater variety of meats than North American shoppers, who choose from meats laid out by animal type—beef, chicken, pork, and so on.[59]

The company must also identify the other brands in the consumer's choice set so that it can plan the appropriate competitive appeals. In addition, marketers should identify the consumer's information sources and evaluate their relative importance. Asking consumers how they first heard about the brand, what information came later, and the relative importance of the different sources will help the company prepare effective communications for the target market.

Evaluation of Alternatives

How does the consumer process competitive brand information and make a final value judgment? No single process is used by all consumers, or by one consumer in all buying situations. There are several processes, and the most current models see the consumer forming judgments largely on a conscious and rational basis.

Some basic concepts will help us understand consumer evaluation processes: First, the consumer is trying to satisfy a need. Second, the consumer is looking for certain benefits from the product solution. Third, the consumer sees each product as a bundle of attributes with varying abilities to deliver the benefits. The attributes of interest to buyers vary by product:

1. *Hotels*—Location, cleanliness, atmosphere, price

2. *Mouthwash*—Colour, effectiveness, germ-killing capacity, taste/flavour, price

3. *Tires*—Safety, tread life, ride quality, price

Consumers will pay the most attention to attributes that deliver the sought-after benefits. We can often segment the market for a product according to attributes and benefits important to different consumer groups.

BELIEFS AND ATTITUDES Through experience and learning, people acquire beliefs and attitudes. These in turn influence buying behaviour. A **belief** is a descriptive thought that a person holds about something. Just as important are **attitudes**, a person's enduring favourable or unfavourable evaluations, emotional feelings, and action tendencies toward some object or idea.[60] People have attitudes toward almost everything: religion, politics, clothes, music, food.

Attitudes put us into a frame of mind: liking or disliking an object, moving toward or away from it. They lead us to behave in a fairly consistent way toward similar objects. Because attitudes economize on energy and thought, they can be very difficult to change. As a general rule, a company is well-advised to fit its product into existing attitudes rather than try to change attitudes. If beliefs and attitudes become too negative, however, more serious steps may be necessary.

EXPECTANCY-VALUE MODEL The consumer arrives at attitudes toward various brands through an attribute evaluation procedure, developing a set of beliefs about where each brand stands on each attribute.[61] The **expectancy-value model** of attitude formation posits that consumers evaluate products and services by combining their brand beliefs—the positives and negatives—according to importance.

Suppose Linda has narrowed her choice set to four laptop computers (A, B, C, and D). Assume she's interested in four attributes: memory capacity, graphics capability, size and weight, and price.

Table 6.4 shows her beliefs about how each brand rates on the four attributes. If one computer dominated the others on all the criteria, we could predict that Linda would choose it. But, as is often the case, her choice set consists of brands that vary in their appeal. If Linda wants the best memory capacity, she should buy C; if she wants the best graphics capability, she should buy A; and so on.

If we knew the weights Linda attaches to the four attributes, we could more reliably predict her laptop choice. Suppose she assigned 40 percent of the importance to the laptop's memory capacity, 30 percent to graphics capability, 20 percent to size and weight, and 10 percent to price. To find Linda's perceived value for each laptop according to the expectancy-value model, we multiply her weights by her beliefs about each computer's attributes. This computation leads to the following perceived values:

$$\text{Laptop A} = 0.4(8) + 0.3(9) + 0.2(6) + 0.1(9) = 8.0$$

$$\text{Laptop B} = 0.4(7) + 0.3(7) + 0.2(7) + 0.1(7) = 7.0$$

$$\text{Laptop C} = 0.4(10) + 0.3(4) + 0.2(3) + 0.1(2) = 6.0$$

$$\text{Laptop D} = 0.4(5) + 0.3(3) + 0.2(8) + 0.1(5) = 5.0$$

An expectancy-model formulation predicts that Linda will favour laptop A, which (at 8.0) has the highest perceived value.[62]

Suppose most laptop computer buyers form their preferences the same way. Knowing this, the marketer of laptop B, for example, could apply the following strategies to stimulate greater interest in brand B:

- *Redesign the laptop computer.* This technique is called *real repositioning.*

- *Alter beliefs about the brand.* Attempting to alter beliefs about the brand is called *psychological repositioning.*

- *Alter beliefs about competitors' brands.* This strategy, called *competitive depositioning,* makes sense when buyers mistakenly believe a competitor's brand has more quality than it actually has.

- *Alter the importance weights.* The marketer could try to persuade buyers to attach more importance to the attributes in which the brand excels.

- *Call attention to neglected attributes.* The marketer could draw buyers' attention to neglected attributes, such as styling or processing speed.

- *Shift the buyer's ideals.* The marketer could try to persuade buyers to change their ideal levels for one or more attributes.[63]

TABLE 6.4	A CONSUMER'S BRAND BELIEFS ABOUT LAPTOP COMPUTERS			
Laptop Computer	Attribute			
	Memory Capacity	Graphics Capability	Size and Weight	Price
A	8	9	6	9
B	7	7	7	7
C	10	4	3	2
D	5	3	8	5

Note: Each attribute is rated from 0 to 10, where 10 represents the highest level on that attribute. Price, however, is indexed in a reverse manner, with 10 representing the lowest price, because a consumer prefers a low price to a high price.

Purchase Decision

In the evaluation stage, the consumer forms preferences among the brands in the choice set and may also form an intention to buy the most preferred brand. In executing a purchase intention, the consumer may make up to five subdecisions: brand (brand A), dealer (dealer 2), quantity (one computer), timing (weekend), and payment method (credit card).

NONCOMPENSATORY MODELS OF CONSUMER CHOICE The expectancy-value model is a compensatory model, in that perceived good things about a product can help to overcome perceived bad things. But consumers often take "mental shortcuts" called **heuristics** or rules of thumb in the decision process.

With **noncompensatory models** of consumer choice, positive and negative attribute considerations don't necessarily net out. Evaluating attributes in isolation makes decision making easier for a consumer, but it also increases the likelihood that he or she would have made a different choice if he or she had deliberated in greater detail. We highlight three choice heuristics here:

1. Using the **conjunctive heuristic**, the consumer sets a minimum acceptable cutoff level for each attribute and chooses the first alternative that meets the minimum standard for all attributes. For example, if Linda decided all attributes had to rate at least 5, she would choose laptop computer B.

2. With the **lexicographic heuristic**, the consumer chooses the best brand on the basis of its perceived most important attribute. With this decision rule, Linda would choose laptop computer C.

3. Using the **elimination-by-aspects heuristic**, the consumer compares brands on an attribute selected probabilistically—where the probability of choosing an attribute is positively related to its importance—and eliminates brands that do not meet minimum acceptable cutoffs.

Our brand or product knowledge, the number and similarity of brand choices and time pressures present, and the social context (such as the need for justification to a peer or boss) all may affect whether and how we use choice heuristics.[64]

Consumers don't necessarily use only one type of choice rule. For example, they might use a noncompensatory decision rule such as the conjunctive heuristic to reduce the number of brand choices to a more manageable number, and then evaluate the remaining brands. One reason for the runaway success of the Intel Inside campaign in the 1990s was that it made the brand the first cutoff for many consumers—they would buy only a personal computer that had an Intel microprocessor. Leading personal computer makers at the time, such as IBM, Dell, and Gateway, had no choice but to support Intel's marketing efforts.

INTERVENING FACTORS Even if consumers form brand evaluations, two general factors can intervene between the purchase intention and the purchase decision (see Figure 6.6).[65] The first factor is the *attitudes of others.* The influence of another person's attitude depends on two things: (1) the intensity of the other person's negative attitude toward our preferred alternative, and (2) our motivation to comply with the other person's wishes.[66] The more intense the other person's negativism and the closer he or she is to us, the more we will adjust our purchase intention. The converse is also true.

Related to the attitudes of others is the role played by infomediaries' evaluations: *Consumer Reports,* which provides unbiased expert reviews of all types of products and services; J. D. Power, which provides consumer-based ratings of cars, financial services, and travel products and services; professional movie, book, and music reviewers; customer reviews of books and music on such sites as Amazon.com; and the increasing number of chat rooms, bulletin boards, blogs, and so on where people discuss products, services, and companies.

Consumers are undoubtedly influenced by these external evaluations, as evidenced by the success of a small-budget movie such as *Paranormal Activity,* which cost only $15 000 to make but grossed over $100 million at the box office in 2009 thanks to a slew of favourable reviews by moviegoers and online buzz at many websites.[67]

FIGURE 6.6

Steps between Evaluation of Alternatives and a Purchase Decision

The second factor is *unanticipated situational factors* that may erupt to change the purchase intention. Linda might lose her job, some other purchase might become more urgent, or a store salesperson may turn her off. Preferences and even purchase intentions are not completely reliable predictors of purchase behaviour.

A consumer's decision to modify, postpone, or avoid a purchase decision is heavily influenced by one or more types of *perceived risk:* [68]

1. *Functional risk*—The product does not perform to expectations.

2. *Physical risk*—The product poses a threat to the physical well-being or health of the user or others.

3. *Financial risk*—The product is not worth the price paid.

4. *Social risk*—The product results in embarrassment in front of others.

5. *Psychological risk*—The product affects the mental well-being of the user.

6. *Time risk*—The failure of the product results in an opportunity cost of finding another satisfactory product.

The degree of perceived risk varies with the amount of money at stake, the amount of attribute uncertainty, and the level of consumer self-confidence. Consumers develop routines for reducing the uncertainty and negative consequences of risk, such as avoiding decisions, gathering information from friends, and developing preferences for national brand names and warranties. Marketers must understand the factors that provoke a feeling of risk in consumers and provide information and support to reduce it.

Post-purchase Behaviour

After the purchase, the consumer might experience dissonance from noticing certain disquieting features or hearing favourable things about other brands and will be alert to information that supports his or her decision. Marketing communications should supply beliefs and evaluations that reinforce the consumer's choice and help him or her feel good about the brand. The marketer's job therefore doesn't end with the purchase. Marketers must monitor post-purchase satisfaction, post-purchase actions, and post-purchase product uses and disposal.

POST-PURCHASE SATISFACTION Satisfaction is a function of the closeness between expectations and the product's perceived performance.[69] If performance falls short of expectations, the consumer is *disappointed;* if it meets expectations, the consumer is *satisfied;* if it exceeds expectations, the consumer is *delighted.* These feelings make a difference in whether the customer buys the product again and talks favourably or unfavourably about it to others.

The larger the gap between expectations and performance, the greater the dissatisfaction. Here the consumer's coping style comes into play. Some consumers magnify the gap when the product isn't perfect and are highly dissatisfied; others minimize it and are less dissatisfied.[70]

POST-PURCHASE ACTIONS A satisfied consumer is more likely to purchase the product again and will also tend to say good things about the brand to others. Dissatisfied consumers may abandon or return the product. They may seek information that confirms its high value. They may take public action by complaining to the company, going to a lawyer, or complaining to other groups (such as business, private, or government agencies). Private actions include deciding to stop buying the product (*exit option*) or warning friends (*voice option*).[71]

Chapter 5 described CRM programs designed to build long-term brand loyalty. Post-purchase communications to buyers have been shown to result in fewer product returns and order cancellations. Computer companies, for example, can send a letter to new owners congratulating them on having selected a fine computer. They can place ads showing satisfied brand owners. They can solicit customer suggestions for improvements and list the location of available services. They can write intelligible instruction booklets. They can send owners a magazine containing articles describing new computer applications. In addition, they can provide good channels for speedy redress of customer grievances.

POST-PURCHASE USES AND DISPOSAL Marketers should also monitor how buyers use and dispose of the product (Figure 6.7). A key driver of sales frequency is product consumption rate—the more quickly buyers consume a product, the sooner they may be back in the market to repurchase it.

Consumers may fail to replace some products soon enough because they overestimate product life.[72] One strategy to speed replacement is to tie the act of replacing the product to a certain holiday, event, or time of year.

FIGURE 6.7

How Customers Use or
Dispose of Products

Source: Jacob Jacoby, et al.,
"What about Disposition?"
Journal of Marketing, July 1977,
p. 23. Reprinted with permission
from the *Journal of Marketing*,
published by the American
Marketing Association.

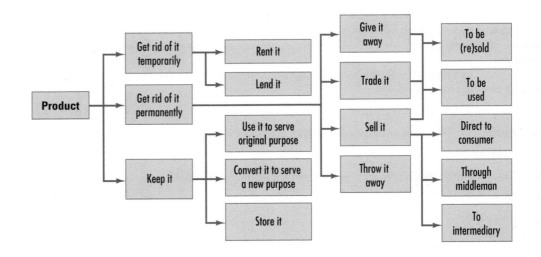

Oral B has tied toothbrush promotions to the springtime switch to daylight savings time. Another strategy is to provide consumers with better information about either (1) the time they first used the product or need to replace it or (2) its current level of performance. Batteries have built-in gauges that show how much power they have left, toothbrushes have colour indicators to indicate when the bristles are worn, and so on. Perhaps the simplest way to increase usage is to learn when actual usage is lower than recommended and persuade customers that more regular usage has benefits, overcoming potential hurdles.

If consumers throw the product away, the marketer needs to know how they dispose of it, especially if—like batteries, beverage containers, electronic equipment, and disposable diapers—it can damage the environment. There also may be product opportunities in disposed products: Vintage clothing shops, such as Savers, resell 2.5 billion pounds of used clothing annually; Diamond Safety buys finely ground used tires and then makes and sells tiles for playgrounds and flooring for athletic fields; and, unlike the usual potato chip maker, which discards some of the spud, Pringles converts the whole potato into dehydrated potato flakes that are rolled and cut into chips.[73]

Moderating Effects on Consumer Decision Making

The manner or path by which a consumer moves through the decision-making stages depends on several factors, including the level of involvement and extent of variety seeking, as follows.

LOW-INVOLVEMENT CONSUMER DECISION MAKING The expectancy-value model assumes a high level of **consumer involvement,** or engagement and active processing that the consumer undertakes in responding to a marketing stimulus.

Richard Petty and John Cacioppo's *elaboration likelihood model,* an influential model of attitude formation and change, describes how consumers make evaluations in both low- and high-involvement circumstances.[74] There are two means of persuasion in their model: The *central route,* in which attitude formation or change stimulates much thought and is based on the consumer's diligent, rational consideration of the most important product information; and the *peripheral route,* in which attitude formation or change provokes much less thought and results from the consumer's association of a brand with either positive or negative peripheral cues. *Peripheral cues* for consumers include a celebrity endorsement, a credible source, or any object that generates positive feelings.

Consumers follow the central route only if they possess sufficient motivation, ability, and opportunity. In other words, they must want to evaluate a brand in detail, have the necessary brand and product or service knowledge in memory, and have sufficient time and the proper setting. If any of those factors is lacking, consumers tend to follow the peripheral route and consider less central, more extrinsic factors in their decisions.

We buy many products under conditions of low involvement and without significant brand differences. Consider salt. If consumers keep reaching for the same brand in this category, it may be out of habit, not strong brand loyalty. Evidence suggests we have low involvement with most low-cost, frequently purchased products.

Marketers use four techniques to try to convert a low-involvement product into one of higher involvement. First, they can link the product to an engaging issue, as when Crest linked its toothpaste to avoiding cavities. Second, they can link the product to a personal situation—for example, fruit juice makers began to include calcium to fortify their drinks. Third, they might design advertising to trigger strong emotions related to personal values or ego defence, as when cereal makers began to advertise to adults the heart-healthy nature of cereals and the importance of living a long time to enjoy family life. Fourth, they might add an important feature—for example, when GE introduced "Soft White" light bulbs. These strategies at best raise consumer involvement from a low to a moderate level; they do not necessarily propel the consumer into highly involved buying behaviour.

If consumers will have low involvement with a purchase decision regardless of what the marketer can do, they are likely to follow the peripheral route. Marketers must give consumers one or more positive cues to justify their brand choice, such as frequent ad repetition, visible **sponsorships**, and vigorous PR to enhance brand familiarity. Other peripheral cues that can tip the balance in favour of the brand include a beloved celebrity endorser, attractive packaging, and an appealing promotion.

VARIETY-SEEKING BUYING BEHAVIOUR Some buying situations are characterized by low involvement but significant brand differences. Here consumers often do a lot of brand switching. Think about cookies. The consumer has some beliefs about cookies, chooses a brand without much evaluation, and evaluates the product during consumption. Next time, the consumer may reach for another brand out of a desire for a different taste. Brand switching occurs for the sake of variety, rather than dissatisfaction.

The market leader and the minor brands in this product category have different marketing strategies. The market leader will try to encourage habitual buying behaviour by dominating the shelf space with a variety of related but different product versions, avoiding out-of-stock conditions, and sponsoring frequent reminder advertising. Challenger firms will encourage variety seeking by offering lower prices, deals, coupons, free samples, and advertising that tries to break the consumer's purchase and consumption cycle and presents reasons for trying something new.

BEHAVIOURAL DECISION THEORY AND BEHAVIOURAL ECONOMICS

As you might guess from low-involvement decision making and variety seeking, consumers don't always process information or make decisions in a deliberate, rational manner. One of the most active academic research areas in marketing over the past three decades has been *behavioural decision theory* (BDT). Behavioural decision theorists have identified many situations in which consumers make seemingly irrational choices.

Table 6.5 summarizes some provocative findings from this research.[75]

What all these and other studies reinforce is that consumer behaviour is very constructive and the context of decisions really matters. Understanding how these effects show up in the marketplace can be crucial for marketers.

The work of behavioural decision theorists and other academics has also challenged predictions from economic theory and assumptions about rationality, leading to the emergence of the field of *behavioural economics*.[76] Here we review some of the issues in three broad areas—decision heuristics, framing, and other contextual effects. "Marketing Insight: Predictably Irrational" summarizes one in-depth treatment of the topic.

Decision Heuristics

Previously, we reviewed some common heuristics that occur with noncompensatory decision making. Other heuristics similarly come into play in everyday decision making when consumers forecast the likelihood of future outcomes or events.[77]

1. The **availability heuristic**—Consumers base their predictions on the quickness and ease with which a particular example of an outcome comes to mind. If an example comes to mind too easily, consumers might overestimate the likelihood of its happening. For example, a recent product failure may lead a consumer to inflate the likelihood of a future product failure and make him or her more inclined to purchase a product warranty.

2. The **representativeness heuristic**—Consumers base their predictions on how representative or similar the outcome is to other examples. One reason package appearances may be so similar for different brands in the same product category is that marketers want their products to be seen as representative of the category as a whole.

TABLE 6.5	SELECTED BEHAVIOURAL DECISION THEORY FINDINGS

- Consumers are more likely to choose an alternative (a home breadmaker) after a relatively inferior option (a slightly better, but significantly more expensive home breadmaker) is added to the available choice set.

- Consumers are more likely to choose an alternative that appears to be a compromise in the particular choice set under consideration, even if it is not the best alternative on any one dimension.

- The choices consumers make influence their assessment of their own tastes and preferences.

- Getting people to focus their attention more on one of two considered alternatives tends to enhance the perceived attractiveness and choice probability of that alternative.

- The way consumers compare products that vary in price and perceived quality (by features or brand name) and the way those products are displayed in the store (by brand or by model type) both affect their willingness to pay more for additional features or a better-known brand.

- Consumers who think about the possibility that their purchase decisions will turn out to be wrong are more likely to choose better-known brands.

- Consumers for whom possible feelings of regret about missing an opportunity have been made more relevant are more likely to choose a product currently on sale than wait for a better sale or buy a higher-priced item.

- Consumers' choices are often influenced by subtle (and theoretically inconsequential) changes in the way alternatives are described.

- Consumers who make purchases for later consumption appear to make systematic errors in predicting their future preferences.

- Consumers' predictions of their future tastes are not accurate—they do not really know how they will feel after consuming the same flavour of yogurt or ice cream several times.

- Consumers often overestimate the duration of their overall emotional reactions to future events (moves, financial windfalls, outcomes of sporting events).

- Consumers often overestimate their future consumption, especially if there is limited availability (which may explain why Black Jack and other gums have higher sales when availability is limited to several months per year than when they are offered year round).

- In anticipating future consumption opportunities, consumers often assume they will want or need more variety than they actually do.

- Consumers are less likely to choose alternatives with product features or promotional premiums that have little or no value, even when these features and premiums are optional (like the opportunity to purchase a collector's plate) and do not reduce the actual value of the product in any way.

- Consumers are less likely to choose products selected by others for reasons they find irrelevant, even when these other reasons do not suggest anything positive or negative about the product's values.

- Consumers' interpretations and evaluations of past experiences are greatly influenced by the ending and trend of events. A positive event at the end of a service experience can colour later reflections and evaluations of the experience as a whole.

3. The **anchoring and adjustment heuristic**—Consumers arrive at an initial judgment and then adjust it based on additional information. For services marketers, a strong first impression is critical to establish a favourable anchor so that subsequent experiences will be interpreted in a more favourable light.

Note that marketing managers also may use heuristics and be subject to biases in their own decision making.

| MARKETING INSIGHT | PREDICTABLY IRRATIONAL |

In a new book, Dan Ariely reviews some of his own research, as well as that of others, that shows that although consumers may think they are making well-reasoned, rational decisions, that is not often the case. As it turns out, a host of mental factors and unconscious cognitive biases conspire to result in seemingly irrational decision making in many different settings. Ariely believes these irrational decisions are not random but are systematic and predictable. As he says, we make the same "mistake" over and over. Here are some of the thought-provoking research insights he highlights:

- When selling a new product, marketers should be sure to compare it with something consumers already know about, even if the new product is literally new-to-the-world with few direct comparisons. Consumers find it difficult to judge products in isolation and feel more comfortable if they base a new decision at least in part on a past decision.

- Consumers find the lure of "free" almost irresistible. In one experiment, consumers were offered normally high-priced Lindt chocolate truffles for 15 cents and ordinary Hershey's Kisses for a penny. Customers had to pick one or the other, not both. Seventy-three percent of the customers went for the truffles. When the prices were cut to 14 cents for the truffles and free for the kisses, however, 69 percent of customers went for the Kisses, even though the truffles were actually a better deal.

- The "optimism bias" or "positivity illusion" is a pervasive effect that transcends gender, age, education, and nationality. People tend to overestimate their chances of experiencing a good outcome (having a successful marriage, healthy kids, or financial security) but underestimate their chances of experiencing a bad outcome (divorce, a heart attack, or a parking ticket).

In concluding his analysis, Ariely notes, "If I were to distill one main lesson from the research described in this book, it is that we are all pawns in a game whose forces we largely fail to comprehend."

Sources: Dan Ariely, *Predictably Irrational* (New York: HarperCollins, 2008); Dan Ariely, "The Curious Paradox of Optimism Bias," *BusinessWeek*, August 24 and 31, 2009, p. 48; Dan Ariely, "The End of Rational Economics," *Harvard Business Review*, July–August 2009, pp. 78–84; "A Manager's Guide to Human Irrationalities," *MIT Sloan Management Review*, Winter 2009, pp. 53–59; Russ Juskalian, "Not as Rational as We Think We Are," *USA Today*, March 17, 2008; Elizabeth Kolbert, "What Was I Thinking?" *New Yorker*, February 25, 2008; David Mehegan, "Experimenting on Humans," *Boston Globe*, March 18, 2008.

Framing

Decision framing is the manner in which choices are presented to and seen by a decision maker. A $200 cell phone may not seem that expensive in the context of a set of $400 phones but may seem very expensive if those phones cost $50. Framing effects are pervasive and can be powerful.

University of Chicago professors Richard Thaler and Cass Sunstein show how marketers can influence consumer decision making through what they call the *choice architecture*—the environment in which decisions are structured and buying choices are made. According to these researchers, in the right environment, consumers can be given a "nudge" via some small feature in the environment that attracts attention and alters behaviour. The researchers maintain that Nabisco is employing a smart choice architecture by offering 100-calorie snack packs, which have solid profit margins, while nudging consumers to make healthier choices.[78]

MENTAL ACCOUNTING Researchers have found that consumers use mental accounting when they handle their money.[79] **Mental accounting** refers to the way consumers code, categorize, and evaluate financial outcomes of choices. Formally, it is "the tendency to categorize *funds* or items of value even though there is no logical *basis* for the categorization, e.g., individuals often segregate their savings into separate accounts to meet different goals even though funds from any of the accounts can be applied to any of the goals."[80]

Consider the following two scenarios:

1. Assume you spend $50 to buy a ticket for a concert.[81] As you arrive at the show, you realize you've lost your ticket. You decide to buy a replacement.

2. Assume you decided to buy a ticket to a concert at the door. As you arrive at the show, you realize somehow you lost $50 along the way. You decide to buy the ticket anyway.

Which one would you be more likely to do? Most people choose scenario 2. Although you lost the same amount in each case—$50—in the first case, you may have mentally allocated $50 for going to a concert. Buying another ticket would exceed your mental concert budget. In the second case, the money you lost did not belong to any account, so you had not yet exceeded your mental concert budget.

According to Thaler, mental accounting is based on a set of core principles:

1. Consumers tend to *segregate gains.* When a seller has a product with more than one positive dimension, it is desirable to have the consumer evaluate each dimension separately. Listing multiple benefits of a large industrial product, for example, can make the sum of the parts seem greater than the whole.

2. Consumers tend to *integrate losses.* Marketers have a distinct advantage in selling something if its cost can be added to another large purchase. House buyers are more inclined to view additional expenditures favourably given the high price of buying a house.

3. Consumers tend to *integrate smaller losses with larger gains.* The "cancellation" principle might explain why withholding taxes from monthly paychecks is less troubling than large, lump-sum tax payments—the smaller withholdings are more likely to be absorbed by the larger pay amount.

4. Consumers tend to *segregate small gains from large losses.* The "silver lining" principle might explain the popularity of rebates on big-ticket purchases such as cars.

The principles of mental accounting are derived in part from prospect theory. **Prospect theory** maintains that consumers frame their decision alternatives in terms of gains and losses according to a value function. Consumers are generally loss-averse. They tend to overweight very low probabilities and underweight very high probabilities.

Mental accounting principles help predict whether consumers will or will not go to an entertainment event having lost a ticket or some money.

SUMMARY

1. Consumer behaviour is influenced by three factors: cultural (culture, subculture, and social class), social (reference groups, family, and social roles and statuses), and personal (age, stage in the life cycle, occupation, economic circumstances, lifestyle, personality, and self-concept). Research into these factors can provide clues to reach and serve consumers more effectively.

2. Five main psychological processes that affect consumer behaviour are motivation, perception, learning, emotions, and memory.

3. The typical buying process consists of the following sequence of events: problem recognition, information search, evaluation of alternatives, purchase decision, and post-purchase behaviour. The marketer's job is to understand the behaviour at each stage. The attitudes of others, unanticipated situational factors, and perceived risk may all affect the decision to buy, as will consumers' levels of post-purchase product satisfaction, use, and disposal, and the company's actions.

4. Consumers are constructive decision makers and subject to many contextual influences. They often exhibit low involvement in their decisions, using many heuristics as a result.

APPLICATIONS

Marketing Debate: Is Target Marketing Ever Bad?

As marketers increasingly tailor marketing programs to target market segments, some critics have denounced these efforts as exploitive. They see the preponderance of billboards advertising cigarettes and alcohol in low-income urban areas as taking advantage of a vulnerable market segment. Critics can be especially harsh in evaluating marketing programs that target African Americans and other minority groups, claiming they often employ stereotypes and inappropriate depictions. Others counter that targeting and positioning is critical to marketing, and that these marketing programs are an attempt to be relevant to a certain consumer group.

Take a position: Targeting minorities is exploitive *versus* Targeting minorities is a sound business practice.

Marketing Discussion: Mental Accounts

What mental accounts do you have in your mind about purchasing products or services? Do you have any rules you employ in spending money? Are they different from what other people do? Do you follow Thaler's four principles in reacting to gains and losses?

MARKETING **EXCELLENCE**

MAPLE LEAF FOODS: NATURAL SELECTIONS

Given today's increasingly hectic lifestyles, precooked meals and processed ingredients are becoming the norm for Canadian families to use in preparing their daily meals. However, these foods are not without their drawbacks and health concerns. For example, a study by the Harvard School of Public Health found that processed meat leads to a significantly higher risk of developing heart disease and Type 2 diabetes. To address the health concerns associated with processed food, Toronto-based Maple Leaf Foods introduced a new line of healthy deli meats called Natural Selections, made without preservatives or artificial ingredients.

Maple Leaf Foods had a difficult year in 2008. A listeriosis outbreak stemming from contamination at a meat processing plant brought the company considerable negative publicity, resulting in damages over $50 million. In an attempt to regain consumer confidence in its products, Maple Leaf responded to consumers' health concerns with the introduction of the Natural Selections line.

A study by Maple Leaf found that 58 percent of consumers couldn't even pronounce the ingredients in the foods they bought regularly. In order to enable consumers to make healthy choices, a large part of the marketing effort for Natural Selections has been focused on "simple ingredients you can actually pronounce." Deli meat isn't the only place where Maple Leaf is making its mark on the family meal. The bakery division has introduced new, healthy lines of bread, and the company has also launched a line of complete, healthy meals for the family on the go. Maple Leaf's goal is to drive these new product lines into the mainstream, and realize the benefits from being an innovator in a product category. By anticipating the needs of its customers and responding to them effectively, Maple Leaf has made significant progress in its image recovery, which may generate considerable rewards in the long run.

QUESTIONS

1. Use Maslow's Hierarchy of Needs to discuss the types of need that Maple Leaf addressed with its introduction of the Natural Selections line.

2. At which stage(s) of the buying-decision process are consumers most likely to pay attention to the ingredients in the foods they buy?

3. From your understanding of the elaboration likelihood model, discuss how the consumer's level of involvement while shopping for groceries would affect the importance they give to the ingredients or nutritional information provided on food packaging.

Sources: "You Are What You Eat...But Only 38 Per Cent of Canadians Know What's in Their Food," *Canada Newswire*, May 26, 2010; Nicole Baute, "Processed Meat Rich in Heart Risk, Study Finds," *Toronto Star*, May 18, 2010, p. 2; Eric Lam, "Maple Leaf Five-Year Plan Aims for 75% Boost in Profit Margin; Food-Processing Company Building Two Plants, Trimming Product Line by 60%," *Edmonton Journal*, October 7, 2010; Maple Leaf Foods website, www.mapleleaf.ca (viewed February 14, 2011).

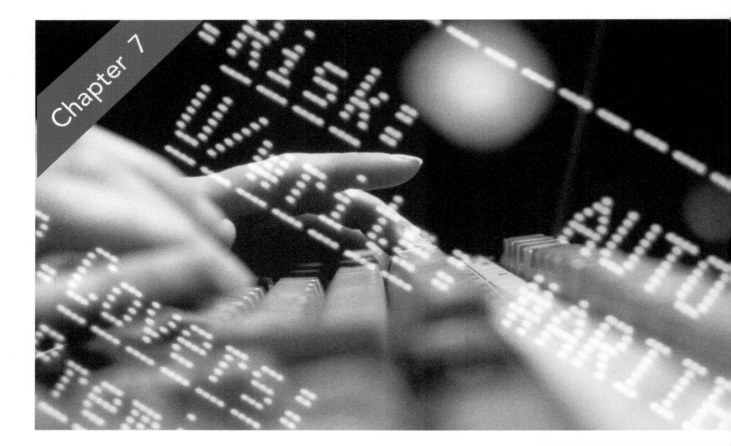

Chapter 7

In This Chapter, We Will Address the Following **Questions**

1. What is the business market, and how does it differ from the consumer market?

2. What buying situations do organizational buyers face?

3. Who participates in the business-to-business buying process?

4. How do business buyers make their decisions?

5. How can companies build strong relationships with business customers?

6. How do institutional buyers and government agencies do their buying?

Great-West Life offers a variety of financial solutions for both business and individual consumer markets.

Analyzing
Business Markets

Business organizations do not only sell; they also buy vast quantities of raw materials, manufactured components, plant and equipment, supplies, and business services. According to Industry Canada, there are over 1.1 million businesses with paid employees in Canada alone.[1] To create and capture value, sellers need to understand these organizations' needs, resources, policies, and buying procedures.

The Great-West Life Assurance Company (GWL), founded in 1891 in Winnipeg, has been helping its clients develop and manage their financial security plans for over a century. GWL provides a variety of insurance, investment, and retirement savings plans for organizational groups as well as individuals in Canada, United States, and Europe.

GWL has long been a leader in the group benefits marketplace in Canada. The company serves over 33 000 plan sponsors and plan members in Canada and handles about 50 million insurance claims for its Canadian plan members and their dependants each year. GWL recognizes the importance of group benefits in helping employers attract and retain employees. Its group plans, featuring benefits such as health, dental, critical illness, accidental death, and disability insurance, can be tailored to fit the specific needs of an organization, regardless of its size.

In offering group benefit plans, GWL shows many of the characteristics typical in business-to-business marketing. For example, GWL has fewer business than individual customers, but its revenue per business account is much larger. Although individuals may purchase their insurance products through an agent, organizations purchase directly from GWL. This, along with the fact that the purchase involves large amounts of money, leads GWL and its customers to develop long-term relationships. When dealing with its group customers, GWL has to be cognizant of the different parties involved in the buying organization. Because the final users of its financial security products are the employees of the customer organization, GWL has to keep their needs in mind while also recognizing that the finance, purchase, and human resource departments in the organization are likely to have different and possibly conflicting priorities. GWL also recognizes that business and individual customers are different in the way they go about making decisions. Dealing with its business customers involves a professional purchase process, and most often a team approach from both parties. Getting a business customer to make the purchase can take months or even years, but at the end, the returns are usually well worth the time and effort.[2]

Some of the world's most valuable brands belong to business marketers: ABB, Caterpillar, DuPont, FedEx, GE, Hewlett-Packard, IBM, Intel, and Siemens, to name a few. This includes some of Canada's largest brands, such as Suncor Energy, Bombardier, Encana, and CN Rail. Many principles of basic marketing also apply to business marketers. They need to embrace holistic marketing principles, such as building strong relationships with their customers, just like any marketer. But they also face some unique considerations in selling to other businesses. In this chapter, we will highlight some of the crucial similarities and differences for marketing in business markets.[3]

WHAT IS ORGANIZATIONAL BUYING?

Frederick E. Webster, Jr., and Yoram Wind define **organizational buying** as the decision-making process by which formal organizations establish the need for purchased products and services and identify, evaluate, and choose among alternative brands and suppliers.[4]

The Business Market versus the Consumer Market

The **business market** consists of all the organizations that acquire goods and services used in the production of other products or services that are sold, rented, or supplied to others. The major industries making up the business market are agriculture, forestry, and fisheries; mining; manufacturing; construction; transportation; communication; public utilities; banking, finance, and insurance; distribution; and services.

More dollars and items change hands in sales to business buyers than to consumers. Consider the process of producing and selling a simple pair of shoes. Hide dealers must sell hides to tanners, who sell leather to shoe manufacturers, who sell shoes to wholesalers, who sell shoes to retailers, who finally sell them to consumers. Each party in the supply chain also buys many other goods and services to support its operations.

Given the highly competitive nature of business-to-business markets, the biggest enemy to marketers here is commoditization.[5] Commoditization eats away margins and weakens customer loyalty. It can be overcome only if target customers are convinced that meaningful differences exist in the marketplace, and that the unique benefits of the firm's offerings are worth the added expense. Thus, a critical step in business-to-business marketing is to create and communicate relevant differentiation from competitors. Here is how a relatively small food distributor has survived competition from major industry players.

Tannis Food Distributors

A Canadian family-owned business operating for over 70 years in eastern Ontario and western Quebec, Tannis Food Distributors has adapted its business model over time to accommodate changing demands from its business customers. Carrying a vast line of food products, the company services business customers such as national/regional food chains, independent restaurants, fast-food operations, convenience stores, health-care units, and recreational centres. To stay ahead of the major food distributors that service all of North America, Tannis Food Distributors has marketed itself as the local and trusted choice. To improve its service and efficiency, the company developed an online web ordering system for its customers. To minimize delivery errors, the company invested in voice-driven software that prompts the staff exactly where to find the product in the warehouse once an order is received. Responding to the marketplace and constant improvement are what keep Tannis Food Distributors growing in a competitive industry.[6]

Business marketers face many of the same challenges as consumer marketers. In particular, understanding their customers and what they value is of paramount importance to both. A survey of top business-to-business firms identified the following as challenges they faced:[7]

1. Understanding deep customer needs in new ways
2. Identifying new opportunities for organic business growth
3. Improving value management techniques and tools
4. Calculating better marketing performance and accountability metrics
5. Competing and growing in global markets, particularly China
6. Countering the threat of product and service commoditization by bringing innovative offerings to market faster and moving to more competitive business models
7. Convincing C-level executives to embrace the marketing concept and support robust marketing programs

Business marketers contrast sharply with consumer markets in some ways, however:

■ *Fewer, larger buyers.* The business marketer normally deals with far fewer, much larger buyers than the consumer marketer does, particularly in such industries as aircraft engines and defence weapons. The fortunes of Goodyear tires, Cummins engines, Delphi control systems, and other automotive part suppliers depend on getting big contracts from just a handful of major automakers.

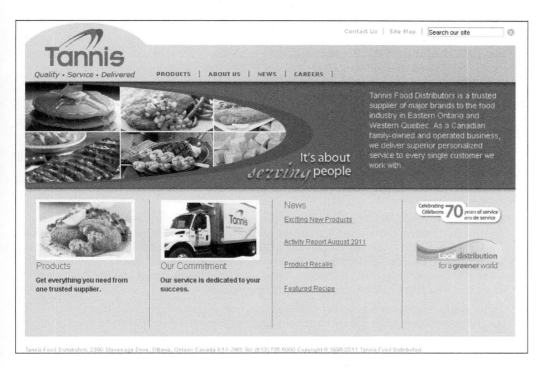

Tannis continuously makes improvements to its business processes.

- *Close supplier–customer relationship.* Because of the smaller customer base and the importance and power of the larger customers, suppliers are frequently expected to customize their offerings to individual business customer needs. Through its Supplier Added Value Effort ($AVE) program, Pittsburgh-based PPG Industries challenges its suppliers of maintenance, repair, and operating (MRO) goods and services to deliver on annual value-added/cost-savings proposals equalling at least 5 percent of their total annual sales to PPG. One preferred supplier submitted a suggestion to $AVE that reduced costs for a lighting project by $160 000 by negotiating discounted prices for new fixtures and fluorescent bulbs.[8] Business buyers often select suppliers that also buy from them. A paper manufacturer might buy from a chemical company that buys a considerable amount of its paper.

- *Professional purchasing.* Business goods are often purchased by trained purchasing agents, who must follow their organizations' purchasing policies, constraints, and requirements. Many of the buying instruments—for example, requests for quotations, proposals, and purchase contracts—are not typically found in consumer buying. Professional buyers spend their careers learning how to buy better. Many belong to the Purchasing Management Association of Canada (PMAC), which seeks to improve professional buyers' effectiveness and status. This means business marketers must provide greater technical data about their product and its advantages over competitors' products.

- *Multiple buying influences.* More people typically influence business buying decisions. Buying committees consisting of technical experts and even senior management are common in the purchase of major goods. Business marketers need to send well-trained sales representatives and sales teams to deal with the well-trained buyers.

- *Multiple sales calls.* A study by McGraw-Hill found that it took four to four-and-a-half calls to close an average industrial sale. In the case of capital equipment sales for large projects, it may take many attempts to fund a project, and the sales cycle—between quoting a job and delivering the product—is often measured in years.[9]

- *Derived demand.* The demand for business goods is ultimately derived from the demand for consumer goods. For this reason, the business marketer must closely monitor the buying patterns of ultimate consumers. For instance, aging of the Canadian population has been leading to an increased demand for condominiums, which in turn has been leading to an increased demand for construction material. Business buyers must also pay close attention to current and expected economic factors, such as the level of production, investment, consumer spending, and the interest rate. In a recession, business buyers reduce their investment in plant, equipment, and inventories. Business marketers can do little to stimulate total demand in this environment. They can only fight harder to increase or maintain their share of demand.

■ *Inelastic demand.* The total demand for many business goods and services is inelastic—that is, not much affected by price changes. Shoe manufacturers are not going to buy much more leather if the price of leather falls, nor will they buy much less leather if the price rises unless they can find satisfactory substitutes. Demand is especially inelastic in the short run because producers cannot make quick changes in production methods. Demand is also inelastic for business goods that represent a small percentage of the item's total cost, such as shoelaces.

■ *Fluctuating demand.* The demand for business goods and services tends to be more volatile than the demand for consumer goods and services. A given percentage increase in consumer demand can lead to a much larger percentage increase in the demand for plant and equipment necessary to produce the additional output. Economists refer to this as the *acceleration effect.* Sometimes a rise of only 10 percent in consumer demand can cause as much as a 200 percent rise in business demand for products in the next period; a 10 percent fall in consumer demand may cause a complete collapse in business demand.

■ *Geographically concentrated buyers.* About 57 percent of all Canadian businesses are located in Ontario and Quebec. Thirty-seven percent of Canada's businesses are in the Western provinces, and 6 percent are located in the Atlantic provinces. Ontario and Quebec are home to the country's auto industry, and Canada's high-tech firms are clustered in Ottawa, Montreal, and Toronto. The petroleum industry calls Calgary and Edmonton home, most grain output comes from the Prairie provinces, and New Brunswick attracts the telemarketing industry.[10]

■ *Direct purchasing.* Business buyers often buy directly from manufacturers rather than through intermediaries, especially items that are technically complex or expensive such as mainframes or aircraft.

Buying Situations

The business buyer faces many decisions in making a purchase. How many depends on the complexity of the problem being solved, newness of the buying requirement, number of people involved, and time required. Three types of buying situations are the straight rebuy, modified rebuy, and new task:[11]

■ *Straight rebuy.* In a straight rebuy, the purchasing department reorders supplies such as office supplies and bulk chemicals on a routine basis and chooses from suppliers on an approved list. The suppliers make an effort to maintain product and service quality and often propose automatic reordering systems to save time. "Out-suppliers" attempt to offer something new or exploit dissatisfaction with a current supplier. Their goal is to get a small order and then enlarge their purchase share over time.

■ *Modified rebuy.* The buyer in a modified rebuy wants to change product specifications, prices, delivery requirements, or other terms. This usually requires additional participants on both sides. The "in-suppliers" become nervous and want to protect the account. The out-suppliers see an opportunity to propose a better offer to gain some business.

■ *New task.* A new-task purchaser buys a product or service for the first time (an office building, a new security system). The greater the cost or risk, the larger the number of participants, and the greater their information gathering, the longer the time to a decision.[12]

The business buyer makes the fewest decisions in the straight rebuy situation and the most in the new-task situation. Over time, new-buy situations become straight rebuys and routine purchase behaviour.

New-task buying is the marketer's greatest opportunity and challenge. The process passes through several stages: awareness, interest, evaluation, trial, and adoption.[13] Mass media can be most important during the initial awareness stage; salespeople often have their greatest impact at the interest stage; and technical sources can be most important during the evaluation stage. Online selling efforts may be useful at all stages.

In the new-task situation, the buyer must determine product specifications, price limits, delivery terms and times, service terms, payment terms, order quantities, acceptable suppliers, and the selected supplier. Different participants influence each decision, and the order in which these decisions are made varies.

Because of the complicated selling required, many companies use a *missionary sales force* consisting of their most effective salespeople. The brand promise and the manufacturer's brand name recognition will be important in establishing trust and the customer's willingness to consider change.[14] The marketer also tries to reach as many key participants as possible and provide helpful information and assistance.

Once a customer has been acquired, in-suppliers are continuously seeking ways to add value to their market offer to facilitate rebuys. Often they do this by giving customers customized solutions, as Magna does.

Magna International

Magna International, based in Aurora, Ontario, is the most diversified automotive-parts supplier in the world. As of September 2010, Magna had 245 manufacturing operations and 80 product-development, engineering, and sales centres in 25 countries on five continents. Magna International's success comes from supplying automobile parts to virtually every major automobile manufacturer, alphabetically from Acura to Volvo. Magna has a history and culture of offering innovation and customization as a key supplier in the automobile industry. For example, thanks to its flexible manufacturing strategy and the MAGNA STEYR Production System (MSPS), Magna offers complete vehicle assembly. Magna can act as the general contractor: a one-stop shop from the idea to the complete vehicle, as Magna has done with popular vehicles such as the Jeep Grand Cherokee, BMW X3, and Chrysler Voyager.[15]

Customers considering dropping six or seven figures on one transaction for big-ticket goods and services want all the information they can get. One way to entice new buyers is to create a customer reference program in which satisfied existing customers act in concert with the company's sales and marketing department by agreeing to serve as references. Technology companies such as HP, Lucent, and Unisys have all employed such programs.

Business marketers are also recognizing the importance of their brand and how they must execute their marketing program well in a number of areas to gain marketplace success. Boeing, which makes everything from commercial airplanes to satellites, implemented the "One Company" brand strategy to unify all its different operations with a one-brand culture. The strategy was based in part on a triple helix representation: (1) enterprising spirit (why Boeing does what it does), (2) precision performance (how Boeing gets things done), and (3) defining the future (what Boeing achieves as a company).[16]

Systems Buying and Selling

Many business buyers prefer to buy a total problem solution from one seller. Called *systems buying*, this practice originated with government purchases of major weapons and communications systems. The government solicited bids from *prime contractors* that, if awarded the contract, would be responsible for bidding out and assembling the system's subcomponents from *second-tier contractors*. The prime contractor thus provided a turnkey solution, so-called because the buyer simply had to turn one key to get the job done. Organizations such as VIA Rail find this kind of buying to be more effective because they can then focus on the aspects of the business they know best.

VIA Rail and Nomad Digital

In December 2010, Canada's passenger train system upgraded its service to keep its customers connected and entertained during their trip. With mobile Internet access an essential part of daily life for many Canadians, especially business travellers, the Government of Canada and VIA Rail Canada chose Nomad Digital to provide its Wi-Fi service. Under the $6.3 million, five-year contract funded by the federal government and its Economic Action Plan, Nomad is responsible for the design, installation, operation, and maintenance of the Wi-Fi infrastructure on VIA's Ontario–Quebec Corridor passenger trains. This addition to VIA's trains will eventually be available on all routes across the country.[17]

Sellers have increasingly recognized that buyers like to purchase in this way, and many have adopted systems selling as a marketing tool. One variant of systems selling is *systems contracting*, in which a single supplier provides the buyer with its entire requirement of MRO supplies. During the contract period, the supplier also manages the customer's inventory. Shell Oil manages the oil inventories of many of its business customers and knows when they require replenishment. The customer benefits from reduced procurement and management costs and from price protection over the term of the contract. The seller benefits from lower operating costs thanks to steady demand and reduced paperwork.

Systems selling is a key industrial marketing strategy in bidding to build large-scale industrial projects, such as dams, steel factories, irrigation systems, sanitation systems, pipelines, utilities, and even new towns. Customers present potential suppliers with a list of project specifications and requirements. Project engineering firms must compete on price, quality, reliability, and other attributes to win contracts. Suppliers, however, are not just at the mercy of customer demands. Ideally, they're active with customers early in the process to influence the actual development of the specifications. Or they can go beyond the specifications to offer additional value in various ways, as the following example shows.

Selling to the Indonesian Government

The Indonesian government requested bids to build a cement factory near Jakarta. A U.S. firm made a proposal that included choosing the site, designing the factory, hiring the construction crews, assembling the materials and equipment, and turning over the finished factory to the Indonesian government. A Japanese firm, in outlining its proposal, included all these services, plus hiring and training the workers to run the factory, exporting the cement through its trading companies, and using the cement to build roads and new office buildings in Jakarta. Although the Japanese proposal involved more money, it won the contract. Clearly, the Japanese viewed the problem as not just building a cement factory (the narrow view of systems selling) but as contributing to Indonesia's economic development. They took the broadest view of the customer's needs, which is true systems selling.

PARTICIPANTS IN THE BUSINESS BUYING PROCESS

Who buys the trillions of dollars' worth of goods and services needed by business organizations? Purchasing agents are influential in straight-rebuy and modified-rebuy situations, whereas other department personnel are more influential in new-buy situations. Engineering personnel usually have a major influence in selecting product components, and purchasing agents dominate in selecting suppliers.[18]

The Buying Centre

Webster and Wind call the decision-making unit of a buying organization *the buying centre*. It consists of "all those individuals and groups who participate in the purchasing decision-making process, who share some common goals and the risks arising from the decisions."[19] The buying centre includes all members of the organization who play any of the following seven roles in the purchase-decision process:

1. *Initiators*—Users or others in the organization who request that something be purchased.

2. *Users*—Those who will use the product or service. In many cases, the users initiate the buying proposal and help define the product requirements.

3. *Influencers*—People who influence the buying decision, often by helping define specifications and providing information for evaluating alternatives. Technical personnel are particularly important influencers.

4. *Deciders*—People who decide on product requirements or on suppliers.

5. *Approvers*—People who authorize the proposed actions of deciders or buyers.

6. *Buyers*—People who have formal authority to select the supplier and arrange the purchase terms. Buyers may help shape product specifications, but they play their major role in selecting vendors and negotiating. In more complex purchases, buyers might include high-level managers.

7. *Gatekeepers*—People who have the power to prevent sellers or information from reaching members of the buying centre. For example, purchasing agents, receptionists, and telephone operators may prevent salespersons from contacting users or deciders.

Several people can occupy a given role, such as user or influencer, and one person may play multiple roles.[20] A purchasing manager, for example, often occupies the roles of buyer, influencer, and gatekeeper simultaneously: he or she can determine which sales reps can call on other people in the organization; what budget and other constraints to place on the purchase; and which firm will actually get the business, even though others (deciders) might select two or more potential vendors that can meet the company's requirements.

The typical buying centre has a minimum of five or six members and often has dozens. Some may be outside the organization, such as government officials, consultants, technical advisers, and other members of the marketing channel. One study found that 3.5 more people on average were engaged in making a business purchase decision in 2005 than in 2001.[21]

Buying Centre Influences

Buying centres usually include several participants with differing interests, authority, status, and persuasiveness, and sometimes very different decision criteria. Engineers may want to maximize the performance of the product; production people may want ease of use and reliability of supply; financial staff focus on the economics of the purchase; purchasing may be concerned with operating and replacement costs; union officials may emphasize safety issues.

Business buyers also have personal motivations, perceptions, and preferences influenced by their age, income, education, job position, personality, attitudes toward risk, and culture. Buyers definitely exhibit different buying styles. There are "keep-it-simple" buyers, "own-expert" buyers, "want-the-best" buyers, and "want-everything-done" buyers. Some younger, highly educated buyers are computer experts who conduct rigorous analyses of competitive proposals before choosing a supplier. Other buyers are "toughies" from the old school who pit competing sellers against one another, and in some companies, the purchasing powers-that-be are legendary.

Webster cautions that ultimately individuals, not organizations, make purchasing decisions.[22] Individuals are motivated by their own needs and perceptions in attempting to maximize the rewards (pay, advancement, recognition, and feelings of achievement) offered by the organization. Personal needs motivate their behaviour, but organizational needs legitimate the buying process and its outcomes. Thus, businesspeople are not buying products. They are buying solutions to two problems: the organization's economic and strategic problem, and their personal need for individual achievement and reward. In this sense, industrial buying decisions are both "rational" and "emotional"—they serve both the organization's and the individual's needs.[23]

Research by one industrial component manufacturer found that although top executives at its small- and medium-size customers were comfortable buying from other companies, they appeared to harbour subconscious insecurities about buying the manufacturer's product. Constant changes in technology had left them concerned about internal effects within the company. Recognizing this unease, the manufacturer retooled its selling approach to emphasize more emotional appeals and how its product line actually enabled the customer's employees to improve their performance, relieving management of the complications and stress of using the manufacturer's components.[24]

Recognizing these extrinsic, interpersonal influences, more industrial firms have put greater emphasis on strengthening their corporate brand. At one time, Emerson Electric, a global provider of power tools, compressors, electrical equipment, and engineering solutions, was a conglomerate of 60 autonomous— and sometimes anonymous—companies. A new CMO aligned the brands under a new global brand architecture and identity, allowing Emerson to achieve a broader presence so it could sell locally while leveraging its global brand name. Record sales and stock price highs soon followed.[25] SAS is another firm that recognized the importance of its corporate brand.

SAS

With sales of more than $2.3 billion and a huge fan club of IT customers, SAS, the business analytics software firm, seemed to be in an enviable position in 1999. Yet its image was what one industry observer called "a geek brand." In order to extend the company's reach beyond IT managers with Ph.D.s in math or statistical analysis, the company needed to connect with C-level executives in the largest companies—the kind of people who either didn't have a clue what SAS's software was and what to do with it, or who didn't think business analytics was a strategic issue. Working with its first outside ad agency ever, SAS emerged with a new logo; a new slogan, "The Power to Know"; and a series of TV spots and print ads in business publications such as *BusinessWeek*, *Forbes*, and *The Wall Street Journal*. One TV spot that exemplifies SAS's rebranding effort ran like this:

> The problem is not harvesting the new crop of e-business information. It's making sense of it. With e-intelligence from SAS, you can harness the information. And put the knowledge you need within reach. SAS. The Power to Know.

Subsequent research showed that SAS had made the transition to a mainstream business decision-making support brand and was seen as both user-friendly and necessary. Highly profitable and now one of the world's largest privately owned software companies, more than doubling its revenue stream since the brand change, SAS has met with just as much success inside the company. For 14 years, *Fortune* magazine has ranked it one of the best U.S. companies to work for; in 2010, the company was number one.[26]

Like many business-to-business firms, software giant SAS emphasizes its corporate brand in its marketing efforts.

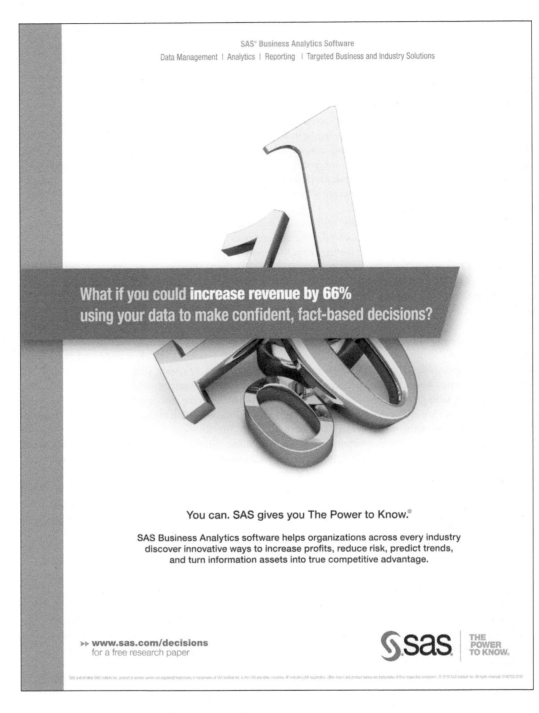

Targeting Firms and Buying Centres

Successful business-to-business marketing requires that business marketers know which types of companies to focus on in their selling efforts, as well as who to concentrate on within the buying centres in those organizations.

TARGETING FIRMS   As we will discuss in detail in Chapter 8, business marketers may divide the marketplace in many different ways to decide on the types of firms to which they will sell. Finding those business sectors with the greatest growth prospects, most profitable customers, and most effective communication channels to reach them is crucial, as Serenic found out.

Serenic Software Inc.

A producer of accounting management software based in Edmonton, Serenic Software Inc. markets its software products to nonprofits, international NGOs, and the public sector. In an attempt to communicate directly with potential business customers, the company switched its entire ad budget from print media (in industry publications) to online. The new marketing strategy focuses on the company's website and hosts regular webinars showcasing Serenic's products. The site also offers advice, demos, case studies, and testimonials. The company advertises the site using online ads including pay-per-click campaigns through Google AdWords. Serenic bids on keywords such as "donation management" to target its ads more effectively. Advertising online allows the company daily performance tracking and the ability to optimize poor-performing campaigns on an ongoing basis.[27]

It's also true, however, that as a slowing economy has put a stranglehold on large corporations' purchasing departments, the small- and midsize business markets are offering new opportunities for suppliers. See "Marketing Insight: Big Sales to Small Businesses" for more on this important B2B market.

In developing selling efforts, business marketers can also consider their customers' customers, or end users, if these are appropriate. Many business-to-business transactions are to firms using the products they purchase as components or ingredients in products they sell to the ultimate end users.

TARGETING WITHIN THE BUSINESS CENTRE Once it has identified the type of businesses on which to focus marketing efforts, the firm must then decide how best to sell to them. To target their efforts properly, business marketers need to figure out the following: Who are the major decision participants? What decisions do they influence? What is their level of influence? What evaluation criteria do they use? Consider the following example:

> A company sells nonwoven disposable surgical gowns to hospitals. The hospital staff who participate in this buying decision include the vice-president of purchasing, the operating-room administrator, and the surgeons. The vice-president of purchasing analyzes whether the hospital should buy disposable gowns or reusable gowns. If the findings favour disposable gowns, then the operating-room administrator compares various competitors' products and prices and makes a choice. This administrator considers absorbency, antiseptic quality, design, and cost, and normally buys the brand that meets functional requirements at the lowest cost. Surgeons influence the decision retroactively by reporting their satisfaction with the particular brand.

The business marketer is not likely to know exactly what kind of group dynamics take place during the decision process, although whatever information he or she can obtain about personalities and interpersonal factors is useful.

Small sellers concentrate on reaching the *key buying influencers*. Larger sellers go for *multilevel in-depth selling* to reach as many participants as possible. Their salespeople virtually live with high-volume customers. Companies must rely more heavily on their communications programs to reach hidden buying influences and keep current customers informed.[28]

Business marketers must periodically review their assumptions about buying centre participants. For years Kodak sold X-ray film to hospital lab technicians, but research indicated that professional administrators were increasingly making purchasing decisions. Kodak revised its marketing strategy and developed new advertising to reach out to these decision makers.

THE PURCHASING/PROCUREMENT PROCESS

In principle, business buyers seek to obtain the highest benefit package (economic, technical, service, and social) in relation to a market offering's costs. To make comparisons, they will try to translate all costs and benefits into monetary terms. A business buyer's incentive to purchase will be a function of the difference

---

Small businesses—defined as those with fewer than 100 employees—are responsible for employing over 5 million Canadians, or 48 percent of the private-sector labour force. According to Industry Canada, as of July 2010 there were over 1.1 million businesses in Canada with fewer than 100 employees, with over 5000 businesses starting up each month. All these new businesses need capital equipment, technology, supplies, and services. Look beyond Canada to small businesses around the world and you have a huge and growing B2B market. Here's how two top companies are reaching it:

■ IBM counts small to midsize customers as 20 percent of its business and has launched Express, a line of hardware, software services, and financing, for this market. IBM sells through regional reps as well as independent software vendors and resellers, and it supports its small–midsize push with millions of dollars in advertising annually, including in publications such as *American Banker* and *Inc.* The company has also directly targeted gay business owners with ads in *The Advocate* and *Out* and has partnered with nonprofits to reach racial and ethnic minority segments.

■ American Express has been steadily adding new features to its credit card for small business, which some small companies use to cover hundreds of thousands of dollars a month in cash needs. It has also created a small-business network called OPEN Forum to bring together various services, web tools, and discount programs with other giants such as FedEx, JetBlue, Hertz, and Hyatt. With OPEN Forum, American Express not only allows customers to save money on common expenses, it also encourages them to do much of their record keeping on its website and gain business insights.

Small and midsize businesses present huge opportunities and huge challenges. The market is large and fragmented by industry, size, and number of years in operation. Small-business owners are notably averse to long-range planning and often have an "I'll buy it when I need it" decision-making style. Here are some guidelines for selling to small businesses:

■ **Don't lump small and midsize businesses together.** There's a big gap between $1 million in revenue and $50 million, or between a start-up with 10 employees and a more mature business with 100 or more employees. IBM distinguishes its offerings to small and medium-sized businesses on its common website for the two.

■ **Do keep it simple.** Simplicity means having one supplier point of contact for all service problems, or one bill for all services and products. AT&T serves millions of small-business customers (fewer than 100 employees) with services that bundle Internet, local phone, long-distance phone, data management, business networking, web hosting, and teleconferencing.

■ **Do use the Internet.** Hewlett-Packard found that time-strapped small-business decision makers prefer to buy, or at least research, products and services online. So it designed a site targeted to small and midsize businesses. The site pulls in visitors through extensive advertising, direct mail, email campaigns, catalogues, and events.

■ **Don't forget about direct contact.** Even if a small-business owner's first point of contact is via the Internet, you still need to offer phone or face time.

■ **Do provide support after the sale.** Small businesses want partners, not pitchmen. When the DeWitt Company, a 100-employee landscaping products business, purchased a large piece of machinery from Moeller, the company's president paid DeWitt's CEO a personal visit and stayed until the machine was up and running properly.

■ **Do your homework.** The realities of small or midsize business management are different from those of a large corporation. Microsoft created a small fictional executive research firm, Southridge, and baseball-style trading cards of its key decision makers to help Microsoft employees tie sales strategies to small-business realities.

Sources: Based on "Key Small Business Statistics—July 2010: How Many Businesses Are There in Canada?" *Industry Canada*, www.ic.gc.ca/eic/site/sbrp-rppe.nsf/eng/rd02493.html (viewed March 3, 2011); Barnaby J. Feder, "When Goliath Comes Knocking on David's Door," *New York Times*, May 6, 2003; Jay Greene, "Small Biz: Microsoft's Next Big Thing?" *BusinessWeek*, April 21, 2003, pp. 72–73; Jennifer Gilbert, "Small But Mighty," *Sales & Marketing Management*, January 2004, pp. 30–35; www.sba.gov; www.openforum.com; www-304.ibm.com/businesscenter/smb/us/en.

between perceived benefits and perceived costs.[29] The marketer's task is to construct a profitable offering that delivers superior customer value to the target buyers.

Business marketers must therefore ensure that customers fully appreciate how the firm's offerings are different and better. *Framing* occurs when customers are given a perspective or point of view that allows the firm to put its best foot forward. Framing can be as simple as making sure customers realize all the benefits or cost savings afforded by the firm's offerings, or becoming more involved and influential in the thought process behind how customers view the economics of purchasing, owning, using, and disposing product offerings. Framing requires understanding how business customers currently think of and choose among products and services, and then determining how they *should* ideally think and choose.

Supplier diversity is a benefit that may not have a price tag but that business buyers overlook at their risk. As the CEOs of many of the country's largest companies see it, a diverse supplier base is a business imperative. Minority suppliers are the fastest-growing segment of today's business landscape. Pfizer is one company that makes use of such suppliers.

Pfizer

One of the biggest names in pharmaceuticals, Pfizer, views its supplier-diversity program as an essential tool in connecting with customers. Chief Diversity Officer Karen Boykin-Towns directs diversity efforts that include recruting and developing talent inside the company, as well as engaging with customers and suppliers outside the company. For leadership, Pfizer also relies on a diversity and inclusion worldwide council and an infrastructure of "ambassadors" throughout the company. Pfizer concentrates its diversity efforts on women, the LGBT community, people with disabilities, Latinos and Hispanics, Asian Pacific Islanders, U.S. Caribbeans, and African Americans. The company has spent about $700 million on 2400 minority and women suppliers. Pfizer has even developed a mentoring program that identifies women and minority suppliers that need help growing, whether it's designing a better website or building a better business plan. Pfizer managers meet with the owners, often on-site, to figure out what they need.[30]

In the past, purchasing departments occupied a low position in the management hierarchy, in spite of often managing more than half the company's costs. Recent competitive pressures have led many companies to upgrade their purchasing departments and elevate administrators to vice-presidential rank. These new, more strategically oriented purchasing departments have a mission to seek the best value from fewer and better suppliers. Some multinationals have even elevated them to "strategic supply departments" with responsibility for global sourcing and partnering. At Caterpillar, purchasing, inventory control, production scheduling, and traffic have been combined into one department. Here are other companies that have benefited from improving their business buying practices.

- Rio Tinto is a world leader in finding, mining, and processing the earth's mineral resources, with a significant presence in North America and Australia. Coordinating with its suppliers was time consuming, so Rio Tinto embarked on an electronic commerce strategy with one key supplier. Both parties have reaped significant benefits from this new arrangement. In many cases, orders are being filled in the supplier's warehouse within minutes of being transmitted, and the supplier is now able to take part in a pay-on-receipt program that has shortened Rio Tinto's payment cycle to around ten days.[31]

- Mitsui & Co. Ltd is a leading Japanese trading firm that owns more than 850 companies and subsidiaries. When the firm took its purchase orders and payments transactions for one group online, it reduced the cost of purchase transactions by 50 percent and increased customer satisfaction due to greater process efficiencies.[32]

- Medline Industries, the largest privately owned manufacturer and distributor of health-care products in the United States, used software to integrate its view of customer activity across online and direct sales channels. The results? The firm enhanced its product margin by 3 percent, improved customer retention by 10 percent, reduced revenue lost to pricing errors by 10 percent, and enhanced the productivity of its sales representatives by 20 percent.[33]

The upgrading of purchasing means business marketers must upgrade their sales staff to match the higher calibre of today's business buyers.

STAGES IN THE BUYING PROCESS

We're ready to describe the general stages in the business buying-decision process. Patrick J. Robinson and his associates identified eight stages and called them *buyphases*.[34] The model in Table 7.1 is the *buygrid* framework.

In modified-rebuy or straight-rebuy situations, some stages are compressed or bypassed. For example, the buyer normally has a favourite supplier or a ranked list of suppliers and can skip the search and proposal solicitation stages. Here are some important considerations in each of the eight stages.

Problem Recognition

The buying process begins when someone in the company recognizes a problem or need that can be met by acquiring a good or service. The recognition can be triggered by internal or external stimuli. The internal stimulus might be a decision to develop a new product that requires new equipment and materials, or a machine that breaks down and requires new parts. Or purchased material turns out to be unsatisfactory and the company searches for another supplier, lower prices, or better quality. Externally, the buyer may get new ideas at a trade show, see an ad, or receive a call from a sales representative who offers a better product or a lower price. Business marketers can stimulate problem recognition by direct mail, telemarketing, and visits to prospects.

General Need Description and Product Specification

Next, the buyer determines the needed item's general characteristics and required quantity. For standard items, this is simple. For complex items, the buyer will work with others—engineers, users—to define characteristics such as reliability, durability, or price. Business marketers can help by describing how their products meet or even exceed the buyer's needs.

The buying organization now develops the item's technical specifications. Often, the company will assign a product value–analysis engineering team to the project. *Product value analysis (PVA)* is an approach to cost reduction that studies whether components can be redesigned or standardized or made by cheaper methods of production *without adversely affecting product performance*. The PVA team will identify overdesigned components, for instance, that last longer than the product itself. Tightly written specifications allow the buyer to refuse components that are too expensive or that fail to meet specified standards. When HP won the Institute of Scrap Recycling Industries' first Design for Recycling Award through an application of PVA methods, it received this accolade:

> HP has worked for many years to design products that are easier to recycle. The firm operates several recycling facilities, which allows it to determine the most effective design features to facilitate product recycling. HP has developed standards that integrate clear design guidelines and checklists into every product's design process to assess and improve recyclability. Hewlett-Packard's design process includes: Using modular design to allow components to be removed, upgraded, or replaced; eliminating glues and adhesives by using, for example, snap-in features; marking plastic parts weighing more than 25g according to ISO 11469 international standards, to

TABLE 7.1	BUYGRID FRAMEWORK: MAJOR STAGES (BUYPHASES) OF THE INDUSTRIAL BUYING PROCESS IN RELATION TO MAJOR BUYING SITUATIONS (BUYCLASSES)			
			Buyclasses	
		New Task	Modified Rebuy	Straight Rebuy
Buyphases	1. Problem recognition	Yes	Maybe	No
	2. General need description	Yes	Maybe	No
	3. Product specification	Yes	Yes	Yes
	4. Supplier search	Yes	Maybe	No
	5. Proposal solicitation	Yes	Maybe	No
	6. Supplier selection	Yes	Maybe	No
	7. Order-routine specification	Yes	Maybe	No
	8. Performance review	Yes	Yes	Yes

speed up materials identification during recycling; reducing the number and types of materials used; using single plastic polymers; using recycled plastic; using moulded-in colours and finishes instead of paint, coatings, or plating.[35]

Suppliers can use product value analysis as a tool for positioning themselves to win an account. Regardless, it is important to eliminate excessive costs. Mexican cement giant Cemex is famed for "The Cemex Way," which uses high-tech methods to squeeze out inefficiencies.[36]

Supplier Search

The buyer next tries to identify the most appropriate suppliers through trade directories, contacts with other companies, trade advertisements, trade shows, and the Internet.[37] The move to Internet purchasing has far-reaching implications for suppliers and will change the shape of purchasing for years to come.[38] Companies that purchase over the Internet are using electronic marketplaces in several forms:

- *Catalogue sites.* Companies can order thousands of items through electronic catalogues distributed by e-procurement software, such as Grainger's.

- *Vertical markets.* Companies buying industrial products such as plastics, steel, or chemicals or services such as logistics or media can go to specialized websites (called e-hubs). Plastics.com allows plastics buyers to search the best prices among thousands of plastics sellers.

- *"Pure Play" auction sites.* Ritchie Bros. Auctioneers is the world's largest industrial auctioneer, with more than 40 auction sites worldwide. It sold $3.5 billion of used and unused equipment at more than 300 unreserved auctions in 2009, including a wide range of heavy equipment, trucks, and other assets for the construction, transportation, agricultural, material handling, mining, forestry, petroleum, and marine industries. While most people prefer to bid in person at Ritchie Bros. auctions, they are also able to bid online in real time at rbauction.com—the company's multilingual website. In 2009, 33 percent of the bidders at Ritchie Bros. auctions bid over the Internet; online bidders purchased $830 million of equipment.[39]

- *Spot (or exchange) markets.* In spot electronic markets, prices change by the minute. ChemConnect.com is an online exchange for buyers and sellers of bulk chemicals such as benzene, and it's a B2B success in an arena littered with failed sites. First to market, it is now the biggest online exchange for chemical trading, with 1 million barrels traded daily. Customers such as Vanguard Petroleum Corp. in Houston conduct about 15 percent of their spot purchases and sales of natural gas liquids on ChemConnect's commodities trading site.

- *Private exchanges.* Hewlett-Packard, IBM, and Walmart operate private exchanges to link with specially invited groups of suppliers and partners over the web.

- *Barter markets.* In barter markets, participants offer to trade goods or services.

- *Buying alliances.* Several companies buying the same goods can join together to form purchasing consortia to gain deeper discounts on volume purchases. TopSource is an alliance of firms in the retail and wholesale food-related businesses.

Online business buying offers several advantages: it shaves transaction costs for both buyers and suppliers, reduces time between order and delivery, consolidates purchasing systems, and forges more direct relationships between partners and buyers. On the downside, it may help to erode supplier–buyer loyalty and create potential security problems. Companies such as Elastic Path are well aware that credibility and customer relationships are important factors when it comes to online buying.

Elastic Path Software Inc.

Elastic Path Software Inc., a Vancouver-based developer of e-commerce systems for online retailers, positions itself as a credible leader in e-commerce by regularly producing reports on best practices in automated checkout processes. To further communicate this credibility to online retailers, the company has developed a blog that regularly reports on trends in online commerce, web design, and search marketing. Elastic Path realized that prospects do not want to be contacted with sales pitches, at least not until the company proves itself as a credible and customer-focused seller. The "Get Elastic" blog offers "no-strings attached" content that informs and entertains its readers. The relationship it has with its readers is built on trust and credibility—a great start to any profitable business relationship. So far the blog has gained 2400 subscribers at the cost of not much more than the blogger's time.[40]

E-PROCUREMENT Websites are organized around two types of e-hubs: *vertical hubs* centred on industries (plastics, steel, chemicals, paper) and *functional hubs* (logistics, media buying, advertising, energy management). In addition to using these websites, companies can use e-procurement in other ways:

- *Set up direct extranet links to major suppliers.* A company can set up a direct e-procurement account at Dell or Office Depot, for instance, and its employees can make their purchases this way.

- *Form buying alliances.* A number of major retailers and manufacturers—such as Acosta, Ahold, Best Buy, Carrefour, Family Dollar Stores, Lowe's, Safeway, Sears, SUPERVALU, Target, Walgreens, Walmart, and Wegmans Food Markets—are part of a data-sharing alliance called 1SYNC. Several auto companies (GM, Ford, Chrysler) formed Covisint for the same reason. Covisint is the leading provider of services that can integrate crucial business information and processes between partners, customers, and suppliers. The company has now also targeted health care to provide similar services.

- *Set up company buying sites.* General Electric formed the Trading Process Network (TPN), where it posts *requests for proposals (RFPs),* negotiates terms, and places orders.

Moving into e-procurement means more than acquiring software; it requires changing purchasing strategy and structure. However, the benefits are many: aggregating purchasing across multiple departments yields larger, centrally negotiated volume discounts; a smaller purchasing staff; and less buying of substandard goods from outside the approved list of suppliers.

LEAD GENERATION The supplier's task is to ensure it is considered when customers are—or could be—in the market and searching for a supplier. Identifying good leads and converting them to sales requires the marketing and sales organizations to take a coordinated, multichannel approach to the role of trusted adviser to prospective customers. Marketing must work together with sales to define what makes a "sales ready" prospect and cooperate to send the right messages via sales calls, trade shows, online activities, PR, events, direct mail, and referrals.[41]

Marketing must find the right balance between the quantity and quality of leads. Too many leads, even of high quality, and the sales force may be overwhelmed and allow promising opportunities to fall through the cracks; too few or low-quality leads and the sales force may become frustrated or demoralized.[42] To proactively generate leads, suppliers need to know about their customers. They can obtain background information from vendors such as Dun & Bradstreet and InfoUSA or information-sharing websites such as Jigsaw and LinkedIn.[43]

Suppliers that lack the required production capacity or suffer from a poor reputation will be rejected. Those that qualify may be visited by the buyer's agents, who will examine the suppliers' manufacturing facilities and meet their staff. After evaluating each company, the buyer will end up with a short list of qualified suppliers. Many professional buyers have forced suppliers to change their marketing to increase their likelihood of making the cut.

Proposal Solicitation

The buyer next invites qualified suppliers to submit proposals. If the item is complex or expensive, the proposal will be written and detailed. After evaluating the proposals, the buyer will invite a few suppliers to make formal presentations.

Business marketers must be skilled in researching, writing, and presenting proposals. Written proposals should be marketing documents that describe value and benefits in customer terms. Oral presentations must inspire confidence and position the company's capabilities and resources so they stand out from the competition. Proposals and selling are often team efforts. Pittsburgh-based Cutler-Hammer developed "pods" of salespeople focused on a particular geographic region, industry, or market concentration. Salespeople can leverage the knowledge and expertise of co-workers instead of working in isolation.[44]

Supplier Selection

Before selecting a supplier, the buying centre will specify and rank desired supplier attributes, often using a supplier-evaluation model such as the one in Table 7.2.

To develop compelling value propositions, business marketers need to better understand how business buyers arrive at their valuations.[45] Researchers studying how business marketers assess customer value found eight different *customer value assessment (CVA)* methods. Companies tended to use the simpler methods, although the more sophisticated ones promise to produce a more accurate picture of customer value propositions (see "Marketing Memo: Developing Compelling Customer Value Propositions").

The choice of attributes and their relative importance varies with the buying situation. Delivery reliability, price, and supplier reputation are important for routine-order products. For procedural-problem products, such as a copying machine, the three most important attributes are technical service,

---

TABLE 7.2 | AN EXAMPLE OF VENDOR ANALYSIS

Attributes		Rating Scale			
	Importance Weights	Poor (1)	Fair (2)	Good (3)	Excellent (4)
Price	0.30				x
Supplier reputation	0.20			x	
Product reliability	0.30				x
Service reliability	0.10		x		
Supplier flexibility	0.10			x	

Total Score: 0.30(4) + 0.20(3) + 0.30(4) + 0.10(2) + 0.10(3) = 3.5

---

supplier flexibility, and product reliability. For political-problem products that stir rivalries in the organization (such as the choice of a computer system), the most important attributes are price, supplier reputation, product reliability, service reliability, and supplier flexibility.

OVERCOMING PRICE PRESSURES The buying centre may attempt to negotiate with preferred suppliers for better prices and terms before making the final selection. Despite moves toward strategic sourcing, partnering, and participation in cross-functional teams, buyers still spend a large chunk of their time haggling with suppliers on price. The number of price-oriented buyers can vary by country, depending on customer preferences for different service configurations and characteristics of the customer's organization.[46]

Marketers can counter requests for a lower price in a number of ways. They may be able to show evidence that the total cost of ownership, that is, the life-cycle cost of using their product, is lower than for competitors' products. They can cite the value of the services the buyer now receives, especially if they are superior to those offered by competitors. Research shows that service support and personal interactions, as well as a supplier's know-how and ability to improve customers' time to market, can be useful differentiators in achieving key-supplier status.[47]

Improving productivity helps alleviate price pressures. Burlington Northern Santa Fe Railway has tied 30 percent of employee bonuses to improvements in the number of railcars shipped per mile.[48] Some firms are using technology to devise novel customer solutions. With web technology and tools, Vistaprint printers can offer professional printing to small businesses that previously could not afford it.[49]

Some companies handle price-oriented buyers by setting a lower price but establishing restrictive conditions: (1) limited quantities, (2) no refunds, (3) no adjustments, and (4) no services.[50]

- Cardinal Health set up a bonus-dollars plan and gave points according to how much the customer purchased. The points could be turned in for extra goods or free consulting.
- GE is installing diagnostic sensors in its airline engines and railroad engines. It is now compensated for hours of flight or railroad travel.
- IBM is now more of a "service company aided by products" than a "product company aided by services." It can sell computer power on demand (like video on demand) as an alternative to selling computers.

Solution selling can also alleviate price pressure and comes in different forms. Here are three examples:[51]

- *Solutions to enhance customer revenues.* Hendrix UTD has used its sales consultants to help farmers deliver an incremental animal weight gain of 5 percent to 10 percent over competitors.
- *Solutions to decrease customer risks.* ICI Explosives formulated a safer way to ship explosives for quarries.
- *Solutions to reduce customer costs.* W. W. Grainger employees work at large customer facilities to reduce materials management costs.

More firms are seeking solutions that increase benefits and reduce costs enough to overcome any low-price concerns.

| MARKETING **MEMO** | DEVELOPING COMPELLING CUSTOMER VALUE PROPOSITIONS |

To command price premiums in competitive B2B markets, firms must create compelling customer value propositions. The first step is to research the customer. Here are a number of productive research methods:

1. **Internal engineering assessment**—Have company engineers use laboratory tests to estimate the product's performance characteristics. However, this approach ignores the fact that the product will have different economic value in different applications.

2. **Field value-in-use assessment**—Interview customers about how costs of using a new product compare with those of using an incumbent. The task is to assess how much each cost element is worth to the buyer.

3. **Focus-group value assessment**—Ask customers in a focus group what value they would put on potential market offerings.

4. **Direct survey questions**—Ask customers to place a direct dollar value on one or more changes in the market offering.

5. **Conjoint analysis**—Ask customers to rank their preferences for alternative market offerings or concepts. Use statistical analysis to estimate the implicit value placed on each attribute.

6. **Benchmarks**—Show customers a benchmark offering and then a new-market offering. Ask how much more they would pay for the new offering or how much less they would pay if certain features were removed from the benchmark offering.

7. **Compositional approach**—Ask customers to attach a monetary value to each of three alternative levels of a given attribute. Repeat for other attributes, then add the values together for any offer configuration.

8. **Importance ratings**—Ask customers to rate the importance of different attributes and their suppliers' performance on each.

Having done this research, you can specify the customer value proposition, following a number of important principles. First, clearly substantiate value claims by concretely specifying the differences between your offerings and those of competitors on the dimensions that matter most to the customer. Rockwell Automation determined the cost savings customers would realize from purchasing its pump instead of a competitor's, by using industry-standard metrics of functionality and performance: kilowatt-hours spent, number of operating hours per year, and dollars per kilowatt hour. Also, make the financial implications obvious.

Second, document the value delivered by creating written accounts of cost savings or added value that existing customers have actually captured by using your offerings. Chemical producer Akzo Nobel conducted a two-week pilot on a production reactor at a prospective customer's facility to document points-of-parity and points-of-difference of its high-purity metal organics product.

Finally, make sure the method of creating a customer value proposition is well-implemented within the company, and train and reward employees for developing a compelling proposition. Quaker Chemical conducts training programs for its managers that include a competition to develop the best proposals.

Sources: James C. Anderson, Nirmalya Kumar, and James A. Narus, *Value Merchants: Demonstrating and Documenting Superior Value in Business Markets* (Boston: Harvard Business School Press, 2007); James C. Anderson, James A. Narus, and Wouter van Rossum, "Customer Value Propositions in Business Markets," *Harvard Business Review*, March 2006, pp. 2–10; James C. Anderson and James A. Narus, "Business Marketing: Understanding What Customers Value," *Harvard Business Review*, November 1998, pp. 53–65.

Risk and gain sharing can offset price reductions that customers request. Suppose Medline, a hospital supplier, signs an agreement with Highland Park Hospital promising $350 000 in savings over the first 18 months in exchange for getting a tenfold increase in the hospital's share of supplies. If Medline achieves less than this promised savings, it will make up the difference. If Medline achieves substantially more than promised, it participates in the extra savings. To make such arrangements work, the supplier must be willing to help the customer build a historical database, reach an agreement for measuring benefits and costs, and devise a dispute resolution mechanism.

NUMBER OF SUPPLIERS Companies are increasingly reducing the number of their suppliers. Ford, Motorola, and Honeywell have cut their number of suppliers 20 percent to 80 percent. These companies want their chosen suppliers to be responsible for a larger component system, they want them to achieve continuous quality and performance improvement, and at the same time they want them to lower prices each year by a given percentage. They expect their suppliers to work closely with them during product development, and they value their suggestions.

There is even a trend toward single sourcing, though companies that use multiple sources often cite the threat of a labour strike as the biggest deterrent to single sourcing. Companies may also fear that single suppliers will become too comfortable in the relationship and lose their competitive edge.

Order-Routine Specification

After selecting suppliers, the buyer negotiates the final order, listing the technical specifications, quantity needed, expected time of delivery, return policies, warranties, and so on. Many industrial buyers lease heavy equipment such as machinery and trucks. The lessee gains a number of advantages: the latest products, better service, the conservation of capital, and some tax advantages. The lessor often ends up with a larger net income and the chance to sell to customers that could not afford outright purchase.

In the case of maintenance, repair, and operating items, buyers are moving toward blanket contracts rather than periodic purchase orders. A blanket contract establishes a long-term relationship in which the supplier promises to resupply the buyer as needed, at agreed-upon prices, over a specified period of time. Because the seller holds the stock, blanket contracts are sometimes called *stockless purchase plans.* The buyer's computer automatically sends an order to the seller when stock is needed. This system locks suppliers in tighter with the buyer and makes it difficult for out-suppliers to break in unless the buyer becomes dissatisfied with prices, quality, or service.

Companies that fear a shortage of key materials are willing to buy and hold large inventories. They will sign long-term contracts with suppliers to ensure a steady flow of materials. DuPont, Ford, and several other major companies regard long-term supply planning as a major responsibility of their purchasing managers. For example, General Motors wants to buy from fewer suppliers, who must be willing to locate close to its plants and produce high-quality components. Business marketers are also setting up extranets with important customers to facilitate and lower the cost of transactions. Customers enter orders that are automatically transmitted to the supplier.

Some companies go further and shift the ordering responsibility to their suppliers in systems called *vendor-managed inventory* (VMI). These suppliers are privy to the customer's inventory levels and take responsibility for replenishing automatically through *continuous replenishment programs.* Plexco International AG supplies audio, lighting, and vision systems to the world's leading automakers. Its VMI program with its 40 suppliers resulted in significant time and cost savings and allowed the company to use former warehouse space for productive manufacturing activities.[52]

Performance Review

The buyer periodically reviews the performance of the chosen supplier(s) using one of three methods. The buyer may contact end users and ask for their evaluations, rate the supplier on several criteria using a weighted-score method, or aggregate the cost of poor performance to come up with adjusted costs of purchase, including price. The performance review may lead the buyer to continue, modify, or end a supplier relationship.

Many companies have set up incentive systems to reward purchasing managers for good buying performance, in much the same way sales personnel receive bonuses for good selling performance. These systems lead purchasing managers to increase pressure on sellers for the best terms.

MANAGING BUSINESS-TO-BUSINESS CUSTOMER RELATIONSHIPS

To improve effectiveness and efficiency, business suppliers and customers are exploring different ways to manage their relationships.[53] Closer relationships are driven in part by supply chain management, early supplier involvement, and purchasing alliances.[54] Cultivating the right relationships with business is paramount for any holistic marketing program.

Business-to-business marketers are avoiding "spray and pray" approaches to attracting and retaining customers, in favour of homing in on their targets and developing one-to-one marketing approaches. They are increasingly using online social media in the form of company blogs, online press releases, and forums or discussion groups to communicate with existing as well as prospective customers.

Some companies deliberately keep their customer lists small to be able to service them more effectively, as the following example shows.

One study found that the closest relationships between customers and suppliers arose when the supply was important to the customer and there were procurement obstacles, such as complex purchase requirements and few alternative suppliers.[61] Another study suggested that greater vertical coordination between buyer and seller through information exchange and planning is usually necessary only when high environmental uncertainty exists and specific investments (described next) are modest.[62]

Business Relationships: Risks and Opportunism

Researchers have noted that establishing a customer–supplier relationship creates tension between safeguarding (ensuring predictable solutions) and adaptation (allowing for flexibility for unanticipated events). Vertical coordination can facilitate stronger customer–seller ties but at the same time may increase the risk to the customer's and supplier's specific investments. *Specific investments* are those expenditures tailored to a particular company and value chain partner (investments in company-specific training, equipment, and operating procedures or systems).[63] They help firms grow profits and achieve their positioning.[64] Xerox worked closely with its suppliers to develop customized processes and components that reduced its copier manufacturing costs by 30 percent to 40 percent. In return, suppliers received sales and volume guarantees, an enhanced understanding of their customer's needs, and a strong position with Xerox for future sales.[65]

Specific investments, however, also entail considerable risk to both customer and supplier. Transaction theory from economics maintains that because these investments are partially sunk, they lock firms into a particular relationship. Sensitive cost and process information may need to be exchanged. A buyer may be vulnerable to holdup because of switching costs; a supplier may be more vulnerable because it has dedicated assets and/or technology/knowledge at stake. In terms of the latter risk, consider the following example:[66]

> An automobile component manufacturer wins a contract to supply an under-hood component to an original equipment manufacturer (OEM). A one-year, sole-source contract safeguards the supplier's OEM-specific investments in a dedicated production line. However, the supplier may also be obliged to work (noncontractually) as a partner with the OEM's internal engineering staff, using linked computing facilities to exchange detailed engineering information and coordinate frequent design and manufacturing changes over the term of the contract. These interactions could reduce costs and/or increase quality by improving the firm's responsiveness to marketplace changes. But they could also magnify the threat to the supplier's intellectual property.

When buyers cannot easily monitor supplier performance, the supplier might shirk or cheat and not deliver the expected value. *Opportunism* is "some form of cheating or undersupply relative to an implicit or explicit contract."[67] It may entail blatant self-serving and deliberate misrepresentation that violates contractual agreements. In creating the 1996 version of the Ford Taurus, Ford Corporation chose to outsource the whole process to one supplier, Lear Corporation. Lear committed to a contract that, for various reasons, it knew it was unable to fulfill. According to Ford, Lear missed deadlines, failed to meet weight and price objectives, and furnished parts that did not work.[68] A more passive form of opportunism might be a refusal or unwillingness to adapt to changing circumstances.

Opportunism is a concern because firms must devote resources to control and monitoring that they could otherwise allocate to more productive purposes. Contracts may become inadequate to govern supplier transactions when supplier opportunism becomes difficult to detect, when firms make specific investments in assets they cannot use elsewhere, and when contingencies are harder to anticipate. Customers and suppliers are more likely to form a joint venture (instead of signing a simple contract) when the supplier's degree of asset specificity is high, monitoring the supplier's behaviour is difficult, and the supplier has a poor reputation.[69] When a supplier has a good reputation, it is more likely to avoid opportunism to protect this valuable intangible asset.

The presence of a significant future time horizon and/or strong solidarity norms typically causes customers and suppliers to strive for joint benefits. Their specific investments shift from expropriation (increased opportunism on the receiver's part) to bonding (reduced opportunism).[70]

New Technology and Business Customers

Top firms are comfortable using technology to improve the way they do business with their business-to-business customers. Here are some examples of how they are redesigning websites, improving search results, leveraging emails, engaging in social media, and launching webinars and podcasts to improve their business performance:

- Chapman Kelly provides audit and other cost containment products to help firms reduce their health-care and insurance costs. The company originally tried to acquire new customers through traditional cold calling and outbound selling techniques. After it redesigned its website and optimized the site's search engine so the company's name moved close to the top of relevant online searches, revenue nearly doubled.[71]

■ Hewlett-Packard launched a "Technology at Work" email newsletter to focus on retention of its current customers. The newsletter's content and format were based on in-depth research to find out what customers wanted. Hewlett-Packard measures the effects of the newsletter carefully and found that emailing product updates helped avoid inbound service calls, saving millions of dollars.[72]

■ Emerson Process Management makes automation systems for chemical plants, oil refineries, and other types of factories. The company blog about factory automation is visited by thousands of readers who like to hear and swap factory war stories. It attracts 35 000 to 40 000 regular visitors each month, generating five to seven leads a week. Given that the systems sell for up to millions, ROI on the blog investment is immense.[73]

■ Machinery manufacturer Makino builds relationships with end-user customers by hosting an ongoing series of industry-specific webinars, producing an average of three a month. The company uses highly specialized content, such as how to get the most out of machine tools and how metal-cutting processes work, to appeal to different industries and different styles of manufacturing. Makino's database created from webinar participants has allowed the firm to cut marketing costs and improve its effectiveness and efficiency.[74]

■ Acquired by IBM in January 2008, Cognos provides business intelligence and performance management software and services to help companies manage their financial and operational performance. To increase visibility and improve customer relations, Cognos launched BI radio, an RSS-enabled series of 30-minute podcasts released every six weeks addressing a range of topics such as marketing, leadership, business management, and "killer apps." Attracting 60 000 subscribers, the podcasts are thought to have directly or indirectly led to $7 million in deals.[75]

INSTITUTIONAL AND GOVERNMENT MARKETS

Our discussion has concentrated largely on the buying behaviour of profit-seeking companies. Much of what we have said also applies to the buying practices of institutional and government organizations. However, we want to highlight certain special features of these markets.

The **institutional market** consists of schools, hospitals, nursing homes, prisons, and other institutions that must provide goods and services to people in their care. Many of these organizations are characterized by low budgets and captive clienteles. For example, hospitals must decide what quality of food to buy for patients. The buying objective here is not profit, because the food is provided as part of the total service package; nor is cost minimization the sole objective, because poor food will cause patients to complain and hurt the hospital's reputation. The hospital purchasing agent must search for institutional-food vendors whose quality meets or exceeds a certain minimum standard and whose prices are low. In fact, many food vendors set up a separate sales division to cater to institutional buyers' special needs and characteristics. Heinz produces, packages, and prices its ketchup differently to meet the requirements of hospitals, colleges, and prisons. ARAMARK, which provides food services for stadiums, arenas, campuses, businesses, and schools, also has a competitive advantage in providing food for prisons across North America, a direct result of refining its purchasing practices and supply chain management.

ARAMARK

Where ARAMARK once merely selected products from lists provided by potential suppliers, it now collaborates with suppliers to develop products customized to meet the needs of individual segments. In the corrections segment, quality has historically been sacrificed to meet food cost limits that operators outside the market would find impossible to work with. "When you go after business in the corrections field, you are making bids that are measured in hundredths of a cent," says John Zillmer, president of ARAMARK's Food & Support Services, "so any edge we can gain on the purchasing side is extremely valuable." ARAMARK sourced a series of protein products with unique partners at price points it never could have imagined before. These partners were unique because they understood the chemistry of proteins and knew how to lower the price while still creating a product acceptable to ARAMARK's customers, allowing ARAMARK to drive down costs. Then ARAMARK replicated this process with 163 different items formulated exclusively for corrections. Rather than reducing food costs by 1 cent or so a meal as usual, ARAMARK took 5 to 9 cents off—while maintaining or even improving quality.[76]

In most countries, government organizations are a major buyer of goods and services. For instance, the Canadian government buys approximately $14 billion worth of goods and services every year from thousands of suppliers. There are over 85 departments, agencies, Crown Corporations, and special operating agencies that purchase millions of dollars of goods and services each year. Public Works and Government Services Canada (PWGSC) is the government's largest purchasing organization, averaging 60 000 contracts totalling $10 billion annually.[77]

Government organizations typically require suppliers to submit bids and often award the contract to the lowest bidder. In some cases, they will make allowance for superior quality or a reputation for completing contracts on time. Governments will also buy on a negotiated contract basis, primarily in complex projects with major R&D costs and risks and those where there is little competition. Many government organizations tend to favour domestic suppliers. A major complaint of multinationals operating in Europe is that each country shows favouritism toward its nationals despite superior offers from foreign firms. Although such practices are fairly entrenched, the European Union is attempting to remove this bias.

Because their spending decisions are subject to public review, government organizations require considerable paperwork from suppliers, who often complain about bureaucracy, regulations, decision-making delays, and frequent shifts in procurement staff.

Many firms complain about selling to governments because of the red tape they perceive to be involved in making a sale. Federal, provincial, and municipal governments are now posting a great deal of information online to help businesses better understand government purchasing processes, supplier-selection criteria, and sales opportunities. For example, on the federal government's Contracts Canada site (http://buyandsell.gc.ca), you can find a wealth of information with only a click of the mouse on such topics as "Government Tendering Sites," which posts opportunities to bid to supply government services, and "How a Bid Is Selected." You can also access information about how to become a registered government supplier. Canada Business: Government Services for Entrepreneurs (www.canadabusiness.ca) is another site established by the government to help Canadian businesses. The site is a gold mine of information on topics as varied as training, importing, and taxation. It features online workshops for small businesses as well as a comprehensive database of government services and programs. Most government and public-sector contracting opportunities can be found on MERX (www.merx.com), a website that provides a list of all public- and private-sector calls for tenders for supplying products and services.

For a number of reasons, many companies that sell to the government have not used a marketing orientation. Some, though, have pursued government business by establishing separate government marketing departments. Companies such as Dell Canada, Kodak, and Goodyear anticipate government needs and projects, participate in the product specification phase, gather competitive intelligence, prepare bids carefully, and produce strong communications to describe and enhance their companies' reputations.

SUMMARY

1. Organizational buying is the decision-making process by which formal organizations establish the need for purchased products and services, then identify, evaluate, and choose among alternative brands and suppliers. The business market consists of all the organizations that acquire goods and services used in the production of other products or services that are sold, rented, or supplied to others.

2. Compared with consumer markets, business markets generally have fewer and larger buyers, a closer customer–supplier relationship, and more geographically concentrated buyers. Demand in the business market is derived from demand in the consumer market and fluctuates with the business cycle. Nonetheless, the total demand for many business goods and services is quite price inelastic. Business marketers need to be aware of the role of professional purchasers and their influencers; the need for multiple sales calls; and the importance of direct purchasing, reciprocity, and leasing.

3. The buying centre is the decision-making unit of a buying organization. It consists of initiators, users, influencers, deciders, approvers, buyers, and gatekeepers. To influence these parties, marketers must be aware of environmental, organizational, interpersonal, and individual factors.

4. The buying process consists of eight stages called buyphases: (1) problem recognition, (2) general need description, (3) product specification, (4) supplier search, (5) proposal solicitation, (6) supplier selection, (7) order-routine specification, and (8) performance review.

5. Business marketers must form strong bonds and relationships with their customers and provide them with added value. Some customers, however, may prefer a transactional relationship. Technology is aiding the development of strong business relationships.

6. The institutional market consists of schools, hospitals, nursing homes, prisons, and other institutions that provide goods and services to people in their care. Buyers for government organizations tend to require a great deal of paperwork from their vendors and to favour open bidding and domestic companies. Suppliers must be prepared to adapt their offers to the special needs and procedures found in institutional and government markets.

APPLICATIONS

Marketing Debate: How Different Is Business-to-Business Marketing?

Many business-to-business marketing executives lament the challenges of business-to-business marketing, maintaining that many traditional marketing concepts and principles do not apply. For a number of reasons, they assert that selling products and services to a company is fundamentally different from selling to individuals. Others disagree, claiming that marketing theory is still valid and only requires some adaptation in marketing tactics.

Take a position: Business-to-business marketing requires a special, unique set of marketing concepts and principles *versus* Business-to-business marketing is really not that different, and the basic marketing concepts and principles apply.

Marketing Discussion: B2C and B2B Concepts

Consider some of the consumer behaviour topics for business-to-consumer (B2C) marketing from Chapter 6. How might you apply them to business-to-business (B2B) settings? For example, how might noncompensatory models of choice work? Mental accounting?

MARKETING EXCELLENCE | HOURSTON GLASCRAFT

While government contracts can be a shot in the arm for a business, navigating the waters to earn that lucrative deal can be a challenge for even the most experienced company. Only those that overcome barriers such as excessive paperwork, bureaucracy, and a highly competitive bidding process earn the right to get a piece of the $14 million worth of goods and services purchased by the Canadian government's 85-plus departments, agencies, and Crown Corporations each year.

Charles Hourston, an inductee in the Canadian Boating Hall of Fame, has been building fibreglass boats since 1949 in North Vancouver. The company he founded, Hourston Glascraft, has sold more than 15 000 fibreglass boats and has done business with the federal government on multiple occasions. Throughout the years, he and his son Bill Hourston, who now manages the company, have learned a thing or two about dealing with this demanding client.

The bidding process for government contracts has become more transparent in recent years but it has also become more complex. Previously, the federal government would shop around with a broad idea, and approach those it thought could competitively bid on the contract. Now, the government posts very specific opportunities online using an electronic tendering service, MERX.com, which creates more transparency, but also more competition.

In 2010, Bill Hourston saw an opportunity listed on the MERX website for four hydrographic survey boats to be supplied to Fisheries and Oceans Canada. The challenge was that the bid was set to close in ten days. Drawing on past experience and his attention to detail, Mr. Hourston took on preparing the 86-page mandatory documentation himself. Although his company had previously supplied police boats to the RCMP and search-and-rescue vessels to the Canadian Coast Guard, the spec requirements of the government for this particular boat were more complex. Based on help from

a naval architect, he gave his proposal an edge over the rest—he added equipment to create navigational charts to the product specifications.

Bill Hourston's ability to provide the necessary paperwork on time and offer an attractive proposal won his company the contract, worth $650 000. Following a hard hit from the recession, Hourston was able to draw on his experience and attention to detail to bring much-needed business to his company. In addition, the contract included an option for the department to order two more boats following contract fulfillment, providing the possibility for more business with the government without having to go through the bidding process.

QUESTIONS

1. What would be some differences in your company trying to sell to another business versus to the government?

2. MERX claims to have levelled the playing field in that businesses of any size have equal access to information on contracting opportunities with the Government of Canada. Is this website helping or hindering the government and Canadian businesses?

3. Are there situations when a government contract could be undesirable?

4. What are some ethical challenges that could arise from pursuing a government contract?

Sources: Virginia Galt, "Navigating Government Contracts Pays Off," *The Globe and Mail*, November 1, 2010, p. B10; MERX website, www.merx.com (viewed January 15, 2011); "B.C. Boat Builder in Hall of Fame," *Vancouver Sun*, May 28, 2005, p. D2; Hourston Glascraft website, www.hourstonglascraft.com (viewed January 15, 2011); Canada Business Ontario, "Government Procurement Guide," www.cbo-eco.ca/en/info-guide/government_procurement_info-guide_1121180832226.cfm (viewed January 2, 2010).

In This Chapter, We Will Address the Following **Questions**

1. What are the different levels of market segmentation?

2. In what ways can a company divide a market into segments?

3. What are the requirements for effective segmentation?

4. How should business markets be segmented?

5. How should a company choose the most attractive target markets?

CANADIAN
Meat Busin
The Beef, Pork & Poultry Industry Maga

Chapter 8

October 2011

AAFC Celebrates
125 Years of Ag
Research

Ginseng-fed
Chicken

Manitoba Pork Industry
vs. Moratorium

In vitro meat &
the yuck factor
pg. 5

meatbusiness.ca $6.00

Canada's meat and poultry industry has adapted to difficult economic times with innovative products and redefined market segmentation.

Identifying Market Segments and Targets

Companies cannot connect with all customers in large, broad, or diverse markets. But they can divide such markets into groups of consumers or segments with distinct needs and wants. A company then needs to identify which market segments it can serve effectively. This decision requires a keen understanding of consumer behaviour and careful strategic thinking. To develop the best marketing plans, managers need to understand what makes each segment unique and different. Identifying and satisfying the right market segments is often the key to marketing success.

Canada's meat producers and processors have gone through rough times over the last few years. The global recession, fears of animal-borne pandemics, rising costs of feed, and a strong loonie have taken a big bite out of the profits of the industry. There is a positive side, however, to the turbulent economic times. A changing and demanding industry forces better market segmentation and targeting in order to stay in business and make profits. Some smart players in Canada's meat industry have been able to do just that by re-evaluating their marketing strategies and being innovative in developing new products targeted to the right segments.

Olymel, a Montreal-based meat processor, has used geographic segmentation to adapt products to regional tastes, adding local ingredients to its traditional products. The company used maple syrup from the Beauce region in one type of ham and cross-marketed another ham made with Boreal, a popular local beer. In addition, segmentation based on benefits sought by the consumer led to products that are convenient to cook, have new flavours, and are healthier. To make meal preparation easier, Olymel introduced foods such as marinated kebabs, precooked roasts, and microwaveable chicken products. To add new flavours, the company found success in serving segments based on ethnicity and taste preferences. Ginger beef, beef strips with an Asian twist, gained great popularity across Canada. Southwest barbecue flavourings also became a favourite. Olymel's healthy foods initiatives include reducing the salt content in its products, and offering them with sea salt instead.

Similarly, Winnipeg-based Granny's Poultry discovered that demographic segments such as baby boomers were more interested in health benefits; behavioural segments such as athletes wanted a leaner protein; and for many moms, chicken was often the meat of choice for the kids. The company is developing new products to deliver the desired benefits to each segment it targets.

Pursuing all consumers with the same marketing mix often results in wasted resources by targeting consumers not receptive to the marketing-mix elements. Market segmentation uncovers profitable and underserved groups of consumers. Properly chosen target segments, combined with tailored marketing campaigns, allow a company to withstand competition and a turbulent economic environment.[1]

To compete more effectively, many companies are now embracing target marketing. Instead of scattering their marketing efforts, they're focusing on those consumers they have the greatest chance of satisfying.

Effective target marketing requires that marketers do the following:

1. Identify and profile distinct groups of buyers who differ in their needs and wants (market segmentation).
2. Select one or more market segments to enter (market targeting).

3. For each target segment, establish and communicate the distinctive benefit(s) of the company's market offering (market positioning).

This chapter will focus on the first two steps. After reviewing some important branding concepts in Chapter 9, Chapter 10 discusses the third step, market positioning.

BASES FOR SEGMENTING CONSUMER MARKETS

Market segmentation divides a market into well-defined slices. A *market segment* consists of a group of customers who share a similar set of needs and wants. The marketer's task is to identify the appropriate number and nature of market segments and decide which one(s) to target.

We use two broad groups of variables to segment consumer markets. Some researchers try to define segments by looking at descriptive characteristics: geographic, demographic, and psychographic. Then they examine whether these customer segments exhibit different needs or product responses. For example, they might examine the differing attitudes of "professionals," "blue collars," and other groups toward, say, "safety" as a product benefit.

Other researchers try to define segments by looking at behavioural considerations, such as consumer responses to benefits, usage occasions, or brands. The researcher then sees whether different characteristics are associated with each consumer-response segment. For example, do people who want "quality" rather than "low price" in an automobile differ in their geographic, demographic, and psychographic makeup?

Regardless of which type of segmentation scheme we use, the key is adjusting the marketing program to recognize customer differences. The major segmentation variables—geographic, demographic, psychographic, and behavioural segmentation—are summarized in Table 8.1.

Geographic Segmentation

Geographic segmentation divides the market into geographical units such as nations, provinces, regions, counties, cities, or neighbourhoods. The company can operate in one or a few areas, or it can operate in all but pay attention to local variations. In that way, it can tailor marketing programs to the needs and wants of local customer groups in trading areas, neighbourhoods, even individual stores. For example, Coast Hotels and Resorts offers full-service hotels with locations in Alberta, British Columbia, and Northwest Territories. In a growing trend called *grassroots marketing,* such activities concentrate on getting as close and personally relevant to individual customers as possible—one of the primary reasons for the success of Canada's credit unions.

Much of Nike's initial success comes from engaging target consumers through grassroots marketing efforts such as sponsorship of local school teams, expert-conducted clinics, and provision of shoes, clothing, and equipment. Citibank provides different mixes of banking services in its branches depending on neighbourhood demographics. Curves, an exercise chain aimed at middle-aged women, places paper bags where consumers can place a form asking for more information about Curves in local businesses such as ice cream shops, pizza parlours, and other places where guilt can strike the weight-conscious shopper. Major retailers such as The Bay, Shoppers Drug Mart, and Bed Bath & Beyond allow store managers to stock products that suit the local community.[2]

Bed Bath & Beyond

The ability of home furnishing retailer Bed Bath & Beyond to cater to local tastes has fuelled its phenomenal growth. The firm's managers pick 70 percent of their own merchandise, and this fierce local focus has helped the chain evolve from bed linens to the "beyond" part—products from picture frames and pot holders to imported olive oil and designer doormats. In some downtown stores, for instance, managers are beginning to stock wall paint. You won't find paint in suburban stores, where customers can go to Home Depot or RONA. One manager says several customers have been surprised to find out the store is part of a national chain and not a mom-and-pop operation. For Bed Bath & Beyond, that's the ultimate compliment.[3]

More and more, regional marketing means marketing right down to a specific postal code.[4] Many companies use mapping software to pinpoint the geographic locations of their customers, learning, say, that most customers are within a four-kilometre radius of the store and are further concentrated within certain LDUs (local delivery units, represented by the last three characters of the postal code). By mapping the densest areas, the retailer can rely on *customer cloning*, assuming the best prospects live where most of the customers already come from.

TABLE 8.1	MAJOR SEGMENTATION VARIABLES FOR CONSUMER MARKETS
Geographic	
Region	Atlantic Provinces, Quebec, Central Provinces, Western Provinces, Northern Territories
City or metro size	Under 5000; 5001–20 000; 20 001–50 000; 50 001–100 000; 100 001–250 000; 250 001–500 000; 500 001–1 000 000; 1 000 001–4 000 000; 4 000 001 or over
Density	Urban, suburban, rural
Climate	Far North, Near North, mountain, maritime, prairie, Great Lakes
Demographic	
Age	Under 6, 6–11, 12–19, 20–34, 35–49, 50–64, 65+
Family size	1–2, 3–4, 5+
Family life cycle	Young, single; young, married, no children; young, married, youngest child under 6; young, married, youngest child 6 or over; older, married, with children; older, married, no children under 18; older, single; other
Gender	Male, female
Income	Under $10 000; $10 001–$15 000; $15 001–$20 000; $20 001–$30 000; $30 001–$50 000; $50 001–$100 000; $100 001 and over
Occupation	Professional and technical; managers, officials, and proprietors; clerical; sales; craftspeople; supervisors; operatives; farmers; retired; students; homemakers; unemployed
Education	Grade school or less, some high school, high-school graduate, some community college, community college graduate, some university, university graduate, graduate degree
Religion	Catholic, Protestant, Jewish, Muslim, Hindu, other
Race	White, Aboriginal, Asian, South Asian, Black
Generation	Baby boomers, Gen Xers, Gen Yers
Nationality	English, French, German, Italian, Chinese, Filipino, Indian, Vietnamese, Middle Eastern
Social class	Lower lowers, upper lowers, working class, middle class, upper middles, lower uppers, upper uppers
Psychographic	
Lifestyle	Culture-oriented, sports-oriented, outdoor-oriented
Personality	Compulsive, gregarious, authoritarian, ambitious
Behavioural	
Occasions	Regular occasion, special occasion
Benefits	Quality, service, economy, speed
User status	Nonuser, ex-user, potential user, first-time user, regular user
Usage rate	Light user, medium user, heavy user
Loyalty status	None, medium, strong, absolute
Readiness stage	Unaware, aware, informed, interested, desirous, intending to buy
Attitude toward product	Enthusiastic, positive, indifferent, negative, hostile

Some approaches combine geographic data with demographic data to yield even richer descriptions of consumers and neighbourhoods. Environics Analytics uses PRIZM, a consumer segmentation system that classifies all 55 000 Canadian neighbourhoods into one of 66 lifestyle types, with names like Cosmopolitan Elite, Electric Avenues, Les Chics, and Lunch at Tim's. The inhabitants in a cluster tend to lead similar lives, drive similar cars, have similar jobs, and read similar magazines. These categories are based on the most important drivers of consumer behaviour: demographics, lifestyles, and values. The groupings also take into consideration 39 factors in five broad categories: (1) education and affluence, (2) family life cycle, (3) urbanization, (4) race and ethnicity, and (5) mobility. Using a cluster analysis of 2006 Census demographics combined with geodemographics, psychographics, and social-values data from Environics Research, the system can be used to understand product preferences and explain consumer behaviour. With PRIZM's ability to link every neighbourhood and postal code to one of 66 segments, the system offers new possibilities with regard to customer profiling and acquisition, cross-selling, site selection, strategic planning, and media buying, and can be used by Canadian marketers from a wide range of industries, including financial services, packaged goods, retail, telecommunications, government, and automotive.[5]

Table 8.2 has examples of four PRIZM clusters.

Marketers can use PRIZM to answer questions such as the following: Which geographic areas (neighbourhoods or postal codes) contain our most valuable customers? How deeply have we already penetrated these segments? Which distribution channels and promotional media work best in reaching our target clusters in each area? Geoclustering captures the increasing diversity of the Canadian population.

A number of organizations have applied this service to their marketing. Canadian Blood Services (CBS) used the PRIZM segmentation system to identify neighbourhoods where blood donation was lower than would be expected based on geodemographics and social values. This allowed the CBS to open clinics where the shortfalls were greatest. The Cancer Research Society (CRS) used the PRIZM lifestyle segmentation to classify donors into 66 lifestyle types, of which three were identified as most likely to donate to

---

TABLE 8.2 | **EXAMPLES OF PRIZM CLUSTERS**

Young Digerati: These young, well-off urban trendsetters are made up of couples or single-headed households living in fashionable in-town neighbourhoods which are typified by high-rise apartments and expensive condos, home offices, casual restaurants, and fitness clubs and which are located in a handful of big cities like Vancouver and Toronto. Affluent, highly educated, and tech-savvy, this group tends to be ethnically mixed. They have deep pockets and like to shop for the latest styles; however, many are also socially conscious consumers who support many causes including environmental groups.

Mini Van & Vin Rouge: These young Quebec families live in comfort in exurban areas beyond the boundaries of Quebec's big cities. Well-educated white-collar professionals with young children, they engage in kid-centred lifestyles like ice skating and boating. They make a point of sitting down to a family dinner every night. When picking media, they favour comedy shows like "Les Simpson" and current-affairs programs.

Lunch at Tim's: These are old and young working-class people living in industrial towns and cities located across southern Ontario. These communities are closely knit and residents like to socialize at local eateries from doughnut shops to pizza parlours to Chinese restaurants. They relax by watching TV, playing video games, or occasionally visiting a casino. They may also be big snowboarding enthusiasts.

Park Bench Seniors: These are downscale seniors in urban high-rises. They tend to lead Canada's oldest lifestyle, live in older, seniors-oriented high-rise apartment buildings and typically get by on modest pensions. Most never made it beyond high school and spent their working lives at blue-collar jobs. Lifestyles are unpretentious. They do support the arts, but concede that they rarely go out to restaurants and aren't too keen on entertaining at home.

Source: Environics Analytics.

cancer research. Using these results, the CRS was able to launch a targeted direct marketing campaign that resulted in a nearly 20 percent increase in revenue among English-speaking prospects and a nearly 70 percent increase in revenue among French-speaking prospects. The Canadian Automobile Association (CAA) in the Maritimes was able to use the PRIZM system to identify groups that would respond to promotional mail the most. As a result of targeting these groups, the CAA realized a 60 percent improvement in the response to its vacation-related mailings.[6]

As database costs decline, software becomes easier to use, and data integration increases, marketing to microsegments has become possible for even small organizations.[7] Those who favour such localized marketing see national advertising as wasteful because it is too arm's length and fails to address local needs. Those against local marketing argue that it drives up manufacturing and marketing costs by reducing economies of scale and magnifying logistical problems. A brand's overall image might be diluted if the product and message are different in different localities.

Demographic Segmentation

In demographic segmentation, we divide the market on variables such as age, family size, family life cycle, gender, income, occupation, education, religion, race, generation, nationality, and social class. One reason demographic variables are so popular with marketers is that they're often associated with consumer needs and wants. Another is that they're easy to measure. Even when we describe the target market in nondemographic terms (say, by personality type), we may need the link back to demographic characteristics in order to estimate the size of the market and the media we should use to reach it efficiently.

Here's how marketers have used certain demographic variables to segment markets.

AGE AND LIFE-CYCLE STAGE Consumer wants and abilities change with age. Toothpaste brands such as Crest and Colgate offer three main lines of products to target kids, adults, and older consumers. Age segmentation can be even more refined. Pampers divides its market into prenatal, new baby (0–5 months), baby (6–12 months), toddler (13–23 months), and preschooler (24 months+). Indirect age effects also operate for some products. One study of kids aged 8–12 found that 91 percent decided or influenced clothing or apparel buys, 79 percent grocery purchases, and 54 percent vacation choices, while 14 percent even made or swayed vehicle decisions.[8]

Nevertheless, age and life cycle can be tricky variables.[9] The target market for some products may be the *psychologically* young. To target 21-year-olds with its boxy Element, which company officials described as a "dorm room on wheels," Honda ran ads depicting sexy college kids partying near the car at a beach. So many baby boomers were attracted to the ads, however, that the average age of Element buyers turned out to be 42! With baby boomers seeking to stay young, Honda decided that the lines between age groups were getting blurred. When it was ready to launch a new subcompact called the Fit, the firm deliberately targeted Gen Y buyers as well as their empty-nest parents.

LIFE STAGE People in the same part of the life cycle may still differ in their life stage. **Life stage** defines a person's major concern, such as going through a divorce, going into a second marriage, taking care of an older parent, deciding to cohabit with another person, deciding to buy a new home, and so on. These life stages present opportunities for marketers who can help people cope with their major concerns. Take the case of the Canadian wedding industry to see how powerful life-stage marketing can be.

The Wedding Industry

Each year, 150 000 brides will walk down the aisle in Canada, and they happily spend an average of $25 883 on their wedding. The price of the gown alone ranges from $1000 to $9000 and up, cakes can cost anywhere from $800 to $12 000, and the reception will set the happy couple back at least $50 per person. All this expense for the "perfect day" translates into a $3.8 billion market. It's not surprising that there are huge trade shows like Canada's Bridal Show and the Total Wedding Show catering to brides and wedding planners. It is estimated that couples spend 250 hours planning their wedding; thus, wedding planners have become a big service industry.[10] Marketing opportunities begin from the point the woman says, "Yes, I will."

GENDER Men and women have different attitudes and behave differently, based partly on genetic makeup and partly on socialization.[11] Women tend to be more communal-minded and men more self-expressive and goal-directed; women tend to take in more of the data in their immediate environment and men to focus on the part of the environment that helps them achieve a goal. A research study examining how men and women shop found that men often need to be invited to touch a product, whereas women are likely to pick it up without prompting. Men often like to read product information; women may relate to a product on a more personal level.[12]

According to some studies, women in Canada, the United States, and the United Kingdom control or influence over 80 percent of consumer goods and services, make 75 percent of the decisions about buying new homes, and purchase outright 60 percent of new cars. Gender differentiation has long been applied in clothing, hairstyling, cosmetics, and magazines. Avon, for one, has built a $6 billion–plus business selling beauty products to women. Marketers can now reach women more easily via media like the WTN, Food Network, and HGTV television networks and scores of women's magazines and websites; men are more easily found at TV channels TSN, The Score, and Spike and through magazines such as *Maxim* and *Men's Health.*[13]

Some traditionally more male-oriented markets, such as the automobile industry, are beginning to recognize gender segmentation and changing the way they design and sell cars.[14] Women shop differently for cars than men do; they are more interested in environmental impact, care more about interior than exterior styling, and view safety in terms of features that help drivers survive an accident rather than help avoid one.[15]

But it's not enough to tout a product as masculine or feminine. Hypersegmentation is now occurring within both male and female personal-care segments. To expand beyond the metrosexual market, Unilever's Axe brand includes Snake Peel Shower Scrub with Desert Minerals + Cactus Oil, the ingredients of which sound more rugged than "exfoliating liquid soap with plant oils."[16] And Unilever earned kudos by targeting women who don't look like (or aspire to look like) fashion models with its award-winning "Dove Campaign for Real Beauty," led largely by its Canadian operation. Following its success, Dove has launched a similar campaign for men.

Dove Men+Care

After the successful "Campaign for Real Beauty," Dove has launched a skin-care line for men. The men's campaign takes a note from the women's version, focusing on the 75 percent of men who feel they are not properly portrayed in advertising. The campaign made its debut during the Super Bowl in 2010, and the Canadian launch took place in the Hockey Hall of Fame. The campaign focuses on men promoting the notion of being "comfortable in their own skin." In order to gain a more masculine and credible image for the Men+Care line, Dove has developed videos about how influential men are comfortable with who they are. The videos show personalities such as New York Yankees manager Joe Girardi and five-time world champ Yankee pitcher Andy Pettitte talking about their journey in life, and how their wives and kids make them comfortable with who they have become.[17]

Dove has launched a line of skin-care products for men, following the success of its Campaign for Real Beauty, which was targeted at women.

INCOME Income segmentation is a long-standing practice in such categories as automobiles, clothing, cosmetics, financial services, and travel. However, income does not always predict the best customers for a given product. Blue-collar workers were among the first purchasers of colour television sets; it was cheaper for them to buy these sets than to go to movies and restaurants.

Many marketers are deliberately going after lower-income groups, in some cases discovering fewer competitive pressures or greater consumer loyalty.[18] Procter & Gamble launched two discount-priced brand extensions in 2005—Bounty Basic and Charmin Basic—whose success led to the introduction in 2009 of Tide Basic, although this extension was later withdrawn from the market. At the same time, other marketers are finding success with premium-priced products. When Whirlpool launched a pricey Duet washer line, sales doubled their forecasts in a weak economy, due primarily to middle-class shoppers who traded up.

Increasingly, companies are finding that their markets are hourglass shaped as middle-market consumers migrate toward both discount *and* premium products.[19] Companies that miss out on this new market risk being "trapped in the middle" and seeing their market share steadily decline. Recognizing that its channel strategy emphasized retailers like Sears selling primarily to the middle class, Levi Strauss introduced premium lines such as Levi's Capital E to upscale retailers Bloomingdales and Nordstrom, and the less-expensive Signature by Levi Strauss & Co. line to mass market retailers Walmart and Target. "Marketing Insight: Trading Up, Down, and Over" describes the factors creating this trend and what it means to marketers.

GENERATION Each generation or *cohort* is profoundly influenced by the times in which it grows up—the music, movies, politics, and defining events of that period. Members share the same major cultural, political, and economic experiences and have similar outlooks and values. Marketers often advertise to a cohort by using the icons and images prominent in its experiences. They also try to develop products and services that uniquely meet the particular interests or needs of a generational target.

Although the beginning and ending birth dates of any generation are always subjective—and generalizations can mask important differences within the group—here are some general observations about the four main generation cohorts of consumers, from youngest to oldest.[20] See Table 8.3 for a summary.

Millennials (or Gen Y) Born in the late 1970s through the mid-1990s, Millennials, also called Gen Y, number 7 million. If you factor in career growth and household and family formation, and multiply by another 53 years of life expectancy, billions of dollars in consumer spending are at stake over Gen Y's life span. It's not surprising that market researchers and advertisers are racing to get a bead on Gen Y's buying behaviour.

TABLE 8.3	PROFILING CANADIAN GENERATION COHORTS		
Generational Cohort	**Birth Range**	**Approximate Size**	**Defining Features**
Millennials (Gen Y)	Late 1970s to mid-1990s	7 million	Raised with relative affluence, technologically plugged in, and concerned with the environment and social issues, they also have a strong sense of independence and a perceived immunity from marketing.
Gen X	Mid-1960s to late 1970s	9.5 million	Sometimes seen as falling between the generational cracks, they bridge the technological savvy of Gen Y with the adult realities of the baby boomers.
Baby Boomers	Mid-1940s to mid-1960s	9.5 million	Still largely in the prime of their consumption cycle, they embrace products and lifestyles that allow them to turn back the hands of time.
Silent Generation	Mid-1920s to mid-1940s	4 million	Defying their advancing age, they maintain active lives, and choose products and marketing that help them to achieve that.

Source: "Estimated Population by Age Group and Sex, Canada, Provinces and Territories, July 1st 2009," *Statistics Canada*, June 18, 2010. Numbers rounded to closest half million.

MARKETING **INSIGHT**	TRADING UP, DOWN, AND OVER

Michael Silverstein and Neil Fiske, the authors of *Trading Up*, observed an increasing number of middle-market consumers periodically trading up to what the authors call "New Luxury" products and services "that possess higher levels of quality, taste, and aspiration than other goods in the category but are not so expensive as to be out of reach." For example, consumers might trade up to such brands as Starbucks coffee, Aveda shampoo, or Viking ranges, depending in part on the emotional benefits they gain in the trade.

Thanks to the trading-up trend, New Luxury goods sell at higher volumes than traditional luxury goods, although priced higher than conventional middle-market items. The authors identify three main types of New Luxury products:

- *Accessible superpremium products,* such as Victoria's Secret underwear and Kettle gourmet potato chips, carry a significant premium over middle-market brands, yet consumers can readily trade up to them because they are relatively low-ticket items in affordable categories.

- *Old Luxury brand extensions* extend historically high-priced brands down-market while retaining their cachet, such as the Mercedes-Benz C-class and the American Express Blue Card.

- *Masstige goods,* such as Kiehl's skin care and Kendall-Jackson wines, are priced between average middle-market brands and superpremium Old Luxury brands. They are "always based on emotions, and consumers have a much stronger emotional engagement with them than with other goods."

To trade up to brands that offer these emotional benefits, consumers often trade down by shopping at discounters such as Walmart and Costco for staple items or goods that confer no emotional benefit but still deliver quality and functionality. As one consumer explained in rationalizing why her kitchen boasted a Sub-Zero refrigerator, a state-of-the-art Fisher & Paykel dishwasher, and a $900 warming drawer but a giant 12-pack of Bounty paper towels from a warehouse discounter, "When it comes to this house, I didn't give in on anything. But when it comes to food shopping or cleaning products, if it's not on sale, I won't buy it."

In a subsequent book titled *Treasure Hunt*, Silverstein notes that 82 percent of U.S. consumers trade down in five or more categories (what he calls "Treasure Hunting"), whereas 62 percent focus on trading up in the two categories that provide the most emotional benefits. This makes the new consumer "part martyr and part hedonist," willingly sacrificing on a number of purchases in order to experience enhanced benefits from a handful of others.

Silverstein believes successful firms will offer one of two kinds of value: New Luxury or Treasure Hunting. Brands that offer opportunities to trade up, such as Coach, Victoria's Secret, Holt Renfrew, and Bath & Body Works, or to trade down, such as Best Value Inn, Giant Tiger, Dollarama, and IKEA, are optimally positioned to deliver the value modern consumers seek. The remaining firms, occupying the middle market and lacking the economic, functional, and emotional value modern consumers are searching for, will see their market share shrink as they get "trapped in the middle." Traditional grocers and department stores are already suffering, with market share declines of 30 percent and 50 percent, respectively.

Market research firm Mintel observes that consumers have also been "trading over" by switching spending from one category to another, buying a new home theatre system, say, instead of a new car. In the recent economic downturn, consumers were "making substitutions that work for recession-minded lifestyles" while still preserving a desired experience. Mintel cites as examples Starbucks VIA Ready Brew coffee, a new, home-based Starbucks experience that's more affordable than coffee at one of the company's outlets, and Tide TOTALCARE, which enables users to obtain certain dry cleaning–type results at home with prices below those of professional dry cleaners.

Sources: Michael J. Silverstein, *Treasure Hunt: Inside the Mind of the New Consumer* (New York: Portfolio, 2006); Jeff Cioletti, "Movin' on Up," *Beverage World*, June 2006, p. 20; Michael J. Silverstein and Neil Fiske, *Trading Up: The New American Luxury* (New York: Portfolio, 2003); Linda Tischler, "The Price Is Right," *Fast Company*, November 2003; Sarah Mahoney, "Top Consumer Trends: Trust, Control,... Playfulness?" *Marketing Daily*, September 4, 2009; David Orgel, "Quality Trumps Quantity in New Product Releases," *Supermarket News*, May 25, 2009.

Also known as the Echo Boomers, these consumers have been "wired" almost from birth—playing computer games, navigating the web, downloading music, connecting with friends via instant messaging and mobile phones. They have a sense of entitlement and abundance from growing up during the economic boom and being pampered by their boomer parents. Yet they are highly socially conscious and concerned about environmental issues. They are selective, confident, and impatient.

Because Gen Y members are often turned off by overt branding practices and hard sell, marketers have tried many different approaches to reach and persuade them:[21]

1. *Online buzz*—Rock band Foo Fighters created a digital street team that sends targeted email blasts to members who "get the latest news, exclusive audio/video sneak previews, tons of chances to win great Foo Fighters prizes, and become part of the Foo Fighters Family."

2. *Student ambassadors*—Red Bull enlisted college students as Red Bull Student Brand Managers to distribute samples, research drinking trends, design on-campus marketing initiatives, and write stories for student newspapers.

3. *Unconventional sports*—Chick-fil-A sponsored the National Amateur Dodgeball Association, "a recreational pursuit for nontraditional sport enthusiasts."

4. *Cool events*—Hurley, which defined itself as an authentic "Microphone for Youth" brand rooted in surf, skate, art, music, and beach cultures, became the title sponsor of the U.S. Open of Surfing. Other sponsors included Casio, Converse, Corona, Paul Mitchell, and Southwest Airlines.

5. *Computer games*—Product placement is not restricted to movies or TV: Mountain Dew, Oakley, and Harley-Davidson all made deals to put logos on Tony Hawk's *Pro Skater 3* from Activision.

6. *Videos*—Burton ensures its snowboards and riders are clearly visible in any videos that are shot.

7. *Street teams*—As part of an antismoking crusade, the American Legacy Foundation hires teens as the "Truth Squad" to hand out T-shirts, bandanas, and dog tags at teen-targeted events.

Gen X Often lost in the demographic shuffle, the 9.5 million or so Canadian Gen X consumers, named for a 1991 novel by Douglas Coupland, are those born in the mid-1960s through the late 1970s. The popularity of Kurt Cobain, rock band Nirvana, and the lifestyle portrayed in the critically lauded film *Slacker* led to the use of terms like *grunge* and *slacker* to characterize Gen X teens and young adults. It was an unflattering image of a disaffected group with short attention spans and little work ethic.

These stereotypes slowly disappeared. Gen X was certainly raised in more challenging times, when working parents relied on day care or left latchkey kids on their own after school, and corporate downsizing led to the threat of layoffs and economic uncertainty. At the same time, social and racial diversity were accepted and technology rapidly changed the way people lived and worked. Although Gen Xers created new norms in educational achievement, they were also the first generation to find surpassing their parents' standard of living a serious challenge.

These realities had a profound impact. Gen Xers feel self-sufficiency and the ability to handle any circumstance are key. Technology is an enabler for them, not a barrier. Unlike the more optimistic, team-oriented Gen Yers, Gen Xers are more pragmatic and individualistic. As consumers, they are wary of hype and pitches that seem inauthentic or patronizing. Direct appeals where value is clear often work best, especially as Gen Xers become parents raising families.[22]

Baby Boomers Baby boomers are the approximately 9.5 million Canadian consumers born in the mid-1940s through the mid-1960s. Though they represent a wealthy target, possessing 55 percent of the country's discretionary spending power and owning 80 percent of the nation's investment wealth, marketers often overlook them.[23] In network television circles, because advertisers are primarily interested in 18- to 49-year-olds, viewers over 50 are referred to as "undesirables."

With many baby boomers moving into their 60s and even the last and youngest wave bearing down on 50, demand has exploded for products to turn back the hands of time. According to one survey, nearly one in five boomers was actively resisting the aging process, driven by the mantra "Fifty is the new thirty." As they search for the fountain of youth, sales of hair replacement and hair colouring aids, health club memberships, home gym equipment, skin-tightening creams, nutritional supplements, and organic foods have all soared.

Interestingly, because so many members of the Gen Y Echo Boomers are living with their boomer parents, parents are being influenced by what demographers are calling a "boom-boom effect." The same products that appeal to 21-year-olds are appealing to youth-obsessed baby boomers. The multiseason success of MTV's reality show *The Osbournes,* starring heavy-metal rocker Ozzy Osbourne and his family, was fuelled as much by boomer parents as by their MTV-loving kids.

Consumers have been "trading over" to Tide TOTALCARE to obtain dry cleaning–type results at home.

Contrary to conventional marketing wisdom that brand preferences of consumers over 50 are fixed, one study found that 52 percent of boomers are willing to change brands, in line with the total population. Although they love to buy things, they hate being sold to, and as one marketer noted, "You have to earn your stripes every day." But abundant opportunity exists. Boomers are also less likely to associate retirement with "the beginning of the end" and see it instead as a new chapter in their lives with new activities, interests, careers, or even relationships.[24]

Silent Generation Those born in the mid-1920s through the mid-1940s—the "Silent Generation"—are redefining what *old age* means. To start with, many people whose chronological age puts them in this category don't see themselves as old. One survey found that 60 percent of respondents over 65 said they felt younger than their actual age. A third aged 65 to 74 said they felt 10 to 19 years younger, and one in six felt at least 20 years younger than their actual age.[25]

Consistent with what they say, many older consumers lead very active lives. As one expert noted, it is as if they are having a second middle age before becoming elderly. Advertisers have learned that older consumers don't mind seeing other older consumers in ads targeting them, as long as they appear to be leading vibrant lives. But marketers have learned to avoid clichés like happy older couples riding bikes or strolling hand-in-hand on a beach at sunset.

Emphasizing this generation's role as grandparents is universally well-received. Many older consumers not only happily spend time with their grandkids, they often provide for their basic needs or at least occasional gifts. The founders of eBeanstalk.com, which sells children's learning toys online, thought their business would be largely driven by young consumers starting families. They were surprised to find that up to 40 percent of their customers were older consumers, mainly grandparents. These customers are very demanding, but also more willing to pay full price than their younger counterparts.[26] See "Marketing Insight: The Grandparent Market" for further details about marketing to grandparents.

RACE AND CULTURE *Multicultural marketing* is an approach recognizing that different ethnic and cultural segments have sufficiently different needs and wants to require targeted marketing activities, and that a mass market approach is not refined enough for the diversity of the marketplace. Consider that McDonald's now does 40 percent of its U.S. business with ethnic minorities. Its highly successful "I'm Lovin' It" campaign was rooted in hip-hop culture but has an appeal that transcends race and ethnicity.[27]

Canada has a highly multicultural mix. Canadians of British and other European origins form the biggest ethnic group, followed by French-Canadians, followed by those of Asian origin and Aboriginal Peoples. Strong immigration to Canada in recent decades has led to a rise in the number of foreign-born people and the portion of the population that they represent. From 1986 to the 2006 Census, the immigrant population in Canada went up by over 2 million, and now represents about 20 percent of the country's population.[28] The non-Aboriginal visible minority segment is growing much faster than any other ethnic group, with numerous submarkets and expanding buying power. Multicultural markets also vary in whether they are first or second (or more) generation, and whether they are immigrants or born and raised in Canada.

The norms, language nuances, buying habits, and business practices of multicultural markets need to be factored into the initial formulation of a marketing strategy, rather than added as an afterthought. All this diversity also has implications for marketing research; it takes careful sampling to adequately profile

---

MARKETING **INSIGHT** | THE GRANDPARENT MARKET

Baby boomers in North America make up one of the largest population groups; in 2006, the first 77 million members of the baby boomer generation turned 60, with an average of 3 million members becoming grandparents every year. As this segment cashes in on retirement savings, its size, combined with large disposable income, makes it a very attractive segment for marketers. North American grandparents are spending an average of over $52 billion per year on their grandkids, with some putting money away to fund their grandkids' college education, and some even buying grandkids their first car. Now that baby boomers are reaching grandparenthood, they are potential consumers for many products oriented around children, such as toys, children's clothes, video games, education-related investments, and small cars.

Sources: Laura Tiffany, "Isn't It Grand?" May 2009, http://findarticles.com/p/articles/mi_m0DTI/is_5_27/ai_54546041/?tag=content;col1; "Grandparents Spending Billions on Their Grandchildren," December 7, 2007, www.marketingcharts.com/television/grandparents-spending-billions-on-their-grandchildren-2653/; "The Power of the Grandparent Economy," www.grandparents.com/gp/content/newsoftheday/news/article/the-power-of-the-grandparent-economy.html (all viewed September 19, 2010).

target markets.[29] See how a financial institution has begun targeting a relatively ignored cultural segment in Canada.

Assiniboine Credit Union

Recognizing the growing population of Muslim immigrants in Canada, Winnipeg-based Assiniboine Credit Union (ACU) was the first in the country to offer a mortgage specifically designed for the Muslim community. The Qur'an prohibits paying interest on loans and doing so is considered a violation of Islamic principles by orthodox Muslims. As a result, many Muslims in Canada are forced to rent homes rather than buy. To serve this growing market, the ACU launched an Islam-friendly mortgage that operates on a "declining partnership agreement." According to this arrangement, the credit union buys the home in partnership with the client. Over the period of the mortgage, the client pays ACU to buy a share of the credit union's ownership of the home plus a profit. At the end of the mortgage period, the client will have completely bought out ACU's ownership of the home and ACU will have earned its profit, in lieu of the traditional interest it would charge on mortgage loans.[30]

Multicultural marketing can result in different marketing messages, media, channels, and so on. Specialized media exist to reach virtually any cultural segment or minority group, though some companies have struggled to provide financial and management support for fully realized programs.

Fortunately, as countries become more culturally diverse, many marketing campaigns targeting a specific cultural group can spill over and positively influence others. An ad for Tide in which an African American man wearing a wedding ring was drying his son off after a bath was well-regarded by both African Americans and the rest of the U.S. market as a whole.[31]

Next, we consider characteristics of the four largest cultural minority markets in Canada—French-Canadian, Aboriginal, South Asian–Canadian, and Chinese-Canadian. Table 8.4 lists some important facts and figures about them.

French Canadians constitute nearly 80 percent of Quebec's and about 22 percent of Canada's population. Studies show that French Canadians, possibly due to their European roots, tend to be more fashion-conscious and engage in hedonic consumption, compared with other Canadians. As a result, products such as cosmetics, fashion accessories, and expensive dresses are more popular with French Canadians than with most other groups.

French Canadians have traditionally emphasized the importance of family, friends, and religion. Consequently, they are more likely to take time off work compared with their Anglo counterparts. Quick-cook foods and TV dinners are less popular among French Canadians, who believe in spending the time to cook meals from scratch for the family. Chain stores are less popular with this group, which prefers smaller independent stores instead. French Canadians are less likely to purchase diet soft drinks and are heavier consumers of wine and beer compared with the rest of Canada.

In terms of media habits, French Canadians watch more TV and read more magazines compared with the rest of Canada. This makes TV and magazine advertising especially important for this market. Some studies have shown higher price-sensitivity among French Canadians and greater response to newspaper promotional flyers, although some other studies have not found a significant difference.[32]

Aboriginal Peoples, with a population of 1.2 million, make up about 4 percent of Canada's population, with 20 percent living in Ontario. There are many Aboriginal languages spoken in Canada, with the primary ones being Cree, Inuktitut, and Ojibwa. Aboriginal Peoples have been concerned about retaining and perpetuating their native culture, which is very important to the group. Marketers have to be careful when marketing to Aboriginal Peoples, as stereotypes

The Assiniboine Credit Union launched an innovative mortgage for the Muslim community—a group that has been ignored by other financial institutions in Canada.

	Canada	French-Canadian	South Asian-Canadian	Chinese-Canadian	Aboriginal
Population—2006	31.6 million	6.9 million	1.3 million	1.2 million	1.2 million
Population growth from 2001 to 2006	5.4%	1.6%	37.7%	18.2%	20.1%
Employment rate	62.4%	63.1%	63.2%	58.5%	53.7%
Unemployment rate	6.6%	6.5%	8.6%	7.5%	14.8%
Bachelor's degree holders	9.6%	11.1%	16.9%	21.9%	5.7%
Master's degree holders	2.8%	3.3%	7.5%	6.3%	1.3%
Average annual income	$36 301	$35 169	$31 757	$32 971	$27 036
Median annual income	$26 850	$26 667	$22 977	$23 349	$20 000
Self-employed proportion of labour force	7.8%	7.0%	6.5%	7.5%	7.2%

TABLE 8.4 | DEMOGRAPHIC POPULATIONS

Source: Adapted from Statistics Canada, *2006 Census of Population.* Catalogue nos. 97-562-XWE2006002, 97-562-XCB2006017, 97-562-XCB2006013, 97-564-XCB2006007, 97-560-XCB2006028, and 92-594-XWE.

and angles such as disrespect for the environment or advertisements making fun of the elderly are likely to be frowned upon by this group and to lead to disastrous consequences for the marketer.

Health concerns have plagued the Aboriginal population with higher incidence of diabetes, heart disease, and cancer compared with non-Aboriginal adults. Some of the reasons identified for this have been the higher consumption of foods and beverages high in fat and calorie content but low in nutrients compared with the rest of the population. For instance, the average Aboriginal adult consumes about twice the daily volume of soft drinks compared with the non-Aboriginal Canadian adult.[33]

South Asian Canadians and **Chinese Canadians** are similar in many respects. Both groups, due to their collectivist nature, value family ties and social relationships. Their outings and travel often tend to be with family and friends. They recognize education as an important factor for career success and have higher proportions of people with university degrees compared with the national average. Both groups, particularly Chinese Canadians, are more likely to engage in conspicuous consumption and are attractive target markets for luxury brands, particularly those from Europe. Due to their relative lack of fluency in English or French, many South Asian Canadians and Chinese Canadians tend to patronize ethnic stores in their neighbourhood communities. Moreover, they are very likely to retain their ethnic food habits at home. Chinese Canadians, much more than South Asian Canadians, are more likely than any other minority group to speak their mother tongue at home. As a result, their Canadian-born children tend to be relatively fluent in Mandarin or Cantonese. Most of the differences between these groups and the majority population get diluted or disappear altogether with the second- and third-generation immigrants.[34] See how Ford Canada targeted its advertising to appeal to Chinese Canadians.

Ford Canada

With one out of six Canadians now belonging to a visible minority, companies such as Ford are making a conscious effort to target immigrant minorities in their marketing campaigns. Ford Canada launched a series of TV and print advertisements featuring expatriate Mark Rowswell, a media superstar in mainland China under the name Dashan. The advertising campaign was simultaneously supported with a Chinese version of the company's website. The ads were shown in both Mandarin and Cantonese in Vancouver and Toronto. Ford's slogan "Powered by You" was translated into meaning "In Your Hand" for the Chinese campaign, based on the Chinese principle of palm reading. One version of the TV advertising showed Dashan driving three separate vehicles with the commercial ending with the three vehicles resting on the three palm lines on Dashan's hand—representing success, relationships, and the lifeline in Chinese culture.[35]

Gay, Lesbian, Bisexual, and Transgender (GLBT) The gay, lesbian, bisexual, and transgender (GLBT) market is estimated to make up about 6 percent of Canada's population and have approximately $100 billion in buying power.[36] Many firms have recently created initiatives to target this market. For example, the major Canadian banks such as BMO, CIBC, and TD Canada Trust have been going after the "pink dollar." BMO opened a branch in Toronto's Gay Village, TD sponsored the Out for Business Conference organized by the gay community in Montreal, and CIBC has established an employee-led GLBT affinity group.[37] Other famous brands such as Tylenol, American Express, and Abercrombie & Fitch have openly targeted the GLBT community in their advertisements. According to one survey of the gay and lesbian community, the most GLBT-friendly businesses were IBM, Google, BT Group, Morgan Stanley, and Cisco Systems.[38]

Some firms, however, worry about backlash from organizations that will criticize or even boycott firms supporting gay and lesbian causes. Although multinationals such as Pepsi and Campbell's have experienced such boycotts, they continue to advertise to the gay community.

Psychographic Segmentation

Psychographics is the science of using psychology and demographics to better understand consumers. In *psychographic segmentation,* buyers are divided into different groups on the basis of psychological/ personality traits, lifestyle, or values. People within the same demographic group can exhibit very different psychographic profiles.

One of the most popular commercially available classification systems based on psychographic measurements is Strategic Business Insight's (SBI) VALS™ framework. VALS, originally signifying values and lifestyles, classifies adults into eight primary groups based on responses to a questionnaire featuring 4 demographic and 35 attitudinal questions. Each year, the VALS system classification questionnaire is integrated into various syndicated and custom surveys about topics such as product ownership, media preferences, environmental attitudes, and financial behaviours. New data from these surveys keeps the VALS system fresh and up to date (see Figure 8.1).[39]

The main dimensions of the VALS framework are psychological motivation (the horizontal dimension) and resources (the vertical dimension). Consumers are inspired by one of three primary motivations: ideals, achievement, and self-expression. Those primarily motivated by ideals are guided by knowledge and principles. Those motivated by achievement look for products and services that demonstrate success to their peers. Consumers whose motivation is self-expression desire social or physical activity, variety, and risk. The VALS concept of resources includes traditional factors of household income, education, and gender in combination with characteristics such as a person's level of self-confidence, willingness to take risks, or express leadership. Different levels of resources enhance or constrain a person's expression of his or her primary motivation.

Here are the four groups with higher resources:

1. *Innovators*—Successful, sophisticated, active, "take-charge" people with high self-esteem. Purchases often reflect cultivated tastes for relatively upscale, niche-oriented products and services.

2. *Thinkers*—Mature, satisfied, and reflective people motivated by ideals and who value order, knowledge, and responsibility. They seek durability, functionality, and value in products.

3. *Achievers*—Successful, goal-oriented people who focus on career and family. They favour premium products that demonstrate success to their peers.

4. *Experiencers*—Young, enthusiastic, impulsive people who seek variety and excitement. They spend a comparatively high proportion of income on fashion, entertainment, and socializing.

Here are the four groups with lower resources:

1. *Believers*—Conservative, conventional, and traditional people with concrete beliefs. They prefer familiar products and are loyal to established brands.

FIGURE 8.1

The VALS Segmentation
System: An Eight-Part
Typology

Source: VALS™ © Strategic
Business Insights (SBI),
www.strategicbusinessinsights.com/
VALS. Used with permission.

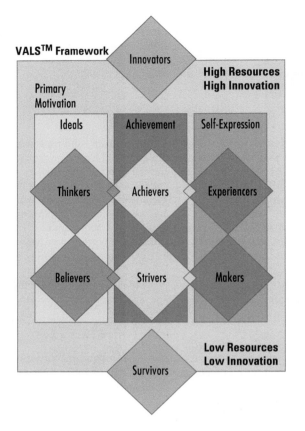

2. *Strivers*—Trendy and fun-loving people who are resource-constrained. They favour stylish products that emulate the purchases of those with greater material wealth.

3. *Makers*—Practical, down-to-earth, self-sufficient people who like to work with their hands. They seek domestic-made products with a practical or functional purpose.

4. *Survivors*—Elderly, passive people concerned about change and loyal to their favourite brands.

Marketers can apply their understanding of VALS segments to marketing planning. For example, Transport Canada, the government department that operates major Canadian airports, found that Innovators, who express independence and taste, made up a disproportionate percentage of air travellers. Given that segment's profile, stores with Innovator appeal such as Sharper Image and Nature Company were invited to set up shop at Canadian airports.

While human psychological traits (such as status or excitement seeking) are relatively constant across cultures, they are expressed differently. Therefore, VALS psychographic frameworks are customized by culture. Japan VALS™ divides society into 10 consumer segments on the basis of two key concepts: primary motivation (tradition, achievement, innovation, and self-expression) and attitudes to social change (sustaining, pragmatic, adapting, and innovating). Venezuela VALS, Nigeria VALS, and Dominican Republic VALS all have similar foundations.

Behavioural Segmentation

In behavioural segmentation, marketers divide buyers into groups on the basis of their knowledge of, attitude toward, use of, or response to a product.

NEEDS AND BENEFITS Not everyone who buys a product has the same needs or wants the same benefits from it. Needs-based or benefits-based segmentation is a widely used approach because it identifies distinct market segments with clear marketing implications. For example, a marketer of wines identified six different benefit segments in the premium wine market ($5.50 a bottle and up):[40]

■ *Enthusiast (12 percent of the market).* Skewing female, their average income is about US$76 000 a year. About 3 percent are "luxury enthusiasts" who skew more male with a higher income.

- *Image Seekers (20 percent).* This is the only segment that skews male, with an average age of 35. They use wine basically as a badge to say who they are, and they're willing to pay more to make sure they're getting the right bottle.

- *Savvy Shoppers (15 percent).* They love to shop and believe they don't have to spend a lot to get a good bottle of wine. They're happy to use the bargain bin.

- *Traditionalist (16 percent).* With very traditional values, they like to buy brands they've heard of and from wineries that have been around a long time. Their average age is 50 and they are 68 percent female.

- *Satisfied Sippers (14 percent).* Not knowing much about wine, they tend to buy the same brands. About half of what they drink is white zinfandel.

- *Overwhelmed (23 percent).* A potentially attractive target market, they find purchasing wine confusing.

DECISION ROLES It's easy to identify the buyer for many products. In North America, men normally choose their shaving equipment and women choose their pantyhose; but even here marketers must be careful in making targeting decisions, because buying roles change. When ICI, the giant British chemical company, discovered that women made 60 percent of decisions on the brand of household paint, it decided to advertise its Dulux brand to women.

People play five roles in a buying decision: *Initiator, Influencer, Decider, Buyer,* and *User.* For example, assume a wife initiates a purchase by requesting a new treadmill for her birthday. The husband may then seek information from many sources, including his best friend who has a treadmill and is a key influencer in what models to consider. After presenting the alternative choices to his wife, he purchases her preferred model, which ends up being used by the entire family. Different people are playing different roles, but all are crucial in the decision process and ultimate consumer satisfaction.

USER AND USAGE—REAL USER AND USAGE-RELATED VARIABLES Many marketers believe variables related to various aspects of users or their usage—occasions, user status, usage rate, buyer-readiness stage, and loyalty status—are good starting points for constructing market segments.

Occasions Occasions mark a time of day, week, month, year, or other well-defined temporal aspects of a consumer's life. We can distinguish buyers according to the occasions when they develop a need, purchase a product, or use a product. For example, air travel is triggered by occasions related to business, vacation, or family. Occasion segmentation can help expand product usage.

User Status Every product has its nonusers, ex-users, potential users, first-time users, and regular users. Blood banks cannot rely only on regular donors to supply blood; they must also recruit new first-time donors and contact ex-donors, using a different marketing strategy for each. The key to attracting potential users, or even possibly nonusers, is understanding the reasons they are not using. Do they have deeply held attitudes, beliefs, or behaviours or just lack knowledge of the product or brand benefits and usage?

Included in the potential-user group are consumers who will become users in connection with some life stage or life event. Mothers-to-be are potential users who will turn into heavy users. Producers of infant products and services learn their names and shower them with products and ads to capture a share of their future purchases. Market share leaders tend to focus on attracting potential users because they stand to gain from that segment the most. Smaller firms focus on trying to attract current users away from the market leader.

Usage Rate We can segment markets into light, medium, and heavy product users. Heavy users are often a small slice but account for a high percentage of total consumption. Heavy beer drinkers account for 87 percent of beer consumption—almost seven times as much as light drinkers. Marketers would rather attract one heavy user than several light users. A potential problem, however, is that heavy users are often either extremely loyal to one brand or never loyal to any brand and always looking for the lowest price. They also may have less room to expand their purchase and consumption.

Buyer-Readiness Stage Some people are unaware of the product, some are aware, some are informed, some are interested, some desire the product, and some intend to buy. To help characterize how many people are at different stages and how well they have converted people from one stage to another, marketers can employ a *marketing funnel* to break down the market into different buyer-readiness stages.

The proportions of consumers at different stages make a big difference in designing the marketing program. Suppose a health agency wants to encourage women to have an annual Pap test to detect cervical cancer. At the beginning, most women may be unaware of the Pap test. The marketing effort should go into awareness-building advertising using a simple message. Later, the advertising should dramatize the benefits of the Pap test and the risks of not getting it. A special offer of a free health examination might motivate women to actually sign up for the test.

Figure 8.2 displays a funnel for two hypothetical brands. Compared with Brand B, Brand A performs poorly at converting one-time users to more recent users (only 46 percent convert for Brand A compared with 61 percent for Brand B). Depending on the reasons consumers didn't use again, a marketing campaign could introduce more relevant products, find more accessible retail outlets, or dispel rumours or incorrect beliefs consumers hold.

Loyalty Status Marketers usually envision four groups based on brand loyalty status:

1. *Hard-core loyals*—Consumers who buy only one brand all the time

2. *Split loyals*—Consumers who are loyal to two or three brands

3. *Shifting loyals*—Consumers who shift loyalty from one brand to another

4. *Switchers*—Consumers who show no loyalty to any brand[41]

A company can learn a great deal by analyzing degrees of brand loyalty: Hard-core loyals can help identify the products' strengths; split loyals can show the firm which brands are most competitive with its own; and by looking at customers who dropped its brand, the company can learn about its marketing weaknesses and attempt to correct them. One caution: what appear to be brand loyal purchasing patterns may reflect habit, indifference, a low price, a high switching cost, or the unavailability of other brands.

Attitude Five consumer attitudes about products are enthusiastic, positive, indifferent, negative, and hostile. Door-to-door workers in a political campaign use attitude to determine how much time to spend with each voter. They thank enthusiastic voters and remind them to vote, reinforce those who are positively disposed, try to win the votes of indifferent voters, and spend no time trying to change the attitudes of negative and hostile voters.

Multiple Bases Combining different behavioural bases can provide a more comprehensive and cohesive view of a market and its segments. Figure 8.3 depicts one possible way to break down a target market by various behavioural segmentation bases.

BASES FOR SEGMENTING BUSINESS MARKETS

We can segment business markets with some of the same variables we use in consumer markets, such as geography, benefits sought, and usage rate, but business marketers also use other variables. Table 8.5 shows one set of these. The demographic variables are the most important, followed by the operating variables—down to the personal characteristics of the buyer.

The table lists major questions that business marketers should ask in determining which segments and customers to serve. A rubber-tire company can sell tires to manufacturers of automobiles, trucks, farm tractors, forklift trucks, or aircraft. Within a chosen target industry, it can further segment by company size and set up separate operations for selling to large and small customers. Small businesses, in particular, are important in the Canadian context, as they account for about 25 percent of Canada's gross domestic product.

FIGURE 8.2

Brand Funnel

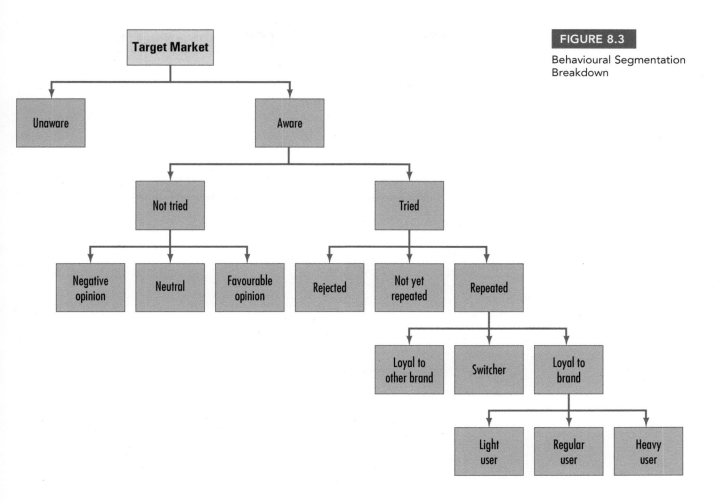

FIGURE 8.3

Behavioural Segmentation
Breakdown

A company can segment further by purchase criteria. Government laboratories need low prices and service contracts for scientific equipment, university laboratories need equipment that requires little service, and industrial labs need equipment that is highly reliable and accurate.

Business marketers generally identify segments through a sequential process. Consider an aluminum company. The company first undertook macrosegmentation. It looked at which end-use market to serve: automobile, residential, or beverage containers. It chose the residential market, and it needed to determine the most attractive product application: semifinished material, building components, or aluminum mobile homes. Deciding to focus on building components, it considered the best customer size and chose large customers. The second stage consisted of microsegmentation. The company distinguished among customers buying on price, service, or quality. Because it had a high-service profile, the firm decided to concentrate on the service-motivated segment of the market.

Business-to-business marketing experts James C. Anderson and James A. Narus have urged marketers to present flexible market offerings to all members of a segment.[42] A **flexible market offering** consists of two parts: a *naked solution* containing the product and service elements that all segment members value, and *discretionary options* that some segment members value. Each option might carry an additional charge. Siemens Electrical Apparatus Division sells metal-clad boxes to small manufacturers at prices that include free delivery and a warranty, but it also offers installation, tests, and communication peripherals as extra-cost options. WestJet offers all economy passengers a seat, a small snack, and soft drinks but charges extra for alcoholic beverages and meals on its domestic and transborder flights.

TABLE 8.5 | MAJOR SEGMENTATION VARIABLES FOR BUSINESS MARKETS

Demographic

1. *Industry:* Which industries should we serve?
2. *Company size:* What size companies should we serve?
3. *Location:* What geographical areas should we serve?

Operating Variables

4. *Technology:* What customer technologies should we focus on?
5. *User or nonuser status:* Should we serve heavy users, medium users, light users, or nonusers?
6. *Customer capabilities:* Should we serve customers needing many or few services?

Purchasing Approaches

7. *Purchasing-function organization:* Should we serve companies with highly centralized or decentralized purchasing organizations?
8. *Power structure:* Should we serve companies that are engineering dominated, financially dominated, and so on?
9. *Nature of existing relationships:* Should we serve companies with which we have strong relationships or simply go after the most desirable companies?
10. *General purchase policies:* Should we serve companies that prefer leasing? Service contracts? Systems purchases? Sealed bidding?
11. *Purchasing criteria:* Should we serve companies that are seeking quality? Service? Price?

Situational Factors

12. *Urgency:* Should we serve companies that need quick and sudden delivery or service?
13. *Specific application:* Should we focus on certain applications of our product rather than all applications?
14. *Size of order:* Should we focus on large or small orders?

Personal Characteristics

15. *Buyer–seller similarity:* Should we serve companies whose people and values are similar to ours?
16. *Attitudes toward risk:* Should we serve risk-taking or risk-avoiding customers?
17. *Loyalty:* Should we serve companies that show high loyalty to their suppliers?

Source: Adapted from Thomas V. Bonoma and Benson P. Shapiro, *Segmenting the Industrial Market* (Lexington, MA: Lexington Books, 1983).

MARKET TARGETING

There are many statistical techniques for developing market segments.[43] Once the firm has identified its market-segment opportunities, it must decide how many and which ones to target. Marketers are increasingly combining several variables in an effort to identify smaller, better-defined target groups. Thus, a bank may not only identify a group of wealthy retired adults but within that group distinguish several segments depending on current income, assets, savings, and risk preferences. This has led some market researchers to advocate a *needs-based market segmentation approach,* as introduced previously. Roger Best proposed the seven-step approach shown in Table 8.6.

Effective Segmentation Criteria

Not all segmentation schemes are useful. We could divide buyers of table salt into blond and brunette customers, but hair colour is undoubtedly irrelevant to the purchase of salt. Furthermore, if all salt buyers buy the same amount of salt each month, believe all salt is the same, and would pay only one price for salt, this market is minimally segmentable from a marketing point of view.

TABLE 8.6 | STEPS IN THE SEGMENTATION PROCESS

	Description
1. Needs-Based Segmentation	Group customers into segments based on similar needs and benefits sought by customers in solving a particular consumption problem.
2. Segment Identification	For each needs-based segment, determine which demographics, lifestyles, and usage behaviours make the segment distinct and identifiable (actionable).
3. Segment Attractiveness	Using predetermined segment attractiveness criteria (such as market growth, competitive intensity, and market access), determine the overall attractiveness of each segment.
4. Segment Profitability	Determine segment profitability.
5. Segment Positioning	For each segment, create a "value proposition" and product-price positioning strategy based on that segment's unique customer needs and characteristics.
6. Segment "Acid Test"	Create "segment storyboard" to test the attractiveness of each segment's positioning strategy.
7. Marketing-Mix Strategy	Expand segment positioning strategy to include all aspects of the marketing mix: product, price, promotion, and place.

Source: *BEST, ROGER, MARKET-BASED MANAGEMENT, 5th ed.,* © 2009. Adapted and Electronically reproduced by permission of Pearson Education, Inc., Upper Saddle River, New Jersey.

To be useful, market segments must rate favourably on five key criteria:

■ *Measurable.* The size, purchasing power, and characteristics of the segments can be measured.

■ *Substantial.* The segments are large and profitable enough to serve. A segment should be the largest possible homogeneous group worth going after with a tailored marketing program. It would not pay, for example, for an automobile manufacturer to develop cars for people who are less than four feet tall.

■ *Accessible.* The segments can be effectively reached and served.

■ *Differentiable.* The segments are conceptually distinguishable and respond differently to different marketing-mix elements and programs. If married and unmarried women respond similarly to a sale on perfume, they do not constitute separate segments.

■ *Actionable.* Effective programs can be formulated for attracting and serving the segments.

Michael Porter has identified five forces that determine the intrinsic long-run attractiveness of a market or market segment: industry competitors, potential entrants, substitutes, buyers, and suppliers. The threats these forces pose are as follows:

1. *Threat of intense segment rivalry*—A segment is unattractive if it already contains numerous, strong, or aggressive competitors. It's even more unattractive if it's stable or declining, if plant capacity must be added in large increments, if fixed costs or exit barriers are high, or if competitors have high stakes in staying in the segment. These conditions will lead to frequent price wars, advertising battles, and new-product introductions and will make it expensive to compete. The cell phone market has seen fierce competition due to segment rivalry.

2. *Threat of new entrants*—The most attractive segment is one in which entry barriers are high and exit barriers are low.[44] Few new firms can enter the industry, and poorly performing firms can easily exit. When both entry and exit barriers are high, profit potential is high, but firms face more risk because poorer-performing firms stay in and fight it out. When both entry and exit barriers are low, firms easily enter and leave the industry, and returns are stable but low. The worst case is when entry barriers are low and exit barriers are high: here firms enter during good times but find it hard to leave during bad times. The result is chronic overcapacity and depressed earnings for all. The airline industry has low entry barriers but high exit barriers, leaving all carriers struggling during economic downturns.

3. *Threat of substitute products*—A segment is unattractive when there are actual or potential substitutes for the product. Substitutes place a limit on prices and on profits. If technology advances or competition increases in these substitute industries, prices and profits are likely to fall. Air travel has severely challenged profitability for Greyhound and VIA Rail.

4. *Threat of buyers' growing bargaining power*—A segment is unattractive if buyers possess strong or growing bargaining power. The rise of retail giants such as Walmart has led some analysts to conclude that the potential profitability of packaged-goods companies will become curtailed. Buyers' bargaining power grows when they become more concentrated or organized, when the product represents a significant fraction of their costs, when the product is undifferentiated, when buyers' switching costs are low, when buyers are price-sensitive because of low profits, or when they can integrate upstream. To protect themselves, sellers might select buyers who have the least power to negotiate or switch suppliers. A better defence is developing superior offers that strong buyers cannot refuse.

5. *Threat of suppliers' growing bargaining power*—A segment is unattractive if the company's suppliers are able to raise prices or reduce quantity supplied. Suppliers tend to be powerful when they are concentrated or organized, when they can integrate downstream, when there are few substitutes, when the supplied product is an important input, and when the costs of switching suppliers are high. The best defences are to build win-win relationships with suppliers or use multiple supply sources.

Evaluating and Selecting the Market Segments

In evaluating different market segments, the firm must look at two factors: the segment's overall attractiveness and the company's objectives and resources. How well does a potential segment score on the five criteria? Does it have characteristics that make it generally attractive, such as size, growth, profitability, scale economies, and low risk? Does investing in the segment make sense given the firm's objectives, competencies, and resources? Some attractive segments may not mesh with the company's long-run objectives, or the company may lack one or more necessary competencies to offer superior value.

Marketers have a range or continuum of possible levels of segmentation that can guide their target market decisions. As Figure 8.4 shows, at one end is a mass market of essentially one segment; at the other are individuals or segments of one person. Between lie multiple segments and single segments. We describe each of the four approaches next.

FULL MARKET COVERAGE With full market coverage, a firm attempts to serve all customer groups with all the products they might need. Only very large firms such as Microsoft (software market), General Motors (vehicle market), and Coca-Cola (nonalcoholic beverage market) can undertake a full market coverage strategy. Large firms can cover a whole market in two broad ways: through differentiated or undifferentiated marketing.

In *undifferentiated* or *mass marketing,* the firm ignores segment differences and goes after the whole market with one offer. It designs a marketing program for a product with a superior image that can be sold to the broadest number of buyers via mass distribution and mass communications. Undifferentiated marketing is appropriate when all consumers have roughly the same preferences and the market shows no natural segments. Henry Ford epitomized this strategy when he offered the Ford Model T in one colour, black.

The argument for mass marketing is that it creates the largest potential market, which leads to the lowest costs, which in turn can lead to lower prices or higher margins. The narrow product line keeps down the costs of research and development, production, inventory, transportation, marketing research, advertising, and product management. The undifferentiated communication program also reduces costs. However, many critics point to the increasing splintering of the market, and the proliferation of marketing channels and communication, which make it difficult and increasingly expensive to reach a mass audience.

FIGURE 8.4

Possible Levels of Segmentation

Although P&G initially targeted very specific segments with its Crest Whitestrips tooth-whitening product, it later expanded both its product offerings and its target markets.

When different groups of consumers have different needs and wants, marketers can define multiple segments. The company can often better design, price, disclose, and deliver the product or service and also fine-tune the marketing program and activities to better reflect competitors' marketing. In *differentiated marketing,* the firm sells different products to all the different segments of the market. Cosmetics firm Estée Lauder markets brands that appeal to women (and men) of different tastes: The flagship brand, the original Estée Lauder, appeals to older consumers; Clinique caters to middle-aged women; M.A.C. to youthful hipsters; Aveda to aromatherapy enthusiasts; and Origins to eco-conscious consumers who want cosmetics made from natural ingredients.[45]

Differentiated marketing typically creates more total sales than undifferentiated marketing. However, it also increases the costs of doing business. Because differentiated marketing leads to both higher sales and higher costs, no generalizations about its profitability are valid.

MULTIPLE-SEGMENT SPECIALIZATION With *selective specialization,* a firm selects a subset of all the possible segments, each objectively attractive and appropriate. There may be little or no synergy among the segments, but each promises to be a moneymaker. When Procter & Gamble launched Crest Whitestrips, initial target segments included newly engaged women and brides-to-be as well as gay males. The multi-segment strategy also has the advantage of diversifying the firm's risk.

Keeping synergies in mind, companies can try to operate in supersegments rather than in isolated segments. A **supersegment** is a set of segments sharing some exploitable similarity. For example, many symphony orchestras target people who have broad cultural interests, rather than only those who regularly attend concerts. A firm can also attempt to achieve some synergy with product or market specialization:

- With *product specialization,* the firm sells a certain product to several different market segments. A microscope manufacturer, for instance, sells to university, government, and commercial laboratories, making different instruments for each and building a strong reputation in the specific product area. The downside risk is that the product may be supplanted by an entirely new technology.

- With *market specialization,* the firm concentrates on serving many needs of a particular customer group, such as by selling an assortment of products only to university laboratories. The firm gains a strong reputation among this customer group and becomes a channel for additional products its members can use. The downside risk is that the customer group may suffer budget cuts or shrink in size.

SINGLE-SEGMENT CONCENTRATION With single-segment concentration, the firm markets to only one particular segment. Porsche concentrates on the sports-car market and Volkswagen on the small-car market—VW's foray into the large-car market with the Phaeton was a failure in the United States. Through concentrated marketing, the firm gains deep knowledge of the segment's needs and achieves a strong market presence. It also enjoys operating economies by specializing its production, distribution, and promotion. If it captures segment leadership, the firm can earn a high return on its investment.

A *niche* is a more narrowly defined customer group seeking a distinctive mix of benefits within a segment. Marketers usually identify niches by dividing a segment into subsegments. Whereas Hertz,

Avis, Alamo, and others specialize in airport rental cars for business and leisure travellers, Enterprise has attacked the low-budget, insurance-replacement market by primarily renting to customers whose cars have been wrecked or stolen. By creating unique associations to low cost and convenience in an overlooked niche market, Enterprise has been highly profitable. Many new products may target broad segments, but as they evolve over the product life cycle new versions of the product begin to target smaller segments, as evidenced even in the case of social networking websites.

SkiThis.ca

After the great success of social networking sites such as Facebook and MySpace, there seems to be a new trend appearing. New social networking sites are beginning to focus on smaller, more homogeneous groups. SkiThis.ca was started by avid skiers from Kelowna, B.C. The goal of the website is to attract and connect passionate skiers across British Columbia through photos, videos, and blog posts. The website is filled with everything ski-related, from snow reports for the major ski areas in B.C. to reviews of the latest ski goggles. People are beginning to find their own groups online based on their interests and hobbies, and marketers are taking notice, making it easier for them to target and communicate with a narrowly defined target market.[46]

Niche marketers aim to understand their customers' needs so well that customers willingly pay a premium. Fairmont Hotels like the Banff Springs and Chateau Lake Louise cater to the personal preferences of their Presidents' Club members so well that members return to these hotels despite the chain's premium pricing.

What does an attractive niche look like? Customers have a distinct set of needs; they will pay a premium to the firm that best satisfies them; the niche is fairly small but has size, profit, and growth potential and is unlikely to attract many competitors; and the niche gains certain economies through specialization. As marketing efficiency increases, niches that were seemingly too small may become more profitable.[47] See "Marketing Insight: Chasing the Long Tail."

INDIVIDUAL MARKETING The ultimate level of segmentation leads to "segments of one," "customized marketing," or "one-to-one marketing."[48] Today, customers are taking more individual initiative in determining what and how to buy. They log on to the Internet; look up information and evaluations of product or service offerings; conduct dialogue with suppliers, users, and product critics; and in many cases design the product they want.

Jerry Wind and Arvind Rangaswamy see a movement toward "customerizing" the firm.[49] **Customerization** combines operationally driven mass customization with customized marketing in a way that empowers consumers to design the product and service offering of their choice. The firm no longer requires prior information about the customer, nor does it need to own manufacturing. It provides a platform and tools and "rents" to customers the means to design their own products. A company is customerized when it is able to respond to individual customers by customizing its products, services, and messages on a one-to-one basis.[50]

Customization is certainly not for every company.[51] It may be very difficult to implement for complex products such as automobiles. It can also raise the cost of goods by more than the customer is willing to pay. Some customers don't know what they want until they see actual products, but they also cannot cancel the order after the company has started to work on it. The product may be hard to repair and have little sales value. In spite of this, customization has worked well for some products.

ETHICAL CHOICE OF MARKET TARGETS Marketers must target carefully to avoid consumer backlash. Some consumers resist being labelled. Singles may reject single-serve food packaging because they don't want to be reminded they are eating alone. Elderly consumers who don't feel their age may not appreciate products that label them "old."

Market targeting also can generate public controversy when marketers take unfair advantage of vulnerable groups (such as children) or disadvantaged groups (such as inner-city poor people) or promote potentially harmful products.[52] The cereal industry has been heavily criticized for marketing efforts directed toward children. Critics worry that high-powered appeals presented through the mouths of lovable animated characters will overwhelm children's defences and lead them to want sugared cereals or poorly balanced breakfasts. Toy marketers have been similarly criticized.

Another area of concern is the millions of kids under the age of 17 who are online. Marketers have jumped online with them, offering freebies in exchange for personal information. Many have come under

---

| MARKETING **INSIGHT** | CHASING THE LONG TAIL |

The advent of online commerce, made possible by technology and epitomized by Amazon, eBay, iTunes, and Netflix, has led to a shift in consumer buying patterns, according to Chris Anderson, editor-in-chief of *Wired* magazine and author of *The Long Tail*.

In most markets, the distribution of product sales conforms to a curve weighted heavily to one side—the "head"—where the bulk of sales are generated by a few products. The curve falls rapidly toward zero and hovers just above it far along the X-axis—the "long tail"—where the vast majority of products generate very little sales. The mass market traditionally focused on generating "hit" products that occupy the head, disdaining the low-revenue market niches composing the tail. The Pareto principle, based on the 80–20 rule that 80 percent of a firm's revenue is generated by 20 percent of a firm's products, epitomizes this thinking.

Anderson asserts that as a result of consumers' enthusiastic adoption of the Internet as a shopping medium, the long tail holds significantly more value than before. In fact, Anderson argues, the Internet has directly contributed to the shifting of demand "down the tail, from hits to niches" in a number of product categories, including music, books, clothing, and movies. According to this view, the rule that now prevails is more like "50–50," with smaller-selling products adding up to half of a firm's revenue.

Anderson's long-tail theory is based on three premises: (1) Lower costs of distribution make it economically easier to sell products without precise predictions of demand; (2) the more products available for sale, the greater the likelihood of tapping into latent demand for niche tastes unreachable through traditional retail channels; and (3) if enough niche tastes are aggregated, a big new market can result.

Anderson identifies two aspects of Internet shopping that support these premises. First, the increased inventory and variety afforded online permit greater choice. Second, the search costs for relevant new products are lowered due to the wealth of information online, the filtering of product recommendations based on user preferences that vendors can provide, and the word-of-mouth network of Internet users.

Some critics challenge the notion that old business paradigms have changed as much as Anderson suggests. Especially in entertainment, they say, the "head" where hits are concentrated is valuable also to consumers, not only to content creators. One critic argued that "most hits are popular because they are of high quality," and another noted that the majority of products and services making up the long tail originate from a small concentration of online "long-tail aggregators."

Although some academic research supports the long-tail theory, other research is more challenging, finding that poor recommendation systems render many very low-share products in the tail so obscure and hard to find they disappear before they can be purchased frequently enough to justify their existence. For companies selling physical products, the inventory, stocking, and handling costs can outweigh any financial benefits of such products.

Sources: Chris Anderson, *The Long Tail* (New York: Hyperion, 2006); "Reading the Tail" (interview with Chris Anderson), *Wired*, July 8, 2006, p. 30; "Wag the Dog: What the Long Tail Will Do," *The Economist*, July 8, 2006, p. 77; Erik Brynjolfsson, Yu "Jeffrey" Hu, and Michael D. Smith, "From Niches to Riches: Anatomy of a Long Tail," *MIT Sloan Management Review*, Summer 2006, p. 67; John Cassidy, "Going Long," *New Yorker*, July 10, 2006; www.longtail.com; "Rethinking the Long Tail Theory: How to Define 'Hits' and 'Niches,'" *Knowledge@Wharton*, September 16, 2009.

fire for this practice and for not clearly differentiating ads from games or entertainment. Establishing ethical and legal boundaries in marketing to children online and offline continues to be a hot topic as consumer advocates decry the commercialism they believe such marketing engenders.

Not all attempts to target children, minorities, or other special segments draw criticism, as illustrated by the following RBC example.

RBC

Aimed at physical-education teachers and community-recreation leaders, Royal Bank's Wicket Cricket program introduces the basics of cricket to kids in grades 2 to 6. Potential participants can register for the program at www.rbc.com/cricket. They receive a free kit that includes youth-sized bats, balls, wickets, and a DVD resource guide that outlines the rules of the game and practice drills. The site also provides coaching tips and information on establishing a house league and tournament play. The program is one manifestation of RBC's commitment to multicultural communities, especially for immigrant customers who are new to Canada and trying to involve their kids in activities that are familiar and bring a sense of home.[53]

Colgate-Palmolive's Colgate Junior toothpaste has special features designed to get children to brush longer and more often. Other companies are responding to the special needs of minority segments. Black-owned ICE Theaters noticed that although moviegoing by blacks had surged, there were few inner-city theatres. Starting in Chicago, ICE partnered with local black communities, using local radio stations to promote films and featuring favourite food items at concession stands.[54] Thus, the issue is not who is targeted, but how and for what. Socially responsible marketing calls for targeting that serves not only the company's interests, but also the interests of those targeted.

This is the case many companies make in marketing to the nation's preschoolers. With nearly 4 million youngsters attending some kind of organized child care, the potential market—including kids and parents—is too great to pass up. So in addition to standards such as art easels, gerbil cages, and blocks, the nation's preschools are likely to have Care Bear worksheets, Pizza Hut reading programs, and Nickelodeon magazines.

Teachers and parents are divided about the ethics of this increasing preschool marketing push. Some side with groups such as Stop Commercial Exploitation of Children, whose members feel preschoolers are incredibly susceptible to advertising and that schools' endorsements of products make children believe the product is good for them—no matter what it is. Yet many preschools and day care centres operating on tight budgets welcome the free resources.[55]

As part of its commitment to multicultural communities, RBC launched its Wicket Cricket program in 2008.

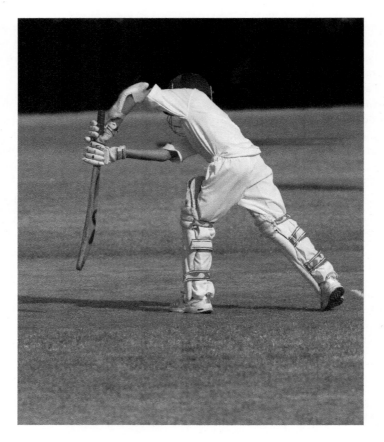

SUMMARY

1. Target marketing comprises three activities: market segmentation, market targeting, and market positioning. Market segments are large, identifiable groups within a market.

2. Two bases for segmenting consumer markets are consumer characteristics and consumer responses. The major segmentation variables for consumer markets are geographic, demographic, psychographic, and behavioural. Marketers use them singly or in combination.

3. Business marketers use all these variables along with operating variables, purchasing approaches, and situational factors.

4. To be useful, market segments must be measurable, substantial, accessible, differentiable, and actionable.

5. We can target markets at four main levels: mass market, multiple segments, single (or niche) segments, and individuals.

6. A mass market targeting approach is adopted only by the biggest companies. Many companies target multiple segments defined in various ways such as various demographic groups who seek the same product benefit.

7. A niche is a more narrowly defined group. Globalization and the Internet have made niche marketing more feasible to many.

8. More companies now practise individual and mass customization. The future is likely to see more individual consumers take the initiative in designing products and brands.

9. Marketers must choose target markets in a socially responsible manner at all times.

APPLICATIONS

Marketing Debate: Is Mass Marketing Dead?

With marketers increasingly adopting more and more refined market segmentation schemes—fuelled by the Internet and other customization efforts—some claim mass marketing is dead. Others counter that there will always be room for large brands employing marketing programs to target the mass market.

Take a position: Mass marketing is dead *versus* Mass marketing is still a viable way to build a profitable brand.

Marketing Discussion: Marketing Segmentation Schemes

Think of various product categories. In each segmentation scheme, to which segment do you feel you belong? How would marketing be more or less effective for you depending on the segment? How would you contrast demographic and behavioural segment schemes? Which one(s) do you think would be most effective for marketers trying to sell to you?

MARKETING EXCELLENCE | CLEARLY CONTACTS

Founded in 2000, Canada's Clearly Contacts Inc. quickly took the eye-care market by storm, becoming the world's largest online retailer of vision-care products in just ten years. Building successful operations in Canada, Clearly Contacts repeated this success abroad, expanding into the United States, Europe, Australia, and much of Asia. A knack for identifying profitable market segments and a bold strategy to enter those markets constitute the recipe behind Clearly Contacts' rapid growth.

Founder and CEO Roger Hardy came up with the idea for an online optical store when he realized he could offer customers an alternative to the large markups optical stores were charging. He set out to create a more affordable and efficient way for consumers to purchase vision care, through an online environment. Offering users quality contact lenses and accessories at lower prices with a 30-day money-back guarantee, his company was able to capture a sizeable segment of online buyers.

Originally selling only contact lenses, Hardy listened to the voice of his customers who told him they wanted eyeglasses as well. The idea was attractive, considering the eyeglass market in the United States alone was worth about US$35 billion, ten times the size of the contact lens market. The question that loomed was whether the company could compete with traditional eye-care retailers in the prescription eyeglass market. Offering lower prices, free shipping, and a money-back guarantee; bundling contact lenses and eyeglasses; offering a wide assortment of brands; and giving customers the ability to shop 24/7 gave the company adequate differentiation from brick-and-mortar competitors. In 2008, Clearly started retailing eyeglasses on the website and to Hardy's surprise, the demand was much larger than anticipated—over 500 pairs of eyeglasses were shipped in one day. Fast forward a few years, and the company now regularly ships over 3000 pairs of eyeglasses each day, with some days seeing sales as high as 5000 pairs.

Targeting the right groups of consumers has allowed Clearly Contacts to attract a loyal following of over 2 million customers worldwide. In order to break into a new geographical segment, the company has used a viral campaign that communicates an upcoming day where consumers in that particular area can order a free pair of glasses. In December 2010, the company gave away free prescription glasses to the first 10 000 customers who lived in and around New York and "liked" the company's Facebook page. Giving away free glasses has proven a successful viral marketing strategy that attracts new visitors to the website and helps create awareness among potential customers in a new geographic area.

Entering new markets has not been done without careful consideration of regional differences. Each nation has its own dedicated website and brand—for example, Clearly Contacts in Canada, Coastal Contacts in the United States, and LensWay in the United Kingdom. Each country's website has a unique design and product offering suited to the country. With a customer base of nearly 3 million customers, the company hopes to become the market leader in all 150 countries it currently serves. This revolutionary company has grown to over 350 employees with sales revenues over $150 million in 2010. With successful segmentation and targeting strategies in place, this Canadian company is well-positioned to become the world's leading vision-care retailer.

QUESTIONS

1. What are the different ways in which Clearly Contacts can segment the vision-care market?

2. By offering a wide assortment of products, is Clearly Contacts behaving like a mass marketer? Justify your answer.

3. What are some possible niche segments in the vision-care market that the company could consider serving?

Sources: "Coastal Contacts Breaks Another Record with Online Eyeglasses and Prepares to Grow Again," *Canada Newswire*, January 21, 2011; Roger Hardy, "Sandbox Solutions," *Profit*, *27*, no. 2 (May 2008): 27; Coastal Contacts Inc., "2010 Annual Report," December 15, 2010; Coastal Contacts Facebook page, www.facebook.com/CoastalContacts.com; Coastal Contacts website, www.coastalcontacts.com; Clearly Contacts website, www.clearlycontacts.ca; LensWay website, www.lensway.co.uk (all viewed March 5, 2011).

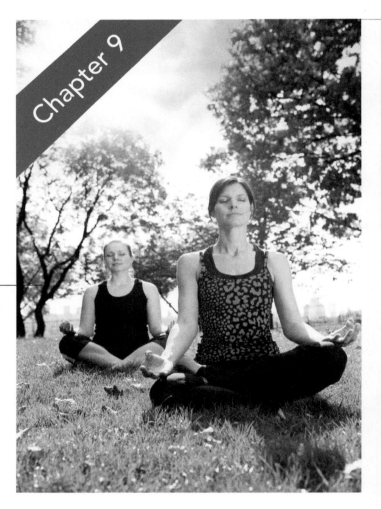

Chapter 9

In This Chapter, We Will Address the Following **Questions**

1. What is a brand and how does branding work?

2. What is brand equity?

3. How is brand equity built, measured, and managed?

4. What are the important decisions in developing a branding strategy?

With a unique concept and shrewd grassroots marketing, lululemon has attracted a loyal customer base and built a strong brand.

Creating Brand Equity

One of the most valuable intangible assets of a firm is its brands, and it is incumbent on marketing to properly manage their value. Building a strong brand is both an art and a science. It requires careful planning, a deep long-term commitment, and creatively designed and executed marketing. A strong brand commands intense consumer loyalty—at its heart is a great product or service.

While attending yoga classes, Canadian entrepreneur Chip Wilson decided the cotton-polyester blends most fellow students wore were too uncomfortable. After designing a well-fitting, sweat-resistant black garment to sell, he also decided to open a yoga studio, and lululemon was born. The company has taken a grassroots approach to growth that creates a strong emotional connection with its customers. Before it opens a store in a new city, lululemon first identifies influential yoga instructors or other fitness teachers. In exchange for a year's worth of clothing, these yogi serve as "ambassadors," hosting students at lululemon-sponsored classes and product sales events. They also provide product design advice to the company. The cult-like devotion of lululemon's customers is evident in their willingness to pay $92 for a pair of workout pants that might cost only $60 to $70 from Nike. lululemon can sell as much as $1800 worth of product per square foot in its approximately 100 stores, three times what other clothing retailers like Abercrombie & Fitch and J.Crew sell. After coping with some inventory challenges, the company is looking to expand beyond yoga-inspired athletic apparel and accessories into similar products in other sports such as running, swimming, and biking.[1]

Marketers of successful twenty-first-century brands must excel at the strategic brand management process. **Strategic brand management** combines the design and implementation of marketing activities and programs to build, measure, and manage brands to maximize their value. The strategic brand management process has four main steps:

- Identifying and establishing brand positioning
- Planning and implementing brand marketing
- Measuring and interpreting brand performance
- Growing and sustaining brand value deals with brand positioning

Chapter 10 deals with brand positioning. The remaining topics are discussed in this chapter.[2] Chapter 11 reviews important concepts for dealing with competition.

WHAT IS BRAND EQUITY?

Perhaps the most distinctive skill of professional marketers is their ability to create, maintain, enhance, and protect brands. Successful brands such as Bell, Dove, Sony, and Nike command a price premium and elicit much loyalty. New brands such as Google, Porter Airlines, and lululemon capture the imagination of consumers and the financial community alike.

The American Marketing Association defines a **brand** as "a name, term, sign, symbol, or design, or a combination of them, intended to identify the goods or services of one seller or group of sellers and to differentiate them from those of competitors."[3] A brand is thus a product or service with added dimensions that differentiate it in some way from other products or services designed to satisfy the same need. These differences may be functional, rational, or tangible—related to product performance of the brand. They may also be more symbolic, emotional, or intangible—related to what the brand represents or means in a more abstract sense.

Branding has been around for centuries as a means to distinguish the goods of one producer from those of another.[4] The earliest signs of branding in Europe were the medieval guilds' requirement that craftspeople put trademarks on their products to protect themselves and consumers against inferior quality. In the fine arts, branding began with artists signing their works. Brands today play a number of important roles that improve consumers' lives and enhance the financial value of firms.

The Role of Brands

Brands identify the source or maker of a product and allow consumers—either individuals or organizations—to assign responsibility to a particular manufacturer or distributor. Consumers may evaluate the identical product differently depending on how it is branded. Consumers learn about brands through past experiences with the product and its marketing program. They find out which brands satisfy their needs and which ones do not. As consumers' lives become more complicated, rushed, and time-starved, the ability of a brand to simplify decision making and reduce risk is invaluable.[5]

Brands also perform valuable functions for firms.[6] First, they simplify product handling or tracing. Brands help to organize inventory and accounting records. A brand also offers the firm legal protection for unique features or aspects of the product.[7] The brand name can be protected through registered trademarks, manufacturing processes can be protected through patents, and packaging can be protected through copyrights and designs. These intellectual property rights ensure that the firm can safely invest in the brand and reap the benefits of a valuable asset.

Brands can signal a certain level of quality so that satisfied buyers can easily choose the product again.[8] Brand loyalty provides predictability and security of demand for the firm and creates barriers to entry that make it difficult for other firms to enter the market. Loyalty also can translate into a willingness to pay a higher price—often 20 to 25 percent more.[9] Although competitors may easily duplicate manufacturing processes and product designs, they cannot easily match lasting impressions in the minds of individuals and organizations from years of marketing activity and product experience. In this sense, branding can be seen as a powerful means to secure a competitive advantage.[10]

Sometimes marketers don't see the real importance of brand loyalty until they change a crucial element of the brand, as the now-classic tale of New Coke illustrates.

Coca-Cola

Battered by a nationwide series of taste-test challenges from the sweeter-tasting Pepsi-Cola, Coca-Cola decided in 1985 to replace its old formula with a sweeter variation, dubbed New Coke. Coca-Cola spent $4 million on market research. Blind taste tests showed that Coke drinkers preferred the new, sweeter formula, but the launch of New Coke provoked a national uproar. Market researchers had measured the taste but failed to measure the emotional attachment consumers had to Coca-Cola. There were angry letters, formal protests, and even lawsuit threats to force the retention of "The Real Thing." Ten weeks later, the company withdrew New Coke and reintroduced its century-old formula as "Classic Coke," a move that ironically might have given the old formula even stronger status in the marketplace.

For better or worse, branding effects are pervasive. One research study that provoked much debate about the effects of marketing on children showed that preschoolers felt that identical McDonald's food items—even carrots, milk, and apple juice—tasted better when wrapped in the familiar McDonald's packaging than in unmarked wrappers.[11]

To firms, brands thus represent enormously valuable pieces of legal property that can influence consumer behaviour, be bought and sold, and provide the security of sustained future revenues. Companies have paid dearly for brands in mergers and acquisitions, often justifying the price premium on the basis of the extra profits that could be extracted and sustained from the brands, as well as the tremendous difficulty and expense of creating similar brands from scratch. The financial industry believes that strong brands result in better earnings and profit performance for firms, which, in turn, create greater value for shareholders.[12]

The Scope of Branding

How, then, do you brand a product? Although firms provide the impetus to brand creation through marketing programs and other activities, ultimately a brand is something that resides in the minds of consumers. A brand is a perceptual entity that is rooted in reality but reflects the perceptions and perhaps even the idiosyncrasies of consumers.

Branding is endowing products and services with the power of a brand. Branding is all about creating differences. To brand a product, it is necessary to teach consumers "who" the product is—by giving it a name and using other brand elements to help identify it—as well as "what" the product does and "why" consumers should care. Branding involves creating mental structures and helping consumers organize their knowledge about products and services in a way that clarifies their decision making and, in the process, provides value to the firm.

For branding strategies to be successful and for brand value to be created, consumers must be convinced that there are meaningful differences among brands in the product or service category. Brand differences often are related to attributes or benefits of the product itself. Bell, Gillette, Merck, RIM, TD, and others have been leaders in their product categories for decades due, in part, to continuous innovation. Other brands create competitive advantages through non-product-related means. Gucci, Louis Vuitton, and others have become leaders in their product categories by understanding consumer motivations and desires and creating relevant and appealing images of their products.

Marketers can apply branding virtually anywhere a consumer has a choice. It is possible to brand a physical good (Campbell's Gardennay Mediterranean Herbed Tomato soup or Molson's Canadian beer), a service (Air Canada travel, Bank of Nova Scotia banking, or Great-West Life insurance), a store (Foot Locker's specialty store or Sobeys' supermarket), a person (Margaret Atwood or Justin Bieber), a place (the city of Sydney, or the province of Newfoundland and Labrador), an organization (Canadian Automobile Association or CARE), or an idea (abortion rights or freedom of speech).[13] See how one young Canadian singer built his brand.[14]

Justin Bieber

The son of a poor single mother, born in London, Ontario, and growing up in Stratford, Ontario—this is not the usual profile of one of the world's hottest pop singers. Justin, however, was one of the first to be discovered on YouTube, where his amateur performances had been posted by his proud mother. Justin and his agent have used social media to continuously build his brand image and his career. His brand has tremendous power, and in early 2011, a music news magazine claimed that Justin was more influential than Barack Obama or the Dalai Lama based on research conducted by Klout. This company "adds together tweets, Facebook likes, pings, mentions on Google, status updates and other social media activity to give a score out of 100, depending on how often what someone has said gets repeated by others online." Justin was given the maximum score of 100, since his tweets are retweeted on average 5 million times each. In contrast, Barack Obama scored 88; his tweets were repeated an average of 250 000 times. It's not surprising that Justin Bieber's popularity (particularly on the Internet) has made him highly attractive as a spokesperson for brands. In August 2010, when "the Biebs" advertisement for Proactiv first aired, the clip received 125 000 views on YouTube and another 500 000 views on Proactiv's website.

Defining Brand Equity

Brand equity is the added value endowed to goods and services. This value may be reflected in how consumers think, feel, and act with respect to the brand, as well as in the prices, market share, and profitability that the brand commands.[15]

Marketers and researchers use various perspectives to study brand equity.[16] Customer-based approaches view brand equity from the perspective of the consumer—either an individual or an organization. The premise of customer-based brand equity models is that the power of a brand lies in what customers have seen, read, heard, learned, thought, and felt about the brand over time.[17]

Customer-based brand equity can be defined as the differential effect that brand knowledge has on consumer response to the marketing of that brand.[18] A brand is said to have positive customer-based brand equity when consumers react more favourably to a product and the way it is marketed when the brand is identified than when it is not. A brand is said to have negative customer-based brand equity if consumers react less favourably to marketing activity for the brand under the same circumstances.

There are three key ingredients of customer-based brand equity:

1. Brand equity arises from differences in consumer response. If no differences occur, the brand-name product is essentially a commodity and competition will probably be based on price.[19]

2. Differences in response are a result of consumers' **brand knowledge**, all the thoughts, feelings, images, experiences, and beliefs associated with the brand. Brands must create strong, favourable,

TABLE 9.1 | MARKETING ADVANTAGES OF STRONG BRANDS

- Improved perceptions of product performance
- Greater loyalty
- Less vulnerability to competitive marketing actions
- Less vulnerability to marketing crises
- Larger margins
- Less elastic consumer response to price increases
- More elastic consumer response to price decreases
- Greater trade co-operation and support
- Increased marketing communications effectiveness
- Possible licensing opportunities
- Additional brand-extension opportunities

and unique brand associations with customers, as have Toyota *(reliability)*, Hallmark *(caring)*, and Amazon.com *(convenience)*.

3. Brand equity is reflected in perceptions, preferences, and behaviour related to all aspects of the marketing of a brand.

Table 9.1 summarizes some key benefits of brand equity. Stronger brands lead to greater revenue.[20]

The challenge for marketers in building a strong brand, therefore, is ensuring that customers have the right type of experiences with goods and services and their marketing programs to create the desired brand knowledge. In an abstract sense, we can think of brand equity as providing marketers with a vital strategic "bridge" from their past to their future.[21]

Marketers should also think of the marketing dollars spent each year on goods and services as investments in consumer brand knowledge. The *quality* of the investment in brand building is the critical factor, not necessarily the *quantity,* beyond some minimal threshold amount. It is actually possible to overspend on brand building if money is not spent wisely.

Brand knowledge dictates appropriate future directions for the brand. A **brand promise** is the marketer's vision of what the brand must be and do for consumers. Consumers will decide, based on what they think and feel about the brand, where (and how) they believe the brand should go and grant permission (or not) to any marketing action or program. New-product ventures such as BENGAY aspirin, Cracker Jack cereal, Frito-Lay lemonade, Fruit of the Loom laundry detergent, and Smucker's premium ketchup all failed because consumers found them inappropriate extensions for the brand.

In contrast is a campaign by Stanfield's that resonated with consumers and added value to its brand.[22]

Stanfield's drew in a new target market and added value to its brand with its "A Guy at Home in His Underwear" campaign.

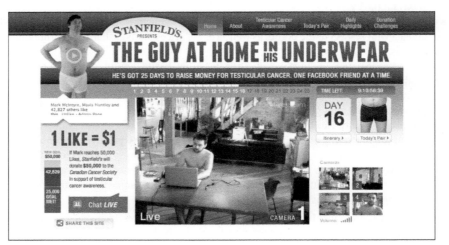

The Guy at Home in His Underwear

To increase the value and relevance of its brand to a younger target market (25- to 40-year-olds), Nova Scotia–based Stanfield's, a men's underwear company, made its first foray into social media with a Facebook campaign launched in October 2010. A live webcam tracked the activities of actor (and testicular cancer survivor) Mark McIntyre, who stayed at home in his underwear for 25 days. Stanfield's donated $1 to the Canadian Cancer Society to help increase awareness of testicular cancer for each "like" vote the site received. Company president Jon Stanfield was very much in favour of linking the brand to an important cause relevant to men and believed the campaign reflected the company's motto, "We Support Men." Although the initial goal was to raise $25 000, consumers were very responsive to the campaign and $50 000 was given to the cause.

Brand Equity Models

Although there is agreement about basic principles, a number of models of brand equity offer some different perspectives. Here we briefly highlight three of the more established ones.

BRAND ASSET VALUATOR Advertising agency Young & Rubicam (Y&R) developed a model of brand equity called Brand Asset Valuator (BAV). Based on research with almost 700 000 consumers in 51 countries, BAV provides comparative measures of the brand equity of thousands of brands across hundreds of different categories. There are four key components—or pillars—of brand equity according to BAV (see Figure 9.1):

- *Energized differentiation* measures the degree to which a brand is seen as different from others, and its perceived momentum and leadership.
- *Relevance* measures the breadth of a brand's appeal.
- *Esteem* measures how well a brand is regarded and respected.
- *Knowledge* measures how familiar and intimate consumers are with a brand.

Energized differentiation and relevance combine to determine *Brand Strength*—a leading indicator that predicts future growth and value. Esteem and knowledge together create *Brand Stature,* a "report card" on past performance and an indicator of current value.

Examining the relationships among these four dimensions—a brand's "pillar pattern"—reveals much about the brand's current and future status. Brand Strength and Brand Stature can be combined to form

FIGURE 9.1

BAV Power Grid

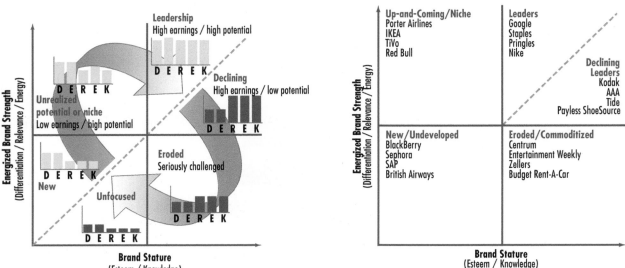

a power grid that depicts the stages in the cycle of brand development—each with its characteristic pillar patterns—in successive quadrants (see Figure 9.1). Strong new brands show higher levels of differentiation and energy than relevance, whereas both esteem and knowledge are lower still. Leadership brands show high levels on all pillars. Finally, declining brands show high knowledge—evidence of past performance—a lower level of esteem, and even lower relevance, energy, and differentiation.

According to BAV analysis, consumers are concentrating their devotion and purchasing power on an increasingly smaller portfolio of special brands—brands with energized differentiation and that keep evolving. These brands connect better with consumers—commanding greater usage loyalty and pricing power, and creating greater shareholder value. A hypothetical $10 000 invested in the top 50 energy-gaining brands gained 12 percent while the S&P 500 index lost nearly 20 percent between December 31, 2001, and June 30, 2009. Some of the latest insights from the BAV data are summarized in "Marketing Insight: Brand Bubble Trouble."

BRANDZ Marketing research consultants Millward Brown and WPP have developed the BRANDZ model of brand strength, at the heart of which is the BrandDynamics Pyramid. According to this model, brand building follows a sequential series of steps, each contingent upon successfully accomplishing the preceding one (see Figure 9.2).

For any one brand, each person interviewed is assigned to one level of the pyramid depending on their responses to a set of questions. The BrandDynamics Pyramid shows the number of consumers who have reached each level:

- *Bonding*—Rational and emotional attachments to the brand to the exclusion of most other brands

- *Advantage*—Belief that the brand has an emotional or rational advantage over other brands in the category

- *Performance*—Belief that it delivers acceptable product performance and is on the consumer's short list

- *Relevance*—Relevance to the consumer's needs, in the right price range or in the consideration set

- *Presence*—Active familiarity based on past trial, saliency, or knowledge of brand promise

"Bonded" consumers, those at the top of the pyramid, build stronger relationships with the brand and spend more on it than those at lower levels. More consumers, however, will be found at the lower levels. The challenge for marketers is to develop activities and programs that help consumers move up the pyramid.

BRAND RESONANCE MODEL The brand resonance model also views brand building as an ascending, sequential series of steps from bottom to top: (1) ensuring customers' identification with the brand and an association of the brand in customers' minds with a specific product class or customer need; (2) firmly establishing the totality of brand meaning in the minds of customers by strategically linking a host of tangible and intangible brand associations; (3) eliciting the proper customer responses in terms of brand-related judgment and feelings; and (4) converting brand response to create an intense, active loyalty relationship between customers and the brand.

FIGURE 9.2

BrandDynamics™ Pyramid

Source: BrandDynamics™ Pyramid. Reprinted by permission of MillwardBrown.

| MARKETING **INSIGHT** | | BRAND BUBBLE TROUBLE |

In *The Brand Bubble*, brand consultants Ed Lebar and John Gerzema use Y&R's historical BAV database to conduct a comprehensive examination of the state of brands. Beginning with data from mid-2004, they discovered several odd trends. For thousands of consumer goods and services brands, key brand value measures such as consumer "top-of-mind" awareness, trust, regard, and admiration experienced significant drops.

At the same time, however, share prices for a number of years were being driven higher by the intangible value the markets were attributing to consumer brands. Digging deeper, Lebar and Gerzema found that the increase was actually due to a very few extremely strong brands, such as Google, Apple, and Nike. The value created by the vast majority of brands was stagnating or falling.

The authors viewed this mismatch between the value consumers see in brands and the value the markets were ascribing to them as a recipe for disaster in two ways. At the macroeconomic level, it implied that stock prices of most consumer companies were overstated. At the microeconomic (company) level, it pointed to a serious and continuing problem in brand management.

Why have consumer attitudes toward brands declined? The research identified three fundamental causes. First, there has been a proliferation of brands. New-product introductions have accelerated, but many fail to register with consumers. Second, consumers expect creative "big ideas" from brands and feel they are just not getting them. Finally, due to corporate scandals, product crises, and executive misbehaviour, trust in brands has plummeted.

Yet vital brands are still being successfully built. Although all four pillars of the BAV model play a role, the strongest brands resonated with consumers in a special way. Amazon.com, Axe, Facebook, Innocent, IKEA, Land Rover, LG, LEGO, Tata, Nano, Twitter, Whole Foods, and Zappos exhibited notable energized differentiation by communicating dynamism and creativity in ways most other brands did not.

Formally, the BAV analysis identified three factors that help define energy and the marketplace momentum it creates:

1. *Vision*—A clear direction and point of view on the world and how it can and should be changed.

2. *Invention*—An intention for the product or service to change the way people think, feel, and behave.

3. *Dynamism*—Excitement and affinity in the way the brand is presented.

The authors offer a five-step framework to infuse brands with more energy:

1. **Perform an "energy audit" on your brand.** Identify the current sources and level of energy to understand your brand's strengths and weaknesses and how well brand management aligns with the dynamics of the new marketplace.

2. **Make your brand an organizing principle for the business.** Find an essential brand idea or thought that can serve as a lens through which you define every aspect of the customer experience, including products, services, and communications.

3. **Create an energized value chain.** Make the organization's goals for the brand real for everyone; all participants must think uniquely from the perspective of the brand and understand how their own actions boost the energy level of the brand and fuel the core.

4. **Become an energy-driven enterprise.** Stakeholders need to transfer their energy and passion to their business units and functions. Once management's aspirations for the brand and business begin becoming part of the culture, the process of building an energized brand enterprise is nearly complete.

5. **Create a loop of constant reinvention.** Finally, keep the organization and its brand in a state of constant renewal. Brand managers must be keenly aware of shifts in consumers' perception and values and be ready to reshape themselves again and again.

Sources: John Gerzema and Ed Lebar, *The Brand Bubble: The Looming Crisis in Brand Value and How to Avoid It* (New York: Jossey-Bass, 2008); Adapted and reprinted with permission from "The Trouble with Brands" by John Gerzema and Ed Lebar from the Summer 2009 issue of *strategy+business* magazine, published by Booz & Company. Copyright © 2009. All rights reserved. www.strategy-business.com.

MasterCard appeals to the head and the heart in its long-running "Priceless" campaign.

snow days: priceless MasterCard

For popcorn, pajamas, movies and more, there's MasterCard? Accepted coast to coast. mastercard.ca

© 2009 MasterCard. ® Registered trademark of MasterCard International.

According to this model, following the four steps involves establishing six "brand building blocks" with customers. These brand building blocks can be assembled into a brand pyramid, as illustrated in Figure 9.3. The model emphasizes the duality of brands—the rational route to brand building is the left-hand side of the pyramid, whereas the emotional route is the right-hand side.[23]

MasterCard is an example of a brand with duality, as it emphasizes both the rational advantage of the credit card, through its acceptance at establishments worldwide, and the emotional advantage through its award-winning "priceless" advertising campaign, which shows people buying items to reach a certain goal. The goal itself—a feeling, an accomplishment, or other intangible—is "priceless" ("There are some things money can't buy. For everything else, there's MasterCard").

Creating significant brand equity involves reaching the top or pinnacle of the brand pyramid and will occur only if the right building blocks are put into place:

- *Brand salience* relates to how often and easily the brand is evoked under various purchase or consumption situations.

- *Brand performance* relates to how the product or service meets customers' functional needs.

- *Brand imagery* deals with the extrinsic properties of the product or service, including the ways in which the brand attempts to meet customers' psychological or social needs.

- *Brand judgments* focus on customers' own opinions and evaluations.

- *Brand feelings* are customers' emotional responses and reactions with respect to the brand.

- *Brand resonance* refers to the nature of the relationship that customers have with the brand and the extent to which customers feel that they are in sync with the brand.

Resonance is characterized in terms of the intensity or depth of the psychological bond customers have with the brand, as well as the level of activity engendered by this loyalty.[24] Brands with high resonance include Harley-Davidson, Apple, and eBay. Fox News has found that the higher levels of resonance and engagement its programs engender often lead to greater recall of the ads it runs.[25]

FIGURE 9.3

Brand Resonance Pyramid

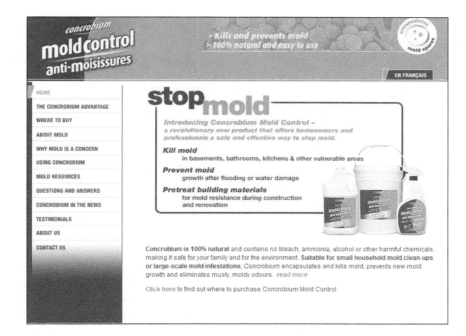

Concrobium carefully chose its brand elements—the colours, lettering, packaging, and label design—when launching its mould-control product.

BUILDING BRAND EQUITY

Marketers build brand equity by creating the right brand knowledge structures with the right consumers. This process depends on *all* brand-related contacts—whether marketer-initiated or not.[26] From a marketing management perspective, however, there are three main sets of *brand equity drivers:*

1. *The initial choices for the brand elements or identities making up the brand* (e.g., brand names, URLs, logos, symbols, characters, spokespeople, slogans, jingles, packages, and signage). Concrobium, a Canadian company that produces mould-control products, carefully chose the blue and green colours (blue for cleanliness, green for environmental friendliness) that characterize both its products and website. Its website also features clean-looking lettering and an uncluttered design. Unlike bleach, which can damage the environment when it goes down the drain, Concrobium is a non-toxic, all-natural product approved by Health Canada.[27]

2. *The product and service and all accompanying marketing activities and supporting marketing programs.* Liz Claiborne's fastest-growing label is Juicy Couture, whose edgy, contemporary sportswear and accessories have a strong lifestyle appeal to women, men, and kids. Positioned as an affordable luxury, the brand creates its exclusive cachet via limited distribution and a somewhat risqué name and rebellious attitude.[28]

3. *Other associations indirectly transferred to the brand by linking it to some other entity* (e.g., a person, place, or thing). The brand name of New Zealand vodka 42 Below refers to both a latitude that runs through New Zealand and the percentage of its alcohol content. All the packaging and other visual cues are designed to leverage the perceived purity of the country to communicate the positioning for the brand.[29]

Choosing Brand Elements

Brand elements are those trademarkable devices that serve to identify and differentiate the brand. Most strong brands employ multiple brand elements. Nike has the distinctive "swoosh" logo, the empowering "Just Do It" slogan, and the mythological "Nike" name based on the winged goddess of victory.

Marketers should choose brand elements to build as much brand equity as possible. The test of the brand-building ability of these elements is what consumers would think or feel about the product if they knew about only the brand element. Based on name alone, for instance, a consumer might expect SnackWell's products to be healthful snack foods and Panasonic Toughbook laptop computers to be durable and reliable.

CRITERIA FOR BRAND ELEMENT CHOICE There are six main criteria for choosing brand elements. The first three (memorable, meaningful, and likable) can be characterized as "brand building" in terms of how brand equity can be built through the judicious choice of a brand element. The latter three (transferable, adaptable, and protectable) are "defensive" and preserve brand equity against challenges.

1. *Memorable.* How easily is the brand element recalled? How easily recognized? Is this true at both purchase and consumption? Short brand names, such as Tide, WestJet, and Shell, can help.

2. *Meaningful.* To what extent is the brand element credible and suggestive of the corresponding category? Does it suggest something about a product ingredient or the type of person who might use the brand? Consider the inherent meaning in names such as Mastercraft tools sold by Canadian Tire, Mop & Glo floor wax, and Lean Cuisine low-calorie frozen entrees.

3. *Likable.* How aesthetically appealing do consumers find the brand element? A recent trend is for playful names that also offer a readily available URL, like Flikr photo sharing, Wakoopa social networking, and Motorola's ROKR and RAZR cell phones.[30]

4. *Transferable.* Can the brand element be used to introduce new products in the same or different categories? To what extent does the brand element add to brand equity across geographic boundaries and market segments? Although initially an online bookseller, Amazon.com was smart enough not to call itself "Books 'R' Us." The Amazon is famous as the world's biggest river, and the name suggests the wide variety of goods that could be shipped, an important descriptor of the diverse range of products the company now sells.

5. *Adaptable.* How adaptable and updatable is the brand element? Betty Crocker has received over eight make-overs in 87 years and she doesn't look a day over 35!

6. *Protectable.* How legally protectable is the brand element? How competitively protectable? Can it be easily copied? It is important that names that become synonymous with product categories—such as Kleenex, Kitty Litter, Jell-O, Scotch Tape, Xerox, and Rollerblade—retain their trademark rights and do not become generic.

DEVELOPING BRAND ELEMENTS Brand elements can play a number of brand-building roles.[31] If consumers do not examine much information in making their product decisions, brand elements should be easily recognized and recalled and inherently descriptive and persuasive. The likability of brand elements may also increase awareness and associations.[32] Often, the less concrete brand benefits are, the more important it is that the brand elements capture the brand's intangible characteristics. Many financial services use symbols of strength (the lion for RBC Financial Group), security (the key for Great-West Life), or symbols of their Canadian roots (the stylized maple leaf used by London Life).

Like brand names, slogans are an extremely efficient means to build brand equity.[33] Slogans can function as useful hooks or handles to help consumers grasp what the brand is and what makes it special. They are an indispensable means of summarizing and translating the intent of a marketing program. Think of the inherent brand meaning in slogans such as "like a good neighbour, State Farm is there," "like a rock" (GM trucks), and "RONA—the Canadian how-to people."

But choosing a name with inherent meaning creates less flexibility, making it harder to add a different meaning or update the positioning.[34]

Designing Holistic Marketing Activities

Brands are not built by advertising alone. Customers come to know a brand through a range of contacts and touch points: personal observation and use, word of mouth, interactions with company personnel, online or telephone experiences, and payment transactions. A **brand contact** can be defined as any information-bearing experience a customer or prospect has with the brand, the product category, or the market that relates to the marketer's product or service.[35] Any of these experiences can be positive or negative. The company must put as much effort into managing these experiences as it puts into producing its ads.[36]

The strategy and tactics behind marketing programs have changed dramatically in recent years.[37] Marketers are creating brand contacts and building brand equity through many avenues, such as clubs and consumer communities, trade shows, event marketing, sponsorships, factory visits, public relations and press releases, and social-cause marketing. To reach the coveted but fickle 12- to 24-year-old target market, Mountain Dew created the multicity Dew Tour, in which athletes compete in different skateboarding, BMX, and freestyle motocross events.[38]

Integrated marketing is about mixing and matching these marketing activities to maximize their individual and collective effects.[39] To achieve it, marketers need a variety of different marketing activities that consistently reinforce the brand promise. The Olive Garden has become the second-largest casual dining restaurant chain in North America, with approximately 650 restaurants, in part through establishing a fully integrated marketing program.

The Olive Garden

The Olive Garden brand promise is "the idealized Italian family meal" characterized by "fresh, simple, delicious Italian food," "complemented by a great glass of wine," served by "people who treat you like family," "in a comfortable homelike setting." To live up to that brand promise, the Olive Garden sends select managers and servers on cultural immersion trips to Italy, launched the Culinary Institute of Tuscany in Italy to inspire new dishes, conducts wine-training workshops for employees and in-restaurant wine sampling for customers, and remodelled restaurants to give them a Tuscan farmhouse look. Communications include in-store, employee, and mass media messages that all reinforce the brand promise and ad slogan, "When You're Here, You're Family."[40]

We can evaluate integrated marketing activities in terms of the effectiveness and efficiency with which they affect brand awareness and create, maintain, or strengthen brand associations and image. Although Volvo may invest in R&D and engage in advertising, promotions, and other communications to reinforce its "safety" brand association, it may also sponsor events to make sure it is seen as contemporary and up-to-date. Marketing programs should be put together so that the whole is greater than the sum of the parts. In other words, marketing activities should work singularly and in combination.

Leveraging Secondary Associations

The third and final way to build brand equity is, in effect, to "borrow" it. That is, create brand equity by linking the brand to other information in memory that conveys meaning to consumers (see Figure 9.4).

These "secondary" brand associations can link the brand to sources such as the company itself (through branding strategies), countries or other geographical regions (through identification of product origin), and channels of distribution (through channel strategy), as well as to other brands (through ingredient or co-branding), characters (through licensing), spokespeople (through endorsements), sporting or cultural events (through sponsorship), or some other third-party sources (through awards or reviews).

For example, assume Burton—makers of snowboards as well as ski boots, bindings, clothing, and outerwear—decided to introduce a new surfboard called "The Dominator." Burton has obtained over a third of the snowboard market by closely aligning itself with top professional riders and creating a strong amateur-snowboarder community. In creating the marketing program to support the new Dominator surfboard, Burton could attempt to leverage secondary brand knowledge in a number of different ways:

FIGURE 9.4

Secondary Sources of Brand Knowledge

■ Burton could leverage associations to the corporate brand by "sub-branding" the product, calling it "Dominator by Burton." Consumers' evaluations of the new product would be influenced by how they felt about Burton and how they felt that such knowledge predicted the quality of a Burton surfboard.

■ Burton could try to rely on its rural New England origins, but such a geographical location would seem to have little relevance to surfing.

■ Burton could also try to sell through popular surf shops in the hope that their credibility would rub off on the Dominator brand.

■ Burton could attempt to co-brand by identifying a strong ingredient brand for its foam or fibreglass materials (as Wilson did by incorporating Goodyear tire rubber on the soles of its ProStaff Classic tennis shoes).

■ Burton could attempt to find one or more top professional surfers to endorse the surfboard or choose to become a sponsor of a surfing competition or even the entire Association of Surfing Professionals (ASP) World Tour.

■ Burton could attempt to secure and publicize favourable ratings from third-party sources like *surfer* and *SURFING* magazines.

Thus, independent of the associations created by the surfboard itself, its brand name, or any other aspects of the marketing program, Burton may be able to build equity by linking the brand to these other entities.

Internal Branding

Marketers must now walk the walk to deliver the brand promise. They must adopt an *internal* perspective to be sure employees and marketing partners appreciate and understand basic branding notions and how they can help—or hurt—brand equity.[41] **Internal branding** consists of activities and processes that help inform and inspire employees.[42] United Airlines learned the hard way what happens when employees are not responsive to consumer complaints.

United Breaks Guitars

Canadian musician Dave Carroll, a member of the band Sons of Maxwell, had to take a flight from Halifax to Omaha, Nebraska, for a gig. While sitting on his United Airlines flight looking out the airplane window as the luggage was being loaded, he watched in horror as baggage handlers threw his guitar about. When he arrived at his destination, he discovered that the neck of his $3500 Taylor guitar was broken. His anger grew over the nine-month period when United refused to compensate him or do anything about his complaint. Frustrated, Dave took action. He posted three YouTube videos featuring original songs about his situation. The lyrics of the first song include the verse "I should have flown with someone else, or gone by car, 'cause United breaks guitars." In the second video, he focuses on his dealings with United's unhelpful customer service employees, and in the final song, he warns United that they must improve customer service or risk losing all their customers. The videos became online sensations, jumping from 150 000 views in their early days over half a million hits just a few weeks later. By July 2010, they had received almost 9 million views. Mass media heavyweights like *The New York Times* and *TIME* soon weighed in. Finally, Rob Bradford, United's managing director of customer solutions, telephoned Carroll to apologize and to ask if the carrier could use the video internally for training. The company finally offered Dave compensation, and United confessed that it hoped to learn from the incident, and to change its customer service policy.[43]

Holistic marketers must go even further and train and encourage distributors and dealers to serve their customers well. Poorly trained dealers can ruin the best efforts to build a strong brand image.

Brand bonding occurs when customers experience the company as delivering on its brand promise. All the customers' contacts with company employees and communications must be positive.[44] *The brand promise will not be delivered unless everyone in the company lives the brand.* Disney is so successful at internal branding that it holds seminars on the "Disney Style" for employees from other companies.

When employees care about and believe in the brand, they're motivated to work harder and feel greater loyalty to the firm. Here are some important principles for internal branding:[45]

1. *Choose the right moment.* Turning points are ideal opportunities to capture employees' attention and imagination. After the gulf oil spill, BP failed to take appropriate actions with regard to either its internal or external communications, which worsened the effects of the spill on its brand reputation.

2. *Link internal and external marketing.* Internal and external messages must match. Société de transport de Montréal (STM) found that it didn't have a green brand image even though public transportation presented a more environmentally friendly alternative to driving. Its research revealed that citizens are willing to adopt more environmentally friendly behaviours if they feel that corporations and public entities are taking similar action. "From this research, we gained the assurance that, with more than 100 environmental actions already to its credit, the STM was well-positioned, [unlike] most corporate citizens, to deliver an environmental promise," its CEO Denise Vaillancourt says. "However, the lack of awareness of the STM's green actions clearly highlighted a need for the STM to communicate" its new brand positioning both internally and externally. Customers were reminded that public transit was the ecofriendly way to get around, and employees were inspired with messages that they were doing noble work. This resulted in a surge in employee motivation, and increases in ridership and customer satisfaction. STM is ranked greener than Greenpeace in Quebec.[46]

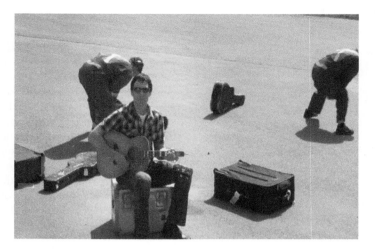

United Airlines learned the hard way what happens when employees are not responsive to consumer complaints.

3. *Bring the brand alive for employees.* Internal communications should be informative and energizing, as was the internal campaign run by STM.

Brand Communities

Thanks to the Internet, companies are interested in collaborating with consumers to create value through communities built around brands. A **brand community** is a specialized community of consumers and employees whose identification and activities focus around the brand.[47] Three characteristics identify brand communities:[48]

1. A "consciousness of kind" or sense of felt connection to the brand, company, product, or other community members

2. Shared rituals, stories, and traditions that help to convey the meaning of the community

3. A shared moral responsibility or duty to both the community as a whole and individual community members

Brand communities come in many different forms.[49] Some arise organically from brand users, such as university alumni associations at Dalhousie or Queen's. Others are company-sponsored and facilitated, such as Discovery Kids Canada, sponsored by the Discovery Channel. One of the most famous brand communities is the Harley-Davidson Owner's Group (H.O.G.).

Harley-Davidson

Founded in 1903 in Milwaukee, Wisconsin, Harley-Davidson opened its first Canadian dealership, Fred Deeley Ltd., in Vancouver in 1917. It is the fourth oldest Harley Davidson dealership in the world. The company has twice narrowly escaped bankruptcy but is today one of the most recognized motor vehicle brands in the world. In dire financial straits in the 1980s, Harley desperately licensed its name to such ill-advised ventures as cigarettes and wine coolers. Although consumers loved the brand, sales were depressed by product-quality problems, so Harley began its return to greatness by improving manufacturing processes. It also developed a strong brand community in the form of an owners' club, called the Harley Owners Group (H.O.G.), which sponsors bike rallies, charity rides, and other motorcycle events and now numbers 1 million members in over 1200 chapters. H.O.G. benefits include a magazine called *Hog Tales*, a touring handbook, emergency road service, a specially designed insurance program, theft reward service, discount hotel rates, and a "fly and ride" program enabling members to rent Harleys on vacation. The company also maintains an extensive website devoted to H.O.G., with information about club chapters and events, and a special members-only section.[50]

A strong brand community results in a more loyal, committed customer base. Its activities and advocacy can substitute to some degree for activities the firm would otherwise have to engage in, creating greater marketing effectiveness and efficiency.[51] A brand community can also be a constant source of inspiration and feedback for product improvements or innovations.

To better understand how brand communities work, one comprehensive study examined communities around brands as diverse as StriVectin cosmeceutical, BMW Mini auto, *Xena: Warrior Princess* television show, Jones soda, Tom Petty & the Heartbreakers rock-and-roll band, and Garmin GPS devices. Using multiple research methods such as "netnographic" research with online forums, participant and naturalistic observation of community activities, and in-depth interviews with community members, the researchers found 11 value-creation practices taking place. They divided them into four categories—social networking, community engagement, impression management, and brand use—summarized in Table 9.2.

Building a positive, productive brand community requires careful thought and implementation. Branding experts Susan Fournier and Lara Lee have identified seven common myths about brand communities and provide the reality in each case (see Table 9.3).

TABLE 9.2 | VALUE-CREATION PRACTICES

Social Networking

Welcoming	Greeting new members, beckoning them into the fold, and assisting in their brand learning and community socialization.
Empathizing	Lending emotional and/or physical support to other members, including support for brand-related trials (e.g., product failure, customizing) and/or for non-brand-related life issues (e.g., illness, death, job).
Governing	Articulating the behavioural expectations within the brand community.

Impression Management

Evangelizing	Sharing the brand "good news," inspiring others to use, and preaching from the mountaintop.
Justifying	Deploying rationales generally for devoting time and effort to the brand and collectively to outsiders and marginal members in the boundary.

Community Engagement

Staking	Recognizing variance within the brand community membership and marking intragroup distinction and similarity.
Milestoning	Noting seminal events in brand ownership and consumption.
Badging	Translating milestones into symbols and artifacts.
Documenting	Detailing the brand relationship journey in a narrative way, often anchored by and peppered with milestones.

Brand Use

Grooming	Cleaning, caring for, and maintaining the brand or systematizing optimal use patterns.
Customizing	Modifying the brand to suit group-level or individual needs. This includes all efforts to change the factory specs of the product to enhance performance.
Commoditizing	Distancing/approaching the marketplace in positive or negative ways. May be directed at other members (e.g., you should sell/ should not sell that) or may be directed at the firm through explicit links or through presumed monitoring of the site (e.g., you should fix this/do this/change this).

Source: Adapted from Hope Jensen Schau, Albert M. Muniz, and Eric J. Arnould, "How Brand Community Practices Create Value," *Journal of Marketing*, 73 (September 2009): 30–51.

TABLE 9.3	THE MYTHS AND REALITIES OF BRAND COMMUNITIES
Myth: Brand community is a marketing strategy.	**Reality:** Brand community is a business strategy. The entire business model must support the community brand.
Myth: Brand communities exist to serve the business.	**Reality:** Brand communities exist to serve the people that constitute them. Brand communities are a means to an end, not the end itself.
Myth: Build the brand, and the community will follow.	**Reality:** Cultivate the community and the brand will grow; engineer the community and the brand will be strong.
Myth: Brand communities should be lovefests for faithful brand advocates.	**Reality:** Communities are inherently political and this reality must be confronted with honesty and authenticity head-on; smart companies embrace the conflicts that make communities thrive.
Myth: Focus on opinion leaders to build a strong community.	**Reality:** Strong communities take care of all of their members; everyone in the community plays an important role.
Myth: Online social networks are the best way to build community.	**Reality:** Social networks are one community tool, but the tool is not the strategy.
Myth: Successful brand communities are tightly managed and controlled.	**Reality:** Control is an illusion; brand community success requires opening up and letting go; of and by the people, communities defy managerial control.

Sources: Susan Fournier and Lara Lee, "The Seven Deadly Sins of Brand Community 'Management,'" Marketing Science Institute Special Report 08-208, 2008; Susan Fournier and Lara Lee, "Getting Brand Communities Right," *Harvard Business Review*, April 2009, pp. 105–111.

MEASURING BRAND EQUITY

How do we measure brand equity? An *indirect* approach assesses potential sources of brand equity by identifying and tracking consumer brand knowledge structures.[52] A *direct* approach assesses the actual impact of brand knowledge on consumer response to different aspects of the marketing. "Marketing Insight: The Brand Value Chain" shows how the two measurement approaches can be linked.[53]

The two general approaches are complementary, and marketers can employ both. In other words, for brand equity to perform a useful strategic function and guide marketing decisions, it is important for marketers to fully understand (1) the sources of brand equity and how they affect outcomes of interest, as well as (2) how these sources and outcomes change, if at all, over time. Brand audits are important for the former; brand tracking is important for the latter.

A **brand audit** is a consumer-focused exercise that involves a series of procedures to assess the health of the brand, uncover its sources of brand equity, and suggest ways to improve and leverage its equity. Marketers should conduct a brand audit whenever they consider important shifts in strategic direction. Conducting brand audits on a regular basis (e.g., annually) allows marketers to keep their fingers on the pulse of their brands so that they can manage them more proactively and responsively. Audits are particularly useful background for managers as they set up their marketing plans.

Brand-tracking studies collect quantitative data from consumers over time to provide consistent, baseline information about how brands and marketing programs are performing. Tracking studies help us understand where, how much, and in what ways brand value is being created, to facilitate day-to-day decision making.

Marketers should distinguish brand equity from **brand valuation**, which is the job of estimating the total financial value of the brand. Table 9.4 displays the world's most valuable brands in 2009 according to one ranking.[54] In these well-known companies, brand value is typically over half the total company market capitalization. John Stuart, co-founder of Quaker Oats, said: "If this business were split up, I would give you the land and bricks and mortar, and I would take the brands and trademarks, and I would fare better than you." U.S. companies do not list brand equity on their balance sheets, in part because of differences in opinion about what constitutes a good estimate. However, companies do give brand equity a value in countries such as the United Kingdom, Hong Kong, and Australia. "Marketing Insight: What Is a Brand Worth?" reviews one popular valuation approach.

MANAGING BRAND EQUITY

Effective brand management requires a long-term view of marketing decisions. Because consumer responses to marketing activity depend on what consumers know and remember about a brand, short-term marketing actions (by changing brand knowledge) necessarily increase or decrease the success of future marketing actions.

Brand Reinforcement

As the company's major enduring asset, a brand needs to be carefully managed so that its value does not depreciate.[55] Many brand leaders of 70 years ago are still today's brand leaders—Wrigley's, Canadian Tire, Coca-Cola, Heinz, and Campbell Soup—but only by constantly striving to improve their goods, services, and marketing.

MARKETING **INSIGHT** | THE BRAND VALUE CHAIN

The **brand value chain** is a structured approach to assessing the sources and outcomes of brand equity and the manner in which marketing activities create brand value. The brand value chain is based on several basic premises.

First, brand value creation begins when the firm targets actual or potential customers by investing in a marketing program to develop the brand, including product research, development, and design; trade or intermediary support; and marketing communications. Next, we assume that customers' mindsets, buying behaviour, and response to price will change as a result of the marketing program; the question is how. Finally, the investment community will consider market performance, replacement cost, and purchase price in acquisitions (among other factors) to assess shareholder value in general and the value of a brand in particular.

The model also assumes that three multipliers moderate the transfer between the marketing program and the subsequent three value stages:

- The *program multiplier* determines the marketing program's ability to affect the customer mindset and is a function of the quality of the program investment.

- The *customer multiplier* determines the extent to which value created in the minds of customers affects market performance. This result depends on competitive superiority (how effective the quantity and quality of the marketing investment of other competing brands are); channel and other intermediary support (how much brand reinforcement and selling effort various marketing partners are putting forth); and customer size and profile (how many and what types of customers, profitable or not, are attracted to the brand).

- The *market multiplier* determines the extent to which the value shown by the market performance of a brand is manifested in shareholder value. It depends, in part, on the actions of financial analysts and investors.

Sources: Kevin Lane Keller and Don Lehmann, "How Do Brands Create Value," *Marketing Management*, May–June 2003, pp. 27–31. See also Rajendra K. Srivastava, Tasadduq A. Shervani, and Liam Fahey, "Market-Based Assets and Shareholder Value," *Journal of Marketing, 62*, no. 1 (1998): 2–18; M. J. Epstein and R. A. Westbrook, "Linking Actions to Profits in Strategic Decision Making," *MIT Sloan Management Review*, Spring 2001, pp. 39–49. For related empirical insights, see Manoj K. Agrawal and Vithala Rao, "An Empirical Comparison of Consumer-Based Measures of Brand Equity," *Marketing Letters, 7*, no. 3 (1996): 237–247; and Walfried Lassar, Banwari Mittal, and Arun Sharma, "Measuring Customer-Based Brand Equity," *Journal of Consumer Marketing, 12*, no. 4 (1995): 11–19.

TABLE 9.4 | THE WORLD'S 10 MOST VALUABLE BRANDS IN 2009

Rank	Brand	2009 Brand Value (billions)
1	Coca-Cola	$68.7
2	IBM	$60.2
3	Microsoft	$56.6
4	GE	$47.8
5	Nokia	$34.9
6	McDonald's	$32.3
7	Google	$32.0
8	Toyota	$31.3
9	Intel	$30.6
10	Disney	$28.4

Source: Interbrand. Used with permission.

MARKETING **INSIGHT** | WHAT IS A BRAND WORTH?

Top brand valuation firm Interbrand has developed a model to formally estimate the dollar value of a brand. Interbrand defines brand value as the net present value of the earnings a brand is expected to generate in the future and believes that both marketing and financial analyses are equally important in determining the value of a brand. Its process follows the following five steps (see Figure 9.5 for a schematic overview):

1. **Market Segmentation.** The first step in the brand valuation process is to divide the market(s) in which the brand is sold into mutually exclusive segments of customers that help to determine the variances in the brand's economic value.

2. **Financial Analysis.** Interbrand assesses purchase price, volume, and frequency to help calculate accurate forecasts of future brand sales and revenues. Specifically, Interbrand performs a detailed review of the brand's equities, industry and customer trends, and historical financial performance across each segment. Once it has established branded revenues, it deducts all associated operating costs to derive earnings before interest and tax (EBIT). It also deducts the appropriate taxes and a charge for the capital employed to operate the underlying business, leaving intangible earnings, that is, the earnings attributed to the intangible assets of the business.

3. **Role of Branding.** Interbrand next attributes a proportion of intangible earnings to the brand in each market segment, by first identifying the various drivers of demand, then determining the degree to which the brand directly influences each. The Role of Branding assessment is based on market research, client workshops, and interviews, and represents the percentage of intangible earnings the brand generates. Multiplying the role of branding by intangible earnings yields brand earnings.

4. **Brand Strength.** Interbrand then assesses the brand's strength profile to determine the likelihood that the brand will realize forecast earnings. This step relies on competitive benchmarking and a structured evaluation of the brand's market, stability, leadership position, growth trend, support, geographic footprint, and ability to be legally protected. For each segment, Interbrand applies industry and brand-equity metrics to determine a risk premium for the brand. The company's analysts derive the overall brand discount rate by adding a brand risk premium to the risk-free rate, represented by the yield on government bonds. The brand discount rate, applied to the brand earnings forecast, yields the net present value of the brand earnings. The stronger the brand, the lower the discount rate, and vice versa.

5. **Brand Value Calculation.** Brand value is the net present value (NPV) of the forecast brand earnings, discounted by the brand discount rate. The NPV calculation comprises both the forecast period and the period beyond, reflecting the ability of brands to continue generating future earnings.

Increasingly, Interbrand uses brand value assessments as a dynamic, strategic tool to identify and maximize return on brand investment across a whole host of areas.

Sources: Interbrand, the Interbrand Brand Glossary, and Interbrand's Nik Stucky and Rita Clifton.

FIGURE 9.5

Interbrand Brand Valuation
Method

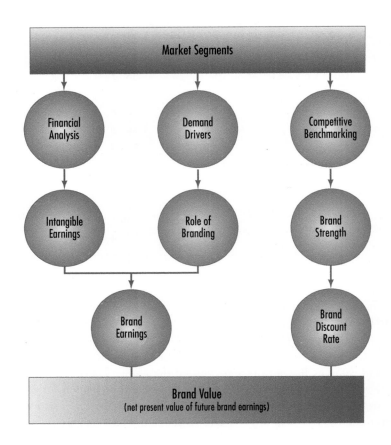

Brand equity is reinforced by marketing actions that consistently convey the meaning of the brand to consumers in terms of (1) what products the brand represents, what core benefits it supplies, and what needs it satisfies; and (2) how the brand makes those products superior and which strong, favourable, and unique brand associations should exist in the minds of consumers.[56] Nivea, one of Europe's strongest brands, has expanded its meaning from a skin-cream brand to a skin-care and personal-care brand through carefully designed and implemented brand extensions reinforcing the Nivea brand promise of "mild," "gentle," and "caring" in a broader arena.

Reinforcing brand equity requires the brand to move forward constantly—in the right direction with new and compelling offerings and ways to market them. In virtually every product category, once-prominent and admired brands—such as Kmart, Eaton's, Oldsmobile, Polaroid—have fallen on hard times or gone out of business.[57]

An important consideration in reinforcing brands is the consistency of the marketing support the brand receives, in terms of both amount and kind. Consistency does not mean uniformity and no changes: many tactical changes may be necessary to maintain the strategic thrust and direction of the brand. Unless there is some change in the marketing environment, however, there is little need to deviate from a successful positioning. When change *is* necessary, marketers should vigorously preserve and defend sources of brand equity. Discovery Communications has successfully done just that while expanding its brand presence.

Discovery Communications

In the hypercompetitive marketplace of cable TV channels, having a consistently clear but evolving identity is critical. One of the most successful cable TV programmers, Discovery Communications, features such signature shows in Canada as *Daily Planet*, *Dirty Jobs*, *Man vs. Wild*, and *MythBusters*. Positioning itself as the number-one nonfiction media company in the world, Discovery Communications is dedicated "to satisfying curiosity and making a difference in people's lives with the highest quality content, services and products that entertain, engage and enlighten—inviting viewers to explore their world." For example, by recognizing that nature and animals harbour mystery and danger, Animal Planet has developed into a compelling brand. New channels in the works include a women's channel with Oprah Winfrey, a kids' channel in partnership with Hasbro, and a possible series of science shows with director Steven Spielberg. Discovery is also increasing its global expansion—including China and India—and now reaches more than 1.5 billion subscribers in 170 countries, generating a third of its revenue from overseas.[58]

In managing brand equity, it is important to recognize the trade-offs between those marketing activities that fortify the brand and reinforce its meaning, such as a well-received new product improvement or a creatively designed ad campaign, and those that attempt to leverage or borrow from existing brand equity to reap some financial benefit, such as a short-term promotional discount that just emphasizes a lower price.[59] At some point, failure to reinforce the brand will diminish brand awareness and weaken brand image.

Brand Revitalization

Any new development in the marketing environment can affect a brand's fortunes. Nevertheless, a number of brands have managed to make impressive comebacks in recent years.[60] After some hard times, Burberry, Fiat, and Volkswagen have all turned their brand fortunes around to varying degrees.

Often, the first thing to do in revitalizing a brand is to understand what the sources of brand equity were to begin with. Are positive associations losing their strength or uniqueness? Have negative associations become linked to the brand? Decisions must then be made as to whether or not to retain the same positioning or create a new positioning and, if the latter, which positioning to adopt.

Sometimes the actual marketing program is the source of the problem because it is failing to deliver on the brand promise. In such instances, a "back to basics" strategy may make sense, as was the case with Harley-Davidson.

In other cases, however, the old positioning is just no longer viable and a "reinvention" strategy is necessary. Mountain Dew completely overhauled its brand image to become a soft drink powerhouse. As its history reveals, it is often easier to reinvent a brand that is alive but has been more or less forgotten. Old Spice is another example.

Old Spice

One of the first mass market fragrances, Old Spice dates back to 1937. Its classic aftershave and cologne combination was the classic Father's Day gift for baby boomers to give, but was largely irrelevant by the time Procter & Gamble acquired the brand in 1990. P&G's revitalization strategy was to abandon the old cologne business to focus on deodorants and other male grooming products. Facing tough competition from Unilever's edgy line of Axe products, the firm reverted to its classic one-two punch of product innovation and new communications to target the 12- to 34-year-old male. New product development resulted in the creation of Old Spice High Endurance, Pro Strength, and Red Zone lines of deodorants, body washes, body sprays, and shaving products. Old Spice's latest line, Ever Clear, arose from focus group participants' "good-bye letters" to their current deodorant. A technological breakthrough allowed Ever Clear to promise the protection of a dry solid without the uncomfortable waxy residue that left white streaks on clothing. All Old Spice products were backed by tongue-in-cheek advertising that stressed the brand's "experience."[61]

There is obviously a continuum involved with revitalization strategies, with pure "back to basics" at one end and pure "reinvention" at the other end, and many combinations in between. Brand revitalizations of almost every kind start with the product.[62] General Motors' turnaround with its fading Cadillac brand was fuelled by new model designs that redefined the Cadillac look and styling, such as the CTS sedan, XLR roadster, and ESV sport utility vehicle.[63] High-end clothing retailer Paul Stuart introduced its first ever sub-brand, the bolder, sleeker Phineas Cole, to update its conservative image for a hipper, younger demographic.[64]

DEVISING A BRANDING STRATEGY

A firm's **branding strategy** reflects the number and nature of common and distinctive brand elements applied to the different products sold by the firm.

Deciding how to brand new products is especially critical. When a firm introduces a new product, it has three main choices:

1. It can develop new brand elements for the new product.
2. It can apply some of its existing brand elements.
3. It can use a combination of new and existing brand elements.

A firm's use of an established brand to introduce a new product is called **brand extension**. When a new brand is combined with an existing brand, the brand extension can also be called a **sub-brand**, as with Hershey's Kisses candy, Adobe Acrobat software, the Toyota Camry automobile, and the CIBC Aerogold Visa. An existing brand that gives birth to a brand extension is referred to as the **parent brand**. If the parent brand is already associated with multiple products through brand extensions, then the parent brand may also be called a **master brand** or **family brand**.

Brand extensions can be classified into two general categories:[65] In a **line extension**, the parent brand is used to brand a new product that targets a new market segment within a product category currently served by the parent brand (e.g., through new flavours, forms, colours, added ingredients, and package sizes). Danone has introduced several types of Danone yogurt line extensions through the years: Fruit on the Bottom, All Natural, and Fruit Blends. In a **category extension**, the parent brand is used to enter a product category different from that currently served by the parent brand (e.g., Swiss Army watches). Honda has used its company name to cover such different products as automobiles, motorcycles, snowblowers, lawnmowers, marine engines, and snowmobiles. This allows Honda to advertise that it can fit "six Hondas in a two-car garage."

A **brand line** consists of all products—original as well as line and category extensions—sold under a particular brand. A **brand mix** (or brand assortment) is the set of all brand lines that a particular seller makes available to buyers. Many companies are now introducing **branded variants**, which are specific brand lines supplied to specific retailers or distribution channels. They result from the pressure retailers put on manufacturers to provide distinctive offerings. A camera company may supply its low-end cameras to mass merchandisers while limiting its higher-priced items to specialty camera shops. Valentino may design and supply different lines of suits and jackets to different department stores.[66]

A **licensed product** is one whose brand name has been licensed to other manufacturers that actually make the product. Corporations have seized on licensing to push their company name and image across a wide range of products—from bedding to shoes—making it a multibillion dollar business.[67] Jeep's licensing program, which now has 600 products and 150 licensees, includes everything from strollers (built for a father's longer arms) to apparel (with Teflon in the denim)—as long they fit the brand's positioning of "Life without Limits." Its global licensing revenue now exceeds $550 million in retail sales. New areas of emphasis include outdoor and travel gear, juvenile products, and sporting goods.[68]

Branding Decisions

ALTERNATIVE BRANDING STRATEGIES Today, branding is such a strong force that hardly anything goes unbranded. Assuming a firm decides to brand its products or services, it must then choose which brand names to use. Three general strategies are often used:

1. *Individual or separate family brand names.* Consumer packaged-goods companies have a long tradition of branding different products by different names. General Mills largely uses individual brand names, such as Bisquick baking mix, Gold Medal flour, Nature Valley granola bars, Old El Paso Mexican foods, Progresso soup, Wheaties cereal, and Yoplait yogurt). If a company produces quite different products, one blanket name is often not desirable. Swift and Company developed separate family names for its hams (Premium) and fertilizers (Vigoro). A major advantage of individual or separate family brand names is that if the product fails or appears to have low quality, the company has not tied its reputation to it. Companies often use different brand names for different quality lines within the same product class. For example, when Air Canada experimented with low-cost fares, it introduced its Tango service. UTC Technologies also relies on individual names.

2. *Corporate umbrella or company brand name.* Many firms, such as Heinz and General Electric, use their corporate brand across their range of products.[69] Development cost is less because there is no need for name research or heavy advertising expenditures to create brand name recognition. Campbell's introduces new soups under its brand name with extreme simplicity and achieves instant recognition. Sales of the new product are likely to be strong if the manufacturer's name is

good. Corporate-image associations of innovativeness, expertise, and trustworthiness have been shown to directly influence consumer evaluations.[70] Finally, a corporate branding strategy can lead to greater intangible value for the firm.[71]

3. *Sub-brand name.* Sub-brands combine two or more of the corporate brand, family brand, or individual product brand names. This sub-branding policy is followed by Kellogg (Kellogg's Rice Krispies, Kellogg's Raisin Bran, and Kellogg's Corn Flakes). Many durable-goods makers such as Honda, Sony, and Hewlett-Packard use sub-brands for their products. The corporate or company name legitimizes, and the individual name individualizes, the new product.

HOUSE OF BRANDS VERSUS A BRANDED HOUSE The use of individual or separate family brand names has been referred to as a "house of brands" strategy, whereas the use of an umbrella corporate or company brand name has been referred to as a "branded house" strategy. These branding strategies represent two ends of a brand relationship continuum. A sub-brand strategy falls somewhere in-between, depending on which component of the sub-brand receives more emphasis. A good example of a house of brands strategy is UTC Technologies.

UTC Technologies

UTC's brand portfolio includes Otis Elevators, Carrier air conditioners, Sikorsky helicopters, and Pratt & Whitney jet engines. Most of its brands are the names of the individuals who invented the product or created the company decades ago—these names have more power and are more recognizable in the business buying marketplace. The parent brand, UTC, is advertised to only small but influential audiences: the financial community and opinion leaders in New York, Toronto, Ottawa, and Washington. After all, the parent trademark dates to 1972, and employees are loyal to the individual companies owned by UTC. "My philosophy has always been to use the power of the trademarks of the subsidiaries to improve the recognition and brand acceptance, awareness, and respect for the parent company itself," said UTC CEO George David.[72]

Two key components of virtually any branding strategy are brand portfolios and brand extensions.

Brand Portfolios

A brand can only be stretched so far, and all the segments the firm would like to target may not view the same brand equally favourably. Marketers often need multiple brands in order to pursue these multiple segments. Some other reasons for introducing multiple brands in a category include the following:[73]

1. Increasing shelf presence and retailer dependence in the store

2. Attracting consumers seeking variety who may otherwise have switched to another brand

3. Increasing internal competition within the firm

4. Yielding economies of scale in advertising, sales, merchandising, and physical distribution

The **brand portfolio** is the set of all brands and brand lines a particular firm offers for sale in a particular category or market segment. Consider the many brands of Starwood Hotels & Resorts.

Starwood Hotels & Resorts

One of the leading hotel and leisure companies in the world, Starwood Hotels & Resorts Worldwide has 850 properties in more than 95 countries and 145 000 employees at its owned and managed properties. In its rebranding attempt to go "beyond beds," Starwood has differentiated its hotels along emotional, experiential lines. Its hotel and call centre operators convey different experiences for the firm's different chains, as does the firm's advertising. This strategy emerged from a major 18-month positioning project, started in 2006, to find brand positions that would establish an emotional connection with consumers. Consumer research suggested these positions for some of the brands:[74]

■ *Sheraton.* With the tagline "You don't stay here, you belong," Sheraton—the largest brand—is warm, comforting, and casual. Its core value centres on "connections," an image aided by the hotel's alliance with Yahoo!, which co-founded the Yahoo! Link@Sheraton lobby kiosks and cyber cafés.

- *Four Points by Sheraton.* For the self-sufficient traveller, Four Points strives to be honest, uncomplicated, and comfortable. The brand is all about providing a high level of comfort and little indulgences like free high-speed Internet access and bottled water. Its ads feature apple pies and talk about providing guests with "the comforts of home."
- *Westin.* Westin's emphasis on "personal, instinctive, and renewal" has led to a new sensory welcome featuring a white tea scent, signature music and lighting, and refreshing towels. Each room features Westin's own Heavenly Beds, sold exclusively in the retail market through Nordstrom, further enhancing the brand's upscale image.

The hallmark of an optimal brand portfolio is the ability of each brand in it to maximize equity in combination with all the other brands in it. Marketers generally need to trade off market coverage with costs and profitability. If they can increase profits by dropping brands, a portfolio is too big; if they can increase profits by adding brands, it's not big enough. The basic principle in designing a brand portfolio is to maximize market coverage so no potential customers are being ignored, but minimize brand overlap so brands are not competing for customer approval. Each brand should be clearly differentiated and appealing to a sizeable enough market segment to justify its marketing and production costs.[75]

Marketers carefully monitor brand portfolios over time to identify weak brands and kill unprofitable ones.[76] Brand lines with poorly differentiated brands are likely to be characterized by much cannibalization and require pruning.[77] There are scores of cereals, beverages, and snacks, and thousands of mutual funds. Students can choose among hundreds of business schools. For the seller, this spells hypercompetition. For the buyer, it may mean too much choice.

Brands can also play a number of specific roles as part of a portfolio.

FLANKERS Flanker or "fighter" brands are positioned with respect to competitors' brands so that more important (and more profitable) *flagship brands* can retain their desired positioning. Celeron helped thwart AMD's competitive challenge to Intel's premium Pentium microprocessor.[78] Marketers walk a fine line in designing fighter brands, which must be neither so attractive that they take sales away from their higher-priced comparison brands nor so cheaply designed that they reflect poorly on those brands.

CASH COWS Some brands may be kept around despite dwindling sales because they manage to maintain their profitability with virtually no marketing support. Companies can effectively "milk" these "cash cow" brands by capitalizing on their reservoir of brand equity. Gillette still sells the older Trac II, Atra, Sensor, and Mach III brands because withdrawing them may not necessarily move customers to another Gillette brand.

LOW-END ENTRY LEVEL The role of a relatively low-priced brand in the portfolio often may be to attract customers to the brand franchise. Retailers like to feature these "traffic builders" because they are able to trade up customers to a higher-priced brand. BMW introduced certain models in its 3 Series automobiles in part as a means of bringing new customers into the brand franchise, with the hope of later moving them to higher-priced models when they decided to trade in their cars.

HIGH-END PRESTIGE The role of a relatively high-priced brand often is to add prestige and credibility to the entire portfolio. One analyst argued that the real value to Chevrolet of its high-performance Corvette sports car was "its ability to lure curious customers into showrooms and at the same time help improve the image of other Chevrolet cars. It does not mean a hell of a lot for GM profitability, but there is no question that it is a traffic builder."[79] Corvette's technological image and prestige cast a halo over the entire Chevrolet line.

Brand Extensions

Recognizing that one of their most valuable assets is their brands, many firms have decided to leverage that asset by introducing a host of new products under some of their strongest brand names. Most new products are in fact line extensions—typically 80 to 90 percent in any one year. For example, winners of the 2010 Best New Product Awards (which recognize the best food, personal-care, and household products launched in Canada based on a survey of 25 000 Canadian consumers) included Astro Zero Superfruit Yogurt, Burt's Bees Replenishing Lip Balm with Pomegranate Oil, Breyers Double Churn Ice Cream, and Purina Beneful Snackin Slices Dog Treats.[80] Nevertheless, many new products are introduced each year as new brands, such as other new-product award winners Tropicana Tropics Mango Citrus, ConAgra's Healthy Choice Gourmet Steamers, Colgate 360° ActiFlex Toothbrush, and Dove Go Fresh Body Mist.

ADVANTAGES OF BRAND EXTENSIONS Two main advantages of brand extensions are that they can facilitate new-product acceptance and provide positive feedback to the parent brand and company.

Improved Odds of New-Product Success Consumers can make inferences and form expectations as to the likely composition and performance of a new product based on what they already know about the parent brand itself and the extent to which they feel this information is relevant to the new product.[81] For example, when Sony introduced Vaio, a new personal computer tailored to multimedia applications, consumers may have been more likely to feel comfortable with its anticipated performance because of their experience with and knowledge of other Sony products.

By setting up positive expectations, extensions reduce risk.[82] Because of the potentially increased consumer demand resulting from introducing a new product as an extension, it also may be easier to convince retailers to stock and promote a brand extension. From a marketing communications perspective, an introductory campaign for an extension does not have to create awareness of both the brand and the new product, but instead can concentrate on the new product itself.[83]

Extensions can thus reduce launch costs, important given that establishing a new brand name in the North American marketplace can cost over $100 million! They also can avoid the difficulty—and expense—of coming up with a new name. Extensions allow for packaging and labelling efficiencies. Similar or virtually identical packages and labels for extensions can result in lower production costs and, if coordinated properly, more prominence in the retail store by creating a billboard effect.[84] For example, Stouffer's offers a variety of frozen entrees with identical orange packaging that increases their visibility when they are stocked together in the freezer. By offering consumers a portfolio of brand variants within a product category, consumers who need a change—because of boredom, satiation, or whatever—can switch to a different product type without having to leave the brand family.

Positive Feedback Effects Besides facilitating acceptance of new products, brand extensions can also provide feedback benefits.[85] They can help to clarify the meaning of a brand and its core brand values or improve consumer perceptions of the credibility of the company behind the extension.[86] Thus, through brand extensions, Crayola means "colourful crafts for kids," Aunt Jemima means "breakfast foods," and Weight Watchers means "weight loss and maintenance."

Line extensions can renew interest and liking for the brand and benefit the parent brand by expanding market coverage. Kimberly-Clark's Kleenex unit has a goal of getting facial tissue in every room of the home. This philosophy has led to a wide variety of Kleenex facial tissues and packaging, including scented, ultra-soft, and lotion-infused tissues; boxes with drawings of dinosaurs and dogs for children's rooms and colourful, stylish designs to match room décor; and a "man-sized" box with tissues 50 percent larger than regular Kleenex.

One benefit of a successful extension is that it may also serve as the basis for subsequent extensions.[87] During the 1970s and 1980s, Billabong established its brand credibility with the young surfing community as a designer and producer of quality surf apparel. This success permitted it to extend into other youth-oriented areas, such as snowboarding and skateboarding.

DISADVANTAGES OF BRAND EXTENSIONS On the downside, line extensions may cause the brand name to not be as strongly identified with any one product.[88] Ries and Trout call this the "line-extension trap."[89] By linking its brand to mainstream food products such as mashed potatoes, dried milk, soups, and beverages, Cadbury ran the risk of losing its more specific meaning as a chocolate and candy brand.[90] **Brand dilution** occurs when consumers no longer associate a brand with a specific product or highly similar products and start thinking less of the brand.

If a firm launches extensions consumers deem inappropriate, they may question the integrity and competence of the brand. Different varieties of line extensions may confuse and perhaps even frustrate consumers: which version of the product is the right one for them? Retailers have to reject many new products and brands because they do not have the shelf or display space for them. And the firm itself may become overwhelmed. The worst possible scenario with an extension is that it not only fails, but also harms the parent brand image in the process. Fortunately, such events are rare. "Marketing failures," where insufficient consumers were attracted to a brand, are typically much less damaging than "product failures," where the brand fundamentally fails to live up to its promise. Even then, product failures dilute brand equity only when the extension is seen as very similar to the parent brand. The Audi 5000 car suffered from a tidal wave of negative publicity and word of mouth in the mid-1980s when it was alleged to have a "sudden acceleration" problem. The adverse publicity also spilled over to the 4000 model. But the Quattro was relatively more insulated from negative repercussions, because it was distanced from the 5000 by its more distinct branding and advertising strategy.[91]

By defining its brand promise in terms of "colourful arts and crafts for kids," Crayola has extended beyond crayons to successfully introduce a range of different products.

Even if sales of a brand extension are high and meet targets, it is possible that this revenue may have resulted from consumers switching to the extension from existing product offerings of the parent brand—in effect *cannibalizing* the parent brand. Intrabrand shifts in sales may not necessarily be so undesirable, as they can be thought of as a form of *pre-emptive cannibalization.* In other words, consumers might have switched to a competing brand instead of the line extension if it had not been introduced into the category. Tide laundry detergent maintains the same market share now as it did 50 years ago because of the sales contributions of the various line extensions (scented and unscented powder, tablet, liquid, and other forms).

One easily overlooked disadvantage to brand extensions is that by introducing a new product as a brand extension, the firm forgoes the chance to create a new brand with its own unique image and equity. Consider the advantages to Disney of having introduced more adult-oriented Touchstone films, to Levi's of having introduced casual Dockers pants, and to Black and Decker of having introduced high-end DeWALT power tools.

SUCCESS CHARACTERISTICS A potential new product extension for a brand must be judged by how effectively it leverages existing brand equity from the parent brand to the new product, as well as how effectively the extension, in turn, contributes to the equity of the parent brand.[92] Crest White-strips leveraged Crest's strong dental-care reputation to provide reassurance in the teeth-whitening arena, while also reinforcing its dental-authority image.

Marketers should ask a number of questions in judging the potential success of an extension:[93]

■ Does the parent brand have strong equity?

■ Is there a strong basis of fit?

■ Will the extension have the optimal points-of-parity and points-of-difference?

■ How can marketing programs enhance extension equity?

■ What implications will the extension have for parent brand equity and profitability?

■ How should feedback effects best be managed?

To help answer these questions, Table 9.5 offers a sample scorecard with specific weights and dimensions that users can adjust for each application.

Table 9.6 lists a number of academic research findings on brand extensions.[94] One major mistake in evaluating extension opportunities is failing to take *all* consumers' brand knowledge structures into account and focusing instead on one or a few brand associations as a potential basis of fit.[95]

TABLE 9.5	BRAND EXTENDIBILITY SCORECARD

Allocate points according to how well the new-product concept rates on the specific dimensions in the following areas:

Consumer Perspectives: Desirability

10 pts. _____ Product category appeal (size, growth potential)

10 pts. _____ Equity transfer (perceived brand fit)

5 pts. _____ Perceived consumer target fit

Company Perspectives: Deliverability

10 pts. _____ Asset leverage (product technology, organizational skills, marketing effectiveness via channels and communications)

10 pts. _____ Profit potential

5 pts. _____ Launch feasibility

Competitive Perspectives: Differentiability

10 pts. _____ Comparative appeal (many advantages, few disadvantages)

10 pts. _____ Competitive response (likelihood, immunity or invulnerability from)

5 pts. _____ Legal/regulatory/institutional barriers

Brand Perspectives: Equity Feedback

10 pts. _____ Strengthens parent brand equity

10 pts. _____ Facilitates additional brand extension opportunities

5 pts. _____ Improves asset base

TOTAL _____ pts.

TABLE 9.6	RESEARCH INSIGHTS ON BRAND EXTENSIONS

- Successful brand extensions occur when the parent brand is seen as having favourable associations and there is a perception of fit between the parent brand and the extension product.

- There are many bases of fit: product-related attributes and benefits, as well as non-product-related attributes and benefits related to common usage situations or user types.

- Depending on consumer knowledge of the categories, perceptions of fit may be based on technical or manufacturing commonalties or on more superficial considerations such as whether the extension is related to the needs or situations associated with the parent brand.

- High-quality brands stretch farther than average-quality brands, although both types of brands have boundaries.

- A brand that is seen as prototypical of a product category can be difficult to extend outside the category.

- Concrete attribute associations tend to be more difficult to extend than abstract benefit associations.

- Consumers may transfer associations that are positive in the original product class but become negative in the extension context.

- Consumers may infer negative associations about an extension, perhaps even based on other inferred positive associations.

- It can be difficult to extend into a product class that is seen as easy to make.

- A successful extension can not only contribute to the parent brand image but also enable a brand to be extended even farther.

- An unsuccessful extension hurts the parent brand only when there is a strong basis of fit between the two.

- An unsuccessful extension does not prevent a firm from "backtracking" and introducing a more similar extension.

- Vertical extensions can be difficult and often require sub-branding strategies.

- The most effective advertising strategy for an extension emphasizes information about the extension (rather than reminders about the parent brand).

Source: *KELLER, KEVIN LANE, STRATEGIC BRAND MANAGEMENT, 2nd Ed.,* © 2003. Reprinted and Electronically reproduced by permission of Pearson Education, Inc., Upper Saddle River, New Jersey.

CUSTOMER EQUITY

Brand equity should be a top priority of any organization. "Marketing Memo: Twenty-First-Century Branding" offers some contemporary perspectives on enduring brand leadership.

Finally, we can relate brand equity to one other important marketing concept: **customer equity**. The aim of customer relationship management (CRM) is to produce high customer equity.[96] Although we can calculate it in different ways, one definition of customer equity is "the sum of lifetime values of all customers."[97] As Chapter 5 explained, customer lifetime value is affected by revenue and cost considerations related to customer acquisition, retention, and add-on spending.[98]

| MARKETING **MEMO** | TWENTY-FIRST-CENTURY BRANDING |

One of the most successful marketers of the past 15 years, Scott Bedbury played a key role in the rise of both Nike and Starbucks. In his insightful book *A New Brand World,* he offers the following branding principles:

1. *Relying on brand awareness has become marketing fool's gold*—Smart brands are more concerned with brand relevance and brand resonance.

2. *You have to know it before you can grow it*—Most brands don't know who they are, where they've been, and where they're going.

3. *Always remember the Spandex rule of brand expansion*—Just because you can, doesn't mean you should.

4. *Great brands establish enduring customer relationships*—They have more to do with emotions and trust than with footwear cushioning or the way a coffee bean is roasted.

5. *Everything matters*—Even your washroom.

6. *All brands need good parents*—Unfortunately, most brands come from troubled homes.

7. *Big is no excuse for being bad*—Truly great brands use their superhuman powers for good and place people and principles before profits.

8. *Relevance, simplicity, and humanity*—Rather than technology, these will distinguish brands in the future.

Source: From A NEW BRAND WORLD by Scott Bedbury, copyright © 2001 by Scott Bedbury. Used by permission of Viking Penguin, a division of Penguin Group (USA) Inc.

- *Acquisition* is affected by the number of prospects, acquisition probability of a prospect, and acquisition spending per prospect.

- *Retention* is influenced by the retention rate and retention spending level.

- *Add-on spending* is a function of the efficiency of add-on selling, the number of add-on selling offers given to existing customers, and the rate of response to new offers.

The brand equity and customer equity perspectives certainly share many common themes.[99] Both emphasize the importance of customer loyalty and the notion that value is created by having as many customers as possible pay as high a price as possible.

In practice, however, the two perspectives emphasize different things. The customer equity perspective focuses on bottom-line financial value. Its clear benefit is its quantifiable measures of financial performance. But it offers limited guidance for go-to-market strategies. It largely ignores some of the important advantages of creating a strong brand, such as the ability to attract higher-quality employees, elicit stronger support from channel and supply chain partners, and create growth opportunities through line and category extensions and licensing. The customer equity approach can overlook the "option value" of brands and their potential to affect future revenues and costs. It does not always fully account for competitive moves and countermoves, or for social network effects, word of mouth, and customer-to-customer recommendations.

Brand equity, on the other hand, tends to emphasize strategic issues in managing brands and creating and leveraging brand awareness and image with customers. It provides much practical guidance for specific marketing activities. With a focus on brands, however, managers don't always develop detailed customer analyses in terms of the brand equity they achieve or the resulting long-term profitability they create.[100] Brand equity approaches could benefit from sharper segmentation schemes afforded by customer-level analyses and more consideration of how to develop personalized, customized marketing programs for individual customers—whether individuals or organizations such as retailers. There are generally fewer financial considerations put into play with brand equity than with customer equity.

Nevertheless, both brand equity and customer equity matter. There are no brands without customers and no customers without brands. Brands serve as the bait that retailers and other channel intermediaries use to attract customers from whom they extract value. Customers serve as the tangible profit engine for brands to monetize their brand value.

SUMMARY

1. A brand is a name, term, sign, symbol, or design, or some combination of these elements, intended to identify the goods and services of one seller or group of sellers and to differentiate them from those of competitors. The different components of a brand—brand names, logos, symbols, package designs, and so on—are brand elements.

2. Brands are valuable intangible assets that need to be managed carefully. The key to branding is that consumers perceive differences among brands in a product category.

3. Brand equity should be defined in terms of marketing effects uniquely attributable to a brand. That is, how do the results of product or service marketing differ with and without brand identification?

4. Building brand equity depends on three main factors: (1) the initial choices of the brand elements or identities making up the brand; (2) the way the brand is integrated into the supporting marketing program; and (3) the associations indirectly transferred to the brand by linking the brand to some other entity (e.g., the company, country of origin, channel of distribution, or another brand).

5. Brand audits measure where the brand has been, and tracking studies measure where the brand is now and whether marketing programs are having the intended effects.

6. A branding strategy for a firm identifies which brand elements a firm chooses to apply across the various products it sells. In a brand extension, a firm uses an established brand name to introduce a new product. Potential extensions must be judged by how effectively they leverage existing brand equity to a new product, as well as how effectively the extension, in turn, contributes to the equity of the existing parent brand.

7. Brands may expand coverage, provide protection, extend an image, or fulfill a variety of other roles for a firm. Each brand name product must have well-defined positioning so that brands can maximize coverage and minimize overlap and thus optimize the portfolio.

8. Customer equity is a concept complementary to brand equity and reflects the sum of lifetime values of all customers for a brand.

APPLICATIONS

Marketing Debate: Are Brand Extensions Good or Bad?

Some critics vigorously denounce the practice of brand extensions, because they feel that too often companies lose focus and consumers become confused. Other experts maintain that brand extensions are a critical growth strategy and source of revenue for firms.

Take a position: Brand extensions can endanger brands *versus* Brand extensions are an important brand-growth strategy.

Marketing Discussion

How can you relate the different models of brand equity presented in this chapter? How are they similar? How are they different? Can you construct a brand equity model that incorporates the best aspects of each model?

MARKETING EXCELLENCE | MCDONALD'S RESTAURANTS OF CANADA LIMITED

McDonald's Restaurants of Canada Limited opened its doors over 40 years ago. By 2010, there were 1434 McDonald's restaurants in Canada. The chain employs 77 000 Canadians, and it is heralded as one of Canada's 50 Best Employers. Two-and-a-half million Canadians are served daily at McDonald's Canada, and it has led the Canadian food service industry for many years, setting the highest standards for food quality and safety. Its formula for success is based on simple principles: quality, service, cleanliness, and value.

It is part of the world's leading hamburger fast-food chain, McDonald's Corporation, which has over 31 000 restaurants that operate in 119 countries. In Canada, more than 80 percent of McDonald's restaurants are owned and operated by franchisees (versus 75 percent franchisee ownership worldwide). Ownership by franchisees decreases the risk associated with expansion and ensures long-term tenants for the company. McDonald's Corporation serves 58 million people each day and promises a simple, easy, and enjoyable food experience for its customers.

The history of the McDonald's Corporation dates back to 1955 when Ray Kroc, a multimixer salesman, franchised a hamburger restaurant from the McDonald brothers, named it McDonald's, and offered simple foods such as the famous 15-cent hamburger. It wasn't long before McDonald's became a household name.

During the 1960s and 1970s, Kroc led McDonald's growth domestically and internationally. The menu expanded to include the Big Mac, Quarter Pounder, Happy Meal, Filet-O-Fish, and breakfast items like the Egg McMuffin. Kroc also understood early on that his core audience consisted of children and families. Therefore, he focused advertising efforts at these groups and introduced Ronald McDonald in 1965 during a 60-second commercial. Soon, characters such as Grimace, the Hamburglar, and Mayor McCheese made their debut in McDonald's advertising campaigns and helped lure children into its restaurants for simple, good-tasting food and a fun experience.

It was also during this time that McDonald's Corporation created the Ronald McDonald House, which opened in 1974 to help children with leukemia. Since then, it has expanded into a global charity effort called Ronald McDonald House Charities, which strives to improve children's lives, health, and well-being. McDonald's Canada has given over $67 million to children's charities and to community sports programs.

McDonald's aggressively expanded overseas throughout the 1980s by adding locations throughout Europe and Asia, including in the Philippines and Malaysia. This rapid expansion, however, led to many struggles during the 1990s and early 2000s. The company lost focus and direction, expanding by as many as 2000 new restaurants a year. New employees weren't trained fast or well enough, all of which led to poor customer service and dirtier restaurants. New competitors popped up and consumer tastes changed, and new products like pizza, the Arch Deluxe, and deli sandwiches failed to connect with consumers, as did tweaks to the current menu, including multiple changes to the Big Mac special sauce. Jim Skinner, McDonald's chief executive officer, explained, "We got distracted from the most important thing: hot, high-quality food at a great value at the speed and convenience of McDonald's."

In 2003, McDonald's implemented a strategic effort called the "Plan to Win." The framework, which still exists today, helped McDonald's restaurants refocus on offering a better, higher-quality consumer experience rather than a quick and cheap fast-food option. The Plan to Win "playbook" provided strategic insight on how to improve on the company's five Ps—people, products, promotions, price, and place—yet allowed local restaurants to adapt to different environments and cultures. For example, McDonald's introduced a Bacon Roll breakfast sandwich in the United Kingdom, a premium M burger in France, and an egg, tomato, and pepper McPuff in China.

Some food changes that helped turn the company around included offering more chicken options as beef consumption started to decline. Other responses included improving drive-through service; introducing more snack options; and refurbishing restaurants by adding leather seats, warmer paint colours, and flat-screen TVs. It removed "Super Size" options after the documentary Super Size Me targeted McDonald's. McDonald's Canada responded to concerns about growing obesity rates and began offering premium salads and apple slices instead of french fries in Happy Meals, as well as all-white-meat McNuggets. Since the introduction of entree and side salads in 2002, McDonald's Canada has sold nearly 10 million salads, making it one of the leading providers of salads in the Canadian food service industry. McDonald's Canada also offers an online nutrition calculator along with in-restaurant nutrition information. Initial results were staggering and its stock price increased by almost 200 percent despite the economic crisis.

McDonald's has continued to innovate and improve its products. It began offering premium Angus burgers and its McCafé coffee line, which directly targeted competitors like Starbucks by offering less expensive specialty coffee drinks. McDonald's also launched a worldwide repackaging effort as a result of intense consumer research. The new packaging aimed to accomplish several tasks, including teaching consumers about McDonald's health consciousness and building awareness of its use of locally grown produce. For example, it purchases $760 million worth of products from Canadian producers including 66 million pounds of beef and 66 million eggs.

Through the years, McDonald's has created a number of successful marketing campaigns and slogans, such as "You Deserve a Break Today," "It's a Good Time for the Great Taste of McDonald's," and "Food, Folks, and Fun." Its current campaign, "I'm Lovin' It," seems on track to join the others by helping the company reach record sales and growth despite difficult economic times. McDonald's Canada's Monopoly promotion continues to be very popular, and its "Free Parking" promotion run in conjunction with the game in Canada's largest cities proved to be a major hit. It's ventured onto Facebook, using social media to involve consumers in a vote on which classic McDonald's burger they prefer: the Big Mac or the Quarter Pounder with Cheese.

QUESTIONS

1. What are the core brand values of McDonald's Restaurants of Canada Limited? Have these changed over the years?

2. McDonald's did very well during the recession in the late 2000s. With the economy turning around for the better, should McDonald's change its strategy? Why or why not?

3. What risks do you feel McDonald's will face going forward?

Sources: Presentation by Sherry MacLauchlan, Director of Public Relations and Sustainability, McDonald's Restaurants of Canada Limited, Dalhousie University, October 15, 2010; Katie Bailey, "McDonald's Floats the Vote," *Strategy Magazine*, July 20, 2010; Katie Bailey, "Spotted! McDonald's Parks New Monopoly Promo," *Media in Canada*, October 7, 2010; Andrew Martin, "At McDonald's, the Happiest Meal Is Hot Profits," *New York Times*, January 10, 2009; Janet Adamy, "McDonald's Seeks Way to Keep Sizzling," *Wall Street Journal*, March 10, 2009; Matt Vella, "McDonald's Thinks About the Box," *BusinessWeek*, December 8, 2008; Jessica Wohl, "McDonald's CEO: Tough Economy, but Some 'Thawing,'" *Reuters*, April 17, 2009; "McDonald's Rolls Out New Generation of Global Packaging," McDonald's Press Release, 2008.

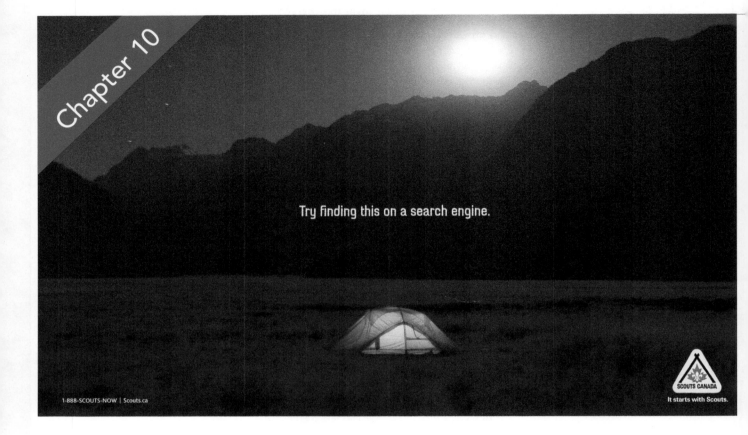

Try finding this on a search engine.

1-888-SCOUTS-NOW | Scouts.ca

It starts with Scouts.

In This Chapter, We Will Address the Following **Questions**

1. How can a firm develop and establish an effective positioning in the market?

2. How do marketers identify and analyze competition?

3. How are brands successfully differentiated?

4. What are the differences in positioning and branding for a small business?

Scouts Canada has worked to reposition itself as a modern, relevant organization through powerful and catchy images.

Crafting the Brand Positioning

No organization can be successful if its products and services resemble every other offering or if they become irrelevant to consumers. As part of the strategic brand management process, each offering must represent the right kinds of things in the minds of the target market. Although successfully positioning a new product or repositioning an existing offering is difficult, it is not impossible. Scouts Canada is currently facing this type of challenge.

Scouts Canada, a venerable volunteer-led organization born in Canada in 1907, decided its image was getting a little worn, because the organization was experiencing a precipitous decline in membership and volunteer support. It needed to think about how it was positioned in the minds of its key stakeholders (parents, volunteers, children, donors), and what it needed to do to reposition itself as a modern, relevant organization. It had to be cautious since it didn't want to alienate its current members.

Scouts Canada took a strategic marketing approach. As its 2009–2010 annual report notes, "It began with a vision. It was nurtured with passion. It will succeed through action." Scouts Canada was very focused in its efforts, developing a new strategic plan around a new positioning strategy which mixed its traditional values with new insights to take it forward during the period 2010 to 2016. Its goals were to remain relevant to Canadian society and ensure its programs were affordable and attractive to both youth and adult volunteers. It began by clearly defining what the organization was all about, the key values at the heart of the new positioning—leadership; healthy, active living; and a clean environment. The values provided a foundation for the new promise of "adventures to come," of Scouting being a "healthier way to live," and of the positive impact that youth can have on society in general and Canada in particular.

Scouts Canada knew that the new values had to be lived, so it undertook an internal marketing campaign. This included a new brand manual designed to ensure that the new brand positioning would be used consistently by all of its management team. The manual not only outlines Scouts Canada's new standards for the brand, it also stresses that "our branding is more than a name and logo." The new brand positioning focuses on scouting as "a positive experience" and the fact that Scouts Canada is "an organization committed to providing children with new adventures and experiences—all of which help them develop into capable and confident individuals, better prepared for success in the world."

As a result of its efforts, Scouts Canada has a new brand logo and motto in both French and English. The English version proclaims, "It starts with Scouts!" The French translation is "Tout commence avec les Scouts." It launched a new print advertising campaign in 2010 to reinforce the new brand positioning externally. Scouts Canada wanted to convey the idea that Scouting is all about great adventures and first-time discoveries. In an age where many children are obese and unfit, it

As the success of the Scouts Canada example demonstrates, all types of organizations can reap the benefits of carving out a unique position in the marketplace. Creating a compelling, well-differentiated brand position requires a keen understanding of consumer needs and wants, customer capabilities, and competitive actions. It also requires disciplined but creative thinking. In this chapter, we outline a process by which marketers can uncover the most powerful brand positioning.

also wanted to stress the benefits children receive from exploring the outdoors. The campaign took a shot at more passive indoor activities involving computer and television screens. One poster, for example, shows a tent in the middle of a field at night, with mountains in the background, along with copy that reads "Try finding this on a search engine." Another poster depicts a sunlit forest accompanied by orders to parents to "Show them where Discovery Channel got its name."

Initial results from the new positioning strategy have been encouraging. By 2010, membership had increased in every province, and almost 600 Scouting groups had increased their membership by over 15 percent.[1]

DEVELOPING AND ESTABLISHING A BRAND POSITIONING

All marketing strategy is built on STP—*segmentation, targeting,* and *positioning.* A company discovers different needs and groups in the marketplace, targets those needs and groups that it can satisfy in a superior way, and then positions its offering so that the target market recognizes the company's distinctive offering and image.

Positioning is the act of designing the company's offering and image to occupy a distinctive place in the mind of the target market.[2] The goal is to locate the brand in the minds of consumers to maximize the potential benefit to the firm. A good brand positioning helps guide marketing strategy by clarifying the brand's essence, what goals it helps the consumer achieve, and how it does so in a unique way. Everyone in the organization should understand the brand positioning and use it as context for making decisions. See how The Bay turned its fortunes around by adopting a new brand positioning.

The Bay

It wasn't long ago that people wondered if The Bay would go the way of other Canadian department stores like Eaton's, but it has revitalized itself through its powerful new positioning strategy. Vice President of Marketing Patrick Dickinson and his 45-member team have been in charge of revitalizing the brand in the minds of Canadians as a go-to fashion destination for the fashion-involved crowd. Extensive research with over 7000 consumers from across Canada was undertaken to better understand purchase behaviours and attitudes. The research revealed that stores needed to reflect local tastes, and in the major Canadian metropolitan markets, like Toronto, Vancouver, and Montreal, people were clamouring for high-end brands. Thus, today The Bay positions itself on a platform of fashion-first thinking and offers its consumers (particularly fashion-forward females) exclusive brands endorsed by celebrities like Jessica Simpson, Jamie Oliver, and Jeanne Beker. Dickinson and his team worked to ensure that The Bay's new position is reflected in all of its communications with its staff and with consumers no matter what media are used—print, TV, or digital ads, or its own *B-Insider's Look Book.* As he notes with pride, "We've made an effort to become a more fashionable destination, present a more edited assortment to customers...and to portray The Bay [as] a rejuvenated brand." The new style-centric strategy has helped The Bay increase its sales, win the Retail Council of Canada's Excellence in Retail Award, and win Dickinson a nomination as *Strategy Magazine*'s Marketer of the Year. Dickinson notes, however, that the best part has been conversations he's had with The Bay customers, who send him 200 letters every week with comments like "Boy, you guys are just doing something special and I'm thinking of The Bay in a whole different way."[3]

A good positioning, like the one designed by The Bay, has a foot in the present and a foot in the future. It needs to be somewhat aspirational so the brand has room to grow and improve. Positioning on the basis of the current state of the market is not forward-looking enough, but, at the same time, the positioning cannot be so removed from reality that it is essentially unobtainable. The real trick in positioning is to strike just the right balance between what the brand is and what it could be.

The Bay has successfully repositioned itself as the go-to place for fashion-conscious Canadians.

The result of positioning is the successful creation of a *customer-focused value proposition*, a cogent reason why the target market should buy the product. Table 10.1 shows how three companies—Butterball, Volvo, and Domino's—have defined their value proposition given their target customers, benefits, and prices.[4]

Positioning requires that similarities and differences among brands be defined and communicated. Specifically, deciding on a positioning requires (1) determining a frame of reference by identifying the target market and the relevant competition, (2) identifying the optimal points-of-parity and points-of-difference brand associations, given that frame of reference, and (3) creating a brand mantra to summarize the positioning and essence of the brand.

Determining a Competitive Frame of Reference

The **competitive frame of reference** defines which other brands a brand competes with and therefore which brands should be the focus of competitive analysis. Decisions about the competitive frame of reference are closely linked to target market decisions. Deciding to target a certain type of consumer can define the nature of competition because certain firms have decided to target that segment in the past (or plan to do so in the future), or consumers in that segment already may look to certain brands in their purchase decisions.

TABLE 10.1	EXAMPLES OF VALUE PROPOSITIONS, DEMAND STATES, AND MARKETING TASKS			
Company and Product	**Target Customers**	**Benefits**	**Price**	**Value Proposition**
Butterball (turkey)	Inexperienced or a time-pressured cooks	Juicy turkey guaranteed	10% premium	Risk- and hassle-free cooking for anyone lacking time or confidence in preparing a weekday or holiday meal
Volvo (station wagon)	Safety-conscious, "upscale" families	Durability and safety	20% premium	The safest, most durable wagon in which your family can ride
Domino's (pizza)	Convenience-minded pizza lovers	Delivery speed and good quality	15% premium	A good pizza, delivered to your door within 30 minutes of ordering, at a moderate price

IDENTIFYING COMPETITORS A good starting point in defining a competitive frame of reference for brand positioning is to determine **category membership**—the products or sets of products with which a brand competes and which function as close substitutes. It would seem a simple task for a company to identify its competitors. PepsiCo knows Coca-Cola's Dasani is a major bottled-water competitor for its Aquafina brand; the Bank of Nova Scotia knows that TD is a major banking competitor; and Petsmart.com knows that a major online retail competitor for pet food and supplies is Petco.com.

The range of a company's actual and potential competitors, however, can be much broader than the obvious. For a brand with explicit growth intentions to enter new markets, a broader or maybe even more aspirational competitive frame may be necessary to reflect possible future competitors. And a company is more likely to be hurt by emerging competitors or new technologies than by current competitors:

- After having spent billions of dollars building their networks, cell phone carriers Bell, Rogers, and Sprint face the threat of new competition emerging as a result of a number of changes in the market-place like the introduction of Skype and the growth of Wi-Fi hotspots and municipal Wi-Fi networks.

- The energy-bar market created by PowerBar ultimately fragmented into a variety of subcategories, including those directed at specific segments (such as Luna bars for women) and some possessing specific attributes (such as the protein-laden Balance and the calorie-control bar Pria). Each represented a subcategory for which the original PowerBar was potentially not as relevant.[5]

Firms should identify their competitive frame in the most advantageous way possible. Consider the competitive frame adopted by Bertolli.[6]

Bertolli

Unilever's Bertolli, a line of frozen Italian food, experienced a steady 10 percent growth in sales through the recent economic recession, in part due to its clever positioning as "restaurant quality Italian food that you can eat at home." Targeting men and women with "discerning palates," Bertolli has aggressively innovated with a stream of high-quality new dishes to keep target customers interested. In its marketing for the brand, Bertolli deliberately chooses to go to places "appropriate for a fine dining brand but not a frozen food brand."

We can examine competition from both an industry and a market point of view.[7] An **industry** is a group of firms offering a product or class of products that are close substitutes for one another. Marketers classify industries according to number of sellers; degree of product differentiation; presence or absence of entry, mobility, and exit barriers; cost structure; degree of **vertical integration**; and degree of globalization.

Using the market approach, we define *competitors* as companies that satisfy the same customer need. For example, a customer who buys a word-processing package really wants "writing ability"—a need that can also be satisfied by pencils, pens, or, in the past, typewriters. Marketers must overcome "marketing myopia" and stop defining competition in traditional category and industry terms.[8] Coca-Cola, focused on its soft drink business, missed seeing the market for coffee bars and fresh-fruit-juice bars and that eventually impinged on its soft drink business.

The market concept of competition reveals a broader set of actual and potential competitors than competition defined in just product category terms. Marketing academics Jeffrey F. Rayport and Bernard J. Jaworski suggest profiling a company's direct and indirect competitors by mapping the buyer's steps in obtaining and using the product. This type of analysis highlights both the opportunities and the challenges a company faces.[9] "Marketing Insight: High Growth through Value Innovation" describes how firms can tap into new markets while minimizing competition from others.

ANALYZING COMPETITORS Chapter 2 described how to conduct a SWOT analysis that includes a competitive analysis. A company needs to gather information about each competitor's real and perceived strengths and weaknesses. Table 10.2 shows the results of a company survey that asked customers to rate its three competitors, A, B, and C, on five attributes. Competitor A turns out to be well-known and respected for producing high-quality products sold by a good sales force, but poor at providing product availability and technical assistance. Competitor B is good across the board and excellent in product availability and sales force. Competitor C rates poor to fair on most attributes. This result suggests that in its positioning the company could attack Competitor A on product availability and technical assistance and Competitor C on almost anything, but it should not attack B, which has no glaring weaknesses. As part of this competitive analysis for positioning, the firm should also ascertain the strategies and objectives of its primary competitors.[10]

MARKETING **INSIGHT**	HIGH GROWTH THROUGH VALUE INNOVATION

INSEAD professors W. Chan Kim and Renée Mauborgne believe that too many firms engage in "red-ocean thinking"—seeking bloody, head-to-head battles with competitors, based largely on incremental improvements in cost, quality, or both. They advocate engaging in "blue-ocean thinking" by creating products and services for which there are no direct competitors. Instead of searching within the conventional boundaries of industry competition, managers should look beyond those boundaries to find unoccupied market positions that represent real value innovation.

The authors cite as one example Bert Claeys, a Belgian company that operates movie theatres, and its introduction of the 25-screen, 7600-seat Kinepolis megaplex. Despite an industry slump, Kinepolis has thrived on a unique combination of features, such as ample and safe free parking; large screens and state-of-the-art sound and projection equipment; and roomy, comfortable, oversized seats with unobstructed views. Through smart planning and economies of scale, Bert Claeys created Kinepolis's unique cinema experience at a lower cost.

This is classic blue-ocean thinking—designing creative business ventures to positively affect both a company's cost structure and its value proposition to consumers. Cost savings result from eliminating and reducing the factors affecting traditional industry competition; value to consumers comes from introducing factors the industry has never before offered. Over time, costs drop even more as superior value leads to higher sales volume, and that generates economies of scale.

Here are other marketers that exhibit unconventional, blue-ocean thinking:

- Callaway Golf designed "Big Bertha," a golf club with a large head and expanded sweet spot that helped golfers frustrated by the difficulty of hitting a golf ball squarely.

- NetJets figured out how to offer private jet service to a larger group of customers through fractional ownership.

- Cirque du Soleil reinvented circus as a higher form of entertainment by eliminating high-cost elements such as animals and enhancing the theatrical experience instead.

Kim and Mauborgne propose four crucial questions for marketers to ask themselves in guiding blue-ocean thinking and creating value innovation:

1. Which of the factors that our industry takes for granted should we eliminate?
2. Which factors should we reduce well below the industry's standard?
3. Which factors should we raise well above the industry's standard?
4. Which factors should we create that the industry has never offered?

They maintain that the most successful blue-ocean thinkers take advantage of all three platforms on which value innovation can take place: *physical product*; *service*, including maintenance, customer service, warranties, and training for distributors and retailers; and *delivery*, meaning channels and logistics.

Sources: W. Chan Kim and Renée Mauborgne, *Blue-Ocean Strategy: How to Create Uncontested Market Space and Make the Competition Irrelevant* (Cambridge, MA: Harvard Business School Press, 2005); W. Chan Kim and Renée Mauborgne, "Creating New Market Space," *Harvard Business Review*, January–February 1999; W. Chan Kim and Renée Mauborgne, "Value Innovation: The Strategic Logic of High Growth," *Harvard Business Review*, January–February 1997.

Once a company has identified its main competitors and their strategies, it must ask, What is each competitor seeking in the marketplace? What drives each competitor's behaviour? Many factors shape a competitor's objectives, including size, history, current management, and financial situation. If the competitor is a division of a larger company, it's important to know whether the parent company is running it for growth or for profits, or milking it.[11]

Finally, based on all this analysis, marketers must formally define the competitive frame of reference to guide positioning. In stable markets with little short-term change likely, it may be fairly easy to define one, two, or perhaps three key competitors. In dynamic categories where competition may exist or arise in a variety of different forms, multiple frames of reference may arise, as we discuss next.

TABLE 10.2	CUSTOMERS' RATINGS OF COMPETITORS ON KEY SUCCESS FACTORS				
	Customer Awareness	Product Quality	Product Availability	Technical Assistance	Selling Staff
Competitor A	E	E	P	P	G
Competitor B	G	G	E	G	E
Competitor C	F	P	G	F	F

Note: E = excellent, G = good, F = fair, P = poor.

Identifying Optimal Points-of-Difference and Points-of-Parity

Once the competitive frame of reference for positioning has been fixed by defining the customer target market and nature of competition, marketers can define the appropriate points-of-difference and points-of-parity associations.[12]

POINTS-OF-DIFFERENCE **Points-of-difference (PODs)** are attributes or benefits consumers strongly associate with a brand, positively evaluate, and believe that they could not find to the same extent with a competitive brand. Strong brands may have multiple points-of-difference. Examples are Apple (*design, ease-of-use,* and *irreverent attitude*) and WestJet (*value, reliability,* and *a fun personality*). Creating strong, favourable, and unique associations as PODs is a real challenge, but essential in terms of competitive brand positioning. See what Cascades is doing.

Cascades

Normally quiet Cascades Inc., headquartered in Kingsey Falls, Quebec, wants to shout out to its customers its unique point of difference—that its products are the "real thing" and truly good for the environment. This change in strategy was brought about by an investigation conducted by an Ottawa-based consulting firm that found that 1018 consumer products sold in North America made unsupportable environmental claims. Only paper towels made by Cascades were found to present truly accurate information. Cascades' towels are really made from 100 percent recycled material, and they are biodegradable and compostable. Until recently, Cascades' consumer products—paper towels, toilet paper, and napkins—have been marketed as private-label brands. But given the growing environmental concerns of consumers, Cascades decided to flaunt its green credentials and labelled its line of products Cascades Enviro® 100% recycled fibres. Cascades has the credentials to support the positioning strategy. It has pursued a green strategy since 1964. Its mills recycle water, thereby using far less water than most paper makers. One of its mills gets most of its heat from a nearby biogas facility, and Cascades has chopped its CO_2 by 66 percent in the past three years.[13]

Three key criteria determine whether a brand association can truly function as a point-of-difference—desirability, deliverability, and differentiability. Some key considerations follow:

■ *Desirable to consumer.* Consumers must see the brand association as personally relevant to them. The Westin Stamford hotel in Singapore advertised that it was the world's tallest hotel, but a hotel's height is not important to many tourists. Consumers must also be given a compelling reason to believe and an understandable rationale for why the brand can deliver the desired benefit. Mountain Dew may argue that it is more energizing than other soft drinks and support this claim by noting that it has a higher level of caffeine. Chanel No. 5 perfume may claim to be the quintessentially elegant French perfume and support this claim by noting the long association between Chanel and haute couture. Substantiators can also come in the form of patented, branded ingredients, such as NIVEA Wrinkle Control Crème with Q10 co-enzyme.

■ *Deliverable by the company.* Companies, like The Bay and Cascades, must have the internal resources and commitment to feasibly and profitably create and maintain the brand association

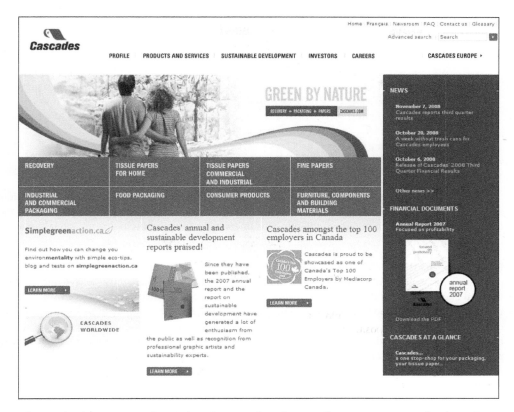

Cascades is communicating its significant point of difference: that it makes from recycled materials products that are truly green, unlike the "greenwashed" products of some other firms.

in the minds of consumers. The product design and marketing offering must support the desired association. Does communicating the desired association require real changes to the product itself, or just perceptual shifts in the way the consumer thinks of the product or brand? Creating the latter is typically easier. General Motors has had to work to overcome public perceptions that Cadillac is not a youthful, modern brand and has done so through bold designs and contemporary images. The ideal brand association is pre-emptive, defensible, and difficult to attack. It is generally easier for market leaders such as Cascades to sustain their positioning, based as it is on demonstrable product or service performance, than it is for market leaders such as The Bay whose positioning is based on fashion and is thus subject to the whims of a more fickle market.

- *Differentiating from competitors.* Finally, consumers must see the brand association as distinctive and superior to relevant competitors. Splenda sugar substitute overtook Equal and Sweet'N Low to become the leader in its category in 2003 by differentiating itself in its authenticity as a product derived from sugar without any of the associated drawbacks.[14]

Any attribute or benefit associated with a product or service can function as a point-of-difference for a brand as long as it is sufficiently desirable, deliverable, and differentiable. The brand must demonstrate clear superiority on an attribute or benefit, however, for it to function as a true point-of-difference. Consumers must be convinced, for example, that Louis Vuitton has the most stylish handbags, Energizer is the longest-lasting battery, and Fidelity Investments offers the best financial advice and planning.

POINTS-OF-PARITY **Points-of-parity (POPs)**, on the other hand, are associations that are not necessarily unique to the brand but may in fact be shared with other brands.[15] These types of associations come in two basic forms: category and competitive.

Category POPs are associations consumers view as essential to be a legitimate and credible offering within a certain product or service category. In other words, they represent necessary—but not necessarily sufficient—conditions for brand choice. Consumers might not consider a travel agency truly a travel agency unless it is able to make air and hotel reservations, provide advice about leisure packages, and offer various ticket-payment and delivery options. Category POPs may change over time due to technological advances, legal developments, or consumer trends, but they are the "greens fees" to play the marketing game.

Competitive POPs are associations designed to negate competitors' PODs. If, in the eyes of consumers, a brand can "break even" in those areas where the competitors are trying to find an advantage *and* can achieve advantages in other areas, the brand should be in a strong—and perhaps unbeatable—competitive position. See how Moores Clothing for Men uses both points-of-parity and points-of-difference.

Moores Clothing for Men

Moores Clothing for Men has grown from one family-owned, Mississauga-based store to be the leading menswear retailer in Canada, with over 1200 employees and almost 120 stores. From the outset, the founders made the commitment to offer the largest selection of quality menswear (its point-of-parity) at the lowest possible prices (its point-of-difference). Unlike other low-priced retailers, however, Moores' other point of difference is its devotion to customer satisfaction and service. For example, if you want alterations made to purchases at other men's retailers, you may have to wait for a week, while Moores offers "while-you-wait hemming." Moores captures its points of parity and difference in its well-known brand slogan "Well Made, Well Priced, Well Dressed."[16]

One good way to uncover key competitive points-of-parity is to role-play competitors' positioning and infer their intended points-of-difference. Competitors' PODs will, in turn, suggest the brand's POPs. Consumer research into the trade-offs consumers make in their purchasing decisions can also be informative.

POINTS-OF-PARITY VERSUS POINTS-OF-DIFFERENCE For an offering to achieve a point-of-parity on a particular attribute or benefit, a sufficient number of consumers must believe that the brand is "good enough" on that dimension. There is a zone or range of tolerance or acceptance with POPs. The brand does not have to be seen as literally equal to competitors, but consumers must feel that the brand does well enough on that particular attribute or benefit. If consumers feel that way, they may be willing to base their evaluations and decisions on other factors potentially more favourable to the brand. A light beer presumably would never taste as good as a full-strength beer, but it would have to taste close enough to be able to effectively compete. Often, the key to positioning is not so much achieving a point-of-difference as achieving points-of-parity! Consider the case of Visa and American Express.

Visa versus American Express

Visa's POD in the credit card category is that it is the most widely accepted card, which underscores the category's main benefit of convenience. American Express, on the other hand, has built the equity of its brand by highlighting the prestige associated with the use of its card. Having established their PODs, Visa and American Express now compete by attempting to blunt each other's advantage for creating POPs. Visa offers gold and platinum cards to enhance the prestige of its brand and advertises "It's Everywhere You Want to Be" in settings that reinforce exclusivity and acceptability. American Express has substantially increased the number of vendors that accept its cards and created other value enhancements while also reinforcing its cachet through advertising that showcases celebrities such as Jerry Seinfeld, Robert De Niro, Tina Fey, Ellen DeGeneres, and Beyoncé.

Visa has established a strong point-of-difference versus American Express on the basis of acceptability.

enjoy exclusive perks at Visa Signature Luxury Hotels.

VISA
SIGNATURE

MULTIPLE FRAMES OF REFERENCE It is not uncommon for a brand to identify more than one actual or potential competitive frame of reference, if competition widens or the firm plans to expand into new categories. For example, Starbucks could define very distinct sets of competitors, suggesting different possible POPs and PODs as a result:

1. *Quick-serve restaurants and convenience shops (McDonald's and Tim Hortons).* Intended PODs might be quality, image, experience, and variety; intended POPs might be convenience and value.

2. *Supermarket brands for home consumption (Folgers and NESCAFÉ).* Intended PODs might be quality, image, experience, variety, and freshness; intended POPs might be convenience and value.

3. *Local cafés.* Intended PODs might be convenience and service quality; intended POPs might be quality, variety, price, and community.

Note that some potential POPs and PODs for Starbucks are shared across competitors; others are unique to a particular competitor.

Under such circumstances, marketers have to decide what to do. There are two main options with multiple frames of reference. One is to first develop the best possible positioning for each type or class of competitors and then see whether there is a way to create one combined positioning robust enough to effectively address them all. If competition is too diverse, however, it may be necessary to prioritize competitors and then choose the most important set of competitors to serve as the competitive frame. One crucial consideration is not to try to be all things to all people; that leads to lowest-common-denominator positioning, which is typically ineffective.

Finally, if there are many competitors in different categories or subcategories, it may be useful to either develop the positioning at the categorical level for all relevant categories ("quick-serve restaurants" or "supermarket take-home coffee" for Starbucks) or with an exemplar from each category (McDonald's or NESCAFÉ for Starbucks).

STRADDLE POSITIONING Occasionally, a company will be able to straddle two frames of reference with one set of points-of-difference and points-of-parity. In these cases, the points-of-difference for one category become points-of-parity for the other and vice versa. Subway restaurants are positioned as offering healthy, good-tasting sandwiches. This positioning allows the brand to create a POP on taste and a POD on health with respect to quick-serve restaurants such as McDonald's and Burger King and, at the same time, a POP on health and a POD on taste with respect to health-food restaurants and cafés. Straddle positions allow brands to expand their market coverage and potential customer base. Another example of a straddle positioning is BMW.

BMW

When BMW first made a strong competitive push into the North American market in the early 1980s, it positioned the brand as being the only automobile that offered both luxury and performance. At that time, American luxury cars were seen by many as lacking performance, and American performance cars were seen as lacking luxury. By relying on the design of its cars, its German heritage, and other aspects of a well-conceived marketing program, BMW was able to simultaneously achieve (1) a POD on luxury and a POP on performance with respect to performance cars, and (2) a POD on performance and a POP on luxury with respect to luxury cars. The clever slogan "The Ultimate Driving Machine" effectively captured the newly created umbrella category—luxury performance cars.

BMW created the slogan "The Ultimate Driving Machine," effectively positioning its cars as both luxury *and* performance vehicles.

Although a straddle positioning often is attractive as a means of reconciling potentially conflicting consumer goals, it also carries an extra burden. If the POPs and PODs with respect to both categories are not credible, the brand may not be viewed as a legitimate player in either category. Many early PDAs that unsuccessfully tried to straddle categories ranging from pagers to laptop computers provide a vivid illustration of this risk.

Choosing POPs and PODs

Marketers typically focus on brand benefits in choosing the points-of-parity and points-of-difference that make up their brand positioning. Brand attributes generally play more of a supporting role by providing "reasons to believe" or "proof points" as to why a brand can credibly claim it offers certain benefits. Marketers of Dove soap, for example, can talk about its attribute of one-quarter moisturizing cream, or its benefit of softer skin. Consumers are usually more interested in benefits and what exactly they will get from a product. Multiple attributes may support a certain benefit, and they may change over time.

For choosing specific benefits as POPs and PODs to position a brand, perceptual maps may be useful. *Perceptual maps* are visual representations of consumer perceptions and preferences. They provide quantitative portrayals of market situations and the way consumers view different products, services, and brands along various dimensions. By overlaying consumer preferences with brand perceptions, marketers can reveal "holes" or "openings" that suggest unmet consumer needs and marketing opportunities.

For example, Figure 10.1(a) shows a hypothetical perceptual map for a beverage category. The four brands—A, B, C, and D—vary in terms of how consumers view their taste profile (light versus strong) and personality and imagery (contemporary versus traditional). Also displayed on the map are ideal point "configurations" for three market segments (1, 2, and 3). The ideal points represent each segment's most preferred ("ideal") combination of taste and imagery.

Consumers in Segment 3 prefer beverages with a strong taste and traditional imagery. Brand D is well-positioned for this segment as it is strongly associated in the marketplace with both these benefits. Given that none of the competitors is seen as anywhere close, we would expect Brand D to attract many of the Segment 3 customers.

Brand A, on the other hand, is seen as more balanced in terms of both taste and imagery. Unfortunately, no market segment seems to really desire this balance. Brands B and C are better positioned with respect to Segments 1 and 2, respectively.

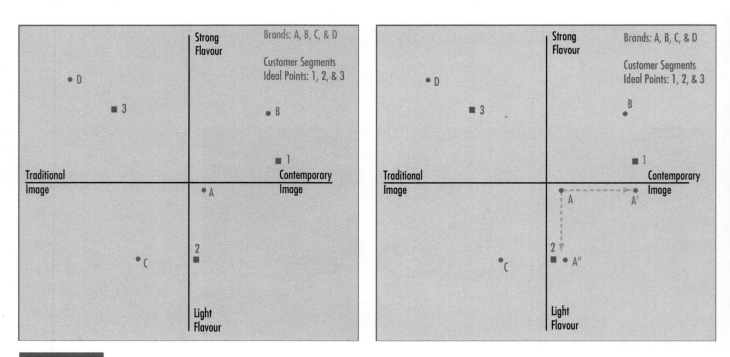

FIGURE 10.1

(a) Hypothetical Beverage Perceptual Map: Current Perceptions

(b) Hypothetical Beverage Perceptual Map: Possible Repositioning for Brand A.

As Figure 10.1(b) suggests, Brand A has two options for repositioning:

- By making its image more contemporary, Brand A could move to A' to target consumers in Segment 1 and achieve a point-of-parity on imagery and maintain its point-of-difference on taste profile with respect to Brand B.

- By changing its taste profile to make it lighter, Brand A could move to A" to target consumers in Segment 2 and achieve a point-of-parity on taste profile and maintain its point-of-difference on imagery with respect to Brand C.

Deciding which repositioning is more promising, A' or A" would require detailed consumer and competitive analysis on a host of factors—including the resources, capabilities, and likely intentions of competing firms—to choose the markets where consumers can profitably be served.

Brand Mantras

To further focus the intent of the brand positioning and the way firms would like consumers to think about the brand, it is often useful to define a brand mantra.[17] A *brand mantra* is an articulation of the heart and soul of the brand and is closely related to other branding concepts like "brand essence" and "core brand promise." Brand mantras are short, three- to five-word phrases that capture the irrefutable essence or spirit of the brand positioning. Their purpose is to ensure that all employees within the organization and all external marketing partners understand what the brand is most fundamentally to represent to consumers so that employees and partners can adjust their actions accordingly.

Brand mantras are powerful devices. They can provide guidance about what products to introduce under the brand, what ad campaigns to run, and where and how to sell the brand. Their influence, however, can extend beyond these tactical concerns. Brand mantras may even guide the most seemingly unrelated or mundane decisions, such as the look of a reception area and the way phones are answered. In effect, they create a mental filter to screen out brand-inappropriate marketing activities or actions of any type that may have a negative bearing on customers' impressions of a brand.

Brand mantras must economically communicate what the brand is and what it is *not*. What makes for a good brand mantra? The brand philosophy of "Food, Folks, and Fun" captures the brand essence and core brand promise of McDonald's. Nike shows the power and utility of a well-designed brand mantra.

Nike

Nike has a rich set of associations with consumers, based on its innovative product designs, its sponsorships of top athletes, its award-winning advertising, its competitive drive, and its irreverent attitude. Internally, Nike marketers adopted the three-word brand mantra, "Authentic Athletic Performance," to guide their marketing efforts. Thus, in Nike's eyes, its entire marketing program—its products and how they are sold—must reflect those key brand values. Over the years, Nike has expanded its brand meaning from "running shoes" to "athletic shoes" to "athletic shoes and apparel" to "all things associated with athletics (including equipment)." Each step of the way, however, it has been guided by its "Authentic Athletic Performance" brand mantra. For example, as Nike rolled out its successful apparel line, one important hurdle for the products was that they could be made innovative enough through material, cut, or design to truly benefit top athletes. At the same time, the company has been careful to avoid using the Nike name to brand products that do not fit with the brand mantra (like casual shoes).

DESIGNING A BRAND MANTRA Brand mantras are designed with internal purposes in mind. A brand slogan is an external translation that attempts to creatively engage consumers. Although Nike's internal mantra was "Authentic Athletic Performance," its external slogan was "Just Do It." Here are the three key criteria for a brand mantra:

- *Communicate*. A good brand mantra should define the category (or categories) of business for the brand and set the brand boundaries. It should also clarify what is unique about the brand.

- *Simplify*. An effective brand mantra should be memorable. For that, it should be short, crisp, and vivid.

- *Inspire*. Ideally, the brand mantra should also stake out ground that is personally meaningful and relevant to as many employees as possible.

Brand mantras typically are designed to capture the brand's points-of-difference, that is, what is unique about the brand. Other aspects of the brand positioning—especially the brand's points-of-parity—may also be important and may need to be reinforced in other ways.

For brands facing rapid growth, it is helpful to define the product or benefit space in which the brand would like to compete, as Nike did with "Athletic Performance." Words that describe the nature of the product or service, or the type of experiences or benefits the brand provides, can be critical for identifying appropriate categories into which to extend. For brands in more stable categories where extensions into more distinct categories are less likely to occur, the brand mantra may focus more exclusively on points-of-difference.

Brand mantras derive their power and usefulness from their collective meaning. Other brands may be strong on one, or perhaps even a few, of the brand associations making up the brand mantra. But for the brand mantra to be effective, no other brand should singularly excel on all dimensions. Part of the key to Nike's success is that for years no competitor could really deliver on the combined promise suggested by its brand mantra.

Establishing Brand Positioning

Once they have determined the brand positioning strategy, marketers should communicate it to everyone in the organization so that it guides their words and actions. One helpful schematic for doing so is a brand positioning bull's-eye. Constructing a bull's-eye for the brand ensures that no steps are skipped in its development. "Marketing Memo: Constructing a Brand Positioning Bull's-Eye" outlines one way marketers can formally express brand positioning.

Establishing the brand positioning in the marketplace requires that consumers understand what the brand offers and what makes it a superior competitive choice. To do so, consumers need to understand in which category or categories it competes and its points-of-parity and points-of-difference with respect to those competitors.

Category membership may be obvious in some cases. Target customers are aware that Maybelline is a leading brand of cosmetics, Cheerios is a leading brand of cereal, Accenture is a leading consulting firm, and so on. Often, however, marketers must inform consumers of a brand's category membership. Perhaps the most obvious situation is the introduction of new products, especially when category identification itself is not apparent. Category membership can be a special problem for high-tech products. For example, should the new electronic book readers be positioned as books or computers?

There are also situations in which consumers know a brand's category membership but may not be convinced the brand is a valid member of the category. They may be aware that Hewlett-Packard produces digital cameras, but they may not be certain whether Hewlett-Packard cameras are in the same class as Sony, Olympus, Kodak, and Nikon. In this instance, HP might find it useful to reinforce category membership.

Brands are sometimes affiliated with categories in which they do *not* hold membership. This approach is one way to highlight a brand's point-of-difference, providing consumers know the brand's actual membership. DiGiorno's frozen pizza has adopted such a positioning strategy. Instead of putting it in the frozen pizza category, the marketers have positioned it in the delivered pizza category with ads that claim, "It's Not Delivery, It's DiGiorno!"

With this approach, however, it's important not to be trapped between categories. Consumers should understand what the brand stands for, and not just what it is not. The typical approach to positioning is to inform consumers of a brand's membership before stating its point-of-difference. Presumably, consumers need to know what a product is and what function it serves before deciding whether it is superior to the brands against which it competes. For new products, initial advertising often concentrates on creating brand awareness, and subsequent advertising attempts to create the brand image.

COMMUNICATING CATEGORY MEMBERSHIP There are three main ways to convey a brand's category membership:

1. *Announcing category benefits.* To reassure consumers that a brand will deliver on the fundamental reason for using a category, marketers frequently use benefits to announce category membership. Thus, industrial tools might claim to have durability, and antacids might announce their efficacy. While Canada Goose outerwear does very little paid media advertising, it receives lots of coverage in sporting and fashion magazines, and it clearly conveys the benefits of its brand by other means.[18]

2. *Comparing to exemplars.* Well-known, noteworthy brands in a category can also help a brand specify its category membership. When Tommy Hilfiger was an unknown, advertising announced his membership as a great U.S. designer by associating him with Geoffrey Beene, Stanley Blacker, Calvin Klein, and Perry Ellis, who were recognized members of that category.

3. *Relying on the product descriptor.* The product descriptor that follows the brand name is often a concise means of conveying category origin. Ford Motor Co. invested more than $1 billion on a radical new 2004 model called the X-Trainer, which combined the attributes of an SUV, a minivan, and a station wagon. To communicate its unique position—and to avoid association with its Explorer and Country Squire models—the vehicle, eventually called Freestyle, was designated a "sports wagon."[19]

MARKETING **MEMO** | CONSTRUCTING A BRAND POSITIONING BULL'S-EYE

A brand bull's-eye provides content and context to improve everyone's understanding of the positioning of a brand in the organization. Here we describe the components of a brand bull's-eye, illustrating with a hypothetical Starbucks example.

In the inner two circles is the heart of the bull's-eye—key points-of-parity and points-of-difference, as well as the brand mantra. In the next circle out are the substantiators or reasons-to-believe (RTB)—attributes or benefits that provide factual or demonstrable support for the points-of-parity and points-of-difference. Finally, the outer circle contains two other useful branding concepts: (1) the brand values, personality, or character—intangible associations that help to establish the tone for the words and actions for the brand; and (2) executional properties and visual identity—more tangible components of the brand that affect how it is seen.

Three boxes outside the bull's-eye provide useful context and interpretation. To the left, two boxes highlight some of the input to the positioning analysis: One includes the consumer target and a key insight about consumer attitudes or behaviour that significantly influenced the actual positioning; the other box provides competitive information about the key consumer need the brand is attempting to satisfy and some competitive products or brands that need suggests. To the right of the bull's-eye, one box offers a big-picture view of the output—the ideal consumer takeaway that would result if the brand positioning efforts were successful.

Canada Goose

Canada Goose prides itself on producing authentic extreme-weather gear. Being produced in Canada is part of the brand's authenticity. Its brand mantra, "Born of Purpose and Function," reflects the fact that its parkas are designed for those who enjoy the confidence that comes from quality. Its parkas are recognized internationally and sold in over 40 countries. Its brand logo, the Arctic Disk, not only symbolizes the fact that the parkas are extreme-weather outerwear, it also stands for the true spirit of exploration. While the outerwear is suitable for wear at either pole, the parkas are also being worn in cities and fashion capitals like New York, Toronto, and Milan.

Canada Goose clearly communicates the benefits of its brand through its distinctive brand logo, its Canadian manufacturing, and its authentic high-quality design.

COMMUNICATING POPS AND PODS One common difficulty in creating a strong, competitive brand positioning is that many of the attributes or benefits that make up the points-of-parity and points-of-difference are negatively correlated. For example, it might be difficult to position a brand as "inexpensive" and at the same time assert that it is "of the highest quality." ConAgra must convince consumers that Healthy Choice frozen foods both taste good and are good for you. Consider these examples of negatively correlated attributes and benefits.

Low price vs. High quality	Powerful vs. Safe
Taste vs. Low calories	Strong vs. Refined
Nutritious vs. Good tasting	Ubiquitous vs. Exclusive
Efficacious vs. Mild	Varied vs. Simple

Moreover, individual attributes and benefits often have positive *and* negative aspects. For example, consider a long-lived brand such as La-Z-Boy recliners, Burberry outerwear, or *The Globe and Mail*. The brand's heritage could suggest experience, wisdom, and expertise. On the other hand, it could also imply being old-fashioned and not up-to-date.[20]

Unfortunately, consumers typically want to maximize *both* of the negatively correlated attributes or benefits. Much of the art and science of marketing is dealing with trade-offs, and positioning is no different. The best approach clearly is to develop a product or service that performs well on both dimensions. GORE-TEX was able to overcome the seemingly conflicting product images of "breathable" and "waterproof" through technological advances. When in-depth and quantitative interviews and focus groups suggested that consumers wanted the benefits of technology without the hassles, Royal Philips launched its "Sense and Simplicity" advertising campaign for its Philips brand of electronics, using print, online, and television advertising.[21]

Some marketers have adopted other approaches to address attribute or benefit trade-offs: launching two different marketing campaigns, each devoted to a different brand attribute or benefit; linking themselves to any kind of entity (person, place, or thing) that possesses the right kind of equity as a means to establish an attribute or benefit as a POP or POD; and even attempting to convince consumers that the negative relationship between attributes and benefits, if they consider it differently, is in fact positive.

DIFFERENTIATION STRATEGIES

To build a strong brand and avoid the commodity trap, marketers must start with the belief that you can differentiate anything. **Competitive advantage** is a company's ability to perform in one or more ways that competitors cannot or will not match. Michael Porter urged companies to build a sustainable competitive advantage.[22] But few competitive advantages are sustainable. At best, they may be leverageable. A *leverageable advantage* is one that a company can use as a springboard to new advantages, much as Microsoft has leveraged its operating system to Microsoft Office and then to networking applications. In general, a company that hopes to endure must be in the business of continuously inventing new advantages.[23]

For a brand to be effectively positioned, however, customers must see any competitive advantage as a *customer advantage*. For example, if a company claims its product works faster than its competitors', the claim won't be a customer advantage if customers don't value speed. Select Comfort has made a splash in the mattress industry with its Sleep Number beds, which allow consumers to adjust the support and fit of the mattress for optimal comfort with a simple numbering index.[24] Companies must also focus on building customer advantages.[25] Then they will deliver high customer value and satisfaction, which leads to high repeat purchases and ultimately to high company profitability. Consider the case of Progressive.

Progressive

Progressive gained a competitive advantage in the mid-1990s when it became one of the first auto insurance companies to sell direct to consumers via the Internet. The company's early adoption of technology enabled it to offer a unique service: in addition to providing free online quotes for its own policies, Progressive also provided quotes from up to three competitors, information that until then had been available only through insurance agents. In addition to saving its customers time, Progressive was able to save them money by showing that, in many cases, its policies were more competitively priced. Once Progressive won new customers' business, it mobilized its army of claims adjusters who will speed right to an accident scene—and often cut a cheque right on the spot. It has further enhanced its competitiveness by adding innovative service features such as an "accident concierge," who handles all aspects of the claims and repair process for customers, and online policy management that enables customers to make payments and change coverage any time. These customer advantages made Progressive the third-largest auto insurer in North America by 2006, up from forty-eighth in 1980, with over 12 million customers.[26]

MEANS OF DIFFERENTIATION The obvious means of differentiation, and often the ones most compelling to consumers, relate to aspects of the product and service (reviewed in Chapters 12 and 13). Swatch offers colourful, fashionable watches; GEICO offers reliable insurance at discount prices. In competitive markets, however, firms may need to go beyond these. Consider these other dimensions, among the many that a company can use to differentiate its market offerings:

- *Employee differentiation.* Companies can have better-trained employees who provide superior customer service. Singapore Airlines is well-regarded in large part because of its flight attendants. Fairmont Hotels are renowned for their high-quality customer service.

- *Channel differentiation.* Companies can more effectively and efficiently design their distribution channels' coverage, expertise, and performance to make buying the product easier and more enjoyable and rewarding. Back in 1946, pet food was cheap, not too nutritious, and available exclusively in supermarkets and the occasional feed store. Iams found success selling premium pet food through regional veterinarians, breeders, and pet stores.

- *Image differentiation.* Companies can craft powerful, compelling images that appeal to consumers' social and psychological needs. The primary explanation for Marlboro's extraordinary worldwide market share (around 30 percent) is that its macho-cowboy image has struck a responsive chord with much of the cigarette-smoking public. Even a seller's physical space can be a powerful image generator. Hyatt Regency hotels developed a distinctive image through their atrium lobbies.

- *Services differentiation.* A service company can differentiate itself by designing a better and faster delivery system that provides more effective and efficient solutions to consumers. There are three levels of differentiation.[27] The first is *reliability:* some suppliers are more reliable in their on-time delivery, order completeness, and order-cycle time. The second is *resilience:* some suppliers are better at handling emergencies, product recalls, and inquiries. The third is *innovativeness:* some suppliers create better information systems, introduce bar coding and mixed pallets, and in other ways help the customer.

EMOTIONAL BRANDING Many marketing experts believe a brand positioning should have both rational and emotional components. In other words, a good positioning should contain points-of-difference and points-of-parity that appeal both to the head and to the heart.

To do this, strong brands often seek to build on their performance advantages to strike an emotional chord with their customers. When research on scar-treatment product Mederma found that women were buying it not just for the physical treatment but also to increase their self-esteem, the marketers of the brand added emotional messaging to what had traditionally been a practical message that stressed physician recommendations: "What we have done is supplement the rational with the emotional."[28]

A person's emotional response to a brand and its marketing will depend on many factors. One increasingly important factor is a brand's authenticity.[29] Brands that are seen as authentic and genuine, such as Canada Goose, Kraft, Crayola, Kellogg's, and Johnson & Johnson, can evoke trust, affection, and strong loyalty.[30] Guinness beer celebrated its heritage, quality, and authenticity with a 250th anniversary marketing campaign whose ads depict consumers all over the world toasting the brand.[31]

Brand consultant Marc Gobé believes emotional brands share three specific traits: (1) a strong, people-focused corporate culture, (2) a distinctive communication style and philosophy, and (3) a compelling emotional hook.[32] Saatchi & Saatchi CEO Kevin Roberts advocates that brands strive to become lovemarks. Brands that are *lovemarks*, according to Roberts, command both respect and love and result from a brand's ability to achieve mystery, sensuality, and intimacy:[33]

1. *Mystery* draws together stories, metaphors, dreams, and symbols. Mystery adds to the complexity of relationships and experiences because people are naturally drawn to what they don't know.

2. *Sensuality* keeps the five senses of sight, hearing, smell, touch, and taste on constant alert for new textures, intriguing scents and tastes, wonderful music, and other sensory stimuli.

3. *Intimacy* means empathy, commitment, and passion—the close connections that win intense loyalty as well as the small perfect gesture.

By successfully differentiating themselves, emotional brands can also provide financial payoffs. As part of its Initial Public Offering (IPO), the U.K. cell phone operator O2 was rebranded from British Telecom's struggling BT Cellnet, based on a powerful emotional campaign about freedom and enablement. When customer acquisition, loyalty, and average revenue soared, the business was acquired by Spanish multinational Telefónica after only five years for more than three times its IPO price.[34]

In general, the firm should monitor three variables when analyzing potential threats posed by competitors:

1. *Share of market*—The competitor's share of the target market.

2. *Share of mind*—The percentage of customers who named the competitor in responding to the statement, "Name the first company that comes to mind in this industry."

3. *Share of heart*—The percentage of customers who named the competitor in responding to the statement, "Name the company from which you would prefer to buy the product."

There's an interesting relationship among these three measures. Table 10.3 shows them as recorded for three hypothetical competitors. Competitor A enjoys the highest market share but is slipping. Its mind share and heart share are also slipping, probably because it's not providing good product availability and technical assistance. Competitor B is steadily gaining market share, probably due to strategies that are increasing its mind share and heart share. Competitor C seems to be stuck at a low level of market, mind, and heart share, probably because of its poor product and marketing attributes. We could generalize as follows: *Companies that make steady gains in mind share and heart share will inevitably make gains in market share and profitability.* Firms such as CarMax, Timberland, Jordan's Furniture, Wegmans, and Toyota are all reaping the benefits of providing emotional, experiential, social, and financial value to satisfy customers and all their constituents.[35]

Alternative Approaches to Positioning

The competitive brand positioning model we've reviewed in this chapter is a structured way to approach positioning based on in-depth consumer, company, and competitive analysis. Some marketers have proposed other, less-structured approaches in recent years that offer provocative ideas on how to position a brand. We highlight a few of those here.

BRAND NARRATIVES AND STORYTELLING Rather than outlining specific attributes or benefits, some marketing experts describe positioning a brand as telling a narrative or story.[36] Canada Goose outerwear uses storytelling to help build its brand. Visit its website, blog, Facebook page, or Twitter feed, and you will find many examples. Recent posts included stories about its partnership with the Porsche Camp4 driving program held near Mont Tremblant, Quebec. It also publishes a limited edition collector's

TABLE 10.3	MARKET SHARE, MIND SHARE, AND HEART SHARE PERCENTAGES								
	Market Share			Mind Share			Heart Share		
	2011	2012	2013	2011	2012	2013	2011	2012	2013
Competitor A	50	47	44	60	58	54	45	42	39
Competitor B	30	34	37	30	31	35	44	47	53
Competitor C	20	19	19	10	11	11	11	11	8

book of stories about 50 people from around the globe, called "Goose People." As Canada Goose's website notes, each person featured "stands for something big, something much bigger than themselves. Some are famous and others you may never have heard of. Their stories will fascinate you. The images will amaze you." People featured range from Warren Faidley, the world's original storm chaser, to Canadian song-writer Chantal Kreviazuk.[37]

Randall Ringer and Michael Thibodeau see *narrative branding* as based on deep metaphors that con-nect to people's memories, associations, and stories.[38] They identify five elements of narrative branding: (1) the brand story in terms of words and metaphors, (2) the consumer journey in terms of how consum-ers engage with the brand over time and touch points where they come into contact with it, (3) the visual language or expression of the brand, (4) the manner in which the narrative is expressed experientially in terms of how the brand engages the senses, and (5) the role/relationship the brand plays in the lives of consumers. Based on literary convention and brand experience, they also offer the following framework for a brand story:

- *Setting.* The time, place, and context
- *Cast.* The brand as a character, including its role in the life of the audience, its relationships and responsibilities, and its history or creation myth
- *Narrative arc.* The way the narrative logic unfolds over time, including actions, desired experiences, defining events, and the moment of epiphany
- *Language.* The authenticating voice, metaphors, symbols, themes, and leitmotifs

Patrick Hanlon developed the related concept of "primal branding" that views brands as complex belief systems. According to Hanlon, diverse brands such as Google, MINI Cooper, Starbucks, Apple, UPS, and Aveda all have a "primal code" or DNA that resonates with their customers and generates their passion awnd fervour. He outlines seven assets that make up this belief system or primal code: a creation story, creed, icon, rituals, sacred words, a way of dealing with nonbelievers, and a good leader.[39]

BRAND JOURNALISM When he was CMO at McDonald's, Larry Light advocated an approach to brand positioning that he called "brand journalism." Just as editors and writers for newspapers and magazines tell many facets of a story to capture the interests of diverse groups of people, Light believes marketers should communicate different messages to different market segments, as long as the messages at least broadly fit within the basic image of the brand:[40]

Brand Journalism is a chronicle of the varied things that happen in our brand world, throughout our day, throughout the years. Our brand means different things to different people. It does not have one brand position. It is positioned differently in the minds of kids, teens, young adults, par-ents and seniors. It is positioned differently at breakfast, lunch, dinner, snack, weekday, weekend, with kids or on a business trip. Brand Journalism allows us to be a witness to the multi-faceted aspects of a brand story. No one communication alone tells the whole brand story. Each com-munication provides a different insight into our brand. It all adds up to a McDonald's journalistic brand chronicle.

CULTURAL BRANDING Oxford University's Douglas Holt believes that for companies to build iconic, leadership brands, they must assemble cultural knowledge, strategize according to cultural branding prin-ciples, and hire and train cultural experts.[41] Even Procter & Gamble, a company that has long orchestrated how shoppers perceive its products, has started on what its chief executive, A. G. Lafley, calls "a learning journey" with the consumer. "Consumers are beginning in a very real sense to own our brands and partici-pate in their creation," he said. "We need to learn to begin to let go."

The University of Wisconsin's Craig Thompson views brands as sociocultural templates, citing research investigating brands as cultural resources that shows how ESPN Zone restaurants tap into com-petitive masculinity, and how American Girl dolls tap into mother–daughter relationships and the cross-generational transfer of femininity.[42] Experts who see consumers actively co-creating brand meaning and positioning even refer to this as "Brand Wikification," given that wikis are written by contributors from all walks of life and all points of view.[43]

Positioning and Branding a Small Business

Building brands for a small business is a challenge because these firms have limited resources and budgets. Nevertheless, numerous success stories exist of entrepreneurs who have built their brands up essentially from scratch to become powerhouse brands, as the history of vitaminwater shows.

vitaminwater

In 1996, J. Darius Bickoff launched an electrolyte-enhanced line of bottled water called smartwater, followed by the introduction two years later of vitaminwater, a vitamin-enhanced and flavoured alternative to plain bottled water, and fruitwater two years after that. Clever marketing, including endorsement deals with rapper 50 Cent, singer Kelly Clarkson, actress Jennifer Aniston, and football star Tom Brady, helped to drive success. Less than ten years after its launch, Bickoff's Energy Brands company, also known as Glacéau, was sold to the Coca-Cola company for $4.2 billion in cash.[44]

In general, with limited resources behind the brand, both focus and consistency in marketing programs are critically important. Creativity is also paramount—finding new ways to market new ideas about products to consumers. Some specific branding guidelines for small businesses are as follows:

- *Creatively conduct low-cost marketing research.* There are a variety of low-cost marketing research methods that help small businesses connect with customers and study competitors. One way is to set up course projects at local colleges and universities to access the expertise of both students and professors.

- *Focus on building one or two strong brands based on one or two key associations.* Small businesses often must rely on only one or two brands and key associations as points-of-difference for those brands. These associations must be consistently reinforced across the marketing program and over time. Rooted in the snowboarding and surfing cultures, Volcom has adopted "Youth Against Establishment" as its credo, which has resulted in steady sales of its music, athletic apparel, and jewellery. Ocean Nutrition is another company that has reaped financial benefits from having a strong brand.

- *Employ a well-integrated set of brand elements.* Tactically, it is important for small businesses to maximize the contribution of each of the three main sets of brand equity drivers. Small businesses should develop a distinctive, well-integrated set of brand elements that enhances both brand awareness and brand image. Brand elements should be memorable and meaningful, with as much creative potential as possible. Innovative packaging can substitute for ad campaigns by capturing attention at the point of purchase. SMARTFOOD introduced its first product without any advertising by means of both a unique package that served as a strong visual symbol on the shelf and an extensive sampling program that encouraged trial. Proper names or family names, which often characterize small businesses, may provide some distinctiveness but can suffer in terms of pronounceability, meaningfulness, memorability, or other branding considerations. If these deficiencies are too great, explore alternative brand elements.

- *Create buzz and a loyal brand community.* Because small businesses often must rely on word of mouth to establish their positioning, public relations, social networking, and low-cost promotions and sponsorship can be inexpensive alternatives. As discussed in Chapter 9, creating a vibrant brand community among current and prospective customers can also be a cost-effective way to reinforce loyalty and help spread the word to new prospects. Web browser Mozilla Firefox is able to compete with Microsoft's Internet Explorer in part because of its dedicated volunteer group of 10 000 programmers who work on its open source coding.

- *Leverage as many secondary associations as possible.* Secondary associations—any persons, places, or things with potentially relevant associations—are often a cost-effective, shortcut means to build brand equity, especially those that help to signal quality or credibility. Canada Goose's brand equity benefits greatly from the company's partnerships with high-quality manufacturers like Porsche.

Ocean Nutrition

Nova Scotia–based Ocean Nutrition Canada Limited has grown to be the world's largest supplier of Omega-3 EPA/DHA ingredients to dietary supplement and food manufacturers. The company stresses its values (integrity, creating value for customers, continuous innovation, quality, difference making, and nimbleness) along with its coastal location and its use of clean, sustainable resources to provide its customers with a competitive edge in a growing marketplace.[45]

Unlike major brands that often have more resources at their disposal, small businesses usually do not have the luxury to make mistakes and must design and implement marketing programs much more carefully.

Ocean Nutrition is a small Nova Scotia company that has grown to be a global player by adhering to its values and unique brand position.

SUMMARY

1. To develop an effective positioning, a company must study competitors as well as actual and potential customers. Marketers need to identify competitors' strategies, objectives, strengths, and weaknesses.

2. Developing a positioning requires the determination of a frame of reference—by identifying the target market and the resulting nature of the competition—and the optimal points-of-parity and points-of-difference brand associations.

3. A company's closest competitors are those seeking to satisfy the same customers and needs and making similar offers. A company should also pay attention to latent competitors, who may offer new or other ways to satisfy the same needs. A company should identify competitors by using both industry- and market-based analyses.

4. Points-of-difference are those associations unique to the brand and that are also strongly held and favourably evaluated by consumers. Points-of-parity are those associations not necessarily unique to the brand but perhaps shared with other brands. Category point-of-parity associations are associations consumers view as being necessary to a legitimate and credible product offering within a certain category. Competitive point-of-parity associations are those associations designed to negate competitors' points-of-difference or overcome perceived weaknesses or vulnerabilities of the brand.

5. The key to competitive advantage is relevant brand differentiation—consumers must find something unique and meaningful about a market offering. These differences may be based directly on the product or service itself or on other considerations related to factors such as employees, channels, image, or services.

6. Emotional branding is becoming an important way to connect with customers and create differentiation from competitors.

7. Although small businesses should adhere to many of the branding and positioning principles larger companies use, they must place extra emphasis on their brand elements and secondary associations and must be more focused and create a buzz for their brand.

APPLICATIONS

Marketing Debate: What Is the Best Way to Position?

Marketers have different views of how to position a brand. Some value structured approaches such as the competitive positioning model described in the chapter, which focuses on specific points-of-parity and points-of-difference. Others prefer unstructured approaches that rely more on stories, narratives, and other flowing depictions. For example, in August 2010 during the annual Rogers Cup, Tennis Canada worked to revitalize its brand by using the tag line "Love Means Nothing." It ran TV advertising using this theme and a website using the same name. In place of a bland presentation of the organization's rules, news releases, and policy archive, the new site was designed to focus more on social elements meant to engage the sport's fans and create a hub for discussion and information.[46]

Take a position: The best way to position a brand is through a structured approach *versus* The best way to position a brand is through an unstructured approach.

Marketing Discussion

Identify other negatively correlated attributes and benefits *not* described in this chapter. What strategies do firms use to try to position themselves on the basis of pairs of attributes and benefits?

MARKETING **EXCELLENCE**	LOUIS VUITTON

Louis Vuitton (LV) is one of the world's most legendary brands and is synonymous with images of luxury, wealth, and fashion. The company is known for its iconic handbags, leather goods, shoes, watches, jewellery, accessories, and sunglasses, and is the highest-ranked luxury brand in the world.

It was 1854 when Louis Vuitton opened his first store in Paris and sold handmade, high-quality trunks and luggage. In the late nineteenth century, Vuitton introduced his signature Damier and Monogram Canvas materials, featuring the famous design still used in most of the company's products today. Throughout the twentieth century, the company that carries his name continued to grow internationally, expanding into the fashion world by the 1950s and reaching $10 million in sales by 1977. In 1987, Louis Vuitton merged with Moët et Chandon and Hennessy, leading manufacturers of champagne and cognac, and created LVMH, a luxury-goods conglomerate.

Louis Vuitton's products are made with state-of-the-art materials, and its designers use a combination of art, precision, and craftsmanship to produce only the finest products. The legendary LV monogram appears on all the company's products and stands for the highest quality, premium status, and luxury travel. Over the years, however, counterfeiting has become a huge problem and one of Louis Vuitton's most difficult challenges. Louis Vuitton is one of the most counterfeited brands in the world, and the company takes the problem very seriously because it feels that counterfeits dilute its prestigious brand image. Louis Vuitton employs a full team of lawyers and fights counterfeiting in a variety of ways with special agencies and investigative teams.

Until the 1980s, Louis Vuitton products were available in a wide variety of department stores. However, to reduce the risk of counterfeiting, the company now maintains tighter control over its distribution channels. Today, it sells its products only through authentic Louis Vuitton boutiques located in upscale shopping areas such as Toronto's Bloor Street and high-end department stores like Holt Renfrew. In the spring of 2011, an additional retailing concept was launched. The Fairmont Hotel Vancouver became the home to Canada's first Louis Vuitton "Maison." As a company spokesperson noted, "It's about the art and the feeling inside the store.

It merges luxury product, leisure, art and culture to provide the ultimate customer experience. Stepping into one of our Maisons is, quite literally, stepping into the home of Louis Vuitton." There are only 11 such concepts worldwide. Prices are never reduced, and only recently did the company start selling through louisvuitton.com in hopes of reaching new consumers and regions.

Over the years, a wide variety of high-profile celebrities have used Louis Vuitton products, including Madonna, Audrey Hepburn, and Jennifer Lopez. In its marketing efforts, the company has used high-fashion celebrities, billboards, print ads, and its own international regatta—the Louis Vuitton Cup. Recently, Louis Vuitton broke tradition and featured celebrities such as Steffi Graf, Mikhail Gorbachev, Buzz Aldrin, and Keith Richards in a campaign entitled "Core Values." The company also launched its first television commercial focused on luxury travel rather than fashion and has formed new partnerships with international artists, museums, and cultural organizations in hopes of keeping the brand fresh. That said, Louis Vuitton still spends up to 60 hours making one piece of luggage by hand—the same way it did 150 years ago.

In 2010, Louis Vuitton held a brand value of $19 billion according to *Forbes* and is ranked the 16th most powerful global brand according to Interbrand. The company is focused on expanding its luxury brand into growing markets such as China and India as well as continuing to grow in strong markets like Japan and Europe. It also continues to add new product lines to its portfolio.

QUESTIONS

1. How does an exclusive brand such as Louis Vuitton grow and stay fresh while retaining its cachet?

2. Is the counterfeiting of Louis Vuitton always a negative? Are there any circumstances where it can be seen as having some positive aspects?

Sources: Kate MacLennan, "Louis Vuitton Opens Canada's First 'Maison,'" *Vancouver Sun*, December 7, 2010; Reena Jana, "Louis Vuitton's Life of Luxury," *BusinessWeek*, August 6, 2007; Eric Pfanner, "Luxury Firms Move to Make Web Work for Them," *New York Times*, November 17, 2009; www.louisvuitton.com.

porter
flying refined

Chapter 11

smile-high club.

...e like to see our passengers happy. That's why we try to make
...rney as smile-inducing as possible, from complimentary snacks
...ed at your roomy leather seat, to the free wine or beer – and most
...portantly of all, the friendliest crew in the clouds.

Book online, call 1-888-619-8622
or contact your travel agent.

flyporter.com

Porter has used a niche strategy, distinctive brand mascot, and extra services in its flight to win customers away from rival Air Canada.

In This Chapter, We Will Address the Following **Questions**

1. How can market leaders expand the total market and defend market share?

2. How should market challengers attack market leaders?

3. How can market followers or nichers compete effectively?

4. What marketing strategies are appropriate at each stage of the product life cycle?

5. How should marketers adjust their strategies and tactics for an economic downturn or recession?

Competitive Dynamics

To be a long-term market leader is the goal of any marketer.

Today's challenging marketing circumstances, however, often dictate that companies reformulate their marketing strategies and offerings several times. Economic conditions change, competitors launch new assaults, and buyer interest and requirements evolve. Different market positions can suggest different market strategies.

Canadian skies have long been dominated by Air Canada. WestJet emerged in the 1990s as a rival, but today, there is a new kid on the block: Porter Airlines. Born in 2006 with just 2 aircraft, Porter has become the small airline that "could" with a fleet of over 20 aircraft. According to one source, Porter has taken an innovative approach to air travel "in an embattled sector whose history is littered with the corpses of companies that challenged Air Canada." Despite considerable opposition, Porter started flying short-haul flights out of the Billy Bishop Toronto City Airport, located on Toronto Island, just a short ferry ride across the lake from the downtown business centre. Porter has a locational advantage—no more long drives or costly cab trips to Pearson International Airport, located almost an hour from downtown.

Porter CEO, Robert Deluce, insightfully tapped into the frustrations of business people who are frequent flyers. Rather than having a lounge and aircraft with seating for only first-class customers, Porter offers all passengers premium treatment—free sandwiches, beer, and wine on flights and access to the lounge at the island airport, with complimentary coffee, biscotti, and Wi-Fi access. Porter flight attendants wear uniforms reminiscent of a period when flying meant glamour, not hassle. Porter has taken a regional niche strategy, focusing on markets in central and Atlantic Canada, including smaller, underserviced cities like Sudbury, Windsor, and Sault Ste. Marie, plus some routes in the eastern United States. Its print, social media (see www.facebook.com/video/video.php?v=186215404749571), and TV advertisements feature clear information on pricing, and the now-well-known Mr. Porter, the company's raccoon brand mascot, who embodies the friendliness and approachability of the airline.

Porter served 300 000 passengers in its first full year of operations, but it now serves over 2 million passengers annually. It is one of the few airlines in the world to have become an official 4 Star Airline in the World Airline Star Rating by Skytrax. Porter has quickly become Canada's most loved airline. Just look on Yelp.ca and you will find customer testimonials with statements like "I have to say it was the best experience on a plane ever!" or "I love, love, love, love Porter."[1]

This chapter examines the role competition plays and how marketers can best manage their brands depending on their market position and stage of the product life cycle. Competition grows more intense every year—from global competitors eager to grow sales in new markets, online competitors seeking cost-efficient ways to expand distribution, private-label and store brands providing low-price alternatives, and brand extensions by megabrands moving into new categories.[2] For these reasons and more, product and brand fortunes change over time, and marketers must respond accordingly.

COMPETITIVE STRATEGIES FOR MARKET LEADERS

Suppose a market is occupied by the firms shown in Figure 11.1. Forty percent is in the hands of a *market leader;* another 30 percent belongs to a *market challenger;* and 20 percent is claimed by a *market follower* willing to maintain its share and not rock the boat. *Market nichers,* serving small segments that larger firms don't reach, hold the remaining 10 percent.

A market leader has the largest market share and usually leads in price changes, new-product introductions, distribution coverage, and promotional intensity. Some historical market leaders are Microsoft (computer software), Gatorade (sports drinks), Best Buy (retail electronics), McDonald's (fast food), Blue Cross and Blue Shield (health insurance), and Visa (credit cards).

Marketers assume well-known brands are distinctive in consumers' minds, but unless a dominant firm, like Air Canada, enjoys a legal monopoly, marketers must maintain constant vigilance. A powerful product innovation may come along; a competitor like Porter Airlines might find a fresh marketing angle or commit to a major marketing investment; or the leader's cost structure might spiral upward. One well-known brand and market leader that has worked to stay on top is Xerox.

Xerox

Xerox has had to become more than just a copier company. Now the blue-chip icon with the name that became a verb sports the broadest array of imaging products in the world and dominates the market for high-end printing systems. And it's making a huge product line transition as it moves from the old light lens technology to digital systems. Xerox is preparing for a world in which most pages are printed in colour (which, not incidentally, generates five times the revenue of black-and-white). Besides revamping its machines, Xerox is beefing up sales by providing annuity-like products and services that are ordered again and again: document management, ink, and toners. It has even introduced the managed print-services business to help companies actually eliminate desktop printers and let employees share multifunction devices that copy, print, and fax. Once slow to respond to the emergence of Canon and the small-copier market, Xerox is doing everything it can to stay ahead of the game.[3]

In many industries, a discount competitor has undercut the leader's prices. "Marketing Insight: When Your Competitor Delivers More for Less" describes how leaders can respond to an aggressive competitive price discounter.

To stay number one, the firm must first find ways to expand total market demand. It must then protect its current share through good defensive and offensive actions. Finally, it should increase market share, even if market size remains constant. Let's look at each strategy.

Expanding Total Market Demand

When the total market expands, the dominant firm usually gains the most. If Heinz can convince more people to use ketchup, or to use ketchup with more meals, or to use more ketchup on each occasion, the firm will benefit considerably because it already sells almost two-thirds of the country's ketchup. In general, the market leader should look for new customers or more usage from existing customers.

NEW CUSTOMERS Every product class has the potential to attract buyers who are unaware of the product or are resisting it because of price or lack of certain features. A company can search for new users among three groups: those who might use it but do not *(market-penetration strategy)*, those who have never used it *(new-market segment strategy)*, or those who live elsewhere *(geographical-expansion strategy)*.

Here is how Starbucks describes its multipronged approach to growth on its corporate website:[4]

Starbucks purchases and roasts high-quality whole bean coffees and sells them along with fresh, rich-brewed, Italian-style espresso beverages, a variety of pastries and confections, and coffee-related accessories and equipment—primarily through its company-operated retail stores. In addition to sales through our company-operated retail stores, Starbucks sells whole bean coffees through a specialty sales group and supermarkets. Additionally, Starbucks produces and sells bottled Frappuccino® coffee drinks and a line of premium ice creams through its joint venture partnerships and offers a line of innovative premium teas produced by its wholly owned subsidiary, Tazo Tea Company. The company's objective is to establish Starbucks as the most recognized and respected brand in the world.

40% Market leader

30% Market challenger

20% Market follower

10% Market nichers

FIGURE 11.1

Hypothetical Market Structure

MARKETING **INSIGHT**	WHEN YOUR COMPETITOR DELIVERS MORE FOR LESS

Companies offering the powerful combination of low prices and high quality are capturing the hearts and wallets of consumers all over the world. In North America, more than half the population now shops weekly at mass merchants such as Walmart and Target. In the United Kingdom, premium retailers such as Boots and Sainsbury's are scrambling to meet intensifying price—and quality—competition from ASDA and Tesco.

These and similar value players, such as ALDI, Dell, E*TRADE Financial, WestJet, Winners, and Canadian chain Dollarama, are transforming the way consumers of nearly every age and income level purchase groceries, apparel, airline tickets, financial services, and computers. Traditional players are right to feel threatened. Upstart firms often rely on serving one or a few consumer segments, providing better delivery or just one additional benefit, and matching low prices with highly efficient operations to keep costs down. These firms have changed consumer expectations about the trade-off between quality and price.

To compete, mainstream companies need to infuse their timeless strategies like cost control and product differentiation with greater intensity and focus, and then execute them flawlessly. Differentiation, for example, becomes less about the abstract goal of rising above competitive clutter and more about identifying openings left by the value players' business models. Effective pricing means waging a transaction-by-transaction perception battle for consumers predisposed to believe that value-oriented competitors are always cheaper.

Competitive outcomes will be determined, as always, on the ground—in product aisles, merchandising displays, reconfigured processes, and pricing stickers. Traditional players can't afford to drop a stitch. The new competitive environment places a new premium on—and adds new twists to—the old imperatives of differentiation and execution.

Differentiation

Marketers need to protect areas where their business models give other companies room to manoeuvre. Instead of trying to compete with Walmart on price, for example, Shoppers Drug Mart (which includes Pharmaprix stores in Quebec) is the leader in Canada's retail drug marketplace. It emphasizes convenience, a growing selection of high-end products, and the promise that consumers can trust its expert advice whether they are buying pharmaceutical products or cosmetics. It has expanded rapidly—it now has approximately 1200 stores from coast to coast—so that its stores are now ubiquitous. It generally locates in malls with easy parking. It overhauled its in-store layouts by renovating and expanding existing locations and building new-format stores that are as large as 14 000 square feet. It has worked to increase the value it offers customers through its Optimum loyalty program, which it launched in 2000. Today Optimum is one of the most successful loyalty programs in Canada, boasting over 9 million members. Optimum members spend 60 percent more than nonmembers. Finally, while pharmacy sales are still Shoppers' mainstay, it is adding many prestige products, from giftware to high-end cosmetics and fragrances.

Execution

Kmart, now defunct in Canada, had a disastrous experience trying to compete head-on with Walmart on price, one that highlights the difficulty of challenging value leaders on their own terms. To compete effectively, firms may instead need to downplay or even abandon some market segments. To compete with Ryanair and easyJet, British Airways has put more emphasis on its long-haul routes, where value-based players are not active, and less on the short-haul routes, where they thrive.

Major airlines, like Air Canada, experimented and introduced their own low-cost carriers, but they have all been unsuccessful. One school of thought is that companies should set up low-cost operations only if (1) their existing businesses will become more competitive as a result, and (2) the new business will derive some advantages it would not have gained if independent. Low-cost operations set up by HSBC, ING, Merrill Lynch, and Royal Bank of Scotland—First Direct, ING Direct, ML Direct, and Direct Line Insurance, respectively—succeed in part thanks to synergies between the old and new lines of business. The low-cost operation must be designed and launched as a money-maker in its own right, not just as a defensive play.

Sources: Adapted from Nirmalya Kumar, "Strategies to Fight Low-Cost Rivals," *Harvard Business Review*, December 2006, pp. 104–112; Robert J. Frank, Jeffrey P. George, and Laxman Narasimhan, "When Your Competitor Delivers More for Less," *McKinsey Quarterly*, Winter 2004, pp. 48–59. See also Jan-Benedict E. M. Steenkamp and Nirmalya Kumar, "Don't Be Undersold," *Harvard Business Review*, December 2009, pp. 90–95; Marina Strauss, "Shoppers' Optimum Program to Offer Less for More," *The Globe and Mail*, June 14, 2010.

MORE USAGE Marketers can try to increase the amount, level, or frequency of consumption. They can sometimes boost the *amount* through packaging or product redesign. Larger package sizes increase the amount of product consumers use at one time.[5] Consumers use more of impulse products such as soft drinks and snacks when the product is made more available.

Increasing *frequency* of consumption, on the other hand, requires either (1) identifying additional opportunities to use the brand in the same basic way or (2) identifying completely new and different ways to use the brand.

Additional Opportunities to Use the Brand A marketing program can communicate the appropriateness and advantages of using the brand. Clorox's ads stress the many benefits of its bleach, such as that it eliminates kitchen odours.

Another opportunity arises when consumers' perceptions of their usage differ from reality. Consumers may fail to replace a short-lived product when they should, because they overestimate how long it stays fresh.[6] One strategy is to tie the act of replacing the product to a holiday, event, or time of year. Another might be to provide consumers with better information about when they first used the product or need to replace it, or the current level of product performance. Gillette razor cartridges feature coloured stripes that slowly fade with repeated use, signalling the user to move on to the next cartridge.

New Ways to Use the Brand The second approach to increasing frequency of consumption is to identify completely new and different applications. Food product companies have long advertised recipes that use their branded products in different ways. After discovering that some consumers used Arm & Hammer baking soda as a refrigerator deodorant, the company launched a heavy promotion campaign focusing on this use and succeeded in getting half the homes in the United States to adopt it. Next, the company expanded the brand into a variety of new product categories such as toothpaste, antiperspirant, and laundry detergent.

Protecting Market Share

While trying to expand total market size, the dominant firm must actively defend its current business: Boeing against Airbus, Staples against Office Depot, and Google against Yahoo! and Microsoft.[7] How can the leader do so? The most constructive response is *continuous innovation.* The front-runner should lead the industry in developing new products and customer services, distribution effectiveness, and cost cutting. Comprehensive solutions increase its competitive strength and value to customers.

PROACTIVE MARKETING In satisfying customer needs, we can draw a distinction between responsive marketing, anticipative marketing, and creative marketing. A *responsive* marketer finds a stated need and fills it. An *anticipative* marketer looks ahead to needs customers may have in the near future. A *creative* marketer discovers solutions customers did not ask for but to which they enthusiastically respond. Creative marketers work for proactive *market-driving* firms, not just market-driven ones.[8]

Many companies assume their job is just to adapt to customer needs. They are reactive mostly because they are overly faithful to the customer-orientation paradigm and fall victim to the "tyranny of the served market." Successful companies instead proactively shape the market to their own interests. Instead of trying to be the best player, they change the rules of the game.[9]

A company needs two proactive skills: (1) *responsive anticipation* to see the writing on the wall, as when IBM changed from a hardware producer to a service business; and (2) *creative anticipation* to devise innovative solutions, as when PepsiCo introduced H2OH! (a soft drink–bottled water hybrid). Note that *responsive anticipation* is performed before a given change, while *reactive response* happens after the change takes place.

Proactive companies create new offers to serve unmet—and maybe even unknown—consumer needs. In the late 1970s, Akio Morita, the Sony founder, was working on a pet project that would revolutionize the way people listened to music: a portable cassette player he called the Walkman. Engineers at the company insisted there was little demand for such a product, but Morita refused to part with his vision. By the 20th anniversary of the Walkman, Sony had sold over 250 million in nearly 100 different models.[10]

Proactive companies may redesign relationships within an industry, like Toyota and its relationship to its suppliers. Or they may educate customers, as The Body Shop does in stimulating the choice of environmentally friendly products.

Companies need to practise "uncertainty management." Proactive firms

- Are ready to take risks and make mistakes,
- Have a vision of the future and of investing in it,
- Have the capabilities to innovate,

- Are flexible and nonbureaucratic, and

- Have many managers who think proactively.

Companies that are *too* risk-averse won't be winners.

DEFENSIVE MARKETING Even when it does not launch offensives, the market leader must not leave any major flanks exposed. The aim of defensive strategy is to reduce the probability of attack, divert attacks to less-threatened areas, and lessen their intensity. Speed of response can make an important difference to profit. A dominant firm can use the six defence strategies summarized in Figure 11.2.[11]

- *Position defence.* Position defence means occupying the most desirable market space in consumers' minds, making the brand almost impregnable, as Procter & Gamble has done with Tide detergent for cleaning, and Pampers diapers for dryness.

- *Flank defence.* The market leader should erect outposts to protect a weak front or support a possible counterattack. Procter & Gamble brands such as Gain and Cheer laundry detergent and Pampers diapers have played strategic offensive and defensive roles.

- *Pre-emptive defence.* A more aggressive manoeuvre is to attack first, perhaps with guerrilla action across the market—hitting one competitor here, another there—and keeping everyone off balance. Another is to achieve broad market envelopment that signals competitors not to attack.[12] Canada's five big banks, with their ubiquitous branches and automated teller machines, provide steep competition to international competitors like HSBC and ING. Yet another pre-emptive defence is to introduce a stream of new products and announce them in advance.[13] Such "pre-announcements" can signal competitors that they will need to fight to gain market share.[14] If Microsoft announces plans for a new-product development, smaller firms may choose to concentrate their development efforts in other directions to avoid head-to-head competition. Some high-tech firms have been accused of selling "vapourware"—announcing products that miss delivery dates or are never introduced.[15]

- *Counteroffensive defence.* In a counteroffensive, the market leader can meet the attacker frontally and hit its flank, or launch a pincer movement so it will have to pull back to defend itself. For example, Canada Post defended itself against large international courier companies by purchasing Purolator. Another common form of counteroffensive is the exercise of economic or political clout. The leader may try to crush a competitor by subsidizing lower prices for the vulnerable product with revenue from its more profitable products, or it may prematurely announce a product upgrade to prevent customers from buying the competitor's product. Or, the leader may lobby legislators to take political action to inhibit the competition.

- *Mobile defence.* In mobile defence, the leader stretches its domain over new territories through market broadening and market diversification. *Market broadening* shifts the company's focus from the current product to the underlying generic need. Thus, "petroleum" companies such as Canadian-owned Nexen have sought to recast themselves as global "energy" leaders. This change required them to research the oil, coal, nuclear, hydroelectric, and chemical industries. *Market diversification* shifts the company's focus into unrelated industries. One of Canada's most successful family businesses, the Bragg Group of Companies, has prospered through savvy diversification. Oxford Frozen Foods was founded by John Bragg in 1968. It remains Canada's largest exporter of blueberries, but today the group is also composed of subunits as diversified as Bragg Communications (including EastLink, Coast Cable, and Delta Cable), Bragg Lumber Co., Pierceys (building materials), and Inland Technologies. It made its first foray outside of Canada in early 2011, when it purchased a data and telecommunications company in Bermuda.

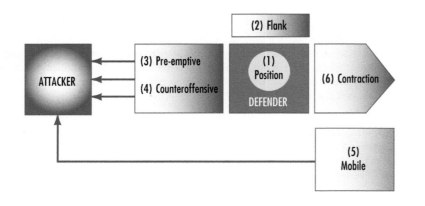

FIGURE 11.2

Six Types of Defence Strategies

■ *Contraction defence.* Sometimes large companies can no longer defend all their territory. In *planned contraction* (also called *strategic withdrawal*), they give up weaker markets and reassign resources to stronger ones. Since 2006, Sara Lee has spun off products that accounted for a large percentage of its revenues—including its strong Hanes hosiery brand and global body care and European detergent businesses—to focus on its core food business.[16]

Purolator

Purolator Courier Ltd. (now Purolator Inc.) is the leading integrated parcel and freight solutions provider in Canada. Purolator has been acknowledged by the National Quality Institute and was recognized as one of Canada's ten most admired companies in 2007, 2008, 2009, and 2010. It has formed key partnerships for deliveries in the United States and elsewhere in the world. Purolator keeps itself visible through its popular annual food drive Tackle Hunger®, conducted in association with the Canadian Football League. At home games, fans bring nonperishable food for collection and distribution by Purolator. Recognizing growing concerns about climate change in 2005, Purolator was the first courier company in Canada to add hybrid electric vehicles to its fleet, and it has won a Canadian Council of Ministers of the Environment Pollution Prevention Award and was a recipient of the Logistics Quarterly Third-Party Logistics Sustainability Award in 2011.[17]

While Canada Post may have first viewed Purolator as a counteroffensive tool, today it is recognized for quality and innovation and is Canada's largest courier and logistics company.

Increasing Market Share

No wonder competition has turned fierce in so many markets: one share point can be worth tens of millions of dollars. Gaining increased share does not automatically produce higher profits, however—especially for labour-intensive service companies that may not experience many economies of scale. Much depends on the company's strategy.[18]

Because the cost of buying higher market share through acquisition may far exceed its revenue value, a company should consider four factors first:

■ *The possibility of provoking antitrust action.* Frustrated competitors are likely to cry "monopoly" and seek legal action from the Canadian Competition Bureau if a dominant firm makes further inroads. Canada's largest banks have long been frustrated by their inability to merge into even larger entities. In the United States, Microsoft and Intel have had to fend off numerous lawsuits and legal challenges around the world as a result of what some feel are inappropriate or illegal business practices and abuse of market power.

■ *Economic cost.* Figure 11.3 shows that profitability might *fall* with market share gains after some level. In the illustration, the firm's *optimal market share* is 50 percent. The cost of gaining further market share might exceed the value if holdout customers dislike the company, are loyal to competitors, have unique needs, or prefer dealing with smaller firms. And the costs of legal work, public relations, and lobbying rise with market share. Pushing for higher share is less justifiable when there are unattractive market segments, buyers who want multiple sources of supply, high exit barriers, and few scale or experience economies. Some market leaders have even increased profitability by selectively *decreasing* market share in weaker areas.[19]

■ *The danger of pursuing the wrong marketing activities.* Companies successfully gaining share typically outperform competitors in three areas: new-product activity, relative product quality, and marketing expenditures.[20] Companies that attempt to increase market share by cutting prices more deeply than competitors typically don't achieve significant gains, because rivals meet the price cuts or offer other values so buyers don't switch.

■ *The effect of increased market share on actual and perceived quality.*[21] Having too many customers can put a strain on the firm's resources, hurting product value and service delivery. Canwest Global Communications Corporation struggled with this dilemma. It was a major media company made up through the mergers of radio, television, and publishing assets. It applied for bankruptcy protection in 2009, and many of its assets were sold to other firms like BCE, the Postmedia Network, and Shaw Communications.[22]

FIGURE 11.3

The Concept of Optimal Market Share

OTHER COMPETITIVE STRATEGIES

Firms that occupy second, third, and lower ranks in an industry are often called runner-up or trailing firms. Some, such as PepsiCo, Ford, and Avis, are quite large in their own right. These firms can adopt one of two postures. They can attack the leader and other competitors in an aggressive bid for further market share as *market challengers,* or they can choose to not rock the boat as *market followers.*

Market-Challenger Strategies

Many market challengers have gained ground or even overtaken the leader. Toyota today produces more cars than General Motors, RONA is putting pressure on Home Depot, and AMD has been chipping away at Intel's market share.[23] While banks have been the primary provider of mortgages in Canada, Dominion Lending Centres, a national network of 1500 independently owned and operated companies, has been challenging that dominance. Dominion offers leasing and mortgage products. About three years ago, the brokerages began to contribute to an advertising fund that enabled it to begin a major offensive against the banks' mortgage business in 2010. Dominion Lending Centres launched a $2 million advertising campaign, which is the largest campaign ever run by a Canadian mortgage broker. The ads feature Don Cherry and are aired during NHL hockey games as well as on various news programs and sports reports, and they have helped Dominion Lending Centres become a household name.[24]

Challengers set high aspirations while market leaders can fall prey to running business as usual. Now let's examine the competitive attack strategies available to challengers.[25]

DEFINING THE STRATEGIC OBJECTIVE AND OPPONENT(S) A market challenger must first define its strategic objective, usually to increase market share. The challenger must decide whom to attack:

- *It can attack the market leader.* This is a high-risk but potentially high-payoff strategy and makes good sense if the leader is not serving the market well. Xerox wrested the copy market from 3M by developing a better copying process. Later, Canon grabbed a large chunk of Xerox's market by introducing desk copiers. This strategy often has the added benefit of distancing the firm from other challengers. When Miller Lite attacked Bud Light on product quality during the mid-2000s, Coors Light was left out of the conversation.

- *It can attack firms its own size that are not doing the job and are underfinanced.* These firms have aging products, are charging excessive prices, or are not satisfying customers in other ways.

- *It can attack small local and regional firms.* Several major banks grew to their present size by gobbling up smaller regional banks, or "guppies."

CHOOSING A GENERAL ATTACK STRATEGY Given clear opponents and objectives, what attack options are available? We can distinguish five: frontal, flank, encirclement, bypass, and guerilla attacks.

- *Frontal attack.* In a pure *frontal attack,* the attacker matches its opponent's product, advertising, price, and distribution. The principle of force says the side with the greater resources will win. A modified frontal attack, such as cutting price, can work if the market leader doesn't retaliate, and if the competitor convinces the market its product is equal to the leader's. Since the founding of its first store in Toronto in 1982, Winners has been highly successful in convincing consumers that they get more value for their money by buying sought-after brands at their stores than through department stores or specialty retailers.

- *Flank attack.* A *flanking* strategy is another name for identifying shifts that are causing gaps to develop, and then rushing to fill the gaps. Flanking is particularly attractive to a challenger with fewer resources and can be more likely to succeed than frontal attacks. In a geographic attack, the challenger spots areas where the opponent is underperforming. Although the Internet has siphoned newspaper readers and advertisers away in many markets, Independent News & Media, a 102-year-old Irish media company, sells a majority of its 175 newspaper and magazine titles where the economy is strong but the Internet is still relatively weak—countries such as Ireland, South Africa, Australia, New Zealand, and India.[26] The other flanking strategy is to serve uncovered market needs. Ariat challenged long-time market leaders Justin Boots and Tony Lama by making cowboy boots that were every bit as ranch-ready, but ergonomically designed to feel as comfortable as a running shoe—a totally new benefit in the category.[27]

- *Encirclement attack. Encirclement* attempts to capture a wide slice of territory by launching a grand offensive on several fronts. It makes sense when the challenger commands superior resources. In making a stand against archrival Microsoft, Sun Microsystems licensed its Java software to hundreds of companies and thousands of software developers for all sorts of consumer devices. As consumer electronic products began to go digital, Java started appearing in a wide range of gadgets.

- *Bypass attack. Bypassing* the enemy altogether to attack easier markets instead offers three lines of approach: diversifying into unrelated products, diversifying into new geographical markets, and leapfrogging into new technologies. Pepsi has used a bypass strategy against Coke by (1) rolling out Aquafina bottled water throughout North America in 1997 before Coke launched its Dasani brand; (2) purchasing orange juice giant Tropicana in 1998, when it owned almost twice the market share of Coca-Cola's Minute Maid; and (3) purchasing the Quaker Oats Company, owner of market leader Gatorade sports drink, in 2000.[28] In *technological leapfrogging,* the challenger patiently researches and develops the next technology, shifting the battleground to its own territory where it has an advantage. Google used technological leapfrogging to overtake Yahoo! and become the market leader in search engines.

- *Guerrilla attack.* Guerrilla attacks consist of small, intermittent attacks, conventional and unconventional, including selective price cuts, intense promotional blitzes, and occasional legal action, to harass the opponent and eventually secure permanent footholds. A guerrilla campaign can be expensive, although less so than a frontal, encirclement, or flank attack, but it typically must be backed by a stronger attack to beat the opponent.

CHOOSING A SPECIFIC ATTACK STRATEGY Any aspect of the marketing program can serve as the basis for attack, such as lower-priced or discounted products, new or improved products and services, a wider variety of offerings, and innovative distribution strategies. A challenger's success depends on combining several, more specific, strategies to improve its position over time.

Market-Follower Strategies

Theodore Levitt argues that a strategy of *product imitation* might be as profitable as a strategy of *product innovation.*[29] In "innovative imitation," as he calls it, the innovator bears the expense of developing the new product, getting it into distribution, and informing and educating the market. The reward for all this work and risk is normally market leadership. However, another firm can come along and copy or improve on the new product. Although it probably will not overtake the leader, the follower can achieve high profits because it did not bear any of the innovation expense. S&S Cycle followed this strategy.

S&S Cycle

S&S Cycle is the biggest supplier of complete engines and major motor parts to more than 15 companies that build several thousand Harley-like cruiser bikes each year. These cloners charge as much as $30 000 for their customized creations. S&S has built its name by improving on Harley-Davidson's handiwork. Its customers are often would-be Harley buyers frustrated by long waiting lines at the dealer. Others simply want S&S's incredibly powerful engines. S&S stays abreast of its evolving market by ordering a new Harley bike every year and taking apart the engine to see what it can improve upon.[30]

Many companies prefer to follow rather than challenge the market leader. Patterns of "conscious parallelism" are common in capital-intensive, homogeneous-product industries such as steel, fertilizers, and chemicals. The opportunities for product differentiation and image differentiation are low, service quality is comparable, and price sensitivity runs high. The mood in these industries is against short-run grabs for market share, because that only provokes retaliation. Instead, most firms present similar offers to buyers, usually by copying the leader. Market shares show high stability.

That's not to say market followers lack strategies. They must know how to hold current customers and win a fair share of new ones. Each follower tries to bring distinctive advantages to its target market—location, services, financing—while defensively keeping its manufacturing costs low and its product quality and services high. It must also enter new markets as they open up. The follower must define a growth path, but one that doesn't invite competitive retaliation. We distinguish four broad strategies:

1. *Counterfeiter*—The counterfeiter duplicates the leader's product and packages and sells it on the black market or through disreputable dealers. Music firms, Apple, and Rolex have been plagued by the counterfeiter problem, especially in Asia.

2. *Cloner*—The cloner emulates the leader's products, name, and packaging, with slight variations. For example, President's Choice laundry detergent is packaged to look much like Tide, Procter & Gamble's famous brand. When P&G introduced new versions of Tide, like 2x Concentrated detergents or Cold Water detergent, President's Choice quickly followed with its own versions.

Telepizza adapted the U.S. pizza home delivery model to Spain with much success.

3. *Imitator*—The imitator copies some things from the leader but differentiates in packaging, advertising, pricing, or location. The leader doesn't mind as long as the imitator doesn't attack aggressively. Leopoldo Fernández Pujals grew up in Fort Lauderdale, Florida, and took the U.S. pizza home delivery model to Spain, where he borrowed $80 000 to open his first store in Madrid. The Telepizza chain, which Pujals sold in 1999, now operates 1220 stores in Europe, Latin America, and the Middle East.

4. *Adapter*—The adapter takes the leader's products and adapts or improves them. The adapter may choose to sell to different markets, but often it grows into a future challenger, as many Japanese firms have done after improving products developed elsewhere.

What does a follower earn? Normally, less than the leader. A study of food-processing companies showed the largest averaging a 16 percent return on investment; the number two firm, 6 percent; the number three firm, –1 percent; and the number four firm, –6 percent. No wonder Jack Welch, former CEO of GE, told his business units that each must reach the number one or two position in its market or else! Being a follower is often not a rewarding path.

Market-Nicher Strategies

An alternative to being a follower in a large market is to be a leader in a small market, or niche, as we introduced in Chapter 8. Smaller firms normally avoid competing with larger firms, by targeting small markets of little or no interest to the larger firms. *Progress Magazine,* for example, is a successful business magazine that concentrates on providing content related to leading-edge trends for entrepreneurs and other business readers working in Atlantic Canada. A recent edition covered stories ranging from how one new start-up is tapping parents' concerns about children's nutrition by creating a line of vending machines that offer healthy choices, to how regional firms can apply theories put forward by Harvard strategic visionary Michael Porter. But even large, profitable firms may choose to use niching strategies for some of their business units or companies.

Firms with low shares of the total market can become highly profitable through smart niching. Such companies tend to offer high value, charge a premium price, achieve lower manufacturing costs, and shape a strong corporate culture and vision. See what one small Nova Scotia firm has done.

LED Roadway Lighting has been highly successful in the environmentally friendly, energy-efficient sector of this worldwide marketplace, with more than 300 clients in 25 countries.

LED Roadway Lighting Ltd.

LED Roadway Lighting Ltd., of Halifax, Nova Scotia, has carved out a profitable niche for itself by designing and manufacturing environmentally friendly street- and area-lighting fixtures. It helps its clients, mainly municipalities and utility companies, from around the globe conserve energy by retrofitting their street-lighting systems. For example, it recently helped Halifax Regional Municipality save more than 50 percent of its energy costs on street lighting, and it just signed a contract with the Province of Nova Scotia to upgrade its highway lighting. The project is forecast to save the province almost $10 million in energy and maintenance costs.[31]

Return on investment for businesses in smaller markets exceeds that in larger markets on average.[32] Why is niching so profitable? The market nicher knows the target customers so well, it meets their needs better than other firms selling to them casually. As a result, the nicher can charge a substantial price over costs. The nicher achieves *high margin,* whereas the mass marketer achieves *high volume.*

Nichers have three tasks: creating, expanding, and protecting niches. The risk is that the niche might dry up or be attacked. The company is then stuck with highly specialized resources that may not have high-value alternative uses.

Because niches can weaken, the firm must continuously create new ones. "Marketing Memo: Niche Specialist Roles" outlines some options. The firm should "stick to its niching" but not necessarily to its niche. That is why *multiple niching* can be preferable to *single niching.* With strength in two or more niches, the company increases its chances for survival.

Firms entering a market should initially aim at a niche rather than the whole market. The cell phone industry has experienced phenomenal growth but is now facing fierce competition as the number of new potential users dwindles. An Irish upstart company, Digicel Group, has successfully tapped into one of the few remaining high-growth segments: poor people without cell phones.

Digicel Group

In 2001, Digicel CEO Denis O'Brien heard that the government of Jamaica was opening its local phone market, long monopolized by British telecom giant Cable & Wireless. O'Brien spent nearly $50 million for a licence, using money from the sale of his first telecom venture, Esat Telecom Group PLC. O'Brien took the plunge because he knew that Jamaicans had to wait over two years for a land line, and only 4 percent of the population had cell phones. Within 100 days, Digicel had signed on 100 000 subscribers, luring them with inexpensive rates and phones and improved service. After eight years, Digicel has more than 8 million customers across its Caribbean and Central American markets, earning a reputation for competitive rates, comprehensive coverage, superior customer care, and a wide variety of products and services. Digicel has also moved into the Pacific in Fiji, Samoa, Papua New Guinea, and other markets. Back in Jamaica, it has become an active sponsor of sports and supporter of causes, befitting for its ascendance as a market leader in the region.[33]

PRODUCT LIFE-CYCLE MARKETING STRATEGIES

A company's positioning and differentiation strategy must change as the product, market, and competitors change over the *product life cycle* (PLC). To say a product has a life cycle is to assert four things:

1. Products have a limited life.
2. Product sales pass through distinct stages, each posing different challenges, opportunities, and problems to the seller.
3. Profits rise and fall at different stages of the product life cycle.
4. Products require different marketing, financial, manufacturing, purchasing, and human resource strategies in each life-cycle stage.

MARKETING **MEMO**   NICHE SPECIALIST ROLES

The key idea in successful nichemanship is specialization. Here are some possible niche roles:

- *End-user specialist.* The firm specializes in one type of end-use customer. For example, a *value-added reseller (VAR)* customizes computer hardware and software for specific customer segments and earns a price premium in the process.

- *Vertical-level specialist.* The firm specializes at some vertical level of the production-distribution value chain. A copper firm may concentrate on producing raw copper, copper components, or finished copper products.

- *Customer-size specialist.* The firm concentrates on either small, medium-sized, or large customers. Many nichers serve small customers neglected by the majors.

- *Specific-customer specialist.* The firm limits its selling to one or a few customers. Many firms sell their entire output to a single company, such as Walmart or General Motors.

- *Geographic specialist.* The firm sells only in a certain locality, region, or area of the world.

- *Product or product line specialist.* The firm carries or produces only one product line or product. A manufacturer may produce only lenses for microscopes. A retailer may carry only ties.

- *Product-feature specialist.* The firm specializes in producing a certain type of product or product feature. Zipcar's car-sharing services target people who live and work in major cities in Canada, the U.S., and the UK, frequently use public transportation, but still need a car a few times a month.

- *Job-shop specialist.* The firm customizes its products for individual customers.

- *Quality-price specialist.* The firm operates at the low- or high-quality ends of the market. Sharp AQUOS specializes in the high-quality, high-price LCD television and component screen market.

- *Service specialist.* The firm offers one or more services not available from other firms. A bank might take loan requests over the phone and hand-deliver the money to the customer.

- *Channel specialist.* The firm specializes in serving only one channel of distribution. For example, a soft drink company makes a very large-sized serving available only at gas stations.

Product Life Cycles

Most product life-cycle curves are portrayed as bell-shaped (see Figure 11.4). This curve is typically divided into four stages: introduction, growth, maturity, and decline.[34]

1. *Introduction*—A period of slow sales growth as the product is introduced in the market. Profits are nonexistent because of the heavy expenses of product introduction.

2. *Growth*—A period of rapid market acceptance and substantial profit improvement.

3. *Maturity*—A slowdown in sales growth because the product has achieved acceptance by most potential buyers. Profits stabilize or decline because of increased competition.

4. *Decline*—Sales show a downward drift and profits erode.

We can use the PLC concept to analyze a product category (telecommunications), a product form (telephone), a product (cell phone), or a brand (Bell). Not all products exhibit a bell-shaped PLC.[35] Three common alternative patterns are shown in Figure 11.5.

Figure 11.5(a) shows a *growth-slump-maturity pattern,* characteristic of, for example, small kitchen appliances such as handheld mixers and breadmakers. Sales grow rapidly when the product is first introduced and then fall to a "petrified" level sustained by late adopters buying the product for the first time and early adopters replacing it.

The *cycle-recycle pattern* in Figure 11.5(b) often describes the sales of new drugs. The pharmaceutical company aggressively promotes its new drug, producing the first cycle. Later, sales start declining, and another promotional push produces a second cycle (usually of smaller magnitude and duration).[36]

Another common pattern is the *scalloped PLC* in Figure 11.5(c). Here, sales pass through a succession of life cycles based on the discovery of new-product characteristics, uses, or users. Sales of nylon have shown a scalloped pattern because of the many new uses—parachutes, hosiery, shirts, carpeting, boat sails, automobile tires—discovered over time.[37]

Common Product Life-Cycle Patterns

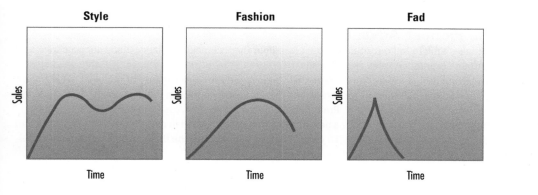

FIGURE 11.6

Style, Fashion, and Fad Life Cycles

Style, Fashion, and Fad Life Cycles

We need to distinguish three special categories of product life cycles—styles, fashions, and fads (see Figure 11.6). A *style* is a basic and distinctive mode of expression appearing in a field of human endeavour. Styles appear in homes (colonial, ranch, Cape Cod), clothing (formal, business casual, sporty), and art (realistic, surrealistic, abstract). A style can last for generations and go in and out of vogue. A *fashion* is a currently accepted or popular style in a given field. Fashions pass through four stages: distinctiveness, emulation, mass fashion, and decline.[38]

The length of a fashion cycle is hard to predict. One view is that fashions end because they represent a purchase compromise, and consumers soon start looking for the missing attributes.[39] For example, as automobiles become smaller, they become less comfortable, and then a growing number of buyers start wanting larger cars. Another explanation is that too many consumers adopt the fashion, thus turning others away. Still another is that the length of a particular fashion cycle depends on the extent to which the fashion meets a genuine need, is consistent with other trends in the society, satisfies societal norms and values, and keeps within technological limits as it develops.[40]

Fads are fashions that come quickly into public view, are adopted with great zeal, peak early, and decline very fast. Their acceptance cycle is short, and they tend to attract only a limited following who are searching for excitement or want to distinguish themselves from others. Fads fail to survive because they don't normally satisfy a strong need. The marketing winners are those who recognize fads early and leverage them into products with staying power. Here's a story of a company that managed to take a fad and make it a long-term success.

Trivial Pursuit

Trival Pursuit was invented by two Canadians, Chris Haney and Scott Abbott. Since its debut at the International Toy Fair in 1982, Trivial Pursuit has sold over 88 million copies in 17 languages in 26 countries, and it remains one of the best-selling adult games. Hasbro Inc. has kept it popular by making a new game with updated questions every year. It also keeps creating offshoots—travel packs, a children's version, Trivial Pursuit Genus IV, and themed versions tapping into niches tied to various sports, movies, and decades— 23 different versions in all. The game is available in a variety of platforms: as an interactive CD-ROM from Virgin Entertainment Interactive, online at its own website (www.trivialpursuit.com), and in a mobile edition accessible via cell phone. If you're having trouble making dinner conversation on a date, no problem: NTN Entertainment Network has put Trivial Pursuit in about 3000 restaurants.[41]

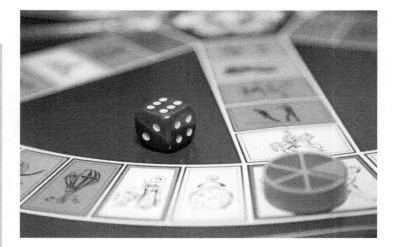

Through countless variations, Trivial Pursuit has proven to be more than a passing fad.

Marketing Strategies: Introduction Stage and the Pioneer Advantage

Because it takes time to roll out a new product, work out the technical problems, fill dealer pipelines, and gain consumer acceptance, sales growth tends to be slow in the introduction stage.[42] Profits are negative or low, and promotional expenditures are at their highest ratio to sales because of the need to (1) inform potential consumers, (2) induce product trial, and (3) secure distribution in retail outlets.[43] Firms focus on buyers who are the most ready to buy. Prices tend to be higher because costs are high.

Companies that plan to introduce a new product must decide when to enter the market. To be first can be rewarding, but risky and expensive. To come in later makes sense if the firm can bring superior technology, quality, or brand strength to create a market advantage.

Speeding up innovation time is essential in an age of shortening product life cycles. Being early has been shown to pay. One study found that products coming out six months late—but on budget—earned an average of 33 percent less profit in their first five years; products that came out on time but 50 percent over budget cut their profits by only 4 percent.[44]

Most studies indicate that the market pioneer gains the greatest advantage.[45] Hudson's Bay, Campbell, Seagrams, Steelco, and Amazon.com developed sustained market dominance. Nineteen of twenty-five market leaders in 1923 were still the market leaders in 1983, 60 years later.[46] In a sample of industrial-goods businesses, 66 percent of pioneers survived at least 10 years, versus 48 percent of early followers.[47]

What are the sources of the pioneer's advantage?[48] Early users will recall the pioneer's brand name if the product satisfies them. The pioneer's brand also establishes the attributes the product class should possess.[49] It normally aims at the middle of the market and so captures more users. Customer inertia also plays a role, and there are producer advantages: economies of scale, technological leadership, patents, ownership of scarce assets, and other barriers to entry. Pioneers can spend marketing dollars more effectively and enjoy higher rates of repeat purchases. An alert pioneer can lead indefinitely by pursuing various strategies.[50]

But the advantage is not inevitable.[51] Bowmar hand calculators, Apple Newton personal digital assistants, WordPerfect word processing software (from Ottawa-based Corel), Reynolds ballpoint pens, and Osborne portable computers were market pioneers overtaken by later entrants. First movers also have to watch out for the "second-mover advantage."

Steven Schnaars studied 28 industries where imitators surpassed innovators.[52] He found several weaknesses among the failing pioneers, including new products that were too crude, were improperly positioned, or appeared before there was strong demand; product-development costs that exhausted the innovator's resources; a lack of resources to compete against entering larger firms; and managerial incompetence or unhealthy complacency. Successful imitators thrived by offering lower prices, improving the product continuously, or using brute market power to overtake the pioneer. None of the companies that now dominate in the manufacture of personal computers—including Dell, HP, and Acer—were first movers.[53]

Peter Golder and Gerard Tellis raise further doubts about the pioneer advantage.[54] They distinguish among an *inventor*, first to develop patents in a new-product category; a *product pioneer*, first to develop a working model; and a *market pioneer*, first to sell in the new-product category. They also include nonsurviving pioneers in their sample. They conclude that although pioneers may still have an advantage, a larger number of market pioneers fail than has been reported, and a larger number of early market leaders (though not pioneers) succeed. Later entrants overtaking market pioneers include IBM over Sperry in mainframe computers, Matsushita over Sony in VCRs, and GE over EMI in CAT scan equipment.

Tellis and Golder more recently identified five factors underpinning long-term market leadership: vision of a mass market, persistence, relentless innovation, financial commitment, and asset leverage.[55] Other research has highlighted the importance of the novelty of the product innovation.[56] When a pioneer starts a market with a really new product, like the Segway Human Transporter, surviving can be very challenging. In the case of incremental innovation, like MP3 players with video capabilities, survival rates are much higher.

The pioneer should visualize the product markets it could enter, knowing it cannot enter all of them at once. Suppose market-segmentation analysis reveals the product market segments shown in Figure 11.7. The pioneer should analyze the profit potential of each product market singly and in combination and decide on a market expansion path. Thus, the pioneer in Figure 11.7 plans first to enter product market P_1M_1, then move the product into a second market (P_1M_2), then surprise the competition by developing a second product for the second market (P_2M_2), then take the second product back into the first market (P_2M_1), then launch a third product for the first market (P_3M_1). If this game plan works, the pioneer firm will own a good part of the first two segments and serve them with two or three products.

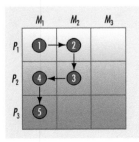

FIGURE 11.7

Long-Range Product-Market Expansion Strategy (P_1 = product 1; M_1 = market 1)

Marketing Strategies: Growth Stage

The growth stage is marked by a rapid climb in sales. Early adopters like the product and additional consumers start buying it. New competitors enter, attracted by the opportunities. They introduce new product features and expand distribution.

Prices stabilize or fall slightly, depending on how fast demand increases. Companies maintain promotional expenditures or raise them slightly, to meet competition and continue to educate the market. Sales rise much faster than promotional expenditures, causing a welcome decline in the promotion–sales ratio. Profits increase as promotion costs are spread over a larger volume, and unit manufacturing costs fall faster than price declines, owing to the producer-learning effect. Firms must watch for a change to a decelerating rate of growth in order to prepare new strategies.

To sustain rapid market share growth now, the firm

- Improves product quality and adds new features and improved styling;
- Adds new models and flanker products (of different sizes, flavours, and so forth) to protect the main product;
- Enters new market segments;
- Increases its distribution coverage and enters new distribution channels;
- Shifts from awareness and trial communications to preference and loyalty communications; and
- Lowers prices to attract the next layer of price-sensitive buyers.

By spending money on product improvement, promotion, and distribution, the firm can capture a dominant position. It trades off maximum current profit for high market share and the hope of even greater profits in the next stage.

Marketing Strategies: Maturity Stage

At some point, the rate of sales growth will slow, and the product will enter a stage of relative maturity. Most products are in this stage of the life cycle, which normally lasts longer than the preceding ones.

The maturity stage divides into three phases: growth, stable, and decaying maturity. In the first, sales growth starts to slow. There are no new distribution channels to fill. New competitive forces emerge. In the second phase, sales per capita flatten because of market saturation. Most potential consumers have tried the product, and future sales depend on population growth and replacement demand. In the third phase, decaying maturity, the absolute level of sales starts to decline, and customers begin switching to other products.

This third phase poses the most challenges. The sales slowdown creates overcapacity in the industry, which intensifies competition. Weaker competitors withdraw. A few giants dominate—perhaps a quality leader, a service leader, and a cost leader—and profit mainly through high volume and lower costs. Surrounding them is a multitude of market nichers, including market specialists, product specialists, and customizing firms.

The question is whether to struggle to become one of the big three and achieve profits through high volume and low cost, or pursue a niching strategy and profit through low volume and high margins. Sometimes the market will divide into low- and high-end segments, and market shares of firms in the middle steadily erode. Here's how Swedish appliance manufacturer Electrolux has coped with this situation.

Electrolux

In 2002, Electrolux faced a rapidly polarizing appliance market. Low-cost Asian companies such as Haier, LG, and Samsung were applying downward price pressure, while premium competitors like Bosch, Sub-Zero, and Viking were growing at the expense of the middle-of-the-road brands. Electrolux's new CEO, Hans Stråberg, decided to escape the middle by rethinking Electrolux customers' wants and needs. He segmented the market according to the lifestyle and purchasing patterns of about 20 different types of consumers. Electrolux now successfully markets its steam ovens to health-oriented consumers, for example, and its compact dishwashers, originally for smaller kitchens, to a broader consumer segment that washes dishes more often. To companies stuck in the middle of a mature market, Stråberg offers this advice: "Start with consumers and understand what their latent needs are and what problems they experience... then put the puzzle together yourself to discover what people really want to have. Henry Ford is supposed to have said, 'If I had asked people what they really wanted, I would have made faster horses' or something like that. You need to figure out what people really want, although they can't express it."[57]

Some companies abandon weaker products to concentrate on new and more profitable ones. Yet they may be ignoring the high potential many mature markets and old products still have. Industries widely thought to be mature—autos, motorcycles, television, watches, cameras—were proved otherwise by the Japanese, who found ways to offer customers new value. Three ways to change the course for a brand are market, product, and marketing program modifications.

MARKET MODIFICATION A company might try to expand the market for its mature brand by working with the two factors that make up sales volume: volume = number of brand users × usage rate per user, as in Table 11.1. However, the volume may also be matched by competitors.

PRODUCT MODIFICATION Managers also try to stimulate sales by improving quality, features, or style. *Quality improvement* increases functional performance by launching a "new and improved" product. *Feature improvement* adds size, weight, materials, supplements, and accessories that expand the product's performance, versatility, safety, or convenience. *Style improvement* increases the product's esthetic appeal. Any of these can attract consumer attention.

MARKETING PROGRAM MODIFICATION Finally, brand managers might also try to stimulate sales by modifying nonproduct elements—price, distribution, and communications in particular. They should assess the likely success of any changes in terms of effects on new and existing customers.

Marketing Strategies: Decline Stage

Sales decline for a number of reasons, including technological advances, shifts in consumer tastes, and increased domestic and foreign competition. All can lead to overcapacity, increased price cutting, and profit erosion. The decline might be slow, as for sewing machines and newspapers, or rapid, as for 5.25 floppy disks and eight-track cartridges. Sales may plunge to zero or petrify at a low level. These structural changes are different from a short-term decline resulting from a marketing crisis of some sort. "Marketing Insight: Managing a Brand Crisis" describes strategies for a brand in temporary trouble.

As sales and profits decline over a long period of time, some firms withdraw. Those remaining may reduce the number of products they offer, withdrawing from smaller segments and weaker trade channels, cutting marketing budgets, and reducing prices further. Unless strong reasons for retention exist, carrying a weak product is often very costly.

Besides being unprofitable, weak products consume a disproportionate amount of management's time, require frequent price and inventory adjustments, incur expensive set-up for short production runs, draw advertising and sales force attention better used to make healthy products more profitable, and cast a negative shadow on the company image. Failing to eliminate them also delays the aggressive search for replacement products, creating a lopsided product mix long on yesterday's breadwinners and short on tomorrow's.

Unfortunately, most companies have not developed a policy for handling aging products. The first task is to establish a system for identifying them. Many companies appoint a product-review committee with

TABLE 11.1	ALTERNATIVE WAYS TO INCREASE SALES VOLUME
Expand the Number of Users	**Increase the Usage Rates among Users**
■ *Convert nonusers.* The key to the growth of air freight service was the constant search for new users to whom air carriers can demonstrate the benefits of using air freight rather than ground transportation.	■ *Have consumers use the product on more occasions.* Serve Campbell's soup for a snack. Use Heinz vinegar to clean windows.
■ *Enter new market segments.* When Goodyear decided to sell its tires via Walmart, Sears, and Discount Tire, it immediately boosted its market share.	■ *Have consumers use more of the product on each occasion.* Drink a larger glass of orange juice.
■ *Attract competitors' customers.* Marketers of Puffs facial tissues are always wooing Kleenex customers.	■ *Have consumers use the product in new ways.* Use Tums antacid as a calcium supplement.

representatives from marketing, R&D, manufacturing, and finance who, based on all available information, make a recommendation for each product—leave it alone, modify its marketing strategy, or drop it.[58]

Some firms abandon declining markets earlier than others. Much depends on the height of exit barriers in the industry.[59] The lower the barriers, the easier for firms to leave the industry, and the more tempting for the remaining firms to stay and attract the withdrawing firms' customers. Procter & Gamble stayed in the declining liquid-soap business and improved its profits as others withdrew.

The appropriate strategy also depends on the industry's relative attractiveness and the company's competitive strength in it. A company in an unattractive industry and that possesses competitive strength should consider shrinking selectively. A company in an attractive industry and that has competitive strength should consider strengthening its investment. Companies that successfully restage or rejuvenate a mature product often do so by adding value to it.

Strategies for harvesting and divesting are quite different. *Harvesting* calls for gradually reducing a product or business's costs while trying to maintain sales. The first step is to cut R&D costs and plant and equipment investment. The company might also reduce product quality, sales force size, marginal services, and advertising expenditures, ideally without letting customers, competitors, and employees know what is happening. Harvesting is difficult to execute, yet many mature products warrant this strategy. It can substantially increase current cash flow.[60]

MARKETING **INSIGHT** | MANAGING A BRAND CRISIS

Marketing managers must assume that a brand crisis will someday arise. Whole Foods, Taco Bell, Maple Leaf Foods, and toy and pet food brands have all experienced potentially crippling brand crises. Widespread repercussions include (1) lost sales, (2) reduced effectiveness of marketing activities for the product, (3) increased sensitivity to rivals' marketing activities, and (4) reduced impact of the firm's marketing activities on competing brands.

In general, the stronger the brand equity and corporate image are—especially credibility and trustworthiness—the more likely the firm can weather the storm. Careful preparation and a well-managed crisis management program, however, are also critical. As Johnson & Johnson's nearly flawless handling of the Tylenol product-tampering incident suggests, the key is that consumers see the firm's response as both *swift* and *sincere*. They must feel an immediate sense that the company truly cares. Listening is not enough.

The longer the firm takes to respond, the more likely consumers can form negative impressions from unfavourable media coverage or word of mouth. Perhaps worse, they may find they don't like the brand after all and permanently switch. Getting in front of a problem with PR, and perhaps ads, can help avoid those problems.

Consider Perrier. In 1994, Perrier was forced to halt production worldwide and recall all existing product when traces of benzene, a known carcinogen, were found in excessive quantities in its bottled water. Over the next weeks it offered several explanations, creating confusion and skepticism. Perhaps more damaging, the product was off shelves for over three months. Despite an expensive relaunch featuring ads and promotions, the brand struggled to regain lost market share, and a full year later sales were less than half what they had been. With its key "purity" association tarnished, Perrier had no other compelling points-of-difference. Consumers and retailers had found satisfactory substitutes, and the brand never recovered. Eventually it was taken over by Nestlé SA.

The more sincere the firm's response—a public acknowledgment of the impact on consumers and willingness to take necessary steps—the less likely consumers will form negative attributions. When consumers reported finding shards of glass in some jars of its baby food, Gerber tried to reassure the public there were no problems in its manufacturing plants but adamantly refused to withdraw products from stores. After market share slumped from 66 percent to 52 percent within a couple of months, one company official admitted, "Not pulling our baby food off the shelf gave the appearance that we aren't a caring company."

Sources: Norman Klein and Stephen A. Greyser, "The Perrier Recall: A Source of Trouble," Harvard Business School Case #9-590-104 and "The Perrier Relaunch," Harvard Business School Case #9-590-130; Harald Van Heerde, Kristiaan Helsen, and Marnik G. Dekimpe, "The Impact of a Product-Harm Crisis on Marketing Effectiveness," *Marketing Science*, 26 (March–April 2007): 230–245; Michelle L. Roehm and Alice M. Tybout, "When Will a Brand Scandal Spill Over and How Should Competitors Respond?" *Journal of Marketing Research*, 43 (August 2006): 366–373; Michelle L. Roehm and Michael K. Brady, "Consumer Responses to Performance Failures by High Equity Brands," *Journal of Consumer Research*, 34 (December 2007): 537–545; Alice M. Tybout and Michelle Roehm, "Let the Response Fit the Scandal," *Harvard Business Review*, December 2009, pp. 82–88; Andrew Pierce, "Managing Reputation to Rebuild Battered Brands," *Marketing News*, March 15, 2009, p. 19; Kevin O'Donnell, "In a Crisis Actions Matter," *Marketing News*, April 15, 2009, p. 22.

When a company decides to divest a product with strong distribution and residual goodwill, it can probably sell the product to another firm. Some firms specialize in acquiring and revitalizing "orphan" or "ghost" brands that larger firms want to divest or that have encountered bankruptcy, such as Linens n' Things, Folgers and Brim coffee, Nuprin pain reliever, and Salon Selective shampoos.[61] These firms attempt to capitalize on the residue of awareness in the market to develop a brand revitalization strategy. Reserve Brands bought Eagle Snacks in part because research showed that six of ten adults remembered the brand, leading Reserve's CEO to observe, "It would take $300 million to $500 million to recreate that brand awareness today."[62]

If the company can't find any buyers, it must decide whether to liquidate the brand quickly or slowly. It must also decide how much inventory and service to maintain for past customers.

Evidence for the Product Life-Cycle Concept

Table 11.2 summarizes the characteristics, marketing objectives, and marketing strategies of the four stages of the product life cycle. The PLC concept helps marketers interpret product and market dynamics, conduct planning and control, and do forecasting. One recent study of 30 product categories unearthed a number of interesting findings concerning the PLC:[63]

- New consumer durables show a distinct takeoff, after which sales increase by roughly 45 percent a year, but they also show a distinct slowdown, when sales decline by roughly 15 percent a year.

- Slowdown occurs at 34 percent penetration on average, well before most households own a new product.

- The growth stage lasts a little over eight years and does not seem to shorten over time.

- Informational cascades exist, meaning people are more likely to adopt the product over time if others already have, instead of by making careful product evaluations. One implication is that product categories with large sales increases at takeoff tend to have larger sales declines at slowdown.

Critique of the Product Life-Cycle Concept

PLC theory has its share of critics, who claim that life-cycle patterns are too variable in shape and duration to be generalized, and that marketers can seldom tell what stage their product is in. A product may appear mature when it has actually reached a plateau prior to another upsurge. Critics also charge that, rather than an inevitable course, the PLC pattern is the self-fulfilling result of marketing strategies, and that skillful marketing can in fact lead to continued growth.[64]

Market Evolution

Because the PLC focuses on what's happening to a particular product or brand rather than the overall market, it yields a product-oriented rather than a market-oriented picture. Firms also need to visualize a *market's* evolutionary path as it is affected by new needs, competitors, technology, channels, and other developments, and change product and brand positioning to keep pace.[65] Like products, markets evolve through four stages: emergence, growth, maturity, and decline. Consider the evolution of the paper towel market.

Paper Towels

Homemakers originally used cotton and linen dishcloths and towels in their kitchens. Then a paper company looking for new markets developed paper towels, crystallizing a latent market that other manufacturers then entered. The number of brands grew and created market fragmentation. Industry overcapacity led manufacturers to search for new features. One manufacturer, hearing consumers complain that paper towels were not absorbent, introduced "absorbent" towels and increased its market share. Competitors produced their own versions of absorbent paper towels, and the market fragmented again. One manufacturer introduced a "superstrength" towel that was soon copied. Another introduced a "lint-free" towel, subsequently copied. The latest innovation is wipes containing a cleaning agent (like Clorox Disinfecting Wipes) that are often surface-specific (for wood, metal, stone). Thus, driven by innovation and competition, paper towels evolved from a single product to one with various absorbencies, strengths, and applications.

| TABLE 11.2 | SUMMARY OF PRODUCT LIFE-CYCLE CHARACTERISTICS, OBJECTIVES, AND STRATEGIES |

	Introduction	Growth	Maturity	Decline
Characteristics				
Sales	Low sales	Rapidly rising sales	Peak sales	Declining sales
Costs	High cost per customer	Average cost per customer	Low cost per customer	Low cost per customer
Profits	Negative	Rising profits	High profits	Declining profits
Customers	Innovators	Early adopters	Middle majority	Laggards
Competitors	Few	Growing number	Stable number beginning to decline	Declining number
Marketing Objectives				
	Create product awareness and trial	Maximize market share	Maximize profit while defending market share	Reduce expenditure and milk the brand
Strategies				
Product	Offer a basic product	Offer product extensions, service, warranty	Diversify brands and items models	Phase out weak products
Price	Charge cost-plus	Price to penetrate market	Price to match or best competitors'	Cut price
Distribution	Build selective distribution	Build intensive distribution	Build more intensive distribution	Go selective: phase out unprofitable outlets
Communications	Build product awareness and trial among early adopters and dealers	Build awareness and interest in the mass market	Stress brand differences and benefits and encourage brand switching	Reduce to minimal level needed to retain hard-core loyals

Sources: Chester R. Wasson, *Dynamic Competitive Strategy and Product Life Cycles* (Austin, TX: Austin Press, 1978); John A. Weber, "Planning Corporate Growth with Inverted Product Life Cycles," *Long Range Planning*, October 1976, pp. 12–29; Peter Doyle, "The Realities of the Product Life Cycle," *Quarterly Review of Marketing*, Summer 1976.

MARKETING IN AN ECONOMIC DOWNTURN

Given economic cycles, there will always be tough times, such as 2008–2010 in many parts of the world. Despite reduced funding for marketing programs and intense pressure to justify them as cost effective, some marketers survived—or even thrived—in the recession. Here are five guidelines to improve the odds for success during an economic downturn.

Explore the Upside of Increasing Investment

Does it pay to invest during a recession? Although the severity of the recent downturn took firms into uncharted territory, 40 years of evidence suggests that those willing to invest during a recession have, on average, improved their fortunes when compared with those that cut back.[66]

The amount of investment isn't all that matters. Firms that received the most benefit from increasing marketing investments during a recession were often those best able to exploit a marketplace advantage such as an appealing new product, a weakened rival, or development of a neglected target market. With such strong evidence, marketers should consider the potential upside and positive payback of an increased investment that seizes market opportunities. Here are two companies that made such a decision:

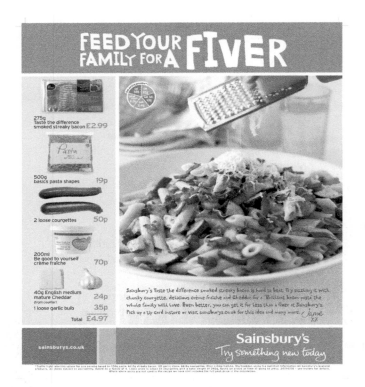

Sainsbury's no-nonsense value appeal was just the right message to send to UK customers in the midst of a recession.

- General Mills increased marketing expenditures for the 2009 fiscal year by 16 percent, increased revenues by 8 percent to $14.7 billion, and increased its operating profit by 4 percent. As CEO Ken Powell explained, "In an environment where you have consumers going to the grocery store more often and thinking more about meals at home, we think that is a great environment for brand building, to remind consumers about our products."[67]

- U.K. supermarket giant Sainsbury's launched an advertising and in-store point-of-sale campaign called "Feed Your Family for a Fiver," one that played off its corporate slogan, "Try Something New Today," to encourage shoppers to try new recipes that would feed families for only £5.

Get Closer to Customers

In tough times, consumers may change what they want and can afford, where and how they shop, even what they want to see and hear from a firm. A downturn is an opportunity for marketers to learn even more about what consumers are thinking, feeling, and doing, especially the loyal customer base that yields so much of a brand's profitability.[68]

Firms should characterize any changes as temporary adjustments versus permanent shifts.[69] In explaining why it is important to look forward during a recession, Eaton CEO Alex Cutler noted, "It is a time when businesses shouldn't be assuming that the future will be like the past. And I mean that in virtually every dimension whether it is economic growth, value propositions, or the level of government regulation and involvement."[70]

The potential value and profitability of some target consumers may change. Marketers should evaluate this factor to fine-tune their marketing program and capitalize on new insights. After unsuccessfully chasing twenty-somethings with trendier clothing, Old Navy refocused its message to target a budget-conscious mom shopping for herself and the family.[71]

Since the Canadian economy weathered the downturn better than did the U.S. economy, many U.S. manufacturers, retailers, and state governments began eyeing Canada with renewed interest. Washington State, for example, located just south of Vancouver, worked to lure Canadian cross-border shoppers with a 10 percent tax break. Major U.S. retailers like Nordstrom, J. Crew, Marshall's, Zumiez, Express Inc., and Ascena Retail Group are planning Canadian ventures. Discount giant Target purchased Zellers locations for $1.8 billion. BCIT marketing instructor Anne Marie Webb-Hughes raises a flag of caution, however, noting that "just because a company does well south of the border doesn't guarantee success here." You have to know your target market, understand how they shop, and what are they looking for. The Canadian Federation of Independent Business says local retailers can be tough competition when it comes to customer service and one-of-a-kind products. Canadians, however, are often familiar with American brands and U.S. stores, so promotion costs may be lower than if these retailers entered a market where consumers were less familiar with the offerings.[72]

Review Budget Allocations

Budget allocations can be sticky and not change enough to reflect a fluid marketing environment. We've seen a dramatic change in marketing communications and channel environment in just five years, with the vast penetration of the Internet, improved functionality of the cell phone, and increased importance of events, experiences, and emotions as marketing opportunities.

A recession provides an opportunity for marketers to closely review how much and in what ways they are spending their money. Budget reallocations can open up promising new options and eliminate sacred-cow approaches that no longer provide sufficient revenue benefits. Underperforming distributors can be weeded out and incentives provided to motivate the more effective product sellers.

Marketing communications allow much experimentation. In London, T-Mobile created spontaneous, large-scale, interactive "happenings" to convey its brand positioning that "Life's for Sharing" and generate massive publicity. Its "Dance" video, featuring 400 dancers getting the whole Liverpool tube station to dance, was viewed millions of times on YouTube.[73]

Put Forth the Most Compelling Value Proposition

One mistake in a recession is to be overly focused on price reductions and discounts, which can harm long-term brand equity and price integrity. Marketers should increase—and clearly communicate— the value their brands offer, making sure consumers appreciate all the financial, logistical, and psychological benefits compared with the competition.[74] The more expensive the item, the more important this value framing becomes. In the recent recession, GE changed its ad messages for the $3500 Profile washer-and-dryer set to emphasize its practicality—it optimizes the use of soap and water per load to reduce waste and saves customers money by being gentle on clothes, extending their life.[75]

Marketers should also review pricing to ensure it has not crept up over time and no longer reflects good value. Procter & Gamble adopted a "surgical" approach to reducing prices in specific categories in which its brands were perceived as costing too much compared with competitive products. At the same time, it launched communications about the innovativeness and value of its many other brands to help ensure consumers would continue to pay premium prices. Ads for Bounty claimed it was more absorbent than a "bargain brand" of paper towels; headlines in print ads for Olay Professional Pro-X Intensive Wrinkle Protocol proclaimed, "As Effective at Wrinkle Reduction as What the Doctor Prescribed. At Half the Price."[76]

To reflect more challenging economic times, GE Profile changed its ad strategy to emphasize practicality.

Fine-Tune Brand and Product Offerings

Marketers must ensure they have the right products to sell to the right consumers in the right places and times. They can review product portfolios and brand architecture to confirm that brands and sub-brands are clearly differentiated, targeted, and supported based on their prospects. Even luxury brands can benefit from lower-priced brands or sub-brands in their portfolios. Take Armani as an example.

Armani

Armani differentiates its product line into three tiers distinct in style, luxury, customization, and price. In the most expensive, Tier I, it sells Giorgio Armani and Giorgio Armani Privé, custom-made couture products that sell for thousands of dollars. In Tier II, it offers Emporio Armani—young, modern, more affordable styles—and Armani jeans that convey technology and ecology. In lowest-priced Tier III are more youthful and street-savvy translations of Armani style, A|X Armani Exchange, sold at retail locations in cities and suburban malls. The brand architecture has been carefully devised so each extension lives up to the core promise of the Armani brand without diluting the parent's image. But clear differentiation also exists, minimizing consumer confusion and brand cannibalization. In tough economic times, the lower end picks up the selling slack and helps maintain profitability.

Because different brands or sub-brands appeal to different economic segments, those that target the lower end of the socioeconomic spectrum may be particularly important during a recession. Value-driven companies, such as McDonald's, Walmart, Costco, Aldi, Dell, E*TRADE, WestJet, and IKEA, are likely to benefit most. Spam, the oft-maligned gelatinous 12-ounce rectangle of spiced ham and pork, found its sales soaring during the recession. Affordably priced and requiring no refrigeration, Spam is, its maker Hormel claims, "like meat with a pause button."[77]

Bad times also are an opportunity to prune brands or products with diminished prospects. In the recession following the 9/11 tragedy, Procter & Gamble divested many stagnant brands, such as Comet cleanser, Folgers coffee, Jif peanut butter, and Crisco oil and shortening, to successfully concentrate on higher-growth opportunities.

SUMMARY

1. A market leader has the largest market share in the relevant product market. To remain dominant, the leader looks for ways to expand total market demand and attempts to protect and perhaps increase its current share.

2. A market challenger attacks the market leader and other competitors in an aggressive bid for more market share. There are five types of general attack; challengers must also choose specific attack strategies.

3. A market follower is a runner-up firm willing to maintain its market share and not rock the boat. It can play the role of counterfeiter, cloner, imitator, or adapter.

4. A market nicher serves small market segments not being served by larger firms. The key to nichemanship is specialization. Nichers develop offerings to fully meet a certain group of customers' needs, commanding a premium price in the process.

5. As important as a competitive orientation is in today's global markets, companies should not overdo the emphasis on competitors. They should maintain a good balance of consumer and competitor monitoring.

6. Because economic conditions change and competitive activity varies, companies normally must reformulate their marketing strategy several times during a

product's life cycle. Technologies, product forms, and brands also exhibit life cycles with distinct stages. The life cycle stages are usually introduction, growth, maturity, and decline. Most products today are in the maturity stage.

7. Each product life cycle stage calls for different marketing strategies. The introduction is marked by slow growth and minimal profits. If successful, the product enters a growth stage marked by rapid sales growth and increasing profits. There follows a maturity stage in which sales growth slows and profits stabilize. Finally, the product enters a decline stage. The company's task is to identify the truly weak products, develop a strategy for each, and phase them out in a way that minimizes impact on company profits, employees, and customers.

8. Like products, markets evolve through four stages: emergence, growth, maturity, and decline.

9. In a recession, marketers must explore the upside of possibly increasing investments, get closer to customers, review budget allocations, put forth the most compelling value proposition, and fine-tune brand and product offerings.

APPLICATIONS

Marketing Debate: Do Brands Have Finite Lives?

Often, after a brand begins to slip in the marketplace or disappears altogether, commentators observe, "All brands have their day," implying brands have a finite life and cannot be expected to be leaders forever. Other experts contend brands *can* live forever, and that their long-term success depends on marketers' skill and insight.

Take a position: Brands cannot be expected to last forever *versus* There is no reason for a brand to ever become obsolete.

Marketing Discussion: Industry Roles

Pick an industry. Classify firms according to the four different roles they might play: leader, challenger, follower, and nicher. How would you characterize the nature of competition? Do the firms follow the principles described in this chapter?

| MARKETING **EXCELLENCE** | SAMSUNG |

Korean consumer electronics giant Samsung has made a remarkable transformation, from a provider of value-priced commodity products that original equipment manufacturers (OEMs) sold under their own brands, to a global marketer of premium-priced Samsung-branded consumer electronics such as flat-screen TVs, digital cameras, digital appliances, semiconductors, and cell phones. Samsung's high-end cell phones have been a growth engine for the company, which has also released a steady stream of innovations, popularizing the PDA phone, the first cell phone with an MP3 player, and the first Blu-ray disc player.

Samsung initially focused on volume and market domination rather than profitability. However, during the Asian financial crisis of the late 1990s, when other Korean *chaebols* collapsed beneath a mountain of debt, Samsung took a different approach. It cut costs and re-emphasized product quality and manufacturing flexibility, which allowed its consumer electronics to go from project phase to store shelves within six months. Samsung invested heavily in innovation and focused intently on its memory-chip business, which established an important cash cow and rapidly made the company the largest chip maker in the world. The company continued to pour money into R&D during the 2000s, budgeting $40 billion for 2005–2010. Its focus on R&D and increasing digital convergence have let Samsung introduce a wide range of electronic products under its strong brand umbrella. The firm also partnered with longtime market leader Sony to create a $2 billion state-of-the-art LCD factory in South Korea and signed a milestone agreement to share 24 000 basic patents for components and production processes.

Samsung's success has been driven not only by successful product innovation, but also by aggressive brand building over the last decade. From 1998 to 2009, the company spent over $7 billion in marketing; sponsored six Olympics; and ran several global ad campaigns themed "Imagine," "Quietly Brilliant," and "YOU," all of which included brand messages such as "technology," "design," and "sensation." In 2005, Samsung surpassed Sony in the Interbrand brand ranking for the first time and continues to outperform Sony today.

The economic downturn during 2008 and 2009 significantly affected the semiconductor industry, overall consumer electronics sales, and Samsung's bottom line. To survive, Samsung slashed profit margins, decreased production, and cut inventories. As a result, the company emerged at the end of 2009 with record-high quarterly profits despite significantly smaller profit margins.

Today, Samsung is the global leader in flat-panel TVs and memory chips, and the number-two player in cell phones. It is focused on growing technologies such as smartphones and has partnered with both Microsoft's Windows Mobile and Google's Android software. In addition, Samsung has formed a green partnership with Microsoft to help create energy-efficient computers.

Unlike rival firms, Samsung has become a global leader by making both components for electronics products and the actual devices sold to consumers, and without acquiring major competitors. It has more than doubled its employees from a decade ago to over 164 000 around the world. With record sales of $110 billion in 2008, the company's CEO, Lee Yoon-woo, announced that the firm hopes to hit $400 billion in revenue by the year 2020. To accomplish this aggressive goal, Samsung will explore areas like health-care and home energy products.

QUESTIONS

1. What are some of Samsung's greatest competitive strengths?

2. Samsung's goal of $400 billion in sales by 2020 would bring it to the same level as Walmart. Is this feasible? Why or why not?

Sources: Moon Ihlwan, "Samsung Is Having a Sony Moment," *BusinessWeek*, July 30, 2007, p. 38; Martin Fackler, "Raising the Bar at Samsung," *New York Times*, April 25, 2006; "Brand New," *Economist*, January 15, 2005, pp. 10–11; Patricia O'Connell, "Samsung's Goal: Be Like BMW," *BusinessWeek*, August 1, 2005; Heidi Brown and Justin Doeble, "Samsung's Next Act," *Forbes*, July 26, 2004; John Quelch and Anna Harrington, "Samsung Electronics Company: Global Marketing Operations," *Harvard Business School*, January 16, 2008; Evan Ramstad, "Samsung's Swelling Size Brings New Challenges," *Wall Street Journal*, November 11, 2009; "Looking Good? LG v. Samsung," *Economist*, January 24, 2009.

In This Chapter, We Will Address the Following **Questions**

Quality, sustainability, and ethical sourcing are the cornerstones of Mountain Equipment Co-op's line of products.

1. What are the characteristics of products, and how do marketers classify products?

2. How can companies differentiate products?

3. Why is product design important and what factors affect a good design?

4. How can a company build and manage its product mix and product lines?

5. How can companies combine products to create strong co-brands or ingredient brands?

6. How can companies use packaging, labelling, warranties, and guarantees as marketing tools?

Setting Product Strategy

At the heart of a great brand is a great product. Product is a key element in the market offering. To achieve market leadership, firms must offer products and services of superior quality and that provide unsurpassed customer value.

Mountain Equipment Co-op (MEC) dedicates itself to providing premium-quality recreation gear and clothes, keeping environmental sustainability and ethical sourcing in mind. MEC was founded in Vancouver, British Columbia, in 1971 by six mountain climbers who had difficulty with customs authorities each time the climbers brought camping equipment bought south of the border into Canada. Starting as a small co-operative, MEC has since expanded, with over 3 million members and stores in 15 Canadian cities across the country.

MEC makes sure that every product is made with care, believing in quality as essential for building innovative, functional, and durable products. While quality is the keystone of the company's success, it takes great care to ensure that its products are ethically sourced and as ecofriendly as possible. MEC strives to minimize environmental and social impact by marketing products that last for a long time—with sustainable materials and suppliers who respect the people involved in the manufacturing process. To meets its quality and sustainability goals, extensive time is spent working with manufacturers on product design, ethical and ecofriendly material sourcing, and testing to ensure that the products are made with sustainable materials without sacrificing quality and durability. For instance, all MEC-label cotton clothing is organic and of the highest quality. It takes approximately 18 months for a product to go from initial design to arrival in a MEC store, and even longer to research and develop new fabrics or technologies.

Mountain Equipment Co-op ensures that products sold in its stores are of superior quality. As a result of this commitment to quality, care for the environment, and respect for humankind, first-time MEC customers often end up becoming loyal repeat customers. Not to mention that every MEC customer is also a member of the co-operative and shares its financial success.[1]

Marketing planning begins with formulating an offering to meet target customers' needs or wants. The customer will judge the offering by three basic elements: product features and quality, services mix and quality, and price (see Figure 12.1). In this chapter we examine product, in Chapter 13 services, and in Chapter 14 price. All three elements must be meshed into a competitively attractive offering.

PRODUCT CHARACTERISTICS AND CLASSIFICATIONS

Many people think a product is tangible, but a **product** is anything that can be offered to a market to satisfy a want or need, including physical goods, services, experiences, events, people, places, properties, organizations, information, and ideas.

Product Levels: The Customer-Value Hierarchy

In planning its market offering, the marketer needs to address five product levels (see Figure 12.2).[2] Each level adds more customer value, and the five constitute a **customer-value hierarchy:**

FIGURE 12.1

Components of the Market Offering

- The fundamental level is the **core benefit**: the service or benefit the customer is really buying. A hotel guest is buying rest and sleep. The purchaser of a drill is buying holes. Marketers must see themselves as benefit providers.

- At the second level, the marketer must turn the core benefit into a **basic product**. Thus, a hotel room includes a bed, bathroom, towels, desk, dresser, and closet.

- At the third level, the marketer prepares an **expected product**, a set of attributes and conditions buyers normally expect when they purchase this product. Hotel guests minimally expect a clean bed, fresh towels, working lamps, and a relative degree of quiet.

- At the fourth level, the marketer prepares an **augmented product** that exceeds customer expectations. In developed countries, brand positioning and competition take place at this level. In developing and emerging markets such as India and Brazil, however, competition takes place mostly at the expected product level.

- At the fifth level stands the **potential product**, which encompasses all the possible augmentations and transformations the product or offering might undergo in the future. Here is where companies search for new ways to satisfy customers and distinguish their offering.

Differentiation arises and competition increasingly occurs on the basis of product augmentation, which also leads the marketer to look at the user's total **consumption system**: the way the user performs the tasks of getting and using products and related services.[3] Each augmentation adds cost, however, and augmented benefits soon become expected benefits and necessary points-of-parity in the category. If today's hotel guests expect satellite television, high-speed Internet access, and a fully equipped fitness centre, competitors must search for still-other features and benefits to differentiate themselves.

As some companies raise the price of their augmented product, others offer a stripped-down version for less. Thus, alongside the growth of fine hotels, such as Four Seasons and Ritz-Carlton, we see lower-cost hotels and motels emerge, such as Motel 6 and Comfort Inn, catering to clients who want simply the basic product. Striving to create an augmented product can be a key for success.

Product Classifications

Marketers classify products on the basis of durability, tangibility, and use (consumer or industrial). Each type has an appropriate marketing-mix strategy.[4]

DURABILITY AND TANGIBILITY Products fall into three groups according to durability and tangibility:

1. **Nondurable goods** are tangible goods normally consumed in one or a few uses, such as beer and shampoo. Because these goods are purchased frequently, the appropriate strategy is to make them available in many locations, charge only a small markup, and advertise heavily to induce trial and build preference.

2. **Durable goods** are tangible goods that normally survive many uses: refrigerators, machine tools, and clothing. Durable products normally require more personal selling and service, command a higher margin, and require more seller guarantees.

3. **Services** are intangible, inseparable, variable, and perishable products that normally require more quality control, supplier credibility, and adaptability. Examples include haircuts, legal advice, and appliance repairs.

FIGURE 12.2

Five Product Levels

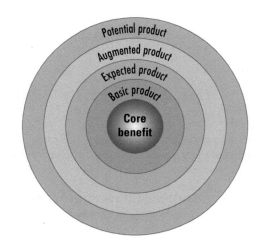

CONSUMER-GOODS CLASSIFICATION When we classify the vast array of consumer goods on the basis of shopping habits, we distinguish among convenience, shopping, specialty, and unsought goods.

The consumer usually purchases **convenience goods** frequently, immediately, and with minimal effort. Examples include soft drinks, soaps, and newspapers. *Staples* are convenience goods consumers purchase on a regular basis. A buyer might routinely purchase Heinz ketchup, Crest toothpaste, and Ritz crackers. *Impulse goods* are purchased without any planning or search effort, like candy bars and magazines. *Emergency goods* are purchased when a need is urgent—umbrellas during a rainstorm, boots and shovels during the first winter snow. Manufacturers of impulse and emergency goods will place them where consumers are likely to experience an urge or compelling need to purchase them.

Shopping goods are those the consumer characteristically compares on such bases as suitability, quality, price, and style. Examples include furniture, clothing, and major appliances. *Homogeneous shopping goods* are similar in quality but different enough in price to justify shopping comparisons. *Heterogeneous shopping goods* differ in product features and services that may be more important than price. The seller of heterogeneous shopping goods carries a wide assortment to satisfy individual tastes and trains salespeople to inform and advise customers.

Specialty goods have unique characteristics or brand identification for which enough buyers are willing to make a special purchasing effort. Examples include cars, stereo components, and men's suits. A Mercedes is a specialty good because interested buyers will travel far to buy one. Specialty goods don't require comparisons; buyers invest time only to reach dealers carrying the wanted products. Dealers don't need convenient locations, although they must let prospective buyers know where to find them.

Unsought goods are those the consumer does not know about or normally think of buying, such as smoke detectors. Classic examples of known but unsought goods are life insurance, cemetery plots, and gravestones. Unsought goods require advertising and personal-selling support.

INDUSTRIAL-GOODS CLASSIFICATION We classify industrial goods in terms of their relative cost and how they enter the production process: materials and parts, capital items, and supplies and business services.

Materials and parts are goods that enter the manufacturer's product completely. They fall into two classes: raw materials, and manufactured materials and parts. *Raw materials* fall into two major groups: *farm products* (wheat, cotton, livestock, fruits, and vegetables) and *natural products* (fish, lumber, crude petroleum, iron ore). Farm products are supplied by many producers, who turn them over to marketing intermediaries, who provide assembly, grading, storage, transportation, and selling services. Their perishable and seasonal nature gives rise to special marketing practices, whereas their commodity character results in relatively little advertising and promotional activity, with some exceptions. At times, commodity groups will launch campaigns to promote their product—potatoes, cheese, and beef. Some producers brand their products—Dole salads, Mott's apples, and Chiquita bananas.

Natural products are limited in supply. They usually have great bulk and low unit value and must be moved from producer to user. Fewer and larger producers often market them directly to industrial users. Because users depend on these materials, long-term supply contracts are common. The homogeneity of natural materials limits the amount of demand-creation activity. Price and delivery reliability are the major factors influencing the selection of suppliers.

Manufactured materials and parts fall into two categories: component materials (iron, yarn, cement, wires) and component parts (small motors, tires, castings). *Component materials* are usually fabricated further—pig iron is made into steel, and yarn is woven into cloth. The standardized nature of component materials usually makes price and supplier reliability key purchase factors. *Component parts* enter the finished product with no further change in form, as when small motors are put into vacuum cleaners, and tires are put on automobiles. Most manufactured materials and parts are sold directly to industrial users. Price and service are major marketing considerations, with branding and advertising less important.

Capital items are long-lasting goods that facilitate developing or managing the finished product. They comprise two groups: installations and equipment. *Installations* consist of buildings (factories, offices) and heavy equipment (generators, drill presses, mainframe computers, elevators). Installations are major purchases. They are usually bought directly from the producer, whose sales force includes technical personnel, and a long negotiation precedes the typical sale. Producers must be willing to design to specification and to supply post-sale services. Advertising is much less important than personal selling.

Equipment includes portable factory equipment and tools (hand tools, lift trucks) and office equipment (personal computers, desks). These types of equipment don't become part of a finished product. They have a shorter life than installations but a longer life than operating supplies. Although some equipment manufacturers sell direct, more often they use intermediaries, because the market is geographically dispersed, buyers are numerous, and orders are small. Quality, features, price, and service are major

Line filling is overdone if it results in self-cannibalization and customer confusion. The company needs to differentiate each item in the consumer's mind with a *just-noticeable difference.* According to Weber's law, customers are more attuned to relative than to absolute difference.[35] They will perceive the difference between boards 20 and 30 centimetres long, and boards 2 and 3 metres long, but not between boards 2.9 and 3 metres long. The proposed item should also meet a market need and not be added simply to satisfy an internal need. The infamous Edsel automobile, on which Ford lost US$350 million in the late 1950s, met Ford's internal positioning need for a car between its Ford and Lincoln lines, but not the market's needs.

LINE MODERNIZATION, FEATURING, AND PRUNING Product lines need to be modernized. The question is whether to overhaul the line piecemeal or all at once. A piecemeal approach allows the company to see how customers and dealers take to the new style. It is also less draining on the company's cash flow, but it lets competitors see changes and start redesigning their own lines.

In rapidly changing markets, modernization is continuous. Companies plan improvements to encourage customer migration to higher-valued, higher-priced items. Microprocessor companies such as Intel and AMD and software companies such as Microsoft and Oracle constantly introduce more-advanced versions of their products. It's important to time improvements so they do not appear too early (damaging sales of the current line) or too late (giving the competition time to establish a strong reputation).[36]

The product line manager typically selects one or a few items in the line to feature. Sears will announce a special low-priced washing machine to attract customers. At other times, managers will feature a high-end item to lend prestige to the product line. Sometimes a company finds one end of its line selling well and the other end selling poorly.

The company may try to boost demand for slower sellers, especially if a factory is idled by lack of demand, but it could be argued that the firm should promote items that sell well rather than prop up weak ones. Nike's Air Force 1 basketball shoe, introduced in the 1980s, is a billion-dollar brand that is still a consumer and retailer favourite and a moneymaker for the company due to collectible designs and tight supplies. Since their introduction, Air Force 1 shoes have been designed or inspired by many celebrities and athletes.[37]

Using sales and cost analysis, product line managers must periodically review the line for deadwood that depresses profits.[38] One study found that for a big Dutch retailer, a major assortment reduction led to a short-term drop in category sales, caused mainly by fewer category purchases by former buyers, but it attracted new category buyers at the same time. These new buyers partially offset the sales losses among former buyers of the delisted items.[39]

In 1999, Unilever announced its "Path to Growth" program designed to get the most value from its brand portfolio by eliminating three-quarters of its 1600 distinct brands by 2003.[40] More than 90 percent of its profits came from just 400 brands, prompting Unilever co-chair Niall FitzGerald to liken the brand reduction to weeding a garden, so "the light and air get in to the blooms which are likely to grow the best." The company retained global brands such as Lipton, as well as regional brands and "local jewels" like Persil, the leading detergent in the United Kingdom.

Multibrand companies all over the world try to optimize their brand portfolios. This often means focusing on core-brand growth and concentrating resources on the biggest and most established brands. Hasbro has designated a set of core toy brands, including GI Joe, Transformers, and My Little Pony, to emphasize in its marketing. Procter & Gamble's "back to basics strategy" concentrated on brands with over US$1 billion in revenue, such as Tide, Crest, Pampers, and Pringles. Every product in a product line must play a role, as must any brand in the brand portfolio.

Product Mix Pricing

Marketers must modify their price-setting logic when the product is part of a product mix. In **product mix pricing**, the firm searches for a set of prices that maximizes profits on the total mix. Pricing is difficult because the various products have demand and cost interrelationships and are subject to different degrees of competition. We can distinguish six situations calling for product mix pricing: product line pricing, optional-feature pricing, captive-product pricing, two-part pricing, by-product pricing, and product-bundling pricing.

PRODUCT LINE PRICING Companies normally develop product lines rather than single products and introduce price steps. A men's clothing store might carry men's suits at three price levels: $300, $600, and $900, which customers associate with low, average, and high quality. The seller's task is to establish perceived quality differences that justify the price differences.[41]

OPTIONAL-FEATURE PRICING Many companies offer optional products, features, and services with their main product. A buyer of the 2010 Subaru Outback 2.5i can order four-way power passenger seats, an all-weather package, and a power moon roof as optional features.

Pricing options is a sticky problem, because companies must decide which to include in the standard price and which to offer separately. Many restaurants price their beverages high and their food low. The food revenue covers costs, and the beverages—especially liquor—produce the profit. This explains why servers often press hard to get customers to order drinks. Other restaurants price their liquor low and food high to draw in a drinking crowd.

CAPTIVE-PRODUCT PRICING Some products require the use of ancillary or **captive products**. Manufacturers of razors and cameras often price them low and set high markups on razor blades and film.[42] Rogers Wireless may give a cell phone free if the person commits to buying three years of phone service. If the captive product is priced too high in the aftermarket, however, counterfeiting and substitutions can erode sales. Consumers now can buy cartridge refills for their printers from discount suppliers and save substantially off the manufacturer's price. Hewlett-Packard shows how captive products can be lucrative for a company.

Hewlett-Packard

In 1996, Hewlett-Packard began drastically cutting prices on its printers, by as much as 60 percent in some cases. HP could afford to make these cuts because customers typically spend twice as much on replacement ink cartridges, toner, and specialty paper as on the printer over the life of the product, and inkjet supplies typically carry 45 percent to 60 percent profit margins. As the price of printers dropped, printer sales rose, and so did aftermarket sales. HP now owns about 46 percent of the worldwide printer business, a share that accounted for 32 percent of HP's $13.4 billion profit in 2008.[43]

TWO-PART PRICING Service firms engage in **two-part pricing**, consisting of a fixed fee plus a variable usage fee. Cell phone users pay a minimum monthly fee plus charges for calls that exceed their allotted minutes. Amusement parks charge an admission fee plus fees for rides over a certain minimum. The service firm faces a problem similar to that of captive-product pricing—namely, how much to charge for the basic service and how much for the variable usage. The fixed fee should be low enough to induce purchase; profit can then come from the usage fees.

BY-PRODUCT PRICING The production of certain goods—meats, petroleum products, and chemicals— often results in by-products that should be priced on their value. Any income earned on the by-products will make it easier for the company to charge a lower price on its main product if competition forces it to do so. Formed in 1855, Australia's CSR was originally named Colonial Sugar Refinery and forged its early reputation as a sugar company. The company began to sell by-products of its sugar cane: waste sugar cane fibre was used to manufacture wallboard. Today, through product development and acquisition, the renamed CSR has become one of the top ten companies in Australia selling building and construction materials.

PRODUCT-BUNDLING PRICING Sellers often bundle products and features. **Pure bundling** occurs when a firm offers its products only as a bundle. A talent agency might insist that a "hot" actor can be signed to a film only if the film company also accepts other talents the agency represents (directors, writers). This is a form of *tied-in sales*.

In **mixed bundling**, the seller offers goods both individually and in bundles, normally charging less for the bundle than if the items were purchased separately. Shaw Communications offers its TV, Internet, and home phone as a bundle at less than the cost of subscribing to all three separately. Tim Hortons offers a soup, sandwich, and coffee combo for less than buying all three separately. Season tickets to CFL home games are priced lower than the cost of buying tickets to each game separately. Customers may not have planned to buy all the components of the product bundle, so savings on the price must be significant enough to induce them to buy the bundle.[44]

Some customers want less than the whole bundle in exchange for a lower price.[45] These customers ask the seller to "unbundle" or "rebundle" its offer. If a supplier saves $100 by not supplying unwanted delivery and reduces the customer's price by $80, it has kept the customer happy while increasing its profit by $20. "Marketing Memo: Product-Bundle Pricing Considerations" offers a few tips.

MARKETING **MEMO**	PRODUCT-BUNDLE PRICING CONSIDERATIONS

As promotional activity increases on individual items in the bundle, buyers perceive less savings on the bundle and are less apt to pay for it. Research suggests the following guidelines for implementing a bundling strategy:

- Don't promote individual products in a package as frequently and cheaply as the bundle. The bundle price should be much lower than the sum of individual products or the consumer will not perceive its attractiveness.

- Limit promotions to a single item in the mix if you still want to promote individual products. Another option is to alternate promotions, one after another, to avoid running conflicting promotions.

- If you offer large rebates on individual products, make them the absolute exception and do it with discretion. Otherwise, the consumer uses the price of individual products as an external reference for the bundle, which then loses value.

- Consider how experienced and knowledgeable your customer is. More knowledgeable customers may be less likely to need or want bundled offerings and prefer the freedom to choose components individually.

- Remember that costs play a role. If marginal costs for the products are low—such as for proprietary software components that can be easily copied and distributed—a bundling strategy can be preferable to a pure component strategy where each component is purchased separately.

- Firms with single products and which are bundling products together to compete against a multiproduct firm may not be successful if a price war ensues.

Sources: Amiya Basu and Padmal Vitharana, "Impact of Customer Knowledge Heterogeneity on Bundling Strategy," *Marketing Science, 28* (July–August 2009): 792–801; Bikram Ghosh and Subramanian Balachnadar, "Competitive Bundling and Counterbundling with Generalist and Specialist Firms," *Management Science, 53* (January 2007): 159–168; Loren M. Hitt and Pei-yu Chen, "Bundling with Customer Self-Selection: A Simple Approach to Bundling Low-Marginal-Cost Goods," *Management Science, 51* (October 2005): 1481–1493; George Wuebker, "Bundles Effectiveness Often Undermined," *Marketing News*, March 18, 2002, pp. 9–12; Stefan Stremersch and Gerard J. Tellis, "Strategic Bundling of Products and Prices," *Journal of Marketing, 66* (January 2002): 55–72.

Co-Branding and Ingredient Branding

CO-BRANDING Marketers often combine their products with products from other companies in various ways. In **co-branding**—also called **dual branding** or **brand bundling**—two or more well-known brands are combined into a joint product or marketed together in some fashion.[46] One form of co-branding is *same-company co-branding*, as when General Mills advertises Trix cereal and Yoplait yogurt. Another form is *joint-venture co-branding*, such as General Electric and Hitachi light bulbs in Japan, and the CIBC Aerogold VISA card. There is *multiple-sponsor co-branding*, such as Taligent, a one-time technological alliance of Apple, IBM, and Motorola.[47] Finally, there is *retail co-branding* in which two retail establishments use the same location to optimize space and profits, such as jointly owned Pizza Hut, KFC, and Taco Bell restaurants.

The main advantage of co-branding is that a product can be convincingly positioned by virtue of the multiple brands. Co-branding can generate greater sales from the existing market and open opportunities for new consumers and channels. It can also reduce the cost of product introduction, because it combines two well-known images and speeds adoption. And co-branding may be a valuable means to learn about consumers and how other companies approach them. Companies in the automotive industry have reaped all these benefits.

The potential disadvantages of co-branding are the risks and lack of control in becoming aligned with another brand in consumers' minds. Consumer expectations of co-brands are likely to be high, so unsatisfactory performance could have negative repercussions for both brands. If the other brand enters a number of co-branding arrangements, overexposure may dilute the transfer of any association. It may also result in a lack of focus on existing brands. Consumers may feel less sure of what they know about the brand.[48]

For co-branding to succeed, the two brands must separately have brand equity—adequate brand awareness and a sufficiently positive brand image. The most important requirement is a logical fit between the two brands, to maximize the advantages of each while minimizing disadvantages. Consumers are more apt to perceive co-brands favourably if they are complementary and offer unique quality, rather than overly similar and redundant.[49]

Managers must enter co-branding ventures carefully, looking for the right fit in values, capabilities, and goals and an appropriate balance of brand equity. There must be detailed plans to legalize contracts, make financial arrangements, and coordinate marketing programs. As one executive at Nabisco put it, "Giving away your brand is a lot like giving away your child—you want to make sure everything is perfect." Financial arrangements between brands vary; one common approach is for the brand more deeply invested in the production process to pay the other a licensing fee and royalty.

Brand alliances require a number of decisions.[50] What capabilities do you *not* have? What resource constraints do you face (people, time, money)? What are your growth goals or revenue needs? Ask whether the opportunity is a profitable business venture. How does it help maintain or strengthen brand equity? Is there any risk of diluting brand equity? Does the opportunity offer extrinsic advantages such as learning opportunities?

INGREDIENT BRANDING **Ingredient branding** is a special case of co-branding.[51] It creates brand equity for materials, components, or parts that are necessarily contained within other branded products. Successful ingredient brands include Dolby noise reduction technology, GORE-TEX water-resistant fibres, and Scotchgard fabrics. Some popular ingredient-branded products are Lunchables lunch combinations with Taco Bell tacos and Lay's potato chips made with KC Masterpiece barbecue sauce.

An interesting take on ingredient branding is "self-branded ingredients" that companies advertise and even trademark. Westin Hotels advertises its own "Heavenly Bed" and "Heavenly Shower." The Heavenly Bed has been so successful that Westin now sells the bed, pillows, sheets, and blankets via an online catalogue, along with other "Heavenly" gifts, bath products, and even pet items. If it can be done well, using self-branded ingredients makes sense because firms have more control over them and can develop them to suit their purposes.[52]

Ingredient brands try to create enough awareness and preference for their product so that consumers will not buy a "host" product that doesn't contain it.[53] DuPont has done so successfully.

DuPont

DuPont has introduced a number of innovative products, such as Corian solid-surface material, for use in markets ranging from apparel to aerospace. Many, such as Tyvek house wrap, Teflon non-stick coating, and Kevlar fibre, became household names as ingredient brands in consumer products manufactured by other companies. Since 2004, DuPont has introduced more than 5000 new products and received over 2400 new patents. One of its recent award winners, Sorona, is a renewably sourced or bio-based polymer for use in carpet and apparel markets.[54]

DuPont's Stainmaster carpets have become a household name.

Many manufacturers make components or materials that enter final branded products but lose their individual identity. One of the few companies that avoided this fate is Intel. Intel's consumer-directed brand campaign convinced many personal computer buyers to buy only brands with "Intel Inside." As a result, major PC manufacturers—IBM, Dell, Compaq—purchase their chips from Intel at a premium price rather than buy equivalent chips from an unknown supplier.

What are the requirements for successful ingredient branding?[55]

1. Consumers must believe that the ingredient matters to the performance and success of the end product. Ideally, this intrinsic value is easily seen or experienced.

2. Consumers must be convinced that not all ingredient brands are the same and that the ingredient is superior.

3. A distinctive symbol or logo must clearly signal that the host product contains the ingredient. Ideally, this symbol or logo functions like a seal and is simple and versatile, credibly communicating quality and confidence.

4. A coordinated "pull" and "push" program must help consumers understand the advantages of the branded ingredient. Channel members must offer full support such as consumer advertising and promotions and—sometimes in collaboration with manufacturers—retail merchandising and promotion programs.

PACKAGING, LABELLING, WARRANTIES, AND GUARANTEES

Some product packages—such as the Coke bottle and Red Bull can—are world famous. Many marketers have called packaging a fifth P, along with price, product, place, and promotion. Most, however, treat packaging and labelling as an element of product strategy. Warranties and guarantees can also be an important part of the product strategy and often appear on the package.

Packaging

Packaging includes all the activities of designing and producing the container for a product. Packages might have up to three layers. Cool Water cologne comes in a bottle (*primary package*) in a cardboard box (*secondary package*) in a corrugated box (*shipping package*) containing six dozen bottles in cardboard boxes.

The package is the buyer's first encounter with the product. A good package draws the consumer in and encourages product choice. In effect, packages can act as five-second commercials for the product. Packaging also affects consumers' later product experiences when they go to open the package and use the product at home. Some packages can even be attractively displayed at home. Distinctive packaging like that for Kiwi shoe polish, Altoids mints, and Absolut vodka is an important part of a brand's equity.[56]

Various factors contribute to the growing use of packaging as a marketing tool:

- *Self-service.* An increasing number of products are sold on a self-serve basis. In an average supermarket, which may stock 15 000 items, the typical shopper passes some 300 products per minute. Given that 50 percent to 70 percent of all purchase decisions are made in the store, the effective package must perform many sales tasks: attract attention, describe the product's features, create consumer confidence, and make a favourable overall impression.

- *Consumer affluence.* Rising affluence means consumers are willing to pay a little more for the convenience, appearance, dependability, and prestige of better packages.

- *Company and brand image.* Packages contribute to instant recognition of the company or brand. In the store, they can create a billboard effect, such as Garnier Fructis with its bright green packaging in the hair-care aisle.

- *Innovation opportunity.* Unique or innovative packaging such as resealable spouts can bring big benefits to consumers and profits to producers.

Packaging must achieve a number of objectives:[57]

1. Identify the brand.
2. Convey descriptive and persuasive information.
3. Facilitate product transportation and protection.
4. Assist at-home storage.
5. Aid product consumption.

Increasingly, marketers are adding a sixth criterion to this list: be made of sustainable materials. To recognize innovation in this regard, the Packaging Association of Canada awards manufacturers that have demonstrated commitment to more sustainable packaging. In 2009, Kraft Canada won awards for switching from glass to plastic for its Miracle Whip mayonnaise and thereby reducing packaging material by 6 million kilograms, and for changing the steel container for its Nabob Coffee to a 50 percent recycled composite material can.[58]

To achieve these objectives and satisfy consumers' desires, marketers must choose the aesthetic and functional components of packaging correctly. Aesthetic considerations relate to a package's size and shape, material, colour, text, and graphics. There are a number of factors and criteria in each area.

Colour is a particularly important aspect of packaging and carries different meanings in different cultures and market segments. Table 12.3 summarizes the beliefs of some visual marketing experts about its role.

Altoids's distinctive packaging, name, and logo are all brand assets.

TABLE 12.3 | THE COLOUR WHEEL OF BRANDING AND PACKAGING

Red is a powerful color, symbolizing energy, passion or even danger. Red works best for action-oriented products or brands, products associated with speed or power, or dominant or iconic brands.

Orange often connotes adventure and fun. Like red, it's an attention-grabber and is thought to stimulate appetites, but it's less aggressive than red can be. Orange has been used to convey value and discounts, and recently has earned young, stylish associations thanks to the fashion industry.

Yellow is equated with sunny warmth and cheeriness. Its more vibrant shades elicit feelings of well-being and are said to stimulate mental activity, so yellow is often associated with wisdom and intellect. Yellow works well for products or brands tied to sports or social activities, or for products or content looking to garner attention.

Green connotes cleanliness, freshness and renewal—and, of course, environmental friendliness—but experts warn that green now is overused in the marketplace. It is one of the most predominant, naturally occurring colors, so it often is associated with wholesome attributes. It works well for organic or recycled products, or for brands associated with health and wellness.

Blue, another naturally predominant color, is regularly associated with security, efficiency, productivity and a clearness of mind. It has become a popular color in the corporate world and particularly in the high-tech industry. Blue also symbolizes cleanliness, openness and relaxation, and works well for everything from cleaning and personal care products to spas and vacation destinations.

Purple, for centuries, has symbolized nobility and wealth, and those associations hold true today. Purple is a powerful color for luxury brands and products, or for companies that want to lend an air of mystery or uniqueness to their wares. Purple is particularly popular with females of all ages.

Pink is a stereotypically girly color associated with frilliness and warmth, and is considered to have soft, peaceful, comforting qualities. Pink works well for personal care products and baby-related brands. Pink also is associated with sweetness and works well for food marketers touting sugary treats.

Brown is a strong, earthy color that connotes honesty and dependability. Brown often is cited as a favorite color among men. Its darker shades are rich and solid, while other shades work well as a foundational color. Brown often works best in conjunction with other colors.

Black is classic and strong, and is a regular fixture in marketers' color schemes as either a primary component or an accent color for font or graphics. Black can convey power, luxury, sophistication and authority, and can be used to market everything from cars and electronics to high-end hotels and financial services.

White, the color of puffy clouds and fresh snow, logically connotes purity and cleanliness. It often is used as a background or accent color to brighten a color scheme, but also it can be used liberally to create clean associations for organic foods or personal care products. White also can symbolize innovation and modernity.

Source: Elisabeth Sullivan, "Color Me Profitable," *Marketing News*, October 15, 2008, p. 8. Reprinted with permission from *Marketing News*, published by the American Marketing Association.

Functionally, structural design is crucial. The packaging elements must harmonize with each other and with pricing, advertising, and other parts of the marketing program.

Packaging updates or redesigns can occur frequently to make the brand more contemporary, relevant, or practical. Club House found success with its redesigned packaging.

Club House launched a line of new herb and spice mixes in redesigned packaging that allows customers to see the mix before purchasing.

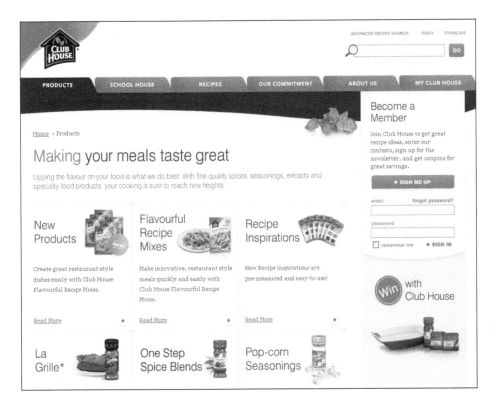

Club House

In business since 1883 in London, Ontario, Club House offers a wide range of spices, herbs, seasoning mixes, and flavourings. In 2010 the company launched Club House Flavourful Recipe Mixes, which feature coarse blends of herbs and spices in a variety of flavours. The package design was key to the launch, as it features an easy-to-store stand-up pouch with a see-through window on the front of the pouch so shoppers can preview the texture and colour of the mix before they buy. Prelaunch test results were positive with strong purchase intent, as 61 percent of consumers stated they would definitely or probably buy, which is significantly higher than the norm of about 40 percent in the food industry.[59]

Although packaging changes can have immediate impact on sales, they are not always positive, as PepsiCo learned the hard way for its Tropicana brand.

Tropicana

PepsiCo experienced great success with its Tropicana brand, acquired in 1998. Then in 2009, the company launched a redesigned package to "refresh and modernize" the brand. The goal was to create an "emotional attachment by 'heroing' the juice and trumpeting the natural fruit goodness." Arnell Group led the extreme makeover that led to an entirely new look, downplaying the brand name, raising the prominence of the phrase "100 percent orange pure & natural," and replacing the "straw in an orange" graphic on the front of the package with a close-up of a glass of orange juice. Consumer response was swift and negative. The package looked "ugly" or "stupid," and some even confused it with a store brand. Sales dropped 20 percent. After only two months, PepsiCo management announced it would revert to the old packaging.[60]

After the company designs its packaging, it must test it. *Engineering tests* ensure that the package stands up under normal conditions; *visual tests*, that the script is legible and the colours harmonious; *dealer tests*, that dealers find the packages attractive and easy to handle; and *consumer tests*, that buyers will respond favourably. Eye tracking by hidden cameras can assess how much consumers notice and examine packages. For Comtrex cold medicine, tracking research was able to confirm that only 50 percent of consumers considered the old package on the shelf, versus 62 percent for a newly redesigned package.[61]

Although developing effective packaging may require several months and several hundred thousand dollars, companies must consider growing environmental and safety concerns about reducing packaging. Fortunately, many companies have gone green and are finding creative new ways to develop packaging. Frito-Lay's Sun Chips multigrain snacks, containing 30 percent less fat than potato chips, are positioned as a healthier, "good for you" snack option. Part of the firm's effort to also support a healthier planet was to unveil a fully compostable bag made from plant-based materials (although it was later withdrawn for some flavours when consumers complained of the noise the bags made) and to run its factory in Modesto, California, on solar power.

Labelling

The label can be a simple attached tag or an elaborately designed graphic that is part of the package. It might carry a great deal of information, or only the brand name. Even if the seller prefers a simple label, the law may require more.

A label performs several functions. First, it *identifies* the product or brand—for instance, the name Sunkist stamped on oranges. It might also *grade* the product; canned peaches are grade-labelled A, B, and C. The label might *describe* the product: who made it, where and when, what it contains, how it is to be used, and how to use it safely. Finally, the label might *promote* the product through attractive graphics. Advanced technology allows 360-degree shrink-wrapped labels to surround containers with bright graphics and accommodate more product information, replacing glued-on paper labels.[62]

Labels eventually need freshening up. The label on Ivory soap has been redone at least 18 times since the 1890s, with gradual changes in the size and design of the letters. As Tropicana found out, companies with labels that have become icons need to tread very carefully when initiating a redesign, to preserve key branding elements.

There is a long history of legal concerns surrounding labels and packaging. In Canada, the Consumer Packaging and Labelling Act makes it mandatory for a label to have three elements: it must identify the product in both English and French, specify the quantity being sold in metric units, and state the producer's name and place of business. There are numerous other regulations affecting labelling practices that vary depending on the type of product being sold. Details can be found on the Government of Canada's Competition Bureau website (www.competitionbureau.gc.ca).

Warranties and Guarantees

All sellers are legally responsible for fulfilling a buyer's normal or reasonable expectations. **Warranties** are formal statements of expected product performance by the manufacturer. Products under warranty can be returned to the manufacturer or designated repair centre for repair, replacement, or refund. Whether expressed or implied, warranties are legally enforceable.

Extended warranties and service contracts can be extremely lucrative for manufacturers and retailers. Analysts estimate that warranty sales have accounted for a large percentage of Best Buy's operating profits.[63] Despite evidence that extended warranties do not pay off, some consumers value the peace of mind.[64] These warranties still generate millions of dollars in revenue for electronic goods in Canada, though the total has declined as consumers have become more comfortable seeking solutions to technical problems online or from friends.

Many sellers offer either general or specific guarantees.[65] A company such as Procter & Gamble promises general or complete satisfaction without being more specific: "if you are not satisfied for any reason, return for replacement, exchange, or refund." A. T. Cross guarantees its Cross pens and pencils for life. The customer mails the pen to A. T. Cross (mailers are provided at stores), and the pen is repaired or replaced at no charge.

Guarantees reduce the buyer's perceived risk. They suggest that the product is of high quality and the company and its service performance are dependable. They can be especially helpful when the company or product is not well-known or when the product's quality is superior to that of competitors. Hyundai's and Kia's highly successful ten-year or 160 000 kilometre powertrain warranty programs were designed in part to assure potential buyers of the quality of the products and the companies' stability.

SUMMARY

1. Product is the first and most important element of the marketing mix. Product strategy calls for making coordinated decisions on product mixes, product lines, brands, and packaging and labelling.

2. In planning its market offering, the marketer needs to think through the five levels of the product: the core benefit; the basic product; the expected product; the augmented product; and the potential product, which encompasses all the augmentations and transformations the product might ultimately undergo.

3. Products can be nondurable goods, durable goods, or services. In the consumer-goods category are convenience goods (staples, impulse goods, emergency goods), shopping goods (homogeneous and heterogeneous), specialty goods, and unsought goods. The industrial-goods category has three subcategories: materials and parts (raw materials and manufactured materials and parts), capital items (installations and equipment), and supplies and business services (operating supplies, maintenance and repair items, maintenance and repair services, and business advisory services).

4. Brands can be differentiated on the basis of product form, features, customization, performance, conformance, durability, reliability, repairability, style, and design, as well as on such service dimensions as ordering ease, delivery, installation, customer training, customer consulting, and maintenance and repair.

5. Design is the totality of features that affect how a product looks, feels, and functions. A well-designed product offers functional and aesthetic benefits to consumers and can be an important source of differentiation.

6. Most companies sell more than one product. A product mix can be classified according to width, length, depth, and consistency. These four dimensions are the tools for developing the company's marketing strategy and deciding which product lines to grow, maintain, harvest, and divest. To analyze a product line and decide how many resources to invest in it, product line managers need to look at sales and profits and market profile.

7. A company can change the product component of its marketing mix by lengthening its product via line stretching (down-market, upmarket, or both) or line filling, by modernizing its products, by featuring certain products, and by pruning its products to eliminate the least profitable.

8. Brands are often sold or marketed jointly with other brands. Ingredient brands and co-brands can add value, assuming they have equity and are perceived as fitting appropriately.

9. Physical products must be packaged and labelled. Well-designed packages can create convenience value for customers and promotional value for producers. Warranties and guarantees can offer further assurance to consumers.

APPLICATIONS

Marketing Debate: With Products, Is It Form or Function?

The form versus function debate applies in many arenas, including marketing. Some marketers believe that product performance is the be-all and end-all. Other marketers maintain that the look, feel, and other design elements of products are what really make the difference.

Take a position: Product functionality is the key to brand success *versus* Product design is the key to brand success.

Marketing Discussion: Product and Service Differentiation

Consider the different means of differentiating products and services. Which ones have the most impact on your choices? Why? Can you think of certain brands that excel on a number of these different means of differentiation?

MARKETING **EXCELLENCE**   CANADA GOOSE

For over 50 years, Canada Goose has been producing cold-weather protective gear that boasts top quality and iconic style. With its signature red Arctic Disk patch displayed on its products, the Canada Goose brand has become synonymous with polar exploration, quality, and craftsmanship. From Antarctic research facilities to the streets of Toronto, New York, Milan, or Tokyo, Canada Goose has become a globally recognized and respected brand.

From humble beginnings in a small Toronto warehouse, 50 years later Canada Goose is a world leader in the manufacturing of extreme-weather outerwear. Made in Canada, the products are tested by those most familiar with the conditions the products must withstand—from Canadian Rangers in the northern territories to oil rig workers in Alaska to researchers stationed in Antarctica. The extreme conditions demand a product on which the wearers must base their survival in some cases. Canada Goose takes that responsibility very seriously, and commitment to quality is at the core of the brand. The products are backed by a free repair or replacement lifetime warranty, showing the company's confidence in its product quality.

Having earned itself a loyal following of customers working and living in extremely cold conditions, the brand attracted a new and dissimilar audience in the world of fashion—in Hollywood. Whether the jackets were onscreen, as on Nicolas Cage in *National Treasure*, or off-screen, as on Rebecca Romijn during the production of *X-Men II*, Hollywood wardrobe consultants, to keep actors warm in cold shooting locations, found that function met fashion in Canada Goose gear. Movies often influence fashion and this case was no exception. Canada Goose recognized the opportunity and began styling its jackets to appeal to a more fashion-conscious target. Without forgetting their core market, they created a new line of fashion-forward outerwear that uses visually appealing fabrics and finishes and more flattering, tailored cuts. The line received good reviews from fashion magazines including *Elle, Flare,* and *GQ.* Today, Canada Goose jackets can be seen in trend-setting cities such as New York, Paris, and Milan, proving that the brand can be functional and aesthetic at the same time.

With the launch of Canada Goose Adventure Tours, the company further legitimizes its product quality and reliability. Every adventure takes visitors to a location where the product is already in use in everyday life, visiting people and wildlife in some of the world's most remote locations. Participants are each given a specially designed Canada Goose jacket to protect them from the elements during their unique adventure and to take home afterward as a souvenir.

With unmatched quality and style, Canada Goose products have conquered the fashionable winter wear market at home and abroad. With loyal customers in over 40 countries, Canada Goose is truly a Made in Canada, worldwide brand.

QUESTIONS

1. Which quality defines the Canada Goose brand—performance or conformance quality?

2. What is Canada Goose's primary differentiation? Did the company dilute its primary differentiation by pursuing the fashion segment?

3. If Canada Goose wanted to expand its product line, what are some new products you would recommend for the company? Should it use the same brand name for those products?

Sources: Canada Goose website, www.canada-goose.com (viewed May 17, 2011); Vivian Vassos, "Canada's Cold-Weather Couture Heats Up on the World Stage," *Calgary Herald,* October 23, 2007, p. C2; Derick Chetty, "Canada Goose Soars above the Rest," *Toronto Star,* January 28, 2010, p. L4; Eric Lam, "Made in Canada Label Has Global Cachet," *Vancouver Sun,* March 16, 2010, p. C8.

In This Chapter, We Will Address the Following **Questions**

1. How do we define and classify services, and how do they differ from goods?

2. What are the new services realities?

3. How can we achieve excellence in services marketing?

4. How can we improve service quality?

5. How can goods marketers improve customer-support services?

The unconventional Cirque du Soleil organization creates memorable experiences for its audiences through its creative redefinition of the circus concept.

Designing and Managing Services

As product companies find it harder and harder to differentiate their physical products, they turn to service differentiation. Many in fact find significant profitability in delivering superior service, whether that means on-time delivery, better and faster answering of inquiries, or quicker resolution of complaints. Top service providers know these advantages well and also know how to create memorable customer experiences.[1]

Since being founded nearly three decades ago in Baie-Saint-Paul, Quebec, by Guy Laliberté, Cirque du Soleil has continuously broken loose from circus convention. It takes traditional ingredients such as trapeze artists, clowns, muscle men, and contortionists and places them in a nontraditional setting with lavish costumes, New Age music, and spectacular stage designs. And it eliminates other commonly observed circus elements— there are no animals. Each production is loosely tied together with a theme such as "a tribute to the nomadic soul" (Varekai) or "a phantasmagoria of urban life" (Saltimbanco). The group has grown from its Quebec street-performance roots to become a half-billion-dollar global enterprise, with 3000 employees on four continents entertaining millions of audience members annually.

Part of its success comes from a company culture that encourages artistic creativity and innovation and carefully safeguards the brand. One new production is created each year, always in-house, and is unique: there are no duplicate touring companies. In addition to Cirque's mix of media and local promotion, an extensive interactive email program targets its million-plus-member Cirque Club and creates an online community of fans—20 percent to 30 percent of all ticket sales come from club members. Generating $800 million in revenue annually, the Cirque du Soleil brand has expanded to encompass a record label, a retail operation, and resident productions in Las Vegas (five in all), Orlando, Tokyo, and other cities.[2]

Because it is critical to understand the special nature of services and what that means to marketers, in this chapter we systematically analyze services and how to market them most effectively.

THE NATURE OF SERVICES

One of the megatrends of recent years has been the phenomenal growth of services. In Canada, the service sector accounts for 72 percent of the GDP, while goods-producing industries account for 28 percent. Manufacturing, which is part of the goods-producing sector, accounts for only 13 percent of the GDP. Service industries in Canada grow faster than both goods-producing industries and the economy as a whole. Service industries in Canada grew 8.4 percent during the five-year period between 2006 and 2010, while goods-producing industries declined 7 percent and overall GDP grew 3.5 percent, fuelled largely by the service sector. Some service sectors grew even more, such as retail trade, finance, and real estate, which all grew at nearly 11 percent.[3]

Similarly, the service sector is a much larger employer than the goods-producing sector. In 2010, the service sector employed 13.3 million Canadians, constituting over 78 percent of all Canadian jobs, compared with the 3.7 million people employed in the goods-producing sector.[4]

Service Industries Are Everywhere

The *government sector,* with its health care, courts, employment services, loan agencies, military services, police and fire departments, postal service, regulatory agencies, and schools, is in the service business. The *private nonprofit sector*—museums, charities, churches, colleges, foundations, and hospitals—is in the service business. A good part of the *business sector,* with its airlines, banks, hotels, insurance companies, law firms, consulting firms, motion picture companies, repair companies, and real estate firms, is in the service business. Many workers in the *manufacturing sector,* such as computer operators, accountants, and legal staff, are really service providers. In fact, they make up a "service factory" providing services to the "goods factory." And those in the *retail sector,* such as cashiers, clerks, salespeople, and customer service representatives, are also providing a service.

A **service** is any act or performance one party can offer to another and that is essentially intangible and does not result in the ownership of anything. Its production may or may not be tied to a physical product. Increasingly, manufacturers, distributors, and retailers are providing value-added services, or simply excellent customer service, to differentiate themselves. Many pure service firms are now using the Internet to reach customers; some are purely online. Monster.com's Webby Award–winning site offers online career advice and employment recruiting. Done right, improvements or innovations in customer service can have a big payoff, as Zipcar found.

Zipcar

Car sharing started in Europe as a means to extend public transportation. In the United States, the appeal of Zipcar, the market leader and pioneer, is both environmental and economic. With a $50 membership fee and rates that total less than $100 a day—which includes gas, insurance, and parking—a typical family could save $3000 to $4000 a year by substituting Zipcar use for car ownership. Zipcar's fleet includes all types of popular models—BMWs, Volvos, pickup trucks, and even MINI Coopers and the Toyota Prius hybrid—and the firm estimates that every car it adds keeps up to 20 private cars off the road. Consumers, and an increasing number of universities and businesses, book online and use a sophisticated reservation system to reserve a specific car in their neighbourhood. There are a number of rules for car care (such as no smoking) and logistics (such as calling to extend a reservation if running late). As CEO Scott Griffith states, "Our business model depends on the kindness of others." To help increase awareness, Zipcar slaps its logo on the side of all but the high-end luxury models. Unusual marketing stunts also help to spread the word, such as a contest to guess how many Swedish meatballs had been stuffed into a MINI Cooper parked in an IKEA parking lot. Targeting major cities and college towns, the company is growing about 30 percent a year.[5]

Zipcar offers its fast-growing customer base a practical, environmentally friendly alternative to car ownership.

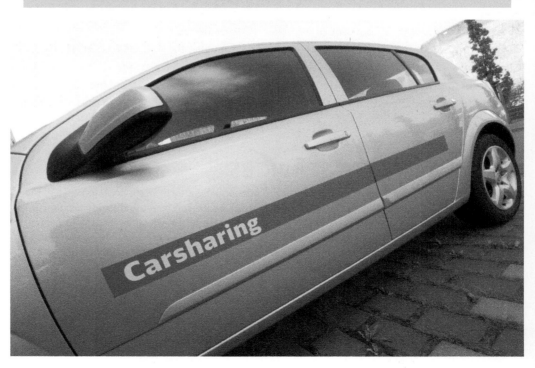

Categories of Service Mix

The service component can be a minor or a major part of the total offering. We distinguish five categories of offerings:

1. *Pure tangible good*—a tangible good such as soap, toothpaste, or salt with no accompanying services.

2. *Tangible good with accompanying services*—a tangible good, like a car, computer, or cell phone, accompanied by one or more services. Typically, the more technologically advanced the product, the greater the need for high-quality supporting services.

3. *Hybrid*—an offering, like a restaurant meal, of equal parts goods and services. People patronize restaurants for both the food and its preparation.

4. *Major service with accompanying minor goods and services*—a major service, like air travel, with additional services or supporting goods such as snacks and drinks. This offering requires a capital-intensive good—an airplane—for its realization, but the primary item is a service.

5. *Pure service*—primarily an intangible service, such as babysitting, psychotherapy, or massage.

The range of service offerings makes it difficult to generalize without a few further distinctions:

■ Services vary as to whether they are *equipment based* (automated car washes, vending machines) or *people based* (window washing, accounting services). People-based services vary by whether unskilled, skilled, or professional workers provide them.

■ Service companies can choose among different *processes* to deliver their service. Restaurants offer cafeteria-style, fast-food, buffet, and candlelight service formats.

■ Some services need the *client's presence*. Brain surgery requires the client's presence, a car repair does not. If the client must be present, the service provider must be considerate of his or her needs. Thus, beauty salon operators will invest in décor, play background music, and engage in light conversation with the client.

■ Services may meet a *personal need* (personal services) or a *business need* (business services). Service providers typically develop different marketing programs for these markets.

■ Service providers differ in their *objectives* (profit or nonprofit) and *ownership* (private or public). These two characteristics, when crossed, produce four quite different types of organizations. The marketing programs of the private Shouldice Hospital in Toronto will differ from those of the public St. Michael's Hospital in the same city.[6]

Customers typically cannot judge the technical quality of some services even after they have received them. Figure 13.1 shows various products and services according to difficulty of evaluation. At the left are goods high in *search qualities*—that is, characteristics the buyer can evaluate before purchase. In the middle are goods and services high in *experience qualities*—characteristics the buyer can evaluate after purchase. At the right are services high in *credence qualities*—characteristics the buyer normally finds hard to evaluate even after consumption.[7]

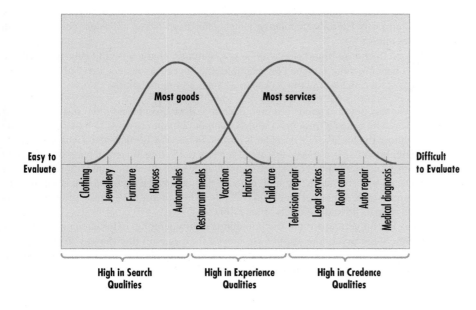

FIGURE 13.1

Continuum of Evaluation for Different Types of Products

Source: Valarie A. Zeithaml, "How Consumer Evaluation Processes Differ between Goods and Services," James H. Donnelly and William R. George, eds., *Marketing of Services* (Chicago: American Marketing Association, 1981). Reprinted with permission of the American Marketing Association.

Because services are generally high in experience and credence qualities, there is more risk in their purchase, with several consequences. First, service consumers generally rely on word of mouth rather than advertising. Second, they rely heavily on price, provider, and physical cues to judge quality. Third, they are highly loyal to service providers who satisfy them. Fourth, because switching costs are high, consumer inertia can make it challenging to entice business away from a competitor.

Distinctive Characteristics of Services

Four distinctive service characteristics greatly affect the design of marketing programs: *intangibility, inseparability, variability,* and *perishability*.[8]

INTANGIBILITY Unlike physical products, services cannot be seen, tasted, felt, heard, or smelled before they are bought. A person getting cosmetic surgery cannot see the results before the purchase, and the patient in the psychiatrist's office cannot know the exact outcome of treatment. To reduce uncertainty, buyers will look for evidence of quality by drawing inferences from the place, people, equipment, communication material, symbols, and price. Therefore, the service provider's task is to "manage the evidence," to "tangibilize the intangible."[9]

Service companies can try to demonstrate their service quality through *physical evidence* and *presentation*.[10] Suppose a bank wants to position itself as the "fast" bank. It could make this positioning strategy tangible through any number of marketing tools:

1. *Place*—The exterior and interior should have clean lines. The layout of the desks and the traffic flow should be planned carefully. Waiting lines should not get overly long.

2. *People*—Employees should be busy, but there should be a sufficient number to manage the workload.

3. *Equipment*—Computers, copy machines, desks, and ATMs should look, and be, state of the art.

4. *Communication material*—Printed materials (text and photos) should suggest efficiency and speed.

5. *Symbols*—The bank's name and symbol could suggest fast service.

6. *Price*—The bank could advertise that it will deposit $5 in the account of any customer who waits in line more than five minutes.

Service marketers must be able to transform intangible services into concrete benefits and a well-defined experience.[11] Disney is a master at "tangibilizing the intangible" and creating magical fantasies in its theme parks; so are companies such as Build-A-Bear and Indigo Books & Music in their respective retail stores.[12]

Table 13.1 measures brand experiences in general along sensory, affective, behavioural, and intellectual dimensions. Applications to services are clear.

Because there is no physical product, the service provider's facilities—its primary and secondary signage, environmental design and reception area, employee apparel, collateral material, and so on—are especially important. All aspects of the service delivery process can be branded, which is why Earl's Restaurants is concerned about the appearance of its wait staff, why UPS has developed such strong equity with its brown trucks, and why Hilton's Doubletree Hotels offer fresh-baked chocolate chip cookies to symbolize care and friendliness.[13]

Service providers often choose brand elements—logos, symbols, characters, and slogans—to make the service and its key benefits more tangible: for example, the "Because Owners Care" of WestJet, the familiar maple leaf logo of Air Canada, and the geckos in all Telus communications.

INSEPARABILITY Whereas physical goods are manufactured, then inventoried, then distributed, and later consumed, services are typically produced and consumed simultaneously.[14] A haircut can't be stored, or produced without the barber. The provider is part of the service. Because the client is also often present, provider–client interaction is a special feature of services marketing. Buyers of entertainment and professional services are very interested in the specific provider. It's not the same concert if Justin Bieber is indisposed and replaced by Usher, although both are very popular, or if a legal defence is supplied by an intern because defence expert James Lockyer is unavailable. When clients have strong provider preferences, the provider can raise its price to ration its limited time.

Several strategies exist for getting around the limitations of inseparability. The service provider can work with larger groups; some psychotherapists have moved from one-on-one therapy to small-group therapy to groups of over 300 people in a large hotel ballroom. The service provider can work faster; the psychotherapist can spend 30 more efficient minutes with each patient instead of 50 less-structured minutes

TABLE 13.1	DIMENSIONS OF BRAND EXPERIENCE

Sensory

- This brand makes a strong impression on my visual sense or other senses.

- I find this brand interesting in a sensory way.

- This brand does not appeal to my senses.

Affective

- This brand induces feelings and sentiments.

- I do not have strong emotions for this brand.

- This brand is an emotional brand.

Behavioral

- I engage in physical actions and behaviors when I use this brand.

- This brand results in bodily experiences.

- This brand is not action-oriented.

Intellectual

- I engage in a lot of thinking when I encounter this brand.

- This brand does not make me think.

- This brand stimulates my curiosity and problem solving.

Source: Joško Brakus, Bernd H. Schmitt, and Lia Zarantonello, "Brand Experience: What Is It? How Is It Measured? Does It Affect Loyalty?" *Journal of Marketing, 73* (May 2009): 52–68. Reprinted with permission from *Journal of Marketing*, published by the American Marketing Association.

and thus see more patients. The service organization can train more service providers and build up client confidence, as H&R Block has done with its national network of trained tax consultants.

Creative artists such as Michael Bublé have developed ways to connect with their customers when the artists are, or are not, providing their service.

Michael Bublé stays in touch with his fans even when he is not on stage.

Michael Bublé

Multiplatinum artist Michael Bublé was born and raised in British Columbia. As a child, he was introduced to music and inspired by his grandfather. In 2003, Bublé's self-titled album was released, earning him numerous awards including two Grammys and a Juno. Bublé is known for his showmanship combined with humbleness. His show is designed to please his fans, and he makes sure that connection is personal by talking to the audience, joking around, and being very casual on stage. His popularity has resulted in sold-out crowds at major stages from Madison Square Garden in New York to the O2 arena in London, England. Bublé has begun a website called "The Daily Bublé," where fans can get up-to-date information on all things Michael Bublé. The site has a presence on Facebook and Twitter, as well as an app for fans to share their tour experiences with him and other fans.[15]

VARIABILITY Because the quality of services depends on who provides them, when and where, and to whom, services are highly variable. Some doctors have an excellent bedside manner; others are less empathic.

Service buyers are aware of this variability and often talk to others before selecting a service provider. To reassure customers, some firms offer *service guarantees* that may reduce consumer perceptions of risk.[16] Here are three steps service firms can take to increase quality control:

1. *Invest in good hiring and training procedures.* Recruiting the right employees and providing them with excellent training is crucial, regardless of whether employees are highly skilled professionals or low-skilled workers. Better-trained personnel exhibit six characteristics: competence, courtesy, credibility, reliability, responsiveness, and communication.[17] Fairmont Hotels demonstrates its commitment to employees through a variety of training opportunities, ranging from courses on finance to food preparation.[18]

2. *Standardize the service-performance process throughout the organization.* A *service blueprint* can map out the service process, the points of customer contact, and the evidence of service from the customer's point of view.[19] Figure 13.2 shows a service blueprint for a guest spending a night at a hotel. Behind the scenes, the hotel must skillfully help the guest move from one step to the next. Service blueprints can be helpful in developing new services, supporting a zero-defects culture, and devising service recovery strategies.

3. *Monitor customer satisfaction.* Employ suggestion and complaint systems, customer surveys, and comparison shopping. Customer needs may vary in different areas, allowing firms to develop region-specific customer satisfaction programs.[20] Firms can also develop customer information databases and systems for more personalized service, especially online.[21]

Because services are a subjective experience, service firms can also design marketing communication and information programs so consumers learn more about the brand than what they get from service encounters alone.

PERISHABILITY Services cannot be stored, so their perishability can be a problem when demand fluctuates. Public transportation companies must own much more equipment because of rush-hour demand than if demand were even throughout the day. Some doctors charge patients for missed appointments because the service value (the doctor's availability) exists only at the time of the appointment.

FIGURE 13.2

Blueprint for Overnight Hotel Stay

Source: Valarie Zeithaml, Mary Jo Bitner, and Dwayne D. Gremler, *Services Marketing: Integrating Customer Focus across the Firm*, 4th ed. (New York: McGraw-Hill, 2006).*

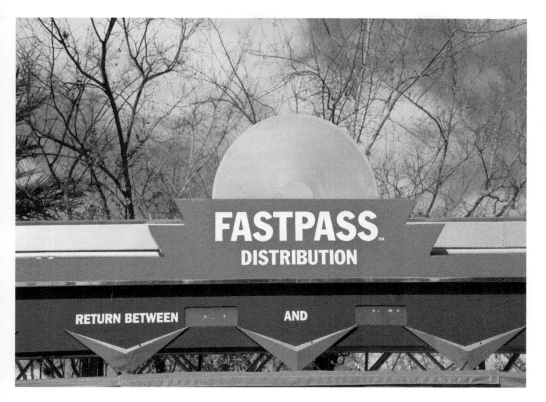

Disney's innovative FASTPASS system helps to match supply and demand for its Disney World theme park rides.

Demand or yield management is critical—the right services must be available to the right customers at the right places at the right times and right prices to maximize profitability. Several strategies can produce a better match between service demand and supply.[22] Here are some demand-side strategies:

- *Differential pricing* will shift some demand from peak to off-peak periods. Examples include low matinee movie prices and weekend discounts for car rentals.[23]

- *Nonpeak demand* can be cultivated. McDonald's pushes breakfast service, and hotels promote mini-vacation weekends.

- *Complementary services* can provide alternatives to waiting customers, such as cocktail lounges in restaurants and automated teller machines in banks.

- *Reservation systems* are a way to manage the demand level. Airlines, hotels, and physicians employ them extensively.

Here are some supply-side strategies:

- *Part-time employees* can serve peak demand. Universities add sessional instructors when enrollment goes up; stores hire extra clerks during holiday periods.

- *Peak-time efficiency* routines can allow employees to perform only essential tasks during peak periods. Paramedics assist physicians during busy periods.

- *Increased consumer participation* frees service providers' time. Consumers fill out their own medical records or bag their own groceries.

- *Shared services* can improve offerings. Several hospitals can share medical-equipment purchases.

- *Facilities for future expansion* can be a good investment. An amusement park buys surrounding land for later development.

Many airlines, hotels, and resorts email short-term discounts and special promotions to self-selected customers. After 40 years of making people stand in line at its theme parks, Disney instituted FASTPASS, which allows visitors to reserve a spot in line and eliminate the wait. Polls revealed 95 percent like the change. Disney's vice-president, Dale Stafford, told a reporter, "We have been teaching people how to stand in line since 1955, and now we are telling them they don't have to. Of all the things we can do and all the marvels we can create with the attractions, this is something that will have a profound effect on the entire industry."[24]

THE NEW SERVICE REALITIES

Service firms once lagged behind manufacturers in their use of marketing because they were small, they were professional businesses that did not use marketing, or they faced large demand or little competition. This has certainly changed. Some of the most skilled marketers now are service firms. One that wins praise for its marketing success is Singapore Airlines.

Singapore Airlines (SIA)

Singapore Airlines is consistently recognized as the world's "best" airline—it wins so many awards, it has to update its website monthly to keep up to date—in large part due to its stellar holistic marketing. Famous for pampering passengers, SIA constantly strives to create a "wow effect" and surpass customers' expectations. It was the first to launch individual video screens for passengers. Thanks to the first-of-its-kind $1 million simulator SIA built to mimic the air pressure and humidity inside a plane, the carrier found that taste buds change in the air and that, among other things, it needed to cut back on spices in its food. SIA places a high value on training; its "Transforming Customer Service (TCS)" program includes staff in five key operational areas: cabin crew, engineering, ground services, flight operations, and sales support. The TCS culture is also embedded in all management training, company-wide. It applies a 40-30-30 rule in its holistic approach to people, processes, and products: 40 percent of resources go to training and invigorating staff, 30 percent to reviewing process and procedures, and 30 percent to creating new product and service ideas. With its innovatively designed Boeing 777-300 ERS and Airbus A380 planes, SIA set new standards of comfort in all classes of service, from eight private minirooms in first class to wider seats, AC power supplies, and USB ports in coach.[25]

A Shifting Customer Relationship

Not all companies, however, have invested in providing superior service, at least not to all customers. In many service industries, such as airlines, banks, stores, and hotels, customer satisfaction has not significantly improved—or in some cases has actually dropped—in recent years.[26] Customers complain about inaccurate information; unresponsive, rude, or poorly trained workers; and long wait times. Even worse, many find their complaints never actually reach a live human being because of slow or faulty phone or online reporting systems.

It doesn't have to be that way. For instance, 55 operators handle 100 000 calls a year on Butterball Turkeys' 1-800 number—10 000 on Thanksgiving Day alone—about how to prepare, cook, and serve turkeys. Trained at Butterball University, the operators have all cooked turkeys dozens of different ways and can handle the myriad queries that come their way, including why customers shouldn't stash turkeys in snowbanks or thaw them in bathtubs.[27]

Savvy service marketers are recognizing the new service realities, such as the importance of the newly empowered customer, customer co-production, and the need to engage employees as well as customers.

CUSTOMER EMPOWERMENT Customers are becoming more sophisticated about buying product support services and are pressing for unbundled services. They may desire separate prices for each service element and the right to select the elements they want. Customers also increasingly dislike having to deal with a multitude of service providers handling different types of equipment. Some third-party service organizations now service a greater range of equipment.

Most importantly, the Internet has empowered customers by letting them vent their rage about bad service—or reward good service—and send their comments around the world with a mouse click. Although a person who has a good customer experience is more likely to talk about it, someone who has a bad experience will talk to more people.[28] Ninety percent of angry customers reported sharing their story with a friend. Now, they can share their stories with strangers too. At PlanetFeedback.com, shoppers can send a complaint, compliment, suggestion, or question directly to a company, with the option to post comments publicly on the site as well.

Most companies respond quickly. Comcast allows contact 24/7 by phone and e-chat but also reaches out to customers and monitors blogs, websites, and social media. If employees see a customer report a problem on a blog, they get in touch and offer help. Email responses to customers must be implemented properly to be effective. One expert believes companies should (1) send an automated reply to tell customers when a more complete answer will arrive (ideally within 24 hours), (2) ensure the subject line always contains the company name, (3) make the message easy to scan for relevant information, and (4) give customers an easy way to respond with follow-up questions.[29]

More important than simply responding to a disgruntled customer, however, is preventing dissatisfaction from occurring in the future. That may mean simply taking the time to nurture customer relationships and give customers attention from a real person. Columbia Records spent $10 million to improve its call centre, and customers who phone the company can now opt out to reach an operator at any point in their call. JetBlue took a service disaster during a storm in New York, when it left hundreds of passengers stranded aboard grounded aircraft, and used it to improve its customer service approach of compensating passengers for such delays.

CUSTOMER CO-PRODUCTION The reality is that customers do not merely purchase and use a service; they play an active role in its delivery.[30] Their words and actions affect the quality of their service experiences and those of others, and the productivity of front-line employees.

Customers often feel they derive more value, and feel a stronger connection to the service provider, if they are actively involved in the service process. This co-production can put stress on employees, however, and reduce their satisfaction, especially if they differ culturally or in other ways from customers.[31] Moreover, one study estimated that one-third of all service problems are caused by the customer.[32] The growing shift to self-service technologies will likely increase this percentage.

Preventing service failures is crucial, since recovery is always challenging. One of the biggest problems is attribution—customers often feel the firm is at fault or, even if not, that it is still responsible for righting any wrongs. Unfortunately, although many firms have well-designed and well-executed procedures to deal with their own failures, they find managing *customer* failures—when a service problem arises from a customer's lack of understanding or ineptitude—much more difficult. Figure 13.3 displays the four broad causes of customer failures. Solutions come in all forms, as these examples show:[33]

1. *Redesign processes and redefine customer roles to simplify service encounters.* One of the keys to Netflix's success was that it charged a flat fee and allowed customers to return DVDs by mail at their leisure, giving customers greater control and flexibility. Now, Netflix has simplified its service even further by live streaming through the subscriber's TV.

2. *Incorporate the right technology to aid employees and customers.* Mountain Equipment Co-op keeps a virtual copy of purchase information in case customers are unable to produce a receipt needed for a return.

3. *Create high-performance customers by enhancing their role clarity, motivation, and ability.* SAP offers training for companies that implement its latest SAP solutions, so that they can get the best out of using them. In addition, training reduces potential frustration with using a new, unfamiliar product.

4. *Encourage "customer citizenship" so that customers help customers.* At golf courses, players can not only follow the rules by playing and behaving appropriately, they can encourage others to do so.

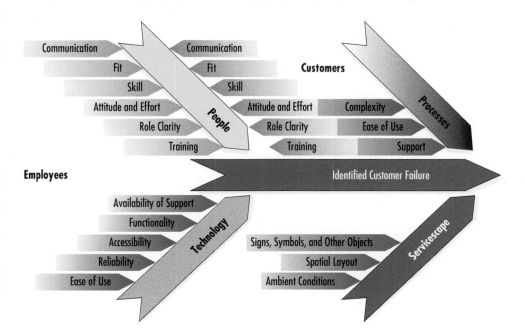

FIGURE 13.3

Root Causes of Customer Failure

Source: Stephen Tax, Mark Colgate, and David Bowen, *MIT Sloan Management Review* (Spring 2006): pp. 30–38. From *MIT Sloan Management* Review © 2006 by Massachusetts Institute of Technology. All rights reserved. Distributed by Tribune Media Services.

SATISFYING EMPLOYEES AS WELL AS CUSTOMERS Excellent service companies know that positive employee attitudes will promote stronger customer loyalty.[34] Instilling a strong customer orientation in employees can also increase their job satisfaction and commitment, especially if they have high customer contact. Employees thrive in customer-contact positions when they have an internal drive to (1) pamper customers, (2) accurately read customer needs, (3) develop a personal relationship with customers, and (4) deliver quality service to solve customers' problems.[35]

Consistent with this reasoning, Sears found a high correlation between customer satisfaction, employee satisfaction, and store profitability. In companies such as Hallmark, John Deere, and Four Seasons Hotels, employees exhibit real company pride. The downside of not treating employees right is significant. A survey of 10 000 employees from 1000 large companies found that 40 percent of workers cited "lack of recognition" as a key reason for leaving a job.[36]

Given the importance of positive employee attitudes to customer satisfaction, service companies must attract the best employees they can find. They need to market a career rather than just a job. They must design a sound training program and provide support and rewards for good performance. They can use an intranet, internal newsletters, daily reminders, and employee roundtables to reinforce customer-centred attitudes. Finally, they must audit employee job satisfaction regularly.

The California-based Panda Express restaurant chain has management turnover that's half the industry average, due in part to a combination of ample bonuses and health benefits with a strong emphasis on worker self-improvement through meditation, education, and hobbies. Special wellness seminars and get-to-know-you events outside work help to create a caring, nurturing atmosphere.[37]

ACHIEVING EXCELLENCE IN SERVICES MARKETING

The increased importance of the service industry has sharpened the focus on what it takes to excel in the marketing of services.[38] Here are some guidelines.

Marketing Excellence

Marketing excellence with services requires excellence in three broad areas: external, internal, and interactive marketing (see Figure 13.4).[39]

- *External marketing* describes the normal work of preparing, pricing, distributing, and promoting the service to customers.

- *Internal marketing* describes training and motivating employees to serve customers well. The most important contribution the marketing department can make is arguably to be "exceptionally clever in getting everyone else in the organization to practice marketing."[40]

- *Interactive marketing* describes the employees' skill in serving the client. Clients judge service not only by its *technical quality* (Was the surgery successful?), but also by its *functional quality* (Did the surgeon show concern and inspire confidence?).[41]

FIGURE 13.4

Three Types of Marketing in Service Industries

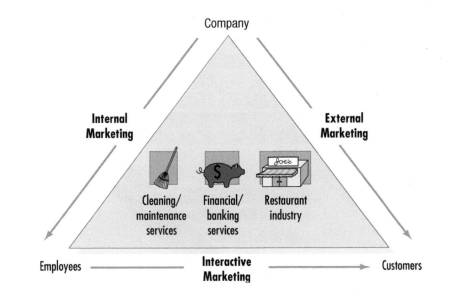

In interactive marketing, teamwork is often key, and delegating authority to front-line employees can allow for greater service flexibility and adaptability through better problem solving, closer employee co-operation, and more efficient knowledge transfer.[42] Sears Canada has invested in workforce automation geared at improving service technician productivity.

Sears Canada

When Sears Canada automated its HomeCentral workforce, it eliminated the burden of paperwork. Real-time, wireless dispatch and mobile workforce automation solution from Mobile Computing Corporation enabled service technicians to connect with company information systems over a secure network. Service technicians have quick access to service information, such as route sheets, and can update information from their handheld units. Sears Canada's goal in implementing automation is to improve productivity, increase customer service, and reduce costs.[43]

Technology also has great power to make service workers more productive. Since Air Canada deployed self-service kiosks across Canadian airports, passenger check-in time has dropped by 80 percent. In addition, the airline has realized significant cost savings due to reduced customer–agent processing interactions, as the kiosk either automates the process or allows passengers to do it themselves.[44]

Sometimes new technology has unanticipated benefits. When BMW introduced Wi-Fi to its dealerships to help customers pass the time more productively while their cars were being serviced, more customers chose to stay rather than use loaner cars, an expensive item for dealers to maintain.[45]

Companies must avoid pushing productivity so hard, however, that they reduce perceived quality. Some methods lead to too much standardization. Service providers must deliver "high touch" as well as "high tech." Amazon.ca has some of the most amazing technological innovations in online retailing, but it also keeps customers extremely satisfied when a problem arises even if they don't actually talk to an Amazon.ca employee.[46]

The Internet lets firms improve their service offerings and strengthen their relationships with customers by allowing for true interactivity, customer-specific and situational personalization, and real-time adjustments of the firm's offerings.[47] But as companies collect, store, and use more information about customers, they have also raised concerns about security and privacy.[48] Companies must incorporate the proper safeguards and reassure customers about company efforts to protect customer privacy and provide a secure online shopping environment.

Best Practices of Top Service Companies

In achieving marketing excellence with their customers, well-managed service companies share a strategic concept, a history of top-management commitment to quality, high standards, profit tiers, and systems for monitoring service performance and customer complaints.

STRATEGIC CONCEPT Top service companies are customer obsessed. They have a clear sense of their target customers and their needs and have developed a distinctive strategy for satisfying these needs. At the Four Seasons luxury hotel chain, employees must pass four interviews before being hired. Each hotel also employs a "guest historian" to track guest preferences.

After surveying more than 200 000 international passengers, the Airports Council International granted the Halifax Stanfield International Airport, which handles over 3 million passengers annually, a 2007 Airport People Award. In fact, in 2010 it was ranked as the world's best airport for overall passenger satisfaction in the under-5-million-passengers category for the seventh straight year. To earn this award, the airport—which has been rated by passengers as having the most courteous and helpful airport, airline, and security staff—had to demonstrate that it had developed a strong customer-service culture across the entire airport community.[49]

TOP-MANAGEMENT COMMITMENT Companies such as Disney, Fairmont, and Canadian Tire have a thorough commitment to service quality. Their management groups look monthly not only at financial performance, but also at service performance. Ray Kroc of McDonald's insisted on continuously measuring each McDonald's outlet on its conformance to QSCV: quality, service, cleanliness, and value. Some companies insert a reminder along with employees' paycheques: "brought to you by the customer." Sam Walton of Walmart required the following employee pledge: "I solemnly swear and declare that every customer that comes within 10 feet of me, I will smile, look them in the eye, and greet them, so help me Sam."

HIGH STANDARDS The best service providers set high quality standards. In 1961, Royal Bank was the first financial institution in Canada to install a computer. Since that time, it has leveraged technology to enable its staff to provide superior customer service anywhere, at any time. The standards must be set *appropriately* high. A 98 percent accuracy standard may sound good, but it would result in 64 000 lost FedEx packages a day; 6 misspelled words on each page of a book; 400 000 incorrectly filled prescriptions daily; 800 000 lost Canada Post mail pieces each day; no phone, Internet, or electricity 8 days per year or 29 minutes per day; 1000 mislabelled or (mispriced) products at a supermarket; and nearly 700 000 people unaccounted for in a Canadian census.

PROFIT TIERS Firms have decided to raise fees and lower services for those customers who barely pay their way, and to coddle big spenders to retain their patronage as long as possible. Customers in high-profit tiers get special discounts, promotional offers, and lots of special service; customers in lower-profit tiers may get more fees, stripped-down service, and voice messages to process their inquiries.

During the recent economic downturn, online retailer Zappos decided to stop offering complimentary overnight shipping to first-time buyers and offer it to repeat buyers only. The money saved was invested in a new VIP service for the company's most loyal customers.[50] Companies that provide differentiated levels of service must be careful about claiming superior service, however—customers who receive lesser treatment will bad-mouth the company and injure its reputation. Delivering services that maximize both customer satisfaction and company profitability can be challenging.

MONITORING SYSTEMS Top firms audit service performance, both their own and competitors', on a regular basis. They collect *voice of the customer (VOC) measurements* to probe customer satisfiers and dissatisfiers. They use comparison shopping, mystery or ghost shopping, customer surveys, suggestion and complaint forms, service-audit teams, and customers' letters to the president.

We can judge services on *customer importance* and *company performance*. *Importance–performance analysis* rates the various elements of the service bundle and identifies required actions.

Table 13.2 shows how customers rated 14 service elements or attributes of an automobile dealer's service department on importance and performance. For example, "Job done right the first time" (attribute 1) received a mean importance rating of 3.83 and a mean performance rating of 2.63, indicating that customers felt it was highly important but not performed well. The ratings of the 14 elements are divided into four sections in Figure 13.5:

■ Quadrant A in the figure shows important service elements that are not being performed at the desired levels: elements 1, 2, and 9. The dealer should concentrate on improving the service department's performance of these elements.

■ Quadrant B shows important service elements that are being performed well; the company needs to maintain the high performance.

FIGURE 13.5

Importance–Performance
Analysis

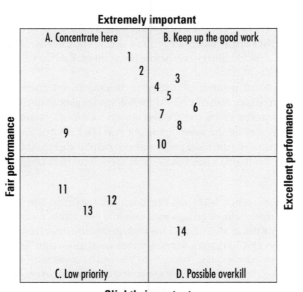

TABLE 13.2	CUSTOMER IMPORTANCE AND PERFORMANCE RATINGS FOR AN AUTO DEALERSHIP		
Attribute Number	Attribute Description	Mean Importance Rating[a]	Mean Performance Rating[b]
1	Job done right the first time	3.83	2.63
2	Fast action on complaints	3.63	2.73
3	Prompt warranty work	3.60	3.15
4	Able to do any job needed	3.56	3.00
5	Service available when needed	3.41	3.05
6	Courteous and friendly service	3.41	3.29
7	Car ready when promised	3.38	3.03
8	Perform only necessary work	3.37	3.11
9	Low prices on service	3.29	2.00
10	Clean up after service work	3.27	3.02
11	Convenient to home	2.52	2.25
12	Convenient to work	2.43	2.49
13	Courtesy buses and cars	2.37	2.35
14	Send out maintenance notices	2.05	3.33

[a] Ratings obtained from a four-point scale of "extremely important" (4), "important" (3), "slightly important" (2), and "not important" (1).

[b] Ratings obtained from a four-point scale of "excellent" (4), "good" (3), "fair" (2), and "poor" (1). A "no basis for judgment" category was also provided.

- Quadrant C shows minor service elements that are being delivered in a mediocre way but do not need any attention.

- Quadrant D shows that a minor service element, "Send out maintenance notices," is being performed in an excellent manner.

Perhaps the company should spend less on sending out maintenance notices and use the savings to improve performance on important elements. Management can enhance its analysis by checking competitors' performance levels on each element.[51]

SATISFYING CUSTOMER COMPLAINTS On average, 40 percent of customers who suffer through a bad service experience stop doing business with the company.[52] But if those customers are willing to complain first, they actually offer the company a gift if the complaint is handled well.

Companies that encourage disappointed customers to complain—and also empower employees to remedy the situation on the spot—have been shown to achieve higher revenues and greater profits than companies without a systematic approach for addressing service failures.[53] Pizza Hut prints its toll-free number on all pizza boxes. When a customer complains, Pizza Hut sends a voice mail to the store manager, who must call the customer within 48 hours and resolve the complaint.

Getting front-line employees to adopt *extra-role behaviours,* and to advocate the interests and image of the firm to consumers, as well as take initiative and engage in conscientious behaviour in dealing with customers, can be a critical asset in handling complaints.[54] Customers evaluate complaint incidents in terms of the outcomes they receive, the procedures used to arrive at those outcomes, and the nature of interpersonal treatment during the process.[55]

Differentiating Services

Finally, customers who view a service as fairly homogeneous care less about the provider than about the price. Marketing excellence requires service marketers to continuously differentiate their brands so that they are not seen as a commodity.

PRIMARY AND SECONDARY SERVICE OPTIONS Marketers can differentiate their service offerings in many ways, through people and processes that add value. What the customer expects is called the *primary service package.* Vanguard, the second-largest U.S. no-load mutual fund company, has a unique client ownership structure that lowers costs and permits better fund returns. Strongly differentiated from many competitors, the brand grew through word of mouth, PR, and viral marketing.[56]

The provider can add *secondary service features* to the package. In the hotel industry, various chains have introduced such secondary service features as merchandise for sale, free breakfast buffets, and loyalty programs.

The major challenge is that most service offerings and innovations are easily copied. Still, the company that regularly introduces innovations will gain a succession of temporary advantages over competitors. See how Amica is differentiating itself in its industry.

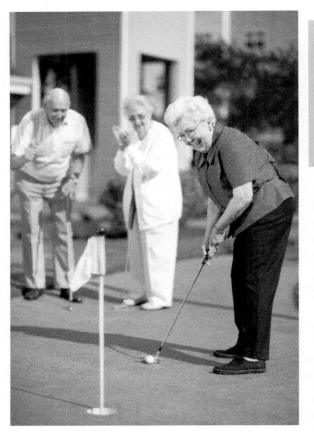

Amica differentiates by offering luxurious, resort-like retirement homes.

Amica Mature Lifestyles

Vancouver-based Amica Mature Lifestyles is redesigning the concept of mature lifestyles and senior homes. There are 25 Amica residences throughout British Columbia and Ontario, with more in the development stage. Amica is dedicated to creating luxurious retirement residences with a more service-oriented focus. Amica residences resemble a five-star resort hotel, with concierge desks, elegant fine dining, outdoor gardens and patios, private dining rooms, English-style pubs, fireside lounges, fitness centres, libraries, corner stores, barber shops, salons, putting greens, pools, greenhouses, and spas.[57]

INNOVATION WITH SERVICES Innovation is as vital in services as in any industry. After years of losing customers to its Hilton and Marriott hotel competitors, Starwood decided to invest $1.7 billion in its Sheraton chain of 400 properties worldwide to give them fresher décor, brighter colours, and more enticing lobbies, restaurants, and cafés. In explaining the need for the makeover, one hospitality industry expert noted, "There was a time when Sheraton was one of the leading brands. But it lagged in introducing new design and service concepts and developed a level of inconsistency."[58]

On the other hand, consider how these relatively new service categories emerged and how, in some cases, organizations offered creative solutions in existing categories:

■ *Online travel.* Online travel agents such as Expedia and Travelocity offer customers the opportunity to conveniently book travel at discount prices. However, they make money only when visitors go to their websites and book travel. Kayak is a newer online travel agency that applies the Google business model of collecting money on a per-click basis. Kayak's marketing emphasis is on building a better search engine by offering more alternatives, flexibility, and airlines.[59]

■ *Banking.* President's Choice Financial, a financial institution of the Loblaw Companies, offers various financial products via a tie-up with CIBC. Through PC Financial's various products, customers can earn PC points, which can be redeemed for products at Loblaw-affiliated stores, drawing those customers into those stores. One can earn even more points by using the PC MasterCard for those purchases. With this bidirectional arrangement, sales of its financial products helps its store sales, and vice versa.

■ *Private aviation.* Initially, private aviation was restricted to owning or chartering a private plane. Fractional ownership pioneered by Ohio-based NetJets allowed customers to pay a percentage of the cost of a private plane plus maintenance and a direct hourly cost. Marquis Jets further innovated with a simple idea of combining prepaid time on NetJets' fleet for as little as 25 hours, offering the consistency and benefits of fractional ownership without the long-term commitment.[60]

Many companies are using the web to offer primary or secondary service features that were never possible before. Salesforce.com uses cloud computing—centralized computing services delivered over the Internet—to run customer management databases for companies. Häagen-Dazs estimated it would have had to spend US$65 000 for a custom-designed database to stay in contact with the company's retail franchises across the country. Instead, it spent only $20 000 to set up an account with Salesforce.com and pays $125 per month for 20 users to remotely monitor franchises via the web.[61]

MANAGING SERVICE QUALITY

The service quality of a firm is tested at each service encounter. If employees are bored, cannot answer simple questions, or are visiting each other while customers are waiting, customers will think twice about doing business there again.

Service outcome and customer loyalty are influenced by a host of variables. One study identified more than 800 critical behaviours that cause customers to switch services.[62] These behaviours fall into eight categories (see Table 13.3).

A more recent study homed in on the service dimensions customers would most like companies to measure. As Table 13.4 shows, good value, first-contact resolution, and knowledgeable employees who ensure that their customers feel valued rose to the top.[63]

Flawless service delivery is the ideal state for any service organization. "Marketing Memo: Recommendations for Improving Service Quality" offers a comprehensive set of guidelines to which top service marketing organizations can adhere. Two important considerations in service delivery are managing customer expectations and incorporating self-service technologies.

Managing Customer Expectations

Customers form service expectations from many sources, such as past experiences, word of mouth, and advertising. In general, customers compare the *perceived service* with the *expected service.*[64] If the perceived service falls below the expected service, customers are disappointed. Successful companies add benefits to their offering that not only *satisfy* customers but also surprise and *delight* them. Delighting customers is a matter of exceeding expectations.[65]

The service-quality model in Figure 13.6 highlights the main requirements for delivering high service quality.[66] It identifies five gaps that cause unsuccessful delivery:

1. *Gap between consumer expectation and management perception*—Management does not always correctly perceive what customers want. Hospital administrators may think patients want better food, but patients may be more concerned with nurse responsiveness.

TABLE 13.3 | FACTORS LEADING TO CUSTOMER SWITCHING BEHAVIOUR

Pricing

- High price
- Price increases
- Unfair pricing
- Deceptive pricing

Inconvenience

- Location/hours
- Wait for appointment
- Wait for service

Core Service Failure

- Service mistakes
- Billing errors
- Service catastrophe

Service Encounter Failures

- Uncaring
- Impolite

- Unresponsive
- Unknowledgeable

Response to Service Failure

- Negative response
- No response
- Reluctant response

Competition

- Found better service

Ethical Problems

- Cheat
- Hard sell
- Unsafe
- Conflict of interest

Involuntary Switching

- Customer moved
- Provider closed

Source: Susan M. Keaveney, "Customer Switching Behavior in Service Industries: An Exploratory Study," *Journal of Marketing*, April 1995, pp. 71–82. Reprinted with permission from *Journal of Marketing*, published by the American Marketing Association.

TABLE 13.4	DIMENSIONS OF SERVICE CUSTOMERS WANT COMPANIES TO DELIVER

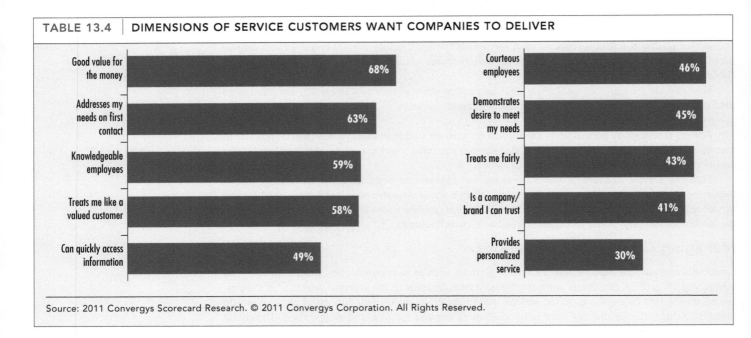

MARKETING **MEMO**	RECOMMENDATIONS FOR IMPROVING SERVICE QUALITY

Pioneers in conducting academic service research, Berry, Parasuraman, and Zeithaml offer 10 lessons they maintain are essential for improving service quality across service industries.

1. *Listening*—Service providers should understand what customers really want through continuous learning about the expectations and perceptions of customers and noncustomers (for instance, by means of a service-quality information system).

2. *Reliability*—Reliability is the single most important dimension of service quality and must be a service priority.

3. *Basic service*—Service companies must deliver the basics and do what they are supposed to do—keep promises, use common sense, listen to customers, keep customers informed, and be determined to deliver value to customers.

4. *Service design*—Service providers should take a holistic view of the service while managing its many details.

5. *Recovery*—To satisfy customers who encounter a service problem, service companies should encourage customers to complain (and make it easy for them to do so), respond quickly and personally, and develop a problem-resolution system.

6. *Surprising customers*—Although reliability is the most important dimension in *meeting* customers' service expectations, process dimensions such as assurance, responsiveness, and empathy are most important in *exceeding* customer expectations, for example, by surprising them with uncommon swiftness, grace, courtesy, competence, commitment, and understanding.

7. *Fair play*—Service companies must make special efforts to *be* fair, and to *demonstrate* fairness, to customers and employees.

8. *Teamwork*—Teamwork is what enables large organizations to deliver service with care and attentiveness by improving employee motivation and capabilities.

9. *Employee research*—Marketers should conduct research with employees to reveal why service problems occur and what companies must do to solve problems.

10. *Servant leadership*—Quality service comes from inspired leadership throughout the organization; from excellent service-system design; from the effective use of information and technology; and from a slow-to-change, invisible, all-powerful, internal force called corporate culture.

Sources: Leonard L. Berry, A. Parasuraman, and Valarie A. Zeithaml, "Ten Lessons for Improving Service Quality," MSI Reports Working Paper Series, No.03-001 (Cambridge, MA: Marketing Science Institute, 2003), pp. 61–82. See also Leonard L. Berry's books *On Great Service: A Framework for Action* (New York: The Free Press, 2006) and *Discovering the Soul of Service* (New York: The Free Press, 1999), as well as some of his articles: Leonard L. Berry, Venkatesh Shankar, Janet Parish, Susan Cadwallader, and Thomas Dotzel, "Creating New Markets through Service Innovation," *Sloan Management Review*, Winter 2006, pp. 56–63; Leonard L. Berry, Stephan H. Haeckel, and Lewis P. Carbone, "How to Lead the Customer Experience," *Marketing Management*, January–February 2003, pp. 18–23; and Leonard L. Berry, Kathleen Seiders, and Dhruv Grewal, "Understanding Service Convenience," *Journal of Marketing*, July 2002, pp. 1–17.

CHAPTER 13 Designing and Managing Services 347

FIGURE 13.6

Service-Quality Model

Source: A. Parasuraman, Valarie A. Zeithaml, and Leonard L. Berry, "A Conceptual Model of Service Quality and Its Implications for Future Research," *Journal of Marketing*, Fall 1985, p. 44. Reprinted with permission of the American Marketing Association. The model is more fully discussed or elaborated in Valarie Zeithaml, Mary Jo Bitner, and Dwayne D. Gremler, *Services Marketing: Integrating Customer Focus across the Firm*, 4th ed. (New York: McGraw-Hill, 2006).*

2. *Gap between management perception and service-quality specification*—Management might correctly perceive customers' wants but not set a performance standard. Hospital administrators may tell the nurses to give "fast" service without specifying it in minutes.

3. *Gap between service-quality specifications and service delivery*—Employees might be poorly trained, or incapable of meeting or unwilling to meet the standard; they may be held to conflicting standards, such as taking time to listen to customers and serving them fast.

4. *Gap between service delivery and external communications*—Consumer expectations are affected by statements made by company representatives and ads. If a hospital brochure shows a beautiful room but the patient finds it to be cheap and tacky looking, external communications have distorted the customer's expectations.

5. *Gap between perceived service and expected service*—This gap occurs when the consumer misperceives the service quality. The physician may keep visiting the patient to show care, but the patient may interpret this as an indication that something really is wrong.

Based on this service-quality model, researchers identified five determinants of service quality, in this order of importance:[67]

1. *Reliability*—The ability to perform the promised service dependably and accurately.

2. *Responsiveness*—Willingness to help customers and provide prompt service.

3. *Assurance*—The knowledge and courtesy of employees and their ability to convey trust and confidence.

4. *Empathy*—The provision of caring, individualized attention to customers.

5. *Tangibles*—The appearance of physical facilities, equipment, personnel, and communication materials.

Based on these five factors, the researchers developed the 21-item SERVQUAL scale (see Table 13.5). They also note there is a *zone of tolerance,* or a range where a service dimension would be deemed satisfactory, anchored by the minimum level consumers are willing to accept and the level they believe can and should be delivered.

The service-quality model in Figure 13.6 highlights some of the gaps that cause unsuccessful service delivery. Subsequent research has extended the model. One *dynamic process model* of service quality is based on the premise that customer perceptions and expectations of service quality change over time, but at any one point they are a function of prior expectations about what *will* and what *should* happen during the service encounter, as well as the *actual* service delivered during the last contact. Tests of the dynamic process model reveal that the two different types of expectations have a similar effect on perceptions of service quality:

1. *Increasing* customer expectations of what the firm *will* deliver can lead to improved perceptions of overall service quality.

2. *Decreasing* customer expectations of what the firm *should* deliver can also lead to improved perceptions of overall service quality.[68]

Much work has validated the role of expectations in consumers' interpretations and evaluations of the service encounter and in the relationship consumers adopt with a firm over time.[69] Consumers are often forward-looking with respect to their decision to keep or switch from a service relationship. Any marketing activity that affects current or expected future usage can help to solidify a service relationship.

With continuously provided services, such as public utilities, health care, financial and computing services, insurance, and other professional, membership, or subscription services, customers have been observed to mentally calculate their *payment equity*—the perceived economic benefits in relationship to the economic costs. In other words, customers ask themselves, "Am I using this service enough, given what I pay for it?"

Long-term service relationships can have a dark side. An ad agency client may feel that over time the agency is losing objectivity, becoming stale in its thinking, or beginning to take advantage of the relationship.[70]

TABLE 13.5 | SERVQUAL ATTRIBUTES

Reliability
- Providing service as promised
- Dependability in handling customers' service problems
- Performing services right the first time
- Providing services at the promised time
- Maintaining error-free records
- Employees who have the knowledge to answer customer questions

Responsiveness
- Keeping customer informed as to when services will be performed
- Prompt service to customers
- Willingness to help customers
- Readiness to respond to customers' requests

Assurance
- Employees who instill confidence in customers
- Making customers feel safe in their transactions
- Employees who are consistently courteous

Empathy
- Giving customers individual attention
- Employees who deal with customers in a caring fashion
- Having the customer's best interests at heart
- Employees who understand the needs of their customers
- Convenient business hours

Tangibles
- Modern equipment
- Visually appealing facilities
- Employees who have a neat, professional appearance
- Visually appealing materials associated with the service

Source: A. Parasuraman, Valarie A. Zeithaml, and Leonard L. Berry, "A Conceptual Model of Service Quality and Its Implications for Future Research," *Journal of Marketing*, Fall 1985, pp. 41–50. Reprinted by permission of the American Marketing Association.

Incorporating Self-Service Technologies (SSTs)

Consumers value convenience in services.[71] Many person-to-person service interactions are being replaced by self-service technologies (SSTs). To the traditional vending machines we can add automated teller machines (ATMs), self-pumping at gas stations, self-checkout at hotels, and a variety of activities on the Internet, such as ticket purchasing, investment trading, and customization of products.

Not all SSTs improve service quality, but they can make service transactions more accurate, convenient, and faster. Obviously, they can also reduce costs. One technology firm founded in Israel, Comverse, estimates the cost to answer a query through a call centre at $7, but only 10 cents online. One of its clients was able to direct 200 000 calls a week to online self-service support, saving US$52 million a year.[72] Every company needs to think about improving its service using SSTs. HMV Canada realized the potential SST had in increasing its music sales.

HMV Canada

HMV is Canada's retail, music, and entertainment go-to store, with over 120 stores from St. John's, Newfoundland, to Victoria, British Columbia. In order to keep up with the trend of downloading music rather than buying it on physical media, HMV released Hmvdigital.ca, Canada's only major music download site. After extensive testing of the online store, HMV was able to develop the technology such that customers can get the music they want in the format they want. One of the major features is the Interac payment option of using a debit card. HMV realized that its core young shoppers are unlikely to have a credit card. As of mid-2011, Hmvdigital.ca remains the only Canadian online music store to accept debit cards as a form of payment.[73]

Some companies have found that the biggest obstacle is not the technology itself, but convincing customers to use it, especially for the first time. Air Canada simplifies the self-check-in process by giving customers the option of entering their booking reference number or Aeroplan number, or swiping their Aeroplan card or credit card. Customers must have a clear sense of their roles in the SST process, see a clear benefit, and feel they can actually use the technology.[74] SST is not for everyone. Although some automated voices are actually popular with customers—the unfailingly polite and chipper voice of Amtrak's "Julie" consistently wins kudos from callers—many can incite frustration and even rage. This is especially true in a multicultural country such as Canada where voice recognition systems have to be capable of understanding a variety of accents. "Marketing Insight: Developing Customer-Interface Systems" discusses how service marketers must re-engineer their customer-interface systems for optimal efficiency and effectiveness.

MANAGING PRODUCT SUPPORT SERVICES

No less important than service industries are product-based industries that must provide a service bundle. Manufacturers of equipment—small appliances, office machines, tractors, mainframes, airplanes—all must provide *product support services.* Product support service is becoming a major battleground for competitive advantage.

Chapter 12 described how products could be augmented with key service differentiators—ordering ease, delivery, installation, customer training, customer consulting, maintenance, and repair. Some equipment companies, such as Caterpillar Tractor and John Deere, make a significant percentage of their profits from these services.[75] In the global marketplace, companies that make a good product but provide poor local service support are seriously disadvantaged.

Many product companies have a stronger web presence than they had before. They must ensure that they offer adequate—if not superior—service online as well. "Marketing Memo: Assessing E-Service Quality" reviews two models of online service quality.

Identifying and Satisfying Customer Needs

Traditionally, customers have had three specific worries about product service:[76]

- They worry about reliability and *failure frequency*. A farmer may tolerate a combine that will break down once a year, but not two or three times a year.
- They worry about *downtime*. The longer the downtime, the higher the cost. The customer counts on the seller's *service dependability*—the seller's ability to fix the machine quickly or at least provide a loaner.[77]

| MARKETING **INSIGHT** | DEVELOPING CUSTOMER-INTERFACE SYSTEMS |

Marketing academics and consultants Rayport and Jaworski believe that companies are facing a crisis in customer interaction and relationship management. Although many companies serve customers through a broad array of interfaces, from retail sales clerks, to websites, to voice-response telephone systems, these more often constitute an interface *collection*, not an actual interface *system*, as the whole set fails to provide superior service and build strong customer relationships. Rising complexity, costs, and customer dissatisfaction can result. Networked technologies, however, such as websites, kiosks, interactive voice-response units, vending machines, and touch screens, let managers successfully introduce machines into front-office roles that have long been held by humans. Here are a few examples the authors note:

- Borders, a book retailer with more than 1100 stores around the world, deployed Title Sleuth self-service kiosks to take the burden of title searches from its employees. The 300 machines handle up to 1.2 million customer searches per week, and customers using these machines spend 50 percent more per store visit and generate 20 percent more special-order sales.

- REI, a chain of premier outdoor-gear stores, uses interactive kiosks in its stores to hold information about its 78 000 SKUs—information that would be impossible for even the most intelligent store clerks to store in their head. Kiosk sales are growing at 30 percent a year, building revenues to the equivalent of one additional 2300-square-foot brick-and-mortar store.

- Rite Aid, the third-largest drugstore chain in the United States, is using prescription-dispensing robots and interactive voice-response units to fulfill an anticipated labour shortage—prescriptions filled in the United States are expected to grow by 30 percent over the next two years while the number of pharmacists is projected to expand by only 6 percent. Automation of rote tasks lets Rite Aid pharmacists use their time to personally attend to customers' needs, providing much-needed brand differentiation in a commoditized category of the retail sector.

According to Rayport and Jaworski, successfully integrating technology into the workforce requires a comprehensive re-engineering of the front office to identify what people do best, what machines do best, and how to deploy them separately and together.

Sources: Jeffrey F. Rayport and Bernard J. Jaworski, *Best Face Forward* (Boston: Harvard Business School Press, 2005); Jeffrey F. Rayport and Bernard J. Jaworski, "Best Face Forward," *Harvard Business Review, 82* (December 2004): 47–58; Jeffrey F. Rayport, Bernard J. Jaworski, and Ellie J. Kyung, "Best Face Forward," *Journal of Interactive Marketing, 19* (Autumn 2005): 67–80.

- They worry about *out-of-pocket costs.* How much does the customer have to spend on regular maintenance and repair costs?

A buyer takes all these factors into consideration and tries to estimate the **life-cycle cost**, which is the product's purchase cost plus the discounted cost of maintenance and repair less the discounted salvage value. A one-computer office will need higher product reliability and faster repair service than an office where other computers are available if one breaks down. An airline needs 100 percent reliability in the air. Where reliability is important, manufacturers or service providers can offer guarantees to promote sales.

To provide the best support, a manufacturer must identify the services customers value most and their relative importance. For expensive equipment, manufacturers offer *facilitating services* such as installation, staff training, maintenance and repair services, and financing. They may also add *value-augmenting services* that extend beyond the functioning and performance of the product itself. Johnson Controls reached beyond its climate control equipment and components business to manage integrated facilities by offering products and services that optimize energy use and improve comfort and security.

A manufacturer can offer, and charge for, product support services in different ways. One specialty organic-chemical company provides a standard offering plus a basic level of services. If the customer wants additional services, it can pay extra or increase its annual purchases to a higher level, in which case additional services are included. Many companies offer *service contracts* (also called *extended warranties*), in which sellers agree to provide free maintenance and repair services for a specified period of time at a specified contract price.

A number of leading manufacturing firms such as IBM, GE, and Xerox generate a considerable portion of their revenues from services that they offer as part of their total business solutions. An increasing number of firms are making a significant transition from being product-centric to becoming "hybrid" companies

---

MARKETING **MEMO** | ASSESSING E-SERVICE QUALITY

Academic researchers Parasuraman, Zeithaml, and Malhotra define online service quality as the extent to which a website facilitates efficient and effective shopping, purchasing, and delivery. They identified 11 dimensions of perceived e-service quality: access, ease of navigation, efficiency, flexibility, reliability, personalization, security/privacy, responsiveness, assurance/trust, site aesthetics, and price knowledge. Some of these service-quality dimensions were the same online as offline, but some specific underlying attributes were different. Different dimensions emerged with e-service quality too. Empathy didn't seem to be as important online, unless there were service problems. Core dimensions of regular e-service quality were efficiency, fulfillment, reliability, and privacy; core dimensions of e-service recovery were responsiveness, compensation, and real-time access to help.

Another set of academic researchers, Wolfinbarger and Gilly, developed a scale of online service quality with four key dimensions: reliability/fulfillment, website design, security/privacy, and customer service. The researchers interpret their study findings to suggest that the most basic building blocks of a "compelling online experience" are reliability and functionality to provide time savings, easy transactions, good selection, in-depth information, and the "right" level of personalization. Their 14-item scale looks like this:

Reliability/Fulfillment

The product that came was represented accurately by the Web site.

You get what you ordered from this Web site.

The product is delivered by the time promised by the company.

Web Site Design

This Web site provides in-depth information.

The site doesn't waste my time.

It is quick and easy to complete a transaction at this Web site.

The level of personalization at this site is about right, not too much or too little.

This Web site has good selection.

Security/Privacy

I feel that my privacy is protected at this site.

I feel safe in my transactions with this Web site.

This Web site has adequate security transactions.

Customer Service

The company is willing and ready to respond to customer needs.

When you have a problem, the Web site shows a sincere interest in solving it.

Inquiries are answered promptly.

Parasuraman, Zeithaml, and Malhotra extended their previous research by examining the dimensions of perceived e-service quality for routine and nonroutine encounters with websites. They argue that e-service quality measurement scales assume that customers have had routine encounters with the website being evaluated and that a different scale is required when customers have nonroutine encounters with the site. They present a three-dimensional (responsiveness, compensation, and contact), 11-item scale of e-service quality measurement specifically for the case when customers evaluate a website's quality of service in handling problems that they experience with the site.

Sources: Mary Wolfinbarger and Mary C. Gilly, "E-TailQ: Dimensionalizing, Measuring, and Predicting E-Tail Quality," *Journal of Retailing, 79* (Fall 2003): 183–198; A. Parasuraman, Valerie Ziethaml, and Arvind Malhotra, "E-S-QUAL: A Multiple-Item Scale for Assessing Electronic Service Quality," *Journal of Service Research, 7*(3) (February 2005), pp. 213–233.

---

that offer both goods and related services, in an attempt to differentiate themselves from the competition. But, does this transition always benefit the firm? Marketing researchers Fang, Palmatier, and Steenkamp examined the relationship between service ratio (proportion of company revenues generated from services) and firm value measured by Tobin's q (ratio of the market value of the firm to the replacement cost of its assets) of 477 manufacturing companies over a 15-year period. They found that across all manufacturing firms, the benefits in terms of firm value are not felt at low service ratios (below 20 percent). When the service ratio goes over 20 percent, the firm value rises at an increasing rate thereon. However, they found that this was true only in low-growth industries. In high-growth industries, a service transition actually hurt firm value.[78] Their results are depicted graphically in Figure 13.7.

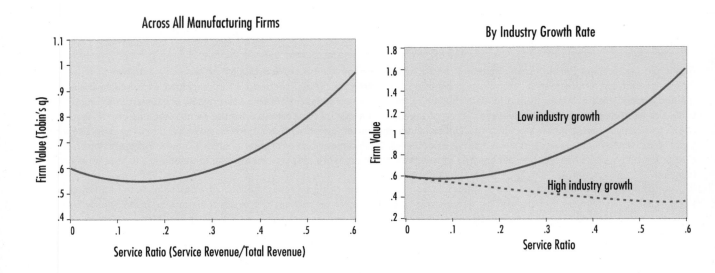

FIGURE 13.7

Service Revenues of
Manufacturing Companies

Source: Reprinted with permission
from *Journal of Marketing*, pub-
lished by the American Marketing
Association, Eric (Er) Fang, Robert
W. Palmatier, Jan-Benedict E. M.
Steenkamp, "Effect of Service
Transition Strategies on Firm
Value," 2008, vol. 72, pp. 1–14,
Fig. 1 and Fig. 3.

Post-sale Service Strategy

The quality of customer service departments varies greatly. At one extreme are departments that simply transfer customer calls to the appropriate person or department for action with little follow-up. At the other extreme are departments eager to receive customer requests, suggestions, and even complaints and handle them expeditiously. Some firms even proactively contact customers to provide service after the sale is complete.[79]

CUSTOMER-SERVICE EVOLUTION Manufacturers usually start by running their own parts-and-service departments. They want to stay close to the equipment and know its problems. They also find it expensive and time consuming to train others, and they discover they can make good money from parts and service if they are the only supplier and can charge a premium price. In fact, many equipment manufacturers price their equipment low and compensate by charging high prices for parts and service.

Over time, manufacturers switch more maintenance and repair services to authorized distributors and dealers. These intermediaries are closer to customers, operate in more locations, and can offer quicker service. Still later, independent service firms emerge and offer a lower price or faster service. A significant percentage of auto-service work is now done outside franchised automobile dealerships by independent garages and chains such as Midas Muffler, Sears, and Canadian Tire. Independent service organizations handle mainframes, telecommunications equipment, and a variety of other equipment lines.

THE CUSTOMER-SERVICE IMPERATIVE Customer-service choices are increasing rapidly, however, and equipment manufacturers increasingly must figure out how to make money on their equipment, independent of service contracts. Some new-car warranties now cover 100 000 kilometres before servicing. The increase in disposable or never-fail equipment makes customers less inclined to pay 2 percent to 10 percent of the purchase price every year for a service. A company with several hundred laptops, printers, and related pieces of equipment might find it cheaper to have its own service people on-site.

SUMMARY

1. A service is any act or performance that one party can offer to another and that is essentially intangible and does not result in the ownership of anything. It may or may not be tied to a physical product.

2. Services are intangible, inseparable, variable, and perishable. Each characteristic poses challenges and requires certain strategies. Marketers must find ways to give tangibility to intangibles, to increase the productivity of service providers, to increase and standardize the quality of the service provided, and to match the supply of services with market demand.

3. Marketing of services faces new realities in the twenty-first century due to customer empowerment, customer co-production, and the need to satisfy employees as well as customers.

4. In the past, service industries lagged behind manufacturing firms in adopting and using marketing concepts and tools, but this situation has changed. Achieving excellence in service marketing calls not only for external marketing but also for internal marketing to motivate employees, as well as interactive marketing to emphasize the importance of both "high tech" and "high touch."

5. Top service companies excel at the following practices: a strategic concept, a history of top-management commitment to quality, high standards, profit tiers, and systems for monitoring service performance and customer complaints. They also differentiate their brands through primary and secondary service features and constant innovation.

6. Superior service delivery requires managing customer expectations and incorporating self-service technologies. Customers' expectations play a critical role in their service experiences and evaluations. Companies must manage service quality by understanding the effects of each service encounter.

7. Even product-based companies must provide post-purchase service. To offer the best support, a manufacturer must identify the services customers value most and their relative importance. The service mix includes both presale services (facilitating and value-augmenting services) and post-sale services (customer service departments, repair and maintenance services).

APPLICATIONS

Marketing Debate: Is Service Marketing Different from Product Marketing?

Some service marketers maintain that service marketing is fundamentally different from product marketing and relies on different skills. Some traditional product marketers disagree, saying "good marketing is good marketing."

Take a position: Product and service marketing are fundamentally different *versus* Product and service marketing are highly related.

Marketing Discussion: Educational Institutions

Colleges, universities, and other educational institutions can be classified as service organizations. How can you apply the marketing principles developed in this chapter to your school? Do you have any advice as to how it could become a better service marketer?

Surgery is often associated with hospital stays, pain, blood loss, healing time, days off work or school, and dependence on caregivers. This is rapidly changing, thanks to advances in medical technology. Now, with the introduction of robotics, surgeons can perform minimally invasive surgery, which would otherwise require deeper incisions, stitches, and scarring. For example, rather than cutting the patient open for heart surgery as done in the past, surgeons simply make tiny incisions and use a robot with a small camera to perform the surgery. The result is less time in the hospital for the patient and a quicker recovery time.

With robots, the surgery can be performed without the surgeon even being in the same room as the patient. In fact, the surgeon could potentially perform the surgery from hundreds of kilometres away! Robotics also improves the quality of surgeries. Robots have finer, steadier control of surgical instruments, and better vision of where they are in the patient's body and where they are headed. In addition, the surgeon can be seated comfortably at a console during the surgery rather than standing in the operating theatre, thus reducing surgeon fatigue.

Canadian medical researchers have been at the forefront of developing robotics to improve the patient's surgical experience. Dr. Mehran Anvari heads the Centre for Surgical Invention & Innovation in Hamilton, Ontario. Dr. Anvari and his centre are world leaders in robotic surgery, making history by performing the first-ever remote surgery in 2003. In 2010, physicians from McGill University were the first in the world to combine a surgical robot with an anaesthesia robot to perform a surgery at the Montreal General Hospital. The Hospital for Sick Children in Toronto is spending $10 million to develop a robot for pediatric surgeries. Dr. Rajni Patel at the University of Western Ontario is designing a robot that will give surgeons the ability to sense the interaction between the surgical tools and the tissues in the patient's body. The list of such medical robotic advancements originating from Canada goes on.

With such innovations, customer satisfaction with health care as a service improves drastically. The current cost of robotic surgery is prohibitive, but as it becomes more widely adopted, it may be no more expensive than regular surgery. With shorter hospital stays, quicker patient recovery, fewer days off work, and the ability for surgeons to perform the surgery remotely, the cost savings to the health-care system and economy at large could far outweigh the cost.

QUESTIONS

1. If medical research advances to a point where a robot can replicate a human surgeon, would that reduce the variability factor of surgeries? Can a service such as a surgery be standardized? Elaborate and justify your answer.

2. What are some other services that are rich in potential for the use of robots?

3. Nowadays, products such as blood pressure monitors, blood sugar monitors, and pregnancy test kits are available for home use. As the Canadian health-care system is constrained by not having enough doctors to meet the demand for medical services, could self-service devices to diagnose and prescribe medications for minor ailments be a workable alternative? Why or why not?

Sources: "Robots in Medicine: UWO Prof Aims to Bring a Sense of Touch to Robot Surgeons," CBCNews.ca, July 18, 2007, www.cbc.ca/news/background/tech/robotics/robot-qa.html (viewed June 17, 2011); Andy Shaw, "Across Canada Physcians and Researchers Develop New Types of Surgical Robots," *Canadian Healthcare Technology*, May 2011, p. 20.

UNDERSTANDING PRICING

Price is not just a number on a tag. It comes in many forms and performs many functions. Rent, tuition, fares, fees, rates, tolls, retainers, wages, and commissions are all the price you pay for some good or service. Price also has many components. If you buy a new car, the sticker price may be adjusted by rebates and dealer incentives. Some firms allow for payment through multiple forms, such as $150 plus 25 000 frequent flier miles for a flight.[3]

Throughout most of history, prices were set by negotiation between buyers and sellers. Bargaining is still a sport in some areas. Setting one price for all buyers is a relatively modern idea that arose with the development of large-scale retailing at the end of the nineteenth century. F. W. Woolworth, Tiffany & Co., John Wanamaker, and others advertised a "strictly one-price policy," because they carried so many items and supervised so many employees.

Traditionally, price has operated as a major determinant of buyer choice. Consumers and purchasing agents who have access to price information and price discounters put pressure on retailers to lower their prices. Retailers in turn put pressure on manufacturers to lower their prices. The result can be a marketplace characterized by heavy discounting and sales promotion.

A Changing Pricing Environment

Pricing practices have changed significantly. At the turn of the twenty-first century, consumers had easy access to credit, so by combining unique product formulations with enticing marketing campaigns, many firms successfully traded consumers up to more expensive products and services. The onset of the global recession in the United States and many other countries around the world changed things, though.

A combination of environmentalism and concern about jobs and home values forced many consumers in recession-hit countries to rethink how they spent their money. They replaced luxury purchases with basics. They bought fewer accessories like jewellery, watches, and bags. They ate at home more often and purchased espresso machines to make lattes in their kitchens instead of buying them at expensive cafés. If they bought a new car at all, they downsized to smaller, more fuel-efficient models. They even cut back spending on hobbies and sports activities.[4]

Downward price pressure from a changing economic environment coincided with some longer-term trends in the technological environment. For some years now, the Internet has been changing how buyers and sellers interact. Here is a short list of how the Internet allows sellers to discriminate between buyers, and buyers to discriminate between sellers.[5]

Buyers can do the following:

■ *Get instant price comparisons from thousands of vendors.* The Comparison Shopper, a service offered by Canada Post, allows Canadian consumers to compare prices of millions of products across hundreds of stores. Pricegrabber.ca lures thousands of visitors to its website every day. Intelligent shopping agents ("bots") take price comparison a step further and seek out products, prices, and reviews from hundreds if not thousands of merchants.

■ *Name their price and have it met.* On Priceline.com, the customer states the price he or she wants to pay for an airline ticket, hotel, or rental car, and Priceline looks for any seller willing to meet that price.[6] Volume-aggregating sites combine the orders of many customers and press the supplier for a deeper discount.

■ *Get products free.* Open source, the free software movement that started with Linux, will erode margins for just about any company creating software. The biggest challenge confronting Microsoft, Oracle, IBM, and virtually every other major software producer is how to compete with programs that can be had for free. "Marketing Insight: Giving It All Away" describes how different firms have been successful with essentially free offerings.

Sellers can do the following:

■ *Monitor customer behaviour and tailor offers to individuals.* GE Lighting, which gets 55 000 pricing requests a year, has web programs that evaluate 300 factors that go into a pricing quote, such as past sales data and discounts, so it can reduce processing time from up to 30 days to 6 hours.

■ *Give certain customers access to special prices.* DirectBuy is a members-only store with 400 000 members, which sells a range of products such as furniture, appliances, home improvement, electronics, and sporting equipment by charging a membership fee to give members prices lower than those available at traditional retail stores. Other business marketers use extranets to get a precise handle on inventory, costs, and demand at any given moment in order to adjust prices instantly.

MARKETING **INSIGHT** | GIVING IT ALL AWAY

Giving away products free via sampling has been a successful marketing tactic for years. Estée Lauder gave free samples of cosmetics to celebrities, and organizers at awards shows lavish winners with plentiful free items or gifts known as "swag." Other manufacturers, such as Gillette and HP, have built their business model around selling the host product essentially at cost and making money on the sale of necessary supplies, such as razor blades and printer ink.

With the advent of the Internet, software companies began to adopt similar practices. Adobe gave away its PDF reader free in 1994, as did Macromedia with its Shockwave player in 1995. These programs became the industry standard, but the firms really made their money selling their authoring software. More recently, Internet start-ups such as Blogger Weblog publishing tool, MySpace online community, and Skype Internet phone calls have all achieved some success with a "freemium" strategy—free online services with a premium component.

Chris Anderson, editor-in-chief of *Wired,* strongly believes that in a digital marketplace, companies can make money with "free" products. As evidence, he offers revenue models involving cross-subsidies (giving away a DVR to sell cable service) and freemiums (offering the Flickr online photo management and sharing application free to everyone while selling the superior FlickrPro to more highly involved users).

Some online firms have successfully moved "from free to fee" and begun charging for services. Under a new participative pricing mechanism that lets consumers decide the price they feel is warranted, buyers often choose to pay more than zero and even enough that the seller's revenues increase over what a fixed price would have yielded.

Offline, profits for discount air carrier Ryanair have been sky-high thanks to its revolutionary business model. The secret? Founder Michael O'Leary thinks like a retailer, charging for almost everything but the seat itself:

1. A quarter of Ryanair's seats are free. O'Leary wants to double that within five years, with the ultimate goal of making all seats free. Passengers currently pay only taxes and fees of about $10 to $24, with an average one-way fare of roughly $52.

2. Passengers pay extra for everything else: for checked luggage ($9.50 per bag), snacks ($5.50 for a hot dog, $4.50 for chicken soup, $3.50 for water), and bus or train transportation into town from the far-flung airports Ryanair uses ($24).

3. Flight attendants sell a variety of merchandise, including digital cameras ($137.50) and iPocket MP3 players ($165). Onboard gambling and cell phone service are projected new revenue sources.

Other strategies cut costs or generate outside revenue:

1. Seats don't recline, window shades and seat-back pockets have been removed, and there is no entertainment. Seat-back trays now carry ads, and the exteriors of the planes are giant revenue-producing billboards for Vodafone Group, Jaguar, Hertz, and others.

2. More than 99 percent of tickets are sold online. The website also offers travel insurance, hotels, ski packages, and car rentals.

3. To reduce maintenance, only Boeing 737-800 jets are flown. Flight crews buy their own uniforms.

The formula works for Ryanair's customers; the airline flies 58 million of them to over 150 airports each year. All the extras add up to 20 percent of revenue. Ryanair enjoys net margins of 25 percent, more than three times Southwest's 7 percent. Some industry pundits even refer to Ryanair as "Walmart with wings!" European discount carrier easyJet has adopted many of the same practices.

Sources: Chris Anderson, *Free: The Future of a Radical Price* (New York: Hyperion, 2009); Peter J. Howe, "The Next Pinch: Fees to Check Bags," *Boston Globe,* March 8, 2007; Katherine Heires, "Why It Pays to Give Away the Store," *Business 2.0,* October 2006, pp. 36–37; Kerry Capel, "'Wal-Mart with Wings,'" *BusinessWeek,* November 27, 2006, pp. 44–45; Matthew Maier, "A Radical Fix for Airlines: Make Flying Free," *Business 2.0,* April 2006, pp. 32–34; Ju-Young Kim, Martin Natter, and Martin Spann, "Pay What You Want: A New Participative Pricing Mechanism," *Journal of Marketing, 73* (January 2009): 44–58; Koen Pauwels and Allen Weiss, "Moving from Free to Fee: How Online Firms Market to Change Their Business Model Successfully," *Journal of Marketing, 72* (May 2008): 14–31; Bruce Myerson, "Skype Takes Its Show on the Road," *BusinessWeek,* October 29, 2007, p. 38.

Both buyers and sellers can do the following:

■ *Negotiate prices in online auctions and exchanges or even in person.* Want to sell hundreds of excess and slightly worn widgets? Post a sale on eBay.ca. Want to purchase vintage baseball cards at a bargain price? Go to www.baseballplanet.com. Looking for tickets below face value for an upcoming concert? Check to see if someone is trying to get rid of theirs on your local Kijiji website.

How Companies Price

Companies do their pricing in a variety of ways. In small companies, the boss often sets prices. In large companies, division and product line managers do. Even there, though, top management sets general pricing objectives and policies and often approves lower management's proposals.

Where pricing is a key factor (aerospace, railroads, oil companies), companies often establish a pricing department to set or assist others in setting appropriate prices. This department reports to the marketing department, finance department, or top management. Others who influence pricing include sales managers, production managers, finance managers, and accountants.

Executives complain that pricing is a big headache—and getting worse by the day. Many companies do not handle pricing well and fall back on "strategies" such as "We determine our costs and take our industry's traditional margins." Other common mistakes are not revising price often enough to capitalize on market changes; setting price independently of the rest of the marketing program rather than as an intrinsic element of market-positioning strategy; and not varying price enough for different product items, market segments, distribution channels, and purchase occasions.

For any organization, effectively designing and implementing pricing strategies requires a thorough understanding of consumer pricing psychology and a systematic approach to setting, adapting, and changing prices.

Consumer Psychology and Pricing

Many economists traditionally assumed that consumers were "price takers" and accepted prices at "face value" or as given. Marketers, however, recognize that consumers often actively process price information, interpreting it from the context of prior purchasing experience, formal communications (advertising, sales calls, and brochures), informal communications (friends, colleagues, or family members), point-of-purchase or online resources, and other factors.[7]

Purchase decisions are based on how consumers perceive prices and what they consider the current actual price to be—*not* on the marketer's stated price. Customers may have a lower price threshold below which prices signal inferior or unacceptable quality, and an upper price threshold above which prices are prohibitive and the product appears not worth the money. The following example helps illustrate the large part consumer psychology plays in determining three different prices for essentially the same item: a black T-shirt.

A Black T-Shirt

The black Armani T-shirt for women looks pretty ordinary. In fact, it's not that different from the black T-shirt sold by Gap and by Swedish discount clothing chain H&M. Yet the Armani T-shirt costs $275.00, whereas the Gap item costs $14.90 and the H&M one $7.90. Customers who purchase the Armani T-shirt are paying for a T-shirt made of 70 percent nylon, 25 percent polyester, and 5 percent elastane, whereas the Gap and H&M shirts are made mainly of cotton. True, the Armani T is a bit more stylishly cut than the other two and sports a "Made in Italy" label, but how does it command a $275.00 price tag? A luxury brand, Armani is primarily known for suits, handbags, and evening gowns that sell for thousands of dollars. In that context, it can sell its T-shirts for more. But because there aren't many takers for $275.00 T-shirts, Armani doesn't make many, thus further enhancing the appeal for status seekers who like the idea of having a limited edition T-shirt. "Value is not only quality, function, utility, channel of distribution," says Arnold Aronson, managing director of retail strategies for Kurt Salmon Associates and former CEO of Saks Fifth Avenue; it's also a customer's perception of a brand's luxury connotations.[8]

With the loonie hovering around parity with the U.S. dollar, pricing of products in Canada has been coming under increased scrutiny by Canadian consumers. It is estimated that Canadians pay 12 to 30 percent higher prices than Americans for exactly the same product. As a result, an increasing number of Canadians have taken their big-ticket shopping south of the border. This is especially true in the case

Developing Pricing Strategies and Programs

of cars, major home appliances, electronics, and alcohol. For instance, luxury automaker Porsche found that for every ten Porsches sold in Canada, seven were being brought from U.S. dealers by Canadians. This prompted Porsche Canada to cut prices on all its models, some by over 10 percent. It also lowered the prices on the options by 16 percent. Such price cuts increased Porsche's Canadian sales by as much as 40 percent in barely a few months.[9]

Even during poor economic times, however, some companies can command a price premium if their offerings are unique and relevant enough to a large enough market segment. Colorado-based Pangea Organics expanded distribution of its pricey $8 soaps and $50 oils, thanks to environmentally friendly organic formulations and clever, seed-infused packaging.[10]

Understanding how consumers arrive at their perceptions of prices is an important marketing priority. Here we consider three key topics—reference prices, price–quality inferences, and price endings.

REFERENCE PRICES Although consumers may have fairly good knowledge of price ranges, surprisingly few can accurately recall specific prices.[11] When examining products, however, they often employ **reference prices**, comparing an observed price to an internal reference price they remember or an external frame of reference such as a posted "regular retail price."[12]

All types of reference prices are possible (see Table 14.1), and sellers often attempt to manipulate them. For example, a seller can situate its product among expensive competitors to imply that it belongs in the same class. Department stores will display women's apparel in separate departments differentiated by price; dresses in the more expensive department are assumed to be of better quality.[13] Marketers also encourage reference-price thinking by stating a high manufacturer's suggested price, indicating that the price was much higher originally, or pointing to a competitor's high price.[14]

When consumers evoke one or more of these frames of reference, their perceived price can vary from the stated price.[15] Research has found that unpleasant surprises—when the perceived price is lower than the stated price—can have a greater impact on purchase likelihood than pleasant surprises.[16] Consumer expectations can also play a key role in price response. On Internet auction sites such as eBay, when consumers know similar goods will be available in future auctions, they will bid less in the current auction.[17]

Clever marketers try to frame the price to signal the best value possible. For example, a relatively expensive item can look less expensive if the price is broken into smaller units, such as a $500 annual membership for "under $50 a month," even if the totals are the same.[18]

PRICE–QUALITY INFERENCES Many consumers use price as an indicator of quality. Image pricing is especially effective with ego-sensitive products such as perfumes, expensive cars, and designer clothing. A $100 bottle of perfume might contain $10 worth of scent, but gift givers pay $100 to communicate their high regard for the receiver.

Price and quality perceptions of cars interact.[19] Higher-priced cars are perceived to possess high quality. Higher-quality cars are likewise perceived to be higher priced than they actually are. When information about true quality is available, price becomes a less significant indicator of quality. When this information is not available, price acts as a signal of quality.

Some brands adopt exclusivity and scarcity to signify uniqueness and justify premium pricing. Luxury-goods makers of watches, jewellery, perfume, and other products often emphasize exclusivity in their communication messages and channel strategies. For luxury-goods customers who desire uniqueness, demand may actually increase price, because they then believe fewer other customers can afford the product.[20]

TABLE 14.1 | **POSSIBLE CONSUMER REFERENCE PRICES**

- "Fair Price" (what consumers feel the product should cost)
- Typical Price
- Last Price Paid
- Upper-Bound Price (reservation price or the maximum most consumers would pay)
- Lower-Bound Price (lower threshold price or the minimum most consumers would pay)
- Historical Competitor Prices
- Expected Future Price
- Usual Discounted Price

Source: Adapted from Russell S. Winer, *Pricing*, MSI Relevant Knowledge Series (Cambridge, MA: Marketing Science Institute, 2006).

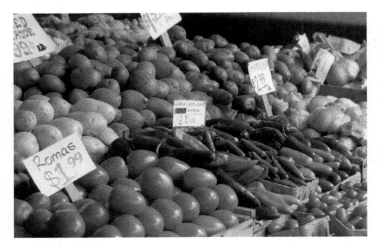

A product priced at $2.99 can be perceived as distinctly less expensive than one priced at $3.00.

PRICE ENDINGS Many sellers believe prices should end in an odd number. Customers see an item priced at $299 as being in the $200 rather than the $300 range; they tend to process prices "left-to-right" rather than by rounding.[21] Price encoding in this fashion is important if there is a mental price break at the higher, rounded price.

Another explanation for the popularity of "9" endings is that they suggest a discount or bargain, so if a company wants a high-price image, it should probably avoid the odd-ending tactic.[22] One study showed that demand actually increased one-third when the price of a dress *rose* from $34 to $39 but was unchanged when it rose from $34 to $44.[23]

Prices that end with 0 and 5 are also popular and are thought to be easier for consumers to process and retrieve from memory.[24] Sale signs next to prices spur demand, but only if not overused: Total category sales are highest when some, but not all, items in a category have sale signs; past a certain point, sale signs may cause total category sales to fall.[25]

Pricing cues such as sale signs and prices that end in 9 are more influential when consumers' price knowledge is poor, when they purchase the item infrequently or are new to the category, and when product designs vary over time, prices vary seasonally, or quality or sizes vary across stores.[26] They are less effective the more they are used. Limited availability (for example, "three days only") also can spur sales among consumers actively shopping for a product.[27]

SETTING THE PRICE

A firm must set a price for the first time when it develops a new product, when it introduces its regular product into a new distribution channel or geographical area, and when it enters bids on new contract work. The firm must decide where to position its product on quality and price.

Most markets have three to five price points or tiers. Marriott Hotels is good at developing different brands or variations of brands for different price points: Marriott Vacation Club—Vacation Villas (highest price), Marriott Marquis (high price), Marriott (high-medium price), Renaissance (medium-high price), Courtyard (medium price), TownePlace Suites (medium-low price), and Fairfield Inn (low price). Firms devise their branding strategies to help convey the price–quality tiers of their products or services to consumers.[28]

The firm must consider many factors in setting its pricing policy.[29] Table 14.2 summarizes the six steps in the process.

Step 1: Selecting the Pricing Objective
The company first decides where it wants to position its market offering. The clearer a firm's objectives, the easier it is to set price. Five major objectives are survival, maximum current profit, maximum market share, maximum market skimming, and product-quality leadership.

SURVIVAL Companies pursue *survival* as their major objective if they are plagued with overcapacity, intense competition, or changing consumer wants. As long as prices cover variable costs and some fixed

TABLE 14.2	STEPS IN SETTING A PRICING POLICY
1.	Selecting the Pricing Objective
2.	Determining Demand
3.	Estimating Costs
4.	Analyzing Competitors' Costs, Prices, and Offers
5.	Selecting a Pricing Method
6.	Selecting the Final Price

costs, the company stays in business. Survival is a short-run objective; in the long run, the firm must learn how to add value or face extinction.

MAXIMUM CURRENT PROFIT Many companies try to set a price that will *maximize current profits.* They estimate the demand and costs associated with alternative prices and choose the price that produces maximum current profit, cash flow, or rate of return on investment. This strategy assumes the firm knows its demand and cost functions; in reality, these are difficult to estimate. In emphasizing current performance, the company may sacrifice long-run performance by ignoring the effects of other marketing variables, competitors' reactions, and legal restraints on price.

MAXIMUM MARKET SHARE Some companies want to *maximize their market share.* They believe that a higher sales volume will lead to lower unit costs and higher long-run profit. They set the lowest price, assuming the market is price sensitive. Texas Instruments (TI) famously practised this **market-penetration pricing** for years. TI would build a large plant, set its price as low as possible, win a large market share, experience falling costs, and cut its price further as costs fell.

The following conditions favour adopting a market-penetration pricing strategy: (1) The market is highly price sensitive and a low price stimulates market growth; (2) production and distribution costs fall with accumulated production experience; and (3) a low price discourages actual and potential competition.

MAXIMUM MARKET SKIMMING Companies unveiling a new technology favour setting high prices to *maximize market skimming.* Sony is a frequent practitioner of **market-skimming pricing**, in which prices start high and slowly drop over time. When Sony introduced the world's first high-definition television (HDTV) to the Japanese market in 1990, it was priced at $43 000. So that Sony could "skim" the maximum amount of revenue from the various segments of the market, the price dropped steadily through the years— a 28-inch Sony HDTV cost just over $6000 in 1993, but a 40-inch Sony HDTV cost only $600 in 2010.

This strategy can be fatal, however, if a worthy competitor decides to price low. When Philips, the Dutch electronics manufacturer, priced its videodisc players to make a profit on each, Japanese competitors priced low and rapidly built their market share, which in turn pushed down their costs substantially.

Moreover, consumers who buy early at the highest prices may be dissatisfied if they compare themselves with those who buy later at a lower price. When Apple dropped the iPhone's price in the United States from $599 to $399 only two months after its introduction, public outcry caused the firm to give initial buyers a $100 credit toward future Apple purchases.[30]

Market skimming makes sense under the following conditions: (1) A sufficient number of buyers have a high current demand; (2) the unit costs of producing a small volume are high enough to cancel the advantage of charging what the traffic will bear; (3) the high initial price does not attract more competitors to the market; and (4) the high price communicates the image of a superior product.

PRODUCT-QUALITY LEADERSHIP A company might aim to be the *product-quality leader* in the market. Many brands strive to be "affordable luxuries"—products or services characterized by high levels of perceived quality, taste, and status and with a price just high enough not to be out of consumers' reach. Brands such as Starbucks, Aveda, Victoria's Secret, BMW, and Bose have positioned themselves as quality leaders in their categories, combining quality, luxury, and premium prices with an intensely loyal customer base.[31] Grey Goose and Absolut carved out a superpremium niche in the essentially odourless, colourless, and tasteless vodka category through clever on-premise and off-premise marketing that made the brands seem hip and exclusive.[32]

OTHER OBJECTIVES Nonprofit and public organizations may have other pricing objectives. A university aims for *partial cost recovery,* knowing that it must rely on private gifts and public grants to cover its remaining costs. A nonprofit hospital may aim for full cost recovery in its pricing. A nonprofit theatre company may price its productions to fill the maximum number of seats. A social service agency may set a service price geared to client income.

Whatever the specific objective, businesses that use price as a strategic tool will profit more than those that simply let costs or the market determine their pricing. For art museums, which earn an average of only 5 percent of their revenues from admission charges, pricing can send a message that affects their public image and the amount of donations and sponsorships they receive.

Step 2: Determining Demand

Each price will lead to a different level of demand and have a different impact on a company's marketing objectives. The normally inverse relationship between price and demand is captured in a demand curve (see Figure 14.1): the higher the price, the lower the demand. For prestige goods, the demand curve sometimes slopes upward. One perfume company raised its price and sold more rather than less. Some consumers take the higher price to signify a better product. However, if the price is too high, demand may fall.

PRICE SENSITIVITY The demand curve shows the market's probable purchase quantity at alternative prices. It sums the reactions of many individuals with different price sensitivities. The first step in estimating demand is to understand what affects price sensitivity. Generally speaking, customers are less price sensitive to low-cost items or items they buy infrequently. They are also less price sensitive when (1) there are few or no substitutes or competitors; (2) they do not readily notice the higher price; (3) they are slow to change their buying habits; (4) they think the higher prices are justified; or (5) price is only a small part of the total cost of obtaining, operating, and servicing the product over its lifetime.

A seller can successfully charge a higher price than competitors if it can convince customers that it offers the lowest *total cost of ownership* (TCO). Marketers often treat the service elements in a product offering as sales incentives rather than as value-enhancing augmentations for which they can charge. In fact, pricing expert Tom Nagle believes that the most common mistake manufacturers have made in recent years is to offer all sorts of services to differentiate their products without charging for them.[33]

Of course, companies prefer customers who are less price sensitive. Table 14.3 lists some characteristics associated with decreased price sensitivity. On the other hand, the Internet has the potential to *increase* price sensitivity. In some established, fairly big-ticket categories, such as auto retailing and term insurance, consumers pay lower prices as a result of the Internet. Car buyers use the Internet to gather information and borrow the negotiating clout of an online buying service.[34] But customers may have to visit multiple sites to realize these savings, and they don't always do so. Targeting only price-sensitive consumers may in fact be leaving money on the table.

ESTIMATING DEMAND CURVES Most companies attempt to measure their demand curves using several different methods:

- *Surveys* can explore how many units consumers would buy at different proposed prices. Although consumers might understate their purchase intentions at higher prices to discourage the company from pricing high, they also tend to actually exaggerate their willingness to pay for new products or services.[35]

- *Price experiments* can vary the prices of different products in a store or charge different prices for the same product in similar territories to see how the change affects sales. Another approach is to use the Internet. An e-business could test the impact of a 5 percent price increase by quoting a higher price to every 40th visitor, to compare the purchase response. However, it must do this carefully and not alienate customers or be seen as reducing competition in any way (and thus violate the Competition Act).[36]

- *Statistical analysis* of past prices, quantities sold, and other factors can reveal their relationships. The data can be longitudinal (over time) or cross-sectional (from different locations at the same time). Building the appropriate model and fitting the data with the proper statistical techniques calls for considerable skill, but sophisticated price optimization software and advances in database management have improved marketers' abilities to optimize pricing.

FIGURE 14.1

Inelastic and Elastic Demand

TABLE 14.3	FACTORS LEADING TO LESS PRICE SENSITIVITY

- The product is more distinctive.
- Buyers are less aware of substitutes.
- Buyers cannot easily compare the quality of substitutes.
- The expenditure is a smaller part of the buyer's total income.
- The expenditure is small compared with the total cost of the end product.
- Part of the cost is borne by another party.
- The product is used in conjunction with assets previously bought.
- The product is assumed to have more quality, prestige, or exclusiveness.
- Buyers cannot store the product.

Source: *NAGLE, THOMAS; HOGAN, JOHN; ZALE, JOSEPH, THE STRATEGY AND TACTICS OF PRICING, 5th ed.,* © 2011. Reprinted and Electronically reproduced by permission of Pearson Education, Inc., Upper Saddle River, New Jersey.

Travel agencies such as Journeys have been selling heavily discounted sun destination packages.

One large retail chain was selling a line of "good–better–best" power drills at $90, $120, and $130 respectively. Sales of the least and most expensive drills were fine, but sales of the midpriced drill lagged. Based on a price optimization analysis, the retailer dropped the price of the midpriced drill to $110. Sales of the low-priced drill dropped 4 percent because it seemed less of a bargain, but the sales of the midpriced drill increased by 11 percent. Profits rose as a result.[37]

In measuring the price–demand relationship, the market researcher must control for various factors that will influence demand.[38] The competitor's response will make a difference. Also, if the company changes other aspects of the marketing program besides price, the effect of the price change itself will be hard to isolate. "Marketing Insight: Parking: There's More to It Than Meets the Eye" discusses the variety of factors that are considered while pricing parking spaces.

Price can affect demand, but at times the reverse also holds true. When demand is low, the industry may lower prices to boost demand, as observed in the sun destination travel industry recently.

Journeys Travel & Leisure SuperCentre

A lack of snow and chilly temperatures can have a negative effect on the demand for vacations in hot spots like Mexico and the Carribean, causing deep price cuts by resorts and cruise lines there. This is exactly what happened in 2010, when the fall weather in Canada lasted longer than expected and the winter was mild. Journeys, a Winnipeg shop for travellers, offers travel bookings, a pre-travel health clinic, passport photos, luggage, travel-related accessories, clothing, books, and a tanning salon all in one location. Journeys encouraged travellers to book immediately because vacation packages were being sold at incredibly low prices. Travellers who took advantage of this lull in the sun destination market also benefited from bundling their airfare and resort booking in a package, sometimes getting a price that was lower than a vacation within Canada.[39]

| MARKETING **INSIGHT** | PARKING: THERE'S MORE TO IT THAN MEETS THE EYE |

Nobody relishes seeing a parking ticket on his or her windshield. Many people don't think of a parking ticket as the penalty for consuming the product (parking, in this case) without adequately paying for it. Not too many people think of the money they feed a parking meter as the "price" they are paying for parking either.

Parking spaces can be a huge source of revenue for city governments. For example, in 2010, Montreal raised $60.9 million in parking meter revenues, not counting revenues from parking tickets. However, revenue generation is not the only reason for providing parking spaces. Parking is provided and parking prices are set by local governments or businesses to reduce vehicle traffic in an area (as part of a traffic management strategy), to reduce parking problems in a certain location (a parking management strategy), to recover facility costs, to generate revenues to fund other projects, to make a profit, or to pursue a combination of these objectives.

The price of parking is determined by taking several factors into account, such as the costs of the facility, equipment, maintenance, and personnel; the expected occupancy rates; and the objective of providing parking in an area. A number of pricing options are possible, each leading to a different outcome and benefit for the management. Here are some examples and considerations that go into them:

- Local governments often practise "congestion pricing," setting prices high during peak-traffic periods and low during other times. The high price during peak periods eases traffic, with a high turnover of vehicles during that time.

- To encourage use of local transit and reduce vehicle traffic in an area (e.g., downtown), parking prices should be set so as to exceed transit fares. For example, daily parking rates must be more than a round-trip ticket on local transit and monthly parking rates must exceed the cost of a monthly transit pass.

- Commercial parking lots price to maximize revenue. That is, they are priced at the highest amount the market will pay. Parking lots in an area often collectively determine the going rate for parking in that area.

- The average price elasticity of parking demand is relatively inelastic at around –0.3. That is, vehicle parking goes down (or up) by 3 percent with a 10 percent increase (or decrease) in parking rates.

- Paid parking is not restricted to vehicles on streets. Even aircraft and ships are charged for parking by airports and ports respectively. Interestingly, the parking rate for aircraft is based on weight and that for ships is based on length. For example, Toronto's Pearson Airport charges a daily parking rate of approximately $300 for a Boeing 747-400 that weighs about 250 tons. The Port of Vancouver has a daily "berthage" (parking) fee of about $5600 for a 300-metre cruise ship.

- Determining how many parking spaces to provide at a store or shopping mall requires marginal analysis (i.e., the additional revenue that will be generated by providing one extra space). Parking is usually free for customers at most shopping malls and off-street stores, but downtown malls often charge for parking. Stores and restaurants benefit from customers staying longer, as those who stay longer tend to buy more. Therefore, a high parking price is not in the best interests of the businesses in the mall, because it would make customers leave quickly. As an incentive to buy more, some stores and malls that have paid parking provide it free to those customers who spend a certain amount.

Underpricing parking can lead to inefficient use of parking facilities and excessive demand. Moreover, it can encourage longer-term parking and, therefore, reduce revenue from parking tickets. Overpricing parking can discourage vehicles from visiting the area, thereby adversely affecting nearby businesses served by the parking facility, which in turn will lower the demand for parking in the area. Considerable thought has to go into pricing any product. Determining how much to charge for parking is no different.

Sources: "Parking Pricing: Direct Charges for Using Parking Facilities," *TDM Encyclopedia*, Victoria Transport Policy Institute, September 2007; Erin Vaca and J. Richard Kuzmyak, "Parking Pricing and Fees," TCRP Report 95, Chapter 13, www.trb.org/publications/tcrp/ tcrp_rpt_95c13.pdf (viewed August 23, 2007); "Parking Meter Revenue up in 2010," *The Gazette*, June 16, 2011, p. A12; "Rates and Charges 2010," Greater Toronto Airports Authority, www.gtaa.com/local/files/en/Business/Rates_and_Charges_2010-2.pdf (viewed June 20, 2011); "Port Metro Vancouver: Fee Schedules," Vancouver Port Authority, www.portmetrovancouver.com/en/users/fees.aspx (viewed June 20, 2011).

PRICE ELASTICITY OF DEMAND Marketers need to know how responsive, or elastic, demand is to a change in price. Consider the two demand curves in Figure 14.1. In demand curve (a), a price increase from $10 to $15 leads to a relatively small decline in demand from 105 to 100. In demand curve (b), the same price increase leads to a substantial drop in demand from 150 to 50. If demand hardly changes with a small change in price, we say the demand is *inelastic*. If demand changes considerably, demand is *elastic*.

The higher the elasticity, the greater the volume growth resulting from a 1 percent price reduction. If demand is elastic, sellers will consider lowering the price. A lower price will produce more total revenue. This makes sense as long as the costs of producing and selling more units do not increase disproportionately.[40]

The effect of not considering the needs of customers for whom demand is most elastic is illustrated by the following example.

Public Transit

Understanding different consumer price elasticities should be an important facet of public-transit pricing. To encourage increased use, many transit authorities like Winnipeg Transit or Saskatoon Transit offer riders monthly passes instead of making riders purchase single-ride tickets. These passes strongly appeal to daily commuters, who receive a significant benefit from the discounted fare. However, since these people are price inelastic, the transit authorities may be leaving money on the table. In fact, the demand curve of many commuters is perfectly inelastic: no matter what happens to the fare, people without alternative means of transportation must get to work or school and get back home. Other commuters have a more elastic demand curve. These are people who have cars or who can walk to work. Shoppers and casual users who use transit for special events may be the most price elastic of all. Given these varying price sensitivities, transit authorities could improve their revenues by reversing their pricing strategies. However, this is rarely done, since transit is seen as a public service and a means of reducing pollution by getting cars off the roads.[41]

Price elasticity depends on the magnitude and direction of the contemplated price change. It may be negligible with a small price change and substantial with a large price change. It may differ for a price cut versus a price increase, and there may be a *price indifference band* within which price changes have little or no effect.

Finally, long-run price elasticity may differ from short-run elasticity. Buyers may continue to buy from a current supplier after a price increase but eventually switch suppliers. Here demand is more elastic in the long run than in the short run, or the reverse may happen: buyers may drop a supplier after a price increase but return later. The distinction between short-run and long-run elasticity means that sellers will not know the total effect of a price change until time passes.

One comprehensive study reviewing a 40-year period of academic research that investigated price elasticity yielded interesting findings:[42]

- The average price elasticity across all products, markets, and time periods studied was –2.62. In other words, a 1 percent decrease in prices led to a 2.62 percent increase in sales.

- Price elasticity magnitudes were higher for durable goods than for other goods, and higher for products in the introduction/growth stages of the product life cycle than in the mature/decline stages.

- Inflation led to substantially higher price elasticities, especially in the short run.

- Promotional price elasticities were higher than actual price elasticities in the short run (although the reverse was true in the long run).

- Price elasticities were higher at the individual item or SKU level than at the overall brand level.

Step 3: Estimating Costs

Demand sets a ceiling on the price the company can charge for its product. Costs set the floor. The company wants to charge a price that covers its cost of producing, distributing, and selling the product, including a fair return for its effort and risk. Yet when companies price products to cover their full costs, profitability isn't always the net result.

TYPES OF COSTS AND LEVELS OF PRODUCTION A company's costs take two forms, fixed and variable. **Fixed costs**, also known as **overhead**, are costs that do not vary with production level or sales revenue. A company must pay bills each month for rent, heat, interest, salaries, and so on regardless of output.

Variable costs vary directly with the level of production. For example, each hand calculator produced by TI incurs the cost of plastic, microprocessor chips, and packaging. These costs tend to be constant per unit produced, but they're called *variable* because their total varies with the number of units produced.

Total costs consist of the sum of the fixed and variable costs for any given level of production. **Average cost** is the cost per unit at that level of production; it equals total costs divided by production. Management wants to charge a price that will at least cover the total production costs at a given level of production.

To price intelligently, management needs to know how its costs vary with different levels of production. Take the case in which a company such as TI has built a fixed-size plant to produce 1000 hand calculators a day. The cost per unit is high if few units are produced per day. As production approaches 1000 units per day, the average cost falls because the fixed costs are spread over more units. Short-run average cost (SRAC) *increases* after 1000 units, however, because the plant becomes inefficient: workers must line up for machines, getting in each other's way, and machines break down more often (see Figure 14.2(a)).

If TI believes it can sell 2000 units per day, it should consider building a larger plant. The plant will use more efficient machinery and work arrangements, and the unit cost of producing 2000 calculators per day will be lower than the unit cost of producing 1000 per day. This is shown in the long-run average cost curve (LRAC) in Figure 14.2(b). In fact, a 3000-capacity plant would be even more efficient according to Figure 14.2(b), but a 4000-daily production plant would be less so because of increasing diseconomies of scale: there are too many workers to manage, and paperwork slows things down. Figure 14.2(b) indicates that a 3000-daily production plant is the optimal size if demand is strong enough to support this level of production.

There are more costs than those associated with manufacturing. To estimate the real profitability of selling to different types of retailers or customers, the manufacturer needs to use activity-based cost (ABC) accounting instead of standard cost accounting, as described in Chapter 5.

ACCUMULATED PRODUCTION Suppose TI runs a plant that produces 3000 hand calculators per day. As TI gains experience producing hand calculators, its methods improve. Workers learn shortcuts, materials flow more smoothly, and procurement costs fall. The result, as Figure 14.3 shows, is that average cost falls with accumulated production experience. Thus, the average cost of producing the first 100 000 hand calculators is $10 per calculator. When the company has produced the first 200 000 calculators, the average cost has fallen to $9. After its accumulated production experience doubles again to 400 000, the average cost is $8. This decline in the average cost with accumulated production experience is called the **experience curve** or **learning curve**.

Now suppose three firms compete in this industry, TI, A, and B. TI is the lowest-cost producer at $8, having produced 400 000 units in the past. If all three firms sell the calculator for $10, TI makes $2 profit per unit, A makes $1 per unit, and B breaks even. The smart move for TI would be to lower its price to $9. This will drive B out of the market, and even A may consider leaving. TI will pick up the business that would have gone to B (and possibly A). Furthermore, price-sensitive customers will enter the market at the lower price. As production increases beyond 400 000 units, TI's costs will drop still further and faster and will more than restore its profits, even at a price of $9. TI has used this aggressive pricing strategy repeatedly to gain market share and drive others out of the industry.

Experience-curve pricing nevertheless carries major risks. Aggressive pricing might give the product a cheap image. It also assumes that competitors are weak followers. The strategy leads the company to build more plants to meet demand, but a competitor may choose to innovate with a lower-cost technology. The market leader is now stuck with the old technology.

Most experience-curve pricing has focused on manufacturing costs, but all costs can be improved on, including marketing costs. If three firms are each investing a large sum of money in marketing, the firm that has used it longest might achieve the lowest costs. This firm can charge a little less for its product and still earn the same return, all other costs being equal.[43]

TARGET COSTING Costs change with production scale and experience. They can also change as a result of a concentrated effort by designers, engineers, and purchasing agents to reduce them through **target costing**.[44] Market research establishes a new product's desired functions and the price at which it will sell, given its appeal and competitors' prices. This price less desired profit margin leaves the target cost the marketer must achieve.

The firm must examine each cost element—design, engineering, manufacturing, sales—and bring down costs so that the final cost projections are in the target range. When ConAgra Foods decided to

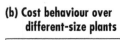

(a) Cost behaviour in a fixed-size plant

(b) Cost behaviour over different-size plants

FIGURE 14.2

Cost per Unit at Different Levels of Production per Period

FIGURE 14.3

Cost per Unit as a Function of Accumulated Production: The Experience Curve

increase the list prices of its Banquet frozen dinners to cover higher commodity costs, the average retail price of the meals increased from $1 to $1.25. When sales dropped significantly, management vowed to return to a $1 price, which necessitated cutting $250 million in other costs through a variety of methods, such as centralized purchasing and shipping, less expensive ingredients, and smaller portions.[45]

Companies can cut costs in many ways.[46] With General Mills, it was as simple as reducing the number of varieties of Hamburger Helper from 75 to 45 and the number of pasta shapes from 30 to 10. Dropping multicoloured Yoplait lids saved $2 million a year. Some companies are applying what they learned from making affordable products with scarce resources in developing countries such as India to cutting costs in developed markets. Cisco blends teams of U.S. software engineers with Indian supervisors. Other companies such as ALDI take advantage of the global scope.

ALDI

Germany's ALDI follows a simple formula globally. It stocks only about 1000 of the most popular everyday grocery and household items, compared with more than 20 000 at a traditional grocer such as Royal Ahold's Albert Heijn. Almost all the products carry ALDI's own exclusive label. Because it sells so few items, ALDI can exert strong control over quality and price and simplify shipping and handling, leading to high margins. With more than 8200 stores worldwide currently, ALDI brings in almost $60 billion in annual sales.[47]

Step 4: Analyzing Competitors' Costs, Prices, and Offers

Within the range of possible prices determined by market demand and company costs, the firm must take competitors' costs, prices, and possible price reactions into account. If the firm's offer contains features not offered by the nearest competitor, it should evaluate their worth to the customer and add that value to the competitor's price. If the competitor's offer contains some features not offered by the firm, the firm should subtract their value from its own price. Now the firm can decide whether it can charge more, the same, or less than the competitor.

The introduction or change of any price can provoke a response from customers, competitors, distributors, suppliers, and even government, as Bell Canada experienced.

Bell Canada

In early 2011, Bell Canada proposed usage-based pricing to the CRTC (Canadian Radio-television Telecommunications Commission) and received a great deal of criticism and concern from the public for proposing such a controversial change. Usage-based billing would have made customers pay based on how much data they upload to and download from the Internet. An online petition opposing the pricing change on OpenMedia.ca gathered nearly half a million digital signatures in just a few days. The CRTC initially ruled in favour of Bell's new pricing strategy, which would have rendered smaller Internet Service Providers (ISPs) unable to offer unlimited usage plans. Consumer and Internet advocacy groups lobbied hard against the decision, claiming that the change would lead to higher prices and violated existing competition laws. After facing a public backlash, parliamentary hearings, and a firm reprimand from the federal Industry Minister, Bell withdrew its proposal. As a compromise, Bell proposed an Aggregated Volume Pricing strategy, or AVP, which would provide wholesale ISPs with complete pricing flexibility on a per-consumer basis. Bell argued that the AVP would allow it to move forward with billions of dollars in investments to make necessary broadband infrastructure improvements that Canadians will need in the near future.[48]

How can a firm anticipate a competitor's reactions? One way is to assume that the competitor reacts in the standard way to a price being set or changed. Another is to assume that the competitor treats each price difference or change as a fresh challenge and reacts according to self-interest at the time. Now the company will need to research the competitor's current financial situation, recent sales, customer loyalty, and corporate objectives. If the competitor has a market share objective, it is likely to match price differences or changes.[49] If it has a profit-maximization objective, it may react by increasing its advertising budget or improving product quality.

The problem is complicated because the competitor can put different interpretations on lowered prices or a price cut: that the company is trying to steal the market, that it is doing poorly and trying to boost its sales, or that it wants the whole industry to reduce prices to stimulate total demand.

Step 5: Selecting a Pricing Method

Given the customers' demand schedule, the cost function, and competitors' prices, the company is now ready to select a price. Figure 14.4 summarizes the three major considerations in price setting: Costs set a floor to the price. Competitors' prices and the price of substitutes provide an orienting point. Customers' assessment of unique features establishes the price ceiling.

Companies select a pricing method that includes one or more of these three considerations. We will examine six price-setting methods: markup pricing, target-return pricing, perceived-value pricing, value pricing, going-rate pricing, and auction-type pricing.

MARKUP PRICING The most elementary pricing method is to add a standard **markup** to the product's cost. Construction companies submit job bids by estimating the total project cost and adding a standard markup for profit. Lawyers and accountants typically price by adding a standard markup on their time and costs.

Suppose a toaster manufacturer has the following costs and sales expectations.

Variable cost per unit	$10
Fixed costs	$300 000
Expected unit sales	50 000

The manufacturer's unit cost is given by:

$$\text{Unit cost} = \text{variable cost} + \frac{\text{fixed cost}}{\text{unit sales}} = \$10 + \frac{\$300\,000}{50\,000} = \$10$$

Now assume that the manufacturer wants to earn a 20 percent markup on sales. The manufacturer's markup price is given by:

$$\text{Markup price} = \frac{\text{unit cost}}{(1 - \text{desired return on sales})} = \frac{\$16}{1 - 0.2} = \$20$$

The manufacturer will charge dealers $20 per toaster and make a profit of $4 per unit. If dealers want to earn 50 percent on their selling price, they will mark up the toaster 100 percent to $40. Markups are generally higher on seasonal items (to cover the risk of not selling), specialty items, slower-moving items, items with high storage and handling costs, and demand-inelastic items, such as prescription drugs.

Does the use of standard markups make logical sense? Generally, no. Any pricing method that ignores current demand, perceived value, and competition is not likely to lead to the optimal price. Markup pricing works only if the marked-up price actually brings in the expected level of sales.

Still, markup pricing remains popular. First, sellers can determine costs much more easily than they can estimate demand. By tying the price to cost, sellers simplify the pricing task. Second, where all firms in the industry use this pricing method, prices tend to be similar and price competition is minimized. Third, many people feel that cost-plus pricing is fairer to both buyers and sellers. Sellers do not take advantage of buyers when the latter's demand becomes acute, and sellers earn a fair return on investment.

High Price
(No possible demand at this price)

Ceiling price
Customers' assessment of unique product features
Orienting point
Competitors' prices and prices of substitutes
Costs
Floor price

Low Price
(No possible profit at this price)

FIGURE 14.4

The Three Cs Model for Price Setting

TARGET-RETURN PRICING In **target-return pricing**, the firm determines the price that yields its target rate of return on investment. Public utilities, which need to make a fair return on investment, often use this method.

Suppose the toaster manufacturer has invested $1 million in the business and wants to set a price to earn a 20 percent ROI, specifically $200 000. The target-return price is given by the following formula:

$$\text{Target-return price} = \text{unit cost} + \frac{\text{desired return} \times \text{invested capital}}{\text{unit sales}}$$

$$= \$16 + \frac{0.20 \times \$1\,000\,000}{\$50\,000} = \$20$$

The manufacturer will realize this 20 percent ROI provided that its costs and estimated sales turn out to be accurate. But what if sales don't reach 50 000 units? The manufacturer can prepare a break-even chart to learn what would happen at other sales levels (see Figure 14.5). Fixed costs are $300 000 regardless of sales volume. Variable costs, not shown in the figure, rise with volume. Total costs equal the sum of fixed and variable costs. The total revenue curve starts at zero and rises with each unit sold.

The total revenue and total cost curves cross at 30 000 units. This is the break-even volume. We can verify it by the following formula:

$$\text{Break-even volume} = \frac{\text{fixed cost}}{(\text{price} - \text{variable cost})} = \frac{\$300\,000}{\$20 - \$10} = 30\,000$$

The manufacturer, of course, is hoping the market will buy 50 000 units at $20, in which case it earns $200 000 on its $1 million investment, but much depends on price elasticity and competitors' prices. Unfortunately, target-return pricing tends to ignore these considerations. The manufacturer needs to consider different prices and estimate their probable impacts on sales volume and profits.

The manufacturer should also search for ways to lower its fixed or variable costs, because lower costs will decrease its required break-even volume. Acer has been gaining share in the netbook market through rock-bottom prices made possible because of its bare-bones cost strategy. Acer sells only via retailers and other outlets and outsources all manufacturing and assembly, reducing its overhead to 8 percent of sales versus 14 percent at Dell and 15 percent at HP.[50]

PERCEIVED-VALUE PRICING An increasing number of companies now base their price on the customer's perceived value. Perceived value is made up of a host of inputs, such as the buyer's image of the product performance, the channel deliverables, the warranty quality, customer support, and softer attributes such as the supplier's reputation, trustworthiness, and esteem. Companies must deliver the value promised by their value proposition, and the customer must perceive this value. Firms use the other marketing program elements, such as advertising, the sales force, and the Internet, to communicate and enhance perceived value in buyers' minds.[51]

Caterpillar uses perceived value to set prices on its construction equipment. It might price its tractor at $100 000, although a similar competitor's tractor might be priced at $90 000. When a prospective customer asks a Caterpillar dealer why he should pay $10 000 more for the Caterpillar tractor, the dealer answers as follows:

$ 90 000	is the tractor's price if it is only equivalent to the competitor's tractor
$ 7 000	is the price premium for Caterpillar's superior durability
$ 6 000	is the price premium for Caterpillar's superior reliability
$ 5 000	is the price premium for Caterpillar's superior service
$ 2 000	is the price premium for Caterpillar's longer warranty on parts
$110 000	is the normal price to cover Caterpillar's superior value
− $ 10 000	discount
$100 000	final price

The Caterpillar dealer is able to show that although the customer is asked to pay a $10 000 premium, he or she is actually getting a $20 000 extra value! The customer chooses the Caterpillar tractor because he or she is convinced its lifetime operating costs will be lower.

Ensuring that customers appreciate the total value of a product or service offering is crucial. Even when a company claims that its offering delivers more total value, not all customers will respond positively. Some care only about price. But there is also typically a segment that cares about quality. The makers of Stag umbrellas in India—umbrellas are essential in the three months of near-nonstop monsoon rain in cities such as Mumbai—found themselves in a bitter price war with cheaper Chinese competitors. After

FIGURE 14.5

Break-Even Chart for
Determining Target-Return
Price and Break-Even
Volume

realizing they were sacrificing quality too much, Stag's managers decided to increase quality with new colours, designs, and features such as built-in high-power flashlights and prerecorded music. Despite higher prices, sales of the improved Stag umbrellas actually increased.[52]

The key to perceived-value pricing is to deliver more unique value than the competitor and to demonstrate this to prospective buyers. Thus, a company needs to fully understand the customer's decision-making process. For example, Goodyear found it hard to command a price premium for its more expensive new tires despite innovative new features to extend tread life. Because consumers had no reference price to compare tires, they tended to gravitate toward the lowest-priced offerings. Goodyear's solution was to price its models on expected miles of wear rather than their technical product features, making product comparisons easier.[53]

The company can try to determine the value of its offering in several ways: managerial judgments within the company, value of similar products, focus groups, surveys, experimentation, analysis of historical data, and conjoint analysis.[54] Table 14.4 contains six key considerations in developing value-based pricing.

VALUE PRICING In recent years, several companies have adopted **value pricing**: they win loyal customers by charging a fairly low price for a high-quality offering. Value pricing is thus not a matter of simply setting lower prices; it is a matter of re-engineering the company's operations to become a low-cost producer without sacrificing quality, to attract a large number of value-conscious customers.

TABLE 14.4	A FRAMEWORK OF QUESTIONS FOR PRACTISING VALUE-BASED PRICING
1.	What is the market strategy for the segment? (What does the supplier want to accomplish? What would the supplier like to have happen?)
2.	What is the differential value that is *transparent* to target customers? (*Transparent* means that target customers easily understand how the supplier calculates the differential value between its offering and the next best alternative, and that the differential value can be verified with the customer's own data.)
3.	What is the price of the next best alternative offering?
4.	What is the cost of the supplier's market offering?
5.	What pricing tactics will be used initially or eventually? ("Pricing tactics" are changes from a price that a supplier has set for its marketing offering—such as discounts—that motivate customers to take actions that benefit the supplier.)
6.	What is the customer's expectation of a "fair" price?

Source: James C. Anderson, Marc Wouters, and Wouter Van Rossum, "Why the Highest Price Isn't the Best Price," *MIT Sloan Management Review*, Winter 2010, pp. 69–76. From *MIT Sloan Management Review* © 2006 by Massachusetts Institute of Technology. All rights reserved. Distributed by Tribune Media Services.

Among the best practitioners of value pricing in Canada are IKEA, Winners, and WestJet. In the early 1990s, Procter & Gamble created quite a stir when it reduced prices on supermarket staples such as Pampers diapers, liquid Tide detergent, and Folgers coffee to value price them. To do so, P&G redesigned the way it developed, manufactured, distributed, priced, marketed, and sold products to deliver better value at every point in the supply chain.[55] Its acquisition of Gillette in 2005 for $57 billion (a record five times Gillette's sales) brought another brand into its fold, one that has also traditionally adopted a value-pricing strategy.

Value pricing can change the manner by which a company sets prices too. One company that sold and maintained switch boxes in a variety of sizes for telephone lines found that the probability of failure—and thus maintenance costs—was proportional to the number of switches customers had in their boxes rather than to the dollar value of the installed boxes. The number of switches could vary in a box, though. Therefore, rather than charging customers based on the total spent on their installation, the company began charging based on the total number of switches needing servicing.[56]

An important type of value pricing is **everyday low pricing (EDLP)**. A retailer that holds to an EDLP pricing policy charges a constant low price with few or no price promotions and special sales. Constant prices eliminate week-to-week price uncertainty and the "high–low" pricing of promotion-oriented competitors. In **high–low pricing**, the retailer charges higher prices on an everyday basis but runs frequent promotions with prices temporarily lower than the EDLP level.[57] These two strategies have been shown to affect consumer price judgments—deep discounts (EDLP) can lead customers to perceive lower prices over time than can frequent, shallow discounts (high–low), even if the actual averages are the same.[58]

In recent years, high–low pricing has given way to EDLP at such widely different venues as Toyota Scion car dealers and upscale department stores such as Nordstrom, but the king of EDLP is surely Walmart, which practically defined the term. Except for a few sale items every month, Walmart promises everyday low prices on major brands.

EDLP provides the customer with benefits of time and money. Toyota believes that its Gen Y target dislikes haggling because it takes too long. These buyers collect a lot of information online anyway, so Toyota cut the time to sell Scions from the industry average of 4.5 hours to 45 minutes by requiring fewer managers to approve negotiated prices and less advertising of sales.[59] Some retailers such as Dollarama base their entire marketing strategy around *extreme* everyday low pricing.

Dollarama

A new breed of price-conscious shoppers are frequenting stores like Dollarama, a dollar store chain with over 650 stores across Canada. Whether shoppers are on a tight budget or are just thrifty, Dollarama attracts both kinds. Recession-related fears have influenced Canadian consumers to become more price-conscious when they shop. Despite the fact that the economy has bounced back, Dollarama continues to thrive, attracting consumers of all incomes. While the industry reported an average of 5.1 percent higher retail sales in Canada in 2010, Dollarama's sales were over twice that at 13.3 percent, with revenues at $1.4 billion. The chain is able to offer low prices by cutting deals with the manufacturers directly rather than the distributors that most retailers deal with. In addition, Dollarama differentiates itself from other dollar stores with its bright, spacious, clean, and neatly organized stores, which make shopping there a pleasant experience.[60]

Dollarama has been thriving as customers become more thrifty during a recession.

The most important reason retailers adopt EDLP is that constant sales and promotions are costly and have eroded consumer confidence in everyday shelf prices. Consumers also have less time and patience for past traditions like watching for supermarket specials and clipping coupons. Yet promotions do create excitement and draw shoppers, so EDLP does not guarantee success. As supermarkets face heightened competition from their counterparts and alternative channels, many supermarkets find that the key is a combination of high–low and everyday low pricing strategies, with increased advertising and promotions.

GOING-RATE PRICING In **going-rate pricing**, the firm bases its price largely on competitors' prices. In oligopolistic industries that sell a commodity such as steel, paper, or fertilizer, all firms normally charge the same price. Smaller firms follow the leader, changing their prices when the market leader's prices change rather than when their own demand or costs change. Some may charge a small premium or discount, but they preserve the difference. Thus, minor gasoline retailers usually charge a few cents less per gallon than the major oil companies, without letting the difference increase or decrease.

Going-rate pricing is quite popular. Where costs are difficult to measure or competitive response is uncertain, firms feel the going price is a good solution because it is thought to reflect the industry's collective wisdom.

AUCTION-TYPE PRICING Auction-type pricing is growing more popular, especially with scores of electronic marketplaces selling everything from pigs to used cars as firms dispose of excess inventories or used goods. These are the three major types of auctions and their separate pricing procedures:

■ *English auctions (ascending bids)* have one seller and many buyers. On sites such as eBay and Amazon.com, the seller puts up an item and bidders raise the offer price until the top price is reached. The highest bidder gets the item. English auctions are used today for selling antiques, cattle, real estate, and used equipment and vehicles. After watching eBay and other ticket brokers, scalpers, and middlemen reap millions by charging what the market would bear, Ticketmaster has overhauled the way it sells tickets to try to gain more of the multibillion-dollar ticket resale industry. It now runs auctions for 30 percent of major music tours, including popular artists such as Christina Aguilera and Madonna, and allows some customers to resell their seats on its website.[61]

■ *Dutch auctions (descending bids)* feature one seller and many buyers, or one buyer and many sellers. In the first kind, an auctioneer announces a high price for a product and then slowly decreases the price until a bidder accepts. In the other, the buyer announces something he or she wants to buy, and potential sellers compete to offer the lowest price. FreeMarkets.com—later acquired by Ariba—helped Royal Mail Group plc, the United Kingdom's public mail service company, save approximately £2.5 million (almost $4 million), in part via an auction where 25 airlines bid for its international freight business.[62]

■ *Sealed-bid auctions* let would-be suppliers submit only one bid; they cannot know the other bids. Governments often use this method to procure supplies. A supplier will not bid below its cost but cannot bid too high for fear of losing the job. The net effect of these two pulls is the bid's *expected profit.*[63]

To buy equipment for its drug researchers, Pfizer uses reverse auctions in which suppliers submit online the lowest price they are willing to be paid. If the increased savings a firm obtains in an online auction translate into decreased margins for an incumbent supplier, however, the supplier may feel the firm is opportunistically squeezing out price concessions.[64] Online auctions with a large number of bidders, greater economic stakes, and more visibility in pricing result in greater overall satisfaction, more positive future expectations, and fewer perceptions of opportunism.

Step 6: Selecting the Final Price

Pricing methods narrow the range from which the company must select its final price. In selecting that price, the company must consider additional factors, including the impact of other marketing activities, company pricing policies, gain-and-risk-sharing pricing, and the impact of price on other parties.

IMPACT OF OTHER MARKETING ACTIVITIES The final price must take into account the brand's quality and advertising relative to the competition. In a classic study, Paul Farris and David Reibstein examined the relationships among relative price, relative quality, and relative advertising for 227 consumer businesses and found the following:[65]

■ Brands with average relative quality but high relative advertising budgets could charge premium prices. Consumers were willing to pay higher prices for known rather than for unknown products.

■ Brands with high relative quality and high relative advertising obtained the highest prices. Conversely, brands with low quality and low advertising charged the lowest prices.

■ For market leaders, the positive relationship between high prices and high advertising held most strongly in the later stages of the product life cycle.

These findings suggest that price is not necessarily as important as quality and other benefits.

COMPANY PRICING POLICIES The price must be consistent with company pricing policies. Yet companies are not averse to establishing pricing penalties under certain circumstances.[66]

Airlines charge $150 to those who change their reservations on discount tickets. Banks charge fees for too many withdrawals in a month or early withdrawal of a guaranteed investment certificate. Dentists, hotels, car rental companies, and other service providers charge penalties for no-shows who miss appointments or reservations. Although these policies are often justifiable, marketers must use them judiciously and not unnecessarily alienate customers.

Many companies set up a pricing department to develop policies and establish or approve decisions. The aim is to ensure that salespeople quote prices that are reasonable to customers and profitable to the company.

GAIN-AND-RISK-SHARING PRICING Buyers may resist accepting a seller's proposal because of a high perceived level of risk. The seller has the option of offering to absorb part or all the risk if it does not deliver the full promised value. Some recent risk-sharing applications include big computer hardware purchases and health plans for big unions.

Baxter Healthcare, a leading medical products firm, was able to secure a contract for an information management system from Columbia/HCA, a leading health-care provider, by guaranteeing the firm several million dollars in savings over an eight-year period. When Queen's School of Business launched its first private MBA program, it guaranteed students that their salaries would increase or their tuition would be refunded. An increasing number of companies, especially business marketers who promise great savings with their equipment, may have to stand ready to guarantee the promised savings but also participate in the upside if the gains are much greater than expected.

IMPACT OF PRICE ON OTHER PARTIES How will distributors and dealers feel about the contemplated price?[67] If they don't make enough profit, they may choose not to bring the product to market. Will the sales force be willing to sell at that price? How will competitors react? Will suppliers raise their prices when they see the company's price? Will the government intervene and prevent this price from being charged?

The Competition Bureau of Canada prohibits sellers from setting prices based on agreements with competitors: price-fixing is illegal and subject to heavy fines. For instance, Panasonic Corporation in 2010 was fined $1.5 million by the Federal Court for price-fixing of its refrigeration products. Many provisions in the Competition Act protect consumers against deceptive pricing practices. For example, it is illegal for a company to set artificially high "regular" prices, then announce a "sale" at prices close to previous everyday prices, as learned the hard way by Suzy Shier, which was fined $1 million in 2003.[68]

ADAPTING THE PRICE

Companies usually do not set a single price but rather develop a pricing structure that reflects variations in geographical demand and costs, market-segment requirements, purchase timing, order levels, delivery frequency, guarantees, service contracts, and other factors. As a result of discounts, allowances, and promotional support, a company rarely realizes the same profit from each unit of a product that it sells. Here we will examine several price-adaptation strategies: geographical pricing, price discounts and allowances, promotional pricing, and differentiated pricing.

Geographical Pricing (Cash, Countertrade, Barter)

In geographical pricing, the company decides how to price its products to different customers in different locations and countries. Should the company charge higher prices to distant customers to cover the higher shipping costs, or a lower price to win additional business? How should it account for exchange rates and the strength of different currencies? A weakening U.S. dollar over recent years has allowed some American companies to mark up prices and still match more expensive imports.[69] In addition, the large number of Canadians making weekend shopping trips down to the States has been a welcome relief for the U.S. retailers, who have seen their sales plummet during the recession.

Another question is how to get paid. This issue is critical when buyers lack sufficient hard currency to pay for their purchases. Many buyers want to offer other items in payment, a practice known as **countertrade**. Companies are often forced to engage in countertrade if they want the business. Countertrade may account for 15 percent to 20 percent of world trade and takes several forms:[70]

- *Barter.* The buyer and seller directly exchange goods, with no money and no third party involved.
- *Compensation deal.* The seller receives some percentage of the payment in cash and the rest in products. A British aircraft manufacturer sold planes to Brazil for 70 percent cash and the rest in coffee.

■ *Buyback arrangement.* The seller sells a plant, equipment, or technology to another country and agrees to accept as partial payment products manufactured with the supplied equipment. A U.S. chemical company built a plant for an Indian company and accepted partial payment in cash and the remainder in chemicals manufactured at the plant.

■ *Offset.* The seller receives full payment in cash but agrees to spend a substantial amount of the money in that country within a stated time period. PepsiCo sold its cola syrup to Russia for rubles and agreed to buy Russian vodka at a certain rate to sell in the United States.

Price Discounts and Allowances

Most companies will adjust their list price and give discounts and allowances for early payment, volume purchases, and off-season buying (see Table 14.5).[71] Companies must do this carefully or find that their profits are much lower than planned.[72]

Discount pricing has become the modus operandi of a surprising number of companies offering both products and services. Salespeople, in particular, are quick to give discounts in order to close a sale. But word can get around fast that the company's list price is "soft," and discounting becomes the norm, undermining the value perceptions of the offerings. Some product categories self-destruct by always being on sale.

Some companies with overcapacity are tempted to give discounts or even begin to supply a retailer with a store-brand version of their product at a deep discount. Because the store brand is priced lower, however, it may start making inroads on the manufacturer's brand. Manufacturers should consider the implications of supplying retailers at a discount, because they may end up losing long-run profits in an effort to meet short-run volume goals.

Only people with higher incomes and higher product involvement willingly pay more for features, customer service, quality, added convenience, and the brand name. So it can be a mistake for a strong, distinctive brand to plunge into price discounting to respond to low-price attacks. At the same time, discounting can be a useful tool if a company can gain concessions in return, such as the customer agreeing to sign a longer contract, order electronically, or buy in truckload quantities.

Sales management needs to monitor the proportion of customers receiving discounts, the average discount, and any salespeople over-relying on discounting. Higher levels of management should conduct a **net price analysis** to arrive at the "real price" of the offering. The real price is affected not only by discounts,

TABLE 14.5	PRICE DISCOUNTS AND ALLOWANCES
Discount	A price reduction to buyers who pay bills promptly. A typical example is "2/10, net 30," which means that payment is due within 30 days and that the buyer can deduct 2 percent by paying the bill within 10 days.
Quantity Discount	A price reduction to those who buy large volumes. A typical example is "$10 per unit for fewer than 100 units; $9 per unit for 100 or more units." Quantity discounts must be offered equally to all customers and must not exceed the cost savings to the seller. They can be offered on each order placed or on the number of units ordered over a given period.
Functional Discount	Discount (also called *trade discount*) offered by a manufacturer to trade-channel members if they will perform certain functions, such as selling, storing, and record keeping. Manufacturers must offer the same functional discounts within each channel.
Seasonal Discount	A price reduction to those who buy merchandise or services out of season. Hotels, motels, and airlines offer seasonal discounts in slow selling periods.
Allowance	An extra payment designed to gain reseller participation in special programs. *Trade-in allowances* are granted for turning in an old item when buying a new one. *Promotional allowances* reward dealers for participating in advertising and sales support programs.

but by other expenses that reduce the realized price (see "Promotional Pricing"). Suppose the company's list price is $3000. The average discount is $300. The company's promotional spending averages $450 (15 percent of the list price). Retailers are given co-op advertising money of $150 to back the product. The company's net price is $2100, not $3000.

Promotional Pricing

Companies can use several pricing techniques to stimulate early purchase:

- *Loss-leader pricing.* Supermarkets and department stores often drop the price on well-known brands to stimulate additional store traffic. This pays if the revenue on the additional sales compensates for the lower margins on the loss-leader items. Manufacturers of loss-leader brands typically object because this practice can dilute the brand image and bring complaints from retailers who charge the list price. Manufacturers have tried to keep intermediaries from using loss-leader pricing through lobbying for retail-price-maintenance laws, but these laws have been revoked.

- *Special event pricing.* Sellers will establish special prices in certain seasons to draw in more customers. Every August, there are back-to-school sales.

- *Special customer pricing.* Sellers will offer special prices exclusively to certain customers. Fairmont Hotels offers its Fairmont President's Club members special room rates that are not available to the general public. In addition, Club members get a number of complimentary services, such as Wi-Fi Internet access, health-club access, shoeshines, local calls, and use of golf clubs, whereas other guests have to pay for these services.[73]

- *Cash rebates.* Auto companies and other consumer-goods companies offer cash rebates to encourage purchase of the manufacturers' products within a specified time period. Rebates can help clear inventories without cutting the stated list price.

- *Low-interest financing.* Instead of cutting its price, the company can offer customers low-interest financing. Automakers have used no-interest financing to try to attract more customers.

- *Longer payment terms.* Sellers, especially mortgage banks and auto companies, stretch loans over longer periods and thus lower the monthly payments. Consumers often worry less about the cost (the interest rate) of a loan, and more about whether they can afford the monthly payment.

- *Warranties and service contracts.* Companies can promote sales by adding a free or low-cost warranty or service contract.

- *Psychological discounting.* This strategy sets an artificially high price and then offers the product at substantial savings, for example, "Was $359, now $299." Discounts from normal prices are a legitimate form of promotional pricing. However, some unscrupulous retailers advertise these types of prices and then try to switch people to higher-priced items by stating the advertised item is sold out. Called "bait and switch," this is illegal under Canada's Competition Act. The Competition Bureau penalizes offenders and the Better Business Bureau represents consumers and fights illegal discount tactics.

"Marketing Memo: Types of Illegal Pricing" discusses pricing strategies that are prohibited.

Promotional-pricing strategies are often a zero-sum game. If they work, competitors copy them and they lose their effectiveness. If they don't work, they waste money that could have been put into other marketing tools, such as building up product quality and service or strengthening product image through advertising.

Differentiated Pricing

Companies often adjust their basic price to accommodate differences in customers, products, locations, and so on. For instance, one could buy a men's white button-down shirt for less than $15 at some stores or as much as $275 for the Canali brand at Harry Rosen.[74]

Price discrimination occurs when a company sells a product or service at two or more prices that do not reflect a proportional difference in costs. In first-degree price discrimination, the seller charges a separate price to each customer depending on the intensity of his or her demand.

In second-degree price discrimination, the seller charges less to buyers of larger volumes. With certain services such as cell phone service, however, tiered pricing results in consumers paying *more* with higher levels of usage. With the iPhone, 3 percent of U.S. users accounted for 40 percent of the traffic on AT&T's network, resulting in costly network upgrades.[75]

MARKETING **MEMO**   TYPES OF ILLEGAL PRICING

In an attempt to increase sales or profits, or simply in order to survive in the marketplace, marketers may be tempted to take their pricing strategies a little too far. According to the Competition Act, here are some pricing tactics considered illegal in Canada:

- Price Fixing—a manufacturer stipulating (rather than just suggesting) what price retailers should sell at, or collaborating with competitors to set prices.
- Predatory Pricing—selling at an unusually low price to eliminate competition.
- False Ordinary Selling Price—promoting product at a sale price with reference to an inflated regular price.
- Bid Rigging—following a call for tenders, collaborating with another bidder on bid amounts or agreeing not to bid.
- Double Ticketing—not selling at the lower of two prices communicated to the customer, displayed in the store or on the product.
- Bait-and-Switch—luring customers into a retail outlet with exceptionally low prices and then switching the customer to a higher priced item, often making the customer believe that the lower-priced product is sold out.

Source: Competition Bureau Canada, "Price-Related Representations," www.competitionbureau.gc.ca/eic/site/cb-bc.nsf/eng/00522.html (viewed June 20, 2011).

In third-degree price discrimination, the seller charges different amounts to different classes of buyers, as in the following cases:

- *Customer-segment pricing.* Different customer groups pay different prices for the same product or service. For example, museums often charge a lower admission fee to students and senior citizens.

- *Product-form pricing.* Different versions of the product are priced differently, but not proportionately to their costs. Evian prices a 1.4-litre bottle of its mineral water at $2.00 and 50 mL of the same water in a moisturizer spray at $6.00.

- *Image pricing.* Some companies price the same product at two different levels based on image differences. A perfume manufacturer can put the perfume in one bottle, give it a name and image, and price it at $20 for 100 mL. The same perfume in another bottle with a different name and image and can sell for $80 for 100 mL.

- *Channel pricing.* Coca-Cola carries a different price depending on whether the consumer purchases it in a fine restaurant, a fast-food restaurant, or a vending machine.

- *Location pricing.* The same product is priced differently at different locations even though the cost of offering it at each location is the same. A theatre varies its seat prices according to audience preferences for different locations.

- *Time pricing.* Prices are varied by season, day, or hour. Public utilities vary energy rates to commercial users by time of day and weekend versus weekday. Restaurants charge less to early bird customers, and some hotels charge less on weekends.

The airline and hospitality industries use yield management systems and **yield pricing**, by which they offer discounted but limited early purchases, higher-priced late purchases, and the lowest rates on unsold inventory just before it expires.[76] Airlines charge different fares to passengers on the same flight, depending on the seating class; the time of day (morning or night coach); the day of the week (workday or weekend); the season; the person's employer, past business, or status (youth, military, senior citizen); and so on.

That's why on a flight from Toronto to Vancouver, you might pay $400 and sit across from someone who paid $800. For instance, Continental Airlines launches 2000 flights a day and each has between 10 and 20 prices. The carrier starts booking flights 330 days in advance, and every flying day is different from every other flying day. At any given moment, the market has more than 7 million prices. And in a system that tracks the difference in prices and the price of competitors' offerings, airlines collectively charge 75 000 different prices a day! It's a system designed to punish procrastinators by charging them the highest possible prices.

The phenomenon of offering different pricing schedules to different consumers and dynamically adjusting prices is exploding.[77] Many companies are using software packages that provide real-time controlled tests of actual consumer response to different pricing schedules. Constant price variation can be tricky, however, where consumer relationships are concerned. Research shows it's most effective when there's no bond between the buyer and the seller. One way to make it work is to offer customers a unique bundle of products and services to meet their needs precisely, making it harder to make price comparisons.

The tactic most companies favour, however, is to use variable prices as a reward rather than a penalty. For instance, most hotels and airlines offer lower prices when customers book early. Customers are also getting savvier about how to avoid buyer's remorse from overpaying. They are changing their buying behaviour to accommodate the new realities of dynamic pricing, where prices vary frequently by channels, products, customers, and time.

Most consumers are probably not even aware of the degree to which they are the targets of discriminatory pricing. For instance, catalogue retailers such as Victoria's Secret routinely send out catalogues that sell identical goods at different prices. Consumers who live in a more free-spending postal code may see only the higher prices. Office product superstore Staples also sends out office supply catalogues with different prices.

Although some forms of price discrimination (in which sellers offer different price terms to different people within the same trade group) are illegal, price discrimination is legal if the seller can prove its costs are different when selling different volumes or different qualities of the same product to different retailers. Predatory pricing—selling below cost with the intention of destroying competition—is unlawful, though.[78] Air Canada has been accused of predatory pricing on a number of occasions by competitors such as former airline Canada 3000, CanJet, and WestJet.

For price discrimination to work, certain conditions must exist. First, the market must be segmentable and the segments must show different intensities of demand. Second, members in the lower-price segment must not be able to resell the product to the higher-price segment. Third, competitors must not be able to undersell the firm in the higher-price segment. Fourth, the cost of segmenting and policing the market must not exceed the extra revenue derived from price discrimination. Fifth, the practice must not breed customer resentment and ill will. Sixth, the particular form of price discrimination must not be illegal, of course.[79]

INITIATING AND RESPONDING TO PRICE CHANGES

Companies often need to cut or raise prices.

Initiating Price Cuts

Several circumstances might lead a firm to cut prices. One is *excess plant capacity*: the firm needs additional business and cannot generate it through increased sales effort, product improvement, or other measures. Companies sometimes initiate price cuts in a *drive to dominate the market through lower costs*. Either the company starts with lower costs than its competitors, or it initiates price cuts in the hope of gaining market share and lower costs.

Cutting prices to keep customers or beat competitors often encourages customers to demand price concessions, however, and trains salespeople to offer them.[80] A price-cutting strategy can lead to other possible traps:

■ *Low-quality trap.* Consumers assume quality is low.

■ *Fragile-market share trap.* A low price buys market share but not market loyalty. The same customers will shift to any lower-priced firm that comes along.

■ *Shallow-pockets trap.* Higher-priced competitors match the lower prices but have longer staying power because of deeper cash reserves.

■ *Price-war trap.* Competitors respond by lowering their prices even more, triggering a price war.[81]

Customers often question the motivation behind price changes.[82] They may assume that the item is about to be replaced by a new model, the item is faulty and is not selling well, the firm is in financial trouble, the price will come down even further, or the quality has been reduced. The firm must monitor these attributions carefully.

TABLE 14.6	PROFITS BEFORE AND AFTER A PRICE INCREASE

	Before	After	
Price	$10	$10.10	(a 1% price increase)
Units sold	100	100	
Revenue	$1000	$1010	
Costs	−970	−970	
Profit	$30	$40	(a 33⅓% profit increase)

Initiating Price Increases

A successful price increase can raise profits considerably. If the company's profit margin is 3 percent of sales, a 1 percent price increase will increase profits by 33 percent if sales volume is unaffected. This situation is illustrated in Table 14.6. The assumption is that a company charged $10 and sold 100 units and had costs of $970, leaving a profit of $30, or 3 percent on sales. By raising its price by 10 cents (a 1 percent price increase), it boosted its profits by 33 percent, assuming the same sales volume.

A major circumstance provoking price increases is *cost inflation*. Rising costs unmatched by productivity gains squeeze profit margins and lead companies to regular rounds of price increases. Companies often raise their prices by more than the cost increase, in anticipation of further inflation or government price controls, in a practice called *anticipatory pricing*.

Another factor leading to price increases is *overdemand*. When a company cannot supply all its customers, it can raise its prices, ration supplies, or both. It can increase price in the following ways, each of which has a different impact on buyers:

- *Delayed quotation pricing.* The company does not set a final price until the product is finished or delivered. This pricing is prevalent in industries with long production lead times, such as industrial construction and heavy equipment.

- *Escalator clauses.* The company requires the customer to pay today's price and all or part of any inflation increase that takes place before delivery. An escalator clause bases price increases on some specified price index. Escalator clauses are found in contracts for major industrial projects, such as aircraft construction and bridge building.

- *Unbundling.* The company maintains its price but removes or prices separately one or more elements that were part of the former offer, such as free delivery or installation. Car companies sometimes add higher-end audio entertainment systems or GPS navigation systems as extras to their vehicles.

- *Reduction of discounts.* The company instructs its sales force not to offer its normal cash and quantity discounts.

Although there is always a chance a price increase can carry some positive meanings to customers—for example, that the item is "hot" and represents an unusually good value—consumers generally dislike higher prices. In passing price increases on to customers, the company must avoid looking like a price gouger.[83] Coca-Cola's proposed smart vending machines that would raise prices as temperatures rose and Amazon.com's dynamic pricing experiment that varied prices by purchase occasion both became front-page news. The more similar the products or offerings from a company, the more likely consumers are to interpret any pricing differences as unfair. Product customization and differentiation and communications that clarify differences are thus critical.[84]

Generally, consumers prefer small price increases on a regular basis to sudden, sharp increases. Their memories are long, and they can turn against companies they perceive as price gougers. Price hikes without corresponding investments in the value of the brand increase vulnerability to lower-priced competition. Consumers may be willing to trade down because they can no longer convince themselves the higher-priced brand is worth it.

Several techniques help consumers avoid sticker shock and a hostile reaction when prices rise. One is maintaining a sense of fairness around any price increase, such as by giving customers advance notice so they can do forward buying or shop around. Sharp price increases need to be explained in understandable terms. Making low-visibility price moves first is also a good technique: eliminating discounts, increasing minimum order sizes, and curtailing production of low-margin products are examples, and contracts or bids for long-term projects should contain escalator clauses based on such factors as increases in recognized national price indexes.[85]

Given strong consumer resistance, marketers go to great lengths to find alternate approaches that avoid increasing prices when they otherwise would have done so. Here are a few popular ones:

- Shrinking the amount of product instead of raising the price. (Tropicana downsized its 1.89-litre [the equivalent of half a gallon] orange juice carton to 1.75 litres in Canada.)
- Substituting less-expensive materials or ingredients. (Many candy bar companies substituted synthetic chocolate for real chocolate to fight cocoa price increases.)
- Reducing or removing product features. (Sears engineered down a number of its appliances so that they could be priced competitively with those sold in discount stores.)
- Removing or reducing product services, such as installation or free delivery.
- Using less-expensive packaging material or larger package sizes.
- Reducing the number of sizes and models offered.
- Creating new economy brands. (Air Canada launched a new regional brand, Air Canada Express, to serve the shorter routes with its smaller aircraft and fewer crew members.)

Telus responded to competitive pressure by introducing a new discount brand.

Telus

In 2011, Telus Communications Company embarked on a new pricing strategy, launching a contract-free, no-activation fee, flat-rate cell phone service under the brand name Clearnet, to be tried in British Columbia and Alberta. This new brand would operate alongside the company's existing Koodo brand, a nationwide lower-cost option. More than just a discount brand, Clearnet offers two simple plans priced at $45 and $55 per month as of mid-2011, with the latter plan offering unlimited text messaging. By launching the Clearnet brand, Telus hopes to protect its subscriber base from new low-cost competitors such as Wind Mobile and Bell's Solo while grabbing a share of the no-contract market. This new brand will also help Telus mitigate lost revenues from land line erosion in its traditional home phone business by moving customers over to its new no-contract cell phone service instead of losing them to other cell phone providers.[86]

Responding to Competitors' Price Changes

How should a firm respond to a competitor's price cut? In general, the best response varies with the situation. The company must consider the product's stage in the life cycle, its importance in the company's portfolio, the competitor's intentions and resources, the market's price and quality sensitivity, the behaviour of costs with volume, and the company's alternative opportunities.

In markets characterized by high product homogeneity, the firm can search for ways to enhance its augmented product. If it cannot find any, it may need to meet the price reduction. If the competitor raises its price in a homogeneous product market, other firms might not match it if the increase will not benefit the industry as a whole. Then the leader will need to roll back the increase.

In heterogeneous product markets, a firm has more latitude. It needs to consider the following issues: (1) Why did the competitor change the price? To steal the market, to use excess capacity, to meet changing cost conditions, or to lead an industry-wide price change? (2) Does the competitor plan to make the price change temporary or permanent? (3) What will happen to the company's market share and profits if it does not respond? Are other companies going to respond? (4) What are the competitors' and other firms' responses likely to be to each possible reaction?

Market leaders often face aggressive price-cutting by smaller firms trying to build market share. Using price, Fuji has attacked Kodak, Schick has attacked Gillette, and AMD has attacked Intel. Brand leaders also face lower-priced store brands. Three possible responses to low-cost competitors are (1) further differentiate the product or service, (2) introduce a low-cost venture, or (3) reinvent as a low-cost player.[87] The right strategy depends on the ability of the firm to generate more demand or cut costs.

An extended analysis of alternatives may not always be feasible when the attack occurs. The company may have to react decisively within hours or days, especially where prices change with some frequency and it is important to react quickly, such as in the meat-packing, lumber, or oil industries. It would make better sense to anticipate possible competitors' price changes and prepare contingent responses.

SUMMARY

1. Despite the increased role of nonprice factors in modern marketing, price remains a critical element of marketing. Price is the only element that produces revenue; the others produce costs. Pricing decisions have become more challenging, however, in a changing economic and technological environment.

2. In setting pricing policy, a company follows a six-step procedure. It selects its pricing objective. It estimates the demand curve, the probable quantities it will sell at each possible price. It estimates how its costs vary at different levels of output, at different levels of accumulated production experience, and for differentiated marketing offers. It examines competitors' costs, prices, and offers. It selects a pricing method, and it selects the final price.

3. Companies usually set not a single price, but rather a pricing structure that reflects variations in geographical demand and costs, market-segment requirements, purchase timing, order levels, and other factors. Several price-adaptation strategies are available: (1) geographical pricing, (2) price discounts and allowances, (3) promotional pricing, and (4) differentiated pricing.

4. Firms often need to change their prices. A price decrease might be brought about by excess plant capacity, an attempt to steal market share, a desire to dominate the market through lower costs, or economic recession. A price increase might be brought about by cost inflation or overdemand. Companies must carefully manage customer perceptions when raising prices.

5. Companies must anticipate competitor price changes and prepare contingent responses. A number of responses are possible in terms of maintaining or changing price or quality.

6. The firm facing a competitor's price change must try to understand the competitor's intent and the likely duration of the change. Strategy often depends on whether a firm is producing homogeneous or heterogeneous products. A market leader attacked by lower-priced competitors can seek to better differentiate itself, introduce its own low-cost competitor, or transform itself more completely.

APPLICATIONS

Marketing Debate: Is the Right Price a Fair Price?

Prices are often set to satisfy demand or to reflect the premium that consumers are willing to pay for a product or service. Some critics shudder, however, at the thought of $2 bottles of water, $150 running shoes, and $500 concert tickets.

Take a position: Prices should reflect the value consumers are willing to pay *versus* Prices should reflect only the cost of making a product or delivering a service.

Marketing Discussion: Pricing Methods

Think about the pricing methods described in this chapter—markup pricing, target-return pricing, perceived-value pricing, value pricing, going-rate pricing, and auction-type pricing. As a consumer, which do you prefer to deal with? Why? If the average price were to stay the same, which would you prefer a firm to do: (1) set one price and not deviate or (2) employ slightly higher prices most of the year but offer slightly discounted prices or specials for certain occasions?

MARKETING **EXCELLENCE**	eBAY

In 1995, Pierre Omidayar, a French-Iranian immigrant, wrote the code for an auction website where everyone would have equal access to a single global marketplace. Omidayar couldn't believe it when a collector bought the first item, a broken laser pointer, for $14.83.* Soon the site grew into a broader auction site where consumers could auction collectibles such as baseball cards and Barbie dolls. The momentum continued when individuals and small businesses discovered that eBay was an efficient way to reach new consumers and other businesses. Large companies began using eBay as a means of selling their bulk lots of unsold inventory. Today, people can buy and sell virtually any product or service on the world's largest online marketplace, as long as it is not illegal and does not violate eBay's rules and policies.

eBay's success truly created a pricing revolution by allowing buyers to determine what they would pay for an item; the result pleases both sides because customers gain control and receive the best possible price while sellers make good margins due to the site's efficiency and wide reach. For years, buyers and sellers used eBay as an informal guide to market value. Even a company with a new-product design and that wanted to know the going price for anything from a copier to a new DVD player checked on eBay.

eBay has evolved to also offer a fixed-price "buy it now" option to those who don't want to wait for an auction and are willing to pay the seller's price. Sellers can also use the fixed price format with a "best offer" option that allows the seller to counteroffer, reject, or accept an offer.

The impact of eBay's global reach is significant. In 2010, over $62 billion worth of goods was sold on eBay—that's over $2000 worth every second. As of mid-2011, the site has over 400 million registered and nearly 96 million active users and receives 81 million unique visitors a month. More than 1 million members make their living from the site. Yet eBay itself doesn't buy any inventory or own the products on its site. It earns its money by collecting fees: an insertion fee for each listing plus a final-value fee based on the auction or fixed price. For example, if an item sells for $60.00, the seller pays 8.75 percent on the first $25.00 ($2.19) plus 3.5 percent on the remaining $35.00 ($1.23). Therefore, the final-value fee for the sale is $3.42. This pricing structure was developed to attract high-volume sellers and deter those who list only a few low-priced items. With eBay's expansion into a wide range of other categories—from boats and cars to travel and tickets to health and beauty to home and garden—collectibles now make up only a small percentage of eBay sales.

eBay's business model is based on connecting individuals who otherwise would not be connected. It was the first example of online social networking, years before Twitter and Facebook existed, and consumer trust is a key element of its success. While skeptics initially questioned whether consumers would buy products from strangers, Omidayar believed people are innately good, and eBay's originators did two things well: they worked hard to make their website a community, and they developed tools to help reinforce trust between strangers. The company tracks and publishes the reputations of both buyers and sellers on the basis of feedback from each transaction. eBay extended its feedback service in 2007 by adding four different seller categories: items as described, communication, shipping time, and shipping and handling rate. The ratings are anonymous but visible to other buyers. Sellers with the highest rankings appear at the top of search results.

eBay's millions of passionate users also have a voice in all major decisions the company makes through its Voice of the Customer program. Every few months, eBay brings in as many as a dozen sellers and buyers and asks them questions about how they work and what else eBay needs to do. At least twice a week, the company holds hour-long teleconferences to poll users on almost every new feature or policy. The result is that users (eBay's customers) feel like owners, and they have taken the initiative to expand the company into ever-new territory.

eBay continues to expand its capabilities to build its community and connect people around the world by adding services, partnerships, and investments. The company acquired PayPal, an online payment service, in 2002 after eBay members made it clear that PayPal was the preferred method of payment. The acquisition lowered currency and language barriers and allowed merchants to easily sell products around the world. eBay now has a presence in 39 markets around the world.

Although eBay was a darling in the dot-com boom and has achieved tremendous success since then, it is not without challenges. These include a worldwide recession, increased competition from Google, and difficulties as it expands globally into tough markets such as China. Its former CEO, Meg Whitman, retired in 2008 after leading the company for ten years and was replaced by John Donahue. Under its new leadership, the company continues to focus on one of its founding beliefs: a strong commitment to investment in technologies that help people connect. Recent efforts to adopt mobile applications, integrate with iPhones, and become greener have helped take the company to the top of such lists such as *Newsweek*'s Greenest Companies in America and *Fortune*'s 100 Best Companies to Work For in back-to-back years.

QUESTIONS

1. Why has eBay succeeded as an online auction marketplace while so many others have failed?

2. Evaluate eBay's fee structure. Is it optimal or could it be improved? Why? How?

3. What's next for eBay? How does it continue to grow when it needs both buyers and sellers? Where will this growth come from?

*Some falsely believe that eBay was created to help Omidayar's girlfriend find and collect Pez candy dispensers. That story, however, was created by an employee to help generate initial interest in the company.

Sources: Douglas MacMillan, "Can eBay Get Its Tech Savvy Back?" *BusinessWeek*, June 22, 2009, pp. 48–49; Catherine Holahan, "eBay's New Tough Love CEO," *BusinessWeek*, February 4, 2008, pp. 58–59; Adam Lashinsky, "Building eBay 2.0," *Fortune*, October 16, 2006, pp. 161–164; Matthew Creamer, "A Million Marketers," *Advertising Age*, June 26, 2006, pp. 1, 71; Clive Thompson, "eBay Heads East," *Fast Company*, July–August 2006, pp. 87–89; Glen L. Urban, "The Emerging Era of Customer Advocacy," *MIT Sloan Management Review*, Winter 2004, pp. 77–82; www.ebay.com; "Who We Are," eBay, www.ebayinc.com/who (viewed June 20, 2011).

MARKETING CHANNELS AND VALUE NETWORKS

Most producers do not sell their goods directly to the final users; between them stands a set of intermediaries performing a variety of functions. These intermediaries constitute a marketing channel (also called a trade channel or distribution channel). Formally, **marketing channels** are sets of interdependent organizations participating in the process of making a product or service available for use or consumption. They are the set of pathways a product or service follows after production, culminating in purchase and consumption by the final end user.[2]

Some intermediaries—such as wholesalers and retailers—buy, take title to, and resell the merchandise; they are called *merchants*. Others—brokers, manufacturers' representatives, sales agents—search for customers and may negotiate on the producer's behalf but do not take title to the goods; they are called *agents*. Still others—transportation companies, independent warehouses, banks, advertising agencies—assist in the distribution process but neither take title to goods nor negotiate purchases or sales; they are called *facilitators*.

Channels of all types play an important role in the success of a company and affect all other marketing decisions. Marketers should judge them in the context of the entire process by which their products are made, distributed, sold, and serviced. We consider all these issues in the following sections.

The Importance of Channels

A **marketing channel system** is the particular set of marketing channels a firm employs, and decisions about it are among the most critical ones management faces. In the United States, channel members collectively have earned margins that account for 30 percent to 50 percent of the ultimate selling price. In contrast, advertising typically has accounted for less than 5 percent to 7 percent of the final price.[3] Marketing channels also represent a substantial opportunity cost. One of their chief roles is to convert potential buyers into profitable customers. Marketing channels must not just *serve* markets, they must also *make* markets.[4]

The channels chosen affect all other marketing decisions. The company's pricing depends on whether it uses online discounters or high-quality boutiques. Its sales force and advertising decisions depend on how much training and motivation dealers need. In addition, channel decisions include relatively long-term commitments with other firms as well as a set of policies and procedures. When an automaker signs up independent dealers to sell its automobiles, it cannot buy them out the next day and replace them with company-owned outlets. But at the same time, channel choices themselves depend on the company's marketing strategy with respect to segmentation, targeting, and positioning. Holistic marketers ensure that marketing decisions in all these different areas are made to collectively maximize value.

In managing its intermediaries, the firm must decide how much effort to devote to push versus pull marketing. A **push strategy** uses the manufacturer's sales force, trade promotion money, or other means to induce intermediaries to carry, promote, and sell the product to end users. A push strategy is particularly appropriate when there is low brand loyalty in a category, brand choice is made in the store, the product is an impulse item, and product benefits are well-understood. In a **pull strategy**, the manufacturer uses advertising, promotion, and other forms of communication to persuade consumers to demand the product from intermediaries, thus inducing the intermediaries to order it. Pull strategy is particularly appropriate when there is high brand loyalty and high involvement in the category, when consumers are able to perceive differences between brands, and when they choose the brand before they go to the store.

Top marketing companies such as Coca-Cola, Intel, and Nike skillfully employ both push and pull strategies. A push strategy is more effective when accompanied by a well-designed and well-executed pull strategy that activates consumer demand. On the other hand, without at least some consumer interest, it can be very difficult to gain much channel acceptance and support, and vice versa.

Hybrid Channels and Multichannel Marketing

Today's successful companies typically employ hybrid channels and multichannel marketing, multiplying the number of "go-to-market" channels in any one market area. **Hybrid channels** or **multichannel marketing** occurs when a single firm uses two or more marketing channels to reach customer segments. HP has used its sales force to sell to large accounts, outbound telemarketing to sell to medium-sized accounts, direct mail with an inbound number to sell to small accounts, retailers to sell to still smaller accounts, and the Internet to sell specialty items. Philips also is a multichannel marketer.

Philips

Royal Philips Electronics of the Netherlands is one of the world's biggest electronics companies and Europe's largest, with sales of approximately 35 billion euros in 2010. Philips's electronics products are channelled toward the consumer primarily through local and international retailers. The company offers a broad range of products from high to low price/value quartiles, relying on a diverse distribution model that includes mass merchants, retail chains, independents, and small specialty stores. To work most effectively with these retail channels, Philips has created an organization designed around its retail customers, with dedicated global key account managers serving leading retailers such as Best Buy, Carrefour, Costco, Dixons, and Tesco. Like many modern firms, Philips also sells via the web through its own online store as well as through a number of other online retailers.[5]

In multichannel marketing, each channel targets a different segment of buyers, or different need states for one buyer, and delivers the right products in the right places in the right way at the least cost. Take the case of Reitmans (Canada) Limited. It operates under a number of different banners including its Reitmans stores, which offer affordable fashion to everybody. Smart Set, another of its banners, is more of a fashion destination for style-savvy women aged 25 to 35, while RW & Co. caters to women aged 18 to 30 interested in moderately priced urban and casual wear. Its Thyme stores serve those looking for maternity clothing, while Penningtons offers plus-size clothing. In addition to the physical stores, the company offers its customers online shopping services.[6]

There can be channel conflict, excessive cost, or insufficient demand if a channel fails to properly target the right customers with the right offerings. Conflict among different parts of a channel may or may not occur. When a major catalogue and Internet retailer invested significantly in brick-and-mortar stores, different results emerged. Customers near the store purchased through the catalogue less frequently, but their Internet purchases were unchanged. As it turned out, customers who liked to spend time browsing were happy to either use a catalogue or visit the store; those channels were interchangeable. Customers who used the Internet, on the other hand, were more transaction focused and interested in efficiency, so they were less affected by the introduction of stores. Returns and exchanges at the stores were found to increase because of ease and accessibility, but extra purchases made by customers returning or exchanging at the store offset any revenue deficit.

Companies that manage hybrid channels clearly must make sure their channels work well together and match each target customer's preferred ways of doing business. Customers expect *channel integration,* which allows them to

- Order a product online and pick it up at a convenient retail location,
- Return an online-ordered product to a nearby store of the retailer, and
- Receive discounts and promotional offers based on total online and offline purchases.

Here's a company that has carefully managed its multiple channels. We discuss the topic of optimal channel integration in greater detail later.

REI

Outdoor supplier REI has been lauded by industry analysts for the seamless integration of its retail store, website, Internet kiosks, mail-order catalogues, value-priced outlets, and toll-free order number. If an item is out of stock in the store, all customers need to do is tap in to the store's Internet kiosk to order it from REI's website. Less Internet-savvy customers can get clerks to place the order for them at the checkout counters. And REI not only generates store-to-Internet traffic, it also sends Internet shoppers into its stores. If a customer browses REI's site and stops to read an REI "Learn and Share" article on backpacking, the site might highlight an in-store promotion on hiking boots. Like many retailers, REI has found that dual-channel shoppers spend significantly more than single-channel shoppers, and tri-channel shoppers spend even more.[7]

Value Networks

A supply chain view of a firm sees markets as destination points, and amounts to a linear view of the flow of ingredients and components through the production process to their ultimate sale to customers. The company should first think of the target market, however, and then design the supply chain backward from that point. This strategy has been called **demand chain planning**.[8]

A broader view sees a company at the centre of a **value network**—a system of partnerships and alliances that a firm creates to source, augment, and deliver its offerings. A value network includes a firm's suppliers and its suppliers' suppliers, and its immediate customers and their end customers. The value network includes valued relationships with others such as university researchers and government approval agencies.

A company like RIM needs to orchestrate these parties in order to deliver superior value to the target market. Partnerships with national and international firms like Rogers Communications Inc., Ericsson GE Mobile Data, Telefónica, Onset Technology Inc., Hewlett-Packard, and Adobe Systems, to name a few, have enabled RIM to design leading-edge products and penetrate markets around the world with its products.[9] Apple's Developer Connection—where developers create iPhone apps and the like—has 50 000 members at different levels of membership.[10] Developers keep 70 percent of any revenue their products generate, and Apple gets 30 percent.

Demand chain planning yields several insights.[11] First, the company can estimate whether more money is made upstream or downstream, in case it can integrate backward or forward. Second, the company is more aware of disturbances anywhere in the supply chain that might change costs, prices, or supplies. Third, companies can go online with their business partners to speed communications, transactions, and payments; reduce costs; and increase accuracy. Ford not only manages numerous supply chains but also sponsors or operates on many B2B websites and exchanges.

Managing a value network means making increasing investments in information technology (IT) and software. Firms have introduced supply chain management (SCM) software and invited such software firms as SAP and Oracle to design comprehensive *enterprise resource planning* (ERP) systems to manage cash flow, manufacturing, human resources, purchasing, and other major functions within a unified framework. They hope to break up departmental silos—where each department acts only in its own self-interest—and carry out core business processes more seamlessly. Most, however, are still a long way from truly comprehensive ERP systems.

Marketers, for their part, have traditionally focused on the side of the value network that looks toward the customer, adopting customer relationship management (CRM) software and practices. In the future, they will increasingly participate in and influence their companies' upstream activities and become network managers, not just product and customer managers.

THE ROLE OF MARKETING CHANNELS

Why would a producer delegate some of the selling job to intermediaries, relinquishing control over how and to whom products are sold? Through their contacts, experience, specialization, and scale of operation, intermediaries make goods widely available and accessible to target markets, usually offering the firm more effectiveness and efficiency than it can achieve on its own.[12]

Many producers lack the financial resources and expertise to sell directly on their own. The William Wrigley Jr. Company would not find it practical to establish small retail gum shops throughout the world or to sell gum by mail order. It is easier to work through the extensive network of privately owned distribution organizations. Even Ford would be hard-pressed to replace all the tasks done by its almost 12 000 dealer outlets worldwide.

Channel Functions and Flows

A marketing channel performs the work of moving goods from producers to consumers. It overcomes the time, place, and possession gaps that separate goods and services from those who need or want them. Members of the marketing channel perform a number of key functions (see Table 15.1).

Some of these functions (storage and movement, title, and communications) constitute a *forward flow* of activity from the company to the customer; other functions (ordering and payment) constitute a *backward flow* from customers to the company. Still others (information, negotiation, finance, and risk taking) occur in both directions. Five flows are illustrated in Figure 15.1 for the marketing of forklift trucks. If these flows were superimposed in one diagram, we would see the tremendous complexity of even simple marketing channels.

TABLE 15.1 | CHANNEL MEMBER FUNCTIONS

- Gather information about potential and current customers, competitors, and other actors and forces in the marketing environment.
- Develop and disseminate persuasive communications to stimulate purchasing.
- Negotiate and reach agreements on price and other terms so that transfer of ownership or possession can be affected.
- Place orders with manufacturers.
- Acquire the funds to finance inventories at different levels in the marketing channel.
- Assume risks connected with carrying out channel work.
- Provide for the successive storage and movement of physical products.
- Provide for buyers' payment of their bills through banks and other financial institutions.
- Oversee actual transfer of ownership from one organization or person to another.

A manufacturer selling a physical product and services might require three channels: a *sales channel,* a *delivery channel,* and a *service channel.* To sell its Bowflex fitness equipment, the Nautilus Group historically has emphasized direct marketing via television infomercials and ads, inbound/outbound call centres, response mailings, and the Internet as sales channels; UPS ground service as the delivery channel; and local repair people as the service channel. Reflecting shifting consumer buying habits, Nautilus now also sells Bowflex through commercial, retail, and specialty retail channels.

The question for marketers is not *whether* various channel functions need to be performed—they must be—but rather *who* is to perform them. All channel functions have three things in common: They use up scarce resources; they can often be performed better through specialization; and they can be shifted among channel members. Shifting some functions to intermediaries lowers the producer's costs and prices, but the intermediary must add a charge to cover its work. If the intermediaries are more efficient than the manufacturer, prices to consumers should be lower. If consumers perform some functions

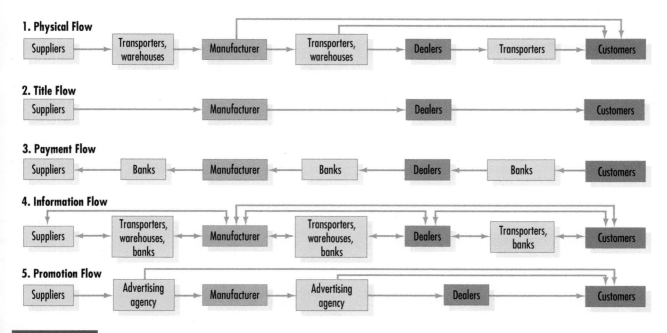

FIGURE 15.1

Five Marketing Flows in the Marketing Channel for Forklift Trucks themselves, they should enjoy even lower prices. Changes in channel institutions thus largely reflect the discovery of more efficient ways to combine or separate the economic functions that provide assortments of goods to target customers.

Channel Levels

The producer and the final customer are part of every channel. We will use the number of intermediary levels to designate the length of a channel. Figure 15.2(a) illustrates several consumer-goods marketing channels of different lengths.

A **zero-level channel**, also called a **direct marketing channel**, consists of a manufacturer selling directly to the final customer. The major examples are door-to-door sales, home parties, mail order, telemarketing, TV selling, Internet selling, and manufacturer-owned stores. Traditionally, Avon sales representatives sell cosmetics door-to-door; the Royal Canadian Mint sells coins to collectors through its website; Veseys (a plant, seed, and gardening equipment company founded in Prince Edward Island) uses the Internet to sell its products to avid gardeners in Canada and the United States; Time Life sells music and video collections through TV commercials or longer infomercials; The Great Canadian Gift Company sells authentic Canadian gifts online to both end consumers and corporate customers; and Apple sells computers and other consumer electronics through its own stores. Many of these firms now sell directly to customers in more ways than one, such as online and through a catalogue.

A *one-level channel* contains one selling intermediary, such as a retailer. A *two-level channel* contains two intermediaries. In consumer markets, these are typically a wholesaler and a retailer. A *three-level channel* contains three intermediaries. In the meat-packing industry, wholesalers sell to **jobbers**, essentially small-scale wholesalers, who sell to small retailers. In Japan, food distribution may include as many as six levels. Obtaining information about end users and exercising control becomes more difficult for the producer as the number of channel levels increases.

Figure 15.2(b) shows channels commonly used in B2B marketing. An industrial-goods manufacturer can use its sales force to sell directly to industrial customers; or it can sell to industrial distributors who sell to industrial customers; or it can sell through manufacturers' representatives or its own sales branches directly to industrial customers, or through its sales branch indirectly to industrial customers through industrial distributors. Zero-, one-, and two-level marketing channels are quite common.

Channels normally describe a forward movement of products from source to user, but *reverse-flow channels* are also important (1) to reuse products or containers (such as refillable chemical-carrying drums), (2) to refurbish products for resale (such as circuit boards or computers), (3) to recycle products (such as paper), and (4) to dispose of products and packaging. Reverse-flow intermediaries include manu-

FIGURE 15.2

Consumer and Industrial Marketing Channels

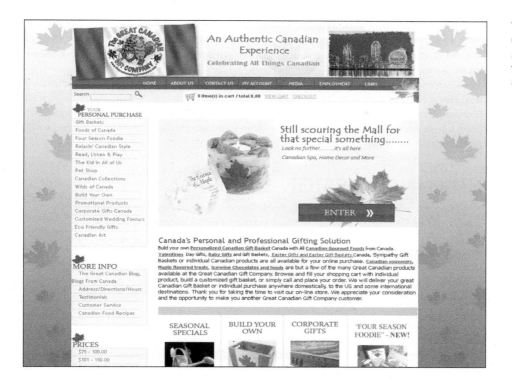

The Great Canadian Gift Company specializes in authentic Canadian gift items for its customers nationally and internationally.

facturers' redemption centres, community groups, trash-collection specialists, recycling centres, trash-recycling brokers, and central processing warehousing.[13] Many creative solutions have emerged in this area in recent years, such as Greenopolis.

Greenopolis

Launched by Waste Management Corporation after it acquired the Code Blue Recycling company, Greenopolis is a new company with an entirely different recycling system that allows consumers and a consortium of consumer packaged goods (CPG) companies to "close the loop" in the recovery and reuse of post-consumer material. With its mantra "Rethink. Recycle. Reward," Greenopolis consists of (1) an extensive set of interactive, on-street recycling kiosks in various retail settings, (2) a number of material reprocessing facilities, (3) a menu of consumer recycling rewards, and (4) a significant online community and social media network. Participating CPG companies use the Greenopolis symbol on their product packaging. The kiosk system is designed to collect those products, track and reward consumers who bring them, and put packaging into reuse or reprocessing. An important feature is that Greenopolis is fully accountable. Innovative kiosk technology allows consumers to follow their recycling contribution, as well as the rewards they earn from the partnering companies. CPG companies, in turn, are able to measure their share of recovery. By achieving sufficient scale and accessibility in the marketplace and making recycling fun, easy, and personally rewarding to consumers, Greenopolis aims to improve recycling rates and make an important environmental difference.[14]

Service Sector Channels

As Internet and other technologies advance, service industries such as banking, insurance, travel, and stock buying and selling are operating through new channels. Kodak offers its customers four ways to print their digital photos—mini-labs in retail outlets, home printers, online services at its Ofoto website, and self-service kiosks. The world leader with 80 000 kiosks, Kodak makes money both by selling the units and by supplying the chemicals and paper they use to make the prints.[15]

Marketing channels also keep changing "person marketing." Besides through live and programmed entertainment, entertainers, musicians, and other artists can reach prospective and existing fans online in many ways—the artists' own websites, social community sites such as Facebook and Twitter, and third-party websites. Politicians also must choose a mix of channels—mass media, rallies, coffee hours, spot TV ads, direct mail, billboards, faxes, email, blogs, podcasts, websites, and social networking sites—for delivering their messages to voters.

Nonprofit service organizations such as schools develop "educational-dissemination systems." Business schools like those at Dalhousie and Queen's offer multiple delivery methods for their programs. Some students attend the university itself; others use online methods to acquire their degrees. Public health providers develop "health-delivery systems." These institutions must figure out agencies and locations for reaching a far-flung population.

CHANNEL-DESIGN DECISIONS

To design a marketing channel system, marketers analyze customer needs and wants, establish channel objectives and constraints, and identify and evaluate major channel alternatives.

Analyzing Customer Needs and Wants

Consumers may choose the channels they prefer based on price, product assortment, and convenience, as well as their own shopping goals (economic, social, or experiential).[16] As with products, segmentation exists, and marketers must be aware that different consumers have different needs during the purchase process.

One study of 40 grocery and clothing retailers in France, Germany, and the United Kingdom found that the retailers served three types of shoppers: (1) *service/quality customers* who cared most about the variety and performance of products and service, (2) *price/value customers* who were most concerned about spending wisely, and (3) *affinity customers* who primarily sought stores that suited people like themselves or groups they aspired to join. The study indicated that customer profiles differed across the three markets: in France, shoppers stressed service and quality, while in the United Kingdom and Germany, affinity was more important, followed by price and value.[17]

Even the same consumer, though, may choose different channels for different functions in a purchase, browsing a catalogue before visiting a store or test driving a car at a dealer before ordering online. Some consumers are willing to trade up to retailers offering higher-end goods such as TAG Heuer watches or Callaway golf clubs and trade down to discount retailers for private-label paper towels, detergent, or vitamins.[18]

Channels produce five service outputs:

1. *Lot size*—The number of units the channel permits a typical customer to purchase on one occasion. In buying cars for its fleet, Hertz prefers a channel from which it can buy a large lot size; a household wants a channel that permits a lot size of one.

2. *Waiting and delivery time*—The average time customers wait for receipt of goods. Customers increasingly prefer faster delivery channels.

3. *Spatial convenience*—The degree to which the marketing channel makes it easy for customers to purchase the product. Toyota offers greater spatial convenience than Lexus because there are more Toyota dealers, helping customers save on transportation and search costs in buying and repairing an automobile.

4. *Product variety*—The assortment provided by the marketing channel. Normally, customers prefer a greater assortment because more choices increase the chance of finding what they need, although too many choices can sometimes create a negative effect.[19]

5. *Service backup*—Add-on services (credit, delivery, installation, repairs) provided by the channel. The greater the service backup, the greater the work provided by the channel.[20]

Providing greater service outputs also means increasing channel costs and raising prices. The success of discount stores such as Walmart and Target and extreme examples like Dollarama and the Great Canadian Dollar Stores indicates that many consumers are willing to accept smaller service outputs if they can save money.

Establishing Objectives and Constraints

Marketers should state their channel objectives in terms of service output levels and associated cost and support levels. Under competitive conditions, channel members should arrange their functional tasks to minimize costs and still provide desired levels of service.[21] Usually, planners can identify several market segments based on desired service and choose the best channels for each.

Channel objectives vary with product characteristics. Bulky products, such as building materials, require channels that minimize the shipping distance and the amount of handling. Nonstandard products, such as custom-built machinery, are sold directly by sales representatives. Products requiring installation or maintenance services, such as heating and cooling systems, are usually sold and maintained by the company or by franchised dealers. High-unit-value products, such as generators and turbines, are often sold through a company sales force rather than intermediaries.

Marketers must adapt their channel objectives to the larger environment. When economic conditions are depressed, producers want to move goods to market using shorter channels and without services that add to the final price. Legal regulations and restrictions also affect channel design. The Canadian Competition Bureau looks unfavourably on channel arrangements that substantially lessen competition or create a monopoly.

In entering new markets, firms often closely observe what other firms are doing. France's Auchan considered the presence of its French rivals Leclerc and Casino in Poland as key to its decision to also enter that market.[22] Apple's channel objective of creating a dynamic retail experience for consumers was not being met by existing channels, so it chose to open its own stores.[23]

Apple Stores

When Apple stores were launched in 2001, many questioned their prospects and *BusinessWeek* published an article titled "Sorry Steve, Here's Why Apple Stores Won't Work." Fast forward ten years, and Apple is celebrating the fact that it has over 300 stores worldwide that generate roughly 20 percent of total corporate revenue. Annual sales per square foot of an Apple store have been estimated at $4700—the Fifth Avenue location is reported to do a staggering $35 000 of business per square foot—compared with Tiffany's $2666, Best Buy's $930, and Saks's $362. Any way you look at it, Apple stores have been an unqualified success. Designed to fuel excitement for the brand, they let people see and touch Apple products—and experience what Apple can do for them—making it more likely they'll become Apple customers. The stores target tech-savvy customers with in-store product presentations and workshops; a full line of Apple products, software, and accessories; and a "Genius Bar" staffed by Apple specialists who provide technical support, often free of charge. Although the stores upset existing retailers, Apple has worked hard to smooth relationships, in part justifying the decision as a natural evolution of its existing online sales channel.

Identifying Major Channel Alternatives

Each channel—from sales forces to agents, distributors, dealers, direct mail, telemarketing, and the Internet—has unique strengths and weaknesses. Sales forces can handle complex products and transactions, but they are expensive. The Internet is inexpensive but may not be as effective with complex products. Distributors can create sales, but the company loses direct contact with customers. Several clients can share the cost of manufacturers' representatives, but the selling effort is less intense than company representatives provide.

Channel alternatives differ in three ways: the types of intermediaries, the number needed, and the terms and responsibilities of each. Let's look at these factors.

TYPES OF INTERMEDIARIES Consider the channel alternatives identified by a consumer electronics company that produces satellite radios. It could sell its radios directly to automobile manufacturers to be installed as original equipment, to auto dealers, to rental car companies, or to satellite radio specialist dealers through a direct sales force or through distributors. It could also sell through company stores, online retailers, mail-order catalogues, or mass merchandisers such as Best Buy.

As Netflix did, companies should search for innovative marketing channels. Canadian banks have been world leaders in offering online services in addition to their traditional branch offerings. See how Sears Canada is using new technology to enhance how people shop.

Sears Canada

Sears Canada understood that many shoppers like to get feedback from friends or family before making a purchase. Now they don't have to bring a buddy along to the store to get this advice. Sears Canada installed wide-screen, webcam-enabled monitors in ten Canadian fashion outlets to allow its shoppers to model potential purchases to friends and family in real time in the store, using Skype. In 2010 alone, sales of brands in Sears stores featuring the Skype online viewing screens grew 32 percent over those of the previous year. This technology has allowed the retailer to draw younger customers to its retail stores and e-commerce site, and overcome its once stuffy image.[24]

Sometimes a company chooses a new or unconventional channel because of the difficulty, cost, or ineffectiveness of working with the dominant channel. One advantage is often reduced competition, at least at first. Years ago, after trying to sell its inexpensive Timex watches through jewellery stores, the U.S. Time Company placed them instead in fast-growing mass-merchandise outlets. Frustrated with a printed catalogue it saw as out-of-date and unprofessional, commercial lighting company Display Supply & Lighting developed an interactive online catalogue that drove down costs, speeded the sales process, and increased revenue.[25]

NUMBER OF INTERMEDIARIES Three strategies based on the number of intermediaries are exclusive distribution, selective distribution, and intensive distribution.

Exclusive distribution means severely limiting the number of intermediaries. It's appropriate when the producer wants to maintain control over the service level and outputs offered by the resellers, and it often includes *exclusive dealing* arrangements. By granting exclusive distribution, the producer hopes to obtain more dedicated and knowledgeable selling. It requires a closer partnership between seller and reseller and is used in the distribution of new automobiles, some major appliances, and some women's apparel brands.

Exclusive deals are becoming a mainstay for specialists looking for an edge in markets increasingly driven by price.[26] When the legendary Italian designer label Gucci found its image severely tarnished by overexposure from licensing and discount stores, it decided to end contracts with third-party suppliers, control its distribution, and open its own stores to bring back some of the lustre.[27] Exclusive distribution is not restricted to high-priced fashion, however, as the strategy of Lee Valley Tools demonstrates.

Lee Valley Tools relies on its own 15 retail outlets to ensure high-quality customer service.

Lee Valley Tools

Lee Valley Tools Ltd. is a family-owned business, founded by Leonard Lee in Ottawa, Ontario, in 1978. This Canadian retailer offers one of the broadest selections of high-quality woodworking and gardening hand tools, and cabinet hardware. Veritas® Tools Inc. (its research, development, and manufacturing arm) continues to be one of the most innovative hand-tool design firms in the world, producing unique and high-quality products. Customers can shop at any of the 15 retail stores across Canada (Halifax, Ottawa, three in Toronto, Burlington, Waterloo, London, Winnipeg, Saskatoon, Edmonton, Calgary, Coquitlam, Vancouver, and Victoria), as well as by catalogue or online at www.leevalley.com. Lee Valley's reputation is based on three principles: customer satisfaction, integrity, and friendship. Customers can return any product for a full refund within three months of purchase, the company's product descriptions are truly what it thinks of the product, and the company treats every customer like a friend. This company listens to its customers; their good advice has helped to improve tools or design new ones in order to continue to meet the needs of the company's customers.[28]

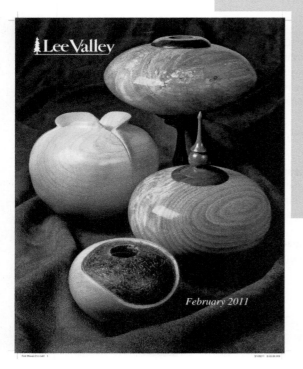

Lee Valley

February 2011

Selective distribution relies on only some of the intermediaries willing to carry a particular product. Whether established or new, the company does not need to worry about having too many outlets; it can gain adequate market coverage with more control and less cost than intensive distribution. Lee Valley Tools is a good example of selective distribution.

Intensive distribution places the goods or services in as many outlets as possible. This strategy serves well for snack foods, soft drinks, newspapers, candies, and gum—products consumers buy frequently or in a variety of locations.

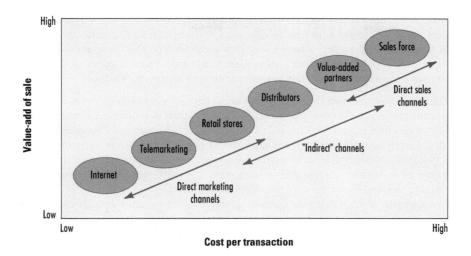

FIGURE 15.3

The Value-Adds versus Costs of Different Channels

Source: Oxford Associates, adapted from Dr. Rowland T. Moriarty. Cubex Corp.

Convenience stores—such as Mac's, 7-Eleven, Circle K, and gas-station-linked stores such as those run by Petro-Canada—have survived by selling items that provide location and convenience.

Manufacturers are constantly tempted to move from exclusive or selective distribution to more intensive distribution to increase coverage and sales. This strategy may help in the short term, but if not done properly, it can hurt long-term performance by encouraging retailers to compete aggressively. Price wars can then erode profitability, dampening retailer interest and harming brand equity. Some firms do not want to be sold everywhere. After Sears acquired discount chain Kmart, Nike pulled all its products from Sears to make sure Kmart could not carry the brand.[29]

TERMS AND RESPONSIBILITIES OF CHANNEL MEMBERS Each channel member must be treated respectfully and given the opportunity to be profitable. The main elements in the "trade-relations mix" are price policies, conditions of sale, territorial rights, and specific services to be performed by each party:

- *Price policy* calls for the producer to establish a price list and schedule of discounts and allowances that intermediaries see as equitable and sufficient.

- *Conditions of sale* refer to payment terms and producer guarantees. Most producers grant cash discounts to distributors for early payment. They might also offer a guarantee against defective merchandise or price declines, creating an incentive to buy larger quantities.

- *Distributors' territorial rights* define the distributors' territories and the terms under which the producer will enfranchise other distributors. Distributors normally expect to receive full credit for all sales in their territory, whether or not they did the selling.

- *Mutual services and responsibilities* must be carefully spelled out, especially in franchised and exclusive-agency channels. McDonald's provides franchisees with a building, promotional support, a record-keeping system, training, and general administrative and technical assistance. In turn, franchisees are expected to satisfy company standards for the physical facilities, co-operate with new promotional programs, furnish requested information, and buy supplies from specified vendors.

Evaluating Major Channel Alternatives

Each channel alternative needs to be evaluated against economic, control, and adaptive criteria.

ECONOMIC CRITERIA Each channel alternative will produce a different level of sales and costs. Figure 15.3 shows how six different sales channels stack up in terms of the value added per sale and the cost per transaction. For example, in the sale of industrial products costing between $2000 and $5000, the cost per transaction could be estimated at $500 (field sales), $200 (distributors), $50 (telesales), and $10 (Internet). A Booz Allen Hamilton study showed that the average transaction at a full-service branch costs the bank $4.07, a phone transaction costs $0.54, and an ATM transaction costs $0.27, but a typical web-based transaction costs only $0.01.[30]

Firms will try to align customers and channels to maximize demand at the lowest overall cost. Clearly, sellers try to replace high-cost channels with low-cost channels as long as the value added per sale is sufficient. Consider the following situation:

A furniture manufacturer located in Laval, Quebec, wants to sell its line to retailers on the West Coast. One alternative is to hire 10 new sales representatives to operate out of a sales office in Vancouver and receive a base salary plus commissions. The other alternative is to use a Vancouver-based manufacturer's sales agency that has extensive contacts with retailers. Its 30 sales representatives would receive a commission based on their sales.

The first step is to estimate how many sales each alternative will likely generate. A company sales force will concentrate on the company's products, be better trained to sell them, be more aggressive because each rep's future depends on the company's success, and be more successful because many customers prefer to deal directly with the company. The sales agency, however, has 30 representatives, not just 10; it may be just as aggressive, depending on the commission level; customers may appreciate its independence; and it may have extensive contacts and market knowledge. The marketer needs to evaluate all these factors in formulating a demand function for the two different channels.

The next step is to estimate the costs of selling different volumes through each channel. The cost schedules are shown in Figure 15.4. Engaging a sales agency is less expensive than establishing a new company sales office, but costs rise faster through an agency because sales agents get larger commissions.

The final step is comparing sales and costs. As Figure 15.4 shows, there is one sales level (*SB*) at which selling costs are the same for the two channels. The sales agency is thus the better channel for any sales volume below *SB*, and the company sales branch is better at any volume above *SB*. Given this information, it is not surprising that sales agents tend to be used by smaller firms, or by large firms in smaller territories where the volume is low.

CONTROL AND ADAPTIVE CRITERIA Using a sales agency can pose a control problem. Agents may concentrate on the customers who buy the most, not necessarily those who buy the manufacturer's goods. They might not master the technical details of the company's product or handle its promotion materials effectively.

To develop a channel, members must commit to each other for a specified period of time. Yet these commitments invariably reduce the producer's ability to respond to change and uncertainty. The producer needs channel structures and policies that provide high adaptability.

CHANNEL MANAGEMENT DECISIONS After a company has chosen a channel system, it must select, train, motivate, and evaluate individual intermediaries for each channel. It must also modify channel design and arrangements over time. As the company grows, it can also consider channel expansion into international markets.

SELECTING CHANNEL MEMBERS To customers, the channels are the company. Consider the negative impression customers would get of McDonald's, Rogers, or Petro-Canada if one or more of their outlets or dealers consistently appeared dirty, inefficient, or unpleasant.

To facilitate channel member selection, producers should determine what characteristics distinguish the better intermediaries—number of years in business, other lines carried, growth and profit record, financial strength, co-operativeness, and service reputation. If the intermediaries are sales agents, producers should evaluate the number and character of other lines carried and the size and quality of the sales force. If the intermediaries are department stores that want exclusive distribution, their locations, future growth potential, and type of clientele will matter.

FIGURE 15.4

Break-Even Cost Chart for the Choice between a Company Sales Force and a Manufacturer's Sales Agency

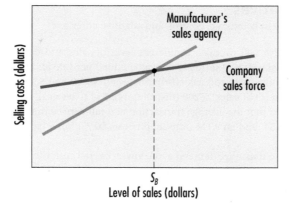

TRAINING AND MOTIVATING CHANNEL MEMBERS A company needs to view its intermediaries the same way it views its end users. It should determine their needs and wants and tailor its channel offering to provide them with superior value.

Carefully implemented training, market research, and other capability-building programs can motivate and improve intermediaries' performance. The company must constantly communicate that intermediaries are crucial partners in a joint effort to satisfy end users of the product. Microsoft requires its third-party service engineers to complete a set of courses and take certification exams. Those who pass are formally recognized as Microsoft Certified Professionals and can use this designation to promote their own business. Other firms use customer surveys rather than exams.

CHANNEL POWER Producers vary greatly in their skill in managing distributors. **Channel power** is the ability to alter channel members' behaviour so that they take actions they would not have taken otherwise.[31] Manufacturers can draw on the following types of power to elicit co-operation:

- *Coercive power.* A manufacturer threatens to withdraw a resource or terminate a relationship if intermediaries fail to co-operate. This power can be effective, but its exercise produces resentment and can lead the intermediaries to organize countervailing power.

- *Reward power.* The manufacturer offers intermediaries an extra benefit for performing specific acts or functions. Reward power typically produces better results than coercive power, but intermediaries may come to expect a reward every time the manufacturer wants a certain behaviour to occur.

- *Legitimate power.* The manufacturer requests a behaviour that is warranted under the contract. As long as the intermediaries view the manufacturer as a legitimate leader, legitimate power works.

- *Expert power.* The manufacturer has special knowledge the intermediaries value. Once the intermediaries acquire this expertise, however, expert power weakens. The manufacturer must continue to develop new expertise so that intermediaries will want to continue co-operating.

- *Referent power.* The manufacturer is so highly respected that intermediaries are proud to be associated with it. Companies such as RIM, Caterpillar, and Hewlett-Packard have high referent power.[32]

Coercive and reward power are objectively observable; legitimate, expert, and referent power are more subjective and depend on the ability and willingness of parties to recognize them.

Most producers see gaining intermediaries' co-operation as a huge challenge. They often use positive motivators, such as higher margins, special deals, premiums, co-operative advertising allowances, display allowances, and sales contests. At times, they will apply negative sanctions, such as threatening to reduce margins, slow down delivery, or terminate the relationship. The weakness of this approach is that the producer is using crude, stimulus-response thinking.

In many cases, retailers hold the power. Manufacturers offer supermarkets between 150 and 250 new items each week, of which store buyers reject over 70 percent. Manufacturers need to know the acceptance criteria that buyers, buying committees, and store managers use. ACNielsen interviews found that store managers were most influenced by (in order of importance) strong evidence of consumer acceptance, a well-designed advertising and sales promotion plan, and generous financial incentives.

CHANNEL PARTNERSHIPS More sophisticated companies try to forge a long-term partnership with distributors.[33] The manufacturer clearly communicates what it wants from its distributors in the way of market coverage, inventory levels, marketing development, account solicitation, technical advice and services, and marketing information, and may introduce a compensation plan for adhering to the policies.

To streamline the supply chain and cut costs, many manufacturers and retailers have adopted *efficient consumer response (ECR) practices* to organize their relationships in three areas: (1) *demand side management* or collaborative practices to stimulate consumer demand by promoting joint marketing and sales activities; (2) *supply side management* or collaborative practices to optimize supply (with a focus on joint logistics and supply chain activities); and (3) *enablers and integrators,* or collaborative information technology and process improvement tools to support joint activities that reduce operational problems, allow greater standardization, and so on.

Research has shown that although ECR has a positive impact on manufacturers' economic performance and capability development, manufacturers may also feel they are inequitably sharing the burdens of adopting it and not getting as much as they deserve from retailers.[34]

EVALUATING CHANNEL MEMBERS Producers must periodically evaluate intermediaries' performance against such standards as sales-quota attainment, average inventory levels, customer delivery time, treatment of damaged and lost goods, and co-operation in promotional and training programs. A producer will occasionally discover it is overpaying particular intermediaries for what they are actually doing. One manufacturer compensating a distributor for holding inventories found that the inventories were actually held in a public warehouse at its own expense. Producers should set up functional discounts in which they pay specified amounts for the trade channel's performance of each agreed-upon service. Underperformers need to be counselled, retrained, motivated, or terminated.

MODIFYING CHANNEL DESIGN AND ARRANGEMENTS   No channel strategy remains effective over the whole product life cycle. In competitive markets with low entry barriers, the optimal channel structure will inevitably change over time. The change could mean adding or dropping individual market channels or channel members or developing a totally new way to sell goods.

CHANNEL EVOLUTION   A new firm typically starts as a local operation selling in a fairly circumscribed market, using a few existing intermediaries. Identifying the best channels might not be a problem; the problem is often to convince the available intermediaries to handle the firm's line.

If the firm is successful, it might branch into new markets with different channels. In smaller markets, the firm might sell directly to retailers; in larger markets, through distributors. In rural areas, it might work with general-goods merchants; in urban areas, with limited-line merchants. It might grant exclusive franchises or sell through all willing outlets. In one country, it might use international sales agents; in another, it might partner with a local firm.

Early buyers might be willing to pay for high-value-added channels, but later buyers will switch to lower-cost channels. Small office copiers were first sold by manufacturers' direct sales forces, later through office equipment dealers, still later through mass merchandisers, and now by mail-order firms and Internet marketers.

In short, the channel system evolves as a function of local opportunities and conditions, emerging threats and opportunities, company resources and capabilities, and other factors. Consider some of the challenges Dell has encountered in recent years.[35]

Dell

Dell revolutionized the personal computer category by selling directly to customers via the telephone and later the Internet. Customers could custom design the exact PC they wanted, and rigorous cost cutting allowed for low everyday prices. Sound like a winning formula? It was for almost two decades. But by 2006, the company was encountering problems that led to a steep stock price decline. First, reinvigorated competitors such as HP narrowed the gap in productivity and price. Always focused more on the business market, Dell struggled to sell effectively to the consumer market. A shift in consumer preferences to buying in retail stores didn't help, but self-inflicted damage from an ultra-efficient supply chain model that squeezed costs—and quality—out of customer service was perhaps the most painful problem. Managers evaluated call centre employees primarily on how quickly they finished each call—a recipe for disaster when scores of customers felt their problems were ignored or not properly handled. A drop in R&D spending that hindered new-product development and led to a lack of differentiation didn't help either. Clearly, Dell had entered a new chapter in its history. A fundamental rethinking of its channel strategy and its marketing approach as a whole would consume the company for the next five years.

CHANNEL MODIFICATION DECISIONS   A producer must periodically review and modify its channel design and arrangements.[36] The distribution channel may not work as planned, consumer buying patterns change, the market expands, new competition arises, innovative distribution channels emerge, and the product moves into later stages in the product life cycle.[37]

Adding or dropping individual channel members requires an incremental analysis. Increasingly detailed customer databases and sophisticated analysis tools can provide guidance into those decisions.[38] A basic question is, What would the firm's sales and profits look like with and without this intermediary?

Perhaps the most difficult decision is whether to revise the overall channel strategy.[39] Avon's door-to-door system for selling cosmetics was modified as more women entered the workforce. Despite the convenience of automated teller machines, online banking, and telephone call centres, many bank customers still want "high touch" over "high tech," or at least they want the choice. Banks are thus opening more branches and developing cross-selling and up-selling practices to capitalize on the face-to-face contact that results.

Global Channel Considerations

International markets pose distinct challenges, including variations in customers' shopping habits, but opportunities at the same time.[40] In India, sales from "organized retail"—hypermarkets, supermarkets, and department stores—make up only 4 percent of the $322 billion market. Most shopping still takes place in millions of independent grocery shops or *kirana* stores, run by an owner and one or perhaps two other people.[41] Many top global retailers such as Germany's Aldi, the United Kingdom's Tesco, and Spain's Zara have tailored their image to local needs and wants when entering a new market.

Franchised companies such as Curves women's fitness centres and Subway sandwich shops have experienced double-digit growth overseas, especially in developing markets such as Brazil and Central and Eastern Europe. In some cases, *master franchisees* pay a significant fee to acquire a territory or country where they operate as a "mini-franchiser" in their own right. More knowledgeable about local laws, customs, and consumer needs than foreign companies, they sell and oversee franchises and collect royalties.[42]

But many pitfalls exist in global expansion. In fact, even entering the U.S. market has been daunting for some Canadian retailers. Tim Hortons failed to dominate an entrenched U.S. competitor, Dunkin' Donuts. Quebec-based pharmacy Jean Coutu Group retreated from the United States, selling the U.S. chains it had acquired. In contrast, ALDO shoes, lululemon, and Roots have had greater success. Why have more Canadian retailers failed than succeeded in this marketplace? Analysts point to several situations that contributed to the retailers' downfall: a failure to understand U.S. consumers, an inability to control costs and deal with razor-thin margins, and an underestimation of how aggressive competition would be.[43]

Retailers must also be able to defend their home turf from the entry of foreign retailers. Selling everything from food to televisions, France's Carrefour, the world's second-biggest retailer, has encountered stiff competition in its home markets from smaller supermarkets for groceries and from specialist retailers such as IKEA or Fnac for other goods. Although strong in parts of Europe, Asia, and Latin America, Carrefour (which means "crossroads" in French) has been forced to cease operations in a number of countries, such as Japan, South Korea, Mexico, Czech Republic, Slovakia, Russia, Switzerland, and Portugal. Another of France's mega-retailers, the Walmart-like Auchan, has been quite successful in entering emerging markets like China while unable to crack markets in the United States or Britain.[44]

The first step in global channel planning, as is often the case in marketing, is to get close to customers. To adapt its clothing lines to better suit European tastes, Philadelphia-based Urban Outfitters set up a separate design and merchandising unit in London before it opened its first store in Europe. Although they increased costs, the blended American and European looks helped the retailer stand out.[45] A good retail strategy that offers customers a positive shopping experience and unique value, if properly adapted, is likely to find success in more than one market. Take Topshop for instance.

Subway has franchise operators all over the world, including in the Doha City Center Shopping Mall in Qatar, shown here.

Topshop

Founded by Sir Richard Green in the United Kingdom in 1994, clothing retailer Topshop is a chain of 310 U.K. stores and 116 international franchisees and that commands intense loyalty from its trendy, style-obsessed customer base. Selling primarily party clothes, accessories, and daywear to women, Topshop blends English street fashion, reasonable prices, and fun services. A higher-end, quirkier version of fast-fashion chains H&M and Zara, Topshop allows middle-market consumers to dress upscale affordably. Partnering with style icons Kate Moss, Stella Vine, and Celia Birtwell to create the latest designs, Topshop offers style advisors, Topshop-to-Go (a Tupperware-type party that brings a style advisor to a customer's home with outfits for up to ten people), and Topshop Express (an express delivery service via Vespa scooters for fashion "emergencies"). In early 2011, The Bay grabbed exclusive franchise rights for Canada and plans to open up to 50 store-within-store and off-site outlets across the country.[46]

CHANNEL INTEGRATION AND SYSTEMS

Distribution channels don't stand still. We'll look at the recent growth of vertical, horizontal, and multichannel marketing systems; the next section examines how these systems co-operate, conflict, and compete.

Vertical Marketing Systems

A **conventional marketing channel** consists of an independent producer, wholesaler(s), and retailer(s). Each is a separate business seeking to maximize its own profits, even if this goal reduces profit for the system as a whole. No channel member has complete or substantial control over other members.

A **vertical marketing system (VMS)**, by contrast, includes the producer, wholesaler(s), and retailer(s) acting as a unified system. One channel member, the *channel captain,* owns or franchises the others or has so much power that they all co-operate. "Marketing Insight: Channel Stewards Take Charge" provides some perspective on how *channel stewards,* a closely related concept, can work.

Vertical marketing systems (VMSs) arose from strong channel members' attempts to control channel behaviour and eliminate conflict over independent members pursuing their own objectives. VMSs achieve economies through size, bargaining power, and elimination of duplicated services. Business buyers of complex products and systems value the extensive exchange of information they can obtain from a VMS,[47] and VMSs have become the dominant mode of distribution in the North American consumer marketplace, serving 70 percent to 80 percent of the market. There are three types: corporate, administered, and contractual.

CORPORATE VMS A *corporate VMS* combines successive stages of production and distribution under single ownership. Sears for years obtained over half the goods it sells from companies it partly or wholly owned. Sherwin-Williams makes paint but also owns and operates 4500 retail outlets.

ADMINISTERED VMS An *administered VMS* coordinates successive stages of production and distribution through the size and power of one of the members. Manufacturers of dominant brands can secure strong trade co-operation and support from resellers. Thus Kodak, Gillette, and the Campbell Soup Company command high levels of co-operation from their resellers in connection with displays, shelf space, promotions, and price policies. The most advanced supply-distributor arrangement for administered VMSs relies on **distribution programming**, which builds a planned, professionally managed vertical marketing system that meets the needs of both manufacturer and distributors.

CONTRACTUAL VMS A *contractual VMS* consists of independent firms at different levels of production and distribution, integrating their programs on a contractual basis to obtain more economies or sales impact than they could achieve alone.[48] Sometimes thought of as "value-adding partnerships" (VAPs), contractual VMSs come in three types:

1. *Wholesaler-sponsored voluntary chains*—Wholesalers organize voluntary chains of independent retailers to help standardize their selling practices and achieve buying economies in competing with large chain organizations.

2. *Retailer co-operatives*—Retailers take the initiative and organize a new business entity to carry on wholesaling and possibly some production. Members concentrate their purchases through the retailer co-op and plan their advertising jointly. Profits pass back to members in proportion to their purchases. Nonmember retailers can also buy through the co-op but do not share in the profits.

3. *Franchise organizations*—A channel member called a *franchisor* might link several successive stages in the production–distribution process. Franchising has been the fastest-growing retailing development in recent years.

| MARKETING **INSIGHT** | CHANNEL STEWARDS TAKE CHARGE |

Harvard's V. Kasturi Rangan believes that companies should adopt a new approach to going to market—channel stewardship. Rangan defines **channel stewardship** as the ability of a given participant in a distribution channel—a steward—to create a go-to-market strategy that simultaneously addresses customers' best interests and drives profits for all channel partners. The channel steward accomplishes channel coordination without issuing commands or directives but by persuading channel partners to act in the best interests of all.

A channel steward might be the maker of the product or service (Procter & Gamble or Air Canada), the maker of a key component (microchip maker Intel), the supplier or assembler (Dell or Arrow Electronics), or the distributor (Sysco) or retailer (The Bay). Within a company, stewardship might rest with the CEO, a top manager, or a team of senior managers.

Channel stewardship should appeal to any organization that wants to bring a disciplined approach to channel strategy. With the customer's point of view in mind, the steward advocates for change among all participants, transforming them into partners with a common purpose.

Channel stewardship has two important outcomes. First, it expands value for the steward's customers, enlarging the market or existing customers' purchases through the channel. A second outcome is to create a more tightly woven and yet adaptable channel, in which valuable members are rewarded and the less valuable members are weeded out.

Rangan outlines three key disciplines of channel management:

1. Mapping at the industry level provides a comprehensive view of the key determinants of channel strategy and how they are evolving. It identifies current best practices and gaps, and it projects future requirements.

2. Building and editing assesses the producer's own channels to identify any deficits in meeting customers' needs and/or competitive best practices to put together a new and improved overall system.

3. Aligning and influencing closes the gaps and works out a compensation package in tune with effort and performance for channel members that add or could add value.

Channel stewardship works at the customer level, not at the level of channel institutions. Thus, channel managers can adapt their fulfillment of customer needs without having to change channel structure all at once. An evolutionary approach to channel change, stewardship requires constant monitoring, learning, and adapting, but all in the best interests of customers, channel partners, and channel steward. A channel steward need not be a huge company or market leader; Rangan cites smaller players, such as Haworth and Atlas Copco, as well as distributors and retailers such as Walmart, Best Buy, and HEB (supermarkets).

Sources: V. Kasturi Rangan, *Transforming Your Go-to-Market Strategy: The Three Disciplines of Channel Management* (Boston: Harvard Business School Press, 2006); Kash Rangan, "Channel Stewardship: An Introductory Guide," www.channelstewardship.com; Partha Rose and Romit Dey, "Channel Stewardship: Driving Profitable Revenue Growth in High-Tech with Multi-Channel Management," *Infosys ViewPoint*, August 2007.

Although the basic idea is an old one, some forms of franchising are quite new. The traditional system is the *manufacturer-sponsored retailer franchise.* Ford licenses independent businesspeople to sell its cars and who agree to meet specified conditions of sales and services. Another system is the *manufacturer-sponsored wholesaler franchise.* Coca-Cola licenses bottlers (wholesalers) in various markets that buy its syrup concentrate and then carbonate, bottle, and sell it to retailers in local markets. A newer system is the *service firm–sponsored retailer franchise,* organized by a service firm to bring its service efficiently to consumers. We find examples in auto rental (Hertz and Avis), fast food (Tim Hortons, McDonald's, and Burger King), and motels (Howard Johnson and Ramada Inn). In a dual distribution system, firms use both vertical integration (the franchisor actually owns and runs the units) and market governance (the franchisor licenses the units to other franchisees).[49]

THE NEW COMPETITION IN RETAILING Many independent retailers that have not joined VMSs have developed specialty stores serving special market segments. The result is a polarization in retailing between large vertical marketing organizations and independent specialty stores, which creates a problem for manufacturers. They are strongly tied to independent intermediaries but must eventually realign themselves with the high-growth vertical marketing systems on less attractive terms. Furthermore, vertical marketing systems constantly threaten to bypass large manufacturers and set up their own manufacturing. The new competition in retailing is no longer between independent business units but between whole systems of centrally programmed networks (corporate, administered, and contractual), competing against one another to achieve the best cost economies and customer response.

Horizontal Marketing Systems

Another channel development is the **horizontal marketing system**, in which two or more unrelated companies put together resources or programs to exploit an emerging marketing opportunity. Each company lacks the capital, know-how, production, or marketing resources to venture alone, or it is afraid of the risk. The companies might work together on a temporary or permanent basis or create a joint venture company.

For example, many supermarket chains have arrangements with local banks to offer in-store banking. Loblaw Companies, for example, formed President's Choice Financial in partnership with CIBC, complete with the President's Choice Financial MasterCard and the PC Points rewards program. Customers are offered a range of financial products, higher interest rates, and lower fees in addition to convenient access to their accounts. They bank online, by telephone, and at President's Choice Financial and CIBC bank machines. When a human face is important, clients can go into an in-store pavilion and talk to a friendly personal banking representative. The partnership has resulted in products and services that won President's Choice Financial services the 2007, 2008, 2009, and 2010 J. D. Power and Associates award for "Highest in Customer Satisfaction Among Midsize Retail Banks."[50]

Integrating Multichannel Marketing Systems

Most companies today have adopted multichannel marketing. Disney sells its DVDs through five main channels: movie rental stores such as Blockbuster, Disney Stores (now owned and run by The Children's Place), retail stores such as Best Buy, online retailers such as Disney's own online stores and Amazon.com, and the Disney catalogue and other catalogue sellers. This variety affords Disney maximum market coverage and enables it to offer its videos at a number of price points.[51] Here are some of the channel options for leather-goods maker Coach.

Coach

> Coach markets a high-end line of luxury handbags, briefcases, luggage, and accessories. Roughly 84 percent of its sales are via the Internet; catalogue; company retail stores in North America, Japan, Hong Kong, Macau, and mainland China; and its North American outlet stores. Coach also has store-in-store offerings in Japan and China inside major department stores. Ten percent of sales are from U.S. department store locations, and five percent are from international wholesalers in 20 countries, mostly department stores. Finally, Coach has licensing relationships with Movado (watches), Jimlar (footwear), and Marchon (eyewear). These licensed products are sometimes sold in other channels such as jewellery stores, high-end shoe stores, and optical retailers.[52]

Luxury-goods maker Coach has a variety of carefully selected and managed channel options.

An **integrated marketing channel system** is one in which the strategies and tactics of selling through one channel reflect the strategies and tactics of selling through one or more other channels. Adding more channels gives companies three important benefits. The first is increased market coverage. Not only are more customers able to shop for the company's products in more places, but those who buy in more than one channel are often more profitable than single-channel customers.[53] The second benefit is lower channel cost—selling by phone is cheaper than personal selling to small customers. The third is more customized selling, such as by adding a technical sales force to sell complex equipment.

There is a trade-off, however. New channels typically introduce conflict and problems with control and co-operation. Two or more may end up competing for the same customers.

Clearly, companies need to think through their channel architecture and determine which channels should perform which functions. Figure 15.5 shows a simple grid to help make channel architecture decisions. The grid consists of major marketing channels (as rows) and the major channel tasks to be completed (as columns).

The grid illustrates why using only one channel is not efficient. Consider a direct sales force. A salesperson would have to find leads, qualify them, presell, close the sale, provide service, and manage account growth. An integrated multichannel approach would be better. The company's marketing department could run a preselling campaign informing prospects about the company's products through advertising, direct mail, and telemarketing; generate leads through telemarketing, direct mail, advertising, and trade shows; and qualify leads into hot, warm, and cool. The salesperson enters when the prospect is ready to talk business and invests his or her costly time primarily in closing the sale. This multichannel architecture optimizes coverage, customization, and control while minimizing cost and conflict.

Companies should use different sales channels for different-sized business customers—a direct sales force for large customers, telemarketing for midsize customers, and distributors for small customers—but be alert for conflict over account ownership. For example, territory-based sales representatives may want credit for all sales in their territories, regardless of the marketing channel used.

Multichannel marketers also need to decide how much of their product to offer in each of the channels. Patagonia views the web as the ideal channel for showing off its entire line of goods, given that its 20 stores and 5 outlets are limited by space to offering a selection only, and even its catalogue promotes less than 70 percent of its total merchandise.[54] Other marketers prefer to limit their online offerings, theorizing that customers look to websites and catalogues for a "best of" array of merchandise and don't want to have to click through dozens of pages.

CONFLICT, CO-OPERATION, AND COMPETITION

No matter how well channels are designed and managed, there will be some conflict, if only because the interests of independent business entities do not always coincide. **Channel conflict** is generated when one channel member's actions prevent another channel from achieving its goal. Software giant Oracle Corp., plagued by channel conflict between its sales force and its vendor partners, decided to roll out new "All Partner Territories," where all deals except for specific strategic accounts would go through select Oracle partners.[55]

FIGURE 15.5

The Hybrid Grid

Source: Adapted from Rowland T. Moriarty and Ursula Moran, "Marketing Hybrid Marketing Systems," *Harvard Business Review*, November–December 1990, p. 150.

Channel coordination occurs when channel members are brought together to advance the goals of the channel, as opposed to their own potentially incompatible goals.[56] Here we examine three questions: What types of conflict arise in channels? What causes conflict? What can marketers do to resolve it?

Types of Conflict and Competition

Suppose a manufacturer sets up a vertical channel consisting of wholesalers and retailers, hoping for channel co-operation and greater profits for each member. Yet horizontal, vertical, and multichannel conflict can occur:

- *Horizontal channel conflict* occurs between channel members at the same level. Some Pizza Inn franchisees complained about others cheating on ingredients, providing poor service, and hurting the overall brand image.

- *Vertical channel conflict* occurs between different levels of the channel. When Estée Lauder set up a website to sell its Clinique and Bobbi Brown brands, some department stores reduced the shelf space they had allocated to Estée Lauder products.[57] Retail concentration is increasing in Canada, especially in industries like grocery retailing. Such concentration may result in conflict between retailers and their suppliers. A recent study reported that the major chains accounted for 60.7 percent of grocery sales. Similarly, the 10 largest U.S. retailers account for over 80 percent of the average manufacturer's business, which has led to increased price pressure and influence from retailers.[58] Walmart, for example, is the principal buyer for many Canadian manufacturers. In any year, approximately 10 000 suppliers apply to become a vendor to Walmart, but only about 2 percent of these are successful. Because of its size and market power, Walmart is able to command reduced prices or quantity discounts from its suppliers. It does recognize the importance of its vendors, however, and it has a monthly program through which it recognizes its best suppliers. In April 2011, for example, Quebec's Ultima Foods, maker of the Yoplait product line, was recognized as the supplier of the month.[59]

- *Multichannel conflict* exists when the manufacturer has established two or more channels that sell to the same market.[60] It's likely to be especially intense when the members of one channel get a lower price (based on larger-volume purchases) or work with a lower margin. When Goodyear began selling its popular tire brands through Sears and Walmart, it angered its independent dealers and eventually placated them by offering exclusive tire models not sold in other retail outlets.

Causes of Channel Conflict

Some causes of channel conflict are easy to resolve, others are not. Conflict may arise from the following:

- *Goal incompatibility.* The manufacturer may want to achieve rapid market penetration through a low-price policy. Dealers, in contrast, may prefer to work with high margins and pursue short-run profitability.

- *Unclear roles and rights.* HP may sell personal computers to large accounts through its own sales force, but its licensed dealers may also be trying to sell to large accounts. Territory boundaries and credit for sales often produce conflict.

- *Differences in perception.* The manufacturer may be optimistic about the short-term economic outlook and want dealers to carry higher inventory. Dealers may be pessimistic. In the beverage category, it is not uncommon for disputes to arise between manufacturers and their distributors about the optimal advertising strategy.

- *Intermediaries' dependence on the manufacturer.* The fortunes of exclusive dealers, such as auto dealers, are profoundly affected by the manufacturer's product and pricing decisions. This situation creates a high potential for conflict.

Managing Channel Conflict

Some channel conflict can be constructive and lead to better adaptation to a changing environment, but too much is dysfunctional.[61] The challenge is not to eliminate all conflict, which is impossible, but to manage it better. There are a number of mechanisms for effective conflict management (see Table 15.2).[62]

STRATEGIC JUSTIFICATION In some cases, a convincing strategic justification that they serve distinctive segments and do not compete as much as they might think can reduce potential for conflict among channel members. Developing special versions of products for different channel members—branded variants as described in Chapter 9—is a clear way to demonstrate that distinctiveness.

TABLE 15.2	STRATEGIES TO MANAGE CHANNEL CONFLICT

- Strategic justification
- Dual compensation
- Superordinate goals
- Employee exchange
- Joint memberships
- Co-optation
- Diplomacy, mediation, or arbitration
- Legal recourse

DUAL COMPENSATION Dual compensation pays existing channels for sales made through new channels. When Allstate started selling insurance online, it agreed to pay agents a 2 percent commission for face-to-face service to customers who got their quotes on the web. Although lower than the agents' typical 10 percent commission for offline transactions, this strategy did reduce tensions.[63]

SUPERORDINATE GOALS Channel members can come to an agreement on the fundamental or superordinate goal they are jointly seeking, whether it is survival, market share, high quality, or customer satisfaction. They usually do this when the channel faces an outside threat, such as a more efficient competing channel, an adverse piece of legislation, or a shift in consumer desires.

EMPLOYEE EXCHANGE A useful step is to exchange people between two or more channel levels. GM's executives might agree to work for a short time in some dealerships, and some dealership owners might work in GM's dealer policy department. Thus, participants can grow to appreciate each other's point of view.

JOINT MEMBERSHIPS Similarly, marketers can encourage joint memberships in trade associations. By working together, various trade associations can have a larger voice in issues affecting the various associations. For example, the StopStickingItToUs Coalition, headed by the Retail Council of Canada, brought together a number of associations—including the Canadian Booksellers Association, the Canadian Convenience Stores Association, the Canadian Council of Grocery Distributors, the Canadian Restaurant and Foodservices Association, the Conseil québécois du commerce de détail, and the Tourism Industry Association of Canada—to protest the escalating credit card fees being levied by the big credit card companies.[64]

CO-OPTATION *Co-optation* is an effort by one organization to win the support of the leaders of another by including them on advisory councils, boards of directors, and the like. If the organization treats invited leaders seriously and listens to their opinions, co-optation can reduce conflict, but the initiator may need to compromise its policies and plans to win outsiders' support.

DIPLOMACY, MEDIATION, AND ARBITRATION When conflict is chronic or acute, the parties may need to resort to stronger means. *Diplomacy* takes place when each side sends a person or group to meet with its counterpart to resolve the conflict. *Mediation* relies on a neutral third party skilled in conciliating the two parties' interests. In *arbitration* two parties agree to present their arguments to one or more arbitrators and accept their decision.

LEGAL RECOURSE If nothing else proves effective, a channel partner may choose to file a lawsuit. When Coca-Cola decided to distribute Powerade thirst quencher directly to Walmart's regional warehouses, 60 bottlers complained the practice would undermine their core direct-store-distribution (DSD) duties and filed a lawsuit. A settlement allowed for the mutual exploration of new service and distribution systems to supplement the DSD system.[65]

Dilution and Cannibalization

Marketers must be careful not to dilute their brands through inappropriate channels, particularly luxury brands whose images often rest on exclusivity and personalized service. Calvin Klein and Tommy Hilfiger took a hit when they sold too many of their products in discount channels.

To reach affluent shoppers who work long hours and have little time to shop, high-end fashion brands such as Dior, Louis Vuitton, and Fendi have unveiled e-commerce sites as a way for customers to research items before walking into a store, and a means to help combat fakes sold on the Internet. Given the lengths to which these brands go to pamper customers in their stores—doormen, glasses of champagne, extravagant surroundings—they have had to work hard to provide a high-quality experience online.[66]

Legal and Ethical Issues in Channel Relations

Companies are generally free to develop whatever channel arrangements suit them as long as they don't use deceptive, exclusionary, or anti-competitive tactics. Canada's Competition Act regulates many channel practices. The first part of the act provides the Competition Bureau with civil powers to deal with potentially anti-competitive practices. Thus, the Competition Bureau investigates many proposed mergers to ensure that they don't substantially lessen competition. It is also concerned with other anti-competitive practices like refusal to deal, tied selling, and exclusive dealing. The second part of the act covers criminal practices such as price fixing and bid rigging, and it places particular emphasis on domestic cartels. The Competition Act also places legal restrictions on some specialized distribution practices such as pyramid selling (also called multilevel marketing plans). In particular, it prohibits schemes that have mandatory participation fees, purchase requirements as a condition of participation, inventory loading, or insufficient buy-back guarantees. It also has rules about the nature of competition between wholesalers and retailers, since they are viewed under the law as direct competitors. New provisions have recently been put in place to govern fraudulent telemarketing practices.[67]

Here we briefly consider the legality of certain practices, including exclusive dealing, exclusive territories, tying agreements, and dealers' rights.

With *exclusive distribution,* only certain outlets are allowed to carry a seller's products. Requiring that these dealers not handle competitors' products is called *exclusive dealing.* Both parties benefit from exclusive arrangements: the seller obtains more loyal and dependable outlets, and the dealers obtain a steady supply of special products and stronger seller support. Exclusive arrangements are legal as long as they do not substantially lessen competition or tend to create a monopoly, and as long as both parties enter into them voluntarily.

Exclusive dealing often includes exclusive territorial agreements. The producer may agree not to sell to other dealers in a given area, or the buyer may agree to sell only in its own territory. The first practice increases dealer enthusiasm and commitment. It is also perfectly legal—a seller has no legal obligation to sell through more outlets than it wishes. The second practice, whereby the producer tries to keep a dealer from selling outside its territory, has become a major legal issue. Producers of a strong brand sometimes sell it to dealers only if they will take some or all of the rest of the line. This practice is called *full-line forcing.* Such **tying agreements** are not necessarily illegal, but they do violate U.S. law if they tend to lessen competition substantially.

Producers are free to select their dealers, but their right to terminate dealers is somewhat restricted. In general, sellers can drop dealers "for cause," but they cannot drop dealers if, for example, the dealers refuse to co-operate in a doubtful legal arrangement, such as exclusive dealing or tying agreements.

E-COMMERCE MARKETING PRACTICES

E-commerce uses a website to transact or facilitate the sale of products and services online. Online retail sales have exploded in recent years, and it is easy to see why. Online retailers can predictably provide convenient, informative, and personalized experiences for vastly different types of consumers and businesses. By saving the cost of retail floor space, staff, and inventory, online retailers can profitably sell low-volume products to niche markets. Online retailers compete in three key aspects of a transaction: (1) customer interaction with the website, (2) delivery, and (3) ability to address problems when they occur.[68]

We can distinguish between online companies, those that have launched a website without any previous existence as a firm, and traditional retailers who added online services for information or e-commerce.

Pure E-Businesses

There are several kinds of pure online companies: search engines, Internet service providers (ISPs), commerce sites, transaction sites, content sites, and enabler sites. Commerce sites sell all types of products and services, notably books, music, toys, insurance, stocks, clothes, and financial services. They use various strategies to compete: Kijiji offers free online classified advertising for a wide range of products in most major cities across Canada; Hotels.com is the information leader in hotel reservations; Trip Advisor provides advice on a wide range of travel options; and Wine Spectator is a single-category specialist.

E-COMMERCE SUCCESS FACTORS Companies must set up and operate their e-commerce websites carefully. Customer service is critical. Online shoppers may select an item for purchase but fail to complete the transaction—one estimate of the conversion rate of Internet shoppers in March 2008 was only about 35 percent. Worse, only 2 percent to 3 percent of visits to online retailers lead to sales, compared with 5 percent of visits to department stores.[69] To improve conversion rates, firms should make the website fast, simple, and easy to use. Something as simple as enlarging product images on-screen can increase perusal time and the amount customers buy.[70]

Consumer surveys suggest that the most significant inhibitors of online shopping are the absence of pleasurable experiences, social interaction, and personal consultation with a company representative.[71] Firms are responding. Many now offer live online chat to give potential customers immediate advice about products and suggest purchasing additional items. When a representative is active in the sale, the average amount per order is typically higher. B2B marketers also need to put a human face on their e-commerce presence, and some are taking advantage of Web 2.0 technologies such as virtual environments, blogs, online videos, and click-to-chat.

To increase customer satisfaction and the entertainment and information value of web-based shopping experiences, some firms are employing *avatars,* graphical representations of virtual, animated characters that act as company representatives, personal shopping assistants, website guides, or conversation partners. Avatars can enhance the effectiveness of a web-based sales channel, especially if they are seen as expert or attractive.[72]

Ensuring security and privacy online remains important. Customers must find the website trustworthy, even if it represents an already highly credible offline firm. Investments in website design and processes can help reassure customers sensitive to online risk.[73] Online retailers are also trying new technologies such as blogs, social networks, and mobile marketing to attract new shoppers.

B2B E-COMMERCE Although business-to-consumer (B2C) websites have attracted much attention in the media, even more activity is being conducted on business-to-business (B2B) sites, which are changing the supplier–customer relationship in profound ways.

In the past, buyers exerted a lot of effort to gather information about worldwide suppliers. B2B sites make markets more efficient, giving buyers easy access to a great deal of information from (1) supplier websites; (2) *infomediaries,* third parties that add value by aggregating information about alternatives; (3) *market makers,* third parties that link buyers and sellers; and (4) *customer communities,* where buyers can swap stories about suppliers' products and services. Firms are using B2B auction sites, spot exchanges, online product catalogues, barter sites, and other online resources to obtain better prices. Ironically, the largest of the B2B market makers is Alibaba, homegrown in China where businesses have faced decades of Communist antipathy to private enterprise.

Alibaba

The brainchild of Jack Ma, Alibaba began in 1999 and grew over the next decade to become the world's largest online B2B marketplace and Asia's most popular online auction site. Its numbers are staggering. The $9 billion company reaches Internet users in 240 countries and regions, has over 45 million registered users, and hosts more than 5.5 million shop fronts; at any moment, more than 4 million businesses are trading. At Alibaba's heart are two B2B websites: alibaba.com, a marketplace for companies around the globe to buy and sell in English, and china.alibaba.com, a domestic Chinese marketplace. The Chinese powerhouse has a nationalist agenda: to build markets for China's vast number of small and medium-sized businesses. Alibaba enables these businesses to trade with each other and link to global supply chains. To establish customer trust, the company set up TrustPass, in which users pay Alibaba a fee to hire a third party that verifies them. Users must have five people vouch for them and provide a list of all their certificates/business licences. Anyone on Alibaba who has done business with a user is encouraged to comment on the firm, in the same way buyers comment on sellers in Amazon.com's or eBay's marketplace. Businesses are even starting to print "TrustPass" on their business cards, a true sign of Alibaba's

Jack Ma has been the visionary force behind the highly successful Chinese online marketplace and auction site Alibaba.

B2B credibility. Global growth has become a priority. Home pages in Spanish, German, Italian, French, Portuguese, and Russian were launched in 2008 to complement Chinese and English options. After its IPO of $1.7 billion in 2007 (second only to Google's among Internet firms), Alibaba, says Jack Ma, will "create the e-commerce platform for 10 million small enterprises creating 100 million jobs around the world and providing an online retail platform to supply the everyday needs of 1 billion people."[74]

The effect of these mechanisms is to make prices more transparent.[75] For undifferentiated products, price pressure will increase. For highly differentiated products, buyers will gain a better picture of the items' true value. Suppliers of superior products will be able to offset price transparency with value transparency; suppliers of undifferentiated products will need to drive down their costs in order to compete.

Traditional Firms with E-Commerce Operations

Although many traditional companies may have initially debated whether to add an online e-commerce channel for fear of channel conflict with their offline retailers, agents, or own stores, most eventually added the Internet as a distribution channel after seeing how much business was generated online.[76] Even Procter & Gamble, which used traditional physical channels of distribution exclusively for years, is selling some big brands such as Tide, Pampers, and Olay online, in part to be able to examine consumer shopping habits more closely.[77] Managing the online and offline channels has thus become a priority for many firms.[78]

Adding an e-commerce channel creates the possibility of a backlash from retailers, brokers, agents, and other intermediaries. The question is how to sell both through intermediaries and online. There are at least three strategies for trying to gain acceptance from intermediaries. One, offer different brands or products on the Internet. Two, offer offline partners higher commissions to cushion the negative impact on sales. Three, take orders on the website but have retailers deliver and collect payment. Harley-Davidson decided to tread carefully before going online.

Harley-Davidson

Given that Harley annually sells more than $860 million worth of parts and accessories to its loyal followers, an online venture was an obvious next step to generate even more revenue. Harley needed to be careful, however, to avoid the wrath of 850 dealers who benefited from the high margins on those sales. Its solution was to send customers seeking to buy accessories online to the company's website. Before they can buy anything, they are prompted to select a participating Harley-Davidson dealer. When the customer places the order, it is transmitted to the selected dealer for fulfillment, ensuring that the dealer still remains the focal point of the customer experience. Dealers, in turn, agreed to a number of standards, such as checking for orders twice a day and shipping promptly. The website now gets more than 1 million visitors a month.[79]

Many traditional retailers are trying to give their customers more control over their shopping experiences by bringing web technologies into the store. This is what Sears Canada has done by using Skype so customers can get the opinions of their family or friends before purchasing. Loblaws has installed self-service scanners so customers can do their own checkout. Chapters has in-store computers that allow customers to search inventory, locate merchandise, and order out-of-stock items. Other retailers are providing Wi-Fi, so consumers can do comparative shopping right in the store. Many retailers resisted allowing consumers to do such searches, but recent research by Deloitte Canada suggests that people will leave the store to check the web, and may never return to make a purchase. If they can use Wi-Fi in the store, they often buy even if the price is four or five dollars less elsewhere. Even if the article is cheaper online, many consumers just don't want to wait the three to five days to get their item delivered.[80]

M-COMMERCE MARKETING PRACTICES

The widespread penetration of cell phones and smartphones—there are currently more cell phones than personal computers in the world—allows people to connect to the Internet and place online orders on the move. Many see a big future in what is now called *m-commerce* (*m* for *mobile*).[81] The existence of mobile channels and media can keep consumers connected and interacting with a brand throughout their day-to-day lives. GPS-type features can help identify shopping or purchase opportunities for consumers for their favourite brands.

By 2011, Rogers, Telus, and Bell had a combined subscriber base of 6.7 million smartphone users. Worldwide sales of smartphones are predicted to reach 468 million units in 2011, a 57.7 percent increase from 2010, according to Gartner Inc. Sales of smartphones in 2010 were just under 297 million units. As smartphone penetration and adoption of 3G increases, and as easy payment options and various apps for mobile phones are developed, m-commerce will take off. By 2015, more people are expected to access the Internet with cell phones than with PCs.[82]

In some countries, m-commerce already has a strong foothold. Millions of Japanese teenagers carry DOCOMO phones. In the United States, mobile marketing is becoming more prevalent and taking all forms.[83] Retailers such as Amazon.com, CVS, and Sears have launched m-commerce sites that allow consumers to buy books, medicine, and even lawn mowers from their smartphones. The travel industry has used m-commerce to target businesspeople who need to book air or hotel reservations while on the move.[84]

While Canadians have been purchasing a lot of smartphones, they are not using many of the more powerful features on their phones. Most use their phones only for calls (89%), for checking the time (56%), text messaging (52%), and reading email (28%). Thus, marketers are cautioned to focus on mobile as only one touch point in their media plans and marketing strategies. Mobile marketing strategies can be successful, however. Many Canadian charities, like the Canadian Red Cross, are finding that they can effectively raise money for causes like the relief for victims of the earthquake in Haiti through text-to-donate programs. Similarly, the Children's Miracle Network raised over $20 000 from text donations during its single-day coast-to-coast radiothon in April 2010. Advertisers can also add QR (Quick Response) codes to print materials. These small black-and-white boxes that look somewhat similar to bar codes can be read by smartphones, and they direct users to online content. Vancouver's Union Gospel Mission added QR codes to bus shelter ads located around the city in 2010. The QR codes allowed donors to give directly to the mission. The ads also included simple print instructions about how to donate, since the ad creators recognized that not everyone is familiar with the black-and-white squares.[85]

While mobile marketing can have clear benefits, the fact that a company can potentially pinpoint a customer or employee's location with GPS technology also raises privacy issues. What if an employer learns an employee is being treated for AIDS at a local clinic, or a wife finds her husband is out clubbing? Like so many new technologies, location-based services have potential for good or harm and ultimately will warrant public scrutiny and regulation.

SUMMARY

1. Most producers do not sell their goods directly to final users. Between producers and final users stands one or more marketing channels, a host of marketing intermediaries performing a variety of functions.

2. Marketing channel decisions are among the most critical decisions facing management. The company's chosen channel(s) profoundly affect all other marketing decisions.

3. Companies use intermediaries when they lack the financial resources to carry out direct marketing, when direct marketing is not feasible, and when they can earn more by doing so. The most important functions performed by intermediaries are information, promotion, negotiation, ordering, financing, risk taking, physical possession, payment, and title.

4. Manufacturers have many alternatives for reaching a market. They can sell direct or use one-, two-, or three-level channels. Deciding which type(s) of channel to use calls for analyzing customer needs, establishing channel objectives, and identifying and evaluating the major alternatives, including the types and numbers of intermediaries involved in the channel.

5. Effective channel management calls for selecting intermediaries and training and motivating them. The goal is to build a long-term partnership that will be profitable for all channel members.

6. Marketing channels are characterized by continuous and sometimes dramatic change. Three of the most important trends are the growth of vertical marketing systems, horizontal marketing systems, and multichannel marketing systems.

7. All marketing channels have the potential for conflict and competition resulting from such sources as goal incompatibility, poorly defined roles and rights, perceptual differences, and interdependent relationships. There are a number of different approaches companies can take to try to manage conflict.

8. Channel arrangements are up to the company, but there are certain legal and ethical issues to be considered with regard to practices such as exclusive dealing or territories, tying agreements, and dealers' rights.

9. E-commerce has grown in importance as companies have adopted hybrid strategies that combine traditional retail stores with Internet shopping sites. Channel integration must recognize the distinctive strengths of online and offline selling and maximize their joint contributions.

10. An area of increasing importance is m-commerce and marketing through smartphones and PDAs.

APPLICATIONS

Marketing Debate: Does It Matter Where You Sell?

Some marketers feel that the image of the particular channel in which they sell their products does not matter—all that matters is that the right customers shop there and the product is displayed in the right way. Others maintain that channel images—such as a retail store—can be critical and must be consistent with the image of the product.

Take a position: Channel images do not much affect the brand images of the products sold in those channels *versus* Channel images must be consistent with the brand image.

Marketing Discussion: Channel Integrations

Think of your favourite retailers. How have they integrated their channel system? How would you like their channels to be integrated? Do you use multiple channels from them? Why or why not?

MARKETING **EXCELLENCE** | PRATT & WHITNEY CANADA

Pratt & Whitney Canada (P&WC), headquartered in Longueil, Quebec (just south of Montreal), is a world leader amongst engine manufacturers for helicopters, and business and regional transport aircrafts. It also has operations in Ontario, Nova Scotia, and Alberta. P&WC has played a major role in shaping and growing the Canadian aerospace industry. Engines produced by the company power the largest fleet of business and regional aircraft and helicopters in the world, with more than 45 000 engines operating in 195 countries. It takes pride in putting its customers first and works hard to provide the high levels of service its customers expect.

P&WC is also an innovative leader in the development of green technologies. It has designed and produced 65 new engines over the last 12 years. Its new generation of engines surpass ICAO standards for low emissions and low noise.

To accomplish this feat, the company spends over $400 million annually on research and development, and it is not surprising that P&WC is the top firm in terms of such investments in the Canadian aerospace industry.

In addition to its Canadian operations, P&WC owns facilities and service centres around the world. It works with a vast range of over 300 national and international suppliers. They provide the company with over 20 000 different parts. Given the quality needed to ensure that P&WC can deliver the best engines possible, managing the supply chain is critical to the company's success. Advanced planning is essential since lead times for complex parts are often a year. Managing inventory is also a huge challenge since P&WC needs to respond to fluctuations in demand while minimizing costs associated with inventory financing.

In its quest for constant improvement, P&WC hired the Createch Group, a Bell Canada Company, which is a leading Canadian firm specializing in supply chain optimization, enterprise resource planning (ERP), and customer relationship management (CRM). Over its 18-year history, the Createch Group has delivered substantial performance improvements to more than 1200 companies.

The objectives of the project were win-win for both P&WC and its suppliers. The project was aimed at improving on-time delivery performance of key suppliers through better synchronization of information flow between P&WC and its suppliers, and encouraging suppliers to adopt simpler manufacturing operations so that manufacturing time required for critical parts could be reduced. Lean manufacturing techniques and synchronization of information flow between the company and its key suppliers helped all members meet their goals.

The project was a success. There was a significant improvement in delivery times and manufacturing lead times, a 30 to 35 percent improvement in on-time deliveries, and a 20 to 30 percent reduction in manufacturing lead times.

QUESTIONS

1. How are channel management and P&WC's commitment to customer service linked?

2. What is unique about P&WC's channel management approach?

Sources: Pratt & Whitney Canada website, www.pwc.ca/en/about/a-global-leader; The Createch Group Success Stories, www.thecreatechgroup.com/success-stories.html (viewed April 2011).

Chapter 16

In This Chapter, We Will Address the Following **Questions**

1. What major types of marketing intermediaries occupy this sector?

2. What marketing decisions do these marketing intermediaries make?

3. What are the major trends with marketing intermediaries?

4. What does the future hold for private-label brands?

Indigo Books & Music revolutionized book selling in Canada with large stores brimming with magazines, gifts, and amenities like couches and coffee shops.

Managing Retailing, Wholesaling, and Logistics

In the previous chapter, we examined marketing intermediaries from the viewpoint of manufacturers who wanted to build and manage marketing channels. In this chapter, we view these intermediaries—retailers, wholesalers, and logistical organizations—as requiring and forging their own marketing strategies in a rapidly changing world. Intermediaries also strive for marketing excellence and can reap the benefits like any other type of company.

Chapters began life in 1995 with the merger of two bookstore chains, Coles and W. H. Smith. The merger created the largest chain of bookstores in Canada. Chapters did more than just merge two existing chains—it changed the face of the book-selling industry in Canada by building large box stores containing a huge product selection to replace the smaller stores favoured by the original chains. Chapters also added features like comfortable chairs and couches and did not discourage the reading of books inside the store. It partnered with Starbucks coffee shops to create a more complete in-store experience. The company soon had 77 superstores branded as Chapters and more than 280 mall-based stores under the original banner names. By 2001, Chapters had aggressively expanded into online book selling with chapters.ca to compete with Amazon, the giant American online retailer.

In 1996, Indigo joined the scene. Indigo was envisioned by Heather Reisman as a book lover's cultural department store with the most inspiring, richly stocked, and inviting retail environment in the world. Fourteen stores soon dotted the Canadian landscape. In 2001, Indigo launched a hostile takeover of Chapters, and the two chains officially merged under the corporate name Indigo Books & Music Inc. By 2003, the chain made music available online and ready to ship within 24 hours. In order to continue its reach, Indigo Books & Music Inc. began to add an ever-widening range of products, from toys to giftware. A recent addition to its line is its proprietary Kobo eReader. It was so popular that the chain ran out of stock during the 2010 Christmas season. Kobo boasts over 5 million users globally, and recently launched the new Kobo Vox Colour eReader.

In 2011, to supplement its traditional fee-based irewards program, Indigo Books & Music Inc. began a new free rewards program, plum rewards, which allows customers to earn ten plum points on every dollar they spend with the chain. "It's so much more than just points, the rewards program really is about connecting with the customer on a very personalized level," said Indigo's VP of marketing, Deirdre Horgan, at a launch event. The move is also aimed at helping the chain fend off competition from other large retailers, like Costco and Walmart. Constant innovation and strong customer relationships are important given the intense rivalry in the field.[1]

While innovative retailers such as Canada's Indigo Books & Music Inc., Sweden's H&M, Spain's Zara and Mango, and Britain's Topshop have thrived in recent years, others such as former Canadian stalwart Eaton's or U.S.-based firms Home Depot and Kmart have struggled. The more successful intermediaries use strategic planning, advanced information systems, and sophisticated marketing tools. They segment their markets, improve their market targeting and positioning, and aggressively pursue market expansion and diversification strategies. In this chapter, we consider marketing excellence in retailing, wholesaling, and logistics.

RETAILING

Retailing includes all the activities in selling goods or services directly to final consumers for personal, nonbusiness use. A **retailer** or **retail store** is any business enterprise whose sales volume comes primarily from retailing.

Any organization selling to final consumers—whether it is a manufacturer, wholesaler, or retailer—is doing retailing. It doesn't matter *how* the goods or services are sold (in person, by mail, by telephone, by vending machine, or on the Internet) or *where* (in a store, on the street, or in the consumer's home).

After reviewing the different types of retailers and the new retail marketing environment, we examine the marketing decisions retailers make. The following are three examples of innovative retail organizations that have experienced market success in recent years.

Innovative Retail Organizations[2]

Gallery1 Furniture Centre.   Winner of the 2010 Retailer of the Year award, Gallery1 Furniture has the largest retail furniture showroom in Atlantic Canada. The chain combines its buying power and experience with an innovative merchandising approach to create a unique shopping experience. It uses creative lifestyle advertising which helps set the company apart from the competition. During his speech at the presentation of the award, the founder of the chain, Joe Ramia, remarked that "it hasn't always been easy. Our company has gone through ups and downs and survived through four recessions." He noted recent trends affecting the industry that his chain has been especially responsive to, such as people's desire to stay closer to home and their growing sensitivity to environmental and global economic issues: "Customers have placed new value on products that are manufactured closer to home. Never before in history has a consumer taken into consideration the environmental cost of shipping a product from another country as part of their purchasing decision." This change presents Gallery1 with a great opportunity to continue to supply these new socially conscientious consumers with the quality goods they want, manufactured closer to home.

Gallery1 Furniture was named Canadian Retailer of the Year because of its innovative, customer-friendly, and community-sensitive approach to furniture retailing.

Gamestop. Video game and entertainment software retailer GameStop has over 6000 locations in malls and shopping strips all over the United States, which is highly convenient for customers. Staffed by hard-core gamers who like to connect with customers, GameStop boasts a trade-in policy that gives customers credit for an old game traded in for a new one.

Net-a-porter. London-based Net-a-Porter is an online luxury clothing and accessories retailer whose website combines the style of a fashion magazine with the thrill of shopping at a chic boutique. Seen by its loyal customers as an authoritative fashion voice, Net-a-Porter stocks over 300 international brands, such as Jimmy Choo, Alexander McQueen, Stella McCartney, Givenchy, and Marc Jacobs. The company ships to 170 countries and offers same-day delivery in London and Manhattan; the average order is $250.

Types of Retailers

Consumers today can shop for goods and services at store retailers, nonstore retailers, and retail organizations.

STORE RETAILERS Perhaps the best-known type of store retailer is the department store. Japanese department stores such as Takashimaya and Mitsukoshi attract millions of shoppers each year and feature art galleries, restaurants, cooking classes, fitness clubs, and children's playgrounds. The most important types of major store retailers are summarized in Table 16.1.

Different formats of store retailers will have different competitive and price dynamics. Discount stores, for example, compete much more intensely with each other than they do with other types of retailers.[3] Retailers also meet widely different consumer preferences for service levels and services. Specifically, they position themselves as offering one of four levels of service:

1. *Self-service*—Self-service is the cornerstone of all discount operations. Many customers are willing to carry out their own "locate-compare-select" process to save money.

TABLE 16.1 | MAJOR TYPES OF STORE RETAILERS

Specialty store: Narrow product line. Running Room, The Body Shop.

Department store: Several product lines. The Bay, Canadian Tire.

Supermarket: Large, low-cost, low-margin, high-volume, self-service store designed to meet total needs for food and household products. Metro, A&P, Sobeys, Safeway.

Convenience store: Small store in residential area, often open 24/7, limited line of high-turnover convenience products plus takeout. 7-Eleven, Mac's.

Drug store: Prescription and pharmacies, health and beauty aids, other personal care, small durable, miscellaneous items. Lawtons, London Drugs, Shoppers Drug Mart.

Discount store: Standard or specialty merchandise; low-price, low-margin, high-volume stores. Walmart, Winners.

Extreme value or hard-discount store: A more restricted merchandise mix than discount stores but at even lower prices. Dollar Store, Army & Navy, Giant Tiger.

Off-price retailer: Leftover goods, overruns, irregular merchandise sold at less than retail. Factory outlets; independent off-price retailers such as TJ Maxx; warehouse clubs such as Costco.

Superstore: Huge selling space, routinely purchased food and household items, plus services (laundry, shoe repair, dry cleaning, cheque cashing). Loblaws Superstores. Category killer (deep assortment in one category) such as PetSmart; combination store such as Staples; hypermarket (huge stores that combine supermarket, discount, and warehouse retailing) such as Carrefour in France and Meijer in the Netherlands.

Source: EW Williams Publications Company; Data from www.privatelabelmag.com.

2. *Self-selection*—Customers find their own goods, although they can ask for assistance.

3. *Limited service*—These retailers carry more shopping goods and services such as credit and merchandise-return privileges. Customers need more information and assistance.

4. *Full service*—Salespeople are ready to assist in every phase of the "locate-compare-select" process. Customers who like to be waited on prefer this type of store. The high staffing cost, higher proportion of specialty goods and slower-moving items, and many services result in high-cost retailing.

NONSTORE RETAILING Although the overwhelming bulk of goods and services—97 percent—is sold through stores, *nonstore retailing* has been growing much faster than store retailing. Nonstore retailing falls into four major categories: direct selling, direct marketing (which includes telemarketing and Internet selling), automatic vending, and buying services:

1. *Direct selling*, also called *multilevel selling* and *network marketing,* is a multibillion-dollar industry, with hundreds of companies selling door-to-door or at home sales parties. Well-known in one-to-one selling are Avon and Electrolux. Tupperware and Mary Kay Cosmetics are sold one-to-many: A salesperson goes to the home of a host who has invited friends; the salesperson demonstrates the products and takes orders. Pioneered by Amway, the multilevel (network) marketing sales system works by recruiting independent businesspeople who act as distributors. The distributor's compensation includes a percentage of sales made by those he or she recruits, as well as earnings on direct sales to customers. These direct-selling firms, now finding fewer consumers at home, are developing multidistribution strategies.

2. *Direct marketing* has roots in direct-mail and catalogue marketing (Tilley Endurables, L.L.Bean); it includes *telemarketing* (1-800-FLOWERS), *television direct-response marketing* (The Shopping Channel), and *electronic shopping* (Chapters.Indigo.ca, Amazon.com). As people become more accustomed to shopping on the Internet, they are ordering a greater variety of goods and services from a wider range of websites, with travel being the biggest category.[4]

3. *Automatic vending* offers a variety of merchandise, including impulse goods such as soft drinks, coffee, candy, newspapers, magazines, and other products such as hosiery, cosmetics, hot food, and paperbacks. Vending machines are found in factories, offices, large retail stores, gasoline stations, hotels, restaurants, and many other places. They offer 24-hour selling, self-service, and merchandise that is stocked to be fresh. Japan has the most vending machines per person—Coca-Cola has over 1 million machines there and annual vending sales of $50 billion—twice its U.S. figures.

4. *Buying services* are storeless retailers serving a specific clientele, usually employees of large organizations, who are entitled to buy from a list of retailers that have agreed to give discounts in return for membership.

CORPORATE RETAILING AND FRANCHISING Although many retail stores are independently owned, an increasing number are part of a **corporate retailing** organization. These organizations offer many economies of scale, greater purchasing power, wider brand recognition, and better-trained employees than independent stores can usually offer alone. The major types of corporate retailing—corporate chain stores, voluntary chains, retailer and consumer co-operatives, franchises, and merchandising conglomerates—are described in Table 16.2.

In a franchising system, individual *franchisees* are a tightly knit group of enterprises whose systematic operations are planned, directed, and controlled by the operation's innovator, called a *franchisor*. Franchises are distinguished by three characteristics:

1. The franchisor owns a trade or service mark and licenses it to franchisees in return for royalty payments.

2. The franchisee pays for the right to be part of the system. Start-up costs include rental and lease equipment and fixtures, and usually a regular licence fee. In Canada, the average franchisee investment is $160 000, but franchisees of McDonald's may invest as much as $1.6 million in total start-up costs and fees. The franchisee then pays McDonald's a certain percentage of sales plus a monthly rent.

3. The franchisor provides its franchisees with a system for doing business. McDonald's requires franchisees to attend "Hamburger University" in Oak Brook, Illinois, for two weeks to learn how to manage the business. Franchisees must follow certain procedures in buying materials.

Franchising benefits both franchisor and franchisee. Franchisors gain the motivation and hard work of employees who are entrepreneurs rather than "hired hands," the franchisees' familiarity with local communities and conditions, and the enormous purchasing power of being a franchisor. Franchisees benefit from buying into a business with a well-known and accepted brand name. They find it easier to borrow

---

TABLE 16.2 | MAJOR TYPES OF CORPORATE RETAIL ORGANIZATIONS

Corporate chain store: Two or more outlets owned and controlled by the same company, employing central buying and merchandising, and selling similar lines of merchandise. Sport Chek, Tim Hortons, Pottery Barn.

Voluntary chain: A wholesaler-sponsored group of independent retailers engaged in bulk buying and common merchandising. Independent Grocers Alliance (IGA).

Retailer co-operative: Independent retailers using a central buying organization and joint promotion efforts. Desjardins (co-operative bank), Ace Hardware.

Consumer co-operative: A retail firm owned by its customers. Members contribute money to open their own store, vote on its policies, elect a group to manage it, and receive dividends. Mountain Equipment Co-op, local co-operative grocery stores that can be found in many markets.

Franchise organization: Contractual association between a franchisor and franchisees, popular in a number of product and service areas. McDonald's, Subway, Pizza Hut, Jiffy Lube, 7-Eleven.

Merchandising conglomerate: A corporation that combines several diversified retailing lines and forms under central ownership, with some integration of distribution and management. Canadian Tire (which includes gas bars and financial services, as well as large stores).

---

money for their business from financial institutions, and they receive support in areas ranging from marketing and advertising to site selection and staffing.

Canada has the second-largest franchise industry in the world, after the United States. According to one website, "Approximately 76,000 individual franchise operations do business in Canada under 900 different brand names." Franchise businesses—such as Kelsey's, pizza pizza, Harvey's, Timothy's World Coffee, Garage Door Depot, Holiday Inn, First Choice Haircutters, and 7-Eleven—represent over $100 billion in sales annually, and the numbers continue to grow. In fact, a Canadian franchise opens every 2 hours, 365 days a year. Approximately one out of five Canadian consumer dollars is spent at a franchise, and franchises employ over 1 million Canadians.[5]

Franchisees do walk a fine line between independence and loyalty to the franchisor. Some franchisors give their franchisees freedom to run their own operations, from personalizing store names to adjusting offerings and price. Great Harvest Bread believes in a "freedom franchise" approach that encourages its franchisee bakers to create new items for their store menus and to share with other franchisees if the new items are successful.[6]

The New Retail Environment

With the onset of the recession in 2008, many retailers had to fundamentally reassess virtually everything they did. Some adopted a cautious, defensive response, cutting stock levels, slowing expansion, and discounting deeply. Others were more creative about managing inventory, adjusting product lines, and carefully avoiding overpromoting. In Canada, there was a resurgence of private-label products as consumers sought lower-priced items. Loblaw, for example, ran controversial ads that pitted its President's Choice products against its national brand rivals. Demand for bargains increased, and clothing prices in Canada dropped as a result. Consumers continued to purchase staples, like household cleaning products, and this category experienced double-digit growth at Canadian Tire Corporation.[7]

Although many of these short-term adjustments were likely to remain longer-term, a number of other long-term trends are also evident in the retail marketing environment. Here are some that are changing the way consumers buy and manufacturers and retailers compete (see Table 16.3 for a summary):

■ *New retail forms and combinations.* To better satisfy customers' need for convenience, a variety of new retail forms have emerged. Bookstores like Indigo Books & Music feature coffee shops. Gas stations include food stores. Loblaws Supermarkets have fitness clubs. Shopping malls and bus and train stations have peddlers' carts in their aisles. Retailers are also experimenting with limited-time "pop-up" stores that let them promote brands to seasonal shoppers for a few weeks in busy areas and create buzz. For the 2009 holiday season, Toys "R" Us set up 350 temporary stores and toy boutiques, in many cases taking over vacant retail space in shopping centres and malls.[8]

TABLE 16.3	RECENT RETAIL DEVELOPMENTS
■ New Retail Forms and Combinations
■ Growth of Intertype Competition
■ Competition between Store-Based and Nonstore-Based Retailing
■ Growth of Giant Retailers
■ Decline of Middle-Market Retailers
■ Growing Investment in Technology
■ Global Profile of Major Retailers
■ Growth of Shopper Marketing

■ *Growth of intertype competition.* Department stores can't worry just about other department stores—discount chains such as Walmart and Tesco are expanding into product areas such as clothing, health, beauty, and electrical appliances. Canada's more stable economy has attracted many new American retailers, like Target, threatening traditional players like Canadian Tire. Different types of stores—discount stores, catalogue showrooms, department stores—all compete for the same consumers by carrying the same type of merchandise.

■ *Competition between store-based and nonstore-based retailing.* Consumers now receive sales offers through direct-mail letters and catalogues, television, cell phones, and the Internet. The nonstore-based retailers making these offers are taking business away from store-based retailers. Store-based retailers have responded by increasing their web presence and finding different ways to sell online, including through their own websites, as well as creating more involving and engaging experiences in their stores. Store-based retailers want their stores to be destinations where consumers enjoy rich experiences that captivate all their senses. Sophisticated lighting, use of appropriate scents, and inviting, intimate designs are all being increasingly employed.[9]

■ *Growth of giant retailers.* Through their superior information systems, logistical systems, and buying power, giant retailers such as Walmart are able to deliver good service and immense volumes of product to masses of consumers at appealing prices. They are crowding out smaller manufacturers that cannot deliver enough quantity, and these giant retailers often dictate to the most powerful manufacturers what to make, how to price and promote, when and how to ship, and even how to improve production and management. Manufacturers need these accounts; otherwise they would lose 10 percent to 30 percent of the market. Some giant retailers are *category killers* that concentrate on one product category, such as pet supplies (PetSmart), home improvement (RONA), or office supplies (Staples). Others are *supercentres* that combine grocery items with a huge selection of non-food merchandise (Loblaws, Walmart).

■ *Decline of middle-market retailers.* We can characterize the retail market today as hourglass or dog-bone shaped: growth seems to be centred at the top (with luxury offerings from retailers such as Holt Renfrew) and at the bottom (with discount pricing from retailers such as Winners and Walmart). As discount retailers improve their quality and image, consumers have been willing to trade down. The Bay is moving more upscale, offering quality merchandise at mid- to upper price points along with new brands like Material Girl. It recently sold its Zellers locations to Target. At the other end of the spectrum, Coach recently converted 40 of its nearly 300 stores to a more upscale format that offers higher-priced bags and concierge services. Opportunities are scarcer in the middle, where one-time successful retailers such as Sears have struggled or even gone out of business.[10] Marks & Spencer in the United Kingdom features in-house brands and has built a strong retail brand image. Although these stores tend to have high operating costs, they command high margins if their in-house brands are both fashionable and popular.[11]

■ *Growing investment in technology.* Almost all retailers now use technology to produce better forecasts, control inventory costs, and order electronically from suppliers. Technology is also affecting what happens inside the store. In-store programming on plasma TVs can run continuous demonstrations or promotional messages. Merchants encountered problems measuring store traffic up and down aisles, however: GPS on shopping carts didn't work, because consumers tended to abandon their carts at times during trips and thermal imaging couldn't tell the difference between turkeys and babies during tests. Since then, bidirectional infrared sensors sitting on store shelves have been successfully introduced. Electronic shelf labelling allows retailers to change price levels instantaneously at any time of the day or week. Retailers are also introducing features to help customers as they shop. Some supermarkets are employing "smart" shopping carts or cell phones that help customers locate items in the store, find out about sales and special offers, and pay for items more easily. As exciting as these new technologies are, their cost and unproven effectiveness in many cases can create significant drawbacks.[12]

High-tech shopping carts allow customers to keep track of their total expenditures, search for products, find out what is on sale, and even pay without waiting in line.

■ *Global profile of major retailers.* Retailers with unique formats and strong brand positioning are increasingly appearing in other countries. Some of Canada's retail giants are also among the 250 largest retailers in the world. Loblaw ranks in 37th place, while convenience store Alimentation Couche-Tard Inc. holds 50th spot.[13] U.S. retailers such as The Limited and the Gap have become globally prominent. Walmart operates over 3600 stores abroad, where it does 25 percent of its business. Dutch retailer Ahold and Belgian retailer Delhaize earn almost two-thirds and four-fifths of their sales, respectively, in nondomestic markets. Other highly recognized global retailers include Italy's Benetton clothing stores, Sweden's IKEA home furnishings stores, and Japan's UNIQLO casual apparel retailer and Yaohan supermarkets.

■ *Growth of shopper marketing.* Buoyed by research suggesting that as many as 70 percent to 80 percent of purchase decisions are made inside the retail store, firms are increasingly recognizing the importance of influencing consumers at the point of purchase.[14] Where and how a product is displayed and sold can have a significant effect on sales.[15] More communication options are available through in-store advertising, such as Walmart TV.[16] Some employ goggle-like devices that record what test customers see by projecting an infrared beam onto the wearer's retina. One finding was that many shoppers ignored products at eye level—the optimum location was between waist and chest level.[17]

Marketing Decisions

With this new retail environment as a backdrop, we will examine retailers' marketing decisions in the areas of target market, channels, product assortment, procurement, prices, services, store atmosphere, store activities and experiences, communications, and location. We discuss the important topic of private labels for retailers in the next section.

TARGET MARKET Until it defines and profiles the target market, the retailer cannot make consistent decisions about product assortment, store décor, advertising messages and media, price, and service levels. Ann Taylor has used a panel of 3000 customers to provide feedback on its merchandise and even its marketing campaign. The firm also solicits employees' input.[18] Whole Foods has found success by offering a unique shopping experience to a customer base interested in organic and natural foods.

Whole Foods Market

With more than 300 stores in Canada, the United States, and the United Kingdom, Whole Foods creates celebrations of food. The markets are bright and well-staffed, and food displays are bountiful and seductive. Whole Foods is the largest organic and natural foods grocer in the world, offering more than 2400 items in four lines of private-label products that add up to 11 percent of sales: the premium Whole Foods Market, Whole Kitchen, and Whole Market lines and the low-priced 365 Everyday Value line. Whole Foods also offers lots of information about its food. If you want to know, for instance, whether the chicken in the display case lived a happy, free-roaming life, you can get a 16-page booklet and an invitation to visit the farm where it was raised. If you can't find the information you need, you have only to ask a well-trained and knowledgeable employee. Whole Foods' approach is working, especially for consumers who view organic and artisanal food as an affordable luxury. From 1991 to 2010, sales grew at a compounded annual growth rate (CAGR) of approximately 28 percent.[19]

Mistakes in choosing or switching target markets can be costly. Many blame the demise of Eaton's on such an error.

To better hit their targets, retailers are slicing the market into ever-finer segments and introducing new lines of stores to exploit niche markets with more relevant offerings. Calgary-based The Forzani Group Ltd., for example, operates under many different banners: Sport Chek, Atmosphere, Athletes World, Sports Experts, Nevada Bob's Golf, and Fitness Source, to name a few. Each has a product mix tailored to meet its particular segment's needs.

CHANNELS Based on a target market analysis and other considerations we reviewed in Chapter 15, retailers must decide which channels to employ to reach their customers. Increasingly, the answer is multiple channels. Staples sells through its traditional retail channel, a direct-response Internet site, virtual malls, and thousands of links on affiliated sites.

As Chapter 15 explained, channels should be designed to work together effectively. Decades-old Canadian Tire has ensured that its Internet, store, flyers, and catalogue businesses are fully intertwined. Although some experts predicted otherwise, catalogues have actually grown in an Internet world, because more firms are using them as branding devices. Victoria's Secret, which expanded into the Canadian marketplace in 2010, has an integrated multichannel approach of retail stores, catalogue, and Internet, which has played a key role in its brand development.

Victoria's Secret

Limited Brands founder Leslie Wexner felt that women would relish the opportunity to have a European-style lingerie shopping experience. "Women need underwear, but women want lingerie," he observed. Wexner's assumption proved correct: a little more than a decade after he bought the business in 1982, Victoria's Secret's average customer was buying eight to ten bras per year, compared with the national average of two. To enhance its upscale reputation and glamorous appeal, high-profile supermodels endorse the brand in ads and fashion shows. To expand its accessibility and offer privacy, the company began to sell directly to consumers. Victoria's Secret used a comprehensive marketing strategy to connect its retail, catalogue, and web sales. Wexner sought to make it "stand [out] as an integrated world-class brand. Across all channels—catalogue, stores, Internet—the same products are launched at the same time, in exactly the same way, with the same quality, and same positioning." Since 1985, Victoria's Secret has delivered 25 percent annual sales growth, selling through its 1000-plus stores, catalogues, and company website. Victoria's Secret ships 400 million catalogues a year, and catalogue and online orders account for nearly 28 percent of its overall revenue, growing at double the rate of sales from its stores.[20]

PRODUCT ASSORTMENT The retailer's product assortment must match the target market's shopping expectations in *breadth* and *depth*. A restaurant can offer a narrow and shallow assortment (small lunch counters), a narrow and deep assortment (delicatessen), a broad and shallow assortment (cafeteria), or a broad and deep assortment (large restaurant).

Identifying the right product assortment can be especially challenging in fast-moving industries such as technology or fashion. Urban Outfitters ran into trouble when it strayed from its "hip, but not too hip" formula, moving to embrace new styles too quickly. Sales fell over 25 percent during 2006.[21] On the other hand, active and casual apparel retailer Aéropostale, which has locations across Canada as well as in the United States, has found success by carefully matching its product assortment to its young teen target market's needs.

Aéropostale

Aéropostale has chosen to embrace a key reality of its target market: 14- to 17-year-olds, especially those on the young end, often want to look like other teens. So while Abercrombie & Fitch and American Eagle might reduce the number of cargo pants on the sales floor, Aéropostale will keep an ample supply on hand at an affordable price. Staying on top of the right trends isn't easy, but Aéropostale is among the most diligent of teen retailers when it comes to consumer research. In addition to running high-school focus groups and in-store product tests, the company launched an Internet-based program that seeks online shoppers' input in creating new styles. It targets 10 000 of its best customers and averages 3500 participants in each of 20 tests a year. Aéropostale has gone from being a lacklustre performer with only 100 stores to a powerhouse with over 900 total stores in the United States, Puerto Rico, and Canada.[22]

Aéropostale's "Teens for Jeans" cause marketing campaign encourages its customers to donate used jeans for homeless teens in North America.

The real challenge begins after defining the store's product assortment, and that is to develop a product-differentiation strategy. To better differentiate themselves and generate consumer interest, some luxury retailers are making their stores and merchandise more varied. Chanel has expanded its "ultralux" goods, including $26 000 alligator bags, while ensuring an ample supply of "must-haves" that are consistently strong sellers.[23] Here are some other possibilities:

- *Feature exclusive national brands that are not available at competing retailers.* Holt Renfrew might get exclusive rights to carry the dresses of a well-known international designer.

- *Feature mostly private-label merchandise.* Benetton and Gap design most of the clothes carried in their stores. Many supermarket and drug chains carry private-label merchandise.

- *Feature distinctive merchandising events.* In 2010, Blockbuster Canada became a sponsor of the annual Toronto International Film Festival and tied the festival into promotions at its retail outlets.[24]

- *Feature surprise or ever-changing merchandise.* Off-price apparel retailer TJ Maxx offers surprise assortments of distress merchandise (goods the owner must sell immediately because it needs cash), overstocks, and close outs, totalling 10 000 new items each week at prices 20 percent to 60 percent below department and specialty store regular prices.

- *Feature the latest or newest merchandise first.* Zara excels in and profits from being first-to-market with appealing new looks and designs.

- *Offer merchandise-customizing services.* Harrods of London will make custom-tailored suits, shirts, and ties for customers, in addition to ready-made menswear.

- *Offer a highly targeted assortment.* Lane Bryant carries goods for the larger woman. Brookstone offers unusual tools and gadgets for the person who wants to shop in a "toy store for grown-ups."

Merchandise may vary by geographical market. Electronics superstore Best Buy reviewed each of its 25 000 SKUs to adjust its merchandise according to income level and buying habits of shoppers. It also puts different store formats and staffs in different areas—a location with computer sophisticates gets a different store treatment than one with less technically sophisticated shoppers.[25] Macy's employs *micromerchandising* and lets managers select a significant percentage of store assortments.[26]

PROCUREMENT After deciding on the product-assortment strategy, the retailer must establish merchandise sources, policies, and practices. In the corporate headquarters of a supermarket chain, specialist buyers (sometimes called *merchandise managers*) are responsible for developing brand assortments and listening to salespersons' presentations.

Retailers are rapidly improving their skills in demand forecasting, merchandise selection, stock control, space allocation, and display. They use computers to track inventory, compute order quantities, order goods, and analyze dollars spent on vendors and products. Supermarket chains use scanner data to manage their merchandise mix on a store-by-store basis.

Some stores are experimenting with radio frequency identification (RFID) systems made up of "smart" tags—microchips attached to tiny radio antennas—and electronic readers. The smart tags can be embedded on products or stuck on labels, and when the tag is near a reader, it transmits a unique identifying number to its computer database. The use of RFIDs has been steadily increasing. Coca-Cola and Gillette use them to monitor inventory and track goods in real time as they move from factories to supermarkets to shopping baskets.[27]

When retailers do study the economics of buying and selling individual products, they typically find that a third of their square footage is tied up in products that don't make an economic profit for them (profit above the cost of capital). Another third is typically allocated to product categories that break even. The final third of the space creates the vast majority of the economic profit, yet many retailers are unaware which third of their products generate this profit.[28]

Stores are using **direct product profitability (DPP)** to measure a product's handling costs (receiving, moving to storage, paperwork, selecting, checking, loading, and space cost) from the time it reaches the warehouse until a customer buys it in the retail store. They learn to their surprise that the gross margin on a product often bears little relation to the direct product profit. Some high-volume products may have such high handling costs that they are less profitable and deserve less shelf space than low-volume products.

Trader Joe's has differentiated itself through its innovative procurement strategy.

Trader Joe's

Los Angeles–based Trader Joe's has carved out a special niche as a "gourmet food outlet discount warehouse hybrid," selling a constantly rotating assortment of upscale specialty food and wine at lower-than-average prices. Roughly 80 percent of what it stocks sells under private labels (compared with only 16 percent at most supermarkets), many with a strong environmentally friendly message. For procurement, Trader Joe's has adopted a "less is more" philosophy. Every store carries about 3000 products, compared with 55 000 at a conventional supermarket, and only what it can buy and sell at a good price, even if that means changing stock weekly. Its 18 expert buyers go directly to hundreds of suppliers, not to intermediaries, and 20 percent to 25 percent of its suppliers are overseas. With thousands of vendor relationships all around the world, Trader Joe's has a success formula that's difficult to copy. In addition, a product finds a space on the shelf only if it's approved by a tasting panel; there is one on each coast to satisfy regional tastes. The company introduces as many as 20 products a week to replace unpopular items. A Facebook page has been started by consumers in an attempt to convince the chain to come to Canada, but currently Canadians have to cross the border if they want to shop at Trader Joe's.[29]

PRICES Prices are a key positioning factor and must be set in relationship to the target market, product-and-service assortment mix, and competition.[30] All retailers would like high *turns × earns* (high volumes and high gross margins), but the two don't usually go together. Most retailers fall into the *high-markup, lower-volume* group (fine specialty stores) or the *low-markup, higher-volume* group (mass merchandisers and discount stores). Within each of these groups are further gradations. Harry Rosen prices suits anywhere from $900 to over $5000. At the other end, Target, which is soon to enter Canada, has skillfully combined a hip image with discount prices to offer customers a strong value proposition.

Target

In the mid-1980s, Zellers and Kmart were the dominant mass retailers, and Walmart was growing rapidly. Sensing a gap in the market for "cheap chic" retail, Target strove to set itself apart from the other big-box retailers by enhancing the design quality of its product selection, focusing on merchandise that was contemporary and unique. The company's team of merchandisers travelled the world looking for the next hot items and trends to bring to the shelves. Target also differentiated its merchandising layout, using low shelves, halogen and track lighting, and wider aisles and avoiding "visual clutter" in stores. With the slogan "Expect More, Pay Less," Target seeks to build an upmarket cachet for its brand without losing price-conscious consumers. It introduced a line of products from world-renowned designers such as Michael Graves, Isaac Mizrahi, Mossimo Giannulli, and Liz Lange and has kept innovating with its merchandising model. In 2006, it introduced consumers to the concept of "fast fashion," already popular in Europe, to help keep the product selection fresh, which in turn led to more frequent shopper visits. Such strategies make Target a formidable competitor, and Canadian retailers ranging from The Bay to Canadian Tire are preparing defensive strategies to counteract its entry into Canada.[31]

Most retailers will put low prices on some items to serve as traffic builders or loss leaders or to signal their pricing policies.[32] They will run storewide sales. They will plan markdowns on slower-moving merchandise. Shoe retailers, for example, expect to sell 50 percent of their shoes at the normal markup, 25 percent at a 40 percent markup, and the remaining 25 percent at cost.

As Chapter 14 noted, some retailers such as Walmart have abandoned "sales pricing" in favour of everyday low pricing (EDLP). EDLP can lead to lower advertising costs, greater pricing stability, a stronger image of fairness and reliability, and higher retail profits. Supermarket chains practising everyday low pricing can be more profitable than those practising high–low sale pricing, but only in certain circumstances.[33]

SERVICES Retailers must decide on the *services mix* to offer customers:

- *Prepurchase services* include telephone and mail orders, advertising, window and interior display, fitting rooms, shopping hours, fashion shows, and trade-ins.

- *Post-purchase services* include shipping and delivery, gift wrapping, adjustments and returns, alterations and tailoring, installations, and engraving.

- *Ancillary services* include general information, cheque cashing, parking, restaurants, repairs, interior decorating, credit, restrooms, and baby-attendant service.

Another differentiator is unerringly reliable customer service, whether face-to-face, across phone lines, or via online chat. When it launched its first Commercial Vehicle Retailers in Canada in 2011, Nissan Canada conducted a rigorous selection process to screen potential retailers. This was essential since these new retailers had to provide consultants who could offer potential business clients expert advice on their commercial vehicle needs. Mark McDade, Director of Market Representation and Vehicle Operations, Nissan Canada Inc., stressed that "Nissan commercial vehicles are a completely new product line-up for Nissan in Canada and we are committed to offering specialized customer support and experience to our commercial customers." For two years, the company worked closely with interested dealers to ensure that those selected to become a Nissan Commercial Vehicle Retailer understood the specialized sales and service support required by business customers.[34] Whatever retailers do to enhance customer service, they must keep women in mind. Women buy or influence the buyer's decision on about approximately 85 percent of everything sold in North America, and women are fed up with the decline in customer service. They are finding every possible way to get around the system, from ordering online to resisting fake sales to just doing without.[35] And when they do shop, they want well-organized layouts, helpful staff, and speedy checkouts.[36]

STORE ATMOSPHERE *Atmosphere* is another element in the store arsenal. Every store has a look, and a physical layout that makes it hard or easy to move around (see "Marketing Memo: Helping Stores to Sell"). Some retailers' floor plans are modelled after a racetrack loop, designed to convey customers smoothly past all the merchandise in the store. They include a middle aisle that hurried shoppers can use as a shortcut, and these layouts yield higher spending levels than do the layouts of many competitors.[37]

Retailers must consider all the senses in shaping the customer's experience. Varying the tempo of music affects average time and dollars spent in the supermarket. Sony Style stores are seasoned with a subtle vanilla-and-mandarin-orange fragrance, and every surface, from countertops to panelling, is designed to be touchable. The famous U.S. chain Bloomingdale's uses different essences in different departments: baby powder in the baby store; suntan lotion in the bathing suit area; lilacs in lingerie; and cinnamon and pine during the holiday season.[38]

STORE ACTIVITIES AND EXPERIENCES The growth of e-commerce has forced traditional brick-and-mortar retailers to respond. In addition to their natural advantages, such as products that shoppers can actually see, touch, and test; real-life customer service; and no delivery lag time for most purchases, stores also provide a shopping experience as a strong differentiator.[39]

The store atmosphere should match shoppers' basic motivations. If customers are likely to be in a task-oriented and functional mindset, then a simpler, more restrained in-store environment may be better.[40] On the other hand, some retailers of experiential products are creating in-store entertainment to attract customers who want fun and excitement.[41] Mountain Equipment Co-op stores allow consumers to test equipment on climbing walls. U.S.-based Bass Pro Shops, a retailer of outdoor sports equipment, features giant aquariums, waterfalls, trout ponds, archery and rifle ranges, fly-tying demonstrations (some with an outdoor pond to test equipment), indoor driving range and putting greens, and classes in everything from ice fishing to conservation—all free.

COMMUNICATIONS Retailers use a wide range of communication tools to generate traffic and purchases. They place ads, run special sales, issue money-saving coupons, run frequent-shopper rewards

MARKETING **MEMO**   HELPING STORES TO SELL

In pursuit of higher sales volume, retailers are studying their store environments for ways to improve the shopper experience. Paco Underhill is managing director of the retail consultant Envirosell, whose clients include McDonald's, Starbucks, Estée Lauder, Blockbuster, Citibank, Gap, Burger King, CVS, and Wells Fargo. Using a combination of in-store video recording and observation, Underhill and his colleagues study 50 000 people each year as they shop. He offers the following advice for fine-tuning retail space:

- *Attract shoppers and keep them in the store.* The amount of time shoppers spend in a store is perhaps the single most important factor in determining how much they buy. To increase shopping time, give shoppers a sense of community; recognize them in some way; give them ways to deal with their accessories, such as chairs in convenient locations for boyfriends, husbands, children, or bags; and make the environment both familiar and fresh each time they come in.

- *Honour the "transition zone."* On entering a store, people need to slow down and sort out the stimuli, which means they will likely be moving too fast to respond positively to signs, merchandise, or sales clerks in the zone they cross before making that transition. Make sure there are clear sight lines. Create a focal point for information within the store. Most right-handed people turn right upon entering a store.

- *Avoid overdesign.* Store fixtures, point-of-sales information, packaging, signage, and flat-screen televisions can combine to create a visual cacophony. Use crisp and clear signage—"Our Best Seller" or "Our Best Student Computer"—where people feel comfortable stopping and facing the right way. Window signs, displays, and mannequins communicate best when angled 10 to 15 degrees to face the direction that people are moving.

- *Don't make them hunt.* Put the most popular products up front to reward busy shoppers and encourage leisurely shoppers to look more. At Staples, ink cartridges are one of the first products shoppers encounter after entering.

- *Make merchandise available to the reach and touch.* It is hard to overemphasize the importance of customers' hands. A store can offer the finest, cheapest, sexiest goods, but if the shopper cannot reach them or pick them up, much of their appeal can be lost.

- *Make kids welcome.* If kids feel welcome, parents will follow. Take a three-year-old's perspective and make sure there are engaging sights at eye level. A virtual hopscotch pattern or dinosaur on the floor can turn a boring shopping trip for a child into a friendly experience.

- *Note that men do not ask questions.* Men always move faster than women do through a store's aisles. In many settings, it is hard to get them to look at anything they had not intended to buy. Men also do not like asking where things are. If a man cannot find the section he is looking for, he will wheel about once or twice, then leave the store without ever asking for help.

- *Remember that women need space.* A shopper, especially a woman, is far less likely to buy an item if her derrière is brushed, even lightly, by another customer when she is looking at a display. Keeping aisles wide and clear is crucial.

- *Make checkout easy.* Be sure to have the right high-margin goods near cash registers to satisfy impulse shoppers. People love to buy candy when they check out, so satisfy their sweet tooth.

Sources: Paco Underhill, *Call of the Mall: The Geography of Shopping* (New York: Simon & Schuster, 2004); Paco Underhill, *Why We Buy: The Science of Shopping* (New York: Simon & Schuster, 1999). See also Kenneth Hein, "Shopping Guru Sees Death of Detergent Aisle," *Brandweek*, March 27, 2006, p. 11; Bob Parks, "5 Rules of Great Design," *Business 2.0*, March 2003, pp. 47–49; Russell Boniface, "I Spy a Shopper!" *AIArchitect*, June 2006; Susan Berfield, "Getting the Most Out of Every Shopper, *BusinessWeek*, February 9, 2009, pp. 45–46; www.envirosell.com.

programs, offer in-store food sampling, and place coupons on shelves or at checkout points. They work with manufacturers to design point-of-sale materials that reflect both the retailer's and the manufacturer's image.[42] Upscale retailers place tasteful, full-page ads in magazines such as *Chatelaine, Vogue,* or *Vanity Fair* and carefully train salespeople to greet customers, interpret their needs, and handle complaints. Off-price retailers will arrange their merchandise to promote bargains and savings, while conserving on service and sales assistance. Retailers are also using interactive and social media to pass on information and create communities around their brands.[43]

LOCATION The three keys to retail success are often said to be "location, location, and location." Department store chains, oil companies, and fast-food franchisers exercise great care in selecting regions of the country, then particular cities, and then particular sites in which to open outlets. Retailers can place their stores in the following locations:

- *Central business districts.* The oldest and most heavily trafficked city areas, often known as "downtown."

- *Regional shopping centres.* Large suburban malls containing 40 to 200 stores, typically featuring one or two nationally known anchor stores, such as Sears or The Bay or a combination of big-box stores such as Payless Shoes, Chapters, or Home Outfitters, and a great number of smaller stores, many under franchise operation.[44]

- *Community shopping centres.* Smaller malls with one anchor store and 20 to 40 smaller stores.

- *Shopping strips.* A cluster of stores, usually in one long building, serving a neighbourhood's needs for groceries, hardware, laundry, shoe repair, and dry cleaning.

- *A location within a larger store.* Certain well-known retailers—McDonald's, Starbucks—locate new, smaller units as concession space within larger stores or operations, such as airports, schools, or department stores.

- *Stand-alone stores.* Some retailers, such as Walmart, avoid malls and shopping centres to locate new stores in free-standing sites on streets, so that they are not connected directly to other retail stores.

In view of the relationship between high traffic and high rents, retailers must decide on the most advantageous locations for their outlets, using traffic counts, surveys of consumer shopping habits, and analyses of competitive locations.

PRIVATE LABELS

A **private-label brand** (also called a reseller, store, house, or distributor brand) is a brand that retailers and wholesalers develop. Shoppers Drug Mart, Benetton, The Body Shop, and Marks & Spencer carry mostly own-brand merchandise. In grocery stores in Europe and Canada, store brands account for as much as 40 percent of the items sold. In Canada, heavy private-label buyers tend to be under 45 years of age and are from larger households with children but have higher incomes (over $70 000). However, this is evolving, and more one-person households made up of people aged 55 to 64, with even higher incomes (over $100 000) are joining the ranks of private-label shoppers. Surprisingly, the heaviest private-label buyers spend more than the average across all product categories, and spend more per shopping trip.[45] In one study, seven of ten shoppers believed that the private-label products they bought were as good as, if not better than, their national brand.

Private labels are rapidly gaining ascendance in a way that has many manufacturers of name brands running scared. Some experts believe, though, that 50 percent is the natural limit for volume of private labels to carry because (1) consumers prefer certain national brands, and (2) many product categories are not feasible or attractive on a private-label basis.[46] Table 16.4 displays the product categories that have the highest private-label sales.

TABLE 16.4 | TOP 10 PRIVATE-LABEL CATEGORIES, 2009 (BILLIONS OF DOLLARS)

- Milk ($8.1)
- Bread & Baked Goods ($4.2)
- Cheese ($3.5)
- Medications/Remedies/Vitamins ($3.4)
- Paper Products ($2.6)
- Eggs—Fresh ($1.9)
- Fresh Produce ($1.5)
- Packaged Meat ($1.5)
- Pet Food ($1.5)
- Unprepared Meat/Frozen Seafood ($1.4)

Source: EW Williams Publications Company; Data from www.privatelabelmag.com. December 9, 2010. Used with permission.

Role of Private Labels

Why do intermediaries sponsor their own brands?[47] First, these brands can be more profitable. Intermediaries search for manufacturers with excess capacity and that will produce private-label goods at low cost. Other costs, such as research and development, advertising, sales promotion, and physical distribution, are also much lower, so private labels can generate a higher profit margin. Retailers also develop exclusive store brands to differentiate themselves from competitors. Many price-sensitive consumers prefer store brands in certain categories. These preferences give retailers increased bargaining power with marketers of national brands.

Private-label or store brands should be distinguished from generics. **Generics** are unbranded, plainly packaged, less expensive versions of common products such as spaghetti, paper towels, and canned peaches. They offer standard or lower quality at a price that may be as much as 20 percent to 40 percent lower than nationally advertised brands and 10 percent to 20 percent lower than the retailer's private-label brands. The lower price is made possible by lower-cost labelling and packaging and minimal advertising, and sometimes lower-quality ingredients. Generics can be found in a wide range of different products, even medicines, as the following example shows.

Generic drugs have become big business as a means to lower health-care costs.

Generic Drugs

Generic drugs have become big business. Branded drug sales actually declined for the first time in 2009. By making knock-offs faster and in larger quantities, Israel's Teva has become the world's biggest generic-drug maker, with revenues of $14 billion. Pharmaceutical giant Novartis is one of the world's top five makers of branded drugs, with such successes as Diovan for high blood pressure and Gleevec for cancer, but it has also become the world's second-largest maker of generic drugs following its acquisition of Sandoz, HEXAL, Eon Labs, and others. Other pharmaceutical companies such as Sanofi-Aventis and GlaxoSmithKline have entered the generic drug market not in North America but in emerging markets in Eastern Europe, Latin America, and Asia, where some consumers cannot afford expensive brand-name drugs but worry about counterfeit or low-quality drugs. These consumers are willing to pay at least a small premium for a drug backed by a trusted company.[48]

Private-Label Success Factors

In the confrontation between manufacturers' labels and private labels, retailers have many advantages and increasing market power.[49] Because shelf space is scarce, many supermarkets charge a *slotting fee* for accepting a new brand, to cover the cost of listing and stocking it. Retailers also charge for special display space and in-store advertising space. They typically give more prominent display to their own brands and make sure they are well-stocked.

Retailers are building better quality into their store brands. Supermarket retailers are adding premium store-brand items like organics or creating new products without direct competition, such as three-minute microwaveable snack pizzas. They are also emphasizing attractive, innovative packaging. Some are even advertising aggressively. Loblaw has found tremendous success with its private-label brands.

Loblaw

Since 1984, when its President's Choice line of foods made its debut, the term *private label* has brought Loblaw instantly to mind. Toronto-based Loblaw's Decadent Chocolate Chip Cookie quickly became a Canadian leader and showed how innovative store brands could compete effectively with national brands by matching or even exceeding their quality. A finely tuned brand strategy for its premium President's Choice line and its no-frills, yellow-labelled No Name line (which the company relaunched with a vengeance during the recent recession) has helped differentiate its stores and built Loblaw into a powerhouse in Canada and the United States. The President's Choice line of products has become so successful that Loblaw is licensing it to noncompetitive retailers in other countries. In 2010, Loblaw introduced a new tier of low-priced store brands, priced slightly above the No Name line, to be made available at its chain of 175 No Frills "hard discount" grocery stores.[50]

Although retailers get credit for the success of private labels, the growing power of store brands has also benefited from the weakening of national brands. Many consumers have become more price sensitive, a trend reinforced by the continuous barrage of coupons and price specials that has trained a generation to buy on price. Competing manufacturers and national retailers copy and duplicate the quality and features of the best brands in a category, reducing physical product differentiation. Moreover, by cutting marketing communication budgets, some firms have made it harder to create any intangible differences in brand image. A steady stream of brand extensions and line extensions has blurred brand identity at times and led to a confusing amount of product proliferation.

Bucking these trends, many manufacturers or national brands are fighting back. "Marketing Insight: Manufacturers' Response to the Private-Label Threat," describes the strategies and tactics being taken to compete more effectively with private labels.

| MARKETING **INSIGHT** | MANUFACTURERS' RESPONSE TO THE PRIVATE-LABEL THREAT |

To maintain their marketplace power, leading brand marketers are investing significantly in R&D to bring out new brands, line extensions, features, and quality improvements to stay a step ahead of the store brands. They are also investing in strong "pull" advertising programs to maintain high consumer brand recognition and preference and overcome the in-store marketing advantage that private labels can enjoy. Top-brand marketers also are seeking to partner with major mass distributors in a joint search for logistical economies and competitive strategies that produce savings for both sides. Cutting all unnecessary costs allows national brands to command a price premium, although it can't exceed the value perceptions of consumers.

University of North Carolina's Jan-Benedict E. M. Steenkamp and London Business School's Nirmalya Kumar offer four strategic recommendations for manufacturers to compete against or collaborate with private labels:

- *Fight selectively* in winnable battles against private labels and add value for consumers, retailers, and shareholders. This is typically when the brand is number one or two in the category or occupying a premium niche position. Procter & Gamble rationalized its portfolio, selling off various brands such as Sunny Delight juice, Jif peanut butter, and Crisco shortening, in part so it could concentrate on strengthening its 20-plus brands with more than $1 billion in sales.

- *Partner effectively* by seeking win-win relationships with retailers through strategies that complement the retailer's private labels. Estée Lauder created four brands (American Beauty, Flirt, Good Skin, and Grassroots) exclusively for Kohl's, to help the retailer generate volume and protect Estée Lauder's own more prestigious brands in the process. Manufacturers selling through hard discounters such as Lidl and ALDI have increased sales by finding new customers who have not previously bought the brand.

- *Innovate brilliantly* with new products to help beat private labels. Continuously launching mildly new products keeps the manufacturer's brands looking fresh, but the firm must also periodically launch radical new products and protect the intellectual property of all brands. Kraft doubled its number of patent lawyers to make sure its innovations were legally protected as much as possible.

- *Create winning value proposition* by imbuing brands with symbolic imagery and functional quality that beats private labels. Too many manufacturer brands have let private labels equal and sometimes better them on functional quality. In addition, to have a winning value proposition, marketers need to monitor pricing and ensure that perceived benefits equal the price premium.

Sources: James A. Narus and James C. Anderson, "Contributing as a Distributor to Partnerships with Manufacturers," *Business Horizons* (September–October 1987); Nirmalya Kumar and Jan-Benedict E. M. Steenkamp, *Private Label Strategy: How to Meet the Store-Brand Challenge* (Boston: Harvard Business School Press, 2007); Nirmalya Kumar, "The Right Way to Fight for Shelf Domination," *Advertising Age*, January 22, 2007; Jan-Benedict E. M. Steenkamp and Nirmalya Kumar, "Don't Be Undersold," *Harvard Business Review*, December 2009, p. 91.

WHOLESALING

Wholesaling includes all the activities in selling goods or services to those who buy for resale or business use. It excludes manufacturers and farmers because they are engaged primarily in production, and it excludes retailers. The major types of wholesalers are described in Table 16.5.

Wholesalers (also called *distributors*) differ from retailers in a number of ways. First, wholesalers pay less attention to promotion, atmosphere, and location because they are dealing with business customers rather than final consumers. Second, wholesale transactions are usually larger than retail transactions, and wholesalers usually cover a larger trade area than retailers. Third, the government deals with wholesalers and retailers differently in terms of legal regulations and taxes.

Why do manufacturers not sell directly to retailers or final consumers? Why are wholesalers used at all? In general, wholesalers are more efficient in performing one or more of the following functions:

- *Selling and promoting.* Wholesalers' sales forces help manufacturers reach many small business customers at a relatively low cost. These sales forces have more contacts, and buyers often trust them more than they trust a distant manufacturer.

TABLE 16.5 | MAJOR WHOLESALER TYPES

Merchant wholesalers: Independently owned businesses that take title to the merchandise they handle. They are full-service and limited-service jobbers, distributors, and mill supply houses.

Full-service wholesalers: Carry stock, maintain a sales force, offer credit, make deliveries, provide management assistance. Wholesale merchants sell primarily to retailers: some carry several merchandise lines, some carry one or two lines, others carry only part of a line. Industrial distributors sell to manufacturers and also provide services such as credit and delivery.

Limited-service wholesalers: *Cash and carry wholesalers* sell a limited line of fast-moving goods to small retailers for cash. *Truck wholesalers* sell and deliver a limited line of semi-perishable goods to supermarkets, grocery stores, hospitals, restaurants, and hotels. *Drop shippers* serve bulk industries such as coal, lumber, and heavy equipment. They assume title and risk from the time an order is accepted to its delivery. *Rack jobbers* serve grocery retailers in nonfood items. Delivery people set up displays, price goods, and keep inventory records; they retain title to goods and bill retailers only for goods sold to the end of the year. *Producers' co-operatives* assemble farm produce to sell in local markets. *Mail-order wholesalers* send catalogues to retail, industrial, and institutional customers; orders are filled and sent by mail, rail, plane, or truck.

Brokers and agents: Facilitate buying and selling, on commission of 2 percent to 6 percent of the selling price; have limited functions; generally specialize by product line or customer type. *Brokers* bring buyers and sellers together and assist in negotiation; they are paid by the party hiring them—food brokers, real estate brokers, insurance brokers. *Agents* represent buyers or sellers on a more permanent basis. Most manufacturers' agents are small businesses with a few skilled salespeople: selling agents have contractual authority to sell a manufacturer's entire output; purchasing agents make purchases for buyers and often receive, inspect, warehouse, and ship merchandise; commission merchants take physical possession of products and negotiate sales.

Manufacturers' and retailers' branches and offices: Wholesaling operations conducted by sellers or buyers themselves rather than through independent wholesalers. Separate branches and offices are dedicated to sales or purchasing. Many retailers set up purchasing offices in major market centres.

Specialized wholesalers: Agricultural assemblers (buy the agricultural output of many farms), petroleum bulk plants and terminals (consolidate the output of many wells), and auction companies (auction cars, equipment, etc., to dealers and other businesses).

- *Buying and assortment building.* Wholesalers are able to select items and build the assortments their customers need, saving them considerable work.

- *Bulk breaking.* Wholesalers achieve savings for their customers by buying large carload lots and breaking the bulk into smaller units.

- *Warehousing.* Wholesalers hold inventories, thereby reducing inventory costs and risks to suppliers and customers.

- *Transportation.* Wholesalers can often provide quicker delivery to buyers because they are closer to the buyers.

- *Financing.* Wholesalers finance customers by granting credit, and finance suppliers by ordering early and paying bills on time.

- *Risk bearing.* Wholesalers absorb some risk by taking title and bearing the cost of theft, damage, spoilage, and obsolescence.

- *Market information.* Wholesalers supply information to suppliers and customers regarding competitors' activities, new products, price developments, and so on.

- *Management services and counselling.* Wholesalers often help retailers improve their operations by training sales clerks, helping with store layouts and displays, and setting up accounting and inventory-control systems. They may help industrial customers by offering training and technical services.

Trends in Wholesaling

Wholesaler-distributors have faced mounting pressures in recent years from new sources of competition, demanding customers, new technologies, and more direct-buying programs by large industrial, institutional, and retail buyers. Manufacturers have several major complaints against wholesalers: They don't aggressively promote the manufacturer's product line and they act more like order takers; they don't carry enough inventory and therefore don't fill customers' orders fast enough; they don't supply the manufacturer with up-to-date market, customer, and competitor information; they don't attract high-calibre managers to bring down their own costs; and they charge too much for their services.

Savvy wholesalers have rallied to the challenge and adapted their services to meet their suppliers' and target customers' changing needs. Wholesalers like Arrow Electronics recognize that they must add value to the channel.

Arrow Electronics

Arrow Electronics is a global provider of products, services, and solutions to the electronic component and computer product industries. Its Canadian operations are located in Halifax. It serves as a supply channel partner for more than 900 suppliers and 125 000 original equipment manufacturers, contract manufacturers, and commercial customers through a global network of 310 locations in 51 countries and territories. With huge contract manufacturers buying more parts directly from suppliers, distributors such as Arrow are being squeezed out. To better compete, Arrow has embraced services, providing financing, on-site inventory management, parts-tracking software, and chip programming. Services helped quadruple Arrow's share price in five years, and the company approached $19 billion in sales in 2010.[51]

Wholesalers have worked to increase asset productivity by managing inventories and receivables better. They're also reducing operating costs by investing in more advanced materials-handling technology, information systems, and the Internet. Finally, they're improving their strategic decisions about target markets, product assortment and services, price, communications, and distribution.

Narus and Anderson interviewed leading industrial distributors and identified four ways they strengthened their relationships with manufacturers:

1. They sought a clear agreement with their manufacturers about their expected functions in the marketing channel.

2. They gained insight into the manufacturers' requirements by visiting their plants and attending manufacturer association conventions and trade shows.

3. They fulfilled their commitments to the manufacturer by meeting the volume targets, paying bills promptly, and feeding back customer information to their manufacturers.

4. They identified and offered value-added services to help their suppliers.[52]

The wholesaling industry remains vulnerable to one of the most enduring trends—fierce resistance to price increases and the winnowing out of suppliers based on cost and quality. The trend toward vertical integration, in which manufacturers try to control or own their intermediaries, is still strong. One firm that succeeds in the wholesaling business is W. W. Grainger.

W.W. Grainger

W. W. Grainger is the leading supplier of facilities maintenance products that help 1.8 million businesses and institutions stay up and running. Grainger serves customers through a network of over 600 branches in North America and China, 18 distribution centres, numerous catalogues and direct-mail pieces, and four websites to guarantee product availability and quick service. Its 4000-plus-page catalogue features 138 000 products such as motors, lighting, material handlers, fasteners, tools, and safety supplies, and customers can purchase over 300 000 products at Grainger.com. The distribution centres are linked by satellite network, which has reduced customer-response time and boosted sales. Helped by more than 3000 suppliers, Grainger offers customers a total of more than 900 000 supplies and repair parts.[53]

MARKET LOGISTICS

Physical distribution starts at the factory. Managers choose a set of warehouses (stocking points) and transportation carriers that will deliver the goods to final destinations in the desired time or at the lowest total cost. Physical distribution has now been expanded into the broader concept of **supply chain management (SCM)**. Supply chain management starts before physical distribution and means strategically procuring the right inputs (raw materials, components, and capital equipment), converting them efficiently into finished products, and dispatching them to the final destinations. An even broader perspective looks at how the company's suppliers themselves obtain their inputs.

The supply chain perspective can help a company identify superior suppliers and distributors and help them improve productivity and reduce costs. Consumer goods manufacturers admired for their supply chain management include P&G, Kraft, General Mills, PepsiCo, and Nestlé; noteworthy retailers include Canadian Tire, Walmart, Target, Zara, Costco, and Meijer.[54]

Firms are also striving to improve the environmental impact and sustainability of their supply chain by shrinking their carbon footprint and using recyclable packaging. Johnson & Johnson switched to Forest Stewardship Council–certified paperboard for its BAND-AID brand boxes. As one executive noted, "Johnson & Johnson and its operating companies are positioned to make paper and packaging procurement decisions that could help influence responsible forest management."[55]

Market logistics includes planning the infrastructure to meet demand, then implementing and controlling the physical flows of materials and final goods from points of origin to points of use, to meet customer requirements at a profit. Market logistics planning has four steps:[56]

1. Deciding on the company's value proposition to its customers. (What on-time delivery standard should we offer? What levels should we attain in ordering and billing accuracy?)

2. Selecting the best channel design and network strategy for reaching the customers. (Should we serve customers directly or through intermediaries? What products should we source from which manufacturing facilities? How many warehouses should we maintain and where should we locate them?)

3. Developing operational excellence in sales forecasting, warehouse management, transportation management, and materials management.

4. Implementing the solution with the best information systems, equipment, policies, and procedures.

Studying market logistics leads managers to find the most efficient way to deliver value. For example, a software company might traditionally produce and package software disks and manuals, ship them to wholesalers, which ship them to retailers, which sell them to customers, who bring them home to download onto their PCs. Market logistics offers two superior delivery systems. The first lets the customer download the software directly onto his or her computer. The second allows the computer manufacturer to download the software onto its products. Both solutions eliminate the need for printing, packaging, shipping, and stocking millions of disks and manuals.

Integrated Logistics Systems

The market logistics task calls for **integrated logistics systems (ILS)**, which include materials management, material flow systems, and physical distribution, aided by information technology (IT). Information systems play a critical role in managing market logistics, especially via computers, point-of-sale terminals, uniform product bar codes, satellite tracking, electronic data interchange (EDI), and electronic funds transfer (EFT). These developments have shortened the order-cycle time, reduced clerical labour, reduced errors, and provided improved control of operations. They have enabled companies to promise "the product will be at dock 25 at 10:00 A.M. tomorrow," and deliver on that promise.

Market logistics encompasses several activities. The first is sales forecasting, on the basis of which the company schedules distribution, production, and inventory levels. Production plans indicate the materials the purchasing department must order. These materials arrive through inbound transportation, enter the receiving area, and are stored in raw-material inventory. Raw materials are converted into finished goods. Finished-goods inventory is the link between customer orders and manufacturing activity. Customers' orders draw down the finished-goods inventory level, and manufacturing activity builds it up. Finished goods flow off the assembly line and pass through packaging, in-plant warehousing, shipping-room processing, outbound transportation, field warehousing, and customer delivery and servicing.

Management has become concerned about the total cost of market logistics, which can amount to as much as 30 percent to 40 percent of the product's cost. In the North American grocery business, waste or "shrink" affects 8 percent to 10 percent of perishable goods, costing over $20 billion annually. To reduce shrinkage, grocery retailers, for example, often order only three days in advance of busy periods, offer price discounts as products start to age, work to improve their receiving policies and procedures, use codes in coolers to ensure that the first-in products are the first ones taken out, and reduce everything from the size of suppliers' boxes to the number of products on display. With these changes, a supermarket chain can cut shrinkage by almost a third, saving over $50 million and eliminating 36 000 pounds of rotten food, improving customer satisfaction at the same time.[57]

Managing global distribution of goods and coordinating supply chain partners around the globe has made logistics and supply chain management (SCM) extremely complex and a strategic issue for decision makers. From 2005 to 2007, total logistics and SCM costs increased by 3 percent for the Canadian economy. Of the three main distribution subsectors, logistics costs increased by close to 22 percent in the retail sector, while manufacturers and wholesalers managed to keep their cost increases closer to 1 percent. Most of the logistics cost increase in retail was attributed to inventory carrying costs. As retailers shift their sourcing to countries with low manufacturing costs, such as China, they have had to increase their inventory levels to help overcome longer shipping times. It's not surprising, therefore, that many experts call market logistics "the last frontier for cost economies," and firms are determined to wring every unnecessary cost out of the system.[58] Even though the cost of market logistics can be high, a well-planned program can be a potent tool in competitive marketing.

Many firms are embracing **lean manufacturing**, originally pioneered by Japanese firms such as Toyota, to produce goods with minimal waste of time, materials, and money. ConMed, a proponent of lean manufacturing, produces disposable devices that are used by a hospital somewhere in the world every 90 seconds to insert and remove fluid around joints during arthroscopic surgery.

By redesigning its production assembly, medical manufacturer ConMed significantly increased productivity.

ConMed

To streamline production, medical manufacturer ConMed set out to link its operations as closely as possible to the ultimate buyer of its products. Rather than moving manufacturing to China, which might have lowered labour costs but could have also risked long lead times, inventory buildup, and unanticipated delays, the firm put new production processes into place to assemble its disposable products only after hospitals placed orders. Some 80 percent of orders were predictable enough that demand forecasts updated every few months could set hourly production targets. As proof of the firm's new efficiency, the assembly area for fluid-injection devices went from covering 3300 square feet and stocking $93 000 worth of parts to 650 square feet and $6000 worth of parts. Output per worker increased 21 percent.[59]

Lean manufacturing must be implemented thoughtfully and monitored closely. Toyota's recent crisis in product safety, which resulted in extensive product recalls, has been attributed in part to the fact that some aspects of the lean manufacturing approach—eliminating overlap by using common parts and designs across multiple product lines, and reducing the number of suppliers to procure parts in greater scale—can backfire when quality-control issues arise.[60]

Market-Logistics Objectives

Many companies state their market-logistics objective as "getting the right goods to the right places at the right time for the least cost." Unfortunately, this objective provides little practical guidance. No system can simultaneously maximize customer service and minimize distribution cost. Maximum customer service implies large inventories, premium transportation, and multiple warehouses, all of which raise market-logistics costs.

Nor can a company achieve market-logistics efficiency by asking each market-logistics manager to minimize his or her own logistics costs. Market-logistics costs interact and are often negatively related, as in the following examples:

- The traffic manager favours rail shipment over air shipment because rail costs less. However, because the railroads are slower, rail shipment ties up working capital longer, delays customer payment, and might cause customers to buy from competitors who offer faster service.

- The shipping department uses cheap containers to minimize shipping costs. Cheaper containers lead to a higher rate of damaged goods and customer ill will.

- The inventory manager favours low inventories. This increases stock-outs, back orders, paperwork, special production runs, and high-cost, fast-freight shipments.

Given that market-logistics activities require strong trade-offs, managers must make decisions on a total-system basis. The starting point is to study what customers require and what competitors are offering. Customers are interested in on-time delivery, supplier willingness to meet emergency needs, careful handling of merchandise, and supplier willingness to take back defective goods and resupply them quickly.

The company must then research the relative importance of these service outputs. For example, service-repair time is very important to buyers of copying equipment. Xerox developed a service delivery standard that "can put a disabled machine anywhere in the continental United States back into operation within three hours after receiving the service request." It then designed a service division of personnel, parts, and locations to deliver on this promise.

The company must also consider competitors' service standards. It will normally want to match or exceed the competitors' service level, but the objective is to maximize profits, not sales. Some companies offer less service and charge a lower price; other companies offer more service and charge a premium price.

The company ultimately must establish some promise it makes to the market. Coca-Cola wants to "put Coke within an arm's length of desire." Lands' End, the giant clothing retailer, aims to respond to every phone call within 20 seconds and to ship every order within 24 hours of receipt. Purolator takes pride in its service standards.

Purolator Courier Ltd.

Purolator is Canada's largest courier company. Every day, it handles 1.1 million pieces. Only 30 percent of these are documents; the remainder are manufactured goods. While you may be more familiar with its trucks that frequent your neighbourhood, Purolator also moves 100 million pounds of air freight each year. Purolator's tag line, "Where Business Is Going," captures the essence of its services. Purolator offers guaranteed delivery by 9 A.M., by 10:30 A.M., or by the end of the second business day to more than 215 countries worldwide. In Canada and the United States, it can respond to more urgent needs, offering clients a range of options like "On & Gone," "Hot," "Rush," "Regular," "Direct Drive," or "Next Flight Out."[61]

Given the market-logistics objectives, the company must design a system that will minimize the cost of achieving these objectives. Each possible market-logistics system will lead to the following cost:

$$M = T + FW + VW + S$$

where M = total market-logistics cost of proposed system
T = total freight cost of proposed system
FW = total fixed warehouse cost of proposed system
VW = total variable warehouse cost (including inventory) of proposed system
S = total cost of lost sales due to average delivery delay under proposed system

Choosing a market-logistics system calls for examining the total cost *(M)* associated with different proposed systems and selecting the system that minimizes *M.* If it is hard to measure *S,* the company should aim to minimize $T + FW + VW$ for a target level of customer service.

Market-Logistics Decisions

The firm must make four major decisions about its market logistics: (1) How should we handle orders (order processing)? (2) Where should we locate our stock (warehousing)? (3) How much stock should we hold (inventory)? (4) How should we ship goods (transportation)?

ORDER PROCESSING Most companies today are trying to shorten the *order-to-payment cycle*—that is, the elapsed time between an order's receipt, delivery, and payment. This cycle has many steps, including order transmission by the salesperson, order entry and customer credit check, inventory and production scheduling, order and invoice shipment, and receipt of payment. The longer this cycle takes, the lower the customer's satisfaction and the lower the company's profits.

WAREHOUSING Every company must store finished goods until they are sold, because production and consumption cycles rarely match. Consumer-packaged-goods companies have been reducing their number of stocking locations from 10 to 15 to about 5 to 7, and pharmaceutical and medical distributors have cut theirs from 90 to about 45. More stocking locations mean goods can be delivered to customers more quickly, but warehousing and inventory costs are higher. To reduce these costs, the company might centralize its inventory in one place and use fast transportation to fill orders.

Some inventory is kept at or near the plant, and the rest in warehouses in other locations. The company might own private warehouses and also rent space in public warehouses. *Storage warehouses* store goods for moderate to long periods of time. *Distribution warehouses* receive goods from various company plants and suppliers and move them out as soon as possible. *Automated warehouses* employ advanced materials-handling systems under the control of a central computer and are increasingly becoming the norm.

Some warehouses are now taking on activities formerly done in the plant. These include assembly, packaging, and constructing promotional displays. Postponing finalization of the offering until the warehousing stage can achieve savings in costs and finer matching of offerings to demand.

INVENTORY Salespeople would like their companies to carry enough stock to fill all customer orders immediately. However, this is not cost-effective. *Inventory cost increases at an accelerating rate as the customer-service level approaches 100 percent.* Management needs to know how much sales and profits would increase as a result of carrying larger inventories and promising faster order fulfillment times, and then make a decision.

As inventory draws down, management must know at what stock level to place a new order. This stock level is called the *order (or reorder) point.* An order point of 20 means reordering when the stock falls to 20 units. The order point should balance the risks of stock-out against the costs of overstock. The other decision is how much to order. The larger the quantity ordered, the less frequently an order needs to be placed. The company needs to balance order-processing costs and inventory-carrying costs. *Order-processing costs* for a manufacturer consist of *set-up costs* and *running costs* (operating costs when production is running) for the item. If set-up costs are low, the manufacturer can produce the item often, and the average cost per item is stable and equal to the running costs. If set-up costs are high, however, the manufacturer can reduce the average cost per unit by producing a long run and carrying more inventory.

Order-processing costs must be compared with *inventory-carrying costs.* The larger the average stock carried, the higher the inventory-carrying costs. These carrying costs include storage charges, cost of capital, taxes and insurance, and depreciation and obsolescence. Carrying costs might run as high as 30 percent of inventory value. This means that marketing managers who want their companies to carry larger inventories need to show that the larger inventories would produce incremental gross profits to exceed incremental carrying costs.

We can determine the optimal order quantity by observing how order-processing costs and inventory-carrying costs sum up at different order levels. Figure 16.1 shows that the order-processing cost per unit decreases with the number of units ordered because the order costs are spread over more units. Inventory-carrying charges per unit increase with the number of units ordered, because each unit remains longer in inventory. We sum the two cost curves vertically into a total-cost curve and project the lowest point of the total-cost curve on the horizontal axis to find the optimal order quantity, Q^*.[62]

Companies are reducing their inventory costs by treating inventory items differently, positioning them according to risk and opportunity. They distinguish between bottleneck items (high risk, low opportunity), critical items (high risk, high opportunity), commodities (low risk, high opportunity), and nuisance items (low risk, low opportunity).[63] They are also keeping slow-moving items in a central location and carrying fast-moving items in warehouses closer to customers. All these strategies give them more flexibility should anything go wrong, as it often does, be it a dock strike in California, a typhoon in Taiwan, a tsunami in Asia, or a hurricane in New Orleans.[64]

The ultimate answer to carrying *near-zero inventory* is to build for order, not for stock. Sony calls it SOMO, "Sell one, make one." Dell's inventory strategy for years has been to get the customer to order a computer and pay for it in advance. Then Dell uses the customer's money to pay suppliers to ship the necessary components. As long as customers do not need the item immediately, everyone can save money. Some retailers are unloading excess inventory on eBay, where, by cutting out the traditional liquidator middleman, they can make 60 to 80 cents on the dollar as opposed to 10 cents.[65]

TRANSPORTATION Transportation choices affect product pricing, on-time delivery performance, and the condition of the goods when they arrive, all of which affect customer satisfaction.

In shipping goods to its warehouses, dealers, and customers, the company can choose rail, air, truck, waterway, or pipeline. Shippers consider such criteria as speed, frequency, dependability, capability, availability, traceability, and cost. For speed, the prime contenders are air, rail, and truck. If the goal is low cost, then the choice is water or pipeline.

Shippers are increasingly combining two or more transportation modes, thanks to containerization. **Containerization** consists of putting the goods in boxes or trailers that are easy to transfer between two transportation modes. *Piggyback* describes the use of rail and trucks; *fishyback,* water and trucks; *trainship,*

FIGURE 16.1

Determining Optimal Order Quantity

water and rail; and *airtruck,* air and trucks. Each coordinated mode offers specific advantages. For example, piggyback is cheaper than trucking alone yet provides flexibility and convenience.

Shippers can choose private, contract, or common carriers. If the shipper owns its own truck or air fleet, it becomes a *private carrier.* A *contract carrier* is an independent organization selling transportation services to others on a contract basis. A *common carrier* provides services between predetermined points on a scheduled basis and is available to all shippers at standard rates.

Organizational Lessons

Market-logistics strategies must be derived from business strategies, rather than solely from cost considerations. The logistics system must be information-intensive and establish electronic links among all the significant parties. Finally, the company should set its logistics goals to match or exceed competitors' service standards and should involve members of all relevant teams in the planning process.

Today's stronger demands from large customers for logistical support will increase suppliers' costs. Customers want more frequent deliveries so that they don't have to carry as much inventory. They want shorter order-cycle times, which means suppliers must have high in-stock availability. Customers often want direct store delivery rather than shipments to distribution centres. They want mixed pallets rather than separate pallets. They want tighter promised delivery times. They may want custom packaging, price tagging, and display building.

Suppliers can't say "no" to many of these requests, but at least they can set up different logistical programs with different service levels and customer charges. Smart companies will adjust their offerings to each major customer's requirements. The company's trade group will set up *differentiated distribution* by offering different bundled service programs for different customers.

SUMMARY

1. Retailing includes all the activities involved in selling goods or services directly to final consumers for personal, nonbusiness use. Retailers can be understood in terms of store retailing, nonstore retailing, and retail organizations.

2. Like products, retail-store types pass through stages of growth and decline. As existing stores offer more services to remain competitive, costs and prices go up, which opens the door to new retail forms that offer a mix of merchandise and services at lower prices. The major types of retail stores are specialty stores, department stores, supermarkets, convenience stores, drug stores, discount stores, extreme value or hard-discount stores, off-price retailers, superstores, and catalogue showrooms.

3. Although most goods and services are sold through stores, nonstore retailing has been growing. The major types of nonstore retailing are direct selling (one-to-one selling, one-to-many party selling, and multilevel network marketing), direct marketing (which includes e-commerce and Internet retailing), automatic vending, and buying services.

4. Although many retail stores are independently owned, an increasing number are falling under some form of corporate retailing. Retail organizations offer many economies of scale, greater purchasing power, wider brand recognition, and better-trained employees. The major types of corporate retailing are corporate chain stores, voluntary chains, retailer co-operatives, consumer co-operatives, franchise organizations, and merchandising conglomerates.

5. The retail environment has changed considerably in recent years; as new retail forms have emerged, intertype competition and store-based versus nonstore-based competition have increased, the rise of giant retailers has been matched by the decline of middle-market retailers, investment in technology and global expansion has grown, and shopper marketing inside stores has become a priority.

6. Like all marketers, retailers must prepare marketing plans that include decisions on target markets, channels, product assortment, procurement, prices, services, store atmosphere, store activities and experiences, communications, and location.

7. Wholesaling includes all the activities in selling goods or services to those who buy for resale or business use. Wholesalers can perform functions better and more cost-effectively than the manufacturer can. These functions comprise selling and promoting, buying and assortment building, bulk breaking, warehousing, transportation, financing, risk bearing, dissemination of market information, and provision of management services and consulting.

8. There are six types of wholesalers: merchant wholesalers, full-service wholesalers, limited-service wholesalers, brokers and agents, manufacturers' and retailers' branches and offices, and specialized wholesalers.

9. Like retailers, wholesalers must decide on target markets, product assortment and services, price, promotion, and place. The most successful wholesalers are those who adapt their services to meet suppliers' and target customers' needs.

10. Producers of physical products and services must decide on market logistics—the best way to store and move goods and services to market destinations; and to coordinate the activities of suppliers, purchasing agents, manufacturers, marketers, channel members, and customers. Major gains in logistical efficiency have come from advances in information technology.

APPLICATIONS

Marketing Debate: Should National Brand Manufacturers Also Supply Private-Label Brands?

Ralston-Purina, Borden, ConAgra, and Heinz have all admitted to supplying products—sometimes lower in quality—to be used for private labels. Other marketers, however, criticize this "if you can't beat them, join them" strategy, maintaining that these actions, if revealed, may create confusion or even reinforce a perception by consumers that all brands in a category are essentially the same.

Take a position: Manufacturers should feel free to sell private labels as a source of revenue *versus* National manufacturers should never get involved with private labels.

Marketing Discussion: Retail Customer Loyalty

Think of your favourite stores. What do they do that encourages your loyalty? What do you like about the in-store experience? What further improvements could they make?

MARKETING **EXCELLENCE**	EMPIRE COMPANY LIMITED

While you may not immediately recognize the name of this company, you will recognize its major banners: Sobeys, IGA, Foodland, FreshCo. (formerly Price Chopper), Thrifty Foods, and Lawtons. The company is a major force and is ranked 67th on the list of the world's major retail companies. According to CEO Paul D. Sobey, the company continues to focus its energy and resources on the businesses it knows best: food retailing and related real estate. Since having convenient locations for shoppers is often the key to retailing success, you should quickly be able to see the link between the two parts of the business. Location is not enough to guarantee success, however. The company also depends on its customer focus, the expertise of its workforce, and their passion for providing top-notch service. It relies on innovation to keep its private-label brands differentiated and in demand.

The Empire Company Limited has demonstrated its ability to weather tough times. Despite weak economic conditions, in 2010 its revenues increased 3.3 percent to $15.5 billion, and the firm's operating earnings were up 8.7 percent.

The company's focus on long-term growth and profitability is led by Sobeys, recognized as the top food retailer in the country. With more than 1300 stores located across Canada, Sobeys is focused on the continued modernization and expansion of its retail store network to better serve customers. Over the last five years alone (2005 to 2010), Sobeys invested more than $2 billion in its stores and their supporting infrastructure.

In addition to having prime locations, an effective and efficient food retailer requires sophisticated distribution and information systems. For example, Empire built a new distribution system in Vaughan, Ontario, as its latest advancement in a journey of continuous supply chain improvement. The warehouse is automated and has a "picking system" that allows the firm to assemble and ship assortments tailored to the needs of individual stores. The new warehouse has also improved the speed and accuracy of the system while reducing overall distribution costs.

Information systems are critical to success in modern retailing. Empire's information systems include productivity tools like the Work Force Management System, which enables scheduling of employees to better align with customers' shopping patterns. Another system enables the planning, ordering, and generating of fresh products to reduce waste while maintaining quality and consistency. A third, the Computer Automated Ordering system, enables the company to better forecast sales and manage inventory so that stock-outs are minimized.

Having powerful customer information may be the most important ingredient in Sobeys' success. Sobeys' system is titled Customer Insight Solution, and it is enabling Sobeys to shift from its traditional one-size-fits-all approach to food retailing, to a localized approach that considers the unique characteristics of customers no matter where they are located across Canada. The system will eventually enable Sobeys to connect more directly with customers and provide them with services and products tailored to their individual needs. Data are captured on millions of daily customer transactions through the Club Sobeys (see the Chapter 5 opener), Club Thrifty, and AIR MILES rewards programs. Analysis of the data provides the company with unique insights about customer motivation, behaviours, and shopping occasions. These insights are helping the firm improve its communications programs, pricing, product assortment, product placement, and merchandising. Above all, Sobeys knows that sustainable growth depends on building its business one relationship at a time: "At Sobeys, there is no such thing as the average customer." In this way, Sobeys resembles the village shopkeeper from days past.

Having powerful information is also helping the firm take a more focused approach to its communications even though it uses a range of traditional and social media. Its research has revealed that Canadians are looking "for inspiration and advice on how to make balanced food choices, while juggling busy schedules and without having to compromise quality." Thus, Sobeys still uses flyers to communicate "hot deals," but it is using more interactive vehicles like Facebook to engage its customers as well. Members of its rewards programs receive customized and relevant electronic offers. Sobeys also produces a quarterly publication which is its highest value-added tool. It is a lifestyle magazine that brings together ideas, information, and education to address consumers' evolving needs.

Empire also believes in embracing a wide range of responsibilities in addition to long-term growth and profitability. It is a contributor to the communities in which it operates. Many of its citizenship programs are designed to align with its core business, and include dozens of health- and food-related programs such as food banks. It is also focused on environmental issues. It is an active supporter of Earth Day and provides donations to many grassroots community groups and local schools to support their environmental initiatives.

QUESTIONS

1. What are the keys to Empire Company Limited's success? What risks does it face going forward?

2. Why is it important that food retailers have a focus on sustainability? Is Sobeys doing enough on this front?

Sources: "Focused on Being the Best . Together," Empire Company Limited 2010 Annual Report, www.empireco.ca/site/media/Empireco/Empire_annual_report_-_FINAL_secured.pdf; Alan Middleton, "Sobey's Unveils a 'More Focused Approach' to Grocery Chain Marketing Communications, Says Schulich Marketing Professor," *Schulich News & Events*, June 16, 2010, http://media.schulich.yorku.ca/ blog/2010/06/16sobeys-unveils-a-more-focused-approach-to-grocery-chain-marketing-communications-says-schulich-marketing-professor/ (accessed July 2011).

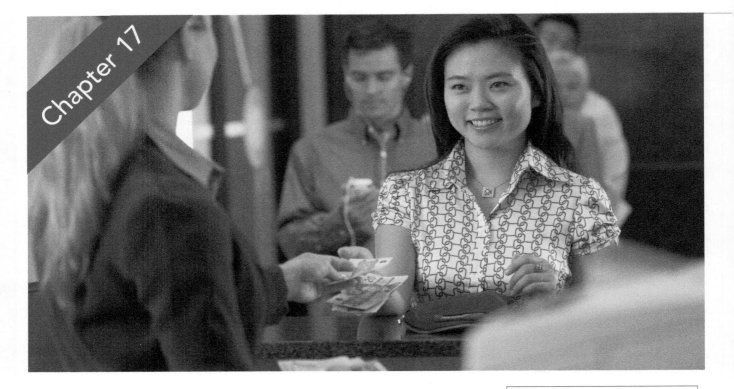

Chapter 17

In all its marketing communications, TD Canada Trust conveys a consistent message that banking with TD is comfortable.

In This Chapter, We Will Address the Following **Questions**

1. What is the role of marketing communications?

2. How do marketing communications work?

3. What are the major steps in developing effective communications?

4. What is the communications mix, and how should it be set?

5. What is an integrated marketing communication program?

Designing and Managing Integrated Marketing Communications

Modern marketing calls for more than developing a good product, pricing it attractively, and making it accessible. Companies must also communicate with their present and potential stakeholders and the general public. For most marketers, therefore, the question is not *whether* to communicate but rather *what* to say, *how* and *when* to say it, to *whom*, and *how often*. Consumers can turn to hundreds of cable and satellite TV channels, thousands of magazines and newspapers, and millions of Internet pages. They are taking a more active role in deciding what communications they want to receive as well as how they want to communicate to others about the products and services they use. To effectively reach and influence target markets, holistic marketers are creatively employing multiple forms of communications.

The Toronto Dominion Bank is Canada's second largest. Its banking operation, TD Canada Trust, with its signature green colour, serves millions of customers through 1100 branches and 2700 ATM machines, along with telephone and online banking.

TD Canada Trust's brand identity is based on the notion of making banking more comfortable, the theme of most TD communications, often with its iconic green armchair to denote comfort. The bank promotes its superior customer service and longer hours of operation, with hundreds of branches open Sundays as well. TD has launched a "Grumpy Old Men" advertising campaign that pokes fun at the older, more traditional view of banking, and then contrasts TD's helpful and comfortable services to traditional banking.

During publicity events, TD has celebrities seated in oversized green armchairs to symbolize the convenience of banking with TD. In the fall of 2010, TD launched "Up Close & Comfortable"—a series of behind-the-scenes chats with writers and directors from major network shows like American Idol, Dancing with the Stars, and Grey's Anatomy. While seated in the green armchair, the series creators talk about comfort within the context of their programs, underscoring the TD brand's positioning while providing viewers with the inside scoop on their favourite shows. TD also uses product placement in Canadian television shows. For instance, MediaCom helped TD partner with CBC to have TD Canada Trust branches worked into the plots of shows such as Being Erica, Heartland, and Little Mosque on the Prairie.

To use the exploding social networking media to communicate with its customers, TD also launched a Twitter account and YouTube page in 2010. Recognizing the importance of such new channels of communication, TD now spends nearly 20 percent of its promotion budget on digital media. With over 11 million customers, TD pays considerable attention to portraying an integrated, consistent image to them via all its online and offline marketing communications.[1]

Done right, marketing communications can have a huge payoff. This chapter describes how communications work and what marketing communications can do for a company. It also addresses how holistic marketers combine and integrate marketing communications. Chapter 18 examines mass (nonpersonal) communications (advertising, sales promotion, events and experiences, and public relations and publicity); Chapter 19 examines personal communications (direct and interactive marketing, word-of-mouth marketing, and personal selling).

THE ROLE OF MARKETING COMMUNICATIONS

Marketing communications are the means by which firms attempt to inform, persuade, and remind consumers—directly or indirectly—about the products and brands they sell. In a sense, marketing communications represent the voice of the company and its brands; they are a means by which the firm can establish a dialogue and build relationships with consumers. By strengthening customer loyalty, marketing communications can contribute to customer equity.

Marketing communications also work for consumers when they show how and why a product is used, by whom, where, and when. Consumers can learn who makes the product and what the company and brand stand for, and they can get an incentive for trial or use. Marketing communications allow companies to link their brands to other people, places, events, brands, experiences, feelings, and things. They can contribute to brand equity—by establishing the brand in memory and creating a brand image—as well as drive sales and even affect shareholder value.[2]

The Changing Marketing Communications Environment

Technology and other factors have profoundly changed the way consumers process communications, and even whether they choose to process them at all. The rapid diffusion of multipurpose smartphones, broadband and wireless Internet connections, and ad-skipping digital video recorders (DVRs) has eroded the effectiveness of the mass media. In 1970, a company could reach a large percentage of women in Canada with one 30-second commercial aired simultaneously on CBC and CTV. Today, the same ad would have to run on numerous channels multiple times to achieve this marketing feat. Consumers not only have more choices of media, they can also decide whether and how they want to receive commercial content. "Marketing Insight: Don't Touch That Remote" describes developments in television advertising.

But as some marketers flee traditional media, they still encounter challenges. Commercial clutter is rampant. The average city dweller is exposed to an estimated 3000 to 5000 ad messages a day. Short-form

---

MARKETING **INSIGHT**	DON'T TOUCH THAT REMOTE

That consumers are more in charge in the marketplace is perhaps nowhere more evident than in television broadcasting, where DVRs allow consumers to skip past ads with a push of the fast-forward button. Estimates had DVRs in 25 percent of Canadian households in mid-2011, and of viewers who use them, 55 percent always fast-forward through commercials (the others either like ads, watch them sometimes, or are not bothered by them).

Is that all bad? Surprisingly, research shows that while focusing on an ad in order to fast-forward through it, consumers actually retain and recall a fair amount of information. The most successful ads in "fast-forward mode" were those consumers had already seen, that used familiar characters, and that didn't have lots of scenes. It also helped to have brand-related information in the centre of the screen, where viewers focus their eyes while skipping through the ads. Although consumers are still more likely to recall an ad the next day if they've watched it live, some brand recall occurs even after an ad was deliberately zapped.

Another challenge marketers have faced for a long time is viewers' tendency to switch channels during commercial breaks. Recently, however, Nielsen, which handles television program ratings, has begun to offer ratings for specific ads. Before, advertisers had to pay based on the rating of the program, even if as many as 5 percent to 15 percent of consumers temporarily tuned away. Now they can pay based on the actual commercial audience available when their ad is shown. To increase viewership during commercial breaks, the major broadcast and cable networks are shortening breaks and delaying them until viewers are more likely to be engaged in a program.

Sources: Jeff Beer, "Canada Lags on PVR Uptake," *Marketing*, September 13, 2010, p. 6; Data from BBM Canada Survey on PVR Penetration Rates, March 2011; S. Adam Brasel and James Gips, "Breaking Through Fast-Forwarding: Brand Information and Visual Attention," *Journal of Marketing*, 72 (November 2008): 31–48; "Watching the Watchers," *Economist*, November 15, 2008, p. 77; Stephanie Kang, "Why DVR Viewers Recall Some TV Spots," *Wall Street Journal*, February 26, 2008; Kenneth C. Wilbur, "How Digital Video Recorder Changes Traditional Television Advertising," *Journal of Advertising*, 37 (Summer 2008): 143–149; Burt Helm, "Cable Takes a Ratings Hit," *BusinessWeek*, September 24, 2007.

video content and ads appear at gas stations, grocery stores, chiropractors' offices, and big-box retailers. Supermarket eggs have been stamped with the name of CBS programs; anti-drinking and driving ads are positioned over urinals; university names are painted on the backside of women's sweatpants; US Airways has sold ads on its motion sickness bags; and anyone who's watched *Casino Royale* has noticed that James Bond uses a Sony VAIO laptop and wears an Omega watch.[3]

Marketing communications in almost every medium and form have been on the rise, and some consumers feel they are increasingly invasive. Marketers must be creative in using technology but not intrude in consumers' lives. Consider what Motorola did to solve that problem.[4]

Motorola

At Hong Kong International Airport, Motorola's special promotion enabled loved ones to "Say Goodbye" via photos and messages sent from their phones to digital billboards in the departure area. When they checked into the gate area, travellers saw photos of the friends and family who had just dropped them off, as part of a digital billboard in the image of a giant Motorola cell phone. The company also offered departing travellers special instructions for using their phones to send a Motorola-branded good-bye video to friends and families, featuring soccer star David Beckham and Asian pop star Jay Chou.

Marketing Communications, Brand Equity, and Sales

In this new communication environment, although advertising is often a central element of a marketing communications program, it is usually not the only one—or even the most important one—for sales and building brand and customer equity. Like many other U.S. firms, over a five-year period from 2004 to 2008 Kimberly-Clark cut the percentage of its marketing budget spent on TV from 60 percent to a little over 40 percent as it invested more heavily in Internet and experiential marketing.[5] However, Canadian firms have been spending a smaller percentage of their advertising budgets on digital media, in comparison to their American and British counterparts.[6]

MARKETING COMMUNICATIONS MIX The **marketing communications mix** consists of eight major modes of communication:[7]

1. *Advertising*—Any paid form of nonpersonal presentation and promotion of ideas, goods, or services by an identified sponsor via print media (newspapers and magazines), broadcast media (radio and television), network media (telephone, cable, satellite, wireless), electronic media (audiotape, video-tape, videodisc, CD-ROM, webpage), or display media (billboards, signs, posters).

2. *Sales promotion*—A variety of short-term incentives to encourage trial or purchase of a product or service including consumer promotions (such as samples, coupons, and premiums), trade promotions (such as advertising and display allowances), and business and sales force promotions (contests for sales reps).

3. *Events and experiences*—Company-sponsored activities and programs designed to create daily or special brand-related interactions with consumers, including sports, arts, entertainment, and cause events as well as less formal activities.

4. *Public relations and publicity*—A variety of programs directed internally to employees of the company or externally to consumers, other firms, the government, and media to promote or protect a company's image or its individual product communications.

5. *Direct marketing*—Use of mail, telephone, fax, email, or Internet to communicate directly with or solicit response or dialogue from specific customers and prospects.

6. *Interactive marketing*—Online activities and programs designed to engage customers or prospects and directly or indirectly raise awareness, improve image, or elicit sales of products and services.

7. *Word-of-mouth marketing*—People-to-people oral, written, or electronic communications that relate to the merits or experiences of purchasing or using products or services.

8. *Personal selling*—Face-to-face interaction with one or more prospective purchasers for the purpose of making presentations, answering questions, and procuring orders.

Table 17.1 lists numerous communication platforms. Company communication goes beyond these. The product's styling and price, the shape and colour of the package, the salesperson's manner and dress, the store's décor, the company's stationery—all communicate something to buyers. Every *brand contact* delivers an impression that can strengthen or weaken a customer's view of a company.[8]

Marketing communication activities contribute to brand equity and drive sales in many ways: by creating brand awareness, forging brand image in consumers' memories, eliciting positive brand judgments or feelings, and strengthening consumer loyalty.

MARKETING COMMUNICATION EFFECTS The way brand associations are formed does not matter. In other words, whether a consumer has an equally strong, favourable, and unique brand association of Subaru with the concepts "outdoors," "active," and "rugged" because of exposure to a TV ad that shows the car driving over rugged terrain at different times of the year, or because Subaru sponsors ski, kayak, and mountain bike events, the impact in terms of Subaru's brand equity should be identical.

But these marketing communications activities must be integrated to deliver a consistent message and achieve the strategic positioning. The starting point in planning marketing communications is a *communication audit* that profiles all interactions customers in the target market may have with the company and all its products and services. For example, someone interested in purchasing a new laptop computer might talk to others, see television ads, read articles, look for information on the Internet, and look at laptops in a store.

TABLE 17.1	COMMON COMMUNICATION PLATFORMS					
Advertising	**Sales Promotion**	**Events and Experiences**	**Public Relations and Publicity**	**Direct and Interactive Marketing**	**Word-of-Mouth Marketing**	**Personal Selling**
Print and broadcast ads	Contests, games, sweepstakes, lotteries	Sports	Press kits	Catalogues	Person-to-person	Sales presentations
Packaging—outer	Premiums and gifts	Entertainment	Speeches	Mailings	Chat rooms	Sales meetings
Packaging inserts	Sampling	Festivals	Seminars	Telemarketing	Blogs	Incentive programs
Cinema	Fairs and trade shows	Arts	Annual reports	Electronic shopping		Samples
Brochures and booklets	Exhibits	Causes	Charitable donations	TV shopping		Fairs and trade shows
Posters and leaflets	Demonstrations	Factory tours	Publications	Fax		
Directories	Coupons	Company museums	Community relations	Email		
Reprints of ads	Rebates	Street activities	Lobbying	Voice mail		
Billboards	Low-interest financing		Identity media	Company blogs		
Display signs	Trade-in allowances		Company magazine	Websites		
Point-of-purchase displays	Continuity programs					
DVDs	Tie-ins					

To implement the right communications programs and allocate dollars efficiently, marketers need to assess which experiences and impressions will have the most influence at each stage of the buying process. Armed with these insights, they can judge marketing communications according to their ability to affect experiences and impressions, build customer loyalty and brand equity, and drive sales. For example, how well does a proposed ad campaign contribute to awareness or to creating, maintaining, or strengthening brand associations? Does a sponsorship improve consumers' brand judgments and feelings? Does a promotion encourage consumers to buy more of a product? At what price premium?

In building brand equity, marketers should be "media neutral" and evaluate *all* communication options on effectiveness (how well does it work?) and efficiency (how much does it cost?). Personal financial website Mint challenged market leader Intuit—and was eventually acquired by the company—on a marketing budget a fraction of what companies typically spend. A well-read blog, a popular Facebook page, and other social media, combined with extensive PR, helped attract the younger crowd the Mint brand was after.[9] Philips also took another tack in launching a new product.[10]

Philips *Carousel*

When Dutch electronics leader Philips wanted to demonstrate the quality of the "world's first cinema proportion" TV, it chose to create *Carousel,* an interactive, long-form Internet film. In this Cannes Grand Prix award–winning effort, online viewers could control the story of a botched robbery while seeing the benefits of the new $3999 home cinema TV. The film showed an epic "frozen moment" cops-and-robbers shootout sequence that included clowns, explosions, a decimated hospital, and lots of broken glass, bullet casings, and money. By clicking hot spots in the video, viewers could toggle between the new set's 21:9 display proportion and a conventional flat screen's 16:9, as well as activate the set's signature Ambilight backlighting. The success of the campaign led Philips to launch a "Parallel Lines" campaign with five short films from the shop of famed director Ridley Scott, promoting the company's whole range of home cinema TVs.

The Communications Process Models

Marketers should understand the fundamental elements of effective communications. Two models are useful: a macromodel and a micromodel.

Figure 17.1 shows a macromodel with nine key factors in effective communication. Two represent the major parties—*sender* and *receiver.* Two represent the major tools—*message* and *media.* Four represent major communication functions—*encoding, decoding, response,* and *feedback.* The last element in the system is *noise,* random and competing messages that may interfere with the intended communication.[11]

Senders must know what audiences they want to reach and what responses they want to get. They must encode their messages so that the target audience can decode them. They must transmit the message through media that reach the target audience and develop feedback channels to monitor the responses. The more the sender's field of experience overlaps that of the receiver, the more effective the message is likely to be. Note that selective attention, distortion, and retention processes—concepts first introduced in Chapter 6—may be operating during communication.

MICROMODEL OF CONSUMER RESPONSES Micromodels of marketing communications concentrate on consumers' specific responses to communications.

Figure 17.2 summarizes four classic *response hierarchy models.*

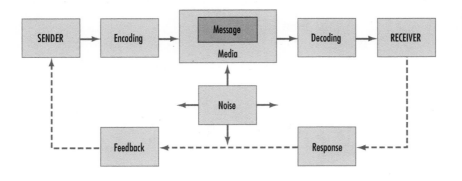

FIGURE 17.1

Elements in the Communications Process

All these models assume that the buyer passes through cognitive, affective, and behavioural stages, in that order. This "learn-feel-do" sequence is appropriate when the audience has high involvement with a product category perceived to have high differentiation, such as an automobile or house. An alternative sequence, "do-feel-learn," is relevant when the audience has high involvement but perceives little or no differentiation within the product category, such as an airline ticket or personal computer. A third sequence, "learn-do-feel," is relevant when the audience has low involvement and perceives little differentiation, such as with salt or batteries. By choosing the right sequence, the marketer can do a better job of planning communications.[12]

Let's assume the buyer has high involvement with the product category and perceives high differentiation within it. We will illustrate the *hierarchy-of-effects model* (the second column of Figure 17.2) in the context of a marketing communications campaign for a small Manitoba college named Prairieville:

- *Awareness.* If most of the target audience is unaware of the object, the communicator's task is to build awareness. Suppose Prairieville seeks applicants from Saskatchewan but has no name recognition there, although 20 000 Saskatchewan high school students could be interested in it. The college might set the objective of making 70 percent of these students aware of its name within one year.

- *Knowledge.* The target audience might have brand awareness but not know much more. Prairieville may want its target audience to know that Prairieville is a four-year college with excellent programs in English, foreign languages, and history. It needs to learn how many people in the target audience have little, some, or much knowledge about the college. If knowledge is weak, Prairieville may select brand knowledge as its communications objective.

- *Liking.* Given that target members know the brand, how do they feel about it? If the audience looks unfavourably on Prairieville College, the communicator needs to find out why. In the case of real problems, Prairieville will need to fix these and then communicate its renewed quality. Good public relations calls for "good deeds followed by good words."

- *Preference.* The target audience might like the product but not prefer it to others. The communicator must then try to build consumer preference by comparing quality, value, performance, and other features to those of likely competitors.

- *Conviction.* A target audience might prefer a particular product but not develop a conviction about buying it. The communicator's job is to build conviction and intent to apply among students interested in Prairieville College.

- *Purchase.* Finally, some members of the target audience might have conviction but not quite get around to making the purchase. The communicator must lead these consumers to take the final step, perhaps by offering the product at a low price, offering a premium, or letting them try it out. Prairieville might invite selected high school students to visit the campus and attend some classes, or it might offer partial scholarships to deserving students.

FIGURE 17.2

Response Hierarchy Models

Sources: [a]E. K. Strong, *The Psychology of Selling* (New York: McGraw-Hill, 1925), p. 9; [b]Robert J. Lavidge and Gary A. Steiner, "A Model for Predictive Measurements of Advertising Effectiveness," *Journal of Marketing*, October 1961, p. 61; [c]Everett M. Rogers, *Diffusion of Innovation* (New York: The Free Press, 1962), pp. 79–86; [d]various sources.

Stages	AIDA Model[a]	Hierarchy-of-Effects Model[b]	Innovation-Adoption Model[c]	Communications Model[d]
Cognitive stage	Attention	Awareness ↓ Knowledge	Awareness	Exposure ↓ Reception ↓ Cognitive response
Affective stage	Interest ↓ Desire	Liking ↓ Preference ↓ Conviction	Interest ↓ Evaluation	Attitude ↓ Intention
Behavioural stage	Action	Purchase	Trial ↓ Adoption	Behaviour

Models

To see how fragile the communications process is, assume that the probability of *each* of the six steps being successfully accomplished is 50 percent. The laws of probability suggest that the likelihood of *all* six steps occurring successfully, assuming they are independent events, is $0.5 \times 0.5 \times 0.5 \times 0.5 \times 0.5 \times 0.5$, which equals 1.5625 percent. If the probability of each step's occurring were, on average, a more moderate 10 percent, then the joint probability of all six events occurring is 0.0001 percent—or only 1 chance in 1 000 000!

To increase the odds for a successful marketing communications campaign, marketers must attempt to increase the likelihood that *each* step occurs. For example, the ideal ad campaign would ensure the following:

1. The right consumer is exposed to the right message at the right place and at the right time.

2. The ad causes the consumer to pay attention but does not distract from the intended message.

3. The ad properly reflects the consumer's level of understanding of and behaviours toward the product and the brand.

4. The ad correctly positions the brand in terms of desirable and deliverable points-of-difference and points-of-parity.

5. The ad motivates consumers to consider purchase of the brand.

6. The ad creates strong brand associations with all these stored communications effects so that they can have an impact when consumers are considering making a purchase.

The challenges in achieving success with communications necessitate careful planning, a topic we turn to next.

DEVELOPING EFFECTIVE COMMUNICATIONS

Figure 17.3 shows the eight steps in developing effective communications. We begin with the basics: identifying the target audience, determining the objectives, designing the communications, selecting the channels, and establishing the budget.

Identify the Target Audience

The process must start with a clear target audience in mind: potential buyers of the company's products, current users, deciders, or influencers; and individuals, groups, particular publics, or the general public. The target audience is a critical influence on the communicator's decisions about what to say, how, when, where, and to whom.

Though we can profile the target audience in terms of any of the market segments identified in Chapter 8, it's often useful to do so in terms of usage and loyalty. Is the target new to the category or a current user? Is the target loyal to the brand, loyal to a competitor, or someone who switches between brands? If a brand user, is he or she a heavy or light user? Communications strategy will differ depending on the answers. We can also conduct *image analysis* by profiling the target audience in terms of brand knowledge.

Determine the Communications Objectives

As we showed with Prairieville College, marketers can set communications objectives at any level of the hierarchy-of-effects model. John R. Rossiter and Larry Percy identify four possible objectives, as follows:[13]

1. *Category need*—Establishing a product or service category as necessary to remove or satisfy a perceived discrepancy between a current motivational state and a desired motivational state. A new-to-the-world product such as electric cars will always begin with a communications objective of establishing category need.

2. *Brand awareness*—Fostering the consumer's ability to recognize or recall the brand within the category, in sufficient detail to make a purchase. Recognition is easier to achieve than recall—consumers asked to think of a brand of frozen entrees are more likely to recognize Stouffer's distinctive orange packages than to recall the brand. Brand recall is important outside the store; brand recognition is important inside the store. Brand awareness provides a foundation for brand equity.

3. *Brand attitude*—Helping consumers evaluate the brand's perceived ability to meet a currently relevant need. Relevant brand needs may be negatively oriented (problem solution, problem avoidance, incomplete satisfaction, normal depletion) or positively oriented (sensory gratification, intellectual stimulation, or social approval). Household cleaning products often use problem solution; food products, on the other hand, often use sensory-oriented ads emphasizing appetite appeal.

FIGURE 17.3

Steps in Developing Effective Communications

4. *Brand purchase intention*—Moving consumers to decide to purchase the brand or take purchase-related action. Promotional offers like coupons or two-for-one deals encourage consumers to make a mental commitment to buy. But many consumers do not have an expressed category need and may not be in the market when exposed to an ad, so they are unlikely to form buy intentions. In any given week, only about 20 percent of adults may be planning to buy detergent, only 2 percent to buy a carpet cleaner, and only 0.25 percent to buy a car.

Design the Communications

Formulating the communications to achieve the desired response requires solving three problems: what to say (message strategy), how to say it (creative strategy), and who should say it (message source).

MESSAGE STRATEGY In determining message strategy, management searches for appeals, themes, or ideas that will tie in to the brand positioning and help establish points-of-parity or points-of-difference. Some of these may be related directly to product or service performance (the quality, economy, or value of the brand), whereas others may relate to more extrinsic considerations (the brand as being contemporary, popular, or traditional).

Researcher John C. Maloney felt buyers expected one of four types of reward from a product: rational, sensory, social, or ego satisfaction.[14] Buyers might visualize these rewards from results-of-use experience, product-in-use experience, or incidental-to-use experience. Crossing the four types of rewards with the three types of experience generates 12 types of messages. For example, the appeal "gets clothes cleaner" is a rational-reward promise following results-of-use experience. The phrase "real beer taste in a great light beer" is a sensory-reward promise connected with product-in-use experience.

CREATIVE STRATEGY Communications effectiveness depends on how a message is being expressed, as well as on its content. If a communication is ineffective, it may mean the wrong message was used, or the right one was poorly expressed. *Creative strategies* are the way marketers translate their messages into a specific communication. We can broadly classify them as either *informational* or *transformational appeals.*[15]

Informational Appeals An **informational appeal** elaborates on product or service attributes or benefits. Examples in advertising are problem solution ads (Excedrin stops the toughest headache pain), product demonstration ads (Michelin winter tires provide better traction and control in snow), product comparison ads (Mac versus PC), and testimonials from unknown or celebrity endorsers (Wayne Gretzky pitching SKECHERS' Shape-ups). Informational appeals assume strictly rational processing of the communication on the consumer's part. Logic and reason rule.

Carl Hovland's research at Yale has shed much light on informational appeals and their relationship to such issues as conclusion drawing, one-sided versus two-sided arguments, and order of argument presentation. Some early experiments supported stating conclusions for the audience. Subsequent research, however, indicates that the best ads ask questions and allow readers and viewers to form their own conclusions.[16] If Honda had hammered away that the Element was for young people, this strong definition might have blocked older drivers from buying it. Some stimulus ambiguity can lead to a broader market definition and more spontaneous purchases.

You might expect one-sided presentations that praise a product to be more effective than two-sided arguments that also mention shortcomings. Yet two-sided messages may be more appropriate, especially when negative associations must be overcome.[17] Two-sided messages are more effective with more educated audiences and those who are initially opposed.[18] Buckley's had remarkable success with the "It tastes awful. And it works" slogan for its cough syrup.

Finally, the order in which arguments are presented is important.[19] In a one-sided message, presenting the strongest argument first arouses attention and interest, important in media where the audience often does not attend to the whole message. With a captive audience, a climactic presentation might be more effective. For a two-sided message, if the audience is initially opposed, the communicator might start with the other side's argument and conclude with his or her strongest argument.[20]

Transformational Appeals An **transformational appeal** elaborates on a nonproduct-related benefit or image. It might depict what kind of person uses a brand (VW advertised to active, youthful people with its famed "Drivers Wanted" campaign) or what kind of experience results from use (Pringles advertised "Once You Pop, the Fun Don't Stop" for years). Transformational appeals often attempt to stir up emotions that will motivate purchase.

Communicators use negative appeals such as fear, guilt, and shame to get people to do things (brush their teeth, have an annual health checkup) or stop doing things (smoking, abusing alcohol, overeating). Fear appeals work best when they are not too strong, when source credibility is high,

Pringles capitalized on the popping sound that occurs when its package is opened to develop a highly successful ad campaign.

and when the communication promises, in a believable and efficient way, to relieve the fear it arouses. Messages are most persuasive when moderately discrepant with audience beliefs. Stating only what the audience already believes at best just reinforces beliefs, and if the messages are too discrepant, audiences will argue with and disbelieve them.[21]

Communicators also use positive emotional appeals such as humour, love, pride, and joy. Motivational or "borrowed interest" devices—such as the presence of cute babies, frisky puppies, popular music, or provocative sex appeals—are often employed to attract attention and raise involvement with an ad. These techniques are thought necessary in the tough new media environment characterized by low-involvement consumer processing and competing ad and programming clutter. Attention-getting tactics are often *too* effective. They may also detract from comprehension, wear out their welcome fast, and overshadow the product.[22] Thus, one challenge is figuring out how to break through the clutter *and* deliver the intended message.

Even highly entertaining and creative means of expression must still keep the appropriate consumer perspective. Toyota was sued in Los Angeles for a promotional campaign designed to create buzz for its youth-targeted Toyota Matrix. The online effort featured a series of emails to customers from a fictitious drunken British soccer hooligan, Sebastian Bowler. In his emails, he announced that he knew the recipient and was coming to stay with his pit bull, Trigger, to "avoid the cops." In her suit, the plaintiff said she was so convinced that "a disturbed and aggressive" stranger was headed to her house that she slept with a machete next to her in bed.[23]

The magic of advertising is to bring concepts on a piece of paper to life in the minds of the consumer target. In a print ad, the communicator must decide on headline, copy, illustration, and colour.[24] For a radio message, the communicator must choose words, voice qualities, and vocalizations. The sound of an announcer promoting a used automobile should be different from one promoting a new Cadillac. If the message is to be carried on television or in person, all these elements plus body language must be planned. For the message to go online, layout, fonts, graphics, and other visual and verbal information must be laid out.

PEI as a tourist destination got considerable advertising mileage from hosting the *LIVE! With Regis & Kelly* TV show.

MESSAGE SOURCE Messages delivered by attractive or popular sources can achieve higher attention and recall, which is why advertisers often use celebrities as spokespeople.

Celebrities are likely to be effective when they are credible or personify a key product attribute. Pretty Julia Roberts for Lancôme, rugged Brett Favre for Wrangler jeans, and *Cheers* star Kirstie Alley for the Jenny Craig weight loss program have all been praised by consumers as good fits. Celine Dion, however, failed to add glamour—or sales—to Chrysler, and even though she was locked into a three-year, $14 million deal, she was let go. Sarah Jessica Parker was found to be too old for Gap and replaced just one year into a three-year contract by 17-year-old Joss Stone.

What *is* important is the spokesperson's credibility. The three most often identified sources of credibility are expertise, trustworthiness, and likability.[25] *Expertise* is the specialized knowledge the communicator possesses to back the claim. *Trustworthiness* describes how objective and honest the source is perceived to be. Friends are trusted more than strangers or salespeople, and people who are not paid to endorse a product are viewed as more trustworthy than people who are paid.[26] *Likability* describes the source's attractiveness. Qualities such as candour, humour, and naturalness make a source more likable.

The most highly credible source would score high on all three dimensions—expertise, trustworthiness, and likability. Pharmaceutical companies want doctors to testify about product benefits because doctors have high credibility. Roots used in its campaigns Canadian Olympic athletes wearing the Roots-designed Olympic uniforms. Another credible pitchman was boxer George Foreman and his multimillion-selling Lean Mean Fat-Reducing Grilling Machine. "Marketing Insight: Celebrity Endorsements as a Strategy" focuses on the use of testimonials.

A well-chosen celebrity endorsement can catapult even the most unlikely product to stardom. Consider how Regis Philbin and Kelly Ripa put Prince Edward Island on the world tourist map.

Regis & Kelly in Prince Edward Island

Regis Philbin and Kelly Ripa, hosts of one of the most popular talk shows in North America, *LIVE! With Regis & Kelly*, recently visited Prince Edward Island to tape four shows filled with celebrity guests, musical performances, and lots of beautiful scenery. Spending $1 million to bring the show to PEI, Premier Robert Ghiz and the federal government saw this opportunity as a great way to build the PEI brand and boost tourism in the province. The campaign featured a wide range of activities that PEI has to offer, showcasing natural beauty, local history, food, and culture. The show was a huge success, reaching nearly 1 million viewers on CTV, making it the most-watched episode ever. Following the show, PEI ranked number two in the top Google searches in the United States, and the traffic on the provincial government website increased 100 percent.[27]

| MARKETING **INSIGHT** | CELEBRITY ENDORSEMENTS AS A STRATEGY |

A well-chosen celebrity can draw attention to a product or brand—as Priceline found when it picked *Star Trek* icon William Shatner to star in campy ads to reinforce its low-price image. The quirky campaigns have run for over a decade, and Shatner's decision to receive compensation in the form of stock options reportedly allowed him to net over $600 million for his work. The right celebrity can also lend his or her image to a brand. To reinforce its high status and prestige image, American Express has used movie legends Robert De Niro and Martin Scorsese in ads.

The choice of celebrity is critical. The person should have high recognition, high positive affect, and high appropriateness or "fit" with the product. Paris Hilton, Howard Stern, and Donald Trump have high recognition but negative affect among many groups. Johnny Depp has high recognition and high positive affect but might not seem relevant, for example, for advertising a new financial service. Tom Hanks and Oprah Winfrey could successfully advertise a large number of products because they have extremely high ratings for familiarity and likability (known as the Q factor in the entertainment industry).

Celebrities can play a more fundamentally strategic role for their brands, not only endorsing a product but also helping to design, position, and sell merchandise and services. Believing elite athletes have unique insights into sports performance, Nike often brings its athletic endorsers in on product design. Tiger Woods, Paul Casey, and Stewart Cink have helped to design, prototype, and test new golf clubs and balls at Nike Golf's Research & Development facility dubbed "The Oven."

Some celebrities lend their talents to brands without directly using their fame. A host of movie and TV stars—including Kiefer Sutherland (Bank of America), Alec Baldwin (Blockbuster), Patrick Dempsey (State Farm), Lauren Graham (Special K), and Regina King (Always)—do uncredited commercial voice-overs. Although advertisers assume some viewers will recognize the voices, the basic rationale for uncredited celebrity voice-overs is the incomparable voice talents and skills they bring from their acting careers.

Using celebrities poses certain risks. The celebrity might hold out for a larger fee at contract renewal or withdraw. And just like movies and album releases, celebrity campaigns can be expensive flops. The celebrity might lose popularity or, even worse, get caught in a scandal or embarrassing situation, as did Tiger Woods in a heavily publicized 2009 episode or Brett Favre in 2010. Besides carefully checking endorsers' backgrounds, some marketers are choosing to use more than one to lessen their brand's exposure to any single person's flaws.

Another solution is for marketers to create their own brand celebrities. Dos Equis beer, imported from Mexico, grew U.S. sales by over 20 percent during the recent recession by riding on the popularity of its "Most Interesting Man in the World" ad campaign. Suave, debonair, with an exotic accent and a silver beard, the character has hundreds of thousands of Facebook friends despite being, of course, completely fictitious. Videos of his exploits log millions of views on YouTube. He even served as the basis of *The Most Interesting Show in the World* tour of the brand's 14 biggest urban markets, which featured one-of-a-kind circus-type performers such as a flaming bowling ball–juggling stunt comedian, a robot-inspired breakdancer, and a contortionist who shoots arrows with her feet. Through a combination of advertising and media coverage, almost 100 million media impressions were achieved on the tour.

Sources: Scott Huver, "Here's the Pitch!," *TV Guide*, May 23, 2010; Linda Massarella, "Shatner's Singing a Happy Tune," *Toronto Sun*, May 2, 2010; "Nike Golf Celebrates Achievements and Successes of Past Year," www.worldgolf.com, January 2, 2009; Piet Levy, "Keeping It Interesting," *Marketing News*, October 30, 2009, p. 8; Keith Naughton, "The Soft Sell," *Newsweek*, February 2, 2004, pp. 46–47; Irving Rein, Philip Kotler, and Martin Scoller, *The Making and Marketing of Professionals into Celebrities* (Chicago: NTC Business Books, 1997).

If a person has a positive attitude toward a source and a message, or a negative attitude toward both, a state of *congruity* is said to exist. But what happens if a consumer hears a likable celebrity praise a brand he or she dislikes? Charles Osgood and Percy Tannenbaum believe that *attitude change will take place in the direction of increasing the amount of congruity between the two evaluations.*[28] The consumer will end up respecting the celebrity somewhat less or the brand somewhat more. If he or she encounters the same celebrity praising other disliked brands, the consumer will eventually develop a negative view of the celebrity and maintain negative attitudes toward the brands. The **principle of congruity** implies that communicators can use their good image to reduce some negative feelings toward a brand but in the process might lose some esteem with the audience.

Multinational companies wrestle with a number of challenges in developing global communications programs. The following are some of them:

1. *Product.* Many products are restricted or forbidden in certain parts of the world. Alcoholic beverages cannot be advertised or sold in many Muslim countries.

2. *Market segment.* North American toy makers were surprised to learn that in many countries (Norway and Sweden, for example) no TV ads may be directed at children under 12. Sweden lobbied hard to extend that ban to all EU member countries in 2001 but failed. To play it safe, McDonald's advertises itself as a family restaurant in Sweden.

3. *Style.* Comparative ads, while legal and even common in Canada and the United States, are less commonly used in the United Kingdom, unacceptable in Japan, and illegal in India and Brazil.

Select the Communications Channels

Selecting an efficient means to carry the message becomes more difficult as channels of communication become more fragmented and cluttered. Communications channels may be personal or nonpersonal. Within each are many subchannels.

PERSONAL COMMUNICATIONS CHANNELS **Personal communications channels** let two or more people communicate face-to-face or person-to-audience through a phone, surface mail, or email. They derive their effectiveness from individualized presentation and feedback and include direct and interactive marketing, word-of-mouth marketing, and personal selling.

We can draw a further distinction between advocate, expert, and social communications channels. *Advocate channels* consist of company salespeople contacting buyers in the target market. *Expert channels* consist of independent experts making statements to target buyers. *Social channels* consist of neighbours, friends, family members, and associates talking to target buyers.

A study by Burson-Marsteller and Roper Starch Worldwide found that one influential person's word of mouth tends to affect the buying attitudes of two other people, on average. That circle of influence, however, jumps to eight online. Word about good companies travels fast; word about bad companies travels even faster. Reaching the right people is key.

More advertisers now seek greater *earned media*—unsolicited professional commentary, personal blog entries, social network discussion—as a result of their paid media marketing efforts. Kimberly-Clark ran a 30-second TV spot prior to the Academy Awards in March 2010 for its Poise brand, which featured Whoopi Goldberg portraying famous women in history who may have suffered from incontinence. The goal was to get people talking, and talk they did! A social media avalanche followed, culminating in a *Saturday Night Live* spoof, which eventually added up to 200 million PR impressions in total.[29] See how Procter & Gamble used social media to reposition its Old Spice brand.

Old Spice

The new Old Spice campaign launched during the Super Bowl XLIV featured Isaiah Mustafa, an ex-football player and actor, performing random and exaggerated acts of manliness with the tag line "The Man Your Man Could Smell Like." The campaign focused on a younger demographic in an attempt to change the image of Old Spice, which had been associated with an older generation. The brand transformation was supported by a YouTube campaign, which showcased Mustafa in nearly two hundred 30- to 90-second videos answering questions sent to him via Facebook, YouTube, and Twitter. The interactive campaign gained considerable attention from the public, media, and celebrities. The Old Spice Man has spoken to Ellen DeGeneres, flirted with Alyssa Milano and Rose McGowan, and even proposed to a woman on behalf of her boyfriend. The Old Spice Guy videos have been viewed nearly 150 million times, and his YouTube site became the most popular sponsored channel ever, with over 100 million followers.[30]

Personal influence carries especially great weight (1) when products are expensive, risky, or purchased infrequently, and (2) when products suggest something about the user's status or taste. People often ask others to recommend a doctor, plumber, hotel, lawyer, accountant, architect, insurance agent, interior decorator, or financial consultant. If we have confidence in the recommendation, we normally act on the referral. Service providers clearly have a strong interest in building referral sources.

Even business-to-business marketers can benefit from strong word of mouth. Here is how John Deere created anticipation and excitement when introducing its 764 High-Speed Dozer, the category's first launch in 25 years.[31]

John Deere

Leading up to the unveiling of its high-speed dozer at the industry's large CONEXPO trade show, John Deere created an extensive PR campaign. First, email announcements were sent to all trade show registrants, with images of the dozer covered in a tarp and teasing headlines, such as "Just a Few Years Ahead of the Competition" and "The Shape of Things to Come." Editors received an invitation to attend a closed-door press conference where they were given a VIP pass and admittance to a special viewing area at the CONEXPO show. Finally, editors were told they could also register for a special, invitation-only press conference with John Deere senior executives, including its CEO. Approximately 2000 people attended the trade show for a rock-star unveiling of the dozer, with about 80 editors present. Customers at the event who declared their desire for the machine helped Deere staff secure more leads. Press reaction was also extremely positive, including several trade magazine cover stories on the dozer and three segments on CNBC. The integrated effort on behalf of John Deere, which included print ads in trade publications, took home the Grand CEBA Award at the American Business Media's annual awards competition and First Prize in the Trade Show category in *B-to-B Magazine*'s "B-to-B's Best" awards competition.

NONPERSONAL (MASS) COMMUNICATIONS CHANNELS Nonpersonal channels are communications directed to more than one person and include advertising, sales promotions, events and experiences, and public relations. Much recent growth has taken place through events and experiences. Events marketers who once favoured sports events are now using other venues such as art museums, zoos, and

Through its print ad and trade show efforts, John Deere created buzz and much word of mouth in anticipation of the launch of its new high-speed dozer.

ice shows to entertain clients and employees. Air Canada sponsors ice sculpting contests, Bell Canada is an active sponsor of the Olympics, and Tim Hortons sponsors Earth Day celebrations in several Canadian cities.

Companies are searching for better ways to quantify the benefits of sponsorship and demanding greater accountability from event owners and organizers. They are also creating events designed to surprise the public and create a buzz. Many efforts amount to guerrilla marketing tactics. As part of a $100 million global advertising and marketing campaign for its line of televisions, LG Electronics developed an elaborate promotion for a fake new TV series, *Scarlet,* including a heavily promoted Hollywood world premiere. Inside, attendees found a new series of actual LG TVs with a red back panel. Teaser TV and online commercials and extensive PR backed the effort.[32]

Events can create attention, although whether they have a lasting effect on brand awareness, knowledge, or preference will vary considerably depending on the quality of the product, the event itself, and its execution. Consider how RONA is increasing its popularity through TV shows.

RONA

RONA sponsored two reality TV series, *Laisse faire, j'vais l'faire!* and *Grin and Build It,* in an effort to reinforce the message that RONA is a good place to shop for home renovations. The Quebec show *Laisse faire, j'vais l'faire!* shows personal stories of women renovating a room in their house, a room they have always wanted to redo. *Grin and Build It* follows couples as they embark on home renovations, where only the less handy of the two is allowed to complete the renovation. The emphasis is on the RONA by Design program, which uses RONA products and design experts to create new looks for rooms following current design trends. RONA's private-label products are featured in each episode, and the audience is encouraged to visit the RONA by Design website for home renovation ideas such as those as seen on the TV shows.[33]

INTEGRATION OF COMMUNICATIONS CHANNELS Although personal communication is often more effective than mass communication, mass media might be the major means of stimulating personal communication. Mass communications affect personal attitudes and behaviour through a two-step process. Ideas often flow from radio, television, and print to opinion leaders, and from these to less media-involved population groups.

RONA has been promoting its store and products through reality TV shows.

This two-step flow has several implications. First, the influence of mass media on public opinion is not as direct, powerful, and automatic as marketers have supposed. It is mediated by opinion leaders, people whose opinions others seek or who carry their opinions to others. Second, the two-step flow challenges the notion that consumption styles are primarily influenced by a "trickle-down" or "trickle-up" effect from mass media. People interact primarily within their own social groups and acquire ideas from opinion leaders in their groups. Third, two-step communication suggests that mass communicators should direct messages specifically to opinion leaders and let them carry the message to others.

Establish the Total Marketing Communications Budget

One of the most difficult marketing decisions is determining how much to spend on marketing communications. John Wanamaker, the department store magnate, once said, "I know that half of my advertising is wasted, but I don't know which half."

Industries and companies vary considerably in how much they spend on marketing communications. Expenditures might be 40 percent to 45 percent of sales in the cosmetics industry, but only 5 percent to 10 percent in the industrial-equipment industry. Within a given industry, there are low- and high-spending companies.

How do companies decide on the communications budget? We will describe four common methods: the affordable method, the percentage-of-sales method, the competitive-parity method, and the objective-and-task method.

AFFORDABLE METHOD Some companies set the communications budget at what they think the company can afford. The affordable method completely ignores the role of promotion as an investment and the immediate impact of promotion on sales volume. It leads to an uncertain annual budget, which makes long-range planning difficult.

PERCENTAGE-OF-SALES METHOD Some companies set communications expenditures at a specified percentage of current or anticipated sales or of the sales price. Automobile companies typically budget a fixed percentage based on the planned car price. Oil companies appropriate a fraction of a cent for each gallon of gasoline sold under their own label.

Supporters of the percentage-of-sales method see a number of advantages. First, communication expenditures will vary with what the company can afford. This satisfies financial managers, who believe expenses should be closely related to the movement of corporate sales over the business cycle. Second, it encourages management to think of the relationship among communications cost, selling price, and profit per unit. Third, it encourages stability when competing firms spend approximately the same percentage of their sales on communications.

In spite of these advantages, the percentage-of-sales method has little to justify it. It views sales as the determiner of communications rather than as the result. It leads to a budget set by the availability of funds rather than by market opportunities. It discourages experimentation with countercyclical communication or aggressive spending. Dependence on year-to-year sales fluctuations interferes with long-range planning. There is no logical basis for choosing the specific percentage, except what has been done in the past or what competitors are doing. Finally, it does not encourage building the communications budget by determining what each product and territory deserves.

COMPETITIVE-PARITY METHOD Some companies set their communications budget to achieve share-of-voice parity with competitors. There are two supporting arguments: that competitors' expenditures represent the collective wisdom of the industry, and that maintaining competitive parity prevents communications wars. Neither argument is valid. There are no grounds for believing that competitors know better. Company reputations, resources, opportunities, and objectives differ so much that communications budgets are hardly a guide. And there is no evidence that budgets based on competitive parity discourage communications wars.

OBJECTIVE-AND-TASK METHOD The objective-and-task method calls upon marketers to develop communications budgets by defining specific objectives, determining the tasks that must be performed to achieve these objectives, and estimating the costs of performing them. The sum of these costs is the proposed communications budget.

Suppose Dr. Pepper Snapple Group wants to introduce a new natural energy drink, called Sunburst, for the casual athlete.[34] Its objectives might be as follows:

1. *Establish the market share goal.* The company estimates 50 million potential users and sets a target of attracting 8 percent of the market—that is, 4 million users.

2. *Determine the percentage of the market that should be reached by advertising.* The advertiser hopes to reach 80 percent (40 million prospects) with its advertising message.

3. *Determine the percentage of aware prospects that should be persuaded to try the brand.* The advertiser would be pleased if 25 percent of aware prospects (10 million) tried Sunburst. It estimates that 40 percent of all triers, or 4 million people, will become loyal users. This is the market goal.

4. *Determine the number of advertising impressions per 1 percent trial rate.* The advertiser estimates that 40 advertising impressions (exposures) for every 1 percent of the population will bring about a 25 percent trial rate.

5. *Determine the number of gross rating points that would have to be purchased.* A gross rating point is one exposure to 1 percent of the target population. Because the company wants to achieve 40 exposures to 80 percent of the population, it will want to buy 3200 gross rating points.

6. *Determine the necessary advertising budget on the basis of the average cost of buying a gross rating point.* To expose 1 percent of the target population to one impression costs an average of $3277. Therefore, 3200 gross rating points will cost $10 486 400 (= $3277 × 3200) in the introductory year.

The objective-and-task method has the advantage of requiring management to spell out its assumptions about the relationship among dollars spent, exposure levels, trial rates, and regular usage.

COMMUNICATIONS BUDGET TRADE-OFFS A major question is how much weight marketing communications should receive in relationship to alternatives such as product improvement, lower prices, or better service. The answer depends on where the company's products are in their life cycle, whether they are commodities or highly differentiable products, whether they are routinely needed or must be "sold," and other considerations. Marketing communications budgets tend to be higher when there is low channel support, much change in the marketing program over time, many hard-to-reach customers, more complex customer decision making, differentiated products and heterogeneous customer needs, and frequent product purchases in small quantities.[35]

In theory, marketers should establish the total communications budget so that the marginal profit from the last communication dollar just equals the marginal profit from the last dollar in the best noncommunication use. Implementing this principle, however, is not easy.

Deciding on the Marketing Communications Mix

Companies must allocate the marketing communications budget over the eight major modes of communication—advertising, sales promotion, public relations and publicity, events and experiences, direct marketing, interactive marketing, word-of-mouth marketing, and the sales force. Within the same industry, companies can differ considerably in their media and channel choices. Avon concentrates its promotional funds on personal selling, whereas Revlon spends heavily on advertising. Electrolux spent heavily on a door-to-door sales force for years, whereas Hoover has relied more on advertising.

Table 17.2 breaks down spending forecasts on some major forms of communication.

Companies are always searching for ways to gain efficiency by substituting one communications tool for others. Many are replacing some field sales activity with ads, direct mail, and telemarketing. One auto dealer dismissed his five salespeople and cut prices, and sales exploded. The substitutability among communications tools explains why marketing functions need to be coordinated.

CHARACTERISTICS OF THE MARKETING COMMUNICATIONS MIX Each communications tool has its own unique characteristics and costs. We briefly review them here and discuss them in more detail in Chapters 18 and 19.

Advertising Advertising reaches geographically dispersed buyers. It can build up a long-term image for a product (Coca-Cola ads) or trigger quick sales (a London Drugs ad for a weekend sale). Certain forms of advertising such as TV can require a large budget, whereas other forms such as newspaper do not. The mere presence of advertising might have an effect on sales: consumers might believe a heavily advertised brand must offer "good value."[36] Because of the many forms and uses of advertising, it's difficult to make generalizations about it.[37] Yet a few observations are worthwhile:

1. *Pervasiveness*—Advertising permits the seller to repeat a message many times. It also allows the buyer to receive and compare the messages of various competitors. Large-scale advertising says something positive about the seller's size, power, and success.

2. *Amplified expressiveness*—Advertising provides opportunities for dramatizing the company and its brands and products through the artful use of print, sound, and colour.

3. *Control*—The advertiser can choose the aspects of the brand and product on which to focus communications.

TABLE 17.2 | ADVERTISING AND DIGITAL MARKETING COMMUNICATIONS FORECAST FOR 2013

Worldwide Advertising Spend Projections	2009–2013 % Change	2013 (US$ billion)	Share of Ad Spending
Cinema	+29.0%	2.72	0.5%
Internet	+76.3%	96.39	18.9%
Magazines	−1.7%	42.91	8.4%
Newspapers	−5.8%	91.33	17.9%
Outdoor	+26.5%	35.12	6.9%
Radio	+10.5%	35.12	6.9%
Television	+29.2%	207.06	40.5%
Total	+22.4%	510.65	100%

Source: Data from "Advertising Expenditures by Medium," *ZenithOptimedia*, October 3, 2011.

U.S. Digital Marketing Communications Spend Projections			
Display Advertising	+105.5%	16.09	32.4%
Email Marketing	+50.2%	1.88	3.8%
Mobile Marketing	+983.9%	4.24	8.5%
Search Marketing	+59.9%	24.61	49.7%
Social Media	+285.5%	2.76	5.6%
Total	+93.8%	49.57	100%

Source: Data from Figure 1 in "US Interactive Marketing Forecast 2011 to 2016," Forrester Research, Inc., September 7, 2011, and Figure 4 in "US Interactive Marketing Forecast 2009 to 2014," Forrester Reseach, Inc., July 30, 2009.

Sales Promotion Companies use sales promotion tools—coupons, contests, premiums, and the like—to draw a stronger and quicker buyer response, including short-run effects such as highlighting product offers and boosting sagging sales. Sales promotion tools offer three distinctive benefits:

1. *Ability to be attention-getting*—They draw attention and may lead the consumer to the product.
2. *Incentive*—They incorporate some concession, inducement, or contribution that gives value to the consumer.
3. *Invitation*—They include a distinct invitation to engage in the transaction now.

Public Relations and Publicity Marketers tend to underuse public relations, yet a well-thought-out program coordinated with the other communications-mix elements can be extremely effective, especially if a company needs to challenge consumers' misconceptions. The appeal of public relations and publicity is based on three distinctive qualities:

1. *High credibility*—News stories and features are more authentic and credible to readers than ads.
2. *Ability to reach hard-to-find buyers*—Public relations can reach prospects who prefer to avoid mass media and targeted promotions.
3. *Dramatization*—Public relations can tell the story behind a company, brand, or product.

Events and Experiences There are many advantages to events and experiences as long as they have the following characteristics:

1. *Relevant*—A well-chosen event or experience can be seen as highly relevant because the consumer is often personally invested in the outcome.

2. *Engaging*—Given their live, real-time quality, events and experiences are more actively engaging for consumers.

3. *Implicit*—Events are typically an indirect soft sell.

Direct and Interactive Marketing Direct and interactive marketing messages take many forms—over the phone, online, or in person. They share three characteristics:

1. *Customized*—The message can be prepared to appeal to the addressed individual.

2. *Up-to-date*—A message can be prepared very quickly.

3. *Interactive*—The message can be changed depending on the person's response.

Word-of-Mouth Marketing Word of mouth also takes many forms both online or offline. The following are three noteworthy characteristics:

1. *Influential*—Because people trust others they know and respect, word of mouth can be highly influential.

2. *Personal*—Word of mouth can be a very intimate dialogue that reflects personal facts, opinions, and experiences.

3. *Timely*—Word of mouth occurs when people want it to and are most interested, and it often follows noteworthy or meaningful events or experiences.

Personal Selling Personal selling is the most effective tool at later stages of the buying process, particularly in building up buyer preference, conviction, and action. Personal selling has three notable qualities:

1. *Personal interaction*—Personal selling creates an immediate and interactive episode between two or more people. Each is able to observe the other's reactions.

2. *Cultivation*—Personal selling also permits all kinds of relationships to spring up, ranging from a matter-of-fact selling relationship to a deep personal friendship.

3. *Response*—The buyer is often given personal choices and encouraged to directly respond.

Here's how one company chose rather unconventional methods to spread its name and generate sales.

Killam Properties

Killam Properties, a property management company owning around 19 000 units in eastern Canada, set out to reduce its vacancy rates with some viral marketing. The campaign introduced Heroic Gatherings, where tenants could order food online from fictional character Landlord Lou and have it delivered to their apartment free. Landlord Lou personally delivered the food, from Boston Pizza and Swiss Chalet, and also gave tenants the option of a themed party. Colour, a marketing agency in Halifax, created three video clips introducing Landlord Lou, depicting him "coming to the rescue" of young student tenants. Another part of the campaign included hiding thousands of toilet plungers around the city and challenging tenants to find them to earn free rent. Finding 50 plungers would earn a tenant a free month's rent and 500 plungers a free year's rent. All these aspects were aimed at getting people to talk about Killam Properties and think about moving to a Killam-managed apartment. The campaign was a huge success and the costs were considerably lower than regular advertising. As a result of the campaign, Killam achieved a zero vacancy rate in almost all of its buildings.[38]

FACTORS IN SETTING THE MARKETING COMMUNICATIONS MIX Companies must consider several factors in developing their communications mix: type of product market, consumer readiness to make a purchase, and stage in the product life cycle.

Type of Product Market Communications-mix allocations vary between consumer and business markets. Consumer marketers tend to spend comparatively more on sales promotion and advertising; business marketers tend to spend comparatively more on personal selling. In general, personal selling is used more with complex, expensive, and risky goods and in markets with fewer and larger sellers (hence, business markets).

Although marketers rely more on sales calls in business markets, advertising still plays a significant role:

■ Advertising can provide an introduction to the company and its products.

■ If the product has new features, advertising can explain them.

■ Reminder advertising is more economical than sales calls.

■ Advertisements offering brochures and carrying the company's phone number or web address are an effective way to generate leads for sales representatives.

■ Sales representatives can use copies of the company's ads to legitimize their company and products.

■ Advertising can remind customers how to use the product and reassure them about their purchase.

Advertising combined with personal selling can increase sales over personal selling alone. Corporate advertising can improve a company's reputation and improve the sales force's chances of getting a favourable first hearing and early adoption of the product.[39] IBM's corporate marketing effort is a notable success in recent years.[40]

IBM Smarter Planet

Working with long-time ad agency Ogilvy & Mather, IBM launched "Smarter Planet" in 2008 as a business strategy and multiplatform communications program to promote the way in which IBM technology and expertise helps industry, government, transportation, energy, education, health care, cities, and other businesses work better and "smarter." The point was that technology has evolved so far that many of the world's problems are now fixable. Emphasizing the United States, the United Kingdom, Germany, China, and Canada, the campaign began internally to inform and inspire IBM employees about how they could contribute to building a "Smarter Planet." An unconventional "Mandate for Change" series offered long-form, content-rich print ads in the business world's top newspapers outlining how IBM would address 25 key issues to make the world work better. Targeted TV ads and detailed interactive online ads provided more support and substance. A "Smarter Cities" tour hosted major events at which IBM and other experts discussed and debated challenges all cities face: transportation, energy, health care, education, and public safety. The success of the overall "Smarter Planet" campaign was evident in the significant improvements in IBM's image as a company "making the world better" and "known for solving its clients' most challenging problems." Despite a global recession, significant increases occurred in new business opportunities and the number of companies interested in doing business with IBM.

On the flip side, personal selling can also make a strong contribution in consumer-goods marketing. Some consumer marketers use the sales force mainly to collect weekly orders from dealers and to see that sufficient stock is on the shelf. Yet an effectively trained company sales force can make four important contributions:

1. *Increase stock position.* Sales reps can persuade dealers to take more stock and devote more shelf space to the company's brand.

2. *Build enthusiasm.* Sales reps can build dealer enthusiasm by dramatizing planned advertising and communications support for the company's brand.

3. *Conduct missionary selling.* Sales reps can sign up more dealers.

4. *Manage key accounts.* Sales reps can take responsibility for growing business with the most important accounts.

FIGURE 17.4

Cost-Effectiveness of Three Different Communication Tools at Different Buyer-Readiness Stages

BUYER-READINESS STAGE Communication tools vary in cost-effectiveness at different stages of buyer readiness.

Figure 17.4 shows the relative cost-effectiveness of three communication tools. Advertising and publicity play the most important roles in the awareness-building stage. Customer comprehension is primarily affected by advertising and personal selling. Customer conviction is influenced mostly by personal selling. Closing the sale is influenced mostly by personal selling and sales promotion. Reordering is also affected mostly by personal selling and sales promotion, and somewhat by reminder advertising.

PRODUCT LIFE-CYCLE STAGE In the introduction stage of the product life cycle, advertising, events and experiences, and publicity have the highest cost-effectiveness, followed by personal selling to gain distribution coverage and sales promotion and direct marketing to induce trial. In the growth stage, demand has its own momentum through word of mouth and interactive marketing. Advertising, events and experiences, and personal selling all become more important in the maturity stage. In the decline stage, sales promotion continues strong, other communication tools are reduced, and salespeople give the product only minimal attention.

Measuring Communications Results

Senior managers want to know the *outcomes* and *revenues* resulting from their communications investments. Too often, however, their communications directors supply only *inputs* and *expenses:* press clipping counts, numbers of ads placed, media costs. In fairness, communications directors try to translate inputs into intermediate outputs such as reach and frequency (the percentage of target market exposed to a communication and the number of exposures), recall and recognition scores, persuasion changes, and cost-per-thousand calculations. Ultimately, behaviour-change measures capture the real payoff.

After implementing the communications plan, the communications director must measure its impact. Members of the target audience are asked whether they recognize or recall the message, how many times they saw it, what points they recall, how they felt about the message, and what their previous and current attitudes are toward the product and the company. The communicator should also collect behavioural measures of audience response, such as how many people bought the product, liked it, and talked to others about it.

Figure 17.5 provides an example of good feedback measurement. We find that 80 percent of the consumers in the total market are aware of brand A, 60 percent have tried it, and only 20 percent who tried it are satisfied. This indicates that the communications program is effective in creating awareness, but the product fails to meet consumer expectations. In contrast, 40 percent of the consumers in the total market are aware of brand B and only 30 percent have tried it, but 80 percent of them are satisfied. In this case, the communications program needs to be strengthened to take advantage of the brand's potential power.

Brand A

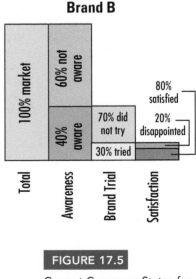

Brand B

FIGURE 17.5

Current Consumer States for Two Brands

MANAGING THE INTEGRATED MARKETING COMMUNICATIONS PROCESS

Many companies still rely on only one or two communication tools. This practice persists in spite of the fragmenting of mass markets into a multitude of minimarkets, each requiring its own approach; the proliferation of new types of media; and the growing sophistication of consumers. The wide range of communication tools, messages, and audiences makes it imperative that companies move toward integrated marketing communications. Companies must adopt a "360-degree view" of consumers to fully understand all the different ways that communications can affect the behaviour of consumers in their daily lives.[41]

The American Marketing Association defines **integrated marketing communications (IMC)** as "a planning process designed to assure that all brand contacts received by a customer or prospect for a product, service, or organization are relevant to that person and consistent over time."[42] This planning process evaluates the strategic roles of a variety of communications disciplines—for example, general advertising, direct response, sales promotion, and public relations—and skillfully combines these disciplines to provide clarity, consistency, and maximum impact through the seamless integration of messages.

Media companies and ad agencies are expanding their capabilities to offer multiplatform deals for marketers. These expanded capabilities make it easier for marketers to assemble various media properties—as well as related marketing services—in an integrated communication program.

Table 17.3 displays the different lines of businesses for marketing and advertising services giant WPP.

Coordinating Media

Media coordination can occur across and within media types, but marketers should combine personal and nonpersonal communications channels through *multiple-vehicle, multiple-stage campaigns* to achieve maximum impact and increase message reach and impact.

Promotions can be more effective when combined with advertising, for example.[43] The awareness and attitudes created by advertising campaigns can increase the success of more direct sales pitches. Advertising can convey the positioning of a brand and benefit from online display advertising or search engine marketing that offers a stronger call to action.[44]

Many companies are coordinating their online and offline communications activities. Web addresses in ads (especially print ads) and on packages allow people to more fully explore a company's products, find store locations, and get more product or service information. Even if consumers don't order online, marketers can use websites in ways that drive consumers into stores to buy. Research has shown that nearly 60 percent of consumers use websites as research tools before making a purchase decision and this percentage is increasing year after year. Retailers such as Future Shop are well-aware of this trend. In response, Future Shop has implemented an interactive "Ask an Expert" system where consumers can conduct research by getting questions answered by a virtual salesperson.[45]

Implementing IMC

In recent years, large ad agencies have substantially improved their integrated offerings. To facilitate one-stop shopping, these agencies have acquired promotion agencies, public relations firms, package-design consultancies, website developers, and direct-mail houses. They are redefining themselves as *communications companies* that assist clients to improve their overall communications effectiveness by offering strategic and practical advice on many forms of communication.[46] Many international clients, such as IBM (Ogilvy), Colgate (Young & Rubicam), and GE (BBDO), have opted to put a substantial portion of their communications work through one full-service agency. The result is integrated and more effective marketing communications at a much lower total communications cost.

Integrated marketing communications can produce stronger message consistency and help build brand equity and create greater sales impact.[47] IMC forces management to think about every way the customer comes in contact with the company, how the company communicates its positioning, the relative importance of each vehicle, and how timing comes into play. It gives someone the responsibility—where none existed before—to unify the company's brand images and messages as they come through thousands of company activities. IMC should improve the company's ability to reach the right customers with the right messages at the right time and in the right place.[48] "Marketing Memo: How Integrated Is Your IMC Program?" provides some guidelines.

TABLE 17.3 | WPP'S LINES OF BUSINESSES

Advertising
Global, national, and specialist advertising services from a range of top international and specialist agencies, amongst them Grey, JWT, Ogilvy & Mather, United Network, and Y&R

Media Investment Management
Above- and below-the-line media planning and buying and specialist sponsorship and branded entertainment services from GroupM companies Maxus, MEC, MediaCom, Mindshare, tenthavenue, and others

Consumer Insight
WPP's Kantar companies, including TNS, Millward Brown, The Futures Company, and many other specialists in brand, consumer, media, and marketplace insight, work with clients to generate and apply great insights

Public Relations & Public Affairs
Corporate, consumer, financial, and brand-building services from PR and lobbying firms Burson-Marsteller, Cohn & Wolfe, Hill & Knowlton, Ogilvy Public Relations Worldwide, RLM Finsbury, and others

Branding & Identity
Consumer, corporate, and employee branding and design services, covering identity, packaging, literature, events, training, and architecture from Addison, The Brand Union, FITCH, Lambie-Nairn, Landor Associates, The Partners, and others

Direct, Promotion & Relationship Marketing
The full range of general and specialist customer, channel, direct, field, retail, promotional, and point-of-sale services from G2, OgilvyOne, OgilvyAction, RTC Relationship Marketing, VML, Wunderman, and others

Health-Care Communications
CommonHealth, GCI Health, ghg, Ogilvy Healthworld, Sudler & Hennessey, and others provide integrated health-care marketing solutions from advertising to medical education and online marketing

Specialist Communications
A comprehensive range of specialist services, from custom media and multicultural marketing to event, sports, youth, and entertainment marketing; corporate and business-to-business; media, technology, and production services

WPP Digital
Through WPP Digital, WPP companies and their clients have access to a portfolio of digital experts including 24/7 Real Media, Blue State Digital, and Possible Worldwide

---

Source: Adapted from WPP, "What We Do," www.wpp.com/wpp/about/whatwedo/ (as at October 2011). Used with permission.

| MARKETING **MEMO** | HOW INTEGRATED IS YOUR IMC PROGRAM? |

In assessing the collective impact of an IMC program, the marketer's overriding goal is to create the most effective and efficient communications program possible. The following six criteria can help determine whether communications are truly integrated:

■ **Coverage.** Coverage is the proportion of the audience reached by each communication option employed, as well as how much overlap exists among communication options. In other words, to what extent do different communication options reach the designated target market and the same or different consumers making up that market?

■ **Contribution.** Contribution is the inherent ability of a marketing communication to create the desired response and communication effects from consumers in the absence of exposure to any other communication option. How much does a communication affect consumer processing and build awareness, enhance image, elicit responses, and induce sales?

■ **Commonality.** Commonality is the extent to which *common* associations are reinforced across communication options; that is, the extent to which the pieces of information conveyed by different communication options share meaning. The consistency and cohesiveness of the brand image is important because it determines how easily existing associations and responses can be recalled and how easily additional associations and responses can become linked to the brand in memory.

■ **Complementarity.** Communication options are often more effective when used in tandem. Complementarity relates to the extent to which *different* associations and linkages are emphasized across communication options. Different brand associations may be most effectively established by capitalizing on those marketing communication options best suited to eliciting a particular consumer response or establishing a particular type of brand association. Many of the TV ads during the Super Bowl—America's biggest media event—are designed to create curiosity and interest so that consumers go online and engage in social media and word of mouth to experience and find more detailed information.[49] A 2010 Super Bowl spot for Snickers candy bar featuring legendary TV comedienne Betty White resulted in over 3.5 million visits to the brand's website after the ad was run.

■ **Versatility.** In any integrated communication program, when consumers are exposed to a particular marketing communication, some will have already been exposed to other marketing communications for the brand, and some will not have had any prior exposure. Versatility refers to the extent to which a marketing communication option is robust and "works" for different groups of consumers. The ability of a marketing communication to work at two levels—effectively communicating to consumers who have and to those who have *not* seen other communications— is critically important.

■ **Cost.** Marketers must weigh evaluations of marketing communications on all these criteria against their cost to arrive at the most effective *and* efficient communications program.

Source: *KELLER, KEVIN, STRATEGIC BRAND MANAGEMENT, 3rd ed., © 2008.* Reprinted and Electronically reproduced by permission of Pearson Education, Inc., Upper Saddle River, New Jersey.

SUMMARY

1. Modern marketing calls for more than developing a good product, pricing it attractively, and making it accessible to target customers. Companies must also communicate with present and potential stakeholders and with the general public.

2. The marketing communications mix consists of eight major modes of communication: advertising, sales promotion, public relations and publicity, events and experiences, direct marketing, interactive marketing, word-of-mouth marketing, and personal selling.

3. The communications process consists of nine elements: sender, receiver, message, media, encoding, decoding, response, feedback, and noise. To get their messages through, marketers must encode their messages in a way that takes into account how the target audience usually decodes messages. They must also transmit the message through efficient media that reach the target audience and develop feedback channels to monitor response to the message.

4. Developing effective communications requires eight steps: (1) identify the target audience, (2) determine the communications objectives, (3) design the communications, (4) select the communications channels, (5) establish the total communications budget, (6) decide on the communications mix, (7) measure the communications results, and (8) manage the integrated marketing communications process.

5. In identifying the target audience, the marketer needs to close any gap that exists between current public perception and the image sought. Communications objectives can be to create category need, brand awareness, brand attitude, or brand purchase intention.

6. Designing the communication requires solving three problems: what to say (message strategy), how to say it (creative strategy), and who should say it (message source). Communications channels can be personal (advocate, expert, and social channels) or nonpersonal (mass media, social promotions, events and experiences, and public relations).

7. Although other methods exist, the objective-and-task method of setting the communications budget, which calls upon marketers to develop their budgets by defining specific objectives, is typically most desirable.

8. In choosing the marketing communications mix, marketers must examine the distinct advantages and costs of each communication tool and the company's market rank. They must also consider the type of product market in which they are selling, how ready consumers are to make a purchase, and the product's stage in the company, brand, and product life cycle.

9. Measuring the effectiveness of the marketing communications mix requires asking members of the target audience whether they recognize or recall the communication, how many times they saw it, what points they recall, how they felt about the communication, and what are their previous and current attitudes toward the company, brand, and product.

10. Managing and coordinating the entire communications process calls for integrated marketing communications (IMC): marketing communications planning that recognizes the added value of a comprehensive plan to evaluate the strategic roles of a variety of communications disciplines, and that combines these disciplines to provide clarity, consistency, and maximum impact through the seamless integration of discrete messages.

APPLICATIONS

Marketing Debate: Has TV Advertising Lost Its Power?

Long deemed the most successful marketing medium, television advertising is increasingly criticized for being too expensive and, even worse, no longer as effective as it once was. Critics maintain that consumers tune out too many ads by zipping and zapping and that it is difficult to make a strong impression. The future, claim some, is with online advertising. Supporters of TV advertising disagree, contending that the multisensory impact of TV is unsurpassed and that no other media option offers the same potential impact.

Take a position: TV advertising has faded in importance *versus* TV advertising is still the most powerful advertising medium.

Marketing Discussion: Communications Audit

Pick a brand and go to its website. Locate as many forms of communication as you can find. Conduct an informal communications audit. What do you notice? How consistent are the different communications?

The BC Hydro and Power Authority, commonly referred to as BC Hydro, is British Columbia's primary electric utility company. It is the second-largest Canadian electric utility company in terms of customers served, with over 1.8 million customers covering 95 percent of British Columbia's population. BC Hydro operates both hydroelectric facilities and natural gas–fuelled thermal power plants. The company's mandate is to provide "reliable power, at low cost, for generations."

BC Hydro has been making changes to its practices to improve its service, but in order for them to be effective, the company requires the support of consumers. For instance, BC Hydro recently proposed a rate increase of 9.73 percent for each of the following three years, amounting to a total increase of 32 percent. Such a large increase was sure to face opposition from consumers, especially if they did not see themselves receiving anything more in terms of service from the provider. In order for customers to accept this rate increase, they had to be made aware of the positive changes BC Hydro is making in the province and subsequently believe they should support the company in its efforts. This is where advertising and public relations come in.

BC Hydro's innovative marketing campaigns have been widely recognized by the media and other utility companies across Canada. BC Hydro was recognized as the 2009 Marketer of the Year—a rare accolade for a utility company, which consumers simply take for granted most of the time.

To promote Power Smart Month, two actors were made to "live" in shipping containers for a week in downtown Vancouver, at the busy corner of Georgia and Granville. The container spaces were furnished to resemble condos, each with a living room and kitchen area that included a refrigerator, TV, and computer. Although the living spaces were identical, the actors' lifestyle behaviours were not—one was wasteful in his power use while the other was energy-efficient. Digital counters on the outside of the containers kept track of the actors' power use and revealed the difference in energy consumption. This public display attracted a great deal of attention and got residents of British Columbia talking about power efficiency. To the publicity stunt, BC Hydro tactfully tied the message that the Power Smart program saves customers millions of dollars each year. The campaign detailed many ways that customers could keep their bills down, communicating to them that the proposed rate increase may not affect their monthly bills if they are power-smart in their lifestyle.

Marketing campaigns such as these by BC Hydro have been proving effective, as evidenced by the BC Utilities Commission approving an interim rate increase of 8 percent effective May 2011.

QUESTIONS

1. Electricity is a service that customers rarely think about until there's a power outage. Because electricity is an essential service, residents often think hydro companies have a duty to serve residents of the province. How can utility companies such as BC Hydro communicate the value of their service to customers?

2. How can BC Hydro utilize digital media to gain support for its proposed rate increase?

3. Discuss the pros and cons of the downtown publicity stunt that BC Hydro carried out. Think of some other creative techniques that are likely to get positive publicity.

Sources: Melinda Mattos, "BC Hydro Regenerates," *Strategy*, April 1, 2011, p. 27; Susan Nelson, "BC Hydro Awaits Decision on Reduced Interim Rate Hike Request," *SNL Energy Power Week Canada*, April 25, 2011; Bill Andrews, "Rate Increases Should Not Be a surprise to the Province," *Vancouver Sun*, April 19, 2011, p. A11; "Residential Rate: What's Happening to Rates," BC Hydro, www.bchydro.com/youraccount/content/residential_rates.jsp#what_s_happening (viewed June 25, 2011).

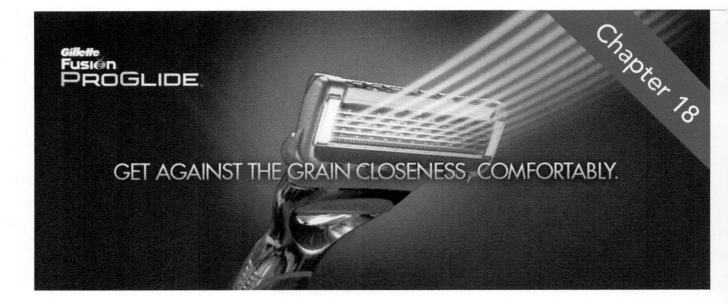

GET AGAINST THE GRAIN CLOSENESS, COMFORTABLY.

Chapter 18

Gillette used a variety of communication channels to generate awareness and interest for its new product.

In This Chapter, We Will Address the Following **Questions**

1. What steps are required in developing an advertising program?

2. How should sales promotion decisions be made?

3. What are the guidelines for effective brand-building events and experiences?

4. How can companies exploit the potential of public relations and publicity?

Managing Mass Communications: Advertising, Sales Promotions, Events and Experiences, and Public Relations

Due to the rapid penetration of the Internet and other factors, there has been an enormous increase in the use of personal communications by marketers in recent years. But the fact remains that mass media, if used correctly, is still an important component of a modern marketing communications program. The old days of "if you build a great ad, they will come," however, are long gone. To generate consumer interest and sales, mass media must often be supplemented and carefully integrated with other communications, as was the case with Gillette.

Consumer product giant Procter & Gamble (P&G) has a large share of the men's personal-care market, with powerful brands such as Gillette, Old Spice, and Braun spanning a portfolio of over 200 products that include razors, shaving cream, hair-care items, body wash, and deodorant. Even though P&G has a significant share of the pie, constant innovation and competitive pressures lead it to continuously find new ways to attract consumers.

With new products such as Unilever's Axe portfolio and Dove's Men+Care line hitting the shelves, competition in the men's personal-care market has intensified. P&G relies on consumer research to help design its communications program so that it keeps consumers interested in its brands. Research showed that Canadian men were some of the hairiest in the world and were more likely to experience skin sensitivity than Americans, due to harsh Canadian winters. Acknowledging the unique needs of Canadian men, P&G designed a communications strategy for the new Gillette Fusion ProGlide razor using TV commercials, social media, online giveaways, and promotional events.

Word of mouth was a key strategic factor through new brand ambassadors who were "real guys" that Canadian men could relate to. Before the Fusion ProGlide launched in June 2010, over 100 000 samples were distributed in person and through online giveaways. Two months prior to launch, P&G took to the streets of Toronto, staging an event that delivered the ProGlide Challenge. The event took the experiential and amplified it digitally: video was streamed live to Gillette's Facebook page so that users could see other men trying the product and post their own reviews.

Using a third medium, Gillette shot its first local television ad in 15 years. In an effort to make the commercial more "relatable," P&G decided to cast a local Canadian man. In the past, the company had seen less-than-impressive results from using pro athletes like American baseball player Derek Jeter and tennis star Roger Federer, whom Canadian men couldn't relate to. The core idea behind the advertising was to show real guys trying the product, loving it, and being converted to believers.

Looking to take their credible and relevant approach one step further, Gillette landed a branded content deal with Canadian sports station The Score to develop Gillette Drafted—a contest that created broadcast segments inspired by reality TV shows. Participants auditioned to become "Canada's next sports-caster" using Gillette products to get ready for their close-up. The winner was granted a job at The Score and a one-year spokesperson contract with Gillette. By the time the product was finally ready to be launched, the company had managed to make over 40 million impressions on Canadian consumers. Such smartly crafted communications strategies have allowed the company to break through the clutter and remain salient in an increasingly competitive industry.[1]

Although Gillette has found great success with its ad campaign, other marketers are trying to come to grips with how to best use mass media in the new—and still changing—communications environment.[2] In this chapter, we examine the nature and use of four mass-communication tools—advertising, sales promotion, events and experiences, and public relations and publicity.

DEVELOPING AND MANAGING AN ADVERTISING PROGRAM

Advertising can be a cost-effective way to disseminate messages, whether to build a brand preference or to educate people. Even in today's challenging media environment, good ads can pay off. P&G has also enjoyed double-digit sales gains in recent years from ads touting the efficacy of Olay Definity anti-aging skin products and Head & Shoulders Intensive Treatment shampoo.[3]

In developing an advertising program, marketing managers must always start by identifying the target market and buyer motives. Then they can make the five major decisions, known as "the five Ms": *Mission:* What are our advertising objectives? *Money:* How much can we spend and how do we allocate our spending across media types? *Message:* What message should we send? *Media:* What media should we use? *Measurement:* How should we evaluate the results? These decisions are summarized in Figure 18.1 and described in the following sections.

Setting the Objectives

The advertising objectives must flow from prior decisions on target market, brand positioning, and the marketing program.

An **advertising objective** (or goal) is a specific communications task and achievement level to be accomplished with a specific audience in a specific period of time:[4]

> To increase among 30 million homemakers who own automatic washers the number who identify brand X as a low-sudsing detergent, and who are persuaded that it gets clothes cleaner, from 10 percent to 40 percent in one year.

We can classify advertising objectives according to whether their aim is to inform, persuade, remind, or reinforce. These objectives correspond to different stages in the *hierarchy-of-effects* model discussed in Chapter 17:

FIGURE 18.1

The Five Ms of Advertising

- *Informative advertising* aims to create brand awareness and knowledge of new products or new features of existing products.[5] To promote its OnStar in-vehicle safety, security, and information service that uses wireless and GPS satellite technology, GM launched the "Real Stories" campaign in 2002. The award-winning TV, radio, and print ad campaign used actual subscriber stories in their own words and voices to share the importance and benefits of OnStar through life-changing experiences. By 2005, the OnStar brand had reached 100 percent awareness among consumers shopping for a new vehicle.[6]

- *Persuasive advertising* aims to create liking, preference, conviction, and purchase of a product or service. Some persuasive advertising uses comparative advertising, which makes an explicit comparison of the attributes of two or more brands. Miller Lite took market share from Bud Light by pointing out that Bud Light had more carbs. Comparative advertising works best when it elicits cognitive and affective motivations simultaneously, and when consumers are processing advertising in a detailed, analytical mode.[7]

- *Reminder advertising* aims to stimulate repeat purchase of products and services. Expensive, four-colour Coca-Cola ads in magazines are intended to remind people to purchase Coca-Cola.

- *Reinforcement advertising* aims to convince current purchasers that they made the right choice. Automobile ads often depict satisfied customers enjoying special features of their new car.

The advertising objective should emerge from a thorough analysis of the current marketing situation. If the product class is mature, the company is the market leader, and brand usage is low, the objective is to stimulate more usage. If the product class is new, the company is not the market leader, but the brand is superior to the leader's, then the objective is to convince the market of the brand's superiority.

Deciding on the Advertising Budget

How does a company know it's spending the right amount? Although advertising is treated as a current expense, part of it is really an investment in building brand equity and customer loyalty. When a company spends $5 million on capital equipment, it may treat the equipment as a five-year depreciable asset and write off only one-fifth of the cost in the first year. When it spends $5 million on advertising to launch a new product, it must write off the entire cost in the first year, reducing its reported profit, even if the effects will persist for many years to come.

FACTORS AFFECTING BUDGET DECISIONS   Here are five specific factors to consider when setting the advertising budget:[8]

1. *Stage in the product life cycle*—New products typically merit large advertising budgets to build awareness and to gain consumer trial. Established brands usually are supported with lower advertising budgets, measured as a ratio to sales.

2. *Market share and consumer base*—High–market share brands usually require less advertising expenditure as a percentage of sales to maintain share. To build share by increasing market size requires larger expenditures.

3. *Competition and clutter*—In a market with a large number of competitors and high advertising spending, a brand must advertise more heavily to be heard. Even simple clutter from advertisements not directly competitive to the brand creates a need for heavier advertising.

4. *Advertising frequency*—The number of repetitions needed to put the brand's message across to consumers has an obvious impact on the advertising budget.

5. *Product substitutability*—Brands in less-differentiated or commodity-like product classes (beer, soft drinks, banks, and airlines) require heavy advertising to establish a unique image.

ADVERTISING ELASTICITY   The predominant response function for advertising is often concave but can be S-shaped. When consumer response is S-shaped, some positive amount of advertising is necessary to generate any sales impact, but sales increases eventually flatten out.[9]

One classic study found that increasing the TV advertising budget had a measurable effect on sales only half the time. The success rate was higher for new products or line extensions than for established brands, and when there were changes in copy or in media strategy (such as an expanded target market). When advertising increased sales, its impact lasted up to two years after peak spending. Moreover, the long-term incremental sales generated were approximately double the incremental sales observed in the first year of an advertising spending increase.[10]

Other studies reinforce these conclusions. In a 2004 IRI study of 23 brands, advertising often didn't increase sales for mature brands or categories in decline. A review of academic research found that advertising elasticities were estimated to be higher for new products (0.3) than for established (0.1).[11]

Developing the Advertising Campaign

In designing and evaluating an ad campaign, marketers employ both art and science to develop the *message strategy* or positioning of an ad—*what* the ad attempts to convey about the brand—and its *creative strategy*—*how* the ad expresses the brand claims. Advertisers go through three steps: message generation and evaluation, creative development and execution, and social-responsibility review.

MESSAGE GENERATION AND EVALUATION Many of today's automobile ads look similar—a car drives at high speed on a curved mountain road or across a desert. Advertisers are always seeking "the big idea" that connects with consumers rationally and emotionally, sharply distinguishes the brand from competitors, and is broad and flexible enough to translate to different media, markets, and time periods.[12] Fresh insights such as how McDonald's created awareness for its new McMini line are important for avoiding using the same appeals and position as others.

McDonald's Canada

In April 2010, McDonald's successfully launched the McMini line in Canada with its "Small Things Matter" campaign. The McMini is a miniature sandwich offered in two gourmet flavours, Thai and pesto, which caters to women looking for a snack option or smaller meal. The advertising campaign depicted men being affectionate to their female partners. Whether it was helping their partner out of the car or leaving a loving note in her purse, the message was that small things matter. McDonalds also partnered with three popular websites targeted at women: CanadianLiving.com, ElleCanada.com, and LaineyGossip.com. The websites became the launching pad for the "Small Things Matter" contest, which was tailored to fit each site. For example, LaineyGossip.com readers were encouraged to submit a photo of their favourite celebrity baby or "Hollywood McMini" while CanadianLiving.com readers were asked to submit entries on small things that matter to them. Rather than just offering new menu items at a lower price point, McDonald's created a differentiated product line and was able to communicate that message effectively through a rather different campaign.[13]

A good ad normally focuses on one or two core selling propositions. As part of refining the brand positioning, the advertiser should conduct market research to determine which appeal works best with its target audience and then prepare a *creative brief,* typically one or two pages. This is an elaboration of the *positioning statement* and includes considerations such as key message, target audience, communications objectives (to do, to know, to believe), key brand benefits, supports for the brand promise, and media.

How many alternative ad themes should the advertiser create before making a choice? The more ad themes explored, the higher the probability of finding an excellent one. Fortunately, an ad agency's creative department can inexpensively compose many alternative ads in a short time by drawing still and video images from computer files. Marketers can also cut the cost of creative dramatically by using consumers as their creative team, a strategy sometimes called "open source" or "crowdsourcing."[14] The following example lists some companies that have engaged in crowdsourcing.

Consumer-Generated Advertising

One of the first major marketers to feature consumer-generated ads was Converse, whose award-winning campaign, "Brand Democracy," used films created by consumers in a series of TV and web ads. Some of the most popular ads during recent Super Bowl broadcasts have been homemade contest winners for Frito-Lay's Doritos tortilla chips. H. J. Heinz ran a "Top This TV Challenge," inviting the public to create the next commercial for its Heinz Ketchup brand and win $57 000. More than 6000 submissions and more than 10 million online views resulted, and sales rose over 13 percent year over year. In addition to creating ads, consumers can help disseminate advertising. In a rather unusual event, Alphabet Photography had a Niagara-based Canadian choir group stage a "flash mob" rendition of a popular Christmas carol at the Seaway Mall in Welland, Ontario. The video instantly went viral and set a YouTube record with over 25 million online views in just seven weeks, generating incredible publicity both for Alphabet and for the choir group, Chorus Niagara.[15]

A Christmas carol sung at an Ontario shopping mall became an online viral marketing sensation.

Although entrusting consumers with a brand's marketing effort can be pure genius, it can also be a regrettable failure. When Kraft sought a hip name for a new flavour variety of its iconic Vegemite product in Australia, it labelled the first 3 million jars "Name Me" to enlist consumer support. From 48 000 entries, however, the marketer selected one that was thrown in as a joke—iSnack 2.0—and sales plummeted. The company had to pull iSnack jars from the shelves and start from scratch in a more conventional fashion, yielding the new name Cheesybite.[16]

CREATIVE DEVELOPMENT AND EXECUTION The ad's impact depends not only on what it says, but often more important, on *how* it says it. Execution can be decisive. Every advertising medium has advantages and disadvantages. Here, we briefly review television, print, and radio advertising media.

Television Ads Television is generally acknowledged as the most powerful advertising medium and reaches a broad spectrum of consumers at low cost per exposure. TV advertising has two particularly important strengths. First, it can vividly demonstrate product attributes and persuasively explain their corresponding consumer benefits. Second, it can dramatically portray user and usage imagery, brand personality, and other intangibles.

Because of the fleeting nature of the ad, however, and the distracting creative elements often found in it, product-related messages and the brand itself can be overlooked. Moreover, the high volume of non-programming material on television creates clutter that makes it easy for consumers to ignore or forget ads. Nevertheless, properly designed and executed TV ads can still be a powerful marketing tool and improve brand equity and affect sales and profits. Standing out above the TV advertising clutter requires creativity, as shown in the Tim Hortons example.

Tim Hortons

Tim Hortons has learned to break through the advertising clutter through real-life stories that touch the heart of Canadians. Its long-standing "True Stories" campaign has created an emotional connection between coffee drinkers and the brand since 1998. The fact that a cup of Tims gives Canadians a sense of belonging with the country is a testament to the success of this campaign. Many of the stories used in the commercials were submitted by customers through the "Every Cup Tells A Story" website launched in 2008. During the 2010 Vancouver Olympics, Tim Hortons aired a "True Story" ad that depicted an African man welcoming his wife and kids home to Canada for the first time with winter jackets and a cup of Tims coffee. The tale was the culmination of many stories submitted by immigrants who found that their journey toward integrating with Canadian society invariably led them to Timmies (as the company is often fondly referred to). By developing ads that reflect the daily lives of their customers, Tim Hortons is able to communicate a strong brand image built on Canadiana.[17]

Print Ads Print media offer a stark contrast to broadcast media. Because readers consume them at their own pace, magazines and newspapers can provide detailed product information and effectively communicate user and usage imagery. At the same time, the static nature of the visual images in print media makes dynamic presentations or demonstrations difficult, and print media can be fairly passive.

The two main print media—magazines and newspapers—share many advantages and disadvantages. Although newspapers are timely and pervasive, magazines are typically more effective at building user and usage imagery. Newspapers are popular for local, especially retailer, advertising. On an average day, roughly one-half to three-quarters of adults read a newspaper, although increasingly that is an online version. Print newspaper circulation has been declining worldwide, with Canada experiencing an overall drop of 5.3 percent in 2010 and U.S. newspapers seeing much steeper declines.[18] Although advertisers have some flexibility in designing and placing newspaper ads, relatively poor reproduction quality and short shelf life can diminish the ads' impact.

Researchers studying print advertisements report that the *picture, headline,* and *copy* matter in that order. The picture must be strong enough to draw attention. The headline must reinforce the picture and lead the person to read the copy. The copy must be engaging and the brand's name sufficiently prominent. Even then, less than 50 percent of the exposed audience will notice even a really outstanding ad. About 30 percent might recall the headline's main point, about 25 percent register the advertiser's name, and fewer than 10 percent will read most of the body copy. Ordinary ads don't achieve even these results.

Given how consumers process print ads, some clear managerial implications emerge, as summarized in "Marketing Memo: Print Ad Evaluation Criteria." One print ad campaign with an important social message is that of WWF Canada.

World Wildlife Fund Canada

Besides preventing the degradation of the natural environment, WWF Canada focuses on protecting the rights of endangered species; this focus can be seen in the organization's print ads. To grab people's attention and make them think about endangered animals, WWF Canada undertook a remarkable print-advertising campaign. One print ad featured an African safari scene with animals represented by cardboard cutouts and a group of hunters pointing rifles at them, conveying the message that there will be no real animals around in the future. Another heart-wrenching print ad included a mother leopard and her cub crossing a grasslands field, with XL and S signs respectively displayed on their backs. WWF hopes that these ads will be a powerful means to jolt readers and bring about a global change in people's attitude toward wildlife. In 2010, WWF Canada had over 150 000 supporters and raised $21 million, with two-thirds of it going toward preservation of habitats and animals.[19]

| MARKETING **MEMO** | PRINT AD EVALUATION CRITERIA |

In judging the effectiveness of a print ad, marketers should consider the communications strategy (target market, communications objectives, and message and creative strategy) and be able to answer yes to the following questions about the ad's execution:

1. Is the message clear at a glance? Can you quickly tell what the advertisement is all about?
2. Is the benefit in the headline?
3. Does the illustration support the headline?
4. Does the first line of the copy support or explain the headline and illustration?
5. Is the ad easy to read and follow?
6. Is the product easily identified?
7. Is the brand or sponsor clearly identified?

Source: Adapted from Scott C. Purvis and Philip Ward Burton, *Which Ad Pulled Best*, 9th ed. (Lincolnwood, IL: NTC Business Books, 2002).

Radio Ads Radio is a pervasive medium: Canadians who listen to the radio listen, on average, about 16 hours a week, a number that has held steady in recent years.[20] Much radio listening occurs in the car and out of home. As streaming Internet access gains ground, traditional AM/FM radio stations are feeling the pressure and account for less than half of all listening at home.[21]

Perhaps radio's main advantage is flexibility—stations are very targeted, ads are relatively inexpensive to produce and place, and short closings allow for quick response. Radio is a particularly effective medium in the morning; it can also let companies achieve a balance between broad and localized market coverage.

The obvious disadvantages of radio are its lack of visual images and the relatively passive nature of the resulting consumer processing. Nevertheless, radio ads can be extremely creative. Some see the lack of visual images as a plus because they feel the clever use of music, sound, and other creative devices can tap into the listener's imagination to create powerfully relevant and liked images.

LEGAL AND SOCIAL ISSUES To break through clutter, some advertisers believe they have to be edgy and push the boundaries of what consumers are used to seeing in advertising. In doing so, marketers must be sure advertising does not overstep social and legal norms[22] or offend the general public, ethnic groups, racial minorities, or special-interest groups.

Two bodies oversee Canadian practices: the federal government's Canadian Radio-television and Telecommunications Commission (www.crtc.gc.ca), best known as the CRTC, and the not-for-profit Advertising Standards Canada (ASC; www.adstandards.ca). The mission of the CRTC is to find a balance between public- and private-sector interests. It governs ownership of broadcasting outlets, licences, and programming content, and it handles complaints about programming and advertising. It works closely with the ASC, which is a national industry association committed to assuring the integrity and viability of advertising through industry self-regulation.

The ASC administers the Canadian Code of Advertising Standards, which was first published in 1963. The code dictates that advertisements must not present inaccurate or deceptive claims, that advertisements must not omit relevant information, and that advertising claims must be supportable. The commercial intent of an advertisement must be obvious to the viewer, listener, or reader. Furthermore, advertisements must not include deceptive price claims or discounts, or unrealistic price comparisons. Advertising to children is subject to a special code, the Broadcast Code for Advertising to Children (it should also be noted that Quebec prohibits advertising to children). The ASC carefully considers and responds to all written consumer complaints submitted to it about advertising that does not comply with the code, and it produces an advertising complaints report.

In addition, groups such as the Media Awareness Network (www.media-awareness.ca) and Better Business Bureau (www.bbb.org/canada) aim to protect Canadians from deceptive or misleading advertising practices. Splenda was challenged on its misleading ads by rival Equal.

Splenda versus Equal

Splenda's tag line for its artificial sweetener was "Made from Sugar, So It Tastes Like Sugar," with "but it's not sugar" in small writing almost as an afterthought. McNeil Nutritionals, Splenda's manufacturer, does begin production of Splenda with pure cane sugar but burns it off in the manufacturing process. However, Merisant, maker of Equal, claimed that Splenda's advertising confused consumers, who were likely to conclude that a product "made from sugar" is healthier than one made from aspartame, Equal's main ingredient. A document used in court and taken from McNeil's own files noted that consumers' perception of Splenda as "not an artificial sweetener" was one of the biggest triumphs of the company's marketing campaign, which began in 2003. Splenda became the runaway leader in the sugar-substitute category with 60 percent of the market, leaving roughly 14 percent each to Equal (in the blue packets) and Sweet'N Low (pink packets). Although McNeil eventually agreed to settle the lawsuit and pay Merisant an undisclosed but "substantial" award (and change its advertising), it may have been too late for consumers to change their perception of Splenda as something sugary *and* sugar-free.[23]

To be socially responsible, advertisers must be careful not to offend the general public or any ethnic groups, racial minorities, or special-interest groups. Ford Canada had to pull a controversial ad that appeared in Manitoba and Saskatchewan. The full-page ad in a Winnipeg newspaper displayed a close-up shot of a truck bumper sticker that read "Drive it like you stole it." In a city already plagued by high auto-theft rates, such an ad was interpreted as condoning the behaviour and considered very inappropriate.[24]

Companies have to be aware that even their overseas advertising is monitored by industry watchdogs and the media. An ad that ran in Europe for Air Canada's first-class seats carried the headline "Sitting comfortabull" and claimed "business chiefs get more moccasin room." This ad was considered offensive to the Aboriginal Peoples in Canada and was withdrawn, with Air Canada issuing an apology.[25]

DECIDING ON MEDIA AND MEASURING EFFECTIVENESS

After choosing the message, the advertiser's next task is to choose media to carry it. The steps here are deciding on desired reach, frequency, and impact; choosing among major media types; selecting specific media vehicles; deciding on media timing; and deciding on geographical media allocation. Then the marketer evaluates the results of these decisions.

Deciding on Reach, Frequency, and Impact

Media selection is finding the most cost-effective media to deliver the desired number and type of exposures to the target audience. What do we mean by the desired number of exposures? The advertiser seeks a specified advertising objective and response from the target audience—for example, a target level of product trial. This level depends on, among other things, level of brand awareness. Suppose the rate of product trial increases, at first quickly and then more slowly, with the level of audience awareness, as shown in Figure 18.2(a). If the advertiser seeks a product trial rate of T^*, it will be necessary to achieve a brand awareness level of A^*.

The next task is to find out how many exposures, E^*, will produce a level of audience awareness of A^*. The effect of exposures on audience awareness depends on the exposures' reach, frequency, and impact:

- *Reach (R).* The number of different persons or households exposed to a particular media schedule at least once during a specified time period

- *Frequency (F).* The number of times within the specified time period that an average person or household is exposed to the message

- *Impact (I).* The qualitative value of an exposure through a given medium (thus a food ad will have a higher impact in *Bon Appetit* than in *Fortune* magazine)

Figure 18.2(b) shows the relationship between audience awareness and reach. Audience awareness will be greater, the higher the exposures' reach, frequency, and impact. There are important trade-offs here. Suppose the planner has an advertising budget of $1 000 000 and the cost per thousand exposures of average quality is $5. This means 200 000 000 exposures ($1 000 000 ÷ [$5/1000]). If the advertiser seeks an average exposure frequency of 10, it can reach 20 000 000 people (200 000 000 ÷ 10) with the given budget. But if the advertiser wants higher-quality media costing $10 per thousand exposures, it will be able to reach only 10 000 000 people unless it is willing to lower the desired exposure frequency.

FIGURE 18.2

Relationship among Trial, Awareness, and the Exposure Function

(a) Relationship between product trial rate and audience awareness level

(b) Relationship between audience awareness level and exposure reach and frequency

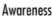

The relationship between reach, frequency, and impact is captured in the following concepts:

- *Total number of exposures (E)*. This is the reach times the average frequency; that is, $E = R \times F$, also called the *gross rating points* (GRP). If a given media schedule reaches 80 percent of homes with an average exposure frequency of 3, the media schedule has a GRP of 240 (80 × 3). If another media schedule has a GRP of 300, it has more weight, but we cannot tell how this weight breaks down into reach and frequency.

- *Weighted number of exposures (WE)*. This is the reach times average frequency times average impact, that is, $WE = R \times F \times I$.

Reach is most important with new products, flanker brands, extensions of well-known brands, or infrequently purchased brands; or when going after an undefined target market. Frequency is most important where there are strong competitors, a complex story to tell, high consumer resistance, or a frequent purchase cycle.[26]

A key reason for repetition is forgetting. The higher the forgetting rate associated with a brand, product category, or message, the higher the warranted level of repetition. However, advertisers should not coast on a tired ad but insist on fresh executions by their ad agency.[27] GEICO has found advertising success by keeping both its campaigns and their executions fresh.

GEICO

Have the hundreds of millions of dollars GEICO has spent on TV advertising been worth it? Warren Buffett, chairman and CEO of GEICO's parent company, Berkshire Hathaway, sure thinks so. He told shareholders he would spend *millions* on GEICO advertising! GEICO has more than quadrupled its revenue over the last decade, from slightly under $3 billion in 1998 to more than $13 billion in 2009—making it the fastest-growing auto insurance company in the United States. The company eschews agents to sell directly to consumers with a basic message, "15 Minutes Could Save You 15% or More on Your Car Insurance." Partnering with The Martin Agency, GEICO has run different award-winning TV campaigns to emphasize different benefits of the brand. Popular TV spots advertising GEICO's claim that its website is "So Easy, a Caveman Can Use It" featured offended Neanderthals expressing indignation at the prejudice they face. TV ads featuring the Cockney-speaking gecko spokescharacter reinforce GEICO's brand image as credible and accomplished. A third campaign, themed "Rhetorical Questions," uses cultural icons and touch points to make it seem obvious that GEICO saves customers money, by asking self-evident questions such as "Does Elmer Fudd have trouble with the letter R?" and "Did the Waltons take way too long to say goodnight?" The multiple campaigns complement each other and build on each other's success; the company dominates the TV airwaves with so many varied car insurance messages that any competitors' ads are lost.[28]

Choosing Among Major Media Types

The media planner must know the capacity of the major advertising media types to deliver reach, frequency, and impact. The major advertising media along with their costs, advantages, and limitations are profiled in Table 18.1. Media planners make their choices by considering factors such as target audience media habits, product characteristics, message requirements, and cost.

Alternative Advertising Options

In recent years, reduced effectiveness of traditional mass media has led advertisers to increase their emphasis on alternative advertising media.

PLACE ADVERTISING **Place advertising**, or **out-of-home advertising**, is a broad category including many creative and unexpected forms that grab consumers' attention. The rationale is that marketers are better off reaching people where they work, play, and, of course, shop. Popular options include billboards, public spaces, product placement, and point of purchase.

Billboards Billboards have been transformed and now use colourful, digitally produced graphics, back-lighting, sounds, movement, and unusual—even 3D—images.[29] In New York, manhole covers have been reimagined as steaming cups of Folgers coffee; in Belgium, eBay posted "Moved to eBay" stickers on empty storefronts; and in Germany, imaginary workers toiling inside vending machines, ATMs, and photo booths were justification for a German job-hunting website to proclaim, "Life Is Too Short for the Wrong Job."[30]

TABLE 18.1	PROFILES OF MAJOR MEDIA TYPES	
Medium	**Advantages**	**Limitations**
Newspapers	Flexibility; timeliness; good local market coverage; broad acceptance; high believability	Short life; poor reproduction quality; small pass-along audience
Television	Combines sight, sound, and motion; appealing to the senses; high attention; high reach	High absolute cost; high clutter; fleeting exposure; less audience selectivity
Direct mail	Audience selectivity; flexibility; no ad competition within the same medium; personalization	Relatively high cost; "junk mail" image
Radio	Mass use; high geographic and demographic selectivity; low cost	Audio presentation only; lower attention than television; nonstandardized rate structures; fleeting exposure
Magazines	High geographic and demographic selectivity; credibility and prestige; high-quality reproduction; long life; good pass-along readership	Long ad purchase lead time; some waste in circulation
Outdoor	Flexibility; high repeat exposure; low cost; low competition	Limited audience selectivity; creative limitations
Yellow Pages	Excellent local coverage; high believability; wide reach; low cost	High competition; long ad purchase creative limitations
Newsletters	Very high selectivity; full control; interactive opportunities; relatively low cost	Runaway costs could occur
Brochures	Flexibility; full control; can dramatize messages	Overproduction could lead to runaway costs
Telephone	Many users; opportunity to give a personal touch	Relatively high cost; increasing consumer resistance
Internet	High selectivity; interactive possibilities; relatively low cost	Increasing clutter

New "Eyes On" measurement techniques allow marketers to better understand who actually has seen their outdoor ads.[31] The right billboard can make all the difference. Chang Soda in Bangkok had enough money in its budget for only one digital billboard. To maximize impact, it built a giant bubbling bottle onto the billboard to illustrate the product's carbonation. Subsequent word-of-mouth buzz quintupled bottle sales from 200 000 to 1 million.[32]

A strong creative message can also break through visual clutter. Snickers' out-of-home program used billboards and taxi-top signs with puns combining the brand's benefits and key locations, such as "Satisflying" at the airport, "Transfer to the Ate Train" in the subway, and "Snackonomics" on cabs in Wall Street.[33]

Public Spaces Advertisers have been increasingly placing ads in unconventional places such as movie screens, airplanes, fitness clubs, classrooms, sports arenas, and office and hotel elevators.[34] Billboard-type poster ads are showing up everywhere. Transit ads on buses, subways, and commuter trains (around for years) have become a valuable way to reach working women. "Street furniture"—bus shelters, kiosks, and public areas—is another fast-growing option.

Advertisers can buy space in stadiums and arenas and on garbage cans, bicycle racks, parking meters, airport luggage carousels, elevators, gasoline pumps, the bottom of golf cups and swimming pools, airline snack packages, and supermarket produce in the form of tiny labels on apples and bananas. They can even buy space in toilet stalls and above urinals which, according to one research study, office workers visit an average of three to four times a day for roughly four minutes per visit.[35]

Product Placement Marketers pay product placement fees of $100 000 to as much as $500 000 so that their products will make cameo appearances in movies and on television.[36] Sometimes placements are the

Creative place advertisements such as these are attention grabbers.

result of a larger network advertising deal, but other times they are the work of small product-placement shops that maintain ties with prop masters, set designers, and production executives. Some firms get product placement at no cost by supplying their product to the movie company (Nike does not pay to be in movies but often supplies shoes, jackets, bags, and so on). Increasingly, products and brands are being woven directly into the story, as the next example demonstrates.[37]

Staples and *The Office*

When Staples introduced a new $69.99 paper-shredding device called the MailMate in 2006, the company struck a two-episode deal with NBC's popular television program *The Office*. In the first episode, the character Kevin Malone was given the responsibility of shredding paper with the MailMate; in the second, another character, Dwight Schrute, took a job at Staples. The writers and producers of the show tried to accommodate Staples' marketing objectives for the product as much as possible. To make sure the shredder looked small enough, it sat on Kevin's desk. To emphasize that the shredder was sturdy, Kevin shredded not only paper but also his credit card. To emphasize that the shredder was available only at Staples, the episode closed with Kevin shredding lettuce and making it into a salad. When a colleague asked where he got the salad, he replied, "Staples."

Product placement is not immune to criticism. Lawmakers are increasingly criticizing its stealth nature, threatening to force more explicit disclosure of participating advertisers. "Marketing Insight: Product Placement in Children's Entertainment" discusses the issue of product placement directed at young consumers.

Point of Purchase   Chapter 16 discussed the importance of shopper marketing and in-store marketing efforts. The appeal of point-of-purchase advertising lies in the fact that in many product categories consumers make the bulk of their final brand decisions in the store, 74 percent according to one study.[38]

There are many ways to communicate with consumers at the **point of purchase** (**P-O-P**). In-store advertising includes ads on shopping carts, cart straps, aisles, and shelves, as well as promotion options such as in-store demonstrations, live sampling, and instant coupon machines.[39] Some supermarkets

| MARKETING **INSIGHT** | PRODUCT PLACEMENT IN CHILDREN'S ENTERTAINMENT |

There is no shortage of marketing attempts to attract young consumers. Kids are being exposed to a growing number of advertising messages through TV, the Internet, video games, in-store advertising, and several other media. For instance, the average North American child watches 38 hours of commercial media each week, being exposed to between 15 and 30 advertisements per hour through TV alone. There is an ongoing ethical debate among parents, advertisers, and regulatory agencies about what is okay to promote and sell to kids and what is not.

Children are strongly influenced by celebrity endorsements of products such as food and toys—an issue that is concerning many parents and the government. The Canadian Radio-television and Telecommunications Commission (CRTC) prohibits celebrity endorsements of products in advertisements targeted toward children. However, marketers are circumventing the law by using product placements in children's TV shows, movies, video games, and other media.

The use of product placements in children's entertainment is becoming increasingly common nowadays. Popular children's movies such as *Despicable Me, The Twilight Saga: Eclipse, The Chronicles of Narnia, Madagascar, Shark Tale*, and even *E.T.* integrated numerous product placements. For instance, *Madagascar* contained ten different product placements from such companies as Coca-Cola, Krispy Kreme, Toys "R" Us, Burger King, Gatorade, and Starbucks.

Product placements used to attract a younger audience are not limited to children's shows or movies. A recent teenage book called *Cathy's Book* included Cover Girl products. Fast-food restaurants such as McDonald's hire agencies to surround their brand with song lyrics and music videos that attract young consumers. Video games are following suit in the form of "advergaming," whereby advertisers create games designed around a product.

Product placement targeted at young consumers is worrisome for many parents, as children find it difficult to distinguish between program content and a promotion. Numerous studies have shown that children under the age of eight are especially vulnerable because they are developmentally unable to understand the intent of advertisements and accept advertising claims as facts.

Parents and numerous organizations are calling on big brand names and governments to make changes. PepsiCo, which includes brands such as Tropicana, Frito-Lay, Gatorade, and Quaker, has pledged not to use product placements in any form of entertainment aimed at children under the age of twelve. Many governments are implementing stricter guidelines regarding advertising to children. Quebec, Norway, and Sweden have completely banned advertising during children's TV programming. The United Kingdom has banned product placement in TV programs. With increasing concern over marketers' targeting of children, it is expected that many other countries will follow suit and ban product placement in children's entertainment in the coming years.

Sources: Simon Hudson, David Hudson, and John Peloza, "Meet the Parents: A Parents' Perspective on Product Placement in Children's Films," *Journal of Business Ethics, 80*, no. 2: 289–304; PepsiCo Inc., "Children's Food and Beverage Advertising Initiative Pledge of PepsiCo, Inc.," www.pepsico.com/PEP_Citizenship/HealthWellness/Philosophy/CARUPEPPLedge.pdf (viewed June 5, 2008); "Product Placement to Triple in Films, TV, Report Says," CBC News, August 20, 2006, www.cbc.ca/arts/story/2006/08/20/productplacement-report.html (viewed July 13, 2008); Corinna Hawkes, "Regulating Food Marketing to Young People Worldwide: Trends and Policy Drivers," *American Journal of Public Health, 97*, no.11 (November 1, 2007): 1962–1973.

are selling floor space for company logos and experimenting with talking shelves. P-O-P radio provides FM-style programming and commercial messages to thousands of food stores and drugstores nationwide. Programming includes a store-selected music format, consumer tips, and commercials. Video screens in some stores allow for TV-type ads to be run. Walmart is taking advantage of this technology.[40]

Walmart SMART Network

One of the in-store advertising pioneers, Walmart replaced its original Walmart TV with its new SMART network in 2008. The new TV network allows Walmart to monitor and control more than 27 000 individual screens in some 2700 stores nationwide, reaching 160 million viewers every four weeks. Its "triple play" feature permits ads to be shown on a large welcome screen at the entrance of the store, a category screen in departments, and endcap screens on each aisle. Those highly visible endcap viewings are not cheap. Advertisers pay $325 000 for 30-second spots per two-week cycle in the grocery section and $650 000 per four-week run in the health and beauty aid department. Five-second ads running every two minutes for two weeks on the welcome screens cost advertisers $80 000, and 10-second spots running twice every six minutes on the full network cost $50 000 per week. By linking the time when ads are shown and when product sales are made, Walmart can estimate how much ads increase sales by department (from 7 percent in electronics to 28 percent in health and beauty) and by product type (mature items increase by 7 percent, seasonal items by 18 percent).

EVALUATING ALTERNATIVE MEDIA   Ads now can appear virtually anywhere consumers have a few spare minutes or even seconds to notice them. The main advantage of nontraditional media is that they can often reach a very precise and captive audience in a cost-effective manner. The message must be simple and direct. Outdoor advertising, for example, is often called the "15-second sell." It's more effective at enhancing brand awareness or brand image than creating new brand associations.

Unique ad placements designed to break through clutter may also be perceived as invasive and obtrusive, however. Consumer backlash often results when people see ads in traditionally ad-free spaces, such as in schools, on police cruisers, and in doctors' waiting rooms. Nevertheless, perhaps because of its sheer pervasiveness, some consumers seem to be less bothered by nontraditional media now than in the past.

The challenge for nontraditional media is to demonstrate its reach and effectiveness through credible, independent research. Consumers must be favourably affected in some way to justify the marketing expenditures. Tropicana chose not only an unusual way to advertise its brand but also a rather remote part of Canada to do so.

Tropicana

PepsiCo's Tropicana Canada combined a stunt with reality advertising to shine a spotlight, quite literally, on its brand. In 2010, the company staged an unusual event in Inuvik, Northwest Territories, during the annual Sunrise Festival—a local celebration of the sun's return after 30 days of 24-hour darkness during the winter months. Tropicana enlisted a documentary crew to chronicle its efforts to raise a giant light-emitting balloon in the town, signifying the "rising of the sun." The 35-foot-wide, helium-filled ball emitted 100 000 lumen, roughly equivalent to the light output of the sun on a clear day, lighting up a radius of about four kilometres. Each household in Inuvik was also given a carton of Tropicana Pure Premium orange juice, to communicate that drinking Tropicana could brighten the morning every day. Allowing consumers nationwide to connect with this hometown story that featured real people, the documentary short was posted on Tropicana's Facebook page and website.[41]

Selecting Specific Media Vehicles

The media planner must search for the most cost-effective vehicles within each chosen media type. The advertiser who decides to buy 30 seconds of advertising on network television can pay around $100 000 for a new show, over $300 000 for a popular prime-time show such as *American Idol, Grey's Anatomy,* or *Desperate Housewives,* or over $2.5 million for an event such as the Super Bowl.[42] Advertising on Canadian networks is a bargain in comparison. Thirty-second commercials on CBC average $6500 while those on Global average $7000. On specialty channels, the average rates can be even lower—$450 on Bravo! and $1250 on YTV. Even wildly popular events in Canada are relatively affordable, such as the Canada–U.S. 2010 Olympics hockey final, where ads went for a record $200 000 for a 30-second spot, or game 6 of the 2011 Stanley Cup Finals between the Vancouver Canucks and Boston Bruins, which brought CBC only $140 000 for such an ad.[43] Choice of media vehicle is critical: the average cost to produce a national 30-second television commercial in 2007 was about $342 000.[44] It can cost as much to run an ad once on network TV as to create and produce the ad to start with!

In making choices, the planner must rely on measurement services that estimate audience size, composition, and media cost. Media planners then calculate the cost per thousand persons reached by a vehicle. In 2011, a full-page, four-colour ad in *Maclean's* cost $38 180 and would reach an estimated readership of 2.4 million people; therefore, the cost of exposing 1000 persons to the ad is about $16.[45] The same ad in *MoneySense* cost less than half of *Maclean's* rates, at $18 915. But, with an estimated readership of 778 000 for *MoneySense,* the cost of exposing the ad to 1000 persons rises to approximately $24.30.[46]

FIGURE 18.3

Classification of Advertising
Timing Patterns

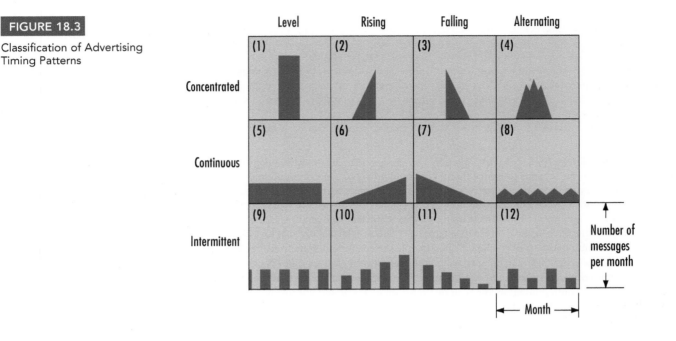

The media planner ranks each magazine by cost per thousand and favours magazines with the lowest cost per thousand for reaching target consumers. The magazines themselves often put together a "reader profile" for their advertisers, describing average readers with respect to age, income, residence, marital status, and leisure activities.

Marketers need to apply several adjustments to the cost-per-thousand measure. First, adjust for *audience quality*. For a baby lotion ad, a magazine read by 1 million young mothers has an exposure value of 1 million; if read by 1 million teenage boys, it has an exposure value of almost zero. Second, adjust the exposure value for the *audience-attention probability*. Readers of *Flare* may pay more attention to ads than may readers of *Canadian Business*. Third, adjust for the medium's *editorial quality* (prestige and believability). People are more likely to believe a TV or radio ad and to become more positively disposed toward the brand when the ad is placed within a program they like.[47] Fourth, consider *ad placement policies and extra services* (such as regional or occupational editions and lead-time requirements for magazines).

Media planners are using more sophisticated measures of effectiveness and employing them in mathematical models to arrive at the best media mix. Many advertising agencies use software programs to select the initial media and make improvements based on subjective factors.[48]

Deciding on Media Timing and Allocation

In choosing media, the advertiser has both a macroscheduling and a microscheduling decision. The *macroscheduling decision* relates to seasons and the business cycle. Suppose 70 percent of a product's sales occur between June and September. The firm can vary its advertising expenditures to follow the seasonal pattern, to oppose the seasonal pattern, or to be constant throughout the year.

The *microscheduling decision* calls for allocating advertising expenditures within a short period to obtain maximum impact. Suppose the firm decides to buy 30 radio spots in the month of September. Figure 18.3 shows several possible patterns. The left side shows that advertising messages for the month can be concentrated ("burst" advertising), dispersed continuously throughout the month, or dispersed intermittently. The top side shows that the advertising messages can be beamed with a level, rising, falling, or alternating frequency.

The chosen pattern should meet the communications objectives set in relationship to the nature of the product, target customers, distribution channels, and other marketing factors. The timing pattern should consider three factors. *Buyer turnover* expresses the rate at which new buyers enter the market; the higher this rate, the more continuous the advertising should be. *Purchase frequency* is the number of times the average buyer buys the product during the period; the higher the purchase frequency, the more continuous the advertising should be. The *forgetting rate* is the rate at which the buyer forgets the brand; the higher the forgetting rate, the more continuous the advertising should be.

In launching a new product, the advertiser must choose among continuity, concentration, flighting, and pulsing:

- *Continuity* means that exposures appear evenly throughout a given period. Generally, advertisers use continuous advertising in expanding market situations, with frequently purchased items, and in tightly defined buyer categories.

- *Concentration* calls for spending all the advertising dollars in a single period. This makes sense for products with one selling season or related holiday.

- *Flighting* calls for advertising during a period, followed by a period with no advertising, followed by a second period of advertising activity. It is useful when funding is limited, the purchase cycle is relatively infrequent, or items are seasonal.

- *Pulsing* is continuous advertising at low-weight levels, reinforced periodically by waves of heavier activity. It draws on the strength of continuous advertising and flights to create a compromise scheduling strategy.[49] Those who favour pulsing believe that the audience will learn the message more thoroughly, and at a lower cost to the firm.

A company must decide how to allocate its advertising budget over space as well as over time. The company makes "national buys" when it places ads on national TV networks or in nationally circulated magazines. It makes "spot buys" when it buys TV time in just a few markets or in regional editions of magazines. These markets are called *areas of dominant influence* (ADIs) or *designated marketing areas* (DMAs). The company makes "local buys" when it advertises in local newspapers, radio, or outdoor sites.

Evaluating Advertising Effectiveness

Most advertisers try to measure the communication effect of an ad—that is, its potential impact on awareness, knowledge, or preference. They would also like to measure the ad's sales effect.

COMMUNICATION-EFFECT RESEARCH **Communication-effect research**, called *copy testing,* seeks to determine whether an ad is communicating effectively. Marketers should perform this test both before an ad is put into media and after it is printed or broadcast. Table 18.2 describes some specific advertising pretest research techniques.

Pretest critics maintain that agencies can design ads that test well but may not necessarily perform well in the marketplace. Proponents maintain that useful diagnostic information can emerge and that pretests should not be used as the sole decision criterion anyway. Widely acknowledged as one of the best advertisers around, Nike is notorious for doing very little ad pretesting.

TABLE 18.2 | ADVERTISING PRETEST RESEARCH TECHNIQUES

For Print Ads

Starch and Gallup & Robinson Inc. are two widely used print pretesting services. Test ads are placed in magazines, which are then circulated to consumers. These consumers are contacted later and interviewed. Recall and recognition tests are used to determine advertising effectiveness.

For Broadcast Ads

In-home tests: A video is taken or downloaded into the homes of target consumers, who then view the commercials.

Trailer tests: In a trailer in a shopping centre, shoppers are shown the products and given an opportunity to select a series of brands. They then view commercials and are given coupons to be used in the shopping centre. Redemption rates indicate commercials' influence on purchase behaviour.

Theatre tests: Consumers are invited to a theatre to view a potential new television series along with some commercials. Before the show begins, consumers indicate preferred brands in different categories; after the viewing, consumers again choose preferred brands. Preference changes measure the commercials' persuasive power.

On-air tests: Respondents are recruited to watch a program on a regular TV channel during the test commercial or are selected based on having viewed the program. They are asked questions about commercial recall.

FIGURE 18.4

Measuring Sales Impact
of Advertising

Share of
expenditures

Share of
voice

Share of
minds and
hearts

Share of
market

Many advertisers use post-tests to assess the overall impact of a completed campaign. If a company hoped to increase brand awareness from 20 percent to 50 percent and succeeded in increasing it to only 30 percent, then the company is not spending enough, its ads are poor, or it has overlooked some other factor.

SALES-EFFECT RESEARCH What sales are generated by an ad that increases brand awareness by 20 percent and brand preference by 10 percent? The fewer or more controllable other factors such as features and price are, the easier it is to measure advertising's effect on sales. The sales impact is easiest to measure in direct marketing situations and hardest in brand or corporate image-building advertising.

Companies are generally interested in finding out whether they are overspending or underspending on advertising. One way to answer this question is to work with the logic shown in Figure 18.4.

A company's *share of advertising expenditures* produces a *share of voice* (proportion of company advertising of that product to all advertising of that product) that earns a *share of consumers' minds and hearts* and, ultimately, a *share of market.*

Researchers try to measure the sales impact by analyzing historical or experimental data. The *historical approach* correlates past sales to past advertising expenditures using advanced statistical techniques.[50] Other researchers use an *experimental design* to measure advertising's sales impact.

A growing number of researchers are striving to measure the sales effect of advertising expenditures instead of settling for communication-effect measures.[51] Millward Brown International has conducted tracking studies for years to help advertisers decide whether their advertising is benefiting their brand.[52]

SALES PROMOTION

Sales promotion, a key ingredient in marketing campaigns, consists of a collection of incentive tools, mostly short term, designed to stimulate quicker or greater purchase of particular products or services by consumers or the trade.[53]

Whereas advertising offers a *reason* to buy, sales promotion offers an *incentive*. Sales promotion includes tools for *consumer promotion* (samples, coupons, cash refund offers, prices off, premiums, prizes, patronage rewards, free trials, warranties, tie-in promotions, cross-promotions, point-of-purchase displays, and demonstrations), *trade promotion* (prices off, advertising and display allowances, and free goods), and *business* and *sales force promotion* (trade shows and conventions, contests for sales reps, and specialty advertising).

Objectives

Sales promotion tools vary in their specific objectives. A free sample stimulates consumer trial, whereas a free management-advisory service aims at cementing a long-term relationship with a retailer.

Sellers use incentive-type promotions to attract new triers, to reward loyal customers, and to increase the repurchase rates of occasional users. Sales promotions often attract brand switchers, who are primarily looking for low price, good value, or premiums. If some of them would not have otherwise tried the brand, promotion can yield long-term increases in market share.[54]

Sales promotions in markets of high brand similarity can produce a high sales response in the short run but little permanent gain in brand preference over the longer term. In markets of high brand dissimilarity, they may be able to alter market shares permanently. In addition to brand switching, consumers may engage in stockpiling—purchasing earlier than usual (purchase acceleration) or purchasing extra quantities. But sales may then hit a post-promotion dip.[55]

Advertising versus Promotion

Sales promotion expenditures increased as a percentage of budget expenditures for a number of years, although growth has recently slowed. Several factors contributed to this growth, particularly in consumer markets. Promotion became more accepted by top management as an effective sales tool, the number of brands increased, competitors used promotions frequently, many brands were seen as similar, consumers became more price-oriented, the trade demanded more deals from manufacturers, and advertising efficiency declined.

But the rapid growth of sales promotion created clutter. Consumers began to tune out promotions. The average U.S. household gets an incredible 2000 to 3000 coupons a year, compared with only about 200 in Canada. As a result, the overall coupon redemption rate in the United States is only 0.5 percent compared with 4 percent in Canada.[56] Incessant price reductions, coupons, deals, and premiums can also devalue the product in buyers' minds. There is a risk in putting a well-known brand on promotion over 30 percent of the time. Having turned to zero percent financing, hefty cash rebates, and special lease programs to ignite sales in the soft post–9/11 economy, auto manufacturers have found it difficult to wean consumers from discounts ever since.[57]

Loyal brand buyers tend not to change their buying patterns as a result of competitive promotions. Advertising appears to be more effective at deepening brand loyalty, although we can distinguish added-value promotions from price promotions.[58] Gain's "Love at First Sniff" campaign used direct mail and in-store scented tear-pads and ShelfVision TV to entice consumers to smell the product, resulting in an almost 500 percent increase in shipments over the goal.[59]

Price promotions may not build permanent total-category volume. One study of more than 1000 promotions concluded that only 16 percent paid off.[60] Small-share competitors may find it advantageous to use sales promotion, because they cannot afford to match the market leaders' large advertising budgets, nor can they obtain shelf space without offering trade allowances or stimulate consumer trial without offering incentives. Dominant brands offer deals less frequently, because most deals subsidize only current users.

The upshot is that many consumer packaged-goods companies feel forced to use more sales promotion than they wish. They blame heavy use of sales promotion for decreased brand loyalty, increased price sensitivity, brand-quality image dilution, and a focus on short-run marketing planning. One review of promotion effectiveness concluded, "When the strategic disadvantages of promotions are included, that is, losing control to the trade and training consumers to buy only on deal, the case is compelling for a reevaluation of current practices and the incentive systems responsible for this trend."[61]

Major Decisions

In using sales promotion, a company must establish its objectives, select the tools, develop the program, pretest the program, implement and control it, and evaluate the results.

ESTABLISHING OBJECTIVES Sales promotion objectives derive from broader communications objectives, which derive from more basic marketing objectives for the product. For consumers, objectives include encouraging purchase of larger-sized units, building trial among nonusers, and attracting switchers away from competitors' brands. Ideally, promotions with consumers would have short-run sales impact as well as long-run brand equity effects.[62] For retailers, objectives include persuading retailers to carry new items and higher levels of inventory, encouraging off-season buying, encouraging stocking of related items, offsetting competitive promotions, building brand loyalty, and gaining entry into new retail outlets. For the sales force, objectives include encouraging support of a new product or model, encouraging more prospecting, and stimulating off-season sales.[63]

SELECTING CONSUMER PROMOTION TOOLS The promotion planner should take into account the type of market, sales promotion objectives, competitive conditions, and each tool's cost-effectiveness. The main consumer promotion tools are summarized in Table 18.3. Examples of *manufacturer promotions* in the auto industry are rebates, gifts to motivate test drives and purchases, and high-value trade-in credit. *Retailer promotions* include price cuts, feature advertising, retailer coupons, and retailer contests or premiums.[64]

We can also distinguish between sales promotion tools that are *consumer franchise building* and those that are not. The former impart a selling message along with the deal, such as free samples; frequency awards; coupons, when they include a selling message; and premiums, when they are related to the product. Sales promotion tools that typically are *not* brand building include price-off packs, consumer premiums not related to a product, contests and sweepstakes, consumer refund offers, and trade allowances.

Consumer franchise-building promotions offer the best of both worlds: they build brand equity while moving product. Sampling has gained popularity in recent years—companies such as McDonald's, Danone, and Starbucks have given away millions of samples of their new products—because consumers like samples and they often lead to higher long-term sales for quality products.[65]

Digital coupons eliminate printing costs, reduce paper waste, are easily updatable, and have higher redemption rates. Coupons.com receives almost 5 million unique visitors a month for money-saving deals. Almost 2 million consumers visit CoolSavings.com each month for money-saving coupons and offers from name brands, as well as helpful tips and articles, newsletters, free recipes, sweepstakes, free trials, free samples, and more. Electronic coupons can arrive by cell phone, Twitter, email, or Facebook.[66]

SELECTING TRADE PROMOTION TOOLS Manufacturers use a number of trade promotion tools (see Table 18.4).[67] Manufacturers award money to the trade (1) to persuade the retailer or wholesaler to carry the brand; (2) to persuade the retailer or wholesaler to carry more units than the normal amount; (3) to induce retailers to promote the brand through features, displays, and price reductions; and (4) to stimulate retailers and their sales clerks to push the product.

TABLE 18.3 | MAJOR CONSUMER PROMOTION TOOLS

Samples: Offer of a free amount of a product or service delivered door-to-door, sent in the mail, picked up in a store, attached to another product, or featured in an advertising offer.

Coupons: Certificates entitling the bearer to a stated saving on the purchase of a specific product: mailed, enclosed in other products or attached to them, or inserted in magazine and newspaper ads.

Cash Refund Offers (rebates): Offers that provide a price reduction after purchase rather than at the retail shop: consumer sends a specified proof of purchase to the manufacturer, who refunds part of the purchase price by mail.

Price Packs (cents-off deals): Offers to consumers of savings off the regular price of a product, flagged on the label or package. A *reduced-price pack* is a single package sold at a reduced price (such as two for the price of one). A *banded pack* is two related products banded together (such as a toothbrush and toothpaste).

Premiums (gifts): Merchandise offered at a relatively low cost or free as an incentive to purchase a particular product. A *with-pack premium* accompanies the product inside or on the package. A *free in-the-mail premium* is mailed to consumers who send in proof of purchase, such as a box top or Universal Product Code (UPC). A *self-liquidating premium* is sold below its normal retail price to consumers who request it.

Frequency Programs: Programs providing rewards related to the consumer's frequency and intensity in purchasing the company's products or services.

Prizes (contests, sweepstakes, games): *Prizes* are offers of the chance to win cash, trips, or merchandise as a result of purchasing something. A *contest* calls for consumers to submit an entry to be examined by a panel of judges, who will select the best entries. A *sweepstakes* asks consumers to submit their names in a drawing. A *game* presents consumers with something every time they buy—bingo numbers, missing letters—which might help them win a prize.

Patronage Awards: Values in cash or in other forms that are proportional to patronage of a certain vendor or group of vendors.

Free Trials: Offers that invite prospective purchasers to try the product without cost in the hope that they will buy.

Product Warranties: Explicit or implicit promises by sellers that the product will perform as specified or that the seller will fix it or refund the customer's money during a specified period.

Tie-In Promotions: Teaming up of two or more brands or companies on coupons, refunds, and contests to increase pulling power.

Cross-Promotions: Use of one brand to advertise another noncompeting brand.

Point-of-Purchase (P-O-P) Displays and Demonstrations: Displays and demonstrations that take place at the point of purchase or sale.

The growing power of large retailers has increased their ability to demand trade promotion at the expense of consumer promotion and advertising.[68] The company's sales force and its brand managers are often at odds over trade promotion. The sales force says local retailers will not keep the company's products on the shelf unless they receive more trade promotion money, whereas brand managers want to spend their limited funds on consumer promotion and advertising.

Manufacturers face several challenges in managing trade promotions. First, they often find it difficult to police retailers to make sure they are doing what they agreed to do. Manufacturers increasingly insist on proof of performance before paying any allowances. Second, some retailers are doing *forward buying*—that is, buying a greater quantity during the deal period than they can immediately sell. Retailers might respond to a 10 percent-off-case allowance by buying a 12-week or longer supply. The manufacturer must then

> **TABLE 18.4 | MAJOR TRADE PROMOTION TOOLS**
>
> **Price-Off (off-invoice or off-list):** A straight discount off the list price on each case purchased during a stated time period.
>
> **Allowance:** An amount offered in return for the retailer's agreeing to feature the manufacturer's products in some way. An *advertising allowance* compensates retailers for advertising the manufacturer's product. A *display allowance* compensates them for carrying a special product display.
>
> **Free Goods:** Offers of extra cases of merchandise to intermediaries who buy a certain quantity or who feature a certain flavour or size.

schedule more production than planned and bear the costs of extra work shifts and overtime. Third, some retailers are *diverting*, buying more cases than needed in a region where the manufacturer offers a deal and shipping the surplus to their stores in nondeal regions. Manufacturers handle forward buying and diverting by limiting the amount they will sell at a discount, or by producing and delivering less than the full order in an effort to smooth production.[69]

Ultimately, many manufacturers feel trade promotion has become a nightmare. It contains layers of deals, is complex to administer, and often leads to lost revenues.

SELECTING BUSINESS AND SALES FORCE PROMOTION TOOLS Companies spend billions of dollars on business and sales force promotion tools (see Table 18.5) to gather leads, impress and reward customers, and motivate the sales force.[70] They typically develop budgets for tools that remain fairly constant from year to year. For many new businesses that want to make a splash to a targeted audience, especially in the B2B world, trade shows are an important tool, but the cost per contact is the highest of all communications options.

DEVELOPING THE PROGRAM In planning sales promotion programs, marketers are increasingly blending several media into a total campaign concept, as Yellow Tail did in Canada.

Reflecting changes in consumer behaviour, digital coupons such as those available at Smart Canucks.ca have grown in importance.

| TABLE 18.5 | MAJOR BUSINESS AND SALES FORCE PROMOTION TOOLS |

Trade Shows and Conventions: Industry associations organize annual trade shows and conventions. Trade shows are a multibillion-dollar business, and business marketers may spend as much as 35 percent of their annual promotion budget on trade shows. Trade show attendance can range from a few thousand people to over 100 000 for large shows. The International Consumer Electronics Show is one of the largest trade shows in the world, with nearly 150 000 attendees and 48 776 exhibitors in its 2011 show.[71] Participating vendors expect several benefits, including generating new sales leads, maintaining customer contacts, introducing new products, meeting new customers, selling more to present customers, and educating customers with publications, videos, and other audiovisual materials.

Sales Contests: A sales contest aims at inducing the sales force or dealers to increase their sales results over a stated period, with prizes (money, trips, gifts, or points) going to those who succeed.

Specialty Advertising: Specialty advertising consists of useful, low-cost items bearing the company's name and address, and sometimes an advertising message, and that salespeople give to prospects and customers. Common items are ballpoint pens, calendars, key chains, flashlights, tote bags, and memo pads.

Yellow Tail

The Australian wine brand Yellow Tail ran a multichannel campaign in 2011 entitled "Goodbye Fridays," which encouraged Canadians to toast away Fridays for good. With increasing competition in the nonpremium wine segment, Yellow Tail felt it needed to reinforce the brand among Canadians. In an effort to make the consumer a part of the campaign, the company ran a contest that would allow the winner to say goodbye to working Fridays for the rest of the year (or receive a $20 000 cash equivalent). Entrants were given the opportunity to post their own "Goodbye Friday" toast for a chance to win a holiday, furniture, and more. The contest brought Yellow Tail's Facebook page 30 000 fans in just over a month. The campaign was supported by digital boards that displayed texted toasts; interactive projections on bar district walls; ads in *Food & Drink, Occasions,* and *Dish* magazines; and a trailer/mobile bar at festivals throughout Ontario.[72]

In deciding to use a particular incentive, marketers must first determine its *size*. A certain minimum is necessary if the promotion is to succeed. Second, the marketing manager must establish *conditions* for participation. Incentives might be offered to everyone or to select groups. Third, the marketer must decide on the *duration* of the promotion. Fourth, the marketer must choose a *distribution vehicle*. A 15-cents-off coupon can be distributed in the product package, in stores, by mail, online, or in advertising. Fifth, the marketing manager must establish the *timing* of promotion, and finally, the *total sales promotion budget*. The cost of a particular promotion consists of the administrative cost (printing, mailing, and promoting the deal) and the incentive cost (cost of premium or cents-off, including redemption costs), multiplied by the expected number of units sold. The cost of a coupon deal would recognize that only a fraction of consumers will redeem the coupons.

IMPLEMENTING AND EVALUATING THE PROGRAM Marketing managers must prepare implementation and control plans that cover lead time and sell-in time for each individual promotion. *Lead time* is the time necessary to prepare the program prior to launching it.[73] *Sell-in time* begins with the promotional launch and ends when approximately 95 percent of the deal merchandise is in the hands of consumers.

Manufacturers can evaluate the program using sales data, consumer surveys, and experiments. Sales (scanner) data help analyze the types of people who took advantage of the promotion, what they bought before the promotion, and how they behaved later toward the brand and other brands. Sales promotions work best when they attract competitors' customers who then switch. *Consumer surveys* can uncover how many consumers recall the promotion, what they thought of it, how many took advantage of it, and how the promotion affected subsequent brand choice behaviour.[74] *Experiments* vary such attributes as incentive value, duration, and distribution media. For example, coupons can be sent to half the households in a consumer panel. Scanner data can track whether the coupons led more people to buy the product and when.

Additional costs beyond the cost of specific promotions include the risk that promotions might decrease long-run brand loyalty. Second, promotions can be more expensive than they appear. Some are inevitably distributed to the wrong consumers. Third, special production runs, extra sales force effort, and handling requirements add costs. Finally, certain promotions irritate retailers, who may demand extra trade allowances or refuse to cooperate.

EVENTS AND EXPERIENCES

The IEG Sponsorship Report projected that US$17.1 billion would be spent on sponsorships in North America during 2010, with 68 percent going to sports; another 10 percent to entertainment tours and attractions; 5 percent to festivals, fairs, and annual events; 5 percent to the arts; 3 percent to associations and membership organizations; and 9 percent to cause marketing.[75] Becoming part of a personally relevant moment in consumers' lives through events and experiences can broaden and deepen a company or brand's relationship with the target market.

Daily encounters with brands may also affect consumers' brand attitudes and beliefs. *Atmospheres* are "packaged environments" that create or reinforce leanings toward product purchase. Law offices decorated with Oriental rugs and oak furniture communicate "stability" and "success."[76] A five-star hotel will use elegant chandeliers, marble columns, and other tangible signs of luxury. Many firms are creating on-site and off-site product and brand experiences. There is Everything Coca-Cola in Las Vegas and M&M World in Times Square in New York.[77]

Many firms are also creating their own events and experiences to generate consumer and media interest and involvement. To showcase its international reach and upgrades in seating, food, and beverage, Delta Airlines created a temporary Sky 360 pop-up retail lounge on West 57th Street in Manhattan. The lounge featured samples of food and wine items from chef Todd English to eat and drink, comfortable leather seats found in coach to sit in, and the seat-back entertainment system to listen to.[78] Given its central business location for the media industry, Manhattan is the site of many events and experiences. GE used a unique event in Manhattan to create buzz for a new product.[79]

A major Times Square event to support the launch of a new line of GE Profile washers and dryers was part of an extensive integrated marketing communications program.

GE Profile

To promote its new GE Profile front-load washer and dryer with SmartDispense technology—designed to optimize the amount of detergent used in any one wash—GE used traditional online and mass media. To create even more buzz, the firm hung 800 feet of jeans and shirts on a massive clothesline in Times Square to represent the six months' worth of washing the new machines could typically handle before needing more detergent. On one of the traffic islands were 20-foot-high inflatable versions of the new washer and dryer. A live celebrity auction to benefit the nonprofit Clothes Off Our Back Foundation was hosted by television mom Alison Sweeney. A small army of 20 representatives handing out product-related goodies (such as bottles of water and colouring books shaped like the appliance's door) added to the spectacle. GE also ran an online promotion. All these efforts combined to attract 150 000 entrants to a washer/dryer giveaway contest.

Events Objectives

Marketers report a number of reasons to sponsor events:

1. *To identify with a particular target market or lifestyle*—Customers can be targeted geographically, demographically, psychographically, or behaviourally according to events. Old Spice sponsors college sports and motor sports—one sponsorship is a ten-year deal with driver Tony Stewart's entries in the Nextel Cup and Busch Series—to highlight product relevance and sample among its target audience of 16- to 24-year-old males.[80]

2. *To increase salience of company or product name*—Sponsorship often offers sustained exposure to a brand, a necessary condition to reinforce brand salience. Top-of-mind awareness for World Cup soccer sponsors such as Emirates, Hyundai, Kia, and Sony benefited from the repeated brand and ad exposure over the month-long tournament.

3. *To create or reinforce perceptions of key brand image associations*—Events themselves have associations that help to create or reinforce brand associations.[81] To toughen its image and appeal to America's heartland, Toyota Tundra elected to sponsor Bass fishing tournaments and a Brooks & Dunn country music tour.

4. *To enhance corporate image*—Sponsorship can improve perceptions that the company is likable and prestigious. Although Visa views its long-standing Olympic sponsorship as a means of enhancing international brand awareness and increasing usage and volume, it also engenders patriotic goodwill and taps into the emotional Olympic spirit.[82]

5. *To create experiences and evoke feelings*—The feelings engendered by an exciting or rewarding event may indirectly link to the brand. Audi models featured prominently in the 2010 blockbuster *Iron Man 2,* including main character Tony Stark's personal R8 Spyder, the A8, Q5 and Q7 SUVs, and A3 hatchback. The event was backed by a month-long marketing blitz, and surveys revealed that positive word of mouth doubled for the brand.[83]

6. *To express commitment to the community or to social issues*—Cause-related marketing sponsors nonprofit organizations and charities. Firms such as RBC, Boston Pizza, Home Depot, Starbucks, and Tim Hortons have made cause-related marketing an important cornerstone of their marketing programs.

7. *To entertain key clients or reward key employees*—Many events include lavish hospitality tents and other special services or activities only for sponsors and their guests. These perks engender goodwill and establish valuable business contacts. From an employee perspective, events can also build participation and morale or serve as an incentive. BB&T Corp., a major banking and financial services player in the South and Southeast United States, used its NASCAR Busch Series sponsorship to entertain business customers and its minor league baseball sponsorship to generate excitement among employees.[84]

8. *To permit merchandising or promotional opportunities*—Many marketers tie contests or sweepstakes, in-store merchandising, direct response, or other marketing activities to an event. L'Oréal Canada used its sponsorship of the hit TV show *Canadian Idol* in this way.

Despite these potential advantages, the result of an event can still be unpredictable and beyond the sponsor's control. Although many consumers will credit sponsors for providing the financial assistance to make an event possible, some may resent the commercialization of events.

Major Sponsorship Decisions

Making sponsorships successful requires choosing the appropriate events, designing the optimal sponsorship program, and measuring the effects of sponsorship.[85]

CHOOSING EVENTS Because of the number of opportunities and their huge cost, many marketers are becoming more selective about choosing sponsorship events.

The event must meet the marketing objectives and communications strategy defined for the brand. The audience must match the target market. The event must have sufficient awareness, possess the desired image, and be capable of creating the desired effects. Consumers must make favourable attributions for the sponsor's engagement. An ideal event is also unique but not encumbered with many sponsors, lends itself to ancillary marketing activities, and reflects or enhances the sponsor's brand or corporate image.[86]

DESIGNING SPONSORSHIP PROGRAMS Many marketers believe the marketing program accompanying an event sponsorship ultimately determines its success. At least two to three times the amount of the sponsorship expenditure should be spent on related marketing activities.

Event creation is a particularly important skill in publicizing fund-raising drives for nonprofit organizations. Fund-raisers have developed a large repertoire of special events, including anniversary celebrations, art exhibits, auctions, benefit evenings, book sales, cake sales, contests, dances, dinners, fairs, fashion shows, phonathons, rummage sales, tours, and walkathons.

More firms are now using their names to sponsor arenas, stadiums, and other venues that hold events. Billions of dollars have been spent over the past decade for naming rights to major North American sports facilities. But as with any sponsorship, the most important consideration is the additional marketing activities.[87]

MEASURING SPONSORSHIP ACTIVITIES It's a challenge to measure the success of events. The *supply-side* measurement method focuses on potential exposure to the brand by assessing the extent of media coverage, and the *demand-side* method focuses on exposure reported by consumers. "Marketing Memo: Measuring High Performance Sponsorship Programs" offers some guidelines critical to issues of sponsorship measurement from industry experts IEG.

Supply-side methods approximate the amount of time or space devoted to media coverage of an event, for example, the number of seconds the brand is clearly visible on a television screen or the column inches of press clippings that mention it. These potential "impressions" translate into a value that is then compared with the dollar cost of actually advertising in the particular media vehicle. Some industry consultants have estimated that 30 seconds of TV logo exposure during a televised event can be worth 6 percent, 10 percent, or as much as 25 percent of a 30-second TV ad spot.

Although supply-side exposure methods provide quantifiable measures, equating media coverage with advertising exposure ignores the content of the respective communications. The advertiser uses media space and time to communicate a strategically designed message. Media coverage and telecasts only expose the brand and don't necessarily embellish its meaning in any direct way. Although some public relations professionals maintain that positive editorial coverage can be worth five to ten times the equivalent advertising value, sponsorship rarely provides such favourable treatment.[88]

The **demand-side method** identifies the effect sponsorship has on consumers' brand knowledge. Marketers can survey event spectators to measure recall of the event as well as resulting attitudes and intentions toward the sponsor.

Creating Experiences

A large part of local, grassroots marketing is experiential marketing, which not only communicates features and benefits but also connects a product or service with unique and interesting experiences. As Pine and Gilmore explain, "The idea is not to sell something, but to demonstrate how a brand can enrich a customer's life."[89]

MARKETING **MEMO**	MEASURING HIGH PERFORMANCE SPONSORSHIP PROGRAMS

1. Measure outcomes, not outputs. Focus on what a sponsorship actually produced rather than what a sponsor got or did—rather than focus on 5,000 people sampled at an event, how many of those people would be classified as members of the target market and what is the likely conversion rate between their trial and future behaviors?

2. Define and benchmark objectives on the front end. Specific objectives help to identify what measures should be tracked. An objective of motivating the sales force and distributors suggests different measures than one of building brand image and key brand benefits. Contrast measures in terms of sponsorship effects and what might have happened if the sponsorship had not occurred.

3. Measure return for each objective against prorated share of rights and activation fees. Rank and rate objectives by importance and allocate the total sponsorship budget against each of those objectives.

4. Measure behavior. Conduct a thorough sales analysis to identify shifts in marketplace behavior as a result of the sponsorship.

5. Apply the assumptions and ratios used by other departments within the company. Applying statistical methods used by other departments makes it easier to gain acceptance for any sponsorship analysis.

6. Research the emotional identities of customers and measure the results of emotional connections. In what ways does a sponsorship psychologically affect consumers and facilitate and deepen long-term loyalty relationships?

7. Identify group norms. How strong of a community exists around the sponsored event or participants? Are there formal groups that share interests that will be impacted by the sponsorship?

8. Include cost savings in ROI calculations. Contrast expenses that a firm has typically incurred in the past achieving a particular objective from those expenses allocated to achieve the objective as part of the sponsorship.

9. Slice the data. Sponsorship affects market segments differently. Breaking down a target market into smaller segments can better identify sponsorship effects.

10. Capture normative data. Develop a core set of evaluation criteria that can be applied across all different sponsorship programs.

Source: IEG, LLC, www.sponsorship.com.

Consumers seem to appreciate that. In one survey, four of five respondents found that participating in a live event was more engaging than all other forms of communication. The vast majority also felt experiential marketing gave them more information than other forms of communication and would make them more likely to tell others about participating in the event and to be receptive to other marketing for the brand.[90]

Companies can even create a strong image by inviting prospects and customers to visit their headquarters and factories. Ben & Jerry's, Boeing, Crayola, and Hershey's all sponsor excellent company tours that draw millions of visitors a year. Companies such as Hallmark, Kohler, and Beiersdorf (makers of NIVEA) have built corporate museums at or near their headquarters and that display their history and the drama of producing and marketing their products.

PUBLIC RELATIONS

Not only must the company relate constructively to customers, suppliers, and dealers, it must also relate to a large number of interested publics. A **public** is any group that has an actual or potential interest in or impact on a company's ability to achieve its objectives. **Public relations (PR)** includes a variety of programs to promote or protect a company's image or individual products.

The wise company takes concrete steps to manage successful relationships with its key publics. Most companies have a public relations department, which monitors the attitudes of the organization's publics and distributes information and communications to build goodwill. The best PR departments counsel top management to adopt positive programs and eliminate questionable practices so that negative publicity doesn't arise in the first place. They perform the following five functions:

1. *Press relations*—Presenting news and information about the organization in the most positive light

2. *Product publicity*—Sponsoring efforts to publicize specific products

3. *Corporate communications*—Promoting understanding of the organization through internal and external communications

4. *Lobbying*—Dealing with legislators and government officials to promote or defeat legislation and regulation

5. *Counselling*—Advising management about public issues and company positions and image during good times and bad

Marketing Public Relations

Many companies are turning to **marketing public relations (MPR)** to support corporate or product promotion and image making. MPR, like financial PR and community PR, serves a special constituency, the marketing department.

The old name for MPR was **publicity**, the task of securing editorial space—as opposed to paid space—in print and broadcast media to promote or hype a product, service, idea, place, person, or organization. MPR goes beyond simple publicity and plays an important role in the following tasks:

- *Launching new products.* The amazing commercial success of toys such as LeapFrog, Beanie Babies, and even the latest kids' craze, Silly Bandz, owes a great deal to strong publicity.

- *Repositioning a mature product.* In a classic PR case study, New York City had extremely bad press in the 1970s until the "I Love New York" campaign.

- *Building interest in a product category.* Companies and trade associations have used MPR to rebuild interest in declining commodities such as eggs, milk, beef, and potatoes and to expand consumption of such products as tea, pork, and orange juice.

- *Influencing specific target groups.* The Vancouver Olympic Bid Committee leveraged PR to build public support for the games and to win the right to hold the Olympics and Paralympics in Vancouver in 2010.

- *Defending products that have encountered public problems.* PR professionals must be adept at managing crises, such as those weathered by well-established brands Tylenol, Toyota, and BP in 2010.

- *Building the corporate image in a way that reflects favourably on its products.* Steve Jobs's heavily anticipated Macworld keynote speeches helped to create an innovative, iconoclastic image for Apple Corporation.

As the power of mass advertising weakens, marketing managers are turning to MPR to build awareness and brand knowledge for both new and established products. MPR is also effective in blanketing local communities and reaching specific groups and can be more cost-effective than advertising. Nevertheless, it must be planned jointly with advertising.[91]

Clearly, creative public relations can affect public awareness at a fraction of the cost of advertising. The company doesn't pay for media space or time but only for a staff to develop and circulate the stories and manage certain events. An interesting story picked up by the media can be worth millions of dollars in equivalent advertising. Some experts say consumers are five times more likely to be influenced by editorial copy than by advertising. The following is an example of an award-winning PR campaign.[92]

Man Lives in IKEA

IKEA showed that a highly successful marketing campaign does not have to cost a lot of money if PR is properly employed. With its PR firm Ketchum, the company created the clever "Man Lives in IKEA" PR campaign. Using a budget of only $13 500, IKEA allowed comedian Mark Malkoff to live in an apartment in the Paramus, New Jersey, store from January 7 to 12, 2008, during which time he was allowed 24-hour access to film anything and everything. The campaign's goals included increasing sales, boosting traffic to IKEA-USA.com, and promoting two key brand messages: "IKEA has everything you need to live and make a home" and "Home is the most important place in the world." Ketchum and IKEA secured interviews with store executives and planned the week's schedule, which included a goodbye party featuring singer Lisa Loeb. Malkoff's team documented his interactions, including with security guards and customers relaxing in his "home," and posted 25 videos during the week. MarkLivesInIKEA.com received more than 15 million hits, and coverage of IKEA's home-related blog rose 356 percent from January 2007 to January 2008. IKEA calculated that the effort generated more than 382 million positive media impressions. Coverage highlights included the AP, *Today*, *Good Morning America*, and CNN. Sales at the Paramus store were up 5.5 percent compared with January 2007, while traffic to the IKEA website was up 6.8 percent.

Major Decisions in Marketing PR

In considering when and how to use MPR, management must establish the marketing objectives, choose the PR messages and vehicles, implement the plan carefully, and evaluate the results. The main tools of MPR are described in Table 18.6.

ESTABLISHING OBJECTIVES MPR can build awareness by placing stories in the media to bring attention to a product, service, person, organization, or idea. It can build *credibility* by communicating the message in an editorial context. It can help boost sales force and dealer *enthusiasm* with stories about a new product before it is launched. It can hold down *promotion cost* because MPR costs less than direct-mail and media advertising.

Whereas PR practitioners reach their target publics through the mass media, MPR is increasingly borrowing the techniques and technology of direct-response marketing to reach target audience members one-on-one.

CHOOSING MESSAGES AND VEHICLES Suppose a relatively unknown college wants more visibility. The MPR practitioner will search for stories. Are any faculty members working on unusual projects? Are any new and unusual courses being taught? Are any interesting events taking place on campus? If there are no interesting stories, the MPR practitioner should propose newsworthy events the college could sponsor. Here the challenge is to create meaningful news. PR ideas include hosting major academic conventions, inviting expert or celebrity speakers, and developing news conferences.

IMPLEMENTING THE PLAN AND EVALUATING RESULTS MPR's contribution to the bottom line is difficult to measure, because it is used along with other promotional tools.

The easiest measure of MPR effectiveness is the number of *exposures* carried by the media. Publicists supply the client with a clippings book showing all the media that carried news about the product and a summary statement such as the following:

Media coverage included 3,500 column inches of news and photographs in 350 publications with a combined circulation of 79.4 million; 2,500 minutes of air time on 290 radio stations and an

TABLE 18.6	MAJOR TOOLS IN MARKETING PR

Publications: Companies rely extensively on published materials to reach and influence their target markets. These materials include annual reports, brochures, articles, company newsletters and magazines, and audiovisual materials.

Events: Companies can draw attention to new products or other company activities by arranging and publicizing special events such as news conferences, seminars, outings, trade shows, exhibits, contests and competitions, and anniversaries that will reach the target publics.

Sponsorships: Companies can promote their brands and corporate name by sponsoring and publicizing sports and cultural events and highly regarded causes.

News: One of the major tasks of PR professionals is to find or create favourable news about the company, its products, and its people and to get the media to accept press releases and attend press conferences.

Speeches: Increasingly, company executives must field questions from the media or give talks at trade associations or sales meetings, and these appearances can build the company's image.

Public Service Activities: Companies can build goodwill by contributing money and time to good causes.

Identity Media: Companies need a visual identity that the public immediately recognizes. The visual identity is carried by company logos, stationery, brochures, signs, business forms, business cards, buildings, uniforms, and dress codes.

estimated audience of 65 million; and 660 minutes of air time on 160 television stations with an estimated audience of 91 million. If this time and space had been purchased at advertising rates, it would have amounted to $1,047,000.[93]

This measure is not very satisfying because it contains no indication of how many people actually read, heard, or recalled the message and what they thought afterward; nor does it contain information about the net audience reached, because publications overlap in readership. It also ignores the effects of electronic media. Publicity's goal is reach, not frequency, so it would be more useful to know the number of unduplicated exposures across all media types.

A better measure is the *change in product awareness, comprehension, or attitude* resulting from the MPR campaign (after allowing for the effect of other promotional tools). For example, how many people recall hearing the news item? How many told others about it (a measure of word of mouth)? How many changed their minds after hearing it?

SUMMARY

1. Advertising is any paid form of nonpersonal presentation and promotion of ideas, goods, or services by an identified sponsor. Advertisers include not only business firms but also charitable, nonprofit, and government agencies.

2. Developing an advertising program is a five-step process: (1) set advertising objectives, (2) establish a budget, (3) choose the advertising message and creative strategy, (4) decide on the media, and (5) evaluate communication and sales effects.

3. Sales promotion consists of mostly short-term incentive tools, designed to stimulate quicker or greater purchase of particular products or services by consumers or the trade.

4. In using sales promotion, a company must establish its objectives, select the tools, develop the program, pretest the program, implement and control it, and evaluate the results.

5. Events and experiences are a means to become part of special and more personally relevant moments in consumers' lives. Events can broaden and deepen the sponsor's relationship with its target market, but only if managed properly.

6. Public relations (PR) includes a variety of programs designed to promote or protect a company's image or its individual products. Marketing public relations (MPR), which support the marketing department in corporate or product promotion and image making, can affect public awareness at a fraction of the cost of advertising and is often much more credible. The main tools of MPR are publications, events, sponsorships, news, speeches, public service activities, and identity media.

APPLICATIONS

Marketing Debate: Should Marketers Test Advertising?

Advertising creatives have long lamented ad pretesting. They believe it inhibits their creative process and results in too much sameness in commercials. Marketers, on the other hand, believe pretesting provides necessary checks and balances to ensure the ad campaign will connect with consumers and be well-received in the marketplace.

Take a position: Ad pretesting in often an unnecessary waste of marketing dollars *versus* Ad pretesting provides an important diagnostic for marketers as to the likely success of an ad campaign.

Marketing Discussion: Television Advertising

What are some of your favourite TV ads? Why? How effective are the message and creative strategies? How are they creating consumer preference and loyalty and building brand equity?

MARKETING EXCELLENCE | COCA-COLA

When it comes to mass marketing, perhaps no one does it better than Coca-Cola. Coke is the most popular and best-selling soft drink in history. With an annual marketing budget of nearly $3 billion and annual sales exceeding $30 billion, the brand tops the Interbrand ranking year after year. Today, Coca-Cola holds a current brand value of $68 billion and reaches consumers in over 200 countries, making it the best-known product in the world. In fact, Coca-Cola is such a global phenomenon that its name is the second-most understood word in the world (after *okay*).

The history of Coke's success is astonishing. The drink was invented in 1886 by Dr. John S. Pemberton, who mixed a syrup of his own invention with carbonated water to cure headaches. The company's first president later turned the product into a pop culture phenomenon by introducing it to pharmacists and consumers around the world and handing out clocks, posters, and other paraphernalia with the Coca-Cola logo.

Coca-Cola believed early on that to gain worldwide acceptance, the brand needed to connect emotionally and socially with the masses, and the product needed to be "within arm's-length of desire." So the company focused on gaining extensive distribution and worked hard at making the product loved by all. In World War II, it declared that "every man in uniform gets a bottle of Coca-Cola for 5 cents, wherever he is, and whatever it costs the company." This strategy helped introduce the soft drink to people around the world as well as connect with them positively in a time of turmoil.

Why is Coca-Cola so much bigger than any other competitor? What Coke does better than everyone else is create highly current, uplifting global campaigns that translate well into different countries, languages, and cultures. Coke's advertising over the years has primarily focused on the product's ability to quench thirst and the brand's magical ability to connect people no matter who they are or how they live. Andy Warhol said it best: "A Coke is a Coke and no amount of money can get you a better Coke than the one the bum on the corner is drinking."

One of Coca-Cola's most memorable and successful commercials was called "Hilltop" and featured the song "I'd Like to Buy the World a Coke." Launched in 1971, the ad featured young adults from all over the world sharing a happy, harmonious moment and common bond (drinking a Coke) on a hillside in Italy. The commercial touched so many consumers emotionally and so effectively showed the worldwide appeal of Coke that the song became a top ten hit single later that year.

Coca-Cola's television commercials still touch upon the message of universal connection over a Coke, often in a lighthearted tone to appeal to a young audience. In one spot, a group of young adults sit around a campfire, playing the guitar, laughing, smiling, and passing around a bottle of Coke. The bottle reaches a slimy, one-eyed alien who joins in on the fun, takes a sip from the bottle, and passes it along. When the next drinker wipes off the slime in disgust, the music stops suddenly and the group stares at him in disappointment. The man hesitantly hands the bottle back to the alien to get re-slimed and then drinks from it, and the music and the party continue in perfect harmony.

Coca-Cola's mass communications strategy has evolved over the years and today mixes a wide range of media including television, radio, print, online, in-store, digital, billboard, public relations, events, paraphernalia, and even its own museum. The company's target audience and reach are so massive that choosing the right media and marketing message is critical. Coca-Cola uses big events to hit huge audiences; it has sponsored the Olympics since 1928 and advertises during the Super Bowl. Red Coke cups are placed front and centre during top-rated television shows like *American Idol,* and the company spends over $1 billion a year on sports sponsorships such as NASCAR and the World Cup. Coca-Cola's global campaigns must also be relevant on a local scale. In China, for example, Coca-Cola has given its regional managers control over its advertising so that they can include appropriate cultural messages.

The delicate balance between Coca-Cola's local and global marketing is crucial because, as one Coca-Cola executive explained, "Creating effective marketing at a local level in the absence of global scale can lead to huge inefficiencies." In 2006, for example, Coca-Cola ran two campaigns during the FIFA World Cup as well as several local campaigns. In 2010, the company ran a single campaign during the same event in over 100 markets. Executives at Coca-Cola estimated that the latter, more global strategy saved the company over $45 million.

Despite its unprecedented success over the years, Coke is not perfect. In 1985, in perhaps the worst product launch ever, Coca-Cola introduced New Coke—a sweeter concoction of the original secret formula. Consumers instantly rejected it and sales plummeted. Three months later, Coca-Cola retracted New Coke and relaunched the original formula under the name Coca-Cola Classic, to the delight of customers everywhere. Then-CEO Roberto Goizueta stated, "The simple fact is that all the time and money and skill poured into consumer research on the new Coca-Cola could not measure or reveal the deep and abiding emotional attachment to original Coca-Cola felt by so many people."

Coca-Cola's success at marketing a product on such a global, massive scale is unique. No other product is so universally available, accepted, and loved. As the company continues to grow, it seeks out new ways to better connect with even more individuals. Referring to itself as a "Happiness Factory," it is optimistic that it will succeed.

QUESTIONS

1. What does Coca-Cola stand for? Is it the same for everyone? Explain.

2. Coca-Cola has successfully marketed to billions of people around the world. Why is it so successful?

3. Can Pepsi or any other company ever surpass Coca-Cola? Why or why not? What are Coca-Cola's greatest risks?

Sources: Natalie Zmuda, "Coca-Cola Lays Out Its Vision for the Future at 2010 Meeting," *Advertising Age*, November 22, 2009; Natalie Zmuda, "Coke's 'Open Happiness' Keeps It Simple for Global Audience," *Advertising Age*, January 21, 2009; John Greenwald, "Will Teens Buy It?" *TIME*, June 24, 2001; "Coca-Cola Still Viewed as Most Valuable Brand," *USA Today*, September 18, 2009; Edward Rothstein, "Ingredients: Carbonated Water, High-Fructose Corniness..." *New York Times*, July 30, 2007; Brad Cook, "Coca-Cola: A Classic," *Brandchannel*, December 2, 2002; Coca-Cola, "Annual Report."

In This Chapter, We Will Address
the Following **Questions**

1. How can companies conduct direct marketing for competitive advantage?

2. How can companies carry out effective interactive marketing?

3. How does word of mouth affect marketing success?

4. What decisions do companies face in designing and managing a sales force?

5. How can salespeople improve their selling, negotiating, and relationship marketing skills?

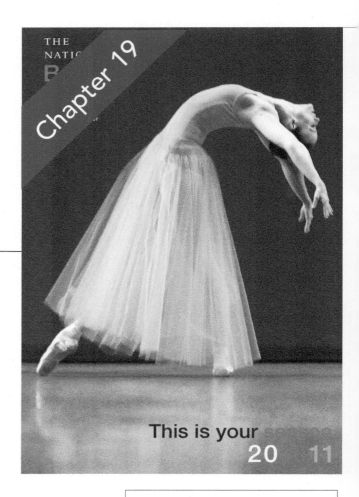

THE
NATIO
B

Chapter 19

This is your

20   11

The National Ballet of Canada uses its website and social media extensively to connect with ballet attendees.

Managing Personal Communications: Direct and Interactive Marketing, Word of Mouth, and Personal Selling

In the face of the Internet revolution, marketing communications today increasingly occur as a kind of personal dialogue between the company and its customers. Companies must ask not only "How should we reach our customers?" but also "How should our customers reach us?" and "How can our customers reach each other?" New technologies have encouraged companies to move from mass communication to more targeted, two-way communications. Consumers now play a much more participatory role in the marketing process.

Offered an entertainment experience rather than a tangible product, consumers walk away with a memory—one that hopefully encourages a repeat purchase. The National Ballet of Canada has found a way to extend the typical one-night ballet experience into an ongoing dialogue and relationship with attendees. Having performed for over 10 million people throughout Canada, the United States, Germany, the Netherlands, Israel, Hong Kong, Japan, Italy, and Mexico, Canada's premier dance company has made a name for itself internationally. By engaging audiences online, the company is able to keep this international status alive, building on existing relationships and creating new ones simultaneously.

Working in partnership with Ektron and Momentum Advanced Solutions, The National Ballet of Canada enhanced video and social integration on its website to create a unique customer experience. The website overhaul included integration with social network services such as Facebook, Twitter, YouTube, and Flickr to keep users up to speed on new performances and gain valuable feedback from them at the same time. For example, those who "fan" the ballet's Facebook page see company updates in their newsfeed. The updates may include an offer for free tickets or a link to recent reviews. Facebook fans have become a tangible asset to the company because fans are much more likely to attend performances and spread good word of mouth among friends than are nonfans.

The social media game is a balancing act of brand values and Internet savviness. The National Ballet of Canada has recognized the challenge it faces with its social media strategy. With a reputation of being both a classical and cutting-edge dance company, the ballet has focused its initiative on preserving the company's brand integrity while encouraging greater audience engagement.[1]

Marketers are trying to figure out the right way to be part of the consumer conversation. Personalizing communications and creating dialogues by saying and doing the right thing to the right person at the right time is critical for marketing effectiveness. In this chapter, we consider how companies personalize their marketing communications to have more impact. We begin by evaluating direct and interactive marketing, then move to word-of-mouth marketing, and finish by considering personal selling and the sales force.

DIRECT MARKETING

Today, many marketers build long-term relationships with customers. They send birthday cards, information materials, or small premiums. Airlines, hotels, and other businesses adopt frequency rewards programs and club programs.[2] **Direct marketing** is the use of consumer-direct (CD) channels to reach and deliver goods and services to customers without using marketing middlemen.

Direct marketers can use a number of channels to reach individual prospects and customers: direct mail, catalogues, telemarketing, interactive TV, kiosks, websites, and mobile devices. They often seek a measurable response, typically a customer order, through **direct-order marketing.**[3] Direct marketing has been a fast-growing avenue for serving customers, partly in response to the high and increasing costs of reaching business markets through a sales force. Sales produced through traditional direct marketing channels (catalogues, direct mail, and telemarketing) have been growing rapidly, along with direct-mail sales, which include sales to the consumer market, B2B sales, and fund-raising by charitable institutions.

The Benefits of Direct Marketing

Market demassification has resulted in an ever-increasing number of market niches. Consumers short of time and tired of traffic and parking headaches appreciate toll-free phone numbers, always-open websites, next-day delivery, and direct marketers' commitment to customer service. In addition, many chain stores have dropped slower-moving specialty items, creating an opportunity for direct marketers to promote these to interested buyers instead.

Sellers benefit from demassification as well. Direct marketers can buy a mailing list containing the names of almost any group: left-handed people, overweight people, millionaires. They can customize and personalize messages and build a continuous relationship with each customer. For example, new parents will receive periodic mailings describing new clothes, toys, and other goods as their child grows.

Direct marketing can reach prospects at the moment they want a solicitation and therefore be noticed by more highly-interested prospects. It lets marketers test alternative media and messages to find the most cost-effective approach. Direct marketing also makes the direct marketer's offer and strategy less visible to competitors. Finally, direct marketers can measure responses to their campaigns to decide which have been the most profitable.

While some companies specialize in selling their product through direct marketing channels only, others have learned to use this approach as part of an integrated marketing plan. These multifaceted campaigns must be aligned with other communications and channel activities.[4] Companies such as Eddie Bauer and Lands' End made fortunes building their brands in the direct marketing mail-order and phone-order business and then opened retail stores. While companies such as HanesBrands Inc. and Molson Canada have both used direct marketing campaigns to communicate new product offerings in a fresh and innovative way, they use these campaigns to cross-promote their stores, catalogues, and websites, by putting their web addresses on packaging materials, for example.[5]

Successful direct marketers view a customer interaction as an opportunity to up-sell, cross-sell, or just deepen a relationship. These marketers make sure they know enough about each customer to customize and personalize offers and messages and develop a plan for lifetime marketing to each valuable customer, based on their knowledge of life events and transitions. They also carefully orchestrate each element of their campaigns.

We next consider some of the key issues that characterize different direct marketing channels.

Direct Mail

Direct-mail marketing means sending an offer, announcement, reminder, or other item to an individual consumer. Using highly selective mailing lists, direct marketers send out millions of mail pieces each year—letters, flyers, foldouts, and other "salespeople with wings." Some direct marketers mail multimedia DVDs to prospects and customers.

Direct mail is a popular medium because it permits target market selectivity, can be personalized, is flexible, and allows early testing and response measurement. Although the cost per thousand is higher than for mass media, the people reached are much better prospects. The success of direct mail, however, has also become its liability—so many marketers are sending out direct-mail pieces that mailboxes are becoming stuffed, leading some consumers to disregard the blizzard of solicitations they receive.

In constructing an effective direct-mail campaign, direct marketers must choose the following: objectives, target markets and prospects, offer elements, means of testing the campaign, and measures of campaign success.

OBJECTIVES   Most direct marketers aim to receive an order from prospects and judge a campaign's success by the response rate. An order-response rate of 2 percent to 4 percent is normally considered good, although this number varies with product category, price, and the nature of the offering.[6] Direct mail can also produce prospect leads, strengthen customer relationships, inform and educate customers, remind customers of offers, and reinforce recent customer purchase decisions.

TARGET MARKETS AND PROSPECTS   Most direct marketers apply the RFM (*recency, frequency, monetary amount*) formula to select customers according to how much time has passed since their last purchase, how many times they have purchased, and how much they have spent since becoming a customer. Suppose the company is offering a leather jacket. It might make this offer to the most attractive customers—those who made their last purchase between 30 and 60 days ago, those who make three to six purchases a year, and those who have spent at least $100 since becoming customers. Points are established for varying RFM levels; the more points, the more attractive the customer.[7]

Marketers also identify prospects on the basis of age, sex, income, education, previous mail-order purchases, and occasion. First-year university students will buy laptop computers, backpacks, and compact refrigerators; newlyweds look for housing, furniture, appliances, and bank loans. Another useful variable is consumer lifestyle or "passions" such as electronics, cooking, and the outdoors. Hilton Hotels identified business travellers in the fall season as its target for a particular promotion.

Hilton Hotels

Hilton is one of the most recognized names in the hospitality industry, with more than 3500 hotels and resorts in 76 countries across six continents. The Hilton HHonors program is a points-and-miles program that awards members points for stays in Hilton Hotels, and miles for over 50 different airline partners. Hilton Hotels began the "Spend a Sunday" HHonors promotion, where members, especially business travellers, are encouraged to extend their trip to include a Sunday in order to gain quadruple points for their stay. The promotion was done during the fall, when business travel increases, and the idea was to encourage business travellers to add a day or two of leisure to their business trips.[8]

Dun & Bradstreet provides a wealth of data for B2B direct marketing. Here the prospect is often not an individual but a group or committee of both decision makers and decision influencers. Each member needs to be treated differently, and the timing, frequency, nature, and format of contact must reflect the member's status and role.

The company's best prospects are customers who have bought its products in the past. The direct marketer can also buy lists of names from list brokers, but these lists often have problems, including name duplication, incomplete data, and obsolete addresses. Better lists include overlays of demographic and psychographic information. Direct marketers typically buy and test a sample before buying more names from the same list. They can build their own lists by advertising a promotional offer and collecting responses.

OFFER ELEMENTS   The offer strategy has five elements—the *product,* the *offer,* the *medium,* the *distribution method,* and the *creative strategy.*[9] Fortunately, all can be tested. The direct-mail marketer also must choose five components of the mailing itself: the outside envelope, sales letter, circular, reply form, and reply envelope. A common direct marketing strategy is to follow up direct mail with an email.

TESTING ELEMENTS   One of the great advantages of direct marketing is the ability to test, under real marketplace conditions, different elements of an offer strategy, such as products, product features, copy platform, mailer type, envelope, prices, or mailing lists.

Response rates typically understate a campaign's long-term impact. Suppose only 2 percent of the recipients who receive a direct-mail piece advertising Samsonite luggage place an order. A much larger percentage became aware of the product (direct mail has high readership), and some percentage may have formed an intention to buy at a later date (either by mail or at a retail outlet). Some may mention Samsonite luggage to others as a result of the direct-mail piece. To better estimate a promotion's impact, some companies measure the impact of direct marketing on awareness, intention to buy, and word of mouth.

MEASURING CAMPAIGN SUCCESS: LIFETIME VALUE   By adding up the planned campaign costs, the direct marketer can determine the needed break-even response rate. This rate must be net of returned merchandise and bad debts. A specific campaign may fail to break even in the short run but can still be profitable in the long run if customer lifetime value is factored in (see Chapter 5) by calculating the average customer longevity, average customer annual expenditure, and average gross margin, minus the average cost of customer acquisition and maintenance (discounted for the opportunity cost of money).[10]

Catalogue Marketing

In catalogue marketing, companies may send full-line merchandise catalogues, specialty consumer catalogues, and business catalogues, usually in print form but also as DVDs or online. Catalogue marketing has a long history in Canada. In the 1880s, Canadians living in isolated regions waited eagerly for catalogues to arrive. So beloved was the Eaton's catalogue, for example, that it was affectionately known by many nicknames, including the "Bible" and the "Wish Book."[11] To this day, many businesses send out catalogues. Companies such as Zellers and Sears send general merchandise catalogues while Victoria's Secret and Harry Rosen send specialty-clothing catalogues. Through its catalogues, Avon sells cosmetics and IKEA sells furnishings. Thousands of small businesses also issue specialty catalogues. Larger businesses such as Staples, Grand & Toy, and Sauder send catalogues to their business prospects and customers.

Catalogues are a huge business in North America. The Direct Marketing Association estimates that there are currently up to 10 000 mail-order catalogues of all kinds. However, the number of catalogues streaming into consumers' mailboxes is not the only measure of growth in this business. Cataloguers have gotten a big boost from the Internet—about three-quarters of catalogue companies present merchandise and take orders over the Internet. Some catalogue marketers, like Sears, are integrating their print editions with online editions. Others, like Nike, are totally replacing their print catalogues with virtual versions. Market research conducted by Canada Post suggests, however, that Canadians overwhelmingly prefer hard-copy catalogues to online versions, and would rather receive catalogues through the mail than pick them up from a store.[12]

The success of a catalogue business depends on managing customer lists carefully to avoid duplication or bad debts, controlling inventory, offering good-quality merchandise so returns are low, and projecting a distinctive image. Some companies add literary or information features, send swatches of materials, operate a special online or telephone hotline to answer questions, send gifts to their best customers, and donate a percentage of profits to good causes. Putting their entire catalogue online also provides business marketers with better access to global consumers than ever before, saving printing and mailing costs. See how IKEA uses its catalogue for more than just informing customers about its products.

IKEA

IKEA began as a small Swedish furniture retailer, and is now a major retail experience around the world. A major part of the IKEA retail experience is its catalogue, printed in 38 different versions, in 17 languages, for 28 countries. Because the catalogue is IKEA's main selling tool, 70 percent of the annual marketing budget is spent on the catalogue alone. In an effort to interact with customers, IKEA Canada developed contests using its catalogue as a major communications medium. A "Capture the Page" contest was developed to hype the arrival of the new catalogue, with contests encouraging consumers to upload pictures of their favourite images from the catalogue for a chance to win IKEA gift cards.[13]

Telemarketing

Telemarketing is the use of telephones and call centres to attract prospects, sell to existing customers, and provide service by taking orders and answering questions. It helps companies increase revenue, reduce selling costs, and improve customer satisfaction. Companies use call centres for *inbound telemarketing*—receiving calls from customers—and *outbound telemarketing*—initiating calls to prospects and customers.

Telemarketing is a major industry in Canada, creating 155 000 new jobs each year. Marketers spend approximately twice as much on telemarketing as they do on advertising, which isn't surprising since telemarketing generates approximately $26 billion in sales. Although outbound telemarketing historically has been a major direct marketing tool, its potentially intrusive nature led the Canadian Radio-television and Telecommunications Commission (CRTC) to establish a National Do Not Call List, similar to one established previously in the United States. Even though the Canadian Marketing Association (CMA) had maintained a voluntary "Do Not Contact" service list since 1988, many agreed that a national list was needed since the CMA's list applied only to member companies and was not legally binding. The CRTC's list reduces the number of telemarketing calls by allowing consumers to register their residential, wireless, fax, and VoIP telephone numbers.[14] Because only political organizations, charities, marketing researchers, or companies with existing relationships with consumers are exempt, consumer telemarketing has lost much of its effectiveness.[15]

Business-to-business telemarketing is increasing, however. Raleigh Bicycles used telemarketing to reduce the personal selling costs of contacting its dealers. In the first year, sales force travel costs dropped 50 percent and sales in a single quarter went up 34 percent. As it improves with the use of videophones, telemarketing will increasingly replace, though never eliminate, more expensive field sales calls.

Other Media for Direct-Response Marketing

Direct marketers use all the major media. Newspapers and magazines carry ads offering books, clothing, appliances, vacations, and other goods and services that individuals can order via toll-free numbers. Radio ads present offers 24 hours a day. Some companies prepare 30- and 60-minute *infomercials* to combine the sell of television commercials with the draw of information and entertainment. Infomercials promote products that are complicated or technologically advanced, or that require a great deal of explanation (Carnival cruises, Mercedes, Universal Studios, and even Monster.com). At-home shopping channels are dedicated to selling goods and services on a toll-free number or via the web for delivery within 48 hours. Kiosks are a popular alternative medium for direct marketing. Curiosk provides kiosks for the wine industry.

Curiosk supplies interactive kiosks to wine stores across Canada.

Curiosk Marketing Solutions

Since 2007, Curiosk Marketing Solutions Inc. has been supplying its in-store touch-screen kiosk to wine stores. At the kiosk, consumers can scan the bar code on a bottle of wine to bring up a display of detailed product information on that particular wine. In addition, consumers are given the option to create a personalized greeting card that fits over the neck of the bottle. The card includes information about their wine selection, such as tasting notes, food pairing suggestions, and cellaring recommendations. The kiosk then allows consumers to preview their card before printing it, and includes a detachable receipt that allows them to pay for the card along with their other purchases.[16]

Public and Ethical Issues in Direct Marketing

Direct marketers and their customers usually enjoy mutually rewarding relationships. Occasionally, however, a darker side emerges:

- *Irritation.* Many people don't like hard-sell direct marketing solicitations.

- *Unfairness.* Some direct marketers take advantage of impulsive or less sophisticated buyers or prey on the vulnerable, especially the elderly.[17]

- *Deception and fraud.* Some direct marketers design mailers and write copy intended to mislead or exaggerate product size, performance claims, or the "retail price." PhoneBusters, a national anti-fraud service jointly operated by the RCMP, the Ontario Provincial Police, and the Competition Bureau, receives thousands of complaints each year about fraudulent telemarketing phone calls.[18]

- *Invasion of privacy.* It seems that almost every time consumers order products by mail or telephone, apply for a credit card, or take out a magazine subscription, their names, addresses, and purchasing behaviour may be added to several company databases. Critics worry that marketers may know too much about consumers' lives, and that they may use this knowledge to take unfair advantage.

People in the direct marketing industry know that, left unattended, such problems will lead to increasingly negative consumer attitudes, lower response rates, and calls for greater provincial and federal regulation. Most direct marketers want the same thing consumers want: honest and well-designed marketing offers targeted to only those who appreciate hearing about them.

INTERACTIVE MARKETING

The newest and fastest-growing channels for communicating and selling directly to customers are electronic.[19] The Internet provides marketers and consumers with opportunities for much greater *interaction* and *individualization.* Soon few marketing programs will be considered complete without a meaningful online component.

Electronic marketing is showing explosive growth. A 2010 Statistics Canada report stated that 92 percent of Canadians households have access to broadband connectivity, necessary for swift downloading of dense digital video and music files. These new capabilities have spurred the growth of rich media ads that combine animation, video, and sound with interactive features.[20]

Online	4:13
TV and video	3:17
Music and radio	1:26
Mobile phone	1:18
Landline phone	0:36
Gaming	0:36
Reading	0:24

FIGURE 19.1

Average Time Spent per Day with Select Media According to U.S. Consumers, 2009 (hrs:mins)

Source: Yankee Group's 2011 U.S. Consumer Survey, September.

Advantages and Disadvantages of Interactive Marketing

The variety of online communication options means companies can send tailored messages that engage consumers by reflecting their special interests and behaviour. The Internet is also highly accountable and its effects can be easily traced by noting how many unique visitors or "UVs" click on a page or ad, how long they spend with it, and where they go afterward.[21]

Marketers can build or tap into online communities, inviting participation from consumers and creating a long-term marketing asset in the process. The web offers the advantage of *contextual placement,* buying ads on sites related to the marketer's offerings. Marketers can also place advertising based on keywords from search engines, to reach people when they've actually started the buying process.

Using the web also has disadvantages. Consumers can effectively screen out most messages. Marketers may think their ads are more effective than they are if bogus clicks are generated by software-powered websites.[22] Advertisers also lose some control over their online messages, which can be hacked or vandalized.

But many feel the pros outweigh the cons, and the web is attracting marketers of all kinds. Beauty pioneer Estée Lauder, who said she relied on three means of communication to build her multimillion-dollar cosmetics business—"telephone, telegraph, and tell a woman"—would now have to add the web, where the company's official site describes new and old products, announces special offers and promotions, and helps customers locate stores where they can buy Estée Lauder products.[23]

Marketers must go where the customers are, and increasingly that's online. In 2011, U.S. consumers spent over 25 percent of their media time online (see Figure 19.1). Customers define the rules of engagement, however, and insulate themselves with the help of agents and intermediaries if they so choose. Customers define what information they need, what offerings they're interested in, and what they're willing to pay.[24]

Online advertising continues to gain on traditional media. Although the global recession saw advertising through traditional media decline, online advertising continues to rise. Total Internet ad spending worldwide grew to almost US$62 billion in 2010, with this number expected to near US$100 billion by 2014.[25] Helping fuel online growth is the emergence of rich media ads that combine animation, video, and sound with interactive features.[26] Consider what Burger King has done online.

Burger King

"If you have a global brand promise, 'Have It Your Way,'" said Russ Klein, Burger King's former President for Global Marketing, Strategy, and Innovation, "it's about putting the customer in charge," even if they say "bad things" about the brand. In competing against McDonald's, with its family-friendly image, "it's more important for us to be provocative than pleasant," added Klein, especially when appealing to a market of mainly teenage boys. Burger King's brash ad campaigns—featuring its creepy bobblehead king and talking chicken—have appeared on YouTube and MySpace, so the company can take advantage of "social connectivity" as consumers react to the ads. Burger King encourages customers to build online communities around their favourite company icons and products. To celebrate the 50th anniversary of its popular Whopper hamburger, the company took over a Burger King restaurant in Las Vegas for a day and told people the Whopper had been permanently removed from the menu. Customers' outraged reactions were filmed as part of an award-winning campaign dubbed "Whopper Freakout," which served as the basis of TV ads and online videos. Over 5 million consumers watched an eight-minute streaming video, another 14 million watched it or the TV spots on YouTube, and millions more heard or read about it via PR or word of mouth.[27]

Interactive Marketing Communication Options

A company chooses which forms of interactive marketing will be most cost-effective in achieving communications and sales objectives.[28] Some of the main categories, discussed next, are (1) websites, (2) search ads, (3) display ads, and (4) emails. After summarizing some developments in mobile marketing, we'll describe social media and word-of-mouth effects.

WEBSITES Companies must design websites that embody or express their purpose, history, products, and vision, and that are attractive on first viewing and interesting enough to encourage repeat visits.[29] Jeffrey Rayport and Bernard Jaworski propose that effective sites feature seven design elements they call the 7Cs (see Figure 19.2). To encourage repeat visits, companies must pay special attention to context and content factors and embrace another "C"—constant change.[30]

- *Context.* Layout and design
- *Content.* Text, pictures, sound, and video the site contains
- *Community.* How the site enables user-to-user communication
- *Customization.* Site's ability to tailor itself to different users or to allow users to personalize the site
- *Communication.* How the site enables site-to-user, user-to-site, or two-way communication
- *Connection.* Degree that the site is linked to other sites
- *Commerce.* Site's capabilities to enable commercial transactions

FIGURE 19.2

Seven Key Design Elements of an Effective Web Site

Source: Jeffrey F. Rayport and Bernard J. Jaworski, *e-commerce* (New York: McGraw-Hill, 2001), p. 116.*

Visitors will judge a site's performance on ease of use and physical attractiveness.[31] *Ease of use* means (1) the site downloads quickly, (2) the first page is easy to understand, and (3) it is easy to navigate to other pages that open quickly. *Physical attractiveness* is assured when (1) individual pages are clean and not crammed with content, (2) typefaces and font sizes are very readable, and (3) the site makes good use of colour (and sound).

Firms such as comScore and Nielsen Online track where consumers go online through page views, unique visitors, length of visit, and so on.[32] Companies must also be sensitive to online security and privacy-protection issues.[33]

Besides their websites, companies may employ **microsites**, individual webpages or clusters of pages that function as supplements to a primary site. They're particularly relevant for companies selling low-interest products. People rarely visit an insurance company's website, but the company can create a micro-site on used-car sites that offers advice for buyers of used cars and at the same time a good insurance deal.

Consider how the Liquor Control Board of Ontario (LCBO) drove consumers online to interact with its website.

LCBO

The Liquor Control Board of Ontario (LCBO) held virtual wine tastings to promote and show the quality and taste of Ontario wines. The wine tastings were a way to get Ontarians excited about wines that are grown right in their backyard. The live webcasts were set on three different days, and featured four different cool-climate wines each week, with wine experts on hand to taste and compare the wines. LCBO consumers were encouraged to participate at home by hosting their own wine tastings and to watch the tastings and email questions or comments in real time to the experts.[34]

SEARCH ADS A hot growth area in interactive marketing is **paid search** or **pay-per-click ads**, which now account for roughly half of all online ad spending.[35] Thirty-five percent of all searches are reportedly for products or services.

In paid search, marketers bid in a continuous auction on search terms that serve as a proxy for the consumer's product or consumption interests. When a consumer searches for any of the words with Google, Yahoo!, or Bing, the marketer's ad may appear above or next to the results, depending on the amount the company bids and an algorithm the search engines use to determine an ad's relevance to a particular search.[36]

Advertisers pay only if people click on the links, but marketers believe consumers who have already expressed interest by engaging in a search are prime prospects. Average click-through is about 2 percent, much more than for comparable online ads. The cost per click depends on how high the link is ranked and the popularity of the keyword. The ever-increasing popularity of paid search has increased competition among keyword bidders, significantly raising search prices and putting a premium on choosing the best possible keywords, bidding on them strategically, and monitoring the results for effectiveness and efficiency.

The LCBO drew customers to its website and engaged them by having them participate in virtual wine-tasting events.

Search engine optimization has become a crucial part of marketing given the large amount of money being spent by marketers on search ads. A number of guidelines have been suggested for more effective search ads.[37] Broader search terms are useful for general brand building; more specific ones—for example, specifying a particular product model or service—are useful for generating and converting sales leads. Search terms need to be spotlighted on the appropriate pages so search engines can easily identify them. Multiple keywords are usually needed for any one product, but each keyword must be bid for according to its likely return on revenue. It also helps to have popular sites link back to the site. Data can be collected to track the effects of paid search.

DISPLAY ADS **Display ads** or **banner ads** are small, rectangular boxes containing text and perhaps a picture, and companies pay to place these ads on relevant websites.[38] The larger the audience, the higher the cost. Some banners are accepted on a barter basis. In the early days of the Internet, viewers clicked on 2 percent to 3 percent of the banner ads they saw, but that percentage quickly plummeted to as little as 0.25 percent and advertisers began to explore other forms of communication.

Given that Internet users spend only 5 percent of their time online actually searching for information, display ads still hold great promise compared with popular search ads. But ads need to be more attention-getting and influential, better targeted, and more closely tracked.[39]

Interstitials are advertisements, often with video or animation, which pop up between changes on a website. For example, ads for Johnson & Johnson's Tylenol headache reliever would pop up on brokers' websites whenever the stock market fell by 100 points or more. Because consumers find pop-up ads intrusive and distracting, many consumers use software to block them.

A popular vehicle for advertising is *podcasts*, digital media files created for playback on portable MP3 players, laptops, or PCs. Sponsors pay roughly $25 per thousand listeners to run a 15- or 30-second audio ad at the beginning of the podcast. Although these rates are higher than for popular radio shows, podcasts are able to reach very specific market segments, and their popularity has grown.[40]

EMAIL Email allows marketers to inform and communicate with customers at a fraction of the cost of a "dmail," or direct mail, campaign. Consumers are besieged by emails, though, and many employ spam filters. Some firms are asking consumers to say whether and when they would like to receive emails. FTD, the flower retailer, allows customers to choose whether to receive email reminders to send flowers for virtually any holiday as well as specific birthdays and anniversaries.[41]

Emails must be timely, targeted, and relevant. For example, Groupon, the online coupon phenomenon that sends deal-of-the-day emails to more than 70 million subscribers worldwide, experienced incredible growth by sending nontraditional offers for coupons. The company has 70 comedy writers on staff who compose absurd write-ups that accompany each daily email, grabbing the attention of readers and encouraging them to visit the Groupon website to purchase that day's coupon.[42] "Marketing Memo: How to Maximize the Marketing Value of Emails" provides some important guidelines for productive email campaigns.

MOBILE MARKETING With cell phones' ubiquitous nature and marketers' ability to personalize messages based on demographics and other consumer behaviour characteristics (see Chapter 15), the appeal of mobile marketing as a communication tool is obvious.[43]

With over 5 billion mobile subscribers in the world in 2010—there are more than twice as many mobile phones in the world as personal computers—cell phones represent a major opportunity for advertisers to reach consumers on the "third screen" (TV and the computer are first and second).[44] Some firms are moving fast into m-space. One mobile pioneer in the banking industry is Bank of America.[45]

Bank of America

Bank of America is using mobile as a communications channel and a means to provide banking solutions for the many ways its customers lead their lives. More than 2 million of its 59 million customers use mobile banking applications, which the bank credits as a significant drawing card given that 8 percent to 10 percent of these mobile users are new customers. Initially, the bank targeted a younger group of users between 18 and 30 years old—with special emphasis on college students—but its mobile banking services increasingly appeal to other groups such as older, higher-income users. Its smartphone apps and traditional browser-based solutions have been praised for clean navigation, ease of use, and reach. The branch and ATM locator, for instance, is used by one in eight mobile customers. Mobile marketing is integrated all through the bank's marketing efforts: The website provides demos and tours of its mobile services; the TV campaigns stress the benefits of its mobile banking. With one click on a mobile banner ad, smartphone users can download the free Bank of America app or just learn more about its mobile banking services.

| MARKETING **MEMO** | HOW TO MAXIMIZE THE MARKETING VALUE OF EMAILS |

- **Give the customer a reason to respond.** Companies should offer powerful incentives for reading email pitches and online ads, such as trivia games, scavenger hunts, and instant-win sweepstakes.

- **Personalize the content of your emails.** Customers who agree to receive IBM's weekly *iSource* newsletter select "the news they choose" from topics on an interest profile.

- **Offer something the customer can't get via direct mail.** Because email campaigns can be carried out quickly, they can offer time-sensitive information. Travelocity sends frequent emails pitching last-minute cheap airfares, and Club Med pitches unsold vacation packages at a discount.

- **Make it easy for customers to unsubscribe.** Online customers demand a positive exit experience. Dissatisfied customers leaving on a sour note are more likely to spread the displeasure to others.

- **Combine with other communications such as social media.** Southwest Airlines found that the highest number of reservations occurs after an email campaign followed by a social media campaign. Papa John's was able to add 45 000 fans to its Facebook page through an email campaign inviting customers to participate in a "March Madness" NCAA basketball tournament contest.

To increase the effectiveness of emails, some researchers are employing "heat mapping," by which they can measure what people read on a computer screen by using cameras attached to a computer that track eye movements. One study showed that clickable graphic icons and buttons that linked to more details of a marketing offer increased click-through rates by 60 percent over links that used just an Internet address.

Sources: Richard Westlund, "Success Stories in eMail Marketing," *Adweek Special Advertising Section to Adweek, Brandweek, and Mediaweek*, February 16, 2010; Suzanne Vranica, "Marketers Give E-Mail Another Look," *Wall Street Journal*, July 17, 2006; Seth Godin, *Permission Marketing: Turning Strangers into Friends and Friends into Customers* (New York: Simon & Schuster, 1999).

As mobile technology develops, the options available to marketers to develop their mobile marketing programs are constantly increasing:

- *Mobile marketing options.* Mobile ad spending was almost $1 billion worldwide in 2009, most of which went into SMS text messages and simple display ads. With the increased capabilities of smartphones, however, mobile ads can be more than just a display medium using static "mini-billboards."[46]

  Much recent interest has been generated in mobile apps—"bite-sized" software programs that can be loaded on to smartphones. In a short time, thousands were introduced by companies large and small. VW chose to launch its GTI in the United States with an iPhone app, receiving 2 million downloads in three weeks. In Europe, it launched the VW Tiguan with a mobile app as well as text messages and an interstitial website. Due to its wide selection of diesel vehicles, VW released a BlackBerry app in Canada allowing users to locate the nearest diesel station relative to their current GPS location or to any Canadian address.[47]

  Smartphones also allow loyalty programs with which customers can track their visits and purchases at a merchant and receive rewards.[48] By tracking the location of receptive customers who opt in to receive communications, retailers can send them location-specific promotions when they are in proximity to shops or outlets. Coca-Cola, Cadbury, Red Bull, and Kraft ran proximity campaigns using Bluetooth technology to send customers ads and coupons for various products while they shopped in one of 1400 Mac's/Couche-Tard convenience stores across Canada.[49]

  With traditional coupon redemption rates declining for years, the ability of cell phones to permit more relevant and timely offers to consumers at or near the point of purchase has piqued the interest of many marketers. These new coupons can take all forms; digital in-store signs can now dispense them to smartphones.[50]

- *Developing mobile marketing programs.* Even with newer-generation smartphones, the web experience can be very different for users, given smaller screen sizes, longer downloads, and the lack of some software capabilities (such as Adobe Flash Player on iPhones). Marketers would be wise to design simple, clear, and clean sites, paying even greater attention than usual to user experience and navigation.[51]

Canadian marketers can learn much about mobile marketing by looking overseas. In developed Asian markets such as Hong Kong, Japan, Singapore, and South Korea, mobile marketing is fast becoming a central component of customer experiences.[52] In developing markets, high cell phone penetration also makes mobile marketing attractive. A pioneer in China, Coca-Cola created a national campaign asking Beijing residents to send text messages guessing the high temperature in the city every day for just over a month, for a chance to win a one-year supply of Coke products. The campaign attracted more than 4 million messages over the course of 35 days.[53]

Although a growing population segment uses mobile phones for everything from entertainment to banking, different people have different attitudes and experiences with mobile technology. "Marketing Memo: Segmenting Tech Users" profiles the role of mobile Internet access in several groups' digital lifestyles.

WORD OF MOUTH

Consumers use *word of mouth* to talk about dozens of brands each day, from media and entertainment products such as movies, TV shows, and publications to food products, travel services, and retail stores.[54]

Companies are acutely aware of the power of word of mouth. Brands such as Hush Puppies shoes, Krispy Kreme doughnuts, the blockbuster movie *The Passion of the Christ,* and, more recently, Crocs shoes have been built through strong word of mouth, as were companies such as The Body Shop, Palm, Red Bull, Starbucks, and Amazon.com.

Positive word of mouth sometimes happens organically with little advertising, but it can also be managed and facilitated.[55] It is particularly effective for locally owned businesses, with whom customers may feel a more personal relationship. Many of these small businesses are investing in various forms of social media at the expense of newspapers, radio, and the Yellow Pages to get the word out. The Winnipeg-based Royal Winnipeg Ballet relies on word of mouth as a way of advertising upcoming events, including its annual Ballet in the Park held each summer, via a community of fans on Facebook and Twitter.[56]

With the growth of social media, marketers sometimes distinguish paid media from earned or free media, as Chapter 17 noted. Although different points of view prevail, many people believe that *paid media*

MARKETING **MEMO**			SEGMENTING TECH USERS
Group Name	**% of Adults**	**What You Need to Know About Them**	**Key Demographic Facts**
Motivated by Mobility (39%)			
Digital Collaborators	8%	With the most tech assets, Digital Collaborators use them to work with and share their creations with others. They are enthusiastic about how ICTs help them connect with others and confident in how to manage digital devices and information.	Mostly male (56%), late 30s, well-educated, and well-off.
Ambivalent Networkers	7%	Ambivalent Networkers have folded mobile devices into how they run their social lives, texting or social networking tools online. They rely on ICTs for entertainment. But they also express worries about connectivity; some find that mobile devices are intrusive and many think it is good to take a break from online use.	Primarily male (60%), they are young (late 20s) and ethnically diverse.

Media Movers	7%	Media Movers have a wide range of online and mobile habits, and they are bound to find or create an information nugget, such as a digital photo, and pass it on. These social exchanges are central to this group's use of ICTs. Cyberspace, as a pathto personal productivity or an outlet for creativity, is less important.	Males (56%) in their mid-30s, many with children and in middle income range.
Roving Nodes	9%	Roving Nodes are active managers of their social and work lives using their mobile device. They get the most out of basic applications with their assets such as e-mail or texting and find them great for arranging the logistics of their lives and enhancing personal productivity.	Mostly women (56%), in their late 30s, well educated and well-off.
Mobile Newbies	8%	This group rates low on tech assets, but its members really like their cell phones. Mobile Newbies, many of whom acquired a cell in the past year, like how the device helps them be more available to others. They would be hard pressed to give up the cell phone.	Mainly women (55%), about age 50, lower educational and income levels.

Stationary Media Majority (61%)

Desktop Veterans	13%	This group of older, veteran online users is content to use a high-speed connection and a desktop computer to explore the Internet and stay in touch with friends, placing their cell phone and mobile applications in the background.	Mainly men (55%), in their mid 40s, well-educated and well-off economically.
Drifting Surfers	14%	Many have the requisite tech assets, such as broadband or a cell phone, but Drifting Surfers are infrequent online users. When they use technology, it is for basic information gathering. It wouldn't bother the typical Drifting Surfer to give up the Internet or a cell phone.	Majority women (56%), in their early 40s, middle income, and average education levels.
Information Encumbered	10%	Most people in this group suffer from information overload and think taking time off from the Internet is a good thing. The Information Encumbered are firmly rooted in old media to get information.	Two-thirds men, in their early 50s, average education, lower-middle income.
Tech Indifferent	10%	Members of this group are not heavy Internet users and although most have cell phones, they don't like their intrusiveness. The Indifferent could easily do without modern gadgets and services.	Mainly women (55%), in their late 50s, low-income and education levels
Off the Network	14%	Members of this group have neither cell phones nor online access, and tend to be older and low-income. But a few have experience with ICTs; some used to have online access and as many as one in five used to have a cell phone.	Low-income senior women, high share of African Americans.

Source: "The Mobile Difference—Tech User Types," Pew Internet & American Life Project, March 31, 2009, www.pewinternet.org/Infographics/The-Mobile-Difference—Tech-User-Types.aspx.

results from press coverage of company-generated advertising, publicity, or other promotional efforts. *Earned media,* sometimes called *free media,* is all the PR benefits a firm receives without having directly paid for anything—all the news stories, blogs, and social network conversations that deal with a brand. Earned media isn't literally free. The company has to invest in products, services, and their marketing to some degree to get people to pay attention to and write and talk about them, but the expenses are not devoted to eliciting a media response.

We first consider how social media promotes the flow of word of mouth before delving into more detail on how word of mouth is formed and travels.

Social Media

Social media are a means for consumers to share text, images, audio, and video information with each other and with companies and vice versa. Social media allow marketers to establish a public voice and presence on the web and reinforce other communications activities. Because of their day-to-day immediacy, social media can also encourage companies to stay innovative and relevant.

There are three main platforms for social media: (1) online communities and forums, (2) blogs (by individuals and networks such as Sugar and Gawker), and (3) social networks (like Facebook, Twitter, and YouTube).

ONLINE COMMUNITIES AND FORUMS Online communities and forums come in all shapes and sizes. Many are created by consumers or groups of consumers with no commercial interests or company affiliations. Others are sponsored by companies whose members communicate with the company and with each other through postings, instant messaging, and chat discussions about special interests related to the company's products and brands. These online communities and forums can be a valuable resource for companies and provide multiple functions by both collecting and conveying key information.

A key for success of online communities is to create individual and group activities that help form bonds among community members. The Idea Center at Kodak Gallery is an online community for exchanging ideas about how to use Kodak products to create personalized gifts and other creative products using digital photos. Kodak has found that peer-to-peer recommendations within the community led to more frequent, larger purchases.[57] Apple hosts a large number of discussion groups organized by product lines and also by consumer versus professional use. These groups are customers' primary source of product information after warranties expire.

Information flow in online communities and forums is two-way and can provide companies with useful, hard-to-get customer information and insights. When GlaxoSmithKline prepared to launch its first weight-loss drug, Alli, it sponsored a weight-loss community. The firm felt the feedback it gained was more valuable than what it could have received from traditional focus groups. Research has shown, however, that firms should avoid too much democratization of innovation. Groundbreaking ideas can be replaced by lowest-common-denominator solutions.[58] MTS Allstream found that its intranet was a useful medium to generate good ideas.

MTS Allstream

As one of Canada's leading national communication solutions companies, MTS Allstream provides innovative communications that complement the ways in which Canadians live and work today. As well, with more than 5500 employees across the country, MTS Allstream has developed an innovative method for communication among its workers. In 2009, the company identified the need for a tool that could be used to facilitate an ongoing conversation between leaders and employees and to support its various face-to-face communication vehicles. From this was created Idea Factory, an idea-sharing social media intranet where employees can submit ideas for improving the business and customer experience, comment and vote on others' ideas, volunteer to be part of the solution, and watch as ideas are turned into action. On average, the site receives more than 1700 visits per month, and 76 percent of employees consider it a functional venue in which they can be heard.[59]

BLOGS *Blogs,* regularly updated online journals or diaries, have become an important outlet for word of mouth. There are millions in existence and they vary widely, some personal for close friends and families, others designed to reach and influence a vast audience. One obvious appeal of blogs is bringing together people with common interests. Blog networks such as Gawker Media offer marketers a portfolio of choices. Online celebrity gossip blog PopSugar has spawned a family of breezy blogs on fashion (FabSugar), beauty (BellaSugar), and romance and culture (TrèsSugar), attracting women aged 18 to 49.[60]

MTS Allstream's Idea Factory brings employees' ideas to the forefront through the use of a social media platform.

Corporations are creating their own blogs and carefully monitoring those of others.[61] Blog search engines provide up-to-the-minute analysis of millions of blogs to find out what's on people's minds.[62] Popular blogs are creating influential opinion leaders. At the TreeHugger site, a team of bloggers tracks green consumer products for 3.5 million unique visitors per month, offering video and reference guides and an average of 35 daily posts.[63]

Studies show that when Canadian consumers research a product online, over 70 percent visit retailer and manufacturer websites. Another 25 percent turn to social media sites or blogs for product- or store-related information.[64] Some consumers use blogs not only for information gathering, but as a means of retribution and revenge on companies for bad service and faulty products. Dell's customer-service shortcomings were splashed all over the Internet through a series of "Dell Hell" postings. Tim Hortons took some heat in 2010 for being associated with an event held by the National Organization for Marriage. The story erupted and spread quickly through bloggers ranting about the company's association with the controversial and politically involved organization and encouraging readers to speak out against the restaurant chain. Within a few days, Tim Hortons issued a statement withdrawing from the event, admitting that the company realized it had gone outside its sponsorship guidelines.[65]

SOCIAL NETWORKS Social networks have become an important force in both business-to-consumer and business-to-business marketing.[66] Major ones include Facebook, which is the world's biggest; MySpace, which concentrates on music and entertainment; LinkedIn, which targets career-minded professionals; and Twitter, which allows members to network via 140-character messages or "tweets." Different networks offer different benefits to firms. For example, Twitter can be an early warning system that permits rapid response, whereas Facebook allows deeper dives to engage consumers in more meaningful ways.[67]

Marketers are still learning how to best tap into social networks and their huge, well-defined audiences. Given networks' noncommercial nature—users are generally there looking to connect with others—attracting attention and persuading are more challenging. Also, given that users generate their own content, ads may find themselves appearing beside inappropriate or even offensive content.[68]

Advertising is only one avenue, however. Like any individual, companies can also join the social groups and actively participate. Having a Facebook page and a presence on Twitter have become a virtual prerequisite for many companies. To create interest for the 2011 Calgary Stampede, a ten-day event that occurs every summer featuring the world's largest rodeo, a parade, concerts, and more, the event planners took to Facebook, Twitter, YouTube, and Flickr to promote the Stampede. In the months leading up to the event, the Stampede's Facebook page advertised scheduled performers, offered giveaways, and welcomed visitors by asking them to pledge to change their Facebook status to "Yahoo" during the days of the Stampede.[69]

CLOSING Closing signs from the buyer include physical actions, statements or comments, and questions. Reps can ask for the order, recapitulate the points of agreement, offer to help write up the order, ask whether the buyer wants A or B, get the buyer to make minor choices such as colour or size, or indicate what the buyer will lose by not placing the order now. The salesperson might offer specific inducements to close, such as an additional service, an extra quantity, or a token gift.

If the client still isn't budging, perhaps the salesperson is not interacting with the right executive—a more senior person may have the necessary authority. The salesperson also may need to find other ways to reinforce the value of the offering and how it alleviates financial or other pressures the client faces.[115]

FOLLOW-UP AND MAINTENANCE Follow-up and maintenance are necessary to ensure customer satisfaction and repeat business. Immediately after closing, the salesperson should cement any necessary details about delivery time, purchase terms, and other matters important to the customer. The salesperson should schedule a follow-up call after delivery to ensure proper installation, instruction, and servicing and to detect any problems, assure the buyer of the salesperson's interest, and reduce any cognitive dissonance. The salesperson should develop a maintenance and growth plan for the account.

Relationship Marketing

The principles of personal selling and negotiation are largely transaction-oriented because their purpose is to close a specific sale. But in many cases the company seeks not an immediate sale but rather a long-term supplier–customer relationship. Today's customers prefer suppliers who can sell and deliver a coordinated set of products and services to many locations, who can quickly solve problems in different locations, and who can work closely with customer teams to improve products and processes.

Salespeople working with key customers must do more than call only when they think customers might be ready to place orders. They should call or visit at other times and make useful suggestions about the business. They should monitor key accounts, know customers' problems, and be ready to serve them in a number of ways, adapting and responding to different customer needs or situations.[116]

Relationship marketing is not effective in all situations. But when it is the right strategy and is properly implemented, the organization will focus as much on managing its customers as on managing its products.

SUMMARY

1. Direct marketing is the use of consumer-direct (CD) channels to reach and deliver goods and services to customers without using marketing middlemen. Direct marketing, especially electronic marketing, is showing explosive growth.

2. Direct marketers plan campaigns by deciding on objectives, target markets and prospects, offers, and prices. Next, they test the campaign and establish measures to determine its success.

3. Major channels for direct marketing include face-to-face selling, direct mail, catalogues, telemarketing, interactive TV, kiosks, websites, and mobile devices.

4. Interactive marketing provides marketers with opportunities for much greater interaction and individualization through well-designed and well-executed websites, search ads, display ads, and emails. Mobile marketing is another growing form of interactive marketing, which relies on text messages, software apps, and ads.

5. Word-of-mouth marketing finds ways to engage customers so that they choose to talk with others about products, services, and brands. Increasingly, word of mouth is being driven by social media in the form of online communities and forums, blogs, and social networks such as Facebook, Twitter, and YouTube.

6. Two notable forms of word-of-mouth marketing are buzz marketing, which seeks to get people talking about a brand by ensuring that a product or service or how it is marketed is out of the ordinary, and viral marketing, which encourages people to exchange online information related to a product or service.

7. Salespeople serve as a company's link to its customers. The sales rep *is* the company to many of its customers, and it is the rep who brings back to the company much-needed information about the customer.

8. Designing the sales force requires choosing objectives, strategy, structure, size, and compensation. Objectives may include prospecting, targeting, communicating, selling, servicing, information gathering, and allocating. Determining strategy requires choosing the most effective mix of selling approaches. Choosing the sales force structure entails dividing territories by geography, product, or market (or some combination of these). To estimate how large the sales force needs to be, the firm estimates the total workload and how many sales hours (and hence salespeople) will be needed. Compensating the sales force entails determining what types of salaries, commissions, bonuses, expense accounts, and benefits to give, and how much weight customer satisfaction should have in determining total compensation.

9. There are five steps in managing the sales force: (1) recruiting and selecting sales representatives; (2) training the representatives in sales techniques and in the company's products, policies, and customer-satisfaction orientation; (3) supervising the sales force and helping reps to use their time efficiently; (4) motivating the sales force and balancing quotas, monetary rewards, and supplementary motivators; (5) evaluating individual and group sales performance.

10. Effective salespeople are trained in the methods of analysis and customer management, as well as the art of sales professionalism. No single approach works best in all circumstances, but most trainers agree that selling is a six-step process: prospecting and qualifying, pre-approach, presentation and demonstration, overcoming objections, closing, and follow-up and maintenance.

APPLICATIONS

Marketing Debate: Are Great Salespeople Born or Made?

One debate in sales is about the impact of training versus selection in developing an effective sales force. Some observers maintain that the best salespeople are born that way and are effective due to personalities and interpersonal skills developed over a lifetime. Others contend that application of leading-edge sales techniques can make virtually anyone a sales star.

Take a position: The key to developing an effective sales force is selection *versus* The key to developing an effective sales force is training.

Marketing Discussion: Corporate Websites

Pick a company and go to its corporate website. How would you evaluate the website? How well does it score on the 7Cs of design elements: context, content, community, customization, communication, connection, and commerce?

MARKETING **EXCELLENCE** | TWITTER

Twitter has taken word-of-mouth advertising to an entirely new level. Imagine a company being able to advertise (or "tweet") an upcoming event, in 140 characters or less, with the click of a mouse or press of a key. Picture that message being delivered to the company's loyal customers in only a few seconds. The message doesn't just stop there—it is just as easy for those customers to turn around and share that message with all of their friends, giving the message a phenomenal reach. The message costs only the time it took to compose the tweet, and marketers are using Twitter to take their message to the world.

With over 200 million registered users in mid-2011 and 460 000 new sign-ups daily, Twitter enables businesses to connect with consumers like never before. Twitter allows companies the opportunity to share information, gather market intelligence and feedback, and build relationships with customers, partners, and influential people—all in real time. Opening up the doors of communication to a company's most valuable consumers, and their friends, Twitter is linking marketers to their target markets in a way never before possible.

In 2009, Best Buy created a Twitter account for the blue-shirted members of its Geek Squad tech support service. Customers could ask technical questions from their Twitter account to an on-the-clock Geek Squad employee. Customers tagged their own tweets, and the answer provided was sent through the Geek Squad account, allowing anyone to search the feed for topics they needed help with. The team received an overwhelming response from Twitter users. Being the first company to use Twitter to offer customer support, Best Buy achieved what it set out to do: humanize the organization. Twitter allowed Best Buy to connect its team of personable employees to customers through an informal online environment.

With almost no cost to it, social network advertising is proving to be the most accessible form of advertising for many Canadian small businesses. Smaller organizations are flocking to Twitter for its ability to reach large groups of prospective customers in a short time. In Victoria, British Columbia, the local fringe festival started tweeting about acts in the months leading up to the festival to create buzz. During the weeks of the festival, organizers tweeted about popular shows and offered links to online reviews. Twitter proved especially helpful when the Festival needed to communicate sudden changes in time, line-up, or venue. With the Victoria Fringe Festival also having its own app for mobile devices, users could connect with the festival in a way no other fringe audiences in Canada could before.

Both small and large service organizations are recognizing the opportunities in electronically delivered word of mouth achieved through social networks like Twitter. Valued at around $10 billion in early 2011, and continuously expanding its services, Twitter will prove to be a force for marketers to harness for years to come.

QUESTIONS

1. Best Buy found success in personalizing customer service on Twitter. In what ways can Twitter be used to further enhance customer service at retail stores?

2. Are there industries where the use of Twitter may be inappropriate?

3. How might Twitter be used to differentiate a company's services from competitors'?

4. What are the risks involved in adopting a social marketing strategy similar to Best Buy's as part of the marketing plan?

Sources: Catherine Wilson, "Word of Mouth, Delivered Digitally," *Dental Practice Management*, Spring 2011, p.5; Amanda Ash, "Virtual Buzz Played Up; Show's Organizers Take to Twitter, Facebook, iPhone to Connect with Audiences," *Times-Colonist*, August 20, 2009, p. D7; Dominic Rushe, "Twitter Valued at $10bn as Google and Facebook Reportedly Vie to Buy It," *The Guardian*, February 11, 2011, p. 3; Kenneth Hein, "Why Best Buy's CMO Judge Sicced His Blue Shirts on Twitter," *Brandweek, 50*, no. 39 (November 2, 2009): 27.

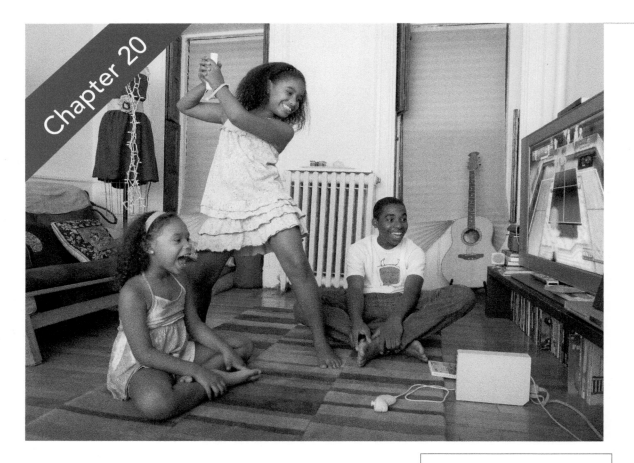

In This Chapter, We Will Address
the Following **Questions**

1. What challenges does a company face in developing
    new products and services?

2. What organizational structures and processes do managers
    use to oversee new-product development?

3. What are the main stages in developing new products and
    services?

4. What is the best way to manage the new-product
    development process?

5. What factors affect the rate of diffusion and consumer
    adoption of newly launched products and services?

With a unique approach to video
game playing, Nintendo's highly
interactive and engaging Wii
became a huge hit.

Introducing New Market Offerings

New-product development shapes a company's future.

Improved or replacement products and services can maintain or build sales; new-to-the-world products and services can transform industries and companies and change lives. But the low success rate of new products and services points to the many challenges they face. Still, companies are doing more than just talking about innovation. They are challenging industry norms and conventions to develop new products and services that delight and engage consumers. Nintendo's Wii is a prime example.[1]

Although Nintendo helped create the $30 billion global video game business and dominated the industry in the 1980s, its worldwide sales had stagnated in the early part of this century due to competition from Sony and Microsoft combined with changes in consumer video-gaming behaviour. Further, Nintendo saw its profitability fall drastically in 2004 to less than a third of what it had been two years prior. CEO Satoru Iwata and game designer Shigeru Miyamoto decided to address two troubling trends in the industry: as players got older and had families and careers, they played less often, and as video game consoles got more powerful, they grew more expensive. Nintendo's solution? Redesign the game controllers and the way they interacted with the consoles. Bucking industry trends, Nintendo chose a cheaper, lower-power chip with fewer graphics capabilities, creating a totally different style of play based on physical gestures. A sleek white design and a new motion-sensitive wireless controller made the video game much more engaging and interactive. Nintendo's decision to embrace outside software developers meant a number of titles quickly became available. Thus Wii was born. Its collaborative nature made it a hit with nongamers drawn by its capabilities and hard-core players seeking to master its many intriguing games.

With new competition from smartphones and tablets serving as gaming devices, Nintendo continues to innovate with its Wii hardware and software to remain a leading force in the video-gaming industry. Besides expanding its array of games, in 2008, Nintendo launched Wii Fit, which effectively combines gaming with physical exercise. This was followed by an enhanced Wii Fit Plus in 2009, and its next generation high-definition version of the Wii console will appear in 2012.

Marketers play a key role in new-product development by identifying and evaluating ideas and working with R&D and other areas in every stage of development. This chapter provides a detailed analysis of the new-product development process. Much of the discussion is equally relevant to new products, services, or business models. Chapter 21 considers how marketers can tap into global markets as another source of long-term growth.

NEW-PRODUCT OPTIONS

There are a variety of types of new products and ways to create them.[2]

Make or Buy

A company can add new products through acquisition or development. When acquiring, the company can buy other companies, patents from other companies, or a licence or franchise from another company. Swiss food giant Nestlé has increased its presence in North America by acquiring such diverse brands as Carnation, Hills Brothers, Stouffer's, Ralston Purina, Dreyer's Ice Cream, Chef America, Jenny Craig, and Gerber.

But firms can successfully make only so many acquisitions. At some point, they need *organic growth*—the development of new products from within. Praxair, worldwide provider of industrial gases, achieved an ambitious goal of US$200 million per year of double-digit new annual sales growth only through a healthy dose of organic growth and a large number of smaller but significant US$5 million projects.[3]

For product development, the company can create new products in its own laboratories, or it can contract with independent researchers or new-product development firms to develop specific new products or provide new technology.[4] Firms such as Samsung, GE, Diageo, Hershey, and USB have engaged new-product consulting boutiques to provide fresh insights and points of view.

Types of New Products

New products range from new-to-the-world products that create an entirely new market to minor improvements or revisions of existing products. Most new-product activity is devoted to improving existing products. Some of the most successful recent new consumer products have been brand extensions: Tide Total Care, Gillette Venus Embrace, iPod Touch, Always Infinity, and Secret Flawless deodorant.[5] At Sony, modifications of established products account for over 80 percent of new-product activity.

It is increasingly difficult to identify blockbuster products that will transform a market, but continuous innovation can force competitors to play catch-up and also broaden the brand meaning.[6] Once a running-shoe manufacturer, Nike now competes with makers of all types of athletic shoes, clothing, and equipment. Pennsylvania-based Armstrong World Industries moved from selling floor coverings to ceilings to total interior surface decoration.

Fewer than 10 percent of all new products are truly innovative and new to the world.[7] These products incur the greatest cost and risk. Although radical innovations can hurt the company's bottom line in the short run, if they succeed they can create a greater sustainable competitive advantage than ordinary products and produce significant financial rewards as a result.[8]

Companies typically must create a strong R&D and marketing partnership to pull off a radical innovation.[9] The right corporate culture is another crucial determinant; the firm must prepare to cannibalize existing products, tolerate risk, and maintain a future market orientation.[10] Few reliable techniques exist for estimating demand for radical innovations.[11] Focus groups can provide perspective on customer interest and need, but marketers may need a probe-and-learn approach based on observation and feedback of early users' experiences and other means such as online chats or product-focused blogs.

High-tech firms in telecommunications, computers, consumer electronics, biotech, and software in particular seek radical innovation.[12] They face a number of product-launch challenges: high technological uncertainty, high market uncertainty, fierce competition, high investment costs, short product life cycles, and scarce funding sources for risky projects.[13] Successes abound, however.[14] BMW is spending more than US$1 billion to develop a small car for urban drivers, including an electric-powered version. In response to growing interest from Canadian institutions, Blackboard e-learning software added a new production facility in Calgary, Alberta, in late 2011.[15] The company brings new technology into the classroom to help professors manage their classes and course materials. Even consumer packaged-goods makers can benefit from a healthy dose of technology. Danone uses sophisticated R&D techniques to study bacteria, coming up with billion-dollar sellers such as Activia yogurt, sold as an aid for regularity.

CHALLENGES IN NEW-PRODUCT DEVELOPMENT

New-product introductions have accelerated, and in retailing, consumer goods, electronics, autos, and other industries, the time to bring a product to market has been cut in half.[16] Luxury leather-goods maker Louis Vuitton implemented a new factory format dubbed Pégase so that it could ship fresh collections to its boutiques every six weeks—more than twice as frequently as in the past—giving customers more new looks to choose from.[17]

The Innovation Imperative

In an economy of rapid change, continuous innovation is a necessity. Highly innovative firms are able to identify and quickly seize new market opportunities. These firms create a positive attitude toward innovation and risk taking, routinize the innovation process, practise teamwork, and allow their people to experiment and even fail. One such firm is W. L. Gore.

W.L. Gore

Best known for its high-performance Gore-Tex fabrics, W. L. Gore has introduced break-through products as diverse as guitar strings, dental floss, medical devices, and fuel cells—while constantly reinventing the uses of the polymer polytetrafluoroethylene (PTFE). Several principles guide the company's new-product development. First, W. L. Gore works with potential customers. Its thoracic graft, designed to combat heart disease, was developed in close collaboration with physicians. Second, it lets employees choose projects and appoints few product leaders and teams. Gore likes to nurture "passionate champions" who convince others a project is worth their time and commitment. Thus, leaders have positions of authority because they have followers. The development of the fuel cell rallied more than 100 of Gore's 9000 research associates. Third, Gore gives employees "dabble" time. All research associates spend 10 percent of their work hours developing their own ideas. Promising ideas are pushed forward and judged according to a "Real, Win, Worth" exercise: Is the opportunity real? Can we win? Can we make money? Fourth, Gore knows when to let go, though dead ends in one area can spark innovation in another: Elixir acoustic guitar strings were the result of a failed venture into bike cables. Even successful ventures may need to move on. Glide shred-resistant dental floss was sold to Procter & Gamble because Gore-Tex knew that retailers want to deal with a company selling a whole family of health-care products.[18]

Companies that fail to develop new products leave their existing offerings vulnerable to changing customer needs and tastes, shortened product life cycles, increased domestic and foreign competition, and especially new technologies. Kodak, long-time leader in the vanishing traditional film market, has worked hard to develop a new business model and product-development processes for a digital-photography world. Its new goal is to do for photos what Apple does for music by helping people organize and manage their personal libraries of images.

Innovation is about "creating new choices" the competition doesn't have access to, says IDEO's CEO Tim Brown. It isn't about brilliant people spontaneously generating new ideas, he argues, but about finding hidden assumptions and ignored processes that can change the way a company does business.[19]

New-Product Success

Most established companies focus on *incremental innovation,* entering new markets by tweaking products for new customers, using variations on a core product to stay one step ahead of the market, and creating interim solutions for industry-wide problems.

When Scott Paper couldn't compete with Fort Howard Paper Co. on price for the lucrative institutional toilet tissue market, it borrowed a solution from European companies: a dispenser that held bigger rolls. Scott made the larger rolls of paper and provided institutional customers with free dispensers, later doing the same thing with paper towels. Scott not only won over customers in a new market, it became less vulnerable to competitors, such as Fort Howard, which could lower prices but weren't offering the larger rolls or tailor-made dispensers.

Newer companies create *disruptive technologies* that are cheaper and more likely to alter the competitive space. Established companies can be slow to react or invest in these disruptive technologies because they threaten their investment. Then they suddenly find themselves facing formidable new competitors, and many fail.[20] To avoid this trap, incumbent firms must carefully monitor the preferences of both customers and noncustomers and uncover evolving, difficult-to-articulate customer needs.[21]

What else can a company do? In a study of industrial products, new-product specialists Cooper and Kleinschmidt found that the number-one success factor is a unique, superior product. Such products succeed 98 percent of the time, compared with products with a moderate advantage (58 percent success) or minimal advantage (18 percent success). Another key factor is a well-defined product concept. The company carefully defines and assesses the target market, product requirements, and benefits before proceeding. Other success factors are technological and marketing synergy, quality of execution in all stages, and market attractiveness.[22]

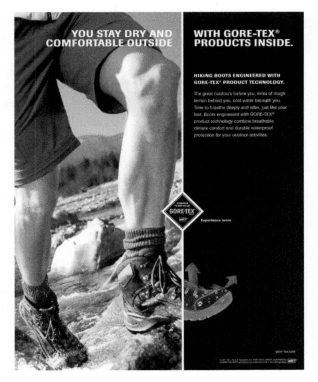

W. L. Gore's thoughtful new-product development strategy has led to many successful innovations over the years, starting with its waterproof, breathable Gore-Tex fabric.

Cooper and Kleinschmidt also found that products designed solely for domestic markets tend to show a high failure rate, low market share, and low growth. Those designed for the world market—or at least neighbouring countries—achieve significantly more profits at home and abroad. Yet only 17 percent of the products in their study were designed with an international orientation.[23] The implication is that companies should consider adopting an international perspective in designing and developing new products, even if only to sell in their home market.

New-Product Failure

New products continue to fail at estimated rates as high as 50 percent or even 95 percent in the United States and 90 percent in Europe. In Canada, according to most industry estimates, 80 percent of new consumer products fail within two years.[24] They fail for many reasons: ignored or misinterpreted market research; overestimates of market size; high development costs; poor design or ineffectual performance; incorrect positioning, advertising, or price; insufficient distribution support; competitors who fight back hard; and inadequate ROI or payback. Additional drawbacks include the following:[25]

- *Shortage of important ideas in certain areas.* There may be few ways left to improve some basic products (such as steel or detergent).

- *Fragmented markets.* Companies must aim their new products at smaller market segments, which can mean lower sales and profits for each product.

- *Social, economic, and governmental constraints.* New products must satisfy consumer safety and environmental concerns. They must also be resilient if economic times are tough.

- *Cost of development.* A company typically must generate many ideas to find just one worthy of development and thus often faces high R&D, manufacturing, and marketing costs.

- *Capital shortages.* Some companies with good ideas cannot raise the funds to research and launch them.

- *Shorter required development time.* Companies must learn to compress development time by using new techniques, strategic partners, early concept tests, and advanced marketing planning.

- *Poor launch timing.* New products are sometimes launched after the category has already taken off or when there is still insufficient interest.

- *Shorter product life cycles.* Rivals are quick to copy success. Sony used to enjoy a three-year lead on its new products. Now Matsushita can copy them within six months, barely leaving Sony time to recoup its investment.

- *Organizational support.* The new product may not mesh with the corporate culture or receive the financial or other support it needs.

But failure comes with the territory, and truly innovative firms accept it as part of what's needed to be successful. Silicon Valley marketing expert Seth Godin maintains, "It is not just OK to fail; it's imperative to fail."[26] Many web companies are the result of failed earlier ventures and experience numerous failures as their services evolve. Dogster.com, a social network site for dog lovers, emerged after the spectacular demise of Pets.com.[27]

Initial failure is not always the end of the road for an idea. Recognizing that 90 percent of experimental drugs are unsuccessful, Eli Lilly looks at failure as an inevitable part of discovery. Its scientists are encouraged to find new uses for compounds that fail at any stage in a human clinical trial. Evista, a failed contraceptive, became a US$1-billion-a-year drug for osteoporosis. Strattera was unsuccessful as an antidepressant, but became a top seller for attention-deficit/hyperactivity disorder. One promising cardiovascular drug in development started as an asthma project.[28]

Frito-Lay found out the hard way that although a product may fail in one geographic market, it can succeed in another.

Frito-Lay SunChips

While "noisy" food might not be appreciated by Americans, Canadians don't seem to mind, at least when it comes to SunChips' new ecofriendly packaging. When SunChips first rolled out its new packaging in the United States, the packaging was met with numerous complaints from customers about how noisy the bag was during handling. After a sales decline of 11 percent, Frito-Lay gave up on its ecofriendly bag in the United States. However, in

Canada, the company capitalized on Canadians' identification with environmental initiatives. SunChips used a new strategy this time around, being upfront about the bag's loudness but explaining why the bag was so noisy. Helmi Ansair, the sustainability leader at Frito-Lay Canada, was used in the campaign to explain the reason behind the bag's noise, and everyone who visited the company's Facebook page was offered a free pair of ear plugs! The campaign received a warm welcome from Canadian customers, who left overwhelmingly positive responses about the ecofriendly bags on Facebook.[29]

ORGANIZATIONAL ARRANGEMENTS

Many companies use *customer-driven engineering* to develop new products, incorporating customer preferences in the final design. Some rely on internal changes to develop more successful new products.

New-product development requires senior management to define business domains, product categories, and specific criteria. One company established the following acceptance criteria:

- The product can be introduced within five years.
- The product has a market potential of at least $50 million and a 15 percent growth rate.
- The product can provide at least 30 percent return on sales and 40 percent on investment.
- The product can achieve technical or market leadership.

Budgeting for New-Product Development

R&D outcomes are so uncertain that it is difficult to use normal investment criteria when budgeting for new-product development. Some companies simply finance as many projects as possible, hoping to achieve a few winners. Other companies apply a conventional percentage-of-sales figure or spend what the competition spends. Still others decide how many successful new products they need and work backward to estimate the required investment.

Table 20.1 shows how a company might calculate the cost of new-product development. The new-products manager at a large consumer packaged-goods company reviewed 64 ideas at a cost of $1000 each. Sixteen passed the screening stage and cost $20 000 each to test. Half of those, or eight, moved on to the product-development stage, at a cost of $200 000 each. Half of those, or four, went on to the test marketing stage, at a cost of $500 000 each. Two did well in the test market, and when they were launched, at a cost of $5 million each, one was highly successful. Thus, this one successful idea cost the company $5 721 000 to develop, while 63 others fell by the wayside for a total development cost of $13 984 000. Unless the company can improve its pass ratios and reduce costs at each stage, it will need to budget nearly $14 million for each successful new idea it hopes to find.

TABLE 20.1	FINDING 1 SUCCESSFUL NEW PRODUCT (STARTING WITH 64 NEW IDEAS)			
Stage	Number of Ideas	Pass Ratio	Cost per Product Idea	Total Cost
1. Idea screening	64	1:4	$ 1 000	$ 64 000
2. Concept testing	16	1:2	20 000	320 000
3. Product development	8	1:2	200 000	1 600 000
4. Test marketing	4	1:2	500 000	2 000 000
5. National launch	2	1:2	5 000 000	10 000 000
			$5 721 000	$13 984 000

Hit rates vary. Inventor Sir James Dyson claims he made 5127 prototypes of his bagless, transparent vacuum cleaner over a 14-year period before getting it right, resulting in the best-selling vacuum cleaner by revenue in the United States, with over 20 million sold and annual revenue of $1 billion. He doesn't lament his failures, though: "If you want to discover something that other people haven't, you need to do things the wrong way... watching why that fails can take you on a completely different path." His latest successes: the Airblade, an energy-efficient hand dryer for public restrooms, and the Air Multiplier, a bladeless table fan.[30]

Fortunately, for companies in Canada, there are many opportunities to obtain financial support from the federal government to fund innovation. Nulogy is one such beneficiary.

Nulogy Corporation

Founded in 2002, Canadian company Nulogy Corporation found a niche for itself in the competitive and growing contract packaging industry. This high-tech company provides cloud computing software that manages inventory, production, and costing, and offers quotes to clients worldwide in real time. Nulogy's newest software, PackShop, allows retailers, marketers, and manufacturers to customize the design of product packaging and displays. In order to successfully develop and launch the new product, the company required significant investment. Looking outside its own organization, the company secured help from the Federal Economic Development Agency (FedDev), which provided a repayable contribution of nearly $1 million. This support gave the company the funds it needed in order to be the first to market, also allowing the hire of an additional 40 full-time employees.[31]

Organizing New-Product Development

Companies handle the organizational aspect of new-product development in several ways.[32] Many assign responsibility to *product managers*. But product managers are often busy managing existing lines and may lack the skills and knowledge to develop and critique new products.

Kraft and Johnson & Johnson employ *new-product managers* who report to category managers. Westinghouse has *growth leaders*—a full-time job for its most creative and successful managers.[33] Some companies have a *high-level management committee* charged with reviewing and approving proposals. Large companies often establish a *new-product department* headed by a manager with substantial authority and access to top management and whose responsibilities include generating and screening new ideas, working with the R&D department, and carrying out field testing and commercialization. Adobe has come up with a unique forum for new-product ideas.

Adobe Systems Inc.

Adobe Systems, a developer of graphic design and publishing software, established a task force to identify the obstacles its employees faced in trying to develop new products. The team discovered that ideas needing a new sales channel, new business model, or even new packaging failed due to the corporate hierarchy. In addition, Adobe had grown so large that ideas originating in branch offices were not getting a fair shake. As a result, Adobe established a New Business Initiatives Group that mimics the venture capital model, backing entrepreneurial people and putting employees in front of their ideas. The group holds quarterly "Idea Champion Showcases," where approximately 20 product managers and other employees (except top executives, who are barred from the proceedings) watch as potential employee-entrepreneurs give brief presentations and Q&A sessions. The ideas are vetted by Adobe Entrepreneurs-in-Residence, and the best ideas are given a first round of funding. But even ideas that are nixed can still get a hearing on the company's brainstorming site. The event has become extremely popular within Adobe—an *American Idol*-style way for good ideas to come to the fore.[34]

CROSS-FUNCTIONAL TEAMS 3M, Dow, and General Mills have assigned new-product development to **venture teams**, cross-functional groups charged with developing a specific product or business. These "intrapreneurs" are relieved of other duties and given a budget, time frame, and "skunkworks" setting. *Skunkworks* are informal workplaces, sometimes garages, where intrapreneurial teams attempt to develop new products.

Cross-functional teams can collaborate and use concurrent new-product development to push new products to market.[35] Concurrent product development resembles a rugby match, with team members passing the new product back and forth as they head toward the goal. Using this system, Allen-Bradley Corporation (a maker of industrial controls) was able to develop a new device in just two years, down from six under its old system. Cross-functional teams help ensure that engineers are not driven to create a better mousetrap when potential customers don't need or want one.

STAGE-GATE SYSTEMS Many top companies use the *stage-gate system* to divide the innovation process into stages, with a gate or checkpoint at the end of each.[36] The project leader, working with a cross-functional team, must bring a set of known deliverables to each gate before the project can pass to the next stage. To move from the business plan stage into product development requires a convincing market research study of consumer needs and interest, a competitive analysis, and a technical appraisal. Senior managers review the criteria at each gate to make one of four decisions: *go, kill, hold,* or *recycle*. Stage-gate systems make the innovation process visible to all and clarify the project leader's and team's responsibilities at each stage.[37] The gates or controls should not be so rigid, however, that they inhibit learning and the development of novel products.[38]

The stages in the new-product development process are shown in Figure 20.1. Many firms have parallel sets of projects working through the process, each at a different stage.[39] Think of the process as a *funnel:* a large number of initial new-product ideas and concepts are winnowed down to a few high-potential products that are ultimately launched. But the process is not always linear. Many firms use a *spiral development process* that recognizes the value of returning to an earlier stage to make improvements before moving forward.[40]

Ansell Healthcare, the world's largest manufacturer of protective gloves and clothing, adopted a stage-gate process and found that the contribution of new products to overall sales jumped from 4.5 percent to 13 percent in a little over two years. Hydro Quebec, one of the world's largest hydroelectricity utilities, implemented a stage-gate system that focused resources on the most valuable projects and reaped over $1 billion in benefits.[41]

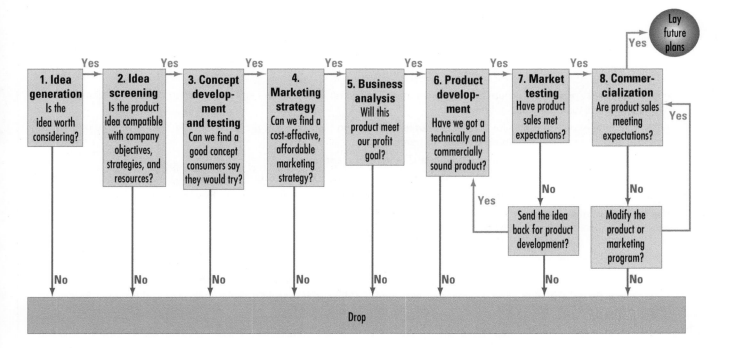

FIGURE 20.1

The New-Product Development Decision Process

MANAGING THE DEVELOPMENT PROCESS: IDEAS

Generating Ideas

The new-product development process starts with the search for ideas. Some marketing experts believe that the greatest opportunities and highest leverage with new products are found by uncovering the best possible set of unmet customer needs or technological innovation.[42] New-product ideas can come from interacting with various groups and using creativity-generating techniques.[43] (See "Marketing Memo: Ten Ways to Find Great New-Product Ideas.")

Erich Joachimsthaler believes that some of the best new-product opportunities are right in front of marketers' eyes. The mistake too many make, he says, is to view the world from the perspective of their own products and services and search for customers for them. His demand-first innovation and growth (DIG) framework is designed to provide companies with an unbiased view and an outside-in perspective of demand opportunities. It has three parts:[44]

1. *The demand landscape*—Use observational, anthropological, and ethnographic methods or consumer self-reports to map consumer needs and wants, and understand their consumption behaviour and decision-making process.

2. *The opportunity space*—Use a conceptual lens and structured innovative-thinking tools to achieve market perspectives from different angles.

3. *The strategic blueprint*—Think about how the new product can fit into customers' lives and how it can be distinguished from competitors' products.

As one DIG-type application, Joachimsthaler notes how Intel famously abandoned its highly competitive memory business to pursue more fertile opportunities with microprocessors.

INTERACTING WITH OTHERS Encouraged by the *open innovation* movement, many firms are going outside their bounds to tap external sources of new ideas, including customers, employees, scientists, engineers, channel members, marketing agencies, top management, and even competitors.[45] "Marketing Insight: P&G's New Connect + Develop Approach to Innovation" describes how Procter & Gamble has made new-product development more externally focused.

MARKETING **MEMO** | TEN WAYS TO FIND GREAT NEW-PRODUCT IDEAS

1. Run informal sessions where groups of customers meet with company engineers and designers to discuss problems and needs and brainstorm potential solutions.

2. Allow time off—scouting time—for technical people to putter on their own pet projects. Google has allowed 20 percent time off; 3M, 15 percent; and Rohm & Haas, 10 percent.

3. Make a customer brainstorming session a standard feature of plant tours.

4. Survey your customers: find out what they like and dislike in your and competitors' products.

5. Undertake "fly-on-the-wall" or "camping out" research with customers, as do Fluke and Hewlett-Packard.

6. Use iterative rounds: a group of customers in one room, focusing on identifying problems, and a group of your technical people in the next room, listening and brainstorming solutions. Immediately test proposed solutions with the group of customers.

7. Set up a keyword search that routinely scans trade publications in multiple countries for new-product announcements.

8. Treat trade shows as intelligence missions, where you view all that is new in your industry under one roof.

9. Have your technical and marketing people visit your suppliers' labs and spend time with their technical people—find out what's new.

10. Set up an idea vault, and make it open and easily accessed. Allow employees to review the ideas and add constructively to them.

Source: Adapted from Robert G. Cooper, *Product Leadership: Creating and Launching Superior New Products* (New York: Perseus Books, 1998). Adapted with permission from the author. See also Robert G. Cooper and Scott J. Edgett, "Ideation for Product Innovation: What Are the Best Methods?" *Visions*, March 2008, pp. 12–17. Product Development Institute www.prod-dev.com.

| MARKETING **INSIGHT** | P&G'S NEW CONNECT + DEVELOP APPROACH TO INNOVATION |

In the first decade of the twenty-first century, one of the fastest-growing major corporations in revenue and profit was Procter & Gamble. Fuelling that growth were successful new products such as Swiffer, Mr. Clean Magic Eraser, and Actonel (a prescription medication for osteoporosis). Many of these new products reflected innovation in what ex-CEO A. G. Lafley calls "the core"—core markets, categories, brands, technologies, and capabilities.

To more effectively develop its core, P&G adopted a "Connect + Develop" model that emphasizes the pursuit of outside innovation. The firm collaborates with organizations and individuals around the world, searching for proven technologies, packages, and products it can improve, scale up, and market on its own or in partnership with other companies. It has strong relationships with external designers, distributing product development around the world to increase what it calls "consumer sensing."

P&G identifies the top ten customer needs, closely related products that could leverage or benefit from existing brand equity, and "game boards" that map the adoption of technology across different product categories. It may consult government and private labs as well as academic and other research institutions, VC firms, individual entrepreneurs, and suppliers, retailers, competitors, and development and trade partners, using online networks to reach thousands of experts worldwide.

P&G has three core requirements for a successful Connect + Develop strategy:

1. Never assume that "ready to go" ideas found outside are truly ready to go. There will always be development work to do, including risky scale-up.

2. Don't underestimate the internal resources required. You'll need a full-time, senior executive to run any Connect + Develop initiative.

3. Never launch without a mandate from the CEO. Connect + Develop cannot succeed if it's cordoned off in R&D. It must be a top-down, company-wide strategy.

Through Connect + Develop—and improvements in product cost, design, and marketing—P&G increased R&D productivity by nearly 60 percent during the decade. The innovation success rate more than doubled, and cost has fallen.

Sources: www.pgconnectdevelop.com; A. G. Lafley and Ram Charan, *The Game Changer: How You Can Drive Revenue and Profit Growth through Innovation* (New York: Crown Business, 2009); Robert Berner, "How P&G Pampers New Thinking," *BusinessWeek,* April 14, 2008, pp. 73–74; Steve Hamm, "Speed Demons," *BusinessWeek,* March 27, 2006, pp. 69–76; Larry Huston and Nabil Sakkab, "Connect and Develop: Inside Procter & Gamble's New Model for Innovation," *Harvard Business Review,* March 2006, pp. 58–66; Geoff Colvin, "Lafley and Immelt: In Search of Billions," *Fortune,* December 11, 2006, pp. 70–72; Rajat Gupta and Jim Wendler, "Leading Change: An Interview with the CEO of P&G," *McKinsey Quarterly,* July 2005.

Customer needs and wants are the logical place to start the search.[46] Griffin and Hauser suggest that conducting 10 to 20 in-depth experiential interviews per market segment often uncovers the vast majority of customer needs.[47] But other approaches can be profitable (see "Marketing Memo: Seven Ways to Draw New Ideas from Your Customers"). One marketer-sponsored café in Tokyo tests products of all kinds with affluent, influential young Japanese women.[48]

The traditional company-centric approach to product innovation is giving way to a world in which companies co-create products with consumers.[49] Companies are increasingly turning to "crowdsourcing" to generate new ideas or, as we saw in the Chapter 18, to create consumer-generated marketing campaigns. *Crowdsourcing* means inviting the Internet community to help create content or software, often with prize money or a moment of glory as an incentive.[50]

This strategy has helped create new products and companies such as Wikipedia, YouTube (which was eventually purchased by Google), and iStockphoto, a "microstock" company. One recent convert to crowdsourcing is Cisco.[51]

Cisco

Cisco's I-Prize, an external innovation competition, gives a team outside the company the chance to join Cisco in heading an emerging technology business while receiving a $250 000 signing bonus and up to $10 million in funding for the first two years. Cisco's rationale for the contest—which drew 1200 entrants from 104 countries—was simple: "In many parts of the world, you have incredibly smart people with incredibly great ideas who have absolutely no access to capital to take a great idea and turn it into a business." Judges applied five main criteria: (1) Does it address a real pain point? (2) Will it appeal to a big enough market? (3) Is the timing right? (4) If we pursue the idea, will we be good at it? (5) Can we exploit the opportunity for the long term? The public judged the entries online, where Cisco found the detailed comments even more useful than the actual votes. The winning entry in the first competition was a plan for a sensor-enabled smart-electricity grid.

Besides producing new and better ideas, co-creation can help customers to feel closer to and more favourably toward the company and to create favourable word of mouth.[52] Getting the right customers engaged in the right way, however, is critical.[53]

Lead users can be a good source of input, even when they innovate products without the consent or knowledge of the companies that produce them. Mountain bikes developed as a result of youngsters taking their bikes to the top of a mountain and riding down. When the bikes broke, the youngsters began building more durable bikes and adding motorcycle brakes, improved suspension, and accessories. They, not the companies, developed these innovations.

MARKETING **MEMO** | SEVEN WAYS TO DRAW NEW IDEAS FROM YOUR CUSTOMERS

1. Observe how customers are using your product. Medtronic, a medical device company, has salespeople and market researchers regularly observe spine surgeons who use their products and competitive products, to learn how theirs can be improved. After living with lower-middle-class families in Mexico City, Procter & Gamble researchers devised Downy Single Rinse, a fabric softener that removed an arduous step from the partly manual laundry process there.

2. Ask customers about their problems with your products. Komatsu Heavy Equipment sent a group of engineers and designers to the United States for six months to ride with equipment drivers and learn how to make products better. Procter & Gamble, recognizing consumers were frustrated that potato chips break and are difficult to save after opening the bag, designed Pringles to be uniform in size and encased in a protective tennis-ball-type can.

3. Ask customers about their dream products. Ask your customers what they want your product to do, even if the ideal sounds impossible. One 70-year-old camera user told Minolta he would like the camera to make his subjects look better and not show their wrinkles and aging. In response, Minolta produced a camera with two lenses, one for rendering softer images of the subjects.

4. Use a customer advisory board to comment on your company's ideas. Levi Strauss uses youth panels to discuss lifestyles, habits, values, and brand engagements; Cisco runs Customer Forums to improve its offerings; and Harley-Davidson solicits product ideas from its one million H.O.G. (Harley Owners Group) members.

5. Use Web sites for new ideas. Companies can use specialized search engines such as Technorati and Daypop to find blogs and postings relevant to their businesses. P&G's site has *We're Listening* and *Share Your Thoughts* sections and Advisory Feedback sessions to gain advice and feedback from customers.

6. Form a brand community of enthusiasts who discuss your product. Harley-Davidson and Apple have strong brand enthusiasts and advocates; Sony engaged in collaborative dialogues with consumers to codevelop Sony's PlayStation 2. LEGO draws on kids and influential adult enthusiasts for feedback on new-product concepts in early stages of development.

7. Encourage or challenge your customers to change or improve your product. Salesforce.com wants its users to develop and share new software applications using simple programming tools. International Flavors & Fragrances gives a toolkit to its customers to modify specific flavours, which IFF then manufactures; LSI Logic Corporation also provides customers with do-it-yourself toolkits so customers can design their own specialized chips; and BMW posted a toolkit on its Web site to let customers develop ideas using telematics and in-car online services.

Source: From an unpublished paper, Philip Kotler, "Drawing New Ideas from Your Customers," 2007.

Some companies, particularly those that want to appeal to hip young consumers, bring their lead users into their product-design process. Technical companies can learn a great deal by studying customers who make the most advanced use of the company's products and who recognize the need for improvements before other customers do.[54] In a business-to-business market, collecting information from distributors and retailers who are not in close contact can provide more diverse insights and information.[55]

Not everyone believes that a customer focus helps to create better new products. As Henry Ford famously said, "If I'd asked people what they wanted, they would have said a faster horse." And some still caution that being overly focused on consumers, who may not really know what they want or what could be possible, can result in short-sighted product development and miss real potential breakthroughs.[56]

Some of the best new-product ideas come from highly involved consumers or lead users, as was the case in the birth of the mountain bike.

INTERACTING WITH EMPLOYEES Employees can be a source of ideas for improving production, products, and services.[57] Toyota claims that its employees submit 2 million ideas annually (about 35 suggestions per employee), over 85 percent of which are implemented. Kodak, Milliken, and other firms give monetary, holiday, or recognition awards to employees who submit the best ideas. Nokia inducts engineers who file for at least ten patents into its "Club 10," recognizing them each year in a formal awards ceremony hosted by the company's CEO.[58] A company can motivate its employees to submit new ideas to an *idea manager* whose name and contact information are widely circulated.

Top management can be another major source of ideas. Some company leaders, such as former CEO Andy Grove of Intel, take personal responsibility for technological innovation in the firm. New-product ideas can come from inventors, patent attorneys, university and commercial laboratories, industrial consultants, advertising agencies, marketing research firms, and industrial publications. However, their chances of receiving serious attention often depend on someone in the organization taking the role of product champion.

STUDYING COMPETITORS Companies can find good ideas by researching the products and services of competitors and other companies. They can find out what customers like and dislike about competitors' products. They can buy their competitors' products, take them apart, and build better ones. Company sales representatives and intermediaries are a particularly good source of ideas. These groups have first-hand exposure to customers and are often the first to learn about competitive developments. Electronic retailer Best Buy actually checks with venture capitalists to find out what start-ups are working on.

ADOPTING CREATIVITY TECHNIQUES Internal brainstorming sessions also can be quite effective—if conducted correctly. "Marketing Memo: How to Run a Successful Brainstorming Session" provides some brainstorming guidelines.

The following list is a sampling of techniques for stimulating creativity in individuals and groups:[59]

- *Attribute listing.* List the attributes of an object, such as a screwdriver. Then modify each attribute, such as replacing the wooden handle with plastic, providing torque power, adding different screw heads, and so on.

- *Forced relationships.* List several ideas and consider each in relationship to each of the others. In designing new office furniture, for example, consider a desk, bookcase, and filing cabinet as separate ideas. Then imagine a desk with a built-in bookcase or a desk with built-in files or a bookcase with built-in files.

- *Morphological analysis.* Start with a problem, such as "getting something from one place to another via a powered vehicle." Now think of dimensions, such as the type of platform (cart, chair, sling, bed), the medium (air, water, oil, rails), and the power source (compressed air, electric motor, magnetic fields). By listing every possible combination, you can generate many new solutions.

- *Reverse assumption analysis.* List all the normal assumptions about an entity and then reverse them. Instead of assuming that a restaurant has menus, charges for food, and serves food, reverse each assumption. The new restaurant may decide to serve only what the chef bought that morning and cooked; may provide some food and charge only for how long the person sits at the table; and may design an exotic atmosphere and rent out the space to people who bring their own food and beverages.

| MARKETING **MEMO** | HOW TO RUN A SUCCESSFUL BRAINSTORMING SESSION |

If done correctly, group brainstorming sessions can create insights, ideas, and solutions that would have been impossible without everyone's participation. If done incorrectly, they are a painful waste of time that can frustrate and antagonize participants. To ensure success, experts recommend the following guidelines:

1. A trained facilitator should guide the session.
2. Participants must feel they can express themselves freely.
3. Participants must see themselves as collaborators working toward a common goal.
4. Rules need to be set up and followed, so conversations don't get off track.
5. Participants must be given proper background preparation and materials so they can get into the task quickly.
6. Individual sessions before and after the brainstorming can be useful for thinking and learning about the topic ahead of time and for reflecting afterward on what happened.
7. Brainstorming sessions must lead to a clear plan of action and implementation, so the ideas that materialize can provide tangible value.
8. Brainstorming sessions can do more than just generate ideas—they can help build teams and leave participants better informed and energized.

Sources: Linda Tischler, "Be Creative: You Have 30 Seconds," *Fast Company*, May 2007, pp. 47–50; Michael Myser, "When Brainstorming Goes Bad," *Business 2.0*, October 2006, p. 76; Robert I. Sutton, "Eight Rules to Brilliant Brainstorming," *BusinessWeek* in *Inside Innovation*, September 2006, pp. 17–21.

- *New contexts.* Take familiar processes, such as people-helping services, and put them into a new context. Imagine helping dogs and cats instead of people with daycare service, stress reduction, psychotherapy, funerals, and so on. As another example, instead of sending hotel guests to the front desk to check in, greet them at curbside and use a wireless device to register them.
- *Mind mapping.* Start with a thought, such as a car, write it on a piece of paper, then think of the next thought that comes up (say Mercedes), link it to car, then think of the next association (Germany), and do this with all associations that come up with each new word. Perhaps a whole new idea will materialize.

Increasingly, new-product ideas arise from *lateral marketing* that combines two product concepts or ideas to create a new offering.[60] Here are some successful examples:

- Gas station stores = gas stations + food
- Cyber-cafés = cafeteria + Internet
- Cereal bars = cereal + snacking
- Kinder Surprise = candy + toy
- Sony Walkman = audio + portable

Using Idea Screening

In screening ideas, the company must avoid DROP-errors. A *DROP-error* occurs when the company dismisses a good idea. It is extremely easy to find fault with other people's ideas (Figure 20.2). Some companies shudder when they look back at ideas they dismissed or breathe sighs of relief when they realize how close they came to dropping what eventually became a huge success. Consider the hit television show *Friends*.

Friends

The NBC situation comedy *Friends* enjoyed a ten-year run from 1994 to 2004 as a perennial ratings powerhouse. But the show almost didn't see the light of day. According to an internal NBC research report, the pilot episode was described as "not very entertaining, clever, or original" and was given a failing grade, scoring 41 out of 100. Ironically, the pilot for an earlier hit sitcom, *Seinfeld*, was also rated "weak," although the pilot for the medical drama *ER* scored a healthy 91. Courteney Cox's Monica was the *Friends* character who scored best with test audiences, but the characters portrayed by Lisa Kudrow and Matthew Perry were deemed to have marginal appeal, and the Rachel, Ross, and Joey characters scored even lower. Adults 35 and over in the sample found the characters as a whole "smug, superficial, and self-absorbed."[61]

The purpose of screening is to drop poor ideas as early as possible. The rationale is that product-development costs rise substantially with each successive development stage. Most companies require new-product ideas to be described on a standard form for a new-product committee's review. The description states the product idea, the target market, and the competition, and roughly estimates market size, product price, development time and costs, manufacturing costs, and rate of return.

The executive committee then reviews each idea against a set of criteria. Does the product meet a need? Would it offer superior value? Can it be distinctively advertised? Does the company have the necessary know-how and capital to implement the idea? Will the new product deliver the expected sales volume, sales growth, and profit? Consumer input may be necessary to tap into marketplace realities.[62]

Management can rate the surviving ideas using a weighted-index method like that in Table 20.2. The first column lists factors required for successful product launches, and the second column assigns importance weights. The third column scores the product idea on a scale from 0 to 1.0, with 1.0 the highest score. The final column multiplies each factor's importance by the product score to obtain an overall rating. In this example, the product idea scores 0.69, which places it in the "good idea" level. The purpose of this basic rating device is to promote systematic evaluation and discussion. It is not supposed to make the decision for management.

As the idea moves through development, the company will need to constantly revise its estimate of the product's overall probability of success, using the following formula:

$$\begin{array}{c}\text{Overall} \\ \text{probability} \\ \text{of success}\end{array} = \begin{array}{c}\text{Probability} \\ \text{of technical} \\ \text{completion}\end{array} \times \begin{array}{c}\text{Probability of} \\ \text{commercialization} \\ \text{given technical} \\ \text{completion}\end{array} \times \begin{array}{c}\text{Probability of} \\ \text{economic} \\ \text{success given} \\ \text{commercialization}\end{array}$$

For example, if the three probabilities are estimated at 0.50, 0.65, and 0.74, respectively, the overall probability of success is 0.24. The company then must judge whether this probability is high enough to warrant continued development.

"I've got a great idea!"

"It won't work here."

"We've tried it before."

"This isn't the right time."

"It can't be done."

"It's not the way we do things."

"We've done all right without it."

"It will cost too much."

"Let's discuss it at our next meeting."

FIGURE 20.2

Forces Fighting New Ideas

Source: © Jerold Panas.

TABLE 20.2 | PRODUCT-IDEA RATING DEVICE

Product-Success Requirements	Relative Weight (a)	Product Score (b)	Product Rating (c = a × b)
Unique or superior product	0.40	0.8	0.32
High performance-to-cost ratio	0.30	0.6	0.18
High marketing-dollar support	0.20	0.7	0.14
Lack of strong competition	0.10	0.5	0.05
Total	1.00		0.69[a]

[a]Rating scale: 0.00–0.30 poor; 0.31–0.60 fair; 0.61–0.80 good. 0.81–1.00 excellent. Minimum acceptance rate: 0.61.

MANAGING THE DEVELOPMENT PROCESS: CONCEPT TO STRATEGY

Attractive ideas must be refined into testable product concepts. A *product idea* is a possible product the company might offer to the market. A *product concept* is an elaborated version of the idea expressed in consumer terms.

Concept Development and Testing

Concept development is a necessary but not sufficient step for new-product success. Marketers must also distinguish winning concepts from losers.

CONCEPT DEVELOPMENT Let us illustrate concept development with the following situation: A large food-processing company gets the idea of producing a powder to add to milk to increase its nutritional value and taste. This is a product *idea,* but consumers don't buy product ideas; they buy product *concepts.*

A product idea can be turned into several concepts. The first question is Who will use this product? It can be aimed at infants, children, teenagers, young or middle-aged adults, or older adults. Second, what primary benefit should this product provide: taste, nutrition, refreshment, or energy? Third, when will people consume this drink: breakfast, midmorning, lunch, midafternoon, dinner, late evening? By answering these questions, a company can form several concepts:

■ *Concept 1.* An instant drink for adults who want a quick, nutritious breakfast without preparation.

■ *Concept 2.* A tasty snack for children to drink as a midday refreshment.

■ *Concept 3.* A health supplement for older adults to drink in the late evening before they go to bed.

Each concept represents a *category concept* that defines the product's competition. An instant breakfast drink would compete against bacon and eggs, breakfast cereals, coffee and pastries, and other breakfast alternatives. A snack drink would compete against soft drinks, fruit juices, sports drinks, and other thirst quenchers.

Suppose the instant-breakfast-drink concept looks best. The next task is to show where this powdered product would stand in relationship to other breakfast products via perceptual mapping.

Figure 20.3(a) uses the two dimensions of cost and preparation time to create a *product-positioning map* for the breakfast drink. An instant breakfast drink offers low cost and quick preparation. Its nearest competitor is cold cereal; its most distant is bacon and eggs. These contrasts can help communicate and promote the concept to the market.

Next, the product concept becomes a *brand concept.* Figure 20.3(b) is a *brand-positioning map,* a perceptual map showing the current positions of three existing brands of instant breakfast drinks (A–C), as seen by consumers. It can also be useful to overlay consumer preferences on to the map in terms of their current or desired preferences. Figure 20.3(b) also shows four segments of consumers (1–4) whose preferences are clustered around the points on the map.

The brand-positioning map helps the company to decide how much to charge and how calorific to make its drink. Three segments (1–3) are well served by existing brands (A–C). The company would not want to position itself next to one of those existing brands, unless that brand was weak or inferior or market demand was high enough to be shared. As it turns out, the new brand would be distinctive in the medium-price, medium-calorie market or in the high-price, high-calorie market. There is a segment of consumers (4) clustered fairly near the medium-price, medium-calorie market, suggesting that this may offer the greatest opportunity.

CONCEPT TESTING Concept testing means presenting the product concept to target consumers, physically or symbolically, and getting their reactions. The more the tested concepts resemble the final product or experience, the more dependable concept testing is. Concept testing of prototypes can help avoid costly mistakes, but it may be especially challenging with radically different, new-to-the-world products.[63] Visualization techniques can help respondents match their mental state with what might occur when they are actually evaluating or choosing the new product.[64]

In the past, creating physical prototypes was costly and time consuming, but today firms can use *rapid prototyping* to design products on a computer and then produce rough models to show potential consumers for their reactions. For example, with an aging population, joint replacements, like artificial knees and hips, are increasingly common. Replacements composed of metal and plastic are often cemented to the bone, where they deteriorate and loosen. Hoping to improve on the 20- to 25-year replacement rate, Toronto's Mount Sinai Hospital used three-dimensional printing at the University of Waterloo's research lab to create a prototype for artificial implants made of materials that the body can absorb without harm. Small pores in the materials allow the body's tissue to grow into and ultimately replace the implant.[65]

(a) Product-Positioning Map (Breakfast Market)

(b) Brand-Positioning Map (Instant Breakfast Market)

FIGURE 20.3

Product and Brand Positioning

Companies are also using *virtual reality* to test product concepts. Virtual reality programs use computers and sensory devices (such as gloves or goggles) to simulate reality. Supercomputers also allow for elaborate product testing to assess changes in performance and supplement consumer input. Kenworth trucks used to test new truck designs with clay models and wind tunnels. Using supercomputer analysis, it can now make more accurate estimates of how much drag and fuel use it can eliminate with new trimmed and tapered mud flaps (answer: $400 of a typical truck's annual gas bill).[66]

Concept testing presents consumers with an elaborated version of the concept. Here is the elaboration of concept 1 in our milk example:

> Our product is a powdered mixture added to milk to make an instant breakfast that gives all the day's needed nutrition along with good taste and high convenience. The product comes in three flavours (chocolate, vanilla, and strawberry) and individual packets, six to a box, at $2.49 a box.

After receiving this information, researchers measure product dimensions by having consumers respond to questions like these:

1. *Communicability and believability*—"Are the benefits clear to you and believable?" If the scores are low, the concept must be refined or revised.

2. *Need level*—"Do you see this product solving a problem or filling a need for you?" The stronger the need, the higher the expected consumer interest.

3. *Gap level*—"Do other products currently meet this need and satisfy you?" The greater the gap, the higher the expected consumer interest. Marketers can multiply the need level by the gap level to produce a *need-gap score*. A high score means the consumer sees the product as filling a strong need not satisfied by available alternatives.

4. *Perceived value*—"Is the price reasonable in relationship to value?" The higher the perceived value, the higher the expected consumer interest.

5. *Purchase intention*—"Would you (definitely, probably, probably not, definitely not) buy the product?" Consumers who answered the first three questions positively should answer "Definitely" here.

6. *User targets, purchase occasions, purchasing frequency*—"Who would use this product, when, and how often?"

Respondents' answers indicate whether the concept has a broad and strong consumer appeal, what products it competes against, and which consumers are the best targets. The need-gap levels and purchase-intention levels can be checked against norms for the product category to see whether the concept appears to be a winner, a long shot, or a loser. One food manufacturer rejects any concept that draws a definitely-would-buy score lower than 40 percent.

CONJOINT ANALYSIS Consumer preferences for alternative product concepts can be measured with **conjoint analysis**, a method for deriving the utility values that consumers attach to varying levels of a product's attributes.[67] Conjoint analysis has become one of the most popular concept-development and testing tools. Consider how the technique is used at Bell Canada.

Bell Canada

As competition in the rapidly growing Canadian telecommunications industry heats up and major telephone companies such as Telus, Bell Canada, and Rogers expand into each other's territories, the rivals compete on price bundling their services. Bundling is a pricing strategy that involves combining different products and services into a package sold at a discount. The trick, of course, is to match these combinations to the right customers. As part of BCE's labyrinth of media companies, Montreal-based Bell Canada has the potential to bundle a wide range of products. Bell's first bundled offer achieved sales 140 percent above the objectives set for the campaign. The key to Bell's success has been careful market research. Bell uses conjoint analysis to test different bundles of services, and then derives optimal groupings that can be aimed at key market segments. One such bundle is Bell Security Solutions, which provides network and information security for communications networks to Canadian organizations.[68]

Bell Canada used conjoint analysis to come up with optimal bundles for its target segments.

With conjoint analysis, respondents see different hypothetical offers formed by combining varying levels of the attributes, then rank the various offers. Management can identify the most appealing offer and its estimated market share and profit. In a classic illustration, academic research pioneers Green and Wind used this approach in connection with developing a new spot-removing, carpet-cleaning agent for home use.[69] Suppose the new-product marketer is considering five design elements:

■ Three package designs (A, B, C—see Figure 20.4)
■ Three brand names (K2R, Glory, Bissell)
■ Three prices ($1.19, $1.39, $1.59)
■ A possible *Good Housekeeping* seal (yes, no)
■ A possible money-back guarantee (yes, no)

Although the researcher can form 108 possible product concepts ($3 \times 3 \times 3 \times 2 \times 2$), it would be too much to ask consumers to rank them all from most to least preferred. A sample of, say, 18 contrasting product concepts is feasible.

The marketer now uses a statistical program to derive the consumer's utility functions for each of the five attributes (see Figure 20.5). Utility ranges between 0 and 1.0; the higher the utility, the stronger the consumer's preference for that level of the attribute. Looking at packaging, package B is the most favoured, followed by C and then A (A hardly has any utility). The preferred names are Bissell, K2R, and Glory, in that order. The consumer's utility varies inversely with price.

A *Good Housekeeping* seal is preferred, but it does not add that much utility and may not be worth the effort to obtain it. A money-back guarantee is strongly preferred.

The consumer's most desired offer is package design B, brand name Bissell, priced at $1.19, with a *Good Housekeeping* seal and a money-back guarantee. We can also determine the relative importance of each attribute to this consumer—the difference between the highest and lowest utility level for that attribute. The greater the difference, the more important the attribute. Clearly, this consumer sees price and package design as the most important attributes, followed by money-back guarantee, brand name, and a *Good Housekeeping* seal.

FIGURE 20.4

Samples for Conjoint Analysis

FIGURE 20.5

Utility Functions Based on Conjoint Analysis

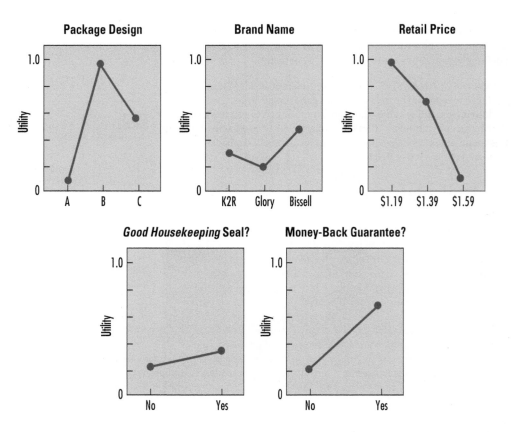

Preference data from a sufficient sample of target consumers helps to estimate the market share any specific offer is likely to achieve, given any assumptions about competitive response. Still, the company may not launch the market offer that promises to gain the greatest market share, because of cost considerations. The most customer-appealing offer is not always the most profitable offer to make.

Under some conditions, researchers will collect the data not with a full-profile description of each offer, but by presenting two factors at a time. For example, respondents may see a table with three price levels and three package types and indicate which of the nine combinations they would like most, second-best, and so on. A further table consists of trade-offs between two other variables. The trade-off approach may be easier to use when there are many variables and possible offers. However, it is less realistic in that respondents are focusing on only two variables at a time. Adaptive conjoint analysis (ACA) is a "hybrid" data collection technique that combines self-explicated importance ratings with pair-wise trade-off tasks.

Marketing Strategy Development

Following a successful concept test, the new-product manager will develop a preliminary three-part strategy plan for introducing the new product into the market. The first part describes the target market's size, structure, and behaviour; the planned product positioning; and the sales, market share, and profit goals sought in the first few years:

> The target market for the instant breakfast drink is families who have children and are receptive to a new, convenient, nutritious, and inexpensive form of breakfast. The company's brand will be positioned at the higher-price, higher-quality end of the instant-breakfast-drink category. The company will aim initially to sell 500 000 cases or to 10 percent of the market, with a loss in the first year not exceeding $1.3 million. The second year will aim for 700 000 cases or 14 percent of the market, with a planned profit of $2.2 million.

The second part outlines the planned price, distribution strategy, and marketing budget for the first year:

> The product will be offered in chocolate, vanilla, and strawberry, in individual packets of six to a box, at a retail price of $2.49 a box. There will be 48 boxes per case, and the case price to distributors will be $24. For the first two months, dealers will be offered one case free for every four cases bought, plus co-operative–advertising allowances. Free samples will be distributed door-to-door. Coupons for 50 cents off will appear in newspapers. The total sales promotional budget will be $2.9 million. An advertising budget of $6 million will be split 50:50 between national and local. Two-thirds will go into television and one-third into online. Advertising copy will emphasize the benefit concepts of nutrition and convenience. The advertising-execution concept will revolve around a small boy who drinks instant breakfast and grows strong. During the first year, $100 000 will be spent on marketing research to buy store audits and consumer-panel information to monitor market reaction and buying rates.

The third part of the marketing strategy plan describes the long-run sales and profit goals and marketing-mix strategy over time:

> The company intends to win a 25 percent market share and realize an after-tax return on investment of 12 percent. To achieve this return, product quality will start high and be improved over time through technical research. Price will initially be set at a high level and lowered gradually to expand the market and meet competition. The total promotion budget will be boosted each year by about 20 percent, with the initial advertising–sales promotion split of 65:35 evolving eventually to 50:50. Marketing research will be reduced to $60 000 per year after the first year.

Business Analysis

After management develops the product concept and marketing strategy, it can evaluate the proposal's business attractiveness. Management needs to prepare sales, cost, and profit projections to determine whether they satisfy company objectives. If they do, the concept can move to the development stage. As new information comes in, the business analysis will undergo revision and expansion.

ESTIMATING TOTAL SALES Total estimated sales are the sum of estimated first-time sales, replacement sales, and repeat sales. Sales-estimation methods depend on whether the product is purchased once (such as an engagement ring or retirement home), infrequently, or often. For one-time products, sales rise at the beginning, peak, and approach zero as the number of potential buyers is exhausted [see Figure 20.6(a)]. If new buyers keep entering the market, the curve will not go down to zero.

(a) One-Time Purchased Product

(b) Infrequently Purchased Product

Replacement sales

(c) Frequently Purchased Product

Repeat purchase sales

FIGURE 20.6

Product Life-Cycle Sales for Three Types of Products

Infrequently purchased products—such as automobiles, toasters, and industrial equipment—exhibit replacement cycles dictated by physical wear or obsolescence associated with changing styles, features, and performance. Sales forecasting for this product category calls for estimating first-time sales and replacement sales separately [see Figure 20.6(b)].

Frequently purchased products, such as consumer and industrial nondurables, have product life-cycle sales resembling Figure 20.6(c). The number of first-time buyers initially increases and then decreases as fewer buyers are left (assuming a fixed population). Repeat purchases occur soon, providing the product satisfies some buyers. The sales curve eventually falls to a plateau representing a level of steady repeat-purchase volume; by this time, the product is no longer a new product.

In estimating sales, the manager's first task is to estimate first-time purchases of the new product in each period. To estimate replacement sales, management researches the product's *survival-age distribution*—that is, the number of units that fail in year one, two, three, and so on. The low end of the distribution indicates when the first replacement sales will take place. Because replacement sales are difficult to estimate before the product is in use, some manufacturers base the decision to launch a new product solely on their estimate of first-time sales.

For a frequently purchased new product, the seller estimates repeat sales as well as first-time sales. A high rate of repeat purchasing means customers are satisfied; sales are likely to stay high even after all first-time purchases take place. Some products and brands are bought a few times and dropped. Colgate's Wisp disposable toothbrush received much trial but repeat sales slowed considerably after that.[70]

ESTIMATING COSTS AND PROFITS Costs are estimated by the R&D, manufacturing, marketing, and finance departments.

Table 20.3 illustrates a five-year projection of sales, costs, and profits for the instant breakfast drink.

Row 1 shows projected sales revenue over the five-year period. The company expects to sell $11 889 000 (approximately 500 000 cases at $24 per case) in the first year. Behind this projection is a set of assumptions about the rate of market growth, the company's market share, and the factory-realized price. *Row 2* shows the cost of goods sold, which hovers around 33 percent of sales revenue. We find this cost by estimating the average cost of labour, ingredients, and packaging per case. *Row 3* shows the expected gross margin, the difference between sales revenue and cost of goods sold.

Row 4 shows anticipated development costs of $3.5 million, including product-development costs, marketing research costs, and manufacturing development costs. *Row 5* shows the estimated marketing costs over the five-year period to cover advertising, sales promotion, and marketing research and an amount allocated for sales force coverage and marketing administration. *Row 6* shows the allocated overhead to this new product to cover its share of the cost of executive salaries, heat, light, and so on.

Row 7, the gross contribution, is gross margin minus the preceding three costs. *Row 8,* supplementary contribution, lists any change in income to other company products caused by the new-product introduction. *Dragalong income* is additional income to them, and *cannibalized income* is reduced income.[71] Table 20.3 assumes no supplementary contributions. *Row 9* shows net contribution, which in this case is the same as gross contribution. *Row 10* shows discounted contribution—that is, the present value of

TABLE 20.3	PROJECTED FIVE-YEAR CASH FLOW STATEMENT (IN THOUSANDS OF DOLLARS)					
	Year 0	Year 1	Year 2	Year 3	Year 4	Year 5
1. Sales revenue	$ 0	$11 889	$15 381	$19 654	$28 253	$32 491
2. Cost of goods sold	0	3981	5150	6581	9461	10 880
3. Gross margin	0	7908	10 231	13 073	18 792	21 611
4. Development costs	−3500	0	0	0	0	0
5. Marketing costs	0	8000	6460	8255	11 866	13 646
6. Allocated overhead	0	1189	1538	1965	2825	3249
7. Gross contribution	−3500	−1281	2233	2853	4101	4716
8. Supplementary contribution	0	0	0	0	0	0
9. Net contribution	−3500	−1281	2233	2853	4101	4716
10. Discounted contribution (15%)	−3500	−1113	1691	1877	2343	2345
11. Cumulative discounted cash flow	−3500	−4613	−2922	−1045	1298	3644

each future contribution discounted at 15 percent per annum. For example, the company will not receive $4 716 000 until the fifth year. This amount is worth only about $2 345 000 today if the company can earn 15 percent on its money through other investments.[72]

Finally, *row 11* shows the cumulative discounted cash flow, the accumulation of the annual contributions in row 10. Two points are of central interest. First is the maximum investment exposure, the highest loss the project can create. The company will be in a maximum loss position of $4 613 000 in year 1. The second is the payback period, the time when the company recovers all its investment, including the built-in return of 15 percent. The payback period here is about three-and-a-half years. Management must decide whether to risk a maximum investment loss of $4.6 million and a possible payback period of three-and-a-half years. As part of their financial analysis, firms may conduct a break-even or risk analysis.

MANAGING THE DEVELOPMENT PROCESS: DEVELOPMENT TO COMMERCIALIZATION

Up to now, the product has existed only as a word description, a drawing, or a prototype. The next step represents a jump in investment that dwarfs the costs incurred so far. The company will determine whether the product idea can translate into a technically and commercially feasible product. If not, the accumulated project cost will be lost, except for any useful information gained in the process.

Product Development

The job of translating target customer requirements into a working prototype is helped by a set of methods known as *quality function deployment* (QFD). The methodology takes the list of desired *customer attributes* (CAs) generated by market research and turns them into a list of *engineering attributes* (EAs) that engineers can use. For example, customers of a proposed truck may want a certain acceleration rate (CA). Engineers can turn this into the required horsepower and other engineering equivalents (EAs). A major contribution of QFD is improved communication between marketers, engineers, and manufacturing people.[73]

PHYSICAL PROTOTYPES The goal of the R&D department is to find a prototype that embodies the key attributes in the product-concept statement, performs safely under normal use and conditions, and can be produced within budgeted manufacturing costs. In the past, developing and manufacturing a successful prototype could take weeks or even years. Sophisticated virtual reality technology and the web now permit more rapid prototyping and more flexible development processes. Simulations, for example, give companies the flexibility to respond to new information and resolve uncertainties by quickly exploring alternatives.

R&D must also decide how consumers will react to different colours, sizes, and weights. Historically, a yellow mouthwash supported an "antiseptic" claim (Listerine), red a "refreshing" claim (Lavoris), and green or blue a "cool" claim (Scope). Marketers need to supply R&D with information about what attributes consumers seek and how they judge whether these are present.

CUSTOMER TESTS When the prototypes are ready, they must be put through rigorous functional and customer tests before they enter the marketplace. *Alpha testing* tests the product within the firm to see how it performs in different applications. After refining the prototype further, the company moves to *beta testing* with customers.[74]

Consumer testing can bring consumers into a laboratory or give them samples to use at home. Procter & Gamble has on-site labs such as a diaper-testing centre where dozens of mothers bring their babies to be studied. To develop its Cover Girl Outlast all-day lip colour, P&G invited 500 women to come to its labs each morning to apply the lipstick, record their activities, and return eight hours later so it could measure remaining lip colour, resulting in a product that came with a tube of glossy moisturizer that women could apply on top of their colour without looking at a mirror. In-home placement tests are common for products from ice cream flavours to new appliances.

Market Testing

After management is satisfied with functional and psychological performance, the product is ready to be branded with a name, logo, and packaging and go into a market test. Canada is becoming the "ultimate" test market for many U.S.-based multinationals that also have operations in Canada. Not only are these companies testing new products, they are testing the marketing campaigns that support the new-product launch. The strategy of such firms is to let Canadian subsidiaries come up with and try out ideas that are more innovative and daring. If an idea works, it can then be rolled out in the United States. Pfizer's New

York–based parent and Montreal-based subsidiary have set the pace with their most recent "Apologies" ad series for VIAGRA, which playfully depicts what happens when guys abandon their buddies and previously planned activities like canoeing and golfing—thanks to VIAGRA.[75]

Not all companies undertake market testing. A company officer at Revlon stated: "In our field—primarily higher-priced cosmetics not geared for mass distribution—it would be unnecessary for us to market test. When we develop a new product, say an improved liquid makeup, we know it's going to sell because we're familiar with the field. And we've got 1500 demonstrators in department stores to promote it." Many companies, however, believe market testing can yield valuable information about buyers, dealers, marketing program effectiveness, and market potential. The main issues are how much market testing should be done, and what kind(s).

The amount is influenced by the investment cost and risk on the one hand, and the time pressure and research cost on the other. High-investment, high-risk products, whose chance of failure is high, must be market tested; the cost will be an insignificant percentage of total project cost. High-risk products that create new-product categories (first instant breakfast drink) or have novel features (first gum-strengthening toothpaste) warrant more market testing than modified products (another toothpaste brand).

CONSUMER-GOODS MARKET TESTING Consumer-product tests seek to estimate four variables: *trial, first repeat, adoption,* and *purchase frequency.* Many consumers may try the product but not rebuy it, or it might achieve high permanent adoption but low purchase frequency (like gourmet frozen foods).

Here are four major methods of consumer-goods market testing, from least to most costly.

Sales-Wave Research Consumers who initially try the product at no cost are re-offered it, or a competitor's product, at slightly reduced prices. The offer may be made as many as five times (sales waves), while the company notes how many customers select it again and their reported level of satisfaction.

Sales-wave research can be implemented quickly, conducted with a fair amount of security, and carried out without final packaging and advertising. However, because customers are preselected, it does not indicate trial rates the product would achieve with different sales incentives, nor does it indicate the brand's power to gain distribution and favourable shelf position.

Simulated Test Marketing Thirty to 40 qualified shoppers are asked about brand familiarity and preferences in a specific product category and attend a brief screening of both well-known and new TV commercials or print ads. One ad advertises the new product but is not singled out for attention. Consumers receive a small amount of money and are invited into a store where they may buy any items. The company notes how many consumers buy the new brand and competing brands. This provides a measure of the ad's relative effectiveness against competing ads in stimulating trial. Consumers are asked the reasons for their purchases or nonpurchases. Those who did not buy the new brand are given a free sample. Some weeks later, they are interviewed by phone to determine product attitudes, usage, satisfaction, and repurchase intention and are offered an opportunity to repurchase any products.

This method can give some surprisingly accurate results on advertising effectiveness and trial rates (and repeat rates if extended) in a much shorter time and at a fraction of the cost of using real test markets.[76] As media and channels grow more fragmented, however, it will become harder to truly simulate market conditions with only traditional approaches.

Controlled Test Marketing The company with the new product specifies the number of stores and geographic locations it wants to test. A research firm delivers the product to a panel of participating stores and controls shelf position, pricing, and number of facings, displays, and point-of-purchase promotions. Electronic scanners measure sales at checkout. The company can also evaluate the impact of local advertising and promotions and interview a sample of customers later to get their impressions of the product. It does not have to use its own sales force, give trade allowances, or "buy" distribution. However, controlled test marketing provides no information about how to sell the trade on carrying the new product. It also exposes the product and its features to competitors' scrutiny.

Test Markets The ultimate way to test a new consumer product is to put it into full-blown test markets. The company chooses a few representative cities and puts on a full marketing communications campaign, and the sales force tries to sell the trade on carrying the product and giving it good shelf exposure. Test marketing also measures the impact of alternative marketing plans by implementing them in different cities. A full-scale test can cost over $1 million, depending on the number of test cities, the test duration, and the amount of data the company wants to collect.

Management faces several decisions:

1. *How many test cities?* Most tests use two to six cities. The greater the possible loss, the number of contending marketing strategies, the regional differences, and the chance of test-market interference by competitors, the more cities management should test.

2. *Which cities?* Selection criteria include good media coverage, co-operative chain stores, and average competitive activity. How representative the city is of other markets must also be considered.

3. *Length of test?* Market tests last a few months to a year. The longer the average repurchase period, the longer the test period.

4. *What information to collect?* Warehouse shipment data will show gross inventory buying but will not indicate weekly sales at the retail level. Store audits will show retail sales and competitors' market shares but will not reveal buyer characteristics. Consumer panels will indicate which people are buying which brands and their loyalty and switching rates. Buyer surveys will yield in-depth information about consumer attitudes, usage, and satisfaction.

5. *What action to take?* If the test markets show high trial and repurchase rates, the marketer should launch the product nationally; if a high trial rate and low repurchase rate, redesign or drop the product; if a low trial rate and high repurchase rate, develop marketing communications to convince more people to try it. If trial and repurchase rates are both low, abandon the product. Many managers find it difficult to kill a project that involved much effort and attention—even if they should—resulting in an unfortunate (and typically unsuccessful) escalation of commitment.[77]

Despite its benefits, many companies today skip test marketing and rely on faster and more economical testing methods. General Mills prefers to launch new products in 25 percent of the country, an area too large for rivals to disrupt. Managers review retail scanner data, which tell them within days how the product is doing and what corrective fine-tuning to do. Colgate-Palmolive often launches a new product in a set of small "lead countries" and keeps rolling it out if it proves successful.

BUSINESS-GOODS MARKET TESTING Business goods can also benefit from market testing. Expensive industrial goods and new technologies will normally undergo alpha and beta testing. During beta testing, the company's technical people observe how customers use the product, a practice that often exposes unanticipated problems of safety and servicing and alerts the company to customer training and servicing requirements. The company can also observe how much value the equipment adds to the customer's operation as a clue to subsequent pricing.

Companies must interpret beta test results carefully, because only a small number of test customers are used, they are not randomly drawn, and tests are somewhat customized to each site. Another risk is that testers unimpressed with the product may leak unfavourable reports about it.

At trade shows, the company can observe how much interest buyers show in the new product, how they react to various features and terms, and how many express purchase intentions or place orders. In distributor and dealer display rooms, products may stand next to the manufacturer's other products and possibly competitors' products, yielding preference and pricing information in the product's normal selling atmosphere. However, customers who come in might not represent the target market, or they might want to place early orders that cannot be filled.

Industrial manufacturers come close to using full test marketing when they give a limited supply of the product to the sales force to sell in a limited number of areas that receive promotion support and printed catalogue sheets.

Commercialization

Commercialization incurs the company's highest costs to date.[78] The firm will need to contract for manufacture or build or rent a full-scale manufacturing facility. To introduce a major new consumer packaged good into the national market can cost $25 million to $100 million in advertising, promotion, and other communications in the first year. For new food products, marketing expenditures typically represent 57 percent of first-year sales. Most new-product campaigns rely on a sequenced mix of market communications tools.

WHEN (TIMING) Suppose a company has almost completed the development work on its new product and learns a competitor is nearing the end of its development work. The company faces three choices:

1. *First entry*—The first firm entering a market usually enjoys the "first mover advantages" of locking up key distributors and customers and gaining leadership. But if rushed to market before it has been thoroughly debugged, the first entry can backfire.

2. *Parallel entry*—The firm might time its entry to coincide with the competitor's entry. The market may pay more attention when two companies are advertising the new product.[79]

3. *Late entry*—The firm might delay its launch until after the competitor has borne the cost of educating the market, and its product may reveal flaws the late entrant can avoid. The late entrant can also learn the size of the market.

If a new product replaces an older product, the company might delay until the old product's stock is drawn down. If the product is seasonal, it might wait until the season arrives; often a product waits for a "killer application" to occur. Many companies are now encountering competitive "design-arounds"—rivals are making their own versions just different enough to avoid patent infringement and royalties.[80]

WHERE (GEOGRAPHIC STRATEGY) Most companies will develop a planned market rollout over time. In choosing rollout markets, the major criteria are market potential, the company's local reputation, the cost of filling the pipeline, the cost of communications media, the influence of the area on other areas, and competitive penetration. Small companies select an attractive city and put on a blitz campaign, entering other cities one at a time. Large companies introduce their product into a whole region and then move to the next. Companies with national distribution networks, such as auto companies, launch new models nationally.

With the web connecting far-flung parts of the globe, competition is more likely to cross national borders. Companies are increasingly rolling out new products simultaneously across the globe. However, masterminding a global launch poses challenges, and a sequential rollout across countries may still be the best option.[81]

TO WHOM (TARGET MARKET PROSPECTS) Within the rollout markets, the company must target initial distribution and promotion to the best prospect groups. Ideally, they should be early adopters, heavy users, and opinion leaders it can reach at low cost.[82] Few groups include all these, so the company should rate prospects and target the best group. The aim is to generate strong sales as soon as possible to attract further prospects.

HOW (INTRODUCTORY MARKET STRATEGY) Because new-product launches often take longer and cost more than expected, many potentially successful offerings suffer from underfunding. It's important to allocate sufficient time and resources—yet not overspend—as the new product gains traction in the marketplace.[83] An increasing number of companies are using online media heavily for the commercialization process, as did PromoHebdo.ca.

PromoHebdo.ca

PromoHebdo.ca is the first group buying website managed entirely by consumers on behalf of their community. The innovative Quebec-based website redefines the group buying concept by enabling consumers to manage the promotions offered online as well as advertising revenues. The site offers a diversified list of product categories including furniture, electronics, and even cars. With a launch date of September 2011, the company was able to build a following prior to launch by offering those who signed up as members a chance to win a trip for two to a Club Med sun destination ($5000 value) or a gift certificate ($25–$100 value) awarded daily to new users. Social media were also used in creating buzz prior to launch: new visitors to the site were greeted by a video explaining the concept behind the website and encouraged to visit and "like" the company's Facebook page.[84]

To coordinate the many tasks in launching a new product, management can use network-planning techniques such as **critical path scheduling (CPS)**, which develops a master chart showing the simultaneous and sequential activities that must take place. By estimating how much time each activity takes, planners estimate completion time for the entire project. Any delay in any activity on the critical path—the shortest route to completion—will delay the project. If the launch must be completed sooner, the planner searches for ways to reduce time along the critical path.[85]

THE CONSUMER ADOPTION PROCESS

Adoption is an individual's decision to become a regular user of a product and is followed by the *consumer-loyalty process*. New-product marketers typically aim at early adopters and use the theory of innovation diffusion and consumer adoption to identify them.

Stages in the Adoption Process

An **innovation** is any good, service, or idea that someone *perceives* as new, no matter how long its history. Everett Rogers defines the **innovation diffusion process** as "the spread of a new idea from its source of invention or creation to its ultimate users or adopters."[86] The *consumer adoption process* is the mental steps through which an individual passes from first hearing about an innovation to final adoption:[87]

1. *Awareness*—The consumer becomes aware of the innovation but lacks information about it.

2. *Interest*—The consumer is stimulated to seek information about the innovation.

3. *Evaluation*—The consumer considers whether to try the innovation.

4. *Trial*—The consumer tries the innovation to improve his or her estimate of its value.

5. *Adoption*—The consumer decides to make full and regular use of the innovation.

The new-product marketer should facilitate movement through these stages. A water filtration system manufacturer might discover that many consumers are stuck in the interest stage; they do not buy, because of their uncertainty and the large investment cost.[88] But these same consumers would be willing to use a water filtration system at home on a trial basis for a small monthly fee. The manufacturer should consider offering a trial-use plan with option to buy.

Factors Influencing the Adoption Process

Marketers recognize the following characteristics of the adoption process: differences in individual readiness to try new products, the effect of personal influence, differing rates of adoption, and differences in organizations' readiness to try new products. Some researchers are focusing on use-diffusion processes as a complement to adoption process models, to see how consumers actually use new products.[89]

READINESS TO TRY NEW PRODUCTS AND PERSONAL INFLUENCE Everett Rogers defines a person's level of innovativeness as "the degree to which an individual is relatively earlier in adopting new ideas than the other members of his social system."[90] Some people are the first to adopt new clothing fashions or new appliances; some doctors are the first to prescribe new medicines. See the adopter categories in Figure 20.7. After a slow start, an increasing number of people adopt the innovation, the number reaches a peak, and then it diminishes as fewer nonadopters remain. The five adopter groups differ in their value orientations and their motives for adopting or resisting the new product:[91]

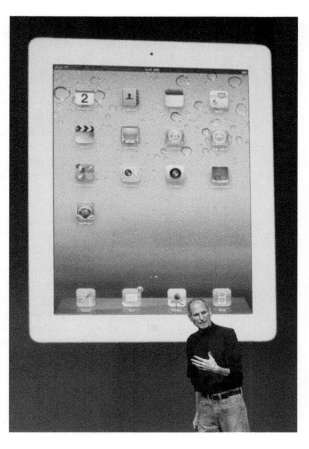

■ *Innovators* are technology enthusiasts; they are venturesome and enjoy tinkering with new products and mastering their intricacies. In return for low prices, they are happy to conduct alpha and beta testing and report on early weaknesses.

■ *Early adopters* are opinion leaders who carefully search for new technologies that might give them a dramatic competitive advantage. They are less price sensitive and are willing to adopt the product if given personalized solutions and good service support.

■ *Early majority* are deliberate pragmatists who adopt the new technology when its benefits are proven and a lot of adoption has already taken place. They make up the mainstream market.

■ *Late majority* are skeptical conservatives who are risk averse, technology shy, and price sensitive.

■ *Laggards* are tradition-bound and resist the innovation until the status quo is no longer defensible.

Each group requires a different type of marketing if the firm wants to move its innovation through the full product life cycle.[92]

Personal influence, the effect one person has on another's attitude or purchase probability, has greater significance in some situations and for some individuals than others, and it is more important in evaluation than in the other stages. It has more power over late than early adopters and in risky situations.

Companies often target innovators and early adopters with product rollouts. When Nike entered the skateboarding market, it recognized that an anti-establishment, big-company bias from the target market could present a sizeable challenge. To gain "street cred" with teen skaters, it sold exclusively to independent shops, advertised nowhere but skate magazines, and gained sponsorships from well-admired pro riders by engaging them in product design.[93]

CHARACTERISTICS OF THE INNOVATION Some products catch on immediately (inline skates), whereas others take a long time to gain acceptance (diesel engine autos). Five main characteristics influence an innovation's rate of adoption. We consider them for personal video recorders (PVRs) for home use, as exemplified by PVR use in Canada.[94]

Many innovators and early adopters were thrilled when Apple CEO Steve Jobs announced the launch of the iPad in January 2010.

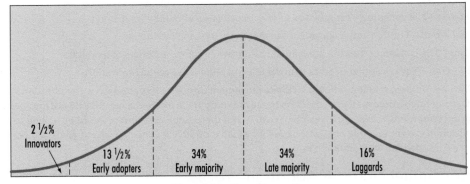

Time of Adoption of Innovations

The first characteristic is *relative advantage*—the degree to which the innovation appears superior to existing products. The greater the perceived relative advantage of using a PVR, say, for easily recording favourite shows, pausing live TV, or skipping commercials, the more quickly it will be adopted. The second is *compatibility*—the degree to which the innovation matches the values and experiences of the individuals. PVRs are highly compatible with the preferences of avid television watchers. Third is *complexity*—the degree to which the innovation is difficult to understand or use. PVRs are somewhat complex and will therefore take a slightly longer time to penetrate into home use. Fourth is *divisibility*—the degree to which the innovation can be tried on a limited basis. This provides a sizeable challenge for PVRs, a product that is relatively difficult to sample, although product demonstration can occur in a retail store or perhaps a friend's house. Fifth is *communicability*—the degree to which the benefits of use are observable or describable to others. The fact that PVRs have some clear advantages can help create interest and curiosity.

Other characteristics that influence the rate of adoption are cost, risk and uncertainty, scientific credibility, and social approval. The new-product marketer must research all these factors and give the key ones maximum attention in designing the product and marketing program.[95]

ORGANIZATIONS' READINESS TO ADOPT INNOVATIONS The creator of a new teaching method would want to identify innovative schools. The producer of a new piece of medical equipment would want to identify innovative hospitals. Adoption is associated with variables in the organization's environment (community progressiveness, community income), the organization itself (size, profits, pressure to change), and the administrators (education level, age, sophistication). Other forces come into play in trying to get a product adopted into organizations that receive the bulk of their funding from the government, such as public schools. A controversial or innovative product can be squelched by negative public opinion.

SUMMARY

1. Once a company has segmented the market, chosen its target customer groups and identified their needs, and determined its desired market positioning, it is ready to develop and launch appropriate new products and services. Marketing should participate with other departments in every stage of new-product development.

2. Successful new-product development requires the company to establish an effective organization for managing the development process. Companies can choose to use product managers, new-product managers, new-product committees, or new-product departments. Increasingly, companies are adopting cross-functional teams, connecting to individuals and organizations outside the company, and developing multiple product concepts.

3. Eight stages take place in the new-product development process: idea generation, screening, concept development and testing, marketing strategy development, business analysis, product development, market testing, and commercialization. At each stage, the company must determine whether the idea should be dropped or moved to the next stage.

4. The consumer adoption process is the process by which customers learn about new products, try them, and adopt or reject them. Today many marketers are targeting heavy users and early adopters of new products, because both groups can be reached by specific media and tend to be opinion leaders. The consumer adoption process is influenced by many factors beyond the marketer's control, including consumers' and organizations' willingness to try new products, personal influences, and the characteristics of the new product or innovation.

APPLICATIONS

Marketing Debate: Whom Should You Target with New Products?

Some new-products experts maintain that getting close to customers through intensive research is the only way to develop successful new products. Other experts disagree and maintain that customers can't possibly provide useful feedback on what they don't know and can't provide insights that will lead to breakthrough products.

Take a position: Consumer research is critical to new-product development *versus* Consumer research may not be all that helpful in new-product development.

Marketing Discussion: Product Innovativeness

Think about the last new product you bought. How do you think its success will be affected by the five characteristics of an innovation: relative advantage, compatibility, complexity, divisibility, and communicability?

MARKETING **EXCELLENCE** | ALDO

Since 1972, Canadian footwear giant Aldo has been serving up stylish shoes and accessories under eight different banners that include Aldo, Feetfirst, Spring, and Little Burgundy. From opening its first Aldo retail location through a partnership with Canadian clothing store le château, the company has grown to 1600 stand-alone stores across 60 countries. Throughout this growth, Aldo has learned to identify opportunities and respond to them. Sensitive to its home market in Canada, Aldo recognized an underserved segment: the mature female shopper looking for both comfort and style.

The target customer in this new market appreciates comfortable footwear with a local flavour, hence the name for the new chain of stores: Locale. Offering a uniquely warm and cultured shopping experience, the stores showcase the works of contemporary artists from local communities. By doing so, Locale stores are clearly differentiated from the shopping experience offered by cookie-cutter chain stores.

By 2011, nine Locale stores were opened in Montreal, Toronto, and Calgary. Aldo recognizes that no matter how attractive the experience of shopping in Locale stores, the brand's success ultimately comes down to the products it offers. Locale staff analyze the weekend sales on Monday mornings to determine which styles to push for the week ahead. While the Locale customer is less fashion-conscious than the Aldo shopper, style is still important. In the Locale product development showroom, the company is able to get a popular new style reproduced and on the shelves in just a few days.

In an effort to provide both style and comfort, Locale products include more padding and richer leathers, and developers have a mandate to keep shoes to "wearable heights" for the slightly older, more sophisticated customer. Locale shoes are also designed to last longer than an Aldo pair, and are priced $20 to $30 higher. As most Locale shoes have a relatively timeless design, they don't go out of style and can be worn year after year.

QUESTIONS

1. In your opinion, is Aldo spreading itself too thin by expanding its portfolio of brands? Justify your answer.

2. If Aldo were to diversify its product line, what are some new products you would recommend the company introduce?

3. Aldo chose three large Canadian cities—Montreal, Toronto, and Calgary—to open its new Locale stores. Should the company have tested its stores in smaller cities instead? Why or why not?

Sources: Eva Friede, "Locale Footprints: Global Shoe Giant Aldo Bets on Wooing Older Consumers," *Ottawa Citizen*, May 25, 2011; Briony Smith, "Aldo Looking to Change the Fashion Game: Can Comfort and Style Ever Exist in the Same Sentence?" TorontoSun.com, June 11, 2011, www.torontosun.com/2011/06/09/aldo-is-looking-to-change-the-fashion-game (viewed June 22, 2011); Locale website, www.localeshoes.com/ca-eng (viewed June 22, 2011).

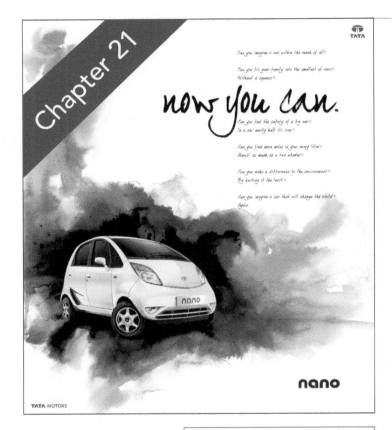

India's Tata Group has a wide range of global businesses, including one that produces the remarkably priced $2500 Tata Nano or the "People's Car."

In This Chapter, We Will Address the Following **Questions**

1. What factors should a company review before deciding to go abroad?

2. How can companies evaluate and select specific foreign markets to enter?

3. What are the differences between marketing in a developing market and in a developed market?

4. What are the major ways of entering a foreign market?

5. To what extent must the company adapt its products and marketing program to each foreign country?

6. How do marketers influence country-of-origin effects?

7. How should the company manage and organize its international activities?

Tapping into Global Markets

With ever-faster communication, transportation, and financial flows, the world is rapidly shrinking. Countries are increasingly multicultural, and products and services developed in one country are finding enthusiastic acceptance in others. A German businessman may wear an Italian suit to meet an English friend at a Japanese restaurant, who later returns home to drink Russian vodka and watch a U.S. movie on a Korean TV. Emerging markets that embrace capitalism and consumerism are especially attractive targets for marketers. These markets are also creating marketing powerhouses all their own.

Tata Group, India's biggest conglomerate, operates successful businesses that range from steel, energy, chemical, telecommunications, and cars to hotels, tea bags, and wristwatches. Its business dealings stretch far and wide and have included purchases of South Korea's Daewoo Motors truck unit, Dutch-British steel giant Corus Group, and U.K.-based Tetley Tea and Jaguar Land Rover. The proprietor of the Taj luxury hotels, Tata also owns or manages the rebranded Ritz-Carlton in Boston, the Pierre in New York City, and Camden Place in San Francisco. Tata Consultancy Services, India's largest tech-services company, collects roughly half its revenues in North America. Tata Motors is also India's largest commercial vehicle maker and created a stir with the recent launch of its $2500 Tata Nano, dubbed the "People's Car." Although impossibly low-priced by Western standards, at 100 000 Indian rupees, the Nano's price is approximately twice India's annual per capita income. The Nano comfortably seats five while running a 35-horsepower engine that gets nearly 50 miles per gallon. Aiming to sell 250 000 units annually, Tata Motors' target customers include the 7 million Indians who buy scooters and motorcycles every year, in part because they cannot afford a car. The market potential is huge—there are just seven automobiles per 1000 people in India. Tata Motors is also targeting other "bottom of the pyramid" markets such as Africa and Southeast Asia and even parts of Eastern Europe and Latin America.[1]

Companies need to be able to cross boundaries within and outside their country. Although opportunities to enter and compete in international markets are significant, the risks can also be high. Companies selling in global industries, however, have no choice but to internationalize their operations. In this chapter, we review the major decisions in expanding into global markets.

COMPETING ON A GLOBAL BASIS

Many companies have been global marketers for decades—firms like Shell, Bayer, and Toshiba have sold goods around the world for years. In luxury goods such as jewellery, watches, and handbags, where the addressable market is relatively small, a global profile is essential for firms like Prada, Gucci, and Louis Vuitton to profitably grow. But global competition is intensifying in more product categories as new firms make their mark on the international stage.[2]

Trade is Canada's primary engine of economic growth. Our domestic market is relatively small, so we depend on international trade for the creation of jobs and the generation of wealth. In 2010, the value of Canadian exports rose 9.6 percent (over 2009 levels) to $404.8 billion.[3] Exports represent approximately 30 percent of our GDP. In comparison, the United States' international sales account for only 9 percent of its GDP, while Japan exports approximately 15 percent of its GDP.[4]

The automotive market is becoming a worldwide free-for-all. In Chile, with no domestic auto manufacturers, imports are coming from all over the world, including 14 different brands of Chinese cars, trucks, and commercial vehicles.[5] In China's fast-moving cell phone market, Motorola found its market share cut in half over a two-year period from inroads by Nokia and Asian competitors.

Competition from developing-market firms is heating up. Mahindra Motors' four-door, diesel-powered short-bed trucks from India are tackling Europe, Asia, and the United States, promising superior fuel economy.[6] Founded in Guatemala, Pollo Campero (Spanish for "country chicken") has expanded into the United States, Europe, and Asia, blending old favourites such as fried plantains and milky *horchata* drinks with traditional North American fare such as grilled chicken and mashed potatoes.[7]

Although some businesses may want to eliminate foreign competition through protective legislation, the better way to compete is to continuously improve products at home and expand into foreign markets. In a **global industry**, competitors' strategic positions in major geographic or national markets are affected by their overall global positions.[8] A **global firm** operates in more than one country and captures R&D, production, logistical, marketing, and financial advantages not available to purely domestic competitors.

Global firms plan, operate, and coordinate their activities on a worldwide basis. Otis Elevator uses door systems from France, small geared parts from Spain, electronics from Germany, and motor drives from Japan; systems integration happens in the United States. Consider the international success of Hyundai.[9]

Hyundai

Once synonymous with cheap and unreliable cars, Hyundai Motor Company has experienced a massive global transformation. In 1999, its new chairman, Mong-Koo Chung, declared that Hyundai would no longer focus on volume and market share but on quality instead. A number of changes were instituted: Hyundai began to benchmark industry leader Toyota, adopted Six Sigma processes, organized product development cross-functionally, partnered more closely with suppliers, and increased quality oversight meetings. From a place near the bottom of J. D. Power's study of U.S. new vehicle quality in 2001—32nd out of 37 brands—Hyundai zoomed to number 4 by 2009, surpassed only by luxury brands Lexus, Porsche, and Cadillac. Hyundai also transformed its marketing. Its "Assurance" campaign, backed by a pricey Super Bowl ad, allowed new buyers to return their cars risk-free if they lost their jobs. Other programs guaranteed customers low gas prices for a year and tax credits in advance of the U.S. government's Cash for Clunkers and Canadian government's Retire Your Ride program. The North American market was not the only one receiving attention from Hyundai and its younger, more affordably priced brand sibling, Kia. Hyundai is the second-largest car-maker in India; it is supplying Europe with a new €1.1 billion factory in the Czech Republic; and in a joint venture with Beijing Automotive, it is targeting China.

Many successful global brands have tapped into universal consumer values and needs—such as Nike with athletic performance, MuchMusic with youth culture, and Coca-Cola with youthful optimism. These firms hire thousands of employees abroad and make sure their products and marketing activities are consistent with local sensibilities.

Global marketing extends beyond products. Services represent the fastest-growing sector of the global economy and account for two-thirds of global output, one-third of global employment, and nearly 20 percent of global trade. Although some countries have erected entry barriers or regulations, the World Trade Organization, consisting of 153 countries, continues to press for more free trade in international services and other areas.[10]

For a company of any size or type to go global, it must make a series of decisions (see Figure 21.1). We'll examine each of these decisions here.[11]

DECIDING WHETHER TO GO ABROAD

Most companies would prefer to remain domestic if their domestic market were large enough. Managers would not need to learn other languages and laws, deal with volatile currencies, face political and legal uncertainties, or redesign their products to suit different customer needs and expectations. Business would be easier and safer. Yet several factors can draw companies into the international arena:

- Some international markets present better profit opportunities than the domestic market.
- The company needs a larger customer base to achieve economies of scale.

- The company wants to reduce its dependence on any one market.
- The company decides to counterattack global competitors in their home markets.
- Customers are going abroad and require international service.

Reflecting the power of these forces, exports accounted for roughly 30 percent of Canadian GDP in 2010.[12] Before making a decision to go abroad, the company must also weigh several risks:

- The company might not understand foreign preferences and could fail to offer a competitively attractive product.
- The company might not understand the foreign country's business culture.
- The company might underestimate foreign regulations and incur unexpected costs.
- The company might lack managers with international experience.
- The foreign country might change its commercial laws, devalue its currency, or undergo a political revolution and expropriate foreign property.

Most countries lament that too few of their companies participate in international trade. This lack of participation keeps the country from earning foreign exchange to pay for needed imports. It also raises the spectre of domestic companies eventually being hurt or taken over by foreign multinationals. Many countries sponsor aggressive export-promotion programs to get their companies to export. These programs require a deep understanding of how companies become internationalized. The Canadian government works hard to convince companies to export and provides services and information essential to their success. In 1997, to better coordinate these efforts, Team Canada Inc. was born. The organization was formed from a network of more than 20 federal government departments and agencies working with the provinces, territories, and other partners to provide a single window of access to export information and services. Its aim is to increase the capabilities, preparedness, and international market development success of Canadian businesses.

Some companies don't act until events thrust them into the international arena. The *internationalization process* typically has four stages:[13]

1. No regular export activities
2. Export via independent representatives (agents)
3. Establishment of one or more sales subsidiaries
4. Establishment of production facilities abroad

The first task is to move from stage 1 to stage 2. Most firms work with an independent agent and enter a nearby or similar country. Later, the firm establishes an export department to manage its agent relationships. Still later, it replaces agents with its own sales subsidiaries in its larger export markets. This increases investment and risk, but also earning potential. Next, to manage subsidiaries, the company replaces the export department with an international department or division. If markets are large and stable, or the host country requires local production, the company will locate production facilities there.

By this time, it's operating as a multinational and optimizing its sourcing, financing, manufacturing, and marketing as a global organization. According to some researchers, top management begins to focus on global opportunities when more than 15 percent of revenue comes from international markets.[14]

DECIDING WHICH MARKETS TO ENTER

In deciding to go abroad, the company needs to define its marketing objectives and policies. What proportion of international to total sales will it seek? Most companies start small when they venture abroad. Some plan to stay small; others have bigger plans.

How Many Markets to Enter

The company must decide how many countries to enter and how fast to expand. Typical entry strategies are the *waterfall* approach, gradually entering countries in sequence, and the *sprinkler* approach, entering many countries simultaneously. Increasingly, firms—especially technology-intensive firms—are *born global* and market to the entire world from the outset.[15]

Matsushita, BMW, General Electric, Benetton, and The Body Shop followed the waterfall approach. It allows firms to carefully plan expansion and is less likely to strain human and financial resources. When first-mover advantage is crucial and a high degree of competitive intensity prevails, the sprinkler approach is better. Microsoft sold over 150 million copies of Windows 7 in 100 countries in the fall of 2009 with only

FIGURE 21.1

Major Decisions in International Marketing

minor tweaks in its marketing. The main risk is the substantial resources needed and the difficulty of planning entry strategies for many diverse markets.[16]

The company must also choose the countries to consider based on the product and on geography, income and population, and political climate.

Developed versus Developing Markets

One of the sharpest distinctions in global marketing is between developed and developing or emerging markets such as Brazil, Russia, India, and China (often called "BRIC" for short).[17] Two other developing markets with much economic and marketing significance are Indonesia and South Africa. The unmet needs of the developing world represent huge potential markets for food, clothing, shelter, consumer electronics, appliances, and many other goods. Market leaders rely on developing markets to fuel their growth. Consider the following:

■ Coca-Cola, Unilever, Colgate-Palmolive, Groupe Danone, and PepsiCo earn 5 percent to 15 percent of their total revenues from the three largest emerging markets in Asia—China, India, and Indonesia.[18]

■ Developing markets make up over 25 percent of Kraft's total business, almost 40 percent of Cadbury's, and over 50 percent of Tupperware's sales.[19]

■ Nestlé estimates that about 1 billion consumers in emerging markets will increase their incomes enough to afford its products within the next decade. The world's largest food company gets about a third of its revenue from emerging economies and aims to lift that to 45 percent within a decade.[20]

Developed nations account for about 20 percent of the world's population. Can marketers serve the other 80 percent, which has much less purchasing power and living conditions ranging from mild deprivation to severe deficiency? This imbalance is likely to get worse, as more than 90 percent of future population growth is projected to occur in the less-developed countries.[21]

Successfully entering developing markets requires a special set of skills and plans. Consider how these companies pioneered ways to serve "invisible" consumers:[22]

■ Grameenphone marketed cell phones to 35 000 villages in Bangladesh by hiring village women as agents who leased phone time to other villagers, one call at a time.

■ Colgate-Palmolive rolled into Indian villages with video vans that showed the benefits of teeth brushing.

■ Corporación GEO builds low-income housing in Mexico. The two-bedroom homes are modular and expandable.

These marketers capitalized on the potential of developing markets by changing their conventional marketing practices.[23] Selling in developing areas can't be business as usual. Economic and cultural differences abound, a marketing infrastructure may barely exist, and local competition can be surprisingly stiff.[24] Here are some examples of "local dynamos."

Local Dynamos

An extensive study by the Boston Consulting Group (BCG) identifies 50 firms in ten emerging economies as "local dynamos." According to BCG, a local dynamo is (1) prospering in its home market, (2) fending off multinational rivals, and (3) not focused on expanding abroad. India's Amul farmers' co-operative sells dairy products through a network of 2.8 million members supported by one of the longest-running and best-loved ad campaigns in India. Its ice cream and chocolate milk businesses have survived the entry of Unilever and Nestlé, respectively. Brazilian budget airline Gol has targeted thrifty Brazilian consumers willing to sacrifice convenience for price; planes often depart at odd hours and make multiple stops. Retailer Grupo Elektra is a Mexican financial and retail corporation owned by Grupo Salinas and is listed on the New York Stock Exchange (EKT), the Bolsa Mexicana de Valores (ELEKTRA), and the Spanish Stock Market Latibex (XEKT). Grupo Elektra sells washing machines, refrigerators, televisions, and other items on credit to people making less than $10 a day. The company's many stores double as bank branches where people can withdraw, deposit, and transmit cash, as well as get loans. According to BCG, local dynamos often combine in-depth understanding of consumer tastes with cost-effective production techniques to create a locally laser-focused business model.[25]

Getting the marketing equation right in developing markets can pay big dividends:

- Smaller packaging and lower sales prices are often critical when incomes and housing spaces are limited. Unilever's 4-cent sachets of detergent and shampoo were a big hit in rural India, where 70 percent of the population still lives.[26]

- Eighty percent of consumers in emerging markets buy their products from tiny bodegas, stalls, kiosks, and mom-and-pop stores not much bigger than a closet, which Procter & Gamble recognizes as "high-frequency stores."[27] In India, Unilever adjusts its distribution strategy, well-aware that 98 percent of food is still purchased from the 12 million neighbourhood mom-and-pop outfits called *kirana* stores.[28]

- Nokia sends marketing, sales, and engineering staff from its entry-level phone group to spend a week in people's homes in rural China, Thailand, and Kenya to observe how they use phones. By developing rock-bottom-priced phones with just the right functionality, Nokia has become the market share leader in Africa and Asia.[29]

- A Western image can be helpful. Coca-Cola's success against local cola brand Jianlibao in China was partly due to its symbolic values of modernity and affluence.[30]

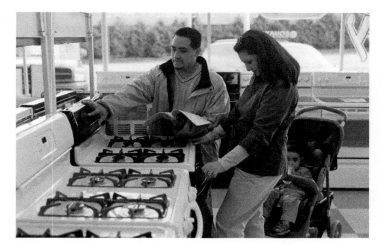

Grupo Elektra's retail stores in Mexico and Latin America sell appliances and offer financial services to low-income consumers.

Competition is growing from companies based in developing markets. China has been exporting cars to Africa, Southeast Asia, and the Middle East. Tata of India, Cemex of Mexico, and PETRONAS of Malaysia have emerged from developing markets to become strong multinationals selling in many countries.[31]

Many firms are using lessons gleaned from marketing in developing markets to better compete in their developed markets (recall the "bottom of the pyramid" discussion from Chapter 3). John Deere's research facility in Pune, India, developed four no-frills tractors whose affordability and manoeuvrability also found a market in North America. About half the tractors Deere makes in India are sold overseas.[32]

Product innovation has become a two-way street between developing and developed markets. The challenge is to think creatively about how marketing can fulfill the dreams of most of the world's population for a better standard of living.[33] Many companies are betting they can do that. "Marketing Insight: Spotlight on Key Developing Markets" highlights some important developments in the BRIC countries plus South Africa and Indonesia.

Regional economic integration—the creation of trading agreements between blocs of countries—has intensified in recent years. This means companies are more likely to enter entire regions at the same time. Certain countries have formed free trade zones or economic communities—groups of nations organized to work toward common goals in the regulation of international trade (see Table 21.1).

Evaluating Potential Markets

However much nations and regions integrate their trading policies and standards, each still has unique features. A nation's or region's readiness for different products and services, and its attractiveness as a market, depend on its demographic, economic, sociocultural, natural, technological, and political-legal environments.

How does a company choose among potential markets to enter? Many prefer to sell to neighbouring countries because companies understand these countries better and can control entry costs more effectively. It's not surprising that the two largest U.S. export markets are Canada and Mexico, or that Swedish companies first sold to their Scandinavian neighbours.

At other times, *psychic proximity* determines choices. Given more familiar language, laws, and culture, many U.S. firms prefer to sell in Canada, England, and Australia rather than in larger markets such as Germany and France. Companies should be careful, however, in choosing markets according to cultural distance. Besides overlooking potentially better markets, companies may only superficially analyze differences and therefore put themselves at a disadvantage.[34]

It often makes sense to operate in fewer countries, with a deeper commitment and penetration in each. In general, a company prefers to enter countries (1) that rank high on market attractiveness, (2) that are low in market risk, and (3) in which it possesses a competitive advantage. Here is how Viterra chooses new locations.

MARKETING **INSIGHT**	SPOTLIGHT ON KEY DEVELOPING MARKETS

Brazil

According to the World Bank, 25 percent of Latin Americans live on less than $2 a day; millions more earn only a few hundred dollars a month. In Brazil, the region's biggest market, low-income groups make up 87 percent of the population but earn only 53 percent of the income. Marketers are finding innovative ways to sell products and services to these poor and low-income residents. Nestlé Brazil boosted sales of Bono cookies 40 percent after shrinking the package from 200 to 140 grams and lowering the price. With illiteracy widespread, Unilever launched a brand of soap in northeast Brazil with the simple name, "Ala."

Brazil experienced some "go-go" growth years in the 1960s and 1970s, when it was the world's second-fastest-growing large economy. As a result, it now boasts large and well-developed agricultural, mining, manufacturing, and service sectors. Brazilian firms that have succeeded internationally include aircraft manufacturer Embraer, sandal maker Havaianas, and brewer and beverage producer AmBev, which merged with Interbrew to form InBev. Brazil also differs from other emerging markets in being a full-blown democracy, unlike Russia and China, and it has no serious disputes with neighbours, unlike India.

A number of obstacles exist, however, that are popularly called *custo Brasil* ("the cost of Brazil"). The cost of transporting products eats up nearly 13 percent of Brazil's GDP, five percentage points more than in the United States. Unloading a container is twice as expensive as in India and takes three times longer than in China. Most observers see Brazil's economic, social, and political transformation as a work in process, although it emerged from the recent economic recession relatively unscathed.

Russia

The 1991 splintering of the Soviet Union transformed Russia's isolated, centrally planned economy to a globally integrated, market-based economy. Russia is the largest exporter of natural gas, the second-largest exporter of oil, and the third-largest exporter of steel and primary aluminum. Reliance on commodities has its downside, however. Russia's economy was hammered in the recent recession by plunging commodity prices and the credit crunch.

Dutch brewer Heineken, Swedish retailer IKEA, U.S. banker Citibank, and more than a dozen car-makers recently ramped up operations in Russia to target its growing middle class, now one-quarter to one-third of the population with fast-rising salaries and access to consumer credit. But the average Russian still earns only $700 a month, a fraction of the U.S. average, and many feel left behind. The economic crisis also saw a significant reduction in foreign investment in the country.

Russia has a dwindling workforce and poor infrastructure. The Organisation for Economic Co-operation and Development (OECD) cautions that economic reforms have stagnated and ranks Russia as one of the most corrupt countries in the world. Many feel Vladimir Putin's government has been unpredictable and difficult to work with.

Still, companies remain optimistic. In 2006, more than 167 000 Motorola handsets were seized on arrival at Moscow airport. The interior ministry supposedly destroyed around 50 000 as smuggled or counterfeit, though some were later reported found on the black market. Eventually, most were returned, but more telling was Motorola's reaction. With Russia as its third-biggest handset market in the world at the time, an unshaken Motorola stayed the course.

India

Reforms in the early 1990s that lowered trade barriers and liberalized capital markets have brought India booming investment and consumption. But it's not all about demand. With many low-cost, high-IQ, English-speaking employees, India is gaining programming and call centre jobs once held by U.S. workers. Its growth has been driven largely by the manufacturing and service sectors where most of its workers are employed.

India's ascent opens a larger market for U.S. and Western goods. Almost two-thirds of the population is under 35, and about 16 million, or 3 percent, are high-earning targets of youth lifestyle brands connoting status and affluence. Luxury cars and shiny motorbikes are the most sought-after status symbols, followed by clothing, food, entertainment, consumer durables, and travel.

India still struggles with poor infrastructure and public services—education, health, and water supply—and restrictive labour laws. Its 28 separate states each have their own policies and tax rules. But global firms such as Mittal, Reliance, Tata, Wipro, and Infosys all have achieved international success, and many outside firms are setting their sights there.

China

China's 1.3 billion people have marketers scrambling to gain a foothold, and competition has heated up between domestic and international firms. Its 2001 entry into the World Trade Organization eased China's manufacturing and investment rules and modernized retail and logistics industries. Greater competition in pricing, products, and channels resulted, but publishing, telecommunications, oil exploration, marketing, pharmaceuticals, banking, and insurance remained fiercely protected or off-limits to foreigners altogether. Foreign businesses complain about subsidized competition, restricted access, conflicting regulations, lack of protection for intellectual property, and opaque and seemingly arbitrary bureaucracy.

Selling in China means going beyond the big cities to the 700 million potential consumers who live in small communities in the rural interior. About half of potential PC buyers live outside major cities; only one-third of overall retail revenues come from China's 24 largest cities. Rural consumers can be challenging; they have lower incomes, are less sophisticated, and often cling to local habits. PC maker Lenovo, cell phone provider TCL, and appliance manufacturer Haier have thrived despite strong foreign competition. Besides their sharp grasp of Chinese tastes, they have vast distribution networks, especially in rural areas.

China's emerging urban middle class is active and discerning, demanding higher-quality products and variety. Although they number four times the U.S. population, Chinese consumers spend a fraction of what U.S. consumers spend. Luxury cars are the fastest-growing auto segment thanks to China's swelling ranks of millionaires.

Indonesia

Indonesia's reputation as a country historically struggling with natural disasters, terrorism, and economic uncertainty is quickly being replaced by a country characterized by political stability and economic growth. The fourth-largest country in the world and the largest Muslim country, it is perhaps no surprise that, given all the country's progress, Morgan Stanley suggested adding Indonesia to the four BRIC countries to make it the BRICI countries.

Indonesia has become the third-fastest-growing economy in the region—behind India and China—largely on the basis of its 240 million consumers. Foreign direct investments account for only 25 percent of gross domestic product. Although half the population live on less than $2 a day, their spending and the spending of an active younger population is driving economic growth.

Some foreign firms are taking advantage of opportunities there. Indonesia is one of Research In Motion's (RIM's) hottest markets, and the BlackBerry has achieved iconic status in the country. RIM has taken advantage of a mobile-friendly environment (broadband service is patchy and expensive) and has also customized its offerings with dozens of applications designed specifically for the Indonesian market. Its success is not without some downside, though: it has inspired scores of knock-offs from China dubbed "Chinaberries" by locals.

Indonesia presents other challenges. Effective, efficient distribution is critical in the country, an archipelago with more than 14 000 islands in a hot and humid climate. Large importers have established extensive distribution networks which allow them to extend beyond the one-third of the population that lives in the six or seven largest cities. Like many developing countries, Indonesia also lacks infrastructure.

But the progress of Indonesia in recent years is noteworthy. As further proof, with over 20 percent of Indonesian Internet users having a Twitter account, Indonesia is the sixth-most-active country in microblogging.

South Africa

Although South Africa is a developed market, it is included here in its role as an access point to the African region as well as an important market in its own right. According to the World Bank, of the 35 least business-friendly countries, 27 are in sub-Saharan Africa; 42 percent of the region's economy is informal. Bad roads, unreliable electricity, and volatile currency fluctuations add logistical and financial challenges. War, famine, AIDS, and disaster are even more significant human difficulties. Most Africans live in poverty, and 60 percent still engage in agriculture for their primary income.

But a recent period of relative stability has coincided with improvements in health, education, and social services. The 2010 World Cup offered a chance to re-examine economic progress in South Africa and other African countries. Many companies are using South Africa as a base to do business in Africa:

- Cell phone operator Celtel invested in rural services by introducing the Me2U service, by which callers could send airtime credit to other cell phones. Because most Africans don't have bank accounts, it became a convenient and cheap way to transfer money, even substituting for cash in some villages.

- South Africa's MTN, the region's largest cell phone company, built its own microwave transmission backbone and power supplies in Nigeria, and the first solar pay phone near Lake Victoria, Uganda.

- South Africa's Net1 has built a customer base of 3.6 million accounts by issuing free smart cards to indigent people who lack bank accounts or credit cards, taking tiny percentages of their transactions for revenue.

The payoff for companies willing to do business in Africa is often large margins and minimal competition. SABMiller, the world's second-largest brewer, enjoys its best operating margins in Africa. Finding a local partner can add expertise and contacts. SABMiller's African operations are joint ventures with locals, some of them government. The Boston Consulting Group has dubbed eight of Africa's strongest economies the "African Lions": Algeria, Botswana, Egypt, Libya, Mauritius, Morocco, South Africa, and Tunisia.

Sources: *Brazil:* Antonio Regalado, "Marketers Pursue the Shallow Pocketed," *Wall Street Journal,* January 26, 2007; "Land of Promise," *Economist,* April 12, 2007; Melissa Campanelli, "Marketing to Latin America? Think Brazil," *DMNews,* June 20, 2006. *Russia:* Jason Bush, "Russia Economy Turns Swiftly Siberian," *BusinessWeek,* December 15, 2008, p. 68; "Risk and Reward in Russia," *BusinessWeek Emerging Market Report,* October 20, 2008; "Dancing with the Bear," *Economist,* February 3, 2007, pp. 63–64; Jason Bush, "Russia: How Long Can the Fun Last?" *BusinessWeek,* December 18, 2006, pp. 50–51; Steven Lee Myers, "Business as Usual, Russian-Style," *International Herald Tribune,* June 13, 2006. *India:* Nandan Nilekani, *Imagining India: The Idea of a Renewed Nation* (New York: Penguin Press, 2009); Anil K. Gupta and Haiyan Wang, "Five Myths about India," *Economic Times,* December 29, 2009; "India on Fire," *Economist,* February 3, 2007, pp. 69–71; "16m. Young High-Earning Consumers Are Targets of High-End Lifestyle Products," *News India Times,* August 4, 2006, p. 16. *China:* Edward Wong, "China's Export Economy Begins Turning Inward, *New York Times,* June 24, 2010; Arthur Kroeber, "Five Myths about the Chinese Economy," *Washington Post,* April 11, 2010; "Impenetrable: Selling Foreign Goods in China," *Economist,* October 17, 2009; Dexter Roberts, "Cadillac Floors It in China," *BusinessWeek,* June 4, 2007, p. 52; Bruce Einhorn, "Grudge Match in China," *BusinessWeek,* April 2, 2007, pp. 42–43; Russell Flannery, "Watch Your Back," *Forbes,* April 23, 2007, pp. 104–105; Dexter Roberts, "Cautious Consumers," *BusinessWeek,* April 30, 2007, pp. 32–34; Seung Ho Park and Wilfried R. Vanhonacker, "The Challenge for Multinational Corporations in China: Think Local, Act Global," *MIT Sloan Management Review,* May 31, 2007; Dexter Roberts, "Scrambling to Bring Crest to the Masses," *BusinessWeek,* June 25, 2007, pp. 72–73. *Indonesia:* Louise Lavabre, "Talking with Our Thumbs: Twitter in Indonesia," *Jakarta Post,* September 22, 2010; Alexandra A. Seno, "Gung-Ho Attitude Delivers Success in Indonesia," *Globe and Mail,* March 25, 2010; Mark MacKinnon, "RIM's Indonesian Bonanza," *Globe and Mail,* March 24, 2010; Peter Geiling, "Will Indonesia Make It BRICI?" *GlobalPost,* July 7, 2009; Margie Bauer, "Indonesia—An Economic Success Story," October 14, 2004, www.fas.usda.gov. *South Africa:* "The Price of Freedom: A Special Report on South Africa," *Economist,* June 5, 2010; "Africa's Dynamo," *BusinessWeek Emerging Market Report,* December 15, 2008; Frank Aquilla, "Africa's Biggest Score: A Thriving Economy," *BusinessWeek,* June 28, 2010; Helen Coster, "Great Expectations," *Forbes,* February 12, 2007, pp. 56–58. *All: CIA World Factbook,* www.cia.gov.

TABLE 21.1 | REGIONAL TRADE AREAS AND AGREEMENTS

The European Union. Formed in 1957, the European Union set out to create a single European market by reducing barriers to the free flow of products, services, finances, and labour among member countries, and by developing trade policies with nonmember nations. Today, it's one of the world's largest single markets, with 27 member countries, a common currency (the euro), and more than 495 million consumers, accounting for 37 percent of the world's exports. Still, companies marketing in Europe face 23 different languages, 2000 years of historical and cultural differences, and a daunting mass of local rules.

NAFTA. In January 1994, the North American Free Trade Agreement (NAFTA) unified the United States, Mexico, and Canada in a single market of 440 million people who produce and consume $16 trillion worth of goods and services annually. Implemented over a 15-year period, NAFTA eliminates all trade barriers and investment restrictions among the three countries. Before NAFTA, tariffs on U.S. products entering Mexico averaged 13 percent, whereas U.S. tariffs on Mexican goods averaged 6 percent.

MERCOSUR. Mercosur (or Mercosul) links Brazil, Argentina, Paraguay, Uruguay, and (soon) Venezuela to promote free trade and the fluid movement of goods, people, and currency. These five countries have 270 million citizens and collective GDP of $2.4 trillion. Bolivia, Chile, Colombia, Ecuador, and Peru are associate members and do not enjoy full voting rights or access to all the same markets. NAFTA will likely eventually merge with this and other arrangements to form an all-Americas free trade zone.

APEC. Twenty-one countries, as well as the NAFTA members and Japan and China, are working to create a pan-Pacific free trade area under the auspices of the Asia-Pacific Economic Cooperation (APEC) forum. These countries account for approximately 40.5 percent of the world's population, approximately 54.2 percent of world GDP, and about 43.7 percent of world trade. Heads of government of APEC members meet at an annual summit to discuss regional economy, co-operation, trade, and investment.

ASEAN. Ten countries make up the Association of Southeast Asian Nations: Brunei Darussalam, Cambodia, Indonesia, Lao PDR, Malaysia, Myanmar, Philippines, Singapore, Thailand, and Vietnam. The region is an attractive market of over 590 million people with $1.2 trillion in GDP. Member countries aim to enhance the area as a major production and export centre.

Sources: www.europa.eu; "World Trade Report 2009," www.wto.org; www.naftanow.org; Council on Foreign Relations, "Mercosur: South America's Fractious Trade Bloc," www.cfr.org; www.apec.org; www.asean.org.

Companies such as Viterra consider a variety of factors when choosing international markets.

Viterra

Regina-based Viterra Inc. is a global agribusiness that specializes in grain handling and marketing agriproducts and value-added processing, with operations across North America, Australia, New Zealand, and Southeast Asia. When looking to expand its international operations, the choice of office location was made taking many factors into account. Kiev, Ukraine, was chosen as the new location for geographical and strategic reasons. Ukraine, in the Black Sea region, is known for its rich soil and is the fifth-largest wheat-exporting nation in the world. The Black Sea region is also known for barley and canola, which are Viterra's core products. By establishing an office in Ukraine, Viterra is able to capitalize on the region's resources and establish itself in the European market.[35]

DECIDING HOW TO ENTER THE MARKET

Once a company decides to target a particular country, it must determine the best mode of entry. Its broad choices are indirect exporting, direct exporting, licensing, joint ventures, and direct investment, shown in Figure 21.2. Each succeeding strategy entails more commitment, risk, control, and profit potential.

Indirect and Direct Export

Companies typically start with export, specifically *indirect exporting*—that is, they work through independent intermediaries. *Domestic-based export merchants* buy the manufacturer's products and then sell them abroad. *Domestic-based export agents,* including trading companies, seek and negotiate foreign purchases for a commission. *Co-operative organizations* conduct exporting activities for several producers—often of primary products such as fruits or nuts—and are partly under their administrative control. *Export-management companies* agree to manage a company's export activities for a fee.

Indirect export has two advantages. First, there is less investment: the firm doesn't have to develop an export department, an overseas sales force, or a set of international contacts. Second, there's less risk: because international marketing intermediaries bring know-how and services to the relationship, the seller will make fewer mistakes.

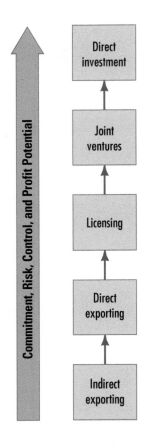

FIGURE 21.2

Five Modes of Entry into
Foreign Markets

Companies may eventually decide to handle their own exports.[36] The investment and risk are somewhat greater, but so is the potential return. Direct exporting happens in several ways:

■ *Domestic-based export department or division.* A purely service function may evolve into a self-contained export department operating as its own profit centre.

■ *Overseas sales branch or subsidiary.* The sales branch handles sales and distribution and perhaps warehousing and promotion as well. It often serves as a display and customer-service centre.

■ *Travelling export sales representatives.* Home-based sales representatives travel abroad to find business.

■ *Foreign-based distributors or agents.* These third parties can hold limited or exclusive rights to represent the company in that country.

Many companies use direct or indirect exporting to "test the waters" before building a plant and manufacturing their product overseas. A company does not necessarily have to attend international trade shows if it can effectively use the Internet to attract new customers overseas, support existing customers who live abroad, source from international suppliers, and build global brand awareness.

Successful companies adapt their websites to provide country-specific content and services to their highest-potential international markets, ideally in the local language. Finding free information about trade and exporting has never been easier. Here are some places to start a search:

■ The Department of Foreign Affairs and International Trade (www.infoexport.gc.ca)

■ Canada Business (www.canadabusiness.ca)

■ Export Development Canada (www.edc.ca)

■ Industry Canada (www.ic.gc.ca)

In addition, most provincial governments provide information to facilitate international trade (e.g., for Ontario, see the International Trade Branch at www.ontarioexports.com). Many provinces' export-promotion offices also have online resources and may allow businesses to link to their sites.

Licensing

Licensing is a simple way to engage in international marketing. The licensor issues a licence to a foreign company to use a manufacturing process, trademark, patent, trade secret, or other item of value for a fee or royalty. The licensor gains entry at little risk; the licensee gains production expertise or a well-known product or brand name.

The licensor, however, has less control over the licensee than over its own production and sales facilities. If the licensee is very successful, the firm has given up profits, and if and when the contract ends, it might find it has created a competitor. To prevent this, the licensor usually supplies some proprietary product ingredients or components (as Coca-Cola does). But the best strategy is to lead in innovation so the licensee will continue to depend on the licensor.

Licensing arrangements vary. Companies such as Hyatt and Marriott sell *management contracts* to owners of foreign hotels to manage these businesses for a fee. The management firm may have the option to purchase some share in the managed company within a stated period.

In *contract manufacturing,* the firm hires local manufacturers to produce the product. When Sears opened department stores in Mexico and Spain, it found qualified local manufacturers to produce many of its products. Contract manufacturing reduces the company's control over the process and risks loss of potential profits. However, it offers a chance to start faster, with the opportunity to partner with or buy out the local manufacturer later.

Finally, a company can enter a foreign market through *franchising,* a more complete form of licensing. The franchisor offers a complete brand concept and operating system. In return, the franchisee invests in and pays certain fees to the franchisor. McDonald's, Ramada, and Avis have entered scores of countries by franchising their retail concepts and making their marketing culturally relevant.

Joint Ventures

Foreign investors may join with local investors to create a joint venture company in which they share ownership and control, as in the following instances:

■ Montreal-based flight-training giant CAE Inc. formed a joint venture with Mitsui & Co. Ltd. of Japan in 2011. The companies worked together to set up a crew and ground services training centre in Japan for Mitsubishi's new 70–90 passenger Regional Jet, due for first delivery in 2014.[37]

■ Vancouver-based Cummins Westport Inc. is a joint venture between leading diesel-engine manufacturer Cummins Inc. and alternative-fuels engine-technology company Westport Innovations

Inc. Cummins Westport develops and markets the world's widest range of high-performance, low-emission engines for transit and commercial vehicles, as well as advanced alternative fuel system technologies for electrical power generation.[38]

Historically, foreign investors have often joined local investors in a **joint venture** company in which they share ownership and control. To reach more geographic and technological markets and to diversify its investments and risk, GE Money—GE's retail lending arm—views joint ventures as one of its "most powerful strategic tools." It has formed joint ventures with financial institutions in South Korea, Spain, Turkey, and elsewhere.[39] Emerging markets, especially large, complex countries such as China and India, see much joint venture action.

A joint venture may be necessary or desirable for economic or political reasons. The foreign firm might lack the financial, physical, or managerial resources to undertake the venture alone, or the foreign government might require joint ownership as a condition for entry. Joint ownership has drawbacks. The partners might disagree over investment, marketing, or other policies. One might want to reinvest earnings for growth, the other to declare more dividends. Joint ownership can also prevent a multinational company from carrying out specific manufacturing and marketing policies on a worldwide basis.

Yet the value of a partnership can extend far beyond increased sales or access to distribution. Good partners share brand values that help maintain brand consistency across markets. For example, the fierce commitment of McDonald's to product and service standardization is one reason its retail outlets are so similar around the world. McDonald's handpicks its global partners one by one to find compulsive achievers who will put forth the desired effort.

Direct Investment

The ultimate form of foreign involvement is direct ownership: the foreign company can buy part or full interest in a local company or build its own manufacturing or service facilities. Cisco had no presence in India before 2005 but opened a second headquarters in Bangalore to take advantage of opportunities in India and other locations such as Dubai.[40]

If the market is large enough, direct investment offers distinct advantages. First, the firm secures cost economies through cheaper labour or raw materials, government incentives, and freight savings. Second, the firm strengthens its image in the host country because it creates jobs. Third, the firm deepens its relationship with government, customers, local suppliers, and distributors, enabling it to better adapt its products to the local environment. Fourth, the firm retains full control over its investment and therefore can develop manufacturing and marketing policies that serve its long-term international objectives. Fifth, the firm assures itself of access to the market in case the host country insists locally purchased goods have domestic content.

Many Canadian retailers have used direct investment to enter the U.S. marketplace. However, they often find the competition is more intense and changes more rapidly than they expect. Moreover, U.S. retailers often have an advantage in size and name recognition over their Canadian rivals. Until recently, only 20 percent of retailers entering the U.S. market succeeded. Mark's Work Wearhouse, Second Cup, Canadian Tire, and People's Jewellers have all tested the U.S. waters only to withdraw in defeat. Today, however, the success rate has risen to 50 percent. Retailers like Harry Rosen, Club Monaco, and Couche-Tard have led the charge. The more successful entrants tend to be smaller, specialized retailers that go for niche markets where they don't have to challenge U.S. competitors head on.[41]

The main disadvantage of direct investment is that the firm exposes a large investment to risks such as blocked or devalued currencies, worsening markets, or expropriation. If the host country requires substantial severance for employees, reducing or closing operations can be expensive.

DECIDING ON THE MARKETING PROGRAM

International companies must decide how much to adapt their marketing strategy to local conditions.[42] At one extreme is a *standardized marketing program* worldwide, which promises the lowest costs; Table 21.2 summarizes some pros and cons. At the other extreme is an *adapted marketing program* in which the company, consistent with the marketing concept, believes consumer needs vary and tailors marketing to each target group.

Global Similarities and Differences

The development of the web, the spread of cable and satellite TV, and the global linking of telecommunications networks have led to a convergence of lifestyles. Increasingly common needs and wants have created

TABLE 21.2	GLOBALLY STANDARDIZED MARKETING PROS AND CONS	

Advantages	**Disadvantages**
Economies of scale in production and distribution	Ignores differences in consumer needs, wants, and usage patterns for products
Lower marketing costs	Ignores differences in consumer response to marketing programs and activities
Power and scope	
Consistency in brand image	Ignores differences in brand and product development and the competitive environment
Ability to leverage good ideas quickly and efficiently	Ignores differences in the legal environment
Uniformity of marketing practices	Ignores differences in marketing institutions
	Ignores differences in administrative procedures

global markets for more standardized products, particularly among the young middle class. Once the butt of jokes, after being acquired by VW, the Czech car-maker ŠKODA used its investments to upgrade its quality and image and offer an affordable option to lower-income consumers worldwide.[43]

At the same time, consumers still vary across markets in significant ways.[44] The median age is about 26 in India, 36 in China, 44 in Italy, and 45 in Japan and Germany.[45] In a particular survey, when asked if they are more concerned with getting a specific brand than the best price, roughly two-thirds of U.S. consumers agreed, compared with around 80 percent in Russia and India.[46] Consider the following beverage consumption facts:

- The United Kingdom, Turkey, and Ireland lead the world in per capita tea consumption, over three times that of China and over ten times that of Canada or the United States.[47]

- When it comes to beer, the Czech Republic leads the pack in Europe with 81.9 litres per capita; Norway is among the lowest at 40.3 litres.[48]

- With bottled water, Canada ranks 17th with 63.5 litres per capita, below the United States at 12th.[49]

Consumer behaviour may reflect cultural differences that can be pronounced across countries.[50] Hofstede identifies four cultural dimensions that differentiate countries:[51]

1. *Individualism versus collectivism*—In collectivist societies, the self-worth of an individual is rooted more in the social system than in individual achievement (high collectivism: Japan; low: United States).

2. *High versus low power distance*—High power distance cultures tend to be less egalitarian (high: Russia; low: Nordic countries).

3. *Masculine versus feminine*—This dimension measures how much the culture is dominated by assertive males versus nurturing females (high masculinity: Japan; low: Nordic countries).

4. *Weak versus strong uncertainty avoidance*—Uncertainty avoidance indicates how risk-aversive people are (high avoidance: Greece; low: Jamaica).

Consumer behaviour differences as well as historical market factors lead marketers to position brands differently in different markets:[52]

- Heineken beer is a high-end superpremium offering in Canada but is middle-of-the-road in its Dutch home market.

- Honda automobiles denote speed, youth, and energy in Japan and quality and reliability in Canada.

- The Toyota Camry is the quintessential middle-class car in Canada but is at the high end in China, though in the two markets the cars differ only in cosmetic ways.

Marketing Adaptation

Because of all these differences, most products require at least some adaptation. Even Coca-Cola is sweeter or less carbonated in certain countries. Rather than assuming it can introduce its domestic product "as is" in another country, a company should review the following elements and determine which add more revenue than cost if adapted:

- Product features
- Labelling
- Colours
- Materials
- Sales promotion
- Advertising media
- Brand name
- Packaging
- Advertising execution
- Prices
- Advertising themes

The best global brands are consistent in theme but reflect significant differences in consumer behaviour, brand development, competitive forces, and the legal or political environment.[53] Oft-heard—and sometimes modified—advice to marketers of global brands is to "think global, act local." In that spirit, HSBC is even explicitly positioned as "The World's Local Bank."

Companies must make sure their brands are relevant to consumers in every market they enter. (See "Marketing Memo: The Ten Commandments of Global Branding.")

We next consider some specific issues in developing global product, communications, pricing, and distribution strategies.

MARKETING **MEMO** | THE TEN COMMANDMENTS OF GLOBAL BRANDING

These guidelines can help a company retain the advantages of global branding while minimizing potential disadvantages:

1. **Understand the global branding landscape.** One international market is rarely identical to or completely different from another in brand development, consumer behaviour, competitive activity, or legal restrictions.
2. **Avoid shortcuts in brand building.** Build from the bottom up, creating awareness before brand image (strategy) and developing the right sources of brand equity (tactics).
3. **Establish a marketing infrastructure.** Build marketing infrastructure from scratch or adapt to and modify existing infrastructure in other countries.
4. **Embrace integrated marketing communications.** Many forms of communication work in overseas markets, not just advertising.
5. **Establish brand partnerships.** Most global brands carefully choose marketing partners that help improve distribution, profitability, and added value.
6. **Balance standardization and customization.** Packaging and brand name can often be standardized, while distribution channels and communications typically require greater customization.
7. **Balance global and local control.** Companies must balance global and local control within the organization and distribute decision making between global and local managers.
8. **Establish operable guidelines.** Brand definition and guidelines let marketers everywhere know what to do and not do. The goal is to communicate and enforce rules for positioning and marketing the brand.
9. **Implement a global brand-equity measurement system.** Information from a global brand-equity system lets marketers make the best short-run tactical and long-run strategic decisions in each market.
10. **Leverage brand elements.** Proper design and implementation of brand name and trademarked identifiers can be an invaluable source of brand equity worldwide.

Source: Adapted from Kevin Lane Keller and Sanjay Sood, "The Ten Commandments of Global Branding," *Asian Journal of Marketing*, 8, no. 2 (2001): 97–108.

Global Product Strategies

Developing global product strategies requires knowing what types of products or services are easily standardized and appropriate adaptation strategies.

PRODUCT STANDARDIZATION Some products cross borders without adaptation better than others. While mature products have separate histories or positions in different markets, consumer knowledge about new products is generally the same everywhere because perceptions have yet to be formed. Many leading Internet brands—Google, eBay, Amazon.com—made quick progress in overseas markets.

High-end products also benefit from standardization, because quality and prestige often can be marketed similarly across countries. Food and beverage marketers find it more challenging to standardize given widely varying tastes and cultural habits. Culture and wealth factors influence how quickly a new product takes off in a country, although adoption and diffusion rates are becoming more alike across countries over time.[54]

A company may emphasize its products differently across markets. IBM takes a two-track approach for its services business: Because U.S. clients often are economizing, it focuses on helping them cut costs; for developing-market clients seeking to modernize and catch up with other countries, IBM helps develop their technology infrastructure. In its medical-equipment business, Philips reserves higher-end, premium products for developed markets and emphasizes products with basic functionality and affordability in developing markets.[55]

PRODUCT ADAPTATION STRATEGIES Warren Keegan has distinguished five product and communications adaptation strategies (see Figure 21.3).[56] We review the product strategies here and the communications strategies in the next section.

Straight extension introduces the product in the foreign market without any change. Tempting because it requires no additional R&D expense, manufacturing retooling, or promotional modification, it's been successful for cameras, consumer electronics, and many machine tools. In other cases, it has been a disaster. Campbell Soup Company lost an estimated $30 million introducing condensed soups in England; consumers saw expensive small-sized cans and didn't realize water needed to be added.

Product adaptation alters the product to meet local conditions or preferences. Flexible manufacturing makes it easier to do so on several levels:

- A company can produce a *regional version* of its product, such as a Western European version. Finnish cell phone superstar Nokia customized its 6100 series phone for every major market. Developers built in rudimentary voice recognition for Asia, where keyboards are a problem, and raised the ring volume to make it audible on crowded Asian streets.

- A company can produce a *country version*. Kraft blends different coffees for the British (who drink coffee with milk), the French (who drink it black), and Latin Americans (who want a chicory taste).

- A company can produce a *city version*—for instance, a beer to meet Munich's or Tokyo's tastes.

- A company can produce different *retailer versions,* such as one coffee brew for the Migros chain store and another for the Cooperative chain store, both in Switzerland.

Some companies have learned adaptation the hard way. The Euro Disney theme park, launched outside Paris in 1992, was harshly criticized as an example of U.S. cultural imperialism that ignored French customs and values, such as serving wine with meals. As one Euro Disney executive noted, "When we first launched, there was the belief that it was enough to be Disney. Now we realize our guests need to

FIGURE 21.3

Five International Product and Communications Strategies

Source: *KEEGAN, WARREN J.; GREEN, MARK C., GLOBAL MARKETING, 4th Ed., © 2005.* Reprinted and Electronically reproduced by permission of Pearson Education, Inc., Upper Saddle River, New Jersey.

		Product		
		Do Not Change Product	Adapt Product	Develop New Product
Communications	Do Not Change Communications	Straight extension	Product adaptation	Product invention
	Adapt Communications	Communication adaptation	Dual adaptation	

be welcomed on the basis of their own culture and travel habits." Renamed Disneyland Paris, the theme park eventually became Europe's biggest tourist attraction—even more popular than the Eiffel Tower—by implementing a number of changes and more local touches.[57]

Product invention creates something new. It can take two forms:

■ **Backward invention** reintroduces earlier product forms well-adapted to a foreign country's needs. The National Cash Register Company reintroduced its crank-operated cash register at half the price of a modern model and sold substantial numbers in Latin America and Africa.

■ **Forward invention** creates a new product to meet a need in another country. Less-developed countries need low-cost, high-protein foods. Companies such as Quaker Oats, Swift, and Monsanto have researched nutrition requirements, formulated new foods, and developed advertising to gain product trial and acceptance.

BRAND ELEMENT ADAPTATION When they launch products and services globally, marketers may need to change certain brand elements.[58] Even a brand name may require a choice between phonetic and semantic translations.[59] When Clairol introduced the "Mist Stick," a curling iron, in Germany, it found that *mist* is slang for *manure*. Brand slogans or ad tag lines sometimes need to be changed too:[60]

■ When Coors put its brand slogan "Turn It Loose" into Spanish, some read it as "suffer from diarrhea."

■ A laundry soap ad claiming to wash "really dirty parts" was translated in French-speaking Quebec to read "a soap for washing private parts."

■ Perdue's slogan—"It Takes a Tough Man to Make a Tender Chicken"—was rendered into Spanish as "It takes a sexually excited man to make a chick affectionate."

■ Electrolux's British ad line for its vacuum cleaners—"Nothing Sucks Like an Electrolux"—would certainly not lure customers in Canada!

Table 21.3 lists some other famous marketing mistakes in this area.

Global Communications Strategies

Changing marketing communications for each local market is a process called **communication adaptation**. If it adapts both the product and the communications, the company engages in **dual adaptation**.

TABLE 21.3	CLASSIC BLUNDERS IN GLOBAL MARKETING

■ Hallmark cards failed in France, where consumers dislike syrupy sentiment and prefer writing their own cards.

■ Philips became profitable in Japan only after reducing the size of its coffee makers to fit smaller kitchens and its shavers to fit smaller hands.

■ Coca-Cola withdrew its big two-litre bottle in Spain after discovering that few Spaniards owned refrigerators that could accommodate it.

■ General Foods' Tang initially failed in France when positioned as a substitute for orange juice at breakfast. The French drink little orange juice and almost never at breakfast.

■ Kellogg's Pop-Tarts failed in Britain because fewer homes have toasters than in the United States, and the product was too sweet for British tastes.

■ Procter & Gamble's Crest toothpaste initially failed in Mexico. Mexicans did not care as much about the decay-prevention benefit as did consumers elsewhere, nor did scientifically oriented advertising appeal to Mexicans.

■ General Foods squandered millions trying to introduce packaged cake mixes to Japan, where only 3 percent of homes at the time were equipped with ovens.

■ S. C. Johnson's wax floor polish initially failed in Japan. It made floors too slippery for a culture where people do not wear shoes at home.

Consider the message. The company can use one message everywhere, varying only the language, name, and perhaps colours to avoid taboos in some countries.[61] Purple is associated with death in Burma and some Latin American nations, white is a mourning colour in India, and in Malaysia green connotes disease.[62]

The second possibility is to use the same message and creative theme globally but adapt the execution. GE's global "Ecomagination" ad campaign substitutes creative content in Asia and the Middle East to reflect the cultural interest there. Even in the high-tech space, local adaptations may be necessary. Consider Apple.

Apple

Apple Computer's highly successful "Mac vs. PC" ad campaign featured two actors bantering. One is hip (Apple), the other nerdy (PC). Apple dubbed the ads for Spain, France, Germany, and Italy but chose to reshoot and rescript for the United Kingdom and Japan—two important markets with unique advertising and comedy cultures. The U.K. ads followed a similar formula but used two well-known actors in character and tweaked the jokes to reflect British humour; the Japanese ads avoided direct comparisons and were more subtle in tone. Played by comedians from a local troupe called the Rahmens, the two characters were more alike and represented work (PC) vs. home (Mac).[63]

The third approach, which Coca-Cola and Goodyear have used, consists of developing a global pool of ads from which each country selects the most appropriate. Finally, some companies allow their country managers to create country-specific ads—within guidelines, of course. The challenge is to make the message as compelling and effective as in the home market.

GLOBAL ADAPTATIONS Companies that adapt their communications wrestle with a number of challenges. They first must ensure their communications are legally and culturally acceptable. Beer, wine, and spirits cannot be advertised or sold in many Muslim countries. Tobacco products are subject to strict regulation in many places. Companies from other countries are sometimes surprised to learn that in many countries (Norway and Sweden, for example) no TV ads may be directed at children under 12. To play it safe, McDonald's advertises itself as a family restaurant in Sweden.

Firms next must check their creative strategies and communication approaches for appropriateness. Comparative ads, although acceptable and even common in the United States and Canada, are less frequent in the United Kingdom, unacceptable in Japan, and illegal in India and Brazil. The EU seems to have a very low tolerance for comparative advertising and prohibits bashing rivals in ads.

Companies also must be prepared to vary their messages' appeal.[64] In advertising its hair-care products, Helene Curtis observed that middle-class British women wash their hair frequently, Spanish women less so. Japanese women avoid overwashing for fear of removing protective oils. Language can vary too, whether the local language, another language such as English, or some combination.[65]

Many messages need adjustment because the brand is at an earlier stage of development in its new market. Consumer education about the product itself may then need to accompany brand development efforts:

- In certain developing markets in Asia, consumers loved the Coca-Cola brand but had never tasted it. They needed to be advised to drink it cold.[66]
- When launching Chik shampoo in rural areas of South India, where hair is washed with soap, CavinKare showed people how to use the product through live "touch and feel" demonstrations and free sachets at fairs.[67]

Personal selling tactics may need to change too. The direct, no-nonsense approach favoured in Canada ("Let's get down to business" and "What's in it for me?") may not work as well in Europe or Asia as an indirect, subtle approach.[68]

In Hong Kong, McDonald's chose to promote the brand with an unusual combo added to its menu—a promotion that is likely to raise eyebrows in many other countries.

McWedding in Hong Kong

Hong Kong will be the first city in the world to offer a McDonald's wedding package for couples. The package includes a layered wedding cake made out of baked apple pies, a dress made out of party balloons, kiddie party favours for guests, and a buffet of McDonald's burgers. Alcohol is not allowed, since the franchise will not shut down the restaurant for the wedding and does not want rowdy guests disturbing the family environment. The fast-food chain got the idea for McWedding from a couple who met and dated at a McDonald's and held their wedding at one of the restaurant's locations.[69]

Global Pricing Strategies

Multinationals selling abroad must contend with price escalation and transfer prices (and dumping charges). Two particularly thorny pricing problems are grey markets and counterfeits.

PRICE ESCALATION   A Gucci handbag may sell for $120 in Italy and $240 in Canada. Why? Gucci must add the cost of transportation, tariffs, importer margin, wholesaler margin, and retailer margin to its factory price. **Price escalation** from these added costs and currency-fluctuation risk might mean that for the manufacturer to earn the same profit, the price must be two to five times as much as in another country.

Companies have three choices for setting prices in different countries:

1. *Set a uniform price everywhere.* PepsiCo might want to charge 75 cents for Pepsi everywhere in the world, but then it would earn quite different profit rates in different countries. Also, this strategy would make the price too high in poor countries and not high enough in rich countries.

2. *Set a market-based price in each country.* PepsiCo would charge what each country could afford, but this strategy ignores differences in the actual cost from country to country. It could also motivate intermediaries in low-price countries to reship their Pepsi to high-price countries.[70]

3. *Set a cost-based price in each country.* Here PepsiCo would use a standard markup of its costs everywhere, but this strategy might price it out of markets where its costs are high.

When companies sell their wares over the Internet, price becomes transparent and price differentiation between countries declines. Consider an online training course. Whereas the price of a classroom-delivered day of training can vary significantly from Canada to France to Thailand, the price of an online-delivered day would be similar everywhere.

In another new global pricing challenge, countries with overcapacity, cheap currencies, and the need to export aggressively have pushed prices down and devalued their currencies. Sluggish demand and reluctance to pay higher prices make selling in these markets difficult. Here is what IKEA did to compete in China's challenging pricing market.[71]

IKEA

IKEA has used market-penetration pricing to get a lock on China's surging market for home furnishings. When the Swedish home furnishings giant opened its first store in Beijing in 2002, shops were selling copies of its designs at a fraction of IKEA's prices. The only way to lure China's frugal customers was to drastically slash prices. Western brands in China usually price products such as makeup and running shoes 20 percent to 30 percent higher than in their other markets, both to make up for China's high import taxes and to give their products added cachet. By stocking its Chinese stores with Chinese-made products, IKEA has been able to slash prices as low as 70 percent below their level outside China. Although it still contends with persistent knock-offs, IKEA maintains sizeable stores in Beijing, Shanghai, Guangzhou, Chengdu, and Tianjin, opening one or two new locations each year.

TRANSFER PRICES   A different problem arises when one unit charges another unit in the same company a **transfer price** for goods it ships to its foreign subsidiaries. If the company charges a subsidiary too *high* a price, it may end up paying higher tariff duties, although it may pay lower income taxes in the foreign country. If the company charges its subsidiary too *low* a price, it can be accused of **dumping**, charging either less than its costs or less than it charges at home, in order to enter or win a market. Various governments are watching for abuses and often force companies to charge the **arm's-length price**—the price charged by other competitors for the same or a similar product.

When the Canada Border Services Agency (CBSA) finds evidence of dumping, anti-dumping and countervailing duties may be enforced. Following a complaint filed by McCain Foods, the CBSA investigated and found Kraft Foods guilty of dumping its frozen DiGiorno Pizza in Canada with a weighted average dumping margin of nearly 30 percent.[72]

GREY MARKETS Many multinationals are plagued by the **grey market**, which diverts branded products from authorized distribution channels either in-country or across international borders. Dealers in the low-price country find ways to sell some of their products in higher-price countries, thus earning more. Often a company finds some enterprising distributors buying more than they can sell in their own country and reshipping the goods to another country to take advantage of price differences.

Research suggests that grey market activity accounts for billions of dollars in revenue each year and makes up about 8 percent of total global IT sales of $725 billion. Information technology manufacturers lose about $10 billion in profits to the grey market each year.[73]

Grey markets create a free-rider problem, making legitimate distributors' investments in supporting a manufacturer's product less productive and selective distribution systems more intensive. They harm distributor relations, tarnish the manufacturer's brand equity, and undermine the integrity of the distribution channel. They can even pose risks to consumers if the seemingly brand-new product they think they are buying is damaged, re-marked, obsolete, without warranty or support, or just counterfeit.

Multinationals try to prevent grey markets by policing the distributors, raising their prices to lower-cost distributors, or altering product characteristics or service warranties for different countries.[74] 3Com successfully sued several companies in Canada (for a total of $10 million) that provided written and oral misrepresentations to get deep discounts on 3Com networking equipment. The equipment, worth millions of dollars, was to be sold to a U.S. educational software company and sent to China and Australia but instead ended up back in the United States.

One research study found that grey market activity was most effectively deterred when penalties were severe, manufacturers were able to detect violations or mete out punishments in a timely fashion, or both.[75]

COUNTERFEIT PRODUCTS Name a popular brand, and chances are a counterfeit version of it exists somewhere in the world.[76] Counterfeiting is estimated to cost over a trillion dollars a year. Counterfeit medication, auto parts, and toys, and DVD and satellite piracy are just some counterfeiting activities that are costing the Canadian economy billions of dollars each year. Satellite signal theft alone accounts for over $300 million in losses per year.[77]

Counterfeit products are a major headache for luxury-goods makers.

Fakes take a big bite of the profits of luxury brands such as Hermès, LVMH Moët Hennessy/Louis Vuitton, and Tiffany, but faulty counterfeits can literally kill people. Cell phones with counterfeit batteries, fake brake pads made of compressed grass trimmings, and counterfeit airline parts pose safety risks to consumers. Virtually every product is vulnerable. As one anti-counterfeit consultant observed, "If you can make it, they can fake it." Defending against counterfeiters is a never-ending struggle; some observers estimate that a new security system can be just months old before counterfeiters start nibbling at sales again.[78]

The web has been especially problematic. After surveying thousands of items, LVMH estimated 90 percent of Louis Vuitton and Christian Dior pieces listed on eBay were fakes, prompting the firm to sue. Manufacturers are fighting back online with web-crawling software that detects fraud and automatically warns apparent violators without the need for any human intervention. Acushnet, maker of Titleist golf clubs and balls, shut down 75 auctions of knock-off gear in one day with just one mouse click.[79]

Web-crawling technology searches for counterfeit storefronts and sales by detecting domain names similar to legitimate brands and unauthorized websites that plaster brand trademarks and logos on their homepages. It also checks for keywords such as *cheap, discount, authentic,* and *factory variants,* as well as colours that products were never made in and prices that are far too low.

Global Distribution Strategies

Too many Canadian manufacturers think their job is done once the product leaves the factory. They should instead note how the product moves within the foreign country and take a whole-channel view of distributing products to final users.

CHANNEL ENTRY Figure 21.4 shows three links between the seller and the final buyer. In the first, *seller's international marketing headquarters,* the export department or international division makes decisions about channels and other marketing activities. The second link, *channels between nations,* gets the products to the borders of the foreign nation. Decisions made in this link include the types of intermediaries (agents, trading companies), type of transportation (air, sea), and financing and risk management. The third link, *channels within foreign nations,* gets products from their entry point to final buyers and users.

When multinationals first enter a country, they prefer to work with local distributors with good local knowledge, but friction often arises later.[80] The multinational complains that the local distributor doesn't invest in business growth, doesn't follow company policy, and doesn't share enough information. The local distributor complains of insufficient corporate support, impossible goals, and confusing policies. The multinational must choose the right distributors, invest in them, and set up performance goals to which they can agree.[81]

CHANNEL DIFFERENCES Distribution channels across countries vary considerably. To sell consumer products in Japan, companies must work through one of the most complicated distribution systems in the world. They sell to a general wholesaler, who sells to a product wholesaler, who sells to a product-specialty wholesaler, who sells to a regional wholesaler, who sells to a local wholesaler, who finally sells to retailers. All these distribution levels can make the consumer's price double or triple the importer's price. Taking these same consumer products to tropical Africa, the company might sell to an import wholesaler, who sells to several jobbers, who sell to petty traders (mostly women) working in local markets.

Another difference is the size and character of retail units abroad. Large-scale retail chains dominate in North America, but much foreign retailing is in the hands of small, independent retailers. Millions of Indian retailers operate tiny shops or sell in open markets. Markups are high, but the real price comes down through haggling. Incomes are low, most homes lack storage and refrigeration, and people shop daily for whatever they can carry home on foot or bicycle. In India, people often buy one cigarette at a time. Breaking bulk remains an important function of intermediaries and helps perpetuate long channels of distribution, a major obstacle to the expansion of large-scale retailing in developing countries.

Sometimes companies mistakenly adapt infrastructure strategies that were critical success factors, only to discover that these changes eroded the brand's competitive advantage. Dell Computer initially abandoned its direct distribution strategy in Europe for a traditional retailer network of existing channels, with poor results. Ignoring critics who claimed the direct distribution model would never work in Europe, Dell then revamped its direct approach, relaunching its personal computer line with a new management team to execute the direct model it had pioneered in the United States, finding greater success as a result.

Increasingly, retailers are moving into new global markets, offering firms the opportunity to sell across more countries and creating a challenge to local distributors and retailers.[82] France's Carrefour, Germany's Metro, and United Kingdom's Tesco have all established global positions. But some of the world's most successful retailers have had mixed success abroad. Despite concerted efforts and earlier success in Latin America and China, Walmart had to withdraw from both the German and South Korean markets.

FIGURE 21.4

Whole-Channel Concept for International Marketing

COUNTRY-OF-ORIGIN EFFECTS

Country-of-origin perceptions are the mental associations and beliefs triggered by a country. Government officials want to strengthen their country's image to help domestic marketers who export, and to attract foreign firms and investors. Marketers want to use positive country-of-origin perceptions to sell their products and services.

Building Country Images

Governments now recognize that the images of their cities and countries affect more than tourism and have important value in commerce. Attracting foreign business can boost the local economy, provide jobs, and improve infrastructure. Image can also help sell products. For its first global ad campaign for Infiniti luxury cars, Nissan chose to tap into its Japanese roots and association with Japanese-driven art and engineering.[83]

Countries are being marketed like any other brand.[84] New Zealand developed concerted marketing programs both to sell its products outside the country, via its New Zealand Way program, and to attract tourists by showing the dramatic landscapes featured in *The Lord of the Rings* film trilogy. Both efforts reinforce the image of New Zealand as fresh and pure.[85]

Another film affected the image of a country in an entirely different way. Although Kazakhstan has a positive story to tell given its huge size, rich natural resources, and rapid modernization, the mock documentary *Borat,* from British comedian Sacha Baron Cohen, portrayed the country in a sometimes crude and vulgar light. As one government official noted, "The only fact of the movie is the geographic location of

Kazakhstan." Fortunately, the tongue-in-cheek film also created awareness and interest in the country and what has been called the "Borat Bounce," an unanticipated surge in tourism.[86]

Attitudes toward countries can change over time. Before World War II, Japan had a poor image, which the success of Sony with its Trinitron TV sets and of Japanese automakers Honda and Toyota helped change. A strong company that emerges as a global player can do wonders for a country's image. Relying partly on the global success of Nokia, Finland campaigned to enhance its image as a centre of high-tech innovation.[87]

Current events can also shape the image of a country. With public unrest and violent protests surrounding the austerity program to address Greece's debt crisis, tourist bookings there dropped as much as 30 percent.[88]

Countries vie to host international sporting events, as they serve as good opportunities to promote the country's image, besides the economic benefits from the event. South Africa left no stone unturned when it hosted the football (soccer) world cup in 2010.

South Africa

Hosting the FIFA World Cup meant more to South Africa than just the entertainment of soccer. The country used the opportunity to change the rest of the world's perception of Africa. Using sports to push a certain image is not a new concept; many countries have done so with global events such as the Olympics and other international championships. South Africa's campaign included television commercials with the slogan "It Starts with You." The country also encouraged people to learn the "diski" dance (a rhythmic soccer dance originating from the towns) ahead of the tournament, in order to generate excitement. Many details were taken into account to change the image of South Africa during the World Cup, such as the flag used on the logo to signify the country's freedom and national pride.[89]

Consumer Perceptions of Country of Origin

Global marketers know that buyers hold distinct attitudes and beliefs about brands or products from different countries.[90] These perceptions can be an attribute in decision making or influence other attributes in the process ("if it's French, it must be stylish"). The mere fact that a brand is perceived as successful on

South Africa got worldwide attention during the FIFA 2010 World Cup.

a global stage—whether it sends a quality signal, taps into cultural myths, or reinforces a sense of social responsibility—may lend credibility and respect.[91] Several studies have found the following:[92]

- People are often ethnocentric and favourably predisposed to their own country's products, unless the people come from a less developed country.

- The more favourable a country's image, the more prominently the "Made in..." label should be displayed.

- The impact of country of origin varies with the type of product. Consumers want to know where a car was made, but not the lubricating oil.

- Certain countries enjoy a reputation for certain goods: Japan for automobiles and consumer electronics; the United States for high-tech innovations, soft drinks, toys, cigarettes, and jeans; France for wine, perfume, and luxury goods.

- Sometimes country-of-origin perception can encompass an entire country's products. In one study, Chinese consumers in Hong Kong perceived U.S. products as prestigious, Japanese products as innovative, and Chinese products as cheap.

Marketers must look at country-of-origin perceptions from both a domestic and a foreign perspective. In the domestic market, these perceptions may stir consumers' patriotic notions or remind them of their past. As international trade grows, consumers may view certain brands as symbolically important in their own cultural heritage and identity.

Patriotic appeals underlie marketing strategies all over the world, but they can lack uniqueness and even be overused, especially in economic or political crises. Many small businesses tap into community pride to emphasize their local roots. To be successful, these businesses need to be clearly local and offer appealing product and service offerings.[93]

Sometimes consumers don't know where brands come from. In surveys, they routinely guess that Heineken is German and Nokia is Japanese (they are Dutch and Finnish, respectively). Few consumers know Häagen-Dazs and Estée Lauder originated in the United States.

With outsourcing and foreign manufacturing, it's hard to know what the country of origin really is anyway. Only 65 percent of the content of a Ford Mustang comes from the United States or Canada, whereas the Toyota Sienna is assembled in Indiana with 90 percent local components. Foreign automakers are pouring money into North America, investing in plants, suppliers, and dealerships as well as design, testing, and research centres. But what makes a product more "American"—having a higher percentage of North American components or creating more jobs in North America? The two measures may not lead to the same conclusion.[94]

Many brands have gone to great lengths to weave themselves into the cultural fabric of their foreign markets. One Coca-Cola executive tells of a young child visiting the United States from Japan and who commented to her parents on seeing a Coca-Cola vending machine, "Look, they have Coca-Cola too!" As far as she was concerned, Coca-Cola was a Japanese brand.

International markets may be more receptive to products from beyond their borders than previously thought. One recent study found that 70 percent of consumers in developing countries, ranging from Argentina to the United Arab Emirates, felt local products weren't as good as international brands.[95] In Saudi Arabia, Kraft packaged cheese, Lay's potato chips, and McDonald's restaurants were all viewed as top brands in their categories. As one American marketer said of the study, "Regardless of all the problems we have as a country, we are still looked to as the consumer capital of the world."[96]

Companies can target niches to establish a footing in new markets. China's leading maker of refrigerators, washing machines, and air conditioners, Haier, is building a beachhead among U.S. college students who loyally buy its mini-fridges at Walmart and elsewhere. Haier's long-term plans are to introduce innovative products in other areas, such as flat-screen TV sets and wine-cooling cabinets.[97]

DECIDING ON THE MARKETING ORGANIZATION

Companies manage their international marketing activities in three ways: through export departments, international divisions, or a global organization.

Export Department

A firm normally gets into international marketing by simply shipping out its goods. If its international sales expand, it organizes an export department consisting of a sales manager and a few assistants. As sales increase, the export department expands to include various marketing services so the company can go after business more aggressively. If the firm moves into joint ventures or direct investment, the export department will no longer be adequate to manage international operations.

International Division

Sooner or later, companies that engage in several international markets and ventures create an international division to handle all this activity. The unit is headed by a division president who sets goals and budgets and is responsible for the company's international growth.

The international division's corporate staff consists of functional specialists who provide services to various operating units. Operating units can be *geographical organizations*. Reporting to the international-division president might be regional vice-presidents for North America, Latin America, Europe, Africa, the Middle East, and the Far East. Reporting to the regional vice-presidents are country managers responsible for a sales force, sales branches, distributors, and licensees in the respective countries. Or the operating units may be *world product groups,* each with an international vice-president responsible for worldwide sales of each product group. The vice-presidents may draw on corporate-staff area specialists for expertise on different geographical areas. Finally, operating units may be *international subsidiaries,* each headed by a president who reports to the president of the international division.

Global Organization

Several firms have become truly global organizations. Their top corporate management and staff plan worldwide manufacturing facilities, marketing policies, financial flows, and logistical systems. The global operating units report directly to the chief executive or executive committee, not to the head of an international division. The firm trains its executives in worldwide operations, recruits management from many countries, purchases components and supplies where it can obtain them at least cost, and makes investments where anticipated returns are greatest.

These companies face several organizational complexities. For example, when the firm is pricing a company's mainframe computers for a large banking system in Germany, how much influence should the headquarters product manager have? And the company's market manager for the banking sector? And the company's German country manager?

When forces for "global integration" (capital-intensive production, homogeneous demand) are strong and forces for "national responsiveness" (local standards and barriers, strong local preferences) are weak, a global strategy that treats the world as a single market can make sense (for example, with consumer electronics). When the reverse is true, a multinational strategy that treats the world as a portfolio of national opportunities can be more appropriate (such as for food or cleaning products).[98]

Korea's globally integrated LG decided to hire a number of top executives from Western firms to help transform it from "an engineering powerhouse that excelled at manufacturing and selling in different parts of the world" to a "globally efficient, trend-setting organization." The new executives were charged with standardizing the hodgepodge of processes and systems LG had developed in different markets in purchasing, the supply chain, marketing, and other areas. A single agency (London's Bartle Bogle Hegarty) was given global responsibility to sell an increasing number of higher-end products.[99]

When both forces prevail to some extent, a "glocal" strategy that standardizes certain elements and localizes others can be the way to go (for instance, with telecommunications). Many firms seek a blend of centralized global control from corporate headquarters with input from local and regional marketers. As one top marketer for global brand icon Jack Daniels described the challenges of managing the world's biggest-selling whiskey brand across 135 countries, "'Not invented' here is a good thing; 'invented here' is also a good thing; 'not invented but improved here' is the best!"[100]

Finding the balance can be tricky, though. Coca-Cola adopted a "think local, act local" philosophy, decentralizing power and responsibility for designing marketing programs and activities. Execution faltered because many local managers lacked the skills or discipline to do the job. Decidedly un-Coke-like ads appeared—such as skinny-dippers streaking down a beach in Italy—and sales stalled. The pendulum swung back, and Coke executives in Atlanta resumed a strong strategic role.[101]

Effectively transferring successful marketing ideas from one region to another is a key priority for many firms. Rather than developing global products for jointly owned Renault and Nissan, CEO Carlos Ghosn has mandated that companies design for local tastes and have the flexibility to export the design to other regions to tap into similar consumer trends. The no-frills Logan was developed by Renault for Eastern Europe and Latin America but found another home in France. When products cross a region, ideas and a way of thinking may also transfer in the process. Ghosn teamed Nissan and Renault with Bajaj Auto to sell a $3000 car in the Indian market, in part to infuse those companies with India's low-cost design thinking: "They understand frugal engineering, which is something we aren't as good at in Europe or Japan."[102]

SUMMARY

1. Despite shifting borders, unstable governments, foreign-exchange problems, corruption, and technological pirating, companies selling in global industries need to internationalize their operations.

2. Upon deciding to go abroad, a company needs to define its international marketing objectives and policies. It must determine whether to market in a few or many countries and rate candidate countries on three criteria: market attractiveness, risk, and competitive advantage.

3. Developing countries offer a unique set of opportunities and risks. The "BRIC" countries—Brazil, Russia, India, and China—plus other significant markets such as Indonesia and South Africa are a top priority for many firms.

4. Modes of entry are indirect exporting, direct exporting, licensing, joint ventures, and direct investment. Each succeeding strategy entails more commitment, risk, control, and profit potential.

5. In deciding how much to adapt their marketing programs at the product level, firms can pursue a strategy of straight extension, product adaptation, or product invention. At the communication level, they may choose communication adaptation or dual adaptation. At the price level, firms may encounter price escalation, dumping, grey markets, and discounted counterfeit products. At the distribution level, firms need to take a whole-channel view of distributing products to the final users. Firms must always consider the cultural, social, political, technological, environmental, and legal limitations they face in other countries.

6. Country-of-origin perceptions can affect consumers and businesses alike. Managing those perceptions to best advantage is a marketing priority.

7. Depending on their level of international involvement, companies manage international marketing activity in three ways: through export departments, international divisions, or a global organization.

APPLICATIONS

Marketing Debate: Is the World Coming Closer Together?

Many social commentators maintain that youth and teens are becoming more alike across countries over time. Others, although not disputing the fact, point out that differences between cultures at even younger ages by far exceed the similarities.

Take a position: People are becoming more and more similar *versus* The differences between people of different cultures far outweigh their similarities.

Marketing Discussion: Country of Origin

Think of some of your favourite brands. Do you know where they come from? Where and how are they made or provided? Do you think knowing these answers would affect your perceptions of quality or satisfaction?

MARKETING EXCELLENCE | NOKIA

Nokia has made a remarkable transformation over the past two decades from an obscure Finnish conglomerate to a cell phone powerhouse. Now the world's largest manufacturer of mobile telephones, it had over 1 billion users and a global market share of 33 percent in 2010, with sales in over 160 countries. The company sells approximately 11 cell phones every second and is the standout leader in Asia, Eastern Europe, and Africa.

Nokia's transformation started in the early 1990s with its strategic decision to divest its product portfolio and focus entirely on telecommunications. Business soon exploded, in part due to Nokia's mastery in innovating telecommunications technologies. Nokia was a key developer of new mobile technologies like GSM (Global System for Mobile Communications) that allow consumers to roam internationally and use new data services like text messaging. Although the firm has struggled in North America—in part because many networks there use a different wireless standard (CDMA) than in Europe (GSM)—its global footprint is still impressive.

Nokia's success also derives from its broad strategic view of how to build a global brand and international consumer base. The company sells a wide range of products and services in all price ranges to different types of consumers all over the world. In short, its approach is "all price points, all markets." Nokia has a practical understanding of what consumers need, value, and can afford depending on their geographical location and demographics. By providing the right products, features, and price, the firm has successfully built long-term brand value all over the world.

With the bulk of industry growth coming from developing markets, Nokia has made sure its cheapest handsets are appealing—and profitable—in markets such as China, India, and Latin America. On the flip side, to sustain its market leadership and compete in challenging markets like Europe and the United States, it has launched a range of high-end handsets with advanced features and applications. This consumer base is so critical to Nokia's growth that it has created a business division focused entirely on creating software and services for this base, including music, videos, games, maps, messaging, and media. Today, Nokia's products range from $30 basic models to $600 smartphones that include video editing, voice-guided navigation, and thousands of applications. Nokia's future also lies in its growing line of mobile computers, devices with the advanced capabilities of a computer but that fit into the palm of your hand.

Nokia takes a broad perspective on competition as well, viewing Apple, Sony, and Canon as threats as much as tradi-tional rivals Motorola and Samsung. Competitors' products like the iPhone, BlackBerry, and Android smartphones have all gained significant market share. Although 84 percent of its sales consist of cell phones, Nokia is focused on making its smartphones durable, reliable, and affordable to consumers in emerging markets, as it did with cell phones.

As a global leader, Nokia understands how critical it is to have a finger on the pulse of countries and cultures all over the world. With research centres in 13 locations across 7 countries, 15 manufacturing plants in 9 countries, and 650 000 points-of-sale—the widest distribution network in the world—Nokia strives to be a global leader that is locally relevant. It forms relationships with local business partners, gets involved in the community, and works to earn consumers' trust on a local level.

In India, for example, the company has increased its local involvement by including in the Nokia Music Store a significant percentage of songs by local and regional artists, adding thousands of local customer-care services, and supporting a local environmental initiative called "Planet Ke Rakhwaale," which encourages consumers to recycle their old phones and batteries. Nokia even added the tag line "Made in India for India."

Valued at nearly $25 billion, Nokia was the eighth-most-valuable global brand in the Interbrand/*BusinessWeek* Best Global Brands 2010 ranking, ahead of strong competitors Apple, BlackBerry, Motorola, and Samsung. The Nokia brand continues to rank well in consumers' minds as high quality, robust, easy to use, and trustworthy—a perfect combination for succeeding in both emerging and mature countries.

QUESTIONS

1. What have been the keys to Nokia's global strength?

2. What can Nokia do to gain market share in North America, where its presence is not as strong?

3. In the ever-changing world of mobile technology, what are the greatest threats to Nokia's global presence?

Sources: Jack Ewing, "Nokia: Lesson Learned, Reward Reaped," *BusinessWeek*, July 30, 2007; "Face Value," *Economist*, May 27, 2006; Oli Pekka Kalasvuo, "Brand Identity: A Delicate Balance between Image and Authenticity," *Economic Times*, August 31, 2010; Kevin J. O'Brien, "Nokia Seeks to Reconnect with the U.S. Market," *New York Times*, August 15, 2010; "Best Global Brands 2010," Interbrand/*BusinessWeek*; Nokia Capital Markets Day presentation, 2009; "Nokia in Brief," www.nokia.com/about-nokia/company; Nokia Research Center, http://research.nokia.com/locations (viewed October 9, 2011).

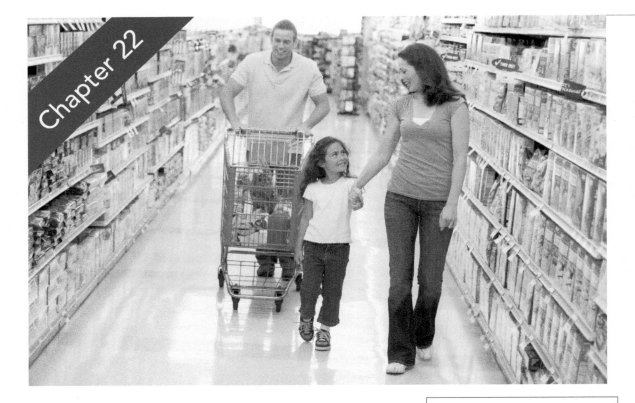

Chapter 22

Loblaw's corporate social responsibility initiatives have contributed to communities, improved the environment, and made its brand distinctive.

In This Chapter, We Will Address the Following **Questions**

1. What are important trends in marketing practices?

2. What are the keys to effective internal marketing?

3. How can companies be socially responsible marketers?

4. How can a company improve its marketing skills?

5. What tools are available to help companies monitor and improve their marketing activities?

Managing a Holistic Marketing Organization for the Long Run

Healthy long-term growth for a brand requires that the marketing organization be managed properly. Holistic marketers must engage in a host of carefully planned, interconnected marketing activities and satisfy an increasingly broader set of constituents and objectives. They must also consider a wider range of effects of their actions. Corporate social responsibility and sustainability have become a priority as organizations grapple with the short-term and long-term effects of their marketing. Some firms have embraced this new vision of corporate enlightenment and made it the very core of what they do. Consider Loblaw Co. Ltd.

Galen G. Weston, the Executive Chairman of Loblaw Co. Ltd., has become an icon of sustainability to many Canadians, through his regular appearances in the firm's advertisements encouraging shoppers to use cloth bags rather than plastic ones. The company's initiatives are more than just hype. Its corporate social responsibility (CSR) efforts are linked to its brand, and its senior management team believes that these initiatives give the grocer a distinct competitive advantage. As the company's fourth corporate social responsibility report declares, "Every day, we work hard to make a positive difference in our communities, in our country and to our planet. Our commitment to corporate social responsibility (CSR) is part of that difference." Such thinking led to Loblaw being named Canada's most responsible firm in the Corporate Knights 2010 ranking. Loblaw's programs are founded on five CSR pillars: Respect the Environment, Source with Integrity, Make a Positive Difference in Our Community, Reflect Our Nation's Diversity, and Be a Great Place to Work.

Loblaw embeds CSR deeply into its operations. Since 2007, Loblaw customers have used 73 percent fewer or 2.5 billion fewer plastic shopping bags, diverting tonnes of waste from landfills. It is also working to reduce by 70 percent overall waste from its operations and thereby from landfills. It has reduced refrigeration leaks by 22 percent, which helps reduce its greenhouse gas emissions. As part of its Grown Close to Home program, Loblaw is sourcing more of its products from Canadian growers. It has continued to develop and market its President's Choice line of green products, and it has an ongoing initiative to decrease its use of nonrecyclable packaging on its private-label products by 50 percent in five years. In 2011, Greenpeace Canada gave Loblaw top marks for its efforts to reduce overfishing and its marketing of sustainable seafood products. Since the grocer accounts for about 40 percent of seafood sales in the Canadian marketplace, this decision alone is having a significant impact toward the development of more stable fish populations.

Many other Canadian firms, such as Bell Canada Enterprises (BCE), Canada Post, Encana, Mountain Equipment Co-op, and TD Bank, have embraced similar philosophies and practices. Successful holistic marketing requires a strong sense of responsibility. It also requires effective relationship marketing, integrated marketing, internal marketing, and performance marketing. Preceding chapters addressed the first two topics and the strategy and tactics of marketing. In this chapter, we consider the latter two topics and how to conduct marketing responsibly. We look at how firms organize, implement, evaluate, and control marketing activities in a context heightened by social responsibility. We begin by examining changes in the way companies conduct marketing today.

Loblaw undoubtedly makes a positive difference in communities. It has donated more than $12.6 million to charities across Canada, and its employees have raised another $22.4 million through in-store fundraising efforts. Its workplace policies make the firm a great place to work, and it is also focusing on having a more diverse workforce that reflects the diversity of Canada, including increasing the number of women managers for its stores. In recognition of these efforts, it was named Canada's top employer by Mediacorp Canada Inc.[1]

TRENDS IN MARKETING PRACTICES

Chapters 1 and 3 described important changes in the marketing macroenvironment, such as globalization, deregulation, consumer empowerment, and environmental concerns.[2] With these and all the remarkable developments in computers, software, the Internet, and cell phones, the world has unquestionably become a very different place for marketers. In earlier chapters, we detailed the many shifts in marketing that dominated the first decade of the twenty-first century.[3] Table 22.1 summarizes some important ones and we briefly review a few next.

Recently, marketers have had to operate in a global, slow-growth economic environment characterized by discriminating consumers, aggressive competition, and a turbulent marketplace. An era of conspicuous consumption has come to an end as many consumers cope with reduced incomes and less wealth.[4] A debt-laden consumer base penalizes companies still promoting a "buy now, pay later" sales philosophy, and consumers and companies alike are increasingly considering the environmental and social consequences of their actions.

As consumers become more disciplined in their spending and adopt a "less is more" attitude, it is incumbent on marketers to create and communicate the true value of their products and services.[5] Marketing can and should play a key role in improving standards of living and quality of life. Marketers must continuously seek to improve what they do.[6]

Companies can't win by standing still. Recent business problems and failures by firms such as Blockbuster, Kodak, and Zellers reflect an inability to adjust to a dramatically different marketing

TABLE 22.1	IMPORTANT SHIFTS IN MARKETING AND BUSINESS PRACTICES

- *Re-engineering.* Appointing teams to manage customer-value-building processes and break down walls between departments
- *Outsourcing.* Buying more goods and services from outside domestic or foreign vendors
- *Benchmarking.* Studying best-practice companies to improve performance
- *Supplier partnering.* Partnering with fewer suppliers, but those who add more value
- *Customer partnering.* Working more closely with customers to add value to their operations
- *Merging.* Acquiring or merging with firms in the same or complementary industries to gain economies of scale and scope
- *Globalizing.* Increasing efforts to think global and act local
- *Flattening.* Reducing the number of organizational levels to get closer to the customer
- *Focusing.* Determining the most profitable businesses and customers and focusing on them
- *Justifying.* Becoming more accountable by measuring, analyzing, and documenting the effects of marketing actions
- *Accelerating.* Designing the organization and setting up processes to respond more quickly to changes in the environment
- *Empowering.* Encouraging and empowering personnel to produce more ideas and take more initiative
- *Broadening.* Factoring the interests of customers, employees, shareholders, and other stakeholders into the activities of the enterprise
- *Monitoring.* Tracking what is said online and elsewhere and studying customers, competitors, and others to improve business practices

environment. Firms must invest instead in improving their offerings and finding big new ideas. Sometimes, even giant firms like BCE, IBM, Microsoft, and Intel may have to fundamentally change their business models. Marketers must collaborate closely and early with product development and R&D, and later with the sales force, to develop and sell products and services that fully satisfy customer needs and wants. They must also work with finance, manufacturing, and logistics to establish a value-creation mindset in the organization.

Emerging markets such as Brazil, India, and China offer enormous new sources of demand—but often only for certain types of products and at certain price points. Across all markets, marketing plans and programs will grow more localized and culturally sensitive, while strong brands that are well-differentiated and constantly improved will remain fundamental to marketing success. Businesses will continue to use social media more and traditional media less. The web allows unprecedented depth and breadth in communications and distribution, and its transparency requires companies to be honest and authentic.

Marketers also face ethical dilemmas and perplexing trade-offs. Consumers may value convenience, but how can companies justify disposable products or elaborate packaging in a world trying to minimize waste? Increasing material aspirations can defy the need for sustainability. However, given increasing consumer sensitivity and government regulation, smart companies are creatively designing with energy efficiency, carbon footprints, toxicity, and disposability in mind. Some are choosing local suppliers over distant ones. Auto companies and airlines must be particularly conscious of releasing CO_2 in the atmosphere. Toyota found success with its environmentally friendly Prius.

Toyota Prius

Some auto experts scoffed when Toyota predicted sales of 300 000 cars within five years of launching its gas-and-electric Prius hybrid sedan in 2001. But by 2004, the Prius had a six-month waiting list, and by 2010, Toyota had sold over 1 million worldwide and 14 000 in Canada. Toyota's winning formula consists of a powerful electric motor and the option for the driver to quickly switch power sources. Striving for constant improvement, Toyota has re-engineered the car to improve its comfort, styling, performance, and fuel economy. It has the roominess and power of a family sedan and an ecofriendly design and look. Base models retail for just under $30 000, but vehicles with lots of options may sell for $40 000. The lesson? Functionally successful products that consumers see as good for the environment can also be good for profit. Toyota is now rolling out hybrids throughout its auto lineup, and North American automakers have followed suit.[7]

Now more than ever, marketers must think holistically and use creative win-win solutions to balance conflicting demands. They must develop fully integrated marketing programs and meaningful relationships with a range of constituents.[8] They must do all the right things inside their company and consider the broader consequences in the marketplace, topics we turn to next.

INTERNAL MARKETING

Traditionally, marketers played the role of middleman, charged with understanding customers' needs and transmitting their voice to various functional areas.[9] But in a networked enterprise, *every* functional area can interact directly with customers. Marketing no longer has sole ownership of customer interactions; rather, it now must integrate all the customer-facing processes so customers see a single face and hear a single voice when they interact with the firm.[10]

Internal marketing requires that everyone in the organization accept the concepts and goals of marketing and engage in choosing, providing, and communicating customer value. Only when *all* employees realize that their job is to create, serve, and satisfy customers does the company become an effective marketer.[11] "Marketing Memo: Characteristics of Company Departments That Are Truly Customer Driven" presents a tool that evaluates which company departments are truly customer driven.

Let's look at how marketing departments are being organized, how they can work effectively with other departments, and how firms can foster a creative marketing culture across the organization.[12]

Organizing the Marketing Department

Modern marketing departments can be organized in a number of different, sometimes overlapping ways: by function, by geography, by product or brand, by market, or in a matrix.

MARKETING **MEMO**	CHARACTERISTICS OF COMPANY DEPARTMENTS THAT ARE TRULY CUSTOMER DRIVEN
R&D	■ They spend time meeting customers and listening to their problems ■ They welcome the involvement of marketing, manufacturing, and other departments on each new project. ■ They benchmark competitors' products and seek best-of-class solutions. ■ They solicit customer reactions and suggestions as the project progresses. ■ They continuously improve and refine the product on the basis of market feedback.
Purchasing	■ They proactively search for the best suppliers rather than choose only from those who solicit their business. ■ They build long-term relationships with fewer but more reliable high-quality suppliers. ■ They do not compromise quality for price savings.
Manufacturing	■ They invite customers to visit and tour their plants. ■ They visit customer factories to see how customers use the company's products. ■ They willingly work overtime when it is important to meet promised delivery schedules. ■ They continuously improve product quality, aiming for zero defects. ■ They meet customer requirements for customization where this can be done profitably. ■ They meet customer requirements for "customization" where this can be done profitably.
Marketing	■ They study customer needs and wants in well-defined market segments. ■ They allocate marketing effort in relationship to the long-run profit potential of the targeted segments. ■ They develop winning offerings for each target segment.. ■ They constantly measure company image and customer satisfaction. ■ They continuously gather and evaluate ideas for new products, product improvements, and services to meet customers' needs. ■ They influence all company departments and employees to be customer-centred in their thinking and practice.
Sales	■ They acquire specialized knowledge of the customer's industry. ■ They strive to give the customer the best solution but make only promises they can keep. ■ They feed customers' needs and ideas back to those in charge of product development. ■ They serve the same customers for a long time.
Logistics	■ They set a high standard for service delivery time and meet it consistently. ■ They operate a knowledgeable and friendly customer service department that can answer questions, handle complaints, and resolve problems in a satisfactory and timely manner.
Accounting	■ They prepare periodic profitability reports by product, market segment, sales territory, order size, and individual customer. ■ They prepare invoices tailored to customer needs and answer customer queries courteously and quickly.
Finance	■ They understand and support marketing investments (like image advertising) that produce long-term customer preference and loyalty. ■ They tailor the financial package to the customer's financial requirements. ■ They make quick decisions on customer creditworthiness.
Public Relations	■ They disseminate favourable news about the company and they handle damage control for unfavourable news. ■ They act as an internal customer and public advocate for better company policies and practices.
Other Customer-Contact Departments	■ They are competent, courteous, cheerful, credible, reliable, and responsive.

FIGURE 22.1

Functional Organization

FUNCTIONAL ORGANIZATION In the most common form of marketing organization, functional specialists report to a marketing vice-president who coordinates their activities. Figure 22.1 shows five specialists. Others might include a customer service manager, a marketing planning manager, a market-logistics manager, a direct marketing manager, and a digital marketing manager.

The main advantage of a functional marketing organization is its administrative simplicity. It can be quite a challenge for the department to develop smooth working relationships, however. This form also can result in inadequate planning as the number of products and markets increases and each functional group vies for budget and status. The marketing vice-president constantly weighs competing claims and faces a difficult coordination problem.

GEOGRAPHIC ORGANIZATION A company selling in a national market often organizes its sales force (and sometimes marketing) along geographic lines.[13] The national sales manager may supervise four regional sales managers, who each supervise six zone managers, who in turn supervise eight district sales managers, who each supervise ten salespeople.

Some companies are adding *area market specialists* (regional or local marketing managers) to support sales efforts in high-volume markets. One such market is Quebec, with its mix of French-speaking, English-speaking, and ethnic markets and distinct set of retail stores. The Quebec specialist would know customer and trade makeup in key centres like Montreal, Hull, Sherbrooke, and Quebec City; help marketing managers at headquarters adjust their marketing mix for these cities; and prepare local annual and long-range plans for selling all the company's products there. Some companies must develop different marketing programs in different parts of the country because geography alters their brand development so much.

PRODUCT OR BRAND MANAGEMENT ORGANIZATION Companies producing a variety of products and brands often establish a product (or brand) management organization. This does not replace the functional organization but serves as another layer of management. A group product manager supervises product category managers, who in turn supervise specific product and brand managers.

A product management organization makes sense if the company's products are quite different or there are more than a functional organization can handle. This form is sometimes characterized as a **hub-and-spoke system**. The brand or product manager is figuratively at the centre, with spokes leading to various departments and representing working relationships (see Figure 22.2). The manager may

- Develop a long-range and competitive strategy for the product;
- Prepare an annual marketing plan and sales forecast;
- Work with advertising and merchandising agencies to develop copy, programs, and campaigns;
- Increase support of the product among the sales force and distributors;
- Continuously gather intelligence about the product's performance, customer and dealer attitudes, and new problems and opportunities; and
- Initiate product improvements to meet changing market needs.

The product management organization lets the product manager concentrate on developing a cost-effective marketing program and react more quickly to new products in the marketplace; it also gives the company's smaller brands a product advocate. However, it has disadvantages too:

- Product and brand managers may lack authority to carry out their responsibilities.
- They become experts in their product area but rarely achieve functional expertise.

(a) Vertical Product Team

(b) Triangular Product Team

(c) Horizontal Product Team

PM = product manager
APM = associate product manager
PA = product assistant
R   = market researcher
C   = communication specialist
S   = sales manager
D   = distribution specialist
F   = finance/accounting specialist
E   = engineer

- The system often proves costly. One person is appointed to manage each major product or brand, and soon more are appointed to manage even minor products and brands.

- Brand managers normally manage a brand for only a short time. Short-term involvement leads to short-term planning and fails to build long-term strengths.

- The fragmentation of markets makes it harder to develop a national strategy. Brand managers must please regional and local sales groups, transferring power from marketing to sales.

- Product and brand managers focus the company on building market share rather than customer relationships.

A second alternative in a product management organization is *product teams*. There are three types: vertical, triangular, and horizontal (see Figure 22.3). The triangular and horizontal product-team approaches let each major brand be run by a **brand-asset management team (BAMT)** consisting of key representatives from functions that affect the brand's performance. The company consists of several BAMTs that periodically report to a BAMT directors committee, which itself reports to a chief branding officer. This is quite different from the way brands have traditionally been handled.

A third alternative is to eliminate product manager positions for minor products and assign two or more products to each remaining manager. This is feasible where two or more products appeal to a similar set of needs. A cosmetics company doesn't need product managers for each product because cosmetics serve one major need—beauty. A toiletries company needs different managers for headache remedies, toothpaste, soap, and shampoo because these products differ in use and appeal.

In a fourth alternative, *category management*, a company focuses on product categories to manage its brands. Procter & Gamble, a pioneer of the brand management system, and other top packaged-goods firms have made a major shift to category management, as have firms outside the grocery channel.[14] P&G cites a number of advantages. By fostering internal competition among brand managers, the traditional brand management system created strong incentives to excel, but also internal competition for resources and a lack of coordination. The new scheme was designed to ensure adequate resources for all categories.

Another rationale for category management is the increasing power of the retail trade, which has thought of profitability in terms of product categories. P&G felt it only made sense to organize along similar lines. Retailers and regional grocery chains such as Walmart and Dominick's embrace category management as a means to define a particular product category's strategic role within the store and address logistics, the role of private-label products, and the trade-offs between product variety and inefficient duplication.[15]

In fact, in some packaged-goods firms, category management has evolved into aisle management and encompasses multiple related categories typically found in the same sections of supermarkets and grocery stores. General Mills' Yoplait yogurt has served as category advisor to the dairy aisle for 24 major retailers, boosting the amount of shelf space allocated to yogurt from four to eight feet and increasing sales of yogurt by 9 percent and category sales in dairy by 13 percent.[16]

MARKET-MANAGEMENT ORGANIZATION Canon sells fax machines to consumer, business, and government markets. Nippon Steel sells to the railroad, construction, and public utility industries. Think about how complicated Montreal-headquartered Bombardier operations can be.

Bombardier

Bombardier has two main divisions: aerospace and transportation. In aerospace, it is a world leader that provides innovative products and services for the commercial, business, and amphibious aircraft markets. It also offers Bombardier Flexjet fractional ownership, aircraft charter and management, technical services, aircraft maintenance and pilot training for business, commercial airline, and military customers. Its transportation division is the global leader in the rail equipment manufacturing and servicing industry for municipal transit systems as well as national passenger rail systems. To meet such diverse demand, Bombardier has manufacturing, engineering, and services facilities in 23 different countries as well as a global network of service and support representatives.[17]

When customers fall into different user groups with distinct buying preferences and practices, as is the case with Bombardier, a **market management organization** is desirable. Market managers supervise several market-development managers, market specialists, or industry specialists and draw on functional services as needed. Market managers of important markets might even have functional specialists reporting to them.

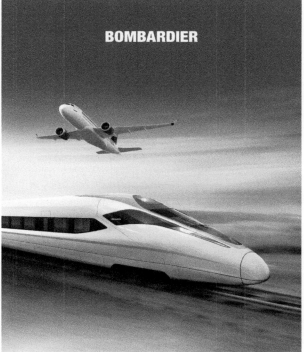

Market managers are staff (not line) people, with duties like those of product managers. They develop long-range and annual plans for their markets and are judged by their market's growth and profitability. Because this system organizes marketing activity to meet the needs of distinct customer groups, it shares many advantages and disadvantages of product management systems. Many companies are reorganizing along market lines and becoming **market-centred organizations**. Xerox converted from geographic selling to selling by industry, as did IBM and Hewlett-Packard.

When a close relationship is advantageous, such as when customers have diverse and complex requirements and buy an integrated bundle of products and services, a **customer-management organization**, which deals with individual customers rather than the mass market or even market segments, should prevail.[18] One study showed that companies organized by customer groups reported much higher accountability for the overall quality of relationships and employees' freedom to take actions to satisfy individual customers.[19]

MATRIX-MANAGEMENT ORGANIZATION Companies that produce many products for many markets may adopt a matrix organization employing both product and market managers. The rub is that it's costly and often creates conflicts. There's the cost of supporting all the managers, and questions about where authority and responsibility for marketing activities should reside—at headquarters or in the division?[20] Some corporate marketing groups assist top management with overall opportunity evaluation, offer divisions consulting assistance on request, help divisions that have little or no marketing, and promote the marketing concept throughout the company.

Bombardier has operations in 23 countries and sales and service teams located around the globe so that it can effectively meet the needs of its diverse customers.

Relationships with Other Departments

Under the marketing concept, all departments need to "think customer" and work together to satisfy customer needs and expectations. Yet departments define company problems and goals from their viewpoint, so conflicts of interest and communications problems are unavoidable. The marketing vice-president, or the CMO, must usually work through persuasion rather than through authority to (1) coordinate the company's internal marketing activities, and (2) coordinate marketing with finance, operations, and other company functions to serve the customer.[21] To help marketing and other functions jointly determine what is in the company's best interests, firms can provide joint seminars, joint committees and liaison employees, employee exchange programs, and analytical methods to determine the most profitable course of action.[22]

Many companies now focus on key processes rather than departments, because departmental organization can be a barrier to smooth performance. They appoint process leaders, who manage cross-disciplinary teams that include marketing and sales people. Marketers thus may have a solid-line responsibility to their teams and a dotted-line responsibility to the marketing department.

Building a Creative Marketing Organization

Many companies realize that they're not yet really market and customer driven—they are product and sales driven. Transforming into a true market-driven company requires the following:

1. Developing a company-wide passion for customers
2. Organizing around customer segments instead of products
3. Understanding customers through qualitative and quantitative research

The task is not easy, but the payoffs can be considerable. It won't happen as a result of the CEO making speeches and urging every employee to "think customer." See "Marketing Insight: The Marketing CEO" for concrete actions a CEO can take to improve marketing capabilities.

MARKETING **INSIGHT** | THE MARKETING CEO

What steps can a CEO take to create a market- and customer-focused company?

1. **Convince senior management of the need to become customer focused.** The CEO personally exemplifies strong customer commitment and rewards those in the organization who do likewise. Such CEOs spend up to a third of their time annually visiting customers in spite of their many strategic, financial, and administrative burdens. Nancy Southern, CEO of Calgary-based ATCO Ltd. (which includes Canadian Utilities Limited), is such a CEO. She is currently ensuring that knowledge gained through serving generations of Alberta's resource-sector customers is translated into ATCO's new Australian venture. Former CEOs Jack Welch of GE and Lou Gerstner of IBM were said to have each spent 100 days a year visiting customers in spite of the CEOs' many strategic, financial, and administrative burdens.

2. **Appoint a senior marketing officer and marketing task force.** The marketing task force should include the CEO; the vice-presidents of sales, R&D, purchasing, manufacturing, finance, and human resources; and other key individuals.

3. **Get outside help and guidance.** Consulting firms have considerable experience helping companies adopt a marketing orientation.

4. **Change the company's reward measurement and system.** As long as purchasing and manufacturing are rewarded for keeping costs low, they will resist accepting some costs required to serve customers better. As long as finance focuses on short-term profit, it will oppose major investments designed to build satisfied, loyal customers.

5. **Hire strong marketing talent.** The company needs a strong marketing vice-president who not only manages the marketing department but also gains respect from and influence with the other vice-presidents. A multidivisional company will benefit from establishing a strong corporate marketing department.

6. **Develop strong in-house marketing training programs.** The company should design well-crafted marketing training programs for corporate management, divisional general managers, marketing and sales personnel, manufacturing personnel, R&D personnel, and others. GE, Motorola, and Accenture run such programs.

7. **Install a modern marketing planning system.** The planning format will require managers to think about the marketing environment, opportunities, competitive trends, and other forces. These managers then prepare strategies and sales-and-profit forecasts for specific products and segments and are accountable for performance.

8. **Establish an annual marketing excellence recognition program.** Business units that believe they've developed exemplary marketing plans should submit a description of their plans and results. Winning teams should be rewarded at a special ceremony and the plans disseminated to the other business units as models of marketing thinking. Becton, Dickinson and Company; Procter & Gamble; and SABMiller follow this strategy.

9. **Shift from a department focus to a process-outcome focus.** After defining the fundamental business processes that determine its success, the company should appoint process leaders and cross-disciplinary teams to re-engineer and implement these processes.

10. **Empower the employees.** Progressive companies encourage and reward their employees for coming up with new ideas and empower them to settle customer complaints to save the customer's business. IBM lets front-line employees spend up to $5000 to solve a customer problem on the spot.

Although it's *necessary* to be customer oriented, it's not *enough*. The organization must also be creative.[23] Companies today copy each others' advantages and strategies with increasing speed, making differentiation harder to achieve and lowering margins as firms become more alike. The only answer is to build a capability in strategic innovation and imagination. This capability comes from assembling tools, processes, skills, and measures that let the firm generate more and better new ideas than its competitors.[24]

Companies must also watch trends and be ready to capitalize on them. Motorola was 18 months late in moving from analogue to digital cell phones, giving Nokia and Ericsson a big lead. Nestlé was late seeing the trend toward coffee houses such as Starbucks. Coca-Cola was slow to pick up beverage trends toward fruit-flavoured drinks such as Snapple, energy drinks such as Gatorade, and designer water brands. Market leaders can miss trends when they are risk averse, obsessed about protecting their existing markets and physical resources, and more interested in efficiency than innovation.[25]

SOCIALLY RESPONSIBLE MARKETING

Effective internal marketing must be matched by a strong sense of ethics, values, and social responsibility.[26] A number of forces are driving companies to practise a higher level of corporate social responsibility, such as rising customer expectations, evolving employee goals and ambitions, tighter government legislation and pressure, investor interest in social criteria, media scrutiny, and changing business procurement practices.[27]

Virtually all firms have decided to take a more active, strategic role in corporate social responsibility, carefully scrutinizing what they believe in and how they should treat their customers, employees, competitors, community, and the environment. Taking this broader stakeholder view is believed to also benefit another important constituency—shareholders. Look at how Walmart Canada is addressing corporate social responsibility.[28]

Walmart Canada

David Cheesewright, President and CEO of Walmart Canada, says, "As a growing company and employer in Canada, we see corporate social responsibility as one of our biggest duties. Our size gives us considerable influence and with it comes considerable responsibility—one that we accept in order to help Canadians save money and live better. Our perspective and priorities fit broadly into four categories of CSR: Environment, People, Responsible Sourcing and Community." David Cheesewright tries to walk the talk—he bikes 20 km to work daily. Since 2005, the company has invested millions in sustainability projects, such as doubling the efficiency of its vehicle fleet, eliminating 30 percent of the energy used in stores, and reducing solid waste generated by stores. To help ensure that it is following the right path, it enlisted long-time environmental champion David Suzuki to provide insight and advice. Walmart Canada did an even more surprising thing in 2010: it started a new initiative, the Walmart Canada Green Business Summit, through which it shared the lessons it has learned about the best sustainable practices with a wide audience, including competitive firms. Held in Vancouver, the summit was attended by 350 senior delegates, who were called to collaborate across industry sectors to accelerate practices that are both profitable and sustainable.

Businesses have not always believed in the value of social responsibility. In 1776, Adam Smith proclaimed, "I have never known much good done by those who profess to trade for the public good." Legendary economist Milton Friedman famously declared social initiatives "fundamentally subversive" because he felt they undermined the profit-seeking purpose of public companies and wasted shareholders' money. Some critics worry that important business investment in areas such as R&D could suffer as a result of a focus on social responsibility.[29]

But these critics are in a tiny minority. Many companies now believe that satisfying customers, employees, and other stakeholders, and achieving business success are closely tied to the adoption and implementation of high standards of business and marketing conduct. A further benefit of being seen as socially responsible is the ability to attract employees, especially younger people who want to work for companies they feel good about.

The most admired—and most successful—companies in the world abide by a code of serving people's interests, not only their own. Procter & Gamble's new CEO Bob McDonald has made "brand purpose" a key component of the company's marketing strategies, noting, "Consumers have a higher expectation of brands and want to know what they are doing for the world. But it has to be authentic with a genuine desire to do it." Downy fabric softener's "Touch of Comfort" cause program, for example, donates 5 cents from purchases to Quilts for Kids, an organization that works with volunteer quilters to make and distribute custom-sewn quilts to children in hospitals.[30] P&G is not alone, as the following demonstrates.

Firms of Endearment

Researchers Raj Sisodia, David Wolfe, and Jag Sheth believe that humanistic companies make great companies. They see "Firms of Endearment" as those with a culture of caring and that serve the interests of their stakeholders, defined by the acronym SPICE: Society, Partners, Investors, Customers, and Employees. Sisodia et al. believe that Firms of Endearment create a love affair with stakeholders. Their senior managers run an open-door policy, are passionate about customers, and earn modest compensation. They pay more to their employees, relate more closely to a smaller group of excellent suppliers, and give back to the communities in which they work. The researchers assert that Firms of Endearment actually spend less on marketing as a percentage of sales yet earn greater profits, because customers who love the company do most of the marketing. The authors see the twenty-first-century marketing paradigm as creating value for all stakeholders and becoming a beloved firm. Table 22.2 lists firms receiving top marks as Firms of Endearment from a sample of thousands of customers, employees, and suppliers.[31]

Corporate Social Responsibility

Raising the level of socially responsible marketing calls for making a three-pronged attack that relies on proper legal, ethical, and social responsibility behaviour. More and more firms are accepting a broader set of responsibilities. Each year, *Corporate Knights*, a magazine founded ten years ago in Canada, ranks the performance of Canada's best companies. It has recently expanded and now offers a ranking of global firms as well. Founder Toby Heaps notes that he was inspired by Peter Drucker's famous adage, "what gets measured, gets managed." In other words, such rankings are one of the drivers of change that have encouraged companies to be better corporate citizens. Topping the 2010 list of Canada's best corporate citizens are the Co-operators Group Ltd., Mountain Equipment Co-op, Domtar Corporation, Loblaw Company Ltd., and BC Hydro and Power Authority.[32]

LEGAL BEHAVIOUR Organizations must ensure every employee knows and observes relevant laws.[33] For example, it's illegal for salespeople to lie to consumers or mislead them about the advantages of buying a product. Salespeople may not offer bribes to purchasing agents or others influencing a B2B sale. Their statements must match advertising claims, and they may not obtain or use competitors' technical or trade secrets through bribery or industrial espionage. Finally, they must not disparage competitors or their products by suggesting things that are not true. Managers must make sure every sales representative knows the law and acts accordingly.

ETHICAL BEHAVIOUR Business practices come under attack because business situations routinely pose ethical dilemmas: it's not easy to draw a clear line between normal marketing practice and unethical behav-

---

TABLE 22.2 | **TOP FIRMS OF ENDEARMENT**

Best Buy	BMW	CarMax	Caterpillar
Commerce Bank	Container Store	Costco	eBay
Google	Harley-Davidson	Honda	IDEO
IKEA	JetBlue	Johnson & Johnson	Jordan's Furniture
L.L.Bean	New Balance	Patagonia	Progressive Insurance
REI	Southwest	Starbucks	Timberland
Toyota	Trader Joe's	UPS	Wegmans
Whole Foods			

Source: *SISODIA, RAJENDRA S.; WOLFE, DAVID B.; SHETH, JAGDISH N., FIRMS OF ENDEARMENT: HOW WORLD-CLASS COMPANIES PROFIT FROM PASSION AND PURPOSE, 1st Ed.,* © 2007. Reprinted and Electronically reproduced by permission of Pearson Education, Inc., Upper Saddle River, New Jersey.

Corporate Knights, a Canadian magazine devoted to clean capitalism, has been one of the drivers of more sustainable business practices in Canada.

iour. Some issues sharply divide critics. For example, 19 Canadian food marketers, such as Burger King, Kellogg Canada Inc., McCain Foods Canada, and McDonald's Restaurants of Canada Ltd., initiated the Canadian Children's Food and Beverage Advertising Initiative, a voluntary industry program that encourages healthier choices and lifestyles for children. However, some watch groups felt that the program was not enough.[34]

Of course, certain business practices are clearly unethical or illegal. These include bribery, theft of trade secrets, false and deceptive advertising, exclusive dealing and tying agreements, quality or safety defects, false warranties, inaccurate labelling, price-fixing or undue discrimination, and barriers to entry and predatory competition.

Companies must adopt and disseminate a written code of ethics, build a company tradition of ethical behaviour, and hold their people fully responsible for observing ethical and legal guidelines.[35] In the past, a disgruntled customer might bad-mouth an unethical or poorly performing firm to 12 other people; today, via the Internet, he or she can reach thousands. Microsoft, for example, has attracted scores of anti-Microsoft sites, including www.msboycott.com and www.ihatemicrosoft.com. Consumers' general distrust of companies is evident in the annual research study conducted by Edelman, an independent public relations firm. Edelman has been conducting these surveys for 11 years, and its Trust Barometer measures firms' trust and credibility around the world. According to the 11th survey, Canada enjoyed stable levels of trust in business, but only 50 percent of Canadians aged 25 to 64 put faith in business. Furthermore, trust is "now different and conditional, and it is premised on what a company does and how it communicates . . . demonstrating a strong need for corporations to create value in a way that aligns with society's interests, not just profits."[36]

SOCIAL RESPONSIBILITY BEHAVIOUR Individual marketers must exercise their social conscience in specific dealings with customers and stakeholders. In addition to the firms noted earlier in this chapter, other top-rated companies for corporate social responsibility, as ranked by Jantzi and Maclean's in 2010, are Bank of Montreal, Cascades Inc., Enbridge Inc., Manulife Financial, Nexen Inc., RBC, Stantec Inc., and Telus Corporation.[37]

Increasingly, people want information about a company's record on social and environmental responsibility to help them decide which companies to buy from, invest in, and work for.[38] It is not surprising, therefore, that McCain Foods Limited, an international leader in the frozen food industry, recognized the importance of winning the annual Corporate Social Responsibility award for its global social responsibility report titled *Our Journey* in 2010 at a ceremony in Washington, D.C. According to Dale Morrison, then McCain's Global President and CEO, the company's journey toward social responsibility began more than 50 years ago. While the term "corporate social responsibility" was not common language when co-founders

McCain was honoured for its first global corporate social responsibility report, produced in 2009.

Harrison and Wallace McCain first ventured out in 1957, "the brothers operated with the philosophy that good ethics is good business as is building mutually beneficial relationships. Even then, the company founders knew that making decisions with a view to social, economic and cultural challenges was the key to sustained success."[39] Once a firm touts itself as a CSR leader, however, it can become a target for criticism. See what happened to Nestlé.[40]

Nestlé

Palm oil was hailed as a renewable fuel for food companies looking to find a solution to a trans-fat ban, until its use was linked to the destruction of tropical rain forests and the extinction of the orangutan and the sun bear. When Greenpeace released a report criticizing Nestlé for purchasing palm oil for its KitKat candy bars from an Indonesian firm linked to rain forest destruction there, a social media war ensued. Protestors posted a negative video on YouTube, bombarded Twitter and Nestlé's Facebook page, and took to the streets outside Nestlé's Jakarta offices. Nestlé cut ties with the firm and took other steps to address the controversy but continued to receive criticism.

Corporate philanthropy also can pose dilemmas. Companies like Bell Canada, RBC, Microsoft Canada, and Canada Newswire have donated millions to charities. Yet good deeds can be overlooked—even resented—if the company is seen as exploitive or fails to live up to a "good guys" image. Philip Morris Company's $250 million ad campaign touting its charitable activities was met with skepticism because of its negative image as a tobacco company. Some critics worry that cause marketing or "consumption philanthropy" may replace virtuous actions with less-thoughtful buying, reduce emphasis on real solutions, or deflect attention from the fact that markets may create many social problems to begin with.[41]

SUSTAINABILITY *Sustainability*—the ability to meet humanity's needs without harming future generations—now tops many corporate agendas. Major corporations outline in great detail how they are trying to improve the long-term impact of their actions on communities and the environment. As one sustainability consultant put it, "There is a triple bottom line—people, planet, and profit—and the people part of the equation must come first. Sustainability means more than being eco-friendly, it also means you are in it for the long haul."[42]

Sustainability ratings exist, but there is no consistent agreement about what metrics are appropriate.[43] One comprehensive study used 11 factors to evaluate and assemble a list of the Top 100 Sustainable Corporations in the World: energy, water, CO_2, and waste productivity; leadership diversity; CEO-to-average-worker pay; taxes paid; sustainability leadership; sustainability pay link; innovation capacity; and transparency. The top 5 firms were GE, PG&E, TNT, H&M, and Nokia.[44]

Some feel companies that score well on sustainability typically exhibit high-quality management in that "they tend to be more strategically nimble and better equipped to compete in the complex, high-velocity, global environment."[45] Consumer interest is also creating market opportunities. Clorox's line of naturally derived Green Works laundry and home cleaners—aided by restrained price premiums and a Sierra Club endorsement—has experienced early success.[46] Another good example is organic products (see "Marketing Insight: The Rise of Organic").

Heightened interest in sustainability has also unfortunately resulted in *greenwashing*, which gives products the appearance of being environmentally friendly without living up to that promise. One study revealed that half the labels on allegedly green products focus on an ecofriendly benefit (such as recycled content) while omitting information about significant environmental drawbacks (such as manufacturing intensity or transportation costs).[47]

Because of insincere firms jumping on the green bandwagon, consumers bring a healthy skepticism to environmental claims, but they are also unwilling to sacrifice product performance and quality.[48] Many firms are rising to the challenge and are using the need for sustainability to fuel innovation. Sales of products emphasizing sustainability remained strong through the recent economic recession.[49]

Socially Responsible Business Models

The future holds a wealth of opportunities, yet forces in the socioeconomic, cultural, and natural environments will impose new limits on marketing and business practices. Companies that innovate solutions and values in a socially responsible way are most likely to succeed.[50]

Many companies are giving social responsibility a more prominent role. Corporate philanthropy is also on the rise, but it has changed from the old "cheque-book" model to one where corporations have taken a more strategic approach to their community investment. In one survey, 50 percent of the companies said that their giving exceeded the 1 percent of profits recommended by Imagine Canada, and the median donation was $340 000.[51] Some companies tie their giving to their marketing activities in the form of cause marketing programs. Others support employee volunteerism programs. Such activities are seen as not just the "right thing" but also the "smart thing to do."[52]

MARKETING **INSIGHT** | THE RISE OF ORGANIC

Organic products have become a strong presence in many food and beverage categories. Since 2006, retail sales of certified organic products in Canada have exceeded $1 billion. Caster & Pollux's success with organic and natural pet foods led to its distribution in major specialty retail chains such as Petco. Pro Organics, founded in Vancouver in 1990, has grown to become Canada's premier distributor of high-quality certified organic fresh food.

Organic and natural are at the core of some brands' positioning. Chipotle Mexican Grill's mission statement, "Food with Integrity," reflects its focus on good food with a socially responsible message. One of the first fast-casual restaurant chains, Chipotle uses natural and organic ingredients and serves more meat from naturally raised animals than any other restaurant. Making each burrito by hand takes time, but the quality of the food and the message behind it are a satisfying payoff for many customers.

Many companies beyond the food industry are embracing organic offerings that avoid chemicals and pesticides to stress ecological preservation. Apparel and other nonfood items make up the second-fastest growth category of the $3.5 billion organic product industry. Organic nonfood grew 9.1 percent in 2009 to $1.8 billion—now 7 percent of the $26.6 billion organic products industry. Organic cotton grown by farmers who fight boll weevils with ladybugs, weed crops by hand, and use manure for fertilizer has become a hot product at retail.

Sources: "Industry Statistics and Projected Growth," *Organic Trade Association*, June 2010; Arianne Cohen, "Ode to a Burrito," *Fast Company*, April 2008, pp. 54–56; Kenneth Hein, "The World on a Platter," *Brandweek*, April 23, 2007, pp. 27–28; Megan Johnston, "Hard Sell for a Soft Fabric," *Forbes*, October 30, 2006, pp. 73–80; Ann Macey, "Retail Sales of Certified Organic Food Products in Canada 2006," Organic Agriculture Centre of Canada, May 2007, http://oacc.info/Docs/RetailSalesOrganic_Canada2006.pdf (viewed July 2011).

Cause-Related Marketing

Many firms blend corporate social responsibility initiatives with marketing activities.[53] **Cause-related marketing** links the firm's contributions to a designated cause, like the Nature Conservancy of Canada, with customers' engaging directly or indirectly in revenue-producing transactions with the firm.[54] Cause marketing is part of *corporate societal marketing (CSM)*, which Minette Drumwright and Patrick Murphy define as marketing efforts "that have at least one noneconomic objective related to social welfare and use the resources of the company and/or of its partners."[55] Drumwright and Murphy also include traditional and strategic philanthropy and volunteerism in CSM.

Table 22.3 summarizes three highly successful cause marketing programs. We next review the pros and cons of such programs and some important guidelines.

CAUSE MARKETING BENEFITS AND COSTS A successful cause marketing program can improve social welfare, create differentiated brand positioning, build strong consumer bonds, enhance the company's public image, create a reservoir of goodwill, boost internal morale and galvanize employees, drive sales, and increase the firm's market value.[56] Consumers may develop a strong, unique bond with the firm, one that transcends normal marketplace transactions.

Specifically, from a branding point of view, cause marketing can (1) build brand awareness, (2) enhance brand image, (3) establish brand credibility, (4) evoke brand feelings, (5) create a sense of brand community, and (6) elicit brand engagement.[57] It has a particularly interested audience in civic-minded 18- to 24-year-old Millennial consumers (see Table 22.4).

Cause-related marketing could backfire, however, if consumers question the link between the product and the cause or see the firm as self-serving and exploitive.[58] Problems can also arise if consumers do not think that a company is consistent and sufficiently responsible in all its behaviour, as happened to KFC.[59]

TABLE 22.3	THREE CLASSIC CAUSE MARKETING PROGRAMS

Tesco

Tesco, a leading U.K. retailer, has created the Tesco for Schools and Clubs program, which dovetails well with its overall corporate brand positioning of "Every Little Bit Helps." Customers receive one voucher for every £10 spent, which they can donate to a school of their choice or any registered amateur club for children under 18. In 2009, the company gave away 540 000 items worth £13.4 million. It also offers vouchers for recycled inkjet cartridges and donated working phones.

Dawn

Procter & Gamble's Dawn, the top dishwashing liquid in the United States, has long highlighted its unusual side benefit—it can clean birds caught in oil spills. A report by the U.S. Fish and Wildlife Service called Dawn "the only bird-cleaning agent that is recommended because it removes oil from feathers; is non-toxic; and does not leave a residue." A website launched in 2006, www.DawnSavesWildlife.com, drew 130 000 people who formed virtual groups to encourage friends and others to stop gas and oil leaks from their cars. After the catastrophic BP oil spill in 2010, P&G donated thousands of bottles. It also placed a code on bottles and donated $1 to wildlife causes for each code customers activated, eventually totalling $500 000. The brand also drew massive publicity and visits to its Facebook site, which outlined the environmental cleanup and relief effort.

Tim Hortons

During catastrophic global emergencies, the iconic Canadian brand Tim Hortons has rallied its customers, staff, and restaurant owners to donate the spare change from their purchases to UNICEF's emergency relief efforts, which saves children's lives through the provision of clean water, nutritious food, and emergency shelters. Through highly cost-effective on-screen advertising and till-side displays in each of its stores during the campaign period, the results have been incredible: More than $750 000 was raised during a two-week period following the devastating earthquake in Haiti in January 2010, and a similar amount was raised following the tsunami in Southeast Asia in 2004. Over the past decade, Tim Hortons has raised more than $2.6 million toward UNICEF's life-saving work for children in emergencies.

Sources: www.tescoforschoolsandclubs.co.uk; www.dawnsaveswildlife.com; Jack Neff and Stephanie Thompson, "Eco-Marketing Has Staying Power This Time Around," *Advertising Age*, April 30, 2007, p. 55.

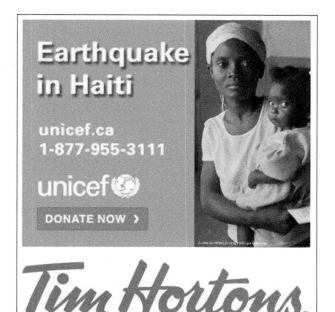

In 2010, Tim Hortons partnered with UNICEF to save lives in the aftermath of the earthquake in Haiti.

TABLE 22.4	MILLENNIAL DATA POINTS: 18- TO 24-YEAR-OLDS' ATTITUDES ABOUT CAUSES

- 85% are likely to switch from one brand to another brand that is about the same in price and quality, if the other brand is associated with a good cause.

- 86% consider a company's social or environmental commitments when deciding which products and services to recommend to others.

- 84% consider a company's social or environmental commitments when deciding what to buy or where to shop.

- 87% consider a company's social or environmental commitments when deciding where to work.

- 86% say when a product or company supports a cause (a social or environmental issue) they care about, they have a more positive image of that product or company.

Source: "2010 Cone Cause Evolution Study"; for additional content, see www.coneinc.com/2010-cone-cause-evolution-study.

KFC

KFC's "Buckets for the Cure" program was to donate 50 cents for every $5 "pink" bucket of fried chicken purchased over a one-month period to the famed Susan G. Komen for the Cure Foundation. The donation was slotted to be the single biggest corporate donation ever to fund breast cancer research—over $8.5 million. One problem: at virtually the same time, KFC also launched its Double Down sandwich with two pieces of fried chicken, bacon, and cheese. Critics immediately pointed out that KFC was selling a food item with excessively high calories, fat, and sodium, one that contributed to obesity, a significant risk factor for breast cancer. On the Susan G. Komen site itself, being overweight was flagged for increasing the risk of breast cancer by 30 percent to 60 percent in post-menopausal women, also leaving the foundation open to criticism over the partnership.

To avoid backlash, some firms take a soft-sell approach to their cause efforts. Nike's alliance with the Lance Armstrong Foundation for cancer research sold over 80 million yellow LIVESTRONG bracelets for $1 from 2004 to 2010, but intentionally the famed Nike swoosh was nowhere to be seen.[60] One interesting recent cause program is the (PRODUCT)RED campaign.[61]

(PRODUCT)^RED

The highly publicized launch of (PRODUCT)^RED in 2006, championed by U2 singer and activist Bono and DATA chairman Bobby Shriver, raised awareness and money for The Global Fund by teaming with some of the world's most iconic branded products—Apple (Canada) iPods, Rogers Wireless, Converse sneakers, Gap T-shirts, and Emporio Armani sunglasses—to produce (PRODUCT)^RED-branded items. Up to 50 percent of the profits from sales of these products go to The Global Fund to help women and children affected by HIV/AIDS in Africa. Each company that becomes (PRODUCT)^RED places its logo in the "embrace" signified by the parentheses and is "elevated to the power of red." Although some critics felt the (PRODUCT)^RED project was overmarketed, in its first 18 months its contribution to The Global Fund surpassed $36 million, more than seven times what businesses had contributed since the fund's founding in 2002. Many well-known brands have joined the cause since then, such as Dell computers, Hallmark cards, and Starbucks coffee.

The knowledge, skills, and resources of a top firm may be even more important to a nonprofit or community group than funding. Nonprofits must be clear about what their goals are, communicate clearly what they hope to accomplish, and devise an organizational structure to work with different firms. Developing a long-term relationship with a firm can take time. As one consultant noted, "What's often a problem between corporations and nonprofits is different expectations and different understanding about the amount of time everything will take."[62]

Firms must make a number of decisions in designing and implementing a cause marketing program, such as how many and which cause(s) to choose and how to brand the cause program.

DESIGNING A CAUSE PROGRAM Some experts believe that the positive impact of cause-related marketing is reduced by sporadic involvement with numerous causes. Cathy Chizauskas, Gillette's Director of Civic Affairs, states, "When you're spreading out your giving in fifty-dollar to one-thousand-dollar increments, no one knows what you are doing.... It doesn't make much of a splash."[63]

Many companies focus on one or a few main causes to simplify execution and maximize impact. McDonald's Ronald McDonald Houses in 30-plus countries offer more than 7200 rooms each night to families needing support while their child is in the hospital, saving them a total of $257 million annually in hotel costs. The program has provided a "home away from home" for nearly 10 million family members since 1974.[64]

Limiting support to a single cause, however, may limit the pool of consumers or other stakeholders who can transfer positive feelings from the cause to the firm. Many popular causes also already have numerous corporate sponsors. Over 300 companies, including Avon, Ford, Estée Lauder, Revlon, Lee Jeans, Polo Ralph Lauren, General Mills' Yoplait, Saks, BMW, and American Express, have associated themselves with breast cancer as a cause.[65] Thus, a brand may find itself overlooked in a sea of symbolic pink ribbons.

Opportunities may be greater with "orphan causes"—diseases that afflict fewer than 200 000 people.[66] Another option is overlooked or invisible diseases: BCE, for example, made an unprecedented multiyear $50 million charitable donation to support mental health across Canada. While such problems are often invisible, one in five Canadians experience a mental illness at some point in their lives; they often have no one to talk to about their problem, so BCE's donation will have a significant impact. It also generated a lot of publicity for the company.[67]

Most firms choose causes that fit their corporate or brand image and matter to their employees and shareholders. LensCrafters' Give the Gift of Sight program—now rebranded as OneSight after the company was purchased by the Italian firm Luxottica—is a family of charitable vision-care programs providing free vision screenings, eye exams, and glasses to more than 6 million needy people in North America and developing countries around the world. All stores are empowered to deliver free glasses in their communities, and two travelling Vision Vans target children in North America and make monthly two-week optical missions overseas. Luxottica pays most of the overhead, so 92 percent of all donations go directly to fund programming.[68]

"Marketing Memo: Making a Difference" provides some tips from a top cause-marketing firm. TOMS shoes is an example of a new firm using cause marketing to successfully build a new business.[69]

MARKETING **MEMO**	MAKING A DIFFERENCE: TOP 10 TIPS FOR CAUSE BRANDING

Cone Communications, a Boston-based public relations and marketing agency specializing in cause branding and corporate responsibility, offers these tips for developing authentic and substantive programs:

1. **Select a focus area that aligns with your mission, goals and organization.**

2. **Evaluate your institutional "will" and resources.** If you, your employees and other allies don't believe or invest in your organization's cause, neither will your audience.

3. **Analyze your competitors' cause positioning.** There are few remaining wide, open spaces, but this may help you locate a legitimate societal need or an untapped element within a more crowded space that you can own.

4. **Choose your partners carefully.** Look for alignment in values, mission and will. Carefully outline roles and responsibilities. Set your sights on a multi-year sustainable relationship, with annual measurement of accomplishments for both partners.

5. **Don't underestimate the name of your program—it's key to the identity of your campaign.** Develop a few words that say exactly what you do and create a visual identity that is simple, yet memorable. The Avon Breast Cancer Crusade, American Heart Association's Go Red for Women and Target Take Charge of Education are good examples.

6. **To create a sustainable and effective program, start by developing a cross-functional strategy team.** Include representatives from the office of the CEO, public affairs, human resources, marketing, public and community relations, research/measurement, volunteer and program management, among others. If you're in silos, you will spend too much valuable time building bridges to other departments to get the real work done.

7. **Leverage both your assets and those of your partner(s) to bring the program to life.** Assets may include volunteers, cash and in-kind donations, special events, in store presence, partner resources and marketing/advertising support. And remember, emotion is one of your greatest assets. It can help you to connect with your audience and differentiate your organization in a crowded marketplace.

8. **Communicate through every possible channel.** Craft compelling words *and* visuals because stirring images can penetrate the heart. Then, take your messages beyond traditional media outlets and become multi-dimensional! Think special events, Web sites, workshops, PSAs, expert spokespersons and even celebrity endorsements.

9. **Go local.** National programs reach the "grass tops," but true transformation begins at the grassroots. Engage citizens/volunteers through hands-on activities at local events, cause promotions and fundraisers.

10. **Innovate.** True cause leaders constantly evolve their programs to add energy, new engagement opportunities and content to remain relevant and to build sustainability.

Source: Cone Communications, "Top 10 Tips for Cause Branding," www.coneinc.com/10-tips-cause-branding. See also Carol L. Cone, Mark A. Feldman, and Alison T. DaSilva, "Cause and Effects," *Harvard Business Review*, July 2003, pp. 95–101.

TOMS Shoes

Although Blake Mycoskie did not win the around-the-world reality show *The Amazing Race*, his return trip to Argentina in 2006 sparked a desire to start a business to help the scores of kids he saw who suffered for one simple reason—they lacked shoes. Shoeless children incur a health risk but are also disadvantaged in that they often are not permitted to go to school. Thus was born TOMS shoes, its name chosen to convey "a better tomorrow," with a pledge to donate a pair of shoes to needy children for each pair of shoes sold. Picked up by stores like Whole Foods, Nordstrom, and Neiman Marcus and also sold online, TOMS shoes are based on the classic *alpargata* footwear of Argentina. As a result of the company's One for One program, the lightweight shoes can also be found on the feet of more than 1 million kids in developing countries such as Argentina and Ethiopia. Using money that would have been used to fund promotional efforts to instead pay for donated shoes has been good marketing too: the firm has garnered heaps of publicity—AT&T even featured Mycoskie in a commercial—and sales revenue for the first five years of the firm's existence has been estimated at $50 million.

Social Marketing

Cause-related marketing supports a cause. **Social marketing** by nonprofit or government organizations *furthers* a cause or helps resolve a social issue, such as "say no to drugs" or "exercise more and eat better."[70]

Social marketing goes back many years. In the 1950s, India started family planning campaigns. In the 1970s, Canada and Sweden introduced social marketing campaigns to turn themselves into nations of non-smokers, the Australian government ran "Wear Your Seat Belt" campaigns, and the Canadian government launched one of its most famous campaigns, "ParticipACTION." The program was internationally recognized for its compelling messages encouraging Canadians to be more physically active.[71] In the 1980s, the World Bank, World Health Organization, and Centers for Disease Control and Prevention started to use the term *social marketing* and promote interest in it. The following are some notable global social marketing successes:

- Oral rehydration therapy in Honduras significantly decreased deaths from diarrhea in children under five.
- Social marketers created booths in marketplaces where Ugandan midwives sold contraceptives at affordable prices.
- Population Communication Services created and promoted two extremely popular songs in Latin America, "Stop" and "When We Are Together," to help young women "say no."

Different types of organizations conduct social marketing in Canada. Federal government departments such as Health Canada and Parks Canada, nonprofit groups such as the Canadian Cancer Society and the Heart and Stroke Foundation, and activist groups such as Greenpeace all use social marketing techniques. Choosing the right goal or objective for a social marketing program is critical. Should a family planning campaign focus on abstinence or birth control? Should a campaign to fight air pollution focus on ride sharing or mass transit? Social marketing campaigns may try to change people's cognitions, values, actions, or behaviours. The following examples illustrate the range of possible objectives.

Cognitive campaigns

- Explain the nutritional values of different foods.
- Demonstrate the importance of conservation.

Action campaigns

- Attract people for mass immunization.
- Motivate people to vote "yes" on a certain issue.
- Inspire people to donate blood.
- Motivate women to take a pap test.

Behavioural campaigns

- Demotivate cigarette smoking.
- Demotivate overuse of popular national parks.
- Demotivate excessive alcohol consumption.

Value campaigns

- Alter ideas about abortion.
- Change attitudes of bigoted people.

While social marketing uses a number of different tactics to achieve its goals, the planning process follows many of the same steps as for traditional products and services (see Table 22.5).[72] Some key success factors for changing behaviour include the following:[73]

- Choose target markets that are most ready to respond.
- Promote a single, doable behaviour in clear, simple terms.
- Explain the benefits in compelling terms.
- Make it easy to adopt the behaviour.
- Develop attention-grabbing messages and media.
- Consider an education–entertainment approach.

One organization that has accomplished most of these goals through the application of modern marketing practices is the World Wildlife Fund.

TABLE 22.5 | THE SOCIAL MARKETING PLANNING PROCESS

Where Are We?
- Determine program focus
- Identify campaign purpose
- Conduct an analysis of strengths, weaknesses, opportunities, and threats (SWOT)
- Review past and similar efforts

Where Do We Want to Go?
- Select target audiences
- Set objectives and goals
- Analyze target audiences and the competition

How Will We Get There?
- Product: Design the market offering
- Price: Manage costs of behaviour change
- Distribution: Make the product available
- Communications: Create messages and choose media

How Will We Stay on Course?
- Develop a plan for evaluation and monitoring
- Establish budgets and find funding sources
- Complete an implementation plan

The World Wildlife Fund uses modern marketing communications and programs to actively support its cause.

World Wildlife Fund

The World Wildlife Fund (WWF) consists of 30 independent World Wildlife organizations around the globe that once operated separately. Its early achievements include helping to form the Forest Stewardship Council in 1993 and co-founding the Marine Stewardship Council with Unilever in 1996. Today it is focused on building a future where people and nature live in harmony through its "Living Planet" campaign. In Canada and the United States, the WWF's annual budget does not allow for lavish marketing expenditures, so it increasingly relies on social media, including its award-winning website and apps for smartphones, to communicate its initiatives, such as the program to conserve polar bears and improve Canada's shorelines. Donations also fund its efforts and research projects. For example, a donation from Donald R. Sobey enabled the WWF and the Marine Affairs Program at Dalhousie University to partner in a new cross-disciplinary research program aimed at helping ocean communities to flourish. The WWF also earns revenue through different types of corporate partnerships with top firms such as Canada Steamship Lines, Bullfrog Power, Loblaws, Coca-Cola, IKEA, Nike, Johnson & Johnson, Cargill, Dole, adidas, Walmart, IBM, and Tyco. Since 1985, the WWF Network has invested over $1.165 billion in more than 11 000 projects in 130 countries.

Social marketing programs are complex; they take time and may require phased programs or actions. You may recall the many steps in discouraging smoking: release of cancer reports, labelling of cigarettes as harmful, bans on cigarette advertising, education about secondary smoke effects, bans on smoking in restaurants and planes, increased taxes on cigarettes to pay for antismoking campaigns, and suits against tobacco companies.

Social marketing organizations should evaluate program success in terms of their objectives. Criteria might include incidence of adoption, speed of adoption, continuance of adoption, low cost per unit of adoption, and absence of counterproductive consequences.

MARKETING IMPLEMENTATION AND CONTROL

Table 22.6 summarizes the characteristics of a great marketing company, great not for what it is but for what it does. Great marketing companies know that the best marketers thoughtfully and creatively devise marketing plans and then bring them to life. Marketing implementation and control are critical to making sure marketing plans have their intended results year after year.

Marketing Implementation

Marketing implementation is the process that turns marketing plans into action assignments and ensures they accomplish the plan's stated objectives.[74] A brilliant strategic marketing plan counts for little if not implemented properly. Strategy addresses the *what* and *why* of marketing activities; implementation addresses the *who, where, when,* and *how*. They are closely related: One layer of strategy implies certain tactical implementation assignments at a lower level. For example, top management's strategic decision to harvest a product must be translated into specific actions and assignments.

Companies today are striving to make their marketing operations more efficient and their return on marketing investment more measurable (see Chapter 4). Marketing costs can amount to as much as a quarter of a company's total operating budget. Marketers need better templates for marketing processes, better management of marketing assets, and better allocation of marketing resources.

Marketing resource management (MRM) software provides a set of web-based applications that automate and integrate project management, campaign management, budget management, asset management, brand management, customer relationship management, and knowledge management. The knowledge management component consists of process templates, how-to wizards, and best practices. Software packages can provide what some have called *desktop marketing*, giving marketers information and decision structures on computer dashboards. MRM software lets marketers improve spending and investment decisions, bring new products to market more quickly, and reduce decision time and costs.

Marketing Control

Marketing control is the process by which firms assess the effects of their marketing activities and programs and make necessary changes and adjustments. Table 22.7 lists four types of needed marketing control: annual-plan control, profitability control, efficiency control, and strategic control.

Annual-Plan Control

Annual-plan control ensures the company achieves the sales, profits, and other goals established in its annual plan. At its heart is management by objectives (see Figure 22.4). First, management sets monthly or quarterly goals. Second, it monitors performance in the marketplace. Third, it determines the causes of serious performance deviations. Fourth, it takes corrective action to close gaps between goals and performance.

This control model applies to all levels of the organization. Top management sets annual sales and profit goals; each product manager, regional district manager, sales manager, and sales rep is committed to attaining specified levels of sales and costs. Each period, top management reviews and interprets the results. Marketers today have better marketing metrics for measuring the performance of marketing plans

TABLE 22.6	CHARACTERISTICS OF A GREAT MARKETING COMPANY

- The company selects target markets in which it enjoys superior advantages and exits or avoids markets where it is intrinsically weak.
- Virtually all the company's employees and departments are customer- and market-minded.
- There is a good working relationship between marketing, R&D, and manufacturing.
- There is a good working relationship between marketing, sales, and customer service.
- The company has installed incentives designed to lead to the right behaviours.
- The company continuously builds and tracks customer satisfaction and loyalty.
- The company manages a value-delivery system in partnership with strong suppliers and distributors.
- The company is skilled in building its brand name(s) and image.
- The company is flexible in meeting customers' varying requirements.

TABLE 22.7 | TYPES OF MARKETING CONTROL

Type of Control	Prime Responsibility	Purpose of Control	Approaches
1. Annual-plan control	Top management Middle management	To examine whether the planned results are being achieved	■ Sales analysis ■ Market-share analysis ■ Sales-to-expense ratios ■ Financial analysis ■ Market-based scorecard analysis
2. Profitability control	Marketing controller	To examine where the company is making and losing money	Profitability by: ■ Product ■ Territory ■ Customer ■ Segment ■ Trade channel ■ Order size
3. Efficiency control	Line and staff management Marketing controller	To evaluate and improve the spending efficiency and impact of marketing expenditures	Efficiency of: ■ Sales force ■ Advertising ■ Sales promotion ■ Distribution
4. Strategic control	Top management Marketing auditor	To examine whether the company is pursuing its best opportunities with respect to markets, products, and channels	■ Marketing-effectiveness rating instrument ■ Marketing audit ■ Marketing excellence review ■ Company ethical and social responsibility review

(see Table 22.8 for some samples).[75] Four tools for the purpose are sales analysis, market share analysis, marketing expense-to-sales analysis, and financial analysis. The chapter appendix outlines them in detail.

Profitability Control

Companies should measure the profitability of their products, territories, customer groups, segments, trade channels, and order sizes to help determine whether to expand, reduce, or eliminate any products or marketing activities. The chapter appendix shows how to conduct and interpret a marketing profitability analysis.

Efficiency Control

Suppose a profitability analysis reveals that the company is earning poor profits on certain products or in certain territories or markets. Are there more efficient ways to manage the sales force, advertising, sales promotion, and distribution?

Some companies have established a *marketing controller* position to work out of the controller's office but specialize in improving marketing efficiency. General Foods, DuPont, and Johnson & Johnson perform a sophisticated financial analysis of marketing expenditures and results. Their marketing controllers examine adherence to profit plans, help prepare brand managers' budgets, measure the efficiency of promotions, analyze media production costs, evaluate customer and geographic profitability, and educate marketing staff on the financial implications of marketing decisions.[76]

Strategic Control

Each company should periodically reassess its strategic approach to the marketplace with a good marketing audit. Companies can also perform marketing excellence reviews and ethical/social responsibility reviews.

THE MARKETING AUDIT The average North American corporation loses half its customers in five years, half its employees in four years, and half its investors in less than one year. Clearly, this points to some weaknesses. Companies that discover weaknesses should undertake a thorough study known as a marketing audit.[77]

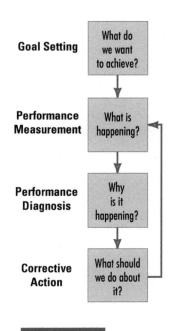

FIGURE 22.4

The Control Process

TABLE 22.8	MARKETING METRICS		

Sales Metrics
- Sales growth
- Market share
- Sales from new products

Customer-Readiness-to-Buy Metrics
- Awareness
- Preference
- Purchase intention
- Trial rate
- Repurchase rate

Customer Metrics
- Customer complaints
- Customer satisfaction
- Ratio of promoters to detractors
- Customer-acquisition costs
- New-customer gains
- Customer losses
- Customer churn
- Retention rate
- Customer lifetime value
- Customer equity
- Customer profitability
- Return on customer

Distribution Metrics
- Number of outlets
- Share in shops' handling
- Weighted distribution
- Distribution gains
- Average stocks volume (value)
- Stocks cover in days
- Out-of-stock frequency
- Share of shelf
- Average sales per point of sale

Communication Metrics
- Spontaneous (unaided) brand awareness
- Top-of-mind brand awareness
- Prompted (aided) brand awareness
- Spontaneous (unaided) advertising awareness
- Prompted (aided) advertising awareness
- Effective reach
- Effective frequency
- Gross rating points (GRP)
- Response rate

A **marketing audit** is a comprehensive, systematic, independent, and periodic examination of a company's or business unit's marketing environment, objectives, strategies, and activities, with a view to determining problem areas and opportunities and recommending a plan of action to improve the company's marketing performance.

Let's examine the marketing audit's four characteristics:

1. *Comprehensive*—The marketing audit covers all the major marketing activities of a business, not just a few trouble spots as in a functional audit. Although functional audits are useful, they sometimes mislead management. Excessive sales force turnover, for example, could be a symptom not of poor sales force training or compensation but of weak company products and promotion. A comprehensive marketing audit usually is more effective in locating the real source of problems.

2. *Systematic*—The marketing audit is an orderly examination of the organization's macro- and micromarketing environments, marketing objectives and strategies, marketing systems, and specific activities. It identifies the most-needed improvements and incorporates them into a corrective-action plan with short- and long-run steps.

3. *Independent*—Self-audits, in which managers rate their own operations, lack objectivity and independence.[78] The 3M Company has made good use of a corporate auditing office, which provides marketing audit services to divisions on request.[79] Usually, however, outside consultants bring the necessary objectivity, broad experience in a number of industries, familiarity with the industry being audited, and undivided time and attention.

4. *Periodic*—Firms typically initiate marketing audits only after failing to review their marketing operations during good times, with resulting problems. A periodic marketing audit can benefit companies in good health as well as those in trouble.

A marketing audit starts with agreement between the company officer(s) and the marketing auditor(s) on the audit's objectives and time frame, and a detailed plan of who is to be asked what questions. The cardinal rule for marketing auditors is Don't rely solely on company managers for data and opinions. Ask customers, dealers, and other outside groups. Many companies don't really know how their customers and dealers see them, nor do they fully understand customer needs.

The marketing audit examines six major components of the company's marketing situation. Table 22.9 lists the major questions.

THE MARKETING EXCELLENCE REVIEW   The three columns in Table 22.10 distinguish among poor, good, and excellent business and marketing practices. The profile that management creates from indicating where it thinks the business stands on each line can highlight where changes could help the firm become a truly outstanding player in the marketplace.

TABLE 22.9 | COMPONENTS OF A MARKETING AUDIT

Part I. Marketing Environment Audit

Macroenvironment

A. Demographic	What major demographic developments and trends pose opportunities or threats to this company? What actions has the company taken in response to these developments and trends?
B. Economic	What major developments in income, prices, savings, and credit will affect the company? What actions has the company been taking in response to these developments and trends?
C. Environmental	What is the outlook for the cost and availability of natural resources and energy needed by the company? What concerns have been expressed about the company's role in pollution and conservation, and what steps has the company taken in response to these concerns?
D. Technological	What major changes are occurring in product and process technology? What is the company's position in these technologies? What major generic substitutes might replace this product?
E. Political	What changes in laws and regulations might affect marketing strategy and tactics? What is happening in the areas of pollution control, equal employment opportunity, product safety, advertising, price control, and so forth that affects marketing strategy?
F. Cultural	What is the public's attitude toward business and toward the company's products? What changes in customer lifestyles and values might affect the company?

Task Environment

A. Markets	What is happening to market size, growth, geographical distribution, and profits? What are the major market segments?
B. Customers	What are the customers' needs and buying processes? How do customers and prospects rate the company and its competitors on reputation, product quality, service, sales force, and price? How do different customer segments make their buying decisions?
C. Competitors	Who are the major competitors? What are their objectives, strategies, strengths, weaknesses, sizes, and market shares? What trends will affect future competition and substitutes for the company's products?
D. Distribution and Dealers	What are the main trade channels for bringing products to customers? What are the efficiency levels and growth potentials of the different trade channels?
E. Suppliers	What is the outlook for the availability of key resources used in production? What trends are occurring among suppliers?
F. Facilitators and Marketing Firms	What is the cost and availability outlook for transportation services, warehousing facilities, and financial resources? How effective are the company's advertising agencies and marketing research firms?
G. Publics	Which publics represent particular opportunities or problems for the company? What steps has the company taken to deal effectively with each public?

TABLE 22.9	COMPONENTS OF A MARKETING AUDIT *(continued)*

Part II. Marketing Strategy Audit

A. Business Mission	Is the business mission clearly stated in market-oriented terms? Is it feasible?
B. Marketing Objectives and Goals	Are the company and marketing objectives and goals stated clearly enough to guide marketing planning and performance measurement? Are the marketing objectives appropriate, given the company's competitive position, resources, and opportunities?
C. Strategy	Has management articulated a clear marketing strategy for achieving its marketing objectives? Is the strategy convincing? Is the strategy appropriate to the stage of the product life cycle, competitors' strategies, and the state of the economy? Is the company using the best basis for market segmentation? Does it have clear criteria for rating the segments and choosing the best ones? Has it developed accurate profiles of each target segment? Has the company developed an effective positioning and marketing mix for each target segment? Are marketing resources allocated optimally to the major elements of the marketing mix? Are enough resources or too many resources budgeted to accomplish the marketing objectives?

Part III. Marketing Organization Audit

A. Formal Structure	Does the marketing vice-president or CMO have adequate authority and responsibility for company activities that affect customers' satisfaction? Are the marketing activities optimally structured along functional, product, segment, end user, and geographical lines?
B. Functional Efficiency	Are there good communication and working relations between marketing and sales? Is the product management system working effectively? Are product managers able to plan profits or only sales volume? Are there any groups in marketing that need more training, motivation, supervision, or evaluation?
C. Interface Efficiency	Are there any problems between marketing and manufacturing, R&D, purchasing, finance, accounting, and/or legal that need attention?

Part IV. Marketing Systems Audit

A. Marketing Information System	Is the marketing information system producing accurate, sufficient, and timely information about marketplace developments with respect to customers, prospects, distributors, dealers, competitors, suppliers, and various publics? Are company decision makers asking for enough marketing research, and are they using the results? Is the company employing the best methods for market measurement and sales forecasting?
B. Marketing Planning System	Is the marketing planning system well-conceived and effectively used? Do marketers have decision support systems available? Does the planning system result in acceptable sales targets and quotas?
C. Marketing Control System	Are the control procedures adequate to ensure that the annual-plan objectives are being achieved? Does management periodically analyze the profitability of products, markets, territories, and channels of distribution? Are marketing costs and productivity periodically examined?
D. New-Product Development System	Is the company well-organized to gather, generate, and screen new-product ideas? Does the company do adequate concept research and business analysis before investing in new ideas? Does the company carry out adequate product and market testing before launching new products?

Part V. Marketing Productivity Audit

A. Profitability Analysis	What is the profitability of the company's different products, markets, territories, and channels of distribution? Should the company enter, expand, contract, or withdraw from any business segments?
B. Cost-Effectiveness Analysis	Do any marketing activities seem to have excessive costs? Can cost-reducing steps be taken?

TABLE 22.9	COMPONENTS OF A MARKETING AUDIT (continued)

Part VI. Marketing Function Audits

A. Products	What are the company's product line objectives? Are they sound? Is the current product line meeting the objectives? Should the product line be stretched or contracted upward, downward, or both ways? Which products should be phased out? Which products should be added? What are the buyers' knowledge and attitudes toward the company's and competitors' product quality, features, styling, brand names, and so on? What areas of product and brand strategy need improvement?
B. Price	What are the company's pricing objectives, policies, strategies, and procedures? To what extent are prices set on cost, demand, and competitive criteria? Do the customers see the company's prices as being in line with the value of its offer? What does management know about the price elasticity of demand, experience-curve effects, and competitors' prices and pricing policies? To what extent are price policies compatible with the needs of distributors, dealers, suppliers, and government regulation?
C. Distribution	What are the company's distribution objectives and strategies? Is there adequate market coverage and service? How effective are distributors, dealers, manufacturers' representatives, brokers, agents, and others? Should the company consider changing its distribution channels?
D. Marketing Communications	What are the organization's advertising objectives? Are they sound? Is the right amount being spent on advertising? Are the ad themes and copy effective? What do customers and the public think about the advertising? Are the advertising media well-chosen? Is the internal advertising staff adequate? Is the sales promotion budget adequate? Is there effective and sufficient use of sales promotion tools such as samples, coupons, displays, and sales contests? Is the public relations staff competent and creative? Is the company making enough use of direct, online, and database marketing?
E. Sales Force	What are the sales force's objectives? Is the sales force large enough to accomplish the company's objectives? Is the sales force organized along the proper principles of specialization (territory, market, product)? Are there enough (or too many) sales managers to guide the field sales representatives? Do the sales compensation level and structure provide adequate incentive and reward? Does the sales force show high morale, ability, and effort? Are the procedures adequate for setting quotas and evaluating performance? How does the company's sales force compare with competitors' sales forces?

TABLE 22.10	THE MARKETING EXCELLENCE REVIEW: BEST PRACTICES

Poor	Good	Excellent
Product driven	Market driven	Market driving
Mass-market oriented	Segment oriented	Niche oriented and customer oriented
Product offer	Augmented product offer	Customer solutions offer
Average product quality	Better than average	Legendary
Average service quality	Better than average	Legendary
End-product oriented	Core-product oriented	Core-competency oriented
Function oriented	Process oriented	Outcome oriented
Reacting to competitors	Benchmarking competitors	Leapfrogging competitors
Supplier exploitation	Supplier preference	Supplier partnership
Dealer exploitation	Dealer support	Dealer partnership
Price driven	Quality driven	Value driven
Average speed	Better than average	Legendary
Hierarchy	Network	Teamwork
Vertically integrated	Flattened organization	Strategic alliances
Shareholder driven	Stakeholder driven	Societally driven

THE FUTURE OF MARKETING

Top management recognizes that marketing requires more accountability than in the past. "Marketing Memo: Major Marketing Weaknesses" summarizes companies' major deficiencies in marketing, and how to find and correct them.

To succeed in the future, marketing must be more holistic and less departmental. Marketers must achieve larger influence in the company, continuously create new ideas, and strive for customer insight by treating customers differently but appropriately. They must build their brands more through performance than promotion. They must go electronic and win through building superior information and communication systems.

The coming years will see several changes:

- The demise of the marketing department and the rise of holistic marketing
- The demise of free-spending marketing and the rise of ROI marketing
- The demise of marketing intuition and the rise of marketing science
- The demise of manual marketing and the rise of both automated *and* creative marketing
- The demise of mass marketing and the rise of precision marketing

To accomplish these changes and become truly holistic, marketers need a new set of skills and competencies in

- Customer relationship management (CRM)
- Partner relationship management (PRM)
- Database marketing and data mining
- Contact centre management and telemarketing
- Public relations marketing (including event and sponsorship marketing)
- Brand building and brand-asset management
- Experiential marketing
- Integrated marketing communications
- Profitability analysis by segment, customer, and channel

The benefits of successful twenty-first-century marketing are many, but they will come only with hard work, insight, and inspiration. New rules and practices are emerging, and it is an exciting time. The words of nineteenth-century U.S. author Ralph Waldo Emerson may never have been more true: "This time like all times is a good one, if we but know what to do with it."

MARKETING **MEMO** | MAJOR MARKETING WEAKNESSES

A number of "deadly sins" signal that the marketing program is in trouble. Here are 10 deadly sins, the signs, and some solutions.

Deadly Sin: The company is not sufficiently market focused and customer driven.

Signs: There is evidence of poor identification of market segments, poor prioritization of market segments, no market segment managers, employees who think it is the job of marketing and sales to serve customers, no training program to create a customer culture, and no incentives to treat the customer especially well.

Solutions: Use more advanced segmentation techniques, prioritize segments, specialize the sales force, develop a clear hierarchy of company values, foster more "customer consciousness" in employees and company agents, and make it easy for customers to reach the company and respond quickly to any communication.

Deadly Sin: The company does not fully understand its target customers.

Signs: The latest study of customers is three years old; customers are not buying your product like they once did; competitors' products are selling better; and there is a high level of customer returns and complaints.

Solutions: Do more sophisticated consumer research, use more analytical techniques, establish customer and dealer panels, use customer relationship software, and do data mining.

Deadly Sin: The company needs to better define and monitor its competitors.

Signs: The company focuses on near competitors, misses distant competitors and disruptive technologies, and has no system for gathering and distributing competitive intelligence.

Solutions: Establish an office for competitive intelligence, hire competitors' people, watch for technology that might affect the company, and prepare offerings like those of competitors.

Deadly Sin: The company does not properly manage relationships with stakeholders.

Signs: Employees, dealers, and investors are not happy; and good suppliers do not come.

Solutions: Move from zero-sum thinking to positive-sum thinking; and do a better job of managing employees, supplier relations, distributors, dealers, and investors.

Deadly Sin: The company is not good at finding new opportunities.

Signs: The company has not identified any exciting new opportunities for years, and the new ideas the company has launched have largely failed.

Solutions: Set up a system for stimulating the flow of new ideas.

Deadly Sin: The company's marketing planning process is deficient.

Signs: The marketing plan format does not have the right components, there is no way to estimate the financial implications of different strategies, and there is no contingency planning.

Solutions: Establish a standard format including situational analysis, SWOT, major issues, objectives, strategy, tactics, budgets, and controls; ask marketers what changes they would make if they were given 20 percent more or less budget; and run an annual marketing awards program with prizes for best plans and performance.

Deadly Sin: Product and service policies need tightening.

Signs: There are too many products and many are losing money; the company is giving away too many services; and the company is poor at cross-selling products and services.

Solutions: Establish a system to track weak products and fix or drop them; offer and price services at different levels; and improve processes for cross-selling and up-selling.

Deadly Sin: The company's brand-building and communications skills are weak.

Signs: The target market does not know much about the company; the brand is not seen as distinctive; the company allocates its budget to the same marketing tools in about the same proportion each year; and there is little evaluation of the ROI impact of promotions.

Solutions: Improve brand-building strategies and measurement of results; shift money into effective marketing instruments; and require marketers to estimate the ROI impact in advance of funding requests.

Deadly Sin: The company is not organized for effective and efficient marketing.

Signs: Staff lacks 21st-century marketing skills, and there are bad vibes between marketing/sales and other departments.

Solutions: Appoint a strong leader and build new skills in the marketing department, and improve relationships between marketing and other departments.

Deadly Sin: The company has not made maximum use of technology.

Signs: There is evidence of minimal use of the Internet, an outdated sales automation system, no market automation, no decision-support models, and no marketing dashboards.

Solutions: Use the Internet more, improve the sales automation system, apply market automation to routine decisions, and develop formal marketing decision models and marketing dashboards.

Source: Philip Kotler, *Ten Deadly Marketing Sins: Signs and Solutions* (Hoboken, NJ: Wiley, 2004). © Philip Kotler. Reprinted with permission of John Wiley & Sons, Inc.

SUMMARY

1. The modern marketing department has evolved through the years from a simple sales department to an organizational structure where marketers work mainly on cross-disciplinary teams.

2. Some companies are organized by functional specialization; others focus on geography and regionalization, product and brand management, or market-segment management. Some companies establish a matrix organization consisting of both product and market managers.

3. Effective modern marketing organizations are marked by customer focus within and strong co-operation among marketing, R&D, engineering, purchasing, manufacturing, operations, finance, accounting, and credit.

4. Companies must practise social responsibility through their legal, ethical, and social words and actions. Cause marketing can be a means for companies to productively link social responsibility to consumer marketing programs. Social marketing is done by a nonprofit or government organization to directly address a social problem or cause.

5. A brilliant strategic marketing plan counts for little unless implemented properly. This includes recognizing and diagnosing a problem, assessing where the problem exists, and evaluating results.

6. The marketing department must monitor and control marketing activities continuously. Marketing plan control ensures that the company achieves the sales, profits, and other goals in its annual plan. The main tools are sales analysis, market share analysis, marketing expense-to-sales analysis, and financial analysis of the marketing plan. Profitability control both measures and controls the profitability of products, territories, customer groups, trade channels, and order sizes. Efficiency control finds ways to increase the efficiency of the sales force, advertising, sales promotion, and distribution. Strategic control periodically reassesses the company's strategic approach to the marketplace using marketing effectiveness and marketing excellence reviews, as well as marketing audits.

7. Achieving marketing excellence in the future will require a new set of skills and competencies.

APPLICATIONS

Marketing Debate: Is Marketing Management an Art or a Science?

Some observers maintain that good marketing is mostly an art and does not lend itself to rigorous analysis and deliberation. Others contend it is a highly disciplined enterprise that shares much with other business disciplines.

Take a position: Marketing management is largely an artistic exercise and therefore highly subjective *versus*

Marketing management is largely a scientific exercise with well-established guidelines and criteria.

Marketing Discussion: Cause Marketing

How does cause or corporate societal marketing affect your personal consumer behaviour? Do you ever buy or not buy any products or services from a company because of its environmental policies or programs? Why or why not?

| MARKETING **EXCELLENCE** | AIR MILES FOR SOCIAL CHANGE—CAN BUSINESS CHANGE THE WORLD? |

Many people blame business and marketing for some of the ills that currently plague the world. Others believe that business can be an agent of positive change. Andreas Souvaliotis, now President of AIR MILES for Social Change, is such a man. He began an innovative rewards program and powerful partnerships with retailers that are moving us toward a more sustainable future.

He originally founded Green Rewards, the world's first environmental consumer loyalty program, a program he saw

as an anti–AIR MILES program. He wanted a program under which people would be rewarded for choosing green options versus more harmful products or services. He wasn't far along in his journey before he realized that it was better to partner with AIR MILES than compete against the program. After all, AIR MILES is the largest loyalty program in Canada and the world. Over two-thirds of Canadian households have an AIR MILES account.

Many retailers have turned to loyalty programs to help retain customers. An astonishing percentage of Canadians—93.6 percent—belong to at least one loyalty program. Loyalty programs also allow retailers to build a large database that can be used to better understand customers' profiles, needs, and shopping behaviours.

The reach and influence of AIR MILES is exceptional. Many retailers have partnered with AIR MILES because they receive the benefits of having a loyalty program without having to bear the costs of setting up and managing a program on their own. By joining with AIR MILES, Andreas knew he had the opportunity to change the behaviour of millions of Canadians. AIR MILES partners with numerous retailers and other service providers but is very careful to partner with only one retailer in any category. In other words, these retailers get category exclusivity, and their competitors can't duplicate this advantage, something very important in a sector where most innovations are visible and can be copied by competitors.

Canadians earn points when they frequent certain retailers or purchase certain products or services. Thus, Andreas knew that he had the opportunity to influence consumer behaviour right at the store level. Canadians are mad about collecting points, which have trophy value that is treasured far more than a coupon or rebate of equal value.

At first, Andreas worked to influence behaviour when consumers redeemed their points. He brought the idea of offering green rewards to AIR MILES. Andreas used the AIR MILES My Planet program, and his objective was to inspire and enable AIR MILES collectors to make more environmentally sustainable choices. Over 140 ecofriendly product options were offered as rewards under the My Planet program. Consumers could also trade in their points for more environmentally sensitive options like passes for Toronto Transit.

Then Andreas had another insight. Why not use AIR MILES for Social Change to influence in-store behaviour in partnership with retailers? With research showing that 53 percent of Canadians said being able to use AIR MILES would be an incentive for them to make greener product choices, retailers were soon on board. Participants included grocery stores (Metro and Safeway), hardware/home centres (RONA and TIM-BR MART), pharmacies (Jean Coutu and Lawtons Drugs), government (Edmonton Transit), renewable energy providers (Bullfrog Power), and financial institu-

tions (AMEX). For example, AIR MILES for Social Change partnered with the LCBO. By allowing consumers to earn more points on beverages that had a lower carbon footprint because they were packaged in lighter containers or shipped only a short distance, consumers were encouraged to favour these products.

Andreas wondered, since these retail partnerships worked so powerfully, what else could be done. Maybe other social issues could be addressed in the same fashion. His next experiment—the first of its kind in the world—was a partnership with the Ontario Power Authority. A small AIR MILES incentive was attached to the authority's annual Power Pledge conservation campaign. The campaign was a huge success, and seven times more Ontarians participated in the program compared with the previous year. Obesity is another huge problem in Canada and around the world. Andreas recently set his sights on making an impact here as well. He partnered with the Heart and Stroke Foundation and grocery retailers so that consumers can earn 50 AIR MILES points for making healthy choices like purchasing fruit and vegetables or low-fat products.

The program has attracted attention around the world. One day, Andreas's phone rang. It was Prince Charles. The Prince invited Andreas to the United Kingdom to explore opportunities for promoting a similar program there. Not every business person gets a chance to meet with a Prince—only those who are working to make a positive change in the world.

QUESTIONS

1. What are the pros and cons of partnering with AIR MILES for Social Change versus establishing an independent, retailer-owned loyalty program?

2. What unique vales does the sub-brand AIR MILES for Social Change bring to retailers, and how has the program helped its retail partners form stronger ties with their customers?

3. Would a similar partnership between retailers and AIR MILES for Social Change elsewhere in the world work as well as it has in Canada? Why or why not?

Sources: Interview with Andreas Souvaliotis, May 5, 2011; "Air Miles Offering More Green Rewards," *Marketing News*, April 17, 2009; "Major Retailers Join Forces to Reward Canadians for Green Purchases," Bullfrog Power Press Release, September 22, 2009.

APPENDIX

TOOLS FOR MARKETING CONTROL

In this appendix, we provided detailed guidelines and insights about how to best conduct several marketing control procedures.

Annual-Plan Control

Four sets of analyses can be useful for annual-plan control.

SALES ANALYSIS **Sales analysis** measures and evaluates actual sales in relationship to goals. Two specific tools make it work.

Sales-variance analysis measures the relative contribution of different factors to a gap in sales performance. Suppose the annual plan called for selling 4000 widgets in the first quarter at $1 per widget, for total revenue of $4000. At quarter's end, only 3000 widgets were sold at $0.80 per widget, for total revenue of $2400. How much of the sales performance gap is due to the price decline, and how much to the volume decline? This calculation answers the question:

Variance due to price decline: ($1.00−$0.80) × (3000) = $ 600   37.5%

Variance due to volume decline: ($1.00) × (4000−3000) = $1000   62.5%

$1600   100.0%

Almost two-thirds of the variance is due to failure to achieve the volume target. The company should look closely at why it failed to achieve expected sales volume.

Microsales analysis looks at specific products, territories, and so forth that failed to produce expected sales. Suppose the company sells in three territories, and expected sales were 1500 units, 500 units, and 2000 units, respectively. Actual volumes were 1400 units, 525 units, and 1075 units, respectively. Thus territory 1 showed a 7 percent shortfall in terms of expected sales; territory 2, a 5 percent improvement over expectations; and territory 3, a 46 percent shortfall! Territory 3 is causing most of the trouble. Maybe the sales rep in territory 3 is underperforming, a major competitor has entered this territory, or business is in a recession there.

MARKET SHARE ANALYSIS Company sales don't reveal how well the company is performing relative to competitors. For this, management needs to track its market share in one of three ways.

Overall market share expresses the company's sales as a percentage of total market sales. **Served market share** is sales as a percentage of the total sales to the served market. The **served market** is all the buyers able and willing to buy the product, and served market share is always larger than overall market share. A company could capture 100 percent of its served market and yet have a relatively small share of the total market. **Relative market share** is market share in relationship to the largest competitor. A relative market share of exactly 100 percent means the company is tied for the lead; over 100 percent indicates a market leader. A rise in relative market share means a company is gaining on its leading competitor.

Conclusions from market share analysis, however, are subject to qualifications:

- *The assumption that outside forces affect all companies in the same way is often not true.* The U.S. Surgeon General's report on the harmful consequences of smoking depressed total cigarette sales, but not equally for all companies.

- *The assumption that a company's performance should be judged against the average performance of all companies is not always valid.* A company's performance is best judged against that of its closest competitors.

- *If a new firm enters the industry, every existing firm's market share might fall.* A decline in market share might not mean the company is performing any worse than other companies. Share loss depends on the degree to which the new firm hits the company's specific markets.

- *Sometimes a market share decline is deliberately engineered to improve profits.* For example, management might drop unprofitable customers or products.

- *Market share can fluctuate for many minor reasons.* For example, it can be affected by whether a large sale occurs on the last day of the month or at the beginning of the next month. Not all shifts in market share have marketing significance.[80]

A useful way to analyze market share movements is in terms of four components:

$$
\begin{matrix}
\textit{Overall} \\
\textit{market} \\
\textit{share}
\end{matrix}
=
\begin{matrix}
\textit{Customer} \\
\textit{penetration}
\end{matrix}
\times
\begin{matrix}
\textit{Customer} \\
\textit{loyalty}
\end{matrix}
\times
\begin{matrix}
\textit{Customer} \\
\textit{selectivity}
\end{matrix}
\times
\begin{matrix}
\textit{Price} \\
\textit{selectivity}
\end{matrix}
$$

where:

Customer penetration	Percentage of all customers who buy from the company
Customer loyalty	Purchases from the company by its customers as a percentage of their total purchases from all suppliers of the same products
Customer selectivity	Size of the average customer purchase from the company as a percentage of the size of the average customer purchase from an average company
Price selectivity	Average price charged by the company as a percentage of the average price charged by all companies

Now suppose the company's dollar market share falls during the period. The overall market share equation provides four possible explanations: The company lost some customers (lower customer penetration); existing customers are buying less from the company (lower customer loyalty); purchases by the company's remaining customers are smaller in size (lower customer selectivity); or the company's price has slipped relative to the competition's (lower price selectivity).

MARKETING EXPENSE-TO-SALES ANALYSIS Annual-plan control requires making sure the company isn't overspending to achieve sales goals. The key ratio to watch is *marketing expense-to-sales*. In one company, this ratio was 30 percent and consisted of five component expense-to-sales ratios: sales force-to-sales (15 percent), advertising-to-sales (5 percent), sales promotion-to-sales (6 percent), marketing research-to-sales (1 percent), and sales administration-to-sales (3 percent).

Fluctuations outside the normal range are cause for concern. Management needs to monitor period-to-period fluctuations in each ratio on a *control chart* (see Figure 22.5). This chart shows that the advertising expense-to-sales ratio normally fluctuates between 8 percent and 12 percent, say 99 of 100 times. In the 15th period, however, the ratio exceeded the upper control limit. Either (1) the company still has good expense control and this situation represents a rare chance event, or (2) the company has lost control over this expense and should find the cause. If there is no investigation, the risk is that some real change might have occurred, and the company will fall behind.

Managers should make successive observations even within the upper and lower control limits. Note in Figure 22.5 that the level of the expense-to-sales ratio rose steadily from the 8th period onward. The probability of encountering six successive increases in what should be independent events is only 1 in 64.[81] This unusual pattern should have led to an investigation sometime before the 15th observation.

FINANCIAL ANALYSIS Marketers should analyze the expense-to-sales ratios in an overall financial framework to determine how and where the company is making its money. They are increasingly using financial analysis to find profitable strategies beyond building sales.

FIGURE 22.5

The Control-Chart Model

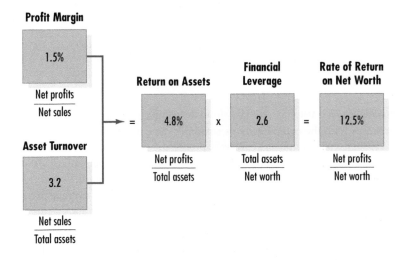

Management uses financial analysis to identify factors that affect the company's *rate of return on net worth*.[82] The main factors are shown in Figure 22.6, along with illustrative numbers for a large chain store retailer. The retailer is earning a 12.5 percent return on net worth. The return on net worth is the product of two ratios, the company's *return on assets* and its *financial leverage*. To improve its return on net worth, the company must increase its ratio of net profits to assets, or increase the ratio of assets to net worth. The company should analyze the composition of its assets (cash, accounts receivable, inventory, and plant and equipment) and see whether it can improve its asset management.

The return on assets is the product of two ratios, the *profit margin* and the *asset turnover*. The profit margin in Figure 22.6 seems low, whereas the asset turnover is more normal for retailing. The marketing executive can seek to improve performance in two ways: (1) increase the profit margin by increasing sales or cutting costs, and (2) increase the asset turnover by increasing sales or reducing assets (inventory, receivables) held against a given level of sales.[83]

Profitability Control

MARKETING PROFITABILITY ANALYSIS We will illustrate the steps in marketing profitability analysis with the following example. The marketing vice-president of a lawn mower company wants to determine the profitability of selling through three types of retail channels: hardware stores, garden supply shops, and department stores. The company's profit-and-loss statement is shown in Table 22.11.

Step 1: Identifying Functional Expenses Assume the expenses listed in Table 22.11 are incurred to sell the product, advertise it, pack and deliver it, and bill and collect for it. The first task is to measure how much of each expense was incurred in each activity.

Suppose most of the salary expense went to sales representatives and the rest to an advertising manager, packing and delivery help, and an office accountant. Let the breakdown of the $9300 be $5100, $1200, $1400, and $1600, respectively. Table 22.12 shows the allocation of the salary expense to these four activities.

TABLE 22.11	A SIMPLIFIED PROFIT-AND-LOSS STATEMENT	
Sales		$60 000
Cost of goods sold		39 000
Gross margin		$21 000
Expenses		
Salaries	$9300	
Rent	3000	
Supplies	3500	
		15 800
Net profit		$ 5200

TABLE 22.12 | MAPPING NATURAL EXPENSES INTO FUNCTIONAL EXPENSES

Natural Accounts	Total	Selling	Advertising	Packing and Delivery	Billing and Collecting
Salaries	$ 9300	$5100	$1200	$1400	$1600
Rent	3000	—	400	2000	600
Supplies	3500	400	1500	1400	200
	$15 800	$5500	$3100	$4800	$2400

Table 22.12 also shows the rent account of $3000 allocated to the four activities. Because the sales reps work away from the office, none of the building's rent expense is assigned to selling. Most of the expenses for floor space and rented equipment are for packing and delivery. The supplies account covers promotional materials, packing materials, fuel purchases for delivery, and home office stationery. The $3500 in this account is reassigned to functional uses of the supplies.

Step 2: Assigning Functional Expenses to Marketing Entities The next task is to measure how much functional expense was associated with selling through each type of channel. Consider the selling effort, indicated by the number of sales in each channel. This number is in the selling column of Table 22.13. Altogether, 275 sales calls were made during the period. Because the total selling expense amounted to $5500 (see Table 22.13), the selling expense averaged $20 per call.

We can allocate advertising expense according to the number of ads addressed to different channels. Because there were 100 ads altogether, the average ad cost $31.

The packing and delivery expense is allocated according to the number of orders placed by each type of channel. This same basis was used for allocating billing and collection expense.

Step 3: Preparing a Profit-and-Loss Statement for Each Marketing Entity We can now prepare a profit-and-loss statement for each type of channel (see Table 22.14). Because hardware stores accounted for half of total sales ($30 000 out of $60 000), charge this channel with half the cost of goods sold ($19 500 out of $39 000). This leaves a gross margin from hardware stores of $10 500. From this we deduct the proportions of functional expenses that hardware stores consumed.

TABLE 22.13 | BASES FOR ALLOCATING FUNCTIONAL EXPENSES TO CHANNELS

Channel Type	Selling	Advertising	Packing and Delivery	Billing and Collecting
Hardware	200	50	50	50
Garden supply	65	20	21	21
Department stores	10	30	9	9
	275	**100**	**80**	**80**
Functional expense	$5500	$3100	$4800	$2400
divided by				
No. of Units	275	100	80	80
Equals	**$ 20**	**$ 31**	**$ 60**	**$ 30**

TABLE 22.14	PROFIT-AND-LOSS STATEMENTS FOR CHANNELS			
	Hardware	Garden Supply	Dept. Stores	Whole Company
Sales	$30 000	$10 000	$20 000	$60 000
Cost of goods sold	19 500	6500	13 000	39 000
Gross margin	$10 500	$ 3500	$ 7000	$21 000
Expenses				
Selling ($20 per call)	$ 4000	$ 1300	$ 200	$ 5500
Advertising ($31 per advertisement)	1550	620	930	3100
Packing and delivery ($60 per order)	3000	1260	540	4800
Billing ($30 per order)	1500	630	270	2400
Total expenses	$10 050	$ 3810	$ 1940	$15 800
Net profit or loss	$ 450	$ (310)	$ 5060	$ 5200

According to Table 22.14, hardware stores received 200 of 275 total sales calls. At an imputed value of $20 a call, hardware stores must bear a $4000 selling expense. Table 22.14 also shows that hardware stores were the target of 50 ads. At $31 an ad, the hardware stores are charged with $1550 of advertising. The same reasoning applies in computing the share of the other functional expenses. The result is that hardware stores gave rise to $10 050 of the total expenses. Subtracting this from gross margin, we find the profit of selling through hardware stores is only $450.

Repeat this analysis for the other channels. The company is losing money in selling through garden supply shops and makes virtually all its profits through department stores. Notice that gross sales is not a reliable indicator of the net profits for each channel.

DETERMINING CORRECTIVE ACTION It would be naïve to conclude that the company should drop garden supply and hardware stores to concentrate on department stores. We need to answer the following questions first:

■   To what extent do buyers buy on the basis of type of retail outlet versus brand?

■   What trends affect the relative importance of these three channels?

■   How good are the company's marketing strategies for the three channels?

Using the answers, marketing management can evaluate five alternatives:

1. Establish a special charge for handling smaller orders.
2. Give more promotional aid to garden supply shops and hardware stores.
3. Reduce sales calls and advertising to garden supply shops and hardware stores.
4. Ignore the weakest retail units in each channel.
5. Do nothing.

Marketing profitability analysis indicates the relative profitability of different channels, products, territories, or other marketing entities. It does not prove that the best course of action is to drop unprofitable marketing entities and does not capture the likely profit improvement of doing so.

DIRECT VERSUS FULL COSTING Like all information tools, marketing profitability analysis can lead or mislead, depending on how well marketers understand its methods and limitations. The lawn mower company chose bases somewhat arbitrarily for allocating the functional expenses to its marketing entities. It used "number of sales calls" to allocate selling expenses, generating less record keeping and computation, when in principle "number of sales working hours" is a more accurate indicator of cost.

A far more serious decision is whether to allocate full costs or only direct and traceable costs in evaluating a marketing entity's performance. The lawn mower company sidestepped this problem by assuming only simple costs that fit with marketing activities, but we cannot avoid the question in real-world analyses of profitability. We distinguish three types of costs:

1. *Direct costs*—We can assign direct costs directly to the proper marketing entities. Sales commissions are a direct cost in a profitability analysis of sales territories, sales representatives, or customers. Advertising expenditures are a direct cost in a profitability analysis of products to the extent that each advertisement promotes only one product. Other direct costs for specific purposes are sales force salaries and travelling expenses.

2. *Traceable common costs*—We can assign traceable common costs only indirectly, but on a plausible basis, to the marketing entities. In the example, we analyzed rent this way.

3. *Nontraceable common costs*—Common costs whose allocation to the marketing entities is highly arbitrary are nontraceable common costs. To allocate "corporate image" expenditures equally to all products would be arbitrary, because all products don't benefit equally. To allocate them proportionately to the sales of the various products would be arbitrary, because relative product sales reflect many factors besides corporate image making. Other examples are top management salaries, taxes, interest, and other overhead.

No one disputes the inclusion of direct costs in marketing cost analysis. There is some controversy about including traceable common costs, which lump together costs that would and would not change with the scale of marketing activity. If the lawn mower company drops garden supply shops, it would probably continue to pay the same rent. Its profits would not rise immediately by the amount of the present loss in selling to garden supply shops ($310).

The major controversy is about whether to allocate the nontraceable common costs to the marketing entities. Such allocation is called the *full-cost approach,* and its advocates argue that all costs must ultimately be imputed in order to determine true profitability. However, this argument confuses the use of accounting for financial reporting with its use for managerial decision making. Full costing has three major weaknesses:

1. The relative profitability of different marketing entities can shift radically when we replace one arbitrary way to allocate nontraceable common costs by another.

2. The arbitrariness demoralizes managers, who feel their performance is judged adversely.

3. The inclusion of nontraceable common costs could weaken efforts at real cost control.

Operating management is most effective in controlling direct costs and traceable common costs. Arbitrary assignments of nontraceable common costs can lead managers to spend their time fighting cost allocations instead of managing controllable costs well.

Companies show growing interest in using marketing profitability analysis, or its broader version, activity-based cost accounting (ABC), to quantify the true profitability of different activities.[84] Managers can then reduce the resources required to perform various activities, make the resources more productive, acquire them at lower cost, or raise prices on products that consume heavy amounts of support resources. The contribution of ABC is to refocus management's attention away from using only labour or material standard costs to allocate full cost, and toward capturing the actual costs of supporting individual products, customers, and other entities.

APPENDIX

SONIC MARKETING PLAN AND EXERCISES

THE MARKETING PLAN: AN INTRODUCTION

As a marketer, you'll need a good marketing plan to provide direction and focus for your brand, product, or company. With a detailed plan, any business will be better prepared to launch an innovative new product or increase sales to current customers. Nonprofit organizations also use marketing plans to guide their fund-raising and outreach efforts. Even government agencies put together marketing plans for initiatives such as building public awareness of proper nutrition and stimulating area tourism.

The Purpose and Content of a Marketing Plan

A marketing plan has a more limited scope than a business plan, which offers a broad overview of the entire organization's mission, objectives, strategy, and resource allocation. The marketing plan documents how the organization's strategic objectives will be achieved through specific marketing strategies and tactics, with the customer as the starting point. It is also linked to the plans of other organizational departments. Suppose a marketing plan calls for selling 200 000 units annually. The production department must gear up to make that many units, finance must arrange funding to cover the expenses, human resources must be ready to hire and train staff, and so on. Without the appropriate level of organizational support and resources, no marketing plan can succeed.

Although the exact length and layout varies from company to company, a marketing plan usually contains the sections described in Chapter 2. Smaller businesses may create shorter or less formal marketing plans, whereas corporations generally require highly structured marketing plans. To guide implementation effectively, every part of the plan must be described in considerable detail. Sometimes a company will post its marketing plan on an internal website so managers and employees in different locations can consult specific sections and collaborate on additions or changes.

The Role of Research

To develop innovative products, successful strategies, and action programs, marketers need up-to-date information about the environment, the competition, and the selected market segments. Often, analysis of internal data is the starting point for assessing the current marketing situation, supplemented by marketing intelligence and research investigating the overall market, the competition, key issues, threats, and opportunities. As the plan is put into effect, marketers use research to measure progress toward objectives and to identify areas for improvement if results fall short of projections.

Finally, marketing research helps marketers learn more about their customers' requirements, expectations, perceptions, satisfaction, and loyalty. This deeper understanding provides a foundation for building competitive advantage through well-informed segmenting, targeting, and positioning decisions. Thus, the marketing plan should outline what marketing research will be conducted and when, as well as how, the findings will be applied.

The Role of Relationships

Although the marketing plan shows how the company will establish and maintain profitable customer relationships, it also affects both internal and external relationships. First, it influences how marketing personnel work with each other and with other departments to deliver value and satisfy customers. Second, it affects how the company works with suppliers, distributors, and partners to achieve the plan's objectives. Third, it influences the company's dealings with other stakeholders, including government regulators, the media, and the community at large. All these relationships are important to the organization's success and must be considered when developing a marketing plan.

From Marketing Plan to Marketing Action

Most companies create yearly marketing plans, although some plans cover a longer period. Marketers start planning well in advance of the implementation date to allow time for marketing research, analysis, management review, and coordination between departments. Then, after each action program begins, marketers monitor ongoing results, investigate any deviation from the projected outcome, and take corrective steps as needed. Some marketers also prepare contingency plans for implementation if certain conditions emerge. Because of inevitable and sometimes unpredictable environmental changes, marketers must be ready to update and adapt marketing plans at any time.

For effective implementation and control, the marketing plan should define how progress toward objectives will be measured. Managers typically use budgets, schedules, and marketing metrics for monitoring and evaluating results. With budgets, they can compare planned expenditures with actual expenditures for a given period. Schedules allow management to see when tasks were supposed to be completed and when they were actually completed. Marketing metrics track the actual outcomes of marketing programs to see whether the company is moving forward toward its objectives.

SAMPLE MARKETING PLAN FOR SONIC

This section takes you inside the sample marketing plan for Sonic, a hypothetical start-up company. The company's first product is the Sonic 1000, a state-of-the-art, fully loaded multimedia smartphone. Sonic will be competing with Apple, BlackBerry, Motorola, Nokia, Samsung, and other well-established rivals in a crowded, fast-changing marketplace where smartphones have many communication and entertainment capabilities. The annotations explain more about what each section of the plan should contain.

1.0 Executive Summary

Sonic is preparing to launch a major new state-of-the-art multimedia smartphone, the Sonic 1000, in a mature market. We can effectively compete with many types of smartphones because our product offers a unique combination of advanced features and functionality at a very competitive value-added price. We are targeting specific segments in the consumer and business markets, taking advantage of the growing interest in a single powerful but affordable device with extensive communication, organization, and entertainment benefits.

The primary marketing objective is to achieve first-year U.S. market share of 1 percent with unit sales of 800 000. The primary financial objectives are to achieve first-year sales revenues of $200 million, keep first-year losses to less than $40 million, and break even early in the second year.

This section summarizes market opportunities, marketing strategy, and marketing and financial objectives for senior managers who will read and approve the marketing plan.

2.0 Situation Analysis

Sonic, founded 18 months ago by two well-known entrepreneurs with telecommunications experience, is about to enter the highly competitive smartphone market. Multifunction cell phones are increasingly popular for both personal and professional use, with more than 320 million smartphones sold worldwide in 2010. Competition is increasingly intense even as technology evolves, industry consolidation continues, and pricing pressures squeeze profitability. Palm, a PDA pioneer, is one of several key players having difficulty adapting to the smartphone challenge. To gain market share in this dynamic environment, Sonic must carefully target specific segments with valued features and plan for a next-generation product to keep brand momentum going.

The situation analysis describes the market, the company's capability to serve targeted segments, and the competition.

2.1 MARKET SUMMARY Sonic's market consists of consumers and business users who prefer to use a powerful but affordable single device for fully functional communication, information storage and exchange, organization, and entertainment on the go. Specific segments being targeted during the first year include professionals, corporations, students, entrepreneurs, and medical users. Exhibit A.1 shows how the Sonic 1000 addresses some of the most basic needs of targeted consumer and business segments in a cost-effective manner. The additional communication and entertainment benefits of the product just enhance its appeal to those segments.

Smartphone purchasers can choose between models based on several different operating systems. The biggest selling smartphone operating system is Symbian OS. Symbian's smaller rivals include Android, BlackBerry OS, iOS, and the Windows Phone OS. Several mobile operating systems including Android and iOS are based on Linux and Unix. Sonic licenses a Linux-based system because it is somewhat less vulnerable to attack by hackers and viruses. Storage capacity (hard drive or flash drive) is an expected feature, so Sonic is equipping its first product with an ultra-fast 64-gigabyte drive that can be supplemented by extra storage. Technology costs are decreasing even as capabilities are increasing, which makes value-priced models more appealing to consumers and to business users with older smartphones and who want to trade up to new, high-end multifunction units.

Market summary includes size, needs, growth, and trends. Describing the targeted segments in detail provides context for marketing strategies and programs discussed later in the plan.

EXHIBIT A.1	NEEDS AND CORRESPONDING FEATURES/BENEFITS OF SONIC SMARTPHONE	
Targeted Segment	**Customer Need**	**Corresponding Feature/Benefit**
Professionals (consumer market)	■ Stay in touch while on the go	■ Wireless email to conveniently send and receive messages from anywhere; cell phone capability for voice communication from anywhere
	■ Record information while on the go	■ Voice recognition for no-hands recording
Students (consumer market)	■ Perform many functions without carrying multiple gadgets	■ Compatible with numerous applications and peripherals for convenient, cost-effective functionality
	■ Express style and individuality	■ Case wardrobe of different colours and patterns allows users to make a fashion statement
Corporate users (business market)	■ Input and access critical data on the go	■ Compatible with widely available software
	■ Use for proprietary tasks	■ Customizable to fit diverse corporate task and networks
Entrepreneurs (business market)	■ Organize and access contacts, schedule details	■ No-hands, wireless access to calendar and address book to easily check appointments and connect with contacts
Medical users (business market)	■ Update, access, and exchange medical records	■ No-hands, wireless recording and exchange of information to reduce paperwork and increase productivity

2.2 STRENGTHS, WEAKNESSES, OPPORTUNITIES, AND THREATS ANALYSIS Sonic has several powerful strengths on which to build, but our major weakness is lack of brand awareness and image. The major opportunity is demand for multifunction communication, organization, and entertainment devices that deliver a number of valued benefits at a lower cost. We also face the threat of ever-higher competition and downward pricing pressure.

Strengths are internal capabilities that can help the company reach its objectives.

Strengths Sonic can build on three important strengths:

1. *Innovative product*—The Sonic 1000 offers a combination of features that are hard to find in single devices, with extensive telecommunications capabilities and the highest-quality digital video, music, TV program storage, and playback.

2. *Security*—Our smartphone uses a Linux-based operating system that is less vulnerable to hackers and other security threats that can result in stolen or corrupted data.

3. *Pricing*—Our product is priced lower than competing smartphones—none of which offer the same bundle of features—which gives us an edge with price-conscious customers.

Weaknesses are internal elements that may interfere with the company's ability to achieve its objectives.

Weaknesses By waiting to enter the smartphone market until considerable consolidation of competitors has occurred, Sonic has learned from the successes and mistakes of others. Nonetheless, we have two main weaknesses:

1. *Lack of brand awareness*—Sonic has no established brand or image, whereas Samsung, Apple, Motorola, and others have strong brand recognition. We will address this issue with aggressive promotion.

2. *Heavier and thicker unit*—The Sonic 1000 is slightly heavier and thicker than most competing models because it incorporates so many telecommunications and multimedia features. To counteract this weakness, we will emphasize our product's benefits and value-added pricing, two compelling competitive strengths.

Opportunities are areas of buyer need or potential interest in which the company might perform profitably.

Opportunities Sonic can take advantage of two major market opportunities:

1. *Increasing demand for state-of-the-art multimedia devices with a full array of communication functions*—The market for cutting-edge multimedia, multifunction devices is growing rapidly. Smartphones are already commonplace in public, work, and educational settings; in fact, users who bought entry-level models are now trading up.

2. *Lower technology costs*—Better technology is now available at a lower cost than ever before. Thus, Sonic can incorporate advanced features at a value-added price that allows for reasonable profits.

Threats We face three main threats at the introduction of the Sonic 1000:

1. *Increased competition*—More companies are offering devices with some but not all of the features and benefits provided by the Sonic 1000. Therefore, Sonic's marketing communications must stress our clear differentiation and value-added pricing.

2. *Downward pressure on pricing*—Increased competition and market share strategies are pushing smartphone prices down. Still, our objective of breaking even with second-year sales of the original model is realistic, given the lower margins in the smartphone market.

3. *Compressed product life cycle*—Smartphones are reaching the maturity stage of their life cycle more quickly than earlier technology products. Because of this compressed life cycle, we plan to introduce an even greater enhanced media-oriented second product during the year following the Sonic 1000's launch.

Threats are challenges posed by an unfavourable trend or development that could lead to lower sales and profits.

2.3 COMPETITION The emergence of well-designed multifunction smartphones, including the Apple iPhone, has increased competitive pressure. Competitors are continuously adding features and sharpening price points. Key competitors include the following:

This section identifies key competitors, describes their market positions, and provides an overview of their strategies.

- *Motorola.* Motorola has a long tradition of successful cell phones—it sold millions and millions of its RAZR clamshell phones worldwide. It has struggled in recent years, however, to keep up with competition.

- *Apple.* The initial iPhone, a smartphone with a 3.5-inch colour screen, was designed with entertainment enthusiasts in mind. It's well-equipped for music, videos, and web access, plus calendar and contact management functions. Apple initially partnered only with the AT&T network and cut the product's price to $399 two months after introduction to speed market penetration.

- *RIM.* Research In Motion makes the lightweight BlackBerry wireless phone/PDA products that are popular among corporate users. RIM's continuous innovation and solid customer service support strengthen its competitive standing as it introduces more smartphones and PDAs.

- *Samsung.* Value, style, function: Samsung is a powerful competitor, offering a variety of smartphones and ultra-mobile PCs for consumer and business segments. Some of its smartphones are available for specific telecommunications carriers, and some are "unlocked," ready for any compatible telecommunications network.

- *Nokia.* With a presence in virtually every possible cell phone market, Nokia is always an experienced, formidable opponent. Having launched one of the early smartphones, it will be expected to aggressively compete in the smartphone market.

Despite strong competition, Sonic can carve out a definite image and gain recognition among targeted segments. Our appealing combination of state-of-the-art features and low price is a critical point of differentiation for competitive advantage. Our second product will be even more media-oriented to appeal to segments where we will have strong brand recognition. Exhibit A.2 shows a sample of competitive products and prices.

2.4 PRODUCT OFFERINGS The Sonic 1000 offers the following standard features:

- Voice recognition for hands-free operation
- Full array of apps
- Complete organization functions, including linked calendar, address book, synchronization
- Digital music/video/television recording, wireless downloading, and instant playback
- Wireless web and email, text messaging, instant messaging
- Four-inch high-quality colour touch screen
- Ultra-fast 64-gigabyte drive and expansion slots
- Integrated 12 megapixel camera with flash and photo editing/sharing tools

First-year sales revenues are projected to be $200 million, based on sales of 800 000 of the Sonic 1000 model at a wholesale price of $250 each. Our second-year product will be the Sonic All Media 2000, stressing enhanced multimedia communication, networking, and entertainment functions. The Sonic All Media 2000 will include Sonic 1000 features plus additional features such as the following:

- Built-in media beaming to share music, video, and television files with other devices
- Webcam for instant video capture and uploading to popular video websites
- Voice-command access to popular social networking websites

EXHIBIT A.2 | SELECTED SMARTPHONE PRODUCTS AND PRICING

	Samsung Galaxy S – Captivate	Apple iPhone 4	Motorola Droid Pro	Nokia N900	BlackBerry Storm 2 9550
Storage	32 GB memory card	32 GB flash drive	Supports up to 32 GB micro SD	Up to 32 GB micro SD (sold separately)	Internal 16 GB 2 GB eMMC 16 MB media card included
Display	WVGA 4" touch screen	Retina display 3.5" (diagonal) widescreen multi-touch screen	HGVA 3.1" touch screen	WVGA 3.5" touch screen	3.25" touch screen
Camera	Auto focus 5.0 MP 4 × digital zoom Video MPEG4, AAC, AAC+ H.263 H.264 Video streaming	Tap to focus 5.0 MP VGA quality photos LED flash Video recording Geotagging	Auto focus 5.0 MP Digital zoom LED flash Image editing tools	Auto focus with two-stage capture key 5 MP Dual LED flash Image editing tools Geotagging	Auto focus 3.2 MP 2 × digital zoom Flash Auto focus Image stabilization Video recording
Price	$449–$599	$723 $199 16 GB $299 32 GB	$449–$489	$349	$349

This section summarizes the main features of the company's various products.

Distribution explains each channel for the company's products and mentions new developments and trends.

2.5 DISTRIBUTION Sonic-branded products will be distributed through a network of retailers in the top 50 U.S. markets. Among the most important channel partners being contacted are the following:

- *Office supply superstores.* Office Max, Office Depot, and Staples will all carry Sonic products in stores, in catalogues, and online.
- *Computer stores.* CompUSA and independent computer retailers will carry Sonic products.
- *Electronics specialty stores.* Best Buy will feature Sonic smartphones in its stores, online, and in its media advertising.
- *Online retailers.* Amazon.com will carry Sonic smartphones and, for a promotional fee, will give Sonic prominent placement on its homepage during the introduction.

Distribution will initially be restricted to the United States, with appropriate sales promotion support. Later, we plan to expand into Canada and beyond.

3.0 Marketing Strategy

3.1 OBJECTIVES We have set aggressive but achievable objectives for the first and second years of market entry.

Objectives should be defined in specific terms so management can measure progress and take corrective action to stay on track.

- *First-Year Objectives.* We are aiming for a 1 percent share of the U.S. smartphone market through a unit sales volume of 800 000.
- *Second-Year Objectives.* Our second-year objective is to achieve break-even on the Sonic 1000 and launch our second model.

All marketing strategies start with segmentation, targeting, and positioning.

3.2 TARGET MARKETS Sonic's strategy is based on a positioning of product differentiation. Our primary consumer target for the Sonic 1000 is middle- to upper-income professionals who need one fully loaded device to coordinate their busy schedules, stay in touch with family and colleagues, and be entertained on the go. Our secondary consumer target is high school, post-secondary, and graduate students who want a multimedia, dual-mode device. This segment can be described demographically by age (16–30) and education status. Our Sonic All Media 2000 will be aimed at teens and twentysomethings who want a device with features to support social networking and heavier, more extensive entertainment media consumption.

The primary business target for the Sonic 1000 is mid- to large-sized corporations that want to help their managers and employees stay in touch and input or access critical data when out of the office. This segment consists of companies with more than $25 million in annual sales and more than 100 employees. A secondary target is entrepreneurs and small-business owners. Also, we will target medical users who want to update or access patients' medical records.

Each of the marketing-mix strategies conveys Sonic's differentiation to these target market segments.

3.3 POSITIONING Using product differentiation, we are positioning the Sonic smartphone as the most versatile, convenient, value-added model for personal and professional use. Our marketing will focus on the value-priced multiple communication, entertainment, and information capabilities differentiating the Sonic 1000.

> Positioning identifies the brand, benefits, points of difference, and parity for the product or line.

3.4 STRATEGIES Positioning identifies the brand, benefits, points of difference, and parity for the product or line.

Product The Sonic 1000, including all the features described in the earlier Product Offerings section and more, will be sold with a one-year warranty. We will introduce the Sonic All Media 2000 during the following year, after we have established our Sonic brand. The brand and logo (Sonic's distinctive yellow thunderbolt) will be displayed on our products and packaging as well as in all marketing campaigns.

> Product strategy includes decisions about product mix and lines, brands, packaging and labelling, and warranties.

Pricing The Sonic 1000 will be introduced at a $250 wholesale price and a $300 estimated retail price per unit. We expect to lower the price of this model when we expand the product line by launching the Sonic All Media 2000, to be priced at $350 wholesale per unit. These prices reflect a strategy of (1) attracting desirable channel partners and (2) taking share from established competitors.

> Pricing strategy covers decisions about setting initial prices and adapting prices in response to opportunities and competitive challenges.

Distribution Our channel strategy is to use selective distribution, marketing Sonic smartphones through well-known stores and online retailers. During the first year, we will add channel partners until we have coverage in all major U.S. markets and the product is included in the major electronics catalogues and websites. We will also investigate distribution through cell phone outlets maintained by major carriers such as Verizon Wireless. In support of channel partners, we will provide demonstration products, detailed specification handouts, and full-colour photos and displays featuring the product. Finally, we plan to arrange special payment terms for retailers that place volume orders.

> Distribution strategy includes selection and management of channel relationships to deliver value to customers.

Marketing Communications By integrating all messages in all media, we will reinforce the brand name and the main points of product differentiation. Research about media consumption patterns will help our advertising agency choose appropriate media and timing to reach prospects before and during product introduction. Thereafter, advertising will appear on a pulsing basis to maintain brand awareness and communicate various differentiation messages. The agency will also coordinate public relations efforts to build the Sonic brand and support the differentiation message. To generate buzz, we will host a user-generated video contest on our website. To attract, retain, and motivate channel partners for a push strategy, we will use trade sales promotions and personal selling. Until the Sonic brand has been established, our communications will encourage purchases through channel partners rather than from our website.

> Marketing communications strategy covers all efforts to communicate to target audiences and channel members.

3.5 MARKETING MIX The Sonic 1000 will be introduced in February. Here are summaries of action programs we will use during the first six months to achieve our stated objectives.

> The marketing mix includes tactics and programs that support product, pricing, distribution, and marketing communications strategy.

■ *January.* We will launch a $200 000 trade sales promotion campaign and participate in major industry trade shows to educate dealers and generate channel support for the product launch in February. Also, we will create buzz by providing samples to selected product reviewers, opinion leaders, influential bloggers, and celebrities. Our training staff will work with retail sales personnel at major chains to explain the Sonic 1000's features, benefits, and advantages.

■ *February.* We will start an integrated print/radio/Internet campaign targeting professionals and consumers. The campaign will show how many functions the Sonic smartphone can perform and emphasize the convenience of a single, powerful handheld device. This multimedia campaign will be supported by point-of-sale signage as well as online-only ads and video tours.

■ *March.* As the multimedia advertising campaign continues, we will add consumer sales promotions such as a contest in which consumers post videos to our website, showing how they use the Sonic in creative and unusual ways. We will also distribute new point-of-purchase displays to support our retailers.

> Programs should coordinate with the resources and activities of other departments that contribute to customer value for each product.

■ *April.* We will hold a trade sales contest offering prizes for the salesperson and retail organization that sells the most Sonic smartphones during the four-week period.

■ *May.* We plan to roll out a new national advertising campaign this month. The radio ads will feature celebrity voices telling their Sonic smartphones to perform functions such as initiating a phone call, sending an email, and playing a song or video. The stylized print and online ads will feature avatars of these celebrities holding their Sonic smartphones. We plan to repeat this theme for next year's product launch.

■ *June.* Our radio campaign will add a new voice-over tag line promoting the Sonic 1000 as a graduation gift. We will exhibit at the semiannual electronics trade show and provide retailers with new competitive comparison handouts as a sales aid. In addition, we will analyze the results of customer satisfaction research for use in future campaigns and product development efforts.

3.6 MARKETING RESEARCH Using research, we will identify specific features and benefits our target market segments value. Feedback from market tests, surveys, and focus groups will help us develop and fine-tune the Sonic All Media 2000. We are also measuring and analyzing customers' attitudes toward competing brands and products. Brand awareness research will help us determine the effectiveness and efficiency of our messages and media. Finally, we will use customer satisfaction studies to gauge market reaction.

4.0 Financials

Total first-year sales revenue for the Sonic 1000 is projected at $200 million, with an average wholesale price of $250 per unit and variable cost per unit of $150 for a unit sales volume of 800 000. We anticipate a first-year loss of up to $40 million. Break-even calculations indicate that the Sonic 1000 will become profitable after the sales volume exceeds 267 500 during the product's second year. Our break-even analysis assumes per-unit wholesale revenue of $250 per unit, variable cost of $150 per unit, and estimated first-year fixed costs of $26 750 000. With these assumptions, the break-even calculation is

$$\frac{26\ 750\ 000}{\$250 - \$150} = 267\ 500 \text{ units}$$

5.0 Controls

Controls are being established to cover implementation and the organization of our marketing activities.

5.1 IMPLEMENTATION We are planning tight control measures to closely monitor quality and customer service satisfaction. This will enable us to react very quickly in correcting any problems that may occur. Other early warning signals that will be monitored for signs of deviation from the plan include monthly sales (by segment and channel) and monthly expenses.

5.2 MARKETING ORGANIZATION Sonic's chief marketing officer, Jane Melody, holds overall responsibility for all of the company's marketing activities. Exhibit A.3 shows the structure of the

This section shows how marketing research will support the development, implementation, and evaluation of marketing strategies and programs

Financials include budgets and forecasts to plan for marketing expenditures, scheduling, and operations.

Controls help management measure results and identify any problems or performance variations that need corrective action.

The marketing department may be organized by function, as in this sample, or by geography, product, customer, or some combination of these.

EXHIBIT A.3

Sonic's Marketing Organization

eight-person marketing organization. Sonic has hired Worldwide Marketing to handle national sales campaigns, trade and consumer sales promotions, and public relations efforts.

SONIC MARKETING PLAN CHAPTER ASSIGNMENTS[1]

Chapter 2

As an assistant to Jane Melody, Sonic's Chief Marketing Officer, you've been assigned to draft a mission statement for top management's review. This should cover the competitive spheres within which the firm will operate and your recommendation of an appropriate generic competitive strategy. Using your knowledge of marketing, the information you have about Sonic, and library or Internet resources, answer the following questions:

- What should Sonic's mission be?
- In what competitive spheres (industry, products and applications, competence, market-segment, vertical, and geographic) should Sonic operate?
- Which of Porter's generic competitive strategies would you recommend Sonic follow in formulating overall strategy?

As your instructor directs, enter your answers and supporting information in a written marketing plan or use *Marketing Plan Pro* software to document your ideas.

Chapter 3

Jane Melody asks you to scan Sonic's external environment for early warning signals of new opportunities and emerging threats that could affect the success of the Sonic 1000 smartphone. Using Internet or library sources (or both), locate information to answer three questions about key areas of the macroenvironment:

- What demographic changes are likely to affect Sonic's targeted segments?
- What economic trends might influence buyer behaviour in Sonic's targeted segments?
- How might the rapid pace of technological change alter Sonic's competitive situation?

Enter your answers about Sonic's environment in the appropriate sections of a written marketing plan or use the *Marketing Plan Pro* software to record your comments.

Chapter 4

Your next task is to consider how marketing research can help Sonic support its marketing strategy. Jane Melody also asks you how Sonic can measure results after the marketing plan is implemented. She wants you to answer the following three questions:

- What surveys, focus groups, observations, behavioural data, or experiments will Sonic need to support its marketing strategy? Be specific about the questions or issues that Sonic needs to resolve using marketing research.
- Where can you find suitable secondary data about total demand for smartphones over the next two years? Identify at least two sources (online or offline), describe what you plan to draw from each source, and indicate how the data would be useful for Sonic's marketing planning.
- What are three specific marketing metrics you would recommend that Sonic apply in determining marketing effectiveness and efficiency?

Enter this information in the marketing plan you've been writing or use the *Marketing Plan Pro* software to document your responses.

Chapter 5

Sonic has decided to focus on total customer satisfaction as a way of encouraging brand loyalty in a highly competitive marketplace. With this in mind, you've been assigned to analyze three specific issues as you continue working on Sonic's marketing plan:

- How (and how often) should Sonic monitor customer satisfaction?
- Would you recommend that Sonic use the Net Promoter method? Explain your reasoning.
- Which customer touch points should Sonic pay particularly close attention to, and why?

Consider your answers in the context of Sonic's current situation and the objectives it has set. Then enter your latest decisions in the written marketing plan or using *Marketing Plan Pro* software.

Chapter 6

You're responsible for researching and analyzing the consumer market for Sonic's smartphone product. Look again at the data you've already entered about the company's current situation and macroenvironment, especially the market being targeted. Now answer these questions about the market and buyer behaviour:

- What cultural, social, and personal factors are likely to most influence consumer purchasing of smartphones? What research tools would help you better understand the effect on buyer attitudes and behaviour?
- Which aspects of consumer behaviour should Sonic's marketing plan emphasize and why?
- What marketing activities should Sonic plan to coincide with each stage of the consumer buying process?

After you've analyzed these aspects of consumer behaviour, consider the implications for Sonic's marketing efforts to support the launch of its smartphone. Finally, document your findings and conclusions in a written marketing plan or with *Marketing Plan Pro*.

Chapter 7

You've been learning more about the business market for Sonic's smartphone. Jane Melody has defined this market as mid- to large-sized corporations that want their employees to stay in touch and be able to input or access data from any location. Respond to the following three questions based on your knowledge of Sonic's current situation and business-to-business marketing:

- What types of businesses appear to fit Melody's market definition? How can you research the number of employees and find other data about these types of businesses?
- What type of purchase would a Sonic smartphone represent for these businesses? Who would participate in and influence this type of purchase?
- Would demand for smartphones among corporate buyers tend to be inelastic? What are the implications for Sonic's marketing plan?

Your answers to these questions will affect how Sonic plans marketing activities for the business segments to be targeted. Take a few minutes to note your ideas in a written marketing plan or using *Marketing Plan Pro*.

Chapter 8

Identifying suitable market segments and selecting targets are critical to the success of any marketing plan. As Jane Melody's assistant, you're responsible for market segmentation and targeting. Look back at the market information, buyer behaviour data, and competitive details you previously gathered as you answer the following questions:

- Which variables should Sonic use to segment its consumer and business markets?
- How can Sonic evaluate the attractiveness of each identified segment? Should Sonic market to one consumer segment and one business segment or target more than one in each market? Why?
- Should Sonic pursue full market coverage, market specialization, product specialization, selective specialization, or single-segment concentration? Why?

Next, consider how your decisions about segmentation and targeting will affect Sonic's marketing efforts. Depending on your instructor's directions, summarize your conclusions in a written marketing plan or use *Marketing Plan Pro*.

Chapter 9

Sonic is a new brand with no prior brand associations, which presents a number of marketing opportunities and challenges. Jane Melody has given you responsibility for making recommendations about three brand equity issues that are important to Sonic's marketing plan:

- What brand elements would be most useful for differentiating the Sonic brand from competing brands?

■   How can Sonic sum up its brand promise for the new smartphone?

■   Should Sonic add a brand for its second product or retain the Sonic name?

Be sure your brand ideas are appropriate in light of what you've learned about your targeted segments and the competition. Then add this information to your written marketing plan or the plan you've been developing with *Marketing Plan Pro* software.

Chapter 10

As before, you're working with Jane Melody on Sonic's marketing plan for launching a new smartphone. Now you're focusing on Sonic's positioning and product life-cycle strategies by answering three specific questions:

■   In a sentence or two, what is an appropriate positioning for the Sonic 1000 smartphone?

■   Knowing the stage of Sonic's smartphone in the product life cycle, what are the implications for pricing, promotion, and distribution?

■   In which stage of its evolution does the smartphone market appear to be? What does this mean for Sonic's marketing plans?

Document your ideas in a written marketing plan or in *Marketing Plan Pro*. Note any additional research you may need to determine how to proceed after the Sonic 1000 has been launched.

Chapter 11

Sonic is a new entrant in an established industry characterized by competitors with relatively high brand identity and strong market positions. Use research and your knowledge of how to deal with competitors to consider three issues that will affect the company's ability to successfully introduce its first product:

■   What factors will you use to determine Sonic's strategic group?

■   Should Sonic select a class of competitor to attack on the basis of strength versus weakness, closeness versus distance, or good versus bad? Why is this appropriate in the smartphone market?

■   As a start-up company, what competitive strategy would be most effective as Sonic introduces its first product?

Take time to analyze how Sonic's competitive strategy will affect its marketing strategy and tactics. Now summarize your ideas in a written marketing plan or using *Marketing Plan Pro* software.

Chapter 12

Introducing a new product entails a variety of decisions about product strategy, including differentiation, ingredient branding, packaging, labelling, warranty, and guarantee. Your next task is to answer the following questions about Sonic's product strategy:

■   Which aspect of product differentiation would be most valuable in setting Sonic apart from its competitors, and why?

■   Should Sonic use ingredient branding to tout the Linux-based operating system that it says makes its smartphone more secure than smartphones based on some other operating systems?

■   How can Sonic use packaging and labelling to support its brand image and help its channel partners sell the smartphone product more effectively?

Once you've answered these questions, incorporate your ideas into the marketing plan you've been writing or document them using the *Marketing Plan Pro* software.

Chapter 13

You're planning customer support services for Sonic's new smartphone product. Review what you know about your target market and its needs; also think about what Sonic's competitors are offering. Then respond to these three questions about designing and managing services:

■   What support services are buyers of smartphone products likely to want and need?

■   How can Sonic manage gaps between perceived service and expected service to satisfy customers?

■   What post-sale service arrangements must Sonic make and how would you expect these to affect customer satisfaction?

Consider how your service strategy will support Sonic's overall marketing efforts. Summarize your recommendations in a written marketing plan or use *Marketing Plan Pro* to document your ideas.

Chapter 14

You're in charge of pricing Sonic's product for its launch early next year. Review the SWOT analysis you previously prepared as well as Sonic's competitive environment, targeting strategy, and product positioning. Now continue working on your marketing plan by responding to the following questions:

- What should Sonic's primary pricing objective be? Explain your reasoning.
- Are smartphone customers likely to be price sensitive? What are the implications for your pricing decisions?
- What price adaptations (such as discounts, allowances, and promotional pricing) should Sonic include in its marketing plan?

Make notes about your answers to these questions and then document the information in a written marketing plan or use *Marketing Plan Pro* software, depending on your instructor's directions.

Chapter 15

At Sonic, you have been asked to develop a marketing channel system for the new Sonic 1000 smartphone. Based on what you know about designing and managing integrated marketing channels, answer the three questions that follow:

- Do you agree with Jane Melody's decision to use a push strategy for the new product? Explain your reasoning.
- How many channel levels are appropriate for Sonic's targeted consumer and business segments?
- In determining the number of channel members, should you use exclusive, selective, or intensive distribution? Why?

Be sure your marketing channel ideas support the product positioning and are consistent with the goals that have been set. Record your recommendations in a written marketing plan or use *Marketing Plan Pro*.

Chapter 16

At this point, you need to make more specific decisions about managing the marketing intermediaries for Sonic's first product. Formulate your ideas by answering the following questions:

- What types of retailers would be most appropriate for distributing Sonic's smartphone? What are the advantages and disadvantages of selling through these types of retailers?
- What role should wholesalers play in Sonic's distribution strategy? Why?
- What market-logistics issues must Sonic consider for the launch of its first smartphone?

Summarize your decisions about retailing, wholesaling, and logistics in the marketing plan you've been writing or in the *Marketing Plan Pro* software.

Chapter 17

Jane Melody has assigned you to plan integrated marketing communications for Sonic's new product introduction. Review the data, decisions, and strategies you previously documented in your marketing plan before you answer the next three questions:

- What communications objectives are appropriate for Sonic's initial campaign?
- How can Sonic use personal communications channels to influence its target audience?
- Which communication tools would you recommend using after Sonic's initial product has been in the market for six months? Why?

Confirm that your marketing communications plans make sense in light of Sonic's overall marketing efforts. Now, as your instructor directs, summarize your thoughts in a written marketing plan or in the *Marketing Plan Pro* software.

Chapter 18

Mass communications will play a key role in Sonic's product introduction. After reviewing your earlier decisions and thinking about the current situation (especially your competitive circumstances), respond to the following questions to continue planning Sonic's marketing communications strategy:

- Once Sonic begins to use consumer advertising, what goals would be appropriate?

- Should Sonic continue consumer and trade sales promotion after the new product has been in the market for six months? Explain your reasoning.

- Jane Melody wants you to recommend an event sponsorship possibility that would be appropriate for the new product campaign. What type of event would you suggest and what objectives would you set for the sponsorship?

Record your ideas about mass communications in the marketing plan you've been writing or use *Marketing Plan Pro*.

Chapter 19

Sonic needs a strategy for managing personal communications during its new product launch. This is the time to look at interactive marketing, word of mouth, and personal selling. Answer these three questions as you consider Sonic's personal communications strategy:

- Which forms of interactive marketing are appropriate for Sonic, given its objectives, mass communications arrangements, and channel decisions?

- How should Sonic use word of mouth to generate brand awareness and encourage potential buyers to visit retailers to see the new smartphone in person?

- Does Sonic need a direct sales force or can it sell through agents and other outside representatives?

Look back at earlier decisions and ideas before you document your comments about personal communications in your written marketing plan or using *Marketing Plan Pro* software.

Chapter 20

Knowing that the smartphone market is likely to remain highly competitive, Jane Melody wants you to look ahead at how Sonic can develop new products outside the smartphone market. Review the competitive situation and the market situation before you continue working on the Sonic marketing plan:

- List three new-product ideas that build on Sonic's strengths and the needs of its various target segments. What criteria should Sonic use to screen these ideas?

- Develop the most promising idea into a product concept and explain how Sonic can test this concept. What particular dimensions must be tested?

- Assume that the most promising idea tests well. Now develop a marketing strategy for introducing it, including a description of the target market; the product positioning; the estimated sales, profit, and market share goals for the first year; your channel strategy; and the marketing budget you will recommend for this new-product introduction. If possible, estimate Sonic's costs and conduct a breakeven analysis.

Document all the details of your new-product development ideas in the written marketing plan or use *Marketing Plan Pro* software.

Chapter 21

As Jane Melody's assistant, you're researching how to market the Sonic 1000 smartphone product outside the United States within a year. You've been asked to answer the following questions about Sonic's use of global marketing:

- As a start-up company, should Sonic use indirect or direct exporting, licensing, joint ventures, or direct investment to enter the Canadian market next year? To enter other markets? Explain your answers.

- If Sonic starts marketing its smartphone in other countries, which of the international product strategies is most appropriate? Why?

■ Although some components are made in Asia, Sonic's smartphones will be assembled in Mexico through a contractual arrangement with a local factory. How are country-of-origin perceptions likely to affect your marketing recommendations?

Think about how these global marketing issues fit into Sonic's overall marketing strategy. Now document your ideas in the marketing plan you've been writing or using *Marketing Plan Pro*.

Chapter 22

With the rest of the marketing plan in place, you're ready to make recommendations about how to manage Sonic's marketing activities. Here are some specific questions Jane Melody wants you to consider:

■ How can Sonic drive customer-focused marketing and strategic innovation throughout the organization?

■ What role should social responsibility play in Sonic's marketing?

■ How can Sonic evaluate its marketing? Suggest several specific steps the company should take.

To complete your marketing plan, enter your answers to these questions in the written marketing plan or in *Marketing Plan Pro* software. Finally, draft the executive summary of the plan's highlights.

ENDNOTES

Chapter 1

1. "Dairy Farmers of Canada First to Launch 3D Advertising Campaign in Canada," June 24, 2009, www.dairyfarmers.ca/news-centre/news (viewed September 13, 2010); "First 3D Ad Campaign in Canada," www.headgearanimation.com/news (viewed October 4, 2010); Rosie Lombardi, "A Big Moo for Social Media," Food in Canada, 69, no. 7 (September 2009): 9; "Dairy Farmers of Canada Wins Big at International Milk Promotions Awards," September 24, 2009, www.dairyfarmers.ca/news-centre/news, (viewed October 4, 2010).

2. Philip Kotler, "Marketing: The Underappreciated Workhorse," Market Leader, Quarter 2 (2009): 8–10.

3. Peter C. Verhoef and Peter S. H. Leeflang, "Understanding the Marketing Department's Influence within the Firm," Journal of Marketing, 73 (March 2009): 14–37.

4. Eric Newman, "To Boost the Bottom Line, Strengthen the Front Line," BrandWeek, June 9, 2008, p. 10.

5. Stephanie Clifford, "A Video Prank at Domino's Taints Brand," New York Times, April 15, 2009; Thom Forbes, "Domino's Takes Cautious Approach to 'Prank' Video," Ad Age, April 15, 2009.

6. Jon Fine, "Marketing's Drift Away from Media," BusinessWeek, August 17, 2009, p. 64.

7. American Marketing Association, "Definition of Marketing," 2007, www.marketingpower.com/AboutAMA/Pages/DefinitionofMarketing.aspx; Lisa Keefe, "Marketing Defined," Marketing News, January 15, 2008, pp. 28–29.

8. Peter Drucker, Management: Tasks, Responsibilities, Practices (New York: Harper and Row, 1973), pp. 64–65.

9. "Gross Domestic Prices at Basic Prices, by Industry," Statistics Canada, Table 379-0027, July 29, 2011.

10. Ibid.

11. B. Joseph Pine II and James Gilmore, The Experience Economy (Boston: Harvard Business School Press, 1999); Bernd Schmitt, Experience Marketing (New York: Free Press, 1999); Philip Kotler, "Dream Vacations: The Booming Market for Designed Experiences," The Futurist, October 1984, pp. 7–13.

12. Irving J. Rein, Philip Kotler, Michael Hamlin, and Martin Stoller, High Visibility, 3rd ed. (New York: McGraw-Hill, 2006).

13. Philip Kotler, Christer Asplund, Irving Rein, and Donald H. Haider, Marketing Places in Europe: Attracting Investments, Industries, Residents, and Visitors to European Cities, Communities, Regions, and Nations (London, England: Financial Times Prentice Hall, 1999); Philip Kotler, Irving J. Rein, and Donald Haider, Marketing Places: Attracting Investment, Industry, and Tourism to Cities, States, and Nations (New York: Free Press, 1993).

14. Michael McCarthy, "Vegas Goes Back to Naughty Roots," USA Today, April 11, 2005; Julie Dunn, "Vegas Hopes for Payoff with Denverites," Denver Post, June 16, 2005; John M. Broder, "The Pied Piper of Las Vegas Seems to Have Perfect Pitch," New York Times, June 4, 2004; Chris Jones, "Las Vegas Tourism: Fewer Visitors, Don't Blame Fuel," Las Vegas Review-Journal, July 15, 2006; Richard Velotta, "Report: Las Vegas Tourism Tumbles 11.9 percent in January," Las Vegas Sun, March 10, 2009.

15. Miro Cernetig, "B.C. Seeks Celebrity Help to Lure Tourists to Visit," The Vancouver Sun, January 15, 2010, p. C1.

16. Carl Shapiro and Hal R. Varian, "Versioning: The Smart Way to Sell Information," Harvard Business Review, November–December 1998, pp. 106–114.

17. John R. Brandt, "Dare to Be Different," Chief Executive, May 2003, pp. 34–38.

18. Jena McGregor, Matthew Boyle, and Peter Burrows, "Your New Customer: The State," BusinessWeek, March 23 and 30, 2009, p. 66.

19. Jeffrey Rayport and John Sviokla, "Exploring the Virtual Value Chain," Harvard Business Review, November–December 1995, pp. 75–85; Jeffrey Rayport and John Sviokla, "Managing in the Marketspace," Harvard Business Review, November–December 1994, pp. 141–150.

20. Mohan Sawhney, Seven Steps to Nirvana (New York: McGraw-Hill, 2001).

21. Nikolaus Franke, Peter Keinz, and Christoph J. Steger, "Testing the Value of Customization: When Do Customers Really Prefer Products Tailored to Their Preferences?" Journal of Marketing, 73 (September 2009), pp. 103–121.

22. "Services, Industry & Specialty Groups," Meyers Norris Penny, www.mnp.ca (viewed September 13, 2010).

23. Lesley Ciarula Taylor, "Lululemon Continues to Roll up Big Profits; Shares in Vancouver Yoga-Wear Maker Soar," Toronto Star, September 11, 2010, p. B8; "lululemon athletica inc.: 2010 Form 10-K," lululemon, http://investor.lululemon.com/financials.cfm (viewed August 10, 2011).

24. Tom Szaky, "Revolution in a Bottle," Portfolio Trade, 2009; Linda M. Castellito, "TerraCycle Founder's Journey Started with Worm Poop," USA Today, September 25, 2009, p. 5B.

25. "Food Site Finds Recipe for Mixing in Sponsors, on the Hot Seat," Boston Globe, September 6, 2009, p. G3; "Allrecipes.com Stirs Up Success," Allrecipes.com Press Release, July 21, 2009, www.allrecipes.com; Eric Engelman, "Questions for Lisa Sharples, President of Allrecipes.com," Puget Sound Business Journal, October 10, 2008.

26. Adam Lashinsky, "Shoutout in Gadget Land," Fortune, November 10, 2003, pp. 77–86; "Computer Industry Trends: Top 100 Companies," www.netvalley.com; Tim Conneally, "Gartner: Acer Gains Big Worldwide, Apple Gains in US," Betanews, October 15, 2008.

27. Anya Kamenetz, "The Network Unbound," Fast Company, June 2006, pp. 69–73.

28. David Kiley, "Advertisers, Start Your Engines," BusinessWeek, March 6, 2006, p. 26; Cameron Wykes, "Making Sense Out of Social Nets," AdweekMedia, July 6, 2009, p. 2.

29. Yankelovich Partners Inc., "2005 Marketing Receptivity Survey," April 18, 2005.

30. Kate Brumbeck, "Alabama Flea Market Owner Turns into YouTube Phenomenon," Associated Press, June 30, 2007.

31. Martin Bosworth, "Loyalty Cards: Rewards or Threats?" ConsumerAffairs.com, July 11, 2005.

32. Antonio Gonsalves, "Dell Makes $3 Million from Twitter-Related Sales," InformationWeek, June 12, 2009.

33. Linda Tischler, "What's The Buzz?" Fast Company, May 2004, p. 76.

34. Valerie Alderson, "Measuring the Value of a Managed WOM Program in Test & Control Markets," BzzAgent Inc., 2007.

35. Suzanne Vranica, "Marketers Aim New Ads at Video iPod Users," Wall Street Journal, January 31, 2006; Kevin Redmond, "GPS + Mobile Marketing = Goodness," Barbarian Blog, February 21, 2009.

36. Bruce Horovitz, "In Trend toward Vanity Food, It's Getting Personal," USA Today, August 9, 2006.

37. Josh Catone, "15 Companies That Really Get Corporate Blogging," www.sitepoint.com.

38. "Intranet Case Study: GM's mySocrates," www.communitelligence.com.

39. Gail McGovern and John A. Quelch, "The Fall and Rise of the CMO," Strategy + Business, Winter 2004.

40. Richard Rawlinson, "Beyond Brand Management," *Strategy + Business*, Summer 2006.

41. Jennifer Rooney, "As If You Didn't Know by Now, It's About the Bottom Line for CMOs," *Advertising Age*, May 5, 2008, pp. 3–57.

42. Elisabeth Sullivan, "Solving the CMO Puzzle," *Marketing News*, March 30, 2009, p. 12.

43. Constantine von Hoffman, "Armed with Intelligence," *BrandWeek*, May 29, 2006, pp. 17–20.

44. "China's Second Biggest PC Maker to Push Windows," April 15, 2006, www.digitalworldtokyo.com.

45. Robert J. Keith, "The Marketing Revolution," *Journal of Marketing, 24* (January 1960): 35–38; John B. McKitterick, "What Is the Marketing Management Concept?" in *The Frontiers of Marketing Thought and Action*, edited by Frank M. Bass (Chicago: American Marketing Association, 1957), pp. 71–82; Fred J. Borch, "The Marketing Philosophy as a Way of Business Life," *The Marketing Concept: Its Meaning to Management* (Marketing series, no. 99; New York: American Management Association, 1957), pp. 3–5.

46. Theodore Levitt, "Marketing Myopia," *Harvard Business Review*, July–August 1960, p. 50.

47. Rohit Deshpande and John U. Farley, "Measuring Market Orientation: Generalization and Synthesis," *Journal of Market-Focused Management, 2* (1998): 213–232; Ajay K. Kohli and Bernard J. Jaworski, "Market Orientation: The Construct, Research Propositions, and Managerial Implications," *Journal of Marketing, 54* (April 1990): 1–18; John C. Narver and Stanley F. Slater, "The Effect of a Market Orientation on Business Profitability," *Journal of Marketing, 54* (October 1990): 20–35.

48. Evert Gummesson, *Total Relationship Marketing* (Boston: Butterworth-Heinemann, 1999); Regis McKenna, *Relationship Marketing* (Reading, MA: Addison-Wesley, 1991); Martin Christopher, Adrian Payne, and David Ballantyne, *Relationship Marketing: Bringing Quality, Customer Service, and Marketing Together* (Oxford: Butterworth-Heinemann, 1991).

49. James C. Anderson, Hakan Hakansson, and Jan Johanson, "Dyadic Business Relationships within a Business Network Context," *Journal of Marketing, 58* (October 15, 1994): 1–15.

50. Larry Selden and Yoko S. Selden, "Profitable Customer: The Key to Great Brands," *Advertising Age*, July 10, 2006, p. S7; Larry Selden and Geoffrey Colvin, *Angel Customers and Demon Customers* (New York: Portfolio, 2003).

51. "Why MTS Bundles?" www.mts.ca (viewed October 17, 2010).

52. Allison Fass, "Theirspace.com," *Forbes*, May 8, 2006, pp. 122–124.

53. Christian Homburg, John P. Workman, Jr., and Harley Krohmen, "Marketing's Influence within the Firm," *Journal of Marketing, 63* (January 1999): 1–15.

54. Robert Shaw and David Merrick, *Marketing Payback: Is Your Marketing Profitable?* (London, England: Pearson Education, 2005).

55. Rajendra Sisodia, David Wolfe, and Jagdish Sheth, *Firms of Endearment: How World-Class Companies Profit from Passion* (Upper Saddle River, NJ: Wharton School Publishing, 2007).

56. If choosing to develop a strategic corporate social responsibility program, see Michael E. Porter and Mark R. Kramer, "Strategy and Society: The Link between Competitive Advantage and Corporate Social Responsibility," *Harvard Business Review*, December 2006, pp. 78–92.

57. Jeffrey Hollender and Stephen Fenichell, *What Matters Most* (New York: Basic Books, 2004), p. 168.

58. Tara Weiss, "Special Report: Going Green," *Forbes.com*, July 3, 2007; Matthew Grimm, "Progressive Business," *BrandWeek*, November 28, 2005, pp. 16–26.

59. www.stonyfield.ca/en/about-us.

60. E. Jerome McCarthy and William D. Perreault, *Basic Marketing: A Global-Managerial Approach*, 14th ed. (Homewood, IL: McGraw-Hill/Irwin, 2002).

Chapter 2

1. Simon Houpt, "Aeroplan Hits Back at Competition," *The Globe and Mail*, March 19, 2010; Rob Carrick, "In a Competitive Landscape, Aeroplan Takes the Gold," *The Globe and Mail*, October 6, 2010; Canadian Press, "Aeroplan Sets Sights on International Expansion," *Marketing*, October 14, 2010; www2.aeroplan.com/learn_more/how_you_benefit.do (viewed October 2010).

2. Nirmalya Kumar, *Marketing as Strategy: The CEO's Agenda for Driving Growth and Innovation* (Boston: Harvard Business School Press, 2004).

3. Michael E. Porter, *Competitive Advantage: Creating and Sustaining Superior Performance* (New York: The Free Press, 1985).

4. For an academic treatment of benchmarking, see Douglas W. Vorhies and Neil A. Morgan, "Benchmarking Marketing Capabilities for Sustained Competitive Advantage," *Journal of Marketing, 69*, no. 1 (January 2005): 80–94.

5. Michael Hammer and James Champy, *Reengineering the Corporation Revolution* (New York: Harper Business, 1993).

6. Ibid.; Jon R. Katzenbach and Douglas K. Smith, *The Wisdom of Teams: Creating the High-Performance Organization* (Boston: Harvard Business School Press, 1993), p. 8.

7. "lululemon athletica Partners with Vitech to Implement Vocollect Voice," Vitech Group Press Release, January 29, 2010, www.your-story.org/lululemon-athletica-partners-with-vitech-to-implement-vocollect-voice-92769/ (viewed October 2010); Marina Strauss, "Lululemon stretched by demand," *The Globe and Mail*, September 10, 2007.

8. C. K. Prahalad and Gary Hamel, "The Core Competence of the Corporation," *Harvard Business Review*, May–June 1990, pp. 79–91.

9. "Transformational Gift to SickKids Cancer Care, Research, and Education," SickKids Foundation News Release, October 25, 2010, www.sickkidsfoundation.com/news/NewsTransformationalGift.asp; www.sickkids.on.ca (viewed October 2010).

10. Canadian Press, "Argos and Bills on Same Team to Make Football More Popular," *Marketing*, August 5, 2010.

11. Pew Internet and American Life Project Survey, November–December 2000.

12. "Aviva Canada on a Mission to 'Change Insurance' in Canada," Aviva Canada Press Release, April 10, 2008, www.avivacanada.com/press/aviva-canada-mission-change-insurance-canada (viewed October 2010).

13. Peter Drucker, *Management: Tasks, Responsibilities and Practices* (New York: Harper and Row, 1973), Ch. 7.

14. "Bioniche Recognized as One of the Top 10 Life Science Companies in Canada," December 4, 2007; "Bioniche Named One of the Top 50 Best Small and Medium Employers in Canada for a Second Time," Bioniche News Release, http://www.bioniche.com/news_item.cfm?id=2235 (viewed October 2010).

15. He also humorously suggests first checking out the mission statement generator of comic strip character Dilbert, if a statement has to be developed by the organization: *Dilbert.com*.

16. www.bioniche.com/products.cfm.

17. www.google.com/about/corporate/company/tenthings.html.

18. Jeffrey F. Rayport and Bernard J. Jaworski, *e-commerce* (New York: McGraw-Hill, 2001), p. 116.

19. Tilman Kemmler, Monika Kubicová, Robert Musslewhite, and Rodney Prezeau, "E-Performance II—The Good, the Bad, and the Merely Average," *mckinseyquarterly.com*, 2001.

20. Bruce Horovitz, "Campbell's 10-Year Goal to Clean Up a Soupy Mess," *USA Today*, January 26, 2009, p. 1B.

21. See Shaw's website, www.shaw.ca/en-ca/AboutShaw (viewed October 2010).

22. This section is based on Robert M. Grant, *Contemporary Strategy Analysis*, 7th ed. (New York: John Wiley & Sons, 2009), Ch. 17.

23. The same matrix can be expanded into nine cells by adding modified products and modified markets. See S. J. Johnson and Conrad Jones, "How to Organize for New Products," *Harvard Business Review*, May–June 1957, pp. 49–62.

24. Tom Lowry, "ESPN's Cell Phone Fumble," *BusinessWeek*, October 30, 2006, p. 26.

25. Jesse Eisinger, "The Marriage from Hell," *Condé Nast Portfolio*, February 2008, pp. 84–88, 132.

26. www.corusent.com/home/Corporate/AboutCorus/tabid/1668/Default.aspx (viewed October 2010).

27. Jena McGregor, "The World's Most Innovative Companies," *BusinessWeek*, April 24, 2006, pp. 63–74.

28. Gary Hamel and C. K. Prahalad, "Corporate Imagination and Expeditionary Marketing," *Harvard Business Review*, 69, no. 4 (1991): 81–92.

29. Paul J. H. Shoemaker, "Scenario Planning: A Tool for Strategic Thinking," *Sloan Management Review*, Winter 1995, pp. 25–40.

30. Ronald Grover, "Hollywood Ponders a Post-DVD Future," *BusinessWeek*, March 2, 2009, p. 56; Brooks Barnes, "Movie Studios See a Threat in Growth of Redbox," *New York Times*, September 7, 2009.

31. Philip Kotler, *Kotler on Marketing* (New York: Free Press, 1999).

32. Ibid.

33. Dominic Dodd and Ken Favaro, "Managing the Right Tension," *Harvard Business Review*, December 2006, pp. 62–74.

34. Michael E. Porter, *Competitive Strategy: Techniques for Analyzing Industries and Competitors* (New York: The Free Press, 1980), Ch. 2.

35. Michael E. Porter, "What Is Strategy?" *Harvard Business Review*, November–December 1996, pp. 61–78.

36. www2.aeroplan.com/earn_miles/our_partners.do.

37. For some readings on strategic alliances, see Peter Lorange and Johan Roos, *Strategic Alliances: Formation, Implementation and Evolution* (Cambridge, MA: Blackwell, 1992); Jordan D. Lewis, *Partnerships for Profit: Structuring and Managing Strategic Alliances* (New York: The Free Press, 1990); John R. Harbison and Peter Pekar, Jr., *Smart Alliances: A Practical Guide to Repeatable Success* (San Francisco, CA: Jossey-Bass, 1998); *Harvard Business Review on Strategic Alliances* (Cambridge, MA: Harvard Business School Press, 2002).

38. Kerry Capell, "Vodafone: Embracing Open Source with Open Arms," *BusinessWeek*, April 20, 2009, pp. 52–53; "Call the Carabiniere," *The Economist*, May 16, 2009, p. 75.

39. Robin Cooper and Robert S. Kaplan, "Profit Priorities from Activity-Based Costing," *Harvard Business Review*, May–June 1991, pp. 130–135.

40. See Robert S. Kaplan and David P. Norton, *The Balanced Scorecard: Translating Strategy into Action* (Boston: Harvard Business School Press, 1996) as a tool for monitoring stakeholder satisfaction.

41. Thomas J. Peters and Robert H. Waterman, Jr., *In Search of Excellence: Lessons from America's Best-Run Companies* (New York: Harper and Row, 1982), pp. 9–12.

42. Terrence E. Deal and Allan A. Kennedy, *Corporate Cultures: The Rites and Rituals of Corporate Life* (Reading, MA: Addison-Wesley, 1982); "Corporate Culture," *BusinessWeek*, October 27, 1980, pp. 148–160; Stanley M. Davis, *Managing Corporate Culture* (Cambridge, MA: Ballinger, 1984); John P. Kotter and James L. Heskett, *Corporate Culture and Performance* (New York: The Free Press, 1992).

43. Marian Burk Wood, *The Marketing Plan: A Handbook* (Upper Saddle River, NJ: Prentice Hall, 2003).

44. Donald R. Lehmann and Russell S. Winer, *Product Management*, 3rd ed. (Boston: McGraw-Hill/Irwin, 2001).

45. David B. Hertz, "Risk Analysis in Capital Investment," *Harvard Business Review*, January–February 1964, pp. 96–106.

Chapter 3

1. "Growth Is in the Bag," *Profit*, 28, no. 6 (December 2009–January 2010): 25; Deborah Aarts, "Beware the Green Skeptic," *Profit*, 29, no. 5 (November 2010): 63–64; Patrick Lejtenyi, "These Bags Save Cows," *Montreal Mirror*, 20, no. 12 (September 9–15, 2004).

2. Susan Warren, "Pillow Talk: Stackers Outnumber Plumpers; Don't Mention Drool," *Wall Street Journal*, January 8, 1998.

3. "Spending Patterns in Canada—2009," *Statistics Canada*, Publication 62-202-X, December 17, 2010.

4. Parks Canada, *2003 Survey of Visitors to Banff, Jasper, Kootenay, and Yoho National Parks of Canada* (Gatineau, QC: Parks Canada, 2004); Dave McVetty, *Understanding Visitor Flows in Canada's Mountain National Parks: The Patterns of Visitor Use Studies in Banff, Jasper, Kootenay, and Yoho National Parks* (Winnipeg, MB: Parks Canada's Western Canada Service Centre, 2004).

5. "Vendor-Managed Inventory in Consumer Electronics and Durables," *The Supply Chain Company*, www.i2.com/industries/consumer_industries/vmi/ vmi_case_study.cfm.

6. William Holstein, "The Dot Com within Ford," *BusinessWeek*, January 30, 2000.

7. Hollie Shaw, "Battle for Grocery Shoppers Heats Up; Sobeys Has You in Its Sights with New Strategy," *Calgary Herald*, July 23, 2010, p. E6.

8. "Predictive Analytics Allows PC Financial to Dramatically Improve Results in Loyalty Marketing," *Angoss Software Corporation*, www.angoss.com/resources/success_stories.php (viewed April 20, 2011).

9. Leonard M. Fuld, "Staying a Step Ahead of the Rest," *Chief Executive*, 218 (June 2006): 32.

10. "Spies, Lies & KPMG," *BusinessWeek*, February 26, 2007.

11. Jennifer Esty, "Those Wacky Customers!" *Fast Company*, January 2004, p. 40.

12. Helen Coster, "Shopping Cart Psychology," *Forbes*, September 7, 2009, pp. 64–65.

13. Sara Steindorf, "Shoppers Spy on Those Who Serve," *Christian Science Monitor*, May 28, 2002; Edward F. McQuarrie, *Customer Visits: Building a Better Market Focus*, 2nd ed. (Newbury Park, CA: Sage Press, 1998).

14. Shirley S. Wang, "Heath Care Taps 'Mystery Shoppers,'" *Wall Street Journal*, August 10, 2006.

15. Heather Green, "It Takes a Web Village," *BusinessWeek*, September 4, 2006, p. 66.

16. Amy Merrick, "Counting on the Census," *Wall Street Journal*, February 14, 2001.

17. Kim Girard, "Strategies to Turn Stealth into Wealth," *Business 2.0*, May 2003, p. 66.

18. "The Blogs in the Corporate Machine," *The Economist*, February 11, 2006, pp. 55–56; also adapted from Robin T. Peterson and Zhilin Yang, "Web Product Reviews Help Strategy," *Marketing News*, April 7, 2004, p. 18.

19. American Productivity & Quality Center, "User-Driven Competitive Intelligence: Crafting the Value Proposition," December 3–4, 2002.

20. Alex Wright, "Mining the Web for Feelings, Not Facts," *New York Times*, August 24, 2009; Sarah E. Needleman, "For Companies, a Tweet in Time Can Avert PR Mess, *Wall Street Journal*, August 3, 2009, p. B6.

21. See *BadFads Museum*, www.badfads.com, for examples of fads and collectibles through the years.

22. John Naisbitt and Patricia Aburdene, *Megatrends 2000* (New York: Avon Books, 1990).

23. "Starbucks VIA Ready Brew: A Breakthrough in Instant Coffee," *Business Wire*, February 17, 2009; "National Coffee Drinking Trends Report: Coffee Proves Resilient in Recession," July 4, 2009, www.vendingmarketwatch.com/web/online/VendingMarketWatch-News/National-Coffee-Drinking-Trends-Report—Coffee-Proves-Resilient-In-Recession/1$24077 (viewed September 12, 2010); John Gillie, "Starbucks VIA Hits Big Sales Mark," *The Olympian*, August 4, 2010.

24. Indata, *IN*, June 2006, p. 27.

25. "World POPClock," *U.S. Census Bureau*, www.census.gov, 2009.

26. See Donella H. Meadows, Dennis L. Meadows, and Jorgen Randers, *Beyond Limits* (White River Junction, VT: Chelsea Green, 1993) for some commentary; http://geography.about.com/od/obtainpopulationdata/ a/worldvillage.htm.

27. "World Development Indicators Database," *World Bank*, http://site resources.worldbank.org/DATASTATISTICS/ Resources/POP.pdf, September 15, 2009; "World Population Growth," www.worldbank.org/depweb/english/beyond/beyondco/beg_03.pdf.

28. "Population Projection for Canada, Provinces, and Territories 2009 to 2036," *Statistics Canada*, Publication 91-520-X, June 18, 2010.

29. Erika Alini, "(Way) Back to the Books: Later-in-Life Schooling 'Is Not Just Growing, It's Growing Exponentially.' Boomers Are the Latest Cash Crop," *Macleans*, 124, no. 6 (February 21, 2011): 47.

30. *Statistics Canada* publications: "Immigration Population by Place of Birth and Period of Immigration (2006 Census)," October 14, 2009; "Canadian Demographics at a Glance," Catalogue no. 91-003-X, January 2008; "Selected Demographic, Cultural, Educational, Labour Force and Income Characteristics for the Population of Canada, Provinces, Territories, Census Divisions and Census Subdivisions, 2006 Census—20% Sample Data," Catalogue no. 97-555-XCB2006057, January 22, 2009; "The Daily," April 2, 2008; "The Daily," December 4, 2007; "Visible Minority Population, by Census Metropolitan Areas (2006 Census)," November 6, 2009.

31. Bobby Siu, "Ethnic Marketing: Demographic Wave Well Worth Riding," *Strategy: The Canadian Marketing Report*, July 6, 1998, p. 15; David Todd, "Special Report: Multicultural Marketing: Nike Takes It to the Streets," *Strategy: The Canadian Marketing Report*, August 17, 1998, p. 26.

32. "Population by Mother Tongue, by Province and Territory (2006 Census)," *Statistics Canada*, December 11, 2007.

33. "The 2006 Participation and Activity Limitation Survey: Disability in Canada," *Statistics Canada*, Catalogue no. 89-628-X, June 22, 2009.

34. *The Central Intelligence Agency's World Factbook*, www.cia.gov/library/publications/the-world-factbook, December 9, 2010.

35. "Census Families by Number of Children at Home, by Province and Territory (2006 Census)," *Statistics Canada*, September 20, 2007.

36. "Healthcare Use among Gay, Lesbian and Bisexual Canadians," *Statistics Canada*, *The Daily*, March 19, 2008.

37. Rebecca Gardyn, "A Market Kept in the Closet," *American Demographics*, November 2001, pp. 37–43.

38. Hollie Shaw, "Pink Money Talks," *Financial Post*, April 18, 2008, www.financialpost.com/news/story.html?id=455619 (viewed June 15, 2008).

39. Hollie Shaw, "Joe Fresh Fashions Low-Cost U.S. Invasion," *National Post*, February 24, 2011, p. A1.

40. Elisabeth Sullivan, "The Age of Prudence," *Marketing News*, April 15, 2009, pp. 8–11; Steve Hamm, "The New Age of Frugality," *BusinessWeek*, October 20, 2008, pp. 55–60; Jessica Deckler, "Never Pay Retail Again," *CNNMoney.com*, May 30, 2008.

41. David Welch, "The Incredible Shrinking Boomer Economy," *BusinessWeek*, August 3, 2009, pp. 27–30.

42. "Assets and Debts Held by Family Units, Median Amounts," Survey of Financial Security (SFS), *Statistics Canada*, December 7, 2006.

43. Julie Schlosser, "Infosys U.," *Fortune*, March 20, 2006, pp. 41–42.

44. Pamela Paul, "Corporate Responsibility," *American Demographics*, May 2002, pp. 24–25.

45. Stephen Baker, "Wiser about the Web," *BusinessWeek*, March 27, 2006, pp. 53–57.

46. Michael Adams, *Fire and Ice: The United States, Canada and the Myth of Converging Values* (Toronto: Penguin Canada, 2003).

47. David MacDonald and Michael Adams, "We Are What We Drive," *Marketing Magazine*, 109, no. 10 (March 15, 2004): 42; Lynn Fletcher, "Under Siege, but Still Upbeat," *Marketing Magazine*, 108, no. 36 (October 27, 2003): 13.

48. Laura Zinn, "Teens: Here Comes the Biggest Wave Yet," *BusinessWeek*, April 11, 2004, pp. 76–86.

49. Chris Taylor, ed., "Go Green. Get Rich," *Business 2.0*, January–February 2007, pp. 68–79.

50. Subhabrata Bobby Banerjee, Easwar S. Iyer, and Rajiv K. Kashyap, "Corporate Environmentalism: Antecedents and Influence of Industry Type," *Journal of Marketing*, 67 (April 2003): 106–122.

51. "Shift! OK, Listen Up. Green Is Not the Colour of Nerds," *Calgary Herald*, December 8, 2010, p. F5; "Enterprise Rent-A-Car to Begin Offering Electric Vehicles in U.S.; Nissan LEAFs Will Be Available in Select Markets Next Year-Extending Enterprise's Commitment to Support Clean, New Technologies," *Marketwire*, July 27, 2010; "Enterprise Rent-A-Car to Offer Electric Cars," *Energy Digital.com*, January 19, 2011, www.energydigital.com/sectors/utilities-electric/enterprise-rent-car-offer-electric-cars (viewed February 26, 2011); Enterprise website, www.enterpriserentacar.ca (viewed February 26, 2011).

52. "Are There High-Tech Industries or Only High-Tech Firms?" *Statistics Canada*, *The Daily*, December 10, 1998.

53. "Apple's App Store Downloads Top 10 Billion," Apple Press Release, January 22, 2011, www.apple.com/pr/library/2011/01/22appstore.html (viewed May 8, 2011).

54. Chris Taylor, ed., "Go Green. Get Rich," *Business 2.0*, January–February 2007, pp. 68–79.

55. Peter O'Neil, "Canada Criticized for Decline in Research Spending," *PostMedia News*, December 14, 2010.

56. "OECD Science, Technology and Industry Outlook 2010 Highlights," *Organisation for Economic Co-operation and Development*, December 14, 2010.

57. See Dorothy Cohen, *Legal Issues on Marketing Decision Making* (Cincinnati, OH: South-Western, 1995).

58. Rebecca Gardyn, "Swap Meet," *American Demographics*, July 2001, pp. 51–55.

59. Pamela Paul, "Mixed Signals," *American Demographics*, July 2001, pp. 45–49.

60. "Excelling in Today's Multimedia World," Conference Summary, Economist Conferences' Fourth Annual Marketing Roundtable, Landor, March 2006.

61. Loblaw Companies Limited,"2010 Annual Report."

62. For a good discussion and illustration, see Roger J. Best, *Market-Based Management*, 4th ed. (Upper Saddle River, NJ: Prentice Hall, 2005).

63. For further discussion, see Gary L. Lilien, Philip Kotler, and K. Sridhar Moorthy, *Marketing Models* (Upper Saddle River, NJ: Prentice Hall, 1992).

64. www.naics.com; www.census.gov/epcd/naics02, December 9, 2010.

65. Brian Sternthal and Alice M. Tybout, "Segmentation and Targeting," in *Kellogg on Marketing*, edited by Dawn Iacobucci (John Wiley & Sons, 2001), pp. 3–30.

66. For an excellent overview of market forecasting, see *Principles of Forecasting: A Handbook for Researchers and Practitioners*, edited by Scott Armstrong (Norwell, MA: Kluwer Academic Publishers, 2001) and Armstrong's website: www.forecastingprinciples.com; also see Roger J. Best, "An Experiment in Delphi Estimation in Marketing Decision Making," *Journal of Marketing Research*, 11 (November 1974): 447–452; Norman Dalkey and Olaf Helmer, "An Experimental Application of the Delphi Method to the Use of Experts," *Management Science*, April 1963, pp. 458–467.

Chapter 4

1. Studentawards Inc. website, www.studentawardsinc.com/default.aspx (viewed September 18, 2010); "Opening Canada's Student Wallet: New Research from Studentawards Inc. Digs Deeper, Uncovers Specific Stage-of-Education Spending Habits, as well as Where, When and on What Students Spend Millions of Dollars Each Month," *Market Wire*, February 16, 2010.

2. See Robert Schieffer, *Ten Key Customer Insights: Unlocking the Mind of the Market* (Mason, OH: Thomson, 2005), for a comprehensive, in-depth discussion of how to generate customer insights to drive business results.

3. Jenn Abelson, "Gillette Sharpens Its Focus on Women," *Boston Globe*, January 4, 2009; A. G. Lafley, "It Was a No-Brainer," *Fortune*, February 21, 2005, p. 96; Naomi Aoki, "Gillette Hopes to Create a Buzz with Vibrating Women's Razor," *Boston Globe*, December 17, 2004; Chris Reidy, "The Unveiling of a New Venus," *Boston Globe*, November 3, 2000.

4. Natalie Zmuda, "Tropicana Line's Sales Plunge 20% Post-Rebranding," *Advertising Age*, April 2, 2009.

5. ESOMAR, Global Market Research 2010: ESOMAR Industry Report (Amsterdam, 2010).

6. Melanie Haiken, "Tuning In to Crowdcasting," *Business 2.0*, November 2006, pp. 66–68.

7. Michael Fielding, "Special Delivery: UPS Conducts Surveys to Help Customers Export to China," *Marketing News*, February 1, 2007, pp. 13–14.

8. "Would You Fly in Chattering Class?" *The Economist*, September 9, 2006, p. 63.

9. "Air Canada Innovations," www.aircanada.com/en/about/media/facts/innovations.html (viewed January 4, 2011); "In-Flight Dogfight," *Business2.Com*, January 9, 2001, pp. 84–91; John Blau, "In-Flight Internet Service Ready for Takeoff," *IDG News Service*, June 14, 2002; "Boeing In-Flight Internet Plan Goes Airborne," *The Associated Press*, April 18, 2004.

10. For a discussion of the decision-theory approach to the value of research, see Donald R. Lehmann, Sunil Gupta, and Joel Steckel, *Market Research* (Reading, MA: Addison-Wesley, 1997).

11. Gregory Solman, "Finding Car Buyers at Their Home (Sites)," *Adweek*, August 21–28, 2006, p. 8.

12. Linda Tischler, "Every Move You Make," *Fast Company*, April 2004, pp. 73–75; Allison Stein Wellner, "Look Who's Watching," *Continental*, April 2003, pp. 39–41.

13. For a detailed review of some relevant academic work, see Eric J. Arnould and Amber Epp, "Deep Engagement with Consumer Experience," in *Handbook of Marketing Research*, edited by Rajiv Grover and Marco Vriens (Thousand Oaks, CA: Sage Publications, 2006). For a range of academic discussion, see "Can Ethnography Uncover Richer Consumer Insights?" *Journal of Advertising Research*, 46 (September 2006). For some practical tips, see Richard Durante and Michael Feehan, "Leverage Ethnography to Improve Strategic Decision Making," *Marketing Research*, Winter 2005.

14. Eric J. Arnould and Linda L. Price, "Market-Oriented Ethnography Revisited," *Journal of Advertising Research*, 46 (September 2006): 251–262; Eric J. Arnould and Melanie Wallendorf, "Market-Oriented Ethnography: Interpretation Building and Marketing Strategy Formulation," *Journal of Marketing Research*, 31 (November 1994): 484–504.

15. "Case Study: Bank of America," *BusinessWeek*, June 19, 2006; Spencer E. Ante, "Inprogress," *IN*, June 2006, pp. 28–29; *Bank of America*, www.bankofamerica.com.

16. Natalia Williams, "Are We Close Enough Yet? How Intimate Research Techniques Are Meaning Cozy Media Plans for Marketers," *Strategy*, July 2005, p. 22; "If Not Now, When? Doritos Launches Innovative inNw? Campaign," Frito-Lay Press Release, March 1, 2005, p. 1.

17. Andrew Kaplan, "Mass Appeal," *Beverage World*, February 2007, pp. 48–49.

18. Michael Fielding, "Shift the Focus," *Marketing News*, September 1, 2006, pp. 18–20.

19. Piet Levy, "In with the Old, In Spite of the New," *Marketing News*, May 30, 2009, p. 19.

20. Eric Schellhorn, "A Tsunami of Surveys Washes over Consumers," *Christian Science Monitor*, October 2, 2006, p. 13.

21. Alexandra Lopez-Pacheco, "Can a Bank Be Youth-Friendly? SCENE Is a Model Program Launched by Cineplex and Scotiabank," *National Post*, August 11, 2009, p.FP11.

22. Ellen Byron, "Wash Away Bad Hair Days—Rinse, Repeat—in the Lab as Procter & Gamble Tries to Figure Out Pantene, Fickle Shampoo Shoppers and Other Marketing Mysteries," *Wall Street Journal (Eastern Edition)*, June 30, 2010, p. D1.

23. Catherine Marshall and Gretchen B. Rossman, *Designing Qualitative Research*, 4th ed. (Thousand Oaks, CA: Sage Publications, 2006); Bruce L. Berg, *Qualitative Research Methods for the Social Sciences*, 6th ed. (Boston: Allyn & Bacon, 2006); Norman K. Denzin and Yvonna S. Lincoln, eds., *The Sage Handbook of Qualitative Research*, 3rd ed. (Thousand Oaks, CA: Sage Publications, 2005); Linda Tischler, "Every Move You Make," *Fast Company*, April 2004, pp. 73–75.

24. Mark Smyka, "Hot for Ice," *Strategy*, September 6, 1993, p. 1.

25. Paula Andruss, "Keeping Both Eyes on Quality," *Marketing News*, September 15, 2008, pp. 22–23.

26. Laurie Burkitt, "Battle for the Brain," *Forbes*, November 16, 2009, pp. 76–77.

27. Stephen Baker, "Wiser about the Web," *BusinessWeek*, March 27, 2006, pp. 54–62.

28. For more information, visit www.innte-dncl.gc.ca.

29. Michael Fielding, "Shift the Focus," *Marketing News*, September 1, 2006, pp. 18–20; Aaron Ukodie, "Worldwide Mobile Phones Reach Four Billion 2008," *allAfrica.com*, http://allafrica.com/stories/200810070774.html, October 6, 2008.

30. "Canadian Internet Use Survey," *Statistics Canada, The Daily*, May 10, 2010.

31. "The Growth of Online Market Research," *B2B International*, www.b2binternational.com/b2b-blog/2009/04/28/the-growth-of-online-market-research (viewed January 6, 2011).

32. Bradley Johnson, "Forget Phone and Mail: Online's the Best Place to Administer Surveys," *Advertising Age*, July 17, 2006, p. 23.

33. Emily Steel, "The New Focus Groups: Online Networks Proprietary Panels Help Consumer Companies Shape Products, Ads," *Wall Street Journal*, January 14, 2008.

34. Elisabeth A. Sullivan, "Delve Deeper," *Marketing News*, April 15, 2008, p. 24.

35. Kate Maddox, "The ROI of Research," *BtoB*, April 5, 2004 pp. 25, 28.

36. Bradley Johnson, "Online Methods Upend Consumer Survey Business," *Advertising Age*, July 17, 2006.

37. "Survey: Internet Should Remain Open to All," *ConsumerAffairs. com*, www.consumeraffairs.com/ news04/2006/01/internet_ survey.html, January 25, 2006; "Highlights from the National Consumers League's Survey on Consumers and Communications Technologies: Current and Future Use," www.nclnet.org/research/ utilities/telecom_highlights.htm, July 21, 2005; Catherine Arnold, "Not Done Net; New Opportunities Still Exist in Online Research," *Marketing News*, April 1, 2004, p. 17; Louella Miles, "Online, on Tap," *Marketing*, June 16, 2004, pp. 39–40; Suzy Bashford, "The Opinion Formers," *Revolution*, May 2004, pp. 42–46; Nima M. Ray and Sharon W. Tabor, "Contributing Factors; Several Issues Affect e-Research Validity," *Marketing News*, September 15, 2003, p. 50; Bob Lamons, "Eureka! Future of B-to-B Research Is Online," *Marketing News*, September 24, 2001, pp. 9–10; Burt Helm, "Online Polls: How Good Are They?" *BusinessWeek*, June 16, 2008, pp. 86–87.

38. Leonard Waverman and Kalyan Dasgupta, "When Behind is Actually Ahead," *The Globe and Mail*, March 6, 2010, p. A23.

39. The Nielsen Company, www.nielsen.com.

40. Elisabeth Sullivan, "Qual Research by the Numb3rs," *Marketing News*, September 1, 2008.

41. Deborah L. Vence, "In an Instant: More Researchers Use IM for Fast, Reliable Results," *Marketing News*, March 1, 2006, pp. 53–55.

42. Catherine Arnold, "Global Perspective: Synovate Exec Discusses Future of International Research," *Marketing News*, May 15, 2004, p. 43; Michael Erard, "For Technology, No Small World after All," *New York Times*, May 6, 2004; Deborah L. Vence, "Global Consistency: Leave It to the Experts," *Marketing News*, April 28, 2003, p. 37.

43. Michael Fielding, "Global Insights: Synovate's Chedore Discusses MR Trends," *Marketing News*, May 15, 2006, pp. 41–42.

44. Kevin J. Clancy and Peter C. Krieg, *Counterintuitive Marketing: How Great Results Come from Uncommon Sense* (New York: The Free Press, 2000).

45. Richard Newman, "Air Canada Giving Wi-Fi a Flight Test; Airlines Making Push to Bring Online World to the Skies," *Calgary Herald*, February 21, 2010, p. C5; "In-Flight Wi-Fi Access with Gogo," www.aircanada.com/en/offers/air/wifi_sep09/wifi_sep09. html (viewed January 5, 2011); Liam Britten, "Air Canada Set to Offer Wifi Access on North American Flights," *TechVibes Blog*, December 31, 2010, www.techvibes.com/blog/air-canada-set-to-offer-wifi-access-on-north-american-flights-2010-12-31 (viewed January 9, 2011).

46. See "Special Issue on Managerial Decision Making," *Marketing Science*, 18 (1999) for some contemporary perspectives; see also John D. C. Little, "Decision Support Systems for Marketing Managers," *Journal of Marketing*, 43 (Summer 1979), p. 11.

47. *Marketing News* can be found at www.marketingpower.com.

48. *The Advertising Research Foundation*, www.thearf.org/assets/ ogilvy-09; "'The Orange Underground' Cheetos," *The 2009 ARF David Ogilvy Awards: Grand Ogilvy Award Case Study*, www. thearf.org/assets/ogilvy-09 (viewed September 21, 2011).

49. Rajiv Grover and Marco Vriens, "Trusted Advisor: How It Helps Lay the Foundation for Insight," *Handbook of Marketing Research* (Thousand Oaks, CA: Sage Publications, 2006), pp. 3–17; Christine Moorman, Gerald Zaltman, and Rohit Deshpandé, "Relationships between Providers and Users of Market Research: The Dynamics of Trust within and between Organizations," *Journal of Marketing Research*, 29 (August 1992): 314–328.

50. Adapted from Arthur Shapiro, "Let's Redefine Market Research," *Brandweek*, June 21, 2004, p. 20; Kevin Ohannessian, "Star Wars: Thirty Years of Success," *Fast Company*, May 29, 2007.

51. Karen V. Beaman, Gregory R. Guy, and Donald E. Sexton, "Managing and Measuring Return on Marketing Investment," *The Conference Board Research Report R-1435-08-RR*, 2008.

52. "Report: Marketers Place Priority on Nurturing Existing Customers," http://directmag.com/roi/0301-customer-satisfaction-retention.

53. Factor TG, www.factortg.com/ideas/CMO_MPM_ Audit__cmo. pdf.

54. Paul Farris, Neil T. Bendle, Phillip E. Pfeifer, and David J. Reibstein, *Marketing Metrics: 50+ Metrics Every Executive Should Master* (Upper Saddle River, NJ: Pearson Education, 2006); John Davis, *Magic Numbers for Consumer Marketing: Key Measures to Evaluate Marketing Success* (Singapore: John Wiley & Sons, 2005).

55. Elisabeth Sullivan, "Measure Up," *Marketing News*, May 30, 2009, pp. 8–11.

56. Michael Krauss, "Which Metrics Matter Most?" *Marketing News*, February 28, 2009, p. 20.

57. Tim Ambler, *Marketing and the Bottom Line: The New Methods of Corporate Wealth*, 2nd ed. (London, England: Pearson Education, 2003).

58. Kusum L. Ailawadi, Donald R. Lehmann, and Scott A. Neslin, "Revenue Premium as an Outcome Measure of Brand Equity," *Journal of Marketing*, 67 (October 2003): 1–17.

59. Tim Ambler, *Marketing and the Bottom Line: The New Methods of Corporate Wealth*, 2nd ed. (London, England: Pearson Education, 2003).

60. Josh Bernoff, "Measure What Matters," *Marketing News, 42*, no. 20 (December 15, 2009): 22; "Kelsey MacDonald is the 2010 Young & Free Alberta Spokester for Servus Credit Union!," www.youtube. com/watch?v=xluzn9kVs0Y (viewed October 30, 2010).

61. Gerard J. Tellis, "Modeling Marketing Mix," in *Handbook of Marketing Research*, edited by Rajiv Grover and Marco Vriens(Thousand Oaks, CA: Sage Publications, 2006).

62. Laura Q. Hughes, "Econometrics Take Root," *Advertising Age*, August 5, 2002, p. S-4.

63. Jack Neff, "P&G, Clorox Rediscover Modeling," *Advertising Age*,March 29, 2004, p. 10.

64. David J. Reibstein, "Connect the Dots," *CMO Magazine*, May 2005.

65. Jeff Zabin, "Marketing Dashboards: The Visual Display of Marketing Data," *Chief Marketer*, June 26, 2006.

66. Robert S. Kaplan and David P. Norton, *The Balanced Scorecard* (Boston: Harvard Business School Press, 1996).

67. Spencer Ante, "Giving the Boss the Big Picture," *BusinessWeek*, February 13, 2006, pp. 48–50.

Chapter 5

1. Emily Wexler, "Club Sobeys Hits a Million," *Strategy*, January 2009, p. 6; Andrea McKenna, "Bank Of Montreal Strikes Deal with Canadian Grocer for No-Fee Cards," *Cardline, 10*, no. 38 (September 17, 2010): 1; "New No Fee BMO Club Sobeys MasterCard Puts Shoppers in the Points Collecting Fast Lane," www.newswire.ca/en/releases/archive/September2010/09/c8191. html (viewed September 26, 2010).

2. Robert Schieffer, *Ten Key Consumer Insights* (Mason, OH: Thomson, 2005).

3. Don Peppers and Martha Rogers, "Customers Don't Grow on Trees," *Fast Company*, July 2005, pp. 25–26.

4. For discussion of some of the issues involved, see Glen Urban, *Don't Just Relate—Advocate* (Upper Saddle River, NJ: Wharton School Publishing, 2005).

5. See Glen L. Urban and John R. Hauser, "'Listening In' to Find and Explore New Combinations of Customer Needs," *Journal of Marketing*, 68 (April 2004): 72–87.

6. "Customer Reviews Drive 196% Increase in Paid Search Revenue for Office Depot," *Bazaarvoice*, www.bazaarvoice.com/cs_rr_ adresults_ officedepot.html, 2008.

7. Glen L. Urban, "The Emerging Era of Customer Advocacy," *Sloan Management Review*, 45 (2004): 77–82.

8. Steven Burke, "Dell's vs. HP's Value," *CRN*, May 15, 2006, p. 46; David Kirkpatrick, "Dell in the Penalty Box," *Fortune*, September 18, 2006, p. 70.

9. Michael Bush, "Consumers Rate Brands That Give Best Bang for Buck," *Advertising Age*, November 3, 2008, p. 8.

10. Irwin P. Levin and Richard D. Johnson, "Estimating Price–Quality Tradeoffs Using Comparative Judgments," *Journal of Consumer Research*, 11 (June 1984): 593–600. Customer-perceived value can be measured as a difference or as a ratio. If total customer value is $20 000 and total customer cost is $16 000, then the customer-perceived value is $4000 (measured as a difference) or 1.25 (measured as a ratio). Ratios that are used to compare offers are often called *value–price ratios*.

11. Alex Taylor, "Caterpillar: Big Trucks, Big Sales, Big Attitude," *Fortune*, August 20, 2007, pp. 48–53; Tim Kelly, "Squash the Caterpillar," *Forbes*, April 21, 2008, pp. 136–141; Jeff Borden, "Eat My Dust," *Marketing News*, February 1, 2008, pp. 20–22.

12. For more on customer-perceived value, see David C. Swaddling and Charles Miller, *Customer Power* (Dublin, OH: Wellington Press, 2001).

13. Richard L. Oliver, *Satisfaction: A Behavioral Perspective on the Consumer* (New York: McGraw Hill, 1997).

14. Michael J. Lanning, *Delivering Profitable Value* (Oxford: Capstone, 1998).

15. Vikas Mittal, Eugene W. Anderson, Akin Sayrak, and Pandu Tadilamalla, "Dual Emphasis and the Long-Term Financial Impact of Customer Satisfaction," *Marketing Science, 24* (Fall 2005): 544–555.

16. Michael Tsiros, Vikas Mittal, and William T. Ross, Jr., "The Role of Attributions in Customer Satisfaction: A Reexamination," *Journal of Consumer Research*, 31 (September 2004): 476–483; for a succinct review, see Richard L. Oliver, "Customer Satisfaction Research," in *Handbook of Marketing Research*, edited byRajiv Grover and Marco Vriens(Thousand Oaks, CA: Sage Publications, 2006), pp. 569–587.

17. For some provocative analysis and discussion, see Praveen K. Kopalle and Donald R. Lehmann, "Setting Quality Expectations When Entering a Market: What Should the Promise Be?" *Marketing Science*, 25 (January–February 2006): 8–24; Susan Fournier and David Glenmick, "Rediscovering Satisfaction," *Journal of Marketing*, 63 (October 1999): 5–23.

18. Jennifer Aaker, Susan Fournier, and S. Adam Brasel, "When Good Brands Do Bad," *Journal of Consumer Research*, 31 (June 2004): 1–16; Pankaj Aggrawal, "The Effects of Brand Relationship Norms on Consumer Attitudes and Behavior," *Journal of Consumer Research*, 31 (June 2004): 87–101.

19. For in-depth discussion, see Michael D. Johnson and Anders Gustafsson, *Improving Customer Satisfaction, Loyalty, and Profit* (San Francisco: Jossey-Bass, 2000).

20. For an interesting analysis of the effects of different types of expectations, see William Boulding, Ajay Kalra, and Richard Staelin, "The Quality Double Whammy," *Marketing Science, 18* (April 1999): 463–484.

21. Renee Alexander, "Yuck: The Taste of Success," *brandchannel*, December 11, 2006, www.brandchannel.com/features_effect. asp?pf_id=345 (viewed September 27, 2010).

22 Neil A. Morgan, Eugene W. Anderson, and Vikas Mittal, "Understanding Firms' Customer Satisfaction Information Usage," *Journal of Marketing*, 69 (July 2005): 131–151.

23. Although for moderating factors, see Kathleen Seiders, Glenn B. Voss, Dhruv Grewal, and Andrea L. Godfrey, "Do Satisfied Customers Buy More? Examining Moderating Influences in a Retailing Context," *Journal of Marketing*, 69 (October 2005): 26–43.

24. See, for example, Christian Homburg, Nicole Koschate, and Wayne D. Hoyer, "Do Satisfied Customers Really Pay More? A Study of the Relationship between Customer Satisfaction and Willingness to Pay," *Journal of Marketing*, 69 (April 2005): 84–96.

25. Claes Fornell, Sunil Mithas, Forrest V. Morgeson III, and M. S. Krishnan, "Customer Satisfaction and Stock Prices: High Returns, Low Risk," *Journal of Marketing*, 70 (January 2006): 3–14. See also Thomas S. Gruca and Lopo L. Rego, "Customer Satisfaction, Cash Flow, and Shareholder Value," *Journal of Marketing*, 69 (July 2005): 115–130; Eugene W. Anderson, Claes Fornell, and Sanal K. Mazvancheryl, "Customer Satisfaction and Shareholder Value," *Journal of Marketing*, 68 (October 2004): 172–185.

26. Thomas O. Jones and W. Earl Sasser, Jr., "Why Satisfied Customers Defect," *Harvard Business Review*, November–December 1995, pp. 88–99.

27. Companies should also note that managers and salespeople can manipulate customer satisfaction ratings. They can be especially nice to customers just before the survey. They can also try to exclude unhappy customers. Another danger is that if customers know the company will go out of its way to please them, some may express high dissatisfaction in order to receive more concessions.

28. "Customer Service Projects," *DPRA*, www.dpra.com/index. cfm/m/260 (viewed January 7, 2011).

29. James C. Ward and Amy L. Ostrom, "Complaining to the Masses: The Role of Protest Framing in Customer-Created Complaint Sites," *Journal of Consumer Research*, 33 (September 2006): 220–230; Kim Hart, "Angry Customers Use Web to Shame Firms," *Washington Post*, July 5, 2006.

30. Eugene W. Anderson and Claes Fornell, "Foundations of the American Customer Satisfaction Index," *Total Quality Management, 11* (September 2000): S869–882; Claes Fornell, Michael D. Johnson, Eugene W. Anderson, Jaaesung Cha, and Barbara Everitt Bryant, "The American Customer Satisfaction Index: Nature, Purpose, and Findings," *Journal of Marketing, 60* (October 1996): 7–18.

31. Andy Holloway, "I'm Down Here, Guys," *Canadian Business Online*, October 28, 2002, www.canadianbusiness.com (viewed July 8, 2004).

32. Technical Assistance Research Programs (Tarp), U.S. Office of Consumer Affairs Study on Complaint Handling in America, 1986.

33. Frederick K. Reichheld, "The One Number You Need to Grow," *Harvard Business Review*, December 2003, pp. 46–54.

34. Stephen S. Tax and Stephen W. Brown, "Recovering and Learning from Service Failure," *Sloan Management Review*, 40 (Fall 1998): 75–88; Ruth Bolton and Tina M. Bronkhorst, "The Relationship between Customer Complaints to the Firm and Subsequent Exit Behavior," *Advances in Consumer Research*, Vol. 22 (Provo, UT: Association for Consumer Research, 1995), pp. 94–100; Roland T. Rust, Bala Subramanian, and Mark Wells, "Making Complaints a Management Tool," *Marketing Management, 1* (March 1992), pp. 40–45; Karl Albrecht and Ron Zemke, *Service America!* (Homewood, IL: Dow Jones–Irwin, 1985), pp. 6–7.

35. Christian Homburg and Andreas Fürst, "How Organizational Complaint Handling Drives Customer Loyalty: An Analysis of the Mechanistic and the Organic Approach," *Journal of Marketing*, 69 (July 2005): 95–114.

36. Philip Kotler, *Kotler on Marketing* (New York: The Free Press, 1999), pp. 21–22.

37. "Basic Concepts," *ASQ*, www.asq.org/glossary/q.html, January 16, 2010.

38. Robert D. Buzzell and Bradley T. Gale, "Quality Is King," *The PIMS Principles: Linking Strategy to Performance* (New York: The Free Press, 1987), pp. 103–134. (PIMS stands for Profit Impact of Market Strategy.)

39. Brian Hindo, "Satisfaction Not Guaranteed," *BusinessWeek*, June 19, 2006, pp. 32–36.

40. Timothy L. Keiningham, Terry G. Vavra, Lerzan Aksoy, and Henri Wallard, *Loyalty Myths* (Hoboken, NJ: John Wiley & Sons, 2005).

41. Werner J. Reinartz and V. Kumar, "The Impact of Customer Relationship Characteristics on Profitable Lifetime Duration," *Journal of Marketing*, 67 (January 2003): 77–99; Werner J. Reinartz and V. Kumar, "On the Profitability of Long-Life Customers in a Noncontractual Setting: An Empirical Investigation and Implications for Marketing," *Journal of Marketing*, 64 (October 2000): 17–35.

42. Rakesh Niraj, Mahendra Gupta, and Chakravarthi Narasimhan, "Customer Profitability in a Supply Chain," *Journal of Marketing*, 65 (July 2001): 1–16.

43. "Easier Than ABC," *Economist*, October 25, 2003, p. 56; Robert S. Kaplan and Steven R. Anderson, *Time-Driven Activity Based Costing* (Boston: Harvard Business School Press, 2007); "Activity-Based Accounting," *Economist*, June 29, 2009.

44. V. Kumar, "Customer Lifetime Value," in *Handbook of Marketing Research*, edited byRajiv Grover and Marco Vriens(Thousand Oaks, CA: Sage Publications, 2006), pp. 602–627; Sunil Gupta, Donald R. Lehmann, and Jennifer Ames Stuart, "Valuing Customers," *Journal of Marketing Research*, 61 (February 2004): 7–18; Rajkumar Venkatesan and V. Kumar, "A Customer Lifetime Value Framework for Customer Selection and Resource Allocation Strategy," *Journal of Marketing*, 68 (October 2004): 106–125.

45. V. Kumar, "Profitable Relationships," *Marketing Research*, 18 (Fall 2006): 41–46.

46. For some recent analysis and discussion, see Michael Haenlein, Andreas M. Kaplan, and Detlef Schoder, "Valuing the Real Option of Abandoning Unprofitable Customers When Calculating Customer Lifetime Value," *Journal of Marketing*, 70 (July 2006): 5–20; Teck-Hua Ho, Young-Hoon Park, and Yong-Pin Zhou, "Incorporating Satisfaction into Customer Value Analysis: Optimal Investment in Lifetime Value," *Marketing Science*, 25 (May–June 2006): 260–277; Peter S. Fader, Bruce G. S. Hardie, and Ka Lok Lee, "RFM and CLV: Using Iso-Value Curves for Customer Base Analysis," *Journal of Marketing Research*, 62 (November 2005): 415–430; V. Kumar, Rajkumar Venkatesan, Tim Bohling, and Denise Beckmann, "The Power of CLV: Managing Customer Lifetime Value at IBM," *Marketing Science*, 27 (2008): 585–599.

47. Nicole E. Coviello, Roderick J. Brodie, Peter J. Danaher, and Wesley J. Johnston, "How Firms Relate to Their Markets: An Empirical Examination of Contemporary Marketing Practices," *Journal of Marketing*, 66 (July 2002): 33–46. For a comprehensive set of articles from a variety of perspectives on brand relationships, see Deborah J. MacInnis, C. Whan Park, and Joseph R. Preister, eds., *Handbook of Brand Relationships* (Armonk, NY: M. E. Sharpe, 2009).

48. For an up-to-date view of academic perspectives, see the articles contained in the "Special Section on Customer Relationship Management," *Journal of Marketing*, 69 (October 2005). For a study of the processes involved, see Werner Reinartz, Manfred Kraft, and Wayne D. Hoyer, "The Customer Relationship Management Process: Its Measurement and Impact on Performance," *Journal of Marketing Research*, 61 (August 2004): 293–305.

49. Nora A. Aufreiter, David Elzinga, and Jonathan W. Gordon, "Better Branding," *The McKinsey Quarterly*, 4 (2003): 29–39.

50. Michael J. Lanning, *Delivering Profitable Value* (New York: Basic Books, 1998).

51. Susan Stellin, "For Many Online Companies, Customer Service Is Hardly a Priority," *New York Times*, February 19, 2001; Michelle Johnson, "Getting Ready for the Onslaught," *Boston Globe*, November 4, 1999.

52. Julie Jargon, "Domino's IT Staff Delivers Slick Site, Ordering System," *Wall Street Journal*, November 24, 2009; Bruce Horovitz, "Where's Your Domino's Pizza? Track It Online," *USA Today*, January 30, 2008; *Domino's Pizza*, www.dominosbiz.com, January 16, 2010.

53. James H. Donnelly, Jr., Leonard L. Berry, and Thomas W. Thompson, *Marketing Financial Services—A Strategic Vision* (Homewood, IL: Dow Jones–Irwin, 1985), p. 113.

54. "North West Company Fund Announces First Quarter Earnings and a Quarterly Distribution," *Marketwire*, June 10, 2010, www.marketwire.com/press-release/North-West-Company-Fund-Announces-First-Quarter-Earnings-Quarterly-Distribution-TSX-NWF.UN-1274294.htm (viewed September 27, 2010).

55. Seth Godin, *Permission Marketing: Turning Strangers into Friends, and Friends into Customers* (New York: Simon & Schuster, 1999). See also Susan Fournier, Susan Dobscha, and David Mick, "Preventing the Premature Death of Relationship Marketing," *Harvard Business Review*, January–February 1998, pp. 42–51.

56. Don Peppers and Martha Rogers, *One-to-One B2B: Customer Development Strategies for the Business-to-Business World* (New York: Doubleday, 2001); Peppers and Rogers, *The One-to-One Future: Building Relationships One Customer at a Time* (London, England: Piatkus Books, 1996); Peppers and Rogers, *The One-to-One Manager: Real-World Lessons in Customer Relationship Management* (New York: Doubleday, 1999); Don Peppers, Martha Rogers, and Bob Dorf, *The One-to-One Fieldbook: The Complete Toolkit for Implementing a One-to-One Marketing Program* (New York: Bantam, 1999); Peppers and Rogers, *Enterprise One to One: Tools for Competing in the Interactive Age* (New York: Currency, 1997).

57. Mark Rechtin, "Aston Martin Woos Customers One by One," *Automotive News*, March 28, 2005.

58. Stuart Elliott, "Letting Consumers Control Marketing: Priceless," *New York Times*, October 9, 2006; Todd Wasserman and Jim Edwards, "Marketers' New World Order," *Brandweek*, October 9, 2006, pp. 4–6; Heather Green and Robert D. Hof, "Your Attention Please," *BusinessWeek*, July 24, 2006, pp. 48–53; Brian Sternberg, "The Marketing Maze," *Wall Street Journal*, July 10, 2006.

59. Rob Walker, "Amateur Hour, Web Style," *Fast Company*, October 2007, p. 87.

60. Ben McConnell and Jackie Huba, "Learning to Leverage the Lunatic Fringe," *Point*, July–August 2006, pp. 14–15; Michael Krauss, "Work to Convert Customers into Evangelists," *Marketing News*, December 15, 2006, p. 6; Ben McConnell and Jackie Huba, *Creating Customer Evangelists: How Loyal Customers Become a Loyal Sales Force* (New York: Kaplan Business, 2003).

61. Jonah Bloom, "The New Realities of a Low Trust Marketing World," *Advertising Age*, February 13, 2006.

62. Mylene Mangalindan, "New Marketing Style: Clicks and Mortar," *Wall Street Journal*, December 21, 2007, p. B5.

63. Nick Wingfield, "High Scores Matter to Game Makers, Too," *Wall Street Journal*, September 20, 2007, p. B1.

64. Candice Choi, "Bloggers Serve Up Opinions," *Associated Press*, March 23, 2008.

65. Elisabeth Sullivan, "Consider Your Source," *Marketing News*, February 15, 2008, pp. 16–19; Mylene Mangalindan, "Web Stores Tap Product Reviews," *Wall Street Journal*, September 11, 2007.

66. Erick Schonfeld, "Rethinking the Recommendation Engine," *Business 2.0*, July 2007, pp. 40–43.

67. Michael Lewis, "Customer Acquisition Promotions and Customer Asset Value," *Journal of Marketing Research*, 63 (May 2006): 195–203.

68. Hamish Pringle and Peter Field, "Why Customer Loyalty Isn't as Valuable as You Think," *Advertising Age*, March 23, 2009, p. 22.

69. "SPC Card Launches to Soaring Membership and New Retail Partners," *Canada Newswire*, August 26, 2010.

70. Werner Reinartz, Jacquelyn S. Thomas, and V. Kumar, "Balancing Acquisition and Retention Resources to Maximize Customer Profitability," *Journal of Marketing*, 69 (January 2005): 63–79.

71. "Service Invention to Increase Retention," *CMO Council*, August 3, 2009, www.cmocouncil.org.

72. Frederick F. Reichheld, "Learning from Customer Defections," *Harvard Business Review*, March–April 1996, pp. 56–69.

73. Frederick F. Reichheld, *Loyalty Rules* (Boston: Harvard Business School Press, 2001); Frederick F. Reichheld, *The Loyalty Effect* (Boston: Harvard Business School Press, 1996).

74. Michael D. Johnson and Fred Selnes, "Diversifying Your Customer Portfolio," *MIT Sloan Management Review*, 46 (Spring 2005): 11–14.

75. Tom Ostenon, *Customer Share Marketing* (Upper Saddle River, NJ: Prentice Hall, 2002); Alan W. H. Grant and Leonard A. Schlesinger, "Realize Your Customer's Full Profit Potential," *Harvard Business Review*, September–October 1995, pp. 59–72.

76. Gail McGovern and Youngme Moon, "Companies and the Customers Who Hate Them," *Harvard Business Review*, June 2007, pp. 78–84.

77. Elisabeth A. Sullivan, "Just Say No," *Marketing News*, April 15, 2008, p. 17.

78. Sunil Gupta and Carl F. Mela, "What Is a Free Customer Worth," *Harvard Business Review*, November 2008, pp. 102–109.

79. Leonard L. Berry and A. Parasuraman, *Marketing Services: Computing through Quality* (New York: The Free Press, 1991), pp. 136–142. For an academic examination in a business-to-business context, see Robert W. Palmatier, Srinath Gopalakrishna, and Mark B. Houston, "Returns on Business-to-Business Relationship Marketing Investments: Strategies for Leveraging Profits," *Marketing Science*, 25 (September–October 2006): 477–493.

80. Frederick F. Reichheld, "Learning from Customer Defections," *Harvard Business Review*, March 3, 2009, pp. 56–69.

81. "Gluten-Free and Thin Crust Highlights Innovation in Boston Pizza's New Menu," *Canadian Newswire*, June 7, 2010.

82. Maxine Clark, "Ask Maxine Clark: Founder, Build-A-Bear Workshop," *Inc.*, 30, no. 7 (July 2008), p. 67.

83. Utpal M. Dholakia, "How Consumer Self-Determination Influences Relational Marketing Outcomes: Evidence from Longitudinal Field Studies," *Journal of Marketing Research*, 43 (February 2006): 109–120.

84. Allison Enright, "Serve Them Right," *Marketing News*, May 1, 2006, pp. 21–22.

85. For a review, see Grahame R. Dowling and Mark Uncles, "Do Customer Loyalty Programs Really Work?" *Sloan Management Review*, 38 (Summer 1997): 71–82.

86. Thomas Lee, "Retailers Look for a Hook," *St. Louis Post-Dispatch*, December 4, 2004.

87. Joseph C. Nunes and Xavier Drèze, "Feeling Superior: The Impact of Loyalty Program Structure on Consumers' Perception of Status," *Journal of Consumer Research*, 35 (April 2009): 890–905; Joseph C. Nunes and Xavier Drèze, "Your Loyalty Program Is Betraying You," *Harvard Business Review*, April 2006, pp. 124–131.

88. Geoff Kirbyson, "Average Member of Gasoline Co-Op in Line for $162 Payout This Year," *Winnipeg Free Press*, February 5, 2010, p. A11.

89. Jacquelyn S. Thomas, Robert C. Blattberg, and Edward J. Fox, "Recapturing Lost Customers," *Journal of Marketing Research*, 61 (February 2004): 31–45.

90. Werner Reinartz and V. Kumar, "The Impact of Customer Relationship Characteristics on Profitable Lifetime Duration," *Journal of Marketing*, 67 (January 2003): 77–99; Werner Reinartz and V. Kumar, "The Mismanagement of Customer Loyalty," *Harvard Business Review*, July 2002, pp. 86–97.

91. V. Kumar, Rajkumar Venkatesan, and Werner Reinartz, "Knowing What to Sell, When, and to Whom," *Harvard Business Review*, March 2006, pp. 131–137.

92. Jeff Zabin, "The Importance of Being Analytical," *Brandweek*, July 24, 2006, p. 21; Stephen Baker, "Math Will Rock Your World," *BusinessWeek*, January 23, 2006, pp. 54–62; Michelle Kessler and Byron Acohido, "Data Miners Dig a Little Deeper," *USA Today*, July 11, 2006.

93. Burt Heim, "Getting Inside the Customer's Mind," *BusinessWeek*, September 22, 2008, p. 88; Mike Duff, "Dunnhumby Complicates Outlook for Tesco, Kroger, Wal-Mart," *bnet.com*, January 13, 2009; Sarah Mahoney, "Macy's Readies New Marketing Strategy, Hires Dunnhumby," *Marketing Daily*, August 14, 2008.

94. Christopher R. Stephens and R. Sukumar, "An Introduction to Data Mining," in *Handbook of Marketing Research*, edited by Rajiv Grover and Marco Vriens(Thousand Oaks, CA: Sage Publications, 2006), pp. 455–486; Pang-Ning Tan, Michael Steinbach, and Vipin Kumar, *Introduction to Data Mining* (Upper Saddle River, NJ: Addison Wesley, 2005); Michael J. A. Berry and Gordon S. Linoff, *Data Mining Techniques: For Marketing, Sales, and Customer Relationship Management*, 2nd ed. (Hoboken, NJ: Wiley Computer, 2004); James Lattin, Doug Carroll, and Paul Green, *Analyzing Multivariate Data* (Florence, KY: Thomson Brooks/Cole, 2003).

95. George S. Day, "Creating a Superior Customer-Relating Capability," *Sloan Management Review*, 44 (Spring 2003): 77–82.

96. Ibid.; George S. Day, "Creating a Superior Customer-Relating Capability," *MSI Report No. 03–101* (Cambridge, MA: Marketing Science Institute, 2003); "Why Some Companies Succeed at CRM (and Many Fail)," *Knowledge at Wharton*, http://knowledge. wharton.upenn. edu, January 15, 2003.

97. Werner Reinartz and V. Kumar, "The Mismanagement of Customer Loyalty," *Harvard Business Review*, July 2002, pp. 86–94; Susan M. Fournier, Susan Dobscha, and David Glen Mick, "Preventing the Premature Death of Relationship Marketing," *Harvard Business Review*, January–February 1998, pp. 42–51.

98. Jon Swartz, "EBay Faithful Expect Loyalty in Return," *USA Today*, July 1, 2002.

Chapter 6

1. "VANOC Thanks Canadians, Fans, for Wearing Hearts on their Hands," *Canada Newswire*, March 5, 2010; "Hudson's Bay Company Combines Canadian Heritage, Sport and Olympic Spirit for Canadian Olympic Team Parade Uniforms at Vancouver 2010 Olympic Winter Games Closing Ceremony," *Canada Newswire*, February 28, 2010; Dana Flavelle, "Olympic Sponsors Strike Gold; While It's Too Early to Say Who Will Bring Home the Bulk of the Corporate Medals, Experts Say Most Companies That Gambled on the Games Are Now Poised for a Payoff," *Toronto Star*, February 25, 2010, p. B1.

2. Michael R. Solomon, *Consumer Behavior: Buying, Having, and Being*, 9th ed. (Upper Saddle River, NJ: Prentice Hall, 2011).

3. Leon G. Schiffman and Leslie Lazar Kanuk, *Consumer Behavior*, 10th ed. (Upper Saddle River, NJ: Prentice Hall, 2010).

4. Shawna Steinberg, "Oh Canada in the Spotlight," *Marketing Magazine*, November 2, 1998, pp. 10–11.

5. Dana Flavelle, "17-Store Chain a Tasty Morsel with Huge Potential for Gain: 'Ethnic Market Is Vast... Our Objective Is to Be No. 1 Player,'" *Toronto Star*, July 25, 2009, p. B1; Jennifer Campbell, "Asian Specialist *T&T* Drives *Loblaw* Profits: Acquisition Helps Fuel Q1 26% Increase," *Calgary Herald*, May 15, 2010, p. C6.

6. For some classic perspectives, see Richard P. Coleman, "The Continuing Significance of Social Class to Marketing," *Journal of Consumer Research*, 10 (December 1983): 265–280; Richard P. Coleman and Lee P. Rainwater, *Social Standing in America: New Dimension of Class* (New York: Basic Books, 1978).

7. The Centre for Canadian Studies, *The Political Voice of Canadian Regional Identities*, 2001, www.mta.ca/faculty/arts/canadian_studies/english/about/study_guide/regional/index.html (viewed October 16, 2004).

8. Leon G. Schiffman and Leslie Lazar Kanuk, *Consumer Behavior*, 10th ed. (Upper Saddle River, NJ: Prentice Hall, 2010).

9. Kimberly L. Allers, "Retail's Rebel Yell," *Fortune*, November 10, 2003, p. 137; Kate Rockwood, "Rock Solid," *Fast Company*, September 2009, pp. 44–48.

10. Elizabeth S. Moore, William L. Wilkie, and Richard J. Lutz, "Passing the Torch: Intergenerational Influences as a Source of Brand Equity," *Journal of Marketing, 66* (April 2002): 17–37; Robert Boutilier, "Pulling the Family's Strings," *American Demographics*, August 1993, pp. 44–48; David J. Burns, "Husband-Wife Innovative Consumer Decision Making: Exploring the Effect of Family Power," *Psychology & Marketing* (May–June 1992), pp. 175–89; Rosann L. Spiro, "Persuasion in Family Decision Making," *Journal of Consumer Research, 9* (March 1983): 393–402. For cross-cultural comparisons of husband–wife buying roles, see John B. Ford, Michael S. LaTour, and Tony L. Henthorne, "Perception of Marital Roles in Purchase-Decision Processes: A Cross-Cultural Study," *Journal of the Academy of Marketing Science, 23* (Spring 1995): 120–131.

11. Kay M. Palan and Robert E. Wilkes, "Adolescent-Parent Interaction in Family Decision Making," *Journal of Consumer Research, 24* (March 1997): 159–169; Sharon E. Beatty and Salil Talpade, "Adolescent Influence in Family Decision Making: A Replication with Extension," *Journal of Consumer Research, 21* (September 1994): 332–341.

12. Lyle V. Harris, "Men Rule the Aisles," *The Globe and Mail*, May 6, 1999, p. C5.

13. Chenting Su, Edward F. Fern, and Keying Ye, "A Temporal Dynamic Model of Spousal Family Purchase-Decision Behavior," *Journal of Marketing Research, 40* (August 2003): 268–281.

14. Hillary Chura, "Failing to Connect: Marketing Messages for Women Fall Short," *Advertising Age*, September 23, 2002, pp. 13–14.

15. Valentyna Melnyk, Stijn M. J. van Osselaer, and Tammo H. A. Bijmolt, "Are Women More Loyal Customers Than Men? Gender Differences in Loyalty to Firms and Individual Service Providers," *Journal of Marketing, 73* (July 2009): 82–96.

16. Michele Miller, *The Soccer Mom Myth* (Austin, TX: Wizard Academy Press, 2008).

17. Susan Krashinsky, "SexTV to Get a Female-Friendly Makeover," *The Globe and Mail*, February 10, 2010, p. B3; "About Corus," *Corus Entertainment*, 2010, www.corusent.com (viewed September 14, 2010); "W Movies," *Corus Entertainment*, 2010, www.corusent.com/home/Television/TelevisionBrands/tabid/1737/Default.aspx?BrandID=95 (viewed September 12, 2010).

18. "YouthPulse: The Definitive Study of Today's Youth Generation," *Harris Interactive*, www.harrisinteractive.com, January 29, 2010.

19. Dana Markow, "Today's Youth: Understanding Their Importance and Influence," *Trends & Tudes, 7*, no. 1, www.harrisinteractive.com, February 2008.

20. Deborah Roedder John, "Consumer Socialization of Children: A Retrospective Look at Twenty-Five Years of Research," *Journal of Consumer Research, 26* (December 1999): 183–213; Lan Nguyen Chaplin and Deborah Roedder John, "The Development of Self-Brand Connections in Children and Adolescents," *Journal of Consumer Research, 32* (June 2005): 119–129; Lan Nguyen Chaplin and Deborah Roedder John, "Growing Up in a Material World: Age Differences in Materialism in Children and Adolescents," *Journal of Consumer Research, 34* (December 2007): 480–493.

21. Mary Orms, "Walmart Potions Promise to Help Keep Tweens Young: 'Anti-aging' Makeup for Girls Raises U.S. Eyebrows," *Toronto Star*, February 3, 2011, p. A1.

22. "Household Size, by Province and Territory," *Statistics Canada*, October 3, 2007.

23. Rex Y. Du and Wagner A. Kamakura, "Household Life Cycles and Lifestyles in the United States," *Journal of Marketing Research, 48* (February 2006): 121–132; Lawrence Lepisto, "A Life Span Perspective of Consumer Behavior," in *Advances in Consumer Research*, Vol. 12, edited by Elizabeth Hirshman and Morris Holbrook (Provo, UT: Association for Consumer Research, 1985), p. 47; also see Gail Sheehy, *New Passages: Mapping Your Life across Time* (New York: Random House, 1995).

24. Harold H. Kassarjian and Mary Jane Sheffet, "Personality and Consumer Behavior: An Update," in *Perspectives in Consumer Behavior*, edited byHarold H. Kassarjian and Thomas S. Robertson(Glenview, IL: Scott Foresman, 1981), pp. 160–180.

25. Jennifer Aaker, "Dimensions of Measuring Brand Personality," *Journal of Marketing Research, 34* (August 1997): 347–356.

26. Jennifer L. Aaker, Veronica Benet-Martinez, and Jordi Garolera, "Consumption Symbols as Carriers of Culture: A Study of Japanese and Spanish Brand Personality Constructs," *Journal of Personality and Social Psychology, 81* (March 2001): 492–508.

27. Yongjun Sung and Spencer F. Tinkham, "Brand Personality Structures in the United States and Korea: Common and Culture-Specific Factors," *Journal of Consumer Psychology, 15* (December 2005): 334–350.

28. M. Joseph Sirgy, "Self Concept in Consumer Behavior: A Critical Review," *Journal of Consumer Research, 9* (December 1982): 287–300.

29. Timothy R. Graeff, "Consumption Situations and the Effects of Brand Image on Consumers' Brand Evaluations," *Psychology & Marketing, 14* (January 1997): 49–70; Timothy R. Graeff, "Image Congruence Effects on Product Evaluations: The Role of Self-Monitoring and Public/Private Consumption," *Psychology & Marketing, 13* (August 1996): 481–499.

30. Jennifer L. Aaker, "The Malleable Self: The Role of Self-Expression in Persuasion," *Journal of Marketing Research, 36* (February 1999): 45–57.

31. LOHAS website, www.lohas.com/about.html (viewed March 20, 2008); Amy Cortese, "They Care about the World (and They Shop Too)," *New York Times*, July 20, 2003, pp. 3–4.

32. Noel C. Paul, "Meal Kits in Home," *Christian Science Monitor*, June 9, 2003, p. 13; Anne D'Innocenzio, "Frugal Times: Hamburger Helper, Kool-Aid in Advertising Limelight," *Seattle Times*, April 29, 2009.

33. For a review of academic research on consumer behaviour, see Barbara Loken, "Consumer Psychology: Categorization, Inferences, Affect, and Persuasion," *Annual Review of Psychology, 57* (2006): 453–495. To learn more about how consumer behaviour theory can be applied to policy decisions, see "Special Issue on Helping Consumers Help Themselves: Improving the Quality of Judgments and Choices," *Journal of Public Policy & Marketing, 25* (Spring 2006).

34. Thomas J. Reynolds and Jonathan Gutman, "Laddering Theory, Method, Analysis, and Interpretation," *Journal of Advertising Research*, February–March 1988, pp. 11–34; Thomas J. Reynolds and Jerry C. Olson, *Understanding Consumer Decision-Making: The Means-Ends Approach to Marketing and Advertising* (Mahwah, NJ: Lawrence Erlbaum, 2001); Brian Wansink, "Using Laddering to Understand and Leverage a Brand's Equity," *Qualitative Market Research, 6* (2003).

35. Ernest Dichter, *Handbook of Consumer Motivations* (New York: McGraw-Hill, 1964).

36. Jan Callebaut et al., *The Naked Consumer: The Secret of Motivational Research in Global Marketing* (Antwerp, Belgium: Censydiam Institute, 1994).

37. Clotaire Rapaille, "Marketing to the Reptilian Brain," *Forbes*, July 3, 2006; Clotaire Rapaille, *The Culture Code* (New York: Broadway Books, 2007).

38. Melanie Wells, "Mind Games," *Forbes*, September 1, 2003, p. 70.

39. Abraham Maslow, *Motivation and Personality* (New York: Harper & Row, 1954), pp. 80–106. For an interesting business application, see Chip Conley, *Peak: How Great Companies Get Their Mojo from Maslow* (San Francisco: Jossey Bass, 2007).

40. Frederick Herzberg, *Work and the Nature of Man* (Cleveland: William Collins, 1966); Thierry and Koopman-Iwema, "Motivation and Satisfaction," in *A Handbook of Work and Organizational Psychology*, edited by P. J. D. Drenth, H. Thierry, P. J. Willems,

and C. J. de Wolff (East Sussex, UK: Psychology Press, 1984), pp. 141–142.

41. Bernard Berelson and Gary A. Steiner, *Human Behavior: An Inventory of Scientific Findings* (New York: Harcourt Brace Jovanovich, 1964), p. 88.

42. J. Edward Russo, Margaret G. Meloy, and Victoria Husted Medvec, "The Distortion of Product Information during Brand Choice," *Journal of Marketing Research*, 35 (November 1998): 438–452.

43. Leslie de Chernatony and Simon Knox, "How an Appreciation of Consumer Behavior Can Help in Product Testing," *Journal of Market Research Society*, July 1990, p. 333. See also Chris Janiszewski and Stiju M. J. Osselar, "A Connectionist Model of Brand–Quality Association," *Journal of Marketing Research*, 37 (August 2000): 331–351.

44. Florida's Chris Janiszewski has conducted fascinating research looking at preconscious processing effects. See Chris Janiszewski, "Preattentive Mere Exposure Effects," *Journal of Consumer Research*, 20 (December 1993): 376–392, as well as some of his earlier and subsequent research. For more perspectives, see John A. Bargh and Tanya L. Chartrand, "The Unbearable Automaticity of Being," *American Psychologist*, 54 (1999): 462–479 and the research programs of both authors. For lively academic debate, see the "Research Dialogue" section of the July 2005 issue of the *Journal of Consumer Psychology*.

45. See Timothy E. Moore, "Subliminal Advertising: What You See Is What You Get," *Journal of Marketing*, 46 (Spring 1982): 38–47 for an early classic discussion; and Andrew B. Aylesworth, Ronald C. Goodstein, and Ajay Kalra, "Effect of Archetypal Embeds on Feelings: An Indirect Route to Affecting Attitudes?" *Journal of Advertising*, 28 (Fall 1999): 73–81 for additional discussion.

46. Patricia Winters Lauro, "An Emotional Connection between Sleeper and Mattress," *New York Times*, July 5, 2007.

47. Ellen Byron, "Tide, Woolite Tout Their Fashion Sense," *Wall Street Journal*, March 11, 2009.

48. Robert S. Wyer, Jr., and Thomas K. Srull, "Person Memory and Judgment," *Psychological Review*, 96 (January 1989): 58–83; John R. Anderson, *The Architecture of Cognition* (Cambridge, MA: Harvard University Press, 1983).

49. For additional discussion, see John G. Lynch, Jr., and Thomas K. Srull, "Memory and Attentional Factors in Consumer Choice: Concepts and Research Methods," *Journal of Consumer Research*, 9 (June 1982): 18–36; and Joseph W. Alba, J. Wesley Hutchinson, and John G. Lynch, Jr., "Memory and Decision Making," in *Handbook of Consumer Theory and Research*, edited byHarold H. Kassarjian and Thomas S. Robertson(Englewood Cliffs, NJ: Prentice Hall, 1992), pp. 1–49.

50. Robert S. Lockhart, Fergus I. M. Craik, and Larry Jacoby, "Depth of Processing, Recognition, and Recall," in *Recall and Recognition*, edited byJohn Brown(New York: John Wiley & Sons, 1976); Fergus I. M. Craik and Endel Tulving, "Depth of Processing and the Retention of Words in Episodic Memory," *Journal of Experimental Psychology*, 104 (September 1975): 268–294; Fergus I. M. Craik and Robert S. Lockhart, "Levels of Processing: A Framework for Memory Research," *Journal of Verbal Learning and Verbal Behavior*, 11 (1972): 671–684.

51. Leonard M. Lodish, Magid Abraham, Stuart Kalmenson, Jeanne Livelsberger, Beth Lubetkin, Bruce Richardson, and Mary Ellen Stevens, "How T.V. Advertising Works: A Meta-Analysis of 389 Real World Split Cable T.V. Advertising Experiments," *Journal of Marketing Research*, 32 (May 1995): 125–139.

52. Elizabeth F. Loftus and Gregory R. Loftus, "On the Permanence of Stored Information in the Human Brain," *American Psychologist*, 35 (May 1980): 409–420.

53. For a comprehensive review of the academic literature on decision making, see J. Edward Russo and Kurt A. Carlson, "Individual Decision Making," in *Handbook of Marketing*, edited byBart Weitz and Robin Wensley(London, England: Sage Publications, 2002), pp. 372–408.

54. Benson Shapiro, V. Kasturi Rangan, and John Sviokla, "Staple Yourself to an Order," *Harvard Business Review*, July–August 1992, pp. 113–122. See also Carrie M. Heilman, Douglas Bowman, and Gordon P. Wright, "The Evolution of Brand Preferences and Choice Behaviors of Consumers New to a Market," *Journal of Marketing Research*, 37 (May 2000): 139–155.

55. Marketing scholars have developed several models of the consumer buying process through the years. See Mary Frances Luce, James R. Bettman, and John W. Payne, *Emotional Decisions: Tradeoff Difficulty and Coping in Consumer Choice* (Chicago: University of Chicago Press, 2001); James F. Engel, Roger D. Blackwell, and Paul W. Miniard, *Consumer Behavior*, 8th ed. (Fort Worth, TX: Dryden, 1994); John A. Howard and Jagdish N. Sheth, *The Theory of Buyer Behavior* (New York: John Wiley & Sons, 1969).

56. William P. Putsis, Jr., and Narasimhan Srinivasan, "Buying or Just Browsing? The Duration of Purchase Deliberation," *Journal of Marketing Research*, 31 (August 1994): 393–402.

57. Chem L. Narayana and Rom J. Markin, "Consumer Behavior and Product Performance: An Alternative Conceptualization," *Journal of Marketing*, 39 (October 1975): 1–6. See also Lee G. Cooper and Akihiro Inoue, "Building Market Structures from Consumer Preferences," *Journal of Marketing Research*, 33 (August 1996): 293–306; and Wayne S. DeSarbo and Kamel Jedidi, "The Spatial Representation of Heterogeneous Consideration Sets," *Marketing Science*, 14 (Summer 1995): 326–342.

58. For a market-structure study of the hierarchy of attributes in the coffee market, see Dipak Jain, Frank M. Bass, and Yu-Min Chen, "Estimation of Latent Class Models with Heterogeneous Choice Probabilities: An Application to Market Structuring," *Journal of Marketing Research*, 27 (February 1990): 94–101. For an application of means-end chain analysis to global markets, see Frenkel Ter Hofstede, Jan-Benedict E. M. Steenkamp, and Michel Wedel, "International Market Segmentation Based on Consumer–Product Relations," *Journal of Marketing Research*, 36 (February 1999): 1–17.

59. Virginia Postrel, "The Lessons of the Grocery Shelf Also Have Something to Say about Affirmative Action," *New York Times*, January 30, 2003.

60. David Krech, Richard S. Crutchfield, and Egerton L. Ballachey, *Individual in Society* (New York: McGraw-Hill, 1962), Ch. 2.

61. Leigh McAlister, "Choosing Multiple Items from a Product Class," *Journal of Consumer Research*, 6 (December 1979): 213–224; Paul E. Green and Yoram Wind, *Multiattribute Decisions in Marketing: A Measurement Approach* (Hinsdale, IL: Dryden, 1973), Ch. 2; Richard J. Lutz, "The Role of Attitude Theory in Marketing," in *Perspectives in Consumer Behavior*, edited byH. Kassarjian and T. Robertson(Lebanon, IN: Scott Foresman, 1981): 317–339.

62. This expectancy-value model was originally developed by Martin Fishbein, "Attitudes and Prediction of Behavior," in *Readings in Attitude Theory and Measurement*, edited by Martin Fishbein (New York: John Wiley & Sons, 1967), pp. 477–492. For a critical review, see Paul W. Miniard and Joel B. Cohen, "An Examination of the Fishbein-Ajzen Behavioral-Intentions Model's Concepts and Measures," *Journal of Experimental Social Psychology*, May 1981, pp. 309–339.

63. Michael R. Solomon, *Consumer Behavior: Buying, Having, and Being*, 9th ed. (Upper Saddle River, NJ: Prentice Hall, 2011).

64. James R. Bettman, Eric J. Johnson, and John W. Payne, "Consumer Decision Making," in *Handbook of Consumer Theory and Research*, edited byKassarjian and Robertson(Upper Saddle River, NJ: Prentice Hall, 1991), pp. 50–84.

65. Jagdish N. Sheth, "An Investigation of Relationships among Evaluative Beliefs, Affect, Behavioral Intention, and Behavior," in *Consumer Behavior: Theory and Application*, edited byJohn U. Farley, John A. Howard, and L. Winston Ring(Boston: Allyn & Bacon, 1974), pp. 89–114.

66. Martin Fishbein, "Attitudes and Prediction of Behavior," in *Readings in Attitude Theory and Measurement*, edited by Martin Fishbein (New York: John Wiley & Sons, 1967), pp. 477–492.

67. Andrew Hampp, "How 'Paranormal Activity,' Hit It Big," *Advertising Age*, October 12, 2009.

68. Margaret C. Campbell and Ronald C. Goodstein, "The Moderating Effect of Perceived Risk on Consumers' Evaluations of Product Incongruity: Preference for the Norm," *Journal of Consumer Research, 28* (December 2001): 439–449; Grahame R. Dowling, "Perceived Risk," in *The Elgar Companion to Consumer Research and Economic Psychology*, edited byPeter E. Earl and Simon Kemp(Cheltenham, UK: Edward Elgar, 1999), pp. 419–424; Grahame R. Dowling, "Perceived Risk: The Concept and Its Measurement," *Psychology and Marketing, 3* (Fall 1986): 193–210; James R. Bettman, "Perceived Risk and Its Components: A Model and Empirical Test," *Journal of Marketing Research, 10* (May 1973): 184–190; Raymond A. Bauer, "Consumer Behavior as Risk Taking," in *Risk Taking and Information Handling in Consumer Behavior*, edited byDonald F. Cox(Boston: Division of Research, Harvard Business School, 1967).

69. Richard L. Oliver, "Customer Satisfaction Research," in *Handbook of Marketing Research*, edited byRajiv Grover and Marco Vriens (Thousand Oaks, CA: Sage Publications, 2006), pp. 569–587.

70. Ralph L. Day, "Modeling Choices among Alternative Responses to Dissatisfaction," *Advances in Consumer Research, 11* (1984): 496–499. Also see Philip Kotler and Murali K. Mantrala, "Flawed Products: Consumer Responses and Marketer Strategies," *Journal of Consumer Marketing*, Summer 1985, pp. 27–36.

71. Albert O. Hirschman, *Exit, Voice, and Loyalty* (Cambridge, MA: Harvard University Press, 1970).

72. John D. Cripps, "Heuristics and Biases in Timing the Replacement of Durable Products," *Journal of Consumer Research, 21* (September 1994): 304–318.

73. Ben Paytner, "From Trash to Cash," *Fast Company*, February 2009, p. 44.

74. Richard E. Petty, *Communication and Persuasion: Central and Peripheral Routes to Attitude Change* (New York: Springer-Verlag, 1986); Richard E. Petty and John T. Cacioppo, *Attitudes and Persuasion: Classic and Contemporary Approaches* (New York: McGraw-Hill, 1981).

75. For an overview of some of the issues involved, see James R. Bettman, Mary Frances Luce, and John W. Payne, "Constructive Consumer Choice Processes," *Journal of Consumer Research, 25* (December 1998), pp. 187–217; and Itamar Simonson, "Getting Closer to Your Customers by Understanding How They Make Choices," *California Management Review, 35* (Summer 1993), pp. 68–84. For examples of classic studies in this area, see the following: Dan Ariely and Ziv Carmon, "Gestalt Characteristics of Experiences: The Defining Features of Summarized Events," *Journal of Behavioral Decision Making, 13* (April 2000), pp. 191–201; Ravi Dhar and Klaus Wertenbroch, "Consumer Choice between Hedonic and Utilitarian Goods," *Journal of Marketing Research, 37* (February 2000), pp. 60–71; Itamar Simonson and Amos Tversky, "Choice in Context: Tradeoff Contrast and Extremeness Aversion," *Journal of Marketing Research, 29* (August 1992), pp. 281–295; Itamar Simonson, "The Effects of Purchase Quantity and Timing on Variety-Seeking Behavior," *Journal of Marketing Research, 27* (May 1990): 150–162.

76. Leon Schiffman and Leslie Kanuk, *Consumer Behavior*, 10th ed. (Upper Saddle River, NJ: Prentice Hall, 2010); Wayne D. Hoyer and Deborah J. MacInnis, *Consumer Behavior*, 5th ed. (Cincinnati, OH: South-Western College Publishing, 2009).

77. For a detailed review of the practical significance of consumer decision making, see Itamar Simonson, "Get Close to Your Customers by Understanding How They Make Their Choices," *California Management Review, 35* (Summer 1993), pp. 78–79.

78. Richard H. Thaler and Cass R. Sunstein, *Nudge: Improving Decisions about Health, Wealth, and Happiness* (New York: Penguin, 2009); Michael Krauss, "A Nudge in the Right Direction," *Marketing News*, March 30, 2009, p. 20.

79. See Richard H. Thaler, "Mental Accounting and Consumer Choice," *Marketing Science, 4* (Summer 1985), pp. 199–214 for a seminal piece; and Richard Thaler, "Mental Accounting Matters," *Journal of Behavioral Decision Making, 12* (September 1999), pp. 183–206 for additional perspectives.

80. Gary L. Gastineau and Mark P. Kritzman, *Dictionary of Financial Risk Management*, 3rd ed. (New York: John Wiley & Sons, 1999).

81. Example adapted from Daniel Kahneman and Amos Tversky, "Prospect Theory: An Analysis of Decision under Risk," *Econometrica, 47* (March 1979), pp. 263–291.

Chapter 7

1. "Key Small Business Statistics-July 2010-How Many Businesses Are There in Canada?" *Industry Canada*, www.ic.gc.ca/eic/site/sbrp-rppe.nsf/eng/rd02493.html (viewed March 3, 2011).

2. www.greatwestlife.com (viewed March 1, 2011); "Evolution Benefits Selected by Great-West Life to Provide Innovative Card Services for First Visa Payment Card for Healthcare Spending Accounts in Canada," *Business Wire*, September 23, 2010.

3. For a comprehensive review of the topic, see James C. Anderson and James A. Narus, *Business Market Management: Understanding, Creating, and Delivering Value*, 3rd ed. (Upper Saddle River, NJ: Prentice Hall, 2009).

4. Frederick E. Webster, Jr., and Yoram Wind, *Organizational Buying Behavior* (Upper Saddle River, NJ: Prentice Hall, 1972), p. 2. For a review of some academic literature on the topic, see Håkan Håkansson and Ivan Snehota, "Marketing in Business Markets," in *Handbook of Marketing*, edited byBart Weitz and Robin Wensley(London, England: Sage Publications, 2002), pp. 513–526; Mark Glynn and Arch Woodside, eds., *Business-to-Business Brand Management: Theory, Research, and Executive Case Study Exercises in Advances in Business Marketing & Purchasing*, Vol. 15 (Bingley, UK: Emerald Group Publishing, 2009).

5. John Low and Keith Blois, "The Evolution of Generic Brands in Industrial Markets: The Challenges to Owners of Brand Equity," *Industrial Marketing Management, 31* (2002): 385–392; Philip Kotler and Waldemar Pfoertsch, *B2B Brand Management* (Berlin: Springer, 2006).

6. Jennifer Campbell, "Team Tannis at 70: Extended Family Keeps It All Together for Food Distributor, but Look No Further Than the Matriarch for the Real Secret Ingredient," *Ottawa Citizen*, September 17, 2010, p. E1.

7. "B-to-B Marketing Trends 2010," *Institute for the Study of Business Markets*, http://isbm.smeal.psu.edu.

8. Susan Avery, *Purchasing, 135* (November 2, 2006): 36; "PPG Honors Six Excellent Suppliers," www.ppg.com, June 16, 2009.

9. Michael Collins, "Breaking into the Big Leagues," *American Demographics*, January 1996, p. 24.

10. Industry Canada, *Report on Key Small Business Statistics*, July 2010, www.strategis.ic.gc.ca (viewed January 2, 2011).

11. Patrick J. Robinson, Charles W. Faris, and Yoram Wind, *Industrial Buying and Creative Marketing* (Boston: Allyn & Bacon, 1967).

12. Michele D. Bunn, "Taxonomy of Buying Decision Approaches," *Journal of Marketing, 57* (January 1993): 38–56; Daniel H. McQuiston, "Novelty, Complexity, and Importance as Causal Determinants of Industrial Buyer Behavior," *Journal of Marketing, 53* (April 1989): 66–79; Peter Doyle, Arch G. Woodside, and Paul Mitchell, "Organizational Buying in New Task and Rebuy Situations," *Industrial Marketing Management*, February 1979, pp. 7–11.

13. Urban B. Ozanne and Gilbert A. Churchill, Jr., "Five Dimensions of the Industrial Adoption Process," *Journal of Marketing Research, 8* (August 1971): 322–328.

14. To learn more about how business-to-business firms can improve their branding, see Philip Kotler and Waldemar Pfoertsch, *B2B Brand Management* (Berlin: Springer, 2006).

15. *Magna 2009 Annual Report,* www.magna.com (viewed February 25, 2011).

16. Elisabeth Sullivan, "Building a Better Brand," *Marketing News,* September 15, 2009, pp. 14–17.

17. "Telecommunications: Coming Soon: Movies and More on VIA Trains—VIA Rail and the Government of Canada Award Contract to Nomad Digital for Wi-Fi Broadband Service on Ontario-Quebec Corridor Trains," *Entertainment Newsweekly,* December 31, 2010, p. 456.

18. Jeffrey E. Lewin and Naveen Donthu, "The Influence of Purchase Situation on Buying Center Structure and Involvement: A Select Meta-Analysis of Organizational Buying Behavior Research," *Journal of Business Research, 58* (October 2005): 1381–1390; R. Venkatesh and Ajay K. Kohli, "Influence Strategies in Buying Centers," *Journal of Marketing, 59* (October 1995): 71–82; Donald W. Jackson, Jr., Janet E. Keith, and Richard K. Burdick, "Purchasing Agents' Perceptions of Industrial Buying Center Influence: A Situational Approach," *Journal of Marketing, 48* (Fall 1984): 75–83.

19. Frederick E. Webster and Yoram Wind, *Organizational Buying Behavior* (Upper Saddle River, NJ: Prentice Hall, 1972), p. 6.

20. James C. Anderson and James A. Narus, *Business Market Management: Understanding, Creating, and Delivering Value,* 3rd ed. (Upper Saddle River, NJ: Prentice Hall, 2009); Frederick E. Webster, Jr., and Yoram Wind, "A General Model for Understanding Organizational Buying Behavior," *Journal of Marketing, 36* (April 1972): 12–19; Frederick E. Webster and Yoram Wind, *Organizational Buying Behavior* (Upper Saddle River, NJ: Prentice Hall, 1972).

21. Allison Enright, "It Takes a Committee to Buy into B-to-B," *Marketing News,* February 15, 2006, pp. 12–13.

22. Frederick E. Webster, Jr., and Kevin Lane Keller, "A Roadmap for Branding in Industrial Markets," *Journal of Brand Management, 11* (May 2004): 388–402.

23. Scott Ward and Frederick E. Webster, Jr., "Organizational Buying Behavior," in *Handbook of Consumer Behavior,* edited by Tom Robertson and Hal Kassarjian(Upper Saddle River, NJ: Prentice Hall, 1991), pp. 419–458.

24. Bob Donath, "Emotions Play Key Role in Biz Brand Appeal," *Marketing News,* June 1, 2006, p. 7.

25. Michael Krauss, "Warriors of the Heart," *Marketing News,* February 1, 2006, p. 7; Brian Hindo, "Emerson Electric's Innovation Metrics," *BusinessWeek,* June 5, 2008.

26. Bob Lamons, "Branding, B-to-B Style," *Sales and Marketing Management, 157* (September 2005): 46–50; David A. Kaplan, "No. 1 SAS," in "The 100 Best Companies to Work For," *Fortune,* February 8, 2010, pp. 56–64.

27. Rick Spence, "Growing with Technology: Great New Marketing," *PROFIT, 27,* no. 3 (June 2008): 81–83.

28. Frederick E. Webster and Yoram Wind, *Organizational Buying Behavior* (Upper Saddle River, NJ: Prentice Hall, 1972), p. 6.

29. James C. Anderson, James A. Narus, and Wouter van Rossum, "Customer Value Proposition in Business Markets," *Harvard Business Review,* March 2006, pp. 2–10; James C. Anderson, "From Understanding to Managing Customer Value in Business Markets," in *Rethinking Marketing: New Marketing Tools,* edited by H. Håkansson, D. Harrison, and A. Waluszewski (London, England: John Wiley & Sons, 2004), pp. 137–159.

30. Susan Caminiti, "Drivers of the Economy," *Fortune,* April 17, 2006, p. C1; "Pfizer Turns Around Its Diversity & Inclusion Initiatives," *Diversity/Careers in Engineering and Information Technology,* December 2009–January 2010; Barbara Frankel, "Pfizer's Newest CDO Represents Transferable Talent," *Diversity Inc.,* November–December 2009; "From One Small Business to Another: Enhancing Community Through Commerce," *Pfizer,* www.pfizer-supplierdiversity.com, February 6, 2010.

31. "Case Studies: Rio Tinto," *Quadrem,* www.quadrem.com, February 6, 2010.

32. "Case Study 2003: Mitsui & Co. Cuts the Cost of Trade Transactions by 50% by Using Trade Card," *Mitsui & Co., Ltd.,* www.tradecard.com.

33. "Best Practices of the Best-Run Sales Organizations: Sales Opportunity Blueprinting," *SAP,* http://download.sap.com, February 6, 2010.

34. Patrick J. Robinson, Charles W. Faris, and Yoram Wind, *Industrial Buying and Creative Marketing* (Boston: Allyn & Bacon, 1967).

35. Institute of Scrap Recycling Industries, www.isri.org.

36. Geri Smith, "Hard Times Ease for a Cement King," *BusinessWeek,* November 9, 2009, p. 28.

37. Rajdeep Grewal, James M. Comer, and Raj Mehta, "An Investigation into the Antecedents of Organizational Participation in Business-to-Business Electronic Markets," *Journal of Marketing, 65* (July 2001): 17–33.

38. "Open Sesame? Or Could the Doors Slam Shut for Alibaba.com?" *Knowledge@Wharton,* July 27, 2005; Julia Angwin, "Top Online Chemical Exchange Is Unlikely Success Story," *Wall Street Journal,* January 8, 2004; Olga Kharif, "B2B, Take 2," *BusinessWeek,* November 25, 2003; George S. Day, Adam J. Fein, and Gregg Ruppersberger, "Shakeouts in Digital Markets: Lessons from B2B Exchanges," *California Management Review, 45* (Winter 2003): 131–151.

39. *Ritchie Bros. Auctioneers,* www.rbauction.com.

40. Rick Spence, "Growing with Technology: Great New Marketing," *PROFIT, 27,* no. 3 (June 2008): 81–83.

41. Brian J. Carroll, *Lead Generation for the Complex Sale* (New York: McGraw-Hill, 2006).

42. "2009–10 B2B Marketing Benchmark Report," *Marketing Sherpa,* www.sherpastore.com, February 6, 2010.

43. Allison Enright, "It Takes a Committee to Buy into B-to-B," *Marketing News,* February 15, 2006, pp. 12–13.

44. Robert Hiebeler, Thomas B. Kelly, and Charles Ketteman, *Best Practices: Building Your Business with Customer-Focused Solutions* (New York: Arthur Andersen/Simon & Schuster, 1998), pp. 122–124.

45. Daniel J. Flint, Robert B. Woodruff, and Sarah Fisher Gardial, "Exploring the Phenomenon of Customers' Desired Value Change in a Business-to-Business Context," *Journal of Marketing, 66* (October 2002): 102–117.

46. Ruth N. Bolton and Matthew B. Myers, "Price-Based Global Market Segmentation for Services," *Journal of Marketing, 67* (July 2003): 108–128.

47. Wolfgang Ulaga and Andreas Eggert, "Value-Based Differentiation in Business Relationships: Gaining and Sustaining Key Supplier Status," *Journal of Marketing, 70* (January 2006): 119–136.

48. Christopher Palmeri, "Serving Two (Station) Masters," *BusinessWeek,* July 24, 2006, p. 46.

49. David Kiley, "Small Print Jobs for Peanuts," *BusinessWeek,* July 17, 2006, p. 58.

50. Nirmalya Kumar, *Marketing as Strategy: Understanding the CEO's Agenda for Driving Growth and Innovation* (Boston: Harvard Business School Press, 2004).

51. Ibid.

52. "Case Study: Automotive Vendor Managed Inventory, Plexco (Australia)," www.marciajedd.com.

53. For foundational material, see Lloyd M. Rinehart, James A. Eckert, Robert B. Handfield, Thomas J. Page, Jr., and Thomas Atkin, "An Assessment of Buyer–Seller Relationships," *Journal of Business*

Logistics, 25 (2004): 25–62; F. Robert Dwyer, Paul Schurr, and Sejo Oh, "Developing Buyer–Supplier Relationships," *Journal of Marketing*, 51 (April 1987): 11–28; and Barbara Bund Jackson, *Winning & Keeping Industrial Customers: The Dynamics of Customer Relations* (Lexington, MA: D. C. Heath, 1985).

54. Arnt Buvik and George John, "When Does Vertical Coordination Improve Industrial Purchasing Relationships?" *Journal of Marketing*, 64 (October 2000): 52–64.

55. Eleanor Beaton, "Mr. Fix-It," *PROFIT*, 27, no. 3 (June 2008): 86–87.

56. Das Narayandas and V. Kasturi Rangan, "Building and Sustaining Buyer–Seller Relationships in Mature Industrial Markets," *Journal of Marketing*, 68 (July 2004): 63–77.

57. Robert W. Palmatier, Rajiv P. Dant, Dhruv Grewal, and Kenneth R. Evans, "Factors Influencing the Effectiveness of Relationship Marketing: A Meta-Analysis," *Journal of Marketing*, 70 (October 2006): 136–153; Jean L. Johnson, Ravipreet S. Sohli, and Rajdeep Grewal, "The Role of Relational Knowledge Stores in Interfirm Partnering," *Journal of Marketing*, 68 (July 2004): 21–36; Fred Selnes and James Sallis, "Promoting Relationship Learning," *Journal of Marketing*, 67 (July 2003): 80–95; Patricia M. Doney and Joseph P. Cannon, "An Examination of the Nature of Trust in Buyer–Seller Relationships," *Journal of Marketing*, 61 (April 1997): 35–51; Shankar Ganesan, "Determinants of Long-Term Orientation in Buyer–Seller Relationships," *Journal of Marketing*, 58 (April 1994): 1–19.

58. William W. Keep, Stanley C. Hollander, and Roger Dickinson, "Forces Impinging on Long-Term Business-to-Business Relationships in the United States: An Historical Perspective," *Journal of Marketing*, 62 (April 1998): 31–45.

59. Joseph P. Cannon and William D. Perreault, Jr., "Buyer–Seller Relationships in Business Markets," *Journal of Marketing Research*, 36 (November 1999): 439–460.

60. Jan B. Heide and Kenneth H. Wahne, "Friends, Businesspeople, and Relationship Roles: A Conceptual Framework and Research Agenda," *Journal of Marketing*, 70 (July 2006): 90–103.

61. Joseph P. Cannon and William D. Perreault, Jr., "Buyer–Seller Relationships in Business Markets," *Journal of Marketing Research*, 36 (November 1999): 439–460.

62. Thomas G. Noordewier, George John, and John R. Nevin, "Performance Outcomes of Purchasing Arrangements in Industrial Buyer–Vendor Arrangements," *Journal of Marketing*, 54 (October 1990): 80–93; Arnt Buvik and George John, "When Does Vertical Coordination Improve Industrial Purchasing Relationships?" *Journal of Marketing*, 64 (October 2000): 52–64.

63. Akesel I. Rokkan, Jan B. Heide, and Kenneth H. Wathne, "Specific Investment in Marketing Relationships: Expropriation and Bonding Effects," *Journal of Marketing Research*, 40 (May 2003): 210–224.

64. Kenneth H. Wathne and Jan B. Heide, "Relationship Governance in a Supply Chain Network," *Journal of Marketing*, 68 (January 2004): 73–89; Douglas Bowman and Das Narayandas, "Linking Customer Management Effort to Customer Profitability in Business Markets," *Journal of Marketing Research*, 61 (November 2004): 433–447; Mrinal Ghosh and George John, "Governance Value Analysis and Marketing Strategy," *Journal of Marketing*, 63 (Special Issue, 1999): 131–145.

65. Sandy Jap, "Pie Expansion Effects: Collaboration Processes in Buyer–Seller Relationships," *Journal of Marketing Research*, 36 (November 1999): 461–475.

66. Arnt Buvik and George John, "When Does Vertical Coordination Improve Industrial Purchasing Relationships?" *Journal of Marketing*, 64 (October 2000): 52–64.

67. Kenneth H. Wathne and Jan B. Heide, "Opportunism in Interfirm Relationships: Forms, Outcomes, and Solutions," *Journal of Marketing*, 64 (October 2000): 36–51.

68. Mary Walton, "When Your Partner Fails You," *Fortune*, May 26, 1997, pp. 151–154.

69. Mark B. Houston and Shane A. Johnson, "Buyer–Supplier Contracts versus Joint Ventures: Determinants and Consequences of Transaction Structure," *Journal of Marketing Research*, 37 (February 2000): 1–15.

70. Aksel I. Rokkan, Jan B. Heide, and Kenneth H. Wathne, "Specific Investment in Marketing Relationships: Expropriation and Bonding Effects," *Journal of Marketing Research*, 40 (May 2003): 210–224.

71. Elisabeth Sullivan, "A Worthwhile Investment," *Marketing News*, December 30, 2009, p. 10.

72. Shar VanBoskirk, "B2B Email Marketing Best Practices: Hewlett Packard," *Forrester*, www.forrester.com, February 21, 2006.

73. Josh Bernoff, "Why B-to-B Ought to Love Social Media," *Marketing News*, April 15, 2009, p. 20; Elisabeth Sullivan, "A Long Slog," *Marketing News*, February 28, 2009, pp. 15–18.

74. Elisabeth Sullivan, "One to One," *Marketing News*, May 15, 2009, pp. 10–12.

75. Elisabeth Sullivan, "Cognos Inc.," *Marketing News*, April 1, 2008, p. 10.

76. Paul King, "Purchasing: Keener Competition Requires Thinking Outside the Box," *Nation's Restaurant News*, August 18, 2003, p. 87.

77. Canada Business Ontario, "Government Procurement Guide," www.cbo-eco.ca/en/info-guide/government_procurement_info-guide_1121180832226.cfm (viewed January 2, 2010).

Chapter 8

1. Rosie Lombardi, "Instant Messaging," *Food in Canada*, 70, no. 2 (March 2010): 29–33; "Canadian Pork Council Report," Canadian Pork Council, Ontario AGM, March 23, 2011.

2. Dale Buss, "Brands in the 'Hood," *Point*, December 2005, pp. 19–24.

3. Nanette Byrnes, "What's Beyond for Bed Bath & Beyond?" *BusinessWeek*, January 19, 2004, pp. 45–50; Andrea Lillo, "Bed Bath Sees More Room for Growth," *Home Textiles Today*, July 7, 2003, p. 2.

4. At MyBestSegments.com, you can enter in a zip code and discover the top five clusters for that area. Note that another leading supplier of geodemographic data is ClusterPlus (Strategic Mapping).

5. See "Environics Analytics PRIZM CE & Links," www.environicsanalytics.ca/prizmce_links.aspx (viewed March 2008).

6. Environics Analytics, *Case Studies*, www.environicsanalytics.ca/case_studies.aspx (viewed March 6, 2011).

7. Michael J. Weiss, "To Be About to Be," *American Demographics*, September 2003, pp. 29–36.

8. "YouthPulse: The Definitive Study of Today's Youth Generation," *Harris Interactive*, 2009, www.harrisinteractive.com.

9. Gina Chon, "Car Makers Talk 'Bout G-G-Generations," *Wall Street Journal*, May 9, 2006.

10. Trevor Cole, "A Day to Remember," *The Globe and Mail*, May 23, 2007; "Planning for Marriage, Not Just a Wedding," *Presbyterian Record*, February 1, 2006.

11. For some practical implications, see Marti Barletta, *Marketing to Women: How to Increase Share of the World's Largest Market*, 2nd ed. (New York: Kaplan Business, 2006); Bridget Brennan, *Why She Buys: The New Strategy for Reaching the World's Most Powerful Consumers* (New York: Crown Business, 2009).

12. For more consumer behaviour perspectives on gender, see Jane Cunningham and Philippa Roberts, "What Woman Want," *Brand Strategy*, December 2006–January 2007, pp. 40–41; Robert J. Fisher and Laurette Dube, "Gender Differences in Responses to Emotional Advertising: A Social Desirability Perspective," *Journal of Consumer Research*, 31 (March 2005): 850–858; Joan Meyers-Levy and Durairaj Maheswaran, "Exploring Males' and Females' Processing

Strategies: When and Why Do Differences Occur in Consumers' Processing of Ad Claims," *Journal of Consumer Research, 18* (June 1991): 63–70; Joan Meyers-Levy and Brian Sternthal, "Gender Differences in the Use of Message Cues and Judgments," *Journal of Marketing Research, 28* (February 1991): 84–96.

13. Dawn Klingensmith, "Marketing Gurus Try to Read Women's Minds," *Chicago Tribune*, April 19, 2006; Elisabeth Sullivan, "The Mother Lode," *Marketing News*, July 15, 2008, p. 28; Claire Cain Miller, "Advertising Woman to Woman, Online," *New York Times*, August 13, 2008; Eric Newman, "The Mook Industrial Complex," *Brandweek*, January 14, 2008, pp. 21–24.

14. Marti Barletta, "Who's Really Buying That Car? Ask Her," *Brandweek*, September 4, 2006, p. 20; Robert Craven, Kiki Maurey, and John Davis, "What Women Really Want," *Critical Eye, 15* (July 2006): 50–53; Michael J. Silverstein and Kate Sayre, "The Female Economy," *Harvard Business Review*, September 2009, pp. 46–53.

15. Aixa Pascual, "Lowe's Is Sprucing Up Its House," *BusinessWeek*, June 3, 2002, pp. 56–57; Pamela Sebastian Ridge, "Tool Sellers Tap Their Feminine Side," *Wall Street Journal*, June 16, 2002.

16. Constantine von Hoffman, "So Long Unisex, Make it His or Hers," *Brandweek, 47*, no. 25 (June 19, 2006): p. S50.

17. Jeff Beer, "From Real Beauty to Real Men," *Marketing*, March 19, 2010, www.marketingmag.ca/news/marketer-news/from-real-beauty-to-real-men-1762 (viewed April 4, 2011); Maisie McCabe, "Campaign for Real Men," *Marketing*, January 20, 2010, p. 18; "The Journey to Comfort," *Dove Men+Care*, http://content.dove.us/mencare/Tv.aspx (viewed September 18, 2010).

18. Ian Zack, "Out of the Tube," *Forbes*, November 26, 2001, p. 200.

19. Gregory L. White and Shirley Leung, "Middle Market Shrinks as Americans Migrate toward the Higher End," *Wall Street Journal*, March 29, 2002.

20. Charles D. Schewe and Geoffrey Meredith, "Segmenting Global Markets by Generational Cohort: Determining Motivations by Age," *Journal of Consumer Behavior, 4* (October 2004): 51–63; Geoffrey E. Meredith and Charles D. Schewe, *Managing by Defining Moments: America's 7 Generational Cohorts, Their Workplace Values, and Why Managers Should Care* (New York: Hungry Minds, 2002); Geoffrey E. Meredith, Charles D. Schewe, and Janice Karlovich, *Defining Markets Defining Moments* (New York: Hungry Minds, 2001).

21. Piet Levy, "The Quest for Cool," *Marketing News*, February 28, 2009, p. 6; Michelle Conlin, "Youth Quake," *BusinessWeek*, January 21, 2008, pp. 32–36.

22. Karen E. Klein, "The ABCs of Selling to Generation X," *BusinessWeek*, April 15, 2004; M. J. Stephey, "Gen-X: The Ignored Generation?" *Time*, April 16, 2008; Tamara Erickson, "Don't Treat Them Like Baby Boomers," *BusinessWeek*, August 25, 2008, p. 64.

23. Sheila McGovern, "One Size Doesn't Fit All for Baby Boomer Shoppers," *CanWest News*, December 5, 2009.

24. Louise Lee, "Love Those Boomers," *BusinessWeek*, October 24, 2005, p. 94; Bob Moos, "Last of Boomers Turn 40," *Dallas Morning News*, January 1, 2005; Linda Tischler, "Where the Bucks Are," *Fast Company*, March 2004, pp. 71–77; Alycia de Mesa, "Don't Ignore the Boomer Consumer," *brandchannel*, www.brandchannel.com, June 25, 2007; Judann Pollack, "Boomers Don't Want Your Pity, but They Do Demand Your Respect," *Advertising Age*, October 8, 2007, p. 24.

25. Mark Dolliver, "Marketing to Today's 65-Plus Consumers," *Adweek*, July 27, 2009.

26. Stuart Elliott, "The Older Audience Is Looking Better Than Ever," *New York Times*, April 19, 2009.

27. Marissa Miley, "Don't Bypass African-Americans," *Advertising Age*, February 2, 2009.

28. "Ethnic Origin and Visible Minorities," 2006 Census of Population, *Statistics Canada*, Catalogue no. 97-562-XCB2006015.

29. Elisabeth Sullivan, "Choose Your Words Wisely," *Marketing News*, February 15, 2008, p. 22; Emily Bryson York, "Brands Prepare for a More Diverse 'General Market,'" *Advertising Age*, November 30, 2009, p. 6.

30. "Islamic Mortgage," Assiniboine Credit Union website, www.assiniboine.mb.ca/My-Finances/Borrowing/Mortgages/Islamic-Mortgage.aspx#cim (viewed March 29, 2011); "Credit Union Offers Solution to Islamic Mortgage Problem," *CanWest News*, May 5, 2010.

31. Emily Bryson York, "Brands Prepare for a More Diverse 'General Market,'" *Advertising Age*, November 30, 2009, p. 6.

32. Charles M. Schaninger, "French-English Canadian Subcultural Consumption Differences," *Journal of Marketing, 49* (Spring 1985): 82.

33. "Eating Habits and Nutrient Intake of Aboriginal Adults Aged 19–50, Living Off-Reserve in Ontario and the Western Provinces," *Health Canada*, 2010, Cat: H164-122/2010E-PDF.

34. Joseph Chen, May Aung, Lianxi Zhou, and Vinay Kanetkar, "Chinese Ethnic Identification and Conspicuous Consumption: Are There Moderators or Mediators Effect of Acculturation Dimensions?" *Journal of International Consumer Marketing, 17*, no. 2 & 3 (2005): 117–136.

35. Rakshande Italia, "Inclusion in Advertising," *Strategy*, October 2008, p. 12.

36. "GLBT Market Overview," International Gay and Lesbian Chamber of Commerce, Montreal, April 2, 2008.

37. Ian Johnson, "Canada Gay Market, *Out Now*, March 23, 2008, http://bx.businessweek.com/gay-business-and-marketing/canada-gay-market/1846945410600052/ (viewed March 25, 2011).

38. "LGBT-Friendly Corporations Revealed: IBM and Google Top the List," *Canadian HR Reporter*, June 22, 2010, www.hrreporter.com/ArticleView.aspx?articleid=7982 (viewed March 25, 2011).

39. *Strategic Business Insights*, www.strategicbusinessinsights.com.

40. Andrew Kaplan, "A Fruitful Mix," *Beverage World*, May 2006, pp. 28–36.

41. This classification was adapted from George H. Brown, "Brand Loyalty: Fact or Fiction?" *Advertising Age*, June 1952–January 1953, a series. See also, Peter E. Rossi, Robert E. McCulloch, and Greg M. Allenby, "The Value of Purchase History Data in Target Marketing," *Marketing Science, 15* (Fall 1996): 321–340.

42. James C. Anderson and James A. Narus, "Capturing the Value of Supplementary Services," *Harvard Business Review*, January–February 1995, pp. 75–83.

43. For a review of many of the methodological issues in developing segmentation schemes, see William R. Dillon and Soumen Mukherjee, "A Guide to the Design and Execution of Segmentation Studies," in *Handbook of Marketing Research*, edited by Rajiv Grover and Marco Vriens(Thousand Oaks, CA: Sage, 2006); and Michael Wedel and Wagner A. Kamakura, *Market Segmentation: Conceptual and Methodological Foundations* (Boston: Kluwer, 1997).

44. Michael E. Porter, *Competitive Strategy* (New York: The Free Press, 1980), pp. 22–23.

45. *Estée Lauder*, www.esteelauder.com.

46. Douglas MacMillan, "The Big Trend in Small Social Sites," *BusinessWeek*, September 9, 2010, www.businessweek.com/magazine/content/10_38/b4195035456823.htm (viewed September 18, 2010); SkiThis.ca website, www.skithis.ca (viewed September 18, 2010); "Ski This Canada," *Facebook*, www.facebook.com/pages/Kelowna-BC/Ski-This-Canada/121565845735?v=info#!/pages/Kelowna-BC/Ski-This-Canada/121565845735?v=wall (viewed September 18, 2010).

47. Robert Blattberg and John Deighton, "Interactive Marketing: Exploiting the Age of Addressability," *Sloan Management Review, 33* (Fall 1991): 5–14.

48. Don Peppers and Martha Rogers, *One-to-One B2B: Customer Development Strategies for the Business-To-Business World* (New York: Doubleday, 2001).

49. Jerry Wind and Arvind Rangaswamy, "Customerization: The Next Revolution in Mass Customization," *Journal of Interactive Marketing*, 15 (Winter 2001): 13–32.

50. James C. Anderson and James A. Narus, "Capturing the Value of Supplementary Services," *Harvard Business Review*, January–February 1995, pp. 75–83.

51. Itamar Simonson, "Determinants of Customers' Responses to Customized Offers: Conceptual Framework and Research Propositions," *Journal of Marketing*, 69 (January 2005): 32–45.

52. Bart Macchiette and Roy Abhijit, "Sensitive Groups and Social Issues," *Journal of Consumer Marketing*, 11 (Fall 1994): 55–64.

53. Kristin Laird, "Royal Bank Sponsors Cricket Program," *Marketing Daily*, February 29, 2008; www.rbc.com/cricket (viewed March 28, 2011).

54. Roger O. Crockett, "They're Lining Up for Flicks in the 'Hood,'" *BusinessWeek*, June 8, 1998, pp. 75–76.

55. Caroline E. Mayer, "Nurturing Brand Loyalty: With Preschool Supplies, Firms Woo Future Customers—and Current Parents," *Washington Post*, October 12, 2003.

Chapter 9

1. Alli McConnon, "Lululemon's Next Workout," *BusinessWeek*, June 9, 2008, pp. 43–44; Danielle Sacks, "Lululemon's Cult of Selling," *Fast Company*, March 2009; Bryant Urstadt, "Lust for Lulu," *New York Magazine*, July 26, 2009.

2. For foundational work on branding, see Jean-Noel Kapferer, *Strategic Brand Management*, 2nd ed. (New York: The Free Press, 2005); David A. Aaker and Erich Joachimsthaler, *Brand Leadership* (New York: The Free Press, 2000); David A. Aaker, *Building Strong Brands* (New York: The Free Press, 1996); and David A. Aaker, *Managing Brand Equity* (New York: The Free Press, 1991).

3. Quoted in "Branding: Defined," *Chicago AMA for Marketing Professionals*, http://chicagoama.org/behind-branding-scenes (viewed September 22, 2011).

4. Interbrand Group, *World's Greatest Brands: An International Review* (New York: John Wiley, 1992). See also Karl Moore and Susan E. Reid, "The Birth of a Brand," Working paper, Desautels Faculty of Management, McGill University, 2006.

5. Rajneesh Suri and Kent B. Monroe, "The Effects of Time Pressure on Consumers' Judgments of Prices and Products," *Journal of Consumer Research*, 30 (June 2003): 92–104.

6. *The Economist on Branding*, edited by Rita Clifton and John Simmons (New York: Bloomberg Press, 2004); Rik Riezebos, *Brand Management: A Theoretical and Practical Approach* (Essex, England: Pearson Education, 2003); Paul Temporal, *Advanced Brand Management: From Vision to Valuation* (Singapore: John Wiley & Sons, 2002).

7. Constance E. Bagley, *Managers and the Legal Environment: Strategies for the 21st Century*, 3rd ed. (Cincinnati, OH: Southwestern College/West Publishing, 2005). For a marketing academic's point of view of some important legal issues, see Judith Zaichkowsky, *The Psychology behind Trademark Infringement and Counterfeiting* (Mahwah, NJ: LEA Publishing, 2006); and Maureen Morrin and Jacob Jacoby, "Trademark Dilution: Empirical Measures for an Elusive Concept," *Journal of Public Policy & Marketing*, 19, no. 2 (May 2000): 265–276.

8. Tulin Erdem, "Brand Equity as a Signaling Phenomenon," *Journal of Consumer Psychology*, 7, no. 2 (1998): 131–157.

9. Scott Davis, *Brand Asset Management: Driving Profitable Growth through Your Brands* (San Francisco: Jossey-Bass, 2000); Mary W. Sullivan, "How Brand Names Affect the Demand for Twin Automobiles," *Journal of Marketing Research*, 35 (May 1998): 154–165; D. C. Bello and M. B. Holbrook, "Does an Absence of Brand Equity Generalize across Product Classes?" *Journal of Business Research*, 34 (October 1996): 125–131; Adrian J. Slywotzky and Benson P. Shapiro, "Leveraging to Beat the Odds: The New Marketing Mindset," *Harvard Business Review*, September–October 1993, pp. 97–107.

10. The power of branding is not without its critics, however, some of whom reject the commercialism associated with branding activities. See Naomi Klein, *No Logo: Taking Aim at the Brand Bullies* (New York: Picador, 2000).

11. "Study: Food in McDonald's Wrapper Tastes Better to Kids," *Associated Press*, August 6, 2007.

12. Natalie Mizik and Robert Jacobson, "Talk about Brand Strategy," *Harvard Business Review*, October 2005, p. 1; Baruch Lev, *Intangibles: Management, Measurement, and Reporting* (Washington, DC: Brookings Institute, 2001).

13. For an academic discussion of how consumers become so strongly attached to people as brands, see Matthew Thomson, "Human Brands: Investigating Antecedents to Consumers' Stronger Attachments to Celebrities," *Journal of Marketing*, 70 (July 2006): 104–119. For some practical branding tips from the world of rock and roll, see Roger Blackwell and Tina Stephan, *Brands That Rock* (Hoboken, NJ: John Wiley & Sons, 2004), and from the world of sports, see Irving Rein, Philip Kotler, and Ben Shields, *The Elusive Fan: Reinventing Sports in a Crowded Marketplace* (New York: McGraw-Hill, 2006).

14. "Justin Bieber Is More Influential Than Barack Obama and Dalai Lama," *NME*, January 2, 2011, www.nme.com/news/justin-bieber/54412; Jo Piazza, "Is Justin Bieber the Best Thing to Ever Happen to Proactiv?" *PopEater*, August 20, 2010, www.popeater.com/2010/08/20/justin-bieber-proactiv/ (viewed January 2011).

15. Kevin Lane Keller, *Strategic Brand Management*, 3rd ed. (Upper Saddle River, NJ: Prentice Hall, 2008); David A. Aaker and Erich Joachimsthaler, *Brand Leadership* (New York: The Free Press, 2000); David A. Aaker, *Building Strong Brands* (New York: The Free Press, 1996); David A. Aaker, *Managing Brand Equity* (New York: The Free Press, 1991).

16. Other approaches are based on economic principles of signalling (e.g., Tulin Erdem, "Brand Equity as a Signaling Phenomenon," *Journal of Consumer Psychology*, 7, no. 2 [1998]: 131–157), or more of a sociological, anthropological, or biological perspective (e.g., Grant McCracken, *Culture and Consumption II: Markets, Meaning, and Brand Management* [Bloomington, IN: Indiana University Press, 2005], or Susan Fournier, "Consumers and Their Brands: Developing Relationship Theory in Consumer Research," *Journal of Consumer Research*, 24 [September 1998]: 343–373).

17. Jennifer L. Aaker, "Dimensions of Brand Personality," *Journal of Marketing Research*, August 1997, pp. 347–356; Jean-Noel Kapferer, *Strategic Brand Management: New Approaches to Creating and Evaluating Brand Equity* (London, England: Kogan Page, 1992), p. 38; Scott Davis, *Brand Asset Management: Driving Profitable Growth through Your Brands* (San Francisco: Jossey-Bass, 2000). For an overview of academic research on branding, see Kevin Lane Keller, "Branding and Brand Equity," in *Handbook of Marketing*, edited by Bart Weitz and Robin Wensley (London, England: Sage Publications, 2002), pp. 151–178; and Kevin Lane Keller and Don Lehmann, "Brands and Branding: Research Findings and Future Priorities," *Marketing Science*, 25 (November–December 2006): 740–759.

18. Kevin Lane Keller, *Strategic Brand Management*, 3rd ed. (Upper Saddle River, NJ: Prentice Hall, 2008); David A. Aaker and Erich Joachimsthaler, *Brand Leadership* (New York: The Free Press, 2000); David A. Aaker, *Building Strong Brands* (New York: The Free Press, 1996); David A. Aaker, *Managing Brand Equity* (New York: The Free Press, 1991).

19. Theodore Levitt, "Marketing Success through Differentiation—of Anything," *Harvard Business Review*, January–February 1980, pp. 83–91.

20. Kusum Ailawadi, Donald R. Lehmann, and Scott Neslin, "Revenue Premium as an Outcome Measure of Brand Equity," *Journal of Marketing*, 67 (October 2003): 1–17.

21. Jon Miller and David Muir, *The Business of Brands* (West Sussex, England: John Wiley & Sons, 2004).

22. Craig McBride, "Stanfield's Goes Social for a Good Cause," *Media in Canada*, September 27, 2010, www.mediaincanada.com/articles/mic/20100927/stanfields.html (viewed January 2011).

23. Kevin Lane Keller, "Building Customer-Based Brand Equity: A Blueprint for Creating Strong Brands," *Marketing Management, 10* (July–August 2001): 15–19.

24. For some academic insights, see Matthew Thomson, Deborah J. MacInnis, and C. W. Park, "The Ties That Bind: Measuring the Strength of Consumers' Emotional Attachments to Brands," *Journal of Consumer Psychology, 15*, no. 1 (2005): 77–91; and Jennifer Edson Escalas, "Narrative Processing: Building Consumer Connections to Brands," *Journal of Consumer Psychology, 14*, nos. 1 & 2 (1996): 168–179. For some managerial guidelines, see Kevin Roberts, *Lovemarks: The Future beyond Brands* (New York: Powerhouse Books, 2004); and Douglas Atkins, *The Culting of Brands* (New York: Penguin Books, 2004).

25. Paul Rittenberg and Maura Clancey, "Testing the Value of Media Engagement for Advertising Effectiveness," www.knowledgenetworks.com, Spring–Summer 2006, pp. 35–42.

26. M. Berk Ataman, Carl F. Mela, and Harald J. van Heerde, "Building Brands," *Marketing Science, 27*, no. 6 (November–December 2008), pp. 1036–1054.

27. Daphne Gordon, "Killing Mold—The Natural Way," *Toronto Star*, January 6, 2006; www.concrobium.com/home.html (viewed March 2008).

28. Rachel Dodes, "From Tracksuits to Fast Track," *Wall Street Journal*, September 13, 2006.

29. "42 Below," www.betterbydesign.org.nz (viewed September 14, 2007).

30. Amanda Baltazar, "Silly Brand Names Get Serious Attention," *Brandweek*, December 3, 2007, p. 4.

31. Alina Wheeler, *Designing Brand Identity* (Hoboken, NJ: John Wiley & Sons, 2003).

32. Pat Fallon and Fred Senn, *Juicing the Orange: How to Turn Creativity into a Powerful Business Advantage* (Cambridge, MA: Harvard Business School Press, 2006); Eric A. Yorkston and Geeta Menon, "A Sound Idea: Phonetic Effects of Brand Names on Consumer Judgments," *Journal of Consumer Research, 31* (June 2004): 43–51; Tina M. Lowery and L. J. Shrum, "Phonetic Symbolism and Brand Name Preference," *Journal of Consumer Research, 34* (October 2007): 406–414.

33. For some interesting theoretical perspectives, see Claudiu V. Dimofte and Richard F. Yalch, "Consumer Response to Polysemous Brand Slogans," *Journal of Consumer Research, 33* (March 2007): 515–522.

34. John R. Doyle and Paul A. Bottomly, "Dressed for the Occasion: Font–Product Congruity in the Perception of Logotype," *Journal of Consumer Psychology, 16*, no. 2 (2006): 112–123; Kevin Lane Keller, Susan Heckler, and Michael J. Houston, "The Effects of Brand Name Suggestiveness on Advertising Recall," *Journal of Marketing, 62* (January 1998): 48–57. For an in-depth examination of how brand names get developed, see Alex Frankel, *Wordcraft: The Art of Turning Little Words into Big Business* (New York: Crown Publishers, 2004).

35. Don Schultz and Heidi Schultz, *IMC: The Next Generation* (New York: McGraw-Hill, 2003); Don E. Schultz, Stanley I. Tannenbaum, and Robert F. Lauterborn, *Integrated Marketing Communications* (Lincolnwood, IL: NTC Business Books, 1993).

36. Mohanbir Sawhney, "Don't Harmonize, Synchronize," *Harvard Business Review*, July–August 2001, pp. 101–108.

37. David C. Court, John E. Forsyth, Greg C. Kelly, and Mark A. Loch, "The New Rules of Branding: Building Strong Brands Faster," *McKinsey White Paper Fall 1999*; Scott Bedbury, *A New Brand World* (New York: Viking Press, 2002).

38. Sonia Reyes, "Cheerios: The Ride," *Brandweek*, September 23, 2002, pp. 14–16.

39. *Kellogg on Integrated Marketing*, edited by Dawn Iacobucci and Bobby Calder (New York: John Wiley & Sons, 2003).

40. Drew Madsen, "Olive Garden: Creating Value through an Integrated Brand Experience," presentation at Marketing Science Institute Conference, *Brand Orchestration*, Orlando, Florida, December 4, 2003.

41. Michael Dunn and Scott Davis, "Building Brands from the Inside," *Marketing Management*, May–June 2003, pp. 32–37; Scott Davis and Michael Dunn, *Building the Brand-Driven Business* (New York: John Wiley & Sons, 2002).

42. Stan Maklan and Simon Knox, *Competing on Value* (Upper Saddle River, NJ: Financial Times, Prentice Hall, 2000).

43. Chris Parry, "United Breaks Guitars—and Loses Luggage: Canadian Musician David Carroll," *Vancouver Sun*, October 29, 2009, www.vancouversun.com/news/United+breaks+guitars+loses+luggage+Canadian+musician+David+Carroll/2159862/story.html (viewed September 2010); "United Breaks Guitars," *Wikipedia*, http://en.wikipedia.org/wiki/United_Breaks_Guitars (viewed September 2010); "United Loses Bags of Broken-Guitar Singer," *CBC News*, October 30, 2009 (viewed September 2010). Lyrics © 2009 Dave Carroll.

44. Coeli Carr, "Seeking to Attract Top Prospects, Employers Brush Up on Brands," *New York Times*, September 10, 2006.

45. The principles and examples from this passage are based on Colin Mitchell, "Selling the Brand Inside," *Harvard Business Review*, January 2002, pp. 99–105. For an in-depth discussion of how two organizations, QuikTrip and Wawa, have developed stellar internal branding programs, see Neeli Bendapudi and Venkat Bendapudi, "Creating the Living Brand," *Harvard Business Review*, May 2005, pp. 124–132.

46. Melinda Mattos, "STM Drives Green Image," *Strategy Magazine*, December 1, 2010, www.strategyonline.ca/articles/magazine/20101201/moystm.html (viewed January 2011).

47. James H. McAlexander, John W. Schouten, and Harold F. Koenig, "Building Brand Community," *Journal of Marketing, 66* (January 2002): 38–54. For some notable examinations of brand communities, see René Algesheimer, Uptal M. Dholakia, and Andreas Herrmann, "The Social Influence of Brand Community: Evidence from European Car Clubs," *Journal of Marketing, 69* (July 2005): 19–34; Albert M. Muniz, Jr., and Hope Jensen Schau, "Religiosity in the Abandoned Apple Newton Brand Community," *Journal of Consumer Research, 31*, no. 4 (2005): 412–432; Robert Kozinets, "Utopian Enterprise: Articulating the Meanings of *Star Trek*'s Culture of Consumption," *Journal of Consumer Research, 28* (June 2001): 67–87; and John W. Schouten and James H. McAlexander, "Subcultures of Consumption: An Ethnography of New Bikers," *Journal of Consumer Research, 22* (June 1995): 43–61.

48. Albert M. Muniz, Jr., and Thomas C. O'Guinn, "Brand Community," *Journal of Consumer Research, 27* (March 2001): 412–432.

49. Susan Fournier and Lara Lee, *The Seven Deadly Sins of Brand Community "Management,"* Marketing Science Institute Special Report 08-208, 2008.

50. Harley-Davidson USA, www.hog.com; Joseph Weber, "Harley Just Keeps on Cruisin'," *BusinessWeek*, November 6, 2006, pp. 71–72.

51. Scott A. Thompson and Rajiv K. Sinha, "Brand Communities and New Product Adoption: The Influence and Limits of Oppositional Loyalty," *Journal of Marketing, 72* (November 2008): 65–80.

52. Deborah Roeddder John, Barbara Loken, Kyeong-Heui Kim, and Alokparna Basu Monga, "Brand Concept Maps: A Methodology for Identifying Brand Association Networks," *Journal of Marketing Research, 43* (November 2006): 549–563.

53. For related empirical insights, see Manoj K. Agrawal and Vithala Rao, "An Empirical Comparison of Consumer-Based Measures of Brand Equity," *Marketing Letters, 7*, no. 3 (July 1996): 237–247;

and Walfried Lassar, Banwari Mittal, and Arun Sharma, "Measuring Customer-Based Brand Equity," *Journal of Consumer Marketing*, 12, no. 4 (1995): 11–19.

54. "The Best Global Brands," *BusinessWeek*, June 19, 2009. The article ranks and critiques the 100 best global brands using the valuation method developed by Interbrand. For more discussion on some brand winners and losers, see Matt Haig, *Brand Royalty: How the Top 100 Brands Thrive and Survive* (London, England: Kogan Page, 2004); and Matt Haig, *Brand Failures: The Truth about the 100 Biggest Branding Mistakes of All Time* (London, England: Kogan Page, 2003). For an academic discussion of valuing brand equity, see V. Srinivasan, Chan Su Park, and Dae Ryun Chang, "An Approach to the Measurement, Analysis, and Prediction of Brand Equity and Its Sources," *Management Science*, 51 (September 2005): 1433–1448.

55. Mark Sherrington, *Added Value: The Alchemy of Brand-Led Growth* (Hampshire, UK: Palgrave Macmillan, 2003).

56. For an up-to-date discussion of what factors determine long-term branding success, see Allen P. Adamson, *Brand Simple* (New York: Palgrave Macmillan, 2006).

57. Nikhil Bahdur and John Jullens, "New Life for Tired Brands," *Strategy+Business*, 50 (February 28, 2008), www.strategy-business.com/article/08101?pg=all.

58. David Lieberman, "Discovery Chief Takes a Network on a Wild Ride," *USA Today*, September 2, 2009, pp. 1B–2B; Discovery Communications, www.corporate.discovery.com; Kenneth Hein, "Consumers Clinging to Old Favorite Brands," *Brandweek*, January 20, 2009; Linda Moss and Linda Haugsted, "Discovery Times New Branding Campaign to 'Deadliest Catch' Debut," *Multichannel News*, March 31, 2008.

59. Natalie Mizik and Robert Jacobson, "Trading Off between Value Creation and Value Appropriation: The Financial Implications of Shifts in Strategic Emphasis," *Journal of Marketing*, 67 (January 2003): 63–76.

60. Larry Light and Joan Kiddon, *Six Rules for Brand Revitalization: Learn How Companies like McDonald's Can Re-Energize Their Brands* (Wharton School Publishing, 2009).

61. Evan West, "Smells Like a Billion Bucks," *Fast Company*, May 2009, pp. 44–46; Patricia Winters Lauro, "Old Spice Begins a Revival as a Body-Care Line for College-Age Men, with Towelettes," *New York Times*, April 29, 2002.

62. Rebecca J. Slotegraaf and Koen Pauwels, "The Impact of Brand Equity and Innovation on the Long-Term Effectiveness of Promotions," *Journal of Marketing Research*, 45 (June 2008): 293–306.

63. Keith Naughton, "Fixing Cadillac," *Newsweek*, May 28, 2001, pp. 36–37.

64. Elizabeth Woyke, "Paul Stuart Tries to Unstuff the Shirts," *BusinessWeek*, October 8, 2007, p. 86.

65. Peter Farquhar, "Managing Brand Equity," *Marketing Research*, 1 (September 1989): 24–33.

66. Steven M. Shugan, "Branded Variants," 1989 AMA Educators' Proceedings (Chicago: American Marketing Association, 1989), pp. 33–38; M. Bergen, S. Dutta, and S. M. Shugan, "Branded Variants: A Retail Perspective," *Journal of Marketing Research*, 33 (February 1996): 9–21.

67. Adam Bass, "Licensed Extension—Stretching to Communicate," *Journal of Brand Management*, 12 (September 2004): 31–38. See also David A. Aaker, *Building Strong Brands* (New York: The Free Press, 1996).

68. Jean Halliday, "Troubled Automakers' Golden Goose," *AutoWeek*, August 14, 2006; Becky Ebenkamp, "The Creative License," *Brandweek*, June 9, 2003, pp. 36–40.

69. For comprehensive corporate branding guidelines, see James R. Gregory, *The Best of Branding: Best Practices in Corporate Branding* (New York: McGraw-Hill, 2004). For some international

perspectives, see *The Expressive Organization: Linking Identity, Reputation, and Corporate Brand*, edited by Majken Schultz, Mary Jo Hatch, and Mogens Holten Larsen (Oxford, UK: Oxford University Press, 2000); and *Corporate Branding: Purpose, People, and Process*, edited by Majken Schultz, Yun Mi Antorini, and Fabian F. Csaba (Denmark: Copenhagen Business School Press, 2005).

70. Guido Berens, Cees B. M. van Riel, and Gerrit H. van Bruggen, "Corporate Associations and Consumer Product Responses: The Moderating Role of Corporate Brand Dominance," *Journal of Marketing*, 69 (July 2005): 35–48; Zeynep Gürhan-Canli and Rajeev Batra, "When Corporate Image Affects Product Evaluations: The Moderating Role of Perceived Risk," *Journal of Marketing Research*, 41 (May 2004): 197–205; Kevin Lane Keller and David A. Aaker, "Corporate-Level Marketing: The Impact of Credibility on a Company's Brand Extensions," *Corporate Reputation Review*, 1 (August 1998): 356–378; Thomas J. Brown and Peter Dacin, "The Company and the Product: Corporate Associations and Consumer Product Responses," *Journal of Marketing*, 61 (January 1997): 68–84.

71. Vithala R. Rao, Manoj K. Agarwal, and Denise Dalhoff, "How Is Manifest Branding Strategy Related to the Intangible Value of a Corporation?" *Journal of Marketing*, 68 (October 2004): 126–141. For an examination of the financial impact of brand portfolio decisions, see Neil A. Morgan and Lopo L. Rego, "The Marketing and Financial Performance Consequences of Firms' Brand Portfolio Strategy," Working paper, Kelley School of Business, Indiana University, 2006.

72. William J. Holstein, "The Incalculable Value of Building Brands," *Chief Executive*, April–May 2006, pp. 52–56.

73. David A. Aaker, *Brand Portfolio Strategy: Creating Relevance, Differentiation, Energy, Leverage, and Clarity* (New York: The Free Press, 2004).

74. Christopher Hosford, "A Transformative Experience," *Sales & Marketing Management*, 158, no. 5 (June 2006): 32–36; Mike Beirne and Javier Benito, "Starwood Uses Personnel to Personalize Marketing," *Brandweek*, April 24, 2006, p. 9.

75. Jack Trout, *Differentiate or Die: Survival in Our Era of Killer Competition* (New York: John Wiley & Sons, 2000); Kamalini Ramdas and Mohanbir Sawhney, "A Cross-Functional Approach to Evaluating Multiple Line Extensions for Assembled Products," *Management Science*, 47, no. 1 (January 2001): 22–36.

76. Nirmalya Kumar, "Kill a Brand, Keep a Customer," *Harvard Business Review*, December 2003, pp. 87–95.

77. For a methodological approach for assessing the extent and nature of cannibalization, see Charlotte H. Mason and George R. Milne, "An Approach for Identifying Cannibalization within Product Line Extensions and Multibrand Strategies," *Journal of Business Research*, 31 (October–November 1994): 163–170.

78. Mark Ritson, "Should You Launch a Fighter Brand?" *Harvard Business Review*, October 2009, pp. 87–94.

79. Paul W. Farris, "The Chevrolet Corvette," Case UVA-M-320, The Darden Graduate Business School Foundation, University of Virginia, Charlottesville.

80. "2010 Best New Product Award Winners Announced," Canadian Living Press Release, January 19, 2010, www.bestnewproductawards.biz/canada/pdf/2010-BNPA-Winners-19-JAN-10.pdf (viewed January 2011).

81. Byung-Do Kim and Mary W. Sullivan, "The Effect of Parent Brand Experience on Line Extension Trial and Repeat Purchase," *Marketing Letters*, 9 (April 1998): 181–193.

82. John Milewicz and Paul Herbig, "Evaluating the Brand Extension Decision Using a Model of Reputation Building," *Journal of Product & Brand Management*, 3, no. 1 (January 1994): 39–47; Kevin Lane Keller and David A. Aaker, "The Effects of Sequential Introduction of Brand Extensions," *Journal of Marketing Research*, 29 (February 1992): 35–50.

83. Valarie A. Taylor and William O. Bearden, "Ad Spending on Brand Extensions: Does Similarity Matter?" *Journal of Brand Management, 11* (September 2003): 63–74; Sheri Bridges, Kevin Lane Keller, and Sanjay Sood, "Communication Strategies for Brand Extensions: Enhancing Perceived Fit by Establishing Explanatory Links," *Journal of Advertising, 29* (Winter 2000): 1–11; Daniel C. Smith, "Brand Extension and Advertising Efficiency: What Can and Cannot Be Expected," *Journal of Advertising Research*, November–December 1992, pp. 11–20; Daniel C. Smith and C. Whan Park, "The Effects of Brand Extensions on Market Share and Advertising Efficiency," *Journal of Marketing Research, 29* (August 1992): 296–313.

84. Ralf van der Lans, Rik Pieters, and Michel Wedel, "Competitive Brand Salience," *Marketing Science, 27*, no. 5 (September–October 2008): 922–931.

85. Subramanian Balachander and Sanjoy Ghose, "Reciprocal Spillover Effects: A Strategic Benefit of Brand Extensions," *Journal of Marketing, 67*, no. 1 (January 2003): 4–13.

86. Bharat N. Anand and Ron Shachar, "Brands as Beacons: A New Source of Loyalty to Multiproduct Firms," *Journal of Marketing Research, 41* (May 2004): 135–150.

87. Kevin Lane Keller and David A. Aaker, "The Effects of Sequential Introduction of Brand Extensions," *Journal of Marketing Research, 29* (February 1992): 35–50. For consumer processing implications, see Huifung Mao and H. Shanker Krishnan, "Effects of Prototype and Exemplar Fit on Brand Extension Evaluations: A Two-Process Contingency Model," *Journal of Consumer Research, 33* (June 2006): 41–49.

88. Maureen Morrin, "The Impact of Brand Extensions on Parent Brand Memory Structures and Retrieval Processes," *Journal of Marketing Research, 36*, no. 4 (November 1999): 517–525; John A. Quelch and David Kenny, "Extend Profits, Not Product Lines," *Harvard Business Review* (September–October 1994): 153–160; "Perspectives from the Editors: The Logic of Product-Line Extensions," *Harvard Business Review*, November–December 1994, pp. 53–62.

89. Al Ries and Jack Trout, *Positioning: The Battle for Your Mind, 20th Anniversary Edition* (New York: McGraw-Hill, 2000).

90. David A. Aaker, *Brand Portfolio Strategy: Creating Relevance, Differentiation, Energy, Leverage, and Clarity* (New York: The Free Press, 2004).

91. Mary W. Sullivan, "Measuring Image Spillovers in Umbrella-Branded Products," *Journal of Business, 63*, no. 3 (July 1990): 309–329.

92. Deborah Roedder John, Barbara Loken, and Christopher Joiner, "The Negative Impact of Extensions: Can Flagship Products Be Diluted?" *Journal of Marketing*, January 1998, pp. 19–32; Susan M. Broniarcyzk and Joseph W. Alba, "The Importance of the Brand in Brand Extension," *Journal of Marketing Research*, May 1994, pp. 214–228 (this entire issue of *JMR* is devoted to brands and brand equity); Barbara Loken and Deborah Roedder John, "Diluting Brand Beliefs: When Do Brand Extensions Have a Negative Impact?" *Journal of Marketing*, July 1993, pp. 71–84. See also Chris Pullig, Carolyn Simmons, and Richard G. Netemeyer, "Brand Dilution: When Do New Brands Hurt Existing Brands?" *Journal of Marketing, 70* (April 2006): 52–66; R. Ahluwalia and Z. Gürhan-Canli, "The Effects of Extensions on the Family Brand Name: An Accessibility-Diagnosticity Perspective," *Journal of Consumer Research, 27* (December 2000): 371–381; Z. Gürhan-Canli and M. Durairaj, "The Effects of Extensions on Brand Name Dilution and Enhancement," *Journal of Marketing Research, 35* (November 1998): 464–473; and S. J. Milberg, C. W. Park, and M. S. McCarthy, "Managing Negative Feedback Effects Associated with Brand Extensions: The Impact of Alternative Branding Strategies," *Journal of Consumer Psychology, 6* (1997): 119–140.

93. See also Franziska Völckner and Henrik Sattler, "Drivers of Brand Extension Success," *Journal of Marketing, 70* (April 2006): 1–17.

94. For recent research on extension evaluations, see Alokparna Basu Monga and Deborah Roedder John, "Cultural Differences in Brand Extension Evaluation: The Influence of Analytical versus Holistic Thinking," *Journal of Marketing Research, 33* (March 2007): 529–536; James L. Oakley, Adam Duhachek, Subramanian Balachander, and S. Sriram, "Order of Entry and the Moderating Role of Comparison Brands in Extension Evaluations," *Journal of Consumer Research, 34* (February 2008): 706–712; Junsang Yeo and Jongwon Park, "Effects of Parent-Extension Similarity and Self Regulatory Focus on Evaluations of Brand Extensions," *Journal of Consumer Psychology, 16*, no. 3 (2006): 272–282; Catherine W. M. Yeung and Robert S. Wyer, "Does Loving a Brand Mean Loving Its Products? The Role of Brand-Elicited Affect in Brand Extension Evaluations," *Journal of Marketing Research, 43* (November 2005): 495–506; Huifang Mao and H. Shankar Krishnan, "Effects of Prototype and Exemplar Fit on Brand Extension Evaluations: A Two-Process Contingency Model," *Journal of Consumer Research, 33* (June 2006): 41–49; Rohini Ahluwalia, "How Far Can a Brand Stretch? Understanding the Role of Self-Construal," *Journal of Marketing Research, 45* (June 2008): 337–350.

95. Pierre Berthon, Morris B. Holbrook, James M. Hulbert, and Leyland F. Pitt, "Viewing Brands in Multiple Dimensions," *MIT Sloan Management Review*, Winter 2007, pp. 37–43.

96. Roland T. Rust, Valerie A. Zeithaml, and Katherine A. Lemon, "Measuring Customer Equity and Calculating Marketing ROI," in *Handbook of Marketing Research*, edited by Rajiv Grover and Marco Vriens (Thousand Oaks, CA: Sage Publications, 2006), pp. 588–601; Roland T. Rust, Valerie A. Zeithaml, and Katherine A. Lemon, *Driving Customer Equity* (New York: The Free Press, 2000).

97. Robert C. Blattberg and John Deighton, "Manage Marketing by the Customer Equity Test," *Harvard Business Review*, July–August 1996, pp. 136–144.

98. Robert C. Blattberg and Jacquelyn S. Thomas, "Valuing, Analyzing, and Managing the Marketing Function Using Customer Equity Principles," in *Kellogg on Marketing*, edited by Dawn Iacobucci (New York: John Wiley & Sons, 2002); Robert C. Blattberg, Gary Getz, and Jacquelyn S. Thomas, *Customer Equity: Building and Managing Relationships as Valuable Assets* (Boston: Harvard Business School Press, 2001).

99. Much of this section is based on Robert Leone, Vithala Rao, Kevin Lane Keller, Man Luo, Leigh McAlister, and Rajendra Srivatstava, "Linking Brand Equity to Customer Equity," *Journal of Service Research, 9* (November 2006): 125–138. This special issue is devoted to customer equity and has a number of thought-provoking articles.

100. Niraj Dawar, "What Are Brands Good For?" *MIT Sloan Management Review*, Fall 2004, pp. 31–37.

Chapter 10

1. Scouts Canada, *Strategic Directions 2006-2016—Creating the Environment for Growth*, www.scouts.ca/media/documents/p15FEB06.pdf (viewed September 2010); Matt Semansky, "Scouts Canada Begins 'Outdoors' Campaign," *Marketing*, September 3, 2010; *Scouts Canada Style Guide*, August 19, 2010, www.scouts.ca/dnn/LinkClick.aspx?fileticket=TC1MvHv0MJs%3d&tabid=133&mid=480; *Scouts Canada 2009–2010 Annual Report*, www.scouts.ca/0910AnnualReport/2009-10%20Annual%20report%20Eng.pdf (viewed January 2011).

2. Al Ries and Jack Trout, *Positioning: The Battle for Your Mind, 20th Anniversary Edition* (New York: McGraw-Hill, 2000).

3. Jonathan Paul, "The Bay's Stylish Makeover," *Strategy Magazine*, December 1, 2010; Kristin Laird, "The Bay Gets Cool with Help from Crush," *Marketing*, October 8, 2010.

4. Michael J. Lanning and Lynn W. Phillips, "Building Market-Focused Organizations," Gemini Consulting White Paper, 1991.

5. David A. Aaker, "The Relevance of Brand Relevance," *Strategy+Business, 35* (Summer 2004): 1–10; David A. Aaker, *Brand Portfolio Strategy: Creating Relevance, Differentiation, Energy, Leverage, and Clarity* (New York: The Free Press, 2004).

6. Elaine Wong, "Unilever Marketer Reveals Bertolli's Secret Sauce," *Brandweek*, August 28, 2009.

7. Allan D. Shocker, "Determining the Structure of Product-Markets: Practices, Issues, and Suggestions," in *Handbook of Marketing*, edited by Barton A. Weitz and Robin Wensley (London, England: Sage, 2002), pp. 106–125. See also Bruce H. Clark and David B. Montgomery, "Managerial Identification of Competitors," *Journal of Marketing*, 63 (July 1999): 67–83.

8. "What Business Are You In? Classic Advice from Theodore Levitt," *Harvard Business Review*, October 2006, pp. 127–137. See also Theodore Levitt's seminal article "Marketing Myopia," *Harvard Business Review*, July–August 1960, pp. 45–56.

9. Jeffrey F. Rayport and Bernard J. Jaworski, *e-Commerce* (New York: McGraw-Hill, 2001), p. 53.

10. Richard A. D'Aveni, "Competitive Pressure Systems: Mapping and Managing Multimarket Contact," *MIT Sloan Management Review*, Fall 2002, pp. 39–49.

11. For discussion of some of the long-term implications of marketing activities, see Koen Pauwels, "How Dynamic Consumer Response, Competitor Response, Company Support, and Company Inertia Shape Long-Term Marketing Effectiveness," *Marketing Science*, 23 (Fall 2004): 596–610; Koen Pauwels, Dominique M. Hanssens, and S. Siddarth, "The Long-Term Effects of Price Promotions on Category Incidence, Brand Choice, and Purchase Quantity," *Journal of Marketing Research*, 34 (November 2002): 421–439; and Marnik Dekimpe and Dominique Hanssens, "Sustained Spending and Persistent Response: A New Look at Long-Term Marketing Profitability," *Journal of Marketing Research*, 36 (November 1999): 397–412.

12. Kevin Lane Keller, Brian Sternthal, and Alice Tybout, "Three Questions You Need to Ask about Your Brand," *Harvard Business Review*, September 2002, pp. 80–89.

13. Bob Weber, "Firms with 'Eco-Friendly' Claims Need to Come Clean: Study," *Canadian Press*, November 19, 2007; Cascades website, www2.cascades.com/en/page/performance-indicators (viewed January 2011); "Cascades Inc.: Company Snapshot," *Gloveinvestor. com*, http://investdb.theglobeandmail.com/invest/investSQL/gx.company_prof?company_id=181649 (viewed March 2008).

14. Michael Applebaum, "Comfy to Cool: A Brand Swivel," *Brandweek*, May 2, 2005, pp. 18–19.

15. Kevin Lane Keller, Brian Stenthal, and Alice Tybout, "Three Questions You Need to Ask about Your Brand," *Harvard Business Review*, 80 (September 2002): 80–89.

16. Lisa D'Innocenzo, "Moores: For Guys Who Hate to Shop," *Strategy*, May 3, 2004; Moores Clothing for Men website, www.mooresclothing.com/english/moores.htm (viewed January 2011).

17. Kevin Lane Keller, *Strategic Brand Management*, 3rd ed. (Upper Saddle River, NJ: Prentice Hall, 2008).

18. Melita Kubras, "Canada Goose Takes Flight at ACC," *Media in Canada*, November 16, 2009; Canada Goose website, www.canada-goose.com/ (viewed January 2011).

19. Keith Naughton, "Ford's 'Perfect Storm,'" *Newsweek*, September 17, 2001, pp. 48–50.

20. Susan M. Broniarczyk and Andrew D. Gershoff, "The Reciprocal Effects of Brand Equity and Trivial Attributes," *Journal of Marketing Research*, 40 (May 2003): 161–175; Gregory S. Carpenter, Rashi Glazer, and Kent Nakamoto, "Meaningful Brands from Meaningless Differentiation: The Dependence on Irrelevant Attributes," *Journal of Marketing Research*, 31 (August 1994): 339–350.

21. Kerry Capell, "Thinking Simple at Philips," *BusinessWeek*, December 11, 2006, p. 50; Philips website, www.philips.com.

22. Michael E. Porter, *Competitive Strategy: Techniques for Analyzing Industries and Competitors* (New York: The Free Press, 1980).

23. Francis J. Kelly, III, and Barry Silverstein, *The Breakaway Brand* (New York: McGraw-Hill, 2005).

24. Willow Duttge, "Counting Sleep," *Advertising Age*, June 5, 2006, pp. 4, 50.

25. Patrick Barwise, *Simply Better: Winning and Keeping Customers by Delivering What Matters Most* (Cambridge, MA: Harvard Business School Press, 2004).

26. Louise Lee, "Can Progressive Stay in Gear?" *BusinessWeek*, August 8, 2004, p. 44; Robert J. Dolan and Hermann Simon, "Power Pricers," *Across the Board*, May 1997, pp. 18–19; Carol J. Loomis, "Sex. Reefer? And Auto Insurance," *Fortune*, August 7, 1995, p. 76; Progressive website, www.progressive.com.

27. William C. Copacino, *Supply Chain Management* (Boca Raton, FL: St. Lucie Press, 1997).

28. Piet Levy, "Express Yourself," *Marketing News*, June 15, 2009, p. 6.

29. James H. Gilmore and B. Joseph Pine, II, *Authenticity: What Consumers Really Want* (Cambridge, MA: Harvard Business School Press, 2007); Lynn B. Upshaw, *Truth: The New Rules for Marketing in a Skeptical World* (New York: AMACOM, 2007).

30. Owen Jenkins, "Gimme Some Lovin'," *Marketing News*, May 15, 2009, p. 19.

31. Heather Landi, "Raise a Glass," *Beverage World*, October 2009, pp. 16–19.

32. Marc Gobé, *Emotional Branding: The New Paradigm for Connecting Brands to People* (New York: Allworth Press, 2001).

33. Kevin Roberts, *Lovemarks: The Future Beyond Brands, Expanded Edition* (New York: Powerhouse Books, 2005); Kevin Roberts, *The Lovemarks Effect: Winning in the Consumer Revolution* (New York: Powerhouse Books, 2005); "The Lovemarks Heart Beat: January 2010," *Lovemarks*, www.lovemarks.com.

34. Hamish Pringle and Peter Field, "Why Emotional Messages Beat Rational Ones," *Advertising Age*, March 2, 2009, p. 13; Hamish Pringle and Peter Field, *Brand Immortality: How Brands Can Live Long and Prosper* (Philadelphia: Kogan Page, 2009).

35. Rajendra S. Sisodia, David B. Wolfe, and Jagdish N. Sheth, *Firms of Endearment: How World-Class Companies Profit from Passion & Purpose* (Upper Saddle River, NJ: Wharton School Publishing, 2007).

36. Ronald Grover, "Selling by Storytelling," *BusinessWeek*, May 25, 2009.

37. See Goose People on Canada Goose's website: www.canada-goose.com/goose-people/ (viewed January 2011).

38. Randall Ringer and Michael Thibodeau, "A Breakthrough Approach to Brand Creation," *Verse, The Narrative Branding Company*, www.versegroup.com.

39. Patrick Hanlon, *Primal Branding: Create Zealots for Your Brand, Your Company, and Your Future* (New York: The Free Press, 2006); ThinkTopia, www.thinktopia.com.

40. Hillary Chura, "McD's Mass Marketing Loses Luster," *Crain's Chicago Business*, June 16, 2004.

41. Douglas Holt, *How Brands Become Icons: The Principle of Cultural Branding* (Cambridge, MA: Harvard Business School Press, 2004); Douglas Holt, "Branding as Cultural Activism," www.zibs.com; Douglas Holt, "What Becomes an Icon Most," *Harvard Business Review*, March 2003, pp. 43–49. See also Grant McKracken, *Culture and Consumption II: Markets, Meaning, and Brand Management* (Bloomington, IN: Indiana University Press, 2005).

42. Craig Thompson, "Brands as Culturally Embedded Resources," 43rd AMA Sheth Foundation Doctoral Consortium, University of Missouri, June 6, 2008. See also research by John Sherry and Robert Kozinets, including John F. Sherry, Jr., Robert V. Kozinets, Adam Duhachek, Benét DeBerry-Spence, Krittinee Nuttavuthisit, and Diana Storm, "Gendered Behavior in a Male Preserve: Role Playing at ESPN Zone Chicago," *Journal of Consumer Psychology*, 14, nos. 1 & 2 (2004): 151–158; Stephen Brown,

Robert V. Kozinets, and John F. Sherry, Jr., "Teaching Old Brands New Tricks: Retro Branding and the Revival of Brand Meaning," *Journal of Marketing*, 67 (July 2003): 19–33.

43. Nick Wreden, *Fusion Branding: How to Forge Your Brand for the Future* (Atlanta: Accountability Press, 2002); Fusion Branding, www.fusionbranding.com.

44. Andrew Ross Sorkin and Andrew Martin, "Coca-Cola Agrees to Buy Vitaminwater," *New York Times*, May 26, 2007.

45. Ocean Nutrition website, www.ocean-nutrition.com/ (viewed January 2011).

46. Jeromy Lloyd, "Tennis Canada Serves up New Brand," *Marketing*, August 5, 2010.

Chapter 11

1. "Mr. Porter Takes Centre Stage," Porter Airlines News Release, March 7, 2011, www.flyporter.com/About/News-Release-Details?id=141&culture=en-CA; Brent Jang, "Porter: The Little Airline That Could," *The Globe and Mail*, November 20, 2009; Brent Jang, "Porter Aviation's IPO: Figuring the Flight Plan," *The Globe and Mail*, April 19, 2010; Porter Airlines News Release, "Porter Airlines Starts Flights to/from Sault Starting Wednesday, May 4," February 25, 2011, www.saultthisweek.com/ArticleDisplay.aspx?e=2995194.

2. For a detailed academic treatment of a number of issues on competition, see "Special Issue on Competitive Responsiveness," *Marketing Science*, 24 (Winter 2005).

3. Sandra Ward, "Warming Up the Copier," *Barron's*, May 1, 2006, pp. 19, 21; William M. Bulkeley, "Xerox Tries to Go Beyond Copiers," *Wall Street Journal*, February 24, 2009, p. B5; Nanette Byrnes and Roger O. Crockett, "An Historic Succession at Xerox," *BusinessWeek*, June 8, 2009, pp. 18–22.

4. Starbucks, www.starbucks.com/aboutus/overview.asp, December 1, 2009.

5. Brian Wansink, "Can Package Size Accelerate Usage Volume?" *Journal of Marketing*, 60 (July 1996): 1–14. See also Priya Raghubir and Eric A. Greenleaf, "Ratios in Proportion: What Should the Shape of the Package Be?" *Journal of Marketing*, 70 (April 2006): 95–107; and Valerie Folkes and Shashi Matta, "The Effect of Package Shape on Consumers' Judgments of Product Volume: Attention as a Mental Contaminant," *Journal of Consumer Research*, 31 (September 2004): 390–401.

6. John D. Cripps, "Heuristics and Biases in Timing the Replacement of Durable Products," *Journal of Consumer Research*, 21 (September 1994): 304–318.

7. George Stalk, Jr., and Rob Lachanauer, "Hardball: Five Killer Strategies for Trouncing the Competition," *Harvard Business Review*, April 2004, pp. 62–71; Richard D'Aveni, "The Empire Strikes Back: Counterrevolutionary Strategies for Industry Leaders," *Harvard Business Review*, November 2002, pp. 66–74.

8. Nirmalya Kumar, Lisa Sheer, and Philip Kotler, "From Market Driven to Market Driving," *European Management Journal*, 18 (April 2000): 129–142.

9. Much of the remaining section on proactive marketing is based on a provocative book by Leonardo Araujo and Rogerio Gava, *The Proactive Enterprise: How to Anticipate Market Changes*, Palgrave Macmillan, 2012(In Press).

10. Jonathan Glancey, "The Private World of the Walkman," *Guardian*, October 11, 1999.

11. These six defence strategies, as well as the five attack strategies, are taken from Philip Kotler and Ravi Singh, "Marketing Warfare in the 1980s," *Journal of Business Strategy*, Winter 1981, pp. 30–41.

12. Michael E. Porter, *Competitive Strategy: Techniques for Analyzing Industries and Competitors* (New York: The Free Press, 1998), pp. 75–87; Jaideep Prabhu and David W. Stewart, "Signaling Strategies in Competitive Interaction: Building Reputations and Hiding the Truth," *Journal of Marketing Research*, 38 (February 2001): 62–72.

13. Roger J. Calantone and Kim E. Schatzel, "Strategic Foretelling: Communication-Based Antecedents of a Firm's Propensity to Preannounce," *Journal of Marketing*, 64 (January 2000): 17–30; Jehoshua Eliashberg and Thomas S. Robertson, "New Product Preannouncing Behavior: A Market Signaling Study," *Journal of Marketing Research*, 25 (August 1988): 282–292.

14. Thomas S. Robertson, Jehoshua Eliashberg, and Talia Rymon, "New-Product Announcement Signals and Incumbent Reactions," *Journal of Marketing*, 59 (July 1995): 1–15.

15. Yuhong Wu, Sridhar Balasubramanian, and Vijay Mahajan, "When Is a Preannounced New Product Likely to Be Delayed?" *Journal of Marketing*, 68 (April 2004): 101–113; Barry L. Bayus, Sanjay Jain, and Ambar G. Rao, "Truth or Consequences: An Analysis of Vaporware and New-Product Announcements," *Journal of Marketing Research*, 38 (February 2001): 3–13.

16. "Sara Lee Cleans Out Its Cupboards," *Fortune*, March 7, 2005, p. 38; Jane Sassen, "How Sara Lee Left Hanes in Its Skivvies," *BusinessWeek*, September 18, 2006, p. 40.

17. "Purolator Corporate History," www.purolator.com/media/corporate/corporate_history.html (viewed March 2011).

18. J. Scott Armstrong and Kesten C. Green, "Competitor-Oriented Objectives: The Myth of Market Share," *International Journal of Business*, 12 (Winter 2007): 115–134; Stuart E. Jackson, *Where Value Hides: A New Way to Uncover Profitable Growth for Your Business* (New York: John Wiley & Sons, 2006).

19. Nirmalya Kumar, *Marketing as Strategy* (Cambridge, MA: Harvard Business School Press, 2004); Philip Kotler and Paul N. Bloom, "Strategies for High-Market-Share Companies," *Harvard Business Review*, November–December 1975, pp. 63–72.

20. Robert D. Buzzell and Frederick D. Wiersema, "Successful Share-Building Strategies," *Harvard Business Review*, January–February 1981, pp. 135–144.

21. Linda Hellofs and Robert Jacobson, "Market Share and Customer's Perceptions of Quality: When Can Firms Grow Their Way to Higher versus Lower Quality?" *Journal of Marketing*, 63 (January 1999), pp. 16–25.

22. Jamie Sturgeon, "CRTC Gives Nod to BCE to Buy CTV's Globemedia," *Postmedia News*, March 8, 2011.

23. Jon Birger, "Second-Mover Advantage," *Fortune*, March 20, 2006, pp. 20–21.

24. Dominion Lending Centres website http://dominionmortgageconnection.ca/careers/careers-brand (viewed March 2011); "View DLC's New Don Cherry ad," *BrokerNews.ca*, November 10, 2010, www.canadianmortgageprofessional.com/news/view-dlcs-new-don-cherry-ad/75648

25. Venkatesh Shankar, Gregory Carpenter, and Lakshman Krishnamurthi, "Late-Mover Advantage: How Innovative Late Entrants Outsell Pioneers," *Journal of Marketing Research*, 35 (February 1998): 54–70; Gregory S. Carpenter and Kent Nakamoto, "The Impact of Consumer Preference Formation on Marketing Objectives and Competitive Second-Mover Strategies," *Journal of Consumer Psychology*, 5 (1996): 325–358; Gregory S. Carpenter and Kent Nakamoto, "Competitive Strategies for Late Entry into a Market with a Dominant Brand," *Management Science*, October 1990, pp. 1268–1278.

26. Megan Johnston, "The Ketchup Strategy," *Forbes*, November 13, 2006, p. 185.

27. Michael V. Copeland, "These Boots Really Were Made for Walking," *Business 2.0*, October 2004, pp. 72–74.

28. Katrina Booker, "The Pepsi Machine," *Fortune*, February 6, 2006, pp. 68–72.

29. Theodore Levitt, "Innovative Imitation," *Harvard Business Review*, September–October 1966, p. 63. Also see Steven P. Schnaars, *Managing Imitation Strategies: How Later Entrants Seize Markets from Pioneers* (New York: The Free Press, 1994).

30. Stuart F. Brown, "The Company That Out-Harleys Harley," *Fortune*, September 28, 1998, pp. 56–57; S&S Cycle, www.sscycle.com.

31. LED Roadway Lighting homepage, www.ledroadwaylighting.com/ (viewed March 2011).

32. Reported in E. R. Linneman and L. J. Stanton, *Making Niche Marketing Work* (New York: McGraw-Hill, 1991).

33. Kathleen Kingsbury, "The Cell Islands," *TIME*, November 20, 2006, p. G20; "Traveling Made Easy with the New BlackBerry Curve 8520," *Digicel-News*, http://digicel-jamaica-news-procomm. blogspot.com, January 12, 2010.

34. Some authors distinguished additional stages. Wasson suggested a stage of competitive turbulence between growth and maturity. See Chester R. Wasson, *Dynamic Competitive Strategy and Product Life Cycles* (Austin, TX: Austin Press, 1978). Maturity describes a stage of sales growth slowdown and saturation, a stage of flat sales after sales have peaked.

35. John E. Swan and David R. Rink, "Fitting Market Strategy to Varying Product Life Cycles," *Business Horizons*, January–February 1982, pp. 72–76; Gerald J. Tellis and C. Merle Crawford, "An Evolutionary Approach to Product Growth Theory," *Journal of Marketing*, 45 (Fall 1981): 125–134.

36. William E. Cox, Jr., "Product Life Cycles as Marketing Models," *Journal of Business*, October 1967, pp. 375–384.

37. Jordan P. Yale, "The Strategy of Nylon's Growth," *Modern Textiles Magazine*, February 1964, p. 32. Also see Theodore Levitt, "Exploit the Product Life Cycle," *Harvard Business Review*, November–December 1965, pp. 81–94.

38. Chester R. Wasson, "How Predictable Are Fashion and Other Product Life Cycles?" *Journal of Marketing*, 32 (July 1968): 36–43.

39. Ibid.

40. William H. Reynolds, "Cars and Clothing: Understanding Fashion Trends," *Journal of Marketing*, 32 (July 1968): 44–49.

41. Bryan Curtis, "Trivial Pursuit," *Slate.com*, April 13, 2005; Patrick Butters, "What Biggest-Selling Adult Game Still Cranks Out Vexing Questions?" *Insight on the News*, January 26, 1998, p. 39.

42. Robert D. Buzzell, "Competitive Behavior and Product Life Cycles," in *New Ideas for Successful Marketing*, edited byJohn S. Wright and Jack Goldstucker(Chicago: American Marketing Association, 1956), p. 51.

43. Rajesh J. Chandy, Gerard J. Tellis, Deborah J. MacInnis, and Pattana Thaivanich, "What to Say When: Advertising Appeals in Evolving Markets," *Journal of Marketing Research*, 38 (November 2001): 399–414.

44. As reported in Joseph T. Vesey, "The New Competitors: They Think in Terms of Speed to Market," *Academy of Management Executive*, 5 (May 1991): 23–33; and Brian Dumaine, "How Managers Can Succeed through Speed," *Fortune*, February 13, 1989, pp. 54–59.

45. Glen L. Urban et al., "Market Share Rewards to Pioneering Brands: An Empirical Analysis and Strategic Implications," *Management Science*, June 1986, pp. 645–659; William T. Robinson and Claes Fornell, "Sources of Market Pioneer Advantages in Consumer Goods Industries," *Journal of Marketing Research*, 22 (August 1985): 305–317.

46. Gregory S. Carpenter and Kent Nakamoto, "Consumer Preference Formation and Pioneering Advantage," *Journal of Marketing Research*, 26 (August 1989): 285–298.

47. William T. Robinson and Sungwook Min, "Is the First to Market the First to Fail? Empirical Evidence for Industrial Goods Businesses," *Journal of Marketing Research*, 39 (February 2002): 120–128.

48. Frank R. Kardes, Gurumurthy Kalyanaram, Murali Chankdrashekaran, and Ronald J. Dornoff, "Brand Retrieval, Consideration Set Composition, Consumer Choice, and the Pioneering Advantage," *Journal of Consumer Research*, 20 (June 1993): 62–75. See also Frank H. Alpert and Michael A. Kamins, "Pioneer Brand Advantage and Consumer Behavior: A Conceptual Framework and Propositional Inventory," *Journal of the Academy of Marketing Science*, 22 (June 1994): 244–253.

49. Kurt A. Carlson, Margaret G. Meloy, and J. Edward Russo, "Leader-Driven Primacy: Using Attribute Order to Affect Consumer Choice," *Journal of Consumer Research*, 32 (March 2006): 513–518.

50. Thomas S. Robertson and Hubert Gatignon, "How Innovators Thwart New Entrants into Their Market," *Planning Review*, September–October 1991, pp. 4–11, 48; Douglas Bowman and Hubert Gatignon, "Order of Entry as a Moderator of the Effect of Marketing Mix on Market Share," *Marketing Science*, 15 (Summer 1996): 222–242.

51. Venkatesh Shankar, Gregory S. Carpenter, and Lakshman Krishnamurthi, "Late Mover Advantage: How Innovative Late Entrants Outsell Pioneers," *Journal of Marketing Research*, 35 (February 1998): 54–70.

52. Steven P. Schnaars, *Managing Imitation Strategies* (New York: The Free Press, 1994). See also Jin K. Han, Namwoon Kim, and Hony-Bom Kin, "Entry Barriers: A Dull-, One-, or Two-Edged Sword for Incumbents? Unraveling the Paradox from a Contingency Perspective," *Journal of Marketing*, 65 (January 2001): 1–14.

53. Victor Kegan, "Second Sight: Second Movers Take All," *The Guardian*, October 10, 2002.

54. Peter N. Golder, "Historical Method in Marketing Research with New Evidence on Long-term Market Share Stability," *Journal of Marketing Research*, 37 (May 2000): 156–172; Peter N. Golder and Gerald J. Tellis, "Pioneer Advantage: Marketing Logic or Marketing Legend?" *Journal of Marketing Research*, 30 (May 1993): 34–46. See also Shi Zhang and Arthur B. Markman, "Overcoming the Early Advantage: The Role of Alignable and Nonalignable Differences," *Journal of Marketing Research*, 35 (November 1998): 1–15.

55. Gerald Tellis and Peter Golder, *Will and Vision: How Latecomers Can Grow to Dominate Markets* (New York: McGraw-Hill, 2001); Rajesh K. Chandy and Gerald J. Tellis, "The Incumbent's Curse? Incumbency, Size, and Radical Product Innovation," *Journal of Marketing Research*, 64 (July 2000): 1–17.

56. Sungwook Min, Manohar U. Kalwani, and William T. Robinson, "Market Pioneer and Early Follower Survival Risks: A Contingency Analysis of Really New Versus Incrementally New Product-Markets," *Journal of Marketing*, 70 (January 2006): 15–35. See also Raji Srinivasan, Gary L. Lilien, and Arvind Rangaswamy, "First In, First Out? The Effects of Network Externalities on Pioneer Survival," *Journal of Marketing*, 68 (January 2004): 41–58.

57. Trond Riiber Knudsen, "Escaping the Middle-Market Trap: An Interview with CEO of Electrolux," *McKinsey Quarterly*, December 2006, pp. 72–79.

58. Rajan Varadarajan, Mark P. DeFanti, and Paul S. Busch, "Brand Portfolio, Corporate Image, and Reputation: Managing Brand Deletions," *Journal of the Academy of Marketing Science*, 34 (Spring 2006): 195–205; Stephen J. Carlotti, Jr., Mary Ellen Coe, and Jesko Perrey, "Making Brand Portfolios Work," *McKinsey Quarterly*, 4 (2004): 24–36; Nirmalya Kumar, "Kill a Brand, Keep a Customer," *Harvard Business Review*, December 2003, pp. 86–95; George J. Avlonitis, "Product Elimination Decision Making: Does Formality Matter?" *Journal of Marketing*, 49 (Winter 1985): 41–52; Philip Kotler, "Phasing Out Weak Products," *Harvard Business Review*, March–April 1965, pp. 107–118.

59. Kathryn Rudie Harrigan, "The Effect of Exit Barriers upon Strategic Flexibility," *Strategic Management Journal*, 1 (February 1980): 165–176.

60. Laurence P. Feldman and Albert L. Page, "Harvesting: The Misunderstood Market Exit Strategy," *Journal of Business Strategy*, Spring 1985, pp. 79–85; Philip Kotler, "Harvesting Strategies for Weak Products," *Business Horizons*, August 1978, pp. 15–22.

61. Rob Walker, "Can Ghost Brands...," *International Herald Tribune*, May 17–18, 2008, pp. 17–18; Peter Carbona, "The Rush to Grab Orphan Brands," *BusinessWeek*, August 3, 2009, pp. 47–48.

62. Stuart Elliott, "Those Shelved Brands Start to Look Tempting," *New York Times*, August 21, 2008.

63. Peter N. Golder and Gerard J. Tellis, "Growing, Growing, Gone: Cascades, Diffusion, and Turning Points in the Product Life Cycle," *Marketing Science, 23* (Spring 2004): 207–218.

64. Youngme Moon, "Break Free from the Product Life Cycle," *Harvard Business Review,* May 2005, pp. 87–94.

65. Hubert Gatignon and David Soberman, "Competitive Response and Market Evolution," in *Handbook of Marketing,* edited byBarton A. Weitz and Robin Wensley(London, England: Sage Publications, 2002), pp. 126–147; Robert D. Buzzell, "Market Functions and Market Evolution," *Journal of Marketing, 63* (Special Issue 1999): 61–63.

66. Raji Srinivasan, Arvind Rangaswamy, and Gary L. Lilien, "Turning Adversity into Advantage: Does Proactive Marketing During Recession Pay Off?" *International Journal of Research in Marketing, 22* (June 2005): 109–125.

67. Jon Fine, "Why General Mills Marketing Pays Off," *BusinessWeek,* July 27, 2009, pp. 67–68; Matthew Boyle, "Snap, Crackle, Pop at the Food Giants," *BusinessWeek,* October 6, 2008, p. 48.

68. Philip Lay, Todd Hewlin, and Geoffrey Moore, "In a Downturn, Provoke Your Customers," *Harvard Business Review,* March 2009, pp. 48–56.

69. John A. Quelch and Katherine E. Jocz, "How to Market in a Downturn," *Harvard Business Review,* April 2009, pp. 52–62.

70. Maria Bartiromo, "Facetime: Inside a Company Resetting for Recovery," *BusinessWeek,* July 13 and 20, 2009, pp. 15–17.

71. Jane Porter and Burt Heim, "Doing Whatever Gets Them in the Door," *BusinessWeek,* June 30, 2008, p. 60.

72. Bill Mann, "U.S. Border Town Flights New Sales-Tax Break for Canadians," July 19, 2010, http://blogs.marketwatch.com/canada/2010/07/19/us-border-town-fights-new-sales-tax-break-for-canadians/ (viewed April 2011); "Nordstrom, J. Crew coming to Canada," *CTV News,* March 30, 2011, www.ctvbc.ctv.ca/servlet/an/local/CTVNews/20110330/bc_shopping_110330/20110330?hub=BritishColumbiaHome; "Metro Merchants Face Space Competiton from U.S. Retailers," *Western Investor,* April 1, 2011, www.western-investor.com/index.php/news/bc/402-metro-retailers-face-space-competition-from-us-retailers (viewed April 2011).

73. David Taylor, David Nichols, Diego Kerner, and Anne Charbonneau, "Leading Brands Out of the Recession," *Brandgym Research Paper 2,* www.brandgym.com, September 2009.

74. Peter J. Williamson and Ming Zeng, "Value for Money Strategies for Recessionary Times," *Harvard Business Review,* March 2009, pp. 66–74.

75. Burt Heim, "How to Sell Luxury to Penny-Pinchers," *BusinessWeek,* November 10, 2008, p. 60.

76. Stuart Elliott, "Trying to Pitch Products to the Savers," *New York Times,* June 3, 2009.

77. Andrew Martin, "In Tough Times, Spam Is Suddenly Appealing," *Boston Globe,* November 16, 2008.

Chapter 12

1. www.mec.ca (viewed January 4, 2011); "Co-op Announces Funding to Get Canadians Active, Protect Environment," *Canada Newswire,* June 23, 2010; Henry Cage, "Retailer Aims for Peak for Ethical Performance: Member-Owned Mountain Co-op Sells Products from Pristine Souces," *National Post,* November 21, 1998, p. D4; "MEC Gifts Give Twice," *Canada Newswire,* November 23, 2005, p.1; "Mountain Equipment Co-op Invites You to Think Big, Tread Lightly in the Outdoors This Summer," *Canada Newswire,* August 19, 2004, p. 1.

2. This discussion is adapted from a classic article: Theodore Levitt, "Marketing Success through Differentiation: Of Anything," *Harvard Business Review,* January–February 1980, pp. 83–91. The first level, core benefit, has been added to Levitt's discussion.

3. Harper W. Boyd, Jr., and Sidney Levy, "New Dimensions in Consumer Analysis," *Harvard Business Review,* November–December 1963, pp. 129–140.

4. For some definitions, see *Dictionary of Marketing Terms,* edited by Peter D. Bennett (Chicago: American Marketing Association, 1995). Also see Patrick E. Murphy and Ben M. Enis, "Classifying Products Strategically," *Journal of Marketing, 50* (July 1986): 24–42.

5. Some of these bases are discussed in David A. Garvin, "Competing on the Eight Dimensions of Quality," *Harvard Business Review,* November–December 1987, pp. 101–109.

6. Marco Bertini, Elie Ofek, and Dan Ariely, "The Impact of Add-On Features on Product Evaluations," *Journal of Consumer Research, 36* (June 2009): 17–28; Tripat Gill, "Convergent Products: What Functionalities Add More Value to the Base," *Journal of Marketing, 72* (March 2008): 46–62; Robert J. Meyer, Sheghui Zhao, and Jin K. Han, "Biases in Valuation vs. Usage of Innovative Product Features," *Marketing Science, 27* (November–December 2008): 1083–1096.

7. Paul Kedrosky, "Simple Minds," *Business 2.0,* April 2006, p. 38; Debora Viana Thompson, Rebecca W. Hamilton, and Roland Rust, "Feature Fatigue: When Product Capabilities Become Too Much of a Good Thing," *Journal of Marketing Research, 42* (November 2005): 431–442.

8. James H. Gilmore and B. Joseph Pine, *Markets of One: Creating Customer-Unique Value through Mass Customization* (Boston: Harvard Business School Press, 2000).

9. Nikolaus Franke, Peter Keinz, Christoph J. Steger, "Testing the Value of Customization: When Do Customers Really Prefer Products Tailored to Their Preferences," *Journal of Marketing, 73* (September 2009): 103–121.

10. Gail Edmondson, "Mercedes Gets Back up to Speed," *BusinessWeek,* November 13, 2006, pp. 46–47; Peter Gumble, "How Dr. Z Plans to Fix Mercedes," *CNNMoney.com,* http://money.cnn.com, July 13, 2009; Chris Shunk, "Paradox: As Quality Improves, Mercedes-Benz Dealership Profits Decline," *Automotive News,* January 27, 2009.

11. Consumer Reports website, www.consumerreports.org/cro/canadaextra/index.htm (viewed November 20, 2010).

12. Bernd Schmitt and Alex Simonson, *Marketing Aesthetics: The Strategic Management of Brand, Identity, and Image* (New York: The Free Press, 1997).

13. Stanley Reed, "Rolls-Royce at Your Service," *BusinessWeek,* November 15, 2005, pp. 92–93; *Rolls-Royce,* www.rolls-royce.com/civil/services/totalcare; "Rolls-Royce Secures USD 4.1 Billion Worth Orders During Paris Air Show," *India Defence,* www.india-defence.com, June 20, 2009; "Rolls-Royce Engine Support," *Aviation Today,* June 1, 2006.

14. Norma Ramage, "Be Our Guest," *Marketing Magazine Online,* September 10, 2007, www.marketingmag.ca.

15. WestJet website, www.westjet.com (viewed November 20, 2010).

16. For a comprehensive discussion of Cemex, see Adrian J. Slywotzky and David J. Morrison, "Digital Innovator: Cemex," *How Digital Is Your Business* (New York: Crown Business, 2000), pp. 78–100. See also Mohanbir Sawhney, Robert C. Wolcott, and Inigo Arroniz, "The 12 Different Ways for Companies to Innovate," *MIT Sloan Management Review,* April 1, 2006.

17. This section is based on a comprehensive treatment of product returns: James Stock, Thomas Speh, and Herbert Shear, "Managing Product Returns for Competitive Advantage," *MIT Sloan Management Review,* Fall 2006, pp. 57–62. See also J. Andrew Petersen and V. Kumar, "Can Product Returns Make You Money?" *MIT Sloan Management Review,* Spring 2010, pp. 85–89.

18. Bruce Nussbaum, "The Power of Design," *BusinessWeek,* May 17, 2004, pp. 88–94; "Masters of Design," *Fast Company,* June 2004, pp. 61–75. Also see Philip Kotler, "Design: A Powerful but Neglected Strategic Tool," *Journal of Business Strategy,* Fall 1984, pp. 16–21.

19. Ravindra Chitturi, Rajagopal Raghunathan, and Vijay Mahajan, "Delight by Design: The Role of Hedonic Versus Utilitarian Benefits," *Journal of Marketing, 72* (May 2008): 48–63.

20. Ulrich R. Orth and Keven Malkewitz, "Holistic Package Design and Consumer Brand Impressions," *Journal of Marketing, 72* (May 2008): 64–81; Mark Borden, "Less Hulk, More Bruce Lee," *Fast Company*, April 2007, pp. 86–91.

21. Steve Hamm and Jay Greene, "That Computer Is So You," *BusinessWeek*, January 14, 2008, pp. 24–26; Damon Darlin, "Design Helps H.P. Profit More on PCs," *New York Times*, May 17, 2007.

22. "New Exporter Winner: Chilliwack Mountain Log Homes Ltd.," *2008 BC Export Awards: Previous Winners 2003*, www. bcexportawards. com/template_bc.asp?p=25 (viewed April 2008); Jessica Murdy, "Locally Built Log Homes Reach around the World," *The Progress*, April 21, 2007.

23. "2010 IDEA Winners," *Fast Company's Co. Design*, www.fast-codesign.com/idea-2010#article_center (viewed May 22, 2011); David Carnoy, "The 20 Most Innovative Products of the Decade," *CNET Reviews*, December 10, 2009; Emily Lambert, "Splash," *Forbes*, July 23, 2007, pp. 66–68.

24. Virginia Postrel, *The Substance of Style: How the Rise of Aesthetic Value Is Remaking Commerce, Culture, and Consciousness* (New York: HarperCollins, 2003).

25. Linda Tischler, "Pop Artist David Butler," *Fast Company*, October 2009, pp. 91–97; Jessie Scanlon, "Coca-Cola's New Design Direction," *BusinessWeek*, August 25, 2008.

26. Todd Wasserman, "Thinking by Design," *Brandweek*, November 3, 2008, pp. 18–21.

27. Jay Green, "Where Designers Rule," *BusinessWeek*, November 5, 2007, pp. 46–51; Deborah Steinborn, "Talking About Design," *Wall Street Journal*, June 23, 2008, p. R6.

28. In reality, Tide's product line is actually deeper and more complex. There are 9 powder products, 16 liquid products, 1 Stain Release product, 1 Tide to Go product, 1 Tide Washing Machine Cleaner, and 9 Tide accessories.

29. A. Yesim Orhun, "Optimal Product Line Design When Consumers Exhibit Choice Set-Dependent Preferences," *Marketing Science, 28* (September–October 2009): 868–886; Robert Bordley, "Determining the Appropriate Depth and Breadth of a Firm's Product Portfolio," *Journal of Marketing Research, 40* (February 2003): 39–53; Peter Boatwright and Joseph C. Nunes, "Reducing Assortment: An Attribute-Based Approach," *Journal of Marketing, 65* (July 2001): 50–63.

30. Adapted from a Hamilton Consultants White Paper, December 1, 2000.

31. Amna Kirmani, Sanjay Sood, and Sheri Bridges, "The Ownership Effect in Consumer Responses to Brand-Line Stretches," *Journal of Marketing, 63* (January 1999): 88–101; T. Randall, K. Ulrich, and D. Reibstein, "Brand Equity and Vertical Product-Line Extent," *Marketing Science, 17* (Fall 1998): 356–379; David A. Aaker, "Should You Take Your Brand to Where the Action Is?" *Harvard Business Review*, September–October 1997, pp. 135–143.

32. Marina Strauss, "The Bay Steps Up Its Game with a Focus on Shoes," *The Globe and Mail*, June 4, 2010, p. B3.

33. Michael Carolan, "InterContinental Hotels Sales up after 18 Months of Falls," *Wall Street Journal*, May 11, 2010; Barbara De Lollis, "Holiday Inn Chain Upgrades with Style," *USA TODAY*, June 24, 2008; Bob Garfield, "What Makes This Commercial Great? The Bacon Bit Says It All," *Advertising Age*, February 25, 2008.

34. Alex Taylor III, "Bavaria's Next Top Model," *Fortune*, March 30, 2009, pp. 100–103; Neal E. Boudette, "BMW's Push to Broaden Line Hits Some Bumps in the Road," *Wall Street Journal*, January 25, 2005; Alex Taylor III, "The Ultimate Fairly Inexpensive Driving Machine," *Fortune*, November 1, 2004, pp. 130–140.

35. Stuart Henderson Britt, "How Weber's Law Can Be Applied to Marketing," *Business Horizons*, February 1975, pp. 21–29.

36. Brett R. Gordon, "A Dynamic Model of Consumer Replacement Cycles in the PC Processor Industry," *Marketing Science, 28* (September–October 2009): 846–867; Raghunath Singh Rao, Om Narasimhan, and George John, "Understanding the Role

of Trade-Ins in Durable Goods Markets: Theory and Evidence," *Marketing Science, 28* (September–October 2009): 950–967.

37. Stanley Holmes, "All the Rage Since Reagan," *BusinessWeek*, July 25, 2005, p. 68.

38. Nirmalya Kumar, "Kill a Brand, Keep a Customer," *Harvard Business Review*, December 2003, pp. 86–95; Brad Stone, "Back to Basics," *Newsweek*, August 4, 2003, pp. 42–44; Sarah Skidmore, "Designers, Makers Tune In to Collectors for New Trends," *Associated Press*, January 21, 2007.

39. Laurens M. Sloot, Dennis Fok, and Peter Verhoef, "The Short- and Long-Term Impact of an Assortment Reduction on Category Sales," *Journal of Marketing Research, 43* (November 2006): 536–548.

40. Patricia O'Connell, "A Chat with Unilever's Niall FitzGerald," *BusinessWeek*, www.businessweek.com, August 2, 2001; John Willman, "Leaner, Cleaner, and Healthier Is the Stated Aim," *Financial Times*, February 23, 2000; "Unilever's Goal: 'Power Brands,'" *Advertising Age*, January 3, 2000.

41. Eric T. Anderson and Duncan I. Simester, "Does Demand Fall When Customers Perceive That Prices Are Unfair? The Case of Premium Pricing for Large Sizes," *Marketing Science, 27* (May–June 2008): 492–500.

42. Ricard Gil and Wesley R. Hartmann, "Empirical Analysis of Metering Price Discrimination: Evidence from Concession Sales at Movie Theaters," *Marketing Science, 28* (November–December 2009): 1046–1062.

43. Connie Guglielmo, "Hewlett-Packard Says Printer Business is 'Healthy,'" *Bloomberg News*, December 22, 2009; "HP Annual Report 2008," *HP*, www.hp.com/hpinfo/investor/; Ben Elgin, "Can HP's Printer Biz Keep Printing Money?" *BusinessWeek*, July 14, 2003, pp. 68–70; Simon Avery, "H-P Sees Room for Growth in Printer Market," *Wall Street Journal*, June 28, 2001.

44. Dilip Soman and John T. Gourville, "Transaction Decoupling: How Price Bundling Affects the Decision to Consume," *Journal of Marketing Research, 38* (February 2001): 30–44; Ramanathan Subramaniam and R. Venkatesh, "Optimal Bundling Strategies in Multiobject Auctions of Complements or Substitutes," *Marketing Science, 28* (March–April 2009): 264–273.

45. Anita Elberse, "Bye-Bye Bundles: The Unbundling of Music in Digital Channels," *Journal of Marketing, 74* (May 2010): 107–123.

46. Akshay R. Rao, Lu Qu, and Robert W. Ruekert, "Signaling Unobservable Quality through a Brand Ally," *Journal of Marketing Research, 36* (May 1999): 258–268; Akshay R. Rao and Robert W. Ruekert, "Brand Alliances as Signals of Product Quality," *Sloan Management Review*, Fall 1994, pp. 87–97.

47. Bernard L. Simonin and Julie A. Ruth, "Is a Company Known by the Company It Keeps? Assessing the Spillover Effects of Brand Alliances on Consumer Brand Attitudes," *Journal of Marketing Research, 35* (February 1998), pp. 30–42. See also C. W. Park, S. Y. Jun, and A. D. Shocker, "Composite Branding Alliances: An Investigation of Extension and Feedback Effects," *Journal of Marketing Research, 33* (November 1996): 453–466.

48. Tansev Geylani, J. Jeffrey Inman, and Frenkel Ter Hofstede, "Image Reinforcement or Impairment: The Effects of Co-branding on Attribute Uncertainty," *Marketing Science, 27* (July–August 2008): 730–744; Ed Lebar, Phil Buehler, Kevin Lane Keller, Monika Sawicka, Zeynep Aksehirli, and Keith Richey, "Brand Equity Implications of Joint Branding Programs," *Journal of Advertising Research, 45* (December 2005).

49. C. W. Park, S. Y. Jun, and A. D. Shocker, "Composite Branding Alliances: An Investigation of Extension and Feedback Effects," *Journal of Marketing Research, 33* (November 1996): 453–466; Lance Leuthesser, Chiranjier Kohli, and Rajneesh Suri, "2 + 2 = 5? A Framework for Using Co-branding to Leverage a Brand," *Journal of Brand Management, 2* (September 2003): 35–47.

50. Based in part on a talk by Nancy Bailey, "Using Licensing to Build the Brand," Brand Masters Conference, December 7, 2000.

51. Philip Kotler and Waldermar Pfoertsch, *Ingredient Branding: Making the Invisible Visible* (Heidelberg, Germany: Springer-Verlag, 2011).

52. Kalpesh Kaushik Desai and Kevin Lane Keller, "The Effects of Brand Expansions and Ingredient Branding Strategies on Host Brand Extendibility," *Journal of Marketing*, 66 (January 2002): 73–93; D. C. Denison, "Ingredient Branding Puts Big Names in the Mix," *Boston Globe*, May 26, 2002.

53. Joe Tradii, "Ingredient Branding: Time to Check That Recipe Again," *Brandweek*, March 29, 2010, p. 44; Piet Levy, "B-to-B-to-C," *Marketing News*, September 30, 2009, pp. 15–20.

54. "DuPont Receives Corporate Innovation Award," *DuPont*, www.dupont.com, November 13, 2009.

55. Kevin Lane Keller, *Strategic Brand Management*, 3rd ed. (Upper Saddle River, NJ: Prentice Hall, 2008); Philip Kotler and Waldemar Pfoertsch, *B2B Brand Management* (New York: Springer, 2006); Paul F. Nunes, Stephen F. Dull, and Patrick D. Lynch, "When Two Brands Are Better Than One," *Outlook*, January 2003, pp. 14–23.

56. Fred Richards, "Memo to CMOs: It's the Packaging, Stupid," *Brandweek*, August 17, 2009, p. 22.

57. Susan B. Bassin, "Value-Added Packaging Cuts through Store Clutter," *Marketing News*, September 26, 1988, p. 21. Reprinted with permission from *Marketing News*, published by the American Marketing Association.

58. "Industry Honours," *Food in Canada*, 69, no. 5 (June 2009), p. 24; "Sustainability," *Kraft Foods Canada*, www.kraftfoodscompany.com/ca/en/responsibility/sustainability/index.aspx (viewed May 23, 2011).

59. "McCormick Canada Launches Six New Flavourful Recipe Mixes," *Marketwire*, November 2010.

60. Stuart Elliott, "Tropicana Discovers Some Buyers Are Passionate about Packaging," *New York Times*, February 23, 2009; Linda Tischler, "Never Mind! Pepsi Pulls Much-Loathed Tropicana Packaging," *Fast Company*, February 23, 2009; Natalie Zmuda, "Tropicana Line's Sales Plunge 20% Post-rebranding," *Advertising Age*, April 2, 2009; Kenneth Hein, "Tropicana Squeezes Out Fresh Design with a Peel," *Brandweek*, January 19, 2009, p. 30.

61. Mya Frazier, "How Can Your Package Stand Out? Eye Tracking Looks Hard for Answers," *Advertising Age*, October 16, 2006, p. 14.

62. Kate Fitzgerald, "Packaging Is the Capper," *Advertising Age*, May 5, 2003, p. 22.

63. Robert Berner, "Watch Out, Best Buy and Circuit City," *BusinessWeek*, November 21, 2005, pp. 46–48.

64. Tao Chen, Ajay Kalra, and Baohung Sun, "Why Do Consumers Buy Extended Service Contracts," *Journal of Consumer Research*, 36 (December 2009): 611–623.

65. Barbara Ettore, "Phenomenal Promises Mean Business," *Management Review*, March 1994, pp. 18–23; "More Firms Pledge Guaranteed Service," *Wall Street Journal*, July 17, 1991. Also see Sridhar Moorthy and Kannan Srinivasan, "Signaling Quality with a Money-Back Guarantee: The Role of Transaction Costs," *Marketing Science*, 14 (Fall 1995): 442–446; and Christopher W. L. Hart, *Extraordinary Guarantees* (New York: AMACOM, 1993).

Chapter 13

1. Leonard L. Berry, *On Great Service: A Framework for Action* (New York: The Free Press, 2006); Leonard L. Berry, *Discovering the Soul of Service: The Nine Drivers of Sustainable Business Success* (New York: The Free Press, 1999); *Customer Service: Extraordinary Results at Southwest Airlines, Charles Schwab, Lands' End, American Express, Staples, and USAA*, edited by Fred Wiersema (New York: HarperBusiness, 1998).

2. Matt Krantz, "Tinseltown Gets Glitzy New Star," *USA TODAY*, August 24, 2009; Linda Tischler, "Join the Circus," *Fast Company*, July 2005, pp. 53–58; "Cirque du Soleil," *America's Greatest Brands*, Vol. 3 (America's Greatest Brands, 2004); Geoff Keighley, "The Factory," *Business 2.0*, February 2004, p. 102;

Robin D. Rusch, "Cirque du Soleil Phantasmagoria Contorts," *Brandchannel.com*, December 1, 2003.

3. Statistics Canada, "Gross Domestic Product at Basic Prices, by Industry," www40.statcan.gc.ca/l01/cst01/econ41-eng.htm (viewed June 7, 2011).

4. Statistics Canada, "Employment by Industry," www40.statcan.ca/l01/cst01/econ40.htm (viewed June 7, 2011).

5. Paul Keegan, "The Best New Idea in Business," *Fortune*, September 14, 2009, pp. 42–52; Adam Ashton, "Growth Galore but Profits Are Zip," *BusinessWeek*, September 8, 2008, p. 62; Alex Frankel, "Zipcar Makes the Leap," *Fast Company*, March 2008, pp. 48–50; Mike Beirne, "Temporary Plates," *Brandweek*, July 9, 2007, pp. 30–34.

6. Further classifications of services are described in Christopher H. Lovelock, *Services Marketing*, 3rd ed. (Upper Saddle River, NJ: Prentice Hall, 1996). Also see John E. Bateson, *Managing Services Marketing: Text and Readings*, 3rd ed. (Hinsdale, IL: Dryden, 1995).

7. Amy Ostrom and Dawn Iacobucci, "Consumer Trade-Offs and the Evaluation of Services," *Journal of Marketing*, 59 (January 1995): 17–28.

8. For discussion of how the blurring of the line distinguishing products and services changes the meaning of this taxonomy, see Christopher Lovelock and Evert Gummesson, "Whither Services Marketing? In Search of a New Paradigm and Fresh Perspectives," *Journal of Service Research*, 7 (August 2004): 20–41; and Stephen L. Vargo and Robert F. Lusch, "Evolving to a New Dominant Logic for Marketing," *Journal of Marketing*, 68 (January 2004): 1–17.

9. Theodore Levitt, "Marketing Intangible Products and Product Intangibles," *Harvard Business Review*, May–June 1981, pp. 94–102; Leonard L. Berry, "Services Marketing Is Different," *Business*, May–June 1980, pp. 24–29.

10. B. H. Booms and M. J. Bitner, "Marketing Strategies and Organizational Structures for Service Firms," in *Marketing of Services*, edited by J. Donnelly and W. R. George (Chicago: American Marketing Association, 1981), pp. 47–51.

11. Lewis P. Carbone and Stephan H. Haeckel, "Engineering Customer Experiences," *Marketing Management*, 3 (Winter 1994): 17.

12. Bernd H. Schmitt, *Customer Experience Management* (New York: John Wiley & Sons, 2003); Bernd H. Schmitt, David L. Rogers, and Karen Vrotsos, *There's No Business That's Not Show Business: Marketing in an Experience Culture* (Upper Saddle River, NJ: Prentice Hall Financial Times, 2004).

13. Chip Heath and Dan Heath, "Give 'Em Something to Talk About," *Fast Company*, June 2007, pp. 58–59.

14. For some emerging research results on the effects of creating time and place service separation, see Hean Tat Keh and Jun Pang, "Customer Reaction to Service Separation," *Journal of Marketing*, 74 (March 2010): 55–70.

15. Stephen Holden, "Becoming Comfortable with Emotional Depth," *New York Times*, March 22, 2010, p. C7; "Michael Bublé," *Michael Bublé Official Site*, www.michaelbuble.com/news (viewed September 30, 2010).

16. Gila E. Fruchter and Eitan Gerstner, "Selling with 'Satisfaction Guaranteed,'" *Journal of Service Research*, 1 (May 1999): 313–323. See also Rebecca J. Slotegraaf and J. Jeffrey Inman, "Longitudinal Shifts in the Drivers of Satisfaction with Product Quality: The Role of Attribute Resolvability," *Journal of Marketing Research*, 41 (August 2004): 269–280.

17. For a similar list, see Leonard L. Berry and A. Parasuraman, *Marketing Services: Competing through Quality* (New York: The Free Press, 1991), p. 16.

18. "The Financial Post's Ten Best Companies to Work For: Fairmont Hotels & Resorts (Profile)," *Canada.com Network*, September 27, 2007, working.canada.com.

19. The material in this paragraph is based in part on Valarie Zeithaml, Mary Jo Bitner, and Dwayne D. Gremler, "Service

Development and Design," *Services Marketing: Integrating Customer Focus across the Firm*, 4th ed. (New York: McGraw-Hill, 2006), Ch. 9; G. Lynn Shostack, "Service Positioning through Structural Change," *Journal of Marketing*, 51 (January 1987): 34–43.

20. Vikas Mittal, Wagner A. Kamakura, and Rahul Govind, "Geographical Patterns in Customer Service and Satisfaction: An Empirical Investigation," *Journal of Marketing*, 68 (July 2004): 48–62.

21. Jeffrey F. Rayport, Bernard J. Jaworski, and Ellie J. Kyung, "Best Face Forward: Improving Companies' Service Interface with Customers," *Journal of Interactive Marketing*, 19 (Autumn 2005): 67–80; Asim Ansari and Carl F. Mela, "E-Customization," *Journal of Marketing Research*, 40 (May 2003), pp. 131–145.

22. W. Earl Sasser, "Match Supply and Demand in Service Industries," *Harvard Business Review*, November–December 1976, pp. 133–140.

23. Steven M. Shugan and Jinhong Xie, "Advance Selling for Services," *California Management Review*, 46 (Spring 2004): 37–54; Eyal Biyalogorsky and Eitan Gerstner, "Contingent Pricing to Reduce Price Risks," *Marketing Science*, 23 (Winter 2004): 146–155; Steven M. Shugan and Jinhong Xie, "Advance Pricing of Services and Other Implications of Separating Purchase and Consumption," *Journal of Service Research*, 2 (February 2000): 227–239.

24. Seth Godin, "If It's Broke, Fix It," *Fast Company*, October 2003, p. 131.

25. James Wallace, "Singapore Airlines Raises the Bar for Luxury Flying, *Seattle Post Intelligencer*, January 18, 2007; Justin Doebele, "The Engineer," *Forbes*, January 9, 2006, pp. 122–124; Stanley Holmes, "Creature Comforts at 30,000 Feet," *BusinessWeek*, December 18, 2006, p. 138; Anonymous, "What Makes Singapore a Service Champion?" *Strategic Direction*, April 2003, pp. 26–28; www.singaporeair.com.

26. Diane Brady, "Why Service Stinks," *BusinessWeek*, October 23, 2000, pp. 119–128.

27. Mary Clingman, "Turkey Talker," *Fortune*, November 27, 2006, p. 70.

28. Elisabeth Sullivan, "Happy Endings Lead to Happy Returns," *Marketing News*, October 30, 2009, p. 20.

29. Hannah Clark, "Customer Service Hell," *Forbes*, March 30, 2006.

30. Stephen S. Tax, Mark Colgate, and David Bowen, "How to Prevent Your Customers from Failing," *MIT Sloan Management Review*, Spring 2006, pp. 30–38; Mei Xue and Patrick T. Harker, "Customer Efficiency: Concept and Its Impact on E-Business Management," *Journal of Service Research*, 4 (May 2002): 253–267; Matthew L. Meuter, Amy L. Ostrom, Robert I. Roundtree, and Mary Jo Bitner, "Self-Service Technologies: Understanding Customer Satisfaction with Technology-Based Service Encounters," *Journal of Marketing*, 64 (July 2000): 50–64.

31. Kimmy Wa Chan, Chi Kin (Bennett) Yim, and Simon S. K. Lam, "Is Customer Participation in Value Creation a Double-Edged Sword? Evidence from Professional Financial Services across Cultures," *Journal of Marketing*, 74 (May 2010): 48–64.

32. Valarie Zeithaml, Mary Jo Bitner, and Dwayne D. Gremler, *Services Marketing: Integrating Customer Focus across the Firm*, 4th ed. (New York: McGraw-Hill, 2006).

33. Stephen S. Tax, Mark Colgate, and David Bowen, "How to Prevent Your Customers from Failing," *MIT Sloan Management Review*, Spring 2006, pp. 30–38; Michael Sanserino and Cari Tuna, "Companies Strive Harder to Please Customers," *Wall Street Journal*, July 27, 2009, p. B4.

34. James L. Heskett, W. Earl Sasser, Jr., and Joe Wheeler, *Ownership Quotient: Putting the Service Profit Chain to Work for Unbeatable Competitive Advantage* (Boston: Harvard Business School Press, 2008).

35. D. Todd Donovan, Tom J. Brown, and John C. Mowen, "Internal Benefits of Service Worker Customer Orientation: Job Satisfaction, Commitment, and Organizational Citizenship Behaviors," *Journal of Marketing*, 68 (January 2004), pp. 128–146.

36. Dan Heath and Chip Heath, "I Love You. Now What?" *Fast Company*, October 2008, pp. 95–96.

37. Evan Hessel, "Kung Pao Chicken for the Soul," *Forbes*, April 21, 2008, pp. 106–107.

38. Frances X. Frei, "The Four Things a Service Business Must Get Right," *Harvard Business Review*, April 2008, pp. 70–80.

39. Christian Gronroos, "A Service-Quality Model and Its Marketing Implications," *European Journal of Marketing*, 18 (1984): 36–44.

40. Leonard Berry, "Big Ideas in Services Marketing," *Journal of Consumer Marketing*, Spring 1986, pp. 47–51. See also Jagdip Singh, "Performance Productivity and Quality of Frontline Employees in Service Organizations," *Journal of Marketing*, 64 (April 2000): 15–34; Detelina Marinova, Jun Ye, and Jagdip Singh, "Do Frontline Mechanisms Matter? Impact of Quality and Productivity Orientations on Unit Revenue, Efficiency, and Customer Satisfaction," *Journal of Marketing*, 72 (March 2008): 28–45; John R. Hauser, Duncan I. Simester, and Birger Wernerfelt, "Internal Customers and Internal Suppliers," *Journal of Marketing Research*, 33 (August 1996): 268–280; and Walter E. Greene, Gary D. Walls, and Larry J. Schrest, "Internal Marketing: The Key to External Marketing Success," *Journal of Services Marketing*, 8 (1994): 5–13.

41. Christian Gronroos, "A Service-Quality Model and Its Marketing Implications," *European Journal of Marketing*, 18 (1984): 36–44; Michael D. Hartline, James G. Maxham III, and Daryl O. McKee, "Corridors of Influence in the Dissemination of Customer-Oriented Strategy to Customer-Contact Service Employees," *Journal of Marketing*, 64 (April 2000): 35–50.

42. Ad de Jong, Ko de Ruyter, and Jos Lemmink, "Antecedents and Consequences of the Service Climate in Boundary-Spanning Self-Managing Service Teams," *Journal of Marketing*, 68 (April 2004): 18–35; Michael D. Hartline and O. C. Ferrell, "The Management of Customer-Contact Service Employees: An Empirical Investigation," *Journal of Marketing*, 60 (October 1996): 52–70; Christian Homburg, Jan Wieseke, and Torsten Bornemann, "Implementing the Marketing Concept at the Employee-Customer Interface: The Role of Customer Need Knowledge," *Journal of Marketing*, 73 (July 2009): 64–81; Chi Kin (Bennett) Yim, David K. Tse, and Kimmy Wa Chan, "Strengthening Customer Loyalty through Intimacy and Passion: Roles of Customer-Firm Affection and Customer-Staff Relationships," *Journal of Marketing Research*, 45 (December 2008): 741–756.

43. "Sears Canada Mobilizes Service Repair Network with Enterprise Wireless Dispatch System from Mobile Computing Corporation," *Canada Newswire*, May 17, 2005, p. 1.

44. "Air Canada Self-Service Kiosk Systems, Canada," www.airport-technology.com/projects/canadiankiosk/ (viewed June 11, 2011).

45. Jena McGregor, "When Service Means Survival," *BusinessWeek*, March 2, 2009, pp. 26–30.

46. Heather Green, "How Amazon Aims to Keep You Clicking," *BusinessWeek*, March 2, 2009, pp. 34–40.

47. Roland T. Rust and Katherine N. Lemon, "E-Service and the Consumer," *International Journal of Electronic Commerce*, 5 (Spring 2001): 83–99. See also Balaji Padmanabhan and Alexander Tuzhilin, "On the Use of Optimization for Data Mining: Theoretical Interactions and ECRM Opportunities," *Management Science*, 49 (October 2003): 1327–1343; and B. P. S. Murthi and Sumit Sarkar, "The Role of the Management Sciences in Research on Personalization," *Management Science*, 49 (October 2003): 1344–1362.

48. Roland T. Rust, P. K. Kannan, and Na Peng, "The Customer Economics of Internet Privacy," *Journal of the Academy of Marketing Science*, 30 (2002): 455–464.

49. "Airport Celebrates Ranking as 'World's Best,'" Halifax Stanfield International Airport Press Release, April 10, 2008.

50. Jena McGregor, "When Service Means Survival," *BusinessWeek*, March 2, 2009, pp. 26–30.

51. John A. Martilla and John C. James, "Importance-Performance Analysis," *Journal of Marketing*, 41 (January 1977): 77–79.

52. Dave Dougherty and Ajay Murthy, "What Service Customers Really Want," *Harvard Business Review*, September 2009, p. 22. For a contrarian point of view, see Edward Kasabov, "The Compliant Customer," *MIT Sloan Management Review*, Spring 2010, pp. 18–19.

53. Jeffrey G. Blodgett and Ronald D. Anderson, "A Bayesian Network Model of the Customer Complaint Process," *Journal of Service Research, 2* (May 2000): 321–338; Stephen S. Tax and Stephen W. Brown, "Recovering and Learning from Service Failures," *Sloan Management Review*, Fall 1998, pp. 75–88; Claes Fornell and Birger Wernerfelt, "A Model for Customer Complaint Management," *Marketing Science, 7* (Summer 1988): 271–286.

54. James G. Maxham III and Richard G. Netemeyer, "Firms Reap What They Sow: The Effects of Shared Values and Perceived Organizational Justice on Customers' Evaluations of Complaint Handling," *Journal of Marketing, 67* (January 2003): 46–62; Jagdip Singh, "Performance Productivity and Quality of Frontline Employees in Service Organizations," *Journal of Marketing, 64* (April 2000): 15–34; Barry J. Rabin and James S. Boles, "Employee Behavior in a Service Environment: A Model and Test of Potential Differences between Men and Women," *Journal of Marketing, 62* (April 1998): 77–91.

55. Stephen S. Tax, Stephen W. Brown, and Murali Chandrashekaran, "Customer Evaluations of Service Complaint Experiences: Implications for Relationship Marketing," *Journal of Marketing, 62* (April 1998): 60–76; Stephen S. Tax and Stephen W. Brown, "Recovering and Learning from Service Failures," *Sloan Management Review*, Fall 1998, pp. 75–88.

56. Amy Barrett, "Vanguard Gets Personal," *BusinessWeek*, October 3, 2005, pp. 115–118; Carolyn Marconi and Donna MacFarland, "Growth by Marketing under the Radar," presentation at Marketing Science Institute Board of Trustees Meeting, *Pathways to Growth*, Tucson, Arizona, November 7, 2002.

57. "Amica Mature Lifestyles Inc.: Samir Manji Named a Winner in the Ernst & Young Entrepreneur of The Year 2010 Awards, BC Region," *Marketwire*, October 1, 2010; "Amenities," *Amica Mature Lifestyles*, www.amica.ca/retirementliving/amenities.html (viewed October 3, 2010).

58. Roger Yu, "Sheraton Has Designs on Fresh Look," *USA TODAY*, August 26, 2008, p. 4B.

59. Robert Levine, "Globe Trotter," *Fast Company*, September 2008, pp. 73–74; Andrew McMains, "Q&A: Kayak's Robert Birge," *Adweek.com*, June 2, 2009.

60. "Kenny Dichter: A Big Idea Takes Off, Special Advertising Supplement, CIT Behind the Business," *Condé Nast Portfolio*, September 2007; www.netjets.com and www.marquisjet.com (viewed June 17, 2011).

61. Jessi Hempel, "Salesforce Hits Its Stride," *Fortune*, March 2, 2009, pp. 29–32.

62. Susan M. Keaveney, "Customer Switching Behavior in Service Industries: An Exploratory Study," *Journal of Marketing, 59* (April 1995): 71–82. See also Jaishankar Ganesh, Mark J. Arnold, and Kristy E. Reynolds, "Understanding the Customer Base of Service Providers: An Examination of the Differences between Switchers and Stayers," *Journal of Marketing, 64* (July 2000): 65–87; Michael D. Hartline and O. C. Ferrell, "The Management of Customer-Contact Service Employees: An Empirical Investigation," *Journal of Marketing, 60* (October 1996): 52–70; Linda L. Price, Eric J. Arnould, and Patrick Tierney, "Going to Extremes: Managing Service Encounters and Assessing Provider Performance," *Journal of Marketing, 59* (April 1995): 83–97; Lois A. Mohr, Mary Jo Bitner, and Bernard H. Booms, "Critical Service Encounters: The Employee's Viewpoint," *Journal of Marketing, 58* (October 1994): 95–106.

63. Dave Dougherty and Ajay Murthy, "What Service Customers Really Want," *Harvard Business Review*, September 2009, p. 22.

64. Glenn B. Voss, A. Parasuraman, and Dhruv Grewal, "The Role of Price, Performance, and Expectations in Determining Satisfaction in Service Exchanges," *Journal of Marketing, 62* (October 1998): 46–61.

65. Roland T. Rust and Richard L. Oliver, "Should We Delight the Customer?" *Journal of the Academy of Marketing Science, 28* (December 2000): 86–94.

66. A. Parasuraman, Valarie A. Zeithaml, and Leonard L. Berry, "A Conceptual Model of Service Quality and Its Implications for Future Research," *Journal of Marketing, 49* (Fall 1985): 41–50. See also Michael K. Brady and J. Joseph Cronin, Jr., "Some New Thoughts on Conceptualizing Perceived Service Quality," *Journal of Marketing, 65* (July 2001): 34–49; and Susan J. Devlin and H. K. Dong, "Service Quality from the Customers' Perspective," *Marketing Research*, Winter 1994, pp. 4–13.

67. Leonard L. Berry and A. Parasuraman, *Marketing Services: Competing through Quality* (New York: The Free Press, 1991), p. 16.

68. William Boulding, Ajay Kalra, Richard Staelin, and Valarie A. Zeithaml, "A Dynamic Model of Service Quality: From Expectations to Behavioral Intentions," *Journal of Marketing Research, 30* (February 1993): 7–27.

69. Roland T. Rust and Tuck Siong Chung, "Marketing Models of Service and Relationships," *Marketing Science, 25* (November–December 2006): 560–580; Katherine N. Lemon, Tiffany Barnett White, and Russell S. Winer, "Dynamic Customer Relationship Management: Incorporating Future Considerations into the Service Retention Decision," *Journal of Marketing, 66* (January 2002): 1–14; Ruth N. Bolton and Katherine N. Lemon, "A Dynamic Model of Customers' Usage of Services: Usage as an Antecedent and Consequence of Satisfaction," *Journal of Marketing Research, 36* (May 1999): 171–186.

70. Kent Grayson and Tim Ambler, "The Dark Side of Long-Term Relationships in Marketing Services," *Journal of Marketing Research, 36* (February 1999): 132–141.

71. Leonard L. Berry, Kathleen Seiders, and Dhruv Grewal, "Understanding Service Convenience," *Journal of Marketing, 66* (July 2002): 1–17.

72. "Help Yourself," *Economist*, July 2, 2009, pp. 62–63.

73. "HMV Launches Brand Into (Cyber) Space with the Introduction of a New Digital Music Store," *Canada Newswire*, July 5, 2010; "About HMV," *HMV*, www.hmv.ca/Info/About.aspx (viewed September 30, 2010).

74. Matthew L. Meuter, Mary Jo Bitner, Amy L. Ostrom, and Stephen W. Brown, "Choosing among Alternative Service Delivery Modes: An Investigation of Customer Trial of Self-Service Technologies," *Journal of Marketing, 69* (April 2005): 61–83.

75. Eric Fang, Robert W. Palmatier, and Jan-Benedict E. M. Steenkamp, "Effect of Service Transition Strategies on Firm Value," *Journal of Marketing, 72* (September 2008): 1–14.

76. Mark Vandenbosch and Niraj Dawar, "Beyond Better Products: Capturing Value in Customer Interactions," *MIT Sloan Management Review, 43* (Summer 2002): 35–42; Milind M. Lele and Uday S. Karmarkar, "Good Product Support Is Smart Marketing," *Harvard Business Review*, November–December 1983, pp. 124–132.

77. For research on the effects of delays in service on service evaluations, see Michael K. Hui and David K. Tse, "What to Tell Consumers in Waits of Different Lengths: An Integrative Model of Service Evaluation," *Journal of Marketing, 60* (April 1996): 81–90; Shirley Taylor, "Waiting for Service: The Relationship between Delays and Evaluations of Service," *Journal of Marketing, 58* (April 1994): 56–69.

78. Eric (Er) Fang, Robert W. Palmatier, and Jan-Benedict E. M. Steenkamp, "Effect of Service Transition Strategies on Firm Value," *Journal of Marketing, 72*(September) (2008): 1–14.

79. Goutam Challagalla, R. Venkatesh, and Ajay K. Kohli, "Proactive Postsales Service: When and Why Does it Pay Off?" *Journal of Marketing, 73* (March 2009): 70–87.

Chapter 14

1. Daniel Girard, "Tickets Too Pricey? Try Later: Team Will Experiment with 'Dynamic Pricing' Where Value Rises, Falls for

Single-Game Seats," *Toronto Star*, October 27, 2010, p. S5; Lori Ewing, "Toronto Raptors Cap Forgettable Season with 97–79 Loss to Miami Heat; Raptors Lose 97-79 to Heat in Finale," *The Canadian Press*, April 13, 2011.

2. "The Price Is Wrong," *Economist*, May 25, 2002.

3. Xavier Dreze and Joseph C. Nunes, "Using Combined-Currency Prices to Lower Consumers' Perceived Cost," *Journal of Marketing Research, 41* (February 2004): 59–72; Raghuram Iyengar, Kamel Jedidi, and Rajeev Kohli, "A Conjoint Approach to Multipart Pricing," *Journal of Marketing Research, 45* (April 2008): 195–201; Marco Bertini and Luc Wathieu, "Attention Arousal Through Price Partitioning," *Marketing Science, 27* (March–April 2008): 236–246.

4. Rick Newman, "The Great Retail Revolution," *U.S. News & World Report*, March 2010, pp. 19–20; Philip Moeller, "Tough Times Are Molding Tough Consumers," *U.S. News & World Report*, March 2010, pp. 22–25; Steve Hamm, "The New Age of Frugality," *BusinessWeek*, October 20, 2008, pp. 55–60; Timothy W. Martin, "Frugal Shoppers Drive Grocers Back to Basics," *Wall Street Journal*, June 24, 2009, p. B1; Daniel Gross, "The Latte Era Grinds Down," *Newsweek*, October 22, 2007, pp. 46–47.

5. Paul Markillie, "A Perfect Market: A Survey of E-Commerce," *Economist*, May 15, 2004, pp. 3–20; David Kirkpatrick, "How the Open-Source World Plans to Smack Down Microsoft, and Oracle, and . . . .," *Fortune*, February 23, 2004, pp. 92–100; Faith Keenan, "The Price Is Really Right," *BusinessWeek*, March 31, 2003, pp. 61–67; Michael Menduno, "Priced to Perfection," *Business 2.0*, March 6, 2001, pp. 40–42; Amy E. Cortese, "Good-Bye to Fixed Pricing?" *BusinessWeek*, May 4, 1998, pp. 71–84. For a discussion of some of the basic academic issues involved, see Florian Zettelmeyer, "Expanding to the Internet: Pricing and Communication Strategies When Firms Compete on Multiple Channels," *Journal of Marketing Research, 37* (August 2000): 292–308; John G. Lynch, Jr., and Dan Ariely, "Wine Online: Search Costs Affect Competition on Price, Quality, and Distribution," *Marketing Science, 19* (Winter 2000): 83–103; and Rajiv Lal and Miklos Sarvary, "When and How Is the Internet Likely to Decrease Price Competition?" *Marketing Science, 18* (Fall 1999): 485–503.

6. Daniel Fisher, "Cheap Seats," *Forbes*, August 24, 2009, pp. 102–103.

7. For a thorough review of pricing research, see Chezy Ofir and Russell S. Winer, "Pricing: Economic and Behavioral Models," in *Handbook of Marketing*, edited byBart Weitz and Robin Wensley(London, England: Sage Publications, 2002).

8. Based on Pia Sarkar, "Which Shirt Costs $275?— Brand Loyalty, Bargain Hunting, and Unbridled Luxury All Play a Part in the Price You'll Pay for a T-Shirt," *Final Edition*, March 15, 2007, p. C1. Reprinted by permission.

9. John Morrissy, "Price Gap Persists after Parity; Consumers Paying at Least 12 Per Cent Too Much, Estimate Suggests," *Edmonton Journal*, January 6, 2011; Michael Bettencourt, "Porsche Cuts Canadian Prices," *The Globe and Mail*, January 7, 2011, p. D11; Michael Bettencourt, "Porsche Price Cuts Boost Sales," *The Globe and Mail*, May 13, 2011, p. D15.

10. Jay Greene, "Selling $8 Soap in an Era of Frugality," *BusinessWeek*, November 30, 2009, p. 66.

11. Peter R. Dickson and Alan G. Sawyer, "The Price Knowledge and Search of Supermarket Shoppers," *Journal of Marketing, 54* (July 1990): 42–53. For a methodological qualification, however, see Hooman Estalami, Alfred Holden, and Donald R. Lehmann, "Macro-Economic Determinants of Consumer Price Knowledge: A Meta-Analysis of Four Decades of Research," *International Journal of Research in Marketing, 18* (December 2001): 341–355.

12. For a comprehensive review, see Tridib Mazumdar, S. P. Raj, and Indrajit Sinha, "Reference Price Research: Review and Propositions," *Journal of Marketing, 69* (October 2005): 84–102. For a different point of view, see Chris Janiszewski and Donald R. Lichtenstein, "A Range Theory Account of Price Perception," *Journal of Consumer Research, 25* (March 1999): 353–368.

13. For a discussion of how "incidental" prices outside the category can serve as contextual reference prices, see Joseph C. Nunes and Peter Boatwright, "Incidental Prices and Their Effect on Willingness to Pay," *Journal of Marketing Research, 41* (November 2004): 457–466.

14. K. N. Rajendran and Gerard J. Tellis, "Contextual and Temporal Components of Reference Price," *Journal of Marketing, 58* (January 1994): 22–34; Gurumurthy Kalyanaram and Russell S. Winer, "Empirical Generalizations from Reference-Price Research," *Marketing Science, 14* (Summer 1995): G161–G169. See also Ritesh Saini, Raghunath Singh Rao, and Ashwani Monga, "Is the Deal Worth My Time? The Interactive Effect of Relative and Referent Thinking on Willingness to Seek a Bargain," *Journal of Marketing, 74* (January 2010): 34–48.

15. Gurumurthy Kalyanaram and Russell S. Winer, "Empirical Generalizations from Reference-Price Research," *Marketing Science, 14* (Summer 1995): 161–169.

16. Glenn E. Mayhew and Russell S. Winer, "An Empirical Analysis of Internal and External Reference-Price Effects Using Scanner Data," *Journal of Consumer Research, 19* (June 1992): 62–70.

17. Robert Ziethammer, "Forward-Looking Buying in Online Auctions," *Journal of Marketing Research, 43* (August 2006): 462–476.

18. John T. Gourville, "Pennies-a-Day: The Effect of Temporal Reframing on Transaction Evaluation," *Journal of Consumer Research, 24* (March 1998): 395–408.

19. Gary M. Erickson and Johny K. Johansson, "The Role of Price in Multi-Attribute Product-Evaluations," *Journal of Consumer Research, 12* (September 1985): 195–199.

20. Wilfred Amaldoss and Sanjay Jain, "Pricing of Conspicuous Goods: A Competitive Analysis of Social Effects," *Journal of Marketing Research, 42* (February 2005); Angela Chao and Juliet B. Schor, "Empirical Tests of Status Consumption: Evidence from Women's Cosmetics," *Journal of Economic Psychology, 19* (January 1998): 107–131.

21. Mark Stiving and Russell S. Winer, "An Empirical Analysis of Price Endings with Scanner Data," *Journal of Consumer Research, 24* (June 1997): 57–68.

22. Eric T. Anderson and Duncan Simester, "Effects of $9 Price Endings on Retail Sales: Evidence from Field Experiments," *Quantitative Marketing and Economics, 1* (March 2003): 93–110.

23. Eric Anderson and Duncan Simester, "Mind Your Pricing Cues," *Harvard Business Review*, September 2003, pp. 96–103.

24. Robert M. Schindler and Patrick N. Kirby, "Patterns of Rightmost Digits Used in Advertised Prices: Implications for Nine-Ending Effects," *Journal of Consumer Research, 24* (September 1997): 192–201.

25. Eric Anderson and Duncan Simester, "Mind Your Pricing Cues," *Harvard Business Review*, September 2003, pp. 96–103.

26. Ibid.

27. Daniel J. Howard and Roger A. Kerin, "Broadening the Scope of Reference-Price Advertising Research: A Field Study of Consumer Shopping Involvement," *Journal of Marketing, 70* (October 2006): 185–204.

28. Robert C. Blattberg and Kenneth Wisniewski, "Price-Induced Patterns of Competition," *Marketing Science, 8* (Fall 1989): 291–309; Katherine N. Lemon and Stephen M. Nowlis, "Developing Synergies between Promotions and Brands in Different Price-Quality Tiers," *Journal of Marketing Research, 39* (May 2002): 171–185. But see also Serdar Sayman, Stephen J. Hoch, and Jagmohan S. Raju, "Positioning of Store Brands," *Marketing Science, 21* (Fall 2002): 378–397.

29. Shantanu Dutta, Mark J. Zbaracki, and Mark Bergen, "Pricing Process as a Capability: A Resource-Based Perspective," *Strategic Management Journal, 24* (July 2003): 615–630.

30. "To All iPhone Customers," *Apple Inc.*, www.apple.com/hot-news/openiphoneletter; Gary F. Gebhardt, "Price Skimming's

Unintended Consequences," Marketing Science Institute Working Paper Series, MSI Report No. 09-109.

31. Michael Silverstein and Neil Fiske, *Trading Up: The New American Luxury* (New York: Portfolio, 2003).

32. Christopher Lawton, "A Liquor Maverick Shakes Up Industry with Pricey Brands," *Wall Street Journal*, May 21, 2003.

33. Timothy Aeppel, "Seeking Perfect Prices, CEO Tears Up the Rules," *Wall Street Journal*, March 27, 2007.

34. Florian Zettelmeyer, Fiona Scott Morton, and Jorge Silva-Risso, "How the Internet Lowers Prices: Evidence from Matched Survey and Automobile Transaction Data," *Journal of Marketing Research*, 43 (May 2006): 168–181; Jeffrey R. Brown and Austan Goolsbee, "Does the Internet Make Markets More Competitive? Evidence from the Life Insurance Industry," *Journal of Political Economy*, 110 (October 2002): 481–507.

35. Joo Heon Park and Douglas L. MacLachlan, "Estimating Willingness to Pay with Exaggeration Bias-Corrected Contingent Valuation Method," *Marketing Science*, 27 (July–August 2008): 691–698.

36. Walter Baker, Mike Marn, and Craig Zawada, "Price Smarter on the Net," *Harvard Business Review*, February 2001, pp. 122–127.

37. Brian Bergstein, "The Price Is Right," *Associated Press*, April 29, 2007.

38. Thomas T. Nagle and Reed K. Holden, *The Strategy and Tactics of Pricing*, 3rd ed. (Upper Saddle River, NJ: Prentice Hall, 2002).

39. Journeys Travel & Leisure SuperCentre website, www.journeystravelgear.com/about-Journeys.cfm (viewed January 3, 2010).

40. For a summary of elasticity studies, see Dominique M. Hanssens, Leonard J. Parsons, and Randall L. Schultz, *Market Response Models: Econometric and Time Series Analysis* (Boston: Kluwer, 1990), pp. 187–191.

41. Gene Epstein, "Economic Beat: Stretching Things," *Barron's*, December 15, 1997, p. 65.

42. Tammo H. A. Bijmolt, Harald J. Van Heerde, and Rik G. M. Pieters, "New Empirical Generalizations on the Determinants of Price Elasticity," *Journal of Marketing Research*, 42 (May 2005): 141–156.

43. William W. Alberts, "The Experience Curve Doctrine Reconsidered," *Journal of Marketing*, 53 (July 1989): 36–49.

44. Michael Sivy, "Japan's Smart Secret Weapon," *Fortune*, August 12, 1991, p. 75.

45. Joseph Weber, "Over a Buck for Dinner? Outrageous," *BusinessWeek*, March 9, 2009, p. 57.

46. Reena Jane, "From India, the Latest Management Fad," *Bloomberg BusinessWeek*, December 14, 2009, p. 57; Julie Jargon, "General Mills Takes Several Steps to Combat High Commodity Costs," *Wall Street Journal*, September 20, 2007; Mina Kimes, "Cereal Cost Cutters," *Fortune*, November 10, 2008, p. 24.

47. Jack Ewing, "The Next Wal-Mart?" *BusinessWeek*, April 26, 2004, pp. 60–62; "German Discounter Aldi Aims to Profit from Belt-Tightening in US," *DW World.de*, www.dw-world.de, January 15, 2009; Aldi website, www.aldi.com.

48. Matt Hartley, "Bell to Drop Usage-Based Billing Plan, Website Says," *Edmonton Journal*, March 29, 2011, p. D1; "CRTC to Review Internet Billing Decision," *CBC.ca*, February 3, 2011, www.cbc.ca/news/canada/story/2011/02/03/crtc-committee.html (viewed April 3, 2011); "Bell's Aggregated Volume Pricing (AVP) Section," Bell Canada website, www.bell.ca/shopping/PrsShp_Bell_Internet_AVP.page (viewed April 3, 2011).

49. Kusum L. Ailawadi, Donald R. Lehmann, and Scott A. Neslin, "Market Response to a Major Policy Change in the Marketing Mix: Learning from Procter & Gamble's Value Pricing Strategy," *Journal of Marketing*, 65 (January 2001): 44–61.

50. Bruce Einhorn, "Acer's Game-Changing PC Offensive," *BusinessWeek*, April 20, 2009, p. 65; Bruce Einhorn and Tim Culpan, "With Dell in the Dust, Acer Chases HP," *Bloomberg BusinessWeek*, March 8, 2010, pp. 58–59.

51. Tung-Zong Chang and Albert R. Wildt, "Price, Product Information, and Purchase Intention: An Empirical Study," *Journal of the Academy of Marketing Science*, 22 (Winter 1994): 16–27. See also G. Dean Kortge and Patrick A. Okonkwo, "Perceived Value Approach to Pricing," *Industrial Marketing Management*, 22 (May 1993): 133–140.

52. Anupam Mukerj, "Monsoon Marketing," *Fast Company*, April 2007, p. 22.

53. Marco Bertini and Luc Wathieu, "How to Stop Customers from Fixating on Price," *Harvard Business Review*, May 2010, pp. 85–91.

54. James C. Anderson, Dipak C. Jain, and Pradeep K. Chintagunta, "Customer Value Assessment in Business Markets: A State-of-Practice Study," *Journal of Business-to-Business Marketing*, 1 (Spring 1993): 3–29.

55. Bill Saporito, "Behind the Tumult at P&G," *Fortune*, March 7, 1994, pp. 74–82. For empirical analysis of its effects, see Kusim L. Ailawadi, Donald R. Lehmann, and Scott A. Neslin, "Market Response to a Major Policy Change in the Marketing Mix: Learning from Procter & Gamble's Value Pricing Strategy," *Journal of Marketing*, 65 (January 2001): 44–61.

56. Elisabeth Sullivan, "Value Pricing," *Marketing News*, January 15, 2008, p. 8.

57. Stephen J. Hoch, Xavier Dreze, and Mary J. Purk, "EDLP, Hi-Lo, and Margin Arithmetic," *Journal of Marketing*, 58 (October 1994): 16–27; Rajiv Lal and R. Rao, "Supermarket Competition: The Case of Everyday Low Pricing," *Marketing Science*, 16 (Winter 1997): 60–80; Michael Tsiros and David M. Hardesty, "Ending a Price Promotion: Retracting It in One Step or Phasing It Out Gradually," *Journal of Marketing*, 74 (January 2010): 49–64.

58. Joseph W. Alba, Carl F. Mela, Terence A. Shimp, and Joel E. Urbany, "The Effect of Discount Frequency and Depth on Consumer Price Judgments," *Journal of Consumer Research*, 26 (September 1999): 99–114; Paul B. Ellickson and Sanjog Misra, "Supermarket Pricing Strategies," *Marketing Science*, 27 (September–October 2008): 811–828.

59. David Welch, "Haggling Starts to Go the Way of the Tail Fin," *BusinessWeek*, October 29, 2007, pp. 71–72.

60. Dana Flavelle and Cynthia Vukets, "New Breed of Bargain Hunters: Dollarama Sales, Profit Rise as Shoppers of All Incomes Seek Deals, but CEO Predicts Higher Prices under Pressure from Suppliers," *Toronto Star*, April 8, 2011, p. B1.

61. Ethan Smith and Sara Silver, "To Protect Its Box-Office Turf, Ticketmaster Plays Rivals' Tune," *Wall Street Journal*, September 12, 2006.

62. "Royal Mail Drives Major Cost Savings through Free Markets," Free Markets Press Release, December 15, 2003.

63. Using expected profit for setting price makes sense for the seller who makes many bids. The seller who bids only occasionally or who needs a particular contract badly will not find it advantageous to use expected profit. This criterion does not distinguish between a $1000 profit with a 0.10 probability and a $125 profit with a 0.80 probability. Yet the firm that wants to keep production going would prefer the second contract to the first.

64. Bernard Condon, "The Haggle Economy," *Forbes*, June 8, 2009, pp. 26–27; Sandy D. Jap, "The Impact of Online Reverse Auction Design on Buyer-Supplier Relationships," *Journal of Marketing*, 71 (January 2007): 146–159; Sandy D. Jap, "An Exploratory Study of the Introduction of Online Reverse Auctions," *Journal of Marketing*, 67 (July 2003): 96–107.

65. Paul W. Farris and David J. Reibstein, "How Prices, Expenditures, and Profits Are Linked," *Harvard Business Review*, November–December 1979, pp. 173–184. See also Makoto Abe, "Price and Advertising Strategy of a National Brand against Its Private-Label Clone: A Signaling Game Approach," *Journal of Business Research*, 33 (July 1995): 241–250.

66. Eugene H. Fram and Michael S. McCarthy, "The True Price of Penalties," *Marketing Management*, October 1999, pp. 49–56.

67. Joel E. Urbany, "Justifying Profitable Pricing," *Journal of Product and Brand Management*, 10 (2001): 141–157; Charles Fishman, "The Wal-Mart You Don't Know," *Fast Company*, December 2003, pp. 68–80.

68. "Panasonic Corporation Pleads Guilty to Price Fixing Conspiracy," Competition Bureau Press Release, November 3, 2010; "Report from the Competition Bureau Deceptive Marketing Practices," Competition Bureau Press Release, October 2–3, 2003.

69. James Mehring, "Let the Markups Begin," *BusinessWeek*, May 19, 2003, p. 100.

70. P. N. Agarwala, *Countertrade: A Global Perspective* (New Delhi: Vikas, 1991); Michael Rowe, *Countertrade* (London, England: Euromoney Books, 1989); Christopher M. Korth, ed., *International Countertrade* (New York: Quorum Books, 1987).

71. For an interesting discussion of a quantity surcharge, see David E. Sprott, Kenneth C. Manning, and Anthony Miyazaki, "Grocery Price Settings and Quantity Surcharges," *Journal of Marketing*, 67 (July 2003): 34–46.

72. Michael V. Marn and Robert L. Rosiello, "Managing Price, Gaining Profit," *Harvard Business Review*, September–October 1992, pp. 84–94. See also Kusum L. Ailawadi, Scott A. Neslin, and Karen Gedenk, "Pursuing the Value-Conscious Consumer: Store Brands versus National-Brand Promotions," *Journal of Marketing*, 65 (January 2001): 71–89; and Gerard J. Tellis, "Tackling the Retailer Decision Maze: Which Brands to Discount, How Much, When, and Why?" *Marketing Science*, 14 (Summer 1995): 271–299.

73. "Fairmont President's Club: Membership Benefits," www.fairmont.com/fpc/MembershipBenefits (viewed June 18, 2011).

74. Harry Rosen website, www.harryrosen.com/eng/products/dress-shirts-ties/dress-shirts/white_twill_dress_shirt?65211131 (viewed June 18, 2011).

75. Peter Burrows and Olga Kharif, "Can AT&T Tame the iHogs," *Bloomberg BusinessWeek*, December 28, 2009, and January 4, 2010, pp. 21–22.

76. Ramarao Deesiraju and Steven M. Shugan, "Strategic Service Pricing and Yield Management," *Journal of Marketing*, 63 (January 1999): 44–56; Robert E. Weigand, "Yield Management: Filling Buckets, Papering the House," *Business Horizons*, 42 (September–October 1999): 55–64.

77. Charles Fishman, "Which Price Is Right?" *Fast Company*, March 2003, pp. 92–102; Bob Tedeschi, "E-Commerce Report," *New York Times*, September 2, 2002; Faith Keenan, "The Price Is Really Right," *BusinessWeek*, March 31, 2003, pp. 62–67; Peter Coy, "The Power of Smart Pricing," *BusinessWeek*, April 10, 2000, pp. 160–164. For a review of some seminal work linking pricing decisions with operational insights, see Moritz Fleischmann, Joseph M. Hall, and David F. Pyke, "Research Brief: Smart Pricing," *MIT Sloan Management Review*, Winter 2004, pp. 9–13.

78. Mike France, "Does Predatory Pricing Make Microsoft a Predator?" *BusinessWeek*, November 23, 1998, pp. 130–132. Also see Joseph P. Guiltinan and Gregory T. Gundlack, "Aggressive and Predatory Pricing: A Framework for Analysis," *Journal of Advertising*, 60 (July 1996): 87–102.

79. For more information on specific types of price discrimination that are illegal, see Henry Cheeseman, *Business Law*, 6th ed. (Upper Saddle River, NJ: Prentice Hall, 2007).

80. Bob Donath, "Dispel Major Myths about Pricing," *Marketing News*, February 3, 2003, p. 10. For an interesting historical account, see Meghan R. Busse, Duncan I. Simester, and Florian Zettelmeyer, "'The Best Price You'll Ever Get': The 2005 Employee Discount Pricing Promotions, in the U.S. Automobile Industry," *Marketing Science*, 29 (March–April 2010): 268–290.

81. Harald J. Van Heerde, Els Gijsbrechts, and Koen Pauwels, "Winners and Losers in a Major Price War," *Journal of Marketing Research*, 45 (October 2008): 499–518.

82. For a classic review, see Kent B. Monroe, "Buyers' Subjective Perceptions of Price," *Journal of Marketing Research*, 10 (February 1973): 70–80. See also Z. John Zhang, Fred Feinberg, and Aradhna Krishna, "Do We Care What Others Get? A Behaviorist Approach to Targeted Promotions," *Journal of Marketing Research*, 39 (August 2002): 277–291.

83. Margaret C. Campbell, "Perceptions of Pricing Unfairness: Antecedents and Consequences," *Journal of Marketing Research*, 36 (May 1999): 187–199.

84. Lan Xia, Kent B. Monroe, and Jennifer L. Cox, "The Price Is Unfair! A Conceptual Framework of Price Fairness Perceptions," *Journal of Marketing*, 68 (October 2004): 1–15; Eric T. Anderson and Duncan Simester, "Does Demand Fall When Customers Perceive That Prices Are Unfair? The Case of Premium Pricing for Larger Sizes," *Marketing Science*, 27 (May–June 2008): 492–500.

85. Eric Mitchell, "How Not to Raise Prices," *Small Business Reports*, November 1990, pp. 64–67.

86. Jamie Sturgeon, "Clearnet to Battle against New-Entrant Threat," *Postmedia News*, April 5, 2011.

87. Nirmalya Kumar, "Strategies to Fight Low-Cost Rivals," *Harvard Business Review*, December 2006, pp. 104–112. See also Michael F. Porter, *Competitive Strategy: Techniques for Analyzing Industries and Competitors* (New York: The Free Press, 1980); Adrian Ryans, *Beating Low Cost Competition: How Premium Brands Can Respond to Cut-Price Rivals* (West Sussex, England: John Wiley & Sons, 2008); and Jack Neff, "How the Discounters Hurt Themsleves," *Advertising Age*, December 10, 2007, p. 12.

Chapter 15

1. "Canadian Tire Retains GENCO Distribution System to Operate Its New Distribution Centre in Coteau-du-Lac Quebec," *Canada Newswire*, June 12, 2008, www.newswire.ca/en/releases/archive/June2008/12/c2358.html; "Canadian Tire Welcomes Government of Canada's Commitment to Reduce Greenhouse Gas Emissions," *Canada Newswire*, May 21, 2010, www.newswire.ca/en/releases/archive/May2010/21/c5976.html (viewed April 2011).

2. Anne T. Coughlan, Erin Anderson, Louis W. Stern, and Adel I. El-Ansary, *Marketing Channels*, 7th ed. (Upper Saddle River, NJ: Prentice Hall, 2007).

3. Louis W. Stern and Barton A. Weitz, "The Revolution in Distribution: Challenges and Opportunities," *Long Range Planning*, 30 (December 1997): 823–829.

4. For an insightful summary of academic research, see Erin Anderson and Anne T. Coughlan, "Channel Management: Structure, Governance, and Relationship Management," in *Handbook of Marketing*, edited by Bart Weitz and Robin Wensley (London, England: Sage, 2002), pp. 223–247. See also Gary L. Frazier, "Organizing and Managing Channels of Distribution," *Journal of the Academy of Marketing Sciences*, 27 (Spring 1999): 226–240.

5. Kerry Capell, "Thinking Simple at Philips," *BusinessWeek*, December 11, 2006, p. 50; "Royal Philips Electronics Annual Report," 2010; "Philips—Unfulfilled," *Brandchannel.com*, June 20, 2005; Jennifer L. Schenker, "Fine-Tuning a Fuzzy Image," *TIMEeurope.com*, Spring 2002.

6. "Our Banners," Reitmans (Canada) Limited website, www.reitmans.ca/about/our_banners.aspx?lang=en (viewed April 2011).

7. Martin Wildberger, "Multichannel Business Basics for Successful E-Commerce," *Electronic Commerce News*, September 16, 2002, p. 1; Matthew Haeberle, "REI Overhauls Its E-Commerce," *Chain Store Age*, January 2003, p. 64.

8. Chekitan S. Dev and Don E. Schultz, "In the Mix: A Customer-Focused Approach Can Bring the Current Marketing Mix into the 21st Century," *Marketing Management*, 14 (January–February 2005).

9. RIM "Company History," www.fundinguniverse.com/company-histories/Research-in-Motion-Ltd-Company-History.html (viewed April 2011).

10. www.apple.com, December 9, 2010.

11. Robert Shaw and Philip Kotler, "Rethinking the Chain," *Marketing Management,* July–August 2009, pp. 18–23.

12. Erin Anderson and Anne T. Coughlan, "Channel Management: Structure, Governance, and Relationship Management," in *Handbook of Marketing*, edited byBart Weitz and Robin Wensley(London, England: Sage, 2002), pp. 223–247.

13. For additional information on backward channels, see Marianne Jahre, "Household Waste Collection as a Reverse Channel: A Theoretical Perspective," *International Journal of Physical Distribution and Logistics, 25* (1995): 39–55; and Terrance L. Pohlen and M. Theodore Farris II, "Reverse Logistics in Plastics Recycling," *International Journal of Physical Distribution and Logistics, 22* (1992): 35–37.

14. Greenopolis website, www.greenopolis.com, December 9, 2010.

15. William M. Bulkeley, "Kodak Revamps Wal-Mart Kiosks," *Wall Street Journal*, September 6, 2006, p. B2; Faith Keenan, "Big Yellow's Digital Dilemma," *BusinessWeek*, March 24, 2003, pp. 80–81.

16. Asim Ansari, Carl F. Mela, and Scott A. Neslin, "Customer Channel Migration," *Journal of Marketing Research, 45* (February 2008): 60–76; Jacquelyn S. Thomas and Ursula Y. Sullivan, "Managing Marketing Communications," *Journal of Marketing,* 69 (October 2005): 239–251; Sridhar Balasubramanian, Rajagopal Raghunathan, and Vijay Mahajan, "Consumers in a Multichannel Environment: Product Utility, Process Utility, and Channel Choice," *Journal of Interactive Marketing, 19* (Spring 2005): 12–30; Edward J. Fox, Alan L. Montgomery, and Leonard M. Lodish, "Consumer Shopping and Spending across Retail Formats," *Journal of Business, 77* (April 2004): S25–S60.

17. For another taxonomy of shoppers, see Paul F. Nunes and Frank V. Cespedes, "The Customer Has Escaped," *Harvard Business Review*, November 2003, pp. 96–105.

18. John Helyar, "The Only Company Wal-Mart Fears," *Fortune,* November 24, 2003, pp. 158–166. See also Michael Silverstein and Neil Fiske, *Trading Up: The New American Luxury* (New York: Portfolio, 2003).

19. Susan Broniarczyk, "Product Assortment," in *Handbook of Consumer Psychology*, edited by Curtis Haugtvedt, Paul Herr, and Frank Kardes (New York: Lawrence Erlbaum Associates, 2008), pp. 755–779; Alexander Chernev and Ryan Hamilton, "Assortment Size and Option Attractiveness in Consumer Choice Among Retailers," *Journal of Marketing Research, 46* (June 2009): 410–420; Richard A. Briesch, Pradeep K. Chintagunta, and Edward J. Fox, "How Does Assortment Affect Grocery Store Choice," *Journal of Marketing Research, 46* (April 2009): 176–189.

20. Anne T. Coughlan, Erin Anderson, Louis W. Stern, and Adel I. El-Ansary, *Marketing Channels*, 7th ed. (Upper Saddle River, NJ: Prentice Hall, 2007).

21. Louis P. Bucklin, *A Theory of Distribution Channel Structure* (Berkeley, CA: Institute of Business and Economic Research, University of California, 1966).

22. Katrijn Gielens and Marnik G. Dekimpe, "The Entry Strategy of Retail Firms into Transition Economies," *Journal of Marketing, 71* (April 2007): 196–212.

23. Alex Frankel, "Magic Shop," *Fast Company*, November 2007, pp. 45–49; "Apple Reports Fourth Quarter Results," www.apple.com, October 19, 2009; Jerry Useem, "Simply Irresistible," *Fortune*, March 19, 2007, pp. 107–112; Nick Wingfield, "How Apple's Store Strategy Beat the Odds," *Wall Street Journal*, May 17, 2006; Alice Z. Cuneo, "Apple Transcends as Lifestyle Brand," *Advertising Age*, June 15, 2003, pp. S2, S6; Tobi Elkin, "Apple Gambles with Retail Plan," *Advertising Age*, June 24, 2001.

24. Marina Strauss, "Does This Blouse Make Sears Look Plugged-In?" *The Globe and Mail*, April 22, 2011, p. B4; Grant Arnott, "Sears Canada Introduces In-Store Skype," *Power Retail*, www.powerretail.com.au/news/sears-canada-introduces-in-store-skype/ (viewed April 2011).

25. Allison Enright, "Shed New Light," *Marketing News*, May 1, 2006, pp. 9–10.

26. "Exclusives Becoming a Common Practice," *DSN Retailing Today*, February 9, 2004, pp. 38, 44.

27. "Trouser Suit," *Economist*, November 24, 2001, p. 56.

28. Lee Valley Tools website, www.leevalley.com/en/home.aspx; "Lee Valley Tools," *Wikipedia*, http://en.wikipedia.org/wiki/Lee_Valley_ Tools (viewed April 2011).

29. "Nike Says No to Blue-Light Specials," *Fortune*, May 4, 2005.

30. Robert K. Heady, "Online Bank Offers Best Rates," *South Florida Sun-Sentinel*, November 22, 2004.

31. Erin Anderson and Anne T. Coughlan, "Channel Management: Structure, Governance, and Relationship Management," in *Handbook of Marketing*, edited by Bart Weitz and Robin Wensley(London, England: Sage Publications, 2002), pp. 223–247; Michaela Draganska, Daniel Klapper, and Sofia B. Villa-Boas, "A Larger Slice or a Larger Pie? An Empirical Investigation of Bargaining Power in the Distribution Channel," *Marketing Science, 29* (January–February 2010): 57–74.

32. These bases of power were identified in John R. P. French and Bertram Raven, "The Bases of Social Power," in *Studies in Social Power*, edited byDorwin Cartwright(Ann Arbor, MI: University of Michigan Press, 1959), pp. 150–167.

33. Joydeep Srivastava and Dipankar Chakravarti, "Channel Negotiations with Information Asymmetries: Contingent Influences of Communication and Trustworthiness Reputations," *Journal of Marketing Research, 46* (August 2009): 557–572.

34. Daniel Corsten and Nirmalya Kumar, "Do Suppliers Benefit from Collaborative Relationships with Large Retailers? An Empirical Investigation of Efficient Consumer Response Adoption," *Journal of Marketing, 69* (July 2005): 80–94. For some related research, see Ashwin W. Joshi, "Continuous Supplier Performance Improvement: Effects of Collaborative Communication and Control," *Journal of Marketing, 73* (January 2009): 133–150.

35. Russ Mitchell, "Can Dell Save Dell?" *Condé Nast Portfolio*, July 2008, pp. 84–90; Cliff Edwards, "Dell's Do-Over," *BusinessWeek*, October 26, 2009, pp. 37–40; Christopher Helman, "The Second Coming," *Forbes*, December 10, 2007, pp. 79–86; David Whitford, "Uh... Maybe I Should Drive," *Fortune*, April 30, 2007, pp. 125–128; Louise Lee, "It's Dell vs. the Dell Way," *BusinessWeek*, March 6, 2006, pp. 61–62; David Kirkpatrick, "Dell in the Penalty Box," *Fortune*, September 18, 2006, pp. 70–78; Nanette Byrnes, Peter Burrows, and Louise Lee, "Dark Days at Dell," *BusinessWeek*, September 4, 2006, pp. 27–30; Elizabeth Corcoran, "A Bad Spell for Dell," *Forbes*, June 19, 2006, pp. 44–46.

36. For a detailed case study example, see Jennifer Shang, Tuba Pinar Yildrim, Pandu Tadikamalla, Vikas Mittal, and Lawrence Brown, "Distribution Network Redesign for Marketing Competitiveness," *Journal of Marketing, 73* (March 2009): 146–163.

37. Xinlei Chen, George John, and Om Narasimhan, "Assessing the Consequences of a Channel Switch," *Marketing Science, 27* (May–June 2008): 398–416.

38. Thomas H. Davenport and Jeanne G. Harris, *Competing on Analytics: The New Science of Winning* (Boston: Harvard Business School Press, 2007).

39. Junhong Chu, Pradeep K. Chintagunta, and Naufel J. Vilcassim, "Assessing the Economic Value of Distribution Channels: An Application to the Personal Computer Industry," *Journal of Marketing Research, 44* (February 2007): 29–41.

40. Bruce Einhorn, "China: Where Retail Dinosaurs Are Thriving," *Bloomberg BusinessWeek*, February 1 and 8, 2010, p. 64.

41. "Unshackling the Chain Stores," *Economist*, May 31, 2008, pp. 69–70.

42. Richard Gibson, "U.S. Franchises Find Opportunities to Grow Abroad," *Wall Street Journal*, August 11, 2009, p. B5.

43. Zena Olijnyk, "Land of Missed Opportunity," *Canadian Business*, September 5, 2006, www.canadianbusiness.com/columnists/

zena_olijnyk/article.jsp?content=20060905_142119_5592 (viewed April 2011).

44. "Crossroads," *Economist*, March 17, 2007, pp. 71–72; "Shopped Around," *Economist*, October 18, 2008, p. 74; Carol Matlack, "A French Wal-Mart's Global Blitz, *BusinessWeek*, December 21, 2009, pp. 64–65.

45. Michael Arndt, "Urban Outfitters Grow-Slow Strategy," *Bloomberg BusinessWeek*, March 1, 2010, p. 56; Michael Arndt, "How to Play It: Apparel Makers," *Bloomberg BusinessWeek*, March 1, 2010, p. 61.

46. Jenifer Reingold, "The British (Retail) Invasion," *Fortune*, July 7, 2008, pp. 132–138; Ruth La Ferla, "But Will It Play in Manhattan," *New York Times*, June 21, 2006; Damien Reece, "Topshop's Injection of True Brit Stirs Up the Big Apple," *Daily Telegraph*, April 2, 2009; Eric Lam, "Topshop Coming to Canada," *Financial Post*, March 9, 2011, www.financialpost.com/Topshop+coming+Canada/4408769/story.html (viewed April 2011).

47. Stefan Wuyts, Stefan Stremersch, Christophe Van Den Bulte, and Philip Hans Franses, "Vertical Marketing Systems for Complex Products: A Triadic Perspective," *Journal of Marketing Research*, 41 (November 2004): 479–487.

48. Russell Johnston and Paul R. Lawrence, "Beyond Vertical Integration: The Rise of the Value-Adding Partnership," *Harvard Business Review*, July–August 1988, pp. 94–101. See also Arnt Bovik and George John, "When Does Vertical Coordination Improve Industrial Purchasing Relationships," *Journal of Marketing*, 64 (October 2000): 52–64; Judy A. Siguaw, Penny M. Simpson, and Thomas L. Baker, "Effects of Supplier Market Orientation on Distributor Market Orientation and the Channel Relationship: The Distribution Perspective," *Journal of Marketing*, 62 (July 1998): 99–111; and Narakesari Narayandas and Manohar U. Kalwani, "Long-Term Manufacturer–Supplier Relationships: Do They Pay Off for Supplier Firms?" *Journal of Marketing*, 59 (January 1995): 1–16.

49. Raji Srinivasan, "Dual Distribution and Intangible Firm Value: Franchising in Restaurant Chains," *Journal of Marketing*, 70 (July 2006): 120–135.

50. "President's Choice Financial," *Wikipedia*, http://en.wikipedia.org/wiki/President's_Choice_Financial; President's Choice Financial website, www.banking.pcfinancial.ca/a/aboutus/aboutUs.page?region=NS&language=en&signinop= (viewed April 2011).

51. www.disney.com, December 9, 2010; Joyceann Cooney, "Mooney's Kingdom," *License*, October 1, 2006.

52. Coach Inc. Form 10-K filed with SEC on August 19, 2009.

53. Rajkumar Venkatesan, V. Kumar, and Nalini Ravishanker, "Multichannel Shopping: Causes and Consequences," *Journal of Marketing*, 71 (April 2007): 114–132.

54. Susan Casey, "Eminence Green," *Fortune*, April 2, 2007, pp. 64–70.

55. Barbara Darow, "Oracle's New Partner Path," *CRN*, August 21, 2006, p. 4.

56. Anne Coughlan and Louis Stern, "Marketing Channel Design and Management," in *Kellogg on Marketing*, edited byDawn Iacobucci(New York: John Wiley & Sons, 2001), pp. 247–269.

57. Nirmalya Kumar, "Some Tips on Channel Management," *rediff.com*, July 1, 2005.

58. Matthew Boyle, "Brand Killers," *Fortune*, August 11, 2003, pp. 51–56; "An Analysis of Canadian Food Industry Concentration," www.ivry.inra.fr/loria/eaaefichiers/ProgCom_fichiers/Criner.pdf (viewed May 2008). For an opposing view, see Anthony J. Dukes, Esther Gal-Or, and Kannan Srinivasan, "Channel Bargaining with Retailer Asymmetry," *Journal of Marketing Research*, 43 (February 2006): 84–97.

59. Jerry Useem, Julie Schlosser, and Helen Kim, "One Nation under Wal-Mart," *Fortune* (Europe), March 3, 2003; Susan Ward, "How to Get Your Products into the Big Box Retailers," *About.com*, undated, http://sbinfocanada.about.com/od/marketing/a/bigboxretail.htm; "Ultima Foods Walmart's Supplier of the Month for April," Yoplait Press Release, www.yoplait.ca/en/quoi_neuf_all.aspx?Id=179 (viewed April 2011).

60. Sreekumar R. Bhaskaran and Stephen M. Gilbert, "Implications of Channel Structure for Leasing or Selling Durable Goods," *Marketing Science, 28* (September–October 2009): 918–934.

61. For an example of when conflict can be viewed as helpful, see Anil Arya and Brian Mittendorf, "Benefits of Channel Discord in the Sale of Durable Goods," *Marketing Science, 25* (January–February 2006): 91–96; and Nirmalya Kumar, "Living with Channel Conflict," *CMO Magazine*, October 2004.

62. This section draws on Anne T. Coughlan, Erin Anderson, Louis W. Stern, and Adel I. El-Ansary, *Marketing Channels*, 7th ed. (Upper Saddle River, NJ: Prentice Hall, 2007), Ch. 9.. See also Jonathan D. Hibbard, Nirmalya Kumar, and Louis W. Stern, "Examining the Impact of Destructive Acts in Marketing Channel Relationships," *Journal of Marketing Research*, 38 (February 2001): 45–61; Kersi D. Antia and Gary L. Frazier, "The Severity of Contract Enforcement in Interfirm Channel Relationships," *Journal of Marketing*, 65 (October 2001): 67–81; James R. Brown, Chekitan S. Dev, and Dong-Jin Lee, "Managing Marketing Channel Opportunism: The Efficiency of Alternative Governance Mechanisms," *Journal of Marketing*, 64 (April 2000): 51–65; Alberto Sa Vinhas and Erin Anderson, "How Potential Conflict Drives Channel Structure: Concurrent (Direct and Indirect) Channels," *Journal of Marketing Research, 42* (November 2005): 507–515.

63. Nirmalya Kumar, "Living with Channel Conflict," *CMO Magazine*, October 2004.

64. "Retail Council of Canada and the Canadian Council of Grocery Distributors to Comment on Senate Investigation of Visa/MasterCard," *Media Advisory*, April 21, 2009.

65. Andrew Kaplan, "All Together Now?" *Beverage World*, March 2007, pp. 14–16.

66. Christina Passriello, "Fashionably Late? Designer Brands Are Starting to Embrace E-Commerce," *Wall Street Journal*, May 19, 2006.

67. Competition Bureau website, www.competitionbureau.gc.ca/epic/site/cb-bc.nsf/en/02542e.html with particular reference to the "Speaking Notes for Sheridan Scott Commissioner of Competition," December 13, 2007.

68. Joel C. Collier and Carol C. Bienstock, "How Do Customers Judge Quality in an E-Tailer," *MIT Sloan Management Review*, Fall 2006, pp. 35–40.

69. *Coremetrics Benchmark December US Retail*, www.coremetrics.com/downloads/coremetrics-benchmark-industry-report-2008-12-us.pdf.

70. Jeff Borden, "The Right Tools," *Marketing News*, April 15, 2008, pp. 19–21.

71. Alexis K. J. Barlow, Noreen Q. Siddiqui, and Mike Mannion, "Development in Information and Communication Technologies for Retail Marketing Channels," *International Journal of Retail and Distribution Management, 32* (March 2004): 157–163; G&J Electronic Media Services, *7th Wave of the GfK-Online-Monitor* (Hamburg: GfK Press, 2001).

72. Martin Holzwarth, Chris Janiszewski, and Marcus M. Newmann, "The Influence of Avatars on Online Consumer Shopping Behavior," *Journal of Marketing*, 70 (October 2006): 19–36.

73. Ann E. Schlosser, Tiffany Barnett White, and Susan M. Lloyd, "Converting Web Site Visitors into Buyers: How Web Site Investment Increases Consumer Trusting Beliefs and Online Purchase Intentions," *Journal of Marketing*, 70 (April 2006): 133–148.

74. "China's Pied Piper," *Economist*, September 23, 2006, p. 80; Alibaba website, www.alibaba.com, December 9, 2010; Garry Barker, "The Treasure Keeps Coming for Alibaba," *The Age*, October 27, 2009; Jessica E. Vascellaro, "Alibaba.com Plans U.S Push," *Wall Street Journal*, August 7, 2009; Bruce Einhorn, "At Alibaba, Investors Come Last," *BusinessWeek*, August 17, 2009, p. 50.

75. For an in-depth academic examination, see John G. Lynch, Jr., and Dan Ariely, "Wine Online: Search Costs and Competition on Price, Quality, and Distribution," *Marketing Science, 19* (Winter 2000): 83–103.

76. Andrea Chang, "Retailers Fuse Stores with E-Commerce," *Los Angeles Times*, June 27, 2010.

77. Anjali Cordeiro, "Procter & Gamble Sees Aisle Expansion on the Web," *Wall Street Journal*, September 2, 2009, p. B6A; Anjali Cordeiro and Ellen Byron, "Procter & Gamble to Test Online Store to Study Buying Habits," *Wall Street Journal*, January 15, 2010.

78. Xubing Zhang, "Retailer's Multichannel and Price Advertising Strategies," *Marketing Science, 28* (November–December 2009): 1080–1094.

79. Susan Fournier and Lara Lee, "Getting Brand Communities Right," *Harvard Business Review*, April 2009, pp. 105–111; "New Harley Davidson Accessory and Clothing Store," *PRLog*, July 21, 2009; Bob Tedeshi, "How Harley Revved Online Sales," *Business x2.0*, December 2002–January 2003, pp. 44; John W. Schouten, and James H. McAlexander, "Market Impact of a Consumption Subculture: The Harley-Davidson Mystique," in *European Advances in Consumer Research*, edited byGary J. Bamossy and W. Fred van Raaij(Provo, UT: Association for Consumer Research, 1993), pp. 389–393.

80. Nanette Byrnes, "More Clicks at the Bricks," *BusinessWeek*, December 17, 2007, pp. 50–51; "Wi-Fi in stores: Deloitte's TMT Predictions 2011," February 8, 2011, http://ideas.deloitte.ca/blog/2011/02/wi-fi-in-stores/ (viewed April 2011).

81. Douglas Lamont, *Conquering the Wireless World: The Age of M-Commerce* (New York: John Wiley & Sons, 2001); Herbjørn Nysveen, Per E. Pedersen, Helge Thorbjørnsen, and Pierre Berthon, "Mobilizing the Brand: The Effects of Mobile Services on Brand Relationships and Main Channel Use," *Journal of Service Research, 7* (2005): 257–276; Venkatesh Shankar and Sridhar Balasubramanian, "Mobile Marketing: A Synthesis and Prognosis," *Journal of Interactive Marketing, 23* (2009): 118–129; Venkatesh Shankar, Alladi Venkatesh, Charles Hofacker, and Prasad Naik, "Mobile Marketing in the Retailing Environment: Current Insights and Future Research Avenues," *Journal of Interactive Marketing, 24* (2010): 111–120.

82. "The Mobile Internet Report," *Morgan Stanley*, www.morganstanley.com, May 7, 2010; "Strength in Numbers . . . How Many Smartphones are There in Canada?" http://getclip.ca/blog/?p=152; Hugh Thompson, "Smartphone Sales Expected to Top 468 million in 2011," *Digital Home*, www.digitalhome.ca/2011/04/smartphone-sales-expected-to-top-468-million-in-2011

83. Adam Cahill, Lars Albright, and Carl Howe, "Mobile Advertising and Branding," session as part of the Britt Technology Impact Series, Tuck School of Business, Dartmouth College, March 31, 2010; Alexandre Mars, "Importing Mobile Marketing Tools," *Brandweek*, February 15, 2010, p. 17.

84. Reena Jana, "Retailers Are Learning to Love Smartphones," *BusinessWeek*, October 26, 2009.

85. Katie Bailey, "Canadians Not So Smart about Smartphones—Study," *Media in Canada*, April 15, 2010, www.mediaincanada.com/articles/mic/20100415/delviniamobile.html; Claire Kerr, "Smartphones & Smart Charities," *Direct Marketing Magazine*, March 14, 2011 (viewed April 2011).

Chapter 16

1. Emily Wester, "Indigo Offers Plum Rewards," *Strategy Magazine*, May 1, 2011; "Chapters," *Wikipedia*, http://en.wikipedia.org/wiki/Chapters; Chapters Indigo website, www.chapters.indigo.ca/ (viewed May 2011).

2. "Gallery1 Furniture Named 'Canadian Retailer of the Year,'" www.gallery1furniture.com/content/retailer-year-0 (viewed May 2011); Devin Leonard, "GameStop Racks Up the Points," *Fortune*, June 9, 2008, pp. 109–122; John Brodie, "The Amazon of Fashion," *Fortune*, September 14, 2009, pp. 86–95.

3. Karsten Hansen and Vishal Singh, "Market Structure across Retail Formats," *Marketing Science, 28* (July–August 2009): 656–673.

4. "US Retail E-Commerce Down 3% in Q4, Up Just 6% in 2008," *Retailer Daily*, February 12, 2009.

5. "Franchise Statistics," undated, www.franchiseek.com/Canada/Franchise_Canada_Statistics.htm (viewed May 2011).

6. Raymund Flandez, "New Franchise Idea: Fewer Rules, More Difference," *Wall Street Journal*, September 18, 2007, p. B4.

7. Marina Strauss, "Store Wars," *The Globe and Mail*, August 21, 2010, p. B3.

8. Joseph Pereira and Ann Zimmerman, "For Toys "R" Us, Holidays Are Open and Shut," *Wall Street Journal*, September 15, 2009, p. B8.

9. Eric Newman, "Retail Design for 2008: Thinking Outside the Box," *Brandweek*, December 17, 2007, p. 26.

10. Scott Cendrowski, "Extreme Retailing," *Fortune*, March 31, 2008, p. 14.

11. "Reinventing the Store—The Future of Retailing," *Economist*, November 22, 2003, pp. 65–68.

12. Matthew Boyle, "IBM Goes Shopping," *Fortune*, November 27, 2006, pp. 77–78; Todd Wasserman, "The Store of the Future," *Brandweek*, December 17, 2007, pp. 23–25; Emma Ritch, "Supermarkets Go Digital," *San Jose Business Journal*, April 11, 2008; Tim Dickey, "Electronic Shelf Labels," *Retail Technology Trends*, February 26, 2010.

13. Barbara Farfan, "2010 World's Largest Retailers—The Biggest and Best Canadian Retail Chains," http://retailindustry.about.com/od/famousretailers/a/canada_2010_largest_retailers_world.htm (viewed May 2011).

14. Michael C. Bellas, "Shopper Marketing's Instant Impact," *Beverage World*, November 2007, p. 18; Richard Westlund, "Bringing Brands to Life: The Power of In-Store Marketing," Special Advertising Supplement to *Adweek*, January 2010.

15. Pierre Chandon, J. Wesley Hutchinson, Eric T. Bradlow, and Scott H. Young, "Does In-Store Marketing Work? Effects of the Number and Position of Shelf Facings on Brand Attention and Evaluation at the Point of Purchase," *Journal of Marketing Research, 73* (November 2009): 1–17.

16. Anthony Dukes and Yunchuan Liu, "In-Store Media and Distribution Channel Coordination," *Marketing Science, 29* (January–February 2010): 94–107.

17. Michael Freedman, "The Eyes Have It," *Forbes*, September 4, 2006, p. 70.

18. Amy Merrick, "Asking 'What Would Ann Do?'" *Wall Street Journal*, September 15, 2006.

19. Charles Fishman, "The Anarchist's Cookbook," *Fast Company*, July 2004, pp. 70–78; "Whole Foods Market 2009 Annual Report," *Whole Foods Market*, www.wholefoodsmarket.com/company/pdfs/ar09.pdf.

20. Louise Lee, "Catalogs, Catalogs, Everywhere," *BusinessWeek*, December 4, 2006, pp. 32–34; Michael J. Silverstein and Neil Fiske, *Trading Up: The New American Luxury* (New York: Portfolio, 2003); "Victoria's Secret," Case #6-0014, Center for Digital Strategies, Tuck School of Business, Dartmouth College, 2002; www.biz.yahoo.com, December 9, 2010.

21. Jessi Hempel, "Urban Outfitters, Fashion Victim," *BusinessWeek*, July 17, 2006, p. 60.

22. Robert Berner, "To Lure Teenager Mall Rats, You Need the Right Cheese," *BusinessWeek*, June 7, 2004, pp. 96–101; Aéropostale website, www.aeropostale.com, December 9, 2010; Jeanine Poggi, "Best in Class: Price Is Right at Aeropostale," *TheStreet*, www.thestreet.com/story/10514026/best-in-class-price-is-right-at-aeropostale.html, June 16, 2009; "Aéropostale, Inc. Seeks New Faces for Fall Ad Campaign with 'Real Teens 2010' Contest," *PR Newswire*, March 15, 2010.

23. Robert Berner, "Chanel's American in Paris," *BusinessWeek*, January 29, 2007, pp. 70–71.

24. Dave Forde, "Blockbuster Canada Prepares for the Toronto International Film Festival," *PR in Canada*, September 8, 2010, www.princanada.com/blockbuster-canada-prepares-for-the-toronto-international-film-festival/ (viewed May 2011).

25. Mark Tatge, "Fun & Games," *Forbes*, January 12, 2004, pp. 138–144.

26. Vanessa O'Connell, "Reversing Field, Macy's Goes Local," *Wall Street Journal*, April 21, 2008.

27. Diane Anderson, "RFID Technology Getting Static in New Hampshire," *Brandweek*, January 23, 2006, p. 13; Mary Catherine O'Conner, "Gillette Fuses RFID with Product Launch," *RFID Journal*, March 27, 2006; "The End of Privacy?" *Consumer Reports*, June 2006, pp. 33–40; Erick Schonfeld, "Tagged for Growth," *Business 2.0*, December 2006, pp. 58–61; "Radio Silence," *Economist*, June 9, 2007, pp. 20–21; Todd Lewan, "The Chipping of America," *Associated Press*, July 29, 2007.

28. Uta Werner, John McDermott, and Greg Rotz, "Retailers at the Crossroads: How to Develop Profitable New Growth Strategies," *Journal of Business Strategy, 25* (2004): 10–17.

29. "Trader Joe's Named a Breakaway Brand for 2009," *Supermarket Industry News*, August 17, 2009; Christopher Palmeri, "Trader Joe's Recipe for Success," *BusinessWeek*, February 21, 2008; Deborah Orr, "The Cheap Gourmet," *Forbes*, April 10, 2006, pp. 76–77; Amy Wu, "A Specialty Food Store with a Discount Attitude," *New York Times*, July 27, 2003.

30. Venkatesh Shankar and Ruth N. Bolton, "An Empirical Analysis of Determinants of Retailer Pricing Strategy," *Marketing Science, 23* (Winter 2004): 28–49.

31. www.target.com, December 9, 2010; Ann Zimmerman, "Staying on Target," *Wall Street Journal*, May 7, 2007; Mya Frazier, "The Latest European Import: Fast Fashion," *Advertising Age*, January 9, 2006, p. 6; Julie Schlosser, "How Target Does It," *Fortune*, October 18, 2004, p. 100; Michelle Conlin, "Look Who's Stalking Walmart," *BusinessWeek*, December 7, 2009, pp. 30–36.

32. Duncan Simester, "Signaling Price Image Using Advertised Prices," *Marketing Science, 14* (Summer 1995): 166–188. See also Jiwoong Shin, "The Role of Selling Costs in Signaling Price Image," *Journal of Marketing Research, 42* (August 2005): 305–312.

33. Frank Feather, *The Future Consumer* (Toronto: Warwick Publishing, 1994), p. 171. Also see David R. Bell and James M. Lattin, "Shopping Behavior and Consumer Preference for Retail Price Format: Why 'Large Basket' Shoppers Prefer EDLP," *Marketing Science, 17* (Spring 1998): 66–68; and Stephen J. Hoch, Xavier Dreeze, and Mary E. Purk, "EDLP, Hi-Lo, and Margin Arithmetic," *Journal of Marketing, 58* (October 1994): 1–15.

34. "Nissan Canada Announces Retail Network for NV Full-Size Commercial Van," Nissan Canada Press Release, March 29, 2011, www.newswire.ca/en/releases/archive/March2011/29/c7403.html (viewed May 2011).

35. Constance L. Hays, "Retailers Seeking to Lure Customers with Service," *New York Times*, December 1, 2003.

36. Amy Gillentine, "Marketing Groups Ignore Women at Their Own Peril," *Colorado Springs Business Journal*, January 20, 2006; Mary Lou Quinlan, "Women Aren't Buying It," *Brandweek*, June 2, 2003, pp. 20–22.

37. Cecile B. Corral, "Profits Pinched, Kohl's Eyes Market Share," *Home Textiles Today*, February 27, 2009; Ilaina Jones, "Kohl's Looking at Spots in Manhattan," *Reuters*, August 19, 2009; Cametta Coleman, "Kohl's Retail Racetrack," *Wall Street Journal*, March 1, 2000.

38. Mindy Fetterman and Jayne O'Donnell, "Just Browsing at the Mall? That's What *You* Think," *USA Today*, September 1, 2006.

39. "Reinventing the Store," *Economist*, November 22, 2003, pp. 65–68; Moira Cotlier, "Census Releases First E-Commerce Report," *Catalog Age*, May 1, 2001; Associated Press, "Online Sales Boomed at End of 2000," *Star-Tribune of Twin Cities*, February 17, 2001; Kenneth T. Rosen and Amanda L. Howard, "E-Tail: Gold Rush or Fool's Gold?" *California Management Review*, April 1, 2000, pp. 72–100.

40. Velitchka D. Kaltcheva and Barton Weitz, "When Should a Retailer Create an Exciting Store Environment?" *Journal of Marketing, 70* (January 2006): 107–118.

41. For more discussion, see Philip Kotler, "Atmospherics as a Marketing Tool," *Journal of Retailing*, Winter 1973–1974, pp. 48–64. Also see B. Joseph Pine II and James H. Gilmore, *The Experience Economy* (Boston: Harvard Business School Press, 1999).

42. Jeff Cioletti, "Super Marketing," *Beverage World*, November 2006, pp. 60–61.

43. Ben Paynter, "Happy Hour," *Fast Company*, March 2010, p. 34; Jessi Hempel, "Social Media Meets Retailing," *Fortune*, March 22, 2010, p. 30.

44. Carol Tice, "Anchors Away: Department Stores Lose Role at Malls," *Puget Sound Business Journal*, February 13, 2004, p. 1.

45. "Insights on the Changing State of Canada's Private Label Consumer," *nielsenwire*, October 19, 2010, http://blog.nielsen.com/nielsenwire/consumer/insights-on-the-changing-state-of-canadas-private-label-consumer/ (viewed May 2011).

46. Kusum Ailawadi and Bari Harlam, "An Empirical Analysis of the Determinants of Retail Margins: The Role of Store-Brand Share," *Journal of Marketing, 68* (January 2004): 147–165.

47. For a detailed analysis of contemporary research on private labels, see Michael R. Hyman, Dennis A. Kopf, and Dongdae Lee, "Review of Literature—Future Research Suggestions: Private Label Brands: Benefits, Success Factors and Future Research," *Journal of Brand Management, 17* (March 2010): 368–389. See also Kusum Ailawadi, Bari Harlam, Jacques Cesar, and David Trounce, "Retailer Promotion Profitability: The Role of Promotion, Brand, Category, and Market Characteristics," *Journal of Marketing Research, 43* (November 2006): 518–535; and Kusum Ailawadi, Koen Pauwels, and Jan-Benedict E. M. Steenkamp, "Private Label Use and Store Loyalty," *Journal of Marketing, 72* (November 2008): 19–30.

48. Natasha Singer, "Drug Firms Apply Brand to Generics," *New York Times*, February 16, 2010; Casey Feldman, "Generic Drug Superstars," *Fortune*, August 5, 2009; Mina Kimes, "Teva: The King of Generic Drugs," *Fortune*, August 5, 2009; Jeanne Whalen, "Betting $10 Billion on Generics, Novartis Seeks to Inject Growth," *Wall Street Journal*, May 4, 2006.

49. Michael Felding, "No Longer Plain, Simple," *Marketing News*, May 15, 2006, pp. 11–13; Rob Walker, "Shelf Improvement," *New York Times*, May 7, 2006.

50. Jim Chrizan, "Loblaw's Reverses Private Label Trend," *Packaging World*, January 22, 2010; "Loblaw Launches a New Line of Discount Store Brands," *Store Brand Decisions*, February 16, 2010; John J. Pierce, "Private Label Stimulus," *Private Label*, March–April 2009.

51. Brett Nelson, "Stuck in the Middle," *Forbes*, August 15, 2005, p. 88; "Arrow Investor Fact Sheet 2010," *Arrow*, www.arrow.com.

52. James A. Narus and James C. Anderson, "Contributing as a Distributor to Partnerships with Manufacturers," *Business Horizons*, September–October 1987. Also see Hlavecek and McCuistion, "Industrial Distributors—When, Who, and How," *Harvard Business Review*, March 1983, pp. 96–101.

53. www.grainger.com/Grainger/wwg/start.shtml, May 8, 2010; Sean Callahan, "Close-Up with Deb Oler, VP-Grainger Industrial Supply Brand, W.W. Grainger," *BtoB*, March 3, 2010; Ian Heller, "The Secret of Being Grainger," www.ezinearticles.com, April 30, 2010.

54. "Who Has the Top Consumer Goods Industry Supply Chains for 2008?" *Supply Chain News*, December 17, 2008; "Who Has the Top Retail Industry Supply Chains for 2008?" *Supply Chain News*, January 5, 2009.

55. "Johnson & Johnson 2007 Sustainability Report"; talk by panelist Chris Hacker, "Production Innovation and Supply Chains: Creating Value for the Next Generation," Tuck School of Business at Dartmouth College, *Business and Society Conference*, January 15, 2009.

56. William C. Copacino, *Supply Chain Management* (Boca Raton, FL: St. Lucie Press, 1997); Robert Shaw and Philip Kotler, "Rethinking the Chain: Making Marketing Leaner, Faster, and Better," *Marketing Management*, July–August 2009, 18–23.

57. "Shrink Rapped," *Economist*, May 17, 2008, p. 80; Romeo Richards, "How to Prevent Perishable Shrinkage," undated, www.articlesnatch.com/Article/How-To-Prevent-Perishable-Shrinkage/1184245 (viewed May 2011).

58. "State of Logistics: The Canadian Report 2008," *Industry Canada*, http://zonecours.hec.ca/documents/H2010-P5-2343553. StateOfLogisticsReport.pdf (viewed May 2011).

59. Pete Engardio, "Lean and Mean Gets Extreme," *BusinessWeek*, March 23 and 30, 2009, pp. 60–62; Traci Gregory, "ConMed Takes Lean Approach," *Central New York Business Journal*, May 22, 2009.

60. Daisuke Wakabayashi, "How Lean Manufacturing Can Backfire," *Wall Street Journal*, January 30, 2010. For some additional discussion of the downside of lean manufacturing, see Brian Hindo, "At 3M, a Struggle between Efficiency and Creativity," *BusinessWeek*, June 11, 2007.

61. "Facts," *Purolator Courier*, April 14, 2010, www.purolator.com/media/corporate/faq.html (viewed May 2011).

62. The optimal order quantity is given by the formula $Q* = 2DS/IC$, where D = annual demand, S = cost to place one order, and I = annual carrying cost per unit. Known as the economic-order quantity formula, it assumes a constant ordering cost, a constant cost of carrying an additional unit in inventory, a known demand, and no quantity discounts. For further reading on this subject, see Richard J. Tersine, *Principles of Inventory and Materials Management*, 4th ed. (Upper Saddle River, NJ: Prentice Hall, 1994).

63. William C. Copacino, *Supply Chain Management* (Boca Raton, FL: St. Lucie Press, 1997), pp. 122–123.

64. "Shining Examples," *Economist: A Survey of Logistics*, June 17, 2006, pp. 4–6.

65. Renee DeGross, "Retailers Try eBay Overstocks, Returns for Sale Online," *Atlanta Journal-Constitution*, April 10, 2004.

Chapter 17

1. Melinda Mattos, "Banking Made Comfy," *Strategy*, Dec. 1, 2010, p. 18; Hollie Shaw, "Marketing Helped Smooth Out TD Merger; Green Armchair," *National Post*, January 19, 2008, p. FP5; TD Canada Trust website, www.td.com/profile.jsp (viewed April 2, 2011); www.youtube.com/user/TDCanada (viewed June 25, 2011).

2. Xueming Luo and Naveen Donthu, "Marketing's Credibility: A Longitudinal Investigation of Marketing Communication Productivity and Shareholder Value," *Journal of Marketing, 70* (October 2006): 70–91.

3. Linda Childers, "Can't-Escape TV," *Fast Company*, July–August 2008, p. 46; Louise Story, "Anywhere the Eye Can See, It's Likely to See an Ad," *New York Times*, January 15, 2007; Laura Petrecca, "Product Placement—You Can't Escape It," *USA Today*, October 11, 2006.

4. Burt Helm, "Attention-Deficit Advertising," *BusinessWeek*, May 5, 2008, p. 50; "Motorola's 'Say Goodbye' Campaign at Hong Kong Airport," *MobiAD News*, February 20, 2008.

5. Vanessa L. Facenda, "Kimberly-Clark's Paper Trail Leads to Creative Marketing," *Brandweek*, January 14, 2008, p. 11.

6. "Google Taps Canadian to Boost Sales," *Times-Colonist*, August 6, 2010, p. B6.

7. Some of these definitions are adapted from Peter D. Bennett, ed., *Dictionary of Marketing Terms* (Chicago: American Marketing Association, 1995).

8. Tom Duncan and Sandra Moriarty, "How Integrated Marketing Communication's 'Touch Points' Can Operationalize the Service-Dominant Logic," in *The Service-Dominant Logic of Marketing: Dialog, Debate, and Directions,* edited by Robert F. Lusch and Stephen L. Vargo(Armonk, NY: M. E. Sharpe, 2006); Tom Duncan, *Principles of Advertising and IMC*, 2nd ed. (New York: McGraw-Hill/Irwin, 2005).

9. Noreen O'Leary, "Mint's Fresh Approach: Marketing on $700 a Year," *Brandweek*, October 12, 2009, p. 4; Coloribus Global Advertising Archive, www.coloribus.com, December 9, 2010.

10. Theresa Howard, "Multiplatform Ads Clean Up at Cannes," *USA Today*, June 29, 2009, p. 3B; Kate Nettleton, "Tribal DDB Amsterdam's 'Carousel' for Philips Scoops Cannes Lions 2009 Film Grand Prix," *Campaign*, June 29, 2009; Daniel Farey-Jones, "Philips Promotes Home Cinema Range with Online Film Premiere," *Campaign*, February 18, 2010.

11. For an alternate communications model developed specifically for advertising communications, see Barbara B. Stern, "A Revised Communication Model for Advertising: Multiple Dimensions of the Source, the Message, and the Recipient," *Journal of Advertising*, June 1994, pp. 5–15. For some additional perspectives, see Tom Duncan and Sandra E. Morarity, "A Communication-Based Marketing Model for Managing Relationships," *Journal of Marketing, 62* (April 1998): 1–13.

12. Demetrios Vakratsas and Tim Ambler, "How Advertising Works: What Do We Really Know?" *Journal of Marketing, 63* (January 1999): 26–43.

13. This section is based on an excellent text by John R. Rossiter and Larry Percy, *Advertising and Promotion Management*, 2nd ed. (New York: McGraw-Hill, 1997).

14. James F. Engel, Roger D. Blackwell, and Paul W. Minard, *Consumer Behavior*, 9th ed. (Fort Worth, TX: Dryden, 2001).

15. John R. Rossiter and Larry Percy, *Advertising and Promotion Management*, 2nd ed. (New York: McGraw-Hill, 1997).

16. James F. Engel, Roger D. Blackwell, and Paul W. Minard, *Consumer Behavior*, 9th ed. (Fort Worth, TX: Dryden, 2001).

17. Ayn E. Crowley and Wayne D. Hoyer, "An Integrative Framework for Understanding Two-Sided Persuasion," *Journal of Consumer Research, 20* (March 1994): 561–574.

18. C. I. Hovland, A. A. Lumsdaine, and F. D. Sheffield, *Experiments on Mass Communication*, Vol. 3 (Princeton, NJ: Princeton University Press, 1949); Ayn E. Crowley and Wayne D. Hoyer, "An Integrative Framework for Understanding Two-Sided Persuasion," *Journal of Consumer Research, 20* (March 1994): 561–574. For an alternative viewpoint, see George E. Belch, "The Effects of Message Modality on One- and Two-Sided Advertising Messages," in *Advances in Consumer Research*, edited byRichard P. Bagozzi and Alice M. Tybout(Ann Arbor, MI: Association for Consumer Research, 1983), pp. 21–26.

19. Curtis P. Haugtvedt and Duane T. Wegener, "Message Order Effects in Persuasion: An Attitude Strength Perspective," *Journal of Consumer Research, 21* (June 1994): 205–218; H. Rao Unnava, Robert E. Burnkrant, and Sunil Erevelles, "Effects of Presentation Order and Communication Modality on Recall and Attitude," *Journal of Consumer Research, 21* (December 1994): 481–490.

20. Brian Sternthal and C. Samuel Craig, *Consumer Behavior: An Information Processing Perspective* (Englewood Cliffs, NJ: Prentice Hall, 1982), pp. 282–284.

21. Michael R. Solomon, *Consumer Behavior*, 7th ed. (Upper Saddle River, NJ: Prentice Hall, 2007).

22. Some recent research on humour in advertising, for example, includes Haseeb Shabbir and Des Thwaites, "The Use of Humor to Mask Deceptive Advertising: It's No Laughing Matter," *Journal of Advertising, 36* (Summer 2007): 75–85; Thomas W. Cline and James J. Kellaris, "The Influence of Humor Strength and Humor Message Relatedness on Ad Memorability: A Dual Process Model," *Journal of Advertising, 36* (Spring 2007): 55–67; H. Shanker Krishnan and Dipankar Chakravarti, "A Process Analysis of

the Effects of Humorous Advertising Executions on Brand Claims Memory," *Journal of Consumer Psychology*, 13 (2003): 230–245.

23. "Follies," *Advertising Age*, December 14, 2009, p. 20.

24. Rik Pieters and Michel Wedel, "Attention Capture and Transfer in Advertising: Brand, Pictorial, and Text-Size Effects," *Journal of Marketing*, 68 (April 2004): 36–50.

25. Herbert C. Kelman and Carl I. Hovland, "Reinstatement of the Communication in Delayed Measurement of Opinion Change," *Journal of Abnormal and Social Psychology*, 48 (July 1953): 327–335.

26. David J. Moore, John C. Mowen, and Richard Reardon, "Multiple Sources in Advertising Appeals: When Product Endorsers Are Paid by the Advertising Sponsor," *Journal of the Academy of Marketing Science*, 13 (Summer 1994): 234–243.

27. "Live! With Regis and Kelly Travels to Prince Edward Island," www.tourismpei.com/regis-kelly-pei (viewed October 9, 2010); "Regis Philbin Calls P.E.I a 'Masterpiece' During Show," *CTV NEWS*, July 12, 2010, www.ctv.ca/CTVNews/Entertainment/20100712/regis-kelly-PEI-100712 (viewed October 9, 2010).

28. C. E. Osgood and P. H. Tannenbaum, "The Principles of Congruity in the Prediction of Attitude Change," *Psychological Review*, 62 (January 1955): 42–55.

29. Brian Morrissey, "Traditional Ads Yield Social Traction," *Adweek*, May 16, 2010.

30. Andrew Potter, "Old Spice Guy (Feb–July 2010)," *Canadian Business*, 83, no. 13–14 (September 13, 2010): 23; Suzanne Vara, "Old Spice Campaign—Could This Be the Best Online Campaign Ever?" July 14, 2010, http://kherize5.com/old-spice-campaign-could-this-be-the-best-online-campaign-ever/ (viewed October 6, 2010); Jack Neff, "America's Hottest Brands," *Advertising Age*, 81, no. 41 (November 15, 2010): 28.

31. "Face-to-Face Report," *American Business Media*, January 2010; "John Deere Face-to-Face Campaign Races Past Competition," *Special Advertising Section to Adweek and Brandweek*, October 14, 2009; Gyro HSR website, www.gyrohsr.com.

32. Suzanne Vranca, "New to the TV Lineup: A Flat-Panel Teaser," *Wall Street Journal*, April 29, 2008.

33. Chris Powell, "Rona Returns to Reality TV with Two New Shows," *Marketing*, September 9, 2010, www.marketingmag.ca/english/news/marketer/article.jsp?content=20100909_152715_6552 (viewed October 9, 2010).

34. Adapted from G. Maxwell Ule, "A Media Plan for 'Sputnik' Cigarettes," *How to Plan Media Strategy* (American Association of Advertising Agencies, 1957 Regional Convention), pp. 41–52.

35. Thomas C. Kinnear, Kenneth L. Bernhardt, and Kathleen A. Krentler, *Principles of Marketing*, 6th ed. (New York: HarperCollins, 1995).

36. K. Sridhar Moorthy and Scott A. Hawkins, "Advertising Repetition and Quality Perceptions," *Journal of Business Research*, 58 (March 2005): 354–360; Amna Kirmani and Akshay R. Rao, "No Pain, No Gain: A Critical Review of the Literature on Signaling Unobservable Product Quality," *Journal of Marketing*, 64 (April 2000): 66–79; Amna Kirmani, "The Effect of Perceived Advertising Costs on Brand Perceptions," *Journal of Consumer Research*, 17 (September 17, 1990): 160–171; Amna Kirmani and Peter Wright, "Money Talks: Perceived Advertising Expense and Expected Product Quality," *Journal of Consumer Research*, 16 (December 1989): 344–353.

37. Demetrios Vakratsas and Tim Ambler, "How Advertising Works: What Do We Really Know?" *Journal of Marketing*, 63 (January 1999): 26–43.

38. Annette Bourdeau, "Free Food, Rent Fuel Viral Buzz," *Strategy*, January 2008, p. 9; "About Killam," *Killam Properties*, www.killamproperties.com/about-killam.asp (viewed June 27, 2011).

39. Theodore Levitt, *Industrial Purchasing Behavior: A Study in Communication Effects* (Boston, MA: Harvard University Division of Research, 1965).

40. "Let's Build a Smarter Planet," *Effie Worldwide*, www.effie.org/winners/showcase/2010/; "IBM Smarter Planet Campaign from Ogilvy & Mather Wins Global Effie," *PRNewswire*, June 9, 2010; Jeffrey M. O'Brien, "IBM's Grand Plan to Save the Planet," *Fortune*, April 21, 2009.

41. Prasad A. Naik and Kalyan Raman, "Understanding the Impact of Synergy in Multimedia Communications," *Journal of Marketing Research*, 40 (November 2003): 375–388. See also Prasad A. Naik, Kalyan Raman, and Russell S. Winer, "Planning Marketing-Mix Strategies in the Presence of Interaction Effects," *Marketing Science*, 24 (January 2005): 25–34.

42. "Dictionary," *American Marketing Association*, www.marketing-power.com/_layouts/Dictionary.aspx?dLetter=I (viewed October 7, 2011).

43. Scott Neslin, *Sales Promotion*, MSI Relevant Knowledge Series (Cambridge, MA: Marketing Science Institute, 2002).

44. Markus Pfeiffer and Markus Zinnbauer, "Can Old Media Enhance New Media?" *Journal of Advertising Research*, March 2010, pp. 42–49.

45. Jim Jansen, "Online Product Research: 58% of Americans Have Researched a Product or Service Online," *Pew Research Center*, September 29, 2010; Future Shop website, www.futureshop.ca (viewed June 25, 2011).

46. Ellen Neuborne, "Ads That Actually Sell Stuff," *Business 2.0*, June 2004, p. 78.

47. Sreedhar Madhavaram, Vishag Badrinarayanan, and Robert E. McDonald, "Integrated Marketing Communication (IMC) and Brand Identity as Critical Components of Brand Equity Strategy," *Journal of Advertising*, 34 (Winter 2005): 69–80; Mike Reid, Sandra Luxton, and Felix Mavondo, "The Relationship between Integrated Marketing Communication, Market Orientation, and Brand Orientation," *Journal of Advertising*, 34 (Winter 2005): 11–23.

48. Don E. Schultz and Heidi Schultz, *IMC, The Next Generation: Five Steps for Delivering Value and Measuring Financial Returns* (New York: McGraw-Hill, 2003); Don E. Shultz, Stanley I. Tannenbaum, and Robert F. Lauterborn, *Integrated Marketing Communications: Putting It Together and Making It Work* (Lincolnwood, IL: NTC Business Books, 1992).

49. Bruce Horovitz, "Super Bowl Marketers Go All Out to Create Hype, Online Buzz," *USA Today*, February 8, 2010.

Chapter 18

1. Melinda Mattos, "Sell Like a Man, Man," *Strategy*, July 1, 2010, p. 12; "Today Shaving Becomes Gliding as Gillete Fusion ProGlide and Gillette Fusion ProSeries Are Available on Store Shelves," *Marketing Weekly News*, June 26, 2010, p. 75.

2. Paul F. Nunes and Jeffrey Merrihue, "The Continuing Power of Mass Advertising," *Sloan Management Review*, Winter 2007, pp. 63–69.

3. Jack Neff, "'Broken' Ad Model Holds Big Advantages for P&G," *Advertising Age*, March 5, 2007.

4. Russell H. Colley, *Defining Advertising Goals for Measured Advertising Results* (New York: Association of National Advertisers, 1961).

5. Wilfred Amaldoss and Chuan He, "Product Variety, Informative Advertising, and Price Competition," *Journal of Marketing Research*, 47 (February 2010): 146–156.

6. Dale Buss, "OnStar First Aid," *Brandchannel*, www.brandchannel.com, February 15, 2010; "OnStar Expands TV Campaign Ads Based on Real-Life Stories," *Road & Travel Magazine*, November 5, 2003.

7. "Responses to Comparative Advertising," *Journal of Consumer Research*, 32 (March 2006): 530–540; Dhruv Grewal, Sukumar Kavanoor, and James Barnes, "Comparative versus Noncomparative Advertising: A Meta-Analysis," *Journal of Marketing*, 61 (October 1997): 1–15; Randall L. Rose, Paul W. Miniard, Michael J. Barone, Kenneth C. Manning, and Brian D. Till, "When Persuasion Goes Undetected: The Case of Comparative

Advertising," *Journal of Marketing Research*, 30 (August 1993): 315–330.

8. Rajesh Chandy, Gerard J. Tellis, Debbie MacInnis, and Pattana Thaivanich, "What to Say When: Advertising Appeals in Evolving Markets," *Journal of Marketing Research*, 38 (November 2001); Gerard J. Tellis, Rajesh Chandy, and Pattana Thaivanich, "Decomposing the Effects of Direct Advertising: Which Brand Works, When, Where, and How Long?" *Journal of Marketing Research*, 37 (February 2000): 32–46; Peter J. Danaher, André Bonfrer, and Sanjay Dhar, "The Effect of Competitive Advertising," *Journal of Marketing Research*, 45 (April 2008): 211–225; Donald E. Schultz, Dennis Martin, and William P. Brown, *Strategic Advertising Campaigns* (Chicago: Crain Books, 1984), pp. 192–197.

9. Demetrios Vakratsas, Fred M. Feinberg, Frank M. Bass, and Gurumurthy Kalyanaram, "The Shape of Advertising Response Functions Revisited: A Model of Dynamic Probabilistic Thresholds," *Marketing Science, 23* (Winter 2004): 109–119. For an excellent review, see Greg Allenby and Dominique Hanssens, "Advertising Response," Marketing Science Institute Special Report 05-200, 2005.

10. Leonard M. Lodish, Magid Abraham, Stuart Kalmenson, Jeanne Livelsberger, Beth Lubetkin, Bruce Richardson, and Mary Ellen Stevens, "How T.V. Advertising Works: A Meta-Analysis of 389 Real-World Split Cable T.V. Advertising Experiments," *Journal of Marketing Research*, 32 (May 1995): 125–139.

11. Greg Allenby and Dominique Hanssens, "Advertising Response," Marketing Science Institute Special Report 05-200, 2005; Jack Neff, "TV Doesn't Sell Package Goods," *Advertising Age*, May 24, 2004, pp. 1, 30.

12. Cleve Langton, "Searching for the Holy Global Ad Grail," *Brandweek*, June 5, 2006, p. 16.

13. Laurel Wentz, "McDonald's Adds McMinis to Menu in Canada," *AdAge.com*, April 7, 2010, http://adage.com/article/global-news/mcdonald-s-adds-mcminis-menu-canada/143162/ (viewed June 9, 2011).

14. Eric Pfanner, "When Consumers Help, Ads Are Free," *New York Times*, June 22, 2009, p. B6; Elisabeth Sullivan, "H. J. Heinz: Consumers Sit in the Director's Chair for Viral Effort," *Marketing News*, February 10, 2008, p. 10; Louise Story, "The High Price of Creating Free Ads," *New York Times*, May 26, 2007; Laura Petrecca, "Madison Avenue Wants You! (or at Least Your Videos)," *USA Today*, June 21, 2007; Eric Pfanner, "Leave It to the Professionals? Hey, Let Consumers Make Their Own Ads," *New York Times*, August 4, 2006.

15. Pat Hewitt, "Ontario Choir That Set Up Flash Mob in Mall Sets YouTube Record for Hits," *Canadian Press*, December 24, 2010.

16. Ruth Lamperd, "Vegemite Product Renamed Vegemite Cheesybite after iSnack 2.0 Was Dumped," *Herald Sun*, October 7, 2009; "Follies," *Advertising Age*, December 14, 2009, p. 20.

17. Jonathan Paul, "A Double-Double for the Nation," *Strategy*, December 2010, p. 45.

18. "Scarborough Writes a Refreshing Headline for the Newspaper Industry: Three-Quarters of Adults Are Reading Newspapers, in Print or Online," *Scarborough Research*, www.scarborough.com; Joseph Plambeck, "Newspaper Circulation Falls Nearly 9%," *New York Times*, April 26, 2010; Chris Powell, "Newspaper Circulation Continues to Decline: ABC," *Marketing Magazine*, May 3, 2011, www.marketingmag.ca/news/media-news/newspaper-circulation-continues-to-decline-abc-26876 (viewed June 28, 2011).

19. "WWF-Canada Annual Review 2010," www.wwf.ca/about_us/annual_report (viewed July 18, 2011).

20. Nick Krewen, "Latest RMB Study Says Radio Is Holding Its Own," *Media in Canada*, January 21, 2010, http://mediaincanada.com/2010/01/21/rmbstudy2010-20100121 (viewed June 28, 2011).

21. "The Infinite Dial 2009," *Arbitron*, April 2009.

22. Kim Bartel Sheehan, *Controversies in Contemporary Advertising* (Thousand Oaks, CA: Sage, 2003).

23. Sarah Hills, "McNeil and Sugar Association Settle Splenda Dispute," *Food Navigator-usa.com*, www.foodnavigator-usa.com, November 18, 2008; James P. Miller, "Bitter Sweets Fight Ended," *Chicago Tribune*, May 12, 2007; Avery Johnson, "How Sweet It Isn't: Maker of Equal Says Ads for J&J's Splenda Misled; Chemistry Lesson for Jurors," *Wall Street Journal*, April 6, 2007. For a discussion of the possible role of corrective advertising, see Peter Darke, Laurence Ashworth, and Robin J. B. Ritchie, "Damage from Corrective Advertising: Causes and Cures," *Journal of Marketing*, 72 (November 2008): 81–97.

24. "Ford Pulls Controversial Ad After Concerns It May Encourage Vehicle Theft," *Canadian Press*, January 18, 2008.

25. Jack Aubry, "Air Canada Apologizes, Then Drops Offensive Advertisement," *Ottawa Citizen*, May 8, 1996, p. A3.

26. Donald E. Schultz et al., *Strategic Advertising Campaigns* (Chicago: NTC/Contemporary Publishing Company, 1994), p. 340.

27. Prashant Malaviya, "The Moderating Influence of Advertising Context on Ad Repetition Effects: The Role of Amount and Type of Elaboration," *Journal of Consumer Research*, 34 (June 2007): 32–40.

28. Elena Malykhina, "GEICO Poses 'Rhetorical Questions,'" *Brandweek*, December 28, 2009; Adam Armbruster, "GEICO Takes Varied Roads to Consumers," *Television Week*, March 12, 2007, p. 10; Rob Walker, "Pop-Culture Evolution," *New York Times Magazine*, April 15, 2007; *Yahoo Finance*, http://biz.yahoo.com/ic/10/10616.html.

29. Sam Jaffe, "Easy Riders," *American Demographics*, March 2004, pp. 20–23.

30. Max Chafkin, "Ads and Atmospherics," *Inc.*, February 2007.

31. Stephanie Clifford, "Billboards That Look Back," *New York Times*, May 31, 2008.

32. Abbey Klaassen and Andrew Hampp, "Inside Outdoor's Digital Makeover," *Advertising Age: Creativity*, June 14, 2010, p. 5.

33. Ibid.

34. Jon Fine, "Where Are Advertisers? At the Movies," *BusinessWeek*, May 25, 2009, pp. 65–66; "Advertisers Go Outside to Play," *AdweekMedia*, March 9, 2009, p. 1; Zack O'Malley Greenburg, "Take Your Brand for a Ride," *Forbes*, March 2, 2009, p. 67.

35. Jeff Pelline, "New Commercial Twist in Corporate Restrooms," *San Francisco Chronicle*, October 6, 1986.

36. Brian Steinberg and Suzanne Vranica, "Prime-Time TV's New Guest Stars: Products," *Wall Street Journal*, January 13, 2004; Michael A. Wiles and Anna Danielova, "The Worth of Product Placement in Successful Films: An Event Study Analysis," *Journal of Marketing*, 73 (July 2009): 44–63; Siva K. Balasubramanian, James Karrh, and Hemant Patwardhan, "Audience Response to Product Placements: An Integrative Framework and Future Research Agenda," *Journal of Advertising*, 35 (2006): 115–141; Cristel A. Russell and Barbara Stern, "Consumers, Characters, and Products: A Balance Model of Sitcom Product Placement Effects," *Journal of Advertising*, 35 (2006): 7–18; Cristel A. Russell and Michael Belch, "A Managerial Investigation into the Product Placement Industry," *Journal of Advertising Research*, 45 (2005): 73–92.

37. Stephanie Clifford, "Product Placements Acquire a Life of Their Own on Shows," *New York Times*, July 14, 2008; "FCC Opens Inquiry into Stealthy TV Product Placement," *Associated Press*, June 26, 2008; Chris Reidy, "Staples Gets an Office Encore," *Boston Globe*, November 4, 2007; James L. Johnston, "Branded Entertainment: The Old Is New Again and More Complicated Than Ever," *Journal of Sponsorship*, 2 (February 2009): 170–175.

38. Popai, www.popai.com (viewed August 22, 2010).

39. Ram Bezawada, S. Balachander, P. K. Kannan, and Venkatesh Shankar, "Cross-Category Effects of Aisle and Display Placements: A Spatial Modeling Approach and Insights," *Journal of Marketing*, 73 (May 2009): 99–117; Pierre Chandon, J. Wesley Hutchinson, Eric T. Bradlow, and Scott H. Young, "Does In-Store Marketing Work? Effects of the Number and Position of Shelf Facings on Brand

Attention and Evaluation at the Point of Purchase," *Journal of Marketing,* 73 (November 2009): 1–17.

40. Bill Yackey, "Walmart Reveals 18-Month Results for SMART Network," *Digital Signage Today,* February 23, 2010; Mark Friedman, "Walmart's New In-Store Ads Turning Heads," *Arkansas Business,* September 22, 2008; Laura Petrecca, "Wal-Mart TV Sells Marketers Flexibility," *USA Today,* March 29, 2007.

41. Hollie Shaw, "Tropicana Adds Shot of Reality to Ads; Joins Trend of Fusing Reality TV and Event Marketing," *Calgary Herald,* January 15, 2010, p. D6.

42. Brian Steinberg, "'Sunday Night Football' Remains Costliest TV Show," *Advertising Age,* October 26, 2009.

43. Chris Zelkovich, "CBC Scores Big Revenue for the Cup," *Toronto Star,* June 15, 2011, p. S5.

44. "4A's Television Production Cost Survey," *4A's,* www.aaaa.org, December 15, 2009.

45. "Maclean's 2011 Advertising Rates: National Rates (Gross)," www.rogersconnect.com/files/Macleans_MediaKit.pdf; www2.macleans.ca (viewed July 14, 2011).

46. *MoneySense* website, www.rogersconnect.com/publication/moneysense (viewed July 14, 2011).

47. Kenneth R. Lord, Myung-Soo Lee, and Paul L. Sauer, "Program Context Antecedents of Attitude toward Radio Commercials," *Journal of the Academy of Marketing Science,* 13 (Winter 1994): 3–15; Kenneth R. Lord and Robert E. Burnkrant, "Attention versus Distraction: The Interactive Effect of Program Involvement and Attentional Devices on Commercial Processing," *Journal of Advertising,* March 1993, pp. 47–60.

48. Roland T. Rust, *Advertising Media Models: A Practical Guide* (Lexington, MA: Lexington Books, 1986).

49. Hani I. Mesak, "An Aggregate Advertising Pulsing Model with Wearout Effects," *Marketing Science,* 11 (Summer 1992): 310–326; Fred M. Feinberg, "Pulsing Policies for Aggregate Advertising Models," *Marketing Science,* 11 (Summer 1992): 221–234.

50. David B. Montgomery and Alvin J. Silk, "Estimating Dynamic Effects of Market Communications Expenditures," *Management Science,* June 1972, pp. 485–501; Kristian S. Palda, *The Measurement of Cumulative Advertising Effect* (Upper Saddle River, NJ: Prentice Hall, 1964), p. 87.

51. Gerard J. Tellis, Rajesh K. Chandy, and Pattana Thaivanich, "Which Ad Works, When, Where, and How Often? Modeling the Effects of Direct Television Advertising," *Journal of Marketing Research,* 37 (February 2000): 32–46; Ajay Kalra and Ronald C. Goodstein, "The Impact of Advertising Positioning Strategies on Consumer Price Sensitivity," *Journal of Marketing Research,* May 1998, pp. 210–224; Anil Kaul and Dick R. Wittink, "Empirical Generalizations about the Impact of Advertising on Price Sensitivity and Price," *Marketing Science,* 14 (Summer 1995): G151–G160; David Walker and Tony M. Dubitsky, "Why Liking Matters," *Journal of Advertising Research,* May–June 1994, pp. 9–18; Abhilasha Mehta, "How Advertising Response Modeling (ARM) Can Increase Ad Effectiveness," *Journal of Advertising Research,* May–June 1994, pp. 62–74; John Deighton, Caroline Henderson, and Scott Neslin, "The Effects of Advertising on Brand Switching and Repeat Purchasing," *Journal of Marketing Research,* 31 (February 1994): 28–43; Karin Holstius, "Sales Response to Advertising," *International Journal of Advertising,* 9 (September 1990): 38–56.

52. Nigel Hollis, "The Future of Tracking Studies," *Admap,* October 2004, pp. 151–153.

53. From Robert C. Blattberg and Scott A. Neslin, *Sales Promotion: Concepts, Methods, and Strategies* (Upper Saddle River, NJ: Prentice Hall, 1990). This text provides a detailed, analytical treatment of sales promotion. A comprehensive review of academic work on sales promotions can be found in Scott Neslin, "Sales Promotion," in *Handbook of Marketing,* edited byBart Weitz and Robin Wensley(London, England: Sage, 2002), pp. 310–338.

54. Kusum Ailawadi, Karen Gedenk, and Scott A. Neslin, "Heterogeneity and Purchase Event Feedback in Choice Models: An Empirical Analysis with Implications for Model Building," *International Journal of Research in Marketing,* 16 (September 1999): 177–198. See also Eric T. Anderson and Duncan Simester, "The Long-Run Effects of Promotion Depth on New versus Established Customers: Three Field Studies," *Marketing Science,* 23 (Winter 2004): 4–20; Luc Wathieu, A. V. Muthukrishnan, and Bart J. Bronnenberg, "The Asymmetric Effect of Discount Retraction on Subsequent Choice," *Journal of Consumer Research,* 31 (December 2004): 652–665; and Praveen Kopalle, Carl F. Mela, and Lawrence Marsh, "The Dynamic Effect of Discounting on Sales: Empirical Analysis and Normative Pricing Implications," *Marketing Science,* 18 (Summer 1999): 317–332.

55. Harald J. Van Heerde, Sachin Gupta, and Dick Wittink, "Is 75% of the Sales Promotion Bump Due to Brand Switching? No, Only 33% Is," *Journal of Marketing Research,* 40 (November 2003): 481–491; Harald J. Van Heerde, Peter S. H. Leeflang, and Dick R. Wittink, "The Estimation of Pre- and Postpromotion Dips with Store-Level Scanner Data," *Journal of Marketing Research,* 37 (August 2000): 383–395. See also Kusum L. Ailawadi, Karen Gedenk, Christian Lutzky, and Scott A. Neslin, "Decomposition of the Sales Impact of Promotion-Induced Stockpiling," *Journal of Marketing Research,* 44 (August 2007).

56. Jerry Langton, "Economics of the Humble Coupon; Coupon Use Spikes During Recessions," *Toronto Star,* July 7, 2008, p. L1.

57. For a good summary of the research on whether promotion erodes the consumer franchise of leading brands, see Robert Blattberg and Scott Neslin, "Sales Promotion: The Long and Short of It," *Marketing Letters,* 1 (December 1989). See also Stephanie Rosenbloom, "In Recession, Even the Holdouts Use Coupons," *New York Times,* September 24, 2009. For a related topic, see Michael J. Barone and Tirthankar Roy, "Does Exclusivity Pay Off? Exclusive Price Promotions and Consumer Response," *Journal of Marketing,* 74 (March 2010): 121–132.

58. Robert George Brown, "Sales Response to Promotions and Advertising," *Journal of Advertising Research,* August 1974, pp. 36–37. Also see Kamel Jedidi, Carl F. Mela, and Sunil Gupta, "Managing Advertising and Promotion for Long-Run Profitability," *Marketing Science,* 18 (Winter 1999): 1–22; Carl F. Mela, Sunil Gupta, and Donald R. Lehmann, "The Long-Term Impact of Promotion and Advertising on Consumer Brand Choice," *Journal of Marketing Research,* 34 (May 1997): 248–261; and Purushottam Papatla and Lakshman Krishnamurti, "Measuring the Dynamic Effects of Promotions on Brand Choice," *Journal of Marketing Research,* 33 (February 1996): 20–35.

59. "2010 REGGIE Awards Shopper Marketing: P&G Gain—Project Gainiac," *Promotion Marketing Association,* www.pmalink.org.

60. Magid M. Abraham and Leonard M. Lodish, "Getting the Most out of Advertising and Promotion," *Harvard Business Review,* May–June 1990, pp. 50–60. See also Shuba Srinivasan, Koen Pauwels, Dominique Hanssens, and Marnik Dekimpe, "Do Promotions Benefit Manufacturers, Retailers, or Both?" *Management Science,* 50 (May 2004): 617–629.

61. Leonard M. Lodish, Magid Abraham, Stuart Kalmenson, Jeanne Livelsberger, Beth Lubetkin, Bruce Richardson, and Mary Ellen Stevens, "How T.V. Advertising Works: A Meta-Analysis of 389 Real World Split Cable T.V. Advertising Experiments," *Journal of Marketing Research,* 32 (May 1995): 125–139.

62. Rebecca J. Slotegraaf and Koen Pauwels, "The Impact of Brand Equity Innovation on the Long-Term Effectiveness of Promotions," *Journal of Marketing Research,* 45 (June 2008): 293–306.

63. For a model for setting sales promotions objectives, see David B. Jones, "Setting Promotional Goals: A Communications Relationship Model," *Journal of Consumer Marketing,* 11 (1994): 38–49.

64. Kusum L. Ailawadi, Bari A. Harlam, Jacques Cesar, and David Trounce, "Promotion Profitability for a Retailer: The Role of Promotion, Brand, Category, and Store Characteristics," *Journal of Marketing Research,* 43 (November 2006): 518–536.

65. Emily Bryson York and Natalie Zmuda, "Sampling: The New Mass Media," *Advertising Age*, May 12, 2008, pp. 3, 56.

66. Sarah Skidmore, "Coupons Evolve for the Digital Age," *Associated Press*, August 30, 2009; "20 Most Popular Comparison Shopping Websites," *eBizMBA*, www.ebizmba.com, June 2010.

67. Miguel Gomez, Vithala Rao, and Edward McLaughlin, "Empirical Analysis of Budget and Allocation of Trade Promotions in the U.S. Supermarket Industry," *Journal of Marketing Research, 44* (August 2007); Norris Bruce, Preyas S. Desai, and Richard Staelin, "The Better They Are, the More They Give: Trade Promotions of Consumer Durables," *Journal of Marketing Research, 42* (February 2005): 54–66.

68. Kusum L. Ailawadi and Bari Harlam, "An Empirical Analysis of the Determinants of Retail Margins: The Role of Store Brand Share," *Journal of Marketing, 68* (January 2004): 147–166; Kusum L. Ailawadi, "The Retail Power-Performance Conundrum: What Have We Learned?" *Journal of Retailing, 77* (Fall 2001): 299–318; Paul W. Farris and Kusum L. Ailawadi, "Retail Power: Monster or Mouse?" *Journal of Retailing*, Winter 1992, pp. 351–369; Koen Pauwels, "How Retailer and Competitor Decisions Drive the Long-Term Effectiveness of Manufacturer Promotions," *Journal of Retailing, 83* (2007): 364–390.

69. James Bandler, "The Shadowy Business of Diversion," *Fortune*, August 17, 2009, p. 65; Rajiv Lal, John Little, and J. M. Vilas-Boas, "A Theory of Forward Buying, Merchandising, and Trade Deals," *Marketing Science, 15* (Winter 1996): 21–37.

70. IBIS World USA, www.ibisworld.com; Noah Lim, Michael J. Ahearne, and Sung H. Ham, "Designing Sales Contests: Does the Prize Structure Matter?" *Journal of Marketing Research, 46* (June 2009): 356–371.

71. "2011 International CES: Attendee Audit Summary Results," www.cesweb.org/aboutces.asp (viewed July 18, 2011).

72. Jonathan Paul, "Yellow Tail Goes 360 to Get Toasted," *Strategy*, June 1, 2011, http://strategyonline.ca/2011/06/01/upfrontyellow-20110601/#ixzz1P6B06NYU (viewed June 12, 2011); Yellow Tail Canada's Facebook page, www.facebook.com/#!/yellowtailcanada (viewed June 12, 2011).

73. Kurt H. Schaffir and H. George Trenten, *Marketing Information Systems* (New York: AMACOM, 1973), p. 81.

74. Joe A. Dodson, Alice M. Tybout, and Brian Sternthal, "Impact of Deals and Deal Retraction on Brand Switching," *Journal of Marketing Research, 15* (February 1978): 72–81.

75. *IEG Sponsorship Report*, as quoted in "Sponsorship Spending Revised, Growth Cut in Half: IEG," *Promo*, June 18, 2009.

76. Philip Kotler, "Atmospherics as a Marketing Tool," *Journal of Retailing*, Winter 1973–1974, pp. 48–64.

77. Kathleen Kerwin, "When the Factory Is a Theme Park," *BusinessWeek*, May 3, 2004, p. 94; Vanessa O'Connell, "'You-Are-There' Advertising," *Wall Street Journal*, August 5, 2002.

78. Jeff Borden, "Tornado: Experiential Marketing Takes the Industry by Storm in 2008," *Marketing News*, January 15, 2008, pp. 23–26.

79. Michael Schmelling, "Creative Mischief," *Fast Company*, November 2008, pp. 134–138; "GE Profile Inflatable Product Replicas Hit Times Square," *Landmark Creations*, www.landmark-creations.com; Laurie Sullivan, "GE Ads Show How to Lighten the Laundry Load," *Marketing Daily*, August 27, 2008.

80. "Personal Care Marketers: Who Does What," *IEG Sponsorship Report*, April 16, 2007, p. 4.

81. Bettina Cornwell, Michael S. Humphreys, Angela M. Maguire, Clinton S. Weeks, and Cassandra Tellegen, "Sponsorship-Linked Marketing: The Role of Articulation in Memory," *Journal of Consumer Research, 33* (December 2006): 312–321.

82. Hilary Cassidy, "So You Want to Be an Olympic Sponsor?" *Brandweek*, November 7, 2005, pp. 24–28.

83. "Brands Suit Up for 'Iron Man 2,'" *Adweek*, May 14, 2010.

84. "BB&T Continues Sponsorship with Clint Bowyer, Richard Childress Racing," *SceneDaily*, January 14, 2010; "BB&T Puts Name on New Winston-Salem Ballpark," *Winston-Salem Journal*, February 24, 2010; "Bank's New Department, Deals Reflect Elevated Sponsorship Status," *IEG Sponsorship Report*, April 16, 2007, pp. 1, 8.

85. The Association of National Advertisers has a useful source, *Event Marketing: A Management Guide*, which is available at www.ana.net/bookstore.

86. T. Bettina Cornwell, Clinton S. Weeks, and Donald P. Roy, "Sponsorship-Linked Marketing: Opening the Black Box," *Journal of Advertising, 34* (Summer 2005).

87. Constantine von Hoffman, "Buying Up the Bleachers," *Brandweek*, February 19, 2007, pp. 18–21.

88. William L. Shankin and John Kuzma, "Buying That Sporting Image," *Marketing Management*, Spring 1992, p. 65.

89. B. Joseph Pine and James H. Gilmore, *The Experience Economy: Work Is Theatre and Every Business a Stage* (Cambridge, MA: Harvard University Press, 1999).

90. "2006 Experiential Marketing Study," *Jack Morton*, www.jackmorton.com.

91. "Do We Have a Story for You!" *Economist*, January 21, 2006, pp. 57–58; Al Ries and Laura Ries, *The Fall of Advertising and the Rise of PR* (New York: HarperCollins, 2002).

92. "*PRWeek* Campaign of the Year," *PRWeek*, March 5, 2009; "Man Lives in IKEA," *Ketchum*, www.ketchum.com; "Man Lives in NYC IKEA Store," *Associated Press*, January 8, 2008.

93. Arthur M. Merims, "Marketing's Stepchild: Product Publicity," *Harvard Business Review*, November–December 1972, pp. 111–112. Also see Katherine D. Paine, "There Is a Method for Measuring PR," *Marketing News*, November 6, 1987, p. 5.

Chapter 19

1. "Social Media Get Analytical Approach; Syncapse Corp.; Company Helps Clients Optimize Facebook, Twitter," *National Post*, July 6, 2010, p. FP4; National Ballet of Canada Facebook page, www.facebook.com/pages/The-National-Ballet-of-Canada/13986327142#!/pages/The-National-Ballet-of-Canada/13986327142 (viewed October 23, 2010); The National Ballet of Canada website, www.national.ballet.ca/ (viewed October 23, 2010); Syncapse website, www.syncapse.com/media/syncapse-value-of-a-facebook-fan.pdf (viewed October 23, 2010); "The National Ballet of Canada Partners with Momentum and Ektron in New Web Design," *Canada Newswire*, October 12, 2010.

2. Ran Kivetz and Itamar Simonson, "The Idiosyncratic Fit Heuristic: Effort Advantage as a Determinant of Consumer Response to Loyalty Programs," *Journal of Marketing Research, 40* (November 2003): 454–467; Ran Kivetz and Itamar Simonson, "Earning the Right to Indulge: Effort as a Determinant of Customer Preferences toward Frequency Program Rewards," *Journal of Marketing Research, 39* (May 2002): 155–170.

3. The term *direct-order marketing* was suggested as a subset of direct marketing by Stan Rapp and Tom Collins in *The Great Marketing Turnaround* (Upper Saddle River, NJ: Prentice Hall, 1990).

4. Stan Rapp and Thomas L. Collins, *Maximarketing* (New York: McGraw-Hill, 1987).

5. "In the Mailbox," *Financial Post Magazine*, April 1, 2009.

6. "DMA Releases 2010 Response Rate Trend Report," *Direct Marketing Association*, www.the-dma.org, June 15, 2010.

7. Bob Stone and Ron Jacobs, *Successful Direct Marketing Methods*, 8th ed. (New York: McGraw-Hill, 2007).

8. Alex Palmer, "Hilton Targets Business Travelers with 'Spend a Sunday' HHonors promotion," October 13, 2010, www.dmnews.com/hilton-targets-business-travelers-with-spend-a-sunday-hhonors-promotion/article/180921/ (viewed October 17, 2010); "About Hilton HHonors," HHonors Hilton Worldwide website, http://hhonors1.hilton.com/en_US/hh/about/index. do?it=Not,TnavAbout (viewed October 17, 2010).

9. Edward L. Nash, *Direct Marketing: Strategy, Planning, Execution*, 4th ed. (New York: McGraw-Hill, 2000).

10. The *average customer longevity* (N) is related to the *customer retention rate* (CR). Suppose the company retains 80 percent of its customers each year. Then the average customer longevity is given by N = 1/(1 − CR) = 1/0.2 = 5 years.

11. "Canadian Mail Order Catalogues," *Library and Archives Canada*, www.collectionscanada.ca/mailorder/index-e.html.

12. "Catalogue Mail: Frequently Asked Questions," *Canada Post*, www.canadapost.ca/business/offerings/catalogue_mail/can/about_faqs-e.asp

13. Matt Semansky, "IKEA Introduces Social Media to Its Marketing Catalogue," *Marketing*, August 13, 2010, www.marketingmag.ca/english/news/marketer/article.jsp?content=20100812_172938_8896 (viewed October 21, 2010); "Student Info," IKEA website, www.ikea.com/ms/en_GB/about_ikea/press_room/student_info.html (viewed October 21, 2010).

14. "Do Not Call: CRTC Rules," *CBC News Online*, www.cbc.ca/news/background/telemarketing/ (viewed July 4, 2011); "National Do Not Call List," www.lnnte-dncl.gc.ca/index-eng; Canadian Radio-television and Telecommunications Commission website, www.lnnte-dncl.gc.ca/faqs-eng (viewed June 28, 2011).

15. "Biennial Report to Congress: Pursuant to the Do Not Call Registry Fee Extension Act of 2007," *Federal Trade Commission*, www.ftc.gov, December 2009.

16. Curiosk Marketing Solutions Inc. website, www.curiosk.com (viewed July 20, 2011).

17. Charles Duhigg, "Telemarketing Thieves Sharpen Their Focus on the Elderly," *New York Times*, May 20, 2007.

18. Government of Canada Anti-Fraud Centre website, www.antifraudcentre-centreantifraude.ca/english/home-eng.html (viewed June 29, 2011).

19. Tony Case, "Growing Up," *Interactive Quarterly*,April 19, 2004, pp. 32–34.

20. "Canadian Internet Use Survey," *Statistics Canada, The Daily*, May 10, 2010.

21. For example, see André Bonfrer and Xavier Drèze, "Real-Time Evaluation of E-mail Campaign Performance," *Marketing Science*, 28 (March–April 2009): 251–263.

22. Kenneth C. Wilbur and Yi Zhu, "Click Fraud," *Marketing Science*, 28 (March–April 2009): 293–308.

23. Ellen Byron, "Estée Lauder Tests Web-Ad Waters," *Wall Street Journal*, September 19, 2006.

24. Asim Ansari and Carl F. Mela, "E-Customization," *Journal of Marketing Research*, 40 (May 2003): 131–145.

25. "Research and Markets: Worldwide Ad Spending—Online Ad Spending Set to Reach $61.8 Billion Worldwide by the End of 2010," *Business Wire*, August 26, 2010.

26. Byron Acohido, "Rich Media Enriching PC Ads," *USA Today*, February 25, 2004.

27. Stuart Elliott, "Letting Consumers Control Marketing: Priceless," *New York Times*, October 9, 2006; Elizabeth Holmes, "On MySpace, Millions of Users Make 'Friends' with Ads," *Wall Street Journal*, August 7, 2006; "2009 Gold Effie Winner: 'Whopper Freakout,'" *Effie Worldwide*, www.effie.org.

28. Allen P. Adamson, *Brand Digital* (New York: Palgrave Macmillan, 2008).

29. John R. Hauser, Glen L. Urban, Guilherme Liberali, and Michael Braun, "Website Morphing," *Marketing Science*, 28 (March–April 2009): 202–223; Peter J. Danaher, Guy W. Mullarkey, and Skander Essegaier, "Factors Affecting Web Site Visit Duration: A Cross-Domain Analysis," *Journal of Marketing Research*, 43 (May 2006): 182–194; Philip Kotler, *According to Kotler* (New York: American Management Association, 2005).

30. Bob Tedeschi, "E-Commerce Report," *New York Times*, June 24, 2002.

31. Jan-Benedict E. M. Steenkamp and Inge Geyskens, "How Country Characteristics Affect the Perceived Value of Web Sites," *Journal of Marketing*, 70 (July 2006): 136–150.

32. Jessi Hempel, "The Online Numbers Game," *Fortune*, September 3, 2007, p. 18.

33. Julia Angwin and Tom McGinty, "Sites Feed Personal Details to New Tracking Industry," *Wall Street Journal*, July 31, 2010.

34. "LCBO Hosts Three Virtual Wine Tastings during 'goLOCAL—It's Seriously Cool' Ontario Wine Promotion," *Canada Newswire*, September 16, 2010.

35. *eMarketer*, www.emarketer.com, May 2010.

36. Emily Steel, "Marketers Take Search Ads Beyond Search Engines," *Wall Street Journal*, January 19, 2009.

37. Paula Andruss, "How to Win the Bidding Wars," *Marketing News*, April 1, 2008, p. 28; Jefferson Graham, "To Drive Traffic to Your Site, You Need to Give Good Directions," *USA Today*, June 23, 2008.

38. Peter J. Danaher, Janghyuk Lee, and Laoucine Kerbache, "Optimal Internet Media Selection," *Marketing Science*, 29 (March–April 2010): 336–347; Puneet Manchanda, Jean-Pierre Dubé, Khim Yong Goh, and Pradeep K. Chintagunta, "The Effects of Banner Advertising on Internet Purchasing," *Journal of Marketing Research*, 43 (February 2006): 98–108.

39. Brian Morrissey, "Big Money Bet on Display Ad Tech," *Adweek*, August 1, 2010; Brian Morrissey, "Beefing Up Banner Ads," *Adweek NEXT*, February 15, 2010, pp. 10–11; Robert D. Hof, "The Squeeze on Online Ads," *BusinessWeek*, March 2, 2009, pp. 48–49; Emily Steel, "Web Sites Debate Best Values for Advertising Dollars," *Wall Street Journal*, August 13, 2009, p. B7.

40. Elisabeth Lewin, "Podcast Audience Growing Faster Than Podcast Advertising," *Podcasting News*, www.podcastingnews.com, May 13, 2009.

41. Natalie Zmuda, "How E-Mail Became a Direct-Marketing Rock Star in Recession," *Advertising Age*, May 11, 2009, p. 27.

42. Brad Stone and Douglas MacMillan, "Are Four Words Worth $25 Billion for Groupon?" *BusinessWeek*, March 21, 2011.

43. Roger Cheng, "Mobile Ads Make Gains, but Pace Slows Sharply," *Wall Street Journal*, April 7, 2009; Mark Walsh, "Gartner: Mobile Advertising to Grow 74 percent in 2009," *MediaPost*, August 31, 2009; Amol Sharma, "Companies Vie for Ad Dollars on Mobile Web," *Wall Street Journal*, January 17, 2007; "Mobile Advertising: The Next Big Thing," *Economist*, October 7, 2007, pp. 73–74.

44. "ITU Statshot," *International Telecommunication Union*, no. 5 (January 2011).

45. Giselle Tsirulnik, "Bank of America Uses Mobile Banners to Drive App Downloads," *Mobile Marketer*, September 4, 2009; Rita Chang, "Consumer Control Brings Brand Loyalty," *Advertising Age*, March 30, 2009, p. 26; Dan Butcher, "Bank of America Campaign Targets Students for Mobile Banking," *Mobile Marketer*, August 28, 2008; Mickey Alam Khan, "Bank of America Surpasses 1M Mobile Banking Customers," *Mobile Marketer*, June 13, 2008.

46. Brian Morrissey, "2009 Really Isn't the Year of Mobile. Here's Why," *Brandweek*, November 16, 2009, p. 6; Douglas MacMillan, Peter Burrows, and Spencer E. Ante, "The App Economy," *BusinessWeek*, November 2, 2009, pp. 44–49.

47. BlackBerry App website, https://appworld.blackberry.com/webstore/vendor/2092?lang=en (viewed June 28, 2011).

48. Peter DaSilva, "Cellphone in New Role: Loyalty Card," *New York Times*, May 31, 2010.

49. Giselle Tsirulnik, "Red Bull Proximity Marketing Campaign Distributes Mobile Coupons via Bluetooth," *Mobile Marketer*, www.mobilemarketer.com/cms/news/database-crm/8924.html (viewed June 28, 2011).

50. Don Clark and Nick Wingfield, "Intel, Microsoft Offer Smart Sign Technology," *Wall Street Journal*, January 12, 2010; Andrew Lavallee, "Unilever to Test Mobile Coupons in Trial at Supermarket, Cellphones Will Be the Medium for Discount Offers," *Wall Street Journal*, May 29, 2009; Bob Tedeschi, "Phone Smart Cents-Off Coupons and Other Special Deals, via Your Cellphone," *New York Times*, December 17, 2008.

51. Piet Levy, "Set Your Sites on Mobile," *Marketing News*, April 30, 2010, p. 6; Tom Lowry, "Pandora: Unleashing Mobile-Phone Ads," *BusinessWeek*, June 1, 2009, pp. 52–53.

52. Elisabeth Sullivan, "The Tao of Mobile Marketing," *Marketing News*, April 30, 2010, pp. 16–20.

53. Loretta Chao, "Cell Phone Ads Are Easier Pitch in China," *Wall Street Journal*, January 4, 2007.

54. Louise Story, "What We Talk About When We Talk About Brands," *New York Times*, November 24, 2006.

55. Robert V. Kozinets, Kristine de Valck, Andrea C. Wojnicki, and Sarah J. S. Wilner, "Networked Narratives: Understanding Word-of-Mouth Marketing in Online Communities," *Journal of Marketing*, 74 (March 2010): 71–89; David Godes and Dina Mayzlin, "Firm-Created Word-of-Mouth Communication: Evidence from a Field Test," *Marketing Science*, 28 (July–August 2009): 721–739.

56. The Royal Winnipeg Ballet's Facebook page, www.facebook. com/#!/pages/Canadas-Royal-Winnipeg-Ballet/111498424376 (viewed June 30, 2011); Jon Swartz, "Small Firms Dive into Social Media," *USA Today*, July 22, 2010, p. 3B.

57. "Effie Awards," *Effie Worldwide*, www.effie.org/downloads/2009_ winners_ list.pdf.

58. Heather Green, "It Takes a Web Village," *BusinessWeek*, September 4, 2006, p. 66; Paul Dwyer, "Measuring the Value of Word of Mouth and Its Impact in Consumer Communities," MSI Report No. 06-118, (Cambridge, MA:Marketing Science Institute); Kelly K. Spors, "The Customer Knows Best," *Wall Street Journal*, July 13, 2009, p. R5.

59. Jeromy Lloyd, "MTS Allstream Uses Social Media Tools for Internal Communication," *Marketing*, July 22, 2010, www. marketingmag.ca/english/news/marketer/article.jsp?conte nt=20100722_152023_6748 (viewed October 19, 2010); "Corporate Profile," *MTS Allstream*, www.mts.ca/portal/site/mts/menuitem.5c 66d997604ae257a1720010408021a0/?vgnextoid=c22e8dca2004111 0VgnVCM1000001342a8c0RCRD (viewed October 19, 2010).

60. Claire Cain Miller, "The Sweet Spot," *Forbes*, April 23, 2007, p. 41.

61. For an academic discussion of chat rooms, recommendation sites, and customer review sections online, see Dina Mayzlin, "Promotional Chat on the Internet," *Marketing Science*, 25 (March–April 2006), pp. 155–163; and Judith Chevalier and Dina Mayzlin, "The Effect of Word of Mouth on Sales: Online Book Reviews," *Journal of Marketing Research*, 43 (August 2006): 345–354.

62. Stephen Baker, "Looking for a Blog in a Haystack," *BusinessWeek*, July 25, 2006, p. 38.

63. Heather Green, "The Big Shots of Blogdom," *BusinessWeek*, May 7, 2007; TreeHugger website, www.treehugger.com/about.

64. "Social Media Overrated as Retail Information Sources: Majority of Consumers Prefer Retailer Websites for Product Info," *Marketwire*, June 28, 2011.

65. Jordan Timm, "Branding by the Masses," *Canadian Business*, May 10, 2010.

66. For a thorough review of relevant academic literature, see Christophe Van Den Bulte and Stefan Wuyts, *Social Networks and Marketing*, Marketing Science Institute Relevant Knowledge Series, (Cambridge, MA: 2007), and for some practical considerations, see "A World of Connections: A Special Report on Social Networking," *Economist*, January 30, 2010.

67. Allen Adamson, "No Contest: Twitter and Facebook Can Both Play a Role in Branding," www.forbes.com, May 6, 2009.

68. "Profiting from Friendship," *Economist*, January 30, 2010, pp. 9–12.

69. Calgary Stampede website, http://cs.calgarystampede.com (viewed June 30, 2011); Calgary Stampede Facebook page, https://www.facebook.com/#!/calgarystampede? (viewed June 30, 2011).

70. Michael Learmonth and Rupal Parekh, "How Influential Are Angry Bloggers? Ask Johnson & Johnson," *Financial Week*, November 19, 2008; Seth Godin, "We Feel Your Pain," *Seth's Blog*, November 17, 2008; Jim Edwards, "J&J Triggers Mommy War with Motrin 'Anti-Baby Sling' Ad," www.bnet.com, November 17, 2008.

71. Stephen Baker, "Beware Social Media Snake Oil," *BusinessWeek*, December 14, 2009, pp. 48–51.

72. Ralf van der Lans, Gerrit van Bruggen, Jehoshua Eliashberg, and Berend Wierenga, "A Viral Branching Model for Predicting the Spread of Electronic Word of Mouth," *Marketing Science*, 29 (March–April 2010): 348–365; Dave Balter and John Butman, "Clutter Cutter," *Marketing Management*, July–August 2006, pp. 49–50.

73. Emanuel Rosen, *The Anatomy of Buzz* (New York: Currency, 2000).

74. George Silverman, *The Secrets of Word-of-Mouth Marketing* (New York: AMACOM, 2001); Emanuel Rosen, *The Anatomy of Buzz* (New York: Currency, 2000), Ch. 12; "Viral Marketing," *Sales & Marketing Automation*, November 1999, pp. 12–14.

75. *Will It Blend?* www.willitblend.com; Blendtec website, www. blendtec.com; Piet Levy, "I Tube, YouTube," *Marketing News*, March 30, 2009, p. 8; Phyllis Berman, "Food Fight," *Forbes*, October 13, 2008, p. 110; Rob Walker, "Mixing It Up," *New York Times*, August 24, 2008; Jon Fine, "Ready to Get Weird, Advertisers?" *BusinessWeek*, January 8, 2007, p. 24.

76. Renée Dye, "The Buzz on Buzz," *Harvard Business Review*, November–December 2000, p. 139.

77. Robert Berner, "I Sold It through the Grapevine," *BusinessWeek*, May 29, 2006, pp. 32–34.

78. Matthew Creamer and Rupal Parekh, "Ideas of the Decade," *Advertising Age*, December 14, 2009.

79. Amar Cheema and Andrew M. Kaikati, "The Effect of Need for Uniqueness on Word of Mouth," *Journal of Marketing Research*, 47 (June 2010): 553–563.

80. Jacqueline Johnson Brown, Peter M. Reingen, and Everett M. Rogers, *Diffusion of Innovations*, 4th ed. (New York: The Free Press, 1995); J. Johnson Brown and Peter Reingen, "Social Ties and Word-of-Mouth Referral Behavior," *Journal of Consumer Research*, 14 (December 1987): 350–362; Peter H. Reingen and Jerome B. Kernan, "Analysis of Referral Networks in Marketing: Methods and Illustration," *Journal of Marketing Research*, 23 (November 1986): 37–78.

81. Malcolm Gladwell, *The Tipping Point: How Little Things Can Make a Big Difference* (Boston: Little, Brown & Company, 2000).

82. Terry McDermott, "Criticism of Gladwell Reaches Tipping Point," *Columbia Journalism Review*, November 17, 2009; Clive Thompson, "Is the Tipping Point Toast?" *Fast Company*, February 1, 2008; Duncan Watts, *Six Degrees: The Science of a Connected Age* (New York: W. W. Norton, 2003).

83. Douglas Atkin, *The Culting of Brands: When Customers Become True Believers* (New York: Penguin, 2004); Marian Salzman, Ira Matathia, and Ann O'Reilly, *Buzz: Harness the Power of Influence and Create Demand* (New York: Wiley, 2003).

84. Bob Greenberg, "A Platform for Life," *Adweek NEXT*, September 14, 2009, p. 38.

85. Michael Trusov, Anand V. Bodapati, and Randolph E. Bucklin, "Determining Influential Users in Internet Social Networks," *Journal of Marketing Research*, 47 (August 2010): 643–658.

86. Suzanne Vranica, "That Guy Showing Off His Hot New Phone May Be a Shill," *The Wall Street Journal* (Eastern Edition), July 31, 2002, p. B1.

87. This section is based in part on an excellent summary, "Is There a Reliable Way to Measure Word-of-Mouth Marketing?" *Marketing NPV*, 3 (2006): 3–9, available at www.marketingnpv.com.

88. Suzanne Vranica, "Social Media Draws a Crowd," *Wall Street Journal*, July 19, 2010; Jessi Hempel, "He Measures the Web," *Fortune*, November 9, 2009, pp. 94–98.

89. Adam L. Penenberg, "How Much Are You Worth to Facebook?" *Fast Company*, October 1, 2009.

90. Rick Lawrence, Prem Melville, Claudia Perlich, Vikas Sindhwani, Steve Meliksetian, Pei-Yun Hsueh, and Yan Liu, "Social Media Analytics," *OR/MS Today*, February 2010, pp. 26–30.

91. "Occupation—National Occupational Classification for Statistics 2006, Class of Worker and Sex for the Labour Force 15 Years and Over of Canada, Provinces, Territories, Census Metropolitan Areas and Census Agglomerations, 2006 Census—20% Sample Data," *Statistics Canada*, Catalogue no. 97-559-XCB2006011.

92. Shrihari Sridhar, Murali K. Mantrala, and Sönke Albers, "Personal Selling Elasticities: A Meta-Analysis," *Journal of Marketing Research*, 47 (October 2010).

93. Adapted from Robert N. McMurry, "The Mystique of Super-Salesmanship," *Harvard Business Review*, March–April 1961, p. 114. Also see William C. Moncrief III, "Selling Activity and Sales Position Taxonomies for Industrial Sales Forces," *Journal of Marketing Research*, 23 (August 1986): 261–270.

94. Lawrence G. Friedman and Timothy R. Furey, *The Channel Advantage: Going to Marketing with Multiple Sales Channels* (Oxford, UK: Butterworth-Heinemann, 1999).

95. Michael Ahearne, Scott B. MacKenzie, Philip M. Podsakoff, John E. Mathieu, and Son K. Lam, "The Role of Consensus in Sales Team Performance," *Journal of Marketing Research*, 47 (June 2010): 458–469.

96. Ashwin W. Joshi, "Salesperson Influence on Product Development: Insights from a Study of Small Manufacturing Organizations," *Journal of Marketing*, 74 (January 2010): 94–107; Philip Kotler, Neil Rackham, and Suj Krishnaswamy, "Ending the War between Sales & Marketing," *Harvard Business Review*, July–August 2006, pp. 68–78; Timothy M. Smith, Srinath Gopalakrishna, and Rubikar Chaterjee, "A Three-Stage Model of Integrated Marketing Communications at the Marketing-Sales Interface," *Journal of Marketing Research*, 43 (November 2006): 546–579.

97. Michael Copeland, "Hits and Misses," *Business 2.0*, April 2004, p. 142.

98. "Sales Performance Benchmarks," *Go-to-Market Strategies*, June 5, 2007. For international tax implications in compensation, see Dominique Rouziès, Anne T. Coughlan, Erin Anderson, and Dawn Iacobucci, "Determinants of Pay Levels and Structures in Sales Organizations," *Journal of Marketing*, 73 (November 2009): 92–104.

99. Tony Ritigliano and Benson Smith, *Discover Your Sales Strengths* (New York: Random House Business Books, 2004).

100. Sönke Albers, "Sales-Force Management—Compensation, Motivation, Selection, and Training," in *Handbook of Marketing*, edited byBart Weitz and Robin Wensley(London, England: Sage, 2002), pp. 248–266.

101. Betsy Cummings, "Wanted: Older Workers," *Sales and Marketing Management*, 158, no. 7: 12; 1-800-GOT-JUNK? website, www.1800gotjunk.com (viewed July 21, 2011).

102. Nanette Byrnes, "Avon Calling—Lots of New Reps," *BusinessWeek*, June 2, 2003, pp. 53–54.

103. Michael R. W. Bommer, Brian F. O'Neil, and Beheruz N. Sethna, "A Methodology for Optimizing Selling Time of Salespersons," *Journal of Marketing Theory and Practice*, Spring 1994, pp. 61–75. See also Lissan Joseph, "On the Optimality of Delegating Pricing Authority to the Sales Force," *Journal of Marketing*, 65 (January 2001): 62–70.

104. Dartnell Corporation, *30th Sales-Force Compensation Survey* (Chicago: Dartnell Corp., 1999). Other breakdowns show that 12.7 percent of time is spent in service calls, 16 percent in administrative tasks, 25.1 percent in telephone selling, and 17.4 percent in waiting/travelling. For analysis of this database, see Sanjog Misra, Anne T. Coughlan, and Chakravarthi Narasimhan, "Salesforce Compensation: An Analytical and Empirical Examination of the Agency Theoretic Approach, *Quantitative Marketing and Economics*, 3 (March 2005): 5–39.

105. Michael Ahearne, Son K. Lam, John E. Mathieu, and Willy Bolander, "Why Are Some Salespeople Better at Adapting to Organizational Change?" *Journal of Marketing*, 74 (May 2010): 65–79.

106. Willem Verbeke and Richard P. Bagozzi, "Sales-Call Anxiety: Exploring What It Means When Fear Rules a Sales Encounter," *Journal of Marketing*, 64 (July 2000): 88–101. See also Douglas E. Hughes and Michael Ahearne, "Energizing the Reseller's Sales Force: The Power of Brand Identification," *Journal of Marketing*, 74 (July 2010): 81–96.

107. Gilbert A. Churchill, Jr., Neil M. Ford, Orville C. Walker, Jr., Mark W. Johnston, and Greg W. Marshall, *Sales-Force Management*, 9th ed. (New York: McGraw-Hill/Irwin, 2009). See also Eric G. Harris, John C. Mowen, and Tom J. Brown, "Reexamining Salesperson Goal Orientations: Personality Influencers, Customer Orientation, and Work Satisfaction," *Journal of the Academy of Marketing Science*, 33 (Winter 2005): 19–35; Manfred Krafft, "An Empirical Investigation of the Antecedents of Sales-Force Control Systems," *Journal of Marketing*, 63 (July 1999): 120–134; and Wujin Chu, Eitan Gerstner, and James D. Hess, "Costs and Benefits of Hard Sell," *Journal of Marketing Research*, 32 (February 1995): 97–102.

108. Noah Lim, Michael J. Ahearne, and Sung H. Ham, "Designing Sales Contests: Does the Prize Structure Matter?" *Journal of Marketing Research*, 46 (June 2009): 356–371.

109. Lisa Vaas, "Oracle Teaches Its Sales Force to Play Nice," *eWeek*, July 28, 2004; Lisa Vaas, "Oracle's Sales Force Reorg Finally Bears Fruit," *eWeek*, December 17, 2003; Ian Mount, "Out of Control," *Business 2.0*, August 2002, pp. 38–44.

110. Philip M. Posdakoff and Scott B. MacKenzie, "Organizational Citizenship Behaviors and Sales-Unit Effectiveness," *Journal of Marketing Research*, 31 (August 1994): 351–363. See also Andrea L. Dixon, Rosann L. Spiro, and Magbul Jamil, "Successful and Unsuccessful Sales Calls: Measuring Salesperson Attributions and Behavioral Intentions," *Journal of Marketing*, 65 (July 2001): 64–78; and Willem Verbeke and Richard P. Bagozzi, "Sales-Call Anxiety: Exploring What It Means When Fear Rules a Sales Encounter," *Journal of Marketing*, 64 (July 2000): 88–101.

111. Neil Rackham, *SPIN Selling* (New York: McGraw-Hill, 1988). Also see his *The SPIN Selling Fieldbook* (New York: McGraw-Hill, 1996); James Lardner, "Selling Salesmanship," *Business 2.0*, December 2002–January 2003, p. 66; Sharon Drew Morgen, *Selling with Integrity: Reinventing Sales through Collaboration, Respect, and Serving* (New York: Berkeley Books, 1999); and Neil Rackham and John De Vincentis, *Rethinking the Sales Force* (New York: McGraw-Hill, 1996).

112. Some of the following discussion is based on a classic analysis in W. J. E. Crissy, William H. Cunningham, and Isabella C. M. Cunningham, *Selling: The Personal Force in Marketing* (New York: Wiley, 1977), pp. 119–129. For some contemporary perspective and tips, see Jia Lynn Yang, "How to Sell in a Lousy Economy," *Fortune*, September 29, 2008, pp. 101–106, and Jessi Hempel, "IBM's All-Star Salesman," *Fortune*, September 29, 2008, pp. 110–119.

113. Stephanie Clifford, "Putting the Performance in Sales Performance," *Inc.*, February 2007, pp. 87–95.

114. Joel E. Urbany, "Justifying Profitable Pricing," *Journal of Product & Brand Management*, 10 (2001): pp.141–159.

115. Jia Lynn Yang, "How Can I Keep My Sales Team Productive in a Recession?" *Fortune*, March 2, 2009, p. 22.

116. V. Kumar, Rajkumar Venkatesan, and Werner Reinartz, "Performance Implications of Adopting a Customer-Focused Sales Campaign," *Journal of Marketing*, 72 (September 2008): 50–68; George R. Franke and Jeong-Eun Park, "Salesperson Adaptive Selling Behavior and Customer Orientation: A Meta-Analysis," *Journal of Marketing Research*, 43 (November 2006):

693–702; Richard G. McFarland, Goutam N. Challagalla, and Tasadduq A. Shervani, "Influence Tactics for Effective Adaptive Selling," *Journal of Marketing*, 70 (October 2006): 103–117.

Chapter 20

1. Brad Stone, "Nintendo Wii to Add Netflix Service for Streaming Video," *New York Times*, January 13, 2010; Eric A. Taub, "Will Nothing Slow Wii?" *New York Times Bits Blog*, October 17, 2008; John Gaudiosi, "How the Wii Is Creaming the Competition," *Business 2.0*, April 25, 2007; Martin Fackler, "Putting the We Back in Wii," *New York Times*, June 8, 2007; "Nintendo Co. Ltd. Annual Report 2006," www.nintendo.com/corp/report/06AnnualReport. pdf; "Nintendo to Launch New Wii in 2012 as Profit Slips," *Edmonton Journal*, April 26, 2012, p. D2.

2. For some scholarly reviews, see Ely Dahan and John R. Hauser, "Product Development: Managing a Dispersed Process," in *Handbook of Marketing*, edited byBart Weitz and Robin Wensley (London, England: Sage, 2002), pp. 179–222; Dipak Jain, "Managing New-Product Development for Strategic Competitive Advantage," in *Kellogg on Marketing*, edited by Dawn Iacobucci (New York: Wiley, 2001), pp. 130–148; Jerry Wind and Vijay Mahajan, "Issues and Opportunities in New-Product Development: An Introduction to the Special Issue," *Journal of Marketing Research*, 34 (February 1997): 1–12. For an overview of different industry approaches, see Frank T. Rothaermel and Andrew M. Hess, "Innovation Strategies Combined," *MIT Sloan Management Review*, Spring 2010, pp. 13–15.

3. Scott Sanderude, "Growth from Harvesting the Sky: The $200 Million Challenge," talk at Marketing Science Institute Conference, *New Frontiers for Growth*, Boston, Massachusetts, April 2005.

4. Stephen J. Carson, "When to Give Up Control of Outsourced New-Product Development," *Journal of Marketing*, 71 (January 2007): 49–66.

5. Elaine Wong, "P&G's '09 Success Hinged on Value, Affordable Luxury," *Brandweek*, March 22, 2010, p. 8.

6. For some academic discussion of the effects of new-product introductions on markets, see Harald J. Van Heerde, Carl F. Mela, and Puneet Manchanda, "The Dynamic Effect of Innovation on Market Structure," *Journal of Marketing Research*, 41 (May 2004): 166–183. For a contrast with radically different new products, see Khaled Aboulnasr, Om Narasimhan, Edward Blair, and Rajesh Chandy, "Competitive Response to Radical Product Innovations," *Journal of Marketing*, 72 (May 2008): 94–110.

7. "Enabling Multifaceted Innovation," *IBM Global Business Services*, 2006, www-935.ibm.com/services/us/ gbs/bus/pdf/g510-6310-executive-brief-enabling-multifaceted.pdf.

8. Shuba Srinivasan, Koen Pauwels, Jorge Silva-Risso, and Dominique M. Hanssens, "Product Innovations, Advertising and Stock Returns," *Journal of Marketing*, 73 (January 2009): 24–43; Alina B. Sorescu and Jelena Spanjol, "Innovation's Effect on Firm Value and Risk: Insights from Consumer Packaged Goods," *Journal of Marketing*, 72 (March 2008): 114–132; Sungwook Min, Manohar U. Kalwani, and William T. Robinson, "Market Pioneer and Early Follower Survival Risks: A Contingency Analysis of Really New versus Incrementally New Product-Markets," *Journal of Marketing*, 70 (January 2006): 15–33; C. Page Moreau, Arthur B. Markman, and Donald R. Lehmann, "'What Is It?' Category Flexibility and Consumers' Response to Really New Products," *Journal of Consumer Research*, 27 (March 2001): 489–498.

9. Stefan Wuyts, Shantanu Dutta, and Stefan Stremersch, "Portfolios of Interfirm Agreements in Technology-Intensive Markets: Consequences for Innovation and Profitability," *Journal of Marketing*, 68 (April 2004): 88–100; Aric Rindfleisch and Christine Moorman, "The Acquisition and Utilization of Information in New-Product Alliance: A Strength-of-Ties Perspective," *Journal of Marketing*, 65 (April 2001): 1–18. See also Raghunath Singh Rao, Rajesh K. Chandy, and Jaideep C. Prabhu, "The Fruits of Legitimacy: Why Some New Ventures Gain More from Innovation Than Others," *Journal of Marketing*, 72 (July 2008): 58–75.

10. Gerard J. Tellis, Jaideep C. Prabhu, and Rajesh K. Chandy, "Radical Innovation across Nations: The Preeminence of Corporate Culture," *Journal of Marketing*, 73 (January 2009): 3–23.

11. Steve Hoeffler, "Measuring Preferences for Really New Products," *Journal of Marketing Research*, 40 (November 2003): 406–420; Glen Urban, Bruce Weinberg, and John R. Hauser, "Premarket Forecasting of Really New Products," *Journal of Marketing*, 60 (January 1996): 47–60.

12. Andy Grove, "Think Disruptive," *Condé Nast Portfolio*, December 2007, pp. 170–175; Ashish Sood and Gerard J. Tellis, "Technological Evolution and Radical Innovation," *Journal of Marketing*, 69 (July 2005): 152–168.

13. For more discussion, see Jakki Mohr, *Marketing of High-Technology Products and Innovations*, 2nd ed. (Upper Saddle River, NJ: Prentice Hall, 2005).

14. Carol Matlack, "How Danone Turns Bacteria into Bucks," *BusinessWeek*, November 15, 2007, pp. 76–77; Jack Ewing, "The Bimmer, Plugged In," *BusinessWeek*, March 23 and 30, 2009, p. 78; Beth Kowitt, "Blackboard Rules the Schools," *Fortune*, November 9, 2009, p. 28.

15. "Blackboard to Open New Data Center in Canada: New Facility Responds to Rising Demand for In-Region Hosting Services," www.blackboard.com/About-Bb/Media-Center/Press-Releases. aspx?releaseid=1562585 (viewed July 10, 2011).

16. Steve Hamm, "Speed Demons," *BusinessWeek*, March 27, 2006, pp. 69–76.

17. Christina Passariello, "Brand New Bag: Louis Vuitton Tries Modern Methods on Factory Lines," *Wall Street Journal*, October 9, 2006.

18. Gary Hamel, "W. L. Gore: Lessons from a Management Revolutionary," *Wall Street Journal*, March 18, 2010; "The World's Most Innovative Companies," *Fast Company*, March 2009; Brad Weiners, "Gore-Tex Tackles the Great Indoors," *Business 2.0*, April 2004, p. 32; Ann Harrington, "Who's Afraid of a New Product," *Fortune*, November 10, 2003, pp. 189–192.

19. Tim Brown, *Change by Design: How Design Thinking Transforms Organizations and Inspires Innovation* (New York: HarperCollins, 2009).

20. Clayton M. Christensen, *Disrupting Class: How Disruptive Innovation Will Change the Way the World Learns* (New York: McGraw-Hill, 2008); Clayton M. Christensen, *The Innovator's Solution: Creating and Sustaining Successful Growth* (Boston: Harvard University Press, 2003); Clayton M. Christensen, *The Innovator's Dilemma: When New Technologies Cause Great Firms to Fail* (Boston: Harvard University Press, 1997).

21. Ely Dahan and John R. Hauser, "Product Development: Managing a Dispersed Process," in *Handbook of Marketing*, edited byBart Weitz and Robin Wensley(London, England: Sage, 2002), pp. 179–222.

22. Robert G. Cooper and Elko J. Kleinschmidt, *New Products: The Key Factors in Success* (Chicago: American Marketing Association, 1990).

23. Ibid., pp. 35–38.

24. Susumu Ogama and Frank T. Piller, "Reducing the Risks of New-Product Development," *MIT Sloan Management Review*, 47 (Winter 2006): 65–71; A. C. Nielsen, "New Product Introduction—Successful Innovation/Failure: Fragile Boundary," A. C. Nielsen BASES and Ernst & Young Global Client Consulting, June 24, 1999.

25. For more discussion, see Dipak Jain, "Managing New-Product Development for Strategic Competitive Advantage," in *Kellogg on Marketing*, edited byDawn Iacobucci(New York: Wiley, 2001).

26. Steve Hamm, "Speed Demons," *BusinessWeek*, March 27, 2006, pp. 69–76.

27. Tom McNichol, "A Start-Up's Best Friend? Failure," *Business 2.0*, March 2007, pp. 39–41.

28. Thomas N. Burton, "By Learning from Failures Lilly Keeps Drug Pipelines Full," *Wall Street Journal*, April 21, 2004.

29. Hollie Shaw, "It's in the Bag: Canada Scores by Sticking with 'Noisy' Chip Bags," *Calgary Herald*, January 7, 2011.

30. Virginia Gardiner, "Dyson Airblade," *Dwell*, March 10, 2010; Reena Jana, "Dyson's Air Multiplier: Flaw as Function," *BusinessWeek*, October 12, 2009; Chuck Salter, "Failure Doesn't Suck," *Fast Company*, May 2007, p. 44.

31. "Government of Canada Announces Support for Two Toronto Start-Up Businesses," *Marketwire, June 2011*.

32. Vijay Govindrajan and Chris Trimble, "Stop the Innovation Wars," *Harvard Business Review*, July–August 2010, pp. 76–83; Doug Ayers, Robert Dahlstrom, and Steven J. Skinner, "An Exploratory Investigation of Organizational Antecedents to New-Product Success," *Journal of Marketing Research, 34* (February 1997): 107–116; David S. Hopkins, *Options in New-Product Organization* (New York: Conference Board, 1974).

33. Brian Hindo, "Rewiring Westinghouse," *BusinessWeek*, May 19, 2008, pp. 48–49.

34. Danielle Sacks, Chuck Salter, Alan Deutschman, and Scott Kirsner, "Innovation Scouts," *Fast Company*, May 2007, p. 90; "Ongoing Innovation: Tom Malloy on Sustaining the Relevance and Impact of Adobe's Advanced Technology Labs," *Knowledge@Wharton*, March 21, 2007; Shantanu Narayen, "Connecting the Dots Isn't Enough," *New York Times*, July 18, 2009.

35. Lisa C. Troy, Tanat Hirunyawipada, and Audhesh K. Paswan, "Cross-Functional Integration and New Product Success: An Empirical Investigation of the Findings," *Journal of Marketing, 72* (September 2008): 132–146; Rajesh Sethi, Daniel C. Smith, and C. Whan Park, "Cross-Functional Product Development Teams, Creativity, and the Innovativeness of New Consumer Products," *Journal of Marketing Research, 38* (February 2001): 73–85.

36. Robert G. Cooper, *Winning at New Products: Accelerating the Process from Idea to Launch* (New York: Perseus Publishing, 2001). See also Robert G. Cooper, "Stage-Gate Systems: A New Tool for Managing New Products," *Business Horizons*, May–June 1990, pp. 44–54; and Robert G. Cooper, "The NewProd System: The Industry Experience," *Journal of Product Innovation Management, 9* (June 1992): 113–127.

37. Robert G. Cooper, *Product Leadership: Creating and Launching Superior New Products* (New York: Perseus Books, 1998).

38. Rajesh Sethi and Zafar Iqbal, "Stage-Gate Controls, Learning Failure, and Adverse Effect on Novel New Products," *Journal of Marketing, 72* (January 2008): 118–134.

39. Ely Dahan and John R. Hauser, "Product Development: Managing a Dispersed Process," in *Handbook of Marketing*, edited byBart Weitz and Robin Wensley (London, England: Sage, 2002), pp. 179–222.

40. Another approach to the funnel process advocates "rocketing." See David Nichols, *Return on Ideas* (West Sussex, England: Wiley, 2007).

41. Michael Zedalis, "Deploying Stage-Gate on a Global Scale—Critical Elements That Drive Performance" and Charles Gagnon, "Driving Value Creation with the Right Portfolio Mix," talks given at Stage-Gate Leadership Summit 2007.

42. John Hauser, Gerard J. Tellis, and Abbie Griffin, "Research on Innovation: A Review and Agenda for Marketing Science," *Marketing Science, 25* (November–December 2006): 687–717.

43. Byron Acohido, "Microsoft Cultures Creativity in Unique Lab," *USA Today*, July 11, 2007; Erich Joachimsthaler, *Hidden in Plain Sight: How to Find and Execute Your Company's Next Big Growth Strategy* (Boston: Harvard Business School Press, 2007); Subin Im and John P. Workman, Jr., "Market Orientation, Creativity, and New-Product Performance in High-Technology Firms," *Journal of Marketing, 68* (April 2004): 114–132.

44. Erich Joachimsthaler, *Hidden in Plain Sight: How to Find and Execute Your Company's Next Big Growth Strategy* (Boston: Harvard Business School Publishing, 2007).

45. Henry Chesbrough, *Open Business Models: How to Thrive in the New-Innovation Landscape* (Boston: Harvard University Press, 2006); Eric Von Hippel, *Democratizing Innovation* (Cambridge, MA: MIT Press, 2005); Burt Helm, "Inside a White-Hot Idea Factory," *BusinessWeek*, January 15, 2005, pp. 72–73; C. K. Prahalad and Venkat Ramaswamy, *The Future of Competition: Cocreating Unique Value with Customers* (Boston: Harvard University Press, 2004); Henry Chesbrough, *Open Innovation: The New Imperative for Creating and Profiting from Technology* (Boston: Harvard University Press, 2003).

46. Bruce Horovitz, "Marketers Zooming in on Your Daily Routines," *USA Today*, April 30, 2007; Ashwin W. Joshi and Sanjay Sharma, "Customer Knowledge Development: Antecedents and Impact on New-Product Performance," *Journal of Marketing, 68* (October 2004): 47–59.

47. Abbie J. Griffin and John Hauser, "The Voice of the Customer," *Marketing Science, 12* (Winter 1993): 1–27.

48. Miho Inada, "Tokyo Café Targets Trend Makers," *Wall Street Journal*, August 24, 2008.

49. Peter C. Honebein and Roy F. Cammarano, "Customers at Work," *Marketing Management, 15* (January–February 2006): 26–31; Peter C. Honebein and Roy F. Cammarano, *Creating Do-It-Yourself Customers: How Great Customer Experiences Build Great Companies* (Mason, OH: Texere Southwestern Educational Publishing, 2005).

50. Jeff Howe, *Crowdsourcing: Why the Power of the Crowd Is Driving the Future of Business* (New York: Crown Business, 2008).

51. Guido Jouret, "Inside Cisco's Search for the Next Big Idea," *Harvard Business Review*, September 2009, pp. 43–45; Anya Kamentz, "The Power of the Prize," *Fast Company*, May 2008, pp. 43–45; Cisco, www.cisco.com/web/solutions/iprize/index.html.

52. Patricia Seybold, *Outside Innovation: How Your Customers Will Codesign Your Company's Future* (New York: Collins, 2006).

53. Helena Yli-Renko and Ramkumar Janakiraman, "How Customer Portfolio Affects New Product Development in Technology-Based Firms, *Journal of Marketing, 72* (September 2008): 131–148; Donna L. Hoffman, Praveen K. Kopalle, and Thomas P. Novak, "The 'Right' Consumers for Better Concepts: Identifying and Using Consumers High in Emergent Nature to Further Develop New Product Concepts," *Journal of Marketing Research, 47* (October 2010).

54. Pioneering work in this area is represented by Eric von Hippel, "Lead Users: A Source of Novel Product Concepts," *Management Science, 32* (July 1986): 791–805. Also see Eric von Hippel, *The Sources of Innovation* (New York: Oxford University Press, 1988); Eric von Hippel, *Democratizing Innovation* (Cambridge, MA: MIT Press, 2005); and Pamela D. Morrison, John H. Roberts and David F. Midgley, "The Nature of Lead Users and Measurement of Leading Edge Status," *Research Policy, 33* (2004): 351–362.

55. John W. Heinke, Jr., and Chun Zhang, "Increasing Supplier-Driven Innovation," *MIT Sloan Management Review*, Winter 2010, pp. 41–46; Eric (Er) Fang, "Customer Participation and the Trade-Off Between New Product Innovativeness and Speed to Market," *Journal of Marketing, 72* (July 2008): 90–104. Note that this research also shows that customer involvement can also slow the development process if a high level of interaction and coordination is required across stages.

56. Kevin Zheng Zhou, Chi Kin (Bennett) Yim, and David K. Tse, "The Effects of Strategic Orientations on Technology- and Market-Based Breakthrough Innovations," *Journal of Marketing, 69* (April 2005): 42–60; Michael Treacy, "Ignore the Consumer," *Advertising Age Point*, September 2005, pp. 15–19.

57. Sharon Machlis, "Innovation and the 20% Solution," *Computerworld*, February 2, 2009.

58. "The World's Fifty Most Innovative Companies," *BusinessWeek*, May 9, 2007.

59. Darren W. Dahl and Page Moreau, "The Influence and Value of Analogical Thinking during New-Product Ideation," *Journal of Marketing Research, 39* (February 2002): 47–60; Michael Michalko,

Cracking Creativity: The Secrets of Creative Genius (Berkeley, CA: Ten Speed Press, 1998); James M. Higgins, *101 Creative Problem-Solving Techniques* (New York: New Management, 1994).

60. Philip Kotler and Fernando Trias de Bes, *Lateral Marketing: New Techniques for Finding Breakthrough Ideas* (New York: Wiley, 2003).

61. NBC Research, "Friends," *Program Test Report,* May 27, 1994; NBC's Failing Grade for "Friends," *The Smoking Gun,* May 10, 2004, www.smokinggun.com.

62. Olivier Toubia and Laurent Florès, "Adaptive Idea Screening Using Consumers," *Marketing Science, 26* (May–June 2007): 342–360; Melanie Wells, "Have It Your Way," *Forbes,* February 14, 2005.

63. David L. Alexander, John G. Lynch, Jr., and Qing Wang, "As Time Goes By: Do Cold Feet Follow Warm Intentions for Really New Versus Incrementally New Products," *Journal of Marketing Research, 45* (June 2008): 307–319; Steve Hoeffler, "Measuring Preferences for Really New Products," *Journal of Marketing Research, 40* (November 2003): 406–420.

64. Min Zhao, Steve Hoeffler, and Darren W. Dahl, "The Role of Imagination-Focused Visualization on New Product Evaluation," *Journal of Marketing Research, 46* (February 2009): 46–55; Raquel Castano, Mita Sujan, Manish Kacker, Harish Sujan, "Managing Customer Uncertainty in the Adoption of New Products: Temporal Distance and Mental Stimulation," *Journal of Marketing Research, 45* (June 2008): 320–336; Darren W. Dahl and Page Moreau, "The Influence and Value of Analogical Thinking during New-Product Ideation," *Journal of Marketing Research, 39* (February 2002): pp. 47–60; Michelle L. Roehm and Brian Sternthal, "The Moderating Effect of Knowledge and Resources on the Persuasive Impact of Analogies," *Journal of Consumer Research, 28* (September 2001): 257–272; Darren W. Dahl, Amitava Chattopadhyay, and Gerald J. Gorn, "The Use of Visual Mental Imagery in New-Product Design," *Journal of Marketing Research, 36* (February 1999): 18–28.

65. Grant Buckler, "Adding a Whole New Dimension to Design," *The Globe and Mail,* March 9, 2010.

66. Jon Fortt, "Heavy Duty Computing," *Fortune,* March 2, 2009, pp. 34–36.

67. For additional information, also see David Bakken and Curtis L. Frazier, "Conjoint Analysis: Understanding Consumer Decision Making," in *The Handbook of Marketing Research,* edited by Rajiv Grover and Marco Vriens (Thousand Oaks, CA: Sage, 2006); Vithala R. Rao and John R. Hauser, "Conjoint Analysis, Related Modeling, and Application," in *Market Research and Modeling: Progress and Prospects: A Tribute to Paul Green,* edited by Yoram Wind and Paul E. Green (New York: Springer, 2004), pp. 141–168; Jordan J. Louviere, David A. Hensher, and Joffre D. Swait, *Stated Choice Models: Analysis and Applications* (New York: Cambridge University Press, 2000); Paul E. Green and V. Srinivasan, "Conjoint Analysis in Marketing: New Developments with Implications for Research and Practice," *Journal of Marketing, 54* (October 1990): 3–19; *Sawtooth Software.* For another approach, see Young-Hoon Park, Min Ding, and Vithala R. Rao, "Eliciting Preference for Complex Products: A Web-Based Upgrading Method," *Journal of Marketing Research, 45* (October 2008): 562–574.

68. Lesley Young, "Peddling Telecom Bundles," *Marketing,* May 7, 2001, www.marketingmag.ca/magazine/current/feature/ article.jsp?content=20010507_17481#; "Bell Canada Launches Bell Security Solutions Inc.," Bell Canada Press Release, February 15, 2005, http://enterprise.bell.ca/en/default.asp?sid=256&did=807.

69. The full-profile example was taken from Paul E. Green and Yoram Wind, "New Ways to Measure Consumers' Judgments," *Harvard Business Review,* July–August 1975, pp. 107–117.

70. Peter N. Golder and Gerald J. Tellis, "Will It Ever Fly? Modeling the Takeoff of Really New Consumer Durables," *Marketing Science, 16* (Summer 1997): 256–270; Glen L. Urban, Bruce D. Weinberg, and John R. Hauser, "Premarket Forecasting of Really New Products," *Journal of Marketing, 60* (January 1996): 47–60; Robert Blattberg and John Golany, "Tracker: An Early Test-Market

Forecasting and Diagnostic Model for New-Product Planning," *Journal of Marketing Research, 15* (May 1978): 192–202.

71. Roger A. Kerin, Michael G. Harvey, and James T. Rothe, "Cannibalism and New-Product Development," *Business Horizons,* October 1978, pp. 25–31.

72. The present value (V) of a future sum (I) to be received t years from today and discounted at the interest rate (r) is given by $V = It/(1 + r)t$. Thus $4\,716\,000/(1.15)5 = \$2\,345\,000$.

73. John Hauser, "House of Quality," *Harvard Business Review,* May–June 1988, pp. 63–73. Customer-driven engineering is also called "quality function deployment." See also Lawrence R. Guinta and Nancy C. Praizler, *The QFD Book: The Team Approach to Solving Problems and Satisfying Customers through Quality Function Deployment* (New York: AMACOM, 1993); and V. Srinivasan, William S. Lovejoy, and David Beach, "Integrated Product Design for Marketability and Manufacturing," *Journal of Marketing Research, 34* (February 1997): 154–163.

74. Tom Peters, *The Circle of Innovation* (New York: Vintage, 1999), p. 96. For more general discussion, see also, Rajesh Sethi, "New Product Quality and Product Development Teams," *Journal of Marketing, 64* (April 2000), pp. 1–14; Christine Moorman and Anne S. Miner, "The Convergence of Planning and Execution Improvisation in New-Product Development," *Journal of Marketing, 62* (July 1998): pp. 1–20; Ravindranath Madhavan and Rajiv Grover, "From Embedded Knowledge to Embodied Knowledge: New Product Development as Knowledge Management," *Journal of Marketing, 62* (1998): 1–12.

75. Jim McElgunn, "The Ultimate Test Market," *Marketing,* February 10, 2003, www.marketingmag.ca/magazine/current/editorial/ article.jsp?content=20030210_24163; "VIAGRA Is All Apologies: Pfizer Canada Sneak Previews New VIAGRA TV Advertisement at VIAGRA.ca," www.pfizer.ca/en/media_centre/news_releases/ article?year=2011&article=356 (viewed July 10, 2011).

76. Kevin J. Clancy, Peter C. Krieg, and Marianne McGarry Wolf, *Marketing New Products Successfully: Using Simulated Test Marketing Methodology* (New York: Lexington Books, 2005); Glen L. Urban, John R. Hauser, and Roberta A. Chicos, "Information Acceleration: Validation and Lessons from the Field," *Journal of Marketing Research, 34* (February 1997): 143–153; V. Mahajan and Jerry Wind, "New Product Models: Practice, Shortcomings, and Desired Improvements," *Journal of Product Innovation Management, 9* (June 1992): 129–139.

77. Eyal Biyalogorsky, William Boulding, and Richard Staelin, "Stuck in the Past: Why Managers Persist with New-Product Failures," *Journal of Marketing, 70* (April 2006): 108–121.

78. Rajesh Chandy, Brigette Hopstaken, Om Narasimhan, and Jaideep Prabhu, "From Invention to Innovation: Conversion Ability in Product Development," *Journal of Marketing Research, 43* (August 2006): 494–508.

79. Remco Prins and Peter C. Verhoef, "Marketing Communication Drivers of Adoption Timing of a New E-Service among Existing Customers," *Journal of Marketing, 71* (April 2007): 169–183.

80. For further discussion, see Feryal Erhun, Paulo Conçalves, and Jay Hopman, "The Art of Managing New Product Transitions," *MIT Sloan Management Review, 48* (Spring 2007): 73–80; Yuhong Wu, Sridhar Balasubramanian, and Vijay Mahajan, "When Is a Preannounced New Product Likely to Be Delayed?" *Journal of Marketing, 68* (April 2004): 101–113; Raji Srinivasan, Gary L. Lilien, and Arvind Rangaswamy, "First In, First Out? The Effects of Network Externalities on Pioneer Survival," *Journal of Marketing, 68* (January 2004): 41–58; Barry L. Bayus, Sanjay Jain, and Ambar Rao, "Truth or Consequences: An Analysis of Truth or Vaporware and New-Product Announcements," *Journal of Marketing Research, 38* (February 2001): 3–13; Thomas S. Robertson, Jehoshua Eliashberg, and Talia Rymon, "New-Product Announcement Signals and Incumbent Reactions," *Journal of Marketing, 59* (July 1995): 1–15; Frank H. Alpert and Michael A. Kamins, "Pioneer Brand Advantages and Consumer Behavior: A Conceptual Framework and Propositional Inventory," *Journal of the Academy of Marketing Science, 22* (Summer 1994): 244–253;

and Robert J. Thomas, "Timing: The Key to Market Entry," *Journal of Consumer Marketing, 2* (Summer 1985): 77–87.

81. Yvonne van Everdingen, Dennis Folk, and Stefan Stremersch, "Modeling Global Spillover in New Product Takeoff," *Journal of Marketing Research, 46* (October 2009): 637–652; Katrijn Gielens and Jan-Benedict E. M. Steenkamp, "Drivers of Consumer Acceptance of New Packaged Goods: An Investigation across Products and Countries," *International Journal of Research in Marketing, 24* (June 2007): 97–111; Marc Fischer, Venkatesh Shankar, and Michael Clement, "Can a Late Mover Use International Market Entry Strategy to Challenge the Pioneer?" Marketing Science Institute Working Paper 05-118 (Cambridge, MA); Venkatesh Shankar, Gregory S. Carpenter, and Lakshman Krishnamukthi, "Late Mover Advantages: How Innovative Late Entrants Outsell Pioneers," *Journal of Marketing Research, 35* (February 1998): 54–70.

82. Philip Kotler and Gerald Zaltman, "Targeting Prospects for a New Product," *Journal of Advertising Research*, February 1976, pp. 7–20.

83. Mark Leslie and Charles A. Holloway, "The Sales Learning Curve," *Harvard Business Review*, July–August 2006, pp. 114–123.

84. "PromoHebdo.Ca Introduces the First Social Web-Based Group-Buying Website to Be Entirely Managed by Consumers for the Community," *Marketwire*, June 9, 2011.

85. For details, see Keith G. Lockyer, *Critical Path Analysis and Other Project Network Techniques* (London, England: Pitman, 1984). See also Arvind Rangaswamy and Gary L. Lilien, "Software Tools for New-Product Development," *Journal of Marketing Research, 34* (February 1997): 177–184.

86. The following discussion leans heavily on Everett M. Rogers, *Diffusion of Innovations* (New York: The Free Press, 1962). Also see his third edition, published in 1983.

87. C. Page Moreau, Donald R. Lehmann, and Arthur B. Markman, "Entrenched Knowledge Structures and Consumer Response to New Products," *Journal of Marketing Research, 38* (February 2001): 14–29.

88. John T. Gourville, "Eager Sellers & Stony Buyers," *Harvard Business Review*, June 2006, pp. 99–106.

89. Chuan-Fong Shih and Alladi Venkatesh, "Beyond Adoption: Development and Application of a Use-Diffusion Model," *Journal of Marketing, 68* (January 2004): 59–72.

90. Everett Rogers, *Diffusion of Innovations* (New York: The Free Press, 2003).

91. Everett M. Rogers, *Diffusion of Innovations* (New York: The Free Press, 1962), p. 192; Geoffrey A. Moore, *Crossing the Chasm: Marketing and Selling High-Tech Products to Mainstream Customers* (New York: HarperBusiness, 1999). For an interesting application with services, see Barak Libai, Eitan Muller, and Renana Peres, "The Diffusion of Services," *Journal of Marketing Research, 46* (April 2009): 163–175.

92. A. Parasuraman and Charles L. Colby, *Techno-Ready Marketing* (New York: The Free Press, 2001); Jakki Mohr, *Marketing of High-Technology Products and Innovations* (Upper Saddle River, NJ: Prentice Hall, 2001).

93. Jordan Robertson, "How Nike Got Street Cred," *Business 2.0*, May 2004, pp. 43–46.

94. Geoff Pevere, "The Death of TV as We Know It," *Toronto Star*, December 24, 2010; Cliff Edwards, "Will Souping Up TiVo Save It?" *BusinessWeek*, May 17, 2004, pp. 63–64; Cliff Edwards, "Is TiVo's Signal Still Fading?" *BusinessWeek*, September 10, 2001, pp. 72–74.

95. Fareena Sultan, John U. Farley, and Donald R. Lehman, "Reflection on 'A Meta-Analysis of Applications of Diffusion Models,'" *Journal of Marketing Research, 33* (May 1996): 247–249; Vijay Mahajan, Eitan Muller, and Frank M. Bass, "Diffusion of New Products: Empirical Generalizations and Managerial Uses," *Marketing Science, 14* (Summer 1995): G79–G89; Minhi Hahn, Sehoon Park, and Andris A. Zoltners, "Analysis of New-Product Diffusion Using a Four-Segment Trial-Repeat Model," Marketing Science, 13 (Summer 1994): 224–247; Hubert Gatignon and Thomas S. Robertson, "A Propositional Inventory for New Diffusion Research," *Journal of Consumer Research*, 11 (March 1985): 849–867.

Chapter 21

1. Mehul Srivastava, "What the Nano Means to India," *BusinessWeek*, May 11, 2009, pp. 60–61; Steve Hamm, "IBM vs. Tata: Which Is More American?" *BusinessWeek*, May 5, 2008, p. 28; Manjeet Kirpalani, "Tata: The Master of the Gentle Approach," *BusinessWeek*, February 25, 2008, pp. 64–66; Kevin Maney, "Model T(ata)," *Condé Nast Portfolio*, February 2008, pp. 35–36; David Welch and Nandini Lakshman, "My Other Car Is a Tata," *BusinessWeek*, January 14, 2008, pp. 33–34; Robyn Meredith, "The Next People's Car," *Forbes*, April 16, 2007, pp. 70–74; Pete Engardo, "The Last Rajah," *BusinessWeek*, August 13, 2007, pp. 46–51.

2. Michael Elliott, "The New Global Opportunity, *Fortune*, July 5, 2010, pp. 96–102.

3. "Exports of Goods on a Balance-of-Payments Basis, by Product," *Statistics Canada*, www40.statcan.ca/l01/cst01/gblec04.htm?.

4. "BEA News Release: Gross Domestic Product," *Bureau of Economic Analysis*, January 28, 2011.

5. Alex Taylor III, "The New Motor City," *Fortune*, October 27, 2008, pp. 166–172.

6. David Kiley, "Baseball, Apple Pie... and Mihindra?" *BusinessWeek*, November 5, 2007, pp. 61–63.

7. Michael Arndt, "Invasion of the Guatemalan Chicken," *BusinessWeek*, March 22 and 29, 2010, pp. 72–73.

8. Michael E. Porter, *Competitive Strategy* (New York: The Free Press, 1980), p. 275.

9. Alex Taylor III, "Hyundai Smokes the Competition," *Fortune*, January 18, 2010, pp. 62–71; Moon Ihlwan and David Kiley, "Hyundai Gains with Marketing Blitz," *BusinessWeek*, September 17, 2009; Moon Ihlwan and David Kiley, "Hyundai Floors It in the U.S.," *BusinessWeek*, February 27, 2009, pp. 30–31.

10. Charles P. Wallace, "Charge!" *Fortune*, September 28, 1998, pp. 189–196; *World Trade Organization*, www.wto.org (viewed July 11, 2011).

11. For a comprehensive treatment, see Philip R. Cateora, Mary C. Gilly, and John L. Graham, *International Marketing* (New York: McGraw-Hill/Irwin, 2009).

12. "Exports of Goods on a Balance-of-Payments Basis, by Product," *Statistics Canada*, www40.statcan.ca/l01/cst01/gblec04.htm?

13. Jan Johanson and Finn Wiedersheim-Paul, "The Internationalization of the Firm," *Journal of Management Studies, 12* (October 1975): 305–322.

14. Michael R. Czinkota and Ilkka A. Ronkainen, *International Marketing*, 9th ed. (Cincinnati, OH: South-Western Cengage Learning, 2010).

15. For a thorough review of academic research on global marketing, see Johny K. Johansson, "Global Marketing: Research on Foreign Entry, Local Marketing, Global Management," in *Handbook of Marketing*, edited byBart Weitz and Robin Wensley(London, England: Sage, 2002), pp. 457–483. Also see Johny K. Johansson, *Global Marketing*, 5th ed. (New York: McGraw-Hill, 2009). For some global marketing research issues, see C. Samuel Craig and Susan P. Douglas, *International Marketing Research*, 3rd ed. (Chichester, UK: John Wiley & Sons, 2005).

16. Marc Gunther, "The World's New Economic Landscape," *Fortune*, July 26, 2010, pp. 105–106.

17. According to the *CIA World Factbook* (www.cia.gov/library/publications/the-world-factbook/index.html), there are 34 developed countries: Andorra, Australia, Austria, Belgium, Bermuda, Canada, Denmark, Faroe Islands, Finland, France, Germany, Greece, Holy See, Iceland, Ireland, Israel, Italy, Japan, Liechtenstein,

Luxembourg, Malta, Monaco, Netherlands, New Zealand, Norway, Portugal, San Marino, South Africa, Spain, Sweden, Switzerland, Turkey, United Kingdom, and United States. They note that DCs are similar to the new International Monetary Fund (IMF) term *"advanced economies"* that adds Hong Kong, Singapore, South Korea, and Taiwan but drops Malta, Mexico, South Africa, and Turkey.

18. Satish Shankar, Charles Ormiston, Nicolas Bloch, Robert Schaus, and Vijay Vishwanath, "How to Win in Emerging Markets," *MIT Sloan Management Review*, April 2008.

19. "Kraft Revamps Developing Markets after Cadbury," *Reuters*, June 30, 2010; Ned Douthat, "Tupperware Seals Up Growth in Emerging Markets," *Forbes*, www.forbes.com, April 21, 2010.

20. Tom Mulier and Shin Pei, "Nestle's $28.1 Billion Payday Gives Google-Size Cash," *BusinessWeek*, June 30, 2010.

21. "World Population to Exceed 9 Billion by 2050," United Nations Press Release, www.un.org, March 11, 2009; "2008 World Population Data Sheet," *Population Reference Bureau*, www.pbr.org.

22. Adapted from Vijay Mahajan, Marcos V. Pratini De Moraes, and Jerry Wind, "The Invisible Global Market," *Marketing Management* (Winter 2000): 31–35. See also Joseph Johnson and Gerard J. Tellis, "Drivers of Success for Market Entry into China and India," *Journal of Marketing*, 72 (May 2008): 1–13; Tarun Khanna and Krishna G. Palepu, "Emerging Giants: Building World-Class Companies in Developing Countries," *Harvard Business Review*, October 2006, pp. 60–69.

23. C. K. Prahalad, *The Fortune at the Bottom of the Pyramid: Eradicating Poverty through Profits* (Upper Saddle River, NJ: Wharton School Publishing, 2005); Niraj Dawar and Amitava Chattopadhyay, "Rethinking Marketing Programs for Emerging Markets," *Long Range Planning*, 35 (October 2002).

24. Bart J. Bronnenberg, Jean-Pierre Dubé, and Sanjay Dhar, "Consumer Packaged Goods in the United States: National Brands, Local Branding," *Journal of Marketing Research*, 44 (February 2007): 4–13; Bart J. Bronnenberg, Jean-Pierre Dubé, and Sanjay Dhar, "National Brands, Local Branding: Conclusions and Future Research Opportunities," *Journal of Marketing Research*, 44 (February 2007): 26–28; Bart J. Bronnenberg, Sanjay K. Dhar, and Jean-Pierre Dubé, "Brand History, Geography, and the Persistence of CPG Brand Shares," *Journal of Political Economy*, 117 (February 2009): 87–115.

25. David Michael and Arindam Bhattacharya, "The BCG 50 Local Dynamos: How Dynamic RDE-Based Companies Are Mastering Their Home Markets—and What MNCs Need to Learn from Them," *BCG Report*, Boston Consulting Group, March 2008; "The Stay-at-Home Giants," *Economist*, March 15, 2008, p. 78; "In Emerging Markets 'Local Dynamos' Are Challenging Big Multinationals," *Manufacturing & Technology News*, April 17, 2008.

26. Vijay Mahajan and Kamini Banga, *The 86% Solution: How to Succeed in the Biggest Market Opportunity of the 21st Century* (Upper Saddle River, NJ: Pearson Education, 2006).

27. Carlos Niezen and Julio Rodriguez, "Distribution Lessons from Mom and Pop," *Harvard Business Review*, April 2008; "Sweet Surrender: Can Kraft's Cadbury Acquisition Help It Tap the Indian Market?" *Knowledge@Wharton*, February 25, 2010; Ellen Byron, "P&G's Global Target: Shelves of Tiny Stores," *Wall Street Journal*, July 16, 2007; "Not So Fizzy," *Economist*, February 23, 2002, pp. 66–67.

28. Sagar Malviya and Maulik Vyas, "Modern Retail Outgrowing Kirana Stores in India," *The Economic Times*, June 16, 2011.

29. Clayton M. Christensen, Stephen Wunker, and Hari Nair, "Innovation vs. Poverty," *Forbes*, October 13, 2008.

30. Rajeev Batra, Venkatram Ramaswamy, Dana L. Alden, Jan-Benedict E. M. Steenkamp, and S. Ramachander, "Effects of Brand Local and Nonlocal Origin on Consumer Attitudes in Developing Countries," *Journal of Consumer Psychology*, 9 (2000): 83–95.

31. Bruce Einhorn, "Grudge Match in China," *BusinessWeek*, April 2, 2007, pp. 42–43; Russell Flannery, "Watch Your Back," *Forbes*, April 23, 2007, pp. 104–105; Steve Hamm and Dexter Roberts, "China's First Global Capitalist," *BusinessWeek*, December 11, 2006, pp. 52–57; "The Fast and the Furious," *Economist*, November 25, 2006, pp. 63–64.

32. Jenny Mero, "John Deere's Farm Team," *Fortune*, April 14, 2008, pp. 119–124.

33. Peter J. Williamson and Ming Zeng, "Value for Money Strategies for Recessionary Times," *Harvard Business Review*, March 2009, pp. 66–74; Vikram Skula, "Business Basics at the Base of the Pyramid," *Harvard Business Review*, June 2008, pp. 53–57.

34. Johny K. Johansson, "Global Marketing: Research on Foreign Entry, Local Marketing, Global Management," in *Handbook of Marketing*, edited by Bart Weitz and Robin Wensley (London, England: Sage, 2002), pp. 457–483.

35. "Viterra Expanding International Marketing Network," *Marketwire*, October 6, 2010.

36. For an academic review, see Leonidas C. Leonidou, Constantine S. Katsikeas, and Nigel F. Piercy, "Identifying Managerial Influences on Exporting: Past Research and Future Directions," *Journal of International Marketing*, 6 (Summer 1998): 74–102.

37. "CAE in Joint Venture with Mitsui of Japan," *Edmonton Journal*, June 20, 2011, www.edmontonjournal.com/story_print.html?id=4975770&sponsor= (viewed July 13, 2011).

38. Cummins Westport website, www.cumminswestport.com/corporate (viewed October 9, 2011).

39. Claudia H. Deutsch, "The Venturesome Giant," *New York Times*, October 5, 2007.

40. Vikram Mahidhar, Craig Giffi, and Ajit Kambil with Ryan Alvanos, "Rethinking Emerging Market Strategies," *Deloitte Review*, no. 4, 2009.

41. Paul Brent, "It's Tough to Make It South of the Border," *Financial Post*, March 10, 1999, C6; Zena Olijnyk, "Plan to Quit U.S. Lifts Future Shop Stock 24%," *Financial Post*, March 10, 1999, p. C6.

42. "Burgers and Fries a la Francaise," *Economist*, April 17, 2004, pp. 60–61; Johny K. Johansson, "Global Marketing: Research on Foreign Entry, Local Marketing, Global Management," in *Handbook of Marketing*, edited byBart Weitz and Robin Wensley(London, England: Sage, 2002), pp. 457–483; Shaoming Zou and S. Tamer Cavusgil, "The GMS: A Broad Conceptualization of Global Marketing Strategy and Its Effect on Firm Performance," *Journal of Marketing*, 66 (October 2002): 40–56; "What Makes a Company Great?" *Fortune*, October 26, 1998, pp. 218–226; Bernard Wysocki, Jr., "The Global Mall: In Developing Nations, Many Youths Splurge, Mainly on U.S. Goods," *Wall Street Journal*, June 26,1997; David M. Szymanski, Sundar G. Bharadwaj, and P. Rajan Varadarajan, "Standardization versus Adaptation of International Marketing Strategy: An Empirical Investigation," *Journal of Marketing*, 57 (October 1993): 1–17; Theodore Levitt, "The Globalization of Markets," *Harvard Business Review*, May–June 1983, pp. 92–102.

43. Gail Edmondson, "Skoda Means Quality. Really," *BusinessWeek*, October 1, 2007, p. 46. Some of the more popular jokes from the past include the following: "How do you double the value of a [[Scaron]]KODA? Fill up the gas tank." "What do you call a [[Scaron]]KODA with a sunroof? A dumpster." "Why do you need a rear-window defroster on a [[Scaron]]KODA? To keep your hands warm when pushing it."

44. For some research method issues in adapting surveys to different cultures, see Martijn G. de Jong, Jan-Benedict E. M. Steenkamp, and Bernard P. Veldkamp, "A Model for the Construction of Country-Specific Yet Internationally Comparable Short-Form Marketing Scales," *Marketing Science*, 28 (July–August 2009): 674–689.

45. *Central Intelligence Agency World Factbook*, www.cia.gov/library/publications/the-world-factbook/fields/2177.html (viewed July 11, 2011).

46. Nigel Hollis, *The Global Brand* (New York: Palgrave Macmillan, 2008); Nigel Hollis, "Going Global? Better Think Local Instead," *Brandweek*, December 1, 2008, p. 14.

47. Benjamin Wallace, "The World's Most Caffeinated Country," *BusinessWeek*, May 3, 2010, p. 74; "Turkey: Second Biggest Tea Market in the World," www.marketresearchworld.net/index2.php?option=com_content&do_pdf=1&id=208 (viewed July 21, 2011).

48. *The Economist: Pocket World in Figures* (London, England: Profile Books, 2009).

49. "Who Drinks What: Identifying International Drinks Consumption Trends 2nd edition," *Euromonitor International*, www.euromonitor.com (viewed July 12, 2011).

50. For some recent examples, see Ana Valenzuela, Barbara Mellers, and Judi Stebel, "Pleasurable Surprises: A Cross-Cultural Study of Consumer Responses to Unexpected Incentives," *Journal of Consumer Research, 36* (February 2010): 792–805; Tuba Üstüner and Douglas B. Holt, "Toward a Theory of Status Consumption in Less Industrialized Countries," *Journal of Consumer Research, 37* (June 2010): 37–56; Praveen K. Kopalle, Donald R. Lehmann, and John U. Farley, "Consumer Expectations and Culture: The Effect of Belief in Karma in India," *Journal of Consumer Research, 37* (August 2010): 251–263.

51. Geert Hofstede, *Culture's Consequences* (Beverley Hills, CA: Sage, 1980).

52. D. A. Aaker and Erich Joachimsthaler, "The Lure of Global Branding," *Harvard Business Review, 37* (November 1999): 137–144.

53. For some in-depth treatments of branding in Asia in particular, see S. Ramesh Kumar, *Marketing & Branding: The Indian Scenario* (Delhi: Pearson Education, 2007); Martin Roll, *Asian Brand Strategy: How Asia Builds Strong Brands* (New York: Palgrave MacMillan, 2006); and Paul Temporal, *Branding in Asia: The Creation, Development, and Management of Asian Brands for the Global Market* (Singapore: John Wiley & Sons, 2001).

54. Deepa Chandrasekaran and Gerard J. Tellis, "Global Takeoff of New Products: Culture, Wealth, or Vanishing Differences?" *Marketing Science, 27* (September–October 2008): 844–860.

55. Leila Abboud, "Philips Widens Marketing Push in India," *Wall Street Journal*, March 20, 2009.

56. Warren J. Keegan and Mark C. Green, *Global Marketing*, 4th ed. (Upper Saddle River, NJ: Prentice Hall, 2005); Warren J. Keegan, *Global Marketing Management*, 7th ed. (Upper Saddle River, NJ: Prentice Hall, 2002).

57. Paulo Prada and Bruce Orwall, "A Certain 'Je Ne Sais Quoi' at Disney's New Park," *Wall Street Journal*, March 12, 2003.

58. Ralf van der Lans, Joseph A. Cote, Catherine A. Cole, Siew Meng Leong, Ale Smidts, Pamela W. Henderson, Christian Bluemelhuber, Paul A. Bottomley, John R. Doyle, Alexander Fedorikhin, Janakiraman Moorthy, B. Ramaseshan, and Bernd H. Schmitt, "Cross-National Logo Evaluation Analysis: An Individual-Level Approach," *Marketing Science, 28* (September–October 2009): 968–985.

59. F. C. (Frank) Hong, Anthony Pecotich, and Clifford J. Shultz II, "Language Constraints, Product Attributes, and Consumer Perceptions in East and Southeast Asia," *Journal of International Marketing, 10* (June 2002): 29–45.

60. Mark Lasswell, "Lost in Translation," *Business 2.0*, August 2004, pp. 68–70; Richard P. Carpenter and the *Globe* Staff, "What They Meant to Say Was...," *Boston Globe*, August 2, 1998.

61. For an interesting distinction based on the concept of global consumer culture positioning, see Dana L. Alden, Jan-Benedict E. M. Steenkamp, and Rajeev Batra, "Brand Positioning through Advertising in Asia, North America, and Europe: The Role of Global Consumer Culture," *Journal of Marketing, 63* (January 1999): 75–87.

62. Thomas J. Madden, Kelly Hewett, and Martin S. Roth, "Managing Images in Different Cultures: A Cross-National Study of Color Meanings and Preferences," *Journal of International Marketing, 8* (Winter 2000): 90–107; Zeynep Gürhan-Canli and Durairaj Maheswaran, "Cultural Variations in Country-of-Origin Effects," *Journal of Marketing Research, 37* (August 2000): 309–317.

63. Geoffrey Fowler, Brian Steinberg, and Aaron O. Patrick, "Globalizing Apple's Ads," *Wall Street Journal*, March 1, 2007; Joan Voight, "Best Campaign of the Year: Apple 'Mac vs. PC,'" *Adweek*, July 17, 2007.

64. See, for example, Haksin Chan, Lisa C. Wan, and Leo Y. M. Shin, "The Contrasting Effects of Culture on Consumer Tolerance: Interpersonal Face and Impersonal Fate," *Journal of Consumer Research, 36* (August 2009): 292–304.

65. Aradhna Krishna and Rohini Ahluwalia, "Language Choice in Advertising to Bilinguals: Asymmetric Effects for Multinationals versus Local Firms," *Journal of Consumer Research, 35* (December 2008): 692–705.

66. Normandy Madden, "Crossing Borders by Building Relationships," *Advertising Age*, October 13, 2008, p. 32.

67. Preeti Khicha, "Building Brands in Rural India," *Brandchannel*, www.brandchannel.com, October 8, 2007.

68. John L. Graham, Alma T. Mintu, and Waymond Rogers, "Explorations of Negotiations Behaviors in Ten Foreign Cultures Using a Model Developed in the United States," *Management Science, 40* (January 1994): 72–95.

69. Joyce Lee, "McWeddings Offered at Hong Kong McDonald's," *CBS*, October 28, 2010, www.cbsnews.com/8301-31749_162-20021022-10391698.html (viewed October 30, 2010); Tiffany Lam, "Would You Like a Wife with That? McDonald's Offers Weddings," October 12, 2010, www.cnngo.com/hong-kong/life/mcdonalds-hong-kong-offers-weddings-494226 (viewed October 30, 2010).

70. Price perceptions may differ too. See Lisa E. Bolton, Hean Tat Keh, and Joseph W. Alba, "How Do Price Fairness Perceptions Differ Across Culture?" *Journal of Marketing Research, 47* (June 2010): 564–576.

71. David Pierson, "Beijing Loves IKEA—But Not for Shopping," *Los Angeles Times*, August 25, 2009; Mei Fong, "IKEA Hits Home in China: The Swedish Design Giant, Unlike Other Retailers, Slashes Prices for the Chinese," *Wall Street Journal*, March 3, 2006, p. B1.

72. "McCain Foods Wins Early Battle in Pizza War: Canadian Agency Imposes Temporary Duty on U.S Imports," *Telegraph-Journal*, May 18, 2004.

73. AGMA, "KPMG/AGMA Survey Projects Global 'Gray Market' of $58 Billion for Information Technology Manufacturers," *KPMG*, www.kpmg.com, December 11, 2008.

74. David Blanchard, "Just in Time—How to Fix a Leaky Supply Chain," *IndustryWeek*, May 1, 2007.

75. Kersi D. Antia, Mark E. Bergen, Shantanu Dutta, and Robert J. Fisher, "How Does Enforcement Deter Gray Market Incidence?" *Journal of Marketing, 70* (January 2006): 92–106; Matthew B. Myers and David A. Griffith, "Strategies for Combating Gray Market Activity," *Business Horizons, 42* (November–December 1999): 2–8.

76. Brian Grow, Chi-Chu Tschang, Cliff Edwards, and Brian Burnsed, "Dangerous Fakes," *BusinessWeek*, October 8, 2008; Brian Burnsed, "The Most Counterfeited Products," *BusinessWeek*, www.businessweek.com, October 8, 2008.

77. "Royal Canadian Mounted Police Counterfeiting Guide," *RCMP*, www.rcmp-grc.gc.ca/fep-pelf/ipr-dpi/booklet-brochure-eng.htm (viewed July 13, 2011).

78. Eric Shine, "Faking Out the Fakers," *BusinessWeek*, June 4, 2007, pp. 76–80.

79. Deborah Kong, "Smart Tech Fights Fakes," *Business 2.0*, March 2007, p. 30.

80. David Arnold, "Seven Rules of International Distribution," *Harvard Business Review*, November–December 2000, pp. 131–137.

81. Ibid.

82. Katrijn Gielens, Linda M. Van De Gucht, Jan-Benedict E. M. Steenkamp, and Marnik G. Dekimpe, "Dancing with a Giant: The Effect of Wal-Mart's Entry into the United Kingdom on the Performance of European Retailers," *Journal of Marketing Research*, 45 (October 2008): 519–534.

83. Noreen O'Leary, "Infiniti Plays Up Japanese Heritage in Global Campaign," *Brandweek*, February 15, 2010, p. 5.

84. "The Shock of Old," *Economist*, July 13, 2002, p. 49.

85. "From Fantasy Worlds to Food," *Economist*, November 11, 2006, p. 73; "A New Sort of Beauty Contest," *Economist*, November 11, 2006, p. 68.

86. Flora Bagenal and John Harlow, "Borat Make Benefit Kazakh Tourist Boom," *Sunday Times*, December 3, 2006; Lisa Minot, "Borat Causes Tourism Boom," *The Sun*, March 5, 2007; "Borat 'Boosted Kazakh Tourism,'" *ABC News*, www.abc.net.au, November 13, 2008.

87. Jim Rendon, "When Nations Need a Little Marketing," *New York Times*, November 23, 2003.

88. Joanna Kakissis, "Vacationers Rethink Greece Amid Debt Crisis," *National Public Radio*, www.npr.org, June 22, 2010; Elena Becatoros, "Greece's Tourism Industry Under Threat," *MSNBC*, www.msnbc.com, June 15, 2010.

89. Jo Roberts, "South Africa United Behind Single Brand," April 29, 2010, www.marketingweek.co.uk/in-depth-analysis/features/south-africa-united-behind-single-brand/3012763.article (viewed October 30, 2010).

90. Zeynep Gurhan-Canli and Durairaj Maheswaran, "Cultural Variations in Country-of-Origin Effects," *Journal of Marketing Research*, 37 (August 2000): 309–317. For some different related issues, see also Lily Dong and Kelly Tian, "The Use of Western Brands in Asserting Chinese National Identity," *Journal of Consumer Research*, 36 (October 2009): 504–523; Yinlong Zhang and Adwait Khare, "The Impact of Accessible Identities on the Evaluation of Global versus Local Products," *Journal of Consumer Research*, 36 (October 2009): 524–537; Rohit Varman and Russell W. Belk, "Nationalism and Ideology in an Anticonsumption Movement," *Journal of Consumer Research*, 36 (December 2009): 686–700.

91. Douglas B. Holt, John A. Quelch, and Earl L. Taylor, "How Global Brands Compete," *Harvard Business Review*, 82 (September 2004): 68–75; Jan-Benedict E. M. Steenkamp, Rajeev Batra, and Dana L. Alden, "How Perceived Brand Globalness Creates Brand Value," *Journal of International Business Studies*, 34 (January 2003): 53–65.

92. Zeynep Gürhan-Canli and Durairaj Maheswaran, "Cultural Variations in Country of Origin Effects," *Journal of Marketing Research*, 37, no. 3 (2000): 309–317; Johny K. Johansson, "Global Marketing: Research on Foreign Entry, Local Marketing, Global Management," in *Handbook of Marketing*, edited by Barton A. Weitz and Robin Wensley (London, England: Sage, 2002): 457–483; "Old Wine in New Bottles," *Economist*, February 21, 1998, p. 45; Johny K. Johansson, "Determinants and Effects of the Use of 'Made in' Labels," *International Marketing Review (UK)*, 6 (January 1989): 47–58; Warren J. Bilkey and Erik Nes, "Country-of-Origin Effects on Product Evaluations," *Journal of International Business Studies*, 13 (Spring–Summer 1982): 89–99.

93. Kimberly Weisul, "Why More Are Buying into 'Buy Local,'" *BusinessWeek*, March 1, 2010, pp. 57–60.

94. Jathon Sapsford and Norihiko Shirouzo, "Mom, Apple Pie and... Toyota?" *Wall Street Journal*, May 11, 2006.

95. Kenneth Hein, "Emerging Markets Still Like U.S. Brands," *Brandweek*, April 16, 2007, p. 4.

96. For additional discussion, see "Strengthening Brand America," *The Burghard Group*, www.strengtheningbrandamerica.com, December 9, 2010.

97. Joel Backaler, "Haier: A Chinese Company That Innovates," *China Tracker*, www.forbes.com, June 17, 2010; Zhang Ruimin, "Voices from China," *Forbes*, September 28, 2009.

98. Rajdeep Grewal, Murali Chandrashekaran, and F. Robert Dwyer, "Navigating Local Environments with Global Strategies: A Contingency Model of Multinational Subsidiary Performance," *Marketing Science*, 27 (September–October 2008): 886–902; Christopher A. Bartlett and Sumantra Ghoshal, *Managing across Borders* (Cambridge, MA: Harvard Business School Press, 1989).

99. Moon Ihlwan, "The Foreigners at the Top of LG," *BusinessWeek*, December 22, 2008, pp. 56–57.

100. Jim Murphy, "The Jack's Eye-View on Marketing a Global Brand Locally," talk given at *The Beverage Forum*, New York, New York, May 20, 2009.

101. Betsy McKay, "Coke Hunts for Talent to Re-establish Its Marketing Might," *Wall Street Journal*, March 6, 2002.

102. David Kiley, "Ghosn Hits the Accelerator," *BusinessWeek*, May 1, 2008.

Chapter 22

1. "Loblaw Companies Limited 2010 Corporate Social Responsibility Report: The Way We Do Business," www.loblaw.ca/English/responsibility/default.aspx (viewed July 2011); Marina Strauss, "Why Loblaw Takes Top Honours for Corporate Social Responsibility," *The Globe and Mail*, June 20, 2010; Mike De Souza, "Loblaws the Best, Costco the Worst for Sustainable Fish Products: Greenpeace," *Postmedia News*, July 8, 2011.

2. Christopher Vollmer, *Always On: Advertising, Marketing, and Media in an Era of Consumer Control* (New York: McGraw-Hill, 2008).

3. For additional analysis and discussion, see Philip Kotler, Hermawan Karatajaya, and Iwan Setiawan, *Marketing 3.0: From Products to Consumers to the Human Spirit* (Hoboken, NJ: Wiley, 2010).

4. Devin Leonard, "The New Abnormal," *Bloomberg BusinessWeek*, August 2–August 10, 2010, pp. 50–55; Noreen O'Leary, "CMOs Face New Reality," *Adweek*, August 11, 2010.

5. John Gerzema and Michael D'Antonio, *Spend Shift: How the Post-Crisis Values Revolution Is Changing the Way We Buy, Sell, and Live* (San Francisco: Jossey-Bass, 2010).

6. John A. Quelch and Katherine E. Jocz, *Greater Good: How Good Marketing Makes for Better Democracy* (Boston: Harvard Business School Press, 2007).

7. Clay Chandler, "Full Speed Ahead," *Fortune*, February 7, 2005, pp. 78–84; "What You Can Learn from Toyota," *Business 2.0*, January–February 2005, pp. 67–72; Keith Naughton, "Red, White, and Bold," *Newsweek*, April 25, 2005, pp. 34–36; John LeBlanc, "2010 Toyota Prius: Polishing the Hybrid Halo," *The Toronto Star Wheels*, March 27, 2009, www.wheels.ca/article/524144 (viewed July 2011).

8. For some thoughtful academic perspectives on marketing strategy and tactics, see *Kellogg on Integrated Marketing*, edited by Dawn Iacobucci and Bobby Calder (New York: Wiley, 2003); and *Kellogg on Marketing*, edited by Dawn Iacobucci (New York: Wiley, 2001).

9. For a broad historical treatment of marketing thought, see D. G. Brian Jones and Eric H. Shaw, "A History of Marketing Thought," in *Handbook of Marketing*, edited by Barton A. Weitz and Robin Wensley (London, England: Sage, 2002), pp. 39–65. For more specific issues related to the interface between marketing and sales, see Christian Homburg, Ove Jensen, and Harley Krohmer, "Configurations of Marketing and Sales: A Taxonomy," *Journal of Marketing*, 72 (March 2008): 133–154.

10. Frederick E. Webster, Jr., "Expanding Your Network," *Marketing Management*, Fall 2010, pp. 16–23; Frederick E. Webster, Jr., Alan J. Malter, and Shankar Ganesan, "Can Marketing Regain Its Seat at the Table?" Marketing Science Institute Report No. 03-113 (Cambridge, MA: Marketing Science Institute, 2003); Frederick E. Webster, Jr., "The Role of Marketing and the Firm," in *Handbook of Marketing*, edited by Barton A. Weitz and Robin Wensley (London, England: Sage, 2002), pp. 39–65.

11. Jan Wieseke, Michael Ahearne, Son K. Lam, and Rolf van Dick, "The Role of Leaders in Internal Marketing," *Journal of Marketing, 73* (March 2009): 123–145; Hamish Pringle and William Gordon, *Beyond Manners: How to Create the Self-Confident Organisation to Live the Brand* (West Sussex, England: John Wiley & Sons, 2001); John P. Workman, Jr., Christian Homburg, and Kjell Gruner, "Marketing Organization: An Integrative Framework of Dimensions and Determinants," *Journal of Marketing, 62* (July 1998): 21–41.

12. Grant McKracken, *Chief Culture Officer: How to Create a Living Breathing Corporation* (New York: Basic Books, 2009).

13. Todd Guild, "Think Regionally, Act Locally: Four Steps to Reaching the Asian Consumer," *McKinsey Quarterly, 4* (September 2009): 22–30.

14. "Category Management Goes beyond Grocery," Cannondale Associates White Paper,www.cannondaleassoc.com, February 13, 2007; Laurie Freeman, "P&G Widens Power Base: Adds Category Managers," *Advertising Age*, October 12, 1999; Michael J. Zenor, "The Profit Benefits of Category Management," *Journal of Marketing Research, 31* (May 1994): 202–213; Gerry Khermouch, "Brands Overboard," *Brandweek*, August 22, 1994, pp. 25–39; Zachary Schiller, "The Marketing Revolution at Procter & Gamble," *BusinessWeek*, July 25, 1988, pp. 72–76.

15. For some further reading on the origins of category management, see Robert Dewar and Don Shultz, "The Product Manager, an Idea Whose Time Has Gone," *Marketing Communications*, May 1998, pp. 28–35; George S. Low and Ronald A. Fullerton, "Brands, Brand Management, and the Brand Manager System: A Critical Historical Evaluation," *Journal of Marketing Research, 31* (May 1994): 173–190; Michael J. Zanor, "The Profit Benefits of Category Management," *Journal of Marketing Research, 31* (May 1994): 202–213.

16. D. Gail Fleenor, "The Next Space Optimizer," *Progressive Grocer*, March 2009; Rajdeep Grewel, Murali Chandrashekaran, and F. Robert Dwyer, "Navigating Local Environments with Global Strategies: A Contingency Model of Multinational Subsidiary Performance," *Marketing Science, 27* (September–October 2008): 886–902; Christopher A. Bartlett and Sumantra Ghoshal, *Managing across Borders* (Cambridge, MA: Harvard Business School Press, 1989).

17. Bombardier website, www.bombardier.com/en/corporate (viewed July 2011).

18. Larry Selden and Geoffrey Colvin, *Angel Customers & Demon Customers* (New York: Portfolio [Penguin], 2003).

19. For an in-depth discussion of issues around implementing a customer-based organization, see George S. Day, "Aligning the Organization with the Market," *MIT Sloan Management Review, 48* (Fall 2006): 41–49.

20. Frederick E. Webster, Jr., "The Role of Marketing and the Firm," in *Handbook of Marketing*, edited byBarton A. Weitz and Robin Wensley(London, England: Sage, 2002), pp. 39–65.

21. For research on the prevalence of CMOs, see Pravin Nath and Vijay Mahajan, "Chief Marketing Officers: A Study of Their Presence in Firms' Top Management Teams," *Journal of Marketing, 72* (January 2008): 65–81. For more discussion on the importance of CMOs, see David A. Aaker, *Spanning Silos: The New CMO Imperative* (Boston: Harvard Business School Press, 2008).

22. For some classic perspectives, see Benson P. Shapiro, "Can Marketing and Manufacturing Coexist?" *Harvard Business Review*, September–October 1977, pp. 104–114. Also see Robert W. Ruekert and Orville C. Walker, Jr., "Marketing's Interaction with Other Functional Units: A Conceptual Framework with Other Empirical Evidence," *Journal of Marketing, 51* (January 1987): 1–19.

23. For more on creativity, see Pat Fallon and Fred Senn, *Juicing the Orange: How to Turn Creativity into a Powerful Business Advantage* (Boston: Harvard Business School Press, 2006); Bob Schmetterer, *Leap: A Revolution in Creative Business Strategy* (Hoboken, NJ: Wiley, 2003); Jean-Marie Dru, *Beyond Disruption: Changing the Rules in the Marketplace* (Hoboken, NJ: Wiley, 2002); Michael Michalko, *Cracking Creativity: The Secrets of Creative Genius* (Berkeley, CA: Ten Speed Press, 1998); James M. Higgins, *101 Creative Problem-Solving Techniques* (New York: New Management Publishing, 1994); and all the books by Edward DeBono.

24. Gary Hamel, *Leading the Revolution* (Boston: Harvard Business School Press, 2000).

25. Jagdish N. Sheth, *The Self-Destructive Habits of Good Companies ... And How to Break Them* (Upper Saddle River, NJ: Wharton School Publishing, 2007).

26. William L. Wilkie and Elizabeth S. Moore, "Marketing's Relationship to Society," in *Handbook of Marketing*, edited byBarton A. Weitz and Robin Wensley(London, England: Sage, 2002), pp. 1–38.

27. "Special Report: Corporate Social Responsibility," *Economist*, January 17, 2008. For a broader academic perspective, see Michael E. Porter and Mark R. Kramer, "Strategy & Society," *Harvard Business Review*, December 2006, pp. 78–82; Clayton M. Christensen, Heiner Baumann, Rudy Ruggles, and Thomas M. Stadtler, "Disruption Innovation for Social Change," *Harvard Business Review*, December 2006, 94–101.

28. "Walmart Canada Social Responsibility Report," www.walmart-csr.ca/; "Share Green Initiative," www.walmartcsr.ca/index.php/en/environment/sharing-best-practices-driving-collaboration; "David Suzuki vs. Walmart CEO: The 2010 Walmart Canada Green Business Summit Recap," *Green Briefs*, February 11, 2010, unicyclecreative.com/wordpress/2010/02/david-suzuki-vs-walmart-ceo-the-2010-walmart-canada-green-business-summit-recap/ (viewed July 2011); Monte Burke, "Mr. Green Jeans," *Forbes*, May 24, 2010; Brian Grow, "The Debate over Doing Good," *BusinessWeek*, August 15, 2005, pp. 76–78.

29. Brian Grow, "The Debate over Doing Good," *BusinessWeek*, August 15, 2005.

30. MaryLou Costa, "P&G Marketing Boss Urges Brands to Move Beyond Traditional Advertising," *Marketing Week*, June 24, 2010; Elaine Wong, "P&G Shows Its Softer Side with Downy Cause Effort," *Brandweek*, February 1, 2010, p. 6; Elaine Wong, "P&G Throws Values into Value Equation," *Brandweek*, March 9, 2009, p. 5.

31. Raj Sisodia, David B. Wolfe, and Jag Sheth, *Firms of Endearment: How World-Class Companies Profit from Passion and Purpose* (Upper Saddle River, NJ: Wharton School Publishing, 2007).

32. Toby Heaps, "The 2011 Best 50 Corporate Citizens in Canada," *Corporate Knights, 35*, wwwcorporateknights.ca/issue/issue-35 (viewed June 2011).

33. Elisabeth Sullivan, "Play by the New Rules," *Marketing News*, November 30, 2009, pp. 5–9. For further reading, see Dorothy Cohen, *Legal Issues in Marketing Decision Making* (Cincinnati, OH: South-Western College Publishing, 1995).

34. "Canadian Children's Food & Beverage Advertising Initiative," www.adstandards.com/en/childrensinitiative/ (viewed July 2011).

35. Shelby D. Hunt and Scott Vitell, "The General Theory of Marketing Ethics: A Retrospective and Revision," in *Ethics in Marketing*, edited byJohn Quelch and Craig Smith (Chicago: Irwin, 1992).

36. "Canadians Place Increasing Trust in NGOs as Trust in Business and Government Remains Steady," *Canada Newswire*, February 14, 2011, www.newswire.ca/en/releases/archive/February2011/14/c2427.html (viewed July 2011).

37. "Top 50 Socially Responsible Corporations, Jantzi-Maclean's Corporate Social Responsibility Report 2010," www2.macleans.ca/tag/canadas-top-50-most-socially-responsible/ (viewed July 2011).

38. Ronald J. Alsop, *The 18 Immutable Laws of Corporate Reputation: Creating, Protecting, and Repairing Your Most Valuable Asset* (New York: The Free Press, 2004); Marc Gunther,

"Tree Huggers, Soy Lovers, and Profits," *Fortune*, June 23, 2003, pp. 98–104; Ronald J. Alsop, "Perils of Corporate Philanthropy," *Wall Street Journal*, January 16, 2002.

39. "McCain's First Global Social Responsibility Report Wins Best Annual Report at CSR Awards," McCain Press Release, February 25, 2010, www.mccain.com/Newsroom/Announcements/Pages/McCainCSRAward.aspx (viewed July 2011).

40. Emily Steel, "Nestlé Takes a Beating on Social-Media Sites," *Wall Street Journal*, March 29, 2010, p. B5; Mya Frazier, "Going Green? Plant Deep Roots," *Advertising Age*, April 30, 2007, pp. 1, 54–55.

41. Angela M. Eikenberry, "The Hidden Cost of Cause Marketing," *Stanford Social Innovation Review*, Summer 2009; Aneel Karnani, "The Case Against Corporate Social Responsibility," *Wall Street Journal*, August 23, 2010.

42. Sandra O'Loughlin, "The Wearin' o' the Green," *Brandweek*, April 23, 2007, pp. 26–27. For a critical response, see also John R. Ehrenfield, "Feeding the Beast," *Fast Company*, December 2006–January 2007, pp. 42–43.

43. Pete Engardio, "Beyond the Green Corporation," *BusinessWeek*, January 29, 2007, pp. 50–64.

44. Global 100 website, www.global100.org.

45. Pete Engardio, "Beyond the Green Corporation," *BusinessWeek*, January 29, 2007, pp. 50–64.

46. Noreen O' Leary, "Marketer of the Year: Jessica Buttimer," *Next*, September 14, 2009, p. 32; Jack Neff, "Marketing 50: Green Works (Jessica Buttimer)," *Advertising Age*, November 17, 2008, p. S-2; Elaine Wong, "CPGs Watch as Clorox Crashes the Green Party," *Brandweek*, April 21, 2008, p. 13; Anya Kamenetz, "Cleaning Solution," *Fast Company*, September 2008, pp. 121–125.

47. David Roberts, "Another Inconvenient Truth," *Fast Company*, March 2008, p. 70; Melanie Warner, "P&G's Chemistry Test," *Fast Company*, July–August 2008, pp. 71–74.

48. Mark Dolliver, "Thumbs Down on Corporate Green Efforts," *Adweek*, August 31, 2010; Betsy Cummings, "A Green Backlash Gains Momentum," *Brandweek*, March 3, 2008, p. 6; Michael Hopkins, "What the 'Green' Consumer Wants," *MIT Sloan Management Review*, Summer 2009, pp. 87–89. For some related consumer research, see Julie R. Irwin and Rebecca Walker Naylor, "Ethical Decisions and Response Mode Compatibility: Weighting of Ethical Attributes in Consideration Sets Formed by Excluding versus Including Product Alternatives," *Journal of Marketing Research*, 46 (April 2009): 234–246.

49. Jack Neff, "Green-Marketing Revolution Defies Economic Downturn," *Advertising Age*, April 20, 2009, pp. 1, 23; Ram Nidumolu, C. K. Prahalad, and M. R. Rangaswami, "Why Sustainability Is Now the Key Driver of Innovation," *Harvard Business Review*, September 2009, p. 57.

50. John A. Quelch and Nathalie Laidler-Kylander, *The New Global Brands: Managing Non-Government Organizations in the 21st Century* (Mason, OH: South-Western, 2006); Philip Kotler and Nancy Lee, *Corporate Social Responsibility: Doing the Most Good for Your Company and Your Cause* (New York: Wiley, 2005); Lynn Upshaw, *Truth: The New Rules for Marketing in a Skeptical World* (New York: AMACOM, 2007).

51. "Imagine Canada Report on Corporate Giving," November 12, 2008, http://lin.ca/resource-details/12927 (viewed July 2011).

52. Robert Berner, "Smarter Corporate Giving," *BusinessWeek*, November 28, 2005, pp. 68–76; Craig N. Smith, "Corporate Social Responsibility: Whether or How?" *California Management Review*, 45 (Summer 2003): 52–76.

53. Larry Chiagouris and Ipshita Ray, "Saving the World with Cause-Related Marketing," *Marketing Management*, 16 (July–August 2007): 48–51; Hamish Pringle and Marjorie Thompson, *Brand Spirit: How Cause-Related Marketing Builds Brands* (New York: Wiley, 1999); Sue Adkins, *Cause-Related Marketing: Who Cares Wins* (Oxford, England: Butterworth-Heinemann, 1999); "Marketing, Corporate Social Initiatives, and the Bottom Line,"

Marketing Science Institute Conference Summary, MSI Report No. 01-106,2001.

54. Rajan Varadarajan and Anil Menon, "Cause-Related Marketing: A Co-Alignment of Marketing Strategy and Corporate Philanthropy," *Journal of Marketing*, 52 (July 1988): 58–74.

55. Minette Drumwright and Patrick E. Murphy, "Corporate Societal Marketing," in *Handbook of Marketing and Society*, edited byPaul N. Bloom and Gregory T. Gundlach (Thousand Oaks, CA: Sage, 2001), pp. 162–183. See also Minette Drumwright, "Company Advertising with a Social Dimension: The Role of Noneconomic Criteria," *Journal of Marketing*, 60 (October 1996): 71–87.

56. C. B. Bhattacharya, Sankar Sen, and Daniel Korschun, "Using Corporate Social Responsibility to Win the War for Talent," *MIT Sloan Management Review*, 49 (January 2008): 37–44; Xueming Luo and C. B. Bhattacharya, "Corporate Social Responsibility, Customer Satisfaction, and Market Value," *Journal of Marketing*, 70 (October 2006): 1–18; Pat Auger, Paul Burke, Timothy Devinney, and Jordan J. Louviere, "What Will Consumers Pay for Social Product Features?" *Journal of Business Ethics*, 42 (February 2003): 281–304; Dennis B. Arnett, Steve D. German, and Shelby D. Hunt, "The Identity Salience Model of Relationship Marketing Success: The Case of Nonprofit Marketing," *Journal of Marketing*, 67 (April 2003): 89–105; C. B. Bhattacharya and Sankar Sen, "Consumer-Company Identification: A Framework for Understanding Consumers' Relationships with Companies," *Journal of Marketing*, 67 (April 2003): 76–88; Sankar Sen and C. B. Bhattacharya, "Does Doing Good Always Lead to Doing Better? Consumer Reactions to Corporate Social Responsibility," *Journal of Marketing Research*, 38 (May 2001): 225–244.

57. Paul N. Bloom, Steve Hoeffler, Kevin Lane Keller, and Carlos E. Basurto, "How Social-Cause Marketing Affects Consumer Perceptions," *MIT Sloan Management Review*, Winter 2006, pp. 49–55; Carolyn J. Simmons and Karen L. Becker-Olsen, "Achieving Marketing Objectives through Social Sponsorships," *Journal of Marketing*, 70 (October 2006): 154–169; Guido Berens, Cees B. M. van Riel, and Gerrit H. van Bruggen, "Corporate Associations and Consumer Product Responses: The Moderating Role of Corporate Brand Dominance," *Journal of Marketing*, 69 (July 2005): 35–48; Donald R. Lichtenstein, Minette E. Drumwright, and Bridgette M. Braig, "The Effect of Social Responsibility on Customer Donations to Corporate-Supported Nonprofits," *Journal of Marketing*, 68 (October 2004): 16–32; Stephen Hoeffler and Kevin Lane Keller, "Building Brand Equity through Corporate Societal Marketing," *Journal of Public Policy and Marketing*, 21 (Spring 2002): 78–89. See also "Special Issue: Corporate Responsibility," *Journal of Brand Management*, 10, nos. 4–5 (May 2003).

58. Mark R. Forehand and Sonya Grier, "When Is Honesty the Best Policy? The Effect of Stated Company Intent on Consumer Skepticism," *Journal of Consumer Psychology*, 13 (2003): 349–356; Dwane Hal Dean, "Associating the Corporation with a Charitable Event through Sponsorship: Measuring the Effects on Corporate Community Relations," *Journal of Advertising*, 31 (Winter 2002): 77–87.

59. Susan Perry, "KFC–Komen 'Buckets for the Cure' Campaign Raises Questions," *MinnPost.com*, www.minnpost.com, April 20, 2010; Chuck English, "Cause Splash vs. Cause Marketing," *Doing Good for Business*, www.doinggoodforbusiness.wordpress.com, May 17, 2010; Nancy Schwartz, "Busted Nonprofit Brand: Anatomy of a Corporate Sponsorship Meltdown (Case Study)," *Getting Attention!* www.gettingattention.org, April 28, 2010.

60. "Nike Announces Global Expansion of LIVESTRONG Product Collection as Lance Armstrong Rides for Hope," *Nike*, www.nike.com, June 30, 2010; Reena Jana, "Nike Goes Green. Very Quietly," *BusinessWeek*, June 22, 2009, p. 56.

61. Mya Frazier, "Costly Red Campaign Reaps Meager $18 Million," *Advertising Age*, March 5, 2007; Bobby Shriver, "CEO: Red's Raised Lots of Green," *Advertising Age*, March 12, 2007; Michelle Conlin, "Shop (in the Name of Love)," *BusinessWeek*, October 2, 2006, p. 9.

62. Todd Cohen, "Corporations Aim for Strategic Engagement," *Philanthropy Journal*, September 20, 2006; John A. Quelch and

Nathalie Laidler-Kylander, *The New Global Brands: Managing Non-Governmental Organizations in the 21st Century* (Cincinnati, OH: South-Western, 2005).

63. Ronald J. Alsop, *The 18 Immutable Laws of Corporate Reputation: Creating, Protecting, and Repairing Your Most Valuable Asset* (New York: The Free Press, 2004), p. 125.

64. "Ronald McDonald House Charities," www.rmhc.org.

65. Susan Orenstein, "The Selling of Breast Cancer," *Business 2.0*, February 2003, pp. 88–94; H. Meyer, "When the Cause Is Just," *Journal of Business Strategy, 20* (November–December 1999): 27–31.

66. Christine Bittar, "Seeking Cause and Effect," *Brandweek*, November 11, 2002, pp. 18–24.

67. "How Bell is Supporting Mental Health," September 21, 2010, http://bce.ca/en/community/mentalhealth/howbellissupportingmentalhealth/ (viewed July 2011).

68. One Sight website, www.onesight.org.

69. Christina Binkley, "Charity Gives Shoe Brand Extra Shine," *Wall Street Journal*, April 1, 2010; "How I Got Started... Blake Mycoskie, Founder of TOMS Shoes," *Fortune*, March 22, 2010, p. 72; Dan Heath and Chip Heath, "An Arms Race of Goodness," *Fast Company*, October 2009, pp. 82–83; Toms website, www.toms.com/movement-one-for-one.

70. Philip Kotler and Nancy Lee, *Social Marketing: Influencing Behaviors for Good* (Thousand Oaks, CA: Sage, 2008); Alan Andreasen, *Social Marketing in the 21st Century* (Thousand Oaks, CA: Sage, 2006); Michael L. Rothschild, "Carrots, Sticks, and Promises: A Conceptual Framework for the Management of Public Health and Social Issue Behaviors," *Journal of Marketing, 63* (October 1999): 24–37.

71. "About ParticipACTION," www.participaction.com/en-us/About-Participaction/About-ParticipACTION.aspx (viewed July 2011).

72. See Michael L. Rothschild, "Carrots, Sticks, and Promises: A Conceptual Framework for the Management of Public Health and Social Issue Behaviors," *Journal of Marketing, 63* (October 1999): 24–37. For an application, see Sekar Raju, Priyali Rajagopal, and Timothy J. Gilbride, "Marketing Healthful Eating to Children: The Effectiveness of Incentives, Pledges, and Competitions," *Journal of Marketing, 74* (May 2010): 93–106.

73. For some relevant recent academic research on developing social marketing programs, see Deborah A. Small and Nicole M. Verrochi, "The Face of Need: Facial Emotion Expression on Charity Advertisements," *Journal of Marketing Research, 46* (December 2009): 777–787; Katherine White and John Peloza, "Self-Benefit versus Other-Benefit Marketing Appeals: Their Effectiveness in Generating Charitable Support," *Journal of Marketing, 73 (July 2009): 109–124; Merel Van Diepen, Bas Donkers, and Philip Hans Franses,* "Dynamic and Competitive Effects of Direct Mailings: A Charitable Giving Application," *Journal of Marketing Research, 46* (February 2009): 120–133; Jen Shang, Americus Reed II, and Rachel Croson, "Identity Congruency Effects on Donations," *Journal of Marketing Research, 45* (June 2008): 351–361.

74. For more on developing and implementing marketing plans, see H. W. Goetsch, *Developing, Implementing, and Managing an Effective Marketing Plan* (Chicago: NTC Business Books, 1993). See also Thomas V. Bonoma, *The Marketing Edge: Making Strategies Work* (New York: The Free Press, 1985). Much of this section is based on Bonoma's work.

75. For other examples, see Paul W. Farris, Neil T. Bendle, Phillip E. Pfeifer, and David J. Reibstein, *Marketing Metrics: 50+ Metrics Every Executive Should Master* (Upper Saddle River, NJ: Wharton School Publishing, 2006); and John Davis, *Measuring Marketing: 103 Key Metrics Every Marketer Needs* (Hoboken, NJ: Wiley, 2006).

76. Sam R. Goodman, *Increasing Corporate Profitability* (New York: Ronald Press, 1982), Ch. 1. See also Bernard J. Jaworski, Vlasis Stathakopoulos, and H. Shanker Krishnan, "Control Combinations in Marketing: Conceptual Framework and Empirical Evidence," *Journal of Marketing, 57* (January 1993): 57–69.

77. Philip Kotler, William Gregor, and William Rodgers, "The Marketing Audit Comes of Age," *Sloan Management Review, 30* (Winter 1989): 49–62. For a discussion of attrition of the figures, see Frederick Reichheld, *The Loyalty Effect* (Boston: Harvard Business School Press, 1996).

78. Useful checklists for a marketing self-audit can be found in Aubrey Wilson, *Aubrey Wilson's Marketing Audit Checklists* (London, England: McGraw-Hill, 1982); and Mike Wilson, *The Management of Marketing* (Westmead, England: Gower Publishing, 1980). A marketing audit software program is described in Ben M. Enis and Stephen J. Garfein, "The Computer-Driven Marketing Audit," *Journal of Management Inquiry, 1* (December 1992): 306–318.

79. Philip Kotler, William Gregor, and William Rodgers, "The Marketing Audit Comes of Age," *Sloan Management Review, 30* (Winter 1989): 49–62.

80. Alfred R. Oxenfeldt, "How to Use Market-Share Measurement," *Harvard Business Review*, January–February 1969, pp. 59–68.

81. There is a one-half chance that a successive observation will be higher or lower. Therefore, the probability of finding six successively higher values is given by 1/2 to the sixth, or 1/64.

82. Alternatively, companies need to focus on factors affecting shareholder value. The goal of marketing planning is to increase shareholder value, which is the present value of the future income stream created by the company's present actions. Rate-of-return analysis usually focuses on only one year's results. See Alfred Rapport, *Creating Shareholder Value*, rev. ed. (New York: The Free Press, 1997).

83. For additional reading on financial analysis, see Peter L. Mullins, *Measuring Customer and Product-Line Profitability* (Washington, DC: Distribution Research and Education Foundation, 1984).

84. Robin Cooper and Robert S. Kaplan, "Profit Priorities from Activity-Based Costing," *Harvard Business Review*, May–June 1991, pp. 130–135. For a recent application to shipping, see Tom Kelley, "What Is the *Real* Cost: How to Use Lifecycle Cost Analysis for an Accurate Comparison," *Beverage World*, January 2010, pp. 50–51.

Appendix

1. Background information and market data adapted from "Gartner Says Worldwide Mobile Phones Sales Grew 35 Percent in Third Quarter 2010; Smartphone Sales Increased 96 Percent," Gartner Press Release, November 18, 2010, www.gartner.com; Joseph Palenchar, "Smartphone Sales Rise as Selection Grows," *TWICE*, June 21, 2010; Sascha Segan, "Motorola RAZR2: The RAZR2 Cuts Four Ways," *PC Magazine*, October 2, 2007, pp. 32–33; Walter S. Mossberg, "Apple's iPod Touch Is a Beauty of a Player Short on Battery Life," *Wall Street Journal*, September 20, 2007, p. B1; "Roam If You Want To," *PC World*, September 2007, p. 134; Sascha Segam, "Exclusive: One RAZR2, Four Ways to Cut It," *PC Magazine Online*, August 13, 2007, www.pcmag.com; "Apple Unlikely to Budge Anytime Soon on iPhone Pricing," *InformationWeek*, July 26, 2007; "Smartphones Get Smarter, Thanks in Part to the iPhone," *InformationWeek*, July 21, 2007; "Nine Alternatives to Apple's iPhone," *InformationWeek*, June 28, 2007; "Hospital Uses PDA App for Patient Transport," *Health Data Management*, June 2007, p.14; Jessica E. Vascellaro and Pui-Wing Tam, "RIM's New Gear Fuels Profit Surge; Palm Sputters," *Wall Street Journal*, June 29, 2007, p. B4; "Smart Phones Force Dell from Handhelds," *MicroScope*, April 23, 2007; "2005 PDA Shipments Set Record," *Business Communications Review*, April 2006, p. 6; "Smartphone Market Grows Fast Despite Challenges," *Appliance*, March 2006, p. 16.

GLOSSARY

activity-based costing (ABC) accounting procedures that can quantify the true profitability of different activities by identifying their actual costs.

adoption an individual's decision to become a regular user of a product.

advertising any paid form of nonpersonal presentation and promotion of ideas, goods, or services by an identified sponsor.

advertising objective a specific communications task and achievement level to be accomplished with a specific audience in a specific period of time.

anchoring and adjustment heuristic when consumers arrive at an initial judgment and then make adjustments of their first impressions based on additional information.

arm's-length price the price charged by other competitors for the same or a similar product.

aspirational groups groups a person hopes or would like to join.

associative network memory model a conceptual representation that views long-term memory as consisting of a set of nodes and interconnecting links, where nodes represent stored information or concepts and links represent the strength of association between the pieces of information or concepts.

attitude a person's enduring favourable or unfavourable evaluations, emotional feelings, and action tendencies toward some object or idea.

augmented product a product that includes features that go beyond consumer expectations and differentiate the product from competitors.

availability heuristic when consumers base their predictions on the quickness and ease with which a particular example of an outcome comes to mind.

available market the set of consumers who have interest, income, and access to a particular offer.

average cost the cost per unit at a given level of production; it is equal to total costs divided by production.

backward invention reintroducing earlier product forms that can be well-adapted to a foreign country's needs.

banner ads (Internet) small, rectangular boxes containing text and perhaps a picture to support a brand.

basic product what specifically the actual product is.

belief a descriptive thought that a person holds about something.

brand a name, term, sign, symbol, or design, or a combination of them, intended to identify the goods or services of one seller or group of sellers and to differentiate them from those of competitors.

brand associations all brand-related thoughts, feelings, perceptions, images, experiences, beliefs, attitudes, and so on that become linked to the brand node.

brand audit a consumer-focused exercise that involves a series of procedures to assess the health of the brand, uncover its sources of brand equity, and suggest ways to improve and leverage its equity.

brand awareness consumers' ability to identify the brand under different conditions, as reflected by their brand recognition or recall performance.

brand community a specialized community of consumers and employees whose identification and activities focus around the brand.

brand contact any information-bearing experience a customer or prospect has with the brand, the product category, or the market that relates to the marketer's product or service.

brand development index (BDI) the index of brand sales to category sales.

brand dilution when consumers no longer associate a brand with a specific product or highly similar products and start thinking less favourably about the brand.

brand elements those trademarkable devices that serve to identify and differentiate the brand, such as a brand name, logo, or character.

brand equity the added value endowed to products and services.

brand extension a company's use of an established brand to introduce a new product.

brand image the perceptions and beliefs held by consumers, as reflected in the associations held in consumer memory.

brand knowledge all the thoughts, feelings, images, experiences, beliefs, and so on that become associated with the brand.

brand line all products, original as well as line and category extensions, sold under a particular brand name.

brand mix the set of all brand lines that a particular seller makes available to buyers.

brand personality the specific mix of human traits that may be attributed to a particular brand.

brand portfolio the set of all brands and brand lines a particular firm offers for sale to buyers in a particular category or market segment.

brand promise the marketer's vision of what the brand must be and do for consumers.

brand valuation an estimate of the total financial value of the brand.

brand value chain a structured approach to assessing the sources and outcomes of brand equity and the manner in which marketing activities create brand value.

brand-asset management team (BAMT) key representatives from functions that affect the brand's performance.

brand-tracking studies collect quantitative data from consumers over time to provide consistent, baseline information about how brands and marketing programs are performing.

branded entertainment using sports, music, arts, or other activities to build brand equity.

branded variants specific brand lines uniquely supplied to different retailers or distribution channels.

branding endowing products and services with the power of a brand.

branding strategy the number and nature of common and distinctive brand elements applied to the different products sold by the firm.

break-even analysis a means by which management estimates how many units of the product the company would have to sell to break even with the given price and cost structure.

brick-and-click describes retailers that add online services to their offerings.

business database complete information about business customers' past purchases, volumes, prices, and profits.

business market all the organizations that acquire goods and services used in the production of other products or services that are sold, rented, or supplied to others.

capital items long-lasting goods that facilitate developing or managing the finished product.

captive products products that are necessary to the use of other products, such as razor blades or film.

category extension using the parent brand to brand a new product outside the product category currently served by the parent brand.

category membership the products or sets of products with which a brand competes and which function as close substitutes.

cause-related marketing marketing that links a firm's contributions to a designated cause with customers' engaging directly or indirectly in revenue-producing transactions with the firm.

channel conflict when one channel member's actions prevent another channel from achieving its goal.

channel coordination when channel members are brought together to advance the goals of the channel, as opposed to their own potentially incompatible goals.

channel power the ability to alter channel members' behaviour so that they take actions they would not have taken otherwise.

channel stewardship the ability of a given participant in a distribution channel—a steward—to create a go-to-market strategy that simultaneously addresses customers' best interests and drives profits for all channel partners.

club membership programs programs open to everyone who purchases a product or service, or limited to an affinity group of those willing to pay a small fee.

co-branding (also dual branding or brand bundling) when two or more well-known brands are combined into a joint product or marketed together in some fashion.

cohorts groups of individuals born during the same time period and who travel through life together.

communication adaptation changing marketing communications programs for each local market.

communication-effect research determining whether an ad is communicating effectively.

company demand the company's estimated share of market demand at alternative levels of company marketing effort in a given time period.

company sales forecast the expected level of company sales based on a chosen marketing plan and an assumed marketing environment.

company sales potential the sales limit approached by company demand as company marketing effort increases relative to that of competitors.

competitive advantage a company's ability to perform in one or more ways that competitors cannot or will not match.

competitive frame of reference the other brands a brand competes with and therefore the focus of competitive analysis.

conformance quality the degree to which all the produced units are identical and meet the promised specifications.

conjoint analysis a method for deriving the utility values that consumers attach to varying levels of a product's attributes.

conjunctive heuristic the consumer sets a minimum acceptable cutoff level for each attribute and chooses the first alternative that meets the minimum standard for all attributes.

consumer behaviour the study of how individuals, groups, and organizations select, buy, use, and dispose of goods, services, ideas, or experiences to satisfy their needs and wants.

consumer involvement the level of engagement and active processing undertaken by the consumer in responding to a marketing stimulus.

consumerist movement an organized movement of citizens and government to strengthen the rights and powers of buyers in relation to sellers.

consumption system the way the user performs the tasks of getting and using products and related services.

containerization putting goods in boxes or trailers that are easy to transfer between two transportation modes.

contractual sales force manufacturers' reps, sales agents, and brokers, who are paid a commission based on sales.

convenience goods goods the consumer purchases frequently, immediately, and with a minimum of effort.

conventional marketing channel an independent producer, wholesaler(s), and retailer(s).

core benefit the service or benefit the customer is really buying.

core competency attribute that (1) is a source of competitive advantage in that it makes a significant contribution to perceived customer benefits, (2) has applications in a wide variety of markets, and (3) is difficult for competitors to imitate.

core values the belief systems that underlie consumer attitudes and behaviour, and that determine people's choices and desires over the long term.

corporate culture the shared experiences, stories, beliefs, and norms that characterize an organization.

corporate retailing corporately owned retailing outlets that offer many economies of scale, greater purchasing power, wider brand recognition, and better-trained employees.

countertrade offering other items in payment for purchases.

critical path scheduling (CPS) network planning techniques to coordinate the many tasks in launching a new product.

cues stimuli that determine when, where, and how a person responds.

culture the fundamental determinant of a person's wants and behaviour.

customer churn customer defection.

customer consulting data, information systems, and advice services that the seller offers to buyers.

customer database an organized collection of comprehensive information about individual customers or prospects that is current, accessible, and actionable for marketing purposes.

customer equity the sum of lifetime values of all customers.

customer lifetime value (CLV) the net present value of the stream of future profits expected over the customer's lifetime purchases.

customer mailing list a set of names, addresses, and telephone numbers.

customer management organization deals with individual customers rather than the mass market or even market segments.

customer profitability analysis (CPA) a means of assessing and ranking customer profitability through accounting techniques such as activity-based costing (ABC).

customer relationship management (CRM) the process of carefully managing detailed information about individual customers and all customer "touch points" to maximize loyalty.

customer training training the customer's employees to use the vendor's equipment properly and efficiently.

customer value the total customer benefit minus the total customer cost.

customer value analysis report of the company's strengths and weaknesses relative to various competitors.

customer-based brand equity the differential effect that brand knowledge has on a consumer response to the marketing of that brand.

customer-perceived value (CPV) the difference between the prospective customer's evaluation of all the benefits and all the costs of an offering and the perceived alternatives.

customer-performance scorecard records how well the company is doing year after year on particular customer-based measures.

customer-value hierarchy five product levels that must be addressed by marketers in planning a market offering.

customerization combination of operationally driven mass customization with customized marketing in a way that empowers consumers to design the product and service offering of their choice.

D

data mining the extracting of useful information about individuals, trends, and segments from the mass of data.

data warehouse a collection of current data captured, organized, and stored by a company's contact centre.

database marketing the process of building, maintaining, and using customer databases and other databases for the purpose of contacting, transacting, and building customer relationships.

declining demand consumers begin to buy the product less frequently or not at all.

deep metaphors basic frames or orientations that consumers have toward the world around them.

delivery how well the product or service is brought to the customer.

demand chain planning the process of designing the supply chain based on adopting a target market perspective and working backward.

demand-side method identifying the effect sponsorship has on consumers' brand knowledge.

design the totality of features that affect how a product looks, feels, and functions to a consumer.

direct (company) sales force full- or part-time paid employees who work exclusively for the company.

direct marketing the use of consumer-direct (CD) channels to reach and deliver goods and services to customers without using marketing middlemen.

direct product profitability (DPP) a way of measuring a product's handling costs from the time it reaches the warehouse until a customer buys it in the retail store.

direct-order marketing marketing in which direct marketers seek a measurable response, typically a customer order.

discrimination the process of recognizing differences in sets of similar stimuli and adjusting responses accordingly.

display ads small, rectangular boxes containing text and perhaps a picture to support a brand.

dissociative groups groups whose values or behaviour an individual rejects.

distribution programming building a planned, professionally managed vertical marketing system that meets the needs of both manufacturer and distributors.

drive a strong internal stimulus impelling action.

dual adaptation adapting both the product and the communications to the local market.

dumping situation in which a company charges either less than its costs or less than it charges in its home market, in order to enter or win a market.

durability a measure of a product's expected operating life under natural or stressful conditions.

durable goods tangible goods that normally survive many uses, such as refrigerators, machine tools, and clothing.

e-commerce when a company or site offers to transact or facilitate the selling of products and services online.

elimination-by-aspects heuristic situation in which the consumer compares brands on an attribute selected probabilistically, and eliminates brands if they do not meet minimum acceptable cutoff levels.

environmental threat a challenge posed by an unfavourable trend or development that would lead to lower sales or profit.

ethnographic research a particular observational research approach that uses concepts and tools from anthropology and other social science disciplines to provide deep cultural understanding of how people live and work.

everyday low pricing (EDLP) in retailing, a constant low price with few or no price promotions and special sales.

exclusive distribution severely limiting the number of intermediaries, in order to maintain control over the service level and outputs offered by resellers.

expectancy-value model consumers evaluate products and services by combining their brand beliefs—positive and negative—according to their weighted importance.

expected product a set of attributes and conditions buyers normally expect when they purchase a given product.

experience curve (learning curve) a decline in the average cost with accumulated production experience.

experimental research the most scientifically valid research, designed to capture cause-and-effect relationships by eliminating competing explanations of the observed findings.

F

fad a craze that is unpredictable, short-lived, and without social, economic, and political significance.

family brand situation in which the parent brand is already associated with multiple products through brand extensions.

family of orientation parents and siblings.

family of procreation spouse and children.

features things that enhance the basic function of a product.

fixed costs (overhead) costs that do not vary with production level or sales revenue.

flexible market offering an offering consisting of two parts: (1) a naked solution containing the product and service elements that all segment members value, and (2) discretionary options that some segment members value.

focus group a gathering of six to ten people who are carefully selected based on certain demographic, psychographic, or other considerations and brought together to discuss various topics of interest.

forecasting the art of anticipating what buyers are likely to do under a given set of conditions.

form the size, shape, or physical structure of a product.

forward invention creating a new product to meet a need in another country.

frequency programs (FPs) programs designed to provide rewards to customers who buy frequently and in substantial amounts.

full demand consumers are adequately buying all products put into the marketplace.

G

generics unbranded, plainly packaged, less expensive versions of common products such as spaghetti, paper towels, and canned peaches.

global firm a firm that operates in more than one country and captures R&D, production, logistical, marketing, and financial advantages in its costs and reputation and that are not available to purely domestic competitors.

global industry an industry in which the strategic positions of competitors in major geographic or national markets are fundamentally affected by their overall global positions.

goal formulation the process of developing specific goals for the planning period.

going-rate pricing pricing based largely on competitors' prices.

grey market branded products diverted from normal or authorized distribution channels in the country of product origin or across international borders.

H

hedonic bias when people have a general tendency to attribute success to themselves and failure to external causes.

heuristics rules of thumb or mental shortcuts in the decision process.

high–low pricing charging higher prices on an everyday basis but then running frequent promotions and special sales.

holistic marketing concept a concept based on the development, design, and implementation of marketing programs, processes, and activities that recognizes their breadth and interdependencies.

horizontal marketing system when two or more unrelated companies put together resources or programs to exploit an emerging marketing opportunity.

hub-and-spoke system product management organization where brand or product manager is figuratively at the centre, with spokes leading to various departments and representing working relationships.

hybrid channels when a single firm uses multiple channels of distribution to reach customers in a defined market.

image the set of beliefs, ideas, and impressions a person holds regarding an object.

industry a group of firms that offer a product or class of products that are close substitutes for one another.

informational appeal elaborates on product or service attributes or benefits.

ingredient branding a special case of co-branding that involves creating brand equity for materials, components, or parts that are necessarily contained within other branded products.

innovation any good, service, or idea that is perceived by someone as new.

innovation diffusion process the spread of a new idea from its source of invention or creation to its ultimate users or adopters.

installation the work done to make a product operational in its planned location.

institutional market schools, hospitals, nursing homes, prisons, and other institutions that must provide goods and services to people in their care.

integrated logistics systems (ILS) materials management, material flow systems, and physical distribution, aided by information technology (IT).

integrated marketing mixing and matching marketing activities to maximize their individual and collective efforts.

integrated marketing channel system system in which the strategies and tactics of selling through one channel reflect the strategies and tactics of selling through one or more other channels.

integrated marketing communications (IMC) a concept of marketing communications planning that recognizes the added value of a comprehensive plan.

intensive distribution placing the goods or services in as many outlets as possible.

internal branding activities and processes that help to inform and inspire employees.

internal marketing an element of holistic marketing, it is the task of hiring, training, and motivating able employees who want to serve customers well.

interstitials advertisements, often with video or animation, that pop up between changes on a website.

irregular demand consumer purchases vary on a seasonal, monthly, weekly, daily, or even hourly basis.

J

jobbers small-scale wholesalers who sell to small retailers.

joint venture a company in which multiple investors share ownership and control.

L

latent demand consumers may share a strong need that cannot be satisfied by an existing product.

lean manufacturing producing goods with minimal waste of time, materials, and money.

learning changes in an individual's behaviour arising from experience.

lexicographic heuristic a consumer chooses the best brand on the basis of its perceived most important attribute.

licensed product one whose brand name has been licensed to other manufacturers who actually make the product.

life stage a person's major concern, such as going through a divorce, going into a second marriage, taking care of an older parent, deciding to cohabit with another person, deciding to buy a new home, and so on.

life-cycle cost the product's purchase cost plus the discounted cost of maintenance and repair less the discounted salvage value.

lifestyle a person's pattern of living in the world as expressed in activities, interests, and opinions.

line extension the parent brand is used to brand a new product that targets a new market segment within a product category currently served by the parent brand.

line stretching when a company lengthens its product line beyond its current range.

long-term memory (LTM) a permanent repository of information.

loyalty a commitment to rebuy or repatronize a preferred product or service.

M

maintenance and repair the service program for helping customers keep purchased products in good working order.

market various groups of customers.

market demand the total volume of a product that would be bought by a defined customer group in a defined geographical area in a defined time period in a defined marketing environment under a defined marketing program.

market forecast the market demand corresponding to the level of industry marketing expenditure.

market logistics planning the infrastructure to meet demand, then

implementing and controlling the physical flows of materials and final goods from points of origin to points of use, to meet customer requirements at a profit.

market management organization organization in which a market manager supervises several market-development managers, market specialists, or industry specialists and draws on functional services as needed.

Market Opportunity Analysis (MOA) system used to determine the attractiveness and probability of success.

market partitioning the process of investigating the hierarchy of attributes consumers use in choosing a brand.

market potential the limit approached by market demand as industry marketing expenditures approach infinity for a given marketing environment.

market share a brand's proportion of the selective demand for a product.

market-buildup method identifying all the potential buyers in each market and estimating their potential purchases.

market-centred organizations companies that are organized along market lines.

marketer someone who seeks a response (attention, a purchase, a vote, a donation) from another party, called the prospect.

marketing the activity, set of institutions, and processes for creating, communicating, delivering, and exchanging offerings that have value for customers, clients, partners, and society at large.

marketing audit a comprehensive, systematic, independent, and periodic examination of a company's or business unit's marketing environment, objectives, strategies, and activities.

marketing channel system the particular set of marketing channels employed by a firm.

marketing channels sets of interdependent organizations involved in the process of making a product or service available for use or consumption.

marketing communications the means by which firms attempt to inform, persuade, and remind consumers—directly or indirectly—about products and brands that they sell.

marketing communications mix advertising, sales promotion, events and experiences, public relations and publicity, direct marketing, interactive marketing, word-of-mouth marketing, and personal selling.

marketing concept involves finding not the right customers for your products, but the right products for your customers

marketing decision support system (MDSS) a coordinated collection of data, systems, tools, and techniques, with supporting software and hardware, by which an organization gathers and interprets relevant information from business and environment and turns it into a basis for marketing action.

marketing funnel identifies the percentage of the potential target market at each stage in the decision process, from merely aware to highly loyal.

marketing implementation the process that turns marketing plans into action assignments and ensures that such assignments are executed in a manner that accomplishes the plan's stated objectives.

marketing information system (MIS) people, equipment, and procedures to gather, sort, analyze, evaluate, and distribute information to marketing decision makers.

marketing insights diagnostic information about how and why we observe certain effects in the marketplace, and what that means to marketers.

marketing intelligence system a set of procedures and sources managers use to obtain everyday information about developments in the marketing environment.

marketing management the art and science of choosing target markets and getting, keeping, and growing customers through creating, delivering, and communicating superior customer value.

marketing metrics the set of measures that helps firms to quantify, compare, and interpret their marketing performance.

marketing network the company and its supporting stakeholders, with whom it has built mutually profitable business relationships.

marketing opportunity an area of buyer need and interest in which there is a high probability that a company can profitably satisfy that need.

marketing plan written document that summarizes what the marketer has learned about the marketplace, indicates how the firm plans to reach its marketing objectives, and helps direct and coordinate the marketing effort.

marketing public relations (MPR) publicity and other activities that build corporate or product image to facilitate marketing goals.

marketing research the systematic design, collection, analysis, and reporting of data and findings relevant to a specific marketing situation facing the company.

market-penetration index a comparison of the current level of market demand to the potential demand level.

market-penetration pricing pricing strategy where prices start low to drive higher sales volume from price-sensitive customers and produce productivity gains.

market-skimming pricing pricing strategy where prices start high and are slowly lowered over time to maximize profits from less price-sensitive customers.

markup pricing an item by adding a standard increase to the product's cost.

mass customization the ability of a company to meet each customer's requirements

master brand situation in which the parent brand is already associated with multiple products through brand extensions.

materials and parts goods that enter the manufacturer's product completely.

media selection finding the most cost-effective media to deliver the desired number and type of exposures to the target audience.

megatrends large social, economic, political, and technological changes that are slow to form and once in place have an influence for seven to ten years or longer.

membership groups groups having a direct influence on a person.

memory encoding how and where information gets into memory.

memory retrieval how and from where information gets out of memory.

mental accounting the manner by which consumers code, categorize, and evaluate financial outcomes of choices.

microsales analysis an examination of specific products, territories, and so forth that fail to produce expected sales.

microsite individual webpages or clusters of webpages that function as supplements to a primary website.

mission statements statements that organizations develop to share with managers, employees, and (in many cases) customers.

mixed bundling when the seller offers goods both individually and in bundles.

motive a need aroused to a sufficient level of intensity to drive us to act.

multichannel marketing when a single firm uses two or more marketing channels to reach one or more customer segments.

multitasking doing two or more things at the same time.

negative demand consumers who dislike the product and may even pay to avoid it.

net price analysis analysis that encompasses company list price, average discount, promotional spending, and co-op advertising to arrive at net price.

noncompensatory models in consumer choice, when consumers do not simultaneously consider all positive and negative attributes in making a decision.

nondurable goods tangible goods normally consumed in one or a few uses, such as beer and shampoo.

nonexistent demand consumers who may be unaware of or uninterested in the product.

O

opinion leader the person in informal, product-related communications who offers advice or information about a specific product or product category.

ordering ease how easy it is for the customer to place an order with the company.

organization a company's structures, policies, and corporate culture.

organizational buying the decision-making process by which formal organizations establish the need for purchased products and services and identify, evaluate, and choose among alternative brands and suppliers.

overall market share the company's sales expressed as a percentage of total market sales.

overfull demand more consumers would like to buy the product than can be satisfied.

P

packaging all the activities of designing and producing the container for a product.

paid search marketers bid on search terms, and when a consumer searches for those words using Google, Yahoo!, or Bing, the marketer's ad will appear on the results page; advertisers pay only if people click on the link.

parent brand an existing brand that gives birth to a brand extension.

partner relationship management (PRM) activities the firm undertakes to build mutually satisfying long-term relations with key partners, such as suppliers, distributors, ad agencies, and marketing research suppliers.

pay-per-click ads see paid search.

penetrated market the set of consumers who are buying a company's product.

perceived value the value promised by the company's value proposition and perceived by the customer.

perception the process by which an individual selects, organizes, and interprets information inputs to create a meaningful picture of the world.

performance marketing understanding the financial and nonfinancial returns to business and society from marketing activities and programs.

performance quality the level at which the product's primary characteristics operate.

personal communications channels channels by which two or more people communicate directly face-to-face or person-to-audience.

personal influence the effect one person has on another's attitude or purchase probability.

personality a set of distinguishing human psychological traits that lead to relatively consistent responses to environmental stimuli.

place advertising (also out-of-home advertising) ads that appear outside of home and where consumers work and play.

point-of-purchase (P-O-P) the location where a purchase is made, typically thought of in terms of a retail setting.

points-of-difference (PODs) attributes or benefits that consumers strongly associate with a brand, positively evaluate, and believe they could not find to the same extent with a competitive brand.

points-of-parity (POPs) attribute or benefit associations that are not necessarily unique to the brand but may in fact be shared with other brands.

positioning the act of designing a company's offering and image to occupy a distinctive place in the minds of the target market.

potential market the set of consumers who profess a sufficient level of interest in a market offer.

potential product all the possible augmentations and transformations the product or offering might undergo in the future.

price discrimination when a company sells a product or service at two or more prices that do not reflect a proportional difference in costs.

price escalation an increase in the price of a product due to added costs of selling it in different countries.

primary groups groups with which a person interacts continuously and informally, such as family, friends, neighbours, and co-workers.

principle of congruity psychological mechanism that states that a consumer likes to see seemingly related objects match in terms of the consumer's attitude toward those objects.

private-label brand brand that retailers and wholesalers develop and market.

product anything that can be offered to a market to satisfy a want or need, including physical goods, services, experiences, events, people, places, properties, organizations, information, and ideas.

product adaptation altering the product to meet local conditions or preferences.

product assortment *see* product mix.

product concept proposes that consumers favour products offering the most quality, performance, or innovative features.

product invention creating something new via product development or other means.

product map competitors' items that are competing against a particular company's items.

product mix the set of all products and items a particular seller offers for sale.

product mix pricing when the firm searches for a set of prices that maximizes profits on the total mix.

product system a group of diverse but related items that function in a compatible manner.

production concept holds that consumers prefer products that are widely available and inexpensive.

product-penetration percentage the percentage of ownership or use of a product or service in a population.

profitable customer a person, household, or company that over time yields a revenue stream that exceeds by an acceptable amount the company's cost stream of attracting, selling, and serving that customer.

prospect a prospective client from whom a purchase, a vote, or a donation is sought.

prospect theory when consumers frame decision alternatives in terms of gains and losses according to a value function.

psychographics the science of using psychology and demographics to better understand consumers.

public any group that has an actual or potential interest in or impact on a company's ability to achieve its objectives.

public relations (PR) a variety of programs designed to promote or protect a company's image or its individual products.

publicity the task of securing editorial space—as opposed to paid space—in print and broadcast media to promote something.

pull strategy when the manufacturer uses advertising and promotion to persuade consumers to ask intermediaries for the product, thus inducing the intermediaries to order it.

purchase probability scale a scale to measure the probability of a buyer making a particular purchase.

pure bundling when a firm offers its products only as a bundle.

pure-click retailers firms that operate online only.

push strategy when the manufacturer uses its sales force and trade promotion money to induce intermediaries to carry, promote, and sell the product to end users.

Q

quality the totality of features and characteristics of a product or service that bear on its ability to satisfy stated or implied needs.

questionnaire a set of questions presented to respondents.

R

reference groups all the groups that have a direct or indirect influence on a person's attitudes or behaviour.

reference prices pricing information a consumer retains in memory or sees posted as an external frame of reference. This pricing information is used to interpret and evaluate a new price.

relationship marketing building mutually satisfying long-term relationships with key parties, in order to earn and retain their business.

relative market share market share in relation to a company's largest competitor.

reliability a measure of the probability that a product will not malfunction or fail within a specified time period.

repairability a measure of the ease of fixing a product when it malfunctions or fails.

representativeness heuristic when consumers base their predictions on how representative or similar an outcome is to other examples.

retailer (or retail store) any business enterprise whose sales volume comes primarily from retailing.

retailing all the activities in selling goods or services directly to final consumers for personal, nonbusiness use.

risk analysis a method by which possible rates of returns and their probabilities are calculated by obtaining estimates for uncertain variables affecting profitability.

role the activities a person is expected to perform.

sales analysis measuring and evaluating actual sales in relation to goals.

sales budget a conservative estimate of the expected volume of sales, used for making current purchasing, production, and cash flow decisions.

sales promotion a collection of incentive tools, mostly short term, designed to stimulate quicker or greater purchase of particular products or services by consumers or the trade.

sales quota the sales goal set for a product line, company division, or sales representative.

sales-variance analysis a measure of the relative contribution of different factors to a gap in sales performance.

satisfaction a person's feelings of pleasure or disappointment resulting from comparing a product's perceived performance or outcome with his or her expectations.

scenario analysis developing plausible representations of a firm's possible future that make different assumptions about forces driving the market and include different uncertainties.

secondary groups groups that tend to be more formal and require less continuous interaction than primary groups, such as religious, professional, and trade-union groups.

selective attention the mental process of screening out certain stimuli while noticing others.

selective distortion a consumer's tendency to interpret product information in a way that fits his or her perceptions.

selective distribution the use of more than a few but less than all of the intermediaries who are willing to carry a particular product.

selective retention process in which a consumer remembers the good points about a product he or she likes and forgets the good points about competing products.

selling concept holds that consumers and businesses, if left alone, won't buy enough of the organization's products.

served market all the buyers who are able and willing to buy a company's product.

served market share a company's sales expressed as a percentage of the total sales to its served market.

service any act or performance that one party can offer to another and that is essentially intangible and does not result in the ownership of anything.

share-penetration index a comparison of a company's current market share with its potential market share.

shopping goods goods that the consumer, in the process of selection and purchase, characteristically compares on such bases as suitability, quality, price, and style.

short-term memory (STM) a temporary repository of information.

social classes homogeneous and enduring divisions in a society, which are hierarchically ordered and whose members share similar values, interests, and behaviour.

social marketing marketing done by a nonprofit or government organization to further a cause or help resolve a social issue, such as "say no to drugs" or "exercise more and eat better."

specialty goods goods with unique characteristics or brand identification for which enough buyers are willing to make a special purchasing effort.

sponsorship financial support of an event or activity in return for recognition and acknowledgment as the sponsor.

stakeholder-performance scorecard a measure to track the satisfaction of various constituencies who have a critical interest in and impact on the company's performance.

status a person's position within his or her own hierarchy or culture.

straight extension introducing a product in a foreign market without any change in the product.

strategic brand management the design and implementation of marketing activities and programs to build, measure, and manage brands to maximize their value.

strategic business units (SBUs) a single business or collection of related businesses that can be planned separately from the rest of the company, with its own set of competitors and a manager who is responsible for strategic planning and profit performance.

strategic group firms pursuing the same strategy directed to the same target market.

strategic marketing plan lays out the target markets and the value proposition that will be offered, based on analysis of the best market opportunities.

strategy a company's game plan for achieving its goals.

style a product's look and feel to the buyer.

sub-brand a new brand combined with an existing brand.

subcultures subdivisions of a culture that provide more specific identification and socialization, such as nationalities, religions, racial groups, and geographical regions.

subliminal perception receiving and processing subconscious messages that affect behaviour.

supersegment a set of segments sharing some exploitable similarity.

supplies and business services short-term goods and services that facilitate developing or managing the finished product.

supply chain management (SCM) procuring the right inputs (raw materials, components, and capital equipment), converting them efficiently into finished products, and dispatching them to the final destinations.

supply-side methods approximating the amount of time or space devoted to media coverage of an event, for example, the number of seconds the brand is clearly visible on a television screen or the column inches of press clippings that mention it.

T

tactical marketing plan lays out marketing tactics, including product features, promotion, merchandising, pricing, sales channels, and service.

target costing deducting the desired profit margin from the price at which a product will sell, given its appeal and competitors' prices.

target market the part of the qualified available market the company decides to pursue.

target-return pricing determining the price that would yield the firm's target rate of return on investment (ROI).

telemarketing the use of telephones and call centres to attract prospects, sell to existing customers, and provide service by taking orders and answering questions.

total costs the sum of the fixed and variable costs for any given level of production.

total customer benefit the perceived monetary value of the bundle of economic, functional, and psychological benefits customers expect from a given market offering because of the product, service, people, and image.

total customer cost the bundle of costs customers expect to incur in evaluating, obtaining, using, and disposing of the given market offering, including monetary, time, energy, and psychological costs.

total market potential the maximum sales available to all firms in an industry during a given period, under a given level of industry marketing effort and environmental conditions.

total quality an organization-wide approach to continuously improving the quality of all the organization's processes, products, and services.

tracking studies collecting information from consumers on a routine basis over time.

transaction a trade of values between two or more parties: A gives X to B and receives Y in return.

transfer in the case of gifts, subsidies, and charitable contributions, A gives X to B but does not receive anything tangible in return.

transfer price the price a unit charges another unit in the same company for goods it ships to foreign subsidiaries.

transformational appeal elaborates on a nonproduct-related benefit or image.

trend a direction or sequence of events that has some momentum and durability.

two-part pricing a fixed fee plus a variable usage fee.

tying agreements agreement in which producers of strong brands sell their products to dealers only if dealers purchase related products or services, such as other products in the brand line.

U

unsought goods goods the consumer does not know about or normally think of buying, like smoke detectors.

unwholesome demand consumers may be attracted to products that have undesirable social consequences.

V

value chain a tool for identifying ways to create more customer value.

value network a system of partnerships and alliances that a firm creates to source, augment, and deliver its offerings.

value pricing winning loyal customers by charging a fairly low price for a high-quality offering.

value proposition the whole cluster of benefits the company promises to deliver.

value-delivery network (supply chain) a company's supply chain and how it partners with specific suppliers and distributors to make products and bring them to markets.

value-delivery system all the experiences the customer will have on the way to obtaining and using the offering.

variable costs costs that vary directly with the level of production.

venture team a cross-functional group charged with developing a specific product or business.

vertical integration situation in which manufacturers try to control or own their suppliers, distributors, or other intermediaries.

vertical marketing system (VMS) the producer, wholesaler(s), and retailer(s) acting as a unified system.

viral marketing using the Internet to create word-of-mouth effects to support marketing efforts and goals.

W

warranties formal statements of expected product performance by the manufacturer.

wholesaling all the activities in selling goods or services to those who buy for resale or business use.

Y

yield pricing situation in which companies offer (1) discounted but limited early purchases, (2) higher-priced late purchases, and (3) the lowest rates on unsold inventory just before it expires.

Z

zero-level channel (direct marketing channel) a manufacturer selling directly to the final customer.

NAME INDEX

COMPANY, BRAND, AND ORGANIZATION INDEX

SUBJECT INDEX

PHOTO CREDITS